D1165069

Short Story Criticism

Guide to Gale Literary Criticism Series

For criticism on	Consult these Gale series
Authors now living or who died after December 31, 1999	*CONTEMPORARY LITERARY CRITICISM (CLC)*
Authors who died between 1900 and 1999	*TWENTIETH-CENTURY LITERARY CRITICISM (TCLC)*
Authors who died between 1800 and 1899	*NINETEENTH-CENTURY LITERATURE CRITICISM (NCLC)*
Authors who died between 1400 and 1799	*LITERATURE CRITICISM FROM 1400 TO 1800 (LC)* *SHAKESPEAREAN CRITICISM (SC)*
Authors who died before 1400	*CLASSICAL AND MEDIEVAL LITERATURE CRITICISM (CMLC)*
Authors of books for children and young adults	*CHILDREN'S LITERATURE REVIEW (CLR)*
Dramatists	*DRAMA CRITICISM (DC)*
Poets	*POETRY CRITICISM (PC)*
Short story writers	*SHORT STORY CRITICISM (SSC)*
Literary topics and movements	*HARLEM RENAISSANCE: A GALE CRITICAL COMPANION (HR)* *THE BEAT GENERATION: A GALE CRITICAL COMPANION (BG)*
Asian American writers of the last two hundred years	*ASIAN AMERICAN LITERATURE (AAL)*
Black writers of the past two hundred years	*BLACK LITERATURE CRITICISM (BLC)* *BLACK LITERATURE CRITICISM SUPPLEMENT (BLCS)*
Hispanic writers of the late nineteenth and twentieth centuries	*HISPANIC LITERATURE CRITICISM (HLC)* *HISPANIC LITERATURE CRITICISM SUPPLEMENT (HLCS)*
Native North American writers and orators of the eighteenth, nineteenth, and twentieth centuries	*NATIVE NORTH AMERICAN LITERATURE (NNAL)*
Major authors from the Renaissance to the present	*WORLD LITERATURE CRITICISM, 1500 TO THE PRESENT (WLC)* *WORLD LITERATURE CRITICISM SUPPLEMENT (WLCS)*

ISSN 0895-9439

Volume 78

Short Story Criticism

Criticism of the Works of Short Fiction Writers

Lawrence J. Trudeau
Project Editor

THOMSON

GALE

Detroit • New York • San Francisco • San Diego • New Haven, Conn. • Waterville, Maine • London • Munich

Short Story Criticism, Vol. 78

Project Editor
Lawrence J. Trudeau

Editorial
Jessica Bomarito, Kathy D. Darrow, Jeffrey W. Hunter, Jelena O. Krstović, Julie Landelius, Michelle Lee, Ellen McGeagh, Thomas J. Schoenberg, Russel Whitaker

Data Capture
Francis Monroe, Gwen Tucker

Indexing Services
Synapse, the Knowledge Link Corporation

Rights and Acquisitions
Margie Abendroth, Denise Buckley, Ann Taylor

Imaging and Multimedia
Dean Dauphinais, Leitha Etheridge-Sims, Lezlie Light, Mike Logusz, Dan Newell, Christine O'Bryan, Kelly A. Quin, Denay Wilding, Robyn Young

Composition and Electronic Capture
Kathy Sauer

Manufacturing
Rhonda Williams

Product Manager
Janet Witalec

LIBRARY OF CONGRESS CATALOG CARD NUMBER 88-641014

ISBN 0-7876-8875-4
ISSN 0895-9439

Printed in the United States of America
10 9 8 7 6 5 4 3 2 1

Contents

Preface vii

Acknowledgments xi

Literary Criticism Series Advisory Board xiii

Isaak Babel 1894-1940 1
Russian short-story writer, novelist, and playwright
Entry devoted to Red Cavalry *(1926)*

Mavis Gallant 1922- 167
Canadian short-story writer, novelist, critic, playwright, and essayist

Olive Senior 1941- 298
Jamaican short-story writer, poet, and nonfiction writer

Literary Criticism Series Cumulative Author Index 373

Literary Criticism Series Cumulative Topic Index 473

SSC Cumulative Nationality Index 485

SSC-78 Title Index 489

Preface

Short Story Criticism (*SSC*) presents significant criticism of the world's greatest short-story writers and provides supplementary biographical and bibliographical materials to guide the interested reader to a greater understanding of the authors of short fiction. This series was developed in response to suggestions from librarians serving high school, college, and public library patrons, who had noted a considerable number of requests for critical material on short-story writers. Although major short-story writers are covered in such Thomson Gale series as *Contemporary Literary Criticism* (*CLC*), *Twentieth-Century Literary Criticism* (*TCLC*), *Nineteenth-Century Literature Criticism* (*NCLC*), and *Literature Criticism from 1400 to 1800* (*LC*), librarians perceived the need for a series devoted solely to writers of the short-story genre.

Scope of the Series

SSC is designed to serve as an introduction to major short-story writers of all eras and nationalities. Since these authors have inspired a great deal of relevant critical material, *SSC* is necessarily selective, and the editors have chosen the most important published criticism to aid readers and students in their research.

Approximately eight to ten authors are included in each volume, and each entry presents a historical survey of the critical response to that author's work. The length of an entry is intended to reflect the amount of critical attention the author has received from critics writing in English and from foreign critics in translation. Every attempt has been made to identify and include the most significant essays on each author's work. In order to provide these important critical pieces, the editors sometimes reprint essays that have appeared elsewhere in Thomson Gale's Literary Criticism Series. Such duplication, however, never exceeds twenty percent of an *SSC* volume.

Organization of the Book

An *SSC* entry consists of the following elements:

- The **Author Heading** cites the name under which the author most commonly wrote, followed by birth and death dates. Also located here are any name variations under which an author wrote, including transliterated forms for authors whose native languages use nonroman alphabets. If the author wrote consistently under a pseudonym, the pseudonym will be listed in the author heading and the author's actual name given in parentheses on the first line of the biographical and critical introduction. Uncertain birth or death dates are indicated by question marks. Single-work entries are preceded by the title of the work and its date of publication.

- The **Introduction** contains background information that introduces the reader to the author and the critical debates surrounding his or her work.

- A **Portrait of the Author** is included when available.

- The list of **Principal Works** is ordered chronologically by date of first publication and lists the most important works by the author. The first section comprises short-story collections, novellas, and novella collections. The second section gives information on other major works by the author. For foreign authors, the editors have provided original foreign-language publication information and have selected what are considered the best and most complete English-language editions of their works.

- Reprinted **Criticism** is arranged chronologically in each entry to provide a useful perspective on changes in critical evaluation over time. All short-story, novella, and collection titles by the author featured in the entry are printed in boldface type. The critic's name and the date of composition or publication of the critical work are given at the beginning of each piece of criticism. Unsigned criticism is preceded by the title of the source in which it appeared. Footnotes are reprinted at the end of each essay or excerpt. In the case of excerpted criticism, only those footnotes that pertain to the excerpted texts are included.

- Critical essays are prefaced by brief **Annotations** explicating each piece.

- A complete **Bibliographical Citation** of the original essay or book precedes each piece of criticism. Source citations in the Literary Criticism Series follow University of Chicago Press style, as outlined in *The Chicago Manual of Style,* 14th ed. (Chicago: The University of Chicago Press, 1993).

- An annotated bibliography of **Further Reading** appears at the end of each entry and suggests resources for additional study. In some cases, significant essays for which the editors could not obtain reprint rights are included here. Boxed material following the further reading list provides references to other biographical and critical sources on the author in series published by Thomson Gale.

Indexes

A **Cumulative Author Index** lists all of the authors that appear in a wide variety of reference sources published by Thomson Gale, including *SSC.* A complete list of these sources is found facing the first page of the Author Index. The index also includes birth and death dates and cross references between pseudonyms and actual names.

A **Cumulative Nationality Index** lists all authors featured in *SSC* by nationality, followed by the number of the *SSC* volume in which their entry appears.

An alphabetical **Title Index** lists all short-story, novella, and collection titles contained in the *SSC* series. Titles of short-story collections, separately published novellas, and novella collections are printed in italics, while titles of individual short stories are printed in roman type with quotation marks. Each title is followed by the author's last name and corresponding volume and page numbers where commentary on the work is located. English-language translations of original foreign-language titles are cross-referenced to the foreign titles so that all references to discussion of a work are combined in one listing.

In response to numerous suggestions from librarians, Thomson Gale also produces an annual paperbound edition of the SSC cumulative title index. This annual cumulation, which alphabetically lists all titles reviewed in the series, is available to all customers. Additional copies of this index are available upon request. Librarians and patrons will welcome this separate index; it saves shelf space, is easy to use, and is recyclable upon receipt of the next edition.

Citing *Short Story Criticism*

When citing criticism reprinted in the Literary Criticism Series, students should provide complete bibliographic information so that the cited essay can be located in the original print or electronic source. Students who quote directly from reprinted criticism may use any accepted bibliographic format, such as University of Chicago Press style or Modern Language Association (MLA) style. Both the MLA and the University of Chicago formats are acceptable and recognized as being the current standards for citations. It is important, however, to choose one format for all citations; do not mix the two formats within a list of citations.

The examples below follow recommendations for preparing a bibliography set forth in *The Chicago Manual of Style,* 14th ed. (Chicago: The University of Chicago Press, 1993); the first example pertains to material drawn from periodicals, the second to material reprinted from books:

Morrison, Jago. "Narration and Unease in Ian McEwan's Later Fiction." *Critique* 42, no. 3 (spring 2001): 253-68. Reprinted in *Short Story Criticism.* Vol. 57, edited by Janet Witalec, 212-20. Detroit: Gale, 2003.

Brossard, Nicole. "Poetic Politics." In *The Politics of Poetic Form: Poetry and Public Policy,* edited by Charles Bernstein, 73-82. New York: Roof Books, 1990. Reprinted in *Short Story Criticism.* Vol. 57, edited by Janet Witalec, 3-8. Detroit: Gale, 2003.

The examples below follow recommendations for preparing a works cited list set forth in the *MLA Handbook for Writers of Research Papers,* 5th ed. (New York: The Modern Language Association of America, 1999); the first example pertains to material drawn from periodicals, the second to material reprinted from books:

Morrison, Jago. "Narration and Unease in Ian McEwan's Later Fiction." *Critique* 42.3 (spring 2001): 253-68. Reprinted in *Short Story Criticism.* Ed. Janet Witalec. Vol. 57. Detroit: Gale, 2003. 212-20.

Brossard, Nicole. "Poetic Politics." *The Politics of Poetic Form: Poetry and Public Policy.* Ed. Charles Bernstein. New York: Roof Books, 1990. 73-82. Reprinted in *Short Story Criticism.* Ed. Janet Witalec. Vol. 57. Detroit: Gale, 2003. 3-8.

Suggestions are Welcome

Readers who wish to suggest new features, topics, or authors to appear in future volumes, or who have other suggestions or comments are cordially invited to call, write, or fax the Product Manager:

Product Manager, Literary Criticism Series
Thomson Gale
27500 Drake Road
Farmington Hills, MI 48331-3535
1-800-347-4253 (GALE)
Fax: 248-699-8054

Acknowledgments

The editors wish to thank the copyright holders of the excerpted criticism included in this volume and the permissions managers of many book and magazine publishing companies for assisting us in securing reproduction rights. We are also grateful to the staffs of the Detroit Public Library, the Library of Congress, the University of Detroit Mercy Library, Wayne State University Purdy/Kresge Library Complex, and the University of Michigan Libraries for making their resources available to us. Following is a list of the copyright holders who have granted us permission to reproduce material in this volume of *SSC*. Every effort has been made to trace copyright, but if omissions have been made, please let us know.

COPYRIGHTED MATERIAL IN *SSC*, VOLUME 78, WAS REPRODUCED FROM THE FOLLOWING PERIODICALS:

Acta Litteraria Academiae Scientiarum Hungaricae, v. 32, no. 3-4, 1990 for "Up and Down, Madonna and Prostitute: The Role of Ambivalence in Red Cavalry" by Zsuzsa Hetenyi. Edited by Tolnai Gabor. Copyright © 1990 by Akademiai Kiado, Budapest. Reproduced by permission.—*America,* v. 176, February 8, 1997. Copyright © 1997. All rights reserved. Reproduced with permission of America Press, Inc., 106 West 56th Street, New York, NY 10019. www.americamagazine.org.— *American Review of Canadian Studies,* v. 24, spring, 1994. Reproduced by permission.—*ARIEL,* v. 24, January 1993 for "The Fiction of Olive Senior: Traditional Society and the Wider World" by Richard F. Patteson; v. 29, October, 1998 for "Registering Woman: Senior's Zig-zag Discourse and Code-Switching in Jamaican Narrative" by Barbara Lalla. Copyright © 1993, 1998 by the Board of Governors, The University of Calgary. Both reproduced by permission of the publisher and the respective authors.—*Callaloo,* v. 11, summer, 1988; v. 16, winter, 1993. Copyright © 1988, 1993 by Charles H. Rowell. All rights reserved. Both reproduced by permission of Johns Hopkins University Press.—*Canadian Slavonic Papers,* v. 33, June, 1991; v. 36, March-June, 1994. Copyright © 1991, 1994 by Canadian Slavonic Papers. All rights reserved. Both reproduced by permission.—*Canadian-American Slavic Studies,* v. 34, no. 2, summer, 2000. Copyright © 2000 by Charles Schlacks, Jr. All rights reserved. Reproduced by permission.—*English in Africa,* v. 25, May, 1998 for "Asian Diasporas, Contending Identities and New Configurations: Stories by Agnes Sam and Olive Senior" by Miki Flockemann. Copyright © 1998 English in Africa. Reproduced by permission of the author.—*English Studies in Canada,* v. 18, September, 1992 for "Mavis Gallant's Apprenticeship Stories, 1944-1950: Breaking the Frame" by Lesley Clement. Reproduced by permission of the publisher and the author.—*Essays in Poetics,* v. 14, September, 1989 for "'Spoil the Purest of Ladies';: Male and Female Imagery in Isaac Babel's *Konarmiya*" by Joe Andrew. Copyright © 1989 by Joe Andrew. Reproduced by permission of the author.—*Essays on Canadian Writing,* no. 42, winter, 1990. Copyright © Canadian Literary Foundation. Reproduced by permission./ no. 80, fall, 2003. Copyright © ECW Press, Ltd. Both reproduced by permission.—*Etudes Canadiennes/ Canadian Studies,* no. 29, 1990. Reproduced by permission.—*Journal of Caribbean Studies,* v. 6, spring, 1988 for "Feminist Consciousness: European/ American Theory, Jamaican Stories" by Evelyn O'Callaghan. Copyright © 1988 by O. R. Dathorne & the Association of Caribbean Studies. All rights reserved. Reproduced by permission of the author.—*Journal of the Short Story in English/ Les Cahiers de la Nouvelle,* no. 32, spring, 1999; no. 35, fall, 2000. Copyright © Université d'Angers, 1999, 2000. All rights reserved. Both reproduced by permission.—*Kunapipi,* v. 16, 1994 for "'Mixed Worlds': Olive Senior's *Summer Lightning*" by John Thieme. Copyright © 1994 by Kunapipi. Reproduced by permission of the author.—*Modern Fiction Studies,* v. 28, spring 1982. Copyright © 1982 by the Purdue Research Foundation. All rights reserved. Reproduced by permission of The Johns Hopkins University.—*New Republic,* v. 212, May 8, 1995. Copyright © 1995 by The New Republic, Inc. Reproduced by permission of the *New Republic.*—*Russian Literature,* v. 15, April, 1984. Copyright © 1984, Elsevier Science Publishers B. V. (North-Holland). All rights reserved. Reprinted with permission from Elsevier.—*Russian Studies in Literature,* v. 37, winter, 2000-2001. English-language translation copyright © 2000 by M. E. Sharpe, Inc. Used with permission. All rights reserved. Not for further reproduction.—*Slavic Review,* v. 53, fall, 1994. Copyright © 1994 *Slavic Review,* by the American Association for the Advancement of Slavic Studies, Inc. Reproduced by permission.—*Slavonica,* v. 3, 1996/97. Copyright © Sheffield Academic Press Limited, 1997. Reproduced by permission.— *Studies in Canadian Literature,* v. 18, summer, 1993. Copyright © 1993 by Danielle Schaub. Reproduced by permission of the editors.—*Third World Quarterly,* v. 10, April, 1988. Copyright © 1988 by *Third World Quarterly.* Reproduced by permission.—*World Literature Today,* v. 70, spring, 1996. Copyright © 1996 by the University of Oklahoma Press. Reproduced by permission of the publisher.

COPYRIGHTED MATERIAL IN *SSC*, VOLUME 78, WAS REPRODUCED FROM THE FOLLOWING BOOKS:

Clement, Lesley D. From *Learning to Look: A Visual Response to Mavis Gallant's Fiction.* McGill-Queen's University Press, 2000. Copyright © 2000 by McGill-Queen's University Press. Reproduced by permission.—Ehre, Milton. From

Thomson Gale Literature Product Advisory Board

The members of the Thomson Gale Literature Product Advisory Board—reference librarians from public and academic library systems—represent a cross-section of our customer base and offer a variety of informed perspectives on both the presentation and content of our literature products. Advisory board members assess and define such quality issues as the relevance, currency, and usefulness of the author coverage, critical content, and literary topics included in our series; evaluate the layout, presentation, and general quality of our printed volumes; provide feedback on the criteria used for selecting authors and topics covered in our series; provide suggestions for potential enhancements to our series; identify any gaps in our coverage of authors or literary topics, recommending authors or topics for inclusion; analyze the appropriateness of our content and presentation for various user audiences, such as high school students, undergraduates, graduate students, librarians, and educators; and offer feedback on any proposed changes/enhancements to our series. We wish to thank the following advisors for their advice throughout the year.

Red Cavalry

Isaak Babel

The following entry presents criticism of Babel's short story collection *Konarmiia* (*Red Cavalry*), which was published in 1926. For discussion of Babel's complete short fiction, see *SSC,* Volume 16.

INTRODUCTION

Regarded as Babel's best work, *Konarmiia* (*Red Cavalry*) is a cycle of thirty-four short stories that initially appeared in periodicals in the Soviet Union between 1923 and 1925. The stories were eventually collected and published in 1926; in 1931, Babel added another story, "Argamak," to a new edition of the book. The pieces in the collection are based on Babel's experiences riding with the Russian Cossacks of the First Cavalry during the Soviet-Polish War of 1920. Diverse in subject matter, these stories are linked through recurring themes of identity, violence, alienation, and morality. *Red Cavalry* is viewed as a major contribution to Soviet literature and Babel's greatest literary achievement.

PLOT AND MAJOR CHARACTERS

Most of the stories in *Red Cavalry* are narrated by Kirill Vasil'evich Liutov, a Jewish intellectual from the south of Russia who joins up with the First Cavalry and serves as a war correspondent during the short, brutal Soviet-Polish War of 1920. Although the stories are not presented in chronological order, they begin in the spring of 1920, when the Poles came to occupy and control the Russian city of Kiev, and continue to the late summer, when Soviet forces were stopped from reaching Warsaw and the First Cavalry was defeated outside of Lvov. As an observer, Liutov records the vicious, ruthless actions of the Cossacks as they sweep across the Polish countryside and encounter two disparate cultures: the Catholics and the Jews. In the opening story, "Perexod cerez Zbruc" ("Crossing the Zbruch"), Liutov juxtaposes the heroic beauty of the Cossack army with the filth and degradation of a Jewish family he is billeted with one night. When he wakes in the morning after a terrible dream, he discovers he has been sleeping next to the corpse of an old man who had been brutally murdered. Babel contrasts the vitality of

revolution and war against the mystery and decay of the Catholic Church in "Kostel v Novograde" ("The Church at Novograd"). When the Cossacks become convinced that the community has hidden valuables in the local Catholic Church, they ransack it. For a moment, the intellectual Liutov is attracted to the Gothic and ornate nature of the surroundings, but rejects the stifling sanctity of the church for the primitive, peripatetic life of a cavalryman.

One of the best-known stories of the collection, "Moj pervyj gus'" ("My First Goose"), finds Liutov struggling to be accepted by the Cossack cavalrymen with whom he is billeted in the house of an old woman. In order to gain their esteem, he brutally kills the old woman's beloved goose and orders her to cook it for them. Although this heartless act earns the approval of the Cossacks, Liutov is haunted by remorse. In "Eskadronnyj Trunov" ("Squadron Commander Trunov"), the Soviet commander of a cavalry unit is killed during a battle with an airplane. As a single man on horseback cannot effectively fight an airplane, critics believe this story signifies the impact of technological progress on human warfare. A deserter who pretends to be deaf in "Ivany" ("Two Ivans") actually becomes deaf after three days of torture at the hands of his guard. "Zizneopisanie Pavlicenki, Matveja Rodionyca" ("The Life of Pavlichenko") chronicles the brutal revenge of Pavlichenko against Nikitinskij, his boss and landowner, for taking advantage of Pavlichenko's wife. After the Russian revolution, Pavlichenko returns to the estate and announces that Lenin has given him the power to kill his former employer. He proceeds to trample him to death, a grotesque scene that borders on black comedy. In "Sol'" ("Salt"), a woman deceives a train full of Cossacks by wrapping a huge lump of salt in blankets and pretending it is a baby. When her deception is revealed, the indignant soldiers throw her off the moving train. When they realize she is unhurt, they shoot and kill her.

MAJOR THEMES

Critics identify the unifying element of *Red Calvary* as the character of Liutov and his search for identity, acceptance, and meaning in a violent, uncaring world. They argue that as a Jew and Soviet sympathizer, the narrator (like Babel himself) is alienated from, but attracted to, the brutal and Darwinian world of the Cossacks, who were known to be anti-Soviet and anti-Semitic. Moreover, as an intellectual, Liutov is unable to fully reconcile himself to the violence and senseless destruction that accompanies warfare. Injustice and discrimination is a key theme of the stories; the numerous pogroms and rampant anti-Semitism, as well as the random and wanton violence perpetrated by the Cossacks, both repels and fascinates Liutov. The impact of war on individuals and society is a major theme in *Red Calvary*. Along with the destruction of human life, critics have pointed to the eradication of spiritual and material culture as a recurring motif in the stories. Feminist critics have focused on the role of women in the tales; some have asserted that, as victims of the idiocy and brutality of men, Babel's female characters engender sympathy for women. The hypocrisy and corruption of organized religion, whether Christianity or Judaism, is another recurring concern in the stories.

CRITICAL RECEPTION

At the time of its publication *Red Cavalry* met with critical controversy. It started with a ferocious condemnation from General Budennyi, who had commanded the First Cavalry during the Soviet-Polish War. In his denunciation Budennyi accused Babel of cowardice, ig-

norance, and the intentional slander of the heroic First Cavalry. As further debate erupted, detractors of Babel's short story collection echoed Budennyi's points, while supporters of the book praised it as an honest and courageous portrayal of the injustices of war. Since that initial controversy, commentators have investigated Babel's use of *skaz* (imitation of spoken storytelling) and his references to oral literature, and traced the parallels between *Red Cavalry* and Babel's *Naplo, 1920* (published 1993; *1920 Diary*). Because of these similarities, many commentators have argued that the stories are autobiographical in nature. The genre of the book has been another topic of critical discussion, with cycle of related stories, episodic novel, prose poem, baroque novel, modern epic all having their proponents. The organization of the stories has been examined; reviewers note that the pieces are not chronologically arranged, but instead placed to gradually reveal Liutov's background, personality, and philosophical maturation. Critics maintain that the events and geography of the stories do not reflect historical reality and that they should be regarded as Babel's artistic interpretation of the truth, contending that the emphasis is not in individual battles or campaigns, but in the dialectical process of history. Some commentators laud Babel's stylistic concern with economy, precision, balance, and detailed imagery. Others underscore his use of words, phrases and syntax typical of the revolutionary period and analyze the intertextuality of the stories, finding allusions to Christian mythology, Russian folk epics, Leo Tolstoy's *War and Peace,* and Nikolai Gogol's *Taras Bulba*. In theme and style, most critics find *Red Cavalry* to be a work of sophisticated maturity and Babel's literary masterpiece.

PRINCIPAL WORKS

Short Fiction

*Rasskazy 1925
Istoriia moei golubiatni 1926
Konarmiia [*Red Cavalry*] 1926
Odesskie rasskazzy [*The Odessa Tales*] 1931
Benya Krik, the Gangster, and Other Stories 1948
The Collected Stories of Isaac Babel 1955
Liubka the Cossack and Other Stories 1963
Chetyre rasskaza 1965
You Must Know Everything: Stories, 1915-1937 1969
Collected Stories 1994

Other Major Works

Korol' (novel) 1926
Zakat [*Sunset*] (play) 1927

Mariia (play) 1935

Isaac Babel: the Lonely Years, 1925-1939 (short stories, letters, essays, and speeches) 1964

I. Babel: Izbrannoe (short stories, plays, autobiography, letters, and speeches) 1966

The Forgotten Prose (short stories and diary excerpts) 1978

Naplo, 1920 [*1920 Diary*] (diary) 1993

The Complete Works of Isaac Babel (short stories, diaries, plays, speeches, and autobiography) 2002

*Expanded editions of this work were published in 1925, 1932, and 1934.

CRITICISM

David A. Lowe (essay date spring 1982)

SOURCE: Lowe, David A. "A Generic Approach to Babel's *Red Cavalry*." *Modern Fiction Studies* 28, no. 1 (spring 1982): 69-78.

[*In the following essay, Lowe explores links between* Red Cavalry *and the Renaissance novella.*]

One would have to search far and wide for a work more emblematic of twentieth-century literary concerns and techniques than Isaak Babel's *Red Cavalry* (*Konarmija*, 1926). The narrator, a revolutionary and an outsider, seeks meaning, purpose, and self-knowledge in a world torn apart by violent upheaval. Adrift in a primordial Darwinian maelstrom, Ljutov has only esthetic irony to rely on as an instrument of cognition. His metaphysics turn on cultural and ethical ambivalence. His insights are evanescent and do not accumulate to form a coherent pattern or system. Significantly, the genre through which Babel explores twentieth-century dilemmas is that of the novella.

A perusal of the substantial body of critical literature devoted to *Red Cavalry* reveals that relatively little attention has been paid to this question of genre. The few critics and scholars who broach the subject do not linger over it, nor do they define their terms. In "Babel's Novella [Novella Babelja]," for instance, Nikolaj Stepanov asserts that in Babel's hands the novella is reduced to a miniature.[1] Here Stepanov may be taking the lead from Babel himself, who called his pieces "miniatures" or "novellas."[2] Neither Babel nor Stepanov, however, tells us precisely what a novella or a miniature is. Fedor Levin, the author of a recent monograph on Babel's works, assures us that Babel is a master of the novella genre.[3] Unfortunately, Levin, too, seems to assume that we all have a clear mental image of the novella in

its Platonically ideal state. Lionel Trilling, frankly admitting his eagerness not to get bogged down in "the problem of definitions," opts out of any serious discussion of genre by labeling Babel's stories "short fictions."[4] Other commentators skirt over the question with silence. Such reticence is all the more quizzical inasmuch as Babel's writings cry out for strict formal analysis. (It is significant, for instance, that seven of the tales that make up *Red Cavalry* were published or republished in the Formalist organ *Lef.*[5]) Moreover, although the Formalists were generally taken with the notion of genre,[6] Stepanov is the only critic to have applied a generic strategy to Babel's prose, with less than satisfactory results. In short, it is quite accurate to say that the question of the genre of the stories in *Red Cavalry* is unresolved. The present article attempts to cast new light on this topic by exploring the many links between Babel's masterpiece and the Renaissance novella.[7]

One of the most obvious traits of the novella is its function as part of a *cycle* of stories. Indeed, as Clements and Gibaldi point out, the typical novella author gave no particular weight to any individual tale; rather, he viewed each one "as a part of a vast tapestry of fiction."[8] The unity of the whole was provided by time, theme, and title (p. 53). Certainly *Red Cavalry* belongs to this tradition. The work is specifically a cycle, although an open-ended one, as both Patricia Carden and Robert Maguire assert.[9] In addition, although the temporal unity in *Red Cavalry* is a function of the historical period being portrayed (the Soviet-Polish War) rather than of the time required for *telling* the stories, still it is interesting to note that Babel considered organizing his tales "by days."[10] Such a diurnal scheme is characteristic of the Renaissance novella. Lastly, the title *Red Cavalry* establishes the same sort of thematic umbrella as does, say, *Canterbury Tales*.

What sets *Red Cavalry* off from the majority of novella collections is the absence of a *frame* or a *cornice*. Such an opening section usually explained the circumstances under which people had gathered together to recount tales. Especially popular was the "disaster cornice," the best known example of which is to be found in Boccaccio's *Decameron*, where escape from the plague serves as a justification for enforced leisure. *Red Cavalry* lacks such a frame, although one might perhaps argue that the opening story, **"Crossing the Zbruch"** [**"Perexod cerez Zbruc"**], fulfills the same function that a cornice would.

Clements and Bigaldi observe that throughout the history of the novella one can see the continuous interaction of literary and oral traditions (p. 8). As they assert, the novella author saw himself as a collector of tales. Thus, for Boccaccio, for instance, a novella could be true or fictional, written or recited (p. 5). We encounter a similar situation in *Red Cavalry*. The mixture of styles there ranges from illiterate *skaz*—an imitation of oral narration (**"Konkin"**)—to inserted letters (**"A Letter"** [**"Pis'mo"**]) to highly ornate authorial speech (**"The Rabbi's Son"** [**"Syn rabbi"**]). Clearly *Red Cavalry* reflects both literary and oral traditions (as does much early twentieth-century Russian experimental prose). Moreover, and this has to do with the notion of the author as a collector or reporter, a comparison of Babel's war diary with the stories contained in *Red Cavalry* reveals the extent to which truth and fiction commingle in Babel's finished literary product.[11]

Another characteristic of the novella, at least in its pre-Cervantes stage of development, is a wide variety of forms. Clements and Gibaldi write: "It is not at all surprising, for instance, to find within a single collection echoes of *fabliau,* chivalric romance, *lai,* beast epic, fable, folktale, fairytale, miracle of the Virgin, and saint's life as well as assorted stories stemming from Biblical, Greco-Roman, Oriental, and historical sources" (p. 14). (Clements and Gibaldi theorize that this variety is probably a function of the novella compiler's awareness of an audience that requires diverse forms of entertainment.) *Red Cavalry* exhibits a similar variegation: first-person authorial accounts (**"Crossing the Zbruch," "My First Goose"** [**"Moj pervyj gus'"**]); *skaz* tales narrated by someone other than Ljutov (**"The Biography of Matvey Rodionych Pavlichenko"** [**"Zizneopisanie Pavlicenki Matveja Rodionyca"**], **"Konkin"**); *skaz* tales in the form of letters (**"A Letter," "Italian Sunshine"** [**"Solnce Italii"**], **"Salt"** [**"Sol'"**], **"Treason"** [**"Izmena"**]); and permutations of the above (**"Berestechko"** [**"Berestecko"**]). In short, the mosaic that *Red Cavalry* comprises is entirely in keeping with Renaissance novella conventions.

It is a cliché of novella criticism that in this genre we see little character development.[12] The novella is populated by flat, static types—no doubt a consequence of the genre's reliance on brevity and plot for its composition. As Clements and Gibaldi suggest, any changes in character are sudden and more in the nature of revolution than evolution (p. 65). The case with *Red Cavalry* is analogous. Stepanov, for instance, states that Babel's characters are conventional and not psychological.[13] Carden concurs.[14]

Although characterization in the novella is severely limited in depth and scope, we do find in novella collections a rich gallery of types—or, more often, stereotypes. Among those enumerated in Clements and Gibaldi's catalogue are the jealous older husband, lively young wife, persistent paramour, magnanimous knight, quick-thinking rogue, lecherous priest, Biblical characters, figures from Classical mythology and ancient history, tragic lovers, comic heroes, simpletons, scamps, rogues, and even contemporary historical figures (pp. 63-90). *Red Cavalry* reveals a similarly luxuriant accumulation of types: violent Cossacks, lecherous priests (**"The Church in Novograd"** [**"Kostel v Novograde"**]), downtrodden Poles, downtrodden Jews, Biblical characters (in **"Pan Apolek"**), roguish artists (**"Pan Apolek"**), rabbis, contemporary historical personages (**"Buddenyj"**), common soldiers, soldiers' wives, cooks, nurses, and so on. In a word, Babel presents us with a colorful cast of nonrounded characters.

The novella is particularly suited to provide glimpses of contemporary society. Indeed, Erich Auerbach considers society the real subject of the novella.[15] And as Clements and Gibaldi remark, the action in a novella is often marked by dynamic interaction, not to say struggle, among varied socioeconomic groups (p. 93). In the Renaissance novella the antagonisms most often at work include man against wife, rich against poor, representatives of the legal system versus law breakers, priests against propriety, and foreigners against native citizens. It would be a mistake, however, to assume that the novella consistently comes down on the side of the insulted and the injured. On the contrary, novella collections are profoundly ambivalent on a number of socioeconomic and cultural issues. Clements and Gibaldi, for instance, come to the conclusion that in the novella one encounters demophobia *and* demophilia, xenophobia *and* xenophilia (p. 109). This notion of the inherent ambivalence of the novella genre will be developed further at the conclusion of this article, when the implications of novella structure are examined.

Certain specific themes that are widespread in novella collections are echoed resoundingly in *Red Cavalry*. Many novella authors took war and warfare as a plot motif. Clements and Gibaldi point out that neither Boccacio nor Chaucer really condemns war, but by the time of Erizzo (*Sei giornate,* 1567), Cinzio (*Ecatommiti,* 1565), and Basile (*Pentamerone,* 1634-36) novelists were anathemizing and satirizing warfare (pp. 122-123). (Incidentally, torture, another form of institutionalized violence, was largely taken for granted by novelists.) *Red Cavalry* focuses on a military campaign, of course; and here Babel seems to embrace the entire novella tradition. Although he at times satirizes the military (see especially **"The Story of a Horse"** [**"Istorija odnoj losadi"**]) and everywhere shows the senseless destruction to which war inevitably leads, Babel stops far short of condemning war outright, particularly inasmuch as it serves as an instrumentality for the Revolution and as a grossly revelatory laboratory of human behavior. Much as one would like to make of Babel an enraged humanist, the text of *Red Cavalry* really does not support such a well-intentioned and comforting interpretation. As James Falen emphasizes, Babel apparently was both repelled *and* fascinated by the violence to which he was a more than willing witness.[16]

Another major topic for novelists is the role and image of women. In general, one must concede that in the vast majority of novellas women appear in a far from favorable light. The unfaithful wife, the concupiscent nun, the inconsolable widow—these are all stock figures. When women are not depicted as vixens and shrews, they are often portrayed as subordinate and subordinated figures. There are exceptions to this strong anti-feminist strain: the most notable is Marguerite de Navarre (*Heptameron,* 1558), who turned the form against itself, so to speak, and portrayed women as intelligent and virtuous.[17] As in the case with warfare, here, too, Babel straddles conflicting novella traditions. Ljutov (**"My First Goose," "Zamoste"**), Balmashev (**"A Letter"**), Levka (**"The Widow"** [**"Vdova"**]), the narrator of **"Treason,"** and most of the other Cossacks to whom we are introduced alternately brutalize women or complacently and wrongly see in them the stereotypical negative traits associated with women in the Renaissance novella. In a manner reminiscent of Marguerite de Navarre, however, Babel turns the tables on his smug male chauvinists. By portraying the macho males in *Red Cavalry* as dangerous dolts, Babel evokes sympathy for women and emerges a feminist author.

Yet another common theme in the novella is the Church, the distinctly antipathetical attitudes toward which originate with Boccaccio and Chaucer. Typical objects of satire include wealthy bishops; avaricious, gluttonous, and randy priests and monks; rapacious nuns; and sham rites, sacraments, and miracles (Clements and Gibaldi pp. 185-197). In this regard such a tale as **"The Church in Novograd"** strikes one as a virtual catalogue of the anti-Church sentiments that one would encounter in the novella. Babel, however, expands the attack on empty, hypocritical, or stagnant religion to include Judaism as well (**"The Rabbi"**). Moreover, just as the Renaissance novella may be interpreted as an attempt to humanize the Church, so in such figures as Pan Apolek and Sandy-the-Christ [**"Saska-Xristos"**] Babel confronts us with blasphemy and sacrilege as liberating moments.

Clements and Gibaldi note that the novella offers a generous catalogue of prejudicial portraits of several nationalities and races (p. 109). The novella is rife with anti-Semitism (particularly in Chaucer and Ser Giovanni Fiorentino), but, in general, foreigners as such are perceived as unsavory and seditious types. Much of the action of *Red Cavalry* turns on precisely such stereotypical prejudices. It is primarily the Jews, of course, who serve as targets for patriotic xenophobes. Jews are slaughtered (**"Crossing the Zbruch," "The Cemetery at Kozin"** [**"Kladbisce v Kozine"**], **"Berestechko"**), accused of treason (**"Treason"**), and generally viewed as pariahs (**"My First Goose"**). Significantly, the narrator's own attitude toward his native culture and religion is not without profound ambiguities. In addition, it might be argued that the portrait of the Cossacks in *Red Cavalry* is highly biased. Certainly Budennyj thought so.[18]

Lastly, a major theme in novella collections is law and justice. The collection in which this is most apparent is the *Gesta Romanorum,* whose narratives feature such titles as "Of the Conflicting Aims of Mercy and Justice," "Story of the Bell of Justice," "How a Certain Lawgiver Induced the People to Abide by His Laws," and so on.[19] Leaving aside the *Gesta,* however, one finds that in the novella tradition judges, lawyers, and officers of the law are generally, if not always, discredited.[20] Clements and Gibaldi write: "In the novella center stage is given to the ambitious, ignorant, greedy, dishonest, servile, concupiscent lawgivers" (p. 163). Many of the tales in *Red Cavalry* also turn on questions of justice—or more often, injustice. Consider, for example, the numerous stories of revenge: **"A Letter," "The Biography of Matvey Rodionych Pavlichenko," "Prishchepa"** [**"Priscepa"**], **"The Story of a Horse," "Afonka Bida," "The Ivans"** [**"Ivany"**]. Examples of gross injustice are too obvious even to need mention. The whole issue of law and justice is crystallized in two tales: **"Gedali"** and **"Berestechko."** Gedali, who believes in the ideals of the Revolution, fails to find any real difference between Revolution and Counter-Revolution in practice. The story **"Berestechko"** concludes with one of the most hideously ironic pronouncements in the entire collection. After the city has been sacked and vandalized, the citizenry demoralized, the Commissar tells the assembled throng: "You are the power. Everything that's here is yours. There are no masters. I will now proceed to the election of a Revolutionary Committee . . . [Vy—vlast'. Vse, cto zdes'—vase. Net panov. Pristupaju k vyboram Revkoma . . .]."[21] These passages show clearly the difference between the treatment of law and justice in the novella and in Babel's *Red Cavalry.* The novella tradition generally assumes the presence of a wise ruler à la Solomon or the existence of natural law which "cannot be abrogated to encourage villainy" (p. 149). In *Red Cavalry,* on the contrary, whatever notion of justice is found there is strictly utilitarian and can be perceived only by someone who places the triumph of the Revolution above any other concerns.

Having established thematic links between *Red Cavalry* and the novella, we are now in a position to go on to address the formal question of novella structure. Perhaps the primary structural characteristic of the novella, other than its brevity, is its emphasis on plot or situation, with the weight of the narrative concentrated on the build-up to an unexpected ending. In this regard Eikhenbaum has likened the novella to "a single equation with one unknown" or to "a riddle."[22] Scherer, perhaps drawing on Petrovskij, identifies four compositional moments in the novella: exposition, entanglement, climax, and denouement.[23] Many of the tales in *Red Cavalry* adhere to just this sort of compositional scheme. As Carden has observed, at the center of every Babel story is an act.[24] In a variation on this notion,

Maguire writes that "most of the stories end in sudden clearings of an atmosphere that has thickened and charged itself to such a point that it can hold nothing more. And this sudden clearing yields a meaning—often underplayed, but always surprising."[25] Significantly, in Babel's rough drafts we find him writing: "Short. Dramatic. Very simple, setting forth the facts without superfluous descriptions."[26] Such an approach is preeminently that of a novelist.

The fact that Babel's stories often turn on sheer narrative interest has not always received sufficient attention. Sidetracked by the haunting imagery and the moral questions raised in the tales, we tend to forget that on the structural level the stories are usually guided by a question mark, as it were: what will happen next? How will the situation be resolved? Why does the narrator seem to recognize the portrait of John the Baptist in **"Pan Apolek"**? How will Ljutov gain the Cossacks' respect in **"My First Goose"**? What has happened to Afonka Bida in the eponymous tale? This sort of situational tension lies at the heart of any novella.

Not all the stories in **Red Cavalry** turn on plot as such, of course. Stepanov argues, for instance, that for Babel plot is not situational (sobitijnaja).[27] Here Stepanov is overstating the case (just as Carden overstates it in asserting that an act stands at the center of every Babel tale), but Stepanov goes on to say that in Babel's narrations situational plot is replaced by linguistic or imagistic intrigue.[28] Certainly this is true in a number of stories. If we take such a seemingly plotless sketch as **"Teaching about the Tachanka"** [**"Ucenie o tacanke"**], for instance, we find that the tension there lies in the images and their resolution. Eventually we understand that the two kinds of carts are being compared with two types of Jewish communities and that the point of the whole story is the illusory quality of surface appearances. Similarly, in **"Crossing the Zbruch"** much of the uneasiness arises from the interplay of imagery: the sun that resembles a lopped-off head, the dream about the brigadier commander being shot. These images of death create a sense of eerie mystery that is both dispelled and intensified when the narrator realizes that the old man with whom he is sharing a bed is dead, murdered at the hands of the Poles. In such cases Babel has estheticized the genre of the novella by displacing sheer plot interest onto mood, imagery, and language. In all other ways, however, the mechanics of exposition, entanglement, climax, and denouement remain in force. Even the estheticized tales still turn on a surprise resolution.

Clements and Gibaldi observe that throughout the history of the novella one finds a tug of war between utility and recreation (pp. 8-9). In other words, the novella author may view his narrations as pure entertainment or as moral edification or as both. The conflict here is between the esthetic and ethical planes. What critics and scholars do not emphasize, however, is the necessary primacy of the esthetic moment. After all, the novella by definition must build to a surprise denouement, point, or resolution, but surprise is an esthetic concept, not an ethical one. Of course the novella may be used for didactic purposes, but one need only examine the moralizing commentaries to the stories in *Gesta Romanorum,* for instance, to see how utterly and incredibly arbitrary such treatments can be. The following excerpt should serve as persuasive evidence:

Tale LVIII

Of Confession

A certain king, named Asmodeus, established an ordinance, by which every malefactor taken and brought before the judge should, if he distinctly declared three truths, against which no exception could be taken, obtain his life and property. It chanced that a certain soldier transgressed the law and fled. He hid himself in a forest, and there committed many atrocities, despoiling and slaying whomever he could lay his hands upon. When the judge of the district ascertained his haunt, he ordered the forest to be surrounded, and the soldier to be seized and brought bound to the seat of judgment. "You know the law," said the judge. "I do," returned the other: "if I declare three unquestionable truths, I shall be free; but if not, I must die." "True," replied the judge; "take then advantage of the law's clemency, or this very day you shall not taste food until you are hanged." "Cause silence to be kept," said the soldier. His wish being complied with, he proceeded in the following manner:—"The first truth is this: I protest before ye all, that from my youth up I have been a bad man." The judge, hearing this, said to the bystanders, "He says true?" They answered, "Else, he had not now been in this situation." "Go on then," said the judge; "what is the second truth?" "I like not," exclaimed he, "the dangerous situation in which I stand." "Certainly," said the judge, "we may credit thee. Now then for the third truth, and thou hast saved thy life." "Why," he replied, "if I once get out of this confounded place, I will never willingly reenter it." "Amen," said the judge, "thy wit hath preserved thee; go in peace." And thus he was saved.

Application

My beloved, the emperor is Christ. The soldier is any sinner; the judge is a wise confessor. If the sinner confess the truth in such a manner as not even demons can object, he shall be saved—that is, if he confess and repent.[29]

The moral application is lame, because the tale is open to absolutely contradictory interpretations. One could argue that it excuses rape and murder, or that it shows the inefficacy of the emperor's legal system, or that it implicitly condemns craft and cleverness. The possibilities are nearly endless as long as one insists on putting the story into any sort of ethical framework. The point is that because of the primacy of esthetic considerations—surprise, cleverness, wit—novella collections seem so ambivalent on so many points. The "moral" lesson of any one novella may be quite contravened by other tales in the same collection. Note, for instance, that the novellas comprising the Sixth Day of Boccaccio's *Decameron* share the common motif of the guilty escaping punishment, whereas all the stories for the First Day tell of wickedness punished or rebuked. The esthetic takes precedence over the ethical.

Esthetic considerations take the upper hand in *Red Cavalry,* too. Hence the profound ambivalence that Falen stresses.[30] Indeed, any attempt to hang any *single* ethical or judgmental shingle on Babel's work is misguided. Budennyj and Grigorij Svirskij view *Red Cavalry* as an anti-Soviet piece, but for the former that is a negative assessment, while for Svirskij it represents a positive one.[31] Both commentators are wrong all the way around, however; or perhaps it would be more accurate to say that they are telling only partial truths. Taken as a totality, *Red Cavalry* is pro-Soviet and anti-Soviet, pro-Semitic and anti-Semitic, pro-Cossack and anti-Cossack, and so on *ad infinitum.* All such ethical categories are useless for interpreting Babel's cycle of tales, however, because the stories are conceived in an esthetic framework rather than an ethical one.

To conclude, Babel's *Red Cavalry* represents a twentieth-century version of a Renaissance novella cycle. The twentieth-century aspects of Babel's work include the narrator's occasionally ornate style (alien to the novella tradition of stylistic simplicity) and the use of the grotesque (particularly in regard to eros). In these respects, Babel has super-estheticized the genre of the novella. In other ways, however—brevity, objectivity, characterization, thematic concerns, and narrative structure—*Red Cavalry* demonstrates a remarkable affinity with Renaissance novella collections. Taking note of this generic link may help forestall discussions of *Red Cavalry* that rely on concepts and language that have no real application to the novella, wherein ethical and metaphysical notions—and hence didacticism—are necessarily superseded by esthetic considerations and exigencies. In a sense, all of *Red Cavalry* is about the twentieth-century rift between ethics and esthetics. Therefore, it is only natural that Babel should couch such a theme in the genre where this divorce was first made plain—the Renaissance novella.[32]

Notes

1. Nikolaj Stepanov, "Novella Babelja," in *I. E. Babel'; stat'i i materialy* (Leningrad: Academia, 1928), p. 14.

2. See Patricia Carden, *The Art of Isaac Babel* (Ithaca, NY: Cornell University Press, 1972), p. 49.

3. Fedor M. Levin, *I. Babel'; ocerk tvorcestva* (Moscow: Khudozh. lit. 1972), p. 141.

4. Lionel Trilling, *Beyond Culture: Essays on Literature and Learning* (New York: Viking Press, 1965), quoted in Carden, p. 49.

5. The stories published or republished in *Lef* were "Pis'mo," "Nacal'nik konzapasa," "Moj pervyj gus'," "Smert' Dolguseva," "Kombrig dva," "Priscepa," and "Sol'."

6. See Victor Erlich, *Russian Formalism* (The Hague: Mouton, 1969), pp. 122, 123, 125, 149, 235, 244, 246-247, 253, 262, 268, and 271.

7. It should be made clear that for the purposes of this article "novella" will be used to refer solely to that genre of short fiction, primarily but not exclusively Italian, that flourished from the early fourteenth century until the early seventeenth. Unless limited to that usage, the term, in fact, becomes meaningless because it can be applied to authors as far apart in time, space, and temperament as Boccaccio, Chaucer, Storm, Keller, Chekhov, and Hemingway. The best single study of the genre, a book from which I will be quoting liberally, is Robert Clements and Joseph Gibaldi, *Anatomy of the Novella* (New York: New York University Press, 1977).

8. Robert Clements and Joseph Gibaldi, p. 20. Further references will be indicated parenthetically within the text.

9. Carden, p. 49; Robert Maguire, *Red Virgin Soil* (Princeton, NJ: Princeton University Press, 1968), p. 348.

10. See Carden, p. 43.

11. See I. A. Smirin, "Na puti k 'Konarmii,'" *Literaturnoe nasledstvo,* 74 (1965), 474-482, 497-482; also L. Livsic, "Materialy k tvorceskoj biografii I. Babelja," *Voprosy literatury,* No. 4 (1964), pp. 110-135. For a discussion in English, see James Falen, *Isaac Babel: Russian Master of the Short Story* (Knoxville: University of Tennessee Press, 1974), p. 150ff.

12. See Clements and Gibaldi, p. 62; Janet M. Ferrier, *Forerunners of the French Novel* (Manchester: Manchester University Press, 1934), p. 1.

13. Stepanov, p. 17.

14. Carden, p. 34.

15. Erich Auerbach, *Zur Technik der Frührenaissancenovella in Italien und Frankreich* (Heidelberg: C. Winter University Verlag, 1971), p. 1.

16. Falen, p. 152.

17. For more on this point, see Chapter II of Ferrier's *Forerunners of the French Novel.*

18. In "Babizm Babelja," *Oktjabr'*, No. 3 (1925), pp. 196-197, General Budennyj accused Babel of slandering the Cossacks and the Red Army in *Red Cavalry*.

19. *Gesta Romanorum,* translated and edited by Charles Swan, revised and corrected by Wynnard Hooper (1894; rpt. London: AMS Press, 1970).

20. There is an echo of this tradition in the seventeenth-century Russian tale "Semjakin sud."

21. Isaak Babel, *Konarmija* (Moscow-Leningrad: Gos. izd., 1928), p. 93.

22. Boris Éjxenbaum, "O. Genri i teorija novelly," *Literatura* (Leningrad: Priboj, 1927), p. 67.

23. Olga Scherer, *The Modern Polish Short Story* (The Hague: Mouton, 1955), p. 6. Scherer's terminology is quite close to formulations in Mixail Petrovskij, "Morfologija novelly," *Ars poetica* (Moscow: GAKhN, 1927), I.

24. Carden, p. 36.

25. Maguire, p. 346.

26. Quoted in Carden, p. 42.

27. Stepanov, p. 33.

28. Stepanov, p. 33.

29. *Gesta Romanorum,* pp. 99-100.

30. Falen, p. 160ff.

31. Grigorij Svirskij, *Russkaja literatura nravstvennogo soprotivlenija* (London: OPI, 1979), pp. 88-92.

32. The role of the Renaissance novella in Russian literature has not been much studied. Among the few works devoted to the question are O. A. Derzavina, *Facecii* (Moscow: AN SSSR, 1962); I. P. Grossman, "Iskusstvo anekdota u Puskina," *Ét-judy o Puskine* (Moscow: Izd. L. D. Frenkel, 1923); and Vaclaw Lednicki, *Bits of Table Talk on Pushkin, Mickiewicz, Goethe, Turgenev, and Sienkiewicz* (The Hague: Mouton, 1956).

Gareth Williams (essay date April 1984)

SOURCE: Williams, Gareth. "The Rhetoric of Revolution in Babel's *Konarmija*." *Russian Literature* 15, no. 3 (April 1984): 279-98.

[*In the following essay, Williams investigates the influence of revolutionary propaganda and language on the stories of* Red Cavalry.]

The **Konarmija** stories are told against the background of the Polish-Soviet war of 1919-20.[1] The military engagements described took place in the period from 3 June 1920 (**"Konkin"**), when the 1st Cavalry Army broke through the Polish lines at Belaja cerkov', to 31 August 1920 (**"Zamost'e"**), when the **Konarmija** were caught in the "Zamość ring".[2] However, **"Konkin"** and **"Zamost'e"** are not the first and last stories respectively. Babel' seems to have had no interest in describing the campaign of the 1st Cavalry Army as a sequence of historical events. Although the stories form a cycle which was carefully arranged by Babel'[3] it is impossible to ascertain from the stories the main events and the main tactical and strategical considerations of the campaign, either from the Polish or from the Soviet side. While there are many scenes of violence, there are few descriptions of battle.

Ever since the book first appeared critics have assumed that the author put the centre of gravity of the cycle as a whole in the figure of Ljutov, the narrator of most of the stories.[4] It has been argued that the need to reveal gradually various aspects of Ljutov's character and philosophy dictated important aspects of the structure of individual stories[5] and of the cycle as a whole. R. Grøngaard, for example, says that Ljutov in **Konarmija** is "both the centripetal and centrifugal force of the composition".[6]

Since Ljutov is a bespectacled Jewish intellectual, a war correspondent writing for *Krasnyj kavalerist,* the newspaper published by the political section of the 1st Cavalry Army, he bears an external resemblance to Babel' and many critics have assumed that Babel' and Ljutov are virtually one and the same person. From this point of view, the events of the Polish-Soviet war are violent stimuli which are important because of the reaction they cause in Babel'/Ljutov but are not important thematic elements in themselves. Polonskij, for example, says that the picture which Babel' gives does not resemble historical reality and that the book is about the author himself, who is the main hero.[7]

The picture which emerges of Babel''s artistic stance is close to that of a lyric poet.[8] His main concern is not with surrounding reality but with his reactions as a poet to reality, which he wants to express in a form, the self-sufficient unity of which will create a buoyant vessel on the ocean of time. The sea-worthiness of this vessel is all-important; if it is well built, it will eventually reach its aim, the reader. The reader is essentially a distant concept, and perhaps not altogether necessary; Babel' might say to his reader, as Lermontov did: "It is not to you, it is to my heart that I am speaking". Babel''s intense concern with economy, precision, balance and polish of style, with creating a surface in which no joins can be seen, reinforces such an impression.

There are elements in **Konarmija,** particularly the story **"Pan Apolek"**, which seem to indicate that Babel' was trying either to redeem the ugliness of reality by turning it into a beautiful work of art[9] or to find beauty in the very essence of ugliness, bestiality and cruelty.[10] The presence of these elements, combined with the various ways in which the author or Ljutov can be seen as of central importance, has tended to lead to a lack of interest in or a lack of attention to the revolution as a theme in *Konarmija* and as one of the determining factors in Babel''s attitude towards the events described. It is the purpose of this article to correct this situation.

The revolution enters the *Konarmija* stories as material from the first words of the first story: "The commander of the sixth division (*načdiv šest'*) reported that Novograd-Volynsk had been taken at dawn today".[11] Here we have an indication both of the abolition of the old Tsarist ranks and of the new passion for business-like abbreviations. The second story, **"Kostel v Novo-grade"**, also contains an abbreviation of this type, *voenkom,* "military commander", in its first sentence. Such words abound in the *Konarmija* stories: *glavkom* (118), *pitpunkt* (139), *načpodiv* (142), *politotdel* (149) etc. These abbreviations may add a certain amount of colour to the speech and writings of the Cossacks (*urevkom* for example in the letter of Chlebnikov to Savickij), and thus represent an element of characterization of the Cossacks, but they are met most frequently in the speech and thoughts of the narrator, Ljutov. These neologisms are not singled out for special attention by devices of contrast, in the manner of Pil'njak, nor are they explained, as though they were exotic. They are used completely neutrally, as though they had always been a part of the author's vocabulary. The way these names are used is a symptom of the fact that the narrator has accepted the new realities created by the revolution. The manner of their use also indicates an assumption that the reader has been affected in the same way.

A law of eccentricity operates in the prose of Babel'. Words, phrases and syntax typical of the revolutionary period are frequently used in a slightly unsuitable context or in a deformed manner. In the story **"Izmena"**, for example, the cavalryman Balmašev describes the doctor Javejn as an animal (*zver'*—135) because the doctor told Balmašev and his wounded comrades to take off their equipment and their clothes and have a bath. Balmašev regards Javejn as an enemy of the revolution because he makes the perfectly reasonable request that the three soldiers, on entering the hospital, should have a bath, and he uses the vituperation typical of revolutionary propaganda when he calls Javejn an animal. In the context the strength of the condemnation is ludicrous, as is the conclusion of his exhortation to the other wounded to maintain their revolutionary vigilance: "But my words bounced off the heroic infantry like sheep droppings off the regimental drum" (136-37). The word "heroic" is used by Balmašev as a stock epithet, he intends no irony by it, but in the context of the contented life of the draughts-playing patients in the

hospital and the simile which is used it appears to be incongruous and one seems to see the ironic smile of Babel'.

The same Nikita Balmašev tells the story **"Sol'"**. Here again the influence of revolutionary propaganda on Balmašev's vocabulary can be seen both in appropriate and inappropriate settings. Balmašev describes how a Cavalry Army "meritorious" (*zaslužennyj*) train stops at the "inveterate" (*zakorenelyj*) railway station of Fastov, which is crowded with petty traders (94). A woman gets on carrying a babe in arms and is treated courteously by the Cossacks. In the morning Balmašev, suspicious because the child has not cried, tears off the swaddling clothes and sees a huge lump of salt. The woman is obviously a speculator, one of the many who traded in salt, butter and other commodities in short supply, but Balmašev reproaches her mainly because she deceived the Cossacks and escaped rape. He pushes her off the train, but she is unharmed:

> And seeing this woman unharmed, and inexpressible (*neskazannuju*) Russia around her, and the peasant fields without an ear of corn, and the girls we had raped, and my comrades, who go a lot to the front but not many come back, I wanted to jump down and kill myself or kill her.

(97)

The mixed vocabulary and mixed motives of Balmašev are incongruous and funny, yet the reader approves when Balmašev shoots the woman, an action which is suggested to him by the other Cossacks and which therefore has communal approval. Balmašev signs his letter: "In the name of all the fighting men of the second company" (97) and one feels that Babel' could well be among those "fighting men".

One of the ways in which Balmašev gains the reader's approval is through his vocabulary and his rhetoric. The words from revolutionary propaganda which he employs may not be used à propos, but the very awkwardness of the way in which they are used seems a proof of the sincerity of Balmašev's belief that these words have an efficacious meaning. Contrary to Horace's dictum,[12] Babel''s "skilful setting" does not "make a well-known word new"; on the contrary, the worn-out nature of the word is particularly noticeable in a fresh setting. Nevertheless, the contrast between the word and its setting is an indication of the hold which this word has on Balmašev's imagination, it shows that for him the word has meaning, even if he has not yet assimilated it fully.

In the revolutionary period much use was made of words which indicated that the revolution was bringing an enormous change, on an unprecedented world-wide scale. In Lenin's first speech at the Second Congress of the Third Communist International (one of Lenin's speeches at this Congress is read out by Ljutov to the Cossacks in **"Moj pervyj gus'"**) he says: "War has brought an unheard-of (*neslychannoe*) exacerbation of the contradictions of capitalism".[13] In his speech to the First All-Russia Congress of Soviets 3-24 June 1917 Lenin uses two such words side by side: "The Soviets are an unheard-of, unprecedentedly strong (*neslychannoe, nevidannoe v mire po sile*) representative institution" (XXXII, 275). In his "Literary Notes", 28 December 1921 Furmanov remarked: "If you read Lenin's speeches you won't find one without the word *neslychannyj*". He notes that other orators, under the influence of Lenin, are using the word more and more frequently.[14] In **"Česniki"** Vorošilov uses the word *nebyvalyj* (139), which is also typical of the revolutionary era. Balmašev introduces his own variant on these words. Instead of *nevidannyj* and *neslychannyj* he uses the word *neskazannyj* to describe Russia, and a conventional poetic epithet seems to acquire a genuinely revolutionary sound,[15] while much of the pathos of the expression derives from the eccentric way in which it is used.

The rhetoric which Balmašev directs against the woman when he first discovers that the "child" is salt is a fine example of revolutionary rhetoric. He tells the woman that he will forgive her:

> But turn to the Cossacks, woman, who elevated you as a working mother in the republic. Turn to these two maidens, who are crying at the moment because of what they suffered during the night. Turn to our wives in the wheat-laden Kuban', who are filled with a woman's strength but have no husbands, and those husbands being just as lonely are forced to rape girls who pass in their life ‹. . .› Turn to Russia, crushed by pain.
>
> (96)

The style of Balmašev's outburst reflects that of his favourite, perhaps only reading, the newspaper *Krasnyj kavalerist,* which he mentions in **"Izmena"**. The word "to crush" or "strangle" (*zadavit'*) is frequently met on its pages. Its leading article, *"učites', tovarišči"*, Saturday 7 August 1920, signed by "Artem Kubanec", says that baron Vrangel' "wants to strangle (*zadavit'*) us with his dirty hands". The anaphora of turn . . . turn . . . is also typical of *Krasnyj kavalerist,* whose main leader-writer, I. Vardin, the *načpoarm* of the 1st Cavalry Army, writes in a style reminiscent of that of Lenin. The word repeated by Balmašev is the key word. Balmašev will forgive her, but the Cossacks, the wives, suffering Russia, to whom she should turn, will not. The repetition of the key word, "turn!" is like the blows of a hammer, as Cejtlin says of Lenin's use of anaphora.[16] In the leading article of *Krasnyj kavalerist,* 12 August 1920, "Почему my idem 'za-granicu'?" Vardin asks: "Of what frontier are we speaking? Of the frontier which was drawn by Tsars, kings, generals, ministers.

Of the frontier created by ravishers and oppressors of the people. Of the frontier which the emperors of Austria and Russia drew between peoples". Balmašev's rhetoric is obviously influenced by his reading, but the eccentric element of it is that he is asking for the woman to apologize, amongst other things, for not having allowed the Cossacks to rape her. Balmašev uses a rhetoric designed to be directed against rape and violence while he accepts rape and violence as a necessary part of the Cossacks' present position.

Balmašev's speech is extremely colourful. Šklovskij once said: "Clever Babel' knows how to justify the beauty of his productions with irony introduced in time".[17] The incongruities of Balmašev's speech do create ironic effects, but that irony does not call into question Balmašev's belief in the cause of the revolution, on the contrary, it underlines the genuine nature of Balmašev's belief. The rhetoric of the revolution has entered Balmašev and is now an essential element in the way he looks at life.

The story which follows **"Sol'"**, **"Večer",** seems to have nothing in common with it except its setting, a train. Galin, one of the contributors to the newspaper *Krasnyj kavalerist,* talks to a laundress, Irina, about the deaths of Russian Tsars. He loves her. She goes to bed with the cook, Vasilij, and while they make love the wall-eyed Galin talks to Ljutov about the need to give political education to the freedom-loving Cossacks. One theme of the story is Galin's ability to conquer his own feelings and submerge them in the common cause. Babel' also indicates the paradox that someone who fights for universal happiness cannot even achieve his own personal happiness, while the cook Vasilij, who despises humanity, achieves personal happiness, The link with **"Sol'"** does not emerge directly from either of these themes. The link is that both Galin and Balmašev are acting in a revolutionary manner under the influence of revolutionary theories. Their personal qualities and their educational backgrounds have resulted in their reaching different stages of development in their understanding of those theories, but they both, in their own way, are contributing actively to the revolution. Balmašev commits an act which is little more than banditry; nevertheless the totality of many such acts does help to create a revolution. His action is the physical expression of his urge to create a revolution. Galin, by sublimating his love for Irina in his work for *Krasnyj kavalerist,* which, says Babel', is "a dynamite fuse put underneath the army" (98), also contributes to the revolution, but in a way which will direct anarchic demonstrations of class hatred into an organized destruction of class-based society. Galin's last words in the story are: "The Cavalry Army is a social focus created by the Central Committee of our party. The arc of the revolution has thrown into the front-line freedom-loving Cossacks steeped in many prejudices but the Central Committee in a flexible manoeuvre will comb them through with an iron comb" (100).

The class hatred of the Cossacks is most vividly shown in **"Žizneopisanie Pavličenki, Matveja Rodionyča"**. Pavličenko works as a cowman for a landowner called Nikitinskij, who seduces Pavličenko's wife. After the revolution Pavličenko returns and kills Nikitinskij very slowly, by trampling on him. This horrible death is given in an almost vaudeville manner by Babel'. Pavličenko's wife, now completely mad, is striding about the room with a drawn sabre, wearing a velvet crown decorated with feathers. Pavličenko reads out to Nikitinskij what he calls "a letter from Lenin": "In the name of the people and in order to found a future happy life I order Pavličenko, Matvej Rodionyč, to deprive various people of their lives as he sees fit" (79). Pavličenko, who cannot read, is pretending to read Lenin's order from what is in fact a blank sheet of paper. The scene is grotesque, and becomes more grotesque in retrospect after the hour-long trampling to death of Nikitinskij. The "letter from Lenin" seems a savage joke. There is, however, a connection between Lenin and Pavličenko's torture of his former landowner. It is only after the revolution that Pavličenko takes his revenge, despite the fact that the original wrong took place long before the revolution. The connection is made more clearly in a story by E. Ščadenko, "Načdiv 6",[18] which tells the story of Apanasenko, the real-life original of Pavličenko, commander of the sixth division, to which Babel' was assigned. In this story, when Apanasenko takes his revenge on the landowner he says to him: "If we don't catch you, you'll catch us tomorrow . . . And this is class war . . . I'll tell you straight, I'm killing you in the name of the people".[19] The revolution made Pavličenko realize the extent of the insult done to him and the way he should avenge it, but whereas Ščadenko tries to justify what was in effect murder Babel', with his usual eccentricity, accentuates the savage elemental violence in Pavličenko's action and thus brings out the fact that revolutions are made not by good people but by people made savage and embittered by want and repression. Such people are the weapons of revolution, and they are taught in which direction to fire by the leaders, such as Lenin, who lack their burning class hatred and have more distant aims.

Ever since the well-known letter of Budennyj to *Pravda* in 1928 Babel' has been depicted as someone who was horrified and repelled by the violence of the revolution. Budennyj asked Gor'kij to agree with him that:

> To describe this heroic class struggle which is unprecedented in all human history one must first of all understand the essence of this struggle and the nature of the classes, that is, one must be a dialectical and Marxist artist, even if one is not completely conscious of one's aims. But Babel' is neither the one nor the other.[20]

Groznova notes the "militant non-receptivity of the artist to the complexities of the revolution".[21] This is not my view. The actions of such men as Pavličenko and Priščepa (in **"Priščepa"**) are not just blind acts of violence, as Struve maintains.[22] They are acts conditioned by the class-consciousness of Pavličenko and Priščepa and as such are completely in accordance with Marxist thinking on the development of the individual consciousness. Babel' shows that a revolution cannot take place without people such as Pavličenko and Priščepa. Babel' accepts such a revolution and can look beyond it. Pavličenko begins his "biography" with a call to his countrymen, comrades and dear brothers to "take cognizance in the name of humanity of the biography of the Red general Matvej Pavličenko" (76). The tone is mocking and throw-away, but why does this Red general tell his story if it is not to inspire others in the struggle against the Poles, which is being waged "in the name of Humanity"? This is the context in which he makes his confession, as part of a revolutionary movement which is gradually becoming more and more organized, as Pavličenko realizes with some regret for his favourite year, 1918 (78).

The two stories which are most frequently quoted to illustrate Ljutov's (and therefore Babel''s) inability to accept the violence which must accompany a revolution are **"Moj pervyj gus'"** and **"Gedali"**.

In **"Moj pervyj gus'"** Ljutov is billeted in a homestead which belongs to an old woman. The Cossack cavalrymen who are also billeted in the homestead only accept him as an equal after he has killed a goose and ordered the old woman to cook it. Ljutov and the five Cossacks sleep together in the hay-loft afterwards. Ljutov has gained acceptance by the Cossacks, but he seems to feel remorse: "My heart, bloodied by murder, creaked and leaked" (56). The words "creaked and leaked" refer back to the way the goose's head was described as he crunched it under his heel. The moral seems obvious. Ljutov, in order to gain acceptance by the Cossacks, has committed a crime. He feels repentance for committing the crime. If he feels repentance for killing a goose, how can he not feel repentance for killing a man? In a revolution, men must be killed. If Ljutov cannot kill, how can he make a revolution? The formal logic of these propositions seems irrefutable. There is, however, another thematic line in **"Moj pervyj gus'"** which makes such logic irrelevant.

When Ljutov reports his arrival to the divisional commander, Savickij, Savickij asks him whether he can read. Ljutov replies that he is a graduate in jurisprudence. Savickij makes mocking comments on Ljutov's puny stature and glasses and mentions that here people get their throats cut because they wear glasses. The quartermaster who takes Ljutov to the homestead repeats this fact. After the Cossacks have shown their dislike for him Ljutov settles down in the yard some way from the Cossacks and reads Lenin's speech at the Second Congress of the Third Communist International in *Pravda*. The Cossacks try to annoy him and he has difficulty in concentrating on what Lenin is saying. He gets up and kills the goose. Shortly afterwards the Cossacks admit him into their circle (they are sitting in a circle around a fire). So far, all the movement of the story, both physical and psychological, has been going in the direction from Ljutov to the Cossacks. The Cossacks have resisted this motion. Now they accept Ljutov and the motion flows from the Cossacks to Ljutov. They offer him pork to eat, thus implicitly recognizing that his Jewishness is no barrier between them, they offer him a spoon, they ask him what is in the newspaper. It was obvious from Savickij's first question to Ljutov that most of the Cossacks could not read. Not only could they not read, they felt hostility towards all intellectuals—people with glasses. Now they listen as Ljutov reads them Lenin's speech. As Ljutov reads to them he rejoices and follows the path of "the secret arc of Lenin's straight line" (56). The final words spoken are by Surovkov, the eldest of the Cossacks: "'Truth tickles every nose' said Surovkov when I had finished, 'but how do you pull it out of the pile of rubbish? But he hits it without fail, like a chicken pecking corn'" (56).

Surovkov has moved from hostility to all intellectuals to acceptance of one particular intellectual, Ljutov, and recognition that what Lenin says in this speech is the truth. Ljutov has achieved what he was urged to do in every issue of *Krasnyj kavalerist*. He has read a newspaper to people who cannot read and he has explained to them in simple terms the essence of the Bolshevik point of view. He has achieved this by doing what was condemned in almost every issue of *Krasnyj kavalerist*, by robbing the civilian population. His killing of the goose may be a crime against the instincts of a man with a traditional Jewish background but it is also a crime against the revolution, one that would be severely punished if it was discovered.[23] Through this crime he has gained acceptance by the Cossacks, whose instincts lead them to commit such crimes. By gaining influence over the Cossacks and introducing them to a Bolshevik way of thinking he is aiding a process which should lead to their becoming conscious (*soznatel'nye*) Bolsheviks who will not commit such crimes.

The speech which Ljutov quotes begins: "We are short of everything" (56). Ljutov is simplifying the speech a little. Lenin made six speeches at this congress, which took place from 19 July-7 August 1920. Ljutov is quoting from the fourth speech. In response to a remark by Krispin that it would be difficult to create a revolution in Germany because the standard of living of workers was higher than it was in Russia, Lenin admitted that the standard of living of Russian workers had fallen since the revolution, but he emphasized that this was purely a temporary phenomenon. Sacrifices had to be made in the present to achieve victory in the future. A paragraph later Lenin talks of the possibility that terror may have to be used against the German capitalists. Again this will be purely a temporary measure (XLI, 250-51). We are not certain how much Ljutov read to the Cossacks or in what ways he simplified it. But the basic position Lenin adopts, which presumably was conveyed by Ljutov, is that if there are difficulties, they must be overcome. This is his straight line. They must be overcome even if one has to do things which run counter to one's principles (lowering the standard of living of workers, terrorizing the civilian population) in order that the greater good of an eventual workers' state may prevail. This is the arc which Ljutov follows, rejoicing. Ljutov's position in accepting the commission of a crime against the people he is supposed to be saving from tyranny is that the end does justify the means. He is thinking dialectically, and the Aristotelian logic of the propositions mentioned earlier is not relevant to the processes which he envisages.

Gedali, in the story of that name, is a Jew who has been blinded by the Poles. His story immediately precedes **"Moj pervyj gus'"**.

Gedali cannot understand why he suffers both at the hands of the Poles and at the hands of the Red Army. His reasoning runs like this: "Good deeds are done by good men. The revolution is a good deed of good men. But good men do not kill. Therefore the revolution is done by evil people" (51). Gedali (the word in Hebrew means "wisdom")[24] is combining here two syllogisms: 1) Good deeds are done by good men; the revolution is a good deed; the revolution is done by good men; 2) It is evil to kill; people kill in revolutions; revolutions are evil.

The main response which Ljutov makes to Gedali seems fatuous: "The sun does not enter closed eyes but we will slash open closed eyes" (51). Slashing eyes does not help them to see. Moreover, Gedali's eyes were closed by the Poles, as he points out. Ljutov's remark sounds like a foolish piece of bravado, in the worst of taste. If Ljutov's remark is looked at a little more closely, however, we see how different it is in structure from the remarks of Gedali, although it seems to mimic the structure and rhythms of Gedali's arguments. It is not as fatuous as it seems. The word "closed" would be more exactly translated "which have closed themselves" (*zakryvšiesja*). To the will of eyes which have closed themselves Ljutov opposes the will of people who want to open those eyes to the sun, that is, to the revolution. This is not Aristotelian logic. This is the dialectic of the class struggle. The second half of his sentence is neither a conclusion from the first nor a rebuttal of the first. It is a dialectical opposition.

Gedali's argument pretends to establish absolute truth through the process of reasoning according to formal classical logic. Lenin always criticized those who used the methods of formal logic. He maintained that everything was relative and in a state of constant flux: "There is no such thing as an abstract truth. Truth is always concrete" he says in "Two Tactics of the Social Democrats in a Democratic Revolution" (XI, 75). Gedali complains that a Red Army soldier took his gramophone and then metamorphoses that soldier into an apotheosis of the revolution: "'I like music, sir' I answer to the revolution. 'You don't know what you like, Gedali, I will shoot at you, then you will know what you like, and I cannot help shooting, because I am the revolution'" (51). The Red Army soldier's response is repeated approvingly by Ljutov. This response indicates that the use of force is inevitable during the period of the dictatorship of the proletariat. This is a concrete fact which cannot be removed by any amount of theorizing (compare the argument of Lenin's article "The Proletarian Revolution and the Renegade Kautskij") and in this way **"Gedali"** links up with **"Moj pervyj gus'"**. The last sentence of the story refers to Gedali as the founder of an International which could not be achieved in real life (*nesbytočnyj*). His logic, dealing as it does with abstractions, cannot have real results. Lenin, in his real speech at a real International, used logic of a different kind.

Throughout the **Konarmija** stories Babel' shows that he thinks of the campaign as being a part of the dialectical process of history, not as something complete in itself. That is why battles, victories or defeats are not portrayed as having any special significance. In the story **"Posle boja"** fighting is taking place with the troops of Budennyj trapped in the "Zamość ring". Ljutov describes how they attack at Česniki. They are opposed by Cossacks who went over to the Poles at the start of the campaign, led by a man called Jakovlev. A gold tooth shines in his mouth and his beard lies on his chest "like an icon on a dead man" (142). Babel' takes us off balance with these details. They seem to be eccentrically selected and to reveal once more his interest in the bizarre and the exotic. But the isolated details of renegade, gold, long beard and icon come together to create a picture of the forces of counter-revolution. Babel', through Ljutov, describes how the Cossack captain "kept his ground this time, and we fled", and refers to the "temporary" victory of the renegade Cossacks (142). This victory was to last all Babel''s lifetime, since from the 31 August 1920 the Konarmija was forced to retreat. In the perspective seen by Babel', however, it is still "temporary".

Babel' introduces us to the way he sees the historical events described in the first story, **"Perechod čerez Zbruč"**. The first line has already been quoted. The story continues: "H.Q. moved out of Krapivno and our

baggage-train stretched out, making a noisy rearguard, along the highway which goes from Brest to Warsaw and which was built on peasants' bones by Nicholas I" (27). It is often commented that these lines read like a military despatch and are neutral in tone.[25] Military despatches are usually concerned with important military facts and with objectives. The only military fact of any significance here is reported in the first line by the commander of the sixth division, that Novograd-Volynsk was taken at dawn. A more valid comparison could be made between these opening lines of the cycle and the opening lines of the stories which soldiers tell of their experiences in the newspaper *Krasnyj kavalerist*, usually in the section "Zametki bojca". Here, for comparison, are the opening lines of some of these anecdotes: "On the 18 July our battery was located above P-village and was shelling the enemy, who had taken up positions on the left bank of the river Sluč'" (8 August 1920, 3); "We stationed ourselves for a rest in M-village; sent out pickets and patrols in all directions" (8 August, 3); "Once we stopped in S-village in a peasant's orchard. We had a chat and ate some cherries" (11 August, 4); "We moved out of T-village and went to O-village, where we had been ordered to make a breakthrough" (12 August, 3); "On the 4 July our valiant 6th cavalry division was ordered to take the town of R at all costs" (13 August, 3).

These Red Army soldiers are, of course, telling their stories to their own comrades, who don't need wordy explanations about the historical context of the war, the conditions in which it is being fought, the strength of the opposing forces, and so on. Hence the typical beginning *in medias res,* the simple factual language and the inclusion of the audience in the common aim of victory over the Poles. The words "we" and "our" are dominant. In the first page of **"Perechod čerez Zbruč"** "we" is used four times and "our" is used twice. The question of the type of reader that Babel' assumes is an extremely complex one, which cannot be dealt with here. It is obvious that he varies his approach to his reader with great skill. Here he creates the implication of a Red Army reader, poorly educated in everything but the art of war, sympathetic to the revolution and receptive to propaganda ("built on peasants' bones by Nicholas I"). Such a reader would have been extremely puzzled by what he reads in the first paragraph of this story.

N. Davies first indicated the geographical and historical inaccuracies in this opening paragraph. Novograd-Volynsk fell on the 27 June 1920, yet the Zbruč was not crossed until mid-July. The river which would have to be crossed to reach Novograd-Volynsk is the Sluč'. The Zbruč at its nearest point to Novograd-Volynsk is some 150 kilometres away. Novograd-Volynsk is hundreds of kilometres from Brest. The 1st Cavalry Army did not get as far north as Brest-Litovsk. Brest-Litovsk was occupied by the Soviet XVIth Army 1 August 1920. Davies can find no explanation for these inaccuracies.[26] Sicher's explanation of the mention of the river Zbruč is that "the Zbrucz is a symbolic boundary which relates the crossing to the Exodus from Egypt, with all the overtones of redemption in the Passover story".[27] He interprets the symbolic nature of the crossing as being linked with the fact that crossing the Zbruč is a "crossing into Poland".[28] The Zbruč is used as a symbolic boundary by Babel', but it did not represent crossing into Poland. The Zbruč only became a part of the official frontier of Poland with Soviet Ukraine after the Treaty of Riga, March 1921.

The significance of the crossing of the Zbruč was indicated in the leading article of *Krasnyj kavalerist,* 12 August 1920, "Počemu my idem 'za-granicu'?", which has already been quoted. In that article Vardin says that they are crossing the frontier which the emperors of Austria and Russia drew between peoples. He is referring to the partitions of Poland. After the first partition of 1772-73 the Zbruč became a part of the Eastern boundary of Austria. In this opening paragraph, which seems so straightforward, Babel' is drawing into one knot the aspirations of the Soviet armies—to create an international revolution. Here we have mingled together the partition of Poland by emperors, the death of serfs at the will of Nicholas I, Bolshevik troops crossing into the territory of the Austro-Hungarian empire and the road from Brest to Warsaw, gateway to the rest of imperialist and capitalist Europe. This seemingly dry, factual statement of the journey of a baggage-train is a lyrical exposition of aspirations, not of facts. Like the "vatic Bojan" of the *Slovo o polku Igoreve* Babel' "ranges in thought [like the nightingale] over the tree".[29] The author's imitation of the style of Bojan shows the extent of this "ranging": "Steeds neigh beyond the Sula; glory rings in Kiev; trumpets blare in Novgorod[-Seversk]; banners are raised in Putivl'".[30] Babel''s introductory passage ranges like Bojan in spirit, but baffles and deceives the reader by its tone.

The inaccuracies are, of course, deliberate. There can be no question that Babel', a war correspondent, might have made mistakes. The inaccuracies, which are few, can be shown to share a common aim. Another illustration of Babel''s use of historical inaccuracy is **"Èskadronnyj Trunov"**. Davies has noted that Trunov is buried in Sokal', which was not taken until 26 August, when the American pilot Cedric Fauntleroy had transferred to the Polish VI Army.[31] Trunov was not, in fact, buried at Sokal', nor was he killed in a duel with an aeroplane. K. A. Trunov, commander of the 34th cavalry regiment, was killed in a cavalry engagement in which he had already killed seven Poles. He was shot from a revolver at close range. He was buried in Dubno 5 August 1920. Babel' knew these details, since he wrote one of the obituaries of Trunov which appeared

in *Krasnyj kavalerist.*[32] Why then does he have Trunov buried in Sokal' and make him die after a battle with an aircraft from the squadron commanded by Fauntleroy?

On the same page of *Krasnyj kavalerist* as Babel''s obituary of Trunov is a description of the shooting down of two enemy aircraft by soldiers in the **Konarmija.** The aircraft were a potent threat to cavalry, cancelling out the advantage of the cavalry's speed of manoeuvre. In his plans for the **Konarmija** stories Babel' noted: "The **Konarmija** is retreating. In the face of whom? In the face of twenty aeroplanes ‹. . .› First meeting with Western European technology".[33] The duel of Trunov with the aeroplanes may recall ancient parallels of heroes duelling with monsters, it undoubtedly is a duel of epic proportions, but the most important feature of it is that it is a duel between a Bolshevik and Western technology flown by Americans. That is why Babel' needed to mention Fauntleroy. It is more difficult to understand why Babel' should choose Sokal'. Perhaps it was because "Gothic Sokal'" (112,117) seemed to him particularly characteristic of Western European culture. According to Brokgauz-Èfron a Cistercian monastery (referred to by Babel' as *sobor*) and an ancient castle were situated in Sokal'. Trunov was not buried in the monastery, as the great men of old would have been buried, but in a public park. Alternatively, Sokal' might have been chosen because it stands on the Bug, which flows through Brest into the heart of Poland and which the **Konarmija** had to cross twice before they could change the direction of their attack from L'vov to Warsaw.

Babel' uses the introduction typical of soldiers' stories again in **"Berestečko"**, in a different manner but with the same purpose as in **"Perechod čerez Zbruč"**. He begins: "We were on a march from Chotin to Berestečko" (91). The implied reader, a cavalryman, would know perfectly well that the village of Chotin was not far from Berestečko. The actual reader would never have heard of the small village of Chotin. On hearing the name Chotin he would think that the "march" (*perechod*) involved was from the town of Chotin, on the Dnjestr, close to where the Zbruč joins the Dnjestr. At that time Chotin was in Rumania, which seemed to be on the verge of intervention in the Soviet Union. There has been a peasant uprising in Chotin in January 1919, the first large-scale revolt of the Bessarabian peasantry.[34] The impression of a long march is continued in the second sentence: "The soldiers dozed in their high saddles" (91). Of course, there can be no question of the march actually being from Chotin to Berestečko, hundreds of kilometres away. But Babel' places the suggestion of the possibility of such a march in the head of the reader, and he links Chotin, the site of two famous battles of the Poles against the Turks, in 1621 and 1673, and Berestečko, where Bogdan Chmel'nickij was defeated by the Poles in 1651. As the Cossacks advance they see corpses left by modern warfare lying on thousand-year old burial mounds and they pass watch-towers set up by Bogdan Chmel'nickij. An old man crawls out from behind a grave-stone and sings them songs of the past glory of the Cossacks. Once again Babel' is ranging like Bojan in time and space. In an ancient castle Ljutov finds a fragment of a letter written in French in 1820 which mentions Napoleon, a letter about the birth of a child.

The implication seems to be that men have always fought and will always fight, the human cycle of birth and death constantly repeats itself, and the lessons of life are never learned. There seems to be here a Tolstoyan fatalism before the facts of human experience. However, the structure and the movement of the story suggest a different conclusion. The closing words of the story belong to the *voenkomdiv* Vinogradov: "You are in power. Everything that is here is yours. There are no masters. I proceed to the election of the revolutionary committee" (93). Babel' mentions ironically that these words are addressed to "bewildered petty traders and plundered Jews" (93). In the central incident of the story a Cossack casually slits the throat of an old Jew, allegedly for spying. The inhabitants were right to close and bolt their shutters when the Red troops entered the hamlet. They have no power, and to say that they are in power is a mockery. The Cossacks are in power. But they are only in power at the moment. The speech which Vinogradov made to the meeting of petty traders and Jews was about the Second Congress of the Comintern, at which Lenin made his speech on the necessity of temporary inconveniences and political terror in the name of a future new society. Throughout the story there are indications that life is changing. The blind old man sings of the former glory of the Cossacks, the way of life of people in Berestečko has faded, the hamlet "stinks as it awaits a new era" (92), the Raciborskij family, the former owners of Berestečko, have no heirs. The reign of terror brought by the Cossacks will be a temporary phenomenon. It is the path which must be followed before the new way of life is established.

While there are lyrical elements in the *Konarmija* stories, these stories, taken as a whole, do not have the atmosphere of "emotions recollected in tranquillity". The stories vary immensely in their approach to the reader, but they all assume on the part of the reader that unquestioning sympathy which the soldiers of the *Konarmija* assumed when they related their experiences in the pages of *Krasnyj kavalerist*. One has the impression that the struggle is still going on and that the events described have not settled into a pattern in the author's consciousness, or in the reader's. All Red Army soldiers, no matter what their faults, have the sympathy of the author, and all Polish soldiers have his unbending hatred. As in the soldiers' own stories, the Polish troops in the pages of *Konarmija* are always referred to as

pane or *šljachta,* they have no faces. In the story which was added to the cycle by Babel' in 1932, **"Argamak",** one can clearly see the difference which the intervening years have made. Now Babel' does not assume that his readers know what he is talking about. He gives, in a consecutive manner, details which amount to a potted history of his life in the cavalry up to the time when the story takes place. He comes to conclusions on and makes considered judgments about the character of the soldiers he mentions, his relationships with them and reasons for the success of the revolution. He describes the difficulties of cavalry life as though they were now over, and he is looking back on them: "We used to have to cover from sixty to eighty kilometres a day" (153). The Poles are no longer *pane* or *šljachta.* They are mentioned three times simply as *poljaki.* **"Poceluj",** which was first published in 1937 and which is not included in the cycle, also deals with the material of this period as something which has long since settled down and can be evaluated.

Ljutov has not finally assimilated the revolutionary reality with which he is in contact in the **Konarmija** stories, and one does not feel that the author, who is masked by Ljutov's presence, has any knowledge more recent than that of Ljutov. Ljutov conveys the collisions of contrasting aspects of reality, and the themes of **Konarmija** are drawn in part from the contrasts themselves.[35] Nevertheless one is aware, despite the consuming interest of Ljutov in all aspects of the reality which he faces, that he realizes that what he sees is fitting into or will fit into the pattern predicted by the leaders of the revolution, principally by Lenin. Either Babel' or Ljutov exclaims in the second story, **"Kostel v Novograde":** "The poor are advancing in hordes on your ancient towns, O Poland, a song telling all slaves to unite rings over them, and woe to you, *Rzeczpospolita,* woe to you, prince Radzivill, and to you, prince Sapega, who have risen for an hour!" (30). Radzivill and Sapega are both members of Pilsudski's government, and both have names famous in Polish history. It seems that history is repeating itself. But the emphasis of this apostrophe is on the fact that their rising is a temporary phenomenon which will be submerged in the tide of freed slaves. Babel', coursing to and fro in history, is not simply intrigued by the exotic aspect of it. He can see a pattern in it and he tries to make this pattern emerge from the stories of **Konarmija.**

The heroes of Babel' have been profoundly influenced by the revolution. We meet them at one moment in their history and we cannot see the changes which are taking place in them in the same way as we could if we were to look back on them after a period of years. But there is no doubt that they are changing. We can be in no doubt that the terms which they use when they speak and the concepts which govern their thoughts are vastly different from what they were before the revolution. The rhetoric of revolution is not just rhetoric for them.

Babel' uses the new terms born in the revolutionary period and the rhetoric typical of that period to characterize his heroes. He may at times permit himself a smile at the way in which his heroes use that rhetoric, but he is not totally distanced from it himself, he has a strong belief in the concepts which led to the creation of that rhetoric and his belief is a deeply embedded feature of the structure of the stories.

Notes

1. I am using the chronology of the war established by N. Davies in *White Eagle, Red Star: The Polish-Soviet War, 1919-20* (London 1972).

2. Polish names mentioned by Babel' are given transliterated from the Russian, with this one exception.

3. See D. A. Furmanov, *Sobranie sočinenij* IV (Moskva 1960-61), 340.

4. See A. Voronskij, "I. Babel'", *Literaturnye portrety* I (Moskva 1928), 159-90. This article was first published in *Krasnaja nov'* No. 5 (1924), 276-300.

5. J. Andrew, "Structure and Style in the Short Story: Babel's 'My First Goose'", *Modern Language Review* 70 (1975), 366-79; M. Falchikov, "Conflict and Contrast in Isaak Babel's *Konarmija*", *Modern Language Review* 72 (1977), 125-33; N. Å. Nilsson, "Isaak Babel's 'Perechod čerez Zbruč'", *Scando-Slavica* 23 (1977), 63-71.

6. R. Grøngaard, *An Investigation of Composition and Theme in Isaak Babel's Literary Cycle 'Konarmija'* (Aarhus 1979), 34.

7. V. Polonskij, "Kritičeskie zametki. O Babele", *O sovremennoj literature,* second edition (Moskva/ Leningrad 1929, reprint The Hague 1967), 45-73 (49-50).

8. A comparison of Babel' to a lyric poet is made by J. E. Falen, *Isaac Babel, Russian Master of the Short Story* (Knoxville, Tennessee 1974), 116.

9. This view is particularly common in Soviet criticism. It can be used both to condemn his attitude towards the revolution and to excuse it as "romantic" or "idealist". One of the first to put forward this view was V. Percov, "Kakaja byla pogoda v èpochu graždanskoj vojny?", *Novyj LEF* No. 7 (1927), 36-45. The fullest and most reasoned presentation of this point of view is given in L. Plotkin, "Tvorčestvo Babelja", *Oktjabr'* No. 3 (1933), 174-84.

10. P. Garden gives a thoughtful interpretation of this aspect of *Konarmija* in her book *The Art of Isaac Babel* (Ithaca, N.Y./London 1972), 133-51.

11. I. Babel', *Izbrannoe* (Moskva 1966), 27. All future references to this edition will be made in the text, by page number only. Translations are my own.

12. "Dixeris egregie notum si callida verbum / reddiderit iunctura novum", *Ars Poetica, 47.*

13. V. I. Lenin, *Polnoe sobranie sočinenij,* fifth edition, XLI (Moskva 1971-75), 224. All future references to this edition will be made by volume and page number in the text. The translations are mine.

14. Furmanov, *op. cit.* IV, 271. Lenin is not always precise in his use of *neslychannyj*. In "Vse na bor'bu s Denikinym" he refers to "the unheard-of yoke ‹. . .› of the capitalists" (XXXIX, 44).

15. See also Afon'ka Bida's promise to his horse to hew down the "neskazannuju šljachtu" (104).

16. A. G. Cejtlin, *Stil' Lenina-publicista* (Moskva 1969), 153. Cejtlin makes the point that Lenin tends to repeat the word which is central to his argument, the key word. Ljutov and Babel', in their own use of anaphora, tend to repeat a word which is slightly off centre.

17. V. Šklovskij, "I. Babel'. (Kritičeskij romans)", *LEF* No. 2 (1924), 154.

18. E. Ščadenko was the third member, with Budennyj and Vorošilov, of the Revolutionary Military Council of the 1st Cavalry Army. He became a member of the *Revvoensovet* of the 2nd Cavalry Army in July 1920. "Načdiv 6" is in *Pervaja konnaja v izobraženii ee bojcov i komandirov* (Moskva/Leningrad 1930), 104-113.

19. Ščadenko, *op.cit.* 110.

20. S. Budennyj, "Otkrytoe pis'mo Maksimu Gor'komu", *Pravda,* 26 October 1928, 4. See also S. Budennyj, "Babizm Babelja iz 'Krasnoj novi'", *Oktjabr'* No. 3 (1924), 196-97.

21. *Russkij sovetskij rasskaz,* edited by V. A. Kovalev (Leningrad 1970), 150. The section on Babel' is by N. A. Groznova.

22. G. Struve, *25 Years of Soviet Russian Literature (1918-1943)* (London 1944), 25.

23. The normal sentence for such crimes was from 6 months to 1 year of hard labour. This was usually suspended if the soldier had a good record. See the section "Revoljucionnyj sud" in *Krasnyj kavalerist,* 7 August 1920, 8 August 1920, 19 August 1920 and 21 August 1920. In cases where

sums of money were taken the sentence might be as much as 10 years hard labour (*Krasnyj kavalerist* 24 August 1920, 4).

24. D. Mendelson, *Metaphor in Babel's Short Stories* (Ann Arbor 1982), 38.

25. See for example T. Stableford, *The Literary Appreciation of Russian writers* (Cambridge 1981), 108.

26. N. Davies, "Izaak Babel''s 'Konarmiya' Stories and the Polish-Soviet War", *Modern Language Review* 67 (1972), 845-57 (849).

27. E. Sicher, "The Road to a Red Cavalry: Myth and Mythology in the Works of Isaak Babel' of the 1920s", *Slavonic and East European Review* 60 (1982), 528-46 (538). See also J. J. van Baak, "The Function of Nature and Space in 'Konarmiya' by I. E. Babel'", *Dutch Contributions to the Eighth International Congress of Slavists, Zagreb, Ljubljana, September 3-9, 1978,* ed. by J. M. Meijer (Amsterdam 1979), 37-55 (54).

28. Sicher, *op.cit.* 545.

29. *The Song of Igor's Campaign,* translated by Vladimir Nabokov (New York 1960), 30.

30. *Ibid,* 32.

31. N. Davies, "Izaak Babel''s 'Konarmiya' Stories and the Polish-Soviet War", *op.cit.,* 852.

32. "Pobol'še takich Trunovych!", signed by "Voennyj korrespondent 6 Kavdivizii K. Ljutov", *Krasnyj kavalerist* 13 August 1920, 3. It was thought that the only extant piece of journalism written by Babel' for *Krasnyj kavalerist* was "Ee den'", published in *Literaturnoe nasledstvo* 74 (Moskva 1965), 488.

33. A. N. Pirožkova, "I. Babel'. Novye materialy", *Literaturnoe nasledstvo* 74 (Moskva 1965), 467-512 (492).

34. See N. V. Bereznjakov, *Bor'ba trudjaščichsja Bessarabii protiv interventov v 1917-20 gg.,* edited by I. M. Razgon (Kišinev 1957), 194-205.

35. See J. van der Eng, "La description poétique chez Babel", *Dutch Contributions to the Fifth International Congress of Slavicists,* Sofia 1963 (The Hague 1963), 79-92 (85).

Jan van der Eng (essay date 1984)

SOURCE: Van der Eng, Jan. "Babel's Short Story 'Zamost'e.'"[1] In *Signs of Friendship: To Honour A. G. F. van Holk,* edited by J. J. van Baak, pp. 419-30. Amsterdam: Rodopi, 1984.

[In the following essay, van der Eng examines narrative aspects of "Zamost'e," particularly the interrelationship of the story's thematic concerns.]

The object of this article is twofold. In the first place it will deal with the erratic thematic pattern of **"Zamost'e"**: the striking metaphors, the suggestive variations on certain themes and combinations of themes, the wide range of the dramatic events and experiences which may create the impression of several interwoven stories (cf. Terras: 149). Of considerable significance in this respect are the various intertextual and extratextual relations: the allusive play with literary motifs, devices and tradition, with different rituals. The fragmentary and cryptic way in which this is done sometimes leads to discordant notes in the text and thus inevitably induces the reader to supply additional information from his literary knowledge and from his acquaintance with various modes of life (cf. van der Eng: 112, 120).

The second object of this article is to uncover the intratextual relations, "the hidden associations" (Stepanov: 33) and thus to lay bare the thematic essence of the at first glance rather capricious sequence of the narrative components. Quite often the fanciful aspect of this sequence rests on textual contrasts. The very first paragraph of the story already has such a contrastive function. It tells about the expected capturing of the town Zamost'e in which the army is supposed to spend the night. This expectation is expressed in simple, straightforward language that is reminiscent of the accounts of soldiers' adventures in the journal *Krasnyj kavalerist* (cf. Williams: 290-291): "The order was that we should spend the night in Zamoste, and the Divisional Commander was awaiting reports of victory". The further course of the story proves these expectations to be totally unfounded. The false expectations reach their culmination point in the laconic conclusion of the story. There the debâcle of the campaign against the Poles is expressed very directly and at the same time very much, as it were, in passing. The story's finale reports a short exchange of words between the narrator and an episodic character, Volkov, the billeting officer: "'We've lost the campaign', muttered Volkov, and snored. 'Yes', I answered".

The addition "and snored" ostensibly affects the gravity of these few spoken words, but at a closer look it will appear to enhance their dramatic impact. This is first of all a result of the intensification of the physiological motif of sleep in the preceding text. Physical exhaustion repeatedly asks its dues and the circumstances in which this happens grow more and more precarious as the story proceeds.

The overpowering need for sleep, despite all physical discomfort, is already present in the second paragraph. The narrator does not conceal his disbelief in the expected capturing of Zamost'e and in being provided with shelter for the night in the town: he decides to lie down on the wet ground, falls asleep and is then dragged along by his horse, the reins of which he had tied to his leg. When he wakes up he has a conversation with an armed peasant who happens to be passing by. Lack of sleep also figures in the description of this peasant: "'You dropped off to sleep, countryman', said the peasant, his sleepless nocturnal eyes smiling. 'Your horse has pulled you along for almost half a verst'".

After the reported conversation with the peasant the story momentarily shifts to the commander preparing the retreat of the troops. His orderlies are almost asleep from exhaustion: "The orderlies were standing at attention before him, sleeping as they stood".

Sleep is mentioned again in the episode describing the narrator's and Volkov's short stay in the hut of an old woman: here it interferes with the narrator's brutal behaviour in order to procure food. The motif of sleep reaches its climax in the story's finale where it is combined with the pithy statement that the war has been lost.

Rain is another motif occurring in many variations. This motif, too, comes to be connected with the disastrous course of the campaign. Again, it is already the second paragraph that is suggestive in this respect, both in its direct statements and in its metaphorical use of language: "Rain fell. Over the flooded earth flew wind and darkness. All the stars were doused in ink-distended clouds".

More than once rain is mentioned in combination with exhaustion and sleep. Somewhat further in the second paragraph, for instance, we read the following simile, based upon the narrator's thought of redeeming death: "The sodden ground offered me the soothing embrace of the tomb".

Rain and death also permeate the following, partly metaphorical description: "More rain fell. Dead mice floated along the roads. Autumn set its ambushes about our hearts, and trees like naked corpses set upright on their feet swayed at the crossroads".

As was the case with the motif of sleep the ending of the story strengthens the impression created by the motif of rain. There we find a variation of a metaphorical expression from the preceding text, indicating the atmospheric phenomenon of rain and at the same time creating an impression of lethal numbness: "The transport-wagons were making off, roaring and sinking in the mud. Morning oozed over us like chloroform over a hospital table".

The endless rain in the story is a historical fact. The Red cavalry was trapped near Zamość and only escaped being wiped out because of the incessant rains. It was the heavy rainfall that provided an opportunity to find an opening in the Zamość Ring (cf. Davies: 846).

An important aspect of the erratic story-line in **"Zamost'e"** is the fact that this story contains various more or less rounded off thematic complexes which can almost be considered to be rivalling stories. This construction occurs in more stories of **Red Cavalry** as, for instance, in **"Crossing the Zbruč"**, **"The Road to Brody"** and **"Squadron Commander Trunov"**. Each one of the in themselves relatively complete components of these stories are in their turn intersected by strongly deviating thematic instances, functioning as contrasts, discordant elements, or even as the stirrings of yet another story.

In **"Zamost'e"** three episodes can be distinguished. Each of these has its own dramatic completeness, with for instance the features arrival and departure, the establishing of contact and its breaking up. Each of them also has its own thematic contrasts and discordant elements, which in one instance in their turn form yet another mosaic pattern. This is the case in the episode describing the narrator's dream after he has fallen asleep on the wet ground in the open air. Here we can almost speak of a story in the story underlining the overall theme of destruction; at the same time, however, the episodic character of this passage is totally different from the surrounding text and it contrasts strongly with certain preceding and following passages. The colourful images of the dream and the corresponding physical and psychological emotions stand out sharply against the bleak images from the beginning of the second paragraph. Another contrast here is the crispy dryness of the hay versus the soaked, wet earth on which the narrator fell asleep: "Then I fell asleep and dreamed of a shed carpeted with hay. Over the shed hummed the dusty gold of threshing", etc.

In the third paragraph the contrast is sharpened because the dream unexpectedly shifts to a beautifully dressed woman entering the silence of the hay shed. In the ensuing erotic scene the emphasis is on life and warm physical contact, evoking a contrast with the preceding awareness of utter discomfort and death. The contrast is the stronger because the narrator's description of the scene in the shed is to some extent reminiscent of the courtly love tradition. The fourth paragraph shows him almost as a knight, willing to undergo the severest ordeals just to be able to see his lady (cf. Mejlach: 257ff.). At the same time he expresses these ordeals in a comparison that ties up with his wretched situation outside the dream. It does not only evoke the disasters of the war, but also pictures the narrator's physical situation at that particular moment: "'Margot', I longed to cry out, 'the earth is dragging me like a jibbering cur by the cord of its calamities. Nevertheless I have seen you, Margot'".

The name Margot might remind the reader of the woman who is cherished by the I in Gor'kij's novel *My Apprenticeship*. He names her Queen Margot and says of her: "I embellished my memories of Queen Margot with all the beauty I had culled from books; I bestowed upon her the finest of what lay within me—all the loveliest fantasies born of my reading" (cf. Borras: 140).

The next paragraph (the fifth), too, brings an interesting development; it introduces an element of frustration, resulting from the fact that the narrator is incapable of actually uttering his words. The rest of the dream is told in three paragraphs (6, 7 and 8). They describe the woman's words and actions. These reveal that she looks upon the narrator as a dead man. What she says and does, however, springs from two different ritual sources: Christian and folkloristic. Meanwhile, the narrator's frustration grows and grows until he finally wakes up: "My moaning vainly beat about inside my clamped jaws . . . I could not force my hands apart . . . and I awoke".

The frustration of the second part of the dream is, of course, connected with the horrors of his (fictional) reality.

The moment of awakening forms the transition to a second, rather substantial and independent text part: the encounter with the peasant. As was said in the above, their conversation begins with the peasant's comment on the grim circumstances under which the narrator had to try and find some sleep. Afterwards, however, this text part focuses upon a gruesome fact of the Polish-Russian war: the persecution of the Jewish population. The shift to this new focus is effected by a number of partly synaesthetic and conflicting images (cf. Mendelson: 360-361). First comes the image of the damp morning which is repeated in the story's finale in almost identical words. Immediately hereafter follows a fairy-like description of the Polish troops opening fire on the Russians. Finally the pogrom in Zamost'e is indicated in a cryptic, metaphorical way (by means of synaesthesia): "The raw dawn flowed over us like waves of chloroform. Green rockets soared above the Polish camp. The shuddered in the air, scattered like rose-leaves beneath the moon, and went out.

And in the stillness I could hear the far-off breath of groaning. The smoke of secret murder strayed around us".

Answering a question of the narrator the peasant then makes it clear that the sounds of murderous violence around them are those of a pogrom going on. He also reveals the grim anti-Semitism behind this violence, an attitude which he apparently shares.

The horrible substance of this conversation strikingly contrasts with the peasant's obvious desire to establish some kind of human contact: "'These nights on the line

are long. There's no end to them. And a man sort of gets a longing to have a talk with someone else . . .'. The peasant made me light a cigarette from his".

The most oppressive part of this episode comes at its end when the peasant remarks that only 200.000 Jews (of the ten million in existence) will survive the war: "'There'll be only two hundred thousand left', cried the peasant, and touched my hand, afraid I would go. But I got into the saddle and galloped off . . .".

The third substantial, more or less independent text part follows after some intermediate passages with impressions of rain, overwhelming sleep and implications of defeat, death, etc. This episode relates how the narrator and billeting officer Volkov flee to Sitanec. In Sitanec the billeting officer finds room for the two of them in the hut of an old woman. The description of their stay focuses upon some rather unedifying actions of the narrator. He orders wine, meat and bread from the old woman, whom he sees sitting on the floor and feeding a calf hidden under the bed. He threatens her, sets fire to a pile of straw on the floor and says": "I'll burn you, old 'un. . . . I'll burn you and your stolen calf". Characteristically he is, while saying this, again overwhelmed by sleep. Even more telling is the totally different occupation of his companion: wedged in the description of the narrator's brutal behaviour is a passage describing Volkov writing a letter to his fiancée: "'Honored Valentina', he wrote, 'do you remember me?'" Later on in the story we find a similar discordant element. After the two men have been forced to leave the house in a great hurry and are on the road again, Volkov suddenly asks: "'Are you married, Lyutov?' . . . 'My wife left me', I answered".

This moment, too, is wedged in between details emphasizing oppressive aspects of the war. In this case these are: the disordered retreat of a great many transport wagons that continually get stuck in the mud, the one horse on which the narrator and Volkov flee from Sitanec (the latter's horse having been shot dead), the both pithy and desperate exchange of words at the end of the story.

Volkov's letter for a moment suggests the introduction of a completely different episode, an intimate emotional story in which he is the central character. The narrator's answer to Volkov's question, too, intimates an—apparently unhappy—emotional experience.

In connection with the emotions dominating the narrator's dream—frustration about the woman thinking him dead and behaving as such—the emotional implications of "my wife left me" even get an extra dimension: the passage becomes significant for the narrator's characterization.

In the context, however, these emotionally divergent elements primarily intensify the reality of the war that is going on. There are other stories in **Red Cavalry** where a comparable contrast with the war can be found. Think for instance of Griščuk's complaints at a moment when he thinks death is near (**"The Death of Dolgušov"**): "'Whatever do women go and give themselves such troubles for? he asked . . . mournfully. 'Whatever do they want engagements and marriages for, and pals to make merry at the wedding?'"

Themes occurring in **"Zamost'e"** have many other parallels in **Red Cavalry** as a whole. The theme of the persecution of the Jews is also present in **"Crossing the Zbruč"**, in **"Gedali"** and in **"Rabbi"**. In **"Zamost'e"** this theme comes to the fore most harrowingly. The same can be said of the narrator's brutal behaviour towards the old woman. Earlier on in the cycle, in **"My First Goose"** he displays a similar behaviour and after **"Zamost'e"** it reoccurs in **"The Song"**. Nowhere, however, does the narrator's behaviour equal his brutality in **"Zamost'e"**.

The disastrous campaign against the Poles was characterized by repression and pogroms. In the finale of **"Zamost'e"** these aspects are expressed more directly than in any of the other stories, though they are also very much present in the preceding stories **"Squadron Commander Trunov"**, **"Two Ivans"**, **"The Story of a Horse Continued"**, **"The Widow"**, and in stories following **"Zamost'e"**, as for instance in **"The Rabbi's Son"**.

In this story, which was to be the last one of the cycle, we again find the chaotic retreat of the cavalry and the recruited peasants. The description here is less direct than in **"Zamost'e"**, but still has the effect of mounting to a climax: "Our troops faltered and mingled in confusion. The Political Section train started crawling over the dead backbone of the fields. And a monstrous and inconceivable Russia tramped in bast shoes on either side of the coaches, like a multitude of bugs swarming in clothes. The typhus-ridden peasantry rolled before them the customary humpback of a soldier's death", etc.

The function of the stories and their themes in the cycle as a whole is, of course, of crucial importance for an analysis and is something which cannot be dealt with in just a few words (cf. van Baak: 145ff.): it is an essential component of the semantic structure of each separate story and of the cycle. For the present article a few remarks on the central position of **"Zamost'e"** in connection with some aspects of the thematic structure of the cycle as a whole must be sufficient.

We may conclude that in **"Zamost'e"** Babel' has created a complex and carefully balanced semantic structure. The sensory suggestiveness of the descriptions is widened and heightened by various metaphorical expressions, both within the scope of the sentence and in successive sentences and paragraphs. The sensory polyvalence is enhanced by certain figures of speech (synaesthesia, oxymoron) and by sudden shifts and contrasts in the perceptions. This is accompanied by shifts in the emotional attitude. The dominant feature in the diverse thematic components, however, is the general atmosphere of disaster. It is implicitly present in the various descriptions of visual, auditive or tactile perceptions, or combinations of these, in the contrasts and incongruities at the visual level, etc.

The impression of disaster also permeates the two recurrent motifs of endless rain and overwhelming sleep. Remarkable in this respect is the contrast between the story's beginning and its ending: expected victory versus catastrophe. The impression of pending disaster is suggestively intensified by the three very different, relatively substantial narrative components, each of them having a clearly marked beginning and ending: the dream, the conversation with the peasant, the short stay in the old woman's hut. These narrative components are thematically more or less complete, but they also contain contrastive passages falling outside their thematic range. Their interrelations, too, show specific contrasts and differentiations of, for instance, certain emotional aspects. As in the story as a whole, we find a more or less mosaic-like pattern of divergent themes and intriguing analogies in each of these text parts.

The most 'baroque' complex in this respect is the dream, primarily because it has moments that contrast shrilly with the disastrous (fictional) reality. It is this text part in particular that—more than the other two—is characterized by intertextual and extratextual relations. Moreover, it is especially the semantic implications of the three longer text segments that are intensified and modified by the various connections with analogous elements in other stories of **Red Cavalry.**

Note

1. Quotations from: Isaac Babel, *The Collected Stories,* ed. and transl. by Walter Morison, with an intr. by Lionel Trilling (New York and Scarborough, Ont., 1974).

Works Cited

Stepanov, Nik. 1928. "Novella Babelja", in: *I. È. Babel': Stat'i i materialy* (Leningrad), 13-41.

Terras, Victor 1966. "Line and Color: The Structure of I. Babel's Short Stories in *Red Cavalry*", in: *Studies in Short Fiction,* III, 2 (Newberry College), 141-156.

Borras, F. M. 1967. *Maxim Gorky the Writer* (Oxford).

Davies, Norman 1972. "Izaak Babel''s 'Konarmiya' Stories, and the Polish-Soviet War", in: *Modern Language Review,* 67, 845-857.

Mejlach, M. B. 1973. "K voprosu o strukture «kurtu-aznogo universuma» trubadurov", in: *Trudy po znak-ovym sistemam,* VI (Tartu), 244-264.

Mendelson, Danuta 1982. *Metaphor in Babel's Short Stories* (Ann Arbor).

Van Baak, J. J. 1983. *The Place of Space in Narration. A Semiotic Approach to the Problem of Literary Space. With an Analysis of the Role of Space in I. E. Babel's Konarmija* (Amsterdam).

Van der Eng, Jan 1983. "Semantic Construction and Semiotic Essentials of the Narrative", in: *American Journal of Semiotics,* Vol. 2, No. 3, 99-129.

Williams, Gareth 1984. "The Rhetoric of Revolution in Babel''s *Konarmija*", in: *Russian Literature,* XV-III (Amsterdam), 279-298.

Milton Ehre (essay date 1986)

SOURCE: Ehre, Milton. "*Red Cavalry.*" In *Isaac Babel,* pp. 63-86. Boston: Twayne Publishers, 1986.

[*In the following essay, Ehre categorizes the major thematic concerns of* Red Cavalry *and views the collection as Babel's attempt "to create an epic of a decisive historical moment."*]

For all their charm, **Odessa Tales** still smack of the provincialism of the genre sketch. **Red Cavalry** is a work of sophisticated maturity. The most important fiction to come out of the Russian Revolution—its only real competitor is a poem, Blok's *The Twelve*—it can advance a claim to stand as the national epic of that momentous event. **Red Cavalry** is to the Russian Revolution what Tolstoy's *War and Peace* is to the Napoleonic invasion, an attempt of the literary imagination to grasp a climactic historical experience in the life of a people. Of course Tolstoy's novel is broader in scope and deeper in its penetration of human experience. Also, the two authors come out of markedly different traditions: Tolstoy is the supreme master of the realistic novel, while Babel proceeds from the imperatives of modernism. Tolstoy offers a microcosm of the world that is comprehensive, exhaustive, and psychologically persuasive. Babel is fragmentary, elliptical, elusive, very much a modernist in his tendency to decompose a text into pastiche. Less confident than his nineteenth-century predecessors about the susceptibility of the world to systematic description, he regards reality more as a mystery to be intuited than a puzzle to be solved. As a result his fiction is metaphoric rather than explicative, suggestive instead of analytical. It narrows character to a figure in a pattern that is at once highly decorative and rich in implication. Even as it presents the world piecemeal, **Red Cavalry** yet betrays a Tolstoyan aspiration to show it in its entirety, to create an epic of a decisive historical moment.

Though **Red Cavalry** may leave an initial impression of a medley of sketches, Babel conceived it as a whole. He worried about the ordering of the individual stories, which he called "excerpts" and "chapters" of a book.[1] A collection on a single topic will inevitably have a kind of unity—that of the cycle or anthology—but **Red Cavalry** is more tightly knit than that. Most of the stories are told by a stand-in for the author, Lyutov (Babel's alias while serving with the First Cavalry Army). Since the actors are mostly unlettered soldiers, Lyutov's mediating consciousness serves to color and complicate bare events with the reflections of a poet's sensibility. As in a travel book, our attention is focused on both scene and narrator. In the setting of the Polish campaign of 1920, the two cultures the Cossack army comes in contact with—Catholic Poland and the Jewish Pale of Settlement—are, like Odessa's Moldavanka, distanced from the reader, made strange.[2] Lyutov guides us through the unfamiliar terrain of war and the exotic landscapes in which it is conducted. His response is a tale in itself. **Red Cavalry** is thirty-five stories, but it is also a single story, a kind of novel relating one man's passage through war and revolution.

The Skaz Tales

Aside from Lyutov, the narrators are soldiers, mostly Cossacks. They speak or write (some of their tales are in the form of letters) in substandard Russian mixed with local dialectisms. In the tradition of *skaz* from Gogol and Leskov through the 1920s, when the manner became highly popular (in the work of Zamyatin, Zoshchenko, Ilf and Petrov), a peculiar idiom is not merely replicated but manipulated for comic and ironic effects. The ironies stem from a deformation of language.

The Cossacks are men of large gesture and small vision. The accidents of history have cast them as actors in an epoch-making drama. Only dimly aware of its awesomeness, their minds cluttered with revolutionary slogans and the bric-a-brac of Communist ideology, they yet insist upon their more tangible claims of personal honor, revenge, and plunder. Their speech resolves into a kind of oxymoron, a comical combination of disparate items: "Let us die for a sour pickle and the world revolution" (*I,* 88).

In **"Pismo"** (**"A letter"**) a callow youth writes to his mother of his father's murder by the boy's brother. The father is in turn the murderer of another brother (the father is a White; the sons, Reds). The young man narrates these brutal events in a chillingly matter-of-fact manner, placing a value on the life of his horse that he denies his father. His language is a concatenation of revolutionary bombast, homely colloquialisms, and Gogolian non sequiturs: "They took me into the expeditionary Political Section where we hand out reading material and newspapers to the positions—the *Moscow*

Izvestiya of the Central Executive Committee, *Moscow Pravda*, and our homebred merciless paper, *The Red Cavalry Man,* which every fighting man on the front lines hungers to read and after that with heroic spirit he cuts down the rotten Poles, and I'm living at Nikon Vasilevich's in grand style."

"Zhizneopisanie Pavlichenki, Matveya Rodionycha" (**"The life and adventures of Matvey Pavlichenko"**) tells of Matvey's vengeance on his pre-Revolutionary master, who had taken advantage of his wife and then struck him when he dared complain. The story is a fable on the making of a revolutionary warrior, detailing Matvey's progress from submissiveness to violent aggression or, to use the tale's metaphors, from herdsman to "wolf" and "jackal." Though the action is terribly brutal, the tone is closer to "black comedy" than melodrama. The language, which plays upon oratorical hyperbole grounded in colloquialisms and folklorish turns, is a richer and more imaginative elaboration of the mock-epic style of *Odessa Tales*:

> Countrymen, comrades, my own dear brothers! In the name of all mankind learn the life story of the Red General Matvey Pavlichenko. He used to be a herdsman, that general did, a herdsman on the Lidino estate, for Nikitinsky the master, and he looked after the master's pigs till life brought stripes to his shoulder straps; and then with those stripes of his Matyushka began to look after horned cattle. And who knows, if this Matvey of ours had been born in Australia, then chances are, my friends, he might have been elevated to elephants, our Matyushka would have come to grazing elephants; only the trouble is where would you find elephants in our district of Stavropol.

In a third example of *skaz*, **"Izmena"** (**"Treason"**), a Cossack accused of disorderly conduct protests his and his comrades' innocence in a letter to a police investigator. The comedy, much like Zoshchenko's, turns on the clash of two cultures: the bureaucratized routines of institutions and the personalistic ethos of people not yet assimilated into modern ways. The Cossacks when sent to a hospital misconstrue conventional regulations as treason to revolutionary militancy, refuse to surrender their arms, and raise havoc. As in much of *skaz* literature, the laugh is, so to speak, behind the back of the narrator. Since we readers move within the normative sphere of rules and regulations, we view the Cossack's complaint from the perspective of his straight victims. From the vantage point of ordinary life and language the narrator appears as comically out of place as a Gargantua among pygmies: "we disarmed the militia in the form of one fellow on horseback, and destroyed with tears in our eyes three mediocre windows in the above-described storeroom. . . . In his short Red life Comrade Kustov was real upset about the treason that is now winking at us from the window, now making game of the common proletariat, but the proletariat, comrades, knows it is common, it hurts us, it does, and our

souls burn and burst with flames the prison of our body. Treason, I tell you, Comrade Investigator Burdenko, treason laughs at us from the window, treason is going about the house barefoot, treason has taken off its boots so the floorboards in the burgled house won't creak."

Though distanced from us by comedy, the Cossacks are not simply objects of ridicule, nor are the author's ironies morally disapproving. Like Benya Krik, their Jewish literary cousin, they are outsized men, sometimes comically odd, sometimes frightening in their violence, but passionate and heroic. Uninhibited by the restraints of conventional society, they yet hold to codes of honor and the dictates of principle. The family of **"A Letter"** is shockingly brutish, but its members act from a sense of justice (*pravda*).[3] Set against each other by politics and personal animosity, both father and sons acquire dignity from the knowledge that were the tables turned, were victim to become victimizer, they would behave no differently. They fully accept the terms of their world. Matvey Pavlichenko's vengeance is horrifying. Underlying his abandon to violence, however, there is again a principle—that a man ought to enter into a personal relationship even with his enemy, no matter at what cost to himself. Not for Matvey are the abstract devices of modern warfare: "Then I stomped on my master Nikitinsky. I trampled him for an hour or maybe more. And in that time I got to know life through and through. With shooting . . . you only can get rid of a man. Shooting's letting him off, and too damn easy for yourself. With shooting you'll never get at the soul, to where it is in a man and how it shows itself. But I don't spare myself. . . . I want to get to know what life really is, what life's like down our way."

EPOS

The stories told by the sophisticated Lyutov-Babel touch a wider range of experience and gamut of styles than the *skaz* tales: factual reportage, naturalistic description, lyrical meditation, poetic evocation, wry irony, heroic hyperbole. Schematically these divide into two—the style of war and the style of culture, corresponding to what Renato Poggioli has called the "epic-heroic" and the "pathetic."[4] War rips a breach in the settled ways of culture, a revolutionary war even more so, since it assaults its very foundations. The dictionary definition of revolution is "momentous change," and change is the stuff of history. Change does violence to the existing order of things. It has its agents and its patients, those who introduce the new and those who suffer it.

The epic mode is one of action. Its rhythms resemble a drum beat—loud, insistent, constant. Armies are on the move, altering the face of history. From the march of revolution and war, running through the book like a line, if interrupted then inevitably resumed, curves veer away to chart scenes from the ordinary life of culture. Here the victims of history are to be found.

In **"Perekhod cherez Zbruch"** (**"Crossing into Poland"**) the Cossacks burst onto the scene (and into the book) in a riot of color, sound, and movement.

> Fields of crimson poppy flower around us, a noon-time breeze plays in the yellowing rye, virginal buckwheat looms on the horizon like the wall of a distant monastery. The silent Volyn bends, the Volyn moves away from us into the pearly haze of birch groves, it crawls into the flowering hills and with loosening arms entangles itself in thickets of hops. An orange sun rolls along the sky like a lopped-off head, a tender light flares in the gorges of clouds, the standards of the sunset fly over our heads. The smell of yesterday's blood and of slaughtered horses drips into the evening chill. The blackened Zbruch roars and twists the foamy knots of its rapids. The bridges are down, and we ford the river. A majestic moon rests on the waves. The horses enter the water to their cruppers, the resounding torrents run through hundreds of horses' legs. Someone sinks and loudly curses the Mother of God. The river is strewn with black squares of wagons, it is full of clamour, whistles, and songs, thundering above the serpentine trails of the moon and the luminous hollows.

Though the imagery associated with the action of war is lush, Babel's syntax is terse, compact, ascetically simple, so that his prose is a counterpoint of ornamental opulence and austere severity. The imagery plunges us into a world of high drama; the phrasing suggests resolute action.[5] Every clause opens with a subject followed by a verb, usually active. Except for the participial phrase, "thundering . . ." (where the style characteristically expands to indicate a conclusion), the passage is without subordination. A panoramic view grows out of a string of discrete images, each given equal weight. This paratactic accumulation has about it the linear inevitability of traditional epic narration. The predominance of active verbs in the present tense, the repetitive drumming of subject followed by verb, the compact phrasing form an extremely assertive style. Babel's epic manner is aggressively masculine.[6]

The dynamism of the prose is heightened by images that animate the scene. As in Russia's great medieval epic *The Song of Igor's Campaign,* or romantic pseudo-epics like Gogol's *Taras Bulba,* natural things by metaphorically assuming human qualities become participants in the movements of men: "an orange sun rolls along the sky like a lopped-off head"; "the breeze plays"; the Volyn twists its "arms." Nature and man blend into a single totality, as the sunset flies over the heads of the warriors like military standards, and the thundering clamor of men merges with the roaring of the river's torrents.

Throughout the book richly colored landscapes, brilliant midday suns, floral sunsets form the backdrop for heroic action: "We were moving to meet the sunset. Its foaming rivers flowed along the embroidered napkins of peasants' fields. The stillness turned pink." "It was after two of an expansive July day. A rainbow web of heat shimmered in the air. Beyond the hilltops glittered a holiday band of uniforms and horses' manes, braided with ribbons." "They rode side by side, in identical jackets and gleaming silver-striped trousers, on tall chestnut horses. Raising a shout the troops moved after them, and pale steel flashed in the ichor of the autumnal sun." Proud military standards regularly accompany these resplendent marches: "The standards of the sunset fly over our heads." "On gilt staffs, bearing velvet tassels, magnificent standards fluttered in fiery pillars of dust" (*I,* 61, 102, 139, 27, 102).

The vivid colors that clothe the Cossacks and the vigorous style that catches their movements separate them from humdrum life. Men without innerness or subjectivity, they inhabit a heroic universe removed from common concerns. Formulaic epithets capture their heroic largeness: "I beheld the masterful indifference of a Tatar Khan and recognized the horsemanship of the celebrated Kniga, the headstrong Pavlichenko, the captivating Savitsky." They stand aloof from ordinary human misery: "To the soothing accompaniment of the peasants' incoherent and desperate clamor, Zh. sought out that gentle pulsing in the brain that portends clarity and energy of thought. Feeling at length the right beat, he snatched the last peasant tear drop, snarled imperiously, and walked off to Headquarters." Unsullied by the squalid and ravaged towns they pass through, indifferent to the suffering of their victims, the heroes reflect in their personal appearance the rarefied atmosphere of their enclosed field of force. The grays of day-to-day existence do not touch them. A Cossack officer, a paragon of masculine beauty, is shown in colors like those of the richly colored sky; the recurrent image of a proudly phallic standard evokes his heroic stature: "I wondered at the beauty of his giant's body. He rose, the purple of his riding breeches, the crimson of his tilted cap, the decorations of his chest cleaving the hut as a standard cleaves the sky. A smell of scent and the cloyingly sweet freshness of soap emanated from him. His long legs were like young girls sheathed to the neck in gleaming boots" (*I,* 70, 37, 53).

Though the Cossacks elicit Babel's respect, they are not spared his ironies. We have observed how in the *skaz* tales he contrasts the pretensions of their speech with the brutality of their natures. His heroes are beautiful, but also theatrical. They are partly observed individuals, partly, like the mobsters of the Moldavanka, products of a hyperbolic literary imagination. Lyutov's admiration for them is sincere, his sexual envy painful, but they smack too much of adolescent daydreams. The ironies create a tension in the image: blown up to mythic proportions, the Cossacks are simultaneously deflated downwards toward comic travesty.[7] In **"Nachalnik konzapasa"** (**"The remount officer"**) Dyakov, a former circus athlete, convinces complaining peasants that the nags they have been given in exchange for their requisitioned horses are serviceable. Dyakov's philosophy of horsemanship is elegantly simple: "If a horse falls and gets up, then it's a horse; if, to put it the other way round, it doesn't get up, then it's not a horse." Dyakov rides into the book as if he were an extra in an opera: "He skillfully swung his well-proportioned athlete's body out of the saddle. Straightening his splendid legs, . . . magnificent and agile, he moved toward the expiring animal, as if he were on stage. Dolefully it fixed its stubborn deep eyes on Dyakov and licked some imperceptible command from his ruddy palm. Immediately the exhausted horse felt a dextrous strength flowing from this gray-haired, vigorous, and dashing Romeo."

Individual Cossacks may be subjected to this type of aesthetic play, "a baring of the device" by which Babel, in Shklovsky's words, "places a heading over his portraits—opera."[8] Their march, however, is always solemn. It is also aimless. As in Tolstoy's *War and Peace,* history is made by men who have no idea what they are making. The Cossacks, not without codes of honor and principles of justice, are yet creatures of impulse. Revolution appeals to them by the opportunity it gives for free exercise of their powers, which they manifest in indiscriminate violence and mindless vengeance. The consciousness of the heroes of **Red Cavalry,** like the prose that conveys their progress, is riveted to the immediate present, the act of the moment, the event as pure event. Consequently, they are children of nature and their march, which is the march of history, is a kind of natural occurrence. Nature is necessity, something given and not made, the weather we live in rather than forms we create. Natural things exhibit motion, whereas humans are capable of action—motions that result from deliberate choice. From the opening passage, where physical nature and human activity merge in a single awesome march, the movement of armies is presented as a spontaneous and ineluctable force, an elemental "Cossack flood" (*I,* 43).

Standing on a border line between nature and culture, part god, part man, part savage, the warrior is threatened by emptiness: "The brilliant sky loomed inexpressibly empty, as it always is in times of danger." Besides the regal standard, another recurring image for war is the desert or wasteland (*pustynya*): "Afonka dragged himself to his squadron, utterly alone, in the blazing desert of the fields." "Beyond the windows horses neighed and Cossacks shouted. The desert of war yawned beyond the window." In the desert of war men suffer "an eternal homelessness." Some turn into beasts. Matvey Pavlichenko has a "jackal's conscience" and was "suckled by a shewolf"; Afonka Bida roams the countryside slaughtering Poles like a "lonely wolf." When life is reduced to pure motion, empty of reflec-

tion and conscious purpose, barren of the nurture and restraints of culture, men turn into wild animals, or they feel themselves "utterly alone" (*I,* 104, 59, 107, 80, 105). The man without a city, Aristotle tells us, becomes either a god or a beast.[9] What escapes him is the specifically human.

PATHOS

"Crossing into Poland," with which we began our discussion of the epic and pathetic modes, is in its structure exemplary of most of the stories that make up **Red Cavalry.** The first half of its brief two pages, devoted to the resplendent march of the Cossack army, is more a prose poem than short story. After the baroque overture, the narrative proper begins, breaking the story, in a way characteristic of Babel, in two. The presentation shifts from the collective "we" of the epic march to the personal "I" of the narrator's story. Lyutov is billeted in a Jewish hovel, goes to sleep, dreams dreams of violence, and is awakened by a pregnant woman, who tells him he has been sleeping next to the corpse of her father. In sharp contrast to the glorious march, the Jewish dwelling is described in sordidly naturalistic detail: "In the room I was given I discovered wardrobes in disarray, scraps of women's fur coats on the floor, human feces, fragments of occult crockery. . . ." The Jews who live in this filth are grotesquely deformed victims of poverty and violence: "They skip about noiselessly, like monkeys, like Japs in a circus, their necks swaying and twisting. . . . The dead old man lies there, thrown on his back. His throat has been torn out, his face ripped in two, blue blood clots his beard like a lump of lead."

Heroic beauty and power are contrasted with the ugliness of suffering. But the story does not end here. In a concluding coda the pregnant Jewess bursts into an impassioned speech: "'Sir, . . . the Poles cut his throat, and he begging them: Kill me in the backyard so that my daughter won't see me die. But they did as suited them. He died in this room, thinking of me. And now I'd like to know,' the woman cried out with sudden and terrible power, 'I'd like to know where in the world you could find another father like my father?'" The epic mode, for all its vigorous insistence, does not displace the pathetic. They make rival claims on the imagination. Competing with the Cossack power of action is "the terrible power" of human suffering, in particular, Jewish suffering, "a power full of somber greatness" (*I,* 64).

The contrasting parts are integral miniatures. Until the conclusion, which reveals a heroic dignity hidden beneath the squalid surface of the Jewish hovel, there is no attempt to bridge the two sections. The narrative is perfunctory—Lyutov visits the Jewish home solely that we may see it. For the expansiveness of narrative Babel substitutes rhapsodic rhetoric and an intense lyric concentration upon images. His story does not move to the denouement of an action but to an epiphany.

"**Crossing into Poland**" veers from the action of war to life on the wayside, from poetic description to a sketchy narrative. "**Kostel v Novograde**" ("**The church at Novograd**") follows an analogous procedure, except that scenes of culture become the object of poetic evocation and the business of war constitutes the narrative. Lyutov goes to report to an army commissar who has been billeted in the Catholic church of the title. The church, the adjacent priest's house, and their denizens are described. Then the story proper begins, as the commissar arrives with a squad of Cossacks, who search the church where they uncover concealed money and valuables.

The church is depicted in the languid style and hothouse imagery of fin de siècle decadence. It is a place of ruin, putrefaction, and silky perversity: "The breath of an invisible order flickered under the ruins of the priest's house, and its insinuating seductions unmanned me. Oh crucifixes, tiny as the talismans of courtesans, parchment of Papal Bulls and satin of women's letters, rotting in the blue silk of waistcoats! . . . I see the wounds of your god, oozing seed, a fragrant poison intoxicating virgins. . . . Beyond the window the garden path shimmered beneath the black passion of the sky. Thirsty roses swayed in the darkness. Flashes of green lightning flamed amid the cupolas. A naked corpse sprawled along the slope. The moonlight streamed over lifeless legs thrust apart. Here is Poland, here is the proud sorrow of the Res Publica!" The heroic march pulses with vitality; places of culture are frozen in immobility. The verbs, mostly intransitive, many reflexive (*mertsalo, perlivaetsya, kolyshutsya, pylayut, valyaetsya, struitsya*), describe motions fixed in place. Where the verbs capturing the epic march place events in time—"a tender light flares," "we ford the river," "the horses enter the water"—these convey states of objects. Their length, the open syllables, and profusion of liquids (*vkradchivye ego soblazny obessilili menya*) slow the tempo and contribute to the "insinuating" quality. Interspersed through the passage are verbless exclamations ("Oh crucifixes") that show the passage for what it is—a static evocation of a world: "Here is Poland . . . !"

Jewish places also languish in stasis. They are pictured, as in "**Crossing into Poland**," in inert catalogs of useless things—broken crockery, scraps of fur, feces—or in a highly evocative manner like that employed for the church at Novograd. "**Kladbishche v Kozine**" ("**The cemetery at Kozin**") is a short prose poem. Almost verbless, it is an incantation, singing through the inscriptions on the gravestones of a dead world surviving only as memory.

> Azrael son of Ananias, lips of Jehovah.
>
> Elijah son of Azrael, a mind waging lonely battle with oblivion.

> Wolff son of Elijah, prince robbed from the Torah in his nineteenth spring.
>
> Judah son of Wolff, Rabbi of Kraków and Prague.
>
> O death, O covetous one, O greedy thief, why couldst thou not have spared us, just for once?

In the second half of "**The Church at Novograd**," the narrative half devoted to the search, the short, clipped accents of Babel's military style assert themselves: "My Commissar still hasn't shown up. I look for him in the Staff, the garden, the church. . . . We make our rounds, searching [*kruzhimsya i ishchem*]. . . ."

As "**Crossing into Poland**" opposed Cossack vigor and Jewish suffering, "**The Church at Novograd**" parallels Catholic mystery and the brusque business of revolution and war. Babel's almost plotless sketches required an ordering principle which he found in contrast. The contrast, which may initially seem schematic, is then complicated. Suffering is ugly and yet has about it an awesome dignity. The decadent charms of Catholicism are "unmanning" and yet "seductive." At the conclusion Lyutov rejects its feminized culture ("crucifixes tiny as the talismans of courtesans, parchment of Papal Bulls and satin of women's letters") to rejoin the world of masculine action: "Away from these winking madonnas deceived by common soldiers!" Nevertheless the mysteries of culture continue to lure his imagination.

"**Berestechko**" combines all three social groupings—Catholic Poland, the Jewish Pale, and the revolutionary army. The pattern of presentation is the same. We are now in the middle of the book, war has muted the songs and darkened the colors of the Cossack march, but it still beats with power: "We were on the march from Khotin to Berestechko. The fighting men dozed in their tall saddles. A song gurgled like a brook running dry. Monstrous corpses lay upon thousand-year-old burial mounds. . . . Divisional Commander Pavlichenko's cloak flew over the Staff like a somber flag. . . . We rode past the Cossack burial mounds, past Bogdan Khmelnitsky's watchtower. An old man with a bandura crept out from behind a gravestone and in a child's voice sang of ancient Cossack glory. We listened to his song in silence and to the sounds of a thundering march burst into Berestechko."

Lyutov wanders into the Jewish quarter, a cramped and sunless ghetto. Excrement, useless waste, is a recurring detail in descriptions of Jewish habitats: "The sun never penetrates here. . . . In wartime the inhabitants seek refuge from bullets and pillage in these catacombs. Human offal and cow dung accumulate here for days. Depression and horror fill the catacombs with the corrosive and foul acidity of excrement."

Depressed by Jewish misery, Lyutov walks off to the deserted castle of a Polish aristocrat, where Gothic moonlight supplants the brilliant sunlight of battle, sinister green hues and watery shades displace the regal purple and bright red, orange, and yellow of the heroic landscape: "The moon, green as a lizard, rose above the pond. From my window I could make out the estate of the Counts Raciborski—meadows and hopfields, hidden by the watery ribbons of twilight." The Raciborski family history is a tale of decay, of a mad ninety-year-old countess, her impotent son, and a "dying family line." A yellowing letter dated 1820 announces the birth of a child and recalls a time when the Raciborskis, still fruitful, could look to the future. In the distance a commissar is heard making a speech.

Lyutov feels the pull of two forces—the commissar's imperious rhetoric and the insinuating seductions of the old order. Building his stories on contrast, Babel is also fond of contrasting syntax, of coordinate sentences whose clauses clash: "He spoke of the Second Congress of the Comintern, while I wandered past walls where nymphs with gouged out eyes were leading an ancient choral dance." Aristocratic culture, though impotent and doomed, still exerts the fascination of art. The story concludes on the notes of power which opened it. "You are in power," the commissar exhorts. "Everything here is yours. There are no more Pans. I now proceed to the election of the Revolutionary Committee." Lyutov ambles in a no-man's land, recognizing the unequivocal voice of power, drawn to the sinuous paths of culture and the pathos of dying ways.

APOCALYPSE

The epic line persists through the book, but its colors gradually darken. By the time of **"Berestechko,"** a little over halfway through, the standard of the sunset has become a "somber flag"; the thundering songs now gurgle "like a brook running dry"; silent Cossacks ride by monstrous corpses. Toward the end, in **"Zamoste,"** the landscape of war turns nightmarish: "Rain fell. Over the flooded earth flew wind and darkness. The stars were blotted out by ink-swollen clouds. . . . The raw dawn flowed over us like waves of chloroform. Green rockets soared above the Polish camp. . . . More rain fell. Dead mice floated along the roads. Autumn set its ambushes about our hearts, and trees like naked corpses set upright on their feet swayed at the crossroads." The imagery accumulates until it forms an apocalyptic vision of the death of things. The story follows the usual pattern, shifting from an extended portrait to specific incidents. However, instead of furnishing contrast now, an encounter with a peasant merely adds to the sense of a world engulfed in total violence.

> The peasant made me light a cigarette from his. "The Jews are to blame for everything, on our side and yours. There'll be mighty few of them left after the war. How many Jews are there in the whole world?"
>
> "Ten million," I answered.
>
> "There'll be only two hundred thousand left," cried the peasant, and touched my hand, afraid I would go.

Much of **Red Cavalry** has a fantastical, at times even hallucinatory quality—moonlit Gothic churches, green skies hovering over deserted manors. **"Zamoste"** alternates between a reality turned nightmare and a dream of escape. Caught up in a maelstrom of destruction, Lyutov, seeking the embrace of the maternal earth, dreams of comfort at a woman's breast. However, to turn back in nostalgia to the mother is also a kind of death:

> The sodden ground offered me the soothing embrace of the tomb. . . . I dreamed of a shed all carpeted with hay. . . . a woman dressed as for a ball came over to me. She freed her breast from the black lace of her bodice and raised it to me, carefully, like a nurse proffering food. She laid her breast against mine. An aching warmth stirred in the depths of my soul, and drops of sweat—live, stirring sweat—seethed between our nipples.
>
> "Margot," I longed to cry out, "the earth is dragging me like a jibbering cur by the cord of its calamities. Nevertheless I have seen you, Margot."
>
> . . . "Jesus," she said, "receive the soul of thy departed servant."
>
> She placed two worn five-kopeck pieces on my eyelids, and stuffed the orifice of my mouth with fragrant hay. My moaning vainly beat about inside my clamped jaws, my failing pupils turned slowly beneath the copper coins, I could not force my hands apart. . . .

Upon awakening, he rejoins the violence. The story concludes in bitter irony: "Silence. 'We've lost the campaign,' muttered Volkov, and snored. 'Yes,' I answered."

Whichever way Lyutov turns, he comes up against unsatisfactory choices, incomplete versions of the self he is struggling to shape. Heroic action and masculine power are compelling, but too often they manifest themselves as hollow theatrical gesture or purposeless cruelty. Violence, understood broadly, is an essential ingredient of creativity: the artist does violence to the language he has inherited, the revolutionist to the social order he lives in. But violence in **Red Cavalry** is always on the edge of becoming an end in itself, barbarism loosed from the humanizing restraints of culture. In its darker moments, as in **"Zamoste,"** Lyutov is the witness, not of a painful birth, but of a cataclysm of death. To retreat to dreams of maternal comfort is to die as a man. The worlds of culture offer the solace of art and the nourishment of community, but these too are dying.

THE JEWS

The double pull of the book—its alternation between attraction and repulsion—is perhaps strongest in the sections devoted to Lyutov's fellow Jews. Gedali, protagonist of the story bearing his name, is the aged and blind proprietor of a curiosity shop, a museum of dead objects: "Here before me is the market and the death of

the market. The fat soul of plenty is dead. Dumb pad-
locks hang upon the booths, and the granite pavement
is as clean as the bald pate of a corpse. . . . There
were buttons and a dead butterfly. . . . [Gedali] wound
in and out of a labyrinth of globes, skulls, and dead
flowers, waving a many colored feather duster of cock's
plumes and blowing dust from the dead flowers. . . . A
vague odor of corruption enfolded me."

Surrounded by death, Gedali, in green frock coat sweeping to the ground and top hat resembling a black tower,
is yet a prophet of life. His eyes have been closed by
Polish anti-Semites, but his ears are attuned to mysterious voices wafting in the night air. (Armies clash in
brilliant sunlight; the cultures of the wayside are
shrouded in twilight or night.) Gedali's prophetic
dreams are of the final "sweet revolution" of joy, of an
"International of Good People," who see to it that there
are no orphans in the house and that every soul receives
"first-category rations." To Gedali's Messianic Revolution, the narrator answers with the voice of the actual
historical Revolution, in clipped accents of violence and
power: "The sunlight doesn't enter eyes that are closed.
But we will cut open those closed eyes."

Lyutov, however, cannot maintain his aggressive posture. The story had begun in tones of elegiac lyricism
and prayerlike incantation, Babel's other way (in addition to naturalistic portraiture) of evoking Jewish places:
"On Sabbath eves I am oppressed by the dense melancholy of memories. In bygone days on these evenings
my grandfather would stroke with his yellow beard the
tomes of Ibn-Ezra. . . . On these evenings my child's
heart rocked like a little ship on enchanted waves. O
the rotted Talmuds of my childhood! O the dense melancholy of memories! I roam Zhitomir in search of a
timid star. . . ." When at the end of the story the Sabbath star rises out of the blue darkness to assume her
throne, Lyutov softens. Throughout *Red Cavalry* the
sharing of food is a token of comradeship and community. **"Gedali"** concludes in an ironic reversal of its initial contrasts. The Revolution has energy but offers
poor nourishment to the starved souls of men; Lyutov,
who had asserted its vitality, turns for nourishment to
the dead world of Gedali.

> "Pan comrade, you don't know what the International
> is eaten with."
>
> "It is eaten with gunpowder and spiced with best-
> quality blood."
>
> And then, from out of the blue dark, the young Sabbath
> ascended to her throne.
>
> "Gedali," I said, "today is Friday, and it's already
> evening. Where are Jewish cakes to be got, and a Jew-
> ish glass of tea, and a bit of that pensioned-off God in
> a glass of tea?"

The stories we have examined reveal the paradoxical
structure of *Red Cavalry*. Built around contrast, they
oppose the epic march of revolution to the suffering of

the old order. The former is described in a style of energy, movement, and color; the latter is pictured in images of decay and death and in a style suggesting stasis.
But if the epic line of the book is vibrant and forceful,
it is also barren—a desert of the heart. The old ways
are rotting but it is among them that Lyutov seeks sus-
tenance. In Catholic Poland he feels the lure of art and
the pathos of a vanished culture; among his fellow Jews,
he experiences nostalgia for familial traditions and the
pathos of suffering.

CULTURE

Culture for Babel is a mysterious thing. It belongs to
night, the moon, and the lonely Sabbath star as opposed
to the sunlight of clamorous events. The shifts from the
clear sunlight and martial rhythms of the epic to the
mysterious moonlit nights and evocative language of
the pathetic mode mark a change in kinds of experience. Language and imagery combine to determine the
book's shape of feeling. In the daylight of the epic-
heroic world, in the arena of history, action is precise,
unreflective, and violent. Life admits of clearcut categorization, as humanity divides into agent and patient, actor and sufferer, forger of the future and remnant of the
dying past. But in the realm of human culture, where
man gives himself to creation and thought, everything
is hopelessly ambiguous: "I went along with the moon,
nursing unrealizable dreams and discordant songs" (I,
45).

The figures representing culture in *Red Cavalry* embody its mysteries and paradoxes. They are incongruous, slightly comic, yet inspired: "Old Gedali, the diminutive proprietor in smoked glasses and a green frock
coat down to the ground, meandered around his treasures in the roseate void of evening. He rubbed his
small white hands, plucked his little grey beard, and listened, head bent, to the mysterious voices wafting down
to him" (I, 50). His Gentile counterpart is the Polish
artist Pan Apolek, of the story bearing his name, who is
also a child of the evening: "On fragrant evenings the
shades of old feudal Poland assembled, the mad
[*yurodivy*] artist at their head." Like Gedali, he has a
touch of the whimsical about him: "In his right hand
Apolek carried a paintbox, and with his left he guided
the blind accordion player. The singing of their nailed
German boots rang out with peace and hope. From
Apolek's thin neck dangled a canary-yellow scarf. Three
little chocolate-colored feathers fluttered on the blind
man's Tyrolean hat. . . . It looked as though . . . the
Muses had settled at the organ side by side in bright,
wadded scarves and hobnailed German boots."

Incongruous in appearance, Apolek leads a life and pursues an art that are exercises in paradox. He is at one
and the same time a decorator of Christian churches
and a heretic. His favorite story is the apocryphal tale

of Jesus lying out of pity with the virgin Deborah. His art carries "a portent of mystery," the mystery of the ways the ordinary can be transformed by art. Apolek spends his life raising the poor and sinful to the condition of saints in icons of glorious color. "He has made saints of you in your lifetime," the indignant church authorities complain.

Apolek's artistic vision is but a variant of the Hasid Gedali's prophetic dream of the coming Revolution of Joy and the International of Good People. Polish village artist and Jewish shopkeeper represent the aesthetic and ethical imaginations, respectively. Engulfed by violence, both cling to dreams of universal compassion. And as in his encounter with Gedali, Lyutov softens in Apolek's presence: "I then made a vow to follow Pan Apolek's example. And the sweetness of a dreamer's malice, my bitter scorn for the curs and swine of mankind, the flame of silent and intoxicating revenge—all this I sacrificed to my new vow."

Even the Cossacks have a visionary bard: Sashka, of **"Sashka Khristos"** (**"Sashka the Christ"**). The tale opens in tones of legend: "Sashka was his name, and he was called Christ on account of his gentleness." This homely hagiography recounts Sashka's passage from a state of sin to sanctity. Away from the heroic march we get glimpses of a Cossack society that is coarse and brutish. In keeping with his mean subject matter Babel tells Sashka's story in a colloquial manner, with much of the speech in dialect. Lyutov's voice momentarily dissolves into the language of the depicted milieu to form a kind of *skaz*.

Sashka is fourteen when his stepfather Tarakanych (the name means cockroach) introduces him to the pleasures of sex through a crippled beggar. They contract a venereal disease, which does not stop the stepfather from intercourse with the boy's mother. As they return from this sexual adventure they pass through a natural world as lovely as the human is ugly. Descriptions of nature in Babel's fiction strive for lyrical expressiveness and metaphorical nuance rather than mimetic exactitude. Built upon formulas, they tend toward abstraction: poppies are crimson, rye is yellow, fog is pearly. However, the imaginativeness of metaphor saves his prose from cliché: "The earth lay in April dampness. In the black hollows emeralds glistened. Green shoots embroidered the earth in intricate stitches."

Sashka soon has enough of Tarakanych's cruelties and asks his permission to follow the ways of the saints and become a shepherd. It would be tempting to say that Sashka has been inspired to take this decision by the beauties of nature, but Babel does not probe the psychology of his characters. Symbolic and poetic vision replaces rational motivation: "The force of his vision held him spellbound. Surrendering to it he rejoiced in

his daydream. It seemed to him that two silver cords . . . were suspended from the sky, and attached to them a cradle—a cradle of rosewood with a floral pattern. It swung high above the earth and far from the skies, and the silver cords swayed and sparkled. Sashka lay in the cradle, and the air wafted over him. The air, resonant as music, blew from the fields, and a rainbow blossomed over the unripe corn. Sashka rejoiced in his day dream. . . ."

Sashka heeds the music of his dreams and becomes the village holy man, **"Sashka the Christ."** Like Gedali and Pan Apolek, he follows a private vision that sets him apart from the common run. He is a gentle child thrown among brutal men. His gentleness may have something to do with his disease; the failed and the hurt seek him out "for his love and his illness." He is also, like Apolek, an artist of sorts, a singer. In battle the Cossacks protect him because men "need songs" (*I*, 147).

In many of the stories of *Red Cavalry* the narrator initially relinquishes his role as character only to resume it at the end. Momentarily granted the status of objective narration, the tale is then converted into food for the narrator's reflections. At the conclusion Sashka's story also becomes Lyutov's, as the sophisticated intellectual discovers in the simple boy a kindred spirit: "I got to know Sashka the Christ. . . . Since then we have often met the dawn and seen the sun set together. And whenever the capricious chance of war has brought us together, we have sat down of an evening on the bench outside a hut, or made tea in the woods in a sooty kettle, or slept side by side in the new-mown fields, the hungry horses tied to his foot or mine."

Grieved by the barbarism of war, Lyutov turns to the paths of culture for solace. He has no illusions about social institutions, which are crumbling under the impact of Revolution. Instead he is attracted to lonely and eccentric men who represent culture's ultimate values. Pan Apolek and Sashka the Christ are artists—one a painter, the other a singer: in time of war men need songs. Gedali is a man of faith, steeped in old familial and communal traditions, who has not forgotten the joy of a Jewish cup of tea. Above all, Jewish Hasidic prophet, heretical Polish painter, and village singer and saint share a capacity for compassion.

As action is the measure of man in the heroic-epic world, so compassion is a cardinal value of culture. It provides the nourishment missing from the deserts of war. Night, which shrouds Catholic churches, Polish estates, and Jewish villages, is a time of comfort. While the images of day are masculine—phallic standards cleaving brilliant sunlit skies—those of night are maternal: "Blue roads flowed past me like streams of milk spurting from many breasts"; "evening wrapped me in the life-giving moisture of its twilight sheets, evening laid a mother's hand upon my burning forehead"; "night comforted us in our sorrows, a light wind wafted over us like a mother's skirt." Gedali exalts the figure of the compassionate mother to a metaphysical principle: "All is mortal. Only the mother is destined for eternal life. And when the mother is no longer among the living, she leaves a memory which no one has yet dared to defile. The memory of the mother nourishes in us a compassion that is like the ocean. The measureless ocean nourishes the rivers that dissect the universe. . . . In the passionate edifice of Hasidism the windows and doors have been knocked out, but it is immortal, like the soul of the mother. With oozing eyes sockets Hasidism still stands at the crossroads of the winds of history" (*I*, 46, 56, 99, 57).

INITIATION

To become fully a man Lyutov must give up the mother. In **"Moy pervy gus"** (**"My first goose"**) he is assigned to Commander Savitsky's division. Confronted by this ideal of manly beauty, he is filled with awe and envy. Derision greets him: "Guys with specs are a drag here. . . . It's no life for high falutin types. But you go and mess up a lady, a real clean one too, and you'll have the boys patting you on the back." Lyutov performs the rape symbolically, by killing the goose of a landlady who had refused to feed him. The act is like a pagan rite of initiation: "The Cossacks in the yard were already sitting around their cauldron. They sat motionless, erect, like heathen priests at a sacrifice. . . ." The results are mixed. In despair at his rejection, Lyutov had sought escape in reading from Lenin, but "the beloved lines came toward me along a thorny path and could not reach me." After the ritual murder he is accepted by the Cossacks and reads to them. He feels the joy of manly camaraderie, and touches a masculine principle: "I read on and exulted, and in my exultation caught the secret curve of Lenin's straight line." But he suffers from guilt. Babel's choice of words points to an identification with the victim that is at the root of Lyutov's conflict: as the goose's head "cracked and oozed" (*tresnula i potekla*), Lyutov's heart, "stained with bloodshed, grated and brimmed over" (*skripelo i teklo*). Overcome by guilt, he longs for maternal comfort: "Evening wrapped about me the life-giving moisture of its twilight sheets, evening laid a mother's hand upon my burning forehead. . . . We slept, all six of us, beneath a torn roof that let in the stars, warming one another, our legs intertwined. I dreamed and in my dreams saw women. But my heart, stained with bloodshed, grated and brimmed over."

Lyutov's conflict admits of no easy solution. To choose Gedali's way, the way of the "compassionate mother," is to deny the imperatives of action and also, in the entanglements of war, even to deny compassion. In

"Smert Dolgushova" (**"The death of Dolgushov"**) the wounded Dolgushov implores Lyutov to finish him off so as to save him from torture at the hands of the Poles. The Cossacks interpret his inability to fulfill the request as a failure of pity: "You guys in specs have about as much pity for us fellows as a cat for a mouse." It is the terrible irony of war that to assume manly responsibility one must learn to kill. In **"Posle boya"** (**"After the battle"**) Lyutov is ashamed when the Cossacks discover that he has gone into battle with an unloaded gun. Taunted as a religious pacifist (*molokan*), he walks off into the night imploring fate to grant him "the simplest of proficiencies—the ability to kill my fellowmen." Violence fills him with guilt, but to stay with the mother is a violence committed upon the self, a denial of one's manly nature. As in **"Zamoste,"** where the dream of a nourishing woman is associated with the hero's death, in **"After the Battle"** night, the time of maternal comfort, is revealed as a time of martyrdom: "Evening flew up to the sky like a flock of birds, and darkness crowned me with its watery wreath. I felt my strength ebbing away. Bent beneath a funeral garland, I walked on. . . ."

RESOLUTION

Isaac Babel's great book continually circles a tragic dilemma. The march of history will not be denied, but it leaves men spiritually famished. The cultures—artistic, religious, moral—which nourish human life are dying. To linger nostalgically in an irretrievable past is to die oneself. The forward march of history and the preservative patterns of culture are never brought into harmony, but the final two stories—**"Syn rabbi"** (**"The rabbi's son"**) and **"Argamak"**—do seek out a middle ground.

The rebellious rabbi's son appears in an earlier sketch, **"Rabbi,"** as "the cursed son, the last son, the recalcitrant son." By the end of *Red Cavalry* this last son of the rabbi's line has joined the Red Army, taken command of a regiment, and been mortally wounded. Like Gedali and Pan Apolek, Ilya is a paradoxical figure. His description combines both male and female features: "a youth . . . with the powerful brow of Spinoza, with the sickly face of a nun." While going through the dying Ilya's belongings, Lyutov discovers that he has lugged off to war emblems of all the opposites of the book: action and poetry, politics and art, things masculine and feminine: "Everything was strewn about pell-mell—mandates of the propagandist and notes of the Jewish poet. The portraits of Lenin and Maimonides lay side by side, the knotted iron of Lenin's skull beside the dull silk of the portraits of Maimonides. A lock of woman's hair had been slipped into a volume of Resolutions of the Sixth Party Congress, and curved lines of Hebrew verse crowded the margins of Communist leaflets. They fell on me in a sparse and mournful rain—pages of the Song of Songs and revolver cartridges."

Ilya has found a way, not to reconcile the contradictions of existence, but to live with them. When he goes off to war, he takes the baggage of culture with him. The tokens of culture lie side by side with those of revolution and war, but they remain antagonistic to the end. A mood of elegiac melancholy sweeps over Lyutov as he once again stands face to face with the tragic incongruity of human life.

That mood is not one in which he or the rabbi's son will permit himself to linger. Explaining to Lyutov why he went off to war, Ilya says that, though formerly he would not abandon his mother, in a revolution a mother is only "an episode." She is also "an episode" for Lyutov. In the course of the book he struggles against the webs of nostalgia that tie him to the mother, and in the final story, **"Argamak,"** he breaks free to join the epic march of the Cossack army. He passes the test of mastering a horse—the sine qua non of Cossack manliness—and the Cossacks finally accept him: "I realized my dream. The Cossacks stopped watching me and my horse."

The maternal image and related images of nurturing have been associated with culture and value. The mother, source of life and center of the family, provides the continuity culture demands. But in **Red Cavalry** culture is also "episodic." The structures in which men and women live—family, nation, religion, and tradition—appear to have a permanence that the juggernaut of history belies. Lyutov rejects the temptations of nostalgia to accept, stoically, the exigencies of history.

However, culture is ultimately not an institution but an idea, and even as its institutions crumble in revolution, its idea is kept alive. For Gedali, the mother, even when dead, "leaves a memory" which is "immortal." It is surely no accident that the representative figures of culture in **Red Cavalry,** Gedali and Pan Apolek, are marginal men—Jewish mystic and Catholic heretic. Less tied than others to temporal institutions and orthodoxies, they remain loyal to visions of compassion in the midst of a crumbling world. Gedali is confident that his values, if not yet realized as actualities, will survive as memories at the "crossroads of history."

At the end the rabbi's son joins these two to become the most important of the work's bearers of culture. As Apolek offered a model of the artist to Lyutov—"I vowed . . . to follow the example of Pan Apolek"—the rabbi's son gives him a model of action. Lyutov feels a kinship with him stronger than any he has known before: "And I—scarcely containing the tempests of my imagination in my ancient body—I received the last breath of my brother." Lyutov joins the Cossacks, but he is too much a man of culture to go completely native. Gedali and Pan Apolek attract him by their commitment to ethical and aesthetic values, but they are dreamers and visionaries, too remote from the realities of history to teach him how to live in the world. The rabbi's son shows him a middle course between mindless violence and Messianic imaginings. While participating in the violence, which he deems necessary, he also keeps alive reminders of other ways: poetry, the thought of Maimonides, a lock of woman's hair. In choosing masculine action, he refuses to deny the feminine part of his nature. He decides to live with the contradictions of culture and force.

The Cossack army Lyutov joins at the end of **Red Cavalry** is not the army that burst into the book in a blaze of color at the start. It now bears the scars of war. From the "standards of the sunset" of **"Crossing into Poland"** through the "somber flag" of Berestechko and the deathly scenes of **"Zamoste"** the fields of war undergo a progressive darkening. Babel starts out with a romantically charged picture of war, then brings us close to its brutal actuality. The cumulative violence has a numbing effect on Lyutov, who for a time dreams of escape in the warm womb of the earth before resolving to ride with the horses of war. In the meantime the Cossacks have moved from the condition of glorious beasts or gods to that of wounded men. As they cross the line separating the poetic idealization of the epic-heroic mode from the grim naturalism of the pathetic, they have begun to resemble their victims. A Cossack warrior, Tikhomolov,

> came wearing galoshes on his bare feet. His fingers had been chopped up, and ribbons of black lint hung down from them, dragging after him like a cloak. . . . Baulin was sitting on the steps of the church, steaming his feet in a tub. His feet were putrescent. . . . Tufts of youthful straw stuck to Baulin's forehead. The sun blazed on the bricks and tiles of the church. . . . Tikhomolov, dragging his mantle of rags, went over to the horses, his galoshes squelching. Argamak stretched out his long neck and neighed toward his master, neighed in a soft squeal, like a horse in the desert. On his back the inflamed lymph twisted lacelike between the strips of torn flesh. Tikhomolov stood next to the horse. The filthy ribbons of bandage trailed unstirring on the ground.
>
> (*I* [*Izbrannoe*], 155)[10]

Ultimately, Cossack, Jew, and Pole are united in suffering.

The unblinking acceptance of tragedy makes **Red Cavalry** a great book. Babel rigorously eschews didacticism or the sentimentalism of synthetic reconciliation. He does not have a lesson to teach but a world to show. His book is imperfect. The prose, though moving and often lovely, sometimes slips into pyrotechnic virtuosity. His Cossacks, if not for his qualifying ironies, would be mere projections of adolescent daydreams. Yet in the long run Babel is not a writer to delude himself. He keeps a hard, cold eye on experience. For a world torn by the rival claims of culture and power, compassion and violence, he finds no comfortable solution. He stands with the rabbi's son, in stoic determination to live with ambiguity. The resolution of **Red Cavalry** does not lie in the triumph of any single allegiance, but in an assertion of the will to live in a discordant world.[11]

Notes

1. *Voprosy literary* (Problems of literature), no. 4 (1964):120.

2. "Babel saw Russia," writes Viktor Shklovskii, "as a French writer attached to Napoleon's army might have seen her" ("I. Babel': kriticheskii romans" [Babel: A critical romance], *LEF,* no. 2 [1924]:154).

3. See A. Voronskii, *Literaturno-kriticheskie stat'i* (Critical articles) (Moscow, 1963), 289-90.

4. Renato Poggioli, "Isaak Babel in Retrospect," in *The Phoenix and the Spider* (Cambridge, Mass., 1957), 235.

5. Albert Cook speaks of "the simple declarative base" of epic and of "the relation between statement and rhythm [that] is one of contrast or counterpoint" (*The Classic Line: A Study in Epic Poetry* [Bloomington: Indiana University Press, 1966], 11).

6. Babel habitually spoke of his language in military terms: style is an "army of words . . . in which all kinds of weapons come into play. No iron can enter the human heart so chillingly as a period put at the right place" (*Izbrannoe* (Moscow, 1966), 273); "A short story must have the precision of a military communique. . . . It must be written in the same firm, straightforward hand one uses for commands . . ." (*Dissonant Voices in Soviet Literature,* ed. Patricia Blake and Max Hayward [London, 1964], 34-35).

7. See Victor Terras, "Line and Color: The Structure of I. Babel's Short Stories in *Red Cavalry,*" *Studies in Short Fiction* 3 (Winter 1966):141-56.

8. Shklovskii, "I. Babel'," 154.

9. Aristotle, *Politics* 1.2.1253a.

10. "Argamak" was not part of the original edition, but was added to the fifth and sixth edition of 1931. Had "The Rabbi's Son" concluded the work, Lyutov would have been left in a state of mourning; as we have *Red Cavalry* now he moves past grief to the threshold of action.

11. See Robert A. Maguire, *Red Virgin Soil: Soviet Literature in the 1920's* (Princeton, 1968), 328-29.

Marc Schreurs (essay date 1988)

SOURCE: Schreurs, Marc. "Intertextual Montage in Babel's *Konarmija.*" In *Dutch Contributions to the Tenth International Congress of Slavists, Sofia, September 14-22, 1988: Literature,* edited by André van Holk, pp. 277-307. Amsterdam: Rodopi, 1988.

[*In the following essay, Schreurs analyzes intertextuality as a montage strategy in* Red Cavalry, *finding allusions to Russian folk epics and nineteenth-century works by Leo Tolstoy and Nikolai Gogol.*]

0.

The phenomenon of intertextuality in literary semantics may be approached in two different ways: in a general sense, as an inherent condition of the poetic word, and, in a more pragmatic sense, as a covert or overt allusion from one text to another. The first approach was launched by Julia Kristeva. She initiated the now widely used term as follows:

> Le mot (le texte) est un croisement de mots (de textes) ou on lit au moins un autre mot (texte).
>
> (Kristeva 1969: 145)

> Il se crée, ainsi, autour du signifié poétique, un espace textuel multiple dont les éléments sont susceptibles d'être appliqués dans le texte poétique concret. Nous appellerons cet espace intertextuel.
>
> (ibid: 255)

Kristeva is mainly concerned with the fact that a literary text as a secondary system of signs is inescapably linked to a multitude of other texts, whether by citations or allusions, by transposition of one system of signs into another, or simply by being connected to a specific stock of literary codes and conventions. She is opposed to using the term intertextuality for describing in concreto the relations of a text with other so-called source texts (ce terme a été souvent entendu dans le sens banal de "critique des sources" (ibid 1974: 60). Her broad and therefore somewhat vague conception of intertextuality is at present frequently criticized. Laurent Jenny, for example, asserts that intertextuality does not concern a vague and mysterious field of influences, but that

> l' intertextualité désigne (. . .) le travail de transformation et d'assimilation de plusieurs textes opéré par un texte centreur qui garde le *leadership* du sens.
>
> (Jenny 1976: 262)

Jenny suggests, that to speak of intertextuality makes sense only if in a specific text the presence of another text can be located in elements which in some respect are alien to their immediate context:

nous proposons de parler d'intertextualité seulement lorsqu'on est en mesure de repérer dans un texte des éléments structurés antérieurement à lui, au-delà du lexème, cela s'entend, mais quel que soit leur niveau de structuration.

(ibid)

Accepting, as Jenny does, the semantic leadership of the alluding text, Wolf Schmid returns to Bachtin's notion of *dialogical relationships* between words (cf. Schmid 1983). As opposed to Kristeva, who used Bachtin's ideas to broaden the concept of intertextuality, Schmid returns to Bachtin in order to circumscribe the process of transformation and (semantic) assimilation. According to Schmid, Bachtin's notion of the literary word (text) as an utterance which expresses the position of a specific "author" is most important:

logičeskie i predmetno-smyslovye otnošenija, čtoby stat' dialogičeskimi, (. . .) dolžny stat' (. . .) vyskaza-niem, i polučit' avtora, to est' tvorca dannogo vyskaza-nija, č'ju poziciju ono vyražaet.

(Bachtin 1929: 314)

Bachtin argues that a dialogical relationship between one utterance (word, text) and another manifests itself in what he terms the "double-voiced word" (dvugolosoe slovo). In the double-voiced word two semantic or ideological orientations collide, interact in the (metaphorical) sense of a dialogue. Schmid calls such a dialogical interaction intersemanticity (Intersemantizität). He approaches intertextuality pragmatically and confines his interest to intersemantical relationships between texts:

Wenn wir uns hier mit den Manifestationen der Inter-textualität nur insoweit beschäftigen als sie sich als "dialogische Beziehungen" darstellen, zielen wir auf Intertextualität nicht einfach als Relation von strukturi-erten *Texten,* sondern (. . .) auf Intertextualität als Relation der in den simultan vergegenwärtigten Texten ausgedruckten *Bedeutungen, Sinnpositionen,* und *Ideologien.*

(1983: 142)

Schmid further maintains that intertextuality is intersemantical only if the presence of a textual source, a 'Prätext' Schmid terms it (pre-text hereafter) can be identified in a text as an intentional significatory aspect of the semantic construction of a text. Submitted to these restrictions, intertextuality largely coincides with what is traditionally known as literary allusion. As far as this device is concerned, reference to intentionality on the part of the author seems to be prerequisite. A text cannot allude to a pre-text unless it can be assumed on reasonable grounds that the author knew the given pre-text.

In his article Schmid discusses four definitions of the literary allusion (cf.: Górski 1962; Johnson 1976; Ben-Porat 1976; Perry 1978). The most comprehensive definition is undoubtedly the one designed by Carmela Perry:

Allusion in literature is a manner of signifying in which some kind of marker (simple or complex, overt or covert) not only signifies unallusively, within the imagined world of the alluding text, but through echo also denotes a source text and specifies some discrete, recoverable property (ies) belonging to the intentions of this source text (. . .), the property (ies) evoked modifies the alluding text, and possibly activates further, larger inter- and intra-textual patterns of properties with consequent further modification of the alluding text.

(Perry 1978: 295)

The present article, which will study intertextuality as a montage strategy in Babel's *Konarmija*-stories subscribes to Perry's definition and Schmid's lucid elaboration. The restricting definitions of intertextuality provided by these scholars are useful in describing manifestations of intertextuality as forms of montage. Montage, as a semantic principle, is based on colliding aspects of "Intersemantizität", in other words, on semantic juxtapositions of initially unrelated elements, selected from heterogeneous contexts. Like inner-stories and digressions, intertextual allusions are traditional phenomena in literature which function according to the "laws" of montage (cf. Schreurs 1987). In what follows I shall use the term intertextual allusion instead of literary allusion. For the qualifier "literary" puts an unnecessary limitation on the field of research. *Konarmija* involves the reader in dialogical patterns not only with other literary texts, but often also with non-literary pretexts.

To regard the insertion of a pre-text into a text as montage makes sense only if the "strange" properties, the marking elements which enable the reader to establish the pre-text have a distinctly conflicting position in their new verbal environment. The inserted marker should create a noticeable effect of discontinuity or contrast. In this respect, the quality of the alluding signal, its material substance, so to speak, is of decisive importance. The chief aim of this study is to describe the attraction-level of the montage, i.e., the conflict status of the marker, and to sketch out the dominant aspects of the hidden dialogical patterns and semantic modifications. The presence of a great variety of pretexts in *Konarmija* has been observed by numerous critics before me. I am happy to be able to start from their excellent work, on which I shall try to elaborate.

1. LITERARY PRE-TEXTS

1.1

One of the traditional literary modes on which Babel draws in his *Konarmija,* is the epic mode of narration. In Babel's hands, the war between Poland and Soviet Russia, or rather the campaign of Budennyj's First Cavalry Army (Konarmija), acquires proportions common to heroic poems of all times. One may even regard

Konarmija in its entirety as a modern epic. It relates to us a series of events which themselves represent a much greater historical event: a radical social change in western civilization, the end of the old world, the coming of a new era, marked by WOI and the October Revolution. Babel's awareness of the long-range significance of his epoch shows itself, among others, in his vivid evocation of an epic mood. James Falen remarked that "Babel's feel for the epic is genuine, and its evocation in his work is extremely effective" (1974: 121). Babel's epic sources are to be found, according to Falen, not only among the ancient classics, but also in the Russian folk-epic—*Slovo o Polku Igoreve (The Igor Tale),* and in the 19th century epic works by Gogol' (*Taras Bulba)* and Tolstoj (*Vojna i mir).*

Konarmija echoes the epic in several ways. Victor Terras describes the reminiscences of the classic epos (Homer) in the cycle pre-eminently on the diegetic level. He sums up typical epic action motifs (the ride to a strange place where adventure, passion, or even death is waiting: the ride to a rendezvous with destiny in, e.g., **"Perechod čerez Zbruč," "Put' v Brody," "Priščepa."** 1966: 142), legendary heroes (the demigods Voroshilov and Budennyj. Ibid), heroic martial scenes (Trunov's duel with Fauntleroy; the cavalry charge in **"Česniki"**), which can be read as "Homeric episodes in travesty". As a result of these epic allusions, the events and characters acquire a mythical meaning. Falen reaches a similar conclusion:

> Interpreting contemporary events in terms of models from the past, Babel describes the Revolution as a "timeless" war, as a part of the unchanging fate of mankind, and its Cossack horsemen—their human traits enlarged to mythic proportions—become Homeric heroes.
>
> (Falen 1974: 191)

According to Falen, Babel's epic vision depends not only on certain diegetic equivalences, on the use of martial themes and a Homeric approach to character, but also involves specific stylistic devices which create an epic mood, devices such as: hyperbolic epithets, apostrophes, and poetic descriptions of the setting (cf. also Murphy 1966: 369-370).

By using these stylistic devices in a specific manner, Babel not only echoes all past epics, but calls to mind one epic pretext in particular: the *Slovo o Polku Igoreve (The Igor Tale).* The presence in the cycle of markers pointing toward this 12th century Russian folk-epos is clear as a day. It has been noted in various studies of Babel's style. Thus, Nilsson (1977) points out that the imagery of **"Perechod čerez Zbruč,"** the poetic description of the crossing of the river, reminds readers familiar with Russian literature of the *Igor Tale* (67). Falen also mentions this work as a source of Babel's

epic vision (1974: 119) but he doesn't go into to much detail. Van Baak pointed out that descriptions of the landscape have functions comparable to those effected descriptions of natural phenomena in the *Igor Tale.* He mentions, for instance, the "epic escorting of individual heroes in the landscape" (cf. 1979: 44; 1983: 182).

The allusions to *Slovo o Polku Igoreve* are detectable predominantly trough equivalences of phraseological material. The alluding signals, the markers, are wrapped in strikingly phrased fragments. It goes without saying, that these moments are alien to their immediate context. As such they can be regarded points of attraction montage. The reader of *Konarmija* is invited to establish a parallel with the *Igor Tale* already in the opening story of the cycle. Through various markers **"Perechod čerez Zbruč"** activates the tale as an intertextual frame of reference to remain operative throughout the cycle.

The *Igor Tale* is referred to in the poetic description of the march toward and the crossing of the river Zbruč. The poetic-ornamental wording of this fragment echoes Bojan's hymnographic style. Several images in Babel's story are closely related to it, for instance: "Štandarty zakata vejut nad našimi golovami" relates to "Už vetry (. . .) vejut s morja strelami". The effects of expressive descriptions of natural phenomena roughly the same: qualifications, similes, metaphors provide nature with an active, personified quality (cf. van Baak 1983: 182). In the *Igor Tale,* nature predicts Igor's lot already at the outset of his ride into the unknown; it even tries to prevent him from going: "Solnce dorogu emu tmoj zastupilo / I rano na drugoj den' krovavye zori svet povedajut." Nature reflects the mourning after Igor's defeat: "Ponikaet trava ot žalosti. A drevo pečalju k zemle priklonilos'."

Throughout the epic personification of nature is an important feature of the ornamental style of narration, particularly in the case of Igor's march toward the Donec and the battles with the Kumany. In **"Perechod čerez Zbruč"** ornamental descriptions of nature have a similar role: they reflect not only the army's movement (Volyn' izgibaetsja, uchodit, vpolzaet, putaetsja), but also the dull and slack atmosphere on a hot day in July. The image of the sun rolling along the sky like a chopped-off head, foreshadows the coming confrontation with death. The river prepares her deadly traps (zakručivaet penistye uzly svoich porogov). The glittering of the cool majestic moon sheds a cold and indifferent light upon the drowning soldier and his comrades who are struggling to come across. Falen suggests (1974: 123) that this type of description may be compared in function with the classical chorus. It gives a kind of indirect comment in response to the depicted events, and expresses the often repressed evaluative perspective of the narrating I.

The allusion to the *Igor Tale* in **"Perechod čerez Zbruč"** is thus primarily effected through imagery reminiscent of Bojan's style in personifying descriptions of spatial elements. The epic passage is an attraction moment, at variance with the rest of the story. It breaks off the tone of the opening paragraph and contrasts sharply with the more laconic phrasing of the next paragraph. The equivalence on the level of phraseological material triggers off additional thematic parallels. Take, for instance, the motif of 'blindness'. Igor fails to recognize the signs of warning expressed by nature, since he is blinded by his eagerness for glory and honour. Unable to form a proper judgement regarding his military capabilities he sets out to fight the enemy by himself instead of fighting them together with other feudal princes. His blindness and conceit leads to a defeat with disastrous consequences. Blindness is also a significant motif in **"Perechod čerez Zbruč."** Like king Igor, the narrator of **Konarmija** goes on a journey into the unknown, filled with great expectations. He too fails to see the implications of the signs of destruction and death. Only in the second part of the story the observing I, confronted with the true state of affairs, is forced to abandon his self-delusion.

Another remarkable concurrence in motifs is the symbolic—meaning of the crossing of the river. In the *Igor Tale,* the Donec does not merely signify the natural boundary between the Russian Soil (Russkaja Zemlja) and the land of the enemy. It is also the borderline between light and darkness, good and evil, heaven and hell, God and the devil (cf. Klein 1976). In Babel's story, too, the river has a symbolical meaning of this type. Apart from being a "crossing into Poland", as is more or less suggested, it is a crossing from day to night, from light to darkness, from color to line and sound. But above all it symbolizes the transition from a peaceful atmosphere to war, and on a mental level, from expectations to realities, from blindness to recognition.

Thus in the opening story of **Konarmija** a firm frame of reference is established by distinct phraseological and diegetic equivalences with the *Igor Tale*. Throughout the cycle, the reader is repeatedly reminded of this epic 'background' through the montage of elements of landscape and nature, particularly the sun, the moon and stars, daybreak and sunset, accompanying martial themes. Some examples are presented by van Baak (cf. 1983: 182-183).

Another montage device linked with the epic is the apostrophe. Apostrophes alluding to the epic genre very strongly can be found in **"Kostel v Novograde."** For instance, the following digression breathes a monumental historicism reminiscent of the historic digressions in the *Igor Tale*:

> Niščie ordy katjatsja na tvoi drevnie goroda, o Pol'ša,
> pesn' ob edinenii vsech cholopov gremit nad nimi, o

> gore tebe, Reč' Pospolitaja, gore tebe, knjaz' Radzivill,
> i tebe, knjaz' Sapega, vstavššie na čas.

Apart from phraseological and diegetic elements, **Konarmija** also has some large-scale compositional idiosyncrasies in common with the *Igor Tale*. The aforementioned epic markers are supported in their alluding function by various elements such as an erratic, anachronical sjužet-composition, deliberate oppositions of different styles and a random approach to fact, setting off the present against the past constantly. On account of what I have been saying so far, we may conclude that Babel undoubtedly intended the many references to the *Igor Tale* as a structural element of the semantic universe of his work. The allusions primarily suggest a historical parallel between the events described in **Konarmija** and the military campaign of Prince Igor Svjatoslavič in 1185. In view of the fact that Igor's plight was a failure, and that his defeat had catastrophical consequences for the internally divided Russia, the parallel may well be regarded as a foreboding of doom.

A more important function of the allusion is, however, that it "reflect(s) a vision of the human condition which is characteristic of a heroic world-view, of a heroic society", clashing with brutal aspects of the war (Terras 1966: 145). The epic allusions operate within a system of colliding points of view, and this turns the cycle into a polyphonic novel in a modernist tradition. Babel's narrator 'imitates' the epic style to create a heroic-epic perspective which stands at variance with other modes of presentation.

1.2

In the second story of the cycle, **"Kostel v Novograde,"** Babel employs some characteristic conventions belonging to the tradition of the *Gothic novel*. Patricia Carden writes:

> Here he (the narrator, M.S.) deals with his attachment
> to the past, exorcising that attachment by showing it
> through the distorting lens of the Gothic.
>
> (1972: 90)

The pre-text to which the story refers cannot be specified. Rather, it consists of a series of texts (novels) which share a number of codes and conventions. The Gothic marker is not restricted to one particular moment in the story, nor does it concern the level of phraseological presentation. The indicator of the literary allusion comprises widely dispersed diegetic elements and narrative-compositional techniques. Therefore, the intertextual correlation with the Gothic pre-text can be established only in retrospect. In such cases the whole text becomes a marker of the source (cf. Schmid 1983: 149).

"Kostel v Novograde" suggests the Gothic tradition in the first place through the presentation of the setting. Carden compares the observing narrator to "that other innocent fascinated by Gothic, Jane Austin's Catherine Morland in *Northanger Abbey*" (ibid). The church in Novograd and the adjacent presbytery are transformed by Ljutov into a conventional Gothic setting, with hidden subterranean rooms, full of strange elements, creating an atmosphere of terror. Some examples in the story:

> Rjadom s domom reveli kolokola . . . ; v zmeinom sumrake; ten' monacha kralas' za mnoj neotstupno; dychanie nevidannogo uklada mercalo pod razvalinami ksendza; vskradčivye ego soblazny obessili menja; vorota kostela raskryty, ja vchožu, i mne navstreču dva čerepa razgorajutsja na kryše slomannogo groba. V ispuge ja brosajus' vniz, v podzemel'e. I ja vižu množestvo ognej, beguščich v vysote u samogo kupola.

Falen describes these "trappings of a Gothic satire" as follows: "through the story's somewhat sinister symbolism, the Christian temple becomes its obverse, a demonic dungeonlike cellar. The search through the temple's crypt suggests the winding quest through a monster's lair—or through the labyrinthine entrails of the monster itself" (1974: 166). It is typical of the Gothic novel that spatial motifs of concealment and horror are psychologically significant.

> One of their (Gothic novels, M.S.) most prominent concerns, though seldom discussed, might grandiosely be called a psychological interest. (. . .) there is a considerable amount of concern for interior mental processes.
>
> (Hume 1969: 283)

The Gothic trappings are a sign of the mental trappings of characters and narrator. Thus the setting in **"Kostel v Novograde"** is a sign of Pan Romual'd's treason, the priest's hidden lusts of the flesh and lustful luxury, of the emotional excitement of the Polish characters (grief, hatred), and the narrator's fascination, fear and moral struggle. Psychic excitement dominates the story on all levels. It not only shows in the spatial presentation, or in the behaviour of the characters (the crazed Robackij, the treacherous Romual'd, the bewildered pani Eliza), or in the narrator's emotional digressions, and even the choice of imagery ("Biskvity pachli kak raspjatie. Lukavyj sok byl zaključen v nich i blagovonnaja jarost' vatikana; pod černoj strast'ju neba; Zazduščie rozy").

One of the reasons why Babel filtered **"Kostel v Novograde"** through a Gothic perspective is, according to Carden, to display the narrator's ambiguous point of view, which oscillates between womanish horror and sensual fascination. Mental ambiguity is indeed a characteristic of the Gothic novel: "It emphasizes psychological reaction to evil and leads into a tangle of moral ambiguity for which no meaningful answers can be found" (Hume 1969: 288). This is a crucial thematic aspect of Babel's story, too. Unable to solve his inner struggle, shifting between moral opposites, the narrator abandons the scene of action.

Another theme which motivates the montage of Gothic elements is Catholicism. Even though there is no concrete 'evidence' in the story, it is not too far-fetched to claim that, within the Gothic pre-textual field, one text is of particular relevance: *The Monk* by M. G. Lewis. This 18th century novel, set in medieval Spain, deals with a Roman Catholic monk Ambrosio, known for his austere way of life and his chastity. However, he falls to the temptations of a woman, and becomes the victim of his sexual desires, which eventually lead him to murder and rape. A similar 'blasphemous' evaluation of religion can be found in other Gothic novels:

> The confusion of evil and good which the Gothic novel reflects in its villain-heroes produces a non-Christian or anticlerical feeling. (. . .) To some extent the feeling is simply anti-Catholic.
>
> (Ibid: 287)

The intertextual correlation thus enhances an essential thematic aspect of Babel's story. The Catholic double morality, as exemplified by the image of the escaped priest, who is embedded in signs of sexual weakness and sinfulness, and whose church is involved in worldly affairs, is intensified by the montage of a Gothic frame of reference. This evaluation is countered by the narrator's apparent fascination with the mystical force of the age-long Catholic culture. The echo of Gothic pre-texts is effectively directed towards the expression of this evaluational ambiguity with great esthetic and emotional force.

1.3

"Kostel v Novograde" alludes to the Gothic tradition through specific themes and narrative-compositional techniques. The marker is not confined to one particular element but is an integral part of the overall construction of the story. In this respect it stands apart from most other stories in which montage of literary allusions is restricted to a structurally and thematically isolated text part. Frequently, the marker is an isolated text segment which includes a quite overt authorial hint.

From **"Solnce Italii"** I now quote the following passage, which refers to Shakespeare's *Romeo and Juliet* staged as an opera:

> Syraja plesen' razvalin cvela, kak mramor opernoj skam'i. I ja ždal potrevožennoj dušoj vychoda Romeo iz-za tuč, atlasnogo Romeo, pojuščego o ljubvi v to vremja kak za kulisami ponuryj elektrotechnik deržit palec na vyključatele luny.

By means of the montage of this attraction-like passage Babel creates a shift from gruesome reality—the ruined city of Novograd—to the enchanting phantasy of an opera-stage. A transformation which is seemingly motivated by the narrator's drunken exaltation, the result of one of his visits to pani Eliza's presbytery:

Duša, nalitaja tomitel'nym chelem mečty, ulybalas' ne-
vedomo komu, i voobraženie, slepaja sčastlivaja baba,
klubilos' vperedi ijul'skim tumanom.

The transformation of the ruins of Novograd to the
stage of Romeo and Juliet is inspired by the effects of a
July-moon which sheds its light on the scene. The tech-
nician holding his finger on the moon-extinguisher emphasizes the moon motif in relation to the narrator's
playful imagination. In Shakespeare's play, July is the
time of action. It is the season of extremes, "where a
balmy moonlit night is dependent on the heat of the
preceding day, its dark, velvet delicacy intensified by
contrast with the sun's unmitigated glare. In the
charmed darkness of silent summer night it is easy to
loose touch with the noisy world of day, so distinct, objective, unveiled" (Gibbons 1980: 60). The montage of
this Shakespearian phantasy passage primarily effects a
double contrast. Harsh every-day reality, the city in ruins, is set off against this Shakespearian moonlit love-
scene. At the same time the scene is ridiculed as a stage-
trick. Then again, the moonlit night is evoked as a
beautiful 'imaginistic' vision of the world, signifying
the narrator's zest for life ("Golubye dorogi tekli mimo
menja, kak strui moloka, bryznuvšie iz mnogich
grudej.").

A dominant thematic aspect of **"Solnce Italii"** is that it
confronts the minds of two dreamers, who seek refuge
from the frustrating misery of their situation: the narrator escapes in his artistic imagination, Sidorov dreams
of starting a Revolution in Italy. The intertextual reference to *Romeo and Juliet* underlines the correspondence between the narrator and Sidorov. The latter's
letter extends the allusion in an ironic manner. Apart
from the fact that he wants to go to Italy, it is noteworthy that the name of his bride is *Viktorija*. Some of Sidorov's remarks shed an ironic light on the segment alluding to Shakespeare's drama:

> (. . .) Viktorija, nevesta, kotoraja nikogda ne budet že-
> noj. Vot i sentimental'nost', nu ee k rasproètakoj materi
> . . . Vot pogladjat po golovke i promjamljat:
> 'romantik'. Skažite prosto,—on bolen, zol, p'jan ot
> toski, on chočet solnca Italii i bananov.

The intertextual correlation furthers the ironic shading
of both the narrator and Sidorov. But what is more, it
accentuates the contra-distinction between them. Lju-
tovs "literary" phantasy is lit by "balmy moonlight",
whereas Sidorov longs for the opposite, the Italian sun.
It adds to the negative evaluation of Sidorov's "common sense madness", and to the narrator's ironic self-
evaluation (the moon-extinguisher; the pink wadding of
my imagination).

1.4

In **"Gedali"** the narrator openly refers to Charles Dickens. Again, this takes place in a singled-out passage in
the story, a digression in which the narrator rhetorically
addresses Dickens:

Dikkens, gde byla v tot den' tvoja laskovaja ten'? Ty
uvidel by v ètoj lavke drevnostej zoločenye tufli i
korabel'nye kanaty, starinnyj kompas i čučela orela,
ochotničij vinčester s vygravirovannoj datoj 1810 i slo-
mannuju kastrjulju.

In this digression the narrator returns to the sweet
memories of childhood, expressed in another digression
at the beginning of the story. The "ship's cables, an ancient compass" point back to that moment, when he remembered how on Sabbath eves "my child's heart was
rocked like a little ship on enchanted waves". A more
or less explicit comparison is drawn between old Gedali's shop and the shop of little Nelly's grandfather in
Dickens' *The Old Curiosity Shop* (Lavka Drevnostej).
We recognize the gloomy atmosphere of Dickens' description of the shop, filled with decaying remnants of
the past:

> There were suits of mail, standing like ghosts in ar-
> mour, here and there; fantastic carvings brought from
> monkish cloisters; rusty weapons of various kinds; dis-
> torted figures in china, and wood, and iron, and ivory;
> tapestry and strange furniture that might have been de-
> signed in dreams.

A similar, almost gothic ambience we find in Gedali's
shop:

> V etoj lavke i est' pugovicy, i mertvaja babočka (. . .).
> I on v'etsja v labirinte iz globusov, čerepov i mertvych
> cvetov.

The montage of this literary reference deepens the
evaluative tension, which is so essential to **"Gedali."**
On the one hand the association with Dickens within
the narrator's mind is apparently generated by a deep
sense of affection, connected with tender memories of
his childhood. The narrator observes Gedali with undis-
guised sympathy, comparable to the way Dickens' narrator meets little Nelly, grandfather and grandchild. The
former is little and old, like Gedali, and has in his face
"marks of deep and anxious thought, which convinced
me that he could not be, as I had been at first inclined
to suppose, in a state of dotage or imbecility". Babel
clearly linked Gedali to the grandfather in Dickens'
novel. They both are figures from the past, and this is
symbolized by the contents of their curiosity shops.
Their worldviews combine wisdom with a childlike na-
ivety, which at first in the case of Nelly's grandfather
obtains elements of senility. In the narrator's presentation, Gedali's somewhat childlike outlook is repeatedly
emphasized through diminutive forms:

> . . . malen'kij chozjain v dymčatych očkach (. . .).
> On potiraet belye ručki, on sciplet sivuju boroden'ku
> (. . .). Eta lavka, kak korobočka ljuboznatel'nogo i
> važnogo mal'čika, iz kotorogo vyjdet professor bot-
> aniki. (. . .) i malen'kogo chozjaina ee zovut Gedali.
> (. . .).

Through his emphasizes of the childlike smallness of
Gedali's appearance, and of the smell of decay and
remnants of the past which dominate Gedali's world,

the narrator counters the straightforward wisdom and ir-refutable logic of his philosophical reasoning with re-gard to the revolution—his "impossible international". Moreover, the montage of the Dickens-allusion throws into relief the nostalgic longing and revolutionary bra-vado of the narrator.

1.5

Another interesting literary allusion occurs in the story **"Ėskadronnyj Trunov,"** which is about the heroic death of squadron commander Pavel Trunov. The story begins with Trunov's military funeral, which includes a funeral speech by Pugačev, the commander of Trunov's regiment "about the dead soldiers of the First Cavalry Army, about that proud phalanx which is beating the hammer of history upon the anvil of future ages". The actual story of Trunov's death and of the events leading up to it is told in reversed order, starting from the de-scription of the funeral. This compositional inversion is all the more emphatic because of two inserted frag-ments which are completely disconnected from the lin-ear action fundament. After giving Trunov's corpse the ritual final kiss the narrator wanders off into "gothic" Sokal. His attention is attracted by "a Galician as lanky and cadaverous as Don Quixote". The association with *Don Quixote* is elaborated in the subsequent description of the Galician:

> Galičanin ètot byl odet v beluju cholščevuju rubachu do pjat. On byl odet kak by dlja pogrebenija ili dlja pričastija i vel na verevke vzlochmačennuju korovenku. Na gigantskoe ego tulovišče byla posažena podvižnaja krochotnaja, probritaja golovka zmei, ona byla prikryta širokopoloj šljapoj iz derevenskoj solomy i pošatyv-alas'. Žalkaja korovenka šla za galičaninom na povodu; on vel ee s važnost'ju i viselicej dlinnych svoich kostej peresekal gorjačij blesk nebes.

The narrator is intrigued by this figure and follows him into a poor Jewish quarter. One striking detail is piled upon another: a lane all smoky with thick and nauseat-ing vapours; little charred houses; squalid kitchens; Jewish women like aged Negresses, with excessive bo-soms; a Gipsy blacksmith with greasy hair. Speaking in terms of actional causality, this passage is in no way re-lated to the actual story. The motivation behind its im-plantation seems to be of a psychological/characterological nature: the narrator shifts from one way of escape to another—his artistic curiosity, ignited by the strange Galician. He hopes to find a new story, but is returned to 'reality' by Seliverstov who suddenly accuses Ljutov of having caused Trunov's death. Ljutov then tells what happened, partly to clear himself from possible guilt.

In the course of reading the second part of the story, which focuses on Trunov's behaviour, it gradually be-comes clear in what way *Don Quixote* as intertextual

frame bears on the main theme. Trunov is a complex character in the story. Heavily wounded, he displays sa-distic cruelty in killing two prisoners without reason. On the other hand, he frantically defends revolutionary justice by preventing a cossack from stealing Polish uniforms (cf.: Darjalova: 118), and he dies like a hero in an epic duel with four enemy aircraft. All his deeds, however, are shaded by a sense of mental distortion: he murders coldbloodedly, almost kills the aforementioned Cossack, and his "heroic" death in battle is a deliberate, suicidal act.

The many signs of death in the description of the strange Galician Don Quixote fall into place. There ex-ists an ironic connection between Trunov and Don Quix-ote, the crazed nobleman who attempts to perform chiv-alrous deeds in the face of reality. Trunov, however, unlike the character of Cervantes, does not win the reader's sympathy. His defence of justice and his heroic death are in contrast with the brutality of the murders he committed. He is in a state of desperation, aware of the fact that the campaign (and possibly the entire Revolution) is at the brink of complete failure. After the killing of the second prisoner he addresses the narrator (the other protagonist of the story), and orders him to remove the prisoner from the list. The narrator refuses and adds that Trunov will have to answer for his deeds:

> —Ne stanu vymaryvat',—otvetil ja, sodrogajas',—Trockij, vidno, ne dlja tebja pišet, Pavel . . . —
>
> Ne stanu vymaryvat',—zakričal ja izo vsech sil,
>
> —Bylo desjat', stalo vosem', v štabe ne posmotrjat na tebja, Paška . . .

The allusion to Cervantes' *Don Quixote* activated by the contrastive description of a Galician peasant deep-ens the story's ambiguity. More specifically, it ironi-cally modifies Trunov's contradictory character, his 'epic' heroism, and the narrator's ethical principles which he holds on to against all odds.

1.6

"Ėskadronnyj Trunov" is a pivotal story in the cycle. It contains clear signs of impending military defeat. The heavily wounded, demoralised Trunov who almost single-handedly fights four modern enemy aircraft, sym-bolically represents the military inferiority of the Konarmija. This is already indicated at the beginning of the story: Trunov is saluted by "our decrepit old little canon", "our old little three-incher champed forth a sec-ond time". In his plans for **Konarmija** Babel made the following remarks:

> The Konarmija is retreating. In the face of whom? In the face of twenty aeroplanes. (. . .) First meeting with western technology.
>
> (cf. Williams 1984: 293)

The story **"Zamost'e"** recounts the final debacle. Near the town Zamość the Konarmija was trapped and defeated by the Polish armies. This historical event is narrated in a very incoherent manner, namely from the focal point of a totally exhausted, demoralized Ljutov. The story is a shocking montage of disparate scenes, which are presented in a detached tone, interspersed by striking metaphoric descriptions providing a sudden insight into the narrator's anxious state of mind.

At some points the imagery of the story reminiscent of modernist poetry such as Russian *Imaginism,* e.g.: "(. . .) i derev'ja, golye mertvecy, postavlennye na obe nogi, zakačalis' na perekrestkach. Spina lošadi černoj perekladinoj rezala nebo, . . .". Concreteness of both comparé and comparant is a typical feature of Babel's metaphorical constructions. It recurs in a great number of his stories. His figures of analogy are frequently built on a sharp collision between concrete perceptions, selected from semantic fields which are far apart in reality. As a result of their startling effects upon the reader, Babel's metaphors often stand out as separate units which attract the reader's full attention. The tendency of the image to function as an end in itself, combined with its opposing concrete versus concrete, connects the author with a group of Russian poets, known as the Imaginists (Šeršenevič; Mariengof). It was the creed of these poets that the image is the sole poetic means to replace logical speech. It should startle, stun, in order to "rouse the reader from his habitual lethargy and set his mind working." (Nilsson 1970: 40).

There are Imaginistic metaphors in other stories from *Konarmija.* We may think again of "the sun rolling down the sky like a chopped-off head" (**"Perechod čerez Zbruč"**) or of "Night flew toward me on mettlesome horses" (**"Ivany"**). Like the Imaginists Babel often selects his images from everyday life, from the trivial and the gross (cf. ibid: 52). The story **"Večer"** provides us with fine examples of this type, for example, when the sun is compared to a lantern and the moon to a splinter:

> Na nebe gasnet kosoglazyj fonar' provincial'nogo solnca.I oni zakryli dver' kuchni, ostaviv Galina nae-dine s lunoj, torčavšej tam, vverchu, kak derzkaja zanosa.

T. S. Eliot's *The Lovesong of J. Alfred Prufrock* can be detected in the following constructions: "Syroj rassvet stekal na nas kak volny chloroforma. (. . .) Utro soči-los' na nas, kak chloroform sočitsja na gospital'nyj stol". It is very likely that Babel read *Prufrock* (published in 1917) and used the beginning of Eliot's poem for his story: "When the evening is spread out against the sky / like a patient etherised upon a table". However, there is another interesting literary allusion that I want to discuss extensively. At the very beginning of **"Zamost'e,"** the narrator lays down in a waterlogged hole, ties his horse to his foot and falls asleep. He has a dream which reveals his subconscious self. This dream is the first large episode in the story, and may be considered an extended inner-story. It is composed of three sections: 1) a pleasantly erotic experience; 2) a sudden outcry; 3) a nightmarish experience of death.

The montage of the dream-story first of all creates an effect of contrast. The preceding motifs of pervading wetness, darkness and exhaustion are replaced by a sense of dryness, abundance and tranquility, which is evoked by an almost hyperbolic description of a hay-barn on an evening in July, a Chagall-like image of sheaves of wheat flying about in the sky. In his dream the narrator is visited by a woman dressed as if for a ball, in black lace. This scene has an erotic impact, it presents an experience of intimate, physical contact:

> Ona vynula grud' iz černych kružev korsaža i ponesla ee mne s ostorožnost'ju, kak kormilica pišču. Ona priložila svoju grud' k moej. Tomitel'naja teplota potr-jasla osnovu moej duši, i kapli pota, živogo, dvižuš-čegosja pota zakipeliimeždu našimi soskami.

At this point a sudden transition takes place in the narrator's mind, expressed in a sort of internal exclamation: "Margo,—chotel ja kriknut',—zemlja menja taščit na verevke svoich bedstvij, kak upirajuščegosja psa, no vse že ja uvidel vas, Margo . . .". The dream becomes a nightmare as it makes the dreamer undergo his own death. The dreaming I cannot escape his fate. The woman who first brought life (food, love) then behaves as if he were a corpse: she falls on her knees and performs a kind of post-mortem ritual which is opposed to the previous wetnurse ritual. Important for the multilayered function of the dream, seen in relation to the encompassing narrative frame, is the fact that it forms a complex knot of intra- and intertextual references. The intratextual relations are based on a series of contrasts in the dream as well in the story as a whole. The contrasts are: heat vs. cold, and physical and emotional fullness of life vs. physical impotence, suffocation, death. As far as the intertextual allusions are concerned, the distinct sensuality of the dream with its hyperbolical impressions of fertility is reminiscent of Guy de Maupassant's work. One may think of such stories as *Histoire d'une Fille de Ferme* with its evocation of physical, sensory experiences of lust and life. But a more concrete allusion is marked by the name Margo. This name relates the dream (and indeed the entire story) to the historical novel *La Reine Margot* by Alexandre Dumas (père). In fact, the dream-utterance might even be a deliberate distortion of a specific scene in Dumas' novel: during Saint Bartholomew's night, a haunted and wounded Hugenot nobleman (la Mole) seeks refuge in the bedroom of queen Marguerite de Valois, the novel's heroine. She embodies an ideal of virtue and beauty; she hides the Hugenot from his persecutors, and proposes to nurse his wounds. In his utter noble-mindedness la Mole is unable to accept this:

> Oh! s'écria la Mole, j' aime mieux mourir que de vous voir, vous, la reine, souiller vos mains d'un sang indigne comme le mien . . . Oh! Jamais! jamais!

The situation of the narrator and, by implication, of the Konarmija with him is thus compared to the fate of la Mole and the Hugenots during Saint Bartholomew's night. The allusion is partly a tacit evaluation of the military situation: the Konarmija is lured into a trap and awaits a large-scale massacre. The same goes for the massacre of the Jews in Zamość, which is subsequently sketched by the narrator.

The allusion to *La Reine Margot* enhances the expectation of imminent catastrophe, perhaps of death. However, it involves more than a situational comparison. Van der Eng relates the dream utterance to the courtly love tradition (1985: 423). Indeed, the narrator's behaviour fits to the romantic image of the nobleman "willing to undergo the severest ordeals just to be able to see his lady" (Ibid). Within the context of **"Zamost'e,"** one may stretch the interpretation of the allusion even further by activating a second pre-text to which Margot refers: Gor'kij's autobiographical novel *V Ljudjach* (Ibid: 424). In this novel, a fairly plain woman enters the base social environment of the adolescent Aleksej, the hero of the novel. In his phantasy he transforms her into an ideal of virtue and beauty:

> She represents for him a dream of regal beauty in the middle of a way of life compounded of his relatives' baseness of soul and the near animal behaviour of the soldiers and washerwomen who work nearby.
>
> (Borras 1967: 140)

He secretly names her *Koroleva Margo* after Dumas' heroine and tries to protect her ideal image, fights the 'slaunderous' remarks people make about her in a manner which suits a courtly nobleman. One day, however, Aleksej's illusions break into pieces as he finds his Margo in the arms of her lover, a rude soldier: "Ja čuvstvoval sebe poterjavši čto-to i prožil neskol'ko dnej v glubokoj pečali."

Seen within the frame of *La Reine Margot* and *V Ljudjach,* Babel's Margo at first seems to signify faith and hope regarding the aspirations of life. But then the dream allegorically shows how the Zamość-encirclement ruins these aspirations. The "utopian" scene in the hay-barn is interrupted by "the earth's calamities", a greater force which renders aspirations illusionary, and brings death. In **"Zamost'e"** the narrator meets with defeat on a military and moral scale. The latter shows itself, throughout the story, in recurrent moments of mental obtusion, estrangement, and the loss of moral control. The narrator pesters a peasant woman for food, for the first time without any sign of remorse.

In sum, the dream is primarily a contrasting unit in the story. It presents a world, abounding in love, safety, food and warmth. This is spatially indicated by the enclosed space of the hay-barn in opposition to the dangerous open space of the field of battle. The intertextual references confined in the dream, and signalled by phraseological (Maupassant) and diegetic markers, on the one hand deepen the contrastive effects of the passage (suggesting love, happiness, beauty). On the other hand, they stress the horror of the situation (St. Bartholomew's night), and involve elements of mental and moral frustration.

2. RELIGIOUS PRE-TEXTS

2.1

An important pre-text to which the **Konarmija** stories regularly refer, is the Bible. As we know from his autobiography, Babel studied the Bible during childhood. This was a result of the ambitions of his father, who wanted his son Isaak to be familiar not only with the Jewish cultural heritage, but also with the Christian tradition. The **Konarmija** stories allude to the Bible through a montage of biblical associations: biblical motifs, themes, phraseological idiosyncrasies. The subject has been extensively dealt with by Zsuzsa Hetényi (1981). According to Hetényi, the frequent recurrence of Biblical motifs in **Konarmija** reflects the author's vision (edinyj vzgljad avtora) not only on the level of poetic language, but also on the scenic level through the presence of churches, popes, frescos, and even on the ideational level of the cycle (v idejnom soderžanii). Moreover, in her study she illustrates how in a number of stories biblical motifs are connected to various characters and events which are thus drawn into a biblical perspective.

Markers indicating intertextual allusions are often attraction-like moments in stories. For instance, in **"Pis'mo,"** Kurdjukov, a primitive cossack, explains in a letter to his mother how one of his brothers was killed by his father, and how his second brother then executed the father in revenge. Hetényi sees a parallel with the following motif in the Bible:

> Brother will betray brother to death, and the father his child, children will turn against their parents and send them to their death.
>
> (Matthew 10, 21)

There are other attraction-like biblical allusions in the inner-stories of **"Pan Apolek"** and **"Put' v brody"**: Apolek's tale of Christ and Deborah, Afon'ka Bida's parable about a bee and Christ upon the cross, and the ballad he sings about a cossack who rides to heaven on the day of the beheading (of John the Baptist). Afon'ka Bida, a key character in several stories, is frequently set off against a background of biblical associations. In the story **"Afon'ka Bida"** his head, resting upon the saddle of his dying horse, is compared to a crucifix (golova— kak raspjataja). There is a considerable tension between these biblical allusions and Bida's violent behaviour: in **"Smert' Dolgušova"** he kills the dying Dolgušov without a blink, and almost murders Ljutov for being unable to do the same; in **"Afon'ka Bida"** we learn of his cruelty from rumours about his violent search for a new horse; in **"U Svjatogo Valenta"** he partakes in an outrage against a Catholic church in the village Berestečko, a provocative desecration of Christian relics.

Babel uses biblical allusions in the representation of quite a few characters. Without doubt, the cossack Saška Christos is the most telling example. His personal history is built on biblical motifs: it is easy to see that Christos is more than just a nickname. His stepfather is a carpenter, like Joseph, he wants to become a shepherd, because "vse svjatiteli iz pastuchov vyšli". On other occasions, the biblical projection of a character and/or his deeds is more hidden. For instance, in **"Načal'nik Konzapasa"** it happens in the episode in which D'jakov rejects the protests of peasants who complain about the bad condition of the horses they received in return for those taken away from them by the Konarmija. To prove that their complaints are unjustified, D'jakov forces an exhausted horse back on his feet. The scene is reminiscent of a scene in the Bible (New Testament: Acts 3) where the apostles Peter and John make a cripple walk again in the name of Jesus Christ. A religious tone is fixed already by D'jakov's first words to the peasant:

Čestnym stervam igumen'e blagosloven'e.

Another 'biblical' character is general Pavličenko. Pavličenko, whose first name is Matvej, like one of the apostles, was a shepherd before the Revolution, like Saška Christos. In the story **"Žizneopisanie Pavličenki, Matveja Rodionyča"** he tells how he executed his former master in revenge for a grave injustice done to him. Pavličenko calls his revenge "the final judgement (poslednij sud)".

The projection of numerous cossack characters on biblical motifs may be explained by the fact that Christianity is the cossack religion. The Bible is an important element of their socio-psychological universe. It is therefore all the more strange that Babel places several Jewish characters in a Christian perspective as well. Take for instance Gedali; Hetényi asserts that Gedali's philosophy of either "yes" or "no" stems from the Bible. In many ways he reminds us of the apostle Paul:

Babel' izobražaet Gedali kak izbrannogo čeloveka: v ego povedenie uže s samogo načala on vvodit apostol'skuju čertu. "On, . . . skloniv golovu, slušaet nevidimye golosa, sletevšiesja k nemu". Nevidimyj golos, po Biblii, prinadležit ili bogu, kogda ego slyšat

Christos i troe apostolov (Matt. 17:5; Mark. 9:7; Luk. 9:35), ili Iisusu, kak, naprimer, v videnii apostola Pavla na puti v Damask (Dejan. 9:5).

(Hetényj 1981: 235)

In **"Rabbi,"** Jews, gathered in prayer, are compared to fishermen and apostles. Il'ja the rebbe's son combines Spinoza's powerful brow with the wan face of a nun. In **"Syn Rabbi,"** the description of Il'ja's body evokes an image of Christ taken down from the cross. The implantation of biblical correspondences in the construction of various characters systematically centers upon effects of contrast. The biblical perspective in which Babel places many of his characters is brought in antithetic opposition to aspects of their behaviour and mental condition. Saška Christos is a syphilitic who betrays his mother; D'jakov deceives the peasants; Afon'ka Bida and Pavličenko are extremely violent characters; Pan Apolek is a heretic. Each of these characters violate the religious values suggested by the biblical frame of reference. Falen asserts that

by representing incongruous characters as figures of a religious import, Babel' is attempting both to humanize the conception of divinity and at the same time to associate the hopes of the Revolution with religious promises.

(1974:180)

This corresponds with Hetényi's interpretation of the biblical allusions with respect to the cossack figures. Since many of these allusions juxtapose characters with apostles, we are led to see the cossacks as "new apostles", bearers of a new myth:

Metod sozdanija novogo mifa svidetel'stvujet o tom, čto pisatel' sčital sobytija 20-ch godov, proischojaščie v Sovetskoj strane, sobytijami mirovogo značenija.

(1981: 240)

This conclusion, however, is somewhat incomplete. In my opinion the creation of a new myth is not so much the expression of the author's view. It should rather be seen as a reflection of a general tendency, provoked by state propaganda, to regard the Revolution as an event of mythical proportions. One is more inclined to interpret the contrasting montage of biblical motifs as a touch of irony regarding this tendency. Babel seems to present his "new apostles" more as debauchers of the old world than as bearers of Utopia.

This is not the case with philosophical characters, such as Pan Apolek, who do not belong to the stratum of cossacks. Apolek's heresy, which comes to expression in his biography, his paintings and blasphemous tale of Christ and Deborah, is an alternative to the traditional teachings of Christianity. Apolek fuses the divine and the earthly into a more humane religion. In this regard he can be compared to the Jewish character Il'ja, who also seems to attempt to reach a synthesis of the Judaistic religious tradition and the ideals of the new order. Il'ja's biblical correspondences partly refer to his heresy, and partly to his ability to combine traditional religious ideologies with the ideology of the new world.

2.2

The narrator's distancing and aesthetically tuned attitude regarding traditional Christianity, in particular Catholicism, is repeated in his views on traditional Judaism (Hassidism and Jewish Orthodoxy). In the world of *Konarmija,* Galicia and Volhynia, Catholicism and Judaism were the main pillars of society. They supported a social configuration consisting of a Catholic community and a Jewish community. Moreover, Christianity and Judaism, more generally, represent the dominant religions in western civilization. These ancient religions largely determined ethical, humanitarian values in the old, pre-WOI societies.

The narrator's viewpoint vis à vis the traditional religions is expressed mostly through montage of lyrical digressions. As far as Judaism is concerned this happens mostly in the stories: **"Gedali"; "Rabbi"; "Syn Rabbi."** In these stories there are direct references to a considerable number of Judaic religiously philosophical scriptures. Twice in **"Gedali"** such references are made through the names of important Jewish philosophers, commentators of the Torah, the Kabbalah, and the Talmud: Ibn-Ezra (1089-1167); Rashi (1040-1105); Maimonides (1135-1204). In **"Rabbi,"** Il'ja, the rebbe's son, is compared to Spinoza, the excommunicated Judaic philosopher. In **"Syn Rabbi,"** Il'ja carries with him a portrait of Maimonides, and ancient Jewish poems, scribbled on the edges of communist leaflets.

Other, more hidden allusions to Judaic texts are, what Maurice Friedberg (1978) calls, echoes of the life and works of Rebbe Nahman, the founder of Hassidism. Nahman was a creative writer who expressed his philosophies in short parables, loaded with symbols. Nahman's creed reminds us of the views of Pan Apolek. Nahman, too, was in his time regarded as a heretic by the orthodox Jewry. He did not care about "saints and miracle rebbes but of princes and shepherds, of anonymous beggars and horsemen, of sages and messengers—and not even Jewish ones at that" (Friedberg 1978: 195). Babel alludes to the pre-text of Rebbe Nahman primarily through his choice of names: Gedali is "a name much favoured among the rebbe's followers" (Ibid: 194); the last name of rebbe Motalè (**"Rabbi"**) is Braclavskij. This too is unmistakably an allusion to rebbe Nahman whose full name was rebbe Nahman ben Simhah of Braclav.

In **"Èskadronnyj Trunov"** the narrator depicts a heated dispute among orthodox and Hassidic Jews about the

mystical teachings of the Kabbalah. The quarrelling Jews mention the gaon of Wilna, Ilija ben Shlomo (1720-1797), a famous talmudist and persecutor of the Hassidim:

> Evrei sporili o Kabbale i pominali v svoich sporach imja Ilii, vilenskogo gaona, gonitelja chasidov . . .
> —Ilija!—kričali oni, izvivajas', i razevali zarosšie rty.

Il'ja (Ilija, or Elijah), the name of the gaon and the rebbe's son, is meant to initiate a referential process in the reader:

> The younger Braclavskij's name, Il'ja, a Russian version of the Hebrew Èlija or Èlijahu, has three major associations. In the Biblical tradition (Kings I and II), Elijah appears as an intransigent prophet, ruthless and fearless in his defence of the faith from unbelievers. In the oral tradition of the Aggadah, Elijah's appearance heralds the advent of the Messiah; it is also in this role that Elijah appears at the Passover ceremony. Finally, in Jewish folklore Elijah is "portrayed as the heavenly emissary sent on earth to combat social injustice. He rewards the poor who are hospitable and punishes the greedy rich.
>
> (Friedberg 1978: 197)

Babel's choice of names usually has semiotic overtones: the triple intertextual allusion, noted by Friedberg, furthers the emblematic quality of the character. Moreover, it shows the narrator's and perhaps the author's attitude towards Il'ja's worldview. I believe that Babel intended Il'ja and Pan Apolek as key-figures on the ideational level of *Konarmija.* Their heresy connects traditional religious philosophies, set in a critical perspective, with a humane standpoint of a socialist type (in Apolek's case this remains implicit). Il'ja and Pan Apolek are placed in antithetic opposition with the primitive cossacks, but also with the backward Hassidic community as described in **"Berestečko."** A dissonant note is struck by the student of Rashi's commentaries and the books of Maimonides: Gedali. His comment of the Revolution in terms of good and evil seems to be based on irrefutable logic. Further complication is created by the narrator's unfavorable qualifications of Gedali (ridiculous) and his reasoning (an impossible International).

3. REVOLUTIONARY PRE-TEXTS

The verbal context of the revolutionary rhetoric, signalled by typical forms of phrasing, is another segment of the intertextual field of reference on which *Konarmija* is built. Numerous examples of revolutionary rhetoric are dispersed over many stories. In all cases the marking signal, of course, consists of phraseological material. "Words, phrases and syntax typical of the revolutionary period are frequently used in a slightly unsuitable context or in a deformed manner" (Williams 1984: 280). At various points the text refers to the specific manner in which the official standpoint of the Communist Party was voiced. After the successful Polish invasion of the Ukraine in April 1920, the Communist Party's Central Committee sent out a call for the defence of Russia, a sudden appeal to nationalism

> addressed, not just to the working class to defend the Soviet Republic, but to 'all workers, peasants, and honourable citizens of Rossiya', that vast, vague, mystical empire which the Revolution was supposed to have destroyed. It succeeded in appealing both to the old-fashioned patriots and to the new-fangled revolutionaries. Its language was heavy with talk of ancient rivalries and foreign invasions, with allusions to 1610 and 1812 and 1914.
>
> (Davies 1972: 115)

This curious mixture of Russian nationalism and Soviet internationalism, as Davies calls it, resounds in the phrasing of passages alluding to the epic. The heroic-epic vision in **Konarmija,** discussed above, partly is on a par with a revolutionary-propagandistic perspective. The *Slovo o Polku Igoreve* is essentially a patriotic work, an appeal to Russia's feudal Princes to join forces (cf. Klein 1972: 133). Nationalism pervades the text and finds expression chiefly in the narrator's digressions in which he stresses the threat to Russia, the bravery of the Princes, and the importance of unity. Babel's use of specific hyperbolic epithets, by which he refers to Lenin's speeches, are worth noticing in this respect. "In the revolutionary period much use was made of words which indicated that the Revolution was bringing an enormous change, on an unprecedented world-wide scale" (Williams 1984: 282). Epithets such as neslychannoe, nevidannoe, neuv''jadaemoe, nebyvaloe, nezabyvaemoe, neskazannoe, which in Falen's view (1974:122) serve as a kind of recurrent leitmotif, fuse the epic perspective and the perspective of Communism, with Russian nationalism as a common denominator.

The idiosyncrasies of revolutionary rhetoric appear within the speech of characters and sometimes of the narrator. A straightforward example is the character Balmasev, the narrator of the inner-stories **"Sol'"** and **"Izmena."** For instance in **"Sol'"** he makes the following statement concerning the dubious killing of a peasant woman:

"I snjav s stenki vernogo vinta, ja smyl ètot pozor s lica trudovoj zemli i Respubliki."

In **"Žizneopisanie Pavličenki, Matveja Rodionyća"** Pavličenko reads aloud a fake letter from Lenin. He composed the letter himself, imitating official jargon:

—Imenem naroda,—čitaju,—i dlja osnovanija buduščej svetloj žizni prikazyvaju Pavličenke, Matveju Rodionyču, lišat' raznych ljudej žizni soglasno ego usmotrenija . . .

"Večer" seems to have revolutionary rhetoric as its central theme. It is a kind of ironic comment on the hollowness of the rhetoric. The narrator, tired of his life in Konarmija, digests the class-struggle in his confused poetic mind. He is reproached by Galin, the political commentator of *Krasnyj Kavalerist,* who shows Ljutov his responsibilities, firing rhetorical slogans at him:

—Konarmija,—skazal mne togda Galin,—konarmija est' social'nyj fokus, proizvodimyj CK našej partii. Krivaja revoljucii brosila v pervyj rjad kazač'ju vol'nicu, propitannuju mnogimi predrassudkami, no CK, manuvriruja, proderet ich železnoju ščetkoju.

The story opens with a digression of the narrator, which directly refers to Galin's speech. It is an ironic comment on the influence of party rhetoric on language: Galin's brush of iron is comparable to the headlong rails in the narrator's statement: "O, Ustav RKP! Skvoz' kisloe testo russkich povestej ty proložil stremitel'nye rel'sy."

The 'curve' in Galin's speech points back to a moment in **"Moj pervyj gus'."** After winning the cossacks' sympathy, the narrator reads to them Lenin's speech, held on the second congress of the Komintern: "Ja čital i likoval i podsteregal, likuja, tainstvennuju krivuju leninskoj prjamoj." Here too we may detect a distinct irony with regard to the straight line of revolutionary rhetoric (the headlong rails and the iron brush) which conceals a secret curve.

The function of the montage of allusions to texts of the Revolution pre-eminently concerns two aims: it inserts the official policy of the Central Committee as a point of view in the polyphony of voices, and, secondly, it communicates the influence of revolutionary ideals wrapped in rhetoric on the speech and mentality of people. An ironic attitude on the part of narrator and author becomes evident in the unsuitable contexts and deformed manners in which rhetorical slogans are used.

4.

Concluding this article, we may repeat that **Konarmija** draws on a variety of heterogeneous intertextual frames (pre-texts). In most cases the references to pre-texts are activated, as we have seen, by markers, that is, phraseological, diegetic, or/and compositional features selected from a pre-text and implanted in the alluding text, markers which are differentiated from their verbal environment by distinct effects of contrast. The markers sometimes also form part of otherwise deviating passages (e.g. inner-stories; digressions; metaphoric constructions). Through these markers thematic properties of the pre-texts are evoked which bring about a semantic modification of the alluding text. These properties of the source primarily affect the meaning of the story under consideration. This particularly applies to more or less overt literary allusions to concrete literary pre-texts (*Romeo and Julia*; *Don Quixote,* etc.). Secondarily, however, the literary allusions also affect the meaning of the cycle as a whole. Dispersed over several stories, the allusions form a systematic representation of an artistic point of view. They frequently lead to an ironic evaluation of events, characters and, at times, of the narrator himself by means of activating parallels with characters and events from literary pre-texts (e.g. **"Solnce Italii"**).

With the exception of the allusion to the *Igor Tale* in **"Perechod čerez Zbruč,"** the significance of the evoked epic properties mostly pertains to long-term strategies, embracing the whole of the cycle. Allusions to the epic draw events and characters into an heroic, mythological perspective. Effects of irony are usually created through juxtaposition of epic properties with antithetic characterological and action elements (senseless violence; destruction; madness; disillusionment). The same applies to the allusions to religious pre-texts and revolutionary texts: Saška Christos is paralleled with Christ, but at the same time he is a syphilitic who betrayed his mother; Galin fervently speaks the language of the Revolution, propagating its ideology, while his fervency is apparently linked up with amorous frustration and his words are put in a perspective of hollow rhetoric.

The semantic properties belonging to diverse pre-texts also contract into a chain corresponding moments dispersed over quite a few stories. Hence the montage functions on two levels of meaning. However, we may establish a third level of meaning where the properties of pre-texts are juxtaposed with each other. The montage of various intertextual frames in the cycle brings in opposition the dominant religious ideologies (Christianity and Judaism) with communism—the "new" ideology, and with an unbound artistic view of the world. These ideational levels in **Konarmija** are brought to the fore with evermore acuity. The juxtaposition of opposed cognitive models is above all materialized, i.e. expressed in the wording of such characters as Pan Apolek, Il'ja, and Ljutov, the primary narrator. Babel made **Konarmija** a battlefield of conflicting worldviews: Judaism, Catholicism (Christianity), Communism, Russian and Polish nationalism, Cossack primitivism and military professionalism are involved in a meaningful dialogue. In particular, the montage of allusions to various intertextual fields (artistic, religious, ideological pre-texts) is essential to the ideational strategy behind the work which presents the world of the Revolution as a crossroads of ideologies.

Works Cited

Baak, J. J. van

1979 "The Function of Nature and Space in *Konarmija* by I. E. Babel'", *Dutch Contributions to the Eighth International Congress of Slavists,* 37-55. Lisse.

1983 *The Place of Space in Narration.* Amsterdam.

Bachtin, M.

1929 *Problemy tvorčestva Dostoevskogo.* Leningrad.

Ben-Porat, Z.

1976 "The Poetics of Literary Allusion", *PTL,* vol. 3, 105-128.

Borras, F. M.

1967 *Maxim Gorky. The Writer. An Interpretation.* Oxford.

Carden, P.

1972 *The Art of Isaac Babel.* Ithaca/London.

Catteau, J.

1973 "L'épopée babélienne", *Communications de la délégation française, VIIe congrès international des slavistes, Varsovie,* 103-118. Paris.

Conte, G. B.

1974 *Memoria dei poeti e sistema letterario. Catullo, Virgilio, Ovidio, Lucano.* Turin.

Davies, N.

1972 *White Eagle, Red Star. The Polish-Soviet War, 1919-1920.* London.

Eng, J. van der

1984 "Babel's Short Story *Zamost'e*", *Signs of Friendship. To Honour A. G. F. van Holk,* 414-435. Groningen.

Falen, J.

1974 *Isaak Babel—Russian Master of the Short Story.* Knoxville.

Friedberg, M.

1978 "Yiddish Folklore Motifs in Isaak Babel's *Konarmija*", *American Contributions to the Eighth International Congress of Slavists, Zagreb and Ljubljana,* 2, 192-203. Ohio.

Gibbons, B.

1980 *Romeo and Juliet.* London.

Górskij, K.

1964 "Aluzja literacka. Istota zjawiska i jego tipologia", *Z hystorii i teorii literatury. Seria druga,* 7-32. Warszawa.

Hetényi, Zs.

1981 "Biblejskie motivy v *Konarmii* Babelja", *Studia Slavica Hung.*, XXVII, 229-240.

Hume, Robert D.

1967 "Gothic versus Romantic: A Revaluation of the Gothic Novel", *PMLA,* vol. 84, 282-290.

Jenny, L.

1976 "La Stratégie de la Forme", *Poétique. Revue de théorie et d'analyse littéraires,* 27, 257-282.

Johnson, A. L.

1976 "Allusion in Poetry", *PTL,* vol. 1, 579-587.

Klein, J.

1972 *Zur Struktur des Igorlieds.* München.

1976 "Donec i Stiks", *Kul'turnoe Nasledie Drevnej Rusi,* 64-69.

Kristeva, J.

1969 *Semeiotikè, recherches pour une sémianalyse.* Paris.

1974 *La Révolution du langage poétique.* Seuil.

Murphy, A. B.

1977 "The Style of Isaac Babel", *The Slavonic Review,* vol. 44, 361-380.

Nilsson, N. Å.

1970 *The Russian Imaginists.* Stockholm.

1977 "Isaak Babel's *Perechod čerez Zbruč*", *Scando-slavica,* vol. 23, 63-71.

Perri, C.

1978 "On Alluding", *Poetics,* 7, 289-307.

Schmid, W.

1983 "Sinnpotentiale der diegetischen Allusion. Aleksandr Puškins *Posthalternovelle* und ihre Prätexte", *Dialog der Texte. WSA, Sonderband 11,* 141-189.

Schreurs, M.

1987 "Two Forms of Montage in Babel's *Konarmija*", *Russian Literature,* XXI, (3), 243-292.

Terras, V.

1968 "Line and Color: the Structure of Isaak Babel's Short Stories in *Red Cavalry*", *Studies in Short Fiction,* 3, 141-156.

Williams, G.

1984 "The Rhetoric of Revolution in Babel's *Konarmija*", *Russian Literature,* XV, (3), 279-298.

Joe Andrew (essay date September 1989)

SOURCE: Andrew, Joe. "'Spoil the Purest of Ladies': Male and Female Imagery in Isaac Babel's *Konarmiya.*" *Essays in Poetics* 14, no. 2 (September 1989): 1-27.

[*In the following essay, Andrew discusses the interplay between male and female characters in* Red Cavalry *and argues that "an understanding of the female char-*acters, their plot roles, the way they are depicted, and, indeed, what they symbolise, is critical in a broadly-based and systematic analysis of the world of war, revolution and violence" which constitutes the collection.]

The purpose of this article is to examine male and female characters in the thirty-five stories that comprise the final version of Babel's **Konarmiya,** or **Red Cavalry,**[1] as well their interplay and what the masculine and feminine principles which are established signify. It may seem strange at first sight to consider female characters at all in these stories. No female character has the status of such as Savitsky, Gedali, or Afonka Bida and the rest, to say nothing of the almost ubiquitous Lyutov. Most are marginal, most are unnamed and women in the stories are generally passed over fleetingly in the critical literature, or else are seen merely as iconic, symbolic or emblematic of something in male destinies, especially Lyutov's.[2] However, as I will argue throughout this paper, an understanding of the female characters, their plot roles, the way they are depicted, and, indeed, what they symbolise, is critical in a broadly-based and systematic analysis of the world of war, Revolution and violence that constitutes **Red Cavalry.**

That most critics tend to ignore or, rather, marginalise female characters in this work is not surprising. I have in mind not merely the male ethos of the work itself, but also the androcentric bias of most literary criticism. Indeed, in order to appreciate the tenor of much of this paper it is necessary to make a brief excursus into the realms of feminist literary criticism.

Since it began to re-emerge as an important cultural and political force in the late 1960s, feminism has presented 'Incontestably the most important challenge'[3] in recent years to accepted academic approaches to literary studies. By now several 'feminisms' have emerged. Each in its own way may be said to have had the aim of radically reinterpreting established literary practices, strategies and analyses. As Carolyn Heilbrunn said of Kate Millett's *Sexual Politics*: 'for the first time we have been asked to look at literature as women; we, men, women, Ph.D.'s have always read it as men'.[4] Underlying this view are a number of assumptions, well summarised by Greene & Kahn:

> Feminist literary criticism is one branch of interdisciplinary enquiry which takes gender as a fundamental organizing category of experience. This enquiry holds two related premises about gender. One is that inequality of the sexes is neither a biological given nor a divine mandate, but a cultural construct, and therefore a proper study for any humanistic discipline. The second is that a male perspective, assumed to be 'universal', has dominated fields of knowledge, shaping their paradigms and methods. Feminist scholarship, then, . . . revises concepts previously thought universal but now seen as originating in particular cultures and serving particular purposes.[5]

The present paper will offer a reading, from a feminist perspective, of a cycle of stories produced in Soviet Russia of the 1920s with a view to understanding the 'particular purposes' of the way women were coded both in this particular work, and, at least by implication, in the culture more broadly. By rereading works, by reproducing meanings in this way, we achieve two things: we see the images of women in a particular culture (and we can assess the purposes of these images); and we derive a new perspective on the world of the work concerned.

It is important to re-evaluate works in this way, especially those which have been 'canonised' as having 'universal' significance.[6] This 'universality' is something of a myth as de Beauvoir maintains: 'Representation of the world, like the world itself, is the work of men; they describe it from their own point of view which they confuse with absolute truth'.[7] We may be trained to read the works of our cultural history as if they were of universal significance, whereas they are usually partial if not distorted representations of humanity.[8]

That **Red Cavalry** is primarily a world of men is no secret. It is equally no secret that it is also a world where violence, death and destruction predominate: these two propositions are closely interconnected, as we shall see. Critic after critic rehearses the themes of morbidity. Murphy notes the common locus of the cycle, namely that of normal lives ruined by war,[9] while Hallett refers to the almost gratuitous blood-letting;[10] Falen talks of 'raging violence' always close to the surface.[11] At times the violence may be seen as merely the product of the particular situation, that is, the Revolutionary war.[12] However, others note that war and its accompanying violence seem to be endemic in this area: as Luplow puts it: 'there is a recurring sense of historical pessimism in **Red Cavalry,** a sense that the Revolution is neither new nor final, but one of an endless series of wars and oppressions.'[13] Lyutov himself makes the point when surveying a scene of particular devastation in *Discourse on the Tachanka*: 'I understood the painful history of this region'.[14]

Yet another aspect of this theme, and one that was common in the literature of the period,[15] was the way in which the Revolution, or war more generally, unleashed all that was worst in human (or rather *man's*) nature, the ferocious cruelty and other irrational forces. In particular, Luplow remarks upon the cycle's seeming 'obsession with violence, death and sex and their interrelationships.'[16] In Falen's view, sexual instincts and violent passions seem to originate in the same common source.[17] Despite these observations, however, few commentators make the simplest and most obvious of connections, namely that all the violence of the cycle is enacted by men. Usually this aggression is directed, fre-

quently in the most ferocious of fashions, towards other men, but we also see instances of violence by men against women. This may be rather bathetic, as in the case of Lyutov's three-fold assaults on powerless old women, to which we shall return, or (literally) deadly earnest, as in **"Salt."** In these instances we see a tendency which is common in the literature of war more generally. As Judith Fetterley observes: 'War simplifies men's relations to women. It erases the distinctions among women that normally keep male hostility under some restraint and it legitimizes aggression against all women.'[18]

But it may be that this violence, aggression or, more particularly, this all-pervasive sadism can be explained not merely by the subject matter (war), but by something rather more fundamental to literature, namely the narrative process itself. Another theoretical digression is necessary at this point, to consider the views of Yury Lotman on plot typologies and, in particular, a feminist re-interpretation of them by Teresa de Lauretis.[19]

In Lotman's article 'The Origin of Plot in the Light of Typology', first published in 1973, and translated in 1979, he proposes a number of basic plot types and character types. His study, in some senses an extension of Propp's work, has much that is relevant for our understanding of men and women in **Red Cavalry,** although Babel's work is not one of the very broadly-based works to which Lotman refers.

We must start, however, with an even more basic proposition, as formulated by Roland Barthes, for whom narrative is an absolutely universal phenomenon: 'Caring nothing for the division between good and bad literature, narrative is international, transhistorical, transcultural: it is simply there, like life itself.'[20] For Lotman, the universal phenomenon of story-telling has a particular relationship with reality: stories re-enact a disturbance: 'The fixing of unique and chance events, crimes, calamities—anything considered the violation of a certain primordial order—was the historical kernel of plot-narration'.[21] From this premise Lotman goes on to establish the basic chain of narrative, from which all stories can be said to be constructed, whether they be primitive anecdotes, nineteenth-century novels, or film:

> The elementary sequence of events in myth can be reduced to a chain: entry into closed space—emergence from it (this chain is open at both ends and can be endlessly multiplied). Inasmuch as closed space can be interpreted as "a cave", "the grave", "a house", "woman" (and correspondingly, be allotted the features of darkness, warmth, dampness), entry into it is interpreted on various levels as "death", "conception", "return home" and so on; moreover all these acts are thought of as mutually identical.[22]

Given this chain of events, narrative also presupposes types of characters, 'those who are mobile, who enjoy freedom with regard to plot-space, who can change their place in the structure of the artistic world and cross the frontier . . . and those who are immobile, who represent, in fact, a function of this space'. The mobile character may be a single individual, or may be 'a paradigm-cluster of different characters on the same plane'[23]. This possibility also applies to the immobile, obstacle, or antagonist character.

If we accept these propositions it is a short and simple step to argue, as Lotman never quite does, but as de Lauretis most definitely does, that all narrative is inherently male. After all, 'woman' is one possible variant of the closed space. In other words it is men who cross the frontier (as Lyutov, of course, does in **Red Cavalry**) while women are merely a feature of the narrative topology, obstacles in the hero's quest. Indeed, the hero *must* be male, because the obstacle is morphologically female.[24] As de Lauretis goes on to argue

> the hero, the mythical subject is constructed as human being and as male; he is the active principle of culture, the establisher of distinction, the creator of differences. Female is what is not susceptible to transformation, to life or death; she (it) is an element of plot-space, a topos, a resistance, matrix and matter.[25]

Furthermore, narrative is, therefore, essentially about a quest for human-becoming, a description of the process of becoming a *man.* Indeed, it can be argued, as we shall see in more detail later, that this is precisely what Lyutov is doing in **Red Cavalry,** and the women are, on the whole, mere elements of the spaces he enters and leaves, or else obstacles in his path, Propp's 'antagonists'.

From this perspective, we can see that **Red Cavalry,** or *any* narrative, is both universal, in the sense that it shares common typological features with other narratives, and not universal, in the more philosophical sense, in that it, like most fiction, fails to take account, or rather to *give an account* of female destinies. However, there is a rather more sinister side to **Red Cavalry,** as we have already briefly related, and to narrative more generally. Lotman's hero '*penetrates* into the other space and *overcomes* the obstacle'. Taking this, and other theories of narrative, de Lauretis comes to see narrative in a way which applies very well to the brutal world of **Red Cavalry**:

> Story demands sadism, depends on making something happen, forcing a change in another person, a battle of will and strength, victory/defeat, all occurring in a linear time with a beginning and an end.[26]

In **Red Cavalry,** as in most narratives, it is, indeed, men who force a change in others, and it is to a consideration of the types of men found in Babel's fiction that we now turn.

Red Cavalry, as we have already noted, is predominantly a man's world. In line with Lotman's theory the male character can be seen as a composite figure, what

Lotman refers to as a 'paradigm-cluster', or what Carden calls more simply 'composite types'.[27] On the one hand are the heroic warriors, on the other is the saintly, but also weak, or maimed type. It is important to remember, however, that both are depicted as heroic. Amongst the first group may be numbered such recurrent characters as Savitsky, Afonka and Balmashev, while Trunov and Baulin (in *Argamak*) bear clear similarities. There are also important links made with real historical characters such as Lenin, Makhno and Budenny.[28] As such a multi-faceted male hero can be pieced together, part-fiction, part-fact and, linking the two worlds of history and literature, part-myth.

Lyutov, as we shall see, strives, and only partially succeeds in his attempts, to ally himself with this group.[29] Also vying for his affiliation is the cluster of saintly or intellectual figures, most notably Gedali, Pan Apolek and the recurrent Sashka Khristos. Not merely for reasons of verisimilitude, this type is rather less common in these tales of war. In other words, what Sinyavsky calls the 'ideal of virile humanism'[30] is given far more attention than those who aspire, like Gedali, to an International of 'Good People'. I too will devote the rest of this section primarily to man's men, while noting in passing that, as in Lotman's paradigm, there are no female heroes.

The group of heroic warriors has many characteristics. All *power,* whether in political or narrative terms, is invested in them. For example, the very opening words of the cycle inform us: 'The commander of the VI Division [i.e. Savitsky] reported that Novograd-Volynsk was taken today at dawn' (27). Savitsky, like many other central male characters is given the power of the word, of organising the discourse. What he reports is also relevant: men acquire or retain power by violent aggression. This theme is immediately echoed by the reference to Nicholas I building the road 'on the bones of peasants' (27). Savitsky is also the central discursive referent in at least two stories which open with his name and rank, **"My First Goose,"**[31] and **"The Story of a Horse."** The nature of male power is particularly clearly illustrated in the latter story. Savitsky is able to dominate the hapless Khlebnikov by the capture of his horse, and, revealingly, by his equally ruthless and imperious possession of the woman, Pavla.[32] Indeed, his imperiousness is made explicit by the grandiose comparison with Peter the Great (84), and, in rather more bathetic terms, by his production of his 'cannon', that is the revolver, 'which was lying on his naked belly' (85).

In Oedipal terms these majestic figures may be interpreted as Father figures to whose stature Lyutov may only aspire.[33] In terms of literary tradition, as has been noted by numerous commentators, they inherit the Cossack tradition of Pushkin and, especially, Gogol and Tolstoy.[34] Lionel Trilling, in particular, comments upon the extent to which Babel's Cossacks echo Tolstoy's *Cossacks,* with the same 'primitive energy, passion and virtue'. For both writers, the Cossack is the man of the body and, significantly, of full sexuality.[35] The critical literature has tended to focus on this very masculine hero (Sinyavsky's 'virile humanism') and many striking phrases have been used to encapsulate the type, as we shall shortly see.

One obvious, and much remarked upon feature, is the close bond between Cossack and horse.[36] At times it seems that their equine companions are the *supreme* value signifying more even than their brothers in arms,—and certainly more than any woman, except the mother. Apart from the two sections relating the dispute between Savitsky and Khlebnikov, **"Afonika Bida"** is the story which most clearly highlights this theme. When Afonka's horse is shot its death is conveyed in terms of great elegiac pathos, which is reinforced by the depiction of Afonka subsequently asleep surrounded by magnificent equestrian trappings, which are itemised in loving detail. An interchange between two minor characters sums up the Cossack view:

> 'A horse is a friend', answered Orlov.
>
> 'A horse is a father', sighed Bitsenko. . . .
>
> 'It's a disaster for Bida without a horse. . . .'
>
> (104)

Despite this eulogy, however, by the end of the cycle, even this highest value is to be desecrated by male violence.

If horses are the Cossacks' highest value, then they themselves are clearly valorised by the narrator and the text more generally. This at least is the common critical view. Particularly striking is their physical beauty. Viktor Shklovsky puts it, as always, pithily and wittily: 'Babel's Cossacks are all insufferably and ineffably handsome'.[37] Probably the most celebrated and oft-quoted instance is the opening paragraph of **"My First Goose,"** in which Savitsky rises before Lyutov's eyes with a peculiarly feminine kind of beauty:[38] in this particular story all Cossacks do indeed seem to be as Shklovsky depicts them. Here we are struck by what Hallett describes as 'the overwhelming feeling of physical strength and attractiveness of the Cossack male'.[39] Another Division Commander, Dyakov (who becomes yet one more member of the cluster-hero) has a no less awesome appearance: 'Dyakov, who used to be a circus athlete, and now the Remount Officer,—red-faced, with grey moustache, in a black cloak and with silver stripes along his red *sharovary*' (37). Rather more contentious, however, is Sinyavsky's assertion that Babel 'makes us see in his Red Cavalry the moral and aesthetic greatness of these men, even though they are stained with blood and mire'.[40] Sinyavsky goes on to term them 'fig-

ures in an epic', a view shared by other critics,[41] and one that is made explicit on several occasions within the text. For example, Makhno, by report is 'as various as nature' (62), while both Trunov and Savitsky are termed 'world-wide hero' (111 and 124), the repeated phrase (from different speakers) being a further instance of the text's reinforcing the similarities of all these heroes.

Although Sinyavsky, and Trilling who talks of the 'lyric joy' involved in the violence of **Red Cavalry,**[42] and grows enthusiastic about the 'ultimate psychic freedom [. . .] to be won through cruelty conceived of as a spiritual exercise',[43] may be able to admire the aesthetic dimensions of these heroes, serious doubts begin to arise when we look at what these 'heroes' actually do and why. In other words, the view of masculinity on offer must surely be seen as both damagingly one-sided, and ultimately dangerous and life-threatening. Thus, the violence may be sometimes for the sake of the Revolutionary cause (**"Salt," "Trunov"**), but it is no less commonly for motives of personal revenge (**"The Letter"**) or completely unmotivated, as Luplow has noted.[44]

Most worrying of all is the view that gradually emerges that to be a man is to kill, and to kill as sadistically as possible, 'to force a change in another person', of the most fundamental kind! In this sense, **Red Cavalry** takes the basic 'sadism' of all stories to gruesome conclusions.

If any man in the stories can be seen as *primus inter pares,* it is Savitsky who appears to significant effect in four stories, including Lyutov's dream in the first of the cycle **"Crossing the Zbruch:"** indeed, he opens the cycle, as we have already noted. In the dream we meet the first of many gruesome killings. As in the later deaths it is not simple death, but extreme, overdetermined savagery.

> I dream of the Commander of the VI Division. On a heavy stallion he pursues the Brigade Commander and plants two bullets in his eyes. The bullets pierce the Brigade Commander's head and his eyes fall to the ground.
>
> (28)

Pavlichenko makes this kind of savagery explicit in his own *skaz* account of personal vengeance. Mere shooting, he asserts, is to let the other man off lightly. To really learn about life, he goes on, you have to trample a man to death for an hour and then you get through to his soul (80). In so doing, he echoes the words used at the end of the **"The Commander of II Brigade."** Lyutov sits and admires several of the members of the cluster-hero:

> That evening in Kolesnikov's quarters I saw the masterful indifference of a Tatar Khan and became aware of the schooling of the celebrated Kniga, the self-willed Pavlichenko, the captivating Savitsky.
>
> (70)

Over and over again Lyutov recounts, or we hear direct *skaz* reportage of quite ferocious, sadistic, overdetermined killings of men by other men. On two occasions at least, Lyutov makes more explicit the meaning of this theme. In a once more oft-quoted line he prays at the end of **"After the Battle"** 'for the simplest of skills—the ability to kill a man'(145), while in **"The Discourse on the Tachanka"** he remarks that 'I ceased being a pariah among the Cossacks'. (62) This is because he is the proud owner of a *tachanka,* which is the basis of the triangle 'to slash—*tachanka*—blood' (ibid.). Apart from the *tachanka* the main emblem of this kind of manhood is a suitably phallic one, namely the sabre, which Lyutov uses to pierce the dead goose (55), which is used to cull honey from the desecrated 'holy republics of bees' (60) in **"The Road to Brody,"** which is wielded by Pavlichenko who reappears in **"Berestechko"** (91), and which is later used by Trunov against the throat of an old man. (114)

More often than not, as I have already noted, men use this kind of extreme and sadistic violence against other men. Thereby, killing becomes an expression not only of manhood but of superiority over other men, a means of 'forcing a change in another person'. And, as I have also already noted, Lyutov prays for this very ability so that he too may be a true man. As Luplow puts it

> The Cossacks often commit violence with such flair, in such a grand manner, that the narrator's fascination and even awe overshadows the horror and moral outrage he feels at their acts.[45]

Certainly I would agree that, although the violence is often gruesome—such as brains being splattered over Lyutov from a blown apart head (115)—it is valorised in a number of ways. Those such as Trunov who takes on the bombers single-handed are accorded the tribute of epic heroism: he is buried 'in a place of honour' (117) at the end of his own story. Moreover, he and others are specifically heroes of the Revolution, which, on the whole, receives a positive 'verdict' in the cycle. Not only does Trunov receive the epithet of 'worldwide hero', and the accolade of a posthumous 'laurel wreath' (112), he is also acclaimed as one of the 'dead warriors of the First Cavalry, this proud phalanx which beats the hammer of history on the anvil of future ages' (111). And after his death the Internationale is played. . . . This identification of male brutality with the progressive forces of history, the Revolution and the Communist Party is echoed and developed by Savitsky in **"The Continuation of the Story of a Horse,"** where he uses equally brutal/sadistic terms for the movement of history. He writes:

> Our Communist party is, comrade Khlebnikov, our iron rank of warriors who give their blood in the first order, and when blood flows from iron, then this is no joke for you, comrade, but victory or death.
>
> (125)[46]

This theme of Revolutionary glory being forged through blood and iron recurs and receives its final accreditation in the last story, in the last of the 'straight-line'[47] men, Baulin, who with thousands like him, we are told, played an important part in the victory of the Revolution. (152)

Whatever recurrent ambivalence there may be in Lyutov's heart as regards violence, it would seem to be ultimately vindicated by the text itself and, beyond that, by history. Yet we must also recognise what else the text tells us, namely that in this world of men, death, gruesome death is everywhere; that male violence (or, simply, masculinity so defined) is dangerous, particularly because, in the end, there is no value that these 'heroic warriors' respect. Male violence is, of course, dangerous to other men, and to women as we shall discuss in more detail. But it presents a very general threat to the world as it is depicted in ***Red Cavalry***: as already noted, this war is merely one of a succession throughout history, stretching right back into pre-history, as is suggested by the sentence near the opening of **"Berestechko:"** 'Monstrous corpses were littered on the thousand-year-old funeral mounds.' (91)[48] In the present, Gedali dreams of an International of 'good people': this must remain a fond hope. Lyutov tells him that 'it [the International] is eaten with gunpowder. . . . and the best blood is used to season it' (52).

The cycle does, indeed, grow gradually darker with corpses piled on corpses, men fighting without ribs (**"Chesnikli"**) and the fields littered with excrement, while dead mice float along the roads (**"Zamost'ye"**). Interestingly, it is one of the few recurrent women, Sashka, who conveys what the cycle as a whole suggests is the essence of maleness: '"Cocks only have one concern", said Sashka, "to smash each other in the face"'. (145) A matter of a few lines later, however, Lyutov prays to fate for the simplest of abilities—to kill another man. Earlier in this story the Cossacks' most sacred values have been harmed: they are now riding on 'utterly exhausted' horses (142) into battle against brother Cossacks who had joined the Poles.[49] This is merely the clearest illustration of internecine strife. If the simplest of abilities is to kill a fellow man, then to be a man is, *ipso facto,* to know how to kill. As a result this apparent paean to masculinity can equally be read as a savage indictment. A story, in de Lauretis's view may demand sadism. This particular cycle of stories suggests that masculinity equally demands sadism as well as desecration of the highest values.

To return briefly to a consideration of the plot typologies of this cycle we can see that many of them do involve precisely this kind of forced change in others' lives, often resulting in gruesome, prolonged violence.

The experience and causation of suffering are commonplaces in the critical literature of the cycle. Falen, for example, speaks of 'a Darwinian jungle in which the strong prevail while the weak are condemned to suffering and destruction'; it is a world, in his view 'of torturers . . . and passive sufferers'.[50] Grongaard, in turn, tells us of the two basic groups of characters, 'the perpetrators of violence and the victims'.[51] Luplow goes even nearer to the truth when she comments that 'the strong victimize the weak and even persecute them for their weakness'.[52] Yet none of the commentators quite catch the centrality of sadism as a plot device, nor, as I have already noted, do they make the obvious connection between masculinity and these plots.

Story after story tells of this sadism. Many are on an individual, man to man basis, as in **"The Letter"** where, in yet another echo of "Taras Bulba," father kills son, only to be killed himself by another son. **"Pavlichenko,"** of course, enacts this plot while in the next story proper the eponymous Prishchepa destroys dogs, a cow, old women and defiles icons. As is often noted, even Lyutov attempts to join this plot by his three attacks on old women, thereby identifying himself with the aforementioned Prishchepa. The plot of sadism is extrapolated to a much more pandemic scale, as in the stealing of village horses (**"The Remount Officer"**), the destruction of the hives, in Trunov's battle and sadistic killing of prisoners. Indeed, it could be argued that the Revolution itself, or history more generally, is depicted in *Red Cavalry* as fitting this paradigm. History as well as a mere story, the view emerges, demands sadism.

If a story demands sadism and, going back one stage, if narrative in Lotman's model is inherently and *by definition* male, what role can women play in plots, and what role do they play in *Red Cavalry*? As we have already seen, following de Lauretis, who in turn develops Lotman and Propp, women are at best obstacles, 'antagonists' to the hero, or else merely a function of the space a hero crosses. De Lauretis develops this theme in her consideration of myth:

> Medusa and the Sphinx, like the other ancient monsters, have survived inscribed in hero narratives, in someone else's story, not their own; so they are figures or markers of positions—places and topoi—through which the hero and his story move to their destination and to accomplish meaning.[53]

With this in mind I will now move to a consideration of women in *Red Cavalry*. If men are heroic and, therefore, valorised by the text, women are almost uniformly denigrated, most usually in terms of their sexuality, although for many other reasons as well. *Red Cavalry* can be read as variations on very traditional stereotyped themes.

To return to some of my opening remarks, no female character has anything like the importance of Savitsky et al., nor even of the 'artist' figures. Only two are re-current, Pani Eliza and Sister Sashka to whom we will return. Most are marginal, and not even named, another link with Gogol's work.[54] Even such significant female characters as the Jewish daughter in **"Crossing the Zbruch,"** the treacherous woman in **"Salt,"** the beggar woman in **"Sashka Khristos"** or the old woman in **"The Song"** remain nameless, a fact which helps to reinforce their status as cyphers or symbolic presences. Women are often weak, and always powerless. The Jewish daughter has 'thin legs' (28), and although she may protest her fate with some dignity she remains impotent. Other instances of female weakness are the mother in **"The Letter"** who is described as a 'tiny peasant woman. . . . with wasted, light and shy features' (36) and Pavlichenko's wife who goes mad.

Women are frequently characterised androcentrically as daughters or mothers (to which we shall return) or as servants. Pani Eliza, as already noted appears in more than one of the early stories, but she is not given any distinct identity and remains locked in her role as housekeeper. As is traditional, women are associated with hospitality, that is, servicing men.

Another such is Braina, the wife of Schmerel who serves the guests raisin vodka and *zrazy* (40). While the men are warriors, saints or artists, and heroes all, the women wait dutifully to be part of some-one else's story. Nurses appear in a number of stories (**"Sun of Italy," "The Death of Dolgushov,"** for example) but are talked of merely as categories. Sashka again is a rare exception to this generic description.

Many of the women are characterised by their old-age, their widowhood or, yet another traditional stereotype, by their weeping and wailing. While men resist their cruel destinies (with some exceptions) women are passive sufferers. Pani Eliza is termed 'the old Polish woman' (29), while in **"Gedali"** we are told of the 'old woman' sitting in the background and 'sweetly sobbing' (50). The housekeeper in **"My First Goose"** is also *starukha,* while the other emblematic housekeeper (also pushed around by Lyutov) in **"The Song"** is described as an 'evil housekeeper. She was a widow, she was poor'. Evil, widow, poor—she becomes an overdetermined antagonist in Lyutov's path. Such piling of traditional image on traditional image can also be seen at the opening of **"Berestechko"**: Lyutov is billeted with 'a red-headed widow, who smelled of a widow's grief' (91): she is, of course, unnamed. We encounter another such emblematic figure in **"In St Valentine's Church,"** who also combines a number of traditional images. There appears in the church 'an old woman with loosened, yellow hair. She moved like a dog with a broken paw, reeling and falling to the ground'. (108) She is blind and begins kissing Lyutov's boots 'with tenderness, embracing them like a baby'. (108)

This *starukha* is old, blind, grotesque, mad, unnamed and mute. Occasionally the short step to becoming a witch is made,[55] as in the disgusting syphilitic beggar-woman who infects Sashka Khristos and his father, and who 'leaped into the room' (71) with remarkable agility for one so described. As well as the other connotations the two *starukha-khozyaka* figures of **"My First Goose"** and **"The Song"** clearly come close to the 'weird sisters' of traditional folk-tales, and their role as antagonists, obstacles in Lyutov's path further endorses this view.

In more mundane terms women are not uncommonly shown to be treacherous, dangerous impediments to men's desires and destinies. Irina the washerwoman (another servant, albeit named) in **"Evening"** is faithless. Galin, weak, half-blind and ineffectual, worships her, but she goes off to make love with Vasily the cook, virtually in public. This story immediately follows, and provides a semi-comic variation on the theme of female duplicity as enacted in **"Salt"** by the false mother (unnamed) who is shot by Balmashev for smuggling salt under the guise of a baby. Balmashev, indeed, opens his *skaz* letter by declaring the theme of his story: 'Dear comrade editor. I want to describe to you about the unconsciousness of women who are harmful to us'. (94) Whereas men die and shed their blood for the Revolution, women—*as a group*—are politically unaroused and dangerous to the cause. Moreover, they betray their own sacred calling of motherhood, to which we shall return.

The danger that women present to men is taken one stage further by the several historical/literary references which characterise women as symbolic castrators. In **"Pan Apolek"** we are presented with a typically gruesome depiction of John the Baptist: 'John's head was jaggedly cut off, with a ragged neck' (39). This image is taken up in **"In St Valentine's Church"** where, lest we miss the point, we are told that other characters' hair shines 'like the beard of Holophernes' (109). The text then, in its usual mosaic way, establishes a series of plots and roles for women to show their danger to men, which is then subtly underscored by an apparently chance series of references.

Given, then, that many of the women are castrators, ugly old witches or merely faithless it is surprising to find at least one woman addressed as a pure love object, in **"The Sun of Italy."** However, here too, in a different way, a woman is objectified and presented as inscribed in someone else's story.

Sidorov 'an anguished murderer' (47) has written to Viktoria telling of the pain of being a man (a murderer) and imploring her assistance in securing his release from his torments. Her name, nearly rhyming with *Italia,* is repeated and repeated, almost like an incantation

or talisman, representing an oasis amidst the death and destruction that Sidorov details. She becomes his Guardian Angel, almost his Muse. 'Save me, Viktoria' (47) he implores, echoing Gogol's Madman, as his letter builds to a lyric crescendo. Other notes are added: she is a fiancée who will never be a wife (an unsullied Virgin, a rarity in these stories). The concluding lines of the letter sum up her significance: 'Italy has entered my heart like an apparition. The thought of this country, which I have never seen, is sweet to me, like the name of a woman, like your name, Viktoria . . .' (48). Unlike many women in the cycle she is given a name. In the end, however, that is all she has, that is all she is, a romantic incantation to ward off the evil spirits of war and masculinity.

If Viktoria represents an oasis for Sidorov, then his love for her, if we can call it this, is a rarity in **Red Cavalry.** Much more commonly sexuality is represented as a 'mere bodily function'[56] and is usually depicted as particularly sordid. Furthermore, women are frequently defined in terms of their sexuality, either as whores, virgins, rape victims, pregnant or with 'monstrous breasts'.

Instances of sordid sexual relations are littered throughout the cycle.[57] The first and one of the most striking instances comes in **"Pan Apolek"** when Jesus and Deborah lie in her vomit. Sashka Khristos and his father both have sex with the disgusting beggar-woman (and, of course, contract syphilis), while later in the story Sashka watches his father and mother, just one of several such voyeuristic scenes. Later on, Sashka is to lie with the 'evil housekeeper' of **"The Song."** As Luplow has noted sex and death are linked in **"Zamost'ye,"** in Lyutov's dream.[58] Women are castrators, diseased and lead to death.

Particularly in the earlier stories, but later on as well, we encounter numerous whores. In **"Pan Apolek"** Lyutov tells us of Apolek's Mary Magdalene. The historical reference is not, however, sufficient to suggest female defilement. The model for the painting had been 'the Jewish girl El'ka, the daughter of unknown parents and the mother of many, illegitimate [lit. under-the-fence] children' (42). Shortly afterwards Lyutov tells us of other paintings by Apolek, including 'village Marys, who had many children, with knees apart'(43). He then returns to Mary Magdalene, to add other touches to the theme of endless generations of female depravity. We can still see in the Novograd church, *inter alia* 'her, the fornicatrix from Magdala, sickly and insane, with a contorted body and sunken cheeks'(43). Deborah, still in the same story, takes up this motif: after lying with Jesus in her own vomit she returns to the wedding-guests 'noisily triumphant, like a woman who is proud of her own fall'(45).

Other whores appear as characters in later stories. Savitsky's woman, the *kazachka* Pavla is apprehended by the narrative combing her luxurious hair, which she tosses over her back, before buttoning up Savitsky's shirt for him, making obvious references to what they have been up to. Sashka, in **"Chesniki"** is described as the 'lady of all the squadrons'(140), while the references to John the Baptist, and, therefore, implicitly, to Salome reinforce the historical dimension to this image. In literature, myth, holy writ, throughout history and in the diegetic present, whores abound and they, like Deborah, and Pavla are 'proud of their fall'.

Female virtue, then, is for sale, or else it is depicted as defiled. This image occurs, quite *en passant,* in the second story of the cycle, **"The Church at Novograd"** when Lyutov remarks in a striking image: 'I see the wounds of your God, oozing semen, a fragrant poison which intoxicates virgins' (30). In similarly casual fashion in **"Discourse on the Tachanka"** Lyutov ruminates on the history of this region, where there were stories 'of girls raped by Polish troopers and over whom Polish magnates shot each other'(64). There is a 'mock rape' of Sashka in **"In St Valentine's Church"** (108), while real, and multiple rape occurs throughout the night train of **"Salt."**[59] As Balmashev berates the false-mother he tells her 'Look at these two girls, who are crying at the present time, having suffered this night' (96). He then goes on to justify this course of events by suggesting that the woman remember the husbands 'also lonely who by evil necessity rape the girls who pass in their lives'(96).

Women are further defined by their sexuality in the frequent references to pregnant women. For Falen, this is a positive image:

> One of the great symbolic images woven through Babel's *oeuvre* is the heroic figure of the pregnant woman, and just as she is destined to give birth in pain and blood so too man, to create, must suffer and sacrifice.[60]

It is highly significant, given the androcentric bias of the text itself, that this critic does not see the women as self-determining, but merely as symbols of something in men's destinies. Certainly, it seems to me, the image of the pregnant woman in *Red Cavalry* is far from positive. For example, just after Lyutov has concluded his surreptitious reading of Sidorov's letter we return to the quotidian: 'On the other side of the wall a pregnant Jewess was sincerely weeping'(48). Here the woman provides a bathetic contrast to Sidorov's romanticism: equally, she, like all her weeping and widowed sisters is an emblem of female weakness and powerlessness, as too in **"Crossing the Zbruch"** where the bereft daughter is also pregnant. This theme is summed up by yet another man who is given a voice, Grishchuk in **"The Death of Dolgushov."** In this story of horrible suffering and Lyutov's fastidiousness, the soldier ruminates: 'Why do women labour . . . Why are there engage-

ments, weddings, why do their friends make merry at weddings?' (67) Women, to interpret these lines, seem to be locked into an endless cycle of births, marriages—and deaths. They stand as an emblem for the futility of life.

Another aspect of female sexuality which has been noted in the critical literature is breasts. Luplow interprets this obsession quite positively: 'Lyutov also reveals his heightened sensuality in his fascination with large-breasted females, who embody for him human animality and sexuality'.[61] I take a rather different reading of some of the grotesquely atomised, indeed, fetishised descriptions of this part of the female anatomy with which Lyutov regales us. To return to Savitsky's Pavla. Tossing back her hair she walks over to her man 'carrying her breasts on high heels, her breasts which were moving like an animal in a bag'(85). Sashka is described in even more outlandish terms. During her 'mock rape' Lyutov offers the following: 'Sashka's body, flowering and strong-smelling like the meat of a newly slaughtered cow' (108). When she reappears in **"The Widow"** he refers to her 'excessive body' (127), while in **"Chesniki"** this 'lady of all the squadrons' is 'swollen' while her 'monstrous breasts swing behind her back' (140). In the next story, **"After the Battle,"** these breasts are 'bouncing about' (145). Given these recurrent fetishistic references it is no surprise that a proffered breast plays a prominent part in one of Lyutov's dreams. He is lying asleep on hay in a barn, when the door opens:

> A woman, dressed for a ball, approached me. She took a breast out of the black lace of her corsage and raised it to me carefully like a wet-nurse offering food.
>
> (130)

However, as we have already noted, the seeming life-giving properties of the nurturing breast prove to be a cruel illusion as sexual ecstasy turns to death.

As we have seen on a number of occasions, the themes of the main body of the text are endorsed by intertextual references and casual remarks by the narrator or other characters. So too here: in **"Trunov,"** Lyutov observes some 'Jewish women, who looked like old negresses, Jewish women with excessive breasts' (112). Indeed, just as the depiction of women almost always denigrates them, so too does the narrator and the text as a whole, through the mechanism of casual, unmotivated misogynistic remarks which are scattered throughout it. For example, in the **"Church at Novograd,"** à propos of nothing in particular, Lyutov tells us of the 'bird-like madness In Pani Eliza's eyes' (31). Lyutov and Pan Apolek discuss, *inter alia* 'the ferocity of women's fanaticism' (43), while in the next story, **"The Sun of Italy"** he observes amidst the ruins of the town the 'crooks of evil old-women's little fingers dug into the ground'(46). In **"Sashka Khristos"** the natural scene is once more remarked upon by our narrator: 'And the earth gave off a sour smell, like from a soldier's wife at dawn' (72). Savitsky in **"The Story of a Horse"** lives in a town 'like a tattered old beggar-woman' (84). In **"In St Valentine's Church"** Lyutov describes the beauty of Apolek's John the Baptist, which is the kind 'for which the concubines of kings lose their already half lost honour' (109). And so it goes on. As a result, the text provides us with a series of demeaning images of women. Moreover, even when not talking of women directly, Lyutov, and other characters help to reinforce this view.

If it may be said that the text *as a whole* defiles femininity then this theme may be extended yet further. Remembering Lotman's basic chain of narrative, within which the hero enters an enclosed space and then leaves it, we may argue that **Red Cavalry** depicts males violating not only women, but space itself, which is often identified as female. The world itself is laid waste by men: space is entered and then left, destroyed.

The title of the opening story is significant in this context. **"Crossing the Zbruch"** implies in Russian the word *reka* (river) a feminine noun. The cycle begins, then, with an army of men crossing a female space. To emphasise the note of violation the river has to be forded, as the bridges are down. Another feminine noun *rodina,* the homeland has been violated throughout history as Lyutov learns in the second story when Romuald tells him in a graphic metaphor of the 'wounds of his homeland' (29), while the third story, **"The Letter"** recounts the violent destruction of yet another feminine entity the *sem'ya* (family).

As Falen has noted, the 'Mother' Church is violated on a number of occasions in the cycle.[62] **"The Church at Novograd"** details broken coffins while the parishioners brassieres have been hung by the priest 'on the nails of the Saviour' (31). The most noteworthy instance of this motif is in the two consecutive stories **"Afon'ka Bida"** and **"In St Valentine's Church"** where Afon'ka celebrates the acquisition of a new horse by desecrating the church dedicated to the patron saint of love, which is eventually closed down.

However, the most pointed and poignant desecration of an enclosed space occurs in the extended, lyrical account of the bee-hives, in **"The Road to Brody."** This story begins with a series of stark statements:

I mourn the bees. They have been mutilated by warring armies. There are no longer any bees in Volhynia.

We have defiled the hives. We exterminated them with sulphur and blew them up with gunpowder.

(60)

In Russian bee (*pchela*) is also a feminine noun. These few lines can be read as a key-note section of the whole cycle. Warring armies (men) enter space, defile it, and then leave it, having exterminated all the (female) inhabitants. The desecration involved in these actions is made explicit in the next sentence when Lyutov remarks that 'Singed rags gave off a foul smell in the *sacred republics of the bees*'. (60-my italics). As noted elsewhere, the maleness of their destructive activity is signalled by the use of the phallic sabres to extract the honey, the property, as it were, of the Queen bee who must also have been exterminated.

There seems to be every justification in reading this extended metaphor as an allegory of the whole cycle, of what men do to their environment. This reading is, however, made absolutely explicit in a rather later story **"Two Ivans."** Surveying the grim landscape (fields strewn with excrement), an emblematic (Tolstoyan?) 'bearded peasant in copper-rimmed glasses'[63] remarks: 'We call ourselves men, but we foul things worse than jackals. You feel ashamed for the earth . . .' (122). In Russian *zemlya* (earth) is yet another feminine noun.

It seems clear, then, that **Red Cavalry** defiles women and femaleness more generally in a variety of ways. Moreover, it marginalises femaleness yet further in that the point of view in the cycle is almost exclusively male.

As Danuta Mendelson has noted, Babel, following Henry James, dispensed with the omniscient narrator, to replace him with a variety of 'truths': 'Thus the truth in **Red Cavalry** is always someone's truth'.[64] However, only very rarely is this 'someone' a woman. Moreover, as already seen, there is what might be called a 'masculinist collective' of voices which denies even the *possibility* of a woman's truth. This is comprised most notably of Balmashev, Pan Apolek as well as Lyutov himself. Most of the stories are about men, who are often valorised, as we have seen. This privileging of the male voice or, quite commonly the voice of violence, is achieved by the frequent use of the *skaz* technique. Because we hear of the acts of violence from the point of view of the men of violence themselves we are led to understand their motivation. Kurdyukov (**"The Letter"**), Pavlichenko and others speak directly to the reader. As Grongaard notes: 'one of Babel's basic principles was that his characters should have the opportunity to express themselves directly'.[65] Consequently, their voices are privileged and as Lermontov noted 'we almost always forgive what we understand'.[66]

Conversely no single story is exclusively or even primarily about a woman. Only one has a female title **"The Widow,"** but even this story deals mainly with male destinies. No women tell their own stories but remain 'inscribed in hero narratives'. For example, Pani

Eliza or the old women in **"My First Goose," "In St Valentine's Church"** and elsewhere could well have had fascinating narratives to relate. Instead, they flicker before us as emblematic presences in Lyutov's destiny.[67]

In fact, women hardly speak at all in *Red Cavalry*. On only three occasions do women have anything significant to say (excluding the duplicitous words of the unnamed woman in **"Salt"**). In the first story the Jewish daughter (unnamed) speaks words of eloquent and dignified protest. But this concerns the death of her father: it is not her *own* story. Sashka, as we have already seen, is allowed to sum up the danger that men's aggression causes (145), while in **"The Song"** the (unnamed) old woman makes similar remarks to Lyutov. Although these are important, if not crucial thematic statements, neither speaks *of herself.* Moreover, as we have also seen, both are profoundly denigrated by the way they are depicted. As a result, the point of view of *Red Cavalry* is almost always male and this aspect of the stories does more than any other to marginalise women.

Obviously the principal speaker and the 'sentient centre' of *Red Cavalry* is the Jewish intellectual and narrator, Lyutov. Most writers on *Red Cavalry* see his plot in terms of a quest. I would now like to examine his plot in these terms, with particular emphasis on his relations with other men, especially the Cossacks, and with women.

The opening story, and especially its title, **"Crossing the Zbruch,"** sets the scene. Lyutov is on a voyage into unknown territory, a voyage of discovery.[68] The 'crossing'[69] of the title, with all its mythic connotations 'implies not only transition, but transformation', to which may be added the equally mythic theme of ritual re-birth.[70] As the cycle unfolds Lyutov 'literally and philosophically wanders'[71] through eastern Poland, the battlefields and mounting corpses.

As Trilling observes, Babel was 'captivated by the vision of two ways of being, the way of violence and the way of peace and he was torn between them'.[72] For Lyutov the central problem is his vacillation between the two, as well as his examination of why men kill violently and why the violated submit.[73] However, the cycle and its progression also mark Lyutov's attempts to become like the Cossacks, that is, to learn the simplest of abilities, how to kill. **"My First Goose,"** as I have noted elsewhere,[74] has as its central theme initiation into the group of Cossacks by means of an act of violence, the slaying of the goose. Other stories show a series of attempts on his part to become one of the boys, a series of temporary successes and then temporary set-backs. In **"The Road to Brody"** it is significant that he declares '*We* have defiled the hives' (60-my italics). But his lyricism, as at the end of **"My First Goose,"** indi-

cates that he is still repelled by his own violence. **"Tachanka"** also marks assimilation ('I stopped being a pariah' (62)) which this time lacks the former ambivalence on his part: 'I experience the rapture of first possession' (63), a phrase of significantly distinct sexual overtones. However, the very next story **"The Death of Dolgushov"** brings renewed alienation following his inability to kill even out of pity. This is marked by the simple elegiac statement: 'Today I lost Afon'ka, my first friend' (68).

Roland Barthes has indicated the Oedipal nature of narrative texts:

> The pleasure of the text is . . . an Oedipal pleasure (to denude, to know, to learn the origin and the end), if it is true that every narrative (every unveiling of the truth) is a staging of the (absent, hidden or hypostatized) father.[75]

This typology tells us much about the nature of Lyutov's quest which is surely to learn how to become a man, and, *ipso facto,* to learn how to *be* the Father, whether he be incarnate in Savitsky (and the others who comprise the cluster-hero) or Makhno or Lenin.[76] (In this sense *Red Cavalry* can be seen as a disguised Russian *Ulysses*). But, as we have seen earlier, to become a man in this world means to be able to kill. As Lionel Trilling notes, Lyutov's initiation centres on the dilemma of 'whether he can endure killing'.[77]

In the text of *Red Cavalry* Lyutov does, indeed, learn how to kill, albeit only a goose and the bees. But he does, by the end of the cycle, learn two other important lessons of manhood as it is depicted here, namely, how to treat women and how to ride. On three occasions, **"My First Goose," "Zamost'ye"** and **"The Song"** he stages attacks on powerless old women. Thereby he rejects the feminine principle so that he may aspire to be the Father.[78] **"The Song"** is the clearest enactment that Lyutov is, finally, learning the lessons of manhood. He presages his attack on the old woman by knocking the locks off her cupboards in the search of food: as in **"The Road to Brody"** he enters and defiles an enclosed space. He later claims: 'But nothing would have saved her, I'd have worn her out with my revolver, if Sashka Konyyaev or, alias, Sashka Khristos, hadn't stopped me' (146). Perhaps, in *Red Cavalry II,* if it had ever been written, Lyutov would have become fully a man, by killing and raping.

The last story, **"Argamak"** marks a beginning as well as an ending. Lyutov declares: 'I decided to transfer to the active forces' (152). The Russian verb *pereiti* (transfer) is exactly cognate with the 'crossing (*perekhod*)' of the opening story. A new story, a new quest begins. In this story Lyutov finally learns to ride properly. Falen sees this as a triumphant ending: 'the bespectacled narrator becomes fit at last to enter a sacred world. Lyutov . . . has triumphed in his quest.'[79] Yet, it must be remembered that he had to maim Arga-mak to learn this skill. His realisation of manhood reen-acts the very plot typology of the cycle in that he des-ecrates one of the highest Cossack values and 'forces a change' in another being.

If any value may be said to stand higher than the horse in the world of *Red Cavalry* then it is the mother. It is with a consideration of women as mothers, as virgins and as the image which unites this seeming contradic-tion in terms, the Madonna, that I will conclude.

Although women characters are not especially impor-tant in the narratives that comprise *Red Cavalry,* the symbolism of women is, and mothers, particularly the Holy Mother, figure as a point of reference in many of the stories. This may be casual references, as in **"The Church at Novograd"** when the soldiers seem to be followed around the church by Mothers of God (30-1), or as in the discussion of Pan Apolek's heretical paint-ings. The mother emerges from these and the other ref-erences as a complex, indeed contradictory symbol. She is seen as a figure commanding respect. Several charac-ters ask that their mother be contacted after their deaths, such as Dolgushov and Shevelyov in **"The Widow."** For Sashka Khristos his mother (the mother of Christ, of course) is an object almost of veneration in that he tells his father 'not to insult mother . . . you're tainted' (74). The clearest illustration of the Cossack view comes, admittedly in a somewhat paradoxical form, in **"Salt."** The woman is allowed to travel on the train of the Revolution, and to be protected by Balmashev, spe-cifically because she is allegedly a mother. He addresses the troops: 'Remember, platoon, your life and how you yourselves were children with your mothers'. (95) He turns to the woman: 'We rely on your conscience that you will bring up others to replace us because the old are getting old and, as you see, there's few young ones'. (95) The mother is, then, an object of veneration, on this occasion because she will produce new fighting men. In these terms Balmashev feels entirely justified in wiping 'this disgrace' (97) from the face of the earth because she had betrayed her sacred calling.

The mother whether earthly or divine is also repre-sented as the source of solace and potentially saving grace. Kurdyukov in **"The Letter"** writes to his mother, using the address 'Dear mother Yevdokiya Fyodorovna' over and over again almost as a ritual, prayer-like in-cantation, as if he were, indeed, beseeching the Holy Mother. In his own way, he allows her honour calling her a 'decent mother' (35). It is, however, the rather more elevated and intellectual Gedali who catches the divine significance of the mother in his remarks which open **"The Rabbi."**

> . . . All is mortal. Only the mother is destined to eter-nal life. And when the mother is no more she leaves

behind a memory which no-one has yet ventured *to de-file.* The memory of the mother nurtures in us compas-sion.

(57—my italics)

The very next story is **"The Road to Brody"** which uses precisely the same word *oskvernit'* (to defile) for the soldiers' destruction of the hives. Indeed, as we have already seen, nothing is sacred, everything may be, and is, defiled in this man's world, up to and in-cluding the Holy Mother of God. Compassion, which stems from the mother cannot be sustained.

Indeed, the Virgin Herself is defiled by the narrator's words on more than one occasion. Fusing the polarities of the traditional Virgin/Whore dichotomy, in *Red Cav-alry* the Virgin is a Whore. Thus, as Lyutov thinks back on the events in the **"Church at Novograd"** he says to himself, 'Away from these winking Madonnas, deceived by soldiers'. (31) The Mother of God is defiled, but she behaves in distinctly whorish fashion! The Virgin Mother, in theological terms, is an attempt to deny sexu-ality.[80] In this metaphor the soldiers, and the narrator who creates the metaphor make her sexual once more. Furthermore the Virgin Mother stands beyond death and therefore time. Even eternity is defiled. Pan Apolek's 'country Marys' (43) with their many children have a similar effect of re-sexualising the Holy Mother of God.

In the Russian language in general blasphemies often invoke the Mother of God and so too in *Red Cavalry.* On the very first page of the cycle this motif of des-ecration is established. Some-one is drowning in the Zbruch and 'loudly defames the Mother of God' (27). On the very last page Baulin berates Lyutov for trying to live without enemies and curses him: 'Clear off, to the damned [lit. dishevelled] mother . . .' (155). Throughout, anger and hatred are expressed in similarly blasphemous, defiling terms. The father of the writer of **"The Letter"** takes the name of the Holy Mother in vain (35), for example. In themselves these may be seen merely as reflections of the coarse colloquialisms to be heard in a war-zone. In the context of the cycle they take on rather greater significance.[81]

As we saw earlier, women are raped and defiled. In this context it is interesting to re-examine Lyntov's initia-tion into the Cossack brotherhood in **"My First Goose."** When he is first rejected the quartermaster advises him: 'If you spoil a lady, the purest of ladies, then you'll be well treated by the lads . . .' (54). In the referential mosaic of *Red Cavalry,* as indeed in theology, the pur-est of ladies is the Virgin Mother of God. By attacking the old woman, and by his other attempts to achieve manhood Lyutov has to learn this particular lesson, namely, that even the 'purest of ladies', the Virgin, must be defiled.

In these terms one of the crucial stories of the cycle is the third last, **"The Song"** which is clearly linked to

"My First Goose" by plot rhyme. The song of the title is one that Sashka Khristos has learned from a hunter and is of special significance to Lyutov. Indeed, Sashka sings it to him precisely to calm Lyutov's anger. Lyutov generalises the importance of such songs inasmuch as they, like the mother, serve as an oasis, a point of rest and respect amid the horrors of war:

> For this we forgave the cunning hunter because we needed his songs: at that time no-one could see an end to the war and Sashka alone could pave our wearisome paths with resonance and tears. Our bloody track went along this path. The song flew over our track.
>
> (147)

At least momentarily, then, this song can erase the bloody trace of men's killing. The refrain of the eponymous song is repeated. "'Star of the fields'", he sang, "star of the fields above my father's house, and *the sad hand of my mother. . . .*'" (146, 147—my italics). The song that soothes man's savage breast is of the mother. The mother grieves: indeed, she is the *Mater Dolorosa.*[82]

Shortly after the singing we see the old-woman with her strange child. She too is a mother, and with her wretched life and 'her dreary complaints' (148) a mother of sorrow. So, in attacking and threatening to kill this old woman Lyutov has desecrated the *Mater Dolorosa.* To him, as to other men, even the Holy Mother of God, Our Lady of Sorrows is not sacred. Indeed, the very events of the cycle and the way in which they are related to us 'spoil the purest of ladies' over and over again.

Notes

1. All references to *Red Cavalry* are to the edition *Babel: Izbrannoye,* (Moscow, 1966), pp. 27-156.

2. See, *inter alia,* G. Williams, 'Two Leitmotifs in Babel's *Konarmiya*' in *Die Welt Der Slaven,* 17 (1972), pp. 308-17, especially 311-2; J. E. Falen, *Issac Babel, Russian Master of the Short Story,* (Knoxville: University of Tennessee Press, 1974), pp. 126, 166, 168 and 179; R. Grongaard, *I. Babel's Red Cavalry: An Investigation of Composition & Theme,* (Aarhus, 1979), p. 45; C. Luplow, *Isaac Babel's Red Cavalry,* (Ann Arbor, 1982), pp. 156 & 35; P. Carden, *The Art of Isaac Babel,* (Ithaca & London, 1972), p. 122; and A. Lee, 'Epiphany in Babel's *Red Cavalry,* in *Russian Literature Triquarterly,* 2 (1972) pp. 249-60, especially pp. 259-60.

3. See K. K. Ruthven, *Feminist Literary Studies. An Introduction,* (Cambridge, 1984), p. 7.

4. Quoted in J. Fetterley, *The Resisting Reader. A Feminist Approach to American Fiction,* (Bloomington & London, 1978), p. xviii.

5. See G. Greene & C. Kahn (eds.), *Making a Difference: Feminist Literary Criticism,* (London & New York, 1985), pp. 2-3.

6. Such claims are made for *Red Cavalry.* See, for example, Luplow, p. 6: the work is described as 'a lasting, universal vision of the paradoxical essence of reality and of human nature and the human condition'.

7. See S. de Beauvoir, *The Second Sex,* (London, 1972), p. 162.

8. For a discussion of this in earlier periods of Russian literature, see J. Andrew, *Women in Russian Literature: 1780-1863,* (London, 1988).

9. See A. B. Murphy 'The Style of Isaac Babel' in *Slavonic & East European Studies,* (1966), pp. 361-80, especially p. 371.

10. See R. Hallett, *Isaac Babel,* (Letchworth, 1972), p. 53.

11. See Falen, p. 122.

12. See Grongaard, pp. 63 & 68.

13. See Luplow, p. 58. Grongaard (p. 64) makes similar remarks.

14. See *Konarmiya,* p. 64. All future references to this work will appear in the text. The translations are my own.

15. See Luplow, pp. 5 & 49.

16. ibid. p. 28.

17. See Falen, p. 121.

18. See Fetterley, p. 49. This remark arises from her discussion of *A Farewell to Arms.*

19. See J. Lotman, 'The Origin of Plot in the Light of Typology' in *Poetics Today,* Vol. 1, Nos. 1-2, (Autumn, 1979), pp. 161-84 and T. de Lauretis, *Alice Doesn't: Feminism, Semiotics, Cinema,* (London, 1984) especially the section 'Desire in Narrative', pp. 103-57. I am much indebted to the latter work for the ensuing discussion.

20. Quoted in de Lauretis, p. 103.

21. See Lotman, p. 163.

22. See Lotman, p. 168. For de Lauretis's discussion of this passage, see de Lauretis, pp. 118ff.

23. See Lotman, p. 167.

24. See de Lauretis, pp. 118-19.

25. See de Lauretis, p. 119.

26. See de Lauretis, pp. 132-3.

27. See Carden, p. 111.

28. For the links established in 'My First Goose' between Savitsky and Lenin, see J. Andrew, 'Babel's "My First Goose"' in J. Andrew (ed.), *The Structural Analysis of Russian Narrative Fiction,* (Keele, 1984), pp. 64-81, especially pp. 76-7.

29. See ibid.

30. See A. Sinyavsky, 'Isaac Babel', in E. J. Brown (ed.), *Major Soviet Writers,* (London, Oxford, New York), pp. 301-9, especially p. 302.

31. For a discussion of Savitsky's significance in this story, see Andrew (1984).

32. For a discussion of this, see Carden, p. 122.

33. See Andrew (1984).

34. For a discussion of these links, see L. Trilling 'Isaac Babel' in *Beyond Culture,* pp. 119-44, especially pp. 127-8; R. Hallett, pp. 50-1 and V. Shklovsky, 'Isaac Babel: A Critical Romance' in E. J. Brown, pp. 295-300, especially p. 299. Shklovsky, like other critics, notes parallels between *Red Cavalry* and Gogol's *Taras Bulba.* For a discussion of women in this latter work, see Andrew (1988) pp. 86-101.

35. See Trilling, p. 128.

36. See Hallett, p. 52 & Falen, p. 198. The latter sees the theme of the cavalry as such as an important dimension of the cycle's poetry:

> As Babel well knew, the Revolution was to be the last great battle in which the cavalry would play an important role, and his nostalgic evocation of its ancient ethos imparts a lyrical tone to his book. The Cossack and his mount, forming a union that is at once both practical and mystic, create an image in which prosaic necessity and poetic form ride together in harmony.

37. See Shklovsky, p. 299.

38. See Andrew (1984) p. 74.

39. See Hallett, p. 55.

40. See Sinyavsky, p. 302.

41. ibid. See also Falen, p. 197.

42. See Trilling, pp. 120 & 126.

43. ibid, p. 138. For a discussion of Babel's Nietzscheanism, see Falen, pp. 160ff.

44. See Luplow, p. 43.

45. ibid., p. 40.

46. See note 28 above.

47. ibid.

48. There are numerous historical references throughout the cycle including Napoleon, Bogdan Khmelnitsky & Nicholas I.

49. Internecine strife among the Cossacks is a further link with Gogol's *Taras Bulba.* See note 34 above.

50. See Falen, p. 133.

51. See Grongaard, p. 89.

52. See Luplow, p. 57.

53. See de Lauretis, p. 109.

54. See Andrew (1988), pp. 79-111.

55. ibid.

56. See Luplow, p. 16.

57. ibid.

58. ibid.

59. Multiple rape also occurs in Babel's *With Old Man Makhno.* The narrator of that story opens the story in the following chillingly clinical terms:

> Six of Makno's lads raped a servant-girl last night. When I got to know of this I decided to find out how a woman looks after a rape repeated six times.

(Quoted in N. Stepanov, 'Novella Babelya' in *I. Babel: Mastera Sovremennoy Literatury, Stat'i i Materialy,* (Leningrad, 1928, reprint London, 1973), p. 21).

60. See Falen, p. 168.

61. See Luplow, p. 15.

62. See Falen, p. 166.

63. No reader of Babel will need reminding that spectacles, worn both by the narrator and the author themselves, are the sign of the intellectual.

64. See D. Mendelson, *Metaphor in Babel's Short Stories,* (Ann Arbor, 1982), p. 116.

65. See Grongaard, p. 62.

66. See M. Lermontov, *Sobraniye Sochineny v Chetyrekh Tomakh,* (Moscow-Leningrad, 1959-62), Vol. 4, p. 340. The remark is by the travelling narrator in his 'Foreword' to Pechorin's Journal.

67. Turgenev's eponymous heroine Asya can be said to fulfil a similar role in the story of N. N. For a discussion of *Asya* in these terms, see Andrew (1988), pp. 113-22, especially, pp. 120-2.

68. See M. Falchikov, 'Conflict & Contrast in Isaac Babel's *Konarmiya* in *Modern Languages Review,* (72), p. 125-33, especially, p. 125.

69. See Falen, p. 137.

70. ibid., p. 141.

71. See Luplow, p. 32.

72. See Trilling, p. 124, and Falchikov, p. 126.

73. See Carden, pp. 93-4.

74. See Andrew (1984).

75. Quoted in de Lauretis, pp. 107-8.

76. See Andrew (1984), pp. 76-7.

77. See Trilling, p. 134.

78. See Andrew (1984), pp. 75-7.

79. See Falen, p. 199.

80. For a discussion of this, see M. Warner, *Alone of All Her Sex. The Myth & Cult of the Virgin Mary,* (London, 1976), especially pp. 3-78.

81. See Andrew (1984) & Carden, pp. 130-1.

82. For a discussion of this, see Warner, pp. 206-23.

Zsuzsa Hetenyi (essay date 1990)

SOURCE: Hetenyi, Zsuzsa. "'Up' and 'Down', Madonna and Prostitute: The Role of Ambivalence in *Red Cavalry* by Isaac Babel." *Acta Litteraria Academiae Scientiarum Hungaricae* 32, nos. 3-4 (1990): 309-26.

[*In the following essay, Hetenyi investigates the role of ambivalence as well as the significance of Christian mythology and biblical allusions in the stories of* Red Cavalry.]

The stories of Isaac Babel, which he combined into a whole in *Red Cavalry,* are united by the author's outlook, a coherent world view. The heroes, objects, landscapes and events become constituents of a system in the artistic method that I have called "the creation of a new myth"[1]. The chief ingredient of this method is its constant allusions to the Christian myth, a parallelism reinforced at a variety of levels within the work. It is a less conspicuous but equally convincing fact that, in precisely twelve of his heroes, Babel, in creating them, employs—directly or indirectly—Biblical parallelisms; I call these "new apostles".

The "new apostles" are all ambivalent figures: in almost all of them, Biblical parallels and allusions to Christian culture constitute a sublime pole, with the "earthly", coarse traits representing the low pole. In the duality of the creation of the new apostles, the Biblical aspects make up a mythicizing system; hence ambivalence is the single element in the cycle that organizes it into a

system, its dominant at the level of textual correspondences; for, counterposed to it, we have, in all cases, the ordinariness of men and soldiers,—an ordinariness obedient to self-interest and the law of the jungle.

Narrative elements admitting of a dual interpretation are essential building blocks of *Red Cavalry.* The scene forming the backbone of the story **"The Remount Officer"** is built, on the one hand, on the elements of the Biblical miracle of "rise and walk"[2]; on the other hand, it is none other than the deception of the peasants by a crafty device—in the interest of a higher cause. Pavlichenko is simply lying when he alleges the existence of a letter empowering him to order executions at his discretion. Making Lenin the object of his new faith, he combines his lie with the belief that he could have been given the instruction contained in the letter, and that it is correct. In a morbid outburst, Akinfiyev, the hero of the story **"Two Ivans,"** prays to Soviet power. His apostolic behaviour and upbringing are, in reality, nothing other than a frightening blend of cruelty, the rule of the vigilante, and a lack of tolerance. Apolek—whose painting is, as has been seen, the key to the whole cycle—lifts into the icons the men and women of the humdrum round of everyday life, which is, of course, also a degradation of the sacred images. Apolek, this new apostle, whose pictures are assigned such a central role in the work, employs high-pressure tactics to sell his own paintings, stating the exact price as he tries to foist off his art on every passer-by;—that is how the counterpoint of the other pole is created. It is no mere accident that, on one and the same page, with a difference of only two lines, the text calls him "icon painter" (or, to take the literal sense, "painter of God"—"богомаз") and "blasphemer" ("богохулъник")(42)[3]. And one could find plenty of other similar details in the work. In each case, one pole represents the aspect of noble deeds, prompted by faith, with the other pole standing for repugnant, contemptible practices; in these instances, ambivalence appears as an artistic pattern that raises the elements of the *fabula* to the level of the *sujet*—it may be conceived of as an artistic device that oscillates between two poles, as simile or metaphor.

In the same way, the art of pan Apolek is built on the structure of ambivalent duality. In the cycle, we encounter the description of all of his pictures. Eight of these appear in the story **"Pan Apolek,"** and they are the pictures of the church at Novograd, with three—in the story **"At St. Valentine's Church"**—being those of the church at Berestechko. Incidentally, the statues, painted with carmine, are also similar in the two churches (31, 110). Their author is unknown, but, as regards their character, they all fit in well with the pictures of Apolek—that is true of the winking Madonna (30), the ruddy-cheeked St. Peter, with its beard painted with carmine, St. Francis and St. Vincent; which explains why the authors of even some more thorough articles mistakenly identify the statue of Christ as a picture of Apolek—it has clearly escaped them that, a paragraph later, Pan Lyudomirsky stands under the *statue* (110)[4]. As far as the individual pictures of Apolek are concerned, the text indicates only the basic contradiction between the subject and the model: the portrait of Pani Eliza is a fleshy-faced, ruddy Virgin Mary; St. Paul is a portrait of Yanek, a Jew with a limp converted to Christianity; Mary Magdalene is a portrait of Elka, a mother of illegitimate children who is herself illegitimate; in the icons hanging in the houses, we see Josephs with sparse hair parted in the middle, pomaded Jesuses and straddling Maries, with bodies bearing the traces of many pregnancies and confinements. The first of the portrayals described in some detail is that of a strange, beheaded St. John, whose head (in the likeness of the sexton) lies on a separate platter, with a small snake in his mouth (39-40). Efraim Sicher interprets the snake as an attribute of John the Baptist and John the Apostle, taking the picture to be emblematic of both Johns simultaneously. "The snake and the lizard combined with the skull, however, form an iconographical unit, meaning the decomposition of Man."[5] In Apolek's picture, the grimness of death is a playful, loveable creature, ("цветисто сияя чешуей, свисало крохотное туловище змеи. Ее головка, нежнорозовая полная оживления . . .") (40) indeed, it is invested with Apolek's colour, pink. A playful memento mori adapted to suit Apolek's disposition, it has an ambivalent content not unlike that of the dummy skeleton, a favourite figure of Mexican carnivals—i.e. it affords a temporary escape from time and from the fear of death.

Efraim Sicher reminds us that the model for the picture, Pan Romuald, is given the world of the snake and the cat to be his medium; while the world of Apolek, who travels the world with two mice, is the antithesis of that. According to Sicher, that is what links his name with Apollo, who is the mouse-god and, *at the same time,* a dragon-slayer—i.e. serpent-slayer. Hence Apolek—whether we regard his mousiness or his attributes as dragon-slayer—is the antithesis of Romuald, who moves in the sphere of the cat and the snake. Sicher sees this contrast as highlighting the opposition between a representative of the Church, on the one hand, and a heretic, on the other[6].

Apolek shows the Novograd priest twelve of his pictures focussing on scriptural themes. His saints, as well as the surrounding scenery, are brilliantly coloured and earthly (41). When painting the new frescoes of the church, Apolek includes a collection of robust animals, throwing a cunningly smiling figure of Louis XIII—i.e. a real, earthly king—in among the Three Magi (41-42). Apolek's apostles, too, have a roguish smile on their faces; on their double chins "огненные бородавки, малиновые бородавки, как редиска в мае" (109). We see the saints going for their execution in the pos-

ture of Italian opera singers (109); while a new John the Baptist astonishes us with its ambiguous beauty (109). This latter description, in my opinion, fits exactly Leonardo da Vinci's picture of John the Baptist, painted between 1513 and 1516. Some scholars detect other influences in the paintings, but that is not the point[7]. The important element here is the conceptual ambivalence with which the workaday round is elevated into the sacred and the sacred images come down to earth. And within the system of the given relationships it is almost irrelevant whether, artistically, we (or others) establish analogies with Rembrandt or with Renaissance painting. The character of linguistic expression, capturing discrete points, is not directed at describing a given picture or author (nor could we, given the discretic limits of linguistic expression, undertake an identification of that sort—i.e. to identify a description of a picture with a particular picture); the object of the analysis can only be the interpretation of the selected parts.

A further analysis of the ambivalent elements brings us closer to the same basic meaning of the work that we managed to determine already during our examination of the "new apostles". Let us consider Sashka, the camp-follower of the company, who is the only nuanced female character in **Red Cavalry.** She cannot be ranged with the new apostles—by no means because of her gender, but because she lacks a belief-like conviction. Nonetheless, revealing the several layers to her personality confirms the method of the creation of a new myth.

Sashka, the company's camp-follower, is a figure encapsulating many of the important motifs that form the second line of the stories. Talking about the ambivalent character of the figure of Sashka, one is immediately struck by one of the two poles to be identified—indeed, its dominance may seem evident: it is the one represented by Sashka's earthly, common traits, dependent on the material-physical principle conceptualized by Bakhtin[8].

With Sashka, being a prostitute is not a character trait or, indeed, a flaw of character; it is simply her lifestyle. An integral part of that lifestyle is the lust for gain—whether she uses her body as a tool, as in the story **"The Widow,"** or she is choosing among the church silks, as in the piece **"At St. Valentine's Church."** She displays feminine cunning—a cunning, that is, characterizing the Cossacks—in the way she finds a worthy mate for her mare (**"Chesniki"**), but equally, her intimate relationship with the horse itself, as well as her participation in the campaign, are singularly masculine—where again, this masculinity is that of a Cossack. On further scrutiny, we also discover some features that are far more indirect and complex. We encounter several references in the cycle underscoring the striking, exaggerated femininity of Sashka's body:

"непомерное тело" (128), "болтающиеся груди" (145), "чудовищная грудъ ее закидывадасъ за спину" (140). According to the formulation, "the images of the body appear in a colossally enlarged, hyperbolic form"[9] in the images of carnival ambivalence. The body of Sashka, invested with exaggerated feminine characteristics, is reminiscent of portrayals and statues of ancient, mythical goddesses of fertility (such as the Venus of Willendorf). This association is reinforced by a scene in **"Chesniki"** where Sashka is just having her mare covered, thereby coming into direct contact—though, of course, not only on this one occasion—with insemination. As she keeps kissing the slobbery cheeks of her mare, rubbing her face against them, this enormous female body appears before us as some primitive natural creature of impulse, in her animal naturality. We are presented with the same animal side of Sashka in one of the episodes in **"At St. Valentine's Church,"** but here the description clearly accentuates the repulsive features. "Тело Сашки, чветущее и вонючее, как мясо только что зарезанной коровы, заголилосъ, поднявшиеся юбки открыли ее ноги зскадронной дамы, чугунные, стройные ноги, и Курдюков, придурковатый малый, усевшисъ на Сашке верхом и трясясъ, притворился объятым страстъю (108). It hardly needs special comment how the description applies to Sashka words referring to horses and riding—how she is identified here with the mare.

In order to get an idea of the ambivalent character of the figure of Sashka, it seems necessary to consider the physical or sexual acts in the stories—a theme that Babel examines from every angle in the cycle, by portraying it in its complexity and contradictoriness. We get the first treatment of the theme in a tale of Pan Apolek, in the story of the same title. Pan Apolek recounts how Christ was united with Deborah to save her marriage, taking upon himself the suffering. It is worth considering what the significance of this profoundly, Biblically symbolic apocryphal scene is for revealing the creation of a new myth as an authorial device. The Biblical Gospels refer to Jesus on several occasions as the bridegroom awaited by the bride—i.e. mankind, preparing to become His church[10]. The bond between the bridegroom and the bride symbolizes the union of God and man in love—an interpretation clearly spelt out by Biblical parables such as the one about the royal wedding and the one about the ten maidens (Mt. 22, 1-15; 25, 1-14). It is interesting that we are directed to this associative correspondence by the text of the story itself: "он . . . удалился в пустынную страну, на Восток от Иудеи, где ждал его Иоанн" (45). The person meant could only have been John the Baptist, author of the famous Biblical sentence: "He who has the bride is the bridegroom" (Jn 3, 29). The—admittedly, rather complicated—dominant meaning of the parable describing the union of Jesus and Deborah—as indeed, the Bibli-

cal parables too—can be explained by accounting for the particular persons and actions in terms of who, or what, they refer to. The bride wallowing in the mud is sinful mankind, preparing to receive the bridegroom—"she yearns for her husband and is afraid of him". In the cycle, Gedali is the exponent of this behaviour: he longs for the revolution and is scared of it. Perhaps we are not wide of the mark in regarding this feeling as the characteristic state of the Russian intelligentsia post 1917. For "Тогда Иисус . . . возложил на себя одежду новобрачного и, полный сострадания, соединился с Деборой." (45) Mankind—or the post-1917 intelligentsia—accepts the revolution in Christ's garb and glove—or, conversely, it perceives the revolution as approaching in the guise of Christ.

Let us now see the concrete interpretation and the poles of the parable. The purity of the self-sacrifice and compassion (cf. 'com-passion' and Russian 'сострадание') expressed in the scene is thrown into sharp relief by the uncleanness—the "vomit"—surrounding Deborah and, in a moral respect, by the spiritual incomprehension of the kinfolk and the guests invited—although, to be sure, it is an incomprehension that stems from traditions. This union served the continuation of life, as "Deborah was delivered of a boy" (26). This ending is like the naive wishes of fairy tales, like a symbolic dream of the presence and continuation of Christ. Let us just recall that the meaning of portraying the physical-bodily sphere is precisely this, that it holds in itself the possibility of rebirth and resurrection[11]. But we may also detect here a parallel with the ancient myths, where the annually recurring vernal renewal was represented as a union of bride and bridegroom, usually with beings incarnating the creative power of vegetation. (Indeed, in some places, the harvest ritual also included the custom, supposed to ensure rebirth in the following year, of feeding the seeds of the last spike to a mare in foal, which directly refers to Sashka's mare taken to horse.[12]) Preeminent among the rites of fertility feasts is the myth of Dionysus, who is a son of God (Zeus), and who rose from the dead. In the Russian literature of the turn of the century, as has been mentioned before, the parallel between Dionysus and Christ was "in the air", so to speak, as a parallel between suffering and resurrecting gods. At the centre of the tempestuous, orgiastic scenes of the rite performed annually in Athens was the union of Dionysus with the Queen, which has quite unequivocal parallels in the wedding of the May King and the May Queen in other myths[13].

Let us digress briefly to try and construe one of the few sentences from *Red Cavalry* that have become common property. The narrator says these words: "Мы оба смотрели на мир, как на луг в мае, как на луг, по которому ходят женщины и кони." (87) It is widely known that Babel was passionately fond of horses; he was capable of spending weeks in a village for the sole reason that he saw some lovely horses there[14]; yet, it is not merely a case of the writer investing one of his heroes with his own personal taste. It is precisely in the semantic sphere of the renewal of nature and fertility that the three concepts featuring in the sentence—the meadow in May, woman and horse—may merge into one. From time immemorial, the figure of the horse has been associated with the concept of fertility, as eloquently attested by the prehistoric cave drawings of the Nordic peoples, as well as by the surviving customs of spring rituals[15]. We have already observed that this is the meaning of the mating of the mare too.

Indeed, if we recall the idea raised by the parable of Deborah—namely, that the bridegroom and the bride, according to the Biblical meaning, symbolize Jesus and his Church—, we may discover, in the story **"Konkin,"** a linking (possessing a stylistical valuation befitting folk poetry) of the Biblical parallel, on the one hand, and the ritual, fertility symbolism of the horse, on the other, where the latter is associated with spring feasts. Moreover, the two have been combined with stunning concreteness: "Конъ под моим тузом, как купчова дочка . . . Нажали я колеса и вкладываюу в коника два заряда. Жалко было жеребча. Большевичок был жеребеч, чистый большевичок. Сам рыжий, как монета, хвост пулей, нога струной. Думал, жлвую *Ле*$_u$ свезу, ан не выЬло. Ликвидировал я зту лошадку. Рухнула она, как невеста . . . (88-89).

The second lovemaking in the book might be termed the antithesis of the first. In the story **"'Sashka the Christ,'"** two people are involved on the male side, Sashka the Christ and his stepfather. The female participant is a rag-gatherer this time, a crippled beggar woman. Her feminine character is underlined by a reference to the moon, the feminine element of myths. This act is a mockery, a deriding of fertility, in the carnivalesque sense of the word. The laughter of the carnival "is ambivalent: it is full of joy, jubilantly happy, but it is also mocking and derisive; it denies and affirms at one and the same time, it buries and restores to life at one and the same time. / . . . / The ambivalent laughter of the people . . . expresses the viewpoint of the perpetually changing world-entirety, which also contains the laughter himself"[16].

In the bed, the ragwoman cries, "Rain for the old woman, I'll give you two hundred puds of crops from one hectare". (72) The interpretation of fertility widens to include, in the true spirit of myth, the fruits of both the earth and woman. This physical encounter is accidental and destructive. It is destructive not only because both men contract venereal disease, but also because Sashka is not yet a man, he is still a child, a boy. In this scene, we witness a clash between youth and old age, chastity and decadence, purity and corruption. The third

encounter, between Sashka's mother and stepfather, also takes place in this story. Its higher significance is given by the fact that, as we may recall, this is the price that Sashka has to pay for being allowed to become a shepherd—that is to say, he responds to his calling, his vocation, and betrays his mother for it[17]. The betrayal itself and the stepfather's egoism in transmitting the disease constitute the pole of base qualities. Yet, even this selfish act is not unequivocally selfish. This love-making is a necessary step for renewal, for maintaining the equilibrium of nature: for, on his arrival home, the father was received with the news that his two small children had died; thus the act represents a counterpole aimed at countervailing death.

To Matvey Pavlichenko and his young wife, sexuality represents a celebration of the freedom of the body. "Всю ночь нам жарко было, всю долгую ночь мы голые ходили и шкуру друг с джужки обрывали." (77) Again we find an oblique reference to the rite of spring fertility, as it is precisely during the spring spawning season that Nastya displays an interest in Matvey. But Nastya is taken away by the landowner, and Matvey only returns after 1918, as a Red general, to take revenge. Before the very eyes of the landowner's wife, he carries out the death sentence that he himself has passed. In the meantime, the landowner's wife, who had gone mad, was sitting in an armchair in the "hall", "на них бархатная корона перъями убрана была, они в кресла бойко сели и шашкой мне на караул сделали." (80) Nadezhda Vasilyevna is provided with all the trappings of a carnival queen; her royal status is indicated by the personal pronoun, the adjective, and the verbs in royal plural referring to her, and also by the designation of the locale, the more archaic "зала" form of the word "зал" ("room", "hall"), which denotes 'audience chamber' or 'throne-room'. The grotesque comicality of the scene provides a counterpoint to the tragedy of the gruesome murder; the madness of Nadezhda Vasilyevna rubs off on Pavlichenko's action too, allowing an insight behind—and, indeed, signifying the madness of—the first-person narrative attitude, the logic of the *skaz* form, a logic of plausibility. The role of the carnival, as defined by Bakhtin, is expressed in the final sentences: Pavlichenko always kills in such a way that, while he does so, his aim is to gain a deeper sense of life.

The direct references of this scene to carnival festivals raise a two-dimensional idea. On the one hand, the carnival shows up from time to time the eternal binary value-system of the world, unaffected by the age, proving thereby the stability, the sternity of mankind (and of the universe). At the same time, the carnival is but a "nine days' wonder", a temporary escape from the workaday round; once the experience is over, every age returns to its wonted routine. If we view from this angle the carnivalesque-theatrical scene of the closing of the short story examined above, the drama of revenge and new value relations are qualified as a temporary show, after which everything and everybody settle back into their old, accustomed lives. It is a fairly bold idea to regard the revolution as a theatrical performance; yet, Babel's short story does allow—nay, it suggests—that interpretation *as well*. That is Babel's dual vision: the pathos of theatricality set on a pedestal and an all-querying skepticism—within the selfsame passage, the one intertwined with the other. As has been mentioned before, we may observe a similar phenomenon in the case of Dyakov, hero of **"The Remount Officer"** who deceives the peasants like a circus juggler in the interest of a higher goal. In the story **"The Widow"** Lyovka, ex-circus rider, light athlete and women's favourite, steps before us in the role of a faithful executor of a will, a defender of justice—after he has stolen from the dead man his lover, and that amid frequent appeals to God and in the name of life. To avoid having to kill a prisoner, Konkin can boast two high ranks: first, that he is а "музыкалъный зксцентрик и салонный чревовещателъ" (89), and secondly, that he is also a "коммунист и комиссар" (90). Accordingly, his pleading with the prisoner is built on the structure of a joke or an anecdote; moreover, it is the only attempt in the cycle to parade for out attention a Cossack who is human, a character who has not yet forgotten the Ten Commandments.

In the story **"Italy's Sun,"** we find additional evidence to support the above interpretation of the circus-like or theatrical elements, which presents the revolution as a temporary changeover to a new set of values, a carnival;—for here the town suddenly appears as an operatic stage setting. "Сырая плесенъ развалин цвела, как мрамор оперной скамъи. И я ждал потвероженной душой выхода Ромео из-за туч, атласного Ромео, поющего о любви, в то время как за кулисами понурый элэктротехник держит палец на выключателе луны." (46)

Suddenly, all the relevant elements of the cycle are seen as part of a pattern: Dyakov is like "an athlete in the arena", a "robust and youthful Romeo", who, as he disappears, "flutters his frock, reminiscent of an operatic costume". Even at his first appearance, reminiscent of an entrance onto the stage, his attire creates a theatrical atmosphere: he arrives on a fiery Arab horse, he is ruddy-cheeked, his frock is black, his red trousers are adorned by silver stripes (37, 38). Gedali's green cloak, his beard and black top hat—among other things—lend him the exterior of a magician or a conjurer. The church at Berestechko "is as dazzling as a stage setting" (108), and in it, the saints in Apolek's pictures go to their death "in the picturesque postures of Italian singers" . . . All these sporadically appearing signals betoken the presence of pretence, of falseness in the incidents and in the characters—they are consequences and

artistic devices of the dual vision of reality. This is a counterpoint to the self-confidence of the Cossacks, the position of the narrator, who admires them, to the pathos and the ideological conditions of the age, which brook no argument. *Alongside* the glorification—which, incidentally, predominates—, the signals enumerated above establish a greater distance between the writer and his heroes, as well as between the narrator and the Cossacks, because the observer becomes an onlooker, an outsider, with the events becoming conditional happenings. The motif of this dual vision, which crops up everywhere, is, in our opinion, the *lense through which Babel's hero looks at things*—he views the world through an intervening layer, through a filter; he has a double vision—and conception—of the universe.

Coming back to the string of bodily acts: to Irina, the washerwoman, and Vasiliy, the cook, love is replaced by the philosophy that evening is there that a man may take a woman to bed—that is the law of nature (the story **"Evening"**). It is by no means coincidental that the preceding conversation is about the assassination and the death of the tsars; therefore this lovemaking is again some kind of response gesture on the part of life. In the description of Vasiliy's outlook upon life, great emphasis is laid on the opposition and unity of life and death, and on how the occupation of a cook embraces everything to do with the body. "Повара—они имеют много дела с мясом мертвых животных и с жадностъю живых . . ." (99)

The first appearance of Sashka, the camp follower of the company, in the story **"At St. Valentine's Church,"** has been quoted already: Kurdyukov has a ride on Sashka, imitating copulation, so as to raise a laugh. On entering the church, the first-person narrator is greeted by that histrionic spectacle, prefaced by only one sentence, conveying the very first impression: "Мертвенный аромат парчи, рассыпавшихся цветов, душистого тления лился в ее трепещущие ноздри, щекоча и отравляя." (108). That image of death, emphasizing lifelessness is in turn, counterbalanced by the boisterous sexuality and earthly animality of the ensuing scene, which also renders psychologically authentic both the simulation of sexual intercourse—that life-affirming, truly carnivalesque happening—and, partly, the subsequent ransacking of the church, as a rebellion against mortality and passing. We may include in the same category the phenomena associated with pillage during war—the priority given, amidst the carnage going on all round, to the here-and-now, to self-interest, to primitive life, with survival as the refuge luring people on. We get a contrasting motif in Prishchepa, who casts everything into the flames; he burns his past to emerge, clean, into the new life, onto the stage of history.

In the story **"The Widow,"** the presence of death is no longer merely hinted at or implied. Shevelyov is dying, and the woman who has been his regular mistress,

Sashka, is rolling about in the bush with his coachman, who uses the name of God as he possesses himself of Sashka's body.

It is also manifest from the text that this is a life-affirming act, whose function is identical with that of eating, for, in the description, the two actions are accompanied by identical noises. Eating, as we shall also see in connection with the story **"The Death of Dolgushov"** is a fairly unequivocal counterbalance to death—indeed, in the custom of funeral feasts, it is a most strongly anchored and widely observed affirmation of life. The abstract idea of the continuation of life could hardly be rendered more palpable than it is by this union in the background to death, with the lover of the dying man shown in the arms of a new man. Moreover, this change of lover has another, by no means abstract facet to it, for Sashka, by using her body, tries to win the favour of Lyova well in advance, as Lyova is expected to become his master's executor, and Sashka wants to get her hands on the part which, by rights, ought to be sent to the mother. Hence this lovemaking—not only in abstract terms but also in a very concrete way—is a means, directed to the future, of preserving life.

We have already touched on some of the aspects of the story **"Chesniki."** The mating of the horse takes up the second half of the story, with the first half treating of the preparation for the battle about to be fought near the town which provides the title for the piece. Nothing further is said here about the battle, though it is clear that, at the end of the story, the fighting is still going on, with an account of the defeat coming only at the beginning of the next story. The defeat, incidentally, is anticipated by the sentence that forms the transition between the two portions of **"Chesniki"**: "Но я не услышал единодушия в казацком вое, и, дожидаясь атаки, я ушел в лес . . ." (139). The mating of the horse is a vivid scene packed with dialogue and incident, whose framework is provided by the hesitant preparation for the battle which is to end in defeat and then the report on the defeat itself. These in turn, serve to heighten the earthy vitality of the intervening part,—a vitality concerned with the future in a very concrete sense. In another respect, we see the same conflict between the important military event and the pursuit of petty individual interests.

An outline of the ninth, and last, physical relationship in line (in the story **"Singing"**) shows a reprise of several of the motifs encountered so far. Three people are lying in bed: Sashka, the Christ, the faded, bony landlady, and his mute, hydrocephalic son beside them. The presence of the boy and the shrivelled old woman recall the trio of the first act, in the story **"Sashka the Christ,"** where Sashka himself was still the young boy; yet, the strand of motif of the union of old age and youth is re-inforced through repetition. Sashka the Christ is at the same time, the comforter of the old woman—he saves her life, scrubs the floor, and treats her humanely. (We may recall that Sashka has comforted others too—first the villagers, and then the company.) The purity of compassion is thus a running thread through the scene, echoing the story of Christ and Deborah; moreover, as regards the physical environment it appears in, here too it is set against a background of squalor (rags, dirty nose, etc.—148). Accordingly, the ninth act, by recalling the motifs of the first and the second acts, closes this theme as if in a frame-like pattern, showing something like the structure of a musical cadenza.

After that string of human relationships and feelings, it would be naive to conceive of the role of the company's camp follower purely in terms of a portrayal of Sashka's individual character or as a case of morality inevitably seduced into vice under the pressures of life in camp. Being everybody's lover means being wife, mother, and sister, all in one person, to everybody for a while. Sashka comforts men—which is the third and most pronounced link between her and Sashka the Christ; indeed, it partly explains why they receive the same name and why they are allied, too, by the same adjective ("эскадронный")—"the camp-follower of the company" (108, 140) and "the singer of the company" (147). Sashka is a nurse; and the concepts of comforting and refuge are inextricably entangled with her very profession. It is worth quoting the old designation of this profession, also featured in the cycle—"сестра милосердия", which translates as Sister of Charity or Sister of Mercy. According to Babel's scheme, physical consolation and nursing are allied concepts; indeed, in the story **"The Widow,"** they follow one another, as Sashka, after making love, immediately changes the bandage of the dying man (128). This motif is not a novelty in Babel's oeuvre, nor is it without parallels. The short story **"Eliya Isaakovich and Margarita Prokofyevna"** may be regarded as the first instance of its use[18], followed by *Doudou*, a journalistic writing[19]. It is conspicuous that here, in *Doudou*, as well, the complex figure of the prostitute—a figure providing consolation—is joined to the figure of a soldier, concretely identifying, at the other pole, the man who struggles or drifts in life, in whose fate the comforter is indispensable. Here too the physical act performs the role of life pitted against death, it is a life-preserving gesture—not only in the face of war, but also in the face of the concretely appearing death throes of the wounded man. Given that knowledge and an acquaintance with the imagery and the conceptual system of **Red Cavalry,** our attention may be attracted by the fact that the French soldier is taken to hospital on the third day of Easter, that is to say, on the festival of the Resurrection. That the date is meant to be a concrete indication of time is to be questioned, if only because the work was published prior to Easter 1917; moreover, in other respects too, it gives the impression of a literary, fictional text, rather than that of a documentary account, as its outward features might suggest. Here the ambivalent character of prostitution still appears explicitly, that is only on the surface (Doudou dances "with tender passion" and "like a virgin"); in the devices pertaining to the relationship with the soldier we may observe a delicacy verging on sentimentalism (silk blouse, lace collar, her fingers trembled).

"Все смертно. Вечная жизнъ суждена толъко матери. И когда матери нет в живых, она оставляет по себе воспоминание, которое никто еще не решился тсквернитъ. Помятъ о матери плтает в нас состраданис, как океан, безмерный океан питает реки, рассекаюющие вселдннную . . . (57). These words of Gedali, the introduction to the story **"The Rabbi,"** are about the eternal force that is the sustainer and perpetuator of life—i.e. motherhood. Christ Sashka and the Rabbi's son subordinated their filial love to their vocation, a motif familiar from the Bible as well. The figure of Kurdyukov's mother, as dimly perceived through the story **"The Letter,"** is one that persists in the memory; in the photo: "крохотная крестьянка . . . с чахлыми светлыми и застенчивыми чертами лица" (36) with three rugged men at her side, two of whom are dead, the members of the family having slaughtered each other from opposing sides of the political divide. In the story **"Salt,"** we may observe an inversion of motherhood, or rather, an abuse of the respect for motherhood. Two consecutive pieces of the cycle, **"The Widow"** and **"Zamostye,"** are the culmination of this theme. In a Freudian dream that Lyutov has, loneliness and the desire for tenderness call up a female figure dressed in festive attire. "Она вынула грудъ из черных кружев корсажа и ионесла ее мне с осторожностъю, как кормилица пишу. Она приложила свою грудъ к моей." (130) This is a complex image of consolation: wife, lover, and mother combined in one person. In his dream, Lyutov is attended on his journey to death by this female figure, and it is she who says a prayer over him. Motherhood and childhood, life and death are intertwined, as has been seen, too, in the figure of Sashka the prostitute.

It is interesting to note that the joining of these opposite poles is a constant theme in the background of the works—in such a way that, counterposed to the deaths and the carnage of the Civil War, we get, from time to time, brief, symbolic appearances—either built into, or as the case may be independent of the plot—of pregnant women signifying that life goes on and there will be new lives (**"Crossing the Zbruch," "The Sun of Italy," "The Rabbi"**). Bakhtin mentions the small terra cotta figures of Kerch, which carry a similar meaning; they portray laughing, pregnant old women, with a deeply mythical symbolism[20]. Apart from the motifs

mentioned so far, associated with Sashka, fertility, as contrasted with the storms of history, receives emphasis elsewhere too—for instance, in a letter in the story **"Berestechko."** Dated exactly a hundred years before the year 1920, the time stated in a few places in the story cycle, the letter, written in French—which serves to heighten the rhetorical effect—mentions together the death of Napoleon and the birth of a child. The motif of pregnant women also raises a Biblical parallel, where in describing the time of the end, there is the ever-recurring idea—"Alas for those who are with child and for those who give suck in those days!" (e.g. Lk 21:23). This role of motherhood, as a sustaining force, and of woman ensuring the continuance of the world is evident in Babel's early works as well. In **"The Palace of Mothers"** and **"The Premature Infants,"** Babel expresses his views on the subject almost in the form of a political precept, explaining the sustaining eternal force of the carnival philosophy: "But the earth keeps turning. People die and people are born."[21] Babel's articles—right from *Doudou* on—were undoubtedly instrumental in the formulation of Gorky's views, which the latter expounded in the same organ scarcely two months later; these, however, show a striking affinity with the hidden meaning of Pan Apolek's picture, the picture of the apostles rocking Jesus: "Женщина в моем представлении прежде всего—матъ, хотя бы Физически она была девушкой . . ."; ". . . и я всем сердцем, всей душой хочу, чтобы вы скорее улыбалисъ улыбкою Богоматери, прижимая к груди своей новорожденного человека России!"; "Россдя сужорожно бъется в страшных муках родов,—вы хотите, чтобы скорее родилосъ новое, прекрасное, доброе, красивое, человеческое?"

The spectacle of Dolgushov dying and the "exultation of destruction" bring a cry to Grishchuk's lips, projecting the senselessness of death onto the birth of life: "Зачем бабы трудаются? . . . Зачем сватання, венчання, зачем кумы на свадъбе гуляют?" (67) The doubly violent death of Dolgushov—for first he is mortally wounded and then he is put out of his misery by a shot from Afonka Bida—and Lyutov's bitterness over the loss of his friend, Afonka Bida, are relieved by a closing which, bringing a change in both tone and subject, offers a characteristic counterpoint—namely, eating, that most palpable, ancient and eternal, consoling confirmation of the sustaining of life.

Thus Sashka unites within her the elements of Lyutov's dream: she uses her femininity to comfort the Cossacks, and, as a nurse, she attends them on their journey to death, right to the very end. Shevelyov died. "Павлик,—сказала она.—Иисус Христос мой,—лег ла на мертвеца боком, прикрыв его своим непомерным телом." (128) That image, worthy of Apolek's brush, is nothing other than an image of motherhood compressed into the Pietà, the prostitute exalted into a

Madonna; while her enormous body suggests heathen and ancient mythical overtones. In conformance with the inner law of the cycle, Sashka appears as mother not just at an abstract and symbolic level, but also in the most grossly materialistic sense of the word, as when she looks upon the property that Shevelyov has bequeathed to his mother as her own. In the final analysis, we may see how, in the light of this Biblical image, the aspects listed above are connected with the figure of the Madonna, as the source of life and the epitome of all that is feminine, with the giver of solace and joy, the silent and sadly resigned observer of death (the act of dying).

Sashka, the everybody's woman raised to become Madonna, is the mirror image and counterpart of Sashka the Christ. Juxtaposed to each other, the camp-follower of the company and the singer of the company also raise the idea that **"Sashka the Christ"** is, above all a comforter of the soul, while Sashka is primarily a comforter of the body. Both of them ambivalent figures in themselves, the relationship they bear to each other is that of the female and male manifestation, respectively, of one and the same meaning—the Madonna and the Saviour of the Christian myth. The figure of Sashka is characterized by the binary connections of masculinity and femininity, animality and humanity, body and mind, love and death.

"Сашка-святитель, у богородицы сиФилис захватил"—is how Sashka the Christ is mocked by his father (72). That is the paradox personified by Sashka, the heroine of the cycle—she is the Blessed Virgin (see the Pietà image) from whom one can contract syphilis. We find a prefiguration or representation of her in one of Apolek's pictures at the end of the story **"The Church at Novograd,"** where the narrator runs away from the "ogling Madonnas".

We have seen, then, that ambivalence—ambivalence, that is, as defined by Bakhtin, which is a vehicle of eternal renewal, and which gains its ultimate meaning in the continuity of life and death—is, as a fundamental perspective, a running thread through the whole cycle.[22] The appearance of ambivalence is, at the same time, a product and a carrier of Babel's dual vision, and in that dual quality it may be regarded as the dominant of the cycle. In Babel, the meaning of ambivalence is manifold: firstly, it suggests that history invariably manifests itself at once in the sublime and in the crassly ordinary; secondly, it raises the intricate unity and interdependence of the eternal and the ephemeral meanings; and thirdly, it illuminates the secret of the writer's method—the view that, in the mythical enstaging of the events of the Civil War, the history of mankind can be regarded as an endless sequence of repetitions, or rather of renewals.

Notes

1. Hetényi, Zsuzsa: Bibliai motívumok Babel "Lovashadsereg"-ében. (The Biblical Motifs in Babel's "Red Cavalry".) Filológiai Közlöny, Nos 1-4, 1985. Хетени, Жужа: Библейские мотивы в "Конармии" И.Бабеля.

2. In the description of the miracle, the emphatic role of the gaze, the eyes, as well as the power of inner strength nourished by faith, echoes Acts 3:4-10 from the Bible. Dyakov says to the doubting peasant: "But you are blaspheming against God, my friend." According to the Bible, doubting the miracles is "blasphemy against the Holy Spirit" (Mt 12:31; Mk 3:29+ Lk 12:10).

3. The page numbers following the quotations refer to the following edition: И. Бабелъ: Избранное. Москва 1966.

4. Sicher, E.: The Road to a Red Calvary. SEER Vol. 60, No. 4. October 1982. 535.

5. Bergström: Disguised Symbolism in "Madonna" Pictures and Still Life. Art Bulletin New York, 1955. 346.

6. See note 4, 533.

7. The names of Murillo, Rubens, Rembrandt, Malevich are mentioned, as well as naive painting and the Polish Baroque. See note 4, and Wiener Slawistischer Almanach, Band 10, 1982. 253-271.

8. Бахтин, М.: Творчество Франсуа Рабле и народная кулътура средневековъя и ренессанса. Москва 1965. 23, 24.

9. Ibid. 23.

10. See Mt 9:15; Mk 2:19; Jn 3:29; 2Cor 11:2.

11. Bakhtin, 26.

12. Frazer, J. G.: The Golden Bough. A Study in Magic and Religion. London[3], 1920-1923. IV/1, 250-252, 266; V/1. 27-30.

13. Ibid. II/97 and sqq.; V/1. 199-202.

14. Иванова, Тамара: Мои современники, какими я их знала. Москва 1984. 293-294.

15. Frazer V/1, 292-294, and Broby-Johansen, R.: Oldnordiske stenbilleder (Gyldendals Ugleborger).

16. Bakhtin, 16.

17. The mother yields in importance to the calling: that is the Bible's system of values. See Mt 12:48-49; Mk 3:33; Lk 8:19 sqq.; Jn 2:4.

18. Лѣтописъ, ноябрь 1916 года.

19. Свободные мысли, 13 марта 1917 года.

20. Bakhtin 31.

21. Горький, М.: Несвоевременные мысли. Paris, 1971. 233, 235, 238. Novaya Zhizhn No. 100. May 13, 1918. It was in "Novaya Zhizhn" that Babel published his short-story-like journalistic pieces about daily life under the revolutionary régime.

22. Bakhtin, 15 and Бахтин, М.: Проблемы поэтики Достоевского. Москва 1972. 304.

Allan Reid (essay date June 1991)

SOURCE: Reid, Allan. "Isaak Babel's *Konarmiia*: Meanings and Endings." *Canadian Slavonic Papers* 33, no. 2 (June 1991): 139-50.

[*In the following essay, Reid notes that over the years there has been little agreement on the style, themes, or genre of* Red Cavalry, *and examines the structure and function of the ending of the collection.*]

Despite its brevity, Isaak Babel's **Konarmiia**[1] has been the victim of a great variety of readings, most of them unsupported textually or extra-textually; few cohere into any intellectually satisfying whole. Fortunately, several recent studies suggest that Babel scholarship—and, in particular, the study of **Konarmiia**—is undergoing serious and profound revisions.[2] Nevertheless, there is still very little agreement about this work's style, themes, or even genre. The problem of genre, for example, betrays itself in translations of the title which frequently carries the dubious epithet "Tales." This implies an autonomy for each of the *parts* making up the work—something which is not obvious at all. While one article cannot reflect on all the problems that have evolved in Babel scholarship over the last six decades, I would like to take up the question of **Konarmiia**'s ending. Under the heading of closure, this paper will examine the internal structure of the ending and discuss its function within the work as a whole.

I

Taking his cue from the leading Soviet theoretician Iurii Lotman, Mark E. Suino writes:

[T]he fact that a verbal work of art, among the many possible kinds of messages which we encounter, has an ending, is important beyond the information that we must cease listening or reading. The ending defines the immediate structure within which the various data—expression, content, and their interrelationship—are active and relevant.[3]

To be sure, Suino's immediate concern is an eight-line poem by Tiutchev. However, he hopes and expects—in time—to be able to produce typological models not only for short poems, but also for longer poetic works and perhaps even for prose. I am not concerned here with typologies or models, but *Konarmiia* provides a rich field for making the move from poetry to prose in reference to closure.

The first complete edition of **Konarmiia** ended with the chapter **"The Rebbe's Son,"** but for the sixth edition Babel added a new chapter, the thirty-fifth, entitled **"Argamak."** For now, let me note that one of the key functions of **"Argamak"** is the creation of a circle, a return to the beginning. It has not been noticed previously that Babel here returns to specific events of at least two other chapters, including the first, **"Crossing the Zbruch"** and **"My First Goose,"** retelling them from a totally different point of view and thereby urging the reader to begin again, as it were. **"Argamak,"** then, provides **Konarmiia** with a cyclical dimension, while **"The Rebbe's Son"** proposes a resolution of certain dominant themes and problems of the work as a whole. According to this reading, **Konarmiia** has features of both an open or linear ending (**"The Rebbe's Son"**), and a closed, circular ending (**"Argamak"**). Ultimately, both work together to form a single ending, creating an uncommon dynamism and making it an uncommonly difficult but, at the same time, exceptionally profound aesthetic achievement.

In the West, traditional Babel scholarship has held that he was fascinated by the violence of the revolution and the civil war, and that this emerged as a sort of moral ambivalence or equivocation in his writing. Soviet scholars have held that he justified the violent excesses of the period by appealing to the great humanistic objectives which they purportedly served. Neither of these standard approaches stands up to close scrutiny. Babel's firsthand experience of fighting and of the front was quite limited,[4] although both Soviet and western scholars often stubbornly assert the opposite. Moreover, what he did see, he neither liked nor approved of, and numerous passages in his diary attest to this. For example:

I went through two weeks of utter despair here. That was because of the ferocious cruelty that never lets up for a minute and because I clearly understood how unfit I am for the business of destruction, how difficult it is for me to break away from the past—from that which was bad, perhaps, but that which smelled of poetry for me as the hive smells of honey. I'm all right now. So what—*some will make the Revolution and I, I will sing that which is off to the side, that which goes deeper. I feel that I can do that* and there will be a place and a time to do it.[5]

I hope to demonstrate how Babel achieves this objective, at least partially, in **"The Rebbe's Son."**

Babel was very deliberate and painstaking in his art. Many are familiar with Paustovskii's anecdote—possibly apocryphal but enlightening nevertheless—according to which one brief story ("**Liubka the Cossack**") went through twenty-two revisions. For Babel, every word was important. He is well known for such statements as "No iron can enter the human heart with the chilling effect of a well-timed period," or "A simile must be as precise and accurate as a logarithm and must be as natural as the smell of dill," and "I think that a noun needs only one adjective, and it must be chosen very carefully." These frequently cited remarks—and there are more like them—have a great bearing on the discussion which follows.

II

"**The Rebbe's Son**" relates in the space of some 500 words the narrator's, i.e., Liutov's, second encounter with Il'ia, the son of Rabbi Motale, and Il'ia's subsequent death. This chapter is organized by paragraphs and divides structurally into three parts, plus an epilog as shown in Table 1.

TABLE 1. ORGANIZATION OF "**THE REBBE'S SON**"

PART I (PARAGRAPHS 1-3)
Refers to previous events, stories, characters
Transition mentions Il'ia

PART II (PARAGRAPHS 4-5)
Time shift to actual encounter, three days prior to telling

PART III (PARAGRAPHS 6-11)
Conversation between Liutov and Il'ia
Reconstructs events from time of previous encounter to present meeting
Bridges parts I and II

EPILOG (PARAGRAPH 12)
Relates Il'ia's death
Associations with parts I and II
Elevates the relationship between the two protagonists to a higher level

Part I refers specifically to previous chapters, events, and characters, mentioning Il'ia in the last sentence. Part II shifts to the time of the narrated events (i.e., of the encounter itself) which occurred three days prior to the telling. Part III is a conversation between Liutov and Il'ia; it briefly reconstructs events between their previous meeting and the present one. As such, it bridges the first two parts, referring to the central events of each. Although it is presented in dialogue form, it is the most strictly narrative part of the story. The epilog relates Il'ia's death and then refers to elements of both the first and second parts, bridging them not by narration but by association. The final sentence of the epilog establishes a deeper, non-circumstantial relationship be-

tween Liutov and Il'ia. I will now turn to an examination of each of the parts.

III

"**The Rebbe's Son**" is one of only two chapters in the entire work that begin with suspension periods. The other chapter which does this is "**The Rebbe.**" The ellipsis in "**The Rebbe's Son**" points back to the latter, the events of which are immediately and specifically summoned up by the narrator. Similarly, in "**The Rebbe**" the ellipsis leads back to the chapter "**Gedali**" and its main character. The latter two take place on the same Sabbath. Thus, Part I of "**The Rebbe's Son**" immediately establishes an explicit association with both these earlier chapters. Incidentally, no other group of chapters is so closely or explicitly linked as is this trio.

Memory is the dominant motif of Part I of "**The Rebbe's Son.**" The narrator harkens back to the events related at Rabbi Motale's house on that Sabbath, but his memory seems less than precise. The tone and atmosphere he evokes have changed, and the characters, furnishings, and events have been rearranged. Only one short passage reflects something unchanged: "Outside the window, horses were neighing and the Cossacks were shrieking. The wasteland of war yawned outside the window." But even this passage seems to work to different ends in each chapter. Memory here seems to be a causal agent. It is not the memory that records details and facts but the memory that organizes and interprets experience. It is also with reference to memory that "**Gedali**" opens. It does so while referring to Liutov's past; thereby, the context developed in Part I of "**The Rebbe's Son**" is widened considerably. That first paragraph from "**Gedali**" also refers to a broader historical and cultural context, calling to mind Jewish tradition in general and Ibn-Ezra (the great twelfth-century Jewish poet, philosopher, and scholar) in particular.

There is one additional, explicit reference in Part I to another chapter in *Konarmiia*. It is to "**The Cemetery in Kozin**," the only other chapter that refers (by means of a gravestone) to a prince of the Bratslav rabbinical dynasty. While the name Il'ia is the second to last mentioned, i.e., it does not figure as the name of the last prince—a term used to refer to Il'ia in "**The Rebbe's Son**"—the association is more deliberate than accidental. Moreover, Babel here constructs conscious anomalies regarding local Jewish history, insofar as the last real Bratslav Rabbi died in 1810, and the Chernobyl dynasty did not belong to this but to the Tver' sect. Still, "**The Cemetery in Kozin**," the shortest yet one of the most important chapters in *Konarmiia*,[6] refers the reader to 300 years of history and, specifically, to the killing of Jews by the Cossacks of Bohdan Khmel'nyts'kyi in the seventeenth century. The only other chapter that bears on that historical period is "**Be-**

restechko." It is intimately connected to **"The Cemetery in Kozin"** and is probably the most explicit statement of Babel's anti-revolutionary views within a broad historical and universalizing perspective.

"The Cemetery of Kozin" closes with an apostrophe to death; **"The Rebbe"** opens with a discussion of it. These are the only two cases in ***Konarmiia*** where there is reference to death in the abstract, although the work veritably overflows with dead and dying bodies. Furthermore, Gedali's discussion of death in the first paragraph of **"The Rebbe"** is given in the central context of memory which, as we saw, is the key element of Part I of **"The Rebbe's Son."** This gives some indication of how skillfully Babel weaves a remarkably subtle and complex pattern from what has been called "associative inner connections" between various parts of the whole.

Part II of **"The Rebbe's Son"** establishes the time of the central events: three days prior to their telling. The first paragraph of Part II (i.e., paragraph four), the longest of the chapter, contains a large number of images and epithets of death and decay, but its central event is clearly the encounter between Liutov and Il'ia. As it crawls along, Liutov idiosyncratically describes the train he is on and the sick and dying soldiers who try to jump on board but either bounce off or are beaten off with rifle butts. Liutov has been giving them potatoes. When none remain, he tosses a pile of leaflets to the soldiers, "but only one of them extended a filthy lifeless hand for a leaflet. And I recognized Il'ia, the son of the Zhitomir Rebbe."

Il'ia is then brought into the car. He is referred to in this paragraph by three terms: Jew or prince (three times); a red soldier (twice); and the neutral "Il'ia" (twice). This sets a context for the following paragraph, the fifth, in which Liutov begins to pick up Il'ia's scattered belongings. What he finds is highly informative: agitator's papers and a book of sayings by a Jewish poet; portraits of Lenin and Maimonides; a lock of woman's hair stuck between the pages of the Resolutions of the VI Party Congress; crooked lines of ancient Hebrew poetry on the margins of communist leaflets; the Song of Songs and revolver cartridges.

Besides the obvious and deliberate pairing of contrasting items (to which I will turn presently), two observations are in order. First, Liutov says he is picking up the scattered belongings of Red Army man Bratslavskii, and that "everything was heaped together." His enumeration of *"everything"* is somewhat limited, given that the reader might reasonably expect other personal and practical items as well. This is important to remember when we arrive at the epilog. Secondly, the tone that develops at the end of the passage, the atmosphere resulting from Liutov's impression of the things he picks up, is gloomy and sad. These objects descend upon him as a "sad and meagre rain."

TABLE 2. THE LAST EFFECTS OF RED ARMY MAN BRATSLAVSKII
PART II, PARAGRAPH 5, *The Rebbe's Son*

GROUP I	GROUP II
Agitator's (propagandist's) papers	A book of sayings of a Jewish poet
A portrait of Lenin	Portraits of Maimonides
Resolutions of the VI Party Congress, into which was inserted . . .	A lock of woman's hair
Communist leaflets on the margins of which were . . .	Crooked lines of ancient Jewish poetry
Revolver cartridges	The Song of Songs

As presented above in Table 2, Il'ia's belongings fall into two groups. Group I includes items referring to communism, the revolution, war, propaganda and violence. Group II contains items suggesting art (poetry), Jewish religious and cultural traditions, rationalism and humanism (Maimonides), love and femininity, and the Hebrew Bible (Christian Old Testament). All objects of Group I refer to contemporary reality and do not establish a wider context except in relation to such chapters as **"The Cemetery in Kozin"** and **"Berestechko"**— where it is implied that the injustices and cruelties inflicted by man upon man, especially upon the downtrodden and weak, are constant features of existence—or to **"Gedali,"** where there is a poignant and powerful condemnation of all violence, whether committed in the name of revolution or any other cause.

Group II creates a broader and more profound context. Jewish culture is associated with art. Maimonides evokes the great achievements of the Jewish traditions of humanism and rationalism; his classic work, *A Guide to the Perplexed,* is contrasted with Lenin's more timely but shallower *What Is To Be Done.*[7] The lock of woman's hair suggests love, maternal and familial relationships, as well as basic, traditional, positive emotions. There is a second reference to Jewish poetry, this time with the additional qualifier "ancient." This is followed by a reference to the "Song of Songs," a great treasure of Jewish and world literature, the most lyrical, secular, and erotic book of the Bible, and also perhaps the most poetic.

Faced with the two groups, the reader is bound to be more impressed by the second, even though the contemporary historical situation and the ascending authority of Group I challenges it. Indeed, Babel has shown various conflicts between the two throughout his work. Most commentators have chosen to see these two series as an unresolved conflict, an ambiguity, or a mysterious synthesis. Others have argued that Il'ia rejects Group II in favor of Group I. My point is that in no other part of the work has Babel employed so straightforward and detailed a confrontation of these two groups of associations and concepts. I would even venture to say that nowhere else has he weighed the evidence so strongly in favor of the second group. As we will see, this becomes even clearer in the epilog. The final sentence of Part II implies a clarification is imminent: "The sad rain of the twilight washed the dust from my hair, and I said to the youth dying in the corner on a ragged mattress . . ." It is not raining inside the train.

Part III briefly relates how Il'ia came from his father's house in Zhitomir to the train in which we find him. It consists of a series of three exchanges between Liutov and Il'ia. The first refers to their original encounter as described in **"The Rebbe"** and seems to correct the false impression Liutov had then of Il'ia. Liutov had assumed he was not a communist; Il'ia says he was—but could not leave his mother. As he says this, Il'ia is *writhing* (*korchas'*). Liutov then asks: "What now?" Il'ia replies in a whisper that a mother is just an episode in the revolution. His number came up and he had to obey his mobilization orders. However, rather than being enthused or determined, or even accepting, he appears resigned. His words—"A mother in a revolution is just an episode"—sound foreign, as if he were repeating an empty phrase; they are not easily reconciled with the things he carries in his knapsack, beginning with the lock of woman's hair. Furthermore, he was *sent* to the front, he did not go voluntarily. In reply to Liutov's last, rhetorical question, "And you ended up in Kovel, Il'ia?" he answers yes or, rather, "*screams [it] in despair.*" At that point he gives a brief description of the battle, his futile efforts, and dies.

During the conversation itself, only the words describing Il'ia's emotional state give meaning to his responses. As he recalls not wanting to leave his mother, he writhes in pain and fever; he seems almost fatalistically resigned to the mobilization and screams in despair when he realizes where he is.

The epilog, which at first glance seems to add little to the story, actually confirms or, at least, lends considerable credence to this reading. The epilog makes no reference to Il'ia as a soldier or communist. He appears only as *the last prince* and as Liutov's *brother*. It contains an image of how he died "amidst verses, phylactery, and foot wrappings." There is no mention of communism, revolution or Lenin, nor even of a soldier's belongings. The verses direct the reader's attention immediately back to Part II, reinforcing the contents of the second Group, especially the allusions to art and civilization. Similarly, the phylactery returns the reader to a context deeply rooted in Jewish tradition, culture, and law; by the same token, he is separated from Lenin and the godless revolution. *The Compact Edition of the Oxford English Dictionary* defines "phylactery" (Russian *filakteriia*) as follows:

> A small leathern box containing four texts of Scripture, Deut. 6: 4-9, 11: 13-21, Exod. 13: 1-10, 11-16, written in Hebrew letters on vellum and, by a literal interpretation of the passages, worn by Jews during morning prayer on all days except the sabbath, as a reminder of the obligation to keep the law.

Clearly, there is an appeal here to the lasting strength and meaning of the past and tradition, and Il'ia is firmly identified with both. Finally, there are his foot wrappings. We know from paragraph four that Il'ia is naked from the waist down, presumably because of typhoid fever. Thus, the foot wrappings reflect his physical suffering and wretchedness, and represent all that remains of his military uniform. This also emphasizes the unmistakable exposure of his Jewishness (in an anatomical sense) to which Babel had explicitly referred earlier.[8]

After Il'ia's burial at some forgotten train station, Liutov says: "And I, barely able to contain in my ancient body the storms of my imagination, I accepted the last breath of my brother." Here, Liutov, a young man in his early twenties, refers to his "ancient" body. The conspicuous choice of the word "ancient," which appears for the second time in this brief chapter, can only refer to tradition: in the first instance of Jewish but also of Western (Judeo-Christian) civilization and culture generally, of which the "Song of Songs," Maimonides and ancient Hebrew poetry (i.e., the core of Group II) are an integral part. Likewise, the storms of his imagination point to his artistic disposition and the affirmation of the positive humanizing value of art.

Liutov accepts the dying breath of his *brother*—not of Red Army man Bratslavskii. This distinction is very important, for throughout the chapter there are several references to Il'ia. In Part I, he is Il'ia, the Rabbi's son, the last prince of the dynasty. This part, we recall, is narrated three days after Il'ia's death, meaning that the narrator's awareness has already been formed. Part II recounts events that transpired three days prior to the narration. Here, the narrator assumes the position of a participant in the events described, thus depriving himself, at least partially, of knowledge and understanding derived from subsequent events. As mentioned above, he refers to Il'ia several times in terms of his military and political affiliations, in terms of his Jewishness, and in neutral terms. There is only one reference to him in paragraph five, after the enumeration of his "paradoxical" possessions, i.e., the statement which forms the transition to part three. Here, Liutov calls him a dying youth (*iunosha*).

In Part III, there are two basically neutral references to Il'ia (as Bratslavskii and as Il'ia) during the conversation between Il'ia and Liutov. They are clearly not on the same level as the discourses of Liutov-the-narrator discussed here. In the course of the conversation, Il'ia informs Liutov of his party affiliations and his concern for his mother. The next time Liutov refers to him as a boy (*mal'chik*), and in the epilog he becomes: first, the last prince and, then, Liutov's brother.

As has already been stated, we know that Babel spent a great deal of time on his stories, revising, refining, concentrating, choosing images, words and compositional features. I think it justifiable to see, in the progressively modified epithets applied to Il'ia, a movement toward the affirmation of the values of tradition, culture, and civilization. Ultimately, both Liutov and Babel (he especially) identify with these values. In the context of *Konarmiia,* this implies an outright, i.e., unambiguous rejection of violence and destruction which, though they may have fascinated Babel, could never satisfy him. This is neither synthesis nor reconciliation; it is a deliberate choice.

IV

My analysis of **"Argamak,"** at this point, follows a different line. Its primary function, in my view, is more compositional-structural than thematic, although both **"Argamak"** and **"The Rebbe's Son"** obviously operate also within the fields of composition and theme. Babel never explained why he added this thirty-fifth chapter. Unfortunately, like **"The Rebbe's Son,"** it has not attracted a great deal of attention. Critics have skirted around both. Typical or, at least, symptomatic of how **"Argamak"** has been read is the following: "In 'Argamak' with which the book closes, the journey of Babel's narrator comes to a close."[9] I will show how wrong, literally, this is.

"Argamak" is ostensibly about Liutov, his struggles with a horse named Argamak, and his desire for acceptance by the Cossacks. However, the chapter begins with Liutov being transferred, on his own request, to a fighting outfit—the Sixth Division. Critics have failed to notice that Liutov has been in the Sixth Division since the first chapter (**"Crossing the Zbruch"**), which begins with the words "The Commander of Division Six reported that Novograd-Volynsk was taken today at dawn." Meanwhile, in **"Argamak,"** it is not until the second page that Liutov relates the taking of Novograd-Volynsk: "The Cavalry captured Novograd-Volynsk. . . ."[10]

As is clear from even a cursory reading, Babel is not concerned in *Konarmiia* with a linear development or any other kind of chronicle. **"My First Goose,"** the eighth chapter, antedates chronologically the first since it relates Liutov's arrival in the Sixth Division—i.e., it is the first version of this arrival. **"Argamak"** is the second. Just as **"The Rebbe's Son,"** especially Part I, presents a different version of events and impressions already related in previous stories, **"Argamak"** presents a different version of the events in **"Crossing the Zbruch"** and **"My First Goose."**

If we consider the two earlier chapters as a unit, we see that there are several elements—in addition to Liutov's arrival and the capture of Novograd-Volynsk—that recur in **"Argamak,"** although with modification, of course. Liutov is oppressed by a dream in both **"Crossing the Zbruch"** and **"Argamak."** The figure of the Divisional Commander, although he is not the same person, figures prominently in **"Argamak"** and **"My First Goose."** However, the key element seems to be Liutov's alienation from this environment of military, Cossacks, horses and violence—a dominant theme also of the entire work. In **"My First Goose,"** it is not satisfactorily resolved. However, the question here is whether it is resolved in **"Argamak,"** and if so, how? I do not pretend to have a completely satisfactory answer; it can only emerge from a more detailed analysis and with reference to a large number of chapters. I will, however, indicate two key elements of **"Argamak"** that are related and which should, in addition to the points mentioned above, suggest a direction for a more complete study.

The first point centres on a passage in which Liutov describes how he tried to ride Argamak.

> . . . Argamak's pace was too long, stretched out, obstinate . . . With this devilish pace he carried me away from my own lines, I got separated from my squadron and, deprived of a sense of orientation, wandered for days at a time searching for my unit; I would fall into the enemy lines, spend nights in ravines, stumble into unfamiliar units and be chased away by them . . . There was nowhere for me to become accustomed—on the move—to the cruel pace of Argamak.

The passage is written almost like a dream sequence. Time/space co-ordinates are stretched and deformed almost to absurdity. Clearly, it is necessary to move to another level of interpretation. It seems entirely reasonable to read this passage as a sort of allegory of the entire work, at least on the level of its moral-psychological analysis of Liutov's alienation, his attempts and failures to understand and come to terms with the violence, the cruelty, and the injustice he sees around him.

To make my second point, I turn to the passage describing Liutov's attempted reconciliation with Tikhomolov. Just before it becomes clear that he will not achieve it, we read: "I was alone amongst these people, whose friendship I was unable to secure (*mne ne udalos' dobit'sia*)." This sentence, inserted unexpectedly in the midst of a conversational sequence, is clearly on a different level than the surrounding text. It is a judgement that is not motivated by and transcends the immediate situation. If it were limited to the context of the exchange between Liutov and Tichomolov, it would surely be better at the end of their conversation, where it would sum up nicely the preceding passage and form a smooth transition to the subsequent exchange with Baulin. Moreover, it has, by virtue of its two perfective verbs, an air of finality. This finality is not overcome by the last paragraph of the text where Liutov suggests his dream of belonging did eventually come true. The Cossacks may have stopped staring at him and his horse, but they certainly have not embraced him as an equal. The reader does not get the impression that any meaningful reconciliation has in fact been achieved. The same impression is suggested by his final conversation with Baulin whose last words to him, euphemistically rendered, were: "Why don't you just get the hell away from us!" This is further reinforced by allusions to **"The Rebbe's Son"** (the chapter which immediately precedes it) and to the entire work, especially if the contention of cyclicity is correct. There is really no doubt that Liutov will never be like these people, i.e., the Cossacks and warmongers. As elucidated by the concept of closure, this is the conclusion that emerges in both **"The Rebbe's Son"** and **"Argamak."** It is with this new perspective that Babel sends his reader back to the beginning.

Notes

1. Isaak Babel, *Konarmiia* (Ann Arbor, 1983). Translations are my own. To allow the use of other editions, and because the chapters are so short, references are by chapter title rather than page number. Babel's name in English is customarily written without the soft sign; I have followed this practice.

2. The leading example of this trend is Galina Belaja, "Tret'ia zhizn' Isaaka Babelia," *Oktiabr'* 10 (1989): 185-197.

3. Mark E. Suino, "Poetic Closure," *Papers in Slavic Philology, I: In Honor of James Ferrell*, ed. Benjamin A. Stolz (Ann Arbor, 1977) 271.

4. This was established in some detail almost twenty years ago. N. Davies, "Izaak Babel's *Konarmija Stories* and the Polish-Soviet War," *Modern Language Review* 62 (1972): 845-857.

5. Isaak Babel, *The Forgotten Prose,* ed. and tr. N. Stroud (Ann Arbor, 1978) 139-140 (my emphasis, A. R.). See also Belaia, "Tret'ia zhizn'."

6. A forthcoming paper by J. J. van Baak will discuss in some detail the richness and centrality of this chapter.

7. My thanks to Peter A. Rolland of the University of Alberta for pointing out to me the implicit contrast between these two texts.

8. "The girls . . . dryly observed his sexual organs, the stunted, curly-haired masculinity of a worn out Semite."

9. J. E. Falen, *Isaac Babel: Russian Master of the Short Story* (Knoxville, Tenn., 1974) 199.

10. Note that in "The Rebbe's Son" the train Liutov is on is heading for Rovno. On the second page of "Argamak" the division he is with is approaching Rovno—on horseback, not by train—and on the next page they attack.

Judith Deutsch Kornblatt (essay date 1992)

SOURCE: Kornblatt, Judith Deutsch. "Isaak Babel and His Red Cavalry Cossacks." In *The Cossack Hero in Russian Literature: A Study in Cultural Mythology,* pp. 107-25. Madison: University of Wisconsin Press, 1992.

[*In the following essay, Kornblatt finds a number of connections between Babel and Nikolai Gogol and analyzes* Red Cavalry *in light of the Cossack myth.*]

In his *A History of Russian Literature,* D. S. Mirsky praises *Taras Bul'ba* with an enthusiasm rare among students of Gogol. The novel is "heroic, frankly and openly heroic," he writes, and "its place in Russian literature is unique—it has had no imitators or followers (except, perhaps, Babel in his stories of the Red Army)."[1] Maksim Gor'kii also suggested the comparison of Gogol and Isaak Babel (1894-41), but with little elaboration. He defended Babel, who had recently been attacked in the press, by claiming that Babel's Cossacks were bolder even than Gogol's.[2]

A critical tradition similarly links Babel with Tolstoi. "Like Tolstoi," writes Steven Marcus, "he [Babel] saw in the Cossacks a conjunction of beauty and fierceness, in which their athleticism gave grace to their aggressiveness."[3] In this reading, Babel's **Red Cavalry** is firmly planted within the Cossack tradition, but the myth is reduced to a unidimensional manifestation of the noble savage.

Babel's own approach was more complex. When asked in 1937 to name his favorite author, Babel expressed his increasing preference for the writings of Tolstoi, and particularly the epic story "Khadzhi Murat."[4] Babel explained his attraction to Tolstoi's work:

> A current flows unobstructed from the earth, directly through his hands, straight to the paper, and completely and mercilessly tears down all veils with the sense of truth. Moreover, as this truth makes its appearance, it clothes itself in transparent and beautiful dress.[5]

In Babel's praise of Tolstoi, we cannot help but remember Gogol's aesthetic statements in "About Little Russian Songs" and "Sculpture, Painting, Music" from *Arabesques.* The art described is spontaneous, like the Cossack songs, and violent like the Cossacks themselves and like music, which Gogol considered the highest form of art. In the same interview, Babel cited Sholokhov, author of *The Quiet Don,* as his favorite contemporary writer, and praised him for writing "heatedly" (*goriacho*), the term Gogol applied to his own work on the Cossacks.

Babel's debt to Gogol, specifically to his early Cossack works, is made explicit in only one story, **"Odessa"**:[6] "It seems to me that there must come—and soon—the productive and life-creating influence of the Russian South." He continues: "Do you remember the fecund sun of Gogol, a writer from the Ukraine? But if such descriptions existed, they were only an episode. That episode was overtaken by 'The Nose,' 'The Portrait,' and 'Notes of a Madman.'"[7] Babel calls for a writer who can recreate the spirit of Gogol's early Ukrainian stories, a spirit absent in the later northern tales, and implicitly issues his challenge as contender for the title of successor to Gogol's "fecund sun."

There can be no question that in creating his own Cossacks, Babel borrowed much of the baggage of Gogol's myth. The heroes of **Red Cavalry** resemble Taras Bul'ba and his Cossack comrades much more closely than they do General Budennyi and the real Cossack cavalry of Babel's own experience in the Red Army. Babel enlisted in the army in 1917 and served on the Romanian front before contracting malaria.[8] He subsequently worked in various capacities for the new government during the early years of the Civil War, including propagandist for the newspaper the *Red Cavalryman*. During the war with Poland in 1920, Babel was assigned to Budennyi's First Cavalry, and spent several months living closely with Budennyi's Cossacks under the assumed name Kiril Vasilevich Liutov, the name he would give to the principal narrator in **Red Cavalry**.[9] He wrote articles for the division's propaganda sheet, as well as drafts of stories (lost during the campaign), and a diary soon transformed into **Red Cavalry**. Claiming instructions from Gor'kii, Babel joined the army in an effort to "go to the people," and to gather material for his craft.[10] The names, places, and situations in which his Cossack characters interact indeed grew from this material, but realism was far from Babel's preferred mode. As Mirsky asserts, his Cossacks are as mythically heroic as Gogol's.

The biographies of Gogol and Babel are strikingly similar. Both writers were born and spent their youth outside Russia proper, in the southwestern region of the empire. Both were exposed to religious tradition and to literature at an early age, impressions that were to shape their future art, and both moved to Petersburg as young men, to integrate into the cultural, Europeanized capital of the Russian state. Neither achieved immediate success as a writer, but both were lucky enough to receive encouragement from the most established writers of the time, Pushkin and Gor'kii, respectively. Ultimately, their works were widely published and duly acclaimed, and they remain popular to this day.[11]

Neither writer produced a large body of work, partly because of their untimely deaths,[12] but more centrally because of their perfectionism. Both were compulsive rewriters. In a letter to his friend Pogodin, Gogol calls his difficulty in writing "mental constipation."[13] And Babel's often quoted line from the story "Guy de Maupassant" ("No iron can enter into the human heart as chillingly as a period accurately placed")[14] suggests the attention that he lavished on the execution of his stories. Konstantin Paustovskii recalls his friend's perfectionism in "A Few Words about Babel":

> He hardly ever said "I am writing," but rather, "I am composing." . . . He wrote slowly and always put off handing in his manuscripts. He lived in a constant panic at the thought of words that could no longer be altered, and he was always trying to gain time—just a few more days, or even hours—so that he could sit over his manuscript a little longer and go on polishing, with no one pressing him or getting in his way.[15]

DVOEDUSHIE

The two writers share an even more salient trait, and one that most likely affected their choice of Cossack heroes. Both Babel and Gogol bore a dual national allegiance: Gogol to Ukraine and to Russia, Babel to Russia and the Jews. As a Ukrainian in Petersburg of the 1830s, Gogol rode the crest of Russia's romantic fascination with its neighbor. *Dvoedushie* (literally, two-souledness, but in some circles carrying the connotation of double-dealing) was extremely fashionable at the time, and Gogol could claim an exotic southern temperament while flaunting his northern sophistication. He asserted that the two sides of his heritage were fully integrated,[16] although we have seen that his choice of Cossack characters would suggest otherwise. The mythic heroes served to reconcile that which is in fact disparate and contradictory.

As was the case with Gogol, Babel's own efforts to reconcile opposing heritages created difficulties in his writing. Although as a child Babel had learned Hebrew and some Yiddish, his parents' mother tongue, he decided to write his first stories in French. The ultimate choice of Russian as his literary language may then have been an attempt, as Renato Poggioli believes, "not merely to escape from the ghetto, but to turn, through Russia, to Europe and the West."[17] But Babel's choice of Russian was as much a matter of tone as theme. At the time he began writing, Yiddish literature was still closely tied to folk sources on the one hand, and to the European realist tradition on the other. But Babel was attracted to modern experimental prose, both Western European and Russian. (Although a modernist school of Yiddish literature did flourish in Kiev in the twenties, Babel was the model for, not student of, those writers.)[18]

Odessa, Babel's hometown, produced a circle of talented writers, some of them Jewish like Babel, who were to form the core of the new Soviet literature when they, and the century, reached their twenties. This group included Babel's friend Konstantin Paustovskii, Valentin Kataev, Iurii Olesha, and I'lf and Petrov, the early Soviet satirists. For all of them, the idiom was Russian.

Like Gogol before him, Babel adopted the dominant cultural idiom of his time not as an escape from his unique experience, but as a mediating gesture that broadened both his readership and his cultural base.[19] Very few of his stories fail to include Jewish references, transformed but not eliminated by his choice of style and language.

Babel never rejected his Jewishness, and the tension of his dual nationality permeates his fiction. Liutov in *Red Cavalry* constantly feels other than any group he confronts. He struggles with the awareness of his Jewishness in the eyes of the Cossacks, and Russianness in the eyes of the Polish Jews and Catholics he meets.[20] As did Gogol, Babel set as a major problem the possible reconciliation of these opposing characteristics, as synecdoche for all alienating oppositions. The Cossack works of both men express a synthetic ideal that contrasts sharply to the fragmented world around them, and the intensity of these two writers thus draws from the centrality of the mythic process in their works.

And yet Babel and his literary predecessor differed in a major way. Although certainly not unique, the Ukrainian Gogol was nonetheless an oddity in Petersburg, where he consciously exploited his otherness as an aesthetic category. Babel, however, was far from unusual. Many members of the revolutionary leadership and the new Soviet intelligentsia were Jews, among them Averbakh, Kamenev, and Zinov'ev. These political leaders were Bolsheviks first, Russians second, and Jews a distant third. Many revolutionaries, among them Lev Davidovich Bronshtein (Trotskii), changed their obviously Jewish-sounding names, and rejected both their religious and their cultural heritage. To be pro-Bolshevik in the first years of the Revolution meant to be internationalist, not parochial and ethnocentric. Later, when internationalism (or cosmopolitanism) became anathema, to be pro-Bolshevik came to mean insularly nationalistic, and largely Russian. It never meant being a Jew. Babel's Jewish heritage was thus far from exotic on the one hand, and allegedly discarded by the Revolution on the other. Yet his stories and letters indicate that he could not escape the contradictions of dual allegiance, and he suffered them in his life as well as his art.

Babel's *dvoedushie*, oscillating between Russian culture and Jewish background, did not encompass any claim to Cossack inheritance. Gogol's family myth included descent from a well-known Cossack, and his Ukrainian affiliation indirectly linked him to the glorious Cossack past. Babel, on the other hand, was a member of an ethnic group persecuted by the historical Cossacks, and ridiculed or condemned in the Cossack fiction that Gogol made famous. His glorification of the Cossack heroes in *Red Cavalry* clearly derives from the tradition of *Trans Bul'ba*; but Babel's Cossacks occupy a much different dimension because of his own cultural and historical situation. Babel went beyond the role of mythologizer, one who naturally accepts and promotes the reconciliation offered by myth, to that of mythologist, or myth analyst. He examined the myth from his Jewish distance, not necessarily rejecting it, but putting it to the test of contemporary reality.

Babel's distanced stance led to adaptations of the myth. Not only did he place a greater emphasis on the relationship between Cossack and creative artist, he also tested the mythic topoi by extending them onto characters other than Cossacks. Gogol wrote of heroes at odds with the manifest aspects of our mundane world; Babel of a heroic world that infuses the otherwise mundane individual. Although he did not spare descriptions of the often grotesque and arbitrary nature of that world, he refused to condemn it. Reality may be cruel, but it is marvelous as well.

THE COSSACK TOPOI DISPERSED

The setting of *Red Cavalry* is a world turned upside down, a liminal realm where all characters, though immersed in destruction, can experience renewal. The tone is set by the first story, **"Crossing the Zbruch."** Nature itself exudes passion, largely marked by the multiplicity of colors: purple poppies (polia purpurnogo maka), yellowing rye (veter igraet v zhelteiushchei rzhi), pearly fog (zhemchuzhnyi tuman), flowery slopes (tsvetistye prigorki), orange sun (oranzhevoe solntse), blackening Zbruch (pochernevshii Zbruch). The vivid visual description gives way to an aural one, with a large number of musical references, the art form previously associated with Cossack vivacity: the sonorous torrents (zvuchnye potoki), someone's ringing defamation (Kto-to tonet i zvonko porochit bogoroditsu), the river full of humming, whistling, and song (Reka useiana chernymi kvadratami teleg, ona polna gula, svista i pesen, gremiashchikh poverkh lunnykh zmei i siiaiushchikh iam) (23).

The first page of the story describes the vibrant landscape at all stages of the day, but the introduction of a temporal element recalls Gogol's technique that destroys instead of establishes historicity. The story begins like a dispassionate military dispatch:

> The commander of Division Six reported that Novograd-Volynsk was taken today at dawn. The staff left Krapivno and our transport stretched out like a noisy rearguard along the highway running from Brest to Warsaw, built on peasant bones by Nicholas the First.

(23)

The first line identifies the division in question and the place of its maneuvers, information that also locates the action in time, for Novograd-Volynsk was a major arena in the Russo-Polish war of 1920. The reference to Nicholas the First widens the historical perspective. The present invasion becomes only one in a repetitive cycle that began even before Nicholas, for the reference to peasant bones also recalls Peter the Great's sacrifice of native labor to the establishment of his westward-looking capital of Sankt Peterburg. This string of associations backward into history forces the reader to lose his grounding in a particular historical moment.

The second paragraph refers in sequence to dawn, noon, evening, and night, setting up for the reader a progression through the day. Yet Babel negates movement through the repetitive ornateness of the paragraph, and the final sense is one of stasis.[21] The atmosphere of Babel's stories has often been compared to the paintings of Chagall:

> The space of both artists is color without a boundary, none even between heaven and earth. In this continuum of color there float images—some beautiful, some sordid; some delicately ethereal, some coarsely naturalistic; images of the peasants and Jews of Red Russia, their little towns, their huts, their horses and their cattle; and the moon in the most incredible, yet so real shades of color.[22]

As Victor Terras observes in this quotation, Babel creates a world that knows no barriers, a type of permanent liminality. Things and people transgress the restrictions normally imposed by gravity, the march of time, or the distinctions between discrete objects. Heaven is juxtaposed with earth, beautiful with sordid, incredible with real, and thus Babel creates a picture of a mythical realm.

Babel frustrates the readers' expectations of temporal progression in **"Crossing the Zbruch"** in order to indicate that the crossing referred to in the title is not from place to place, and certainly not simply from Russia into Poland as sometimes suggested (the title has been incorrectly translated as "Crossing into Poland"), but into a new realm altogether. The transgression of the spatial boundary represented by the river is the first of many in the cycle. That the actual crossing takes place at sunset, as does the action in so many of the stories,[23] suggests as well the temporal threshold between clear day and obscure night. On the other side, we find ourselves abandoned by normal referents, in a place where characters differ from our mundane world, and where all share in liminal aspects before associated only with the Cossacks.[24] The myth of the Cossacks, with its boundlessness, wholeness, and vitality, extends throughout the world of **Red Cavalry.**

Provoked by mention of the Jewish holiday of Passover in the story ("shards of secret pottery used by Jews once a year, on the Passover," 24), one critic suggests we compare the Zbruch to the biblical Red Sea: "The Zbruch is a symbolic boundary which relates the crossing to the Exodus from Egypt, with all the overtones of

redemption in the Passover story."[25] Although he does not draw the parallel, in light of the myth we must recall the Cossacks of *Taras Bul'ba* who cross the Dnestr, like the Red Sea, and exit out of history into myth.

At Passover, Jews remember the historical Exodus from Egypt, but relate the story as if it were in the present. The Passover narrative is told largely in the first person; each year the participants in the seder recite: "In every generation one must look upon himself as if he personally had come out of Egypt, as the Bible says: 'And thou shalt tell thy son on that day, saying, it is because of that which the Eternal did to *me* when *I* went forth from Egypt.'"[26] Passover offers ritual renewal, when historical events are placed in an atemporal light. To have the Cossacks' transgression of their first boundary in **Red Cavalry** take place during this mythic time raises them as well to the level of myth. They cross over into a realm in which we confront reminders of at least ritual messianic reunion.[27]

"Crossing the Zbruch" ends with a Jewish girl's rhetorical cry, spoken "with terrible strength" (24). We would expect both the rhetoric and the potency from a Cossack, not a Jew. Yet Cossack heroism in this particular story appears only in a dream, albeit one that contains a reference to the heroes of *The Iliad* in the eyes that fall out of the head of the warrior, a common epic wound: "I dream about the commander of the sixth division. He is chasing the brigade commander on a heavy stallion and plunges two bullets between his eyes. The bullets pierce the brigade commander's head and both eyes fall out onto the earth" (24). But the Cossacks all appear puppetlike in this story, including the narrator, whom ironically we assume at this point to be a Cossack like his fellow cavalrymen. He is fidgety and negative, and frightened by his own nightmare.

By conferring a heroic stance on the girl instead of on the Cossack, Babel blurs the boundaries between the characters. On the one hand each character seems chosen from a stock repertory, almost like eighteenth-century puppet plays in which Cossacks play a clearly defined brave and exotic role.[28] The Jews "jump about in silence like monkeys or Japanese at the circus" (24); the Cossack Savitskii pursues an enemy on a heavy stallion and "plunges two bullets into his eyes" (24). Yet already here in the first story Babel merges traits from one group onto another, a form of barrier crossing but one that could confuse the mythic image rather than clarify it. The girl is the one who embodies rebirth in the midst of destruction, for she carries a child in her womb as she cares for the corpse of her father. She is the one who calls out the challenge for heroism.

Babel's mythic motifs in **Red Cavalry** are wandering motifs. All the elements are present but they do not relate always to the Cossacks alone, as though his world as a whole is boundless and confers majesty on the heroes instead of the heroes on the world. In the second story, Babel presents us with a Polish Catholic who shares Cossack qualities: he moves "fiercely" (*iarostno*); his size is like a giant (*ispolin*); he acts "without pity" (*bez sozhaleniia*); he drinks and wears a "costume." (The wearing of strange clothing in *Red Cavalry* is generally associated with the Cossacks.)[29] The narrator in this story is first called *pan* as though he were Polish, then *tovarishch* as though he were Bolshevik. And we still do not know in this story that he is not a Cossack and, as we will discover, in many ways is the antithesis of the Cossack heroes. Yet here he calls himself a "violent intruder" and goes off, ironically into a church, to rejoin his comrades.

We can best discover the diffusion of topoi into non-Cossack characters in a cycle of stories—**"Gedali,"** **"The Rebbe," "The Rebbe's Son"**—that is embedded within *Red Cavalry*. These three stories present the Jews of Poland, ugly and pathetic, but inexplicably attractive to Liutov, and made so to the readers as well. Critics often claim that Babel uses the Jewish characters to demonstrate his true allegiance to the values of his own past. Or, conversely, they assert that the portrayal of dying Jewish culture proves Babel's effort to embrace the new secular world of the Revolution. On more careful examination, we find that Gedali and his friends share many traits with the Cossacks, including their essential spirit of life. They are not contrasted to but compared with the mythic Cossacks. Babel makes the connection between Jew and Cossack explicit elsewhere, for certainly the Jews of Babel's Odessa stories, written at about the same time as *Red Cavalry,* differ from the Cossacks in name only. Benia Krik, the Jewish gangster of **"The King"** and **"How It Was Done in Odessa,"** "was passionate, and passion rules the universe" (162).

The three stories of the mini-cycle describe the Hasidim of Eastern Europe. The title character of the central story is himself a Hasidic rebbe. A rebbe (*rabbi,* not *ravvin* or *ravvi,* in Russian) is the charismatic leader of a Hasidic community, not a traditional Jewish rabbi, as usually translated.[30] He represents the Hasidic movement that swept through Ukraine and Poland in the eighteenth century, still the heyday of Cossackdom, with its message of renewal and of the access of all human beings to the divine life-force. Hasidic Jews retained the practices of traditional observance, but claimed to reinfuse them with life, music, and joy. They rebelled against the ossified old order, as did the latter-day revolutionaries to whom they are here compared.

Liutov's attraction to these particular Jews stems from his general desire to participate in the paradoxical intensity of their world, just as he yearns to join the Cossacks in their immediate experience of life. "I roam around Zhitomir," says the narrator in **"Gedali,"** "in search of the shy star [of Sabbath devotion]. Jews with beards like the prophets, with passionate rags (s borodami prorokov, so strastnymi lokhmot'iami) on their sunken chests sell chalk, blueing, and wicks by the yellow and indifferent walls of the ancient synagogue" (46). Here Liutov meets Gedali, the old Jew who proclaims a revolution that will be integrated with the Sabbath. As one critic notices, Babel finds a vital connection between the Cossacks of *Red Cavalry* and "elements of the Jewish tradition he could accept, elements of prophetic fervor and revolutionary awareness."[31]

Like the Cossacks, the Hasidic Jews of *Red Cavalry* form an all-male community. Both Gedali and the rebbe's son refer to "Mother," but only as an abstraction, a compelling force much like the fiancée-steppe of the Cossacks. Women play little role in the public or communal aspects of traditional Judaism. Babel stresses the Hasidic male's self-sufficiency when he presents a scenario in which life itself passes from male to male, as Il'ia Bratislavskii, the rebbe's son, dies practically in the arms of Liutov. In the process, however, the latter breathes in the breath of the former, adding strength to the "storm of imagination" already bursting out of his ancient body (147). The dying Jew reinvigorates Liutov; "I received the last breath of my brother" (147).

ADOPTION OR ADAPTATION OF THE COSSACK TOPOI?

To understand why Babel may have chosen Cossack characters only to disperse their traditional heroic topoi over the rest of his fictional world, and more important, to clarify the effects of the mythic dispersal, we need to take a closer look at *Red Cavalry* specifically in light of the Cossack myth.

Babel's diary from his summer with Budennyi's Cossacks reveals his distance from the exotic but nonetheless flesh-and-blood soldiers. Babel was disgusted by war, deadened by the dull and destructive campaigns, and stricken by the insensitivity of the Cossack warriors to their environment. That Babel's association with the Cossacks occasionally tormented him is evidenced by an entry from July 24 when he describes being billeted with the Cossack Prishchepa in the home of some Polish Jews on the Sabbath. The Cossacks ordered their hosts to cook a meal, an activity forbidden to religious Jews on their day of rest. Babel writes that he was forced to remain silent for in that context he was a Russian like the Cossacks, not a Jew like his hosts. The following day would be Tisha b'Av, a holy fast day in the Jewish calendar commemorating the destruction of the First and Second Temples. Babel notes here the parallel between the Polish campaign and, as he writes, the "frightful words of the prophet—they eat manure, the girls are raped, the men slain, Israel destroyed, angry, wailing words. The lamp smokes, the old woman howls, outside is Demidovka, Cossacks, everything like the time when the Temple fell. . . ."[32]

Babel modeled his heroes on men whom he actually knew in the early 1920s, and who participated in historical events well known to his reading public. We might be led to believe we are reading a war report. Reality and artifice, however, are inextricably tangled, as Babel uses the facts to create the impression of historicity only then to destroy it. He confuses chronology, as Gogol did, so we can no longer follow the march of the army as we might in his nonmythic diary.

Babel begins apparently objectively, but immediately introduces surreal descriptions into his war report.[33] And like Gogol, Babel makes veiled reference to the epics of Homer and *The Lay of Igor's Campaign,* as in the "standards of sunset" that "blow above our heads" in **"Crossing the Zbruch."**[34] The struggle in *Red Cavalry* becomes a mock-epic battle, as the Russo-Polish war definitely was not.

Babel's frequent references to song in general and bards in particular further associate his cycle with epic. The Cossacks' song "hums like a stream running dry" (**"Berestechko"** 87), and an epic songster joins the Cossacks as they ride past Cossack burial mounds from the time of Khmel'nitskii. The reference to the famous Cossack leader reminds the reader of history, and the bard then transforms that history into myth. He plays a bandura and sings of ancient Cossack glory (*slava/ kleos*).

Yet *Red Cavalry* is no more a true epic than *Taras Bul'ba.* Homer created literature as we know it by writing down a linear narrative told in time and existing throughout time, but the mythic consciousness from which it had evolved saw the world spatially, not temporally.[35] Myth knew only space; postmythic thought learned both time and space. According to Joseph Frank, modern literature has the distinction of recapturing that mythic imagination for which historical time does not exist.[36] The relationship of Babel's *Red Cavalry* to myth becomes much clearer in this light, for the destruction of time associated with epic in the stories grows directly from and leads directly back into myth.

Many critics have pointed to the spatial quality of Babel's stories. Victor Terras speaks of static space, filled with vivid, sensuous images. In this connection he compares Babel and Chagall. Patricia Carden remarks on Babel's interest in art as well as on the spatial aspect of his stories in Joseph Frank's special sense: "the Babel story is a carefully limited space, a canvas into which he paints the significant world-objects before our eyes."[37]

We must apprehend that space in an instant, not through time. Like Gogol's work, Babel's cycle uses epic elements to point beyond epic, to mythic consciousness.

The very form of a fragmented cycle emphasizes its timelessness. Babel first published many of the stories separately, destroying their development as a temporal narrative. They are infinitely reorderable. And Babel specifically broke up the two mini-cycles within the larger cycle: **"Gedali"—"The Rebbe"—"The Rebbe's Son"** and **"Story of a Horse"—"Continuation of Story of a Horse."** In the cycle as a whole there is no progression, development, or maturity on the part of any of the characters. *Red Cavalry* does not take the reader through a narrative in which event follows event. Rather it forces the reader into a reading act that, in total, suspends linear time and causal expectations. The narrator himself must continuously refight his battle to be accepted by the Cossacks, only to lose the security of community he might have gained in the very next story. Only in **"Argamak,"** the last story as now published, are we, and the narrator, allowed the satisfaction born of progress for any length of time. Babel added this story, however, long after he had completed the rest of the cycle. It functions as a demythologizing force and did not grow from the same artistic impulse as the rest of *Red Cavalry.*

Babel put date and place markers at the end of many of his stories in the space one would expect to find the date of composition. Instead, the markers refer to the month in which the action of the story supposedly occurred.[38] This practice in itself mythologizes by destroying the distance between event and literary recreation. To this day, many scholars confuse the sequence of writing and publication of Babel's stories. Babel creates the illusion that the "true" stories were written down as they were actually experienced, producing the "juxtaposition of past and present" that makes "history become unhistorical."[39]

Babel no doubt learned from Gogol one of the important techniques for crossing temporal barriers: the establishment of fluctuating distances between the narrator, reader, and heroes. The rapid alternation of narrative styles (lyrical, bureaucratic, dramatic, terse, florid, *skaz*) works in a similar fashion to Gogol's narrative technique in *Evenings.* Eventually we lose our bearings and do not know whom to take as an authority.

The stories told in first person, presumably from the mouths (or pens) of Cossacks themselves, particularly cause us to question our position, moral as well as temporal. We are uncertain, for example, how to evaluate a character like Matvei Pavlichenko (**"The Life Story of Pavlichenko, Matvei Rodionych"**), who returns to his home to seek vengeance on Nikitinskii, the man who has stolen his wife. He tells his story with such ardor and conviction that we are drawn to him. Yet how can we condone murder, and particularly a murder so personal, so physical, and so graphic as that of his former landlord? The devoted husband and revolutionary Cossack stomps another human being into a pulverized mass. The narrator, with whom we can usually associate quite easily, yearns desperately for just this ability to destroy.

We do not know how to feel about war in general. Babel associates it often with the bright sun, as though its raw violence is itself the fecund power he sought in "Odessa." The lyrical tone he uses to describe horrible acts of destruction disarms us of an immediate negative and moralistic response. Ultimately we must recognize that the world of *Red Cavalry* is mythic, and thus beyond the limits of our moral judgment. The characters play by different rules, rules which attract and repulse at the same time.

Most readers notice a lack of resolution in *Red Cavalry.* They feel ill at ease over Babel's apparent failure to choose between two opposing lifestyles, whether "Cossack ethos versus Jewish ethos," "way of violence versus way of peace," "sun versus moon," or "outdoor world versus indoor world."[40] Many critics make the choice for Babel, despite his ambivalent messages, claiming that the author favored nostalgia for his Jewish roots over the future-oriented revolutionary fervor of the Cossacks, or vice versa.

Some critics do recognize the continued ambiguity of Babel's portrayal by allowing for conflict not simply between two groups, Cossack and Jew, but within each group itself.[41] The conflict between Jews is most apparent. Liutov, the Russian Jew, wanders through remnants of the dying Polish culture and yearns for the life of Odessa. Yet the Hasidim who confront him in the person of Gedali exude the life he associates only with the Jews of his youth. It is not necessary to determine which side of any opposition the author ultimately supports if we recognize that the combination of opposites itself is an aspect of the myth he evokes.

Even more significant for his adaptation of the myth, Babel adopts many of the elements involving regeneration through violence. The Cossacks of **"Crossing the Zbruch"** not only traverse the river but actually submerge themselves in it. The horses march in up to their backs, and one Cossack sinks. The submersion suggests baptism, further supporting the view already discussed of the crossing as a transgression of barriers between two metaphysical or in this case even religious realms. On the other side the narrator confronts a pregnant woman, the first figure described in Novograd. Despite the death around her, including that of her own father,

she represents new life. The remnants of Passover dishes, although broken, also suggest new life through the symbol of the spring celebration of liberation and hope.

The human feces included in the list of debris in **"Crossing the Zburch"** foreshadows the manure into which Liutov grinds the head of the goose in **"My First Goose."** In this latter story his act of violence and murder, no matter how debased or ridiculous, marks a transition into a new state, into Cossackdom, if only temporarily. The juxtaposition of death (in the goose) and life (in the manure that provides fodder for new growth out of refuse) metaphorically parallels Liutov's rebirth as a member of the Cossack band.[42]

The stomping to death of the goose in turn suggests the death of Nikitinskii by the hand, or literally the feet, of Matvei Rodionovych Pavlichenko in the story already cited. In this case also the physical destruction leads to a form of rebirth, for the Cossack experiences the essence of life through his act of murder: "But ya know, I don't pity myself. So, ya know, I stomp on my enemy for an hour or so. I want to know life, to know it as it really is" (76).

In the second story of the cycle, **"The Catholic Church at Novograd,"** the narrator dashes into the crypt of the church after having been frightened by two skulls. His action obviously deepens the morbid mood instead of annulling it. Once below, however, he notices a staircase leading up to the altar, and sees lights "running in the heights, in the very dome" (26). The lights, we learn, belong to candles held by the narrator's fellow Cossacks. The Cossacks then serve as metaphoric guides from darkness to light, from underground to high above ground, from death to new life.

Babel's portrayal of women in *Red Cavalry,* like the rebirth imagery, also derives from the Cossack myth. In his diary Babel expressed sympathetic interest in the women who traveled with the Cossack division.[43] In the stories, however, the question of sex and the Cossacks takes a different turn. Many critics have noted the strong sexuality of Babel's Cossacks. Like their violence, it lends intensity and urgency. The sexual tension attached specifically to women characters, however, always carries a sense of sickness or perversion, not life-giving force. Venereal disease is a recurrent motif (**"The Ivans," "Sashka the Christ," "Continuation of Story of a Horse"**), and any heterosexual union leads to grief. Irina's relations with Vasilii in **"Evening"** breathe corruption; in a scene of Gogolian fragmentation, we are told how her fat-heeled feet and his black crooked nail stick out from the kitchen door while the two make love. As cook, Vasilii deals with "the meat of dead animals and the greed of living ones" (95)—neither appetizing, much less life-engendering, images. Neither women's sexuality nor their particular nurturing aspects have any place in the real Cossack world.[44]

The Cossacks' sexuality, and the intensity derived from it, thus do not come from their association with women. Even the goose murdered by Liutov in **"My First Goose"** as a substitute for "spoiling a dame" (50) is actually a gander. In the Cossack myth, it is a male-male union that characterizes the true Cossacks; men are their own source of life and nurture.

The very male Cossack hero Savitskii in **"My First Goose"** has "long legs like girls sheathed to the neck in shining riding boots," and here we are not so far from *Taras Bul'ba* and the potent celibacy of the Cossack "monk." The Cossack army invades a virginal field in the very first story, and repeatedly unites with and is embraced by nature. As an added twist, Matvei calls the Revolution "sweetheart," suggesting a sexual union with the epic history of the cycle, and not only with its environment.

Much of the Cossacks' vitality in **Red Cavalry** takes the form of an immediate understanding of life itself. Matvei understands it through his involvement with death. On the other hand, the Cossack Afon'ka Bida condemns Liutov, the Jewish intellectual, for his misunderstanding of it (**"The Death of Dolgushov"**); Liutov cannot kill. Paradoxically, as in all of the Cossack myth, violence is a productive act.

The Violence of Creation

By stressing the sexual and regenerating topoi of the Cossack myth, Babel further adapts the Cossack hero. The historical Cossacks were enemies of his people, and by the twentieth century had come to represent repression for all citizens, not only Jews. The small percentage of Cossacks who joined the Red Army did not change this reputation, for they excelled in anarchic behavior and merciless retribution. Babel turned to the traditional hero despite, or in fact on account of, the disparity between the Cossacks he knew and his own sensibilities.

Babel operated, and attempted to reconcile the polar experiences of his life, in the world of literature, or creative art as a whole. Although Gogol was no stranger to this world, his primary concern was the "Russian soul," a category under which he subsumed vitality, productivity, and art itself. Babel's Cossacks are manifestations not so much of his Russianness as of his creative potential. They represent the energy necessary to write. That Babel believed energy is violent is suggested in the quote about Tolstoi's art cited at the beginning of this chapter, or in the famous simile from "Guy de Maupassant": the placement of a period is like a sword thrust. The harmony of violence and life in the Cossack myth provided a metaphor for Babel's own creative impulse.

Babel's most obvious artist character in **Red Cavalry** is Pan Apolek, the errant Pole who drew from the citizens of Novograd to create religious paintings labeled sacrilegious by the official Church. His renditions of holy persons resemble too naturalistically the profane models that inspired them. When he paints, Apolek ignores the boundary between human and divine, doing violence to the letter of the ecclesiastic law. That the painter's transgression in fact demonstrates the spiritual quality of our own world does not impress the Church authorities, but it is Babel's major preoccupation. The artist reconciles the spirit and the flesh; he makes the physical holy and the holy physical.

Here is yet another character who unexpectedly resembles the Cossack hero; a violent creator, he too must be understood in light of the Cossack myth. Speaking of Pan Apolek, a Polish character exclaims: "O, this man! This man'll never die in his bed" (40). One would expect such words only in praise of a Cossack warrior like Taras Bul'ba. But the artist Pan Apolek shares the energy and contradictory destructive creativity of the Cossacks. His name itself suggests both Apollo, god of sun and order, and Apol'lyon, demon of destruction and the bottomless pit.[45] The name also recalls Apollinarius and the Church controversy that attempted to determine the relationship of the two opposing natures in the person of Christ, human and divine.[46]

Yet, the difference between Gogol's creative destroyers and Babel's violent artist is one we have already seen. Gogol's Cossacks embody the ideal essence of the Russian soul that is hidden by mundane reality. Babel's characters, in that they all—Cossack, Jew, artist—resemble one another, show the ideal essence uncovered in the world around us.

To follow Apolek's example, as he vows to do at the beginning of the story, the narrator plays the role of his own bard. He is a wanderer, moving from Cossack to Cossack or hero to hero, collecting stories, like **"Pan Apolek"** itself, and eternalizing the glory of the events. His craft—storytelling—is his own creative act, juxtaposed with the physical violence of the Cossacks, the spiritual creativity of the Hasids, and Pan Apolek's heretical painting.

Babel must assume that the creative image of his mythic Cossacks is strong enough to prevent any confusion resulting from its presence among his other characters. He is mostly correct, for the non-Cossacks rise to the level of myth. The diffusion of topoi is, however, a profound adaptation of the myth. No longer are the Cossack heroes contrasted to mere mortals. Instead the world as a whole joins them in timeless grandeur.

Babel risks loss of clarity and, in turn, the disintegration of the myth. By this point, however, the Cossacks have a fixed identity. By spilling over their characteristics onto other heroes, Babel need not fear for their integrity. Rather, he points to a profound identity vacuum in the rest of the world. Like the metaphysical emptiness of Gogol's Poles, the weakness in a character such as Liutov makes him vulnerable to attack. He might not survive the incursion of the Cossacks, or he might manage to imbibe their spirit. Although he does not become a Cossack (or a Hasid or a religious painter), he does befriend all, and ultimately expresses himself through a violently creative act—the stories he tells through the pen of Babel.

It would be misleading, however, to conclude on such an unambiguous note. A sense of distance, which some interpret as simple nostalgia but is more likely complex irony, pervades *Red Cavalry*. The reticence of the cycle as a whole to take a positive stand about its portrait of the ideal may well point back to Tolstoi more than Gogol. *Red Cavalry*, as does *The Cossacks*, balances precariously between mythic affirmation and ironic malaise, so that some readers are led to see Liutov's desire to join the Cossacks as not only vain but pathetic. Liutov says one thing, but Babel "means" the other.

The irony, as has been noted, however, is "double-edged";[47] it is "a battle in which both sides win and lose."[48] In a sense, all the characters in *Red Cavalry* are both unappealing and extremely attractive. Wavering between parody and myth, Babel suggests the possible affinity of destruction and progress, war and wonder. He adopts the Cossack myth not so much to glorify the heroes themselves as to emphasize the applicability to his own chaotic world of the creative power he recognizes they wield.[49]

Conclusion: Story of a Horse

Babel's adaptations attest to the continued power of the Cossack myth, but they reorder its priorities, placing an increased emphasis on the topoi of regeneration as it relates to the creative artist. Babel's understatement of the Cossacks' role as Russian national symbol is not necessarily typical of his contemporaries, but he does share with the poets to be discussed in the following chapter his association of Cossack and artist.

An analysis of the two-part story within *Red Cavalry*, **"Story of a Horse"** and **"Continuation of Story of a Horse,"** can best recapitulate the differences and common ground between Gogol's and Babel's Cossacks. The story presents Savitskii—the same Cossack who shoots out his adversary's eyes in the opening story and sends Liutov to his Cossack tormentors in **"My First Goose"**—in the role of renegade Cossack. Abusing his authority as division chief, he appropriates a white stallion from Khlebnikov, commander of the First Squadron. The horse in question "had a magnificent yet untamed form" (perhaps a little heavy, from the narrator's

non-Cossack point of view) (80). Khlebnikov received in exchange "a smooth-gaited dark mare from a not-so-bad line," that is, a domesticated, dull female for the brilliant male. Considering the emphasis placed on the horse as an extension of the Cossack in *Red Cavalry* and in all of the Cossack myth, it is clear that Khlebnikov felt deprived of that which symbolized his own masculine, Cossack essence.

Khlebnikov thirsts for revenge. He writes to the Army Staff for just retribution and receives back an order, written in dry official language, for the return of his horse. Meanwhile Savitskii has been replaced and sent to the reserves. He now lives in a Polish town with the horse and a Cossack woman previously found with a Jew. By this time he owns twenty other thorough-breds, looked on as his own property. The former division chief lives alone, separated from the other Cossacks. In fact, Savitskii seems to have abandoned Cossackdom altogether. By settling in Poland he defies the Cossacks' traditional rejection of fixed home and their antagonism toward the Polish enemy; his association with a woman—and one already defiled by a Jew—ignores the Cossack bachelor tradition in which the warriors take the "virgin field and the good steed" for their tenderness and the sabre for their mother.[50] His possession of an entire stable ridicules the Cossack disregard for material wealth; as Gogol has shown, a real Cossack will drink away any gold in his pockets or carelessly forget the spot in which he buried his booty. Babel spares no details. Savitskii's residence is a "ragged slut," a "maimed little town," thus both defiled and miniature in contrast to the vast virginal steppe. "Drenched in perfume and resembling Peter the Great [the historical character associated earlier with the bridling of southern, Cossack freedom], he lived in disgrace" (80).

The whole environment suggests anti-Cossack domesticity: foals greedily suck the teats of their mothers, and Savitskii's Cossack woman lazily cares for her physical appearance and walks "carrying her breasts on high heels, breasts that wriggled about like an animal in a sack" (81). Savitskii calls not for *gorelka*, the traditional Cossack vodka, and not even for a samovar, but for a "little samovar," a diminutive that renders his request precious.

Savitskii turns a "deadened face" toward Khlebnikov when the latter comes to retrieve his horse, and utters a line of rhetoric that, albeit still Cossacklike, can only strike us as ironic given the description of his visage. "'I still live,' he said, embracing his woman. 'Yet can my legs march, yet can my steeds gallop, yet can my arms reach you and does this cannon of mine burn near my body . . .'" (81). He reaches for the gun that lies across his naked stomach, a feeble effort to prove his male potency, but enough to frighten Khlebnikov.

The remainder of the first episode of the story concerns Khlebnikov's reaction to Savitskii's refusal to honor the order of the letter from Army Staff, and the narrator's reaction to Khlebnikov. Like other "creative" Cossacks in the collection, Khlebnikov lays down his revolver and takes up his pen, becoming consumed in the writing of a letter voicing his grievances.

Khlebnikov's recourse to letter writing cannot help but recall the turn taken by the two antiheroes in Gogol's "The Tale of How Ivan Ivanovich Quarreled with Ivan Nikiforovich," discussed in the conclusion of Chapter 3. In "The Tale," the two Ivans, both descendents of Cossacks who renounced all heroic blood, argue over possession of a useless gun and the flinging of childish epithets. Babel's Khlebnikov chooses to solve his dispute through official channels rather than in battle with his fellow Cossack. Ivan Nikiforovich and Ivan Ivanovich similarly play out their quarrel with paper and pen instead of bullet and blood. And the outcome for each is equally unrewarding. Gogol informs us that the dispute stagnated in legal proceedings and stretched on interminably. Babel tells us that the chief of staff refused to listen to Khlebnikov's second plea since "your case has been decided. . . . Your stallion has been returned by me . . ." (81). Having fulfilled the letter of the law by writing the first order, the official feels that the matter is done. In both Gogol and Babel, action stops when writing begins.

"Continuation of Story of a Horse" is nothing more than a series of letters. Khlebnikov and Savitskii have apparently changed places, the former leaving the army, the latter returning. As in Gogol's story, the preliminary apparent difference between the two characters blurs as the story progresses.

Savitskii's letter that closes the episode ends on a curious note. The white stallion has died and the Cossack, too, will probably die soon in battle, he claims, but

> We will see each other, to give it to you straight, in the kingdom of heaven. But, as rumor has it, the old man in heaven doesn't have a kingdom, but a regular brothel. . . . There's gonorrhea enough as it is on earth, so maybe we won't see each other. With that, comrade Khlebnikov, I'll take my leave.
>
> (121)

Savitskii's discussion of divine venereal disease raises the suggestion that death may be nothing more than a continuation of life on earth. Thus, if Gogol ended "The Tale" with the narrator's declaration that "It is boring in this world, gentlemen" (Skuchno na etom svete, gospoda), Babel could have his narrator retort, "And in *that* one, too, I'm afraid." "Story of a Horse" can be read as an amplification of Gogol's travesty of the Cossack myth: two Cossacks exhibit non-Cossack behavior;

one desires an object, a symbol of masculine Cossack power, that belongs to the other; they turn to documents instead of weapons to resolve their differences; and the dispute remains unresolved. Boredom reigns. This mini-cycle in **Red Cavalry** seems, on the surface, to deny the vibrancy of the Cossack myth. To be reborn means nothing, for life has no spirit anywhere, and no mythic world is possible.

Yet Babel's version may be read in another way as well. Gogol's story, which ends the *Mirgorod* collection of his southern stories and points to his "northern" fiction, is an inversion of the Cossack myth. **Red Cavalry,** as we have seen, represents rather a dispersion. The cycle does not end on **"Continuation of Story of a Horse."** Instead, the reader is sent back into the Cossacks' strange and wondrous world in the next story.

And Babel does *not* bring in his narrator for an ironic comment at the end of **"Continuation of Story of a Horse,"** although this device is not unknown in **Red Cavalry.** In Gogol's story, the narrator's comment reinforces a clear ironic distance between the readers and the two Ivans, closing the door forever on our erstwhile relationship to the inhabitants of *Mirgorod.* Babel will not allow even this reassurance about the disjunction of fiction and reality. Babel originally published the story as **"Timashenko and Mel'nikov,"** apparently having based it on an event he witnessed between those two members of the Sixth Division of the cavalry. Mel'nikov complained that the story misrepresented his case. Babel apologized in a letter to the editor of the journal *October,* and simply changed the names.[51] That this story is grounded in experience—and that contemporaries often reacted as though Babel's works were meant as documentary evidence—seems only too appropriate. Babel gives us a clear proof that truth is stranger than fiction. Or myth is truer than reality.

So, parody is not ruled out, but neither is the possibility that the wonder of the Cossacks and their fellow characters in **Red Cavalry** is an antidote to the metaphysical boredom of the two Ivans. Such mythic energy is not found in particular characters, however, who could repudiate it as does Savitskii, but is rather diffused in the world around them. Pan Apolek recognizes this fact and needs no other inspiration for his representations of a higher reality than the motley Poles and Jews that he meets in towns and villages of his own homeland.

The energy of a mythic realm can therefore be exploited by those who enter it. The distance or nostalgia perceived by readers of **Red Cavalry** is but a product of the difficulty of Liutov's continued search for a door into what is, in fact, the very world around him.

Notes

1. D. S. Mirsky, *A History of Russian Literature,* ed. Francis J. Whitfield (New York: Alfred A. Knopf,

1949), 151. Babel's Red Army stories comprise the cycle *Konarmiia,* an abbreviation for Horse Army or Cavalry, but generally translated as *Red Cavalry.*

2. Maksim Gor'kii, "Rabselkoram i voenkoram o tom, kak uchilsia pisat'," *Pravda,* Sept. 30, 1928, 3. See also Patricia Carden, *The Art of Isaac Babel* (Ithaca: Cornell University Press, 1972), 59, 76, 127; James E. Falen, *Isaac Babel, Russian Master of the Short Story* (Knoxville: University of Tennessee Press, 1974), 52-54; Martin B. Klotz, "Poetry of the Present: Isaak Babel's *Red Cavalry,*" *Slavic and East European Journal* 18 (1974):160; Judith Stora-Sandor, *Isaac Babel', 1894-1941, l'homme et l'oeuvre* (Paris: Klincksieck, 1968), 77; I. A. Smirin, "Na puti k *Konarmii,*" *Literaturnoe nasledstvo* 74 (Moscow: Nauka, 1965):482.

3. Steven Marcus, "The Stories of Isaac Babel," *Partisan Review* 22, no. 3 (Summer 1955):403. See also Lionel Trilling, Introduction to *Isaac Babel: The Collected Stories,* trans. and ed. Walter Morrison (Cleveland and New York: New American Library, 1955), 18, published also in Trilling, *Beyond Culture: Essays on Literature and Learning* (New York: Viking Press, 1965); Ragna Grøngaard, *An Investigation of Composition and Theme in Isaak Babel's Literary Cycle Konarmija* (Aarhus: Arkona, 1979), 87; R. W. Hallett, *Isaac Babel* (Letchworth, Hertfordshire: Bradda Books, 1972), 51.

4. Although Khadzhi Murat is not a Cossack, he can be understood as an extension of the highly ambivalent heroes portrayed in *The Cossacks,* as discussed in Chapter 6. Renato Poggioli claims that *Red Cavalry* resembles *Khadzhi Murat* much more than it does *The Cossacks.* "Isaak Babel in Retrospect," *The Phoenix and the Spider* (Cambridge: Harvard University Press, 1957), 234.

5. Interview during a celebratory evening at the Writers' Union, Sept. 28, 1937, first published in *Nash Sovremennik* 4(1964). Reprinted as "O tvorcheskom puti pisatelia," in *Zabytyi Babel',* ed. Nikolai Stroud (Ann Arbor: Ardis, 1979), 267.

6. From "Moi Listki," an early story published in *Zhurnal zhurnalov,* no. 51 (1917):4-5, under the transparent pseudonym Bab-El'. Republished in *Zabytyi Babel'* 48-51.

7. *Zabytyi Babel'* 48-49, 50.

8. The best available biography of Babel is by Judith Stora-Sandor, *Isaac Babel',* cited above. Babel's own autobiography is fascinating, but not necessarily accurate.

9. Babel thus concealed his obviously Jewish name from the traditionally anti-Semitic Cossacks. But he could not adopt a pseudo-character as well. If his stories are any indication of his experience, the Cossacks were painfully aware of "Liutov's" intellectualism, symbolized by his glasses and associated with the educated Jewish population.

10. Patricia Carden feels Gor'kii's advice may be apocryphal, or at least exaggerated by Babel as he developed a "self-created legend," but that his search for material among the Cossacks was real (*Art of Isaac Babel* 11, 12-13).

11. Babel of course suffered a period of about twenty-five years when his works did not appear in the Soviet Union. He was 'rehabilitated' after Stalin's death.

12. Gogol died at the age of forty-three, apparently from self-starvation. Babel, at the age of forty-seven, fell victim to the Stalinist purges.

13. Gogol', Letter of Feb. 1, 1833, *PSS* 10:257.

14. I. Babel', *Konarmiia. Odesskie rasskazy. P'esy* (Letchworth, Hertfordshire: Bradda Books, 1965), 262. Page numbers in the text will refer to this edition unless otherwise cited.

15. Konstantin Paustovskii, "Neskol'ko slov o Babele: Memuary," first published in *Nedelia,* nos. 11-17 (Sept. 1966). Translated in *Isaac Babel: You Must Know Everything,* trans. Max Hayward, ed. Nathalie Babel (New York: Farrar, Straus and Giroux, 1966):281.

16. See Gogol's December 24, 1844, letter to Smirnova quoted in Chapter 3, above.

17. Poggioli, *Phoenix and the Spider* 230. Cited in Carden, *Art of Isaac Babel* 8.

18. To this date, Soviet-Yiddish writers have been insufficiently studied. For some background, see *Ashes out of Hope: Fiction by Soviet-Yiddish Writers,* edited and introduction by Irving Howe and Eliezer Greenberg (New York: Schocken Books, 1977).

19. As Donald Fanger writes about Gogol: "Gogol capitalized on this appeal [the exoticism of Ukraine] as a mediator; by embracing his Ukrainian heritage, he became a Russian writer." *Creation of Nikolai Gogol* 87-88.

20. See Stora-Sandor's comment in *Isaac Babel'* 85, 92.

21. Nils Åke Nilsson suggests that the passage appears as a temporal chain on a metonymic plane, but that when experienced metaphorically it is detached from either temporal or causal progression. "Isaak Babel's 'Perechod čerez Zbruč,'" *Scando-Slavica* 23 (1977):69-70.

22. Victor Terras, "Line and Color: The Structure of I. Babel's Short Stories in *Red Cavalry,*" *Studies in Short Fiction* 3, no. 2 (1966):153. See also Rochelle H. Ross, "The Unity of Babel's Konarmija," *South Central Bulletin* 41, no. 4 (Winter 1981):116; Toby W. Clyman, "Babel' as Colorist," *Slavic and East European Journal* 21 (1977):333.

23. See "The Road to Brody," "My First Goose," "Gedali," "The Rebbe," "The Death of Dolgushov," "The Brigade Commander," "Konkin," and "Berestechko." For the suggestion that sunset also refers to the traditional symbol of demarcation of temporal power and the beginning of the sacred Sabbath, see Efraim Sicher, "The Road to a Red Calvary: Myth and Mythology in the Works of Isaak Babel' of the 1920's," *Slavonic and East European Review* 60, no. 4 (Oct. 1982):540.

24. Nilsson, "Perekhod" 65, and Falen, *Isaac Babel* 137, also read the crossing, as Nilsson states, as "a transition from one world to another."

25. Sicher, "Road to a Red Calvary" 538.

26. From the traditional Passover Haggadah. Italics mine.

27. Passover falls in spring, not early summer, when the Polish campaign actually began. The dishes may be scattered because the invading soldiers removed them from storage, but Babel's choice to mention them specifically, and not other stored items, gives credence to this interpretation. Babel was not interested in temporal fidelity here.

28. See Elizabeth A. Warner, *The Russian Folk Theater* (The Hague and Paris: Mouton, 1977), 95-98, for a discussion of the Cossack in Russian and Ukrainian folk theater. For an early-nineteenth-century play strongly influenced by the eighteenth-century folk plays, see *Kazak-stikhotvorets* by A. A. Shakhovskoi (1812).

29. Carden, *Art of Isaac Babel* 49, 112-13.

30. For a discussion of the specific Hasidic references in these stories, see Maurice Friedberg, "Yiddish Folklore Motifs in Isaak Babel's *Konarmija,*" *American Contributions to the Eighth International Congress of Slavists,* Vol. 2 (Columbus, Ohio: Slavica, 1978), 192-203.

31. Herbert Marder, "The Revolutionary Art of Isaac Babel," *Novel: A Forum on Fiction* 7(1973):56.

32. Babel, *The Forgotten Prose,* ed. and trans. Nicholas Stroud (Ann Arbor: Ardis, 1978), 129-30.

33. Or: "Hyperbolic, surrealistic elements," according to Michael Falchikov, "Conflict and Contrast in Isaak Babel's *Konarmiya,*" *Modern Language Review* 72 (1977):128.

34. J. J. van Baak, "The Function of Nature and Space in *Konarmija* by I. E. Babel'," in *Dutch Contributions to the Eighth International Congress on Slavists: Zagreb, Ljubljana, 1978* (Amsterdam: Benjamins, 1979), 44. Many critics have noticed Babel's use of epic. Terras's article "Line and Color" sees a travesty of epic (142), and Sicher claims Babel's use of myth gives the illusion of epic while mocking it ("Road to a Red Calvary" 531). See also Carol Luplow, *Isaac Babel's "Red Cavalry"* (Ann Arbor: Ardis, 1982), 40; Carden, *Art of Isaac Babel* 118, 126; Falen, *Isaac Babel* 80, 83-84, 119, 191-25; J. Catteau, "L'épopée dans la *Cavalerie Rouge* de I. Babel," in *VII Między-narodowy Kongres Slawistów w Warszawie.* 1973: Streszczenia referatów i komunikatów (Warsaw: PAN, 1973), 700-701; Milton Ehre, "Babel's *Red Cavalry*: Epic and Pathos, History and Culture," *Slavic Review* 40, no. 2(1981):228-40; Martin B. Klotz, "Poetry of the Present: Isaak Babel's *Red Cavalry,*" *Slavic and East European Journal* 18(1974):160-69; A. B. Murphy, "The Style of Isaak Babel'," *Slavonic and East European Review* 44(1966):369.

35. John G. Gunnell, *Political Philosophy and Time* (Middletown, Conn.: Wesleyan University Press, 1968), 11.

36. Frank, "Spatial Form in Modern Literature" 393.

37. Terras, "Line and Color" 152; Carden, *Art of Isaac Babel* 48.

38. L. Livshits, "Materialy k tvorcheskoi biografii I. Babelia," *Voprosy literatury* 4(1964):122.

39. Frank, "Spatial Form in Modern Literature" 392.

40. Raymond Rosenthal, "The Fate of Isaak Babel," *Commentary* 3, no. 2 (Feb. 1947); Trilling, Introduction to *Collected Stories,* and Falchikov, "Conflict and Contrast"; Gareth Williams, "Two Leitmotifs in Babel's *Konarmija,*" *Die Welt der Slaven* 17(1972):308-17; van Baak, "Function of Nature and Space" 37-55.

41. As Patricia Carden states, "the easy division between Cossack and Jew is inadequate" (*Art of Isaac Babel* 121). Louis Irabarne writes of the paradox of the "beautiful-bad Cossack" vs. "ugly-good Jew," in "Babel's *Red Cavalry* as a Baroque Novel," *Contemporary Literature* 14(1973):68; see also Stanley Edgar Hyman, "The Problem of Jewish Identity: Identities of Isaac Babel," *The Promised End* (New York: World Publishing, 1963), 322; and Luplow, *Isaac Babel's "Red Cavalry"* 10.

42. See Falen, *Isaac Babel* 141, on the theme of rebirth, and Hyman, "Problem of Jewish Identity" 321, who sees changes of identity through rituals of rebirth as a major theme of *Red Cavalry.*

43. Livshits, "Materialy k tvorcheskoi biographii I. Babelia" 131.

44. Milk, a typically female symbol, is frequently associated with non-Cossack behavior in *Red Cavalry*. Matvei Pavlichenko describes himself in his young life as wasting away as a herdsman—not a warrior—surrounded by and infused with the smell of milk, for he has not yet entered true adult Cossackdom (73). The Polish enemy cries "white tears, real human milk" ("Konkin" 85) to express his fear of death. And the Cossack Akinfiev calls Liutov a *molokan* (a member of a pacifist sect named from the word *moloko* or milk) when he fails to act like a Cossack and cannot kill without regret ("After the Battle" 140).

45. My thanks to Robert A. Maguire for suggesting this allusion.

46. See Carden, *Art of Isaac Babel* 135-36.

47. Klotz, "Poetry of the Present" 161.

48. Terras, "Line and Color" 145.

49. In his autobiography, Babel describes his schoolboy world in just such chaotic and creative terms: "[At my school] studied the sons of foreign merchants, the children of Jewish brokers, imposing Poles, Old-Believers, and many overgrown billiard players. During breaks I would go out to the pier at the port or to the Greek coffee houses to play billiards, or to the Moldavanka to drink cheap Bessarabian wine in the cellars" (*Konarmiia* 19).

50. Cf. Gogol, *Taras Bul'ba, PSS* 2:43.

51. *Oktiabr'*, no. 4(1924):224. See also Budennyi's outraged remarks in "Babizm Babelia," *Oktiabr'*, no. 3(1924):196-97 and "Otkrytoe pis'mo M. Gor'komu," in *Pravda*, Oct. 26, 1928.

David K. Danow (essay date March-June 1994)

SOURCE: Danow, David K. "The Paradox of Red Cavalry." *Canadian Slavonic Papers* 36, nos. 1-2 (March-June 1994): 43-54.

[*In the following essay, Danow considers the stories of* Red Cavalry *to be full of depictions of mindless violence coupled with futile attempts to understand such behavior.*]

In *Red Cavalry* the first story sets the tone: horrific violence thrust upon the unsuspecting narrator and reader, accompanied by a question at the end for which there is, and can be, no response. "And now I should wish to know . . . I should wish to know where in the whole world you could find another father like my father?"

asks the daughter whose father has been butchered before her eyes.[1] The question itself, we are told, is delivered "with sudden and terrible violence." In Babel's cycle of stories, violence that is sudden and terrible appears generic to the world he describes. That disturbing feature generates an equally compelling need to understand; these two aspects of the tales are inextricably united in the minds of both teller and reader. The focus of this essay will be on this fearful, human union, born of that need for understanding linked to mindless brutality.

Like questions pervade the cycle. While Liutov, the most prominent consciousness of the work, is clearly and most consistently seeking to understand, throughout the tales there are numerous other seekers posing their own questions to which there are no answers. Old Gedali wants to know how he is to say Yes to the Revolution, when it "sends out in front nought but shooting . . ." In frustration the old man articulates in querying paraphrase what it is that he does not understand: "I cannot do without shooting, because I am the Revolution." In response to his implicit question (How can that be? How can the idea of universal brotherhood be squared with universal shooting?), the old man hears only his own paraphrase directed back at him, with added ironic overtones: "She cannot do without shooting, Gedali . . . because she is the Revolution." Pointing out that both sides are principally occupied with shooting, Gedali asks: "Then how is Gedali to tell which is Revolution and which is Counter-Revolution? . . . Woe unto us, where is the joy-giving Revolution?" (70-71). He gets no answer; both urgent questioner and author of ironic rejoinders fall into silence. As a further, deeper irony, not only does the old man receive no response, but Liutov as well must do without answers. Finally, since Liutov, as the principal voice, can provide little understanding, the reader is also left essentially on his own to unravel the terrible enigma of human being that Babel repeatedly and variously poses within the collection as a whole.

The question raised by the daughter in the first story of the cycle concludes that story. There is nothing further that can be said; having gleaned only sparse and brutal detail, the reader learns nothing more. In **"Gedali,"** likewise, there are no answers. Thus silence appears as the predominant mode in these stories, governed by a poetics that perversely inverts the Socratic mode of attaining understanding. Here questions do not beget answers; the persistent seeking for understanding (Gedali, for instance, is certainly persistent) leads nowhere. In this world of cruel and murderous havoc, the primary teller of the tales and the reader, as well as numerous other fugitive seekers populating the stories, are all left to attain their own answers in what remains perhaps the quintessential existential situation of modern times. Briefly put, the ruling governance of that contemporaneity that was Babel's, and is now our own, dictates that we either acquire our understandings privately and independently—or we do without.

Having taken the horrendous situation of civil war as his subject, Babel projects his world *in extremis* impassively, as a kind of norm—in a sense, operating on the well-founded assumption that people can get used to just about anything—and thereby models contemporary reality which, likewise, provides neither a set of recognized truths nor an undisputed source from which the seeker may attain "true" understanding (as opposed to a certain ephemeral solace). In this crucial respect, the tales, situated in an outlandish, horrific setting, model, paradoxically, the prosaic, everyday life that constitutes ordinary existence.

In a related respect, the inverted poetics of the cycle serves also to negate, in effect, the possibility of achieving understanding through dialogue. What Bakhtin designates in his most profound meaning-producing model as the "self and other," engaged in shared dialogue, is entirely negated here. That model bears the potential to produce answers. In contrast, in Babel's stories, where such a model is dissolved into isolated speakers lacking a counterpart, simple talk is at once elevated to a higher "poetic" sphere, as stylized speech of an order that no one could actually speak.[2] Affording little or no understanding, it exists solely to exemplify its own formalized, stylized, self-indulgent form. Its principal virtue is thus precisely its form, which makes such speech the perfect exemplar of the autotelic sign (designed to designate itself alone) by which art is made.

This is not to suggest that among Babel's characters there is no desire to talk. Apart from such garrulous and disparate types as Gedali and Matthew Pavlichenko, the one challenging the Revolution while the other extols it, all the while indulging in florid rhetoric, there is, for instance, the solitary (and nameless) figure, who utters the plaint: "These nights on the line are long. There's no end to them. And a man sort of gets a longing to have a talk with someone else, but where's one to get someone else, I'd like to know?" (170). Typically, the speaker here receives no response, yet his query serves as counterpoise to "the fierce and wordless brigandage" (136) that typifies this hellish world. There is, in other words, at least the occasional desire to communicate and that desire is not limited to this speaker alone. Aside from Liutov, after all, there is a veritable profusion of storytellers and letter writers, who articulate their respective word and seek to be heard. Not only, then, is there the human bent toward violence, but a like inclination in the need to talk and to tell, which, one hopes, even more conclusively defines our kind. But that latter, distinctively human element is one that Babel can only grasp at among the "fierce and wordless brigandage" that affords so little potential for dialogue.

As a result, the word uttered in solitude, the desire for verbal exchange, remains essentially unanswered. The speaker in Babel's world is generally a solo speaker. The letter writer, likewise, pens his word with little expectation of response. In rare counterpoise, the retired and disillusioned Khlebnikov receives an answer from his former commander Savitskii (**"The Story of a Horse, Continued"** [**"Продолжение истории одной лошади"**]), who tells him, in effect, that if they meet again, it will be in Hell.

The question most often left unanswered has to do with violence, perpetrated or threatened, implicit or explicit. The young woman of the first story was forced to witness her father's murder, contrary to his last wish. Gedali was blinded by the dark force of Counter-Revolution, but feels an even worse threat from the supposedly "joy-giving Revolution" that has so far failed to calm his fear. To say that the crux of the stories is centered in violence amounts to a critical cliché. Violence is clearly at the core of what Liutov, in particular, struggles to understand, even as he perpetrates it himself, both physically and psychologically. He crushes the goose with his boot, shoves and punches a crippled epileptic, and threatens first one landlady ("I'll burn you . . . I'll burn you and your stolen calf" [171]), then another ("I smelt meat in that cabbage soup of hers, and laid my revolver on the table . . ." [187]). Food, of course, is the essential thing; its absence is frequently a primary factor in dislocating character. Yet how are the individual manifestations of violence that focus the tales effected? What makes them so distinctive and profoundly affecting? Is there, in the cycle, a hidden understanding that somehow redeems these tales?

First, as noted, there is virtually no informed response to questions, whether implicit or explicit, centered on violence. The landlady, obliged to cook the goose, articulates obliquely (in mournful terms that suggest helplessness and further recourse to violence): "Comrade . . . I want to go and hang myself" (76). The shoved and punched epileptic makes no response, but Sasha, the regimental whore who leads the beaten man away, expresses it thus: "Cocks have only one thought in life—to go and tear at one another . . . And everything that's gone on today makes me want to go and hide my face" (186-87). While, in response to Sandy's offer to comfort her ("I don't mind laying myself out to be nice to you, if you like"), the other threatened landlady laments:

> Never see no cabbage soup . . . It's gone, my cabbage soup has. People only go and show me weapons, and when there does come along a decent chap I could have a bit of fun with, I'm so sick of everything I couldn't get no pleasure out of sinning.

(190)

Not nearly so oblique as the response of the old woman deprived of her goose, this equally plaintive remark nevertheless jibes with Sasha's general deploring of what she sees. For these women, as for Gedali and, to a certain extent, for Liutov as well, there is and can be no explanation for the violence that "never lets up." Neither they, nor Liutov, nor the reader can get a clear grasp of what it is that motivates a man to kill. As partial recompense, however, we do encounter a kind of global response to the entire problem, uttered in summative fashion, as one figure (characterized only as "a sort of lively humpback") puts it: "Nowadays everybody judges everybody else . . . And condemns to death—it's as simple as that" (157). Seemingly, for the Cossack it *is* simple; there are no entangling questions, no extraneous circumstances that would prevent Matthew Pavlichenko, for instance, from carrying out his self-appointed task, nor stop Prishchepa from taking his vengeance. Similarly, there are no extenuating circumstances that would allow Afonka Bida to forgive or even understand Liutov's failure to put Dolgushov out of his misery.

The desire for vengeance is simple; from one otherwise inarticulate perspective, it is also simply human and perhaps stronger than the desire for talk heralded earlier. The same incontrovertible argument applies, it would seem, in the case of Dolgushov. He needs to be shot; since that is the only possible solution, there can be no attendant questions. For the Cossack riders, as distinct from Liutov and his counterparts, questions of life and death are fully codified. The matter, regardless of its complexity, is clear; correct and proper behavior have long ago been both prescribed and proscribed: one takes vengeance for harm perpetrated against oneself or one's family; one does not leave a helpless comrade to suffer further at the hands of the enemy. Thus it cannot be fathomed how Liutov can go into battle without cartridges in his pistol. For once, then, the question of violence is posed by one of those for whom, presumably, there are no questions: "The Poles go after you, and you don't go after them . . . What for?" And the response he gets, prior to receiving a punch in the face, is the same mimicking paraphrase that Gedali had heard: "The Poles go after me and I don't go after them . . ." (186)—a response that once again answers nothing and resolves nothing.

Moral and ethical resolution on the philosophical plane is alien to the Cossack; it is central to the Jew. The latter seeks intellectual resolution—an idea that takes recourse in law, tradition, humane conduct. Rather than resolution, the Cossack seeks retribution, whatever the cost. After the loss of his horse, Afonka Bida wails: "No, I won't give in to accursed fate! . . . Now I'll go and butcher the bloody Poles without mercy. I'll do them in right to the heart, do them damned well in . . ." (134). The Cossack will go one better than an eye

for an eye; he will go an eye for a horse. "Where his left eye had been, a pink swelling gaped repulsively in his charred face" (137). No matter now the loss of a horse, nor the loss of an eye; retribution has been effected. For the Jew, what counts is the idea: Is it moral/ethical? For the Cossack, what matters is the act: Have I paid my enemy out? Whether it is termed an act of retribution or of vengeance is of no consequence; as the fundamental tenet of such a code, one must act. In other words, one responds—to the vagaries of fate, to the distressing hand dealt by (mis)fortune—wordlessly. In clear opposition to the life of the mind that guides the principal consciousness of the stories is the life of the body which, seeking no approbation, remains the governing ethos of the cycle. Intellect is subordinated to brute force, the idea to the act. Were Babel to have had it otherwise, the reader would have had less. In this existential universe of free choice, in which all that one has is the code and a horse (or the need of one), the man who tears at life trudges off "alone, utterly alone . . ." (135).

Afonka Bida, Matthew Pavlichenko, Prishchepa all ride out alone. Their individual aim is the same—to maim and to kill. Yet their respective projects are not conducted in secret. Rather, each has his ready audience, witnesses as eager spectators or avid listeners. In proclaiming his murderous exploit, Matthew Pavlichenko, who serves both as chief protagonist and "chorus," relates to his fellow "Stavropol boys" in lyrical, poetic fashion how he took his enemy "by the body and by the throat and by the hair" in order "to get to know what life really is, what life's like down our way" (106). While Prishchepa goes about the task of settling his accounts, "The inhabitants of the settlement watched his progress sullenly . . . The young Cossacks were scattered over the steppe, keeping the score" (108-9). In the case of Afonka Bida, we read: "Only the menacing murmurs from the countryside—traces of rapacious plundering showed us his arduous course . . . Echoes of that ferocious and single-handed struggle reached our ears, echoes of those despairing, lonewolf attacks upon the masses" (136). In each case, there is no possibility of shame, criminality, or of conducting oneself otherwise. Further, the possibility of such behavior even being perceived as heinous is at once precluded.

Echoes of the "lonewolf" going at others alone appears a kind of tautology. Yet in this world of vengeance not talked about but acted upon, what might not readily appear tautological may nonetheless be akin. That each of these attackers goes out alone to get his own represents not only "facts" but unquestioned acts. The Cossack may ask how (in an incomprehensible act of inverted courage) a man rides into battle with an unloaded gun. But he does not question how one can be so pitiless as to leave a helpless comrade for the enemy "to play their dirty tricks." Certain conduct brooks no mitigating possibility. Behavior that obviates the code necessarily obviates the need to question circumstance. Entirely self-evident, then, the lack of a question suffices to explain the corresponding lack of an answer. Yet the reader, as well as the writer of ***Red Cavalry,*** presumes the need to pose one question at least: namely, how to explain the violence? For the ***Red Cavalry*** riders there is no such need. There is an enemy and there are themselves. There is the universal military code that proclaims unequivocally that one must kill or be killed. And, coupled with these irreversible facts, there is the desire to live. So, from the Cossack perspective, what question can there be? Such reasoning is as clearly evident as any tautology.

Yet the paradox remains; thoroughly engaging and all-pervasive, like the violence that engenders it in the first place, paradox is definitively a part of the work. As a principal fundament of the cycle, it is generated by Babel's unflinching ability to present images that nonetheless cause the reader to flinch, producing, in turn, the need to understand. For the main protagonists there is no such need; there is no uncertainty and no ambiguity. Thus Dolgushov says simply: "You'll have to waste a cartridge on me" (89), taking for granted what he considers his due and his comrade's duty. Conversely, but drawing on the same understanding in the same situation, Commander Trunov writes: "Having to die today, I consider it my duty to fire a couple of shots toward the possible bringing down of the enemy . . ." (150-51). Matthew Pavlichenko explains coolly: "Then I stamped on my master Nikitinsky, trampled on him for an hour or maybe more. And in that time I got to know life through and through" (106); of that he is sure. In the same fearful spirit, the closing of **"Two Ivans"** (**"Два Ивана"**) promises like cruelty: "Well, now I'm going to have sport with you, Ivan, and no mistake. You just wait and see the sport I'll have with you" (160). Whether the act is already performed or projected into the future, there is the same unwavering sense of certainty, as though it were already an accomplished fact.

The sense of a strong will in action derives precisely from such certainty. Even the idiot Kurdiukov (**"A Letter"**) *knows* that "father was a dog" (51); Diakov (**"The Remount Officer"** [**"Начальник конзапаса"**]) never doubts that he will demonstrate to the poor supplicating peasant that the dying mare he received in return for his own horse is indeed "a mount" (54); Sidorov (**"Italian Sunshine"** [**"Солнце Италии"**]) is certain that "The King [of Italy] must be sent to join his forebears" (67); Afonka Bida is close to doing the same thing for Liutov (**"The Death of Dolgushov"** [**"Смерть Долгушова"**])—out of absolute certainty that his murder would be just ("Get out of my sight . . . or I'll kill you" 90). Resulting from a like surety, "that stain from the face of the workers' land and the republic" is, in

fact, "washed away" (126) in a contrastively completed act of perceived justice (**"Salt"** [**"Соль"**]). Similarly, Khlebnikov knows that he has a right to keep his horse (**"The Story of a Horse"** [**"История одной лошади"**])—or resign; Afonka Bida knows he must get a horse—or die. Pavlichenko and Prishchepa are certain that their death-dealing missions are just. Not one of these self-willed figures experiences doubt, uncertainty, or pity. Such sentiments are left for others. Questions of life and death—in their immediate concrete application—are immediately settled.

This quick "settlement" precludes all other considerations: questions of morality, ethics, law. Yet, for Liutov, who bemoans the fate of the bees (in the opening line of **"The Road to Brody"** [**"Путь в Броды"**]), whose hives offer the only opportunity for purloined sweetness in bitter civil war, and who himself expresses in analogous fashion virtually the only sentiment registered in the entire cycle, such problems are not raised either. Rather, the horror of violence and brutality is mitigated by expressions of feeling, concern, and the sustained lyricism that frames many of the stories of the cycle.[3] Hence, in the depiction of yet another grotesquely sad image, we read: "I lit my little lantern, turned back, and saw lying on the ground the corpse of a Pole I had splattered with my urine. . . . I wiped the skull of my unknown brother, and went on, bent beneath the weight of the saddle" (155-56). That same democratic acknowledgement of brotherhood is extended in a more likely direction by Liutov when he encounters the dying "Red Army man Bratslavsky" (192), whom he had met earlier, designated then as "the cursed son, the last son, the unruly son" (79) in the court of the Hasidic Rabbi Motale, the father. Now, lying naked and dying in a railroad car, that "cursed" son is buried "at some forgotten station. And I, who can scarce contain the tempests of my imagination within this age-old body of mine, I was there beside my brother when he breathed his last" (193).

Originally intended as the concluding passage to the cycle,[4] these words bear considerable significance. On the one hand, they underscore the all-pervasive violence documented in the stories; on the other, they tentatively suggest a certain hope—tinged, nonetheless, with attendant irony—that Gedali's desire for "an International of good people" (71) eventually will be realized. His wish implies the need for brotherhood, which is expressed in the stories in the two instances just noted. Yet the twin objects of Liutov's expressed sentiment are dead in both cases, giving good reason for pause rather than for optimism. Nonetheless, the sense of a relentless paradox emerges as not entirely negative but as also bearing a positive correlative. Since the very existence of a voice that expresses humane sentiment serves as counterpoise to those that exist solely to sound a war cry.

Further, the presence of figures who either sing, paint, or make music (Sandy the Christ, Pan Apolek, blind Gottfried) augment that barely audible sentiment in the face of the terrible despair expressed by the war-weary women of the cycle. In addition, those who practice their religious beliefs—Gedali, the Rabbi and his court, "the all-powerful body of the Catholic Church" (59)— and who maintain faith in the midst of unflagging carnage, offset the seemingly hopeless rage of war. Art performs a similar function. Suffering and Spirit are thus united in the religious imagery produced by "Apolek's heretical and intoxicating brush."

> There was in this Berestechko church an individual and alluring way of looking upon the mortal sufferings of the sons of men. Saints in this temple went to their deaths with all the picturesqueness of Italian singers, and the black hair of the executioners was as glossy as Holophernes' beard.
>
> (141)

Liutov's commentary here heightens the impression made by art. His first statement draws our attention, as it were, to the work. His second constitutes a verbal inlay of metaphor and simile that establish relations that are his alone. The pictorial image is thus enhanced, in the process, by the imagery of verbal art.

As a pronounced, greatly sustained element of the stories, Liutov's intellectual and cultural preoccupations, appearing as individual but repeated fragments in an otherwise unrelentingly blood-red mosaic, serve to remind one that the world of art, history, and learning have not entirely relinquished their place to the seeming death of culture. In **"My First Goose"** (**"Мой первый гусь"**), if Liutov initially wins over his bloody "brethren" through brutal behavior, he later makes a greater inroad into their ranks by reading to them. Conversely, in **"The Song"** (**"Песня"**), Sandy mollifies a hungry, threatening Liutov by dispelling the need for food ("So it was that . . . I was thwarted of my landlady's cabbage soup") and the use of a gun.

> He turned away and, knowing full well what would give me pleasure, began a Kuban song. . . . I love that song. Sandy knew this. . . . And I listened to him, stretched out in the corner on the fusty hay. Reverie broke my bones, reverie shook the rotting hay beneath me."
>
> (188-89)

In sober reflection, Liutov observes: "we needed his songs. At that time no one could see an end to the war. . . . Those songs are indispensable to us. No one can see an end to the war . . ." (189). In the more global terms that his "reverie" invites, we may conclude that it is art in general that is indispensable as the paramount feature of human being most clearly juxtaposed to the mentality that promotes war.

It would be tempting but facile to say that the paradox of **Red Cavalry** is resolved through art—that art in the multifarious forms by which it is repeatedly manifested and reflected upon in the stories provides the resolution to the riddle of life, the misery of war. Nonetheless, by its very presence and, indeed, proliferation in this world ravaged by war, it provides a partial resolution, at least a tentative understanding that being human entails not only savagery but the capacity to create beauty. That ability emerges from within hidden corners and unsuspected quarters. One of the least likely is the bruised and battered bludgeoner, Afonka Bida. The third paragraph of **"In St. Valentine's Church"** (**"У святого Валента"**) begins: "I was amazed to hear the organ peal forth." Further, we read: "The sounds of the organ floated across to us, now slow and ponderous, now light and nimble. Their flight was laborious, and their reverberations rang on plaintively and long" (139). Appended to the description of Apolek's painting, certain "traces of destruction" that Liutov had not noted earlier are remarked—followed by the words: "And Afonka Bida was still playing the organ." While the reader had already been made aware of its plaintive peals, it is not until now that we learn that it is Afonka Bida who was *still* playing. That unexpected fact is accompanied by more predictable detail:

> He was drunk and wild and hacked to pieces, having returned only the day before with the horse he had seized from the peasants. . . . the Cossack would not stop, and his songs were many. Each sound was a song, and all the sounds were torn from one another. The song—its dense strain—lasted a second, then gave place to another.
>
> (141)

Coupled, then, with the expected description of Afonka Bida as "drunk and wild" is the entirely unexpected indication that "each sound was a song" and that music might be a part of his sphere. The man who tears at life not surprisingly produces sounds that "were torn from one another." That the realm of art is not exclusionary, however, comes to us as something newly revealed, an epiphanic moment that confirms life even in the midst of death, just as the Cossack plays in the midst of those "traces of destruction" which he, sometime organist, undoubtedly wrought.

The sounds of Sandy's songs, the dissonant notes of the organ, as well as snippets of history, emerge periodically as part of Babel's chronicle of death and destruction. Those snippets appear as "folios in which were printed hosannas to the Most Excellent and Illustrious Head of State, Joseph Pilsudski" (45); as the tombstone markings ("Carved gray stones with inscriptions three centuries old" (107) that essentially compose the brief lyric piece, **"The Cemetery at Kozin"** (**"Кладбище в Козине"**); as a song sung by "an old fellow with a bandore" that tells of "the ancient glory of the Cossacks" (118-19); and as "a fragment of a letter yellow with age" dated 1820, that asks if the Emperor Napoleon is really dead. Immediately counterposed to that yellowed page rooted in the past is the voice of the Commissar proclaiming (to "the bewildered townsfolk and the plundered Jews") an enigmatic future: "You are in power. Everything here is yours. No more Pans" (121). History is revealed as mystery; analogous to the hidden chambers in **"The Church at Novograd"** (**"Костел в Новограде"**), it extends outward into the unknown:

> We went around and around, searching. Bone buttons sprang beneath our fingers, icons split down the middle and opened out, revealing subterranean passages and mildewed caverns. The temple was an ancient one, and full of secrets. In its glossy walls lay hidden passages, niches, doors that moved noiselessly aside.

(46)

At times, however, history may appear in *Red Cavalry* as both immediate and very much known, as in the following personal and lyrical phrasing that clearly surmises the end: "Tardy has been killed, Lukhmannikov has been killed, Lykoshenko has been killed, Gulevoy has been killed, Trunov has been killed, and the white stallion is no longer beneath me" (161). Here, through poetic refrain, commemorating the killing of both man and beast, there emerges a certain metonymy born of a peculiarly hellish logic that succinctly communicates the sense of one's own inevitable violent death. On a more global, historical plane, a like surmise is encompassed by another warrior's clearly dispassionate remark: "'We've lost the campaign,' muttered Volkov, and snored" (172). For the man who no longer has the white stallion beneath him, for the one who cannot remain awake, and for all the others—in that sound is expressed the utter exhaustion that no one expresses.

As an instance of further, unobtrusive historical account, rendered in more fully developed fashion, **"Discourse on the Tachanka"** (**"Учение о тачанке"**) provides a survey of the innovative and effective use of a small battle wagon, "a mobile and formidable instrument of warfare" that is likened to "the Ukrainian village of not long ago—savage, rebellious, and grasping" (83-4). The sketch concludes on a note, inspired by a fleeting reference to the Jews of Volhynia and Galicia ("their capacity for suffering was full of a somber greatness") that is both historical and lyrical: "Watching them, I understood the poignant history of this region: the stories of Talmudists renting taverns, of Rabbis carrying on usury, of young girls raped by Polish troopers and over whom Polish magnates fought pistol duels" (86). That brief concluding frame documents the history of disparate peoples fairly tripping over themselves in an unceasing effort to commit mayhem and folly, much

as *Red Cavalry* itself recounts essentially the same detail on a grand scale. As a significant redeeming factor of a work pervaded by a single-minded preoccupation with violence and death, part of that "grandness" of scale may be attributed to the intermittent historical detail, whether projected in stone or song, that provides a sense of continuance; the hellish time of the present thus exists within an artistic framework that acknowledges the diachronic over the synchronic. The sense of history that also pervades *Red Cavalry* provides a counterbalance to the alternative of a static synchrony inexorably promising the certainty of a frightening, unchanging reality. Instead, there is the feeling of a continuum, affording the possibility of flux and consequent change. The carnage that is now present, in other words, need not exist indefinitely. The stones that populate the cemetery at Kozin need not proclaim the future but only signify the past.

Nonetheless, while the intermittent linked presence of art, history, and especially a sustained lyricism serves to mitigate a dismal present, *Red Cavalry* is permeated by the sense of an ever-present death that makes itself felt in Babel's striking imagery. "More rain fell. Dead mice floated along the roads. Autumn set its ambushes about our hearts, and trees like naked corpses set upright on their feet swayed at the crossroads" (170).

The past, in its own (lyrical) way, also fares poorly. Thus, we read: "Woe unto you, *Res Publica*; woe unto you, Prince Radziwill, and unto you, Prince Sapieha, risen for the space of an hour!" (45). Woe unto the past; but is there allotted to the present more than "the space of an hour?" That is a question that *Red Cavalry* does not take up. Instead, we are told, regarding Berestechko, for instance, that "The little town reeks on, awaiting a new era . . ." (120). The cycle indulges neither in speculation nor optimism for the new "republic" or man in general. There is only the paradox of contemporary historical fact. What Babel describes is both contemporary and historical; the reader never doubts the immediacy or the veracity of what is depicted. The stories convey a joint sense of history being lived at the level of individual biography and of history being made collectively—now, at the present moment of narration. Just as there can be no possible answer to the young woman's question that concludes the opening story, which sets the tone for what follows, the final lines of the entire cycle sound a hopeful note in only a very minor key. "Months passed, and my dream came true. The Cossacks stopped watching me and my horse" (200). Yet those words follow the wistful observation, "I was alone among these men whose friendship I had not succeeded in gaining" (199), emblematic of the commitment to a vision of existential reality that focuses the stories, affording the paradoxical sense of the contemporary merging with the historical in a troubled present that is now.

Paradox is thus at the core of the stories in a temporal sense: what is past appears present; history is made immediate. Paradox is also central both thematically and philosophically, with the question of violence and how it is to be understood, situated—multi-leveled—at the core of the paradox itself. Thus the question, 'How are we to understand violence?' entails the related, embedded problem of 'Who is "we"?' For the perpetrator of violence—the Cossack who is protagonist—does not "perpetrate" the question. To do so would constitute a kind of indulgence on his part equivalent to the writer's unlikely projection of a false optimism. The Cossacks' answers are ready-made—by the code, the need to survive, and, in effect, by the nature of war itself. Hence, only the outsider has the need for an answer; the insider seeks only to live or, if need be, to die without shame. As a final paradox, then, **Red Cavalry** makes of the reader—much as we find in the author—a vicarious seeker, who can never partake of the code, never participate in the violence it condones, and, ultimately, never understand. Yet in all this negation, there remains the sustained desire to live, impressive and instructive in itself, linked to the power of art, at which, also paradoxically, and as here shown, both "outsider" and Cossack are able to marvel. As a final illustrative instance, in **"Berestechko,"** the Cossack appreciation for song is followed, subsequently, by more music—this time the sound of war:

> From behind a burial stone an old fellow with a bandore crept forth and, plucking the strings, sang to us in a childish treble of the ancient glory of the Cossacks. We listened to his songs in silence; then unfurled the standards and burst into Berestechko to the sounds of a thundering march.

(118-19)

The passage, in effect, is peculiarly emblematic both of **Red Cavalry,** as a striking encapsulation of its principal themes, and of the present topic. For here the merging of art, history, and (potential) violence is manifested in a way that is undeniably and inexplicably human. But if violence is itself human, a fact that Babel so ably shows and cannot subsequently deny, then art is, perhaps, what unites us in our otherwise disparate humanity.

Notes

1. Isaac Babel, *The Collected Stories* (New York, 1955) 43. All translated references to *Red Cavalry* are from this collection, and will be subsequently noted in the text. The original is found in I. Babel', *Sochineniia,* vol. II (Moscow 1992).

2. Consider, for example, "The Letter" (Письмо), which includes one of the most extraordinary exchanges reported in *Red Cavalry,* as the brother Simon converses with his father just prior to the latter's execution at his own son's behest.

3. For an extended discussion of this characteristic lyricism, in a companion study to the present essay, see David K. Danow, "A Poetics of Inversion: The Non-Dialogic Aspect in Isaac Babel's *Red Cavalry,*" *Modern Language Review* 86 (October 1991): 939-53.

4. Babel later added "Argamak" as the final story.

Yuri K. Shcheglov (essay date fall 1994)

SOURCE: Shcheglov, Yuri K. "Some Themes and Archetypes in Babel's *Red Cavalry.*" *Slavic Review* 53, no. 3 (fall 1994): 653-70.

[*In the following essay, Shcheglov examines the plot, symbolism, and major themes of "My First Goose," focusing on the "archetypal patterns," the "literary motifs of ancient, ritualistic, and mythological origin which serve as a kind of concealed amplifier enhancing the paradigmatic effect of the story's events."*]

It is an established fact that the so-called "Southern" (mainly Odessa-based) school of writers enriched Soviet literature of the 1920s with a number of "European" dimensions neglected by the then dominant Russian realist tradition, such as (to name but a few) intertextuality, a focus on language and style, and a sharpened sensitivity to plot and composition. It can be said that in Babel' criticism some of these aspects are just beginning to receive the full measure of attention that they merit. However, the rich fabric of Russian and western cultural subtexts in Babel''s prose and its intricate relationships with various literary and mythological prototypes remain largely unexplored. Among recent studies that begin to fill this gap, the forthcoming monograph in Russian by Yampolsky and Zholkovsky deserves special mention as one of the most comprehensive to date.

The diversity of functions of archetypal and literary motifs utilized by different members of the "Southern" school is readily apparent. While some of them (like Il'f and Petrov) made ample and ostensible use of such elements to parody and debunk traditional "literariness," others (like Valentin Kataev) imbued them with marxist content in endeavors to create Soviet action prose à la Stevenson or Mark Twain; still others (such as Babel' and Olesha) used mythological and literary sources subtly, unobtrusively and highly selectively, building up subliminal support for their philosophical messages, thematic idiosyncrasies or personal myths. It is this last case that I will demonstrate with regard to one of the most popular stories of Babel's **Konarmiia** (**Red Cavalry**), **"My First Goose."** First, however, a brief reminder of some relevant elements of Babel''s thematic core is in order.

One can argue that the narrator of **Red Cavalry,** Kirill Vasil'evich Liutov, is not endowed with the same unique and "dense" individuality as are the other characters in the book, even those who are minor and episodical. Much of the time he appears as a more or less formal figure, subject to various elements of authorial voice and outlook. In this Liutov resembles those nominal narrators who are not given a voice noticeably distinct from the author's. We tend to be oblivious of their mediatorial presence, let alone of their names and occupations: who remembers such characters of Russian fiction as Anton Lavrent'evich (*The Possessed*) or Colonel I.L.P. ("The Shot")? Only occasionally does Liutov thicken from a purely functional figure into a semblance of a hero in his own right. Then we begin to see that, although he may not possess a character so colorful or sharply etched as most heroes of **Red Cavalry,** he at least has a *problem* that isolates him from the Cossacks at the same time as it affiliates him with another family of heroes—the troubled Soviet intellectuals of the revolutionary era, such as Olesha's Nikolai Kavalerov. As we know, these characters' feelings with respect to the revolution are irreconcilably split between the desire to play an active role in the creation of a new world and the inability to part with the humanitarian and cultural "superstitions" that they have inherited from the past.

In Liutov's case this dilemma is complicated by his ethnic and cultural background. As critics point out, the narrator of **Red Cavalry** "is caught between these groups as he tries to define his position in relation to the humanist tradition of his Jewish heritage and the new values of the Revolution."[1] As Markish aptly has remarked, while Liutov must not be identified with the author, he is one of the author's halves—the Jewish one, "desperately wishing to join the other, revolutionary, Bolshevik one, but without losing the former." According to Markish, Liutov's desire to reconcile tradition and revolution is cerebral and coexists with an estranged and distant view of both. Heritage and novelty are "accepted and rejected simultaneously." The narrator depicts old-style Jewry with the cold preciseness of an aesthete, "often balancing on the brink of active hostility." Nor is he particularly sympathetic towards his bolshevik comrades, who often evoke in him "fear and bewilderment." It is this double allegiance combined with "a position of consistent and uncompromising nonconformism" that ensures a sharp and unbiased view of both sides that constitutes, for Markish, the main strength of **Red Cavalry,** which "was to be Babel''s greatest success, precisely because in no other work did he lean on both of his supports with such confidence and force."[2]

A somewhat different view of Babel''s/Liutov's duality figures in Lionel Trilling's introduction to the English translation of Babel''s works. Even though this critic has failed to discriminate between the author and his hero and rather incautiously quoted Babel''s stories about his allegedly unhappy and humiliated Odessa childhood as a reliable biographical source, the psychological invariants he sees in Babel' are quite relevant. One of Babel''s most persistent motivations, in Trilling's view, was his desire to be "submitted to a test, to be initiated."[3] Detached from the realities of life and painfully conscious of his own fragility and weakness ("spectacles on his nose and autumn in his heart"), Babel''s hero is fascinated by a world imbued with strength, boldness, passion, "sensual freedom," "conscienceless self-assertion," "animal grace," "simplicity," "directness," etc. To partake of this ideal mode of living (whether in Budennyi's Red Cavalry or in the world of old Odessa gangsters), Babel''s hero has to learn violence, to prove to himself and others his ability to commit violent acts, since they are inseparable from the "genuine life" that he craves. However, violence does not come easily to him; the other half of his being is attracted by a wholly different ideal of "realness," whose features—spirituality, compassion, sacrificial humility, "the denial of the pride of the glory of the flesh"—are embodied in such figures as the delicate little sage, Gedali, or the pathetic and helpless Christ in the fresco by Pan Apolek (**"In St. Valentine's Church"**). Concluded Trilling, "The opposition of these two images made his art—but it was not a dialectic that his Russia could permit."[4]

In discussing the ingredients of Babel''s involvement with the revolution, we must not forget *curiosity,* which the writer's biographers and acquaintances unanimously point to as the most salient personal feature of Babel', the "main moving force" of his life.[5] At times Babel''s curiosity is difficult to distinguish from his trademark as seen by Trilling, the "necessity of submitting to [a] test." Falen correctly has pointed out this thirst for experience: "For Babel' the key to both life and art is immersion in experience . . . **Red Cavalry** reflects his continuing desire to subject the individualism and self-absorption of the middle-class intellectual to the test of living . . . Almost all of the reminiscences . . . emphasize his insatiable curiosity about life in the raw."[6] Similarly, Carden has merged the two motivations together by explaining Babel''s enlistment in the army as his "curiosity and desire to experience everything from which he had been excluded by the circumstances of his upbringing."[7] However, there need not be a link between the writer's curiosity and his presumed inferiority complex, his need of self-testing, etc. It appears from memoirs about Babel' that he was as interested in watching and listening as he was in being directly involved in life, and that he appreciated conversations with talkative old women and housekeepers no less avidly than the company of romantic heroes like Betal Kalmykov.[8] Obviously, curiosity was an integral part of that wise joie de vivre which, according to the painter Valentina Khodasevich, made Babel' "an adornment of life for anyone who was lucky enough to know him."[9]

The willingness of a curious Babel' to penetrate forbidden and dangerous zones of life is amply illustrated by biographical data—from his early years when the future author of *Odessa Stories* took up his quarters at the center of Moldavanka, the district of mob hangouts,[10] to his last years, when he played with fire visiting the "militiamen," as he conspiratorially called the entourage of the chief of the secret police Ezhov, in order, in his words, "to sniff out what is brewing."[11]

It is not irrelevant for this analysis to know to what extent Babel''s curiosity is reflected in his heroes, specifically Liutov. Since Liutov is not defined with any finality and assumes various faculties and features of his creator (such as the knowledge of French in **"Berestechko"**), it would not be unreasonable to credit him with some degree of curiosity as well. And we find it in **"Italian Sunshine"**: the moment that his roommate, the anarchist Sidorov, leaves the room, Liutov hurries to his desk, with trembling hands turns the pages of his books, avidly reads another man's letter . . . It is probably also curiosity that impels Liutov to wander through the curved streets of old Berestechko, peering at the unprepossessing remains of local antiquity and picking up century-old letters, rather than to attend a propaganda meeting organized by his Red Cavalry comrades. Would it not also be natural to assume some of Babel''s curiosity in the intellectual Liutov, if it can be observed even in some of the Cossacks, who explain their violence by a passion for experimentation: "You see, I want to get to know what life really is, what life's like down our way" (**"The Life of Pavlichenko"**)?

Although this article is not the place for a full synopsis of the definitions proposed by Babel' scholars regarding his real-life and literary persona or the main themes of his work, it can be said by way of summing up that Babel''s prose is seen by most critics as highly ambivalent with respect to all values, including the revolution and other manifestations of "raw," elemental life. On the one hand, attraction alternates or mingles with revulsion, the admiration for the revolution's force and genuineness is mixed with horror at its cruelty and dirt. On the other, Liutov's desire to be admitted to the epicenter of this "genuine life" as a spontaneous and equal participant blends with the pathos of an explorer and experimenter, moved by sheer intellectual curiosity and preserving the attitude of a detached viewer even in the midst of turbulent events.

Babel''s **"My First Goose"** displays this ambivalence with exemplary clarity. It is a story of a desire and its fulfillment, enclosed between those two fundamental emotions of the Soviet intellectual of the 1920s, envy and remorse. *Zavist'*, "envy" (towards the new masters of life) and *sovest'*, "conscience" (its pangs) mark the initial and final points of the plot. No less symptomatic is the chain of events connecting them—the hero's mim-

icry and oppression of kindred human beings in order to get close to those in power, to be invited to their meal. As Carden justly has pointed out, the *bespectacled* old woman whom Liutov pushes in the chest is a creature of the same species as himself, who calls for his sympathy but is rejected because he wants to please the Cossacks.[12] (This old woman has a somewhat different kinship at another level of the story, as I shall try to show later.)

"My First Goose" is a paradigmatic text in more ways than one. Liutov's two encounters—first with the dazzling Savitskii and then with the ruthless and hostile warriors by the fire—illustrate the insoluble duality not only of the hero but of the new reality itself in which there are two inseparable and constantly overlapping facets that can roughly be called "romantic" and "barbaric." This is a dilemma confronted by many heroes of early Soviet fiction who are spontaneously drawn to the revolution yet are dismayed by the discrepancy between the realm of its enthusiastic theorists, poets and visionaries; and that of barbarians, fanatics, dullards or bureaucrats who violently and thoughtlessly translate exciting ideals into disappointing realities. This theme has a wide spectrum of variations in the Soviet fiction dealing with the revolution and its aftermath, socialism; apart from **"My First Goose,"** we recognize it in Olesha's *Envy* in which Kavalerov may secretly desire to join the charismatic Andrei Babichev but is repelled by the narrow-minded brutality of his disciple, Volodia Makarov. This duality of the revolution is famously presented in Sholokhov's *Quiet Flows the Don,* as well as in Pasternak's *Doctor Zhivago,* in the novels of Il'f and Petrov[13] and in other major works of Soviet fiction.

I shall not discuss in detail how this duality of the new world and the ambiguous stance of the *Red Cavalry* narrator translate into the complex imagery and plot of **"My First Goose"** (these more explicit layers of the story's structure have been rather extensively studied). Instead, I shall dwell upon just one or two points which may have some relevance for my immediate topic.

Reading the story in a sound realistic key (that is, temporarily leaving aside its rich literary and archetypal subtext), one cannot fail to notice that the narrator deliberately treats his hosts to a rather coarse, slapstick show. The theatricality of his performance is manifest from the sheer redundancy of the sword that Liutov picks up from the ground to no apparent use, as well as from the exaggerated belligerence of his gesticulation and speech, rather comic in a little, bespectacled civilian addressing an old woman, yet accepted at face value by his viewers.[14] Liutov's mimicry and calculated simulation as a means of recognition distinguishes him rather sharply from the majority of the intelligentsia heroes of early Soviet fiction, both those who are locked in a love-hate relationship with the revolution and those who just hate it but feign loyalty for survival. Suffice it to compare Liutov with Olesha's Kavalerov, whose behavior in a similar context, whether demanding admission to the Soviet aviation parade or showering venomous philippics upon his nemesis, Andrei Babichev, is always passionate and straightforward. Liutov's vacillation between his readiness to exploit the simplicity of the Red Cavalry heroes, to gain their favors by cunning, on the one hand, and his secret envy for the "flower and iron of their youth," on the other, is a more complex stance. It reminds us not so much of the dismayed intellectuals of a Kavalerov type as of the wise, thoroughly experienced Ostap Bender of the last part of *The Golden Calf,* who, when confronted with the army of enthusiastic builders of the great Turksib railway, is not sure which he desires more, to continue playing his picaresque tricks and manipulating their still rather simple souls for his personal gain, or to lay down his arms and tearfully beg for admission into their happy community.

Another curious detail in the surface plot of **"My First Goose"** is the role played by Lenin's name and text as a form of lingua franca which functions as the final mediator between Liutov and the Cossacks after they have been sufficiently "mollified" by his cavalier treatment of the landlady. In early Soviet mythology the name "Lenin" tends to figure as a password that overcomes distances and class/race barriers (e.g. in Vsevolod Ivanov's *Armored Train 14-69* where the partisans intone the word "Lenin" to get their message across to their American prisoner; in Nikolai Tikhonov's poem, "Sami," etc.). As many other details of the story, this one has an obvious realistic motivation, since Lenin's persona embraced the contrasting halves of the revolution, both theory and practice, and appealed to individuals otherwise divided, educated fellow travelers and brutal bolshevik warriors.[15] At the same time, serving as a kind of magic "sesame," the name preserves a subdued aura of mystique that agrees well with the mythologizing, ritualistic and fairy-tale-like connotations of the story.

Although more could be said about the plot, symbolism and other aspects of **"My First Goose,"** I shall now focus on my main topic, its *archetypal* patterns, that is, literary motifs of ancient, ritualistic and mythological origin which serve as a kind of concealed amplifier enhancing the paradigmatic effect of the story's events. The narrator's ambivalent attitude to the Red Cavalry warriors obviously influenced the selection of these archetypes, which fall into two categories. For that part of the narrator's soul which craves to be tested and accepted into the Cossack brotherhood, the appropriate archetypal counterpart is *Initiation* with its various ritualistic concomitants. The word "initiation" has been used previously in Babel' criticism (by Trilling, Andrew and others), but in a more figurative than terminological sense, that is, without sufficient awareness of those features in **Red Cavalry** which actually reflect the tradi-

tional ordeals that adolescents had to undergo to become full-fledged members of their society.

For the other half of his hero's persona, which responds to the revolution with a mixture of intellectual curiosity, estrangement, fear, revulsion and mimicry, Babel' drew not so much on ritualistic sources as on legendary and literary ones; more specifically, on motifs that have to do with *Visiting the Otherworld.* This is a well known topos whose protagonist is an individualist, an outsider who undertakes a journey to forbidden regions to obtain something for himself—an object, a human being, a benefit, a piece of arcane wisdom, etc. To achieve his objective, the hero may have to play the games of the inhabitants of the otherworld, to spy out their secrets, to use stratagems, to cheat and to flee for his life.

Since the initiation rites also imply a journey to the country of the dead, some degree of overlap between the two sets of archetypal motifs is to be expected. However, each of the two groups includes some motifs that are distinctly its own, i.e., either initiatory or demonic par excellence. More importantly, even identical motifs may acquire different overtones depending on which set is activated: with *Initiation* the stress is likely to be on the hero's desire to be assimilated, to submit to ordeals, to fraternize with his new companions and to obey his seniors; while *Visiting the Otherworld* will highlight the dangers and risks of the enterprise, that realm's basic viciousness and hostility to man, and the hero's independence.

To identify initiatory and otherworldly patterns in Babel''s story, I will draw relevant parallels from artistic and literary works rather than from actual myths and rituals, focusing on those texts in which these motifs either appear in their original form or are adapted ("displaced") in more or less recurrent and familiar ways. For *Visiting the Otherworld,* the list of exemplary works, rather predictably headed by Dante's *Divine Comedy* and Gogol's "The Lost Letter," will include such Russian Romantic stories as Karamzin's "The Isle of Bornholm" and Lermontov's "Taman'." Besides sharing with **"My First Goose"** several collateral details of plot and description, these two narratives resemble Babel''s story in that each features a curious intruder who tries to explore an alien, closed world but who finds it difficult to gain access to it and to establish a common language with its inhabitants. *Initiation* is exemplified by a Spanish picaresque novel and some modern American short stories. Besides these "model" texts, I will also consider several other works of art and fiction and, occasionally, some "raw" anthropological data. Needless to say, this miniature anthology of parallels to **"My First Goose"** is open and can be expanded by additional illustrations from world literature, art and mythology.

After these somewhat prolonged preliminaries, let me recapitulate the motifs in **"My First Goose"** that can be related to one or both archetype clusters:

1) *Sunset.* The sun is setting as the narrator of **"My First Goose"** is led to the lodging of the Cossacks: "The dying sun . . . was giving up its roseate ghost to the skies." In the romantic tradition twilight and the evening landscape constitute a borderline chronotope in which the otherworldly is at its closest to the terrestrial. Whenever a hero ventures into a domain of dark forces, the transition usually takes place in the ambiguous light of the setting sun, at that disturbing and nostalgic hour when the friendly luminary is quickly departing the scene, leaving man alone and helpless in the face of the mysterious forces of the night. The prototype of all such scenes may well be the opening passage of Dante's *Inferno*: "Guardai in alto e vidi le sue spalle / vestite già de' raggi del planeta / che mena dritto altrui per ogni calle" (I.16-18) and "Lo giorno se n'andava, e l'aere bruno / toglieva li animai che sono in terra / da le fatiche loro . . ." (II.1-3). Abundant illustrations are provided by romanticism and the gothic genres. In Gogol's "Vii" the wanderers arrive at the sinister wayside farm when "the sky was already quite dark, and only a red gleam lingered on the western horizon."[16] In "The Lost Letter" "the sun had set; here and there streaks of red glowed in the sky . . . The farther they went, the darker it grew";[17] in "St. John's Eve" "the sun was gone. There was only a streak of red on one side of the sky. And that, too, was fading. It turned colder";[18] in "A Bewitched Place" "the sun had begun to set."[19] In Radcliffe's *The Mysteries of Udolpho* the macabre castle that the heroine is approaching is "lighted up by the setting sun" and "as she gazed, the light died away on its walls" (II.5). In Lüdwig Tieck's tale "The Blond Ekbert" the traveler meets a mysterious old woman in the dusk and accompanies her to her hut as night falls; a similar evening encounter with an otherworldly stranger occurs in his "Runenberg." A picture of twilight—the last rays of light on the snowy summits, darkness and cold gradually descending on the mountainous landscape—unfolds in Bram Stoker's *Dracula* as the hero nears his destination, the fateful castle, in a coach (chap. 1). The demonic visitor in Bulgakov's *The Master and Margarita* enters Moscow "at the hour of an incredibly hot sunset" when "the windowpanes dazzlingly reflected the fragmented sun that was departing from Mikhail Alexandrovich forever" (chap. 1). Lermontov's "Taman'" slightly deviates from the stereotype in that the narrator drives up to his new lodging late at night by moonlight. On the whole, however, the constancy of the motif is so obvious that no further examples need be cited.

2) *The frightened guide.* Babel''s narrator is led to the Cossacks' camp by the quartermaster. He warns Liutov of the danger and hints at a possible way of averting it: "Nuisance with specs. Can't do anything to stop it, ei-ther. Not a life for the brainy type here. But you go and mess up a lady, and a good lady too, and you'll have the boys patting you on the back." Having introduced the novice to the Cossacks, "the quartermaster, purple in the face, left us without looking back." Narratives with "infernal" overtones often include guides who conduct the heroes to the border of the other world but refuse to accompany them further, sometimes with signs of superstitious fear: "My guide, afraid of he knew not what, implored me to return to the village . . . I looked back, but the boy, my guide, had disappeared" ("The Isle of Bornholm"). "Here our ways must part," says the mysterious companion who has led Christian to the foot of the mountain towards which the latter is attracted by a mysterious force (Tieck, "Runenberg"). An inferno metaphor and the figure of a guide deserting his protégés can be found in *Dead Souls*: meandering through the rooms of government offices, Chichikov and Manilov are helped by a civil servant ironically compared to Virgil: "He took them to the president's office, in which . . . sat the president in solitary majesty, like the sun. In this place the new Virgil was so overawed that he did not venture to set his foot in it, but turned back, displaying his back worn as threadbare as a bit of matting and with a hen's feather sticking to it" (chap. 7).

Such moments as the hero's parting with the normal world, abandoning the warmth and security of human company, are quite often highlighted, as are actions that block the hero's way back to safety. Sometimes, as in Babel''s story, the guide literally hands over his charge to his new, ghostly hosts. The vehicle departs from the scene and the newcomer is left alone with his belongings whose bulk, impeding his mobility, ties him to the place. In Stoker's novel the coach driver unloads the passenger's luggage as the carriage sent for him from the castle arrives (cf. "The quartermaster . . . set my little trunk down on the ground"), then hurriedly leaves; the young man "felt a strange chill, and a lonely feeling came over me" (*Dracula,* chap. 1). Pechorin tells his orderly to "unload the trunk and let the cabby go" ("Taman'"). The goat who has brought Ruprecht to the Sabbath "descended low, almost to the earth, and, riding me right up to the crowd, he suddenly tipped me off to the ground . . . and disappeared" (Valerii Briusov, *The Fiery Angel,* chap. 2).

Warnings and advice can come from the guide or other persons whom the traveler meets before embarking on his journey. "We don't go there, and God knows what is going on there," says the boy in "The Isle of Bornholm." "There is one other place, sir, but you wouldn't fancy it. Unwholesome, it is" ("Taman'"). In *Dracula* it is the frightened looks of the peasants and the passengers in the coach that serve as a warning to Harker of the sinister nature of his destination. In Gogol's "The Lost Letter" the grandfather receives his itinerary to hell from the innkeeper, who, "saying this . . . went off to his corner and would not say another word."[20] Cf. "the quartermaster, purple in the face, left us without looking back."

3) *The inhospitable people by the fire.* In the yard where Liutov is left by the quartermaster "the Cossacks were sitting, shaving one another." Supper is being prepared near by: "Near the hut, on a brick stove, stood a cauldron in which pork was cooking. The steam that rose from it was like the far-off smoke of home in the village." The next time that we see them the Cossacks are "already sitting around their cauldron . . . motionless, stiff as priests." Figures seated around the fire remind us of Goethe's *Faust* where participants of the Walpurgisnacht sit by numerous fires (Mephistopheles to Faust: "Einhundert Feuer brennen in der Reihe . . . Komm nur! von Feuer gehen wir zu Feuer . . .") and of "The Lost Letter": "Only now [Grandad] saw that there were people sitting around a fire . . ." The Cossacks' less than friendly response to Liutov's military salute is close to the gogolian scene in that in neither case do the hosts deign to look at the novice, let alone speak with him:[21]

> So Grandad tossed off a low bow, saying: 'God help you, good people!' No one nodded his head; they all sat in silence and kept dropping something into the fire . . . No one of them glanced at him . . . To this speech, too, there was not a word. But one of the pig-faces thrust a hot brand straight into Grandad's face . . .[22]

Such unanimous, as if by agreement, failure to notice a newcomer may originate either from the hostility and disgust that the dead are known to feel for the living[23] or from the ritualistic notion that the novice is still "unborn" and therefore "invisible" until he is initiated. The latter explanation seems to be more applicable to "The Fourth Day Out from Santa Cruz" by Paul Bowles, a story with no noticeable infernal overtones (see below, 7), while **"My First Goose,"** with its double set of background archetypes, is open to both kinds of associations (see below, 9).

4) *Harassment.* Disregarding Liutov's advances, the Cossacks keep harassing him, throw out his little trunk and tread on his feet. Treating novices in this manner is a familiar fact of army and school life, where the infamous customs of "zuck" and "grandfatherism" (hazing) most probably go back to the ritual harassment and torture that are known from studies on initiation. Typical of all such scenes are disparaging remarks about the novice's hothouse upbringing, in which the tutors or elders often take the lead: "A new one! From the town! Mommy's son!" or "A little nobleman! Brought up on candies!" (Nikolai Pomialovskii, *Sketches from the Seminary*; Ivan Kushchevskii, *Nikolai Negorev*). Savitskii's taunt "You are one of those kinderbalsams"

clearly continues the same tradition. Mocking references to the novice's home and the upbringing he has received there reflect one of the central notions of initiation, a young man's "passing from his mother and the women-folk into the society of the warriors of his tribe."[24] It is therefore no accident that harassment and *derisory references* to the youngster's home are often complemented by another expression of the same archetypal idea, the novice's *longing* for his home. We find this *Heimweh* motif immediately following the mockery in both Russian seminary tales quoted above, as well as in **"My First Goose"**: "The steam that rose from [the pork] was like the far-off smoke of home in the village, and it mingled hunger with desperate loneliness in my head."

5) *Indecent gestures and sounds.* Harassments that the hero has to endure are manifold. In Grimmelshausen's *Simplizissimus* the novice suffers from hunger and is subjected to distasteful practical jokes, when his new companions contrive to make him smell malodorous emissions of their bowels (I.28). This leads us to the gestures of the young Cossack in Babel''s story: "He turned his back on me and with remarkable skill emitted a series of shameful noises." The devil's delight in impudent behavior, such as showing his backside, offering it for kisses, etc., is well known.[25] In one of Hieronimus Bosch's paintings a beautiful woman looks at her mirror reflection in the devil's behind. In Briusov's *The Fiery Angel* a newcomer at the Sabbath is required to kiss the devil's backside, "black and emitting a nauseating odor, but yet strangely reminiscent of a human face" (chap. 2). Such acts, in which the hind quarters perform functions normally reserved for the face, are easily explained in terms of "invertedness," another well known characteristic of the underworld.[26] The "backside = face" equation is implied in Nabokov's commentary on Chichikov, whose figure, following Merezhkovskii, he interprets in demonic terms: "Chichikov . . . ecstatically hitting his chubby behind—*his real face*—with the pink heel of his bare foot"[27] (my emphasis). This paradigmatic exchange of roles between face and backside in demonic behavior is evoked in Babel's story by their conspicuous syntagmatic juxtaposition: "A lad with a beautiful Ryazan *face*. . . . turned his *back* on me," etc.

The blond Cossack's pranks recall to us the memorable demon in Dante who "made a trumpet out of his behind" ("ed egli avea del cul fatto trombetta"; *Inferno* XXI.139). This line from Dante serves as an associative link between the behavior of the young Cossack (which, let it be noted in passing, is also described metaphorically, although with a different instrument as vehicle: "To your guns—number double-zero . . . , running fire") and yet another type of activity frequently attributed to demonic creatures: those rather widespread scenes in art and literature where demons use the body (their own, other people's, animals') and its various parts to perform music. Satan's music is body music par excellence. Gogol''s musicians in hell "beat on their cheeks with their fists as if they were tambourines, and whistled with their noses as if they were horns."[28] In Grimmelshausen's novel the devils "trumpeted with their noses till the whole wood resounded therewith"; other musicians at the sabbath play on adders, cats, bitches, horses' skulls, etc. (*Simplizissimus* II.17). A contemporary caricature of Luther presents his body as a bagpipe played by Satan; his nose has the shape of a flute. The Walpurgisnacht musicians mentioned in Goethe's *Faust*—crickets and frogs—presumably use their own bodies as instruments. Some Bosch paintings feature a monster playing its own long nose as a trumpet ("The Hay-cart") and devils blowing into sinners' bodies as if they were wind instruments ("The Garden of Earthly Delights"); one of these sinners has a trumpet sticking from his anus. The elegance of those scenes in which the hind quarters rather than nose, lips or other parts do the job of wind instruments, is in their combination of two otherwise independent demonic features— "music performed on the body" and the previously mentioned "backside-face" inversion.

6) *The hero bespattered with faeces.* The meaning of the young Cossack's motions can be understood in light of yet another series of motifs, also related to the otherworld but this time from a primarily initiatory angle. Some of Liutov's ordeals are prefigured in the picaresque novel "The Story of a Rogue Called Don Pablos" by Francisco de Quevedo, a classic of Spanish baroque. The novel abounds in scenes more or less obviously related to the rites of initiation, including various forms of metaphorical death and rebirth. In chapter 5, as Pablos enrolls in a university, a crowd of fellow students for no visible reason subjects him to a series of cruel jokes. Exclaiming, "This Lazarus must be ready for raising from the dead judging by the way he smells," these new companions surround Pablos and assiduously spit and blow their noses all over him, so that in the end "I was snow-white from head to foot" with saliva and mucus.[29] This procedure is followed by an even more nauseating one: "That crowd of devils let out such a shout that it made me dizzy, and I, to judge from the way they had emptied their stomachs all over me, decided they must use new students as a form of purge to save going to the doctor or druggist." Taking flight, the hero is pursued and kicked by everyone he encounters on his way home. But this is not the end of his calvary: when he returns home the servants, feigning friendly concern, defecate into his bed at night. Significantly, when these ritualistic tortures are over, peace and harmony sets in between the hero and his tormentors: "We all became friends and from then on all of us in the house lived together like brothers, and neither in class nor on the campus did anyone trouble me again."

Excrement, defecation and urination often figure in initiation rituals and are not uncommon as attributes of the lower world, presumably symbolizing death and decomposition. In some versions of Russian tales Baba Iaga has a "shit leg" (*govnianaia noga*) instead of her proverbial "bone leg." In some initiatory traditions neophytes were subjected to loathsome procedures: "they had to drink the urine of their mentor, etc. They were put into a pit filled with excrement and water, bespattered with animals' faeces . . . They had to endure and overcome disgust as well as pain."[30]

7) *"When in Rome, do as the Romans do." Slaughtering birds and animals.* Having endured these trials and fraternized with the students and servants, Pablos decides that he must stick to the same norms of behavior as those around him. In fulfillment of this plan, "I resolved to become a rogue among rogues and to better them if possible . . . First of all I passed a death sentence on all the pigs that wandered into the house, and on all the housekeeper's chickens who strayed from their coop into my room" (chap. 6). We see that both in Quevedo's novel and in Babel''s story the novice's harassment with nauseating body emissions is followed by his hunt after domestic animals and fowl. It is known that in some tribes initiatory tests included killing an enemy, a successful hunt, rapine or cattle stealing, acts "assimilating the members of the warrior band to carnivora." In Sparta an adolescent was sent away to live for a whole year on what he could steal.[31] If the killing of geese, chickens and pigs by Pablos and Liutov can indeed be regarded as a reflection of these ancient customs, Babel''s hero appears to be even closer to the ritualistic prototype than Quevedo's picaro, the goose-killing in the former taking place as part of the test itself, rather than after its successful conclusion, as in the latter.

Several parallels with **"My First Goose"** in "The Fourth Day Out from Santa Cruz" by Paul Bowles are particularly valuable since there are no visible traces of Babel''s direct influence on the American author. The story is placed in the "Initiation" section of Evans and Finestone's anthology of literary archetypes.

> Members of the ship's crew refuse to speak with the new scullery boy Ramon, do not invite him to their meals, give no sign of recognition when he meets them in the port, in short, "behave as if he did not exist." He decides to change this state of affairs at any cost. One day in the open sea he sees a group of sailors at the stern amusing themselves with the plight of a bird flying after the boat. The exhausted bird desperately wants to land on the deck but is afraid of the people. The sailors make bets on whether the bird will make it or perish. "Ramon's first thought was to tell the men to step back a little from the rail so that the bird might have the courage to land," but then he thinks better of it, considering the ridicule that would have been directed at him for such sentimentality. He runs to the

galley, brings the ship's cat and shows him the bird. The animal lies in wait for the bird and leaps at it as it tries to land; the men watch with fascination; seeing the futility of its efforts, the bird stops flying and falls to the sea. The sailors pay their bets; one of them brings from his cabin a bottle of cognac and fills glasses, offering one of them to Ramon: "Have some?"

The killing of a domestic animal takes place in Richard Wright's story "The Man Who Was Almost a Man," which Evans and Finestone also classify as initiatory. The young hero secretly buys a gun and, while trying to shoot, unintentionally kills a horse. When the adults tell him he will have to work two years to compensate the horse's owner, he jumps on a cargo train to flee "away, away to somewhere, somewhere where he could be a man . . ." These parallels support the view that Liutov's actions regarding the goose and the landlady have initiatory overtones and provide a ritualistic motivation for his theatrically exaggerated gestures, in addition to his "realistic" mimicry and desire to impress his none too sophisticated hosts.[32]

8) *The blind old woman with a bird.* Blindness is one of the best known features of Baba Iaga, the guardian of the realm of the dead.[33] More generally, blindness in one or both eyes is a frequent characteristic of various types of otherworld and borderline creatures.[34] One such figure is the blind boy in "Taman'," about whom Pechorin—not without reason, considering the sinister nature of the place—remarks, "I confess I am strongly prejudiced against the blind, one-eyed, deaf, dumb, legless, armless, hunch-backed and so on." On the other hand, the "diffused whites of her purblind eyes" that the woman raises to Liutov evoke both initiation and the realm of the dead since "white [in which some tribes paint neophites, rubbing it, among other parts, over the eyes] is the color of death and invisibility." Other facets of initiation may also apply, such as the neophyte demanding and eating Iaga's food in many folktales and rites.[35] As "hostess" of the otherworld (note Babel''s use of the terminological *khoziaika*), Iaga presides over the animal kingdom; wise or prophetic birds quite often accompany demonic female figures in literature and folklore. In Tieck's "The Blond Ekbert" the heroine runs away from such a woman, stealing and eventually killing her bird, which later reappears as the symbol of her guilty conscience (the killing of a bird is generally considered a crime that brings disaster and requires expiation—see *The Ancient Mariner*). The standard features of Iaga's residence in Russian folklore are a hut, a yard, a fence, a gate—all of which are present in Babel''s story. Another intriguing attribute of the old woman in the latter is spinning ("I . . . went out to the landlady who was spinning on the porch"), a detail rich in mythological connotations, including otherworldly ones: "Yarn and spinning are often associated with the hostess of the lower world."[36]

9) *Ceremony.* "They sat motionless, stiff as heathen priests, and did not look at the goose." This comparison of the Cossacks to priests overtly points to the ritualistic nature of the entire proceeding and has been noticed by commentators.[37] Ceremonial overtones of the Cossacks' behavior are no less obvious in their *not looking* at the goose (or at Liutov), despite the fact that the hero has already accomplished his anti-feat and aroused their sympathetic attention. Why not look? Probably because at this point it is still too *early* to look. Had the Cossacks been overtly watching and discussing Liutov's manipulations with the bird, their conduct would have been little more than just natural and "realistic." However, their actions, as well as Liutov's, have an archetypal facet that imposes a certain amount of ceremony; recognition does not come spontaneously and at once but unfolds in discrete stages following each other in a fixed order. Up to a certain point the warriors "do not see" the novice; after his successful endurance of trials, they will of course begin "to see" him, but not before some final formalities—such as a verbal statement—are performed ("The lad's all right . . . Hey, brother, come down and feed with us . . .").

Having passed the test, the hero reads the newspaper "loudly, like a triumphant man hard of hearing," i.e., he adopts the ceremonious manner of his new comrades, participating with them in the celebration of his transition to a new status. Not only ritualistically solemn, Liutov's metaphorical deafness is yet another hint at his temporary association with the realm of death, whose inhabitants and visitors are prone to sensory deficiencies.[38]

10) *Safe conduct.* In light of the previously mentioned motifs, it is possible to discern an archetypal aspect in Liutov's encounter with divisional commander Savitskii, who has been characterized at the "realistic" level as personifying the attractive, "romantic" facet of the revolution. A hero embarking on a journey to the otherworld can obtain a permission and a safe conduct from some supreme authority to whom those dangerous realms are subordinated. Thus, Dante and his guide often have to explain to the demons and other guardians of the lower world that their peregrination is authorized in the spheres "where they can what they want" ("Vuolsi cosí colà dove si puote / Ciò che si vuole, e piú non dimandare"; *Inferno* III.94-95). As a result of this warning, the devils and monsters, while doing their best to intimidate and hamper the strangers, stop well short of causing them direct physical harm. Something very similar occurs in **"My First Goose"**: the Cossacks throw out the visitor's trunk as a substitute for the man, but do not actually touch its owner, protected by the quartermaster's announcement that "Comrade Savitskii's orders are that you're to take this chap in your billets, so no nonsense about it." The story's prologue is largely designed to create around Savitskii the aura

of a powerful lord presiding over hosts of obedient subjects. This purpose is well served by the grandiose metaphors describing Savitskii's appearance as well as by his thunderous letter to the lesser commander, Ivan Chesnokov.

Besides the two motif clusters outlined above, I would like to point out another possible subtext of Babel''s story that stands in a different relation to it: not an archetypal "amplifier" of its events and images, but a contrasting version, outlining an alternative course of action under identical circumstances.

Maksim Gor'kii's forgotten story "On the Salt" ("Na soli") was published in "The Samara Newspaper" in 1895 and never reprinted until 1968.[39] It is possible, but not necessary, to conjecture that Gor'kii might have shown or told the story to Babel' at an early stage of their acquaintance. Comparing texts with a different treatment of similar themes or plots can make sense regardless of whether their authors were aware of each other's work, engaged in conscious dialogues or polemics, etc., for the stock of recurrent themes, *fabulas*, character types and other ready-made artistic paradigms that "exist" in the anonymous unwritten vocabulary of literature is far greater than it may appear. We should always be ready to allow for the possibility of their unrelated use and even independent generation by various writers.[40]

Gor'kii's hero and first-person narrator comes to look for a job to the salt mines of which he had heard horror stories as a place of back-breaking, unrewarding labor. The assortment of hoboes and jailbirds who work there meet the hero with hostility, shower him with insults and threats, tease him for his spectacles ("Hello, Glass-eyes!"), mockingly deny him access to the common meal ("With us, Maksims are not admitted to the kettle on the first day of work. With us, Maksims eat their own grub on the first day . . . Get the hell out of here!") and subject him to cruel jokes. In his despair the hero addresses them with an angry speech, calling on their conscience and declaring that "I am a human being just like them, that I too want to eat and must work, that I came to them as my equals:—We are all in the same boat,—I said to them,—and must understand each other . . ." In response the workers give him a handful of pennies and ask him to leave, saying he does not belong here. "Nothing will come out of it between you and us . . . Go your way and be thankful you have not been beaten up."

This story apparently does not contain initiatory or otherworldly subtexts, is four times longer than **"My First Goose"** and has limited artistic merit. However, the two narratives have enough common points (including eyeglasses and cauldron) to warrant comparison. The most salient difference between them is their protagonists' contrasting conducts in a basically similar situation.

Gor'kii's characters, incorrigible idealists and romantics, respond to the world's evils and injustices with moral exhortations; if these have no effect, they turn to thundering denunciations or extreme, self-destructive acts (cf. the endings of *The Three* or *Foma Gordeev*). The "calculating wisdom of a snake" (Tiutchev: "zmeinoi mudrosti raschet"), to which Liutov has recourse, reflects a new age that has replaced the romantic norms of humanity and common sense with cynicism, violence and absurdity on an unprecedented scale. Open defiance is no longer a viable option, since it is incapable not only of changing the state of affairs but even of producing waves, leaving a trace, setting an example. Any relationships with the new system of power must take into consideration its essential impermeability to moral and rational discourse. Hence the predominance in the twentieth century of more indirect and sly forms of coping, such as mimicry, acting and overzealous conformism, used by many for survival under a repressive world order, and by others for its subtle, ironic debunking.

The latter has its classic examples in such characters as Hašek's Švejk, Erenburg's Julio Jurenito and Il'f and Petrov's Ostap Bender. In Babel''s **"Goose"** we encounter a hybrid case, where the hero is deeply ambivalent vis-à-vis the new order, is painfully conscious of the necessity to lie and dissimulate, yet does so out of motives that are ultimately idealistic and intellectual rather than either purely opportunistic or mocking and subversive. The conciseness and density of **"My First Goose,"** reinforced by its wealth of archetypal connotations, make this story an almost emblematic prototype of many works of later Soviet fiction that address analogous themes.

Notes

1. Carol Luplow, *Isaac Babel's Red Cavalry* (Ann Arbor: Ardis, 1982), 32.

2. S. Markish, "Russko-evreiskaia literatura i Isaak Babel'," in I. Babel', *Detstvo i drugie rasskazy* (Jerusalem: Biblioteka "Aliia," 1979), 332, 343.

3. Lionel Trilling, "Introduction," in Isaac Babel, *The Collected Short Stories* (New York: New American Library, 1975), 20.

4. *Ibid.,* 37.

5. A. N. Pirozhkova and N. N. Iurgeneva, eds., *Vospominaniia o Babele* (Moscow: Knizhnaia palata, 1989), 62, 64, 181, 198, 274, 289, etc.

6. James E. Falen, *Isaac Babel: Russian Master of the Short Story* (Knoxville: University of Tennessee Press, 1974), 126-27.

7. Patricia Carden, *The Art of Isaac Babel* (Ithaca: Cornell University Press, 1972), 11.

8. *Vospominaniia o Babele,* 62.

9. *Ibid.,* 63.

10. *Ibid.,* 15.

11. N. Mandel'shtam, *Vospominaniia* (Paris: YMCA-Press, 1970), I: 341.

12. Carden, 130-31. The analogies between Liutov and the landlady are also noticed by Andrew, who adds important nuances to their interpretation: "The narrator and the old woman are quite clearly linked: they both wear glasses, they are both pushed around . . . By pushing the Old Woman around, the narrator is rejecting what he sees of himself in her, he is deciding that *he* will not be an Eternal Victim." See Joseph Andrew, "Structure and Style in the Short Story: Babel's 'My First Goose'," *Occasional Papers* (Colchester: University of Essex Language Centre, 1974), 14: 18.

13. The relationship between the ideal and real, "earthly" socialism in Il'f and Petrov is discussed in Iu. K. Shcheglov, *Romany I. Il'fa i E. Petrova* (Wien: *Wiener Slawistischer Almanach,* Sonderband 26/1 and 26/2, 1990-91), 11-24.

14. In a similar manner the hero of Babel''s "My First Honorarium" (1928) wins a prostitute's personal sympathy and successfully passes his *sexual* initiation by making her believe a fictional story of his life (note the parallelism of titles).

15. Ironically, it is the same duality of Lenin that enables Liutov to maintain his inner distance: far from merging with his audience in a cathartic co-experience, he leaves it to the Cossacks to enjoy the sheer force and directness of Lenin's speech ("he goes and strikes at it straight off like a hen pecking at a grain") while secretly relishing Lenin's more recondite dialectics ("I read on and rejoiced, spying out exultingly the secret curve of Lenin's straight line"). The issue of "straight line" vs. "curve" in connection with Liutov's duality and with the compromise between him and the Cossacks is convincingly discussed by Andrew ("Structure and Style in the Short Story," 19).

16. Nikolai Gogol', *The Complete Tales,* ed. Leonard J. Kent (Chicago: University of Chicago Press, 1985), I: 136.

17. *Ibid.,* 79.

18. *Ibid.,* 40.

19. *Ibid.,* 199.

20. *Ibid.,* 82.

21. This scene seems to have been a persistent personal symbol in Babel's life. It reappears with a somewhat different meaning in "Argamak," a story written several years after "My First Goose." "Every night I had the same dream. I am dashing along on Argamak at a fast trot. By the roadside *bonfires are burning,* the Cossacks are cooking their food. I ride past them, and they do not raise their eyes to me. Some salute, others pay no attention: they're not concerned with me. What's the meaning of all this? Their indifference means that there is nothing special about the way I ride. I ride like everybody else, so there's no point in looking at me. I gallop on my way and am happy" (my emphasis). Note the multiple *bonfires* around which the Cossacks are sitting—a more explicit parallel with the Walpurgisnacht scene in *Faust* than the single fire of "My First Goose."

22. Gogol', *The Complete Tales,* 83.

23. V. Ia. Propp, *Istoricheskie korni volshebnoi skazki* (Leningrad: Izd. LGU, 1946), 52-53.

24. Oliver Evans and Harry Finestone, eds., *The World of the Short Story: Archetypes in Action* (New York: Knopf, 1971), 446.

25. In two scenes of Goethe's *Faust* (part 1, sc. 6, with the witch; scene 14, with Faust) Mephistopheles "makes an indecent gesture" ("macht eine unanständige Gebärde"; "mit einer Gebärde"), provoking his partner's admiration in the former case, shock and disgust in the latter. The character of the gesture is not specified.

26. The inversion of human and earthly phenomena typical of the otherworld is discussed and illustrated in S. Iu. Nekliudov, "O krivom oborotne (k issledovaniiu mifologicheskoi semantiki fol'klornogo motiva)," in *Problemy slavianskoi etnografii* (Leningrad: Nauka, 1979); and in Iu. K. Shcheglov, "Dve variatsii na temu smerti i vozrozhdeniia: Chekhov, 'Skripka Rotshil'da' i 'Dama s sobachkoi,'" *Russian Language Journal* (1994, forthcoming).

27. Vladimir Nabokov, *Nikolai Gogol* (New York: New Directions, 1961), 71.

28. Gogol', *The Complete Tales,* 84.

29. White in some initiatory rites is the color of a neophyte who is forcibly painted white from head to toe; white represents blindness and invisibility; see Propp, *Istoricheskie korni volshebnoi skazki,* 60.

30. *Ibid.,* 58, 75.

31. Mircea Eliade, *Rites and Symbols of Initiation* (New York: Harper Torchbooks, 1975), 81, 83, 109.

32. In Wright's story the actual shooting of the horse is preceded by a long episode of buying the gun. The instrument of initiation is thereby "enlarged," the reader's attention is drawn to it, its presenta-

tion is "prolonged." Would it not be right to see a similar function in the sword episode of Babel''s story? The narrator picks up the sword without any practical need, just for the sake of pomp (he does not use it to kill the goose). Again, we have explained it "realistically" as showing off but it may also pertain to a ritualistic archetype.

33. Propp, *Istoricheskie korni volshebnoi skazki,* 58-59.

34. See Nekliudov, "O krivom oborotne . . ."

35. Propp, *Istoricheskie korni volshebnoi skazki,* 58-61, 65.

36. V. N. Toporov, "Prizha," *Mify narodov mira* (Moscow: Sovetskaiia entsiklopediia, 1982), 11:344. Andrew has perspicaciously pointed out the symbolic and mythical connotations of the old woman's figure: "The Old Woman is even more emblematic and mask-like than the other characters, and she seems to fulfil a purely symbolic role in the story. It is rather difficult to be precise as to exactly what she symbolizes, but . . . she is central to the narrator's Fate, almost as if she were a supernatural being, meeting the hero at the symbolic cross-roads of his life" ("Structure and Style in the Short Story," 17).

37. *Ibid.,* 12-13.

38. Interestingly, in one of later Chekhov's prose masterpieces, "At Christmas Time" (1899), a pose similar to that of Babel''s Cossacks is associated with blindness: "He stood staring fixedly ahead of him like a blind man" ("on stoial i gliadel nepodvizhno i priamo, kak slepoi"; the sentence is later repeated). It can be said that the "whites of [the old woman's] purblind eyes," the Cossacks sitting "motionless [and] stiff" and Liutov reading "like a triumphant man hard of hearing" form a chain of details that subtly "infect" each other with the seme of blindness through a series of intra- and intertextual similarities and transitions.

39. M. Gor'kii, *Polnoe sobranie sochinenii* (Moscow: Nauka, 1968), I: 189-201, 545-48.

40. Iurii Tynianov used the term "convergence" for this kind of spontaneous growth of identical motifs out of similar thematic functions. He says that in such cases "the chronological question—'who was the first to say it?'—turns out to be irrelevant." See Iu. N. Tynianov, *Poetika. Istoriia Literatury. Kino* (Moscow: Nauka, 1977), 280.

Carol J. Avins (essay date fall 1994)

SOURCE: Avins, Carol J. "Kinship and Concealment in *Red Cavalry* and Babel's *1920 Diary.*" *Slavic Review* 53, no. 3 (fall 1994): 694-710.

[*In the following essay, Avins elucidates the relationship between Babel's diary and the stories of* Red Cavalry, *and she investigates identity and the expression of kinship as key thematic concerns in the book.*]

To begin, three encounters, and then some ruminations about two deaths, the veiling of identity and the expression of kinship. The encounters are from the diary Isaac Babel' kept during his service with Budenny's First Cavalry Army in the Polish campaign of 1920; the deaths are those that frame the work of fiction he drew from this experience, ***Red Cavalry.***[1] That book begins and ends with the narrator contemplating a corpse—in each instance, the body of a Jewish man whose passing leads the narrator to confront the meanings of kinship and loss. In the first case, he witnesses bereavement; in the second, he experiences it. On one important level, the narrator's trajectory in ***Red Cavalry*** is captured in the contrast between his links to the first death and to the last. Reading the story cycle against the background of the diary, one can see this feature of the cycle's design in terms of the central dilemma for Babel' (bearing papers in the name of Kirill Vasilievich Liutov, the name he bequeaths to his narrator) in his dealings with the civilians of the heavily Jewish towns through which his division passed: whether or not to reveal that he was himself a Jew.

It is a question at issue in ***Red Cavalry***'s opening story, which shows the narrator's entry into war entailing intrusion into a Jewish home. That story, and the one that concluded the book in its original redaction, will be the subject of much of this essay. Though a good deal of attention has been paid to these two stories, there is more to be said about their symmetries and asymmetries, particularly about how they deal with the matter of Jewishness acknowledged or concealed. Broadly speaking, the cycle moves (though not in a straight path) from the narrator's concealment in **"Crossing the Zbruch"** to his acknowledgment in **"The Rebbe's Son"** of Jewish identity. The end point is not quite that simple, however: the final story brings an encoded and hitherto undeciphered dimension—in the person of a mysterious addressee—to the cycle's treatment of the masking of self.[2]

The movement observed in ***Red Cavalry*** characterizes the diary as well, both as a whole and within some entries. It should be said at the outset that in juxtaposing Babel's diary and his fiction—two entirely different kinds of texts—I am seeing the former as a source of ideas about the choices he made in designing ***Red Cavalry*** rather than as a source of facts that show one or another element of the fiction to be "true" or "made up." I turn first to the diary episodes promised above because they illustrate in telling ways the dual impulse in Babel''s interaction with the Jews of eastern Poland, showing how an experience of concealing his Jewishness could be followed by a desire to express or examine it. The first incident—they proceed in chronological order—provides a particularly sharp example.

One Monday in early July, Babel' spent the night at the home of a Jewish family in the Volhynian town of Hoszcza on the Horyn River, between Zhitomir and Rovno.³ The war between Poland and Soviet Russia, begun eighteen months before, was in full force following the Polish occupation of Kiev in early May. Soviet troops were meeting with success in their drive to push the Poles back westward toward Warsaw. Babel', assigned to the political section of the Sixth Division as a correspondent for the army newspaper, had just spent two days in Zhitomir and had heard stories of the pogrom that accompanied the battle for the town. The Jews of Hoszcza had experienced brutal treatment as well, and the family urging the young correspondent to make their home his billet served up their story along with supper and tea. The Poles had looted; then the conquering Cossacks, having driven out the Poles, descended again on the family for good measure. While the father told the story, his six-year-old daughter, a wise-eyed child still shivering from the trauma, sat on his lap and stared at the visitor. Interrupting the account of the pogrom, she directed at him a blunt and poignantly relevant question: "aren't you a Jew?"

Babel''s answer is not given; apparently he told his self-protective lie. The account contains his response to another question, however: that of what Soviet control would mean for the Jews. "I tell them everything will be all right, explain what the revolution means, I talk on and on," he recorded. Later in the evening, however, he decided to drop his cover. Many townsfolk were out on this summer night and he felt drawn to join their conversation and absorb their words. Toward the end of the passage quoted below, which incorporates echoes of their speech, it becomes evident that one reason Babel admitted his Jewishness was to account for his willingness to help his distraught host (one Duvid Uchenik) resolve a conflict with the patrolling Cossacks.

> The Horyn, Jewish men and old women on their porches. Hoszcza has been sacked, Hoszcza is cleaned out, Hoszcza is silent. A nice clean job. In a whisper— they lifted everything, and shed not a tear, real experts. The Horyn, a network of lakes and tributaries, evening light, the battle for Rovno took place here. Talking to the Jews, I feel close to them, they think I'm Russian, and my soul is laid bare. We sit on the steep river bank. Peace and soft sighs behind my back. I go off to defend Uchenik. I told them my mother was Jewish, a whole story. . . .⁴

The entry has many stories in it (those of the local Jews, those of Babel' himself). It has in common with the other episodes that form my preamble several elements: a masked outsider ambivalent about his not entirely successful disguise, the rhetoric of hope and renewal he voices (though increasingly troubled about its truth value), a shift from concealing Jewish identity to acknowledging or reflecting upon it. We see this again a few weeks later, in the course of a day that holds visits to two Jewish homes, with a synagogue service inbetween.

The diarist had just marked his twenty-sixth birthday; it was a Friday in late July. The place was Dubno, at this time a town of about 9,000. Once again Babel' found himself in a Jewish household; this visit, though, was a social call of an unusual sort. He was brought along by a Cossack member of his division named Prishchepa, who had taken up with the flirtatious young wife. Babel' himself sat politely, feeling ridiculous, while he was stared at and pointedly asked his surname. He evidently gave his standard camouflage answer. (Babel' invariably sought to maintain the fiction of his Russian identity when among Cossacks; as the Hoszcza incident shows, however, he did not always drop his cover even when on his own.) The husband also posed the question Babel' was asked repeatedly by the many tradesmen concerned that Sovietization would destroy their livelihood. And to this question he gave what he described as his standard answer as well: ". . . everything's changing for the better—my usual system—miraculous things are happening in Russia. . . . They listen with delight and disbelief."⁵

In the evening, as in Hoszcza, we see a voluntary unmasking. If at times Babel' dispensed facile and comforting visions, he sought for himself a different kind of comfort and a deeper understanding both of the Jewish history to which he belonged and the revolutionary future he was helping to make. In Dubno he found relief from subterfuge and occasion for meditation in the synagogue. Sitting through the service, he did not idealize what he saw—nor did he wholly identify with it, aesthetically or spiritually (though choosing to be there is itself a form of identification). "Of all the Jews in Dubno the most repulsive-looking seem to have gathered here," he wrote of the "misshapen little figures" around him—and the aesthetic judgment he passed on the people finds an equivalent in his description of the setting. "There are no adornments in the building," he continued, "everything is white and plain to the point of asceticism, everything is fleshless, bloodless, to a grotesque degree, you have to have the soul of a Jew to sense what it means. But what does that soul consist of? Can ours be the century in which they perish?"

His musings about the nature and future of the Jewish soul gave way as, after the service, he shifted back into his Russian persona and went to the billet (again in a Jewish home) he shared with Prishchepa. He maintained it the next day as the two continued on the road together. What happened that day, a bit farther west in the town of Demidovka, is my encounter number three.

In Dubno, as elsewhere, Babel' could find respite in the synagogue, in shifting from the mode of cavalry staffer to that of traveling Jew. Demidovka posed a greater challenge. There he found himself pulled simultaneously towards his camouflaged and Jewish selves, for the home where he was billeted with his Cossack companion was both a domestic setting and a place of prayer. It was the eve of Tisha b'Av, a day of fasting to commemorate the destruction in ancient times of the First and Second Temples in Jerusalem. Babel' knew the significance of the holiday and was troubled by his participation in yet another act of desecration. Prishchepa raged, demanding a meal; "I keep silent," wrote Babel' later that evening, "because I'm a Russian." Privately appalled, he nonetheless ate too, then recorded: "We sweat, they keep serving us, all this is terrible, I tell them fairy tales about Bolshevism . . . I entertain all these tormented people" (24 July).

His polished visions of the future yielded to dark images of the past, as his performance was followed by that of a young man who chanted the liturgy traditional to the holiday: Lamentations. In describing the text and the setting Babel' drew the analogy between past and present drawn traditionally by Jews with each successive period of destruction: "The lamp smokes, the old woman wails, the young man sings melodiously, girls in white stockings, outside—Demidovka, night, Cossacks, all just as it was when the Temple was destroyed."[6] One passage he would have heard recited, Lamentations 5:1-3, helps one understand his perception of an analogy between past and present: "Remember, O Lord, what is come upon us; / Behold, and see our reproach. / Our inheritance is turned unto strangers, / Our houses unto aliens."

The episode in Demidovka, which occurs about one third of the way into the diary, is one of the central experiences Babel' recounted and something of a turning point. He never dropped his cover that evening—or the next morning, when the abusive behavior of Prishchepa and others continued. His notes make clear, however, his discomfort in playing a role counter to the tradition of which he was part. What he wrote a day later, though not explicitly about himself as a Jew, further indicates that his experience in Demidovka occasioned some soul-searching. Settled in the town of Leszniow in a quite different Jewish home ("prosperity, cleanliness, quiet, splendid coffee, clean children"), he reflected: "I feel anguished, I need to think about it all, Galicia, the world war, my own destiny" (26 July).

The dynamic one sees recurring in each of these episodes—a denial of Jewish identity followed by a turning to or reflection upon it—also marks, as I have indicated, the movement of the diary as a whole. (My claim refers to the textual evidence, not to the life: of course we have not a complete picture of Babel''s experience but only what this already professional and supremely self-conscious writer chose to record.) As the weeks went on, the devastation he saw intensified his depression about the course of the war in particular and the situation of the region's Jews in general. From early summer to early fall (the period covered, with gaps of missing text) one can discern a decreasing incidence of

Babel''s concealing his origins among the Jews he encountered and an increasing tendency to see their situation in traditional, historical terms. By "traditional" terms I mean those of the realities of anti-Semitism and its threat to Jewish survival, rather than the utopian terms of an internationalist revolution that would de-problematize religious differences. The episodes recounted show that, as one allied with the bolshevik cause, Babel' played the role of bearer of a modern ideology—and also the role of an assimilated, secular Jew whose mentality placed him at odds with the small-town eastern European Jews (especially the Hasidim) whom he encountered. But although he retained some distance, perceiving himself as a Soviet, an Odessaite, a different kind of Jew, he seems to have felt a deepening sense of identification with these Jews and their crisis.[7]

A few final words on the diary. The trajectory I have described is something of an oversimplification, because a degree of ambivalence characterizes Babel''s stance throughout. The very first entry, for example, shows him trying to have it both ways, telling a Jew (who later took him to see the Zhitomir tsaddik whose fictional version we have in **"The Rebbe"**): "I'm Russian, of course, my mother's Jewish, why do you ask?" Describing the evening gathering at the tsaddik's, he wrote: "I feel happy, enormous faces, hooked noses, black beards streaked with gray, I think about many things, good-bye, dead men." That last phrase (*do svidan'ia, mertvetsy*) is a startling characterization, given the satisfaction Babel' seems to have drawn from being among these living "dead men" and given that he had just learned of the many lives lost in the recent pogrom. He meant, I think, not that these men at prayer were doomed to the same fate but rather that they were part of a dying world. Earlier in the entry, describing his encounters in the market (including one with the prototype of his character Gedali), he used nearly the same expression: "Sweat, anaemic tea, I'm beginning to get my teeth into life, farewell, dead men." As the campaign continued and he saw an increasing number of real corpses, Jewish and non-Jewish, the somewhat flippant sense of his distance from such *mertvetsy* as these faded.

The peak of the carnage and of Babel''s sense of identification can be seen at what one might call the diary's nadir, the most gruesome scene he witnessed. On 28 August his unit entered the town of Komarów. A pogrom had been carried out the previous day by Cossacks who had gone over to the Polish side. There were many casualties. Here is part of Babel''s account in the day's entry:

> Captain Yakovlev's Cossacks were here yesterday. A pogrom. The family of David Zis, in their rooms, a naked, barely breathing prophet of an old man, a hacked-up old woman, a child with fingers chopped

off, many people still breathing, stench of blood, everything turned upside down, chaos, a mother sitting over her hacked-up son, an old woman lying twisted up like a pretzel, four people in one hovel, filth, blood under a black beard, they're still lying there bloody.

The survivors told their story, anxious that the correspondent see the extent of the atrocities ("The Jews on the square, an agonized Jew showing it all to me, a tall Jew takes over from him"). Babel' contributed to the publicity by writing a piece for *The Red Cavalryman* in which he recounted the incident in gory detail and described his horror as a reaction shared by all his fellow soldiers.[8] The article ends with an avenging battle cry, exhorting the troops to strike back at the savage dogs who could commit such base crimes. This rousing ending differs starkly from the despairing passage that concludes Babel''s diary entry for the day. In the evening, resting in his lodgings, he had no kind words for the Soviet side and not even the consolation of imagined revenge to offer. "The hatred is the same," he reflected, "the Cossacks just the same, the cruelty the same, it's nonsense to think one army is different from another. The life of these little towns. There's no salvation." What he went on to say shows that he sensed the historical as well as the immediate significance of what he was seeing: "What a mighty and marvelous life of a nation existed here. The fate of Jewry. At our place in the evening, supper, tea, I sit and drink in the words of the Jew with the little beard, wistfully asking me whether it will be possible to trade."

The melancholy pleasure Babel' derived from this sort of intimacy with the Jewish population is evident also in the last visit the diary records to a Jewish home (the third from last entry, 13 September, in the town of Kivertsy). It was Rosh Hashanah, the Jewish New Year. A few days earlier (8 September), billeted with a Russian in the home of an elderly Jewish couple, Babel' had remained aloof, eavesdropping on the family's conversations and noting in his diary, "They think I don't understand Yiddish." On the morning of Rosh Hashanah, he went off alone and shed his disguise. He was treated to the hospitality of a woman in her holiday silk dress who took him into her tidy house, shared with him her bread and butter, and told him her story. "I am moved to tears," he wrote, "only language [Yiddish, presumably] could help here, we talk for a long time, her husband is in America, a sensible, steady Jewish woman." The incident makes a telling contrast to the Demidovka episode seven weeks earlier, when, in the company of Cossacks, he ambivalently participated in desecrating the observance of a more solemn holiday. It contrasts sharply, too, with the one instance in *Red Cavalry* in which Babel''s narrator, Liutov (whose distinction from the author should be kept in mind), finds himself in a Jewish woman's home: the opening story, the first of those frame stories to which I now turn.

The encounters that frame the book are both with Jews roughly of Liutov's generation: one (the young woman in the opening story who has seen her civilian father murdered by the Poles) to whom no end could be great enough to justify her suffering, the other (the tsaddik's son turned committed combatant) willing to be martyred for the Soviet cause. Babel''s many nights lodged in Jewish households are distilled in that first story, **"Crossing the Zbruch,"** as are all the times he hid his Jewishness and felt the strain of doing so. *Red Cavalry* has a number of stories in which the narrator openly reveals his Jewishness; this is one of two (**"Zamosc"** is the other) in which his concealing it is at issue. That the narrator is a Jew pretending to be a non-Jew is made clear to the reader but not to the Jews among whom the narrator finds himself. They are in the position of those Babel' encountered who were uninitiated into his secret.

The reader starting *Red Cavalry* with no preconceptions about the narrator is shocked by his behavior when, on arriving in the occupied town and entering the billet he has been assigned—the home of Jews obviously victimized by a pogrom—he insultingly orders them to put things in order:

> Far on in the night we reached Novograd. In the house where I was billeted I found a pregnant woman and two red-haired, scraggy-necked Jews; a third was asleep, huddled to the wall with his head covered up. In the room I was given I found turned-out wardrobes, scraps of women's fur coats on the floor, human excrement, and shards of the secret crockery that Jews use only once a year—at Passover.
>
> "Clear this up," I said to the woman. "What a filthy way to live!"[9]

Though the narrator is new to the front, he is not so naive that he fails to recognize the aftermath of a pogrom. He realizes that the home has been looted by the Poles but purposely does not acknowledge the status of these people as victims, blaming them for their situation. One could say that he plays the role of "Cossack" to the role imposed on them as "Jew"—except that the narrative's description of the scene reveals him to be a Jew as well. The crucial detail is his description of the broken china: who else but a Jew would identify a smashed set of packed-up dishes in these terms?[10]

This description reveals the narrator's Jewishness to the reader; it remains concealed, however, from his hosts. Consumed by his own anxieties, the narrator maintains his distance from them, hiding behind callous bluster. That distance is breached toward the end of the story, when he sees that the "sleeping" Jew is dead and is confronted with the young woman's anguished account of her father's murder in this room. All the stories of pogroms that Babel' had heard are summed up in the story's final lines: "'And now I should wish to know,' cried the woman with sudden and terrible violence, 'I should wish to know where in the whole world you could find another father like my father?'" The daughter's question is, of course, not so much a question as a lament, a cry of outrage. In the diary, when confronted with such suffering and with questions about what hope lay beyond it, Babel' described himself offering comforting visions in response, particularly early in the summer. It is one mark of the many differences between Isaac Babel'-as-Liutov and the fictional Liutov that Babel' never put such words in his narrator's mouth—perhaps because he had grown uncomfortable with such utopian rhetoric. In this opening story he made his narrator speechless—both in the sense that the story is ended before he has a chance to respond, and in the sense that the question he is asked has no adequate answer.

The words of the bereaved daughter force the narrator to revise his interpretation of his surroundings, to see the people and the setting through a different lens. That much is obvious—as it is obvious that the reader is meant to engage in the same process. Babel''s restraint is such that one is left to infer the narrator's horror; Liutov's ambivalence is such that he does not, either here or in subsequent stories, make any gesture of empathy or sentimentalize the woman's grief. She and her husband—presumably one of the two "red-haired, scraggy-necked Jews" of the opening story—are mentioned twice again. A few stories later, at the end of **"Pan Apolek,"** Liutov recounts: "I said goodbye to all and went to spend the night at home with my plundered Jews." That use of the possessive is proprietary—the "my" of an occupation force—rather than reflective of any felt kinship. And it is significant that the Jews are marked as "plundered" rather than "bereaved," as if to discount the lost life relative to lost possessions.

The following story, **"Italian Sunshine,"** is set in that same home and in the same room (cleaned presumably of filth if not of all traces of invasion) where Liutov sleeps in the opening episode. He shares the room with Sidorov, the bloodthirsty dreamer who yearns for distant Rome. Sidorov's fantasies are implicitly contrasted not only with Liutov's concerns but with the woes of the bereaved daughter and her husband. "On the other side of the wall the pregnant Jewess was crying her heart out," Liutov narrates, "and her long-bodied husband was muttering moaning replies. They were going over their stolen possessions and bickering about their ill fortune." Again, the murder is not explicitly mentioned (though it is reflected in the woman's tears) and there is no sense that Liutov feels any kind of connection to the experience of those on the other side of the wall.

The juxtaposition of stories in *Red Cavalry* carries an important component of the book's meaning. In **"Gedali,"** which directly follows **"Italian Sunshine,"**

Liutov himself seeks a connection to Jewish life in these towns (though on his own terms). The shift from self-estrangement to self-exposure that recurs in the diary can be observed here. Though in **"Gedali"** one has moved on from Novograd to Zhitomir, the story makes implicit reference to those Novograd Jews who have been left behind. The story opens with the narrator's first explicit expression of his Jewishness, a lyrical, sentimental passage that evokes his childhood experience of sweet and melancholy Sabbath piety. "On Sabbath eves I am oppressed by the dense melancholy of memories," it begins. "In bygone days on these occasions my grandfather would stroke the volumes of Ibn Ezra with his yellow beard. . . . On those evenings my child's heart was rocked like a little ship upon enchanted waves." The recollection of intergenerational intimacy evokes its destruction in the cycle's first story, where one encounters a grandchild (carried by the pregnant woman) who will have no grandfather.

It is not until nearly the middle of the cycle, with **"The Cemetery at Kozin,"** that Babel' put the problem of Jewish loss in a historical context which includes the narrator himself. The inscriptions on the burial vault of Rabbi Azrael, murdered by the Cossacks of Bogdan Khmelnitsky but progenitor of a long line, speak of continuity as well as breached continuity. The last line quoted from the tombstone—"'O death, O covetous one, O greedy thief, why couldst thou not have spared us, just for once?'"—is felt, though marked as a quotation, to be uttered in Liutov's voice, modulating here from first-person singular to first-person plural.

The matter of Liutov's belonging to a vulnerable collectivity is raised again in **"Zamość,"** five stories before the book's conclusion.[11] In this story the sphere of those dead and at risk widens beyond one home, one dynasty and one town to encompass the globe—and thus, even more directly than in **"The Cemetery at Kozin,"** to include Liutov himself. The story explicitly shows us Liutov concealing his Jewishness from a non-Jew and provides one explanation of why he engages in the deception.

"Zamość" is set outside the town of that name. Liutov, with the troops of his division, spends the night in a field on the outskirts, awaiting orders to attack. He ties his horse's bridle to his foot, gets dragged by the horse away from the others and awakes from an erotic dream turned nightmare to find before him a peasant fighting on the side of the Reds. The man smiles and addresses him familiarly; Liutov, before responding, looks around to get his bearings. He is closer now to the front line and has a better vantage point on the town: "I could see the chimneys of Zamość, stealthy lights in the defiles of its ghetto, the watchtower with its broken lantern. . . . And in the stillness I could hear the far-off breath of groaning. The smoke of secret murder strayed around us." The peasant, who takes him for a Russian, confirms his realization that killing is going on in the town and articulates what Liutov must know about identities of killer and victim: "The Poles are slaughtering the Yids." Liutov is silent. He has not been in those particular households but he has seen the aftermath of such rampages in others (in Novograd, to begin with) and thus imaginatively supplies—as does the reader—the details kept out of the text. He listens in silence as the peasant talks on, remarking fondly on the satisfaction of having found a fellow soul to ease his loneliness and boredom. That Liutov is no soul mate he does not let on. The peasant's small talk and comradely gestures continue:

> The peasant made me light a cigarette from his. "The Yids are to blame for everything, on our side and yours. There'll be mighty few of them left after the war. How many Yids are there in the whole world?"
>
> "Ten million," I answered, putting the bridle on my horse.
>
> "There'll be only two hundred thousand left," cried the peasant, and touched my hand, afraid I would go. But I got into the saddle and galloped off to the spot where the Staff had been.

Quantifying the Jews as a people, Liutov is surely conscious both of counting himself in their number and of the hazards of doing so. There is, of course, an exquisite irony in the peasant's affectionate treatment, particularly in the detail of his touching Liutov's hand to keep from losing him as he approvingly predicts the decimation of the earth's Jews. The death designated for the narrator contrasts eerily with the death of which he dreams earlier in the story, while he is being dragged along the rough ground by the horse. (The dream itself may be seen as having to do with concealed identity, though it is unclear whether Liutov's dream persona is non-Jewish or concealing the fact that he is a Jew.) In the dream he is taken for dead and for a Christian—and as prayers are said over him and he is suffocated by a mourner, he struggles to stay alive. Awakening, he can be said to find little relief—for he wakes to be confronted with what it means in this setting to be a Jew.

"Zamość," while focused on anti-Semitic violence in one Polish town, carries the reminder that in at least one sense the differences among Jews are less significant than the element of identity they share. The story functions to broaden the stage and to prepare the ground for the final story, **"The Rebbe's Son."**

The death of a Jew in this story is set apart in important ways from the murders thus far discussed. Il'ia Bratslavskii, the title character, is not a victim of Polish pogroms but a revolutionary who believes in the Soviet cause and joins the Red Army's fight against the Poles. He dies not of war wounds but of typhus, though he is clearly a casualty of the war nonetheless. Liutov, riding on the Political Section train retreating from a decisive defeat, notices the youth among the mass of refugees and, aided by others on the train, pulls him up into the car. Encountering him, Liutov is brought back to the time of their first meeting four months before. Then he was a visitor to the Bratslavskii home; this second encounter, though, takes place on Liutov's turf. One can see the episode as a kind of inverted version of Liutov's mode of seeking release among Jews—a reversal of the visit-to-a-Jewish-setting pattern that obtains in **"Crossing the Zbruch," "Gedali"** and **"The Rebbe."**

The scene is a variant of Liutov's visit to Il'ia's home in another way as well: that earlier episode, as recalled here, takes on an aura sharply different from the original. The setting of **"The Rebbe"** is marked by starkness and absence ("We entered a room, stony and empty, like a morgue"). Of ritual objects there is nothing but some prayerbooks, of ritual nothing but moaning men in a corner. Il'ia, characterized by a local as "the cursed son, the last son, the disobedient [*nepokornyi*] son," sits smoking and shuddering like a prisoner, entirely estranged from his surroundings. In memory, however, the setting gains a different aesthetic and spiritual valence. The key sentence that carries it reads as follows: "Then the curtain of the Ark was drawn aside, and we saw in the funereal gleam of the candles the Torah scrolls sheathed in covers of purple velvet and blue silk and, bowed over the Torah, the lifeless, obedient [*pokornyi*], beautiful face of Il'ia, the rebbe's son, last prince of the dynasty." The portrait of Il'ia is not entirely transformed but it is made more complex: he joins in a ritual that has beauty and warmth as well as a dark side (the candle flames look predatory, the candlelight has a funereal gleam); his expression, "lifeless and obedient," shows him to be at once both detached and bound. That the scene gains an elegiac tone in this reprise is a function largely of the fact that at the time of telling Il'ia is dead. Babel' fashioned the account of the life Il'ia has left to contrast maximally with the setting in which he leaves life. The sense of bereavement experienced by Liutov finds expression in his description of Il'ia as he was when still within his father's world.

What emotion Liutov feels in Il'ia's presence during their final meeting is beneath the surface of the words he speaks to the youth who lies dying in a corner. Liutov's first words inform Il'ia of the circumstances in which he first saw him; the three things he goes on to say challenge Il'ia to explain what has taken him from Zhitomir to this point. One could say, though, that sentiment and sympathy have already been conveyed by the passage quoted above and by another passage that precedes the conversation: the description of Il'ia's pathetic body and the often-cited catalogue of his belongings, which include in equal parts Hebrew poetry and philosophy, on the one hand, and the booklets and bullets of revolution, on the other.

The story's coda, which follows their conversation, is emotionally charged as well. This final paragraph reads: "He died before we reached Rovno. He died, the last of the princes, amid his poetry, phylacteries, and footwrappings. We buried him at some forgotten station. And I—who can scarce contain the tempests of my imagination within this ancient body—I received the last breath of my brother." The tension between concealing and acknowledging Jewishness are seemingly resolved in that concluding word, that acknowledgment (one could even say embrace) of kinship. We can now see that this story, like **"Crossing the Zbruch,"** deals with a bereaved Jew's response to the death of a kinsman—a term that in the first case is literal (a daughter mourning a father), in the second, self-defined. That self-definition as "brother" bears examination, for its resolution of ambivalence is apparent rather than real.

In what sense does Liutov feel himself to be this man's brother, and with what sort of irony does the declaration resonate? The word "brother," by virtue of its previous usage in the book, carries among other meanings the universalist sense of "brotherhood of man" and especially "brotherhood-of-combatants," for Il'ia is not the first one to be called brother by Liutov. In **"Two Ivans"** Liutov unwittingly urinates in the dark on what turns out to be the corpse of a Pole surrounded by belongings that those of Il'ia will echo (fragments of Pilsudski's proclamations instead of Lenin's, traces of secular pastimes—a list of plays to be given at the Cracow theater—instead of Hebrew texts). "My unknown brother," Liutov calls him. Il'ia, of course, is also "brother" in the sense of comrade and fellow believer in the Soviet cause, as well as in the sense of coreligionist. But as soldier-propagandist and as Jew he is entirely different from Liutov, aggressive in combat and devoted (though not to his father's brand of faith) to ancient Jewish texts as well as to the latest party resolutions. That he carries in his pack evidence of his Jewishness contrasts with Liutov's effort to conceal the difference between himself and the non-Jews with whom he is surrounded.

Il'ia is buried along with the mark of his Jewishness (his Hebrew verses and phylacteries go into the grave); Liutov continues with the mark of his difference still upon him. If this original final story has to do with the problematics of Liutov's acknowledging his difference, the story subsequently added to conclude *Red Cavalry,* **"Argamak,"** is about the desire to erase difference, to simulate kinship with Cossacks by acquiring traits—principally, riding a horse as Cossacks do—that can be viewed as equivalent to inherited. The highest value there, for the narrator, is concealment of identity by means of a form of camouflage. In **"The Rebbe's Son"** Liutov proclaims his identity—but not publicly. Camouflage is at issue in this story as well, in a way that itself entails a form of concealment.

"The Rebbe's Son" as a whole, and the meaning of the word "brother" in the final sentence, must finally be understood in relation to the mysterious addressee to whom this confession of kinship is directed. Among the stories in **Red Cavalry** narrated by Liutov this one is unique in being addressed not simply to a presumed reader but to a specific person. The episode is told to someone named Vasilii. Who this Vasilii is the reader arriving after 33 stories at the end of **Red Cavalry** has no idea.

There are three people in the book given that name: Vasilii Kurdiukov, the naive, illiterate boy who dictates the letter of the third story; Vasilii the cook, lover of Irina the washerwoman in **"Evening"**; and the narrator of the story told in **"Konkin"** (translated as **"Konkin's Prisoner"**). The last, a political commissar of a cavalry brigade and a colorful storyteller, lightheartedly (and in a highly colloquial Russian) entertains a group including Liutov with a tale about an old Polish general whom he takes prisoner and then kills. He is referred to only as Vas'ka or Vasia, Liutov has no apparent personal tie to him, and—though the story indicates that Liutov has heard him tell other yarns—he does not appear again in the book.

It is implausible that Liutov would tell the story of Il'ia the rebbe's son to any of these men and likely that the reader is not meant to know the addressee's identity. Having traveled this far with Liutov, it is unsettling to find introduced a heretofore unseen character who is evidently important enough to take, in this final episode, the place of confidant. One feels that one should know him and wonders at the urgency with which Liutov directs the account to him, insistently repeating his name. The story begins: "Do you remember Zhitomir, Vasilii? Do you remember the Teterev, Vasilii . . . ?"; the name punctuates the narrative three more times: "Do you remember that night, Vasilii?"; "Well, the day before yesterday, Vasilii . . ."; "I recognized him at once, Vasilii." What makes this particularly unsettling is that Liutov describes Vasilii as having been with him and Gedali at the tsaddik's on that evening in Zhitomir, though in the story about this, **"The Rebbe,"** there is no such character. There Liutov's narrative uses the singular (". . . Gedali . . . took me [*povel menia*] to Rebbe Motale's"); here the same verb governs a plural ("Queer old Gedali . . . took us [*vel nas*] to Rebbe Motale Bratslavskii's . . .").

We have already seen how, describing that evening in the later story, Babel' substantially recast Liutov's perception of the scene in **"The Rebbe."** Vasilii's presence in that scene appears to further contradict the earlier account. But why did it suit Babel''s purpose to place Vasilii at the rebbe's and to use him in the final story as Liutov's addressee? An addressee to whom the narrator relates a previous episode is a convenient expositional device but not an indispensable one: Babel' could have had Liutov recalling Zhitomir in his own thoughts. Instead we have an addressee about whom nothing is revealed except that he was (maybe) with Liutov in Zhitomir and is named Vasilii. The name, though it may seem incidental, is a key element of Babel''s device—because it is one of those Russian names that marks a person as someone who could not be a Jew.

If one assumes Vasilii to be Russian, then his role as listener gives Liutov's (partly ironic) confessional gesture—the declaration of kinship carried in the final word, "brother"—particular force. The other stories in which Liutov refers to his Jewishness are all "private," so to speak, written "for himself" in the diaristic style of most of the book. This is the first time we see Liutov reveal himself to someone other than a fellow Jew. Since Vasilii knows about the Zhitomir evening at the tsaddik's, he already knows that Liutov is Jewish. What can be seen as new is the explicit act of self-revelation in the final passage (however ironically one reads it) to someone apparently not a Jew. One problem with this way of construing the story, however, is that Vasilii is addressed as if he *were* a Jew, as if he understood the milieu of hasidic Zhitomir and could fully understand Liutov's experience. This factor, and the insistent repetition of Vasilii's name (as if to keep flashing the message that there is something encoded in this "Vasilii"), lead me to offer instead a reading better grounded in textual evidence: Vasilii *is* a Jew, but one who, like Liutov, uses a conspicuously Russian pseudonym.[12]

It is a pseudonym linked to Liutov: in the nom de guerre shared by narrator and author, the patronymic chosen to follow the markedly Russian first name is Vasilievich. (Only the surname appears in *Red Cavalry,* however, so the reader is not handed this connection.) Even leaving aside this name coincidence, Vasilii can be seen as an alter ego whose similarity to Liutov reconciles the apparent contradiction between saying that one or both were taken to the rebbe's. Vasilii, properly understood, is a "brother" type more kindred to Liutov than the uncamouflaged Il'ia Bratslavskii. The masked identity of both narrator and addressee contrast with the exposure to which Il'ia is subjected, his naked body and his belongings open to view. Babel''s narrator, who in the cycle's opening story engages in deliberate estrangement from a fellow Jew, feels for this dying man a complicated kind of kinship. The person to whom he confides this feeling is chosen for his capacity to understand that sense of kinship and the need for self-concealment that coexists with it. Liutov's baring of self at the end of *Red Cavalry* is undercut by a reminder of the masking

of self—the surface expression of which is the use of a non-Jewish pseudonym—that is practiced by both the narrator and his addressee.

In the diary episodes one sees victims of anti-Semitic violence anxious about their ability to survive, and one sees Babel''s awareness of this as both an individual and historical issue. At the end of *Red Cavalry,* the narrator himself accepts the position of Jewish survivor, as one who buries and mourns Il'ia Bratslavskii. But it is important to remember that Bratslavskii the bolshevik has himself rejected the particular Jewish world that is his inheritance: he is the last of a hasidic dynasty not in that he dies without progeny, but in that he has chosen a different path. That his gravesite is "a forgotten station" (a phrase not meant to be taken literally—would the journalist Liutov, chronicler of so many towns along the route, fail to note the place?) underlines the difference between this death and those marked in the cemetery at Kozin. The Kozin inscriptions speak of a continuity that endures though Cossacks and wars may come and go across the centuries. One inscription tells of an Iliia (Elijah, the biblical form of the name), son of a rabbi killed by Cossacks, whose grandson became Rabbi of Cracow and Prague. That kind of continuity has been broken, with the violence of Cossacks and Poles compounded by the powerful winds of historical change.

The windswept metaphor is used by Gedali in the opening of **"The Rebbe."** Hasidism has been shaken but not shattered, he says; it is immortal: "With oozing orbits, Hasidism still stands at the crossroads of the furious winds of history." These historical forces are part of Babel''s concern in *Red Cavalry,* but it is telling that the storms at whose mercy Liutov ultimately finds himself are those not of history but of imagination. The first part of the final sentence—"And I, who can scarce contain the tempests of my imagination within this ancient body"—is a summary characterization of Liutov that informs and complicates the meaning of what follows ("I received the last breath of my brother"). The phrases "tempests of my imagination" and "ancient body" are in tension with each other, a tension that bespeaks the ambivalence Liutov feels about his Jewish identity.

The word "ancient" (*drevnii*) has appeared once earlier in the story, in the compound *"drevneevreiskii"* (Hebrew). Liutov's description of his body as "ancient" expresses his identification with an ancient people and implies that his single self embodies the whole. This identification is tempered, however, by his self-characterization as an individual possessed of—and by—a turbulent imagination that leads him into an idiosyncratic relation to all that he experiences, whether alien or kindred. One expects in this line uncontainable grief for a fallen kinsman, not uncontainable and tempestuous imagination. The focus on imagination points to Liutov's individualism and detachment, as well as to the tensions of self-fashioning in which we have seen him engaged. Those tensions find different but related forms of expression in Babel''s diary and fiction. More remains to be understood about the subtleties of kinship and concealment in both.

Notes

1. Here and elsewhere in this essay, the edition of *Red Cavalry* referred to is the first (*Konarmiia* [Moscow-Leningrad: Gosizdat, 1926]). My source is the most readily available text of that edition, in Isaak Babel', *Detstvo i drugie rasskazy,* ed. Efraim Sicher (Jerusalem: Biblioteka Aliya, 1979). From the 1st through the 6th editions, the final story in the cycle was "Syn rebbe"; in the 7th and 8th editions (1933) "Argamak" was added, becoming the final story. The most recent publication of *Red Cavalry* (Isaak Babel', *Sochineniia,* 2 vols. [Moscow: Khudozhestvennaia literatura, 1990], 2:5-140) adds another story at the end, "Potselui," first published separately in 1937 and not included in the cycle during Babel's lifetime. According to his widow (*Sochineniia,* 2:561n), Babel' intended to add it to the next edition. It does not seem to fit, however, particularly as a conclusion. My focus on the 1926 redaction reflects my view that this original version has the greatest compositional unity.

   The diary first appeared in full in the above-cited 1990 *Sochineniia,* 1:362-435. The manuscript was given in the mid-1950s to Babel''s widow, Antonina Nikolaevna Pirozhkova, by the writer's friend, T. O. Stakh, who had received it (along with other papers) from another Kiev friend, M. Ia. Ovrutskaya. Pirozhkova surmises that Babel' might have left the papers with Ovrutskaya circa 1927, when he closed up the Kiev home of his first wife's family after her father's death and her mother's emigration (interview with A. N. Pirozhkova, Moscow, 8 May 1993). Fragmentary excerpts were first published in Ia. Smirin, "Na puti k 'Konarmii' (Literaturnye iskaniia Babelia)," *Literaturnoe nasledstvo* (Moscow: Nauka, 1965), 74:467-82, and in Smirin's notes (497-98) to the drafts of stories published in the same volume. More substantial portions appeared, with an introduction by Galina Belaya, in *Druzhba narodov,* no. 4 (1989):238-52 and 5:247-60. A complete English edition, translated by H. T. Willetts and with my introductory essay and notes, is forthcoming from Yale University Press.

2. I translate Babel''s titles directly from the Russian rather than using the less accurate translations ("Crossing into Poland," "The Rabbi's Son") commonly used.

There is a substantial critical literature on *Red Cavalry,* on Babel''s depiction of Jews there and elsewhere in his work, and on Babel''s identity as a Jew. While I cannot give here a complete bibliography, I refer readers to the most complete one available, that of Efraim Sicher in his *Style and Structure in the Prose of Isaak Babel'* (Columbus Ohio: Slavica, 1986). Among the studies relevant to my subject (though not, by and large, to my approach) are Sicher's book itself; his article on the diary (cited in n. 3 below); E. A. Dobrenko, "Logika tsikla," in G. A. Belaia, E. A. Dobrenko and I. A. Esaulov, *"Konarmiia" Isaaka Babelia* (Moscow: Rossiiskii universitet, 1993), 33-101; Alice Stone Nakhimovsky, *Russian-Jewish Literature and Identity* (Baltimore: Johns Hopkins University Press, 1992); Milton Ehre, *Isaac Babel* (Boston: Twayne, 1986); Arkady Lvov, "Babel the Jew," *Commentary* (March 1983):40-49; Carol Luplow, *Isaac Babel''s "Red Cavalry"* (Ann Arbor: Ardis, 1982); Simon Markish, "The Example of Isaac Babel," *Commentary* (November 1977):36-45; James Falen, *Isaac Babel: Master of the Short Story* (Knoxville: University of Tennessee Press, 1974); and Patricia Carden, *The Art of Isaac Babel* (Ithaca: Cornell University Press, 1972). A number of useful studies are included in Harold Bloom, ed., *Isaac Babel: Modern Critical Views* (New Haven: Chelsea House, 1987). An overview with useful insights is Gregory Freidin, "Isaac Babel," *European Writers of the Twentieth Century* (New York: Scribner's, 1991), 11:1885-1914.

3. The date given in the diary is 3 June but it seems probable that Babel' slipped and meant 3 July since this area in early June was still held by the Poles. Norman Davies in "Izaak Babel''s 'Konarmiia' Stories, and the Polish-Soviet War" (*Modern Language Review* 67, no. 4 [October 1972]:847) and Efraim Sicher in "The Jewish Cossack": Isaac Babel in the First Red Cavalry" (*Studies in Contemporary Jewry* IV [1988]:131) agree on this point. Sicher argues, further, that given Babel''s use of Roman numerals to indicate months, the difference between June and July is merely one stroke; also, the entry at issue clearly takes place on a Saturday and, while 3 July 1920 was a Saturday, 3 June was not.

4. Babel', "Dnevnik 1920 g.," *Sochineniia,* 1:366.

5. *Ibid.,* 1:385 (entry for 23 July). Subsequent references to the diary are given parenthetically in the text. Most entries are so short that only dates are cited, not page numbers.

6. On interpretations over the centuries of the significance of Tisha b'Av and its paradigm of destruction, see David G. Roskies, *Against the*

Apocalypse: Responses to Catastrophe in Modern Jewish Culture (Cambridge: Harvard University Press, 1984). Roskies briefly discusses Babel''s experience in Demidovka on 136-37.

7. One could explore further here the dichotomy between Babel' as "Westernized" Jew and the "Ostjuden" (the German term is typically used in discussing these categories) of small-town Volhynia and Galicia. (Geography was obviously not the only relevant criterion of one's status as "Ostjude" or "Westjude": though Odessa was east of Poland, the relatively assimilated Jewish milieu from which Babel' came was "western" relative to that of the eastern European shtetl.) On the matters of Judaism and modern ideologies, and of western vs. eastern Jewry, see (among many other sources) John Murray Cuddihy, *The Ordeal of Civility: Freud, Marx, Levi-Strauss and the Jewish Struggle for Modernity* (New York: Basic Books, 1974); Sander L. Gilman, *Jewish Self-Hatred: Anti-Semitism and the Hidden Language of the Jews* (Baltimore: Johns Hopkins University Press, 1986); and the fascinating and more historically relevant book by Joseph Roth, *Juden auf Wanderschaft* (Berlin: Verlag die Schmiede, 1927).

8. K. Liutov (Babel''s pseudonym), "Nedobitye ubiitsy," *Krasnyi kavalerist,* 17 September 1920, reprinted in *Sochineniia,* 1:205-6.

9. Isaak Babel', "Perekhod cherez Zbruch," *Detstvo i drugie rasskazy,* ed. Efraim Sicher (Jerusalem: Biblioteka Aliya, 1979), 102. Because the stories are so short, I have thought it unnecessary to give page references to subsequent quoted passages. My translations differ, when accuracy requires, from those in the standard English translation by Walter Morison (Isaac Babel, *The Collected Stories* [Cleveland: World, 1960]).

10. The Morison translation gives that line as "fragments of the occult crockery the Jews use only once a year, at Eastertime." The translation is inaccurate on two counts. There is nothing occult in "*sokrovennyi,*" which connotes something secret, hidden and precious. The most difficult problem for a translator is what do with the word "*paskha,*" which can refer to either the Christian or the Jewish holiday. Morison leads the reader to see the narrator as knowing that these are Passover dishes (which only a Jew would be likely to do), but purposely distancing himself by using the Christian rather than the Jewish term.

11. Those who know *Red Cavalry* will see that I am not attempting to deal with every story that involves Jews or Liutov's identity as a Jew (nor is each of the stories mentioned analyzed fully). That would entail probing more problems and more stories than is possible here. It would include, for example, an analysis of one of the cycle's most complex stories, "Squadron Commander Trunov," in which Liutov, disturbed by Trunov's murder of two Polish prisoners, his dispute with Trunov over refusing to cover it up and the commander's suicidal death, goes off to lose himself among the Hasidim arguing on the synagogue square.

12. I am indebted to Vera Proskurina, Michael Denner, Julia Volpe and Alina Chesnokova for stimulating discussions of this element of the story. To my knowledge, the first—and almost only—study to give any attention to the identity of Vasilii is the above-cited essay by Simon Markish, "The Example of Isaac Babel." Markish (41) agrees that the character is previously unseen and that his name identifies him as a non-Jew ("*chuzhoi*" is the term he uses). However, he interprets the repetition of the name to indicate that Vasily is so alien as to be unable to understand the story being told. The only other scholar to note the use of Vasilii, E. A. Dobrenko ("Logika tsikla," 93), follows Markish in this view.

Cynthia Ozick (essay date 8 May 1995)

SOURCE: Ozick, Cynthia. "The Year of Writing Dangerously." *New Republic* (8 May 1995): 31-8.

[*In the following essay, Ozick investigates autobiographical aspects of the stories in* Red Cavalry *and elucidates the relationship between the short story collection and his* 1920 Diary.]

> Identity, at least, is prepared to ask questions.
>
> —Leon Wieseltier

A year or so before the Soviet Union imploded, S.'s mother, my first cousin, whose existence until then had been no more than a distant legend, telephoned from Moscow. "Save my child!" she cried, in immemorial tones. So when S. arrived in New York, I expected a terrified refugee on the run from the intolerable exactions of popular anti-Semitism; at that time the press was filled with such dire reports. For months, preparing for her rescue, I had been hurtling from one agency to another, in search of official information on political asylum.

But when S. finally turned up, in black tights, a miniskirt and the reddest lipstick, it was clear she was indifferent to all that. She didn't want to be saved. What she wanted was an American holiday, a fresh set of boyfriends and a leather coat. She had brought with her a sizable cosmetics case, amply stocked, and a vast, rattling plastic bag stuffed with hundreds of cheap tin Komsomol medals depicting Lenin as a boy. She was scornful of these; they were worthless, she said. She had paid pennies for the lot. Within two weeks S., a natural entrepreneur, had established romantic relations with the handsome young manager of the local sports store and had got him to set up a table at Christmas in his heaviest traffic location. She sold the tin Lenin medals for $3 each, made $300 in a day, and bought the leather coat.

Of course she was a great curiosity. Her English was acutely original, her green eyes gave out ravishing ironic lightnings, her voice was as dark as Garbo's in *Ninotchka,* and none of us had ever seen an actual Soviet citizen up close before. She thought the telephone was bugged. She thought the supermarket was a public exhibition. Any show of household shoddiness—a lamp, say, that came apart—would elicit from her a comical crow: "Like in Soviet!" She was, emphatically, no atheist: she had an affinity for the occult, believed that God could speak in dreams (she owned a dream book, through which Jesus often walked), adored the churches of old Russia and lamented their destruction by the Bolsheviks. On the subject of current anti-Semitism she was mute; that was her mother's territory. Back in Moscow, her boyfriend, Gennadi, had picked her up in the subway *because* she was Jewish. He was in a hurry to marry her. "He want get out of Soviet," she explained.

At home she had been a Sportsdoktor: she traveled with the Soviet teams, roughneck country boys, and daily tested their urine for steroids. (Was this to make sure her athletes were properly dosed?) She announced that *everybody* hated Gorbachev, only the gullible Americans liked him, he was a joke like all the others. A historically minded friend approached S. with the earnest inquiry of an old-fashioned liberal idealist: "We all know, obviously, about the excesses of Stalinism," she said, "but what of the *beginning*? Wasn't Communism a truly beautiful hope at the start?" S. laughed her cynical laugh; she judged my friend profoundly stupid. "Communism," she scoffed, "what Communism? Naïve! Fairy tale, always! No Communism, never! Naïve!"

And leaving behind five devastated American-as-apple-pie boyfriends (and wearing her leather coat), S. returned to Moscow. She did not marry Gennadi. Her mother emigrated to Israel. The last I heard of S., she was in business in Sakhalin, buying and selling—and passing off as the real thing—ersatz paleolithic mammoth tusks.

Well, it is all over now—the Great Experiment, as the old brave voices used to call it—and S. is both symptom and proof of how thoroughly it is over. She represents the Soviet Union's final heave, its last generation. S. is the consummate New Soviet Man: the unfurled future of its seed. If there is an axiom here, it is that ide-

alism squeezed into utopian channels will generate a cynicism so profound that no inch of human life—not youth, not art, not work, not romance, not introspection—is left untainted. The S. whom I briefly knew trusted nothing. In her world, there was nothing to trust. The primal Communist fairy tale had cast its spell: a *baba yaga*'s birth-curse.

In college I read *The Communist Manifesto,* a rapture-bringing psalm. I ought to have read Isaac Babel's **Red Cavalry** stories, if only as a corrective companion text. Or antidote. "But what of the beginning?" my friend had asked. S. answered better than any historian, but no one will answer more terrifyingly than Isaac Babel. If S. is the last generation of New Soviet Man, Babel is the first, the *Manifesto*'s primordial manifestation.

That Babel favored the fall of the Czarist regime is no anomaly. He was a Jew from Odessa, the child of an enlightened family, hungry for a European education; he was subject to the *numerus clausus,* the Czarist quota that kept Jews as a class out of the universities, and Babel in particular out of the University of Odessa. As a very young writer, he put himself at risk when, to be near Maxim Gorky, his literary hero, he went to live illegally in St. Petersburg, a city outside the Pale of Settlement (the area to which Jews were restricted). What Jew would not have welcomed the demise of a hostile and obscurantist polity that, as late as 1911, tried Mendel Beiliss in a Russian court on a fantastic blood libel charge, and what Jew in a time of government-sanctioned pogroms would not have turned with relief to forces promising to topple the oppressors? In attaching himself to the Bolshevik cause, Babel may have been more zealous than many, but far from aberrant. If the choice were either Czar or Bolshevism, what Jew could choose Czar? (A third possibility, which scores of thousands sought, was escape to America.) But even if one were determined to throw one's lot in with the Revolution, what Jew would go riding with Cossacks?

In 1920 Isaac Babel went riding with Cossacks. It was the third year of the Civil War, revolutionary Reds versus Czarist Whites; he was 26. Babel was not new to the military. Two years earlier, during the First World War, he had been a volunteer—in the Czar's army—on the Romanian front, where he contracted malaria. In 1919 he fought with the Red Army to secure St. Petersburg against advancing government troops. And in 1920 he joined ROSTA, the Soviet wire service, as a war correspondent for the newspaper *Red Cavalryman.*

Poland, newly independent, was pressing eastward, hoping to recover its eighteenth-century borders, while the Bolsheviks, moving westward, were furiously promoting the Communist salvation of Polish peasants and workers. The Polish-Soviet War appeared to pit territory against ideology. In reality, territory—or, more precisely, the conquest of impoverished villages and towns and their wretched inhabitants—was all that was at stake for either side. Though the Great War was over, the Allies, motivated by fear of the spread of communism, went to the aid of Poland with equipment and volunteers. (Ultimately the Poles prevailed and the Bolsheviks retreated, between them despoiling whole populations.)

In an era of air battles, Babel was assigned to the First Cavalry Army, a Cossack division led by General Semyon Budyonny. The Cossack image—glinting sabers, pounding hooves—is indelibly fused with Czarist power, but the First Cavalry Army was, perversely, Bolshevik. Stalin was in command of the southern front, the region abutting Poland, and Budyonny was in league with Stalin. Ostensibly, then, Babel found himself among men sympathetic to Marxist doctrine. Yet Red Cossacks were no different from White Cossacks: untamed riders, generally illiterate, boorish and brutish, suspicious of ideas of any kind, attracted only to horseflesh, rabid looting and the quick satisfaction of hunger and lust. "This isn't a Marxist revolution," Babel privately noted; "it's a rebellion of Cossack wild men." Polish and Russian cavalrymen clashing in ditches while warplanes streaked overhead was no more incongruous than the raw sight of Isaac Babel—a writer who had already published short stories praised by Gorky—sleeping in mud with Cossacks.

Lionel Trilling, in a highly nuanced (though partially misinformed) landmark introduction to a 1955 edition of *The Collected Stories of Isaac Babel* (which included the *Red Cavalry* stories), speaks of "the joke of a Jew who is a member of a Cossack regiment." A joke, Trilling explains, because

> traditionally the Cossack was the feared and hated enemy of the Jew. The principle of his existence stood in total antithesis to the principle of the Jew's existence. The Jew conceived of his own ideal character as intellectual, pacific, humane. The Cossack was physical, violent, without mind or manners . . . the natural and appropriate instrument of ruthless oppression.

Yet Trilling supplies another, more glamorous, portrait of the Cossack, which he terms Tolstoyan: "He was the man as yet untrammeled by civilization, direct, immediate, fierce. He was the man of enviable simplicity, the man of the body—the man who moved with speed and grace." In short, "our fantasy of the noble savage." And he attributes this view to Babel.

As it turns out, Babel's tenure with Budyonny's men was more tangled, and more intricately psychological, than Trilling—for whom the problem was tangled and psychological enough—could have known or surmised. For one thing, Trilling mistakenly believed that Babel's

job was that of a supply officer—i.e., that he was actually a member of the regiment. But as a correspondent for a news agency (which meant grinding out propaganda), Babel's position among the troops was from the start defined as an outsider's, Jew or no. He was there as a writer. Worse, in the absence of other sources, Trilling fell into a crucial—and surprisingly naïve—second error: he supposed that the "autobiographical" tales were, in fact, autobiographical.

Babel, Trilling inferred from Babel's stories, "was a Jew of the ghetto" who "when he was 9 years old had seen his father kneeling before a Cossack captain." He compares this (fictitious) event to Freud's contemplation of his father's "having accepted in a pacific way the insult of having his new fur cap knocked into the mud by a Gentile who shouted at him, 'Jew, get off the pavement.'" "We might put it," Trilling concludes, that Babel rode with Budyonny's troops because he had witnessed his father's humiliation by "a Cossack on a horse, who said, 'At your service,' and touched his fur cap with his yellow-gloved hand and politely paid no heed to the mob looting the Babel store."

There was no Babel store. This scene—the captain with the yellow glove, the Jew pleading on his knees while the pogrom rages—is culled from Babel's story **"First Love."** But it was reinforced for Trilling by a fragmentary memoir, published in 1924, wherein Babel calls himself "the son of a Jewish shopkeeper." The truth was that Babel was the son of the class enemy: he came from a well-off family. His father sold agricultural machinery and owned a warehouse in a business section of Odessa where numerous import-export firms were located. In the same memoir Babel records that, since he had no permit allowing him residence in St. Petersburg, he hid out "in a cellar on Pushkin Street which was the home of a tormented, drunken waiter." This was pure fabrication: in actuality Babel was taken in by a highly respectable engineer and his wife, with whom he was in correspondence. The first invention was to disavow a bourgeois background in order to satisfy Communist dogma. The second was a romantic imposture.

It did happen, nevertheless, that the young Babel was witness to a pogrom. He was in no way estranged from Jewish suffering or sensibility or, conversely, from the seductive winds of contemporary Europe. Odessa was modern, bustling, diverse, cosmopolitan; its very capaciousness stimulated a certain worldliness and freedom of outlook. Jewish children were required to study the traditional texts and commentaries, but they were also sent to learn the violin. Babel was early on infatuated with Maupassant and Flaubert, and wrote his first stories in fluent literary French. In his native Russian he lashed himself mercilessly to the discipline of an original style, the credo of which was burnished brevity. At the time of his arrest by the NKVD in 1939—he had failed to conform to Socialist Realism—he was said to be at work on a Russian translation of Sholem Aleichem.

Given these manifold intertwinings, it remains odd that Trilling's phrase for Babel was "a Jew of the ghetto." Trilling himself had characterized Babel's Odessa as "an eastern Marseilles or Naples," observing that "in such cities the transient, heterogeneous population dilutes the force of law and tradition, for good as well as for bad." One may suspect that Trilling's cultural imagination (and perhaps his psyche as well) was circumscribed by a kind of either/or: either worldly sophistication or the ghetto; and that, in linking Jewish learning solely to the ghetto, he could not conceive of its association with a broad and complex civilization.

This partial darkening of mind, it seems to me, limits Trilling's understanding of Babel. An intellectual who had mastered the essentials of rabbinic literature, Babel was an educated Jew not "of the ghetto" but of the world. And not "of both worlds," as the divisive expression has it, but of the great and variegated map of human thought and experience. Trilling, after all, in his own youth had judged the world to be rigorously divided. In 1933, coming upon one of Hemingway's letters, he wrote in his notebook:

> [A] crazy letter, written when he was drunk—self-revealing, arrogant, scared, trivial, absurd; yet [I] felt from reading it how right such a man is compared to the "good minds" of my university life—how he will produce and mean something to the world . . . how his life which he could expose without dignity and which is anarchic and "childish" is a better life than anyone I know could live, and right for his job. And how far—far—far—I am going from being a writer.

Trilling envied but could not so much as dream himself into becoming a version of Hemingway—rifle in one hand and pen in the other, intellectual Jew taking on the strenuous life; how much less, then, could he fathom Babel as Cossack. Looking only to Jewish constriction, what Trilling vitally missed was this: coiled in the bottom-most pit of every driven writer is an impersonator, protean, volatile, restless, relentless. Trilling saw only stasis, or, rather, an unalterable consistency of identity: either lucubration or daring, never both. But Babel imagined for himself an identity so fluid that, having lodged with his civilized friend, the St. Petersburg engineer, it pleased him to invent a tougher Babel consorting underground with a "tormented, drunken waiter." A drunken waiter would have been adventure enough—but ah, that Dostoyevskian "tormented"!

"He loved to confuse and mystify people," his daughter Nathalie wrote of him, after decades spent in search of his character. Born in 1929, she lived with her mother in Paris, where her father was a frequent, if raffish, visi-

tor. In 1935 Babel was barred from leaving the Soviet Union, and never again saw his wife and child. Nathalie Babel was 10 when Babel was arrested. In 1961 she went to look for traces of her father in Moscow,

> where one can still meet people who loved him and continue to speak of him with nostalgia. There, thousands of miles from my own home in Paris, sitting in his living room, in his own chair, drinking from his glass, I felt utterly baffled. Though in a sense I had tracked him down, he still eluded me. The void remained.

In a laudatory reminiscence published in a Soviet literary magazine in 1964—a time when Babel's reputation was undergoing a modicum of "rehabilitation"—Georgy Munblit, a writer who had known Babel as well as anyone, spoke of "this sly, unfaithful, eternally evasive and mysterious Babel"; and though much of this elusiveness was caution in the face of Soviet restriction, a good part of it nevertheless had to do with the thrill of dissimulation and concealment. In a speech in Moscow in the mid-1960s at a meeting championing Babel's work, Ilya Ehrenburg, the literary Houdini who managed to survive every shift of Stalinist whim, described Babel as liking to "play the fool and put on romantic airs. He liked to create an atmosphere of mystery about himself; he was secretive and never told anybody where he was going."

Other writers (all of whom had themselves escaped the purges) came forward with recollections of Babel's eccentricities in risky times: Babel as intrepid wanderer; as trickster, rapscallion, ironist; penniless, slippery, living on the edge, off the beaten track, down and out; seduced by the underlife of Paris, bars, whores, cabdrivers, jockeys. All this suggests Orwellian experiment and audacity. Babel relished Villon and Kipling, and was delighted to discover that Rimbaud, too, was an "adventurer." Amusing and mercurial, "he loved to play tricks on people," according to Lev Nikulin, who was at school with Babel and remembered him "as a bespectacled boy in a rather shabby school coat and a battered cap with a green band and badge depicting Mercury's staff."

Trilling, writing in 1955, had of course no access to observations such as these; and we are as much in need now as Trilling was of a valid biography of Babel. Still, it is clear even from such small evidences and quicksilver portraits that Babel's connection with the Cossacks was, if not inevitable, more natural than not; and that Trilling's Freudian notion of the humiliated ghetto child could not have been more off the mark. For Babel, lamp oil and fearlessness were not antithetical. He was a man with the bit of recklessness between his teeth. One might almost ask how a writer so given to disguises and role-playing could *not* have put on a Cossack uniform.

"The Rebbe's Son," one of the *Red Cavalry* tales, is explicit about this fusion of contemplative intellect and physical danger. Ilya, the son of the Zhitomir Rebbe, "the last prince of the dynasty," is a Red Army soldier killed in battle. The remnants of his possessions are laid out before the narrator:

> Here everything was dumped together—the warrants of the agitator and the commemorative booklets of the Jewish poet. Portraits of Lenin and Maimonides lay side by side. Lenin's nodulous skull and the tarnished silk of the portraits of Maimonides. A strand of female hair had been placed in a book of the resolutions of the Sixth Party Congress, and in the margins of Communist leaflets swarmed crooked lines of ancient Hebrew verse. In a sad and meager rain they fell on me—pages of the Song of Songs and revolver cartridges.

Babel was himself drawn to the spaciousness and elasticity of these unexpected combinations. They held no enigma for him. But while the Rebbe's son was a kind of double patriot, loyal to the God of Abraham, Isaac and Jacob and loyal to a dream of the betterment of Russia, Babel tended toward both theological and (soon enough) political skepticism. His *amor patriae* was, passionately, for the Russian mother tongue. Before the Stalinist prison clanged shut in 1935, Babel might easily have gone to live permanently in France, with his wife and daughter. Yet much as he reveled in French literature and language, he would not suffer exile from his native Russian.

A family can be replaced, or duplicated; but who can replace or duplicate the syllables of Pushkin and Tolstoy? And in fact (though his wife in Paris survived until 1957, and there was no divorce) Babel did take another wife in the Soviet Union, who gave birth to another daughter. A second family was possible; a second language was not. (Only consider what must be the intimate sorrows—even in the shelter of America, even after the demise of Communism—of Czeslaw Milosz, Joseph Brodksy, Norman Manea and countless other literary refugees.) By remaining in the Soviet Union, and refusing finally to bend his art to Soviet directives, Babel sacrificed his life to his language.

It was a language he did not allow to rest. He meant to put his spurs to it, and run it to unexampled leanness. He quoted Pushkin: "precision and brevity." "Superior craftsmanship," Babel told Munblit, "is the art of making your writing as unobtrusive as possible." Ehrenburg recalled a conversation in Madrid with Hemingway, who had just discovered Babel. "I find that Babel's style is even more concise than mine. . . . It shows what can be done," Hemingway marveled. "Even when you've got all the water out of them, you can still clot the curds a little more." Such idiosyncratic experiments in style were hardly congruent with official pressure to honor the ascent of socialism through prescriptive prose about the beauty of collective farming. Babel did not dissent from party demands; instead he fell mainly into silence, writing in private and publishing almost nothing. His attempts at a play and a filmscript met convulsive party criticism; the director of the film—an adaptation of a story by Turgenev—was forced into a public apology.

The *Red Cavalry* stories saw print, individually, before 1924. Soviet cultural policies in those years were not yet consolidated; it was a period of post-revolutionary leniency and ferment. Russian modernism was sprouting in the shape of formalism, acmeism, imagism, symbolism; an intellectual and artistic avant-garde flourished. Censorship, which had been endemic to the Czarist regime, was reintroduced in 1922, but the restraints were loose. Despite a program condemning elitism, the early Soviet leadership, comprising a number of intellectuals—Lenin, Bukharin, Trotsky—recognized that serious literature could not be wholly entrusted to the sensibilities of party bureaucrats.

By 1924, then, Babel found himself not only famous, but eligible eventually for Soviet rewards: an apartment in Moscow, a dacha in the country, a car and chauffeur. Yet he was increasingly called on to perform (and conform) by the blunter rulers of a darkening repression. Why was he not writing in praise of New Soviet Man? Little by little a perilous mist gathered around Babel's person: though his privileges were not revoked (he was at his dacha on the day of his arrest), he began to take on a certain pariah status. When a leftist Congress for the Defense of Culture and Peace met in Paris, for example, Babel was deliberately omitted from the Soviet delegation, and was grudgingly allowed to attend only after the French organizers brought their protests to the Soviet Embassy.

Certain manuscripts he was careful not to expose to anyone. Among these was the remarkable journal he had kept, from June to September 1920, of the actions of Budyonny's First Cavalry Army in eastern Poland. Because it was missing from the papers seized by the secret police at the dacha and in his Moscow flat, the manuscript escaped destruction, and came clandestinely into the possession of Babel's (second) wife only in the 1950s. Ehrenburg was apparently the journal's first influential reader, though very likely he did not see it until the 1960s, when he mentioned it publicly, and evidently spontaneously, in his rehabilitation speech:

> I have been comparing the diary of the *Red Cavalry* with the stories. He scarcely changed any names, the events are all practically the same, but everything is illuminated with a kind of wisdom. He is saying: this is how it was. This is how the people were—they did terrible things and they suffered, they played tricks on others and they died. He made his stories out of the facts and phrases hastily jotted down in his notebook.

It goes without saying that the flatness of this essentially evasive summary does almost no justice to an astonishing historical record set down with godlike prowess in a prose of frightening clarity. In Russia the complete text of the journal finally appeared in 1990. Yale University Press brings it to us now in an electrifying translation, accompanied by an indispensable introduction. (It ought to be added that an informative introduction can be found also in the new Penguin **Collected Stories**; but the reader's dependence on such piecemeal discussions only underscores the irritating absence of a formal biography.) In 1975 Ardis Publishers made available the first English translation of excerpts from the journal (*Isaac Babel: Forgotten Prose*). That such a manuscript existed had long been known in the Soviet Union, but there was plainly no chance of publication; Ehrenburg, in referring to it, was discreet about its contents.

The *Diary* may count, then, as a kind of secret document; certainly as a suppressed one. But it is "secret" in another sense as well. Though it served as raw material for the **Red Cavalry** stories, Babel himself, in transforming private notes into daring fiction, was less daring than he might have been. He was, in fact, circumspect and selective. One can move from the notes to the stories without surprise—or rather, the surprise is in the masterliness and shock of a ripe and radical style. Still, as Ehrenburg reported, "the events are all practically the same," and what is in the *Diary* is in the stories.

But one cannot begin with the stories and then move to the journal without the most acute recognition of what has been, substantively and for the most part, shut out of the fiction. And what has been shut out is the calamity (to say it in the most general way) of Jewish fate in Eastern Europe. The *Diary* records how the First Cavalry Army, and Babel with it, went storming through the little Jewish towns of Galicia, in Poland, towns that had endured the Great War, with many of their young men serving in the Polish Army, only to be decimated by pogroms immediately afterward, at the hands of the Poles themselves. And immediately after that, the invasion of the Red Cossacks.

The Yale edition of the *Diary* supplies maps showing the route of Budyonny's troops; the resonant names of these places, rendered half-romantic through the mystical tales of their legendary hasidic saints, rise up with the nauseous familiarity of their deaths: Brody, Dubno, Zhitomir, Belz, Chelm, Zamosc and so on. Only two decades after the Red Cossacks stampeded through them, their Jewish populations fell prey to the Germans and were destroyed. Riding and writing, writing and riding, Babel saw it all: saw it like a seer. "Ill-fated Galicia, ill-fated Jews," he wrote. "Can it be," he wrote, "that ours is the century in which they perish?"

True: everything that is in the stories is in the *Diary*— priest, painter, widow, gun-cart, soldier, prisoner; but

the heart of the *Diary* remains secreted in the *Diary*. When all is said and done—and much is said and done in these blistering pages: pillaged churches, ruined synagogues, wild Russians, beaten Poles, mud, horses, hunger, looting, shooting—Babel's journal is a Jewish lamentation: a thing the Soviet system could not tolerate, and Ehrenburg was too prudent to reveal. The merciless minds that snuffed the identities of the murdered at Babi Yar would hardly sanction Babel's whole and bloody truths.

Nor did Babel himself publicly sanction them. The **Red Cavalry** narratives include six stories (out of thirty-five) that touch on the suffering of Jews; the headlong *Diary* contains scores. An act of authorial self-censorship, and not only because Babel was determined to be guarded. Impersonation, or call it reckless play, propelled him at all points. The *Diary* can muse, "The Slavs—the manure of history?"—but Babel came to the Cossacks disguised as a Slav, having assumed the name K. L. Lyutov, the name he assigns also to his narrator. And in the *Diary* itself, encountering terrified Polish Jews, he again and again steers them away from the knowledge that rides in his marrow, and fabricates deliberate revolutionary fairy tales (his word): he tells his trembling listeners how

> everything's changing for the better—my usual system—miraculous things are happening in Russia—express trains, free food for children, theaters, the International. They listen with delight and disbelief. I think—you'll have your diamond-studded sky, everything and everyone will be turned upside down and inside out for the umpteenth time, and [I] feel sorry for them.

"My usual system": perhaps it is kind to scatter false consolations among the doomed. Or else it is not kindness at all, merely a writer's mischief or a rider's diversion: the tormented mice of Galicia entertained by a cat in Cossack dress. Sometimes he is recognized (once by a child) as a Jew, and then he half-lies and explains that he has a Jewish mother. But mainly he is steadfast in the pretense of being Lyutov. And nervy: the *Diary* begins on June 3, in Zhitomir, and on July 12, one day before Babel's twenty-sixth birthday, he notes: "My first ride on horseback." In no time at all he is, at least on horseback, like all the others: a skilled and dauntless trooper. "The horse galloped well," he says on that first day.

Enchanted, proud, he looks around at his companions: "red flags, a powerful, well-knit body of men, confident commanders, calm and experienced eyes of topknotted Cossack fighting men, dust, silence, order, brass band." But moments later the calm and experienced eyes are searching out plunder in the neat cottage of an immigrant Czech family, "all good people." "I took nothing, although I could have," the new horseman comments.

"I'll never be a real Budyonny man." The real Budyonny men are comely, striking, stalwart. Turning off a highway, Babel catches sight of "the brigades suddenly appear[ing], inexplicable beauty, an awesome force advancing." Another glimpse:

> Night . . . horses are quietly snorting, they're all Kuban Cossacks here, they eat together, sleep together, a splendid silent comradeship . . . they sing songs that sound like church music in lusty voices, their devotion to horses, beside each man a little heap—saddle, bridle, ornamental saber, greatcoat, I sleep in the midst of them.

Babel is small, his glasses are small and round, he sets down secret sentences. And meanwhile his dispatches, propaganda screeches regularly published in *Red Cavalryman,* have a different tone: "Soldiers of the Red Army, finish them off! Beat down harder on the opening covers of their stinking graves!" And: "That is what they are like, our heroic nurses! Caps off to the nurses! Soldiers and commanders, show respect to the nurses!" (In the *Diary* the dubious propagandist writes satirically, "Opening of the Second Congress of the Third International, unification of the peoples finally realized, now all is clear. . . . We shall advance into Europe and conquer the world:")

And always there is cruelty, and always there are the Jews. "Most of the rabbis have been exterminated." "The Jewish cemetery . . . hundreds of years old, gravestones have toppled over . . . overgrown with grass, it has seen Khmelnitsky, now Budyonny . . . everything repeats itself, now that whole story—Poles, Cossacks, Jews—is repeating itself with stunning exactitude, the only new element is Communism." "They all say they're fighting for justice and they all loot." "Life is loathsome, murderers, it's unbearable, baseness and crime." "I ride along with them, begging the men not to massacre prisoners. . . . I couldn't look at their faces, they bayoneted some, shot others, bodies covered by corpses, they strip one man while they're shooting another, groans, screams, death rattles." "We are destroyers . . . we move like a whirlwind, like a stream of lava, hated by everyone, life shatters, I am at a huge, never-ending service for the dead . . . the sad senselessness of my life."

The Jews: "The Poles ransacked the place, then the Cossacks." "Hatred for the Poles is unanimous. They have looted, tortured, branded the pharmacist with a red-hot iron, put needles under his nails, pulled out his hair, all because somebody shot at a Polish officer." "The Jews ask me to use my influence to save them from ruin, they are being robbed of food and goods. . . . The cobbler had looked forward to Soviet rule—and what he sees are Jew-baiters and looters. . . . Organized looting of a stationer's shop, the proprietor in tears, they tear up everything. . . . When night comes the whole town will be looted—everybody knows it."

The Jews at the hands of the Poles: "A pogrom . . . a naked, barely breathing prophet of an old man, an old woman butchered, a child with fingers chopped off, many people still breathing, stench of blood, everything turned upside down, chaos, a mother sitting over her sabered son, an old woman lying twisted up like a pretzel, four people in one hovel, filth, blood under a black beard, just lying there in the blood."

The Jews at the hands of the Bolsheviks: "Our men nonchalantly walking around looting whenever possible, stripping mangled corpses. The hatred is the same, the Cossacks just the same, it's nonsense to think one army is different from another. The life of these little towns. There's no salvation. Everyone destroys them." "Our men were looting last night, tossed out the Torah scrolls in the synagogue and took the velvet covers for saddlecloths. The military commissar's dispatch rider examines phylacteries, wants to take the straps." The *Diary* mourns, "What a mighty and marvelous life of a nation existed here. The fate of Jewry."

And then: "I am an outsider." And again: "I don't belong, I'm all alone, we ride on . . . five minutes after our arrival the looting starts, women struggling, weeping and wailing, it's unbearable, I can't stand these never-ending horrors. . . . [I] snatch a flatcake out of the hands of a peasant woman's little boy." He does this mechanically, and without compunction. "How we eat," he explains. "Red troops arrive in a village, ransack the place, cook, stoves crackling all night, the householders' daughters have a hard time" (a comment we will know how to interpret). Babel grabs the child's flatcake—a snack on the fly—on August 3.

On July 25, nine days earlier, he and a riding companion, Prishchepa, a loutish syphilitic illiterate, have burst into a pious Jewish house in a town called Demidovka. It is the Sabbath, when lighting a fire is forbidden; it is also the eve of the Ninth of Av, a somber fast day commemorating the destruction of the Temple in Jerusalem. Prishchepa demands fried potatoes. The dignified mother, a flock of daughters in white stockings, a scholarly son, are all petrified: on the Sabbath, they protest, they cannot dig potatoes, and besides, the fast begins at sundown. "Fucking Yids," Prishchepa yells; so the potatoes are dug, the fire to cook them is lit.

Babel, a witness to this anguish, says nothing. "I keep quiet, because I'm a Russian." Will Prishchepa discover that Lyutov is only another Yid? "We eat like oxen, fried potatoes and five tumblersful of coffee each. We sweat, they keep serving us, all this is terrible, I tell them fairy tales about Bolshevism." Night comes, the mother sits on the floor and sobs, the son chants the liturgy for the Ninth of Av, Jeremiah's Lamentations: "they eat dung, their maidens are ravished, their menfolk killed, Israel subjugated." Babel hears and understands every Hebrew word. "Demidovka, night, Cossacks," he sums it up, "all just as it was when the Temple was destroyed. I go out to sleep in the yard, stinking and damp."

And there he is, New Soviet Man: stinking, a sewer of fairy tales, an unbeliever—and all the same complicit. Nathalie Babel said of her father that nothing "could shatter his feeling that he belonged to Russia and that he had to share the fate of his countrymen. What in so many people would have produced only fear and terror, awakened in him a sense of duty and a kind of blind heroism." In the brutal light of the *Diary,* violation upon violation, it is hard to yield to this point of view. Despair and an abyss of cynicism do not readily accord with a sense of duty; and whether or not Babel's travels with the Cossacks, and with Bolshevism altogether, deserve to be termed heroic, he was anything but blind. He saw, he saw, and he saw.

It may be that the habit of impersonation, the habit of deception, the habit of the mask, will in the end lead a man to become what he impersonates. Or it may be that the force of "I am an outsider" overwhelms the secret gratification of having got rid of a fixed identity. In any case, the *Diary* tells no lies. These scenes in a journal, linked by commas quicker than human breath, run like rapids through a gorge—on one side the unrestraint of violent men, on the other the bleaker freedom of unbelonging. Each side is subversive of the other; and still they embrace the selfsame river.

To venture yet another image, Babel's *Diary* stands as a tragic masterwork of breakneck cinematic "dailies," those raw, unedited rushes that expose the director to himself. If Trilling, who admitted to envy of the milder wilderness that was Hemingway, had read Babel's *Diary*—what then? And who, in our generation, should read the *Diary*? Novelists and poets, of course; specialists in Russian literature, obviously; American innocents who define the world of the '20s by jazz, flappers and Fitzgerald. And also those who protested Claude Lanzmann's *Shoah* as unfair to the psyche of the Polish countryside; but, most of all, the cruelly ignorant children of the left who still believe that the Marxist utopia requires for its realization only a more favorable venue, and another go.

No one knows when or exactly how Babel perished. Some suppose he was shot immediately after the NKVD picked him up and brought him to Moscow's Lyubanka Prison, on May 15, 1939. Others place the date of his murder in 1941, following months of torture. More than fifty years later, as if the writer were sending forth phantoms of his first and last furies, Babel's youthful *Diary* emerges. What it attests to above all is not simply that fairy tales can kill—who doesn't understand this?—but that Bolshevism was lethal in its very cradle.

Which is just what S., my ironical Muscovite cousin, found so pathetically funny when, laughing at our American stupidity, she went home to Communism's graveyard.

Efraim Sicher (essay date 1995)

SOURCE: Sicher, Efraim. "The Jewishness of Babel." In *Jews in Russian Literature after the October Revolution: Writers and Artists between Hope and Apostasy,* pp. 70-111. Cambridge: Cambridge University Press, 1995.

[*In the following excerpt, Sicher chronicles Babel's time with Russian Cossacks in the First Cavalry in 1920, maintaining that by exploring "the conflict of Russian and Jew in the writer's identity, we . . . see how Babel came to form his image of the post-Revolutionary Jewish intellectual, torn between Judaism and Communism, alienated from his past and unable to come to terms with the future."*]

As a war correspondent attached to Budyonny's First Cavalry (*Pervaia konnaia armiia*) from May until September 1920, Babel adopted the pseudonym Liutov and passed himself off as a Russian. The name Liutov itself speaks for the ironic contrast between its connotation of fierceness in Russian and Babel's meek appearance. Babel found himself a Jew among Cossacks whose animosity toward the Jews was as awesome as their ferocity and horsemanship. If we now examine the conflict of Russian and Jew in the writer's identity, we will see how Babel came to form his image of the post-Revolutionary Jewish intellectual, torn between Judaism and Communism, alienated from his past and unable to come to terms with the future.

The legendary First Cavalry had been formed in November 1919 out of Cossack and peasant horsemen in the Red Army. Its command, under Semyon Mikhailovich Budyonny (1883-1973), grew out of Stalin's faction which had defied Trotsky at Tsaritsyn. After a phenomenal march through Makhno country of 750 miles in a month, the First Cavalry crossed the Dnieper on 6 May 1920, in time for the opening of the Soviet counter-offensive in the Ukraine.[1] Babel accompanied them as a war correspondent for the South Russia Telegraph Agency during the Polish campaign of summer 1920, but was apparently never a regular soldier in a combat unit. He talked with many Jewish local residents who had been subjected to pogroms and extortion under a number of occupying powers including Reds, Whites, Poles, supporters of Petliura, anarchists and peasant bands. Much of the fighting was waged in the heart of the former Pale of Settlement, territory disputed for centuries by Russians, Poles and Ukrainians. Yet, despite his assumed Russian identity, Babel's true sympathies for the victims of looting and pogroms are revealed in his Diary and in the articles he wrote for the front-line propaganda news-sheet, *Krasnyi kavalerist*.[2] His testimony is unusual for two reasons. First, Babel was a chance witness in areas under Bolshevik control (unlike for example, the members of the international investigating commission which had visited Poland in 1919). Second, Babel intended to use his experiences for literary purposes, and in the Diary which he kept he writes as an objective bystander, even though he himself records his deeply emotional affinity with his Jewish brethren.[3]

In 1921-1922 Babel was working on the drafts of stories about the First Cavalry[4] and in 1923 the completed stories began to appear in the Odessa Party newspaper *Izvestiia* and then in Moscow literary journals. They were later included in a controversial and extraordinary collection, **Konarmiia (Red Cavalry)**, which was published by the State Publishing House in Moscow in 1926. The published stories merge and transform the plotlines in the drafts and occasionally they revert to the material in the Diary. It seems that Babel returned to the Diary after abandoning about half the plots in the drafts,[5] despite his promises to his editor Dmitri Furmanov, author of the Civil War epic *Chapaev*, that he would introduce in the completed book more of the masses and militant communists.[6] A comparison of the Diary entries with the fictional stories helps explain the position of the diarist vis à vis the Cossacks, the local Jews and his own historical situation as a Jew.

Written by hand in an accounting book, Babel's 1920 Diary was preserved by friends in Kiev during his years of wandering and it thereby escaped confiscation with the rest of Babel's papers when he was arrested by the NKVD on 15 May 1939. It is clear from several instructions to himself to 'remember' or 'describe' that Babel had in mind a literary work which would be based on the material he recorded; there is no trace of the 'voennyi zhurnal' (military journal) which he mentions in the Diary. Some fragments and draft versions of short stories on Red Cavalry themes were written on pages torn from the Diary, so that the manuscript may be more complete than has previously been thought. In addition, pencil and red ink marks were made over Diary entries, probably at a later date, as part of the transfer of material to literary form. The Diary is written in elliptic phrases, aides-memoire not intended for publication, and its hurried style makes obvious that it was written during the campaign at the time of the events which it describes. Each entry is headed with a date, mostly also with a place name; however, it should be noted that the date and place given at the end of the stories in their early published versions, and retained in

several cases in **Red Cavalry,** do not always relate to those in the Diary but were added to enhance the illusion of authenticity and the journal style of some of the stories.

The personal tone of the Diary conveys Babel's bitter cynicism from the first weeks of his stay in the First Red Cavalry, as well as his shrewd assessment of the military situation and of the behaviour of the Soviet rank and file. By September he is ill and hates the war. It is worth quoting at length from an unsent personal letter of mid-August 1920, found between the pages of the Diary, to get an idea of Babel's mood and his attitude to the Revolution, as well as to his writing:

> Today's heading should read, Forest Clearing North-West of Starye Maidany. Since morning the divisional staff has been here in the forest with the squadron command . . . For days on end we ride from one brigade to another, watch the fighting, compose dispatches, spend the night at . . . [one word indecipherable] in the woods, run away from the aeroplanes which drop bombs on us. Above us are captivating skies, a cool sun, around us it smells of pine trees, hundreds of Steppe horses snort, this is where to live but all our thoughts are on killing. These words of mine sound trite, but war is actually sometimes beautiful, though in every case destructive.

> I have gone through here two weeks of complete despair; this was because of the brutal cruelty which does not let up for a moment here and because of my clear realization of how unfit I am for the business of destruction, how difficult it is to wrench myself away from the old times, from . . . [indecipherable]; from what was perhaps bad, but for me breathed with poetry like a hive with honey, I am going away now, but so what,—some will make the revolution, and I shall, I shall sing of what is to be found to one side, what is to be found deeper; I have felt that I can do this, and there will be a time and a place for this. . . . [indecipherable] woke up, one hundred horsepower throbbing in my chest, I again start athinking and two demons, that is, two bombs which went off half-an-hour ago a hundred paces from us, cannot disturb me.

> I often write to you but there is no answer, I live in tense anxiety, they say there are some letters and telegrams for me wandering around, that means trouble; with what close ties [here the MS breaks off].[7]

Although Babel was aware of the irreparable decay of the East European *shtetl*, these petty-bourgeois Jews were his 'kin' and he opened his heart to them (Diary, 5 July 1920). The first entry in the Diary mentions the pogrom by the Poles at Zhitomir, in which 43 Jews had perished and two were buried alive.[8] Babel suffered from no illusions that the Jewish population could expect any better treatment from the Cossacks:

> The Zhitomir pogrom was initiated by the Poles, later, of course, by the Cossacks.

> After the appearance of our advance guard the Poles came into the town for 3 days, Jewish pogrom, they cut

off beards, that's usual, they assembled 45 Jews on the market square, they led them away to the cattle slaughterhouse, tortures, they cut off tongues, wailing all over the square.

(Diary, 3 July 1920)

Babel had to travel quickly in order to catch up with the divisional command, owing to the rapid Soviet advance after the breakthrough of 5 June at Zhitomir, and he visited a number of Jewish communities. On the way to Równe he spent the night in Hoszcza. Despite the dissuasion of Russian soldiers Babel insisted on staying with a Jewish family, the Ucheniks. Their six-year-old daughter was not slow to guess their guest was a Jew and Babel told them something of his family, saying he had a Jewish mother. Throughout the campaign Babel tried to maintain the guise of a Russian who did not understand Yiddish, though he realized his Jewish hosts were not easily fooled, while his heart was bursting from emotion at the plight of his brethren. The Jews' apprehensions are justified: the soldiers' intentions are clear towards the women of the house and Hoszcza is pillaged in the dead silence of night, 'chistaia rabota' (a professional job). Not even crying can be heard (Diary, 5 July 1920).[9] Eavesdropping on a Jewish family in Równe after the arrival of a Cossack brigade, Babel hears of the robberies committed by Budyonny's men (Diary, 6 July 1920). A number of Jews believed that their livelihood was threatened by Soviet restrictions on free trade, an understandable fear considering the precarious economic structure of *shtetl* life, and Babel noticed the pervasive fear of rape and requisitions.

Support for the Bolsheviks is found only among the Jewish youth (a column of Jewish 'midgets' appears in the drafts and we recall the Jewish *ataman* with the face of a Talmud student in **'Afonka Bida'**); the old Jews are indifferent. The local Jews are, however, oriented toward Russian culture and have little love for the Poles, especially after the recent pogroms. Babel quotes the saying that it is better to starve under the Bolsheviks than eat white bread under the Poles. It should be remembered that joining the Reds afforded a chance of revenge for the pogroms and that the Bolsheviks had overturned the old order responsible for Jewish suffering, promising a new social justice for all.

The general picture in the Diary of the destruction of a once bountiful Jewish life full of tradition is confirmed by Babel's visit to Brody (30 July 1920, 31 July 1920). After the successful Polish defence of Warsaw—the 'Miracle on the Vistula'—there is little change in the picture; at Laszków Babel hears the 'usual stories' of the degradation of rabbis (9 August 1920). In the four-hundred-year-old *shtetl* of Korec Babel finds the synagogues and other buildings in ruins. The graves give mute testimony to the Jews who fell in the First World

War. No atrocities are recorded here, although the Cossacks empty a local store (21 July 1920). Dubno passes from hand to hand in July 1920, but does not seem to Babel to have been the scene of looting; on his arrival there, however, he finds the synagogues wrecked (23 July 1920). At Sokal' (26 August 1920) Babel is witness to organized looting but he finds time to visit the local synagogues, observing the two-hundred-year dispute between Hasidim and the anti-Hasidic *mitnagdim*, between followers of the Husiatyn and Belz rebbes (the latter had fled to Vienna). The dispute is featured in the story **'Eskadronnyi Trunov'** (**'Squadron Commander Trunov'**) and it suggests to Babel the unchanging and unshakable traditional Jewish way of life that continues despite war and revolution.

In Demidowka the Red Cossacks force the local Jews to desecrate the Sabbath by digging potatoes. A Jewish dentist resists. The fact that it is the eve of the Fast of the Ninth of Av increases the tragedy in Babel's mind, for on this day Jews read the lament of Jeremiah and sit on the floor in mourning for the destruction of the Temple in Jerusalem; now they must relive that destruction:

> Ninth of Av. An old woman sobs, sitting on the floor; her son, who adores his mother and says that he believes in God to make her feel good, sings in a pleasant tenor and explains the story of the Destruction of the Temple. The terrible words of the prophets—the people eat dung, the maidens dishonoured, the men killed, Israel destroyed, angry melancholy words. The lamp smokes, the old woman howls, the young man sings melodiously, girls in white stockings; outside the window is Demidowka, night, Cossacks, everything as it was when they were destroying the Temple.

(24 July 1920)

The prophecies of Isaiah and Jeremiah have always been part of the Jewish response to national and communal calamities, commemorated on the Fast of Av by a liturgy of communal repentance and prayers for spiritual as well as historical redemption. The Destruction of Jerusalem was the archetypal paradigm of the catastrophes of Jewish history that renewed the meaning of the Ninth of Av, especially instances of martyrdom in the Crusades and the Khmelnitsky massacres; in fact, some Polish communities used to prepare for the Fast by reading Hannover's elegy for Khmelnitsky's victims, *Yeven metsulah*. In the First World War, just a few years before, Cossacks had pillaged and wrecked Jewish homes in these and adjacent areas of dense Jewish population. When An-sky toured Galicia in a Russian uniform as representative of the State Duma committee to aid war victims, the Destruction of Jerusalem was very much in his mind. At Sadgora in 1917 he found an icon placed in the Holy Ark of the synagogue, *tselem be-heikhal* ('an idol in the sanctuary'), just as in the Talmudic narrative of the desecration of the Temple.[10] In

Babel's drafts we read: 'Ninth of Av—Destruction of Jerusalem . . . Lament of Jeremiah . . . about the Ninth of Av—to structure [the story] on the correspondence of the prayers and what is on the other side of the wall.' Babel began writing a story about the *shtetl* of Demidowka which centred on the national tragedy of the Jews symbolized by the destruction of the Temple and the prophecy of Jeremiah, but he gave it up, apparently in favour of a more subtle approach that would not require a Jewish literary focus yet would retain the importance of the experience at Demidowka, whose centrality is indicated in a number of drafts on the subject.

The shift in focus is reflected in **'The Cemetery at Kozin'**, a brief miniature quoted at the end of the previous chapter, which is based on impressions in the Diary of overgrown Jewish cemeteries where the victims of Khmelnitsky were now joined by those of another Cossack hero, Budyonny: 'Everything is repeating itself; now this story—Poles—Cossacks—Jews—is being repeated with striking accuracy; what is new is Communism' (Diary, 18 July 1920). In the stories Babel stresses that nothing has changed for the three centuries of victims of Poles and Cossacks, but he does this surreptitiously, by flanking the description of the graves of the *unavenged* Jews in **'The Cemetery at Kozin'** with two stories of horrifying Cossack vengeance.[11]

Babel makes no mention of the Bolshevik Party line, which discriminated between the Jewish bourgeoisie and the Jewish proletariat, and we know from other sources that often the Cossacks on the Bolshevik side made no such distinction.[12] In the stories **'Sol'' ('Salt')** and **'Izmena' ('Treason')** the Cossacks think of the Jews as non-fighting intellectuals; Balmashev goes as far as to defend Trotsky (the Minister of War) from the charge of being a 'zhid' by identifying him as the son of the governor of Tambov province who went over to the workers![13]

A Putilov worker sees little point in dragging prisoners along only to put their lives into the hands of the convoys (Diary, 30 August 1920), and one may presume that these carters who transported prisoners to headquarters for further investigation meted out the sort of rough justice described in **'Ivany' ('The Two Ivans')**. One healthy prisoner was wounded by two bullets without any provocation whatsoever (27 July 1920). Babel notes a massacre of prisoners (17 August 1920) and records another incident in which ten prisoners perished (30 August 1920). Drafts entitled **'Ikh bylo deviat'' ('There Were Nine')** and **'Ikh bylo desiat'' ('There Were Ten')** describe in detail the shooting of Polish prisoners who had undressed before capture in order to conceal the identity of their officers. A pitiful scene in **'There, Were Nine'** is one in which a beaten Jewish prisoner, Adolf Shulmeister, a Łódź shop-assistant, rec-

ognizes the narrator as a fellow-Jew and begs for his life. The narrator tears himself away with some difficulty:

> He kept pressing up against my horse and stroked and caressed my boot with trembling fingers. His leg had been broken with a rifle butt. It left a thin trail of blood like that of a wounded dog, and sweat, glistening in the sun bubbled on his cracked, yellowish bald pate.
>
> 'You are a *Jude,* sir!' he whispered, frantically fondling my stirrup. 'You are—' he squealed, the spittle dribbling from his mouth, and his whole body convulsed with joy.
>
> 'Get back into line, Shulmeister!' I shouted at the Jew, and suddenly, overcome by a deathly feeling of faintness, I began to slip from the saddle and, choking, I said, 'How did you know?'
>
> 'You have that nice Jewish look about you,' he said in a shrill voice, hopping on one leg and leaving the thin dog's trail behind him. 'That nice Jewish look, sir.'
>
> His fussing had a sense of death about it, and I had quite a job fending him off. It took me some time to come to, as though I had had a concussion.[14]

In the story **'Squadron Commander Trunov'** the incident is incorporated into the more ironic context of the martyrdom of Trunov at the hands of American bomber pilots, while the narrator (who quotes Trotsky's orders not to shoot prisoners) cannot join him. More subtly, the raid on the beehives, mentioned in the Diary in connection with the massacre of prisoners, is transferred in *Red Cavalry* to **'Put' v Brody' ('The Road to Brody')** where it introduces the unending litany of death and the 'chronicle of daily atrocities'.

The capture of an American pilot provided Babel with an indication of the anti-Semitic image of the Bolsheviks disseminated on the Polish side. The pilot, who had enlisted in the Kosciuszko Squadron of the Polish Air Force, pretended to be a Jew called Frank Mosher in the hope that he could thus enlist the sympathy of the Bolsheviks, who were thought to be predominantly Jews. The Soviet armies were virtually defenceless against the reconnaissance and bombing raids of the Polish aeroplanes, whose pilots included a group of Americans who had volunteered for an adventure in Poland rather than return home from the Western Front.[15] Babel, who was pretending *not* to be a Jew, interrogated the captured pilot, and displayed special interest in the pilot as a representative of Western culture. From him, and from a letter found on him written by Major Fauntleroy, Babel learned details of the unstable political situation in Poland and of the Poles' exaggerated idea of Bolshevik strength, as well as their belief in communist intentions to 'annihilate' (*sic!*) national minorities and their customs (14 July 1920). Nothing further is recorded of the American pilot in the Diary, but the planes of his commanding officer, Major Fauntleroy, are the ones in action in the story **'Squadron Commander Trunov'**.

Babel considers Bolshevik propaganda to have a much greater effect on the Cossacks than the sentimental patriotic Polish appeals, and an unspecified number come over to the Soviet side (15 July 1920). However, the low level of understanding among the Cossacks of the aims of the Revolution is quite evident; but now that they have been organized by the Soviets they present a formidable sight, professional yet also bestially cruel. They regard the local population as a natural target for looting and they make use of the opportunity for unleashing their promiscuity. Babel regards the Cossacks as scavengers (he calls them 'barakhol'shchiki') and also remarks: 'A terrible truth—all the soldiers suffer from syphilis' (28 July 1920). The moan of peasants who have been robbed of their pigs and chickens or given emaciated nags in exchange for their healthy mounts (16 July 1920) is described in the story **'Nachal'nik konzapasa'** (**'The Remount Officer'**). The Cossacks are not at all impressed, as they cross into Galicia, by the order from South-West Command which tells them to treat the local population well because they are not coming as a conquering army but in order to assist the Galician workers and peasants in the establishment of Soviet power (18 July 1920). A commissar warns Babel not to take anything from 'our region' during forced requisitioning in a Czech colony (12 July 1920); a commissar who remonstrates with soldiers in one of the drafts for the stories is met by obscene abuse from the soldiers who justify pillaging. Instead of Bolshevik 'salvation' the bewildered Jews are greeted by Cossack whips and shouts of 'zhidy'; they tell the 'usual stories' of pillage. They are, of course, not the only ones to suffer: horses and fodder are forcibly taken from peasants and Czech colonists. Babel sums up, 'Budyonny's men are bringing Communism, an old peasant woman cries' (14 July 1920).

On his visits to the Zhitomir rebbe or to Hasidic synagogues Babel ponders his own fate, and he has no illusions about the significance of the Revolution for the battered Jewish communities. By the end of August the Soviet forces are in retreat and Babel complains in his Diary of his illness and depression. The Jewish New Year finds him in Kiwercy, homesick, hungry and weary. He finds a Jewish housewife, a proverbial 'eshet khayil', Woman of Valour, who gives him bread: 'I am moved to tears; here only my tongue helped; we talked for a long time' (13 September 1920). 'My tongue' can equally be 'language', meaning Yiddish, the common tongue of the Odessa Jew and the *shtetl*, and this gives a clue to the conflict of self on the part of a Jew in a Revolution that was hastening the destruction of the *shtetl*.

It might be thought that Babel wished to become a Cossack and that this ridiculous form of self-hate explains the nonchalance towards Cossack acts of brutality in *Red Cavalry* and in such stories as **'First Love'**. The

Diary suggests a rather different conclusion. During the Polish campaign Babel was deeply interested in whatever remnants he could find in Poland of Western culture, whether in bookshops or the Catholic churches. However, his sympathy for the Jewish families with whom he billets overrides all other sentiments.[16] 'How everything strikes a chord in my heart,' he remarks in Zhitomir when he talks to local Jews, including a philosophic shopkeeper, who says of both Revolution and Counter-Revolution that each side pillages and who wishes that there was one government that was good (3 July 1920). This idealistic shopkeeper was to be the prototype of Gedali in the *Red Cavalry* story that bears his name, the imaginary founder of the Fourth International of Good People.

Babel's Diary represents anti-Jewish incidents as part of the lot of Russian Jewry, not just sporadic outbursts of anarchic elements or the inevitable effects of the war. The personal agony of the writer is unmistakable, for he was only too aware of the historical symbolism of the incursion of semi-literate, barbaric Cossacks to the heart of the former Jewish Pale of Settlement, to those same areas decimated by their heroic forbear Bogdan Khmelnitsky in 1648 and recently subjected to brutal pogroms by Ukrainians, Poles and other warring factions. This was not merely the 'back garden' of two armies, as might be thought from Budyonny's wrathful outburst of 1924 when he accused Babel of bawdy babbling about women's breasts in some kitchen in the rear.[17] Jews were a common enemy of Poles and Cossacks, an easy, defenceless target for quick retribution and an immediate outlet for low morale, as well as for the more corrupt and base instincts of the semi-literate professional Cossack soldiers, who did not usually share the ideological motivation of the foot-slogging revolutionary volunteers. Retribution against the Jewish population from all sides involved in the conflict was extraordinarily swift, even when fighting was still in progress. Zamość was the scene of a pogrom perpetrated during the battle for the town in the days from 30 August to 1 September 1920; it was to be described in the *Red Cavalry* story **'Zamość'**. Dragged in his sleep by his horse to the front-line, the narrator can hear clearly the screams of the Jews in Zamość. A peasant soldier on the Soviet side comments approvingly to his visitor, whom he apparently takes for a Russian intellectual:

> 'Everything is the Jew's fault, for what has happened to us and to you. There will be a very small number of them left after the war. How many Jews are there in the world?'
>
> 'Ten million,' I replied and began to bridle my horse.
>
> 'There'll be two hundred thousand left,' the peasant shouted and touched my arm, afraid I might go away. But I managed to climb into the saddle and galloped to the place where staff headquarters were.
>
> (210)

During the Polish campaign Babel posed as a Russian, an identity which had come naturally during the Revolution when he wrote of 'our fighters' in Gorky's anti-Bolshevik *Novaia zhizn'* ('About the Horses') or presented himself as a Russian ('Finns'). But here he was among his own people, and it would not have been as natural for him to pretend to be a non-Jew as it was for Ehrenburg in *Viza vremeni* ('Visa of Time') to represent himself as Russian vis à vis the Polish Hasidim. These were his kith and kin (*rodnoe*), whereas among his comrades-in-arms, 'our lads' (*nashi*), he felt forever 'alien' ('ia chuzhoi,' he writes on 26 July 1920). Nevertheless he steeled himself to go through with the ordeal. After his horse went lame, for example, he chided himself for being 'too weak' (29 August 1920). Somehow he managed to stand by and watch defenceless Jews being harassed or maltreated, 'And I am silent, because I am a Russian' (24 July 1920).

On entering the *shtetl,* Babel had warned himself to 'be on my guard' and had tried to restrain Prishchepa, a communist Cossack whose terrible vengeance on his home village is immortalized in the story bearing his name. Now Babel notes the pain of the situation in which he is an involuntary accomplice to the desecration of the Sabbath and—of all days—the Fast of Av: 'They all hate us and me' (24 July 1920). However, as he had done when his conscience was similarly affected three days previously during the ransacking of a Jewish shop in Korec, he told the poor tormented Jews yarns of the communist utopia ('nebylitsy o bol'shevizme', 24 July 1920). Babel applied what he called 'the usual system' and his fantastic stories of a better future were heard eagerly by the local Jews, whom Babel pitied for their credulity (23 July 1920). He preferred to 'pour balm' (as he put it in the Diary entry for 21 July) on the wounds of the pogrom victims, telling them of the socialist utopia in Moscow, and he apparently did nothing when Cossacks attacked Jews and prisoners, looted Jewish and other local property, or desecrated synagogues and Polish churches.

If the avoidance of direct involvement was dictated by self-preservation, in the *Red Cavalry* stories the observer's distancing of self becomes an aesthetic device which exposes the brutality natural to the Cossacks, as well as parodying the alienated Jewish intellectual who thought he could live among them. The admiration for the Cossacks' professionalism contradicts the integrity of the self who identifies with their Jewish victims. In the story called '**Beresteczko**' the town is the setting for a callous execution 'for spying' of an old Jew by Soviet Cossacks:

> Right in front of my windows a few Cossacks were shooting an old silver-bearded Jew for spying. The old man was wriggling and screaming. Then Kudria from the machine-gun team grabbed his head and hid it under his armpit. The Jew quietened down and spread his legs. With his right hand Kudria drew a knife and carefully cut the old man's throat, taking care not to splash himself. Then he knocked on the shuttered window, 'If anyone's interested,' he said, 'they can come and get him.'

(168)

The narrator watches, apparently dispassionately, as the Cossacks turn the corner, but the absence of comment underlines the personal trauma akin to that of the boy in '**First Love**' watching his father's victimization by Cossacks in a pogrom. In both cases our attention is diverted to the professional confidence of the Cossacks. It could be that the fascination with the aesthetics of the perpetrators conceals a repressed guilt for impotence in not preventing a violent act which also threatens his own ethnic and artistic identity. However, sufficient irony is contained in the Cossacks' epic march from the nearby village of Chotin, past the watchtower where Bogdan Khmelnitsky was routed by the Poles, for us to notice the unspoken authorial message. The town greets the 'heroes' with silent, barred windows, and at the end of the story the pillaged Jewish burghers elect a Revolutionary Committee, which supposedly puts all power in their hands. The election is held in the garden of the castle of the mad Polish countess, a description based directly on the Diary entry, and, although the Diary does not record the execution, it confirms that the suspicion of espionage fell on the Jewish population with the entry of Soviet as well as Polish forces.

The Diary records that Babel could not help thinking seriously about his own destiny in view of what he experienced in Galicia (26 July 1920), but he nevertheless maintained his false identity even though he knew that the Cossacks would never accept him, an intellectual in spectacles and a Jew. Such deception raises serious questions concerning Babel's stance as a Jew and a writer.

To achieve artistic self-restraint can be both physically and psychologically dangerous. We know from the 1920 Diary and from his private correspondence of later years how much it exhausted Babel. Indeed, curiosity has been known to kill the cat, though in this case it gave birth to an *alter ego*, the fictional Liutov of the *Red Cavalry* stories. Liutov is a composite figure who was apparently added at a late stage of composition to embody a Jewish intellectual distinct from the authorial voice who adopts differing standpoints in relation to other protagonists. He appears most obviously in confrontation with the Cossacks in '**Squadron Commander Trunov**' and during the retreat of the Bolshevik forces in '**Zamość**' when he assaults his Polish landlady. Liutov can also be identified with the bespectacled law graduate in '**My First Goose**', who is at first rejected by the Cossacks, and with the unnamed Jewish intellectual who yearns for his Jewish past in the ruined Jewish quarter of Zhitomir in **'Gedali'** and **'The Rebbe'**.

At the beginning of **'Gedali'** the narrator sadly recalls his childhood when the Sabbath candles were kindled and his grandfather would read the Bible commentator Ibn Ezra: 'On these evenings my child's heart rocked like a little ship on enchanted waves.[18] Oh, the rotted Talmuds of my childhood! Oh, the heavy melancholy of memories!' (125). He wanders around the former market of Zhitomir—the thematic and biographic association with Bialik is striking—in search of a 'shy star' that marks the beginning of the Sabbath, a 'Jewish glass of tea' and a bit of that 'retired God' in the glass of tea.[19] The narrator's search brings him to the junk store of old Gedali who has witnessed the cruelty both of the Poles and the Bolsheviks. With Talmudic logic Gedali examines the warring camps, but neither offers him salvation. The Revolution cannot accommodate Jewish values: '"To the Revolution we say 'yes', but are we to say 'no' to the Sabbath?" Thus Gedali begins and winds round me the silken straps of his smoky eyes. "Yes, I shout to the Revolution, yes, I shout, but the Revolution hides from Gedali and sends forth naught but shooting . . ."' (126). The narrator retorts in Bolshevik propaganda slogans that the Revolution will open closed eyes and the story ends with the narrator returning to the brightly lit propaganda train. However, Gedali's eyes have been closed by *pogromshchiki*, not by ideological blindness or hostility to Communism. On the contrary, he believes in the coming of Messiah and universal justice, like all devout Jews who read Maimonides' Thirteen Principles daily. The 'straps' he winds around the narrator are the phylacteries which ought to bind him to Judaism and the Jewish people. The straps are 'silken' rather than leather perhaps because Gedali is a *zadener mentsh*, a 'silken man', exceptionally learned, and Gedali's words recall those of Moses in Deuteronomy relating the redemption story of the Exodus from Egyptian bondage: 'And we all, learned people [*anashim nevonim*] we prostrate ourselves and cry out loud: woe to us, where is the sweet revolution?' (126). If the Revolution kills and requisitions private property (his gramophone, for example) then it cannot be the real revolution. Since Gedali is a petty-bourgeois shopkeeper who does not believe that pogroms are a symptom of the class struggle, he is an enemy of the Revolution, so that most commentators have failed to see that it is the Jewish communist who does not resolve the contradiction of violence and revolution, Jewish identity and Communism.

A similar dilemma was faced by many Jewish intellectuals who had forsaken Jewish life and pledged allegiance to the Revolution, but could not be totally indifferent to the destruction of the *shtetl* and its values. Nor could they ignore the bestial violence unleashed in the Revolution and Civil War or the common soldier's frequent ignorance of Marxism. It is not by chance that Babel's stories, including **'Gedali'**, were the only translations to be included in the short-lived Soviet Hebrew journal *Bereshit*.[20] The dilemma is presented by Babel with subtle irony. Gedali, who has studied the Talmud and loves Rashi and Maimonides, departs for the synagogue, a lone figure in the setting sun which symbolizes the end of the *shtetl*, but which also heralds the inauguration of the Sabbath—day of rest and foretaste of the messianic age. As he departs in the setting sun, Gedali dreams of an 'International of Good People' who will distribute first-class rations to all.

The subjective first-person narrator of **'Gedali'** recalls his Jewish childhood when he wanders around Zhitomir on a Sabbath eve searching for symbols of the Jewish past and his own identity. He recalls his grandfather's yellow beard and the old woman's almost occult ritual of lighting candles. This typological model of ethnic-cultural identity places Judaism on an estranged distanced plane, a generation removed, coloured in an oppressive black and yellow melancholy, lifeless and doomed like the *rotted* Talmuds of the narrator's childhood. Yellow is the colour of the grandfather's beard which brushes the open pages of Ibn Ezra, the culture of the medieval Jewish past, and yellow are the 'indifferent' walls of the 'ancient' synagogue. The narrator's return to his grandparents' past continues as a search for that same point in time which began the story, the Sabbath eve, for the 'shy star' that will inaugurate the day of rest, a Jewish space of communal identity and belief. The search and the return culminate at sunset in the shop of a ridiculous old *shtetl* philosopher, a microcosm of the outdated values of the enclosed Jewish world and the impasse which it represents for the narrator. The spatial metaphors and the attributes, especially those of colour and smell, accruing to the enclosed areas underscore the recurrent typology of constriction and repulsion. Gedali's shop is hidden away in the tightly closed stalls of the dead town market. The shop is a 'labyrinth' of all kinds of useless junk and dead things, secluded from the real world and closer to the spirit of Dickens's *Old Curiosity Shop* than the present day. A hunter's rifle is dated 1810. Gedali is blind, his hands are white, his beard is narrow and grey; he wears a black top hat and a green coat. There is a slight rotting smell.

Yet if the narrator enters Gedali's store armed with the hostile stereotypes of Judaism as repulsive, dying and confining, he soon encounters a revelation which undermines his position and questions his apparent non-identification with his Jewish brethren, a revelation foreshadowed in **'Crossing the Zbrucz'** and here by the metaphorical and not so metaphorical blood of sunset. The narrator answers Gedali's complaint that the Revolution sends forth only shooting with a Party line retort that 'we' will rip open eyes that have closed to the sun. Yet in a whisper the old man reveals that his eyes were closed not by ideological error in blindness to the truth but by anti-Semitism in a pogrom, an event which identifies both Gedali and the narrator as Jews. The dialectic rages between the narrator and his Jewishness, between his writing 'I' and the collective 'we,' not between Gedali and the Revolution. The Revolution is supposed to bring justice to the world and it is dealing retribution to the anti-Semitic Pole, yet it requisitions Gedali's gramophone. Where then, asks Gedali, identifying himself with the culture of the narrator's grandfather, with Rashi and Maimonides, where is the just Revolution welcomed by God-fearing Jews? The narrator must awake to the irreconcilable contradiction between the violent Revolution and humane Judaism. As the sun sets over Zhitomir and over Jewry, the narrator turns to Gedali, the dreamer of a Fourth International and a believer in the messianic Sabbath, and he asks to share Jewish experience with him. But it is too late. The Jewish cake and the Jewish glass of tea, in which there is 'a little of that retired God', are not to be had. The ravages of war and revolution have devastated the Jewish population, long resigned to their tragic fate.

The Sabbath begins and Gedali departs for the synagogue alone, although the narrator will also go there as the bystander and detached observer of **'The Rebbe'**. However, interposed between the two stories, **'Gedali'** and **'The Rebbe'**, is **'My First Goose,'** an ironic comment on the inability of the narrator to reconcile his Judaism with the hostile outside world of violence and maturity, war and revolution. The topology of **'My First Goose'** is consistent with the opposition between enclosed Judaism and the outer space of aspired acceptability. Savitsky, the Cossack commander, expresses the violence with which spatial barriers must be broken open when he does not simply stand in the middle of the hut but rather splits it in two. His *raspberry* hat links him with the men of action of the Odessa stories, the Jewish gangsters who sport raspberry waistcoats, while Savitsky's astonishing physicality and his explicitly feminine sexuality arouse the narrator's envy. The semi-literate Cossack does not rate very high the chances of the bespectacled intellectual's survival among the Cossacks ('specs get your throat cut around here'), and he consigns him to the quartermaster who warns the young Jew he will be accepted only if he breaks the Judaic humanitarian code: 'But you mess up a lady, the cleanest lady, then the boys will be kind to you' (130).

The road is round and yellow 'like a pumpkin', images of lifeless vegetation and alienation. The sun is dying. The first act of the Cossacks is to kick the intellectual's suitcase of manuscripts, his synecdochal identity, out of the courtyard, a transitory space between home and the non-bounded outside. In an obscenely offensive way

one young Cossack disrupts his reading of Lenin's speech to the second congress of the Comintern. The narrator responds by taking up the quartermaster's challenge and symbolically raping a virgin: he abuses a fellow-victim, the bespectacled landlady, and defiles a *white*-necked goose. As I have noted elsewhere in my analysis of estrangement in this story,[21] he first takes someone else's (*chuzhoi*) sword and, lured by the homely smoke of the *unkosher* pork in the Cossacks' cooking-pot, he commits an act of violence in order to win the admiration of the Cossacks as well as acceptance into their ritual communion. Only then do they allow him to resume the role of intellectual and to read them Lenin's speech.

Yet despite the dreams of women and the warmth of the Cossacks' bodies, that might be interpreted as surrogate sexual fulfilment of the earlier envy of Savitsky, the narrator's Judaic conscience cannot be at peace with wanton killing. The contextual setting of maternal Nature, and the semantic as well as rhythmic repetition of the description of the killing of the goose, suggest that this 'first kill' has violated something within the narrator: 'Only my heart, crimson with killing, squealed and bled' (132). The tension between the past tense of the Jewish home (*svoi*) and the alluring outer space of the Cossacks (*chuzhoi*) creates a dramatic conflict in the estranged vision of the intellectual between what he is and what he cannot be.

'The Rebbe' opens with Gedali speaking of Hasidism as an immortal, if battered, building at the crossroads of history. Judaism, he is saying, will weather the storm. In the story **'The Rebbe'** the narrator seems to have found his 'shy star', and Sabbath peace has descended on the crooked roofs of Zhitomir. The rebbe's room is stone-built and empty 'like a morgue' (in the Diary the surroundings were ordinary, bourgeois, and even spacious). The rebbe has a yellow beard and sits at his table surrounded by 'fools and madmen', attended by the eccentric deformed beggar, the ragged Reb Mordecai (details absent from the Diary). The imagery of constriction is reinforced by the sudden glimpse of the rebbe's son, Ilia Bratslavsky, a sort of recaptured fugitive from 'prison'. The messianic role of Ilia, which was mentioned in the previous chapter, is thwarted by images of emaciation and impotence: Ilia's face is compared with that of an emaciated nun, a simile with strong Christian associations as incongruous as the likening of the Jews to 'fishermen and apostles', while the attribute of impotence (*chakhloe*) links Ilia with the Jewish ataman in **'Afonka Bida'**; later it describes the dying Ilia's genitals in **'Syn rabbi'** (**'The Rebbe's Son'**). The New Testament allusion, Ilia's 'powerful forehead of Spinoza' and his desecration of the Sabbath clash with the rebbe's blessing (the Sabbath *kiddush*, normally pronounced over wine) which praises the Creator for singling out the Chosen People from all the nations.

The silent enclosedness of this doomed world is juxtaposed with the hostile noises of war outside, the wilderness beyond the window-frame: 'The desert of war yawned outside the window' (135). The window-frame is the imprisoning frame of the Jewish space threatened by the violent outdoor gentile world, by war and by anti-Semitism. The window is a framing device as well as a threshold between the hostile exterior, where the alienated Jew would like to belong, and the enclosed interior of Judaism where his sympathies secretly lie but from which he has attempted to sever his roots.

The narrator of 'The Rebbe' is the first to leave the rebbe's house and returns to his unfinished task of writing an article for *Krasnyi kavalerist,* the Russian propaganda newspaper. He returns to the bright lights and the machinery of the Propaganda Train, an antithesis of his Judaic heritage in imagery but also in cultural and linguistic values. The 'I' rejoins the collective, but he makes no friends or allies, apart from Grishchuk, a former prisoner-of-war and a fellow-victim. As becomes apparent in 'Smert' Dolgushova' ('Death of Dolgushov') and 'Posle boia' ('After the Battle'), he fails to acquire the Cossacks' 'simplest of abilities': to kill. Here Babel might be mocking Tolstoyan non-resistance, but the ability to kill can be simple only for the Cossack. The Judaic prohibition of murder is absolute and unconditional, just as the disrespect for a father (in addition to anti-Semitic prejudices) is most evident to a Jewish sensibility when the Cossack lad in 'Pis'mo' ('The Letter') enquires after his horse before casually relating his tale of parricide. Liutov's acceptance of the taunt of 'Molokan', a sectarian who will not shed blood, is merely yet another example of self-mocking narration which serves to foreground the complex questions of violence in the name of a better future.

'Crossing the Zbrucz'—the opening story of *Red Cavalry,* often translated as 'Crossing into Poland'—will serve to illustrate the device of the detached narrator used to pinpoint the menace of anti-Semitism while calling into question the ethnic and ethical identity of the narrator. The first-person narrator separates himself from the rearguard in Novograd-Volynsk and billets with a Jewish family. What meets his eye is the disgusting filth in which the Jews live—a typical stereotyped perception from a non-Jewish point of view—but when the third sleeping Jew turns out to be a horrifying corpse the reader must correct this perspective. Here is the aftermath of a pogrom carried out by the Poles. Just as in the ironic lyricism describing the march, when the sky reflected the bloody deeds of men, here too Nature proves a more impartial witness. The moon is homeless, like the Wandering Jew. The story ends with the same plea for justice and mercy which closes 'The Cemetery at Kozin': why has the Angel of Death never spared the Jews?

If Babel had had any doubts it was now clear to him what was the price in blood of war and revolution. He could not avoid seeing the impossibility of wedding Judaism to Communism, of welding together the ideals and traditions juxtaposed in the last effects of the dying Ilia Bratslavsky in 'The Rebbe's Son':

> Here everything was thrown together—propaganda manifestos and the jottings of a Jewish poet. The portraits of Lenin and Maimonides lay next to each other. Lenin's knotted iron skull and the dull silk of the portrait of Maimonides. A lock of a woman's hair was placed in a copy of the Resolutions of the Sixth Party Congress and in the margins of communist leaflets were crowded the crooked lines of Hebrew verse. They descended on me in a sad and tedious rainfall, pages from the Song of Songs and revolver cartridges.
>
> (229)[22]

This story is addressed to someone called Vasily, who has not previously been introduced as an interlocutor. This would suggest that the narrator's memories of the Friday evening with Gedali and the Rebbe (inaccurate memories, incidentally) and his lament over Ilia, the last prince of a Hasidic dynasty turned revolutionary, are directed to a Russian audience. It is to his aspired-towards Russian identity that the narrator turns at the end of *Red Cavalry* to explain his own attachment to the 'ancient body' of Judaism and Jewish culture (Maimonides, Hebrew poetry) while he is writing in Russian. By the time *Red Cavalry* was written it was clear how irreconcilable were Lenin and Maimonides, love and Party resolutions, Hebrew verse and communist propaganda, the Bible and war. The paradox is that among the hordes of typhus ridden peasantry, 'monstrous Russia, incredible like a swarm of fleas' (228), the Jewish renegade Ilia is the only one to stretch out an emaciated hand for Trotsky's leaflets, and that he dies having failed to win the battle for the Revolution.

As the failed Jewish revolutionary lies dying, the narrator recognizes him as his spiritual brother, a similar type of dreamer who has severed his roots in the dying Jewish past, which nevertheless remains nostalgically and poisonously attractive. Ilia is Elijah, the prophet who will herald the messianic age, and he also brings to mind his namesake Elijah the Vilna Gaon, the staunch opponent of Hasidism in the eighteenth century, whose name is shouted by the *mitnagdim* at Sokal' in 'Squadron Commander Trunov'. The narrator—who himself can barely contain within his ancient Judaic consciousness the 'storms' of his imagination—thus ends *Red Cavalry* with an ambivalent portrait of the Jewish intellectual who wished to reconcile love and violence, Judaism and Communism. Only in 'Argamak,' the later addition to the cycle in 1933, does Liutov succeed in riding a horse without attracting the hostile stares of the Cossacks, though not before making more enemies. Nevertheless, the dialectic of Jewish intellectual and Revolution, Jew and Cossack, remains unresolved.

Notes

1. For an account of the hostilities between the Bolsheviks and Poland see Norman Davies, *White Eagle, Red Star: The Polish-Soviet War, 1919-20* (London: Macdonald, 1972).

2. See 'Rytsari tsivilizatsii' ('Knights of Civilization'), *Krasnyi Kavalerist,* 14 August 1920 and 'Nedobitye ubiitsy' ('Unvanquished Killers'), *Krasnyi Kavalerist,* 17 September 1920. Reprinted in *Sochineniia* [Moscow, 1990], I, 203-6. An English translation can be found in Efraim Sicher, 'The "Jewish Cossack": Isaac Babel in the First Red Cavalry', *Studies in Contemporary Jewry,* 4 (1988): 127-33.

3. The manuscripts of the Diary and of the drafts for the *Red Cavalry* stories are kept in the private collection of Babel's widow Antonina Nikolaevna Pirozhkova in Moscow. The Diary entries run from 3 July 1920 to 6 July 1920, followed by a break from pages 69 to 88, which are missing from the manuscript; the Diary continues from 11 July 1920 to 15 September 1920, covering most of Babel's stay in the First Red Cavalry. The Diary was published in full after many difficulties for the first time in *Sochineniia,* I, 362-435. This publication and other commentators read 'June' for the first entries, which must be a mistake, because, as Norman Davies points out, Zhitomir had not yet been taken on 3 June ('Isaak Babel's *Konarmiia* stories and the Polish-Soviet War', *Modern Language Review,* 67, 4 [1972]: 847); in any case, the first entry was evidently written on a Saturday, which makes it without doubt 3 July 1920. I have given the correct dates throughout. I have previously discussed the Diary in 'The "Jewish Cossack": Isaak Babel' in the First Red Cavalry', 113-34, An English translation of the Diary by H. T. Willetts is available in Isaac Babel, *1920 Diary,* ed. Carol Avins (New Haven: Yale University Press, 1995); the translations in this chapter are my own.

4. Partly published in *Literaturnoe nasledstvo* LXXIV (Moscow: Akademiia nauk, 1965), 490-9. I refer to the complete manuscripts in the collection of Antonina Pirozhkova.

5. In 1938 Babel avowed that the stories were based directly on the Diary, much of which he claimed to have lost and supplemented from memory of the events (transcript of an address to young writers from the national republics, 30 December 1938, in the archives of A. N. Tolstoi, Institut Mirovoi Literatury i Iskusstva, fond 43, opis' I, edinitsa khraneniia 944, 2b, l. 33). I. Smirin has discussed the transfer of Diary material to the stories in his 'Na puti k *Konarmii*: Literaturnye iskaniia Babelia', *Literaturnoe nasledstvo,* LXXIV, 467-82.

6. See Furmanov's diaries in his *Sobranie sochinenii,* IV (Moscow, 1961), and L. K. Kuvanova, 'Furmanov i Babel'', *Literaturnoe nasledstvo* LXXIV, 500-12.

7. The Russian original appears in Smirin, 'Na puti k *Konarmii*: Literaturnye iskaniia Babelia', *Literaturnoe nasledstvo* LXXIV, 467-82.

8. *Jewish Chronicle,* 16 July 1920, 11-12. It goes without saying that the outrages of summer 1920 pale in comparison with the unspeakable horrors of 1918-19 committed by Petliura's forces, including the Zhitomir pogroms of January 1919, after the suppression of the local Soviet, and of March 1919, after a brief Bolshevik occupation. The retreating Petliura forces also carried out atrocities in areas of Eastern Galicia not under Bolshevik occupation in August-September 1920 (L. Motzkin, *Les Pogromes en Ukraine sous les gouvernements ukrainiens, 1917-1920* [Paris: Comité des délégations juives, 1927], 82-9; cf. appendices 17, 36, 45, 46). See also I. Cherikover, *Di ukrainer pogromen in yor 1919* (New York: YIVO 1965), and *Antisemitizm i pogromy na Ukraine, 1917-1918* (Berlin: Ostjudisches Historisches Archiv, 1923); I. Shekhtman, *Pogromy Dobrovol'cheskoi armii na Ukraine: K istorii antisemitizma na Ukraine v 1919-1920 gody* (Berlin: Ostjudisches Historisches Archiv, 1932).

9. For corroboration of Babel's account see the memoirs of Holocaust survivors from Hoszcza in B. Ayalon-Baranik and A. Yaron-Kricmar, *Hoshtsh: Sefer zikaron* (Tel-Aviv: Irgun yotsei hoshtsh, 1957), 25-9.

10. 'The Destruction of Galicia', in *The Literature of Destruction: Jewish Responses to Catastrophe,* ed. David G. Roskies (Philadelphia: Jewish Publication Society, 1988), 225. An-sky's testimony is relevant here also because of the examples of Jewish medical officers who repressed their identity and did not react to anti-Semitic incidents, as well as of Jewish conscripts who surreptitiously aided the victims of their Cossack comrades-in-arms. A Jewish medical officer serving in the Tsarist army also evoked the Destruction of Jerusalem when he saw Husiatyn razed to the ground by Russian troops in 1916 (Gershon Levin, *In velt krig* [Warsaw, 1923]). These texts and the vast literary tradition of which they form a part are discussed in Roskies, *Against the Apocalypse.*

11. A contemporary observer of the massacres in the Ukraine also compared them in scale and location to those committed by Khmelnitsky, and concluded that there was little left of the hopes of the *maskilim* for an enlightened attitude to the Jews (Shimon Bernfeld, *Sefer hadema'ot* [Berlin: Eshkol, 1923], 74-7).

12. First Cavalry recruits included former soldiers in Denikin's army, responsible for massacres in the Ukraine, and Budyonny is alleged to have permitted his cavalry to organize several pogroms in the provinces of Ekaterinoslav and Volhynia, notably at Korsun, the Cossacks declaring they must 'beat the Jews and save Russia' (*Jewish Chronicle,* 23 July 1920, 15). Bolsheviks were reported responsible for rape and the brutal murder of women and children at Brody (*Jewish Chronicle,* 27 August 1920, 10-11), though it is not always easy to establish responsibility in view of the charges and counter-charges of Polish and Soviet war propaganda. After Budyonny had received orders from Tukhachevsky to transfer to the front against Wrangel, First Cavalry troops carried out pogroms (designated as such in Soviet sources) during the march to the Dnieper. Budyonny arrested two brigadiers of the Sixth Cavalry Division whose chief of staff was responsible, and a purge was carried out (Norman Davies, *White Eagle, Red Star,* 232). Relevant archival material may be found in Piotr S. Wandycz, *Soviet-Polish Relations, 1917-1921* (Cambridge MA: Harvard University Press, 1969). Sergei Shtern cites an order by Budyonny of 20 October 1920: 'We must take the Crimea come what may, and we will take it, in order to begin the life of peace. The German Baron is making desperate efforts to stay in the Crimea but he will not succeed. Traitors to the revolution are helping him—the Jews and bourgeois. But a decisive blow from our glorious cavalry will suffice and the traitors will be wiped out. Stand firm and have no mercy. The Crimea will be ours' (*V ogne grazhdanskoi voiny* [Paris: Russkoe knigoizdatel'stvo Ia. Povoloskaia, 1922], 187).

13. Trotsky confirms the existence of this common misconception (*My Life* [New York: Charles Scribner's Sons, 1930], 361).

14. Isaac Babel, *You Must Know Everything: Stories, 1915-1937,* translated by Max Hayward (New York: Farar, Straus & Giroux, 1969), 131-2. The word *Jude* is German, not Yiddish, which can be explained by the fact that many assimilated Jews preferred German to Yiddish. In the Diary Babel records a number of such phrases, including one very similar to the one uttered by Shulmeister, but directed at himself (Diary, 23 July), so that this scene could be a projection of Babel's own fear of penetration of his mask, as well as of his guilt about the shooting of prisoners, bringing together his moral and Jewish identity.

15. Mosher's real name was Lt.-Col. Merian C. Cooper and he came from Florida, not New York. See K. M. Murray, *Wings Over Poland* (New York:

Appleton, 1932); J. B. Cynk, *History of the Polish Air Force, 1918-1968* (Reading: Osprey Publishing, 1972).

16. In some of the conversations which Babel had with local Jewish youth he displayed open admiration for the Zionist pioneers and did not hide his identity. This is according to the memoirs of Akiva Govrin, 'Vstrechi s I. Babelem', serialized in *Nasha strana* between 8 March 1974 and 5 April 1974; a Hebrew translation appeared as 'Pegishot 'im Yitskhak Babel', *Moznayim* 38, 1-2 (1973-4): 42-9. In the Diary entry for 26 August 1920 Babel mentions being shown around Sokal' by a local Zionist, and he had probably had experience of the Zionist movement in Odessa before the Revolution (as mentioned above).

17. S. M. Budyonny, 'Babizm Babelia iz *Krasnoi novi',* Oktiabr', 3 (1924): 196-7. Babel countered in a letter to the editor in the next issue of *Oktiabr'* that his descriptions of the First Cavalry were essentially authentic, and cited a letter from First Cavalry veteran S. Melnikov. Melnikov had been surprised to find himself described along with Timoshenko, commander of the Sixth Division, in one of Babel's stories ('Melnikov and Timoshenko', later retitled 'Story of a Horse' and 'Continuation of Story of a Horse'; the heroes were also renamed, as were other real personages in *Red Cavalry*). Melnikov thanked Babel for his story, but pointed out that he had never resigned from the Party as stated in the story, though it was true that Timoshenko had abused his power and taken his white steed. Melnikov also noted there were 'negative features' of Budyonny's army which the author did not mention, such as the looting in Równe (archive of *Krasnaia nov',* Rossiiskii Gosudarstvennyi Arkhiv Literatury i Iskusstva, fond 602, opis' I, edinitsa khraneniia 1718). See also Melnikov's later memoir, 'Pervaia konnaia', *Krasnaia niva,* 6 (1930): 6-7. In 1928 Gorky entered into debate with Budyonny over the absence of communists and the masses in Babel's stories, and the question of ideological commitment is one that dogged the treatment of Babel in the Soviet press ever after. A former doctor in the First Cavalry made a relevant point about the transcendence of art when he attested to the fundamental truth portrayed in *Red Cavalry*: 'Babel saw more than we. What can one do if in a certain sense all of us, witnesses and participants in Budyonny's campaigns, remember "after Babel"?' (I. Kassirskii, 'Nikto puti proidennogo', *Znanie—sila,* 6 [1967]: 12-14). Needless to say, Babel's portrait of Budyonny's First Cavalry and of Budyonny himself was hardly flattering, at a time when songs and popular legend, as well as literary publications such as Aseev's 1923 poem *Budyonny,*

were already establishing the Cossack commander's reputation as an epic hero. Unfortunately,
evaluation of the fictional picture has been obscured by criticism of Babel for historical
'discrepancies', such as the confusion of the rivers
Słucz and Zbrucz or the impossible deployment of
forces in 'Crossing the Zbrucz' (see Norman
Davies, 'Isaak Babel's *Konarmiia* Stories and the
Polish-Soviet War', 845-57).

18. The 'ship' and 'waves' presumably refer to the
'sea' of the Talmud in the commonplace Jewish
idiom.

19. The 'shy star' recalls a reference to lechery in a
1908 poem by Bialik, 'Be'erev hakayits' ('Summer
Evening'), while in his well-known poem
'Hamatmid' ('The Talmud Student') the twinkling
stars evoke a lyrical world of nature outside which
both describes and undermines the student's situation amid the rotted Talmuds, memories of lost
youth and longing for the Messiah. As already
noted in Chapter 1, there is a common theme of
breaking out of the dying Jewish world and the
pull of a lyrical eroticism likewise pulls the narrator toward the gentile world. Babel could have expected his Jewish readers to be acquainted with
Bialik's verse and with his pre-Revolutionary lec-
turing and publishing activities in Odessa. Bialik
prayed at the Brody Synagogue, frequented by
Babel's father (as Babel remembered in his Diary),
and it is very likely this would have been a personal memory for Babel himself.

20. 'Reshimot', *Bereshit*, 1 (1926): 15-38. Babel authorized these translations personally. See Y. A.
Gilbo'a, *Oktobraim 'ivriim* (Tel Aviv: Sifriyat
hapo'alim, 1974) and also above p. 23.

21. Efraim Sicher, *Style and Structure in the Prose of
Isaak Babel* (Columbus OH: Slavica, 1986), 87-9.

22. Zvi Gitelman compares Babel with Shlomo Ya'a-
kov Nepomniashchii, who had served in the Cheka
and in the Red Army during the Soviet-Polish War,
having earlier studied in *yeshivas* and worked for
the Zionist movement (*Jewish Nationality and Soviet Politics: The Jewish Sections of the CPSU,
1917-1930* [Princeton University Press, 1972],
283-4). Gitelman cites private correspondence in
which Nepomniashchii evokes the conflicts reflected in this passage, and confides how difficult
it was to break with the past and to reconcile Hebrew and Judaism with communist ideology: 'I
will say, in Gordon's words, "I am a slave to Hebrew forever." No-one will be able to uproot
"khumash-and-Rashi" from my soul. I gave my
best years to these old writings.' Giving back the
Torah on Mount Sinai, he knows he will be naked
without it but looks forward to the new Genesis

(letter to David Charney of 1925, cited in Zvi
Gitelman, *A Century of Ambivalence: The Jews of
Russia and the Soviet Union, 1881 to the Present*
[New York: Viking, 1990], 115). The similarity to
Ilia Bratslavsky is remarkable, as is the resonance
of the imagery of returning the covenant and ex-
pectation of a new genesis discussed in the previ-
ous chapter.

Charles Rougle (essay date 1996)

SOURCE: Rougle, Charles. "Isaac Babel and His Od-
yssey of War and Revolution." In *Red Cavalry,* edited
by Charles Rougle, pp. 5-65. Evanston, Ill: Northwestern University Press, 1996.

[*In the following excerpt, Rougle provides a stylistic
analysis of the stories of* Red Cavalry *and argues that
Babel does not focus on accurate descriptions of the
military and historical aspects of the Soviet-Polish War,
but rather on* "the effect of violence on human life,
morals, and culture."]

RED CAVALRY AND THE POLISH-SOVIET WAR

Relations between revolutionary Russia and the newly
created Republic of Poland had been smoldering for
more than a year before Babel arrived on the scene.
They erupted into a major conflict in late April and
early May 1920, when the Poles occupied Kiev, then
the capital of the shaky Ukrainian People's Republic
recognized by the 1918 Treaty of Brest-Litovsk. The
principals are still debating whether the move was a
preemptive strike prompted by fear of Russian designs
now that the civil war had turned in favor of the Bolsheviks or an aggressive gambit to regain historically
Polish territories. At any rate, the Soviets quickly responded to this challenge along a front extending from
the Ukraine to the Baltic, and they were initially quite
successful. By the end of May the Poles had been driven
out of Kiev. By June they were steadily retreating, pursued in the south by Budyonny, in the center by Tukhachevsky, and in the north by Ghai. The offensive
pressed on into July, and by mid-August the Red forces
were threatening Warsaw in the center and Lvov in the
south. They never reached either. The armies advancing
on the Polish capital were repulsed by 20 August. Budyonny's cavalry suffered a decisive defeat on 31 August
and was fortunate even to escape the so-called Za-
moshch Ring. The Battle of the Niemen gave the Poles
another decisive victory on the central and northern
fronts in September, and by the mid-October cease-fire
the Bolsheviks had been pushed back almost to their
positions of six months before. The Treaty of Riga,
signed in March 1921, was a victory for Poland, which
gained a huge section of present-day western Ukraine

and Belarus and considerable other indemnities. For Soviet Russia it was a painful defeat that would not be forgotten when borders were redrawn once again at the end of World War II.

No war is ever as neat and orderly as the generals' chessboards or the crisply sweeping arrows of a military map, but this particular conflict was messier than most. Norman Davies, who has written one of the most authoritative accounts, describes it as follows:

> Warfare in the Borders had a quality all of its own. The immensity of the theatre of operations, the impossibility of garrisoning it efficiently, turned the attention of armies to specific, limited objectives—rivers, railways, and small towns. Rivers formed the only lines of natural defence. . . . Fighting, for psychological as well as for logistical reasons, proceeded by fits and starts, jerking from one township to the next perhaps fifty miles on, like sparks building up energy in a terminal before jumping the gap. Action followed the lines of communication in a game of generals' leapfrog, back and forward between one station and another. . . . The line was too thin to be held for long. The flank was always exposed. To attack was easy; to retreat was always possible. . . . When the historian writes of "a general offensive" or "an advance on a wide front," he is rationalizing a thousand individual engagements. Border warfare was essentially local and fragmentary, spasmodic and infinitely confused.[1]

As guerilla wars in our own day may suggest, such mobile, fluid conflicts generate conditions that are more than usually conducive to excesses. Davies again:

> The fighting in the Polish-Soviet War was undoubtedly vicious. The Poles frequently shot captured commissars outright. The Soviets shot captured officers and cut the throats of priests and landlords. On occasion, both sides murdered Jews. The atmosphere was somehow ripe for atrocity. The soldier was surrounded by confusion and insecurity. He rarely found himself in a comfortable trench, or in the reassuring company of his regiment. More often he was on his own out in the forest, or standing guard on the edge of a village, never knowing whether the surprise attack would come from in front or behind, never knowing whether the frontline had moved forward or back. Ambushes and raids bred panic, and invited vengeance. Meetings with the enemy were infrequent but bloodthirsty.[2]

Even allowing for exaggeration and unverifiable rumor, it is not difficult to believe that, for example, the entire Polish garrison at Zhitomir was put to the sword or that the hospital there containing six hundred Polish wounded and their Red Cross nurses was burned to the ground[3] or that in Grodno the Poles murdered sixty Jewish families, blinded seventeen young men, cut the breasts off women and raped young girls.[4] The stories of **Red Cavalry** abound in such violence against the defenseless. Particularly memorable and evidently common brutalities are the cold-blooded murder or mutilation of civilians ("**Crossing into Poland,**" "**Gedali,**" "**The Life and Adventures of Matthew Pavlichenko,**" "**Prishchepa's Vengeance,**" "**Salt,**" "**Afonka Bida,**" "**Berestechko**") and the killing of prisoners ("**A Letter,**" "**Konkin's Prisoner,**" "**Squadron Commander Trunov**"). Babel's campaign diary, which was never intended for publication, clearly shows that these incidents are not mere hearsay events inserted or embellished for the sake of fictional shock value. In one entry he relates the story of a pharmacist who was tortured by the Poles with a red-hot iron and needles under his fingernails.[5] The shooting of prisoners in another diary entry may well have served as the basis of the scene in "**Squadron Commander Trunov**":

> There is a thundering hurrah, the Poles have been crushed, we ride on to the battlefield, a little Pole with polished nails rubs his rosy head and thinning hair, answers evasively, beats around the bush, bleats, well yes, Sheko [a commander] animated and pale: answer, who are you—I, he mumbles—a warrant officer, sort of; we are leaving, they take him away, behind his back a fellow with a handsome face loads, I shout Yakov Vasilevich! He pretends he doesn't hear, rides farther, a shot, the little Pole in underwear falls on his face writhing. Life is repulsive; murderers, unbearable, baseness and crime.
>
> They drive the prisoners, undress them, a strange sight—they undress terribly quickly, shaking their heads, all this in the sun, a minor awkwardness, officers right there, awkwardness, just a trifle, though, through their fingers. I will never forget this treacherously murdered "sort of" warrant officer.
>
> Ahead—terrible things. We crossed the railroad at Zadvurdze. The Poles are breaking through along the rail line to Lvov. Attack in the evening near a farm. Carnage. We ride with a commander along the line, plead not to kill prisoners; Apanasenko [commander of the Sixth Division who replaced Timoshenko—Ed.] washes his hands. Sheko says casually, cut them down, this played a terrible role. I did not look at the faces; bayoneting, shooting, corpses covered by bodies, one is being undressed, another is being shot, groans, cries, wheezing, it was our squadron which mounted the attack, Apanasenko on the sidelines, the squadron properly dressed now, Matusevich's horse killed, he runs around with an awful, filthy face looking for a horse. A hell. The freedom we bring, terrible. They search the farm, drag people out, Apanasenko: don't waste cartridges, cut their throats. Apanasenko always says: cut the nurse's throat, cut the Poles' throats.[6]

It is artistically reworked scenes such as this which force even many of Babel's critics to concede that he succeeded in capturing the very special atmosphere and rich human interest of this war. To that extent the stories are true not in the external "but in the internal sense,"[7] surely the one that matters most to us. This is not to say that "external" truth should simply be dismissed as entirely irrelevant, however, and here it is appropriate to address some questions that have been raised regarding the historical reality depicted in Babel's cycle. How much did he actually see firsthand, and how accurate are the accounts of what he claims to have witnessed? He was attacked on both points by Budyonny, who called him a "creature of the army's back yard" who lacked substantial eyewitness experience of the action and was therefore ill-suited to judge the heroism of the Cossacks. Davies basically concurs, noting that with few exceptions, all the locations Babel mentions are twenty to thirty miles behind the front line at any given time, and that contrary to the impression given in the stories, "Babel much preferred to drink coffee with his Jewish friends in the taverns of Zhitomir and Berestechko than to ride into battle with his Cossack heroes."[8]

Certain comments are in order here. First of all, if Babel himself seldom actually came under enemy fire (he mentions his first battle on 17 August),[9] the extensive excerpts from his diary now available indicate that on numerous occasions he was much closer to hostilities than twenty or thirty miles. Especially as the Poles began to press the Soviets in mid-July, the headquarters to which he was attached switched back and forth just ahead or behind the enemy within the triangle around Brody, and he also seems to have been very close to the fighting in the advance on Busk.[10] As noted above, the front was in any case very mobile, and the rear, although undoubtedly much more secure, was probably not the cozy, tranquil haven detractors seem to imply. More important than the total number of engagements Babel may have taken part in or witnessed, however, is the philosophical question of what, exactly, should be defined as the essential "reality" of this or any other conflict. For understandable reasons, military commanders and historians perceive the locus of meaning in the actual fighting and the behavior of its participants, and in the impact of the outcome on further political and military decisions. That may be a legitimate and important view, but it is not the only possible one, nor is it the most productive approach to a work of imaginative literature. Babel was neither a soldier nor a historian; there is little reason, therefore, to be either surprised or disappointed that, like many artists before and after him, he has chosen to leave the military facts to others and to focus instead on the aspects of war that are most important to him: the effect of violence on human life, morals, and culture. As Viktor Shklovsky noted in Babel's defense during the debate, Budyonny was unhappy with Babel, but Kutuzov (the general who drove Napoleon out of Russia in 1812) would also have been unhappy with Tolstoy in *War and Peace*.[11]

That being said, it must still be admitted that in a few places Babel is not adverse to manipulating facts if he has compelling aesthetic reasons for doing so. Perhaps the most glaring example is in the very first paragraph of **Red Cavalry**:

Comdiv six reported that Novograd-Volynsk was taken today at dawn. Headquarters moved out of Krapivno, and our supply wagons stretched out in a boisterous rearguard along the highway, the immortal highway running from Brest to Warsaw that was built on peasant bones by Nicholas I.

(41)[12]

As Davies points out, the geography and chronology here are entirely inaccurate.[13] Budyonny's cavalry did indeed take Novograd-Volynsk, but the city is some two hundred miles to the southeast of Brest, which means that the "rearguard" would hardly be strung out in front to the west. Moreover, it was not Budyonny's but Tukhachevsky's forces that marched along this famous highway, and not in June (Novograd was occupied on 27 June) but in the first week of August as the Russians advanced on Warsaw.

There is more. Novograd-Volynsk is on the west bank of the Sluch rather than the Zbruch. It lies some eighty miles to the north of the latter river, which is nowhere near a line of march to the city. Budyonny's cavalry, in fact, probably never crossed the Zbruch at all, because the Dniester region to which it belongs was the responsibility of the Soviet Fourteenth Army under Uborevich throughout the summer of 1920. The error is repeated in the story "Italian Sunshine," where the narrator speaks of the "noiseless Zbruch" in the ravine below Novograd-Volynsk (64).

Wrong time, wrong river, wrong highway, wrong cities, wrong armies—one can sympathize with the historian who laments such "burglary" of history, but perhaps one can stop short of accusing the author of "gratuitous vandalism."[14] Babel's manipulation of his historical material is anything but gratuitous; nor are these alterations merely designed to convey "an atmosphere of apparent reality."[15] After all, if that were the intent, surely he could have found some "real" facts that would have served just as well. The reasons for the discrepancies in this and a few other passages lie deeper, and must be considered in their full context to be properly appreciated.

Viewed from the broader perspective of European history, the Polish-Soviet War has been all but eclipsed by the larger conflicts that frame it, and perhaps for this reason it is easy to overlook its tremendous significance in the eyes of its participants. On the Russian side, the immediate contemporary issues at stake concerned the very survival of the revolution. Since at this point in time, at least, the Bolshevik leaders believed that Russia was not likely to endure unless similar revolutions were ignited in Europe, and since Poland lay directly in the path of any such spreading conflagration, the nature of the regimes in these border areas was of the utmost significance.

Poland was also an infant state struggling to survive, but was otherwise a very different country indeed. A parliamentary democracy ruled by men committed to Catholicism, private property, class interests, and patriotism, it was in many respects the exact opposite of Russia at the time, and the Borders were no less significant to Polish aspirations. This was the first time since 1772 that Poland had existed as a sovereign nation, and that was a gain its leaders were extremely anxious to consolidate, by territorial aggrandizement if necessary. Russia had more than once crushed such ambitions—twice in the nineteenth century alone—but even more distant history played an important role. Psychologically, the border areas were surrounded by a romantic aura of centuries past, when Poland stretched from the Baltic to the Black Sea and was the outpost of Christendom standing against the Turks and Tartars in defense of the Faith and warring with the Muscovites for control of the steppes.[16] The Russians made similar claims. Kiev was the cradle of Eastern Slavic civilization, and it had been ruled by Poland until late in the seventeenth century. In 1605 Polish forces took advantage of dynastic confusion in Muscovy to occupy Moscow and set their own candidate on the throne. This abortive attempt was followed by another in 1608, and not until ten years later were the foreign invaders finally completely driven out of Russia, marking the beginning of Russian nationhood. Added to this, of course, was the religious factor, for the Pope was regarded by many Orthodox as none other than the Antichrist.

To the principals, then, the conflict of 1919-20 was more than a border squabble. Babel skillfully exploits this emotionally charged, semimythical background in his opening paragraph to comment on the central issues raised in the cycle as a whole. The road from Brest to Warsaw, for example, was a symbolical high road to the heart of Europe, the road along which internationalist ambitions would most likely proceed. Russian soldiers had taken the route before—in pursuit of Napoleon, for example; in fact the very title of the story, **"The Crossing of the Zbruch,"**[17] recalls two poems by K. N. Batiushkov, who was with the army in that earlier campaign: "The Crossing of the Nieman by Russian Forces on 1 January 1813" and "The Crossing of the Rhine."[18] A Polish reader might instead recall the highway as a military road by which Nicholas I and his successors kept Poland in check after the abortive insurrection of 1830. The note that it was "built on the bones of serfs" further reinforces the political dimension—once a symbol of absolutist tyranny, the road is now serving to bring liberation from the social injustices of the past. (Or is it? The ambivalence of Babel's position will be discussed below.)

The River Zbruch serves a similar function. Although, as mentioned above, it played no role whatsoever in the taking of Novograd-Volynsk and seems to have been of minor importance throughout the war, it had considerable symbolical value as a border. First, it had been the boundary between Russia and Austria since 1772, and contemporary commentators made much of that fact as the Soviets pushed the Poles westward. I. Vardin (Babel's colleague on *The Red Cavalryman* and later among the most militant of his proletarian critics) wrote a leading article in August 1920 in which he declared to his readers that the old borders drawn by tsars and oppressors were no longer valid.[19] Second, there is the fact that the Zbruch was also reestablished as the border between Russia and Poland by the 1921 Treaty of Riga. This immediately evokes what is to become a dominant theme in the story and the cycle as a whole, namely, doom and defeat, as the optimistic note sounded at the beginning yields to more ominous allusions and imagery. In the second paragraph, personifications of nature recall the Igor Tale,[20] which is also a story of defeat, and the narrative goes on to present a vivid picture of defiled nature, surrealistic details of blood, death, and confusion, desecrated human dignity, cold-blooded murder. The setting must also have raised questions in the mind of the contemporary reader as to the meaning of the entire conflict, since in context it seems to be suggesting that at least as far as Russia is concerned, all the suffering and bloodshed has really changed very little.

There are a few other "quasi-facts"—fictional details that are deliberately made to coincide partially with real ones. Thus there really was a squadron commander by the name of Trunov connected with the story of that name; in fact Babel wrote his obituary for *The Red Cavalryman*.[21] His first name, however, was not Pasha, as in the story, but Konstantin; he was not killed in a duel with an airplane piloted by an American (he calls him Major Reginald Fauntleroy—his real name was Colonel Cedric Fauntleroy), and he is not buried in Sokal. These details, of course, would not have been familiar to the contemporary reader, who might, however, have heard of the hero Trunov. Babel has taken an incident he probably knew only by hearsay[22] and transformed it into an epic battle between one (far from entirely positive) hero and a monster machine; or, if you will, between the outdated swashbuckling of the past and the new cavalry technology of the West.

In all these cases, facts have been tampered with in various degrees to serve thematic demands. Babel needed the symbolism of the Zbruch and a duel with an airplane more than he needed accuracy in details which for almost half a century no one seems to have noticed anyway. The discrepancies, in any case, are not very numerous, and the deeper truth that they help to convey is so consummately and convincingly presented that even if other errors should come to light, they are not likely to challenge the claim of **Red Cavalry** to stand not only as the chronicle of this conflict but as the national epic of the Russian Revolution.

RED CAVALRY: NOTES ON STYLE AND STRUCTURE

Anyone at all familiar with **Red Cavalry** will probably agree that it is not the sort of work that easily yields its meanings on a first reading. There is a continual feeling that even that which can be readily grasped is somehow intimating or pointing toward something else that is possibly more significant, whereas at other places the text seems puzzling, ambiguous, or downright opaque. It is perhaps no wonder that so many different explications and interpretations continue to be offered. There is a very good reason for this difficulty: it is intentional and very much a part of the author's aesthetic and philosophical attitude. Babel is a modernist, an important exponent of the consciousness that dominated Russian art and literature between the last decade of the nineteenth century and roughly 1930. Central to the modernist aesthetic position is a shift away from the objective reality which the nineteenth-century realists had attempted to capture as unobtrusively as possible to a focus on the subjective vision of the artist and to the artist's material itself, which in the case of literature is of course language. This overall tendency was reinforced in Russia by the supremacy of poetry over prose during this period. The formerly rigid distinctions between the two became blurred as prose writers turned their attention to verbal fabric, exploring and exploiting its phonetic, semantic, and syntactical potential through rhetorical and prosodic devices, word play, the use of dialectal, archaic, and other distinctive lexicon, and the incorporation into fiction of all sorts of literary and nonliterary genres and discourses. Two of the innovators here were Aleksei Remizov and Andrei Belyi, who are often regarded as the seminal influences on the so-called ornamental prose practiced, besides Babel, by 1920s writers such as Evgenii Zamiatin, Boris Pilniak, and Vsevolod Ivanov.[23] Although there are considerable differences between them, all the ornamentalists display a penchant for phonetic, lexical, syntactical and structural devices that tend to undermine mimetic purpose and draw attention instead to the fact that before the reader is a consciously, deliberately, and painstakingly *made* work of art.

Compared to the prose of traditional realism, this prose is denser, more charged, more "poetic," more dedicated to evoking moods and associations than to producing recognizable descriptions of reality. Unfortunately, some of the most important devices contributing to this effect are phonetic and syntactical and next to impossible to demonstrate on the basis of even a very good translation, which, alas, the most commonly cited one by Walter Morison is not. Readers who have access to the original, however, can turn to almost any descriptive passage and discover some of these features for themselves. The second paragraph of **"Crossing into Poland,"** for example, contains several interesting examples of alliteration, assonance, onomatopoeia, and sound orchestration. A syntactic and prosodic analysis would reveal a meticulously crafted arrangement of long and short clauses and sentences supported on a symmetric triadic structure and substructures. Reading and rereading such passages, it is easy to believe Babel's own report that an important stage of composition consisted in declaiming passages aloud to achieve optimal rhythmic and sonic effect.[24]

Other features can be captured more easily in translation. These include the use of repetition and parallelism, rhetorical devices, and imagery. Note, for example, the following sentences in the above-mentioned passage from the first story, which opens with three parallel subject-verb constructions using different subjects, then a triad of another three subjects in which one (Volhynia) is repeated and concluded with a pronominal reference:

> Fields of purple poppies bloom around us, the midday wind plays in the yellowing rye, virgin buckwheat rises on the horizon like the wall of a distant monastery. Quiet Volhynia curves, Volhynia moves away from us into the pearly mist of groves of birch, she creeps into flowery hillocks and with weakened arms entangles herself in thickets of hops.
>
> (41)[25]

Almost every story contains verbatim or slightly varied repetitions that heighten cadence and lyricism: "the ocean, the boundless ocean" (77); "rest—Sabbath rest" (78); "silence, sovereign silence" (119); "the tireless wind, the clean wind of night" (163); "the Sabbath, the young Sabbath" (193). In some places this sort of repetition extends to longer passages of equal or nearly equal material, as in the song refrain in **"The Song"** (188, 189) or the beginning and ending of **"Squadron Commander Trunov"** (143, 152).

Contributing to the pathos and emotional intensity of many stories are rhetorical apostrophes: "Destitute hordes roll on toward your ancient cities, oh Poland . . . woe unto you, *Res Publica,* woe unto you, Prince Radziwill, and unto you Prince Sapieha, who have risen for an hour!" (45); "O the rotted Talmuds of my childhood!" (69); "O Brody!" (82); "O regulations of the Russian Communist Party!" (127).

Babel is the acknowledged master of the striking image, which not infrequently relies for its effect on an original exploitation of color, sensory impressions, synaesthesia, animation and deanimation, and unusual combinations of the concrete and the abstract. Examples are far too numerous even to mention briefly, but one does not soon forget the orange sun rolling across the sky like a lopped-off head and the smell of blood and dead horses dripping into the cool of evening (42), blue roads flowing by like streams of milk spurting from many breasts (65), sponge-cakes spiced with cunning juice and the fragrant fury of the Vatican (43), bullets striking and swarming in the earth, quivering with impatience (87), the moon loitering like a beggar-woman in the sky (164).

Although a pull toward lyricism can be felt throughout the text of **Red Cavalry,** that is not the only defining feature of its language. Five stories (**"A Letter," "The Life and Adventures of Matthew Pavlichenko," "Konkin's Prisoner," "Salt,"** and **"Treason"**), for example, are in what is known as *skaz*—stylized narrative imitating oral speech, often an incongruous mixture of styles resulting from the efforts of an uneducated speaker to use bookish language. Dialogue is infrequent, but many lines are in colloquial or substandard speech whereas others are elevated. Still other passages are decidedly laconic, matter-of-fact, unemotional statements. In a manner typical of Babel, these often convey very brutal material, which produces an effect of striking incongruity. What gives Babel's prose its distinctive quality is that these various registers and levels of discourse are so often juxtaposed, several of them often occurring in the same story or even paragraph. The result is a veritable mosaic of variegated verbal fragments that forces the reader constantly to adjust his or her inner ear to catch the fluctuating rhythms, accents, and flavors of the language.

Reading such texts is of course more difficult than reading prose in a more uniform key. What makes it even harder, however, is that this contrastive mixture of language elements is not merely stylistic pyrotechnics but reflects the overall principle on which the stories are structured. This organization is in turn related to meanings and says a great deal about the vision that underlies it. Carol Luplow summarizes the main features of story structure in **Red Cavalry** as follows: (1) a radically different proportioning of the three basic story parts, especially an extended development of the exposition; (2) a tendency toward nondramatic rendering of plot, where verbal elaboration dominates over even sometimes quite violent events; (3) a weakening of causal and sequential links in favor of associational connections between theme, imagery, and style; (4) a "kaleidoscopic" arrangement of heterogeneous elements: inner tales, peripheral anecdotes, dreams, letters, notes, reminiscences, and so on.[26] All these features represent departures from the "realistic," mimetic mode of discourse, where narrative is more typically organized along spatiotemporal and causal progressions. In some respects, in fact, the strategy represents a transition into the nonliterary medium of cinema: the stories of **Red**

Cavalry, as one extensive monograph analyzes in detail, are excellent examples of the cinematic technique of montage—the juxtaposition of disparate elements—which exercised an enormous influence on modernist literature.[27]

We have already seen some of these techniques at work in **"Crossing into Poland."** The opening sentence begins in the voice of a soldier recounting a recent military operation, perhaps in a newspaper report.[28] By the middle of the second sentence, however, an abrupt change occurs, with the introduction of a historical perspective ringing of revolutionary and nationalist propaganda as the Red Cavalry marches west to eradicate the social injustice of the Old World and Russia marches to reclaim her rightful territory from her ancient enemy Poland. This and the expectations aroused by the title seem to point toward victory.

The second paragraph marks an abrupt shift, as an intensely lyrical and subjective voice introduces a string of vivid images and sensory impressions that progress from dominantly visual at midday, to olfactory and tactile in the evening, to audial at night. The narrator is no longer only a soldier or a propagandist but an artist as well, and his incongruous voices already seem to suggest some underlying inconsistency in his character.

The third paragraph introduces another voice and viewpoint. The cavalry arrives in Novograd and the scene switches abruptly to the unnamed narrator and his quarters with a Jewish family. Noticeable here are two shifts—from the first-person plural "we" of the opening to the singular "I" in which the remainder of the story is told, and a palpable change of tone from lyrical description to a detached listing of the ravaged interior of the home. This is followed by the narrator's expression of disgust at the filth and his contemptuous description of the Jews hopping around "like monkeys, like Japanese in the circus."

These shifts in tone and voice are crucial to the theme we can now see developing. On the other side of the river, in both the literal and figurative senses, we begin to get a glimpse of war that has been stripped of the disturbing if colorful lyricism of the second paragraph. There is nothing at all "poetic" about overturned wardrobes, tatters of clothing, and Passover crockery desecrated (it seems to be suggested) by human excrement. The emerging narrator is also of interest. Until now he was a member of the military collective, its "voice," in a way, who seemed to be proposing to report to the world on its movements, set its exploits in the proper ideological perspective, and sing of its victories and defeats. Here he steps forth and begins to assume more individual contours. He still regards himself as part of the collective—his behavior toward the pregnant woman is insensitive at best, and he barely accords the other

Jews human status. Yet at the same time is dropped the first clue that he is also a Jew. Who among his fellow soldiers would recognize the broken crockery used exclusively at Passover?[29]

The identity conflict taking shape in this passage is central to the overall theme of *Red Cavalry* and will be shown at work below in other stories as well. It is accentuated further here by another sharp transition back into a lyrical voice. In the oxymoronic image of the moon wandering about in the dead silence outside the window clutching her "carefree" head in her hands—a typical gesture of despair—we can sense the estrangement and loneliness hidden behind the narrator's mask of uncaring conqueror.

The next clearly demarcated fragment is a dream, itself a kind of inner tale or "text within the text"[30] in which the narrator sees the commander Savitsky—Comdiv six of the opening paragraph—shoot the eyes out of the brigade commander for retreating. Death draws closer still, as does the threat of defeat. The Jewess awakens him, for he has been tossing and turning and kicking the man "sleeping" in the corner. Following swiftly upon this is the horrible revelation, rendered even more striking by the laconic and matter-of-fact details with which it is conveyed, that the narrator has been lying the whole while next to the mutilated corpse of her father.

The final paragraph is yet another distinct fragment told in an entirely different voice, this time that of the Jewess. Her tale of the Poles cutting her father's throat is restrained, if not quite as dispassionate as the preceding section, but it and the story end in an emotional outburst that brings the tragedy and horror lurking below the surface to a concluding crescendo. The glaring contrast it provides with the rhetoric of the opening is itself a statement of a major theme, namely, the conflict between the forces of history and the fate of the individual.[31]

Beneath the seemingly fractured and disjointed surface, then, there are coherent themes and motifs, but it is largely up to the reader to find the relevant links. What of the work as a whole? Clearly, many stories can be read individually, and several of them have been anthologized as self-contained narratives. There is in fact some disagreement as to how the book is to be approached in its entirety, and depending on how vague or definite the connections between stories are perceived to be, observers have called it everything from a loose collection of stories, to a cycle of short stories, to a poem in prose divided into chapters, to an episodic novel, to a baroque novel.[32] The question of the exact genre of *Red Cavalry* need not be decided here, but there is more than intuitive evidence to recommend approaching it as a unity. From the beginning Babel conceived of his project as a single work of art, and not merely as a disjunctive series of stories that could be arranged more or less arbitrarily. He spoke with irritation of the material necessity that forced him to publish the stories separately: "To get money I've published in the local *Izvestiya* several wretched fragments, wretched precisely because they are fragments," he wrote a friend in 1923.[33] In his conversations and correspondence with his editor Dmitry Furmanov during the two years before the appearance of the first book edition, he repeatedly referred to the stories as "chapters" or "chapter-stories" (*glavy-novelly*), and he was personally responsible for their original order.[34] Furmanov reports that Babel described to him the final composition of the work as consisting of "at least twenty chapters which are already written and published, twenty written but not published—these will simply serve as links, cementing the others. Ten chapters are being written—these are long, serious chapters; they will present the positive side of the cavalry, fill the gaps . . . Altogether, fifty chapters."[35]

The components of narrative can cohere in a number of different ways. To return to a point made above, there is first of all the sequencing of spatiotemporal and causal events. As in the case of individual stories, this type of link is relatively weak on the level of the collection, but it is not insignificant. On the basis of direct or indirect references in the stories themselves and on a knowledge of the general movements of the First Cavalry, the stories as presented in the outline below follow a chronology broken by some flashbacks and flashforwards from mostly June (stories 1-9) through July and late August (10-28) to the end of August and into the middle of September (29-34). Story 35, added later, spans almost the whole campaign. These more or less correspond to the three stages of the First Cavalry's involvement—advance in June, advance with increasing resistance and some defeats in July-August, retreat in late August and in September—and they also tend to group in three general arenas: Novograd-Volynsk/Zhitomir, Brody/Berestechko, Zamoste/Chesniki. As will be suggested below, these spatiotemporal blocks coincide with thematic divisions.

The datelines that Babel originally provided some of the stories tended to focus more attention on time and place of action or writing, but even then the unity thus created is fairly loose. Much more important than any such sequential principle is the associative one mentioned above, which relies on repetition or parallelism based on similarity or contrast. Among these devices may be mentioned recurring characters, recurring imagery, and repeated and varied themes, situations, subplots, and so on. Thus a majority of all the important and minor characters figure or are mentioned in more than one episode. To list them alphabetically: *Afonka Bida* (**"Afonka Bida," "The Death of Dolgushov,"**

"The Road to Brody," "In St. Valentine's Church"); *Akifiniev* ("Two Ivans," "Chesniki," "After the Battle"); *Balmashev* ("Salt," "Treason"); *Gedali* ("Gedali," "The Rabbi," "The Rabbi's Son"); *Grishchuk* ("Discourse on the Tachanka," "The Death of Dolgushov"); *Ilya Bratslavsky* ("The Rabbi," "The Rabbi's Son"); *Khlebnikov* ("The Story of a Horse," "The Story of a Horse, Continued"); *Kurdyukov* ("The Letter," "In St. Valentine's Church"); *Pan Romuald* ("The Church at Novograd," "Pan Apolek"); *Pan Apolek* ("Pan Apolek," "In St. Valentine's Church"); *Pani Eliza* ("The Church at Novograd," "Italian Sunshine"); *Pan Robacki* ("The Church at Novograd," "Pan Apolek"); *Pavlichenko* ("The Brigade Commander," "The Life and Adventures of Matthew Pavlichenko," "Berestechko," "Chesniki"); *Sandy (Sasha) the Christ* ("Sandy the Christ," "After the Battle," "The Song"); *Sasha* (the nurse) ("In St. Valentine's Church," "The Widow," "Chesniki," "After the Battle"); *Savitsky* ("Crossing into Poland," "My First Goose," "The Story of a Horse," "The Story of a Horse, Continued"); *Vinogradov* ("Berestechko," "After the Battle"). The significance of these recurrences should perhaps not be overemphasized—only exceptionally (in "Gedali," "The Rabbi," and "The Rabbi's Son," in "The Story of a Horse" and "The Story of a Horse, Continued," and in "Afonka Bida" and "In St. Valentine's Church") is there any real narrative connection between them. They do, however, invite us to look for thematic links between the episodes in which they appear, and they serve a cohesive function themselves by providing a familiar cast of characters.

Recurring imagery works in a similar fashion. Nature imagery is particularly prominent in this regard, and, among these many metaphors, the sun and moon are important both for providing a sense of temporal progression and for indicating psychic and thematic shifts. Thus we cannot help but notice the similarities between the colorful banners ("Crossing into Poland"), orange strife ("The Rabbi") and overflowing goblets ("Zamoste") of sunset, or between the moribund, roseate void ("Gedali"), ghost ("My First Goose"), and haze ("The Rabbi") of evening, or between the moon loitering like a beggar-woman ("The Widow"), the vagrant wandering outside the window ("Crossing into Poland"), and the homeless moon of "Pan Apolek." Structurally, these and other details create motif chains that provide atmospheric unity and cross-reference episodes. They simultaneously serve an important thematic function, as there is an observable tendency to link natural phenomena with certain types of thematic oppositions, and it has even been argued that such cadenced reappearances are intended to evoke a longing for the lost human involvement in the rhythmical patterns of nature and to suggest an almost paganly animistic universe.[36]

Themes, motifs, situations, and events echo one another throughout the cycle. One example discussed by van Baak is the important motif of crossing a river. Dominant in the first story, it recurs explicitly (although not as prominently) in "Afonka Bida," and implicitly in "Berestechko" and "In St. Valentine's Church." In all places it is connected with the notion of a threshold and the changes in character or perception accompanying the crossing of such boundaries.[37] Other such situations include Lyutov's inability to kill in "The Death of Dolgushov" and "After the Battle," which in both cases causes a rupture between him and the Cossacks; acts of revenge and revolutionary justice link "A Letter," "The Life and Adventures of Matthew Pavlichenko," "Prishchepa's Revenge," "Konkin's Prisoner," "Salt," and "Two Ivans"; Lyutov mistreats the women with whom he is billeted in "Crossing into Poland," "My First Goose," and "The Song"; Cossacks and their lost horses unite "The Story of a Horse," "Afonka Bida," and "The Story of a Horse, Continued"; old Jews have their throats cut in "Crossing into Poland" and "Berestechko"; prisoners are executed in "Konkin's Prisoner," "Squadron Commander Trunov," and (probably) "Two Ivans."

The role that these and other elements play will become more obvious as we attempt below to determine a more precise internal structure. First, however, a few words about the most important unifying element by far, which is the single consciousness that narrates or presents all the stories. The world of *Red Cavalry* is the narrator's world, and it is his biographical, cultural, and spiritual identity and experiences that select, organize, and refract the thematic material. Who, then, is he? The first-time reader of the work can be excused for not having an exhaustive answer ready, for even the external details are scattered in bits and pieces over the entire book. His name, Kirill Vasilevich Lyutov, is not entirely revealed until nine-tenths of the way through, and then not in a single story (the surname first occurs in "Squadron Commander Trunov" (146) and the name and patronymic in "Chesniki").[38] As can be gathered from explicit information supplied at scattered points, he is a Jewish intellectual from the south of Russia and a recent graduate of the Law School of St. Petersburg University ("Gedali," "My First Goose," "Discourse on the Tachanka"), which means he is in his early to mid-twenties. He claims his wife deserted him ("Zamoste"). He has served in the army for more than two years, since he fought against the Germans no later than March 1918 (the date of the signing of the Brest-Litovsk Treaty ending World War I for Russia; "Argamak"), and has been on the Red side in the civil war since at least the spring of 1919. He has taken part in campaigns in the Kuban against Denikin and the "Greens" (anti-Bolshevik peasant partisans), he may have gone through the siege of Uralsk in May-July 1919,[39] and he has evidently been with Budyonny's First Cavalry in the Caucasus, the arena from which the unit was transferred to the Polish front (**"The Song"**). Until shortly before the taking of Novograd-Volynsk, however, he was not attached to a combat unit (**"Argamak"**). The English-speaking reader should also be aware that the name Kirill Vasilevich Lyutov is very definitely Russian rather than Jewish, that there is considerable irony in the meaning of the surname ("lyutyi" = ferocious, savage, cruel), and that Babel himself used the pseudonym for his dispatches from the front. Again like his real-life namesake, Lyutov is attached to the army newspaper *The Red Cavalryman*. His official functions in that capacity include observing and reporting on the war and explaining the revolution to the soldiers, and at various points he explicitly or implicitly assumes these professional roles of reporter and political interpreter. He is never very convincing in either, however, because if he possesses the journalist's curiosity and keenness of observation and the agitator's flair for the pithy phrase, these talents are harnessed to a purpose that is emphatically aesthetic rather than informative or persuasive in nature. For Lyutov is above all an artist. He openly declares as much in **"Pan Apolek,"** but his heightened aesthetic sensibility is overwhelmingly obvious anyway in his lyricism, his appreciation of both natural and created beauty, the strongly metaphorical mode of his vision, the important role he allots to dreams and imagination, the sensitivity he displays to sense impressions and the sensual phenomena of life, and of course the self-consciously crafted style of the narrative itself.

Lyutov's biography is thus sketchy at best. It is adequate, however, for he is not so much an individualized psychological portrait as a type shaped by the roles his background, situation, and temperament have imposed on him. All three of the main aspects of his persona—Jew, intellectual, and artist—define him as an outsider. In the reality of the 1920 war, of course, this is an entirely believable position, as Babel himself could personally testify. The type also has important literary antecedents extending back at least to romanticism and its estranged hero confronted with the contradictory need to identify with some larger collective or purpose without sacrificing his exclusive cultural, moral, and aesthetic sensibility. In Russian literature of the 1920s the intellectual hero torn between old and new was a common figure, and Lyutov is one of the most memorable of this series.[40] Emotionally and culturally rooted in the world of Jewish tradition and Western humanist values, he at the same time recognizes that that world is dying, and he wants to belong to the new reality promised by the Revolution. The bearers of the future are the Cossacks, and whereas he admires their vitality and masculinity, he is repulsed by their brutality. In its most basic contours, then, **Red Cavalry** is a work of quest for identity, understanding, and meaning on the individual, historical, and metaphysical levels, and all the component parts explicitly or implicitly address the questions

that arise in the course of the search: ends and means, old and new culture and values, freedom and necessity, the meaning of history.

Notes

1. Davies, *White Eagle, Red Star,* 35-36.

2. Ibid., 38. Jews were murdered more than "on occasion": between 1918 and 1921, pogroms in the Ukraine claimed 60,000 killed, 100,000 wounded, and 200,000 orphans (Nora Levin, *The Jews in the Soviet Union since 1917,* vol. 1 [New York: New York University Press, 1988], 43). Babel wrote about atrocities by both sides in articles for *The Red Cavalryman* ("The Unvanquished Killers" and "Knights of Civilization"). For an account of Babel's position and a translation of the articles, see Efraim Sicher, "The 'Jewish Cossack': Isaac Babel in the First Red Cavalry," *Studies in Contemporary Jewry: An Annual,* vol. 4 (The Jews and the European Crisis, 1914-1921), edited by Jonathan Frankel (New York: Oxford University Press, 1988), 113-34. The Russian text is in Babel', *Sochineniia,* vol. 1, 203-6.

3. Davies, *White Eagle, Red Star,* 125.

4. Joseph Roth, *Berliner Saisonbericht* (Cologne: Kiepenheuer and Witsch, 1984), 45.

5. Isaak Babel', *Socheniniia,* vol. 2, 403-4 (diary entry of 7 August).

6. Babel', *Sochineniia,* vol. 2, 415-16 (diary entry of 18 August). See also the original version of the Trunov episode "Ikh bylo deviat'" (Babel', *Sochineniia* vol. 1, 437-39), translated as "And Then There Were None" in Isaac Babel, *You Must Know Everything. Stories 1915-1937,* translated by Max Hayward, edited with notes by Nathalie Babel (New York, 1969), 125-34.

7. Norman Davies, "Izaak Babel's 'Konarmiya' Stories, and the Polish-Soviet War," *Modern Language Review* 67, no. 4 (1972): 848.

8. Davies, "'Konarmiya' Stories," 848-49.

9. Babel', *Sochineniia,* vol. 1, 415.

10. See Babel', *Sochineniia,* vol. 1, 378-401, 410, 418.

11. Quoted in G. S. Merkin, "S. Budennyi i I. Babel' (k istorii polemiki)," *Filologicheskie nauki* 4 (1990): 97-103.

12. My translation. Here and in numerous other places the most commonly used English edition leaves much to be desired. Numbers in parentheses within the body of the text are to the corresponding passages in *The Collected Stories of Isaac Ba-*

bel, translated by Walter Morison (New York: New American Library, 1974). The phrase "the immortal highway" (*po neuviadshemu shosse*) was later deleted by Babel.

13. Davies, "'Konarmiya' Stories," 848.

14. Ibid.

15. Ibid., 849

16. Davies, *White Eagle, Red Star,* 29.

17. In one of many examples of insensitivity to the patterns of the text, the title of the story is rendered by Morison as "Crossing into Poland," which completely conceals the original intent. Several other titles tamper with the original: "Rabbi" in "The Rabbi" and "The Rabbi's Son" should read "Rebbe," as this is a much different, charismatic type of Hasidic leader. (Most scholars have perpetuated the error in their studies.) "Prishchepa's Revenge" and "Konkin's Prisoner" are merely "Prishchepa" and "Konkin." Morison also insists on Anglicizing Russian names, as in "Sandy the Christ" (for "Sasha") and "The Life and Adventures of Matthew Pavlichenko" (for "Matvei"). Since this is the only translation with which most readers are familiar, however, I have retained his titles here. The presently out-of-print version by Andrew MacAndrew (*Lyubka the Cossack and Other Stories* [New York: American Library, 1963]) and the new translation by David McDuff (*Collected Stories* [New York: Penguin, 1995]) address these shortcomings (although especially MacAndrew adds distortions of his own; see n. 33 below).

18. Nils Åke Nilsson, "Isaak Babel's 'Perechod čerez Zbruč,'" *Scando-Slavica* 23 (1977): 65; Marc Schreurs, *Procedures of Montage in Isaak Babel's* Red Cavalry (Amsterdam: Rodopi, 1989), 175. Incidentally, the Russians crossed the Nieman in this war as well, but now it was in retreat from the Poles, who won a major victory on that river.

19. Gareth Williams, "The Rhetoric of Revolution in Babel's *Konarmija,*" *Russian Literature* 15, 3 (1984): 283. It has even been suggested that Vardin was the ghostwriter of Budennyi's attack on Babel (Alice Stone Nakhimovsky, *Russian-Jewish Literature and Identity* (Baltimore: The Johns Hopkins University Press, 1992), 230, n. 38.

20. Schreurs, *Procedures of Montage,* 102-3.

21. "Pobol'she takikh Trunovykh!" (More such Trunovs!), *Sochineniia,* vol. 1, 202.

22. Davies, "'Konarmiya' Stories," 852. Gareth Williams makes the interesting observation ("The Rhetoric of Revolution," 293) that on the same page of *The Red Cavalryman* as Babel's obituary of Trunov was a description of the shooting down of two enemy aircraft by soldiers in the First Cavalry. This real-life montage is surely what gave Babel the idea of including the episode in the story.

23. See Gary L. Browning, "Russian Ornamental Prose," *Slavic and East European Journal* 23, 3 (Fall 1979): 346-53.

24. Isaak Babel', *Sochineniia* vol. 2, 373, 378.

25. Morison ignores this parallelism almost completely, and he and MacAndrew both mistranslate Volhynia as a river, when in fact it is a region. McDuff's "the quiet Volyn" seems to perpetuate the error.

26. Carol Luplow, *Isaac Babel's Red Cavalry* (Ann Arbor, 1982), 99-100.

27. On the relationship between especially Sergei Eisenstein's theory of montage and literature, see Schreurs, *Procedures of Montage,* 1-36.

28. See Williams, "The Rhetoric of Revolution," 279-98.

29. The Morison translation (42) obscures this connection. "Sacred" (or at least "special"—*sokrovennyi*) crockery becomes alien "occult" crockery, and the narrator is made to seem an ignorant Christian when he says that the Jews celebrate Easter rather than Passover. Corrected by MacAndrew and McDuff.

30. See Schreurs, *Procedures of Montage,* 46, and Jan van der Eng, "Types of Inner Tales in *Red Cavalry,*" *Text and Context* (Stockholm: Almquist and Wiksell, 1987), 128-38.

31. For more detailed analyses of "Crossing into Poland," see Schreurs, *Procedures of Montage,* 171-99; Nilsson, "Isaak Babel's *Perechod čerez Zbruč,*" 63-71; and Richard Young, "Theme in Fictional Literature: A Way into Complexity," *Language and Style* 13, 3 (1980): 61-71.

32. On the question of genre, see Jan van der Eng, "Red Cavalry: A Novel of Stories," *Russian Literature* 33 (1993): 249-64; Agnes Gereben, "Über die Kohärenz einer epischen Gattung," *Studia Slavica Academiae Scientarum Hungaricae* 27 (1981): 213-28; Agnes Gereben, "Some Aspects of Narration in the Composition of Cycles of Short Stories," *Studia Slavica Academiae Scientarum Hungaricae* 28 (1982): 333-47; Agnes Gereben, "The Syntactics of Cycles of Short Stories," *Essays in Poetics* 11, 1 (1986): 44-75; Louis Iribarne, "Babel's *Red Cavalry* as a Baroque Novel," *Contemporary Literature* 14, 1 (1973): 58-77;

Erzhebet Kaman, "Kompozitsiia knigi rasskazov I. Babelia 'Konarmiia,'" *Studia Slavica Academiae Scientarum Hungaricae* 25 (1979): 207-15; N. I. Khimukhina, "O zhanrovoi spetsifike 'Konarmii' I. Babelia," *Vestnik Moskovskogo universiteta,* seriia 9, *Filologiia,* 3 (1991): 26-32; David Lowe, "A Generic Approach to Babel's *Red Cavalry,*" *Modern Fiction Studies* 28, 1 (Spring 1982): 69-78; R. Ross, "The Unity of Babel's *Konarmija,*" *South Central Bulletin* 41, 4 (1981): 114-19. The use of the words *collection* and *cycle* here is for convenience and does not imply any rigorous generic classification.

33. Babel', *Sochineniia,* vol. 1, 238. MacAndrew evidently disagrees with the author, since he treats the stories as disjointed fragments when he takes the liberty of rearranging them in what he feels is their "proper" chronological and narrative order.

34. Babel', *Sochineniia,* vol. 1, 244.

35. Dmitrii Furmanov, *Sobranie sochinenii v chetyrekh tomakh,* vol. 4 (Moscow, 1961), 340.

36. James Falen, *Isaac Babel: Russian Master of the Short Story* (Knoxville, Tenn., 1974), 123-24. On nature imagery, especially the sun and the moon, see also Gareth Williams, "Two Leitmotifs in Babel's *Konarmija,*" *Die Welt der Slaven* 17, 2 (1972): 308-17.

37. See Jan van Baak, *The Place of Space in Narration. A Semiotic Approach to the Problem of Literary Space. With an Analysis of the Role of Space in I. E. Babel's Konarmija* (Amsterdam: Rodopi, 1983), 150-51.

38. The English translation omits the name and patronymic. It should occur on page 80, after the line "he called out to me in despair." Corrected by McDuff (216).

39. Uralsk is incorrectly translated as "the Urals" (189). Corrected by McDuff (223).

40. See Robert Maguire, *Red Virgin Soil. Soviet Literature in the 1920s* (Ithaca: Cornell University Press, 1987), 327-29, 336-37.

Stephen Brown (essay date 1996-1997)

SOURCE: Brown, Stephen. "The Jew among the Cossacks: Isaac Babel and the Red Cavalry in the Soviet-Polish War of 1920." *Slavonica* 3, no. 1 (1996-1997): 29-43.

[*In the following essay, Brown discusses the autobiographical nature of the stories of* Red Cavalry, *asserting that "Babel's depiction of a Cossack Red Cavalry should be viewed not as a mere recounting of the facts of the writer's wartime experience but as an integral part of his pessimistic account of war and revolution."*]

For the historian, Isaac Babel's literary masterpiece, *Konarmiia,* represents an intriguing blend of historical fact, autobiography and literary fantasy. *Konarmiia* is set amid a strange and nightmarish world of brutal Cossack cavalrymen, plundered Jewish settlements and the failure of the Soviet government's first attempt to bring about the export of communism during the Soviet-Polish War of 1920. The *Konarmiia* of the title refers to Semen Budennyi's First Cavalry Army, the Red Army's elite cavalry unit with which Babel served during summer and autumn 1920.[1] The name of Liutov which Babel gave to the narrator of *Konarmiia* was the *nom de guerre* Babel himself used while riding with the Red cavalry. Like Liutov in *Konarmiia,* Babel was born to Jewish parents, wore spectacles, and wrote for *Krasnyi kavalerist,* the newspaper of the First Cavalry Army.

At the heart of *Konarmiia* is the paradox of a Jew and sympathizer of the Soviet government riding alongside Cossacks, representatives of a military caste celebrated for its opposition to the Soviet government in 1918-20 and notorious for its anti-Semitism. Liutov's predicament is all the more poignant for the fact that the action of *Konarmiia* takes place in the Ukrainian and Polish borderlands where, in 1648-49, Zaporozhian Cossacks led by Bogdan Khmelnitskii murdered tens of thousands of Jews during an uprising against Polish rule. While Babel's critics have recognised the fact that the stories of *Konarmiia* are autobiographical only up to a point, there is widespread acceptance of Babel's depiction of a 'Cossack' Red cavalry as a fact of history. This is true even of those charged with describing the historical background to Babel's œuvre.[2] The present paper draws attention to the fact that it was not history that threw up this strange image of the Cossack Red cavalry with its lone Jewish conscience but Babel's artistic imagination. Babel's depiction of a Cossack Red cavalry should be viewed not as a mere recounting of the facts of the writer's wartime experience but as an integral part of his pessimistic account of war and revolution.

It has long been recognized that the relationship between *Konarmiia* and the historical events that were its inspiration is a complex one.[3] Babel was a mysterious character, an habitual story teller whose autobiographical sketches are no more a reliable guide to his life story than his fiction.[4] Our most valuable source for Babel's wartime experiences is the diary he kept during the summer and autumn of 1920, the surviving portion of which was recently published in full.[5] Babel, short-sighted and lacking in cavalry training, was not called upon to serve as a front-line soldier of the Red cavalry. He was one of several hundred 'political workers' attached to the eighteen-thousand strong First Cavalry Army. The brief of the political worker was to sharpen the soldiers' will to fight, heighten their political consciousness and to transform them into loyal citizens of the Soviet state. In his capacity as a contributor to *Krasnyi kavalerist*, Babel was able to move easily between the front and the rear. Babel witnessed cavalry battles, interviewed prisoners, spoke with the inhabitants of the borderland towns and experienced the hunger, boredom and terror that were the ordinary soldier's lot; Babel observed the commanders of the Red cavalry and heard the stories of its rank-and-file soldiers. It was the cavalrymen of the First Cavalry Army who provided Babel with many of the prototypes for the heroes of *Konarmiia.*

An elite, mainly volunteer force, the First Cavalry Army suffered more than fourteen thousand casualties during summer 1920, a much higher rate of attrition than that for the Red Army as a whole during the Russian Civil War of 1918-20. Reinforcements replenished the ranks but, even so, the nine thousand sabres of the First Cavalry Army in August 1920 represented half its size of the previous May.[6] The soldiers who died were mostly young men; the median age for rank-and-file soldiers was twenty three and for commanders twenty four.[7] Babel would remark that service with the Red cavalry was like attending 'a never-ending requiem for the dead'.[8]

Babel's *Konarmiia* was an unusual Soviet publication for in place of the chivalrous and politically-conscious fighters who adorn the pages of so many Soviet accounts of the historical First Cavalry Army, Babel's cavalrymen heroes seem to have little or no connection to the ideals of the revolution under whose banners they fought. They are disdainful of their political teachers, sometimes sadistic, mostly anti-Semitic and often motivated by personal vengeance or the search for loot. The unflattering portrait of the Red cavalrymen found in *Konarmiia* gave rise to howls of protest from Babel's fellow veterans.[9] The opening of Soviet archives has corroborated a great deal of Babel's picture of the Red cavalry; the anti-Semitism of the Red cavalrymen, the shooting of prisoners, plunder of the civilian population and hostility of the soldiery to political education described or alluded to by Babel can all be confirmed as based on real events.[10] At the same time, Babel changed aspects of the setting provided for him by history in order to write a literary masterpiece that illuminates not only the misdeeds of the Red cavalry but deeper ironies and paradoxes that Babel felt lay just below the surface of the Soviet revolution.

In *Konarmiia*, Babel makes use of a great many historical facts, describes real military units, battles and cavalry tactics and employs commanders of the historical First Cavalry Army as characters in his stories. Babel thought it important to use the names of actual cavalry-

men of the First Cavalry Army, names that were widely known in Russia in the 1920s. The facts of history were important to Babel both as a framework for his fiction and because they anchored the *Konarmiia* stories firmly within the context of the Soviet-Polish War. Were it not for Babel's ability to suffuse his fiction with a strong sense of time and place, his stories, with their strange characters and outlandish images, might have struck the reader as too fantastic to have been based on real events. Using the names of real people, places and events imparted to the stories of *Konarmiia* a sense of authenticity that Babel believed important to their success.

Babel wanted his stories to have an authentic feel but did not consider himself bound to remain faithful to the facts of his experience. The narrator of *Konarmiia* appears as a solitary Jew who survives by using the Russian-sounding name of Liutov. While no precise figures on the number of Jews in the First Cavalry Army are available, we need only examine Babel's diary to discover the presence of Jewish comrades in the Red cavalry.[11] We know from archival sources that Jews served in the Red cavalry as commanders, rank-and-file cavalrymen and political commissars.[12] Jews were sufficiently well represented for Babel to be able to distinguish between those Jews who had joined the Communist Party and those, like Babel himself, who had not.[13] The educated and urbane Babel was an outsider in the world of the Red cavalry but the fact of his Jewishness did not make him unique.

On more than ninety occasions in *Konarmiia,* Babel makes reference to the Red cavalrymen as Cossacks; by contrast, there is only a single occasion when a cavalryman is described as a peasant and, in this instance, the identification is made not by the narrator but by a character in the story.[14] Lionel Trilling summed up the astonishment of many of Babel's readers when he marvelled at 'the vagary of the military mind' that could have placed a Jew in a Cossack cavalry regiment.[15] But this anomaly of a Jew among the Cossacks had much more to do with Babel's imagination than the Soviet military mind. To create the impression of a Cossack Red cavalry, Babel had to turn the facts of history on their head. According to the census of the First Cavalry Army carried out in 1920, Cossacks made up only fourteen per cent of the fighters of the First Cavalry Army. Peasants, with sixty two per cent of the total, comprised the largest group in the Red cavalry. Twenty per cent fell into the category of worker and four per cent were listed as intelligentsia.[16] Fully twenty per cent of the cavalrymen listed their place of origin as the Ukraine where no Cossack host had existed since the eighteenth century.[17] If only front-line cavalrymen of the First Cavalry Army were to be counted, the proportion of peasants and Cossacks would rise and that of workers and intelligentsia decline. Even so, the historical and memoir literature of the Soviet era described the First Cavalry Army as a mainly peasant fighting force,[18] while the only study produced by a Russian historian writing since the opening of Soviet archives also stressed the fact that the First Cavalry Army was a peasant rather than a Cossack army.[19] The only credible source to describe a Cossack Red cavalry was Babel.[20]

Two possible objections might be raised at this point. One is that those who surveyed the Red Army in 1920, wrote Soviet histories, and compiled the documents found in Soviet archives had an interest in proving that the heroic and successful Red cavalry arose from the peasant masses and not from the privileged Cossacks. Thus, Babel's description of a Cossack Red cavalry, while out of step with other accounts, may represent the more accurate picture. A second objection might be that Babel, a Jew from Odessa, may have found it difficult to distinguish between Cossacks and peasants whose appearance, speech and prejudices were so similar. Thus, even if the Red cavalry were not a Cossack fighting force, this information sheds little light on the concerns of Babel who genuinely believed that all, or nearly all, the cavalrymen around him were Cossacks. Neither objection stands up to close scrutiny.

In tsarist Russia, Cossacks comprised a separate legal estate whose members were required to serve in the imperial cavalry. The original Cossacks were runaway serfs and Tartar freebooters who came to the southern steppe at the end of the Mongol era. The Cossack's special burden of military service brought with it rewards of land ownership and self-government. The Cossack did not pay feudal dues or the soul tax and, like the nobility, was entitled to distil vodka. While he belonged to the Orthodox faith and spoke a version of the Russian language, the Cossack looked upon himself and was looked upon by others as different to his peasant neighbours. Cossacks became an even more select group from 1827 when entrance to the Cossack estate was closed to newcomers. The Cossack could not leave his estate nor could he marry an outsider without permission. By 1914 there were some four million Cossacks, divided into eleven hosts; the largest and most important hosts were those of the Don and Kuban situated in the south-east corner of Russia.

The impression Babel created of a Cossack Red cavalry was superficially plausible, to Russian literary critics as much as to their Western counterparts, because it played upon the fact that a majority of the soldiers of the real First Cavalry Army were drawn from in and around the Cossack lands of south-east Russia. Yet Cossacks were not the sole inhabitants of these lands. The Don Cossacks had long been in the habit of bringing peasants to the Cossack lands as serfs. Following the Emancipation, peasants from central Russia and the Ukraine flooded into the reputedly rich and underpopulated lands of the Don, Kuban' and the neighbouring Stavropol'

plateau. These new migrants to the Cossacks lands were known as *inogorodnie* (literally, people from another town). Cossacks tolerated the *inogorodnie* as a source of hired labour, taxes and rent. The number of non-Cossacks in the Don region increased from 320,000 to 1,783,000 between 1860 and 1912, or from thirty four per cent to fifty six per cent of the total population of the region.[21] The ratio of Cossacks to non-Cossacks in the Kuban by World War One was similar to that in the Don region while in the lands of the small Terek Host, non-Cossacks made up eighty per cent of the total. *Inogorodnie* came to share the Cossack's speech and dress but not his burden of military service, nor his privileges of land ownership and self-government. While Cossacks in 1914 made up only slightly more than forty per cent of the population of the Don and Kuban regions, they owned some eighty per cent of the land.[22] Non-Cossacks who resented Cossack privileges and coveted Cossack lands constituted an important wellspring of support for 'Soviet power' during 1917-20.[23]

The commander of the First Cavalry Army, Semen Budennyi, was one of the most famous Red Army soldiers of the early Soviet period. Budennyi is often described in introductions to Babel's work as a Don Cossack.[24] In reality, Budennyi was no more a Cossack than Babel. Budennyi's paternal grandfather came from Voronezh in central Russia and moved to the Don following the Emancipation of 1861. Babel's mother was the daughter of a Ukrainian serf.[25] Budennyi was therefore not a 'Red Cossack' but the most famous product of the Don *inogorodnie*. The *inogorodnie* were overrepresented in the Red cavalry during the Civil War just as Cossacks were over-represented in the White cavalry. The only two references to *inogorodnie* in **Konarmiia** come in the stories **'Sashka the Christ'** and **'Agramak'**. In **'Agramak'**, the reference is to peasant civilians not cavalrymen. The reference in **'Sashka the Christ'** to *inogorodnie* might easily be missed by those who read **Konarmiia** in translation for Babel's editors offer no explanation as to who these 'peasants from another town' might be.

In his diary Babel tended to describe any cavalryman he did not know as a Cossack. Yet Babel was forced to rein in his imagination when describing cavalrymen with whom he was personally acquainted or whose origins he was required to investigate. In an article which appeared in *Krasnyi kavalerist* in August 1920, Babel described the fallen hero, Konstantin Trunov, a regimental commander of the Sixth Cavalry Division, as a peasant from Stavropol' (*stavropol'skii krestianin*).[26] It is a description that accords with other accounts that we have of the Sixth Cavalry Division.[27] The Stavropol' plateau was a region populated by land-hungry peasants who sought to redistribute the lands of their Kuban Cossack neighbours; it was these peasants who came to form the backbone of the Sixth Cavalry Division with which Babel served.[28] Another cavalryman, Diakov, is described by Babel not as a Cossack but as a *stavropolets* in the diary entry for 13 July 1920.[29]

Further evidence of the fact that Babel was well aware that many of the prototypes for his cavalrymen heroes were not Cossacks comes from *Konarmiia* itself. There is a pattern to Babel's application of the term Cossack to his cavalrymen heroes in *Konarmiia*. Babel studiously avoided applying the label of Cossack to any of his cavalrymen heroes who carry the name of a famous real-life cavalryman of the First Cavalry Army. By contrast, the nameless secondary characters who inhabit the background of Babel's stories are invariably described as Cossacks. Babel was careful too to ensure that he attached the label of peasant to the rural inhabitants of the areas through which the First Cavalry Army passed, thus emphasizing the distinction between peasant civilians and the Cossack cavalrymen of the Red cavalry.[30]

The list of famous cavalrymen who appear as characters in *Konarmiia* includes army commanders, Semen Budennyi (**'Chesniki', 'Uchenie o tachanke',** and **'Kombrig dva'**) and Klim Voroshilov (**'Chesniki'**); divisional commander Semen Timoshenko, renamed as Boris Savitskii in later editions of *Konarmiia,* (**'Perekhod cherez Zbruch''**, **'Moi pervyi gus''**, **'Kombrig dva',** and **'Istoriia odnoi loshadi'**); brigade commanders Vasilii Kniga (**'Kombrig dva'**) and Masliakov (**'Afon'ka Bida'**); and the squadron commander, Oleko Dundich (**'Agramak'**). None is described by Babel as a Cossack. Nor does Babel describe as a Cossack Matthew Pavlichenko,[31] a character in his stories who is easily recognised as Iosef Apanasenko, Timoshenko's replacement as commander of the Sixth Cavalry Division, or Diakov, the remount officer in *Konarmiia* who closely resembles the Stavropol' peasant of the same name found in the diary.[32]

The reason Babel does not describe Budennyi, Voroshilov, Timoshenko or Kniga as Cossacks is quite straightforward. Babel knew that his stories would be controversial enough without inviting criticism that his knowledge of the Red cavalry was so poor that he had mistaken its leaders for Cossacks. The real Budennyi was a Don peasant, Voroshilov was a metalworker from Ekaterinoslav,[33] Timoshenko/Savitskii was born in Bessarabia,[34] Dundich was a Serb, while Apanasenko/Pavlichenko[35] and Kniga[36] hailed from Stavropol'. The only famous Cossack cavalryman of the First Cavalry Army whose name appears in *Konarmiia* is Masliakov. Babel could not, on the one hand, employ the names of Budennyi, Timoshenko and Kniga for the purpose of linking his stories to the historical First Cavalry Army and, on the other, relate obvious falsehoods concerning their backgrounds. Babel's caution in not describing these cavalrymen heroes as Cossacks suggests strongly that he was well aware of their peasant origins.

Why have Babel's readers and critics so often assumed that Budennyi, Timoshenko, and Pavlichenko were Cossacks if they are not so described by Babel? The answer is that Babel employed a simple but effective ruse. He immersed his cavalrymen heroes in a Cossack milieu. Thus, while Timoshenko/Savitskii is nowhere labelled a Cossack directly, we discover that he has a Cossack wife,[37] Budennyi makes speeches to the Cossacks,[38] Diakov finds horses for the Cossacks,[39] and Pavlichenko wears a bright red Cossack coat.[40] They are surrounded by Cossacks and they act in a manner that might be expected of Cossacks. They are athletic, brave, exotic, and brutal. Babel's tactics succeeded brilliantly; without committing any direct violence to the historical record, Babel was able to convey the impression to his general readers that the depiction of a Cossack Red cavalry in *Konarmiia* was a simple reflection of historical fact.

While the value of *Konarmiia* as a literary classic or indeed as a commentary on real events is not dependent upon the accuracy of the historical material found in its pages, disentangling fact from fiction in Babel's writings provides us with clues as to Babel's central concerns. Babel delighted in ironies and contrasts; the creation of a Cossack Red cavalry undoubtedly suited more than one of his artistic purposes. The term Cossack is an evocative one especially when placed alongside that of Jew. Babel's Cossack cavalrymen, creatures of passion and violence, make for a sharp contrast with the humane Liutov and the civilized but defenceless Jews who inhabit the borderland towns. Liutov's position as a Jew among the Cossacks conveys beautifully the sense of the narrator as an outsider and represents the most enduring image of the *Konarmiia* stories. At the same time, Babel was able to play upon the irony that the Soviet government was relying upon Cossacks, long-time enemies of the revolution, to achieve its goals.

It would be unfair to claim that Babel's transformation of the Red cavalry into a purely Cossack fighting force was an act of surrender, an admission that he found it impossible to comprehend the behaviour of the Red cavalrymen and so stereotyped them as Cossacks. Babel sought to locate the behaviour of the Red cavalrymen within the Cossack heritage with its complexities and contradictions. In Russian and Ukrainian history, the Cossack appeared first as a freedom fighter and later as janissary of the tsar. The Cossack claimed membership of an egalitarian community but saw himself as different and superior to his peasant neighbours. He displayed great valour on the battlefield yet committed bestial crimes against innocent and helpless civilians. Babel was fascinated by the physical attributes, recklessness, bravery, and revolutionary enthusiasm of the Red cavalrymen. He was intrigued as to how these qualities might coexist with a brazen disregard for the rights of others, a capacity to torment the weak and cowardly acts of murder and robbery. By applying the term Cossack to his cavalrymen, Babel suggests that the answer to the puzzle of the cavalrymen's behaviour lay deep in the history of the southern steppe with its tradition of backwardness, violence, and prejudice.

Babel's attitude towards the Red cavalrymen has long been a matter of dispute.[41] Some commentators consider that Babel portrayed his cavalrymen as revolutionary heroes while at least one critic has found in *Konarmiia* an endorsement of revolutionary war.[42] The facts of history provided Babel with ample opportunity to describe the story of the Red cavalry as one of heroic class struggle on the part of poor peasants risen up against Cossack oppressors and Polish landowners. It is precisely in those terms that the story of the Red cavalry was presented to the Soviet public in more conventional works of Soviet military history and literature.[43] By inventing a Cossack Red cavalry, Babel was able to undermine simple Soviet formulas of a class war between rich and poor, of violence in the service of a just cause.

Babel's notion of the Cossack was not the romanticized one of a community of warriors committed to freedom and equality favoured by some Russian and Ukrainian writers of the nineteenth century. Babel's diary entry for 21 July 1920 described the Cossack in the following terms:

> What sort of person is our Cossack? Many-layered; looting, reckless daring, professionalism, revolutionary spirit, bestial cruelty. We are the advance guard—but of what? The population awaits its deliverers, the Jews freedom . . . the Cossacks from the Kuban arrive.[44]

Babel's diary returns again and again to the theme of murder and robbery committed by the Red cavalrymen in the name of the revolution. On 6 September 1920, Babel made one of many diary entries in which he despaired of the robbery and violence;

> A nurse, a proud, dim-witted nurse in tears, a doctor outraged by yells of 'Smash the Yids. Save Russia'. They are stunned, the quartermaster has been thrashed with a whip, the contents of the clinic tossed out, pigs requisitioned and dragged off without receipt . . . that's Budennyi's warriors for you.[45]

It is likely that Babel's wartime service proved even more traumatic for the twenty-six-year-old political worker than a reading of his diary would suggest. We cannot be sure precisely when Babel joined the First Cavalry Army, nor do we know when his tour of duty came to an end. It is sometimes assumed that Babel left the Red cavalry in mid-September 1920.[46] But this assumption is based purely on the fact that mid-September 1920 is the date at which Babel's diary and the *Konarmiia* stories break off. The evidence of Babel's daughter suggests that her father in all probability stayed with the Red cavalry until at least the end of 1920. As

she recalled, 'at the end of that year [1920] he was reported dead, but ultimately returned'.[47] The diary provides no clues as to why or how Babel left the First Cavalry Army in mid-September 1920. The last diary entry, for 15 September 1920, has Babel still with the Red cavalry in western Ukraine and about to sit down to supper.[48]

The matter is an important one for between mid-September and mid-October 1920, Babel's Sixth Cavalry Division was responsible for some of the most appalling crimes against civilians committed by the Red Army during the Russian Civil War of 1918-20. As they retreated from Poland, the Red cavalrymen mutinied, declaring war on the 'Communists and Jews' of the rear. The mutiny affected all units of the First Cavalry Army but was led by soldiers of the thirty-first, thirty-second and thirty-third regiments of the Sixth Cavalry Division, the unit with which Babel served; it soon degenerated into a three-week spree of looting, rape and murder inflicted upon the Jewish settlements of western Ukraine. The soldiers involved were mainly peasants from the Stavropol' region and, when the violence subsided, more than eight hundred of them were put on trial.[49] The pogroms gave rise to an investigation by the Politburo and resulted in the execution of between one hundred and four hundred soldiers of the Sixth Cavalry Division and the sentencing to death of the division's commanders, including Apanasenko and Kniga; the standards and honours bestowed upon the Sixth Cavalry Division were removed and its name eradicated from the Red Army's Tables of Organization.[50] The details of the mutiny were kept secret from the Soviet public for seventy years.

We can only speculate as to whether, in September and October 1920, Babel, as a Jew and a political worker, came under fire from his own soldiers. If Babel were not directly involved, he could not have remained ignorant of these outrages for long; the stories of the pogroms spread rapidly among other units of the Red Army and were common knowledge among veterans of the Red cavalry. It is hard to imagine that the horrendous events of September and October 1920 did not play an important part in the bleak portrait of the behaviour of the Red cavalrymen which we find in *Konarmiia*.

Babel presents a gloomy vision of the Soviet revolution in *Konarmiia*. Babel's Jewish shopkeeper, Gedali, sees much more than the Cossacks for he knows that 'the revolution is the good deed of good men'; yet he is powerless even to prevent the Cossacks from requisitioning his gramophone.[51] Meanwhile, the reader is invited to witness the death of the revolutionary dream in the second-to-last story of the rabbi's son, the young, idealistic Jew who joined the Communist Party and went to the front to serve the Red Army. The campaign has gone badly, and the rabbi's son, having succumbed to typhus, is destined to be buried at 'some forgotten station', mourned only by Babel's narrator.[52]

In *Konarmiia,* the Red cavalrymen bring death and destruction to the borderlands under the guise of liberation. Babel's Cossack heroes seem to enjoy killing, to consider rape as normal and never to show remorse or compassion. Trunov sabres prisoners in cold blood,[53] Pavlichenko executes his former master by trampling him to death for more than an hour,[54] while the Kurdiukov brothers experience no remorse during the torture and execution of their own father.[55] The only mild-mannered cavalryman we encounter in *Konarmiia* is Sashka the Christ whose gentleness appears to have been the result of his being struck down with syphilis at the age of fourteen.[56] The Cossacks of *Konarmiia* are well versed in the rhetoric of revolution but use it as a cover for actions aimed at personal gain or vengeance.[57] Their violence is often directed at individuals who are either innocent or aging and pathetic. Balmashev's victim is an old woman who has deceived him,[58] Pavlichenko's victim is an odious yet seemingly defenceless landowner,[59] Akinfiev tortures the cowardly Aggev,[60] while unnamed Cossacks cut the throat of an elderly Jewish 'spy'.[61]

It is not that Babel's Cossacks lack courage; the Cossacks described in *Konarmiia* are often brave to the point of recklessness. It is the mentality of the Red cavalryman, well illustrated in the story **'Afon'ka Bida',** that undermines his contribution to the revolution. The Cossack for whom the story was named had set out on a desperate search for a horse to replace the one shot from under him. During his travels, Afon'ka Bida terrorizes the local population, shoots Polish farmers and has his eye smashed out in a fight.[62] Eventually he returns to his squadron with a new horse, to be admired by his fellow Cossacks who look upon his mission as a success. The Cossack fails to understand that his self-serving violence is discrediting the revolution for which he fights. It is a theme that runs through Babel's diary as well. As Babel put it, on 11 August 1920, 'this isn't a Marxist revolution, it's a Cossack rebellion out to win all and lose nothing'.[63]

The Cossack Red cavalry depicted in *Konarmiia* should be looked upon not as a fact of history but as another of Babel's artistic achievements. By inventing a Cossack Red cavalry, Babel sought to unsettle his Soviet readers, in much the same way that he was unsettled by his wartime experiences. On the one hand, Cossacks, who belonged to what was on the whole a relatively privileged caste, represented an anomaly in what Soviet propaganda usually described as an army of the poor and oppressed. On the other hand, Babel's transformation of the Red cavalry into a Cossack fighting force linked the Soviet revolution to Cossack rebellions of centuries past. Babel came to view the Soviet revolution as symptomatic of Russia's backwardness not as the forward-looking vehicle of Russia's transformation for which he had hoped when he volunteered for service in the Red Army in May 1920. The experience of the Polish campaign impressed upon Babel how unlikely it was that the revolutionary dream of freedom and equality would be realized by the likes of those who fought with the Red cavalry. Turning the Red cavalrymen into Cossacks was one of the means by which Babel sought to convey that experience, and his doubts about the Soviet project, to his readers.

Notes

1. First Cavalry Army is a slightly inaccurate translation of Pervaia konnaia armiia (literally, First Horse Army), which, in Soviet military parlance, was often shortened to Konarmiia. I will refer to the military unit as the First Cavalry Army and to Babel's fictional work as *Konarmiia.*

2. See, for example, Isaac Babel, *1920 Diary,* edited and with an introduction and notes by Carol J. Avins (New Haven, Yale University Press, 1995), pp. xxii-xxiii.

3. The relationship between *Konarmiia* and the historical events of the Soviet-Polish War is discussed in Norman Davies, 'Izaak Babel''s "Konarmiya" Stories and the Polish-Soviet War', *Modern Language Review,* 64 (October 1972) and Ragna Grongaard, *An Investigation of Composition and Theme in Isaak Babel's Literary Cycle Konarmija,* trans. D. R. Frickleton (Aarhus, Arkona, 1979).

4. On this point, see I. Babel, *The Lonely Years: 1925-1939,* edited by Nathalie Babel, trans. Andrew R. MacAndrew and Max Hayward (Noonday Press, New York, 1964), pp. ix-xxviii.

5. See Isaac Babel', *Sochineniia,* 2 vols. (Khudozhestvennaia literatura, Moscow, 1991), 1, pp. 362-436.

6. S. Prisiazhnyi, *Pervaia konnaia armiia na pol'skom fronte v 1920 godu* (Izdatel'stvo rostovskogo universiteta, Rostov-na-donu, 1992), p. 57.

7. The relevant archive for the First Cavalry Army is Moscow, *Rossiiskii gosudarstvennyi voennyi arkhiv.* On this point, see *RGVA,* f. 245, op. 4, d. 183, p. 26.

8. *Sochineniia,* 1, p. 402.

9. See, for example, the protest by Semen Budennyi, commander of the First Cavalry Army, in *Pravda,* 28 October 1928.

10. See Stephen Brown, 'Communists and the Red cavalry; the political education of the *Konarmiia*

in the Russian Civil War of 1918-20', *Slavonic and East European Review,* 73 (January 1995), pp. 82-99.

11. This point is made by Carol J. Avins in Babel, *1920 Diary,* p. xxx.

12. See, for example, *RGVA,* f. 245, op. 9, d. 4, p. 9.

13. See Babel, *1920 Diary,* p. xxx.

14. See the story, 'Sashka the Christ', Babel, *Sochineniia,* 2, p. 50.

15. See Isaac Babel, *Collected Stories,* trans. David McDuff (Penguin, London, 1994), p. 348.

16. The results of this survey are quoted in a number of Soviet sources, including I. Tiulenev, *Pervaia konnaia v boiakh za sotsialisticheskuiu rodinu* (Voennoe izdatel'svo ministerstva oborony Soiuza SSR, Moscow, 1957), p.2 2.

17. Prisiazhnyi, *Pervaia konnaia,* p. 20.

18. See, for example, V. Sidorov, *Pervaia konnaia armiia* (Voennoe izdatel'svo ministerstva vooruzhenyikh sil soiuza SSR, Moscow, 1949), p. 5, or S. Budennyi, 'Prazdnik RKKA i krasnoi konnitsy', *Krasnaia konnitsa,* 2 (1935), p. 4.

19. S. Prisiazhnyi, *Pervaia konnaia,* p. 20.

20. Babel did find an unreliable ally in some Soviet literature of the late 1930s. As part of a propaganda campaign aimed at restoring the glories of Russia's military past, the First Cavalry Army was sometimes described as an example of 'Red Cossack cavalry'. For a discussion, see Albert Seaton, *The Horsemen of the Steppes* (The Bodley Head, London, 1985), p. 233.

21. Robert. H. McNeal Neal, *Tsar and Cossack, 1855-1914,* (Macmillan, Basingstoke, 1987), p. 14.

22. K. Khmelevskii, *Krakh krasnovshchiny i nemetskoi interventsii na Donu (aprel' 1918-mart 1919 goda)* (Izdatel'stvo rostovskogo universiteta, Rostov, 1965), pp. 20-22.

23. For a description of the conflict between Cossacks and *inogorodnie,* see P. Kenez, *Civil War in South Russia, 1919-1920: The Defeat of the Whites* (University of California Press, Berkeley, 1977). pp. 86-87.

24. See, for example, I. Babel, *Red Cavalry* (Bristol Classical Press, Bristol, 1994), edited with introduction and notes by Christopher Luck, p. 124, and Isaac Babel, *Collected Stories* (1994), p. 317.

25. See S. Budennyi, *Proidennyi put',* 3 vols. (Moscow, 1958-73), 3, pp. 9-10, and Seaton, *The Horsemen of the Steppes,* p. 233.

26. Babel, *Sochineniia,* 1, p. 202.

27. See, for example, Prisiazhnyi, *Pervaia konnaia,* p. 20.

28. See *Stavropol'e za 40 let Sovetskoi vlasti 1917-1955 gg. (Materialy po izucheniiu Stavropol'skogo kraiia)* (Stavropol'skoe knizhnoe izdatel'stvo, Stavropol', 1957) and Prisiazhnyi, *Pervaia konnaia,* p. 20.

29. *Sochineniia,* 1, p. 372.

30. See, for example, the description of the Volhynian peasants in the story 'Afon'ka Bida', *Sochineniia,* 2, p. 80.

31. Pavlichenko appears in the stories 'Zhizneopisanie Pavlichenki, Matveia Rodionycha', 'Chesniki', and 'Afon'ka Bida' and 'Kombrig dva'.

32. Diakov appears in the story 'Nachal'nik konzapasa'.

33. For an account of Voroshilov's origins, see *The Modern Encyclopaedia of Russian and Soviet History,* ed. J. Wieczynski, 48 vols. (Academic International Press, USA, 1976-88), 43, p. 67.

34. For Timoshenko's origins, see *The Modern Encyclopaedia,* 39, p. 66.

35. For Apanasenko's origins, see *The Modern Encyclopaedia,* 2, p. 64.

36. For Kniga's origins, see Budennyi, *Proidennyi put',* 1, p. 327.

37. See the story 'Istoriia odnoi loshadi', *Sochineniia,* 2, p. 62.

38. See the story 'Chesniki', *Sochineniia,* 2, p. 119.

39. See the story 'Nachal'nik konzapasa', *Sochineniia,* 2, p. 16.

40. See the story 'Chesniki', *Sochineniia,* 2, p. 119.

41. For a summary of this debate, see C. Luplow, *Isaac Babel's 'Red Cavalry'* (Ardis, Ann Arbor, 1982), pp. 33-34.

42. See Gareth Williams, 'The rhetoric of revolution in Babel's Konarmija', *Russian Literature,* 15 (1984), pp. 285-86.

43. See, for example, Semyon Budyonnyi, *The Path of Valour* (Progress Publishers, Moscow, 1972), Vsevolod Vishnevskii, *Pervaia konnaia* (Gosudarstvennoe izdatel'stvo khudozhestvennoi literatury, Moscow, 1931) or Semen Krivoshein, *Chongartsy* (Sovetskaia Rossiia, Moscow, 1975).

44. *Sochineniia,* 1, pp. 381-82.

45. Here, I have used the translation in Babel, *1920 Diary,* p. 93.

46. Norman Davies, 'Izaak Babel''s 'Konarmiya' stories', p. 847.

47. Babel, *The Lonely Years,* p. xviii.

48. *Sochineniia,* 1, p. 435.

49. See Brown, 'Communists and the Red Cavalry', pp. 85-86 and Prisiazhnyi, *Pervaia konnaia,* pp. 16-19. A summary of the investigator's report is to be found in *RGVA,* f. 245, op. 9, d. 2.

50. See S. Budennyi, *Proidennyi put',* 3, pp. 38-41. The brigades of the Sixth Cavalry Division were reorganized as 'march battalions' for the war against Baron Wrangel's White Army in the Crimea in November and December 1920. Having acquitted themselves well in this fight, the division was renamed as *Chongarskaia 6-aia kavaleriiskaia diviziia* and its standards were returned. Apanasenko and Kniga were sentenced to death but not executed.

51. *Sochineniia,* 2, p. 30.

52. *Sochineniia,* 2, p. 129.

53. *Sochineniia,* 2, p. 92.

54. *Sochineniia,* 2, p. 59.

55. *Sochineniia,* 2, p. 14.

56. *Sochineniia,* 2, p. 50.

57. See Luplow, *Isaac Babel's 'Red Cavalry',* p. 34.

58. See the story 'Sol'', *Sochineniia,* 2, p. 76.

59. See the story, 'Zhizneopisanie Pavlichenki, Matveia Rodionycha', *Sochineniia,* 2, p. 59.

60. See the story 'Ivany', *Sochineniia,* 2, p. 101.

61. See the story 'Berestechko', *Sochineniia,* 2, p. 69.

62. *Sochineniia,* 2, p. 84.

63. *Sochineniia,* 1, p. 409.

Janet Tucker (essay date summer 2000)

SOURCE: Tucker, Janet. "*Skaz* and Oral Usage as Satirical Devices in Isaak Babel's *Red Calvary.*"[1] *Canadian-American Slavic Studies* 34, no. 2 (summer 2000): 201-10.

[*In the following essay, Tucker considers Babel's use of* skaz *and the oral tradition in* Red Cavalry *as parodic devices.*]

Given the density and intricacy of his short story collection **Red Cavalry,** justifiably regarded as one of the great prose works of twentieth-century Russian literature, Isaak Babel' is notoriously difficult to pin down. Even the briefest of his tales masterfully develops the subject central to all of them: the violence inherent in the October Revolution and the civil war that followed it. No writer explores this theme more cogently than Babel'. There is no single element in his stories that more strikingly underscores the horror of this violence than Babel's use of *skaz* and images from the folktale.

Babel's employment of *skaz,* coupled with his references to oral literature, reminds us that he is writing about semi- or illiterate people who are still immersed in traditional culture. The very word *skaz,* from *skazat'* ("to say" or "to tell") suggests oral usage, which itself can variously encompass oral folk narrative (typically, in folktales, in prose) or can appear as the speech of a semi- or uneducated narrator quoted by the actual author.[2] Oral usage incorporates the epithets, turns of phrase and images typically encountered in Russian oral literature, whether heroic tales or *skazki* (folk-tales or fairy tales); for reasons of space, only *skazki* will be considered here. Since no discussion of *skazki* would be complete without consulting Vladimir Propp's *Morphology of the Folktale,* that work will also figure in my analysis. Propp considers the actions/functions of characters in the *skazki* to be the central element, the key to understanding these tales.[3] The purpose of this essay is to pinpoint examples of *skaz* and oral motifs in Babel', to attempt to discover his reasons for incorporating these motifs, and to discuss them as parodic/satirical devices.[4]

Skaz figures prominently in two **Red Cavalry** stories: **"Pis'mo"** (**"The Letter"**) and **"Sol'"** (**"Salt"**).[5] In the first, Babel's narrator Liutov reproduces for his readers a letter dictated by the youngest son of a family in which, in a microcosmic version of the Civil War, the father has killed one of three brothers and is in turned executed by another. Sub- or non-standard forms abound, emphasizing the oral or traditional orientation of this tale: "Ia est'" for "I am," "zdesia" instead of "zdes'" for "here," "prosiu" for "proshu" ("I ask, request").[6] So does the traditional discourse associated with the *skaz-ka:* "A takzhe nizhaiushche vam klaniaius' ot bela litsa do syroi zemli. . . ." ("And likewise do I bow down low to you from my white face to the damp earth," with "matka syraia zemlia," "mother damp earth," understood here, **"Pis'mo,"** 12).

In **"Sol',"** the narrator Balmashev repeatedly says "Raseiu" ("Russia") instead of the standard literary form "Rossiiu" (**"Sol',"** 97), "anteresnoe" ("interesting," "odd," a foreign word) rather than "interesnoe" (**"Sol',"** 97), "prosiut" for "prosiat" ("to request," "ask for") (**"Sol',"** 98). The *skazka* appears linguistically rather than situationally in the introduction of Balmashev's letter to the "comrade editor": "za trideviat' zemel', v nekotorom gosudarstve, na nevedomon prostranstve" ("beyond the thrice ninth land, in a certain country, in an unknown place"). (**"Sol',"** 94).[7] This pattern would be right at home in Afanas'ev's collection; in "Ivan Bykovich," the formula is: "V nekotorom tsarstve, v nekotorom gosudarstve, zhil-byl tsar' s tsaritseiu" ("In a certain kingdom, in a certain country, there dwelled a tsar' with a tsaritsa").[8] Balmashev recites the story teller's typical formulaic hint at a reward for his/her efforts, but with a twist: in "ia tam byl, myod pil, usy obmochil, v rot ne zaskochil" ("I was there, drank mead, wet my mustache, didn't jump into my mouth"), the mead becomes "samogon-pivo," home-brewed beer (**"Sol',"** 94). Such banal transformational lowering of the original folk pattern reappears throughout the story.[9]

In each story, sub-standard locution and—even more strikingly, the language of the folktale—are combined with the most appalling event of all: killing. Murder within the family context makes **"The Letter"** especially horrific. In **"Salt,"** the "stain" that Balmashev wipes out is a woman smuggling salt, crucial in the smelting of steel and hence for the war effort (**"Sol',"** 98). Her salt disguised in swaddling clothes is, of course, no infant, but because the reader sees her initially with a bundle disguised as a baby, she still bears the imprint of mother. She could be *any* mother, and mothers still command respect, which is why she has not been raped after a night of riding in a train car full of soldiers; hence, Balmashev seems to have committed matricide. The image of "mother," which links **"The Letter"** with **"Salt,"** has folkloric as well as societal and familial overtones. In "Vasilisa prekrasnaia" ("Vasilisa the Beautiful"), for example, Vasilisa's dying mother gives her a doll, a magical agent, that saves Vasilisa in her moments of greatest need and even seems, in dispensing wisdom to Vasilisa ("the morning is wiser than the evening"), to take her mother's place.[10]

What sort of impression does this nexus of the language of traditional culture plus savagery produce in Babel's reader? We know that these people have not lost all their values. In **"The Letter,"** the young Kudriukov respectfully addresses his mother as Evdokiia Fedorovna and bows to the "damp earth" before her, conflating his own mother with the folk image of "Mother Damp Earth" ("Matka syraia zemlia"). One assumes that he is not merely taking advantage of their relationship to get her to care for his horse Styopa, whom he genuinely loves and worries about (**"Pis'mo,"** 13). Other familial relationships, after all, seem to count for very little in this story! In **"Sol',"** Balmashev still retains that regard for motherhood that is inherent in any culture. Yet something has clearly been lost, and that intangible "something" is the freshness, the innocence that the educated and jaded intellectual assumes should still exist in any traditional culture, especially *Russian* culture. If we consider the *narod*, the folk, in nineteenth-century works as disparate as Pushkin's *Eugene Onegin* and

Tolstoi's *War and Peace,* we can hear their voices functioning as counterweights to the limitations and dubious worth of a culture modeled on that of the West. That sense of traditional values is ruined by the violence of a revolution and war that the *narod* but dimly understand.[11] *Skaz,* in which Babel's narrator Liutov stands to one side to let his readers hear the voice of the people directly, unadulterated by an outsider's views, underscores this loss.[12]

Because Babel' focuses on the cavalry from which the collection takes its name and on *Cossack* cavalry at that, the horse inevitably plays a central role. In all of these stories, the "heroes" have left home on horses (in Propp, the hero *abandons* home), and the narrator attempts to be a horseman like them, sometimes with disastrous results (**"Argamak,"** 172-76).[13] Even where horses do not literally appear, as in the *skaz* masterpiece **"The Letter,"** they intrude into the text. In **"The Letter,"** young Kudriukov twice mentions his horse to his mother, thus underscoring the link between traditional family structure, oral usage, and the horse. That the soap for washing his horse is kept behind the icon elevates the horse still further, and the very act of washing here suggests baptism. Horses and riders form a nexus, with the Cossacks of the tales frequently exhibiting the swaggering bravado and confident nobility that links them with the "knights" or "heroes" of the heroic tales and *skazki* (folktales). *Skaz* and the horse operate in tandem as the "medium" and "message," respectively, of Babel's **Red Cavalry.** The *function* of the horse is what Babel' stresses here and serves as a reminder of the fact that Propp considered function to be the basic unit of the folktale.[14]

Nowhere does the horse play a more dramatic role than in **"Afon'ka Bida,"** about a bullying cossack whose horse is shot from beneath him by the Poles, and who goes on a mad rampage to avenge the death of his mount and acquire a new one. His abduction of a "replacement" mount serves as a reminder that the horse is part of his identity, not merely property or a means of transportation. Clearly, the horse functions here as a sort of magical agent indispensable for the Cossack.[15] Afon'ka Bida's later abduction of a replacement recalls the abductions perpetrated by villains—not heroes—in the *skazki*.[16] After Maslak has put Afon'ka's critically wounded horse out of his misery, a chorus of Cossacks comments on Afon'ka's loss.[17] "'He brought his horse (literally "steed," "kon',") from home,' said the long-mustached Bitsenko." Note the word "steed," "kon'," hinting at the heroic tale. "'A steed—he's a friend ("drug," suggesting "other," "bosom buddy"),' responded Orlov. A steed—he's a father,' sighed Bitsenko" (**"Afon'ka Bida,"** 108), thus giving the horse the stature of an authority figure. As a mark of its great value, Afon'ka Bida pays for his new horse with his left eye (110). Clearly more than just a horse, it has acquired the characteristics of the talisman/magical agent noted by Propp.[18] Afon'ka's theft of the horse, combined with his rapacious plundering of the church and surrounding countryside (**"Afon'ka Bida,"** 109-10) links him with the villains of the *skazki*[19] and blurs the line between Cossack heroism and Cossack villainy. (Magical agents in **Red Cavalry** are not necessarily restricted to horses; the Hasid Gedali's shop is full of "dead" ones, wondrous objects that have now lost their magical power) (**"Gedali,"** 36-37).[20]

Nor are horses and other magical agents the only folkloric components of these stories; other folkloric elements, typically related to the functions of the characters, figure as well. One of the most significant of these is the interdiction, sometimes in the form of the interdiction plus the proposal. In **"My First Goose,"** Liutov's traditional Jewish interdiction against gratuitous slaughter collides with the traditional Cossack dictum that in wartime (the Cossack milieu) one *should* or *must* kill. It is only after having accepted the suggestion to "ruin" a lady, which he does circuitously by killing her goose (specifically, a gander) and using boorish language, that is, by accepting a cossack *proposal,* that Liutov is able to gain a degree of acceptance—at a price (**"Moi pervyi gus',"** 41-44).[21]

Interdiction and the difficult task are central to **"The Rabbi"** and especially to **"The Rabbi's Son,"** where the last son of the "dynasty" forsakes his Hasidic heritage to serve the revolution. The young man desecrates the Sabbath by lighting a cigarette in **"The Rabbi"** (47), and the narrator encounters him in **"The Rabbi's Son"** near death, with his talismanic objects from the Jewish world and the world of the revolution clustered around him (**"Syn rabbi,"** 169-70).[22]

Interdiction overlaps with the difficult task not only in **"My First Goose," "The Rabbi"** and **"The Rabbi's Son,"** but in **"The Death of Dolgushev"** (58-60) as well, where Liutov, once again torn between Jewish and Cossack codes of behavior, turns down the dying Dolgushev's plea for a mercy killing and, almost shot by his friend Afon'ka Bida, suffers "banishment" (a traditional *skazka* form of punishment) as a consequence.[23] The request for mercy, a natural component of war stories, appears also in **"Konkin"** (86-89) and **"The Ivans"** (126-34).[24]

Babel's stories reveal *skazka* roots not only in their characters and the events in which these characters are involved, but also in their imagery. Nowhere is this particular link between the *skazki* and Babel's stories more pronounced than in **"Salt,"** and even here we have the suggestion of horsemen, as can be seen below. The narrator/author has just intruded into the *skaz* narrator Balmashev's letter with the lines: "And the third bell having rung, the train started to move. And a glorious

little night spread like a tent. And in that tent (note the repetition of three) were star-lanterns." Then Balmashev reappears with the sentence: "After some time passed, when night changed its guard and the little red drummers played reveille on their red drums, then the Cossacks came over to me. . . ." (**"Sol',"** 96) The red drummers not only have the obvious political (Marxist) overtones but also echo figures from the *skazki.*[25]

In the tale **"Vasilisa the Beautiful,"** her cruel stepmother has sent the heroine to the hut of the witch Baba Iaga ostensibly to get a light, but actually to get her killed off. Aided by her magic doll, the girl performs all the tasks assigned to her ("the difficult task") and survives. As Vasilisa walks trembling to Baba Iaga's hut, she encounters three horsemen: the first one gallops past, a white man dressed in white, on a white horse with white reins, and it begins to get light. Then the second one comes and flashes by; he himself is red, wearing red and on a red horse, and the sun starts to rise. The third horseman is black, is clad all in black, and gallops by on a black horse. When he rides by, night falls. Babel's readers would surely have recalled this tale from childhood and would remember the additional scary details of the fence made of human bones, the skulls with eyes that light up the night darkness, and the witch who is a cannibal.[26]

Babel' has transformed the horsemen of the tale to drummers, perhaps because the noise of the train wheels over the sleepers is more akin to the sound of a drum (these horsemen "ride" a train). The connection with the sun, however, still holds, even though the white and black figures, part of the triad of riders, are missing from **"Salt."** In **"Vasilisa the Beautiful,"** we have a picture of innocent beauty, of goodness aided by the magic helper (the doll her late mother has left her) and persecuted by a cruel stepmother and stepsisters, maltreatment that becomes even more severe during her father's long absence. In **"Salt"** the "doll" proves the false mother's undoing. The contrast of goodness versus depravity climaxes when Vasilisa and Baba Iaga, eater of human flesh, are together.[27]

"Salt" contains a similar juxtaposition. When Balmashev notes the essential innocence of his young soldiers, their ruined lives, and the ruined lives of their wives and the girls they have raped (97), the reader who remembers the *skazka* can supply the missing component: like Baba Iaga, the war "eats" human flesh and human souls. As with Babel's use of *skaz,* traditional culture as embodied in the *skazki* encounters is ultimately corrupted by the forces of revolution and war. It is this very use of contrast, of the combination of opposites that runs through virtually all of his stories, the Odessa tales as well as **Red Cavalry,** that may well be Babel's most striking and significant stylistic characteristic.[28] "The world of man," notes Karen Luplow in her

essay on *Red Cavalry,* "consists of antithetical and irreconcilable ways of life based on conflicting, incom-
patible value systems."[29]

What effect does Babel's incorporation of *skaz* and of
skazka motifs or situations have on *Red Cavalry*? On
the most basic level, of course, the use of *skaz* directly
relates the revolution and civil war to the immediate experience of the *narod* and demonstrates that on at least
one level—the level of gratuitous violence—the revolution can be defined as "popular revolution." Revolution
certainly is manifested most savagely in those tales of
familial (and symbolically familial) violence, **"The Letter"** and **"Salt,"** in which *skaz* is central. The use of
skaz and of *skazka* motifs and images, combined with
Babel's employment of striking color combinations, en-
dows *Red Cavalry* with the sort of vitality identified
with the world of Russian popular culture, so readily
apparent in the painter Filipp Andreevich Maliavin's
red-clad, exuberant, dancing peasant women.[30] This is
the same sort of vigor that characterized the popular
Cossack revolts that rocked Russia in the seventeenth
and eighteenth centuries.[31]

The combination of the violence of revolution and war
with the energy and innocence of traditional culture,
when associated with an incomplete or unclear comprehension of the aims of that revolution for those very
men who are fighting for it (see **"My First Goose,"**
mentioned above) creates the impression of a cause that
somehow, for all the dynamism of its appeal, has gone
horribly wrong. The brutality of the civil war shreds
families (**"The Letter"**) or surrogate families (**"Salt"**),
turns a "hero" into a villain (**"Afon'ka Bida"**), and defiles magical objects (**"Gedali"**) and "magic people"
(**"The Rabbi," "The Rabbi's Son"**). Violation of the
interdiction and acceptance of the proposal leads to loss
instead of the expected redemption, as in the last sentence of **"My First Goose"** when the narrator, having
killed the goose, records how his "heart . . . crimsoned
with murdered, creaked and flowed out" (like the brains
of the murdered goose, 44). An attempt to fulfill the
difficult task, which typically leads to success in the
skazki—marrying a princess, acquiring wealth, merely
staying alive[32]—leads instead to failure and death (**"The
Rabbi's Son"**). The narrator's inability to accept the
plea of a dying man, an acceptance which typically results in some sort of reward for the hero of the *skazka,*
instead nearly causes Liutov's death at the hands of
Afon'ka Bida (**"The Death of Dolgushev"**). The traditional values of the *skazki* are violated or overturned
countless times in *Red Cavalry* and, always, the revolution and civil war are depicted as the cause.

How do *skaz* and elements of the *skazki,* which enable
Babel' to analyze and castigate the revolution and the
civil war that followed in its wake, function as satirical
devices? Satire is a mode rather than a genre, a means

of making a form of art out of the examination and
criticism of, to cite Karen Ryan, "the social, political or
moral life of the culture it treats." She comments further that the parody of genre conventions is a significant component of contemporary Russian satire.[33] There
is also a precedent for such parody in nineteenth-century
Russian literature, as in Dostoevskii's parodies of
Gogol', described by the Formalist critic Iurii
Tynianov.[34]

Babel' provides a prime example of such parody during
the 1920s, but are *skaz* narrators parodies of the traditional story tellers and his stories, in turn, mere parodies of the *skazki*? Since, as Karen Ryan notes, satire
attacks such external targets as politics, societal codes
of behavior and "cultural institutions,"[35] then Babel's
Red Cavalry tales manage at once to function as both
parody and satire.

First of all, Babel' uses *skaz* to mock the figure of the
narrator himself. If the conventional narrator of the *skazki* recounts his/her tales to uphold the traditional values of the Russian oral tradition, then Babel's *skaz* narrators instead find themselves in the midst of a
bewildering world in which these traditional values are
perilously close to being lost forever. Nor are narrators
always reliable in *Red Cavalry*; even the non-*skaz*
"frame" narrator of **"The Letter,"** who swears that he
is recounting young Kudriukov's message to his mother
in its entirely, makes a parenthetical aside to the reader
about leaving out the young man's enumeration of his
various relations and godparents (12) and, hence, undermines his own position. Most significantly for our purposes, *skaz,* which typically functions as a droll mode
of discourse (as in the stories of Nikolai Leskov or
Mikhail Zoshchenko), is completely stripped of any humorous aspects in the grim world of *Red Cavalry. Skazki* that figure in Babel's stories are similarly undermined and lampooned (although once again, without
any humorous overtones), devoid of the ingenuous
charm that distinguished the original models of
Afanas'ev's collection.

If satire can be understood as a means of exposing societal shortcomings or flaws, then the tales of *Red Cavalry* certainly qualify as satirical. Unlike Mikhail Zoshchenko, who satirized a more settled Soviet community
of the NEP period of the 1920s, Babel' instead assailed
a society that was undergoing the painful, horrific transition of revolution and civil strife, a world in which
the accepted norms were in the process of being turned
upside down or even destroyed. Hence, a Jew could
ride with the Cossacks, nay, almost *become* a Cossack
(as in **"Argamak"**). A family could devour itself, divided between the two sides in the revolution (**"The
Letter"**). Most significantly, the common, traditional
values of an entire civilization, as epitomized by the
oral culture of its folk, its *narod,* could be fatally com-

promised by revolutionary upheaval, in which the civil war functions as a violent component. Babel' parodies the traditional teller of tales and the tales themselves in order to comment satirically on the wasteful violence of revolution and the Civil War. As in Olesha's 1927 novel *Envy,* Babel' employs imagery, motifs and narrators to express his doubts about the efficacy and legitimacy of the Soviet revolution.[36] It was a revolution that, however lofty its design, nonetheless managed to discredit its goals in the course of a violent genesis.

Notes

1. The present essay is based on a paper presented at a panel on satire and parody in Russian literature, at the annual meeting of the American Association of Slavic Studies, Boca Raton, Florida, in September 1998. I would like to thank Professor Karen Ryan for graciously inviting me to be on that panel. Dr. Joyce Story from Glendale Community College, Glendale, Arizona, provided many helpful comments. The insightful observations of Professor Anna Brodsky of Washington and Lee University improved this essay immeasurably.

2. Hugh McLean, "Skaz," in *Handbook of Russian Literature,* ed. Victor Terras (New Haven, CT: Yale Univ. Press, 1985), p. 420.

3. V. Ia. Propp, *Morfologiia skazki,* 2nd ed. (Moscow: Nauka, 1969), pp. 24-28.

4. Victor Erlich notes that Vladimir Propp's *Morfologiia skazki* was originally published in Leningrad in 1928. Victor Erlich, *Russian Formalism: History—Doctrine,* 3rd ed. (New Haven, CT: Yale Univ. Press, 1981), p. 29n. That publication of *Morfologiia skazki* postdated the appearance of Babel's *Konarmiia* has no bearing on Babel''s own undoubted familiarity with the collection of A. N. Afanas'ev (1826-1871). For information on Afanas'ev's career and publications, see Yu. M. Sokolov, *Russian Folklore,* trans. Catherine Ruth Smith (Hatboro, PA: Folklore Associates, 1966), pp. 69, 70n., 71-74, *passim.*

5. There is even a story called "Salt" (#242) in Afanas'ev's collection. A. N. Afanas'ev, *Narodnye russkie skazki v trekh tomakh* (Moscow: Goslitizdat, 1938), 2: 341-44.

6. "Pis'mo," in Isaak Babel', *Konarmiia,* 3rd ed. (Moscow: Gosudarstvennoe izdatel'stvo, 1928; reprint London: Flegon Press, n.d.), pp. 12-13. Further references to Babel's stories will be in the text.

7. For an excellent examination of the Ukrainianisms, southern Russianisms, Oddessisms and Yiddishisms in Babel, see Efraim Sicher, *Style and Structure in the Prose of Isaak Babel'* (Columbus,

OH: Slavica Publishers, 1986), pp. 72-79. Maurice Friedberg's "Yiddish Folklore Motifs in Isaak Babel's *Konarmija*" (in Harold Bloom, ed., *Modern Critical Views* [New York: Chelsea House Publishers, 1987], pp. 191-98) contains a fine discussion of Babel''s treatment of the Hasidism.

8. "Ivan Bykovich," in A. N. Afanas'ev, *Narodnye russkie skazki v trekh tomakh* (Moscow: Gosudarstvennoe izdatel'stvo khudozhestvennoi literatury, 1957), 1: 278.

9. Nor should we forget that the imperfective of "zaskochit'" ("to jump") is "zaskakivat'," related to "skakat'," "to gallop." Even where no horses appear *physically,* they are present *etymologically.*

10. A. N. Afanas'ev, *Narodnye russkie skazki* (Moscow: Akademiia, 1936), 1: 176-77, 179. In the *skazka* "Salt" from Afanas'ev's collection, Russian salt is a valuable commodity that makes a youngest son's fortune (as Joyce Story has reminded me). Significantly, the revolutionary train, with sometimes negative associations, is juxtaposed to the ship of the *skazka.*

11. See, for instance, Babel's "Moi pervyi gus'," from the same collection. Joyce Story has noted to me that, while the hero of the traditional tale is transformed (for the better), young Kudriukov from "The Letter" remains naive while, at the same time, causing his mother suffering with his letter.

12. There is a precedent for the narrator as outsider among Cossacks in early nineteenth-century Russian literature. In "Kavalerist-devitsa," Nadezhda Durova rides with the cavalry disguised as a man, her deception echoed later in *Red Cavalry* as Babel's narrator Liutov attempts to merge with the Cossacks, overcoming two significant stigmas: being a Jew and an intellectual in glasses. Horses, of course, play a significant role in Durova's work; see N. A. Durova, "Kavalerist-devitsa," *Izbrannye sochineniia* (Moscow: Moskovskii rabochii, 1983), pp. 31, 33, 46, 53, 55. Durova rides into battle with the Cossacks (46) and arouses the suspicions of a woman who sees through her disguise (48). Like Babel's descriptions of nature just over a century later, Durova's seem to mirror her narrator's mood: "Spring . . . was . . . sad, wet, cold, windy, dirty. . . ." (147). The Cossack Platov, who reappears in Nikolai Leskov's short story "The Steel Flea," makes a cameo appearance in Durova's memoirs (47). I am grateful to Anna Brodsky for her valuable suggestion to consult Durova's "Kavalerist-devitsa."

13. Propp, *Morfologiia skazki,* p. 40. For a discussion of the heroic in *Red Cavalry,* not only among the Cossacks but in the Jewish characters as well, see

Judith Deutsch Kornblatt, *The Cossack Hero in Russian Literature: A Study in Cultural Mythology* (Madison: Univ. of Wisconsin Press, 1992), pp. 113-14.

14. Propp, *Morfologiia skazki,* pp. 24-28; Erlich, *Russian Formalism,* pp. 249-50.

15. Propp, *Morfologiia skazki,* pp. 40-41.

16. *Ibid.,* pp. 32-34.

17. Interestingly this horse, like the one in "Pis'mo," is also named Stepan, although Babel' use the full name here rather than the nickname.

18. *Ibid.,* pp. 43-44. Other stories with "magical" or special horses include "Istoriia odnoi loshadi," "Nachal'nik konzapasa" and "Zamost'e."

19. See *ibid.,* p. 34.

20. *Ibid.,* p. 42.

21. On the deceitful proposal, see *ibid.,* pp. 32-33.

22. In his incisive discussion of both stories, Friedberg reminds us that Spinoza, whom this youth resembles, was a rebel who was excommunicated and that Maimonides, whose portrait the rabbi's son carries along with that of Lenin, was forbidden fruit for the Hasidism who followed *Rebbe* Nahman of Braclav. Friedberg, "Yiddish Folklore Motifs," pp. 195-96.

23. Propp, *Morfologiia skazki,* pp. 30-31, 38-39, 41, 56-57. Interdiction also figures in "Sashka Khristos'."

24. *Ibid.,* p. 41.

25. The color red ("krasnyi") here echoes the root for "prekrasnyi," ("beautiful").

26. Afanas'ev, *Narodnye russkie skazki,* 1: 178.

27. See Propp, *Morfologiia skazki,* p. 36. The villain of the folktale frequently threatens or even engages in cannibalism.

28. Kornblatt discusses the combination of opposites as an aspect of Babelian myth. Kornblatt, *The Cossack Hero,* p. 118.

29. Karen Luplow, "Paradox and the Search for Value in Babel's *Red Cavalry,*" in Charles Rougle, ed., *Red Cavalry: A Critical Companion* (Evanston, IL: Northwestern Univ. Press, 1996), p. 70.

30. Babel' has been compared more than once with Chagall (see, for example, Victor Terras, "Line and Color: The Structure of I. Babel's Short Stories in *Red Cavalry,*" in Bloom, ed., *Modern Critical Views,* p. 108; Toby W. Clyman, "Babel' as Colorist," *Slavic and East European Journal,* 21

[Fall 1977], 333; Rochelle H. Ross, "The Unity of Babel's *Konarmija,*" *South Central Bulletin,* 41, no. 4 [Winter 1981], 116 (this last item cited in Kornblatt, *The Cossack Hero,* pp. 202, 22n). Clyman not only mentions Chagall (pp. 333-34) but also observes that "Babel' was aware of Kandinsky's theoretical stance" on color. Clyman, pp. 337-39).

31. The horses' names Styopa (from "The Letter") and Stepan (from "Afon'ka Bida") recall Stepan Razin, leader of a great Cossack revolt in the seventeenth century. For a discussion of Stepan Razin in oral literature, see Patricia Krafcik, "Stenka Razin in Russian Historical Folksongs: A Robin Hood of the Volga," Ph.D. dissertation, Columbia Univ., 1980.

32. Propp, *Morfologiia,* pp. 58-60.

33. Karen Ryan-Hayes, *Contemporary Russian Satire: A Genre Study* (Cambridge: Cambridge Univ. Press, 1995), pp. 3-4.

34. Iurii Tynianov, "Dostoevskii i Gogol' (k teorii parodii)," in Iu. N. Tynianov, *Poetika, istoriia literatury, kino* (Moscow: Nauka, 1977), p. 293.

35. Ryan-Hayes, *Contemporary Russian Satire,* p. 4.

36. See Janet Tucker, *Revolution Betrayed: Jurij Olesa's* Envy (Columbus, OH: Slavica Publishers, 1996).

Robert A. Maguire (essay date 2000)

SOURCE: Maguire, Robert A. "Ekphrasis in Isaak Babel." In *Depictions: Slavic Studies in the Narrative and Visual Arts in Honor of William E. Harkins,* edited by Douglas M. Greenfield, pp. 14-23. Dana Point, Calif.: Ardis, 2000.

[*In the following essay, Maguire examines Babel's use of ekphrasis, or elaborate description, in the stories of* Red Cavalry.]

Toward the beginning of Babel's **"Pan Apolek,"** one of the longest and most complex stories in *Red Cavalry,* the narrator, Liutov, pauses to describe a painting he sees hanging on the wall of a fugitive priest's house in Novograd-Volynsk:

> I remember: the spiderweb stillness of a summer morning hung between the straight and bright walls. A straight shaft of light had been placed at the bottom of the picture by the sun. In it swarmed sparkling dust. The long figure of John [the Baptist] was descending straight down upon me out of the dark-blue depths of the niche. A black cloak hung in triumph from that implacable, repulsively thin body. Drops of blood glit-

tered in the round clasps of the cloak. John's head had been cut off at an angle from the flayed neck. It lay upon an earthenware dish that was held tightly by the large yellow fingers of a warrior. The dead man's face looked familiar to me. I felt a touch of mystery in the offing. On the earthenware dish lay a head that had been copied from that of Pan Romuald, the fugitive priest's assistant. From between the bared teeth of the mouth hung the tiny body of a snake, its scale glittering colorfully. Its small head, delicately pink, full of animation, powerfully set off the deep background of the cloak.[1]

This is an instance of the device known in Greek (and usually in English) as *ekphrasis,* in Latin as *descriptio.* Ernst Robert Curtius has defined it succinctly as "the elaborate 'delineation,'" verbally, of "people, places, buildings, works of art."[2] It takes its origin in the Greek and Roman classics. We all remember famous instances like Achilles's shield in Book 18 of the *Iliad,* or the murals depicting the fall of Troy in the temple of Venus in Book 1 of the *Aeneid.* So graphic are these instances that they can be readily translated into paintings and drawings.[3] And they serve more specifically literary purposes too: varying the narrative pace, furthering the characterization of the heroes involved, invoking a larger world that lies outside the text.

Over the centuries, writers have borrowed lavishly from Homer and Virgil, replicating or varying the famous scenes, and taking for granted that readers would remember the originals. No such assumption is possible today, of course. Yet the classics live silently on in literature, and ekphrasis is as vigorous as ever. We are often surprised at the lengths to which writers of the late twentieth century will go to give it prominence. In ancient times, ekphrasis could serve as a visual record of things otherwise unrecordable and therefore unpreservable. Obviously that is no longer the case; yet writers apparently still feel the need to create verbal equivalents of that which can be registered on film, canvas, or computer disk, and made available, through inexpensive reproductions and the internet, to millions of people throughout the world. We must also wonder why ekphrasis, as both a literary and rhetorical device, has recently engendered an enormous resurgence of interest— along with the related topic of *ut pictura poesis*—among critics and theorists. During the past ten years alone, many books and articles have been devoted to explorations of a device whose very name, a generation ago, would have been unfamiliar to most scholars who were not professional classicists.[4]

Broad questions of this kind can best be addressed through specifics, like the passage I have just quoted from **"Pan Apolek."** It not only draws on some of the traditional uses of classical ekphrasis, but gives them a modern spin. One of these uses is to amplify the personage most closely associated with the object being described. In the *Iliad,* for example, the new shield marks the true coming-of-age of Achilles. In the *Aeneid,* the murals reassure Aeneas that he is on friendly territory, and also embed some of the paradoxes and ironies that will complicate his physical and psychological journey to Italy. The Liutov who contemplates the painting of John seems more self-aware than his classical predecessors—at least, more neurotically self-preoccupied—but he is not very perceptive about ways of dealing with the chaotic world of war he encounters in *Red Cavalry.* The fact that it is he who describes the painting, and not an anonymous narrator, as in Homer and Virgil, subjects what he sees to his own limitations. Perhaps, then, he is not much "fuller" a character at this point than Achilles or Aeneas toward the beginning of their stories. Yet precisely because his perspective is narrow, and because any specimen of ekphrasis tends to take on a life independent of its observer, the "real" author, Babel, can enter silently into the narrative and show us sides of Liutov that would otherwise remain dim, if not invisible. In the process, Liutov does become fuller, and we readers gain in our understanding of certain issues that inform the book as a whole.

Liutov tells us that the "dead man's face looked familiar." Presently he connects it with Pan Romuald. But the word "mystery" suggests a more important connection, which he does not see but may intuit. As every reader of the Bible knows, John the Baptist was the last of the prophets of Israel, a transitional figure between an old way of life and a new one, often called the Kingdom, where there would be no differences between Jew and Gentile. Specifically, his role was to prepare the way of the Lord, by preaching repentance and administering baptism. Some parallels with Liutov immediately suggest themselves. He too is a Jew, and in his role as a Bolshevik political officer he preaches repentance, as it were, of the old ways of life as a prerequisite to entering a new order, where all distinctions of class, social standing, ethnic origin, and religion will disappear. The first story, **"Crossing the Zbruch"** (**"Perekhod cherez Zbruch"**) has already evoked mythologies of initiation and baptism, in its emphasis on the water-crossing and the entrance into a new realm (Poland) that is very different from the ones in which the Cossacks, not to speak of Liutov himself, have passed their lives. And the immersion in the river contains one specifically Christian reference, albeit blasphemous, which points ahead to the subject of the "icon" just a few pages later: "Someone was drowning, and loudly defaming the Mother of God." (23) We remember that Mary is told by the Angel Gabriel not only that she will bear a son, but that her cousin, Elizabeth, "has conceived a son in her old age." (Luke 1:36-63) That son is John, and the most important baptism he performs is that of Jesus himself (Matthew 3:13-17). But ironies abound. John the Baptist never doubted for a moment what his mission was, succeeded in accomplishing it brilliantly, and was fully prepared to die for it. Liutov quickly discovers that the Cossacks are singularly unreceptive to his message, and he progressively loses confidence in the validity of his mission. Finally, if anyone is a candidate for baptism in this book, it is Liutov himself, as the "old" identities he brings to the land across the river—Jew, Russian, Bolshevik, urbanite, intellectual—are challenged and found wanting; yet every step he takes toward a "new" life is marked by a hesitation and fear that make regeneration impossible. Whether he sees either the parallels or the ironies is unclear. But we readers do, and we understand that the painting of John the Baptist stands in mute reproach to a vocation imperfectly conceived and incompetently pursued, and as a challenge to rethink and remake it in creative and productive ways.

The problem of Liutov's vocation is preponderantly a problem of language. Let us recall how the first story begins: "The Sixth Divcom reported that Novograd-Volynsk was taken today at dawn" ("Nachdiv shest' dones o tom, chto Novograd-Volynsk vziat segodnia na rassvete"). This has all the gray impersonality of any military dispatch. In its colorless certitude, the language conveys the kind of impersonal, abstract actuality that can account for all situations, because it ignores the messiness of actual experience. It is a language that generals and commissars understand well. But the rest of the story deconstructs this statement, as Liutov (who as yet has no name) comes to understand that it is inadequate to the many ways in which a town's capture can be described. He tells the same story over and over again in a variety of styles and from different points of view, without arriving at any definitive version. Struggling with the soul of the ideologue is the soul of the poet, which understands that reality is composed of particulars, each of which has a name that the poet feels bound to find, record, and communicate. This struggle creates the main dynamic of the book. But it is a dynamic that inspires profound disquiet in Liutov; for as an ideologue, he has been trained, to reapply the apt words of E. H. Gombrich, to cultivate "the art of imposing a pattern on reality, and to impose it so successfully that the victim can no longer conceive it in different terms."[5] One reason he is drawn to visual artifacts, like the painting of John, is that they do not move, and are thus more susceptible to receiving prefabricated patterns than is the welter of experience which imposes itself on him in baffling, often dangerous ways.

"My First Goose" (**"Moi pervyi gus'"**) deals with this struggle in an especially rich and nuanced way. Liutov's task is to bring the word of Bolshevism to the Cossack division commanded by Savitskii. But he is frustrated from the outset as Savitskii and other soldiers make it brutally clear that he is out of place. Assailed by "an unparalleled feeling of loneliness," he then "lay down on the ground to read in *Pravda* Lenin's speech at the Second Congress of the Comintern." That is to

say, he resorts to the soothingly familiar rhetoric of ideology. But to no avail: "the beloved lines came toward me along a thorny path and could not reach me," (50-51) because they do not account for the situation with which he must deal in this particular Cossack camp at this particular time. The seemingly helpful quartermaster proposes what amounts to an initiation (already hinted at by the word "first" in the title): "Just go and mess up a lady, a real pure lady, and the boys will treat you good." Liutov does no more than kill a goose, but that apparently suffices. The Cossacks now listen to him read the speech and even comment on it: "Truth tickles everyone's nostrils." What really matters to Liutov, however, is the pleasure he derives from "spying out exultingly the secret curve of Lenin's straight line," a pleasure he cares nothing about communicating to his audience, as he himself suggests when he tells us that he declaimed the speech "loudly, like a triumphant deaf man," a man, that is, who remains "deaf" and presumably blind as well (his eyes being fixed on the "secret curve" of the speech) to the still elusive realities of this particular slice of Cossack life, and who has therefore not found a language that can convey them.

As an ideologue, Liutov has learned a language which purports to explain everything about the world. As a highly sensitive observer, he understands that this is not the case, that other languages must be sought and found, but that none of them suffices. Whether the fault lies in the way he perceives the world or in the linguistic resources at his command is never offered as an alternative in these stories. In his famous essay on the Laokoön group (1776), Lessing had argued that literature and the visual arts reflected different modes of perceiving the world, the one sequential, the other spatial, and therefore required different means of expression. The distinction has not prevented writers from attempting to employ the perceptions and techniques of the visual arts as one way of coping with the problems posed by the slippery, elusive ways of language. Babel is one such writer. Many of the stories in *Red Cavalry,* like "Crossing the Zbruch," rely heavily on the kind of spatial juxtapositions we associate with painting.[6] The use of ekphrasis, as in the painting of John, is technically less sophisticated, but psychologically more gratifying to Liutov. It represents a verbal imitation of a solid object, which, as an "icon," has the additional advantage of incorporating the eternal and unchanging truths of religion. Babel may not have been thinking of Gogol; but the parallel is intriguing, for painting, in particular religious painting, attracted Gogol as a wish-fulfilling alternative to the verbal medium he found increasingly unsuited to the kind of iconic art he wished to create. It functions as a wish-fulfillment for Liutov too, a vivid and colorful affirmation of the rightness of the mind-set of the ideologue.

But why does Liutov call it an "icon?" This term has long been reserved to designate a particular kind of Eastern Orthodox religious art, and is not now properly used of Western art at all, regardless of subject-matter. Liutov's misuse of the term hints at a failure to understand not only what icons are all about, but what this particular painting could reveal to him if he had the eyes to see. Least of all is an icon intended to serve as a mirror of an individual's psyche. Rather, in Egon Sandler's words, it "introduces another dimension to the image, transcendence, and thus projects itself beyond the forms of our world, making God's world present. . . . The icon points to a dimension which goes beyond the natural; it pushes out toward the ineffable. This ascension toward the Beyond is a communion with eternity."[7] Babel's non-Jewish Russian readers are presumably more competent than Liutov. They also know that even though the painting in question is Roman Catholic in origin, the decollation of John the Baptist is a frequent subject of Orthodox icons too. But Babel may be inviting us to "read" this painting as we would an icon, appealing to what any Orthodox Russian reader would know: that, as Leonid Ouspensky puts it, the Church "attributes to the icon the same dogmatic, liturgic and educational significance as it does to the Holy Scriptures. As the word of the Holy Scriptures is an image, so the image is also a word."[8] The equation extends to the creative act too, as suggested by the verb *pisat'*, which means both "paint" and "write." In these ways we are instructed that whatever the "icon" of John "means," that meaning informs Liutov's acts of verbal creation as well.

Presently the title character, Pan Apolek, appears. The name is charmingly odd. "Pan" is of course the normal Polish word for "mister." "Apolek" is an affectionate diminutive of the name of Apollo, who is associated with the arts and with the sun, among other things, and who therefore epitomizes two of this wandering painter's main qualities. Once the mythological subtext has been brought into play, however, "Pan" becomes more than just an honorific, and summons up yet another ancient Greek figure. Half-man and half-goat, Pan is a pastoral god who is famously lustful, a quality that in his Polish namesake has been sublimated into a joyous celebration of the sensualities of nature and ordinary human life. "Pan" is supposedly derived from a word designating "feeding" or "nourishing," but readers ignorant of the niceties of classical philology will almost certainly associate it with the word for "all," as did the Greeks themselves. "Allness" hints at Apolek's ability to meld, through his art, puzzlingly different realms of being, particularly the spiritual and the fleshly, into an integral and apparently authentic whole.

But there are troubling things about his names. We soon learn that he was baptized "Apollinarius." This is a peculiar name for a Christian, since it is most notably borne by the exponent of the first great Christological heresy (fourth century). Apollinarius taught that "in man there coexist body, soul, and spirit. In Christ, however, were to be found the human body and soul, but no human spirit, the spirit being replaced by the Divine Logos." What this means is that "while He possessed perfect Godhood, He lacked complete manhood." This is inimical to Roman Catholic teaching because "if there is no complete manhood in Christ, He is not a perfect example for us, nor did He redeem the whole of human nature but only its spiritual elements." In what sense might Apolek/Apollinarius be a "heretic" in this story? Presumably we are being invited to seek a parallel in the painter's life and work that would show him to be favoring the spiritual over the fleshly, or the saintly over the merely human. Yet his religious pictures appear to combine all those qualities successfully, most of all in the "icon" of John the Baptist, which we soon learn is a product of his brush. A hint may lurk in the Vicar's objection to Apolek's making "saints" of the townsfolk "in their lifetime." Our first impulse is to dismiss him as narrow-minded and formalistic. After all, Roman Catholic artists have for centuries been using live models for works commissioned by the highest ecclesiastical authorities, without much fuss about their manners or morals. What he specifies as the sins that disqualify those who have sat for Apolek—"disobedience, secret distillers, pitiless moneylenders, makers of false weights, and sellers of the innocence of your own daughters"—are mere rhetorical tinsel, the stuff of bad Sunday sermons: we are offered no evidence that these people are any worse than human beings generally. (39) Even so, the Vicar may have a point. His outrage suggests that he is not concerned with these paintings as much as with the danger that at a stroke of the brush, anyone can be turned into a saint, human qualities aside. Catholics know that only the Church can make saints, and only posthumously. Quite apart from questions of sin, true personhood is regarded as a process which ends only with death. A human being who is incomplete in the eyes of the Church would be passed off as complete, and in that sense, would represent a counterpart of the operation performed upon Christ by the fourth-century Apollinarius. To a man like Liutov, who is uncomfortable with the ambiguities of raw experience and yearns for quick solutions, Apolek's way is tempting. But we see that it is dangerous because it brings spiritual death, as Faust, among the many literary prototypes of Liutov, discovered. Can it be mere coincidence that Apolek/Apollinarius is also phonically suggestive of Apollyon or Abbadon, "the angel in charge of the abyss" in Revelation 9:11?[9]

Troubling too is the way in which Apolek tells the Jesus/Deborah story. Of course he wants to shock Robatskii, the beadle, and he succeeds; but it does not take a very sensitive ear to detect a smacking of the lips, and to wonder whether Apolek is not just an esthetic lecher, who ogles life as material for his paintings, paintings which, furthermore, are rendered according to formulas, and thus are mere cartoons, not even imitations of life. The fakery is hard to see because it is so engagingly brought off—who can fail to like Apolek?—and it represents still another temptation to Liutov because it is the way of the ideologue too. Yet Liutov is constantly forced to experience more authentic versions of sensuality, because they are more immediate, and often life-threatening.

Once again, the first story poses the problem in a dramatic way. The pregnant Jewess removes a blanket from what the narrator thinks is her sleeping father, and reveals "a dead old man," whose "throat had been ripped out, and his face cleft in two, and dark blue blood lay in his beard like a piece of lead." She then tells the narrator that it was the Poles who had cut his throat, while he begged them to kill him "'in the back yard so that my daughter won't see me die.'" The old man is anxious that his daughter *not* see what is being done to him. But she does see, and in seeing, achieves the kind of wisdom expressed in her final cry: "where on all the earth will you find another father like my father?" (24) In effect she seems to be saying that it is only as a result of violent death that the otherwise insignificant, anonymous old Jew becomes special, a "father," someone whose memory will be perpetuated in and through the child that is yet to be born. This particular episode does not seem to touch Liutov personally; he remains an onlooker, as nameless at this point as the daughter and the father. In the three stories that follow—**"The Church at Novograd"** (**"Kostel v Novograde"**), **"A Letter"** (**"Pis'mo"**), and **"The Remount Officer"** (**"Nachal'nik konzapasa"**)—he comments, muses, reports, but feels at best an intruder into an alien world. The fourth story, however, is **"Pan Apolek,"** and the icon of John, with which it opens, poses the problem of sensuality and violence in a way that begins to touch him more deeply and directly.

The beheading of John, and the events that led up to it, are related in Matthew (14:1-12), Mark (6:14-29), and Luke (9:7-9), and are commemorated by the Church on August 29. For all its brevity, it is one of the most fruitful stories of the New Testament, as countless paintings, novels and operas attest. The Gospel tells us only that Herodias's marriage to Herod is illegal, since he is her brother-in-law, and (in Mark) that her daughter, Salome, performs a dance, which "delighted" her stepfather, and for which she is rewarded by being given John's head on a platter. What most readers remember, however—Babel surely among them—are the later, secular versions, where Herodias takes a carnal interest in John (as in Flaubert's story), or where Salome is depicted as a Lolita type (as in the Oscar Wilde play and the Richard Strauss opera based on it). For all but the most literal-minded readers of the Bible, a sexual ele-

ment is subtextually present in the painting that Liutov contemplates. We will remember that in the first story, **"Crossing the Zbruch,"** violence is also directed at the head and inflicted with a blade, and that the result is the ennoblement of the victim, and a flash of wisdom in the daughter, who is also the "victim" of the thrusting, sword-like act of sex that produces a new life. Where is the "wisdom" of the event portrayed in the painting? Perhaps it is suggested in the detail of the snake that hangs from the mouth of the decapitated head. Of course, we associate the snake with temptation and evil, which certainly figure in the death of John. But the snake is also a traditional emblem of wisdom and healing. The fact that the snake is leaving the head, however, suggests that wisdom and healing do not depend on cerebral activity, as an ideologue like Liutov might wish them to, but are bound up with sensuality, especially in the form of sex and violence.

It is not until **"My First Goose,"** however, that Liutov is compelled by circumstances to act upon these dimly intuited verities. As the story opens, he stands in the presence of Savitskii, the commander of the Sixth Division, and "marveled at the beauty of his giant's body. He rose, and with the purple of his riding-breeches, with the little crimson cap that had been knocked to one side, with the decorations hammered into his chest, he clove the hut in two, as a standard cleaves the sky. From him wafted the smell of perfume and the cloying coolness of soap. His long legs were like girls who had been sheathed up to the shoulders in gleaming jackboots." (49) The sexuality is blatant and violent ("knocked," "hammered," "clove," "sheathed"); but because it is also predominantly homoerotic—we might easily encounter it in a specimen of gay sadomasochistic fiction—it cannot be biologically productive. As such, it is admirably expressive of the voyeuristic proclivities of Liutov. His glasses keep him safely distanced from Savitskii, the object of his fantasy; yet they instantly mark him as an ogler, and open him to discovery and danger. "People get their throats cut for wearing glasses," Savitskii observes contemptuously, the implication being that not only is Liutov an outsider of an especially undesirable kind—Jew, intellectual, and propagandist—and as such is incapable of taking the kinds of action incumbent on a real soldier in this war, but that he cannot even properly see—in the sense of observing and understanding—how things really are, or, in the homoerotic context of the opening paragraph, possess what Savitskii represents: manliness, strength, beauty, and membership in a vital collective.

Possession is also denied a few paragraphs later when Liutov encounters "a young lad with long flaxen hair and a beautiful Riazan' face," who "turned his rear end toward me and with special skill began emitting shameful sounds" from it, which an onlooking Cossack laughingly compares to the firing of a cannon. (50) It is as if

Liutov's homoerotic contemplation of Savitskii is being mocked by the lad, who announces in effect that this particular rear end is unavailable for any purpose other than that for which it was originally designed. The lad's actions also reinforce the solution that the quartermaster has just proposed to enable Liutov to win acceptance by the Cossacks. "Just go and mess up a lady, a real pure lady, and the boys will treat you good." Liutov is hereby put on notice that the male bonding of the Cossacks, which he yearns to share, is not an expression of homo-eroticism, but requires an assertion of maleness in the most obvious way. His response is curious, because it does not literally fulfill the requirements of the statement. The only female present is the old Polish land-lady, who, being almost blind too, is another version of Liutov himself and therefore cannot be directly as-saulted. Instead he picks a goose, whose whiteness en-dows it with symbolic purity, crushes its head beneath his boot, impales it on "someone else's sword" ("chuzhuiu sabliu"), and orders the landlady to cook it for him. The Cossacks watch this series of ritual dis-placements "like pagan priests" ("kak zhretsy"), and ap-pear to extend acceptance, as they invite him to share their meal, and then listen to him read aloud from Le-nin's speech.

In the final scene, the Cossacks allow him to sleep with them, legs intertwined. As he sleeps he dreams that he "saw women, and only my heart, blood-stained with murder, squeaked and flowed over." (51) "Murder" (*ubiistvo*) is of course too strong a word for the killing of a goose. But it is no more of a mismatch than Liu-tov's response to the quartermaster's challenge. We are prompted to ask: what *is* being "murdered," if not the goose? The fact that the Cossack "priests" "did not look at the goose" suggests that their "acceptance" of Liutov is provisional at best, condescending at worst. This is a truth he sees in the discomfiting dream, and it tells him that his debut as a man of action is bogus, that the goose-killing is perverse sexuality, with its hints at fe-tishism and cannibalism, and that the intertwined legs represent not bonding, but the temporary gratification of an adolescent fantasy of belonging. Ironically, Liutov has declined to violate his self in the alter-ego of the landlady, only to violate, or "murder" it far more funda-mentally in the substitution he chooses.

Yet Liutov does act, however absurdly. That is why his experience is more authentic than Apolek's, and why it brings him closer to the figure of John in the icon than to the painter who created him. He is beginning to see that spirituality grows out of the lives of ordinary people, especially those who are violated in one way or another, and that he must accept his own ordinari-ness—as Jew, Russian, and soldier—if he is to achieve integration into the human community as represented, with all its imperfections, in these stories. Spirituality cannot be imposed by formula, whether iconographic or

verbal. As one who imposes, Apolek is a heretic, as his baptismal name suggests, and so is Liutov whenever his psychological need for certainty draws him to ideologi-cal solutions. From this point on, he displays a greater willingness to engage himself, though never fully, and with frequent and disastrous setbacks, as in **"The Death of Dolgushov"** (**"Smert' Dolgushova"**). Never does he attain the level of fearless commitment exemplified by John, which depends on an order of spiritual maturity he never even approaches. Nor does he ever understand that a true sense of mission inescapably involves know-ing what that mission is *not*. John certainly does, as a particularly vivid account in the Fourth Gospel attests. His initial responses to the question "Who are you?" are framed as denials: "I am not the Christ . . . I am not [Elijah] . . . No, [not the Prophet]." This opens the way for a clear statement of who he is and what he does: "I baptize with water," in preparation for the one "who comes after me, the thong of whose sandal I am not worthy to untie" (John 1:19-27, Revised Standard Version). Liutov knows that he is not a Cossack, of course, but it is the Cossacks themselves who provide constant reminders of that, while he wishes with all his heart that he were one of them. What makes his emo-tional and moral flaccidity even more striking, and rather funny too, is his name. It is obviously one of those revolutionary pseudonyms that were in vogue among the early Bolsheviks. Being derived from *liutyi*, "fierce"—a word often used of predatory animals—it attributes to its bearer qualities which in this case he certainly does not possess, but would like to. What he admires about Savitskii and the Cossacks is their *liu-tost'* (although he does not call it that), their capacity for direct, purposeful, and, if need be, "fierce" action. He has to learn, again and again, that such qualities, in this story and throughout the cycle, spring from an hon-est understanding of one's purpose in life and a willing-ness to see it through, with no concern for unpleasant consequences.

He must also learn to endure the knowledge that this self is actually two. One is the self which believes in, yearns for, and strives toward essences. The other is the self which is obsessed with observing the existential world and trying to render it as precisely as possible. The two selves have opposite aims, and are inevitably in conflict. Liutov is tormented by the anxiety that the world before his eyes may disappear into a rhetorical sea of ideological dicta and military dispatches, two of the prime genres of essentialism. (It is useful to remem-ber that Babel was a contemporary of the Acmeist po-ets, who were intent on celebrating the thinginess of the world.) Conversely, he often seems overwhelmed by the plethora of particulars, and fearful that nothing can knit them together. This conflict takes many forms, among them his increasingly troubled questioning of his Jewish identity: Judaism is not only a religion of rules and practices, and thus a rival to the new religion of Bolshevism, but is also a religion of the book, that is, of the word.

In any event, Liutov begins to find a voice in the process of creating these stories. Babel's brilliant touch is to make him a reluctant creator, who is thrown into situations for which his gift seems utterly inadequate, yet for which it could not be better suited. Quite against Liutov's will, words become the vehicles of flux and process; they cannot create an iconic reality. Probably no Russian writer since Gogol has had a keener sense of the flaws of the verbal medium in which he is condemned to work. For Gogol, however, the icon was perfect and exemplary, and because he could not translate its lessons into the terms of his own art, he ended by abandoning his writing and dying shortly thereafter. By contrast, Liutov discerns the limitations of the visual media—whether the "icon" in **"Pan Apolek"** or the stagecraft in **"Italian Sunshine"** (**"Solntse Italii"**)—yet reaches a solution, one that is not satisfying to most readers, who tend to perceive it as a cop out. In **"Argamak,"** a story added to the 1931 edition of ***Red Cavalry,*** he finally learns to ride like a Cossack, whereupon "[my] dream came true. The Cossacks stopped following me and my horse with their eyes." (152) The writer disappears into his material, and the stories must come to an end.

Isaak Babel was not the only Russian writer of the 1920s to explore the tensions between word and image. We could profitably look at Evgenii Zamiatin's *We* (*My,* 1920) or Iurii Olesha's *Envy* (*Zavist',* 1927), among many interesting instances. Nor was this a uniquely Russian preoccupation. It had surfaced internationally around the turn of the century, and was engaging the talents of some first-class writers. Virginia Woolf's *To the Lighthouse,* for example, appeared in 1927, one year after the first publication in book form of ***Red Cavalry.*** It bears many similarities, albeit coincidental, to Babel's story-cycle: the prominence of mythic motifs, including water-crossings; the crucial importance of "moments"—scenes in Woolf, whole stories in Babel—in which private sensibilities and disparate images of the outside world meld to create an integral, albeit fleeting vision. Other similarities can be detected in the ways Woolf uses her characters to represent different ways of perceiving reality. For Mrs. Ramsay, words serve to register the ebb and flow of the minutiae, mental and physical, that comprise the world yet are "ephemeral as a rainbow." Her husband, Mr. Ramsay, is a professional philosopher of great repute, obsessed with creating a grand scheme of thought as represented by the twenty-six letters of the alphabet, and bitterly frustrated that in his intellectual quest he may possibly move beyond "Q" to reach "R," but never the "Z" of full understanding, let alone the sudden "flash" which "lump[s] all the letters together." (part 1, section 6) In short, he is an essentialist, who, like Liutov, is aware

not only of the limitations of his mind, but also of his inability to deal with the necessary bustle of life he affects to despise yet desperately craves. It is he who most resists undertaking the "expedition" to the Lighthouse, "distant and austere," which the children and Mrs. Ramsay constantly urge, in their deeply rooted sense that such an undertaking confirms one's commitment to life as a journey in all its puzzling variety, and its inevitable finiteness.

The third major character, whom we might conveniently if inaccurately call the "heroine," is the painter Lily Briscoe. She is shown throughout the novel attempting to paint a picture of Mrs. Ramsay and her young son James. It is not to be representational but abstract; and the purple triangle that represents a first effort is promising. But she cannot make it come right. The reason is that she is unable, until nearly the end of the novel, to understand that art is not a question of personal feelings and emotions, but of insight born of detachment, distance, and impersonality. (Coleridge's famous distinction, in *Biographia Litteraria,* between "fancy" and "imagination" works very well here.) As that begins to happen, the particulars of her vision arrange themselves in shapes and lines that move as if by an inner rhythm and strike the eye as "greens and blues," "brown running nervous lines," "a red, a grey." The result, she hopes, comprises something "[b]eautiful and bright . . . on the surface, feathery and evanescent, one colour melting into another like the colours on a butterfly's wing." (Part 3, Section 5) Painting does seem to be privileged; but it is meant to stand for all art, regardless of medium. Woolf uses a painter to make her point perhaps because a painting, especially if abstract, more readily stands apart from the creator and the viewer, who are otherwise tempted to "read" art in terms of personal needs, aspirations, and urgings. But the same should be true of a work of verbal art, as the method Woolf employs in *To the Lighthouse* is meant to demonstrate. No doubt that is why we do not really know what Lily's painting looks like: there is no ekphrasis where we expect it. The denial of visual specificity further makes the point that painting should convey none of the sense of permanence that a describable artifact would, for each work of art is unique and unrepeatable, being the product of a specific time and place. Lily's slow arrival at that truth is the mark of her achievement. Her picture "would be hung up in the attics, [Lily] thought; it would be destroyed." But she knows that this does not matter: "It [the painting] was done; it was finished . . . I have had my vision." (Part 3, Section 13)

Undoubtedly Woolf's novel is more "modernist" than Babel's story-cycle in its calm acknowledgment of ambiguity and impermanence, in its strong but unspoken conviction that there is a "language" common to both graphic and verbal discourse, but reducible to neither, and in its cultivation of distance and impersonality as the only way the artist—represented in Woolf by an anonymous third-person narrator with no describable personality—can achieve the right kind of vision. Detachment and impersonality may often be desiderata for Liutov, but in his passionate, agonized attempts to make sense of life and his place in it, he can never rise above his insatiable involvement with the immediacies of situations and people, as the very fact of his being his own narrator emphasizes. Still, his yearning for mutually exclusive alternatives strikes us as modern, if not modernist. Perhaps **"Argamak,"** written when Stalinism was already ascendant, can be read as a prophecy of things to come: not only does the wielder of words disappear into the mute mass of the Cossacks, but their "eyes" cease to register his existence, as his do theirs. With the imposition, a mere three years later, of socialist realism as the official and therefore exclusive guide to artistic creation, word was made iconic, and privileged over image, which became merely illustrative of truths that supposedly could find full expression verbally. (In an even grimmer irony, Babel began complaining about his inability to write fiction, and put his talent to the service of a visual art, in the form of film scenarios.) Not surprisingly, ekphrasis virtually disappeared. The only striking instances in all of Stalinist literature that I can recall are associated with "negative," that is, anti-Soviet characters and situations, precisely because the kind of graphic detail essential to ekphrasis was deemed alien to the esthetics of socialist realism.[10]

With the passing of socialist realism, the graphic arts are reappearing in Russia with a vigor that they have not displayed since the 1920s. It remains to be seen whether the complex relationship between word and image, which Babel so brilliantly explored more than seventy-five years ago, will also revive, and whether ekphrasis will again take an honored place in the arsenal of literary devices.

Notes

1. In *Konarmiia. Odesskie rasskazy. P'esy.* Letchworth (Hertfordshire): Bradda Books, 1965. 35-36. (Reprinted from *Izbrannoe.* Moscow, 1957.) Hereafter, page references will be given in the text.

2. *European Literature and the Latin Middle Ages.* Trans. Willard R. Trask. London: Routledge and Kegan Paul, 1979. 69.

3. See, e.g., the drawing of Achilles's shield in Malcolm W. Willcock, *A Companion to the Iliad.* Chicago and London: The University of Chicago Press, 1976. 210.

4. On ekphrasis, three books have recently appeared from the University of Chicago Press alone: James A. W. Heffernan, *Museum of Words. The Poetics of Ekphrasis from Homer to Ashbery* (1993); John Hollander, *The Gazer's Spirit. Poems Speaking to Silent Works of Art* (1995); W. J. T. Mitchell, *Picture Theory. Essays on Verbal and Visual Representation* (1994). On *ut pictura poesis,* see Wesley Trimpi, "Horace's 'Ut pictura poesis:' The Argument for Stylistic Decorum." *Traditio* 34 (1978): 29-73. For Russian literature, see Amy Mandelker, *Framing Anna Karenina. Tolstoi, the Woman Question, and the Victorian Novel.* Columbus: The Ohio State University Press, 1993, esp. Ch. 5. Of the many books on rhetoric that have appeared in the last fifteen years or so, one of the best is Brian Vickers, *In Defence of Rhetoric.* Oxford: Clarendon Press, 1988.

5. "Renaissance and Golden Age." *Studies in the Art of the Renaissance.* Vol. I. Chicago: University of Chicago Press, 1985. 31.

6. Cf., e.g., Joseph Frank, "Spatial Form in Modern Literature." *The Widening Gyre.* New Brunswick (NJ): Rutgers University Press, 1963. 3-62.

7. *The Icon. Image of the Invisible.* Trans. Steven Bingham. Redondo Beach (CA): Oakwood Publications, 1988. 1-2.

8. Ouspensky, Leonid and Vladimir Lossky. "The Meaning of Icons." *The Meaning of Icons.* Trans. G. E. H. Palmer and E. Kadloubovsky. Crestwood (NY): St. Vladimir's Seminary Press, 1983. 30.

9. For the characterization of Apollinarius, see *The Oxford Dictionary of the Christian Church.* Ed. F. L. Cross. London: Oxford University Press, 1958. 70. The quotation from Revelation comes from *The New American Bible,* which defines the Hebrew "Abaddon" as "destruction or ruin," and the Greek Apollyon as "destroyer."

10. See Robert A. Maguire, "Literary Conflicts in the 1920's." *Survey* 18.3 (1972): 98-127.

Igor' Sukhikh (essay date winter 2000-2001)

SOURCE: Sukhikh, Igor'. "About Stars, Blood, People, and Horses." *Russian Studies in Literature* 37, no. 1 (winter 2000-2001): 6-26.

[*In the following essay, Sukhikh offers a thematic and stylistic examination of* Red Cavalry *and chronicles the writing of the book, which he asserts happened in "three steps, over three stages of transformation of the raw material of life into a work of art."*]

In the seventh year of the new era (A.D. 1924), Army Commander Budennyi, "having rode into literature on horseback, and criticizing it from the height of his horse" (Gorky), discovered that serving under his command was a slanderer, sadist, and literary degenerate: citizen Babel'.

> Under the fine-sounding, patently speculative title, "*Iz knigi Konarmiia*" [from the book *Red Cavalry*], the hapless author has attempted to depict the life, mores, and traditions of the First Cavalry Army during the hectic period of its heroic struggle on the Polish and other fronts. To describe the heroic struggle of classes never before seen in the history of mankind, one must first understand the essence of that struggle and the nature of classes, that is, one must be a dialectic, a Marxist artist. The author is neither. . . . Citizen Babel' tells us old-wives' tales about the Red Army, he rummages in old-wives' trash and clothes, he recounts with old-wives' horror how a hungry Red Army man takes a loaf of bread and a chicken somewhere; he concocts cock-and-bull stories, slings mud at the best Communist commanders, fantasizes, and simply lies.

Six years later, "rank-and-file Budennyi man" Vsevolod Vishnevskii, when sending to Comrade Gorky his own version—the drama *Pervaia Konnaia* [*The First Cavalry Army*]—honked the same horn.

> Babel''s misfortune is that he is not a soldier. He was stunned and frightened when he came to us, and this strangely morbid impression of an intellectual is reflected in his *Red Cavalry*. Budennyi could well have been offended and indignant. We former rank-and-file men, too. Babel' gave the wrong thing! He missed a lot. He gave only a tiny bit: a Red Cavalry worn out in battle on the Polish Front. And even then, not in its entirety but *fragments*. Believe a soldier: Our Red Cavalry was not what Babel' has depicted.

The future commander-in-chief of Soviet writers fought with Budennyi for Babel'. The author himself did not fight back; instead, he explained and agreed with him.

"What I saw at Buddennyi's is what I gave. I see that I failed to give any political workers, and, in general, I failed to give a lot about the Red Army; I will, if I can, later." This is what he said in 1925 to Dmitrii Furmanov, the author of *Chapaev* and publisher-editor, using the same lexicon as in the as yet unwritten epistle of Vishnevskii (gave—did not give).

In the early 1930s, at a writers' meeting, he even allied himself with the army commander himself: "I stopped writing because I came to dislike all I had written before. I can't write like before anymore, not one line. It's a pity that S. M. Budennyi didn't think of turning to me at the time to form an alliance against my *Red Cavalry,* because I don't like *Red Cavalry*." The promises to reform and change it, to give "the right thing," remained—perhaps fortunately—unfulfilled.

The book of thirty-four stories (although Babel' had spoken of fifty to Furmanov) was put together in three years and then republished unchanged. In the 1930s,

Babel' published two "follow-ups" ("**Argamak**," dated 1924-30, and "**Potselui**" ["**The kiss**"], 1937), and he even managed to include the former in the next edition. Stylistically, the stories were written "like before." Their subject matter in part duplicates other pieces ("**Argamak**"—"**Istoriia odnoi loshadi**" ["**The story of a horse**"] and "**My First Goose**"; and "**The Kiss**"— "**Perekhod cherez Zbruch**" ["**Crossing the Zbruch**"] and "**Vdova**" ["**The widow**"]). Those texts could possibly have found their place somewhere in the middle of the collection. Their mechanical placement at the end disrupts the conceived and already developed structure. Today, their place is in an appendix. The *book* gets along nicely without them. These stories merely supplement the "basic text," just as the "Odessa stories" are supplemented by other works on the same topic.

Babel' arrived at the completed, classical *Red Cavalry* in three steps, over three stages of transformation of the raw material of life into a work of art.

The Polish campaign was the penultimate significant episode of the civil war (to be followed by the storming of the Perekop isthmus) and the last desperate attempt to export the Russian revolution to the West. The capture of Kiev by the Poles, the following advance of the First Cavalry Army on Warsaw, the terrible defeat ("'We've lost the campaign,' mutters Volkov, and snores. 'Yes,' I answer." ["**Zamost'fe**"]), the rollback to the Ukraine, the peace treaty and demarcation of the borders (until 1939)—by the mid-twenties all this had become recent history, still bleeding, but already setting, coated in storybook glaze (hence the protests of Budennyi and "rank-and-file Budennyi men").

The author of the future *Red Cavalry* participated in the Polish campaign (May-November 1920) with documents issued to Kirill Vasil'evich Liutov. The newspaper *Krasnyi kavalerist* [*Red Cavalryman*] printed reports from its "Sixth Cavalry Division war correspondent" about heroic soldiers, heroic nurses, and heinous enemies.

> Another name, unforgettable for the Sixth Division, must be entered into our heroic, bloody, and sorrowful lists, the name of Konstantin Trunov, commander of the Thirty-fourth Cavalry Regiment, killed August 3, in combat at K. Another grave will be hidden in the shade of the dense Volhynia forests, another noted life, filled with selflessness and devotion to duty, has been sacrificed for the cause of the oppressed, one more proletarian heart has been broken for its hot blood to color the red banners of revolution. The Polish army has gone mad. The mortally wounded pans,[1] meeting their end, are thrashing in mortal agony, piling crime upon stupidity, perishing as they ingloriously enter the grave to their own curses and those of others.

This style of ideological slogans and banalities, flowery metaphors and rhetorical figures of speech would, of course, appeal to the commander of the First Cavalry

Army. But then, could an army newspaper print anything else? But in Babel''s stories, such style became an episodic "alien word," an object of detached inspection and refined aesthetic play.

> "Men," then said Pugachev, the regiment's commander, looking at the dead man and standing on the edge of the pit. "Men," he said, trembling and straightening himself out with his arms stiff against his trouser seams, "we are burying Pashka Trunov, the world hero; we are giving Pasha the last honors." And raising to the sky his eyes, inflamed by lack of sleep, Pugachev shouted a speech about the dead soldiers of the First Cavalry regiment and about the proud column that was beating the hammer of history on the anvil of future generations.
>
> ("**Eskadronnyi Trunov**" ["**Squadron Commander Trunov**"], 155-56)

At the same time, Babel' kept a diary, "for himself." It was lost, miraculously retrieved, and published many years after its author's death. It provides a detailed chronicle of the campaign, with candid assessments of friends and foes. The heroic formulas of newspaper articles are emended with scenes of viciousness, plunder, drunken debauchery, and wantonness.

> The Zhitomir pogrom, launched by the Poles and then, of course, the Cossacks. After the appearance of our forward units, the Poles entered the city for three days; Jewish pogrom; cut beards, that's usual; assembled forty-five Jews at the marketplace, then herded them to the slaughterhouse, torture, cut-out tongues, wails all over the square.—Terrible event. Church plundered, ripped raiments, precious, glittering fabrics shredded, on the floor, a nurse dragged away three bundles. . . . Animals, they came to plunder, it's so clear, the old gods are being destroyed.—Must get into the soldier's soul, I do, it's all so awful, animals with principles.— Conversation with artillery battalion commander Maksimov, our army is out to earn, not a revolution, an uprising, a free-for-all. It's just a means that the Party condones.

Also preserved are plans and sketches of **Red Cavalry**. While echoing the diary in content, they contain important comments about the form and artistic structure of the future book. "The story swift and fast.—Short chapters filled with content.—One day at a time. Short. Dramatic.—No reflections.—Careful choice of words.— Form of episodes—half a page.—No comparisons or historical parallels.—Simply story.—Style, meter.— Poem in prose." The last definition repeated three times.

Repeating himself, groping, Babel' seeks and ultimately finds an aesthetic formula in which to fit the material of battles and campaigns so common in the 1920s: a poem in prose, a headlong, fast-moving narrative that becomes poetry.

> Babel' fits in well with the Soviet literary landscape of the twenties. Subject-wise, **Red Cavalry** ranks along with the partisan stories and short novels of Vsevolod

> Ivanov, with Furmanov's *Chapaev*, with Fadeev's *Razgrom* [*The Rout*], and with a great variety of other works about the civil war. Its naturalism and cruelty, the unruliness of dark, elemental forces let loose by the revolution are no more noteworthy and no more shocking than that same Vsevolod Ivanov's, or Artem Veselyi's. His florid style is no more florid or vivid than the magic verbal fabric of Andrei Platonov or the fearless experiments of the *Serapion Brothers,* or the inimitable color of *Tikhii Don* [*And quiet flows the Don*].
>
> (Sh. Markish)

This is true and at the same time not true at all. While coinciding with many of his contemporaries subject-wise, Babel' veers away from them aesthetically, and first of all genre-wise.

Chapaev, The Rout, Rossiia, krov'iu umytaia [*Russia, washed in blood*], *And Quiet Flows the Don,* and Platonov's main books (*Chevengur* and *Kotlovan* [*The pit*]) were different transformations of the novel. Apparent in Ivanov's partisan short novels and a great number of other works on the civil war was a naturalist, essayist foundation. Such "military physiologies" also on the whole inherited the psychological detail, ramification, and unhurried pace of larger forms and were, genre-wise, amorphous. It is quite impossible to apply to them criteria of brevity, thorough word choice, or rhythm. The closest *aesthetic* ally of the author of **Red Cavalry** was a writer who started out a little earlier and differed widely in subject matter. "To the thunder of cannons and the clanging of sabers, Zoshchenko begat Babel'," was how a limerick of the twenties recorded that link. The fate of both is linked with the short-story genre of Russian prose.

In 1937, in a talk with young writers, Babel', while stating that, from his point of view, Lev Tolstoy was the leading Russian writer, went on to explain, almost physiologically, why he could not follow Tolstoy's method.

> The thing is that Lev Nikolaevich Tolstoy had the temperament to describe all twenty-four hours of the day, moreover, remembering all that had happened to him, while I, apparently, have only enough temperament to describe the most interesting five minutes I had experienced. Hence the appearance of this novella genre.

Babel' realized only too well that "this genre" was somewhat alien to the Russian soil.

> I think it would be useful to talk about the story technique, because this genre is not well regarded in our country. It must be said that this genre never flourished especially here, and the French were well ahead of us. Actually, our real novella writer is Chekhov. With Gorky, most of his stories are abbreviated novels. Tolstoy's, too, were abbreviated novels, except for "Posle bala" ["After the ball"]. This is a real story. In general, here people do not write stories very well; they are more inclined to novels.

Naturally, he finds the working definition of the novella not "here" but "there."

> I read the definition of the novella in a letter from Goethe to Eckermann: a small story of the genre in which I feel more comfortable than in others. His definition of the novella is very simple: it is a story about an unusual event. Maybe that's not correct, I don't know. Goethe thought so.

With his involvement with the new, searing subject matter ("Why do I have this unending anguish? Because I am far from home, because we are destroying, moving like a whirlwind, like lava, hated by all, life is torn asunder, I am present at a never-ending wake"), Babel' became the creator of a new type of story combining the poetics of everyday "novelty" with modernist expressiveness and eccentricity.

Red Cavalry is a book of "unusual events," of five-minute novellas. In this context, as a genre, Babel' is closer not to Fadeev and Platonov but to Zoshchenko, the author of *Rasskazy Sinebriukhova* [*Stories of Sinebriukhov*], with his idea of the indescribability of the new reality by old creative means.

Babel' takes great pains to arrange neatly this small, fragmentary genre, diversifying it and making it rich in opportunities and perspectives.

The book contains novellas in the precise sense of the word: jokes, anecdotes, unusual events with a required *pointe,* a totally unexpected ending that leaves the reader shocked.

In a strange house, the totally unsuspecting narrator sleeps alongside a dead body (**"Crossing the Zbruch"**). An infant tenderly nursed all night by another cavalryman turns out to be a sack of salt—and Balmashov "gives it" to the scheming woman black-marketeer (**"Sol'"** [**"Salt"**]). A deacon-deserter who shams deafness, after three days of torture at the hands of his guard actually becomes deaf (**"Ivany"** [**"Two Ivans"**]).

In other cases, there is no unusual event in the story. People are simply traveling somewhere, conversing, writing letters, singing . . . But here, too, the plot is constructed according to the laws of the novella rather than of the abbreviated novel. The novella's eventful *pointe* is replaced by a *mot,* a word ("Has *a word* been found?"), a striking aphorism, which flares up at the end and relieves the intensity and expectation mounting throughout the novella.

"And we heard the great noiselessness of a cavalry attack" (**"Kombrig dva"** [**"Combrig 2"**]). "O, death, O, covetous one, O, greedy thief, why have you not spared us, just for once?" (**"Kladbishche v Kozine"** [**"The Kozino cemetery"**]). "[B]ut we will see each other in the Kingdom of Heaven, to put it bluntly, though there is a rumor going around that the old fellow up in heaven has not got a Kingdom but a real whorehouse, and since there's enough clap here on earth, so, perhaps, we will not see each other" (**"Prodolzhenie istorii odnoi loshadi"** [**"The story of a horse, continued]"**).

"With Babel', just one little word, or some magic formula, becomes the gravitational center of an episode," notes E. Kogan, a researcher of the *Red Cavalry* drafts. "In some cases, such a verbal clot appears a priori, before the situation. It drifts from episode to episode, and the author has to try out different plot settings before it merges with a precious find."

In *Red Cavalry,* the traditional novella-situation and novella-anecdote come along with the novella-formula and novella-aphorism. Naturally, there are cases when a word bolsters and reaffirms a novella's point.

Here is how the hero concludes his story of gruesome revenge against his merry *barin* [landlord], Nikitinski, in the novella **"Zhizneopisanie Pavlichenki, Matveia Rodionycha"** [**"The life and adventures of Matvei Pavlichenko"**]:

> "With shooting—I'll put it that way—with shooting you only get rid of a chap. Shooting's letting him off and too damn easy for yourself. With shooting you'll never get at the soul, to where it is in a fellow and how it goes and shows itself. But I don't spare myself, and I've more than once trampled an enemy for more than an hour. You see, I want to get to know what life really is and how it is inside me."

(90)

In **"Smert' Dolgusheva"** [**"Death of Dolgushev"**], after shooting Dolgushev Afon'ka Bida growls: "You people in specs take about as much pity on our brothers as a cat on a mouse."

Another method Babel' uses to achieve creative diversity is through different narrators.

The greater part of the book (twenty-three of the thirty-four novellas) is written in the style of a personal narrative as told by the principal character—the "autopsychological hero"—a witness of, and participant in, the events. In only four cases he is named Liutov. In the other novellas he is just "I," with occasionally varying biographical details. The later **"Argamak"** is done in the same manner.

In seven novellas Babel' displays a classical narrative style. We have the word of the hero, a picturesque, paradoxical character created not just through action but by purely linguistic means. This is Vas'ka Kurdiukov's letter in **"Pis'mo"** [**"A letter"**] about how they "finished off" two enemies—father and son (variations of *Taras Bulba*); another letter from the gloomy and enigmatic Sokolov with a request to send him to make revolution in Italy (**"Solntse Italii"** [**"Italian sunshine"**]; another letter and an explanatory note to a magistrate from Nikita Balmashov (**"Salt," "Izmena"** [**"Treason"**]); an exchange of messages between Savitskii and Khlebnikov (**"The Story of a Horse," "The Story of a Horse, Continued"**); and Pavlichenko's story-confession (**"The Life and Adventures of Matvei Pavlichenko"**).

"The Kiss," written later and appended to the book, is essentially an alien idiom. Although Liutov is commonly considered to be the hero, actually the narrator differs significantly from "people in specs" (he is a squadron commander, he "unsaddled two Polish officers in battle," and flaunts his brutality) and should be regarded as an objective hero with an intellectual rather than common-folk vocabulary.

In the novella **"Prishchepa,"** the narrator refers to the hero's story but recounts it himself, presenting the central character's thoughts, but not his speech.

Finally, three novellas (**"Nachal'nik konzapasa"** [**"The remount officer"**], **"The Kozino Cemetery,"** and **"The Widow"**) have no narrator or storyteller. They are presented objectively, in the third person. But here, too, the pure anecdote about the clever D'iakov (the most carefree and "problem-free" novella of the book) differs markedly from the poem in prose, a lyrical sigh at a Jewish cemetery (the shortest and "non-plot" novella).

Babel' rallies the hidden possibilities of the small genre, testing its strength, diversity, and depth.

Although Babel' published his first writings God knows where (in the Odessa newspaper *Izvestiia*, the magazine *Shkval, Pravda, Prozhektor, Lef, Krasnaia nov'*), he always had in mind, as R. Bush demonstrates, an integrated image: The first newspaper and magazine publications, at the level of novella compatibility, compositionally reflect the structure of the final version of *Red Cavalry*.

The book of poetry, with its specific structure, became an accepted form already in the nineteenth century (Baratynskii's *Sumerki* [*Dusk*] and Fet's *Vechernie ogni* [*Evening lights*]) and really took hold in the Silver Age (Annenskii, Blok, Akhmatova, Pasternak, and many others).

One of the first to start building books of stories was, I think, Chekhov (*Khmurie liudi* [*Gloomy people*], *V sumerkakh* [*At dusk*], and *Detvora* [*Children*]). But then, were there not also [Pushkin's] *Povesti Belkina* [*Tales by Belkin*] and the experiments of the romanticists (V. Odoevsky's *Russkie nochi* [*Russian nights*])?!

Red Cavalry, as a book of novellas, becomes a metagenre, an analogue and rival of the novel (another example of this kind is Zoshchenko's *Sentimental'nye povesti* [*Sentimental stories*]).

Sergei Eisenstein, the director of *Bronenosets "Potemkin"* [*Battleship Potemkin*], who had already worked with Babel' on the script of *Benia Krik,* fully realized the novelty of Babel''s structure. In an article written in 1926, he stated:

> The understanding of the cinema is now entering a *"second literary period,"* a phase of drawing closer to the symbolism of language. Of speech. Of speech, which gives symbolic (meaning not literal) and "imagery" to a very concrete material connotation through *contextual juxtaposition,* that is, *montage.* In some cases—in unexpected or unusual juxtaposition—it acts as a "poetic image." "Bullets whine and scream. Their complaint builds up intolerably. Bullets strike the earth and fumble in it, quivering with impatience."
>
> (Babel')

The example from **"Death of Dolgushev"** is not serendipitous; it is basic. Two years later, Eisenstein would say that Babel' "will forever remain an irreplaceable supplementary 'reader' for the new *cinematic imagery.*"

The structure of *Red Cavalry* can thus be organically described in the language of another art form: as a montage of frame bits within the novella and a montage of novella episodes in the whole of the book. Here, many of the opening frames ("The Comdiv 6 communicated today that Novograd-Volynsk was taken at dawn" [8]; "The Sixth Division was mustered together in the wood outside the village of Chesniki, awaiting the signal to attack" [191]) and formulae-aphorisms ("We'll die for a sour pickle and the world revolution"—"A horse is a friend . . . A horse is a father" [193]) can be interpreted as captions of this colorful silent film.

In any artistic arrangement the most significant, demarcated parts are the beginning and end. *Red Cavalry* starts with **"Crossing the Zbruch."** This page-and-a-half text presents almost all the topics and motifs that provide the structural basis of the book.

"'Crossing the Zbruch' doesn't have this crossing" (F. Levin). To be fair, we should note that the novella does have a crossing, but with just one colorful, graphic frame, half a paragraph:

> The blackened Zbruch roars, twisting itself into foamy knots at the falls. The bridges are destroyed, and we wade across the river on which rests a majestic moon. The horses are in to their cruppers and the torrent gurgles past hundreds of horses' legs. Somebody sinks, calling out loudly against the Mother of God. The river is dotted with square black patches—the carts—and is full of confused sounds, of whistling and singing that rise above the bright hollows and the serpentine trails of the moon.
>
> (8-9)

With respect to the *pointe* of each novella, its title is indeed "misleading," camouflaging. It is a notch for the memory, a point on the map, a formal place marker (compare **"Kostel v Novograde"** [**"The Novograd Church"**], **"Put' v Brody"** [**"The road to Brody"**], **"The Kozino Cemetery,"** **"Berestechko,"** **"Zamost'e,"** and **"Chesniki"**). But from the perspective of the book, the title introduces an important timeframe: the roads along which shouting, cursing, singing people are traveling somewhere on horseback.

A luxurious noon is followed by evening, then night. The sun, moon, and stars become anchor details of landscape descriptions, no longer detailed, as in the first novella, but concisely packaged into one or two sentences, or even just into a comparison or epithet.

The road leads to a house, moreover, a strange one—a place to spend the night, a chance shelter (compare the image of the family home in M. Bulgakov's *Belaia gvardiia* [*White Guard*]).

It is a Jewish home, and the fate of the Jewish world and the philosophy behind it becomes a constant theme of the book (**"Ghedali,"** **"Rabbi,"** and **"Syn rabbi"** [**"The rabbi's son"**].

In passing, an instantaneous punch in the very first paragraph-frame provides a historical parallel: "Our noisy rearguard convoy is spread out over the road from Brest to Warsaw built by Nicholas I over the bones of peasants" (8).

From here begins the motif of death persistently pursued throughout the entire novella: the orange sun rolls down the sky like a decapitated head; the evening coolness drips with the smell of yesterday's blood and of killed horses; silence overpowers all; Comdiv 6 is pursuing the Combrig on a heavy stallion, firing at him twice between the eyes.

Death flows like water through nature and through history, seeping even into dreams, thus preparing for the shocking finale, the novella's full stop: "She . . . removes the blanket from the sleeping man. Lying on his back is an old man, dead. His glottis has been torn out and his face split in two; his beard is clotted with blue blood resembling a piece of lead" (10).

The words of the pregnant daughter concluding the novella (another connective joint: a coming birth with a past death) project not grief or sorrow but an almost preternatural pride.

> "The Poles killed him," says the Jewess, shaking the mattress, "and he begged them: 'Kill me in the back yard so that my daughter doesn't see how I die.' But they did as it was most convenient to them. He died in this room and thought of me. And now I'd like to know," cried the woman with sudden terrible violence, "I'd like to know where you'd find in the whole world another father like my father!"
>
> (10)

Beyond the unemotional words of a military report lies a world of overwhelming beauty and Shakespearean passions.

The first killers in the book are Poles, the nominal enemy. But then everything intermixes, diffuses, and turns into one bloody mess. ***Red Cavalry*** has not got a single natural death (save for an old man in the later story **"The Kiss,"** who does die suddenly, albeit without outside help). On the other hand, plenty of people are shot, cut down, and mutilated. The thirty-four novellas offer twelve firsthand accounts of deaths, with many other mass slaughters mentioned in passing. "Prishchepa went from neighbor to neighbor, leaving behind him the trail of his blood-stained footprints. He set fire to villages and shot Polish headmen for hiding" (94).

In "Stikhi o neizvestnom soldate" ["Verses about an unknown soldier"], O. Mandel'shtam would later write about "millions killed for nothing . . . massive, wholesale deaths in the sky." The action in Babel''s book takes place under this sky.

A father *rezhet* [slashes] his Red-Armyman son, while another son *konchaet* [finishes off] his dad (**"A Letter"**). Pavlichenko *topchet* [tramples] the former landlord (**"Life and Adventures of Matvei Pavlichenko"**). Konkin *kroshit* [wipes out] Poles, then, together with a fellow soldier, *snimaet vintami* two men [put them out of action with rifles], while Spir'ka *vedet* [conducts] another man to Dukhonin's headquarters to check his documents, and, finally, the narrator *oblegchaet* [relieves] a proud old Pole (*Konkin*). Nikita Balmashov, with the help of his trusted rifle, also *konchaet* [gives it] to a deceitful black-marketeer woman (**"Salt"**). Trunov *vsunul sabliu v glotku* of a prisoner [thrusts his sword into the prisoner's neck], Pashka *raznes cherep* of a lad [sends his skull flying], then enemy airplanes *rasstreliali* [shoot], first Andriushka, then Trunov, with their machine guns (**"Squadron Commander Trunov"**). Galin with the white spot in his eye, a contributor to the newspaper *Krasnyi kavalerist,* savors the violent deaths of emperors.

> "Last time," says Galin, narrow-shouldered, pale and blind, "last time, Irina, we considered the shooting of Nicholas the Bloody by the Ekaterinburg proletariat. Now we will go on to another tyrant who died the death of a dog. Peter III was strangled by Orlov, his wife's lover, and Paul was torn to pieces by his courtiers and his own son. Nicholas the Rod poisoned himself; his son fell on March 1, and his grandson died of drunkenness. You need to know all that, Irina."
>
> (**"Vecher"** [**"Evening"**], 132)

What a diversity of synonyms! And not one of them that denotes a simple, natural death.

In the world of ***Red Cavalry*** it is difficult to escape and survive not only for people. "I grieve over the bees. The fighting armies have treated them most brutally. There are no bees left in Volhynia now" (**"The Road to Brody"**). "All torn and singed and dragging his feet, he led a cow out of the stall, put his revolver in its mouth, and fired" (**"Prishchepa,"** 94).

Most pages of the book are painted in the brightest color—red. That is why the sun here looks like a decapitated head, the blazing sunset reminds one of approaching death, the autumn trees oscillate at the crossroads like naked corpses.

Blood and death are equalizers for friend and foe, for right and wrong. "Pashka is dead, and there is no one to judge him on earth, and I would be the last to judge him" (**"Squadron Commander Trunov,"** 159).

"What is our Cossack?" Babel' writes in his diary. "Many things: looting, daring, professionalism, revolutionary zeal, brutal cruelty. We are the vanguard, but of what?"

The novella frames in ***Red Cavalry*** are arranged by contrast and juxtaposition, with no comforting connectors or soothing reflections.

One character strips prisoners and corpses; another plunders a church; the third tortures an unfortunate deacon, his unrecognized double; the fourth dies heroically in an encounter with airplanes; the fifth sees treason even in a hospital, among the doctors treating him; the sixth suddenly becomes an able brigade commander with the "imperious indifference of a Tartar khan"; the seventh dreams of killing the king of Italy to spark a revolutionary fire; the eighth, a Red Cavalry Christ, travels quietly and peacefully with the rearguard convoy playing an accordion; the ninth issues inane orders to flog his own infantry, the common soldiery; the tenth prefers his favorite horse over the [Communist] Party . . .

On rereading Babel' in the late 1950s, film director G. Kozintsev (another director!) was carried away by "the burning instant of life observed" in his books, noting that the writer had discovered an entire "continent": "the soldier of the civil war."

The inhabitants of Babel''s continent are people on horses, moral centaurs. They are united by an intensity of external manifestations, unbridled feelings, passion—for horses, the Party, women, the revolution. Participants in the just ended civil war, they are hyperbolized, enlarged, and presented in remote epic perspective.

Like Gogol's Zaporozhye Cossacks, or perhaps "Achaean menfolk" embarking on a campaign to Warsaw in search of Helen—the world revolution.

It was Gorky who compared Babel''s Cossacks with the Zaporozhye Cossacks: "Babel' illuminated the fighting men . . . from within and, in my view, better and more truthfully than Gogol did the Zaporozhye Cossacks." E. Pomianowski, the Polish literary scholar and Babel' translator, did not agree and elaborated:

> No, he did not illuminate them. He simply transferred them to another level, to the level of a *skaz* [tale], the epic form of which ennobles the heroes by its very method of narration. Even the beginning of the *Iliad* would have been but the story of a row between two unwashed *atamans* [chieftains] in a hand-to-hand fight over a wench, had it not been for the seriousness and brilliance that Homer, with his hexameter, forces us to see in this brawl.

An objective, epic view explains much in the poetics of ***Red Cavalry***: the unflappability, the superficial impartiality with which tragic events are recounted, specifically, death. The most famous example, which shocked so many, is from **"Berestechko"**:

> Right under my window some Cossacks were shooting an old, silver-bearded Jew for spying. The old man was uttering piercing screams and struggling to get away. Then Kudria, of the machine-gun section, took hold of his head and tucked it under his arm. The Jew stopped screaming and set his legs apart. Kudria drew out his dagger with his right hand and carefully, without splashing himself, cut the old man's throat. Then he knocked on the closed casement.
>
> "Anyone who cares may come and fetch him," he said, "You're free to do so."
>
> The Cossacks disappeared behind a corner.
>
> (120)

Naturalism in descriptions and in object details—an extreme, indicative frame in the novella **"Two Ivans"**: "Loading my saddle on my back, I went along the overturned edge of a field and stopped at a turning to satisfy a natural need. Having relieved myself, I buttoned up and felt drops on my hand. I lit a little lantern, turned around and saw, lying on the ground, the corpse of a Pole spattered with my urine." In the first editions there was another detail, later removed by either the author or the censor: "It dripped from his mouth, trickled between his teeth, and pooled in his empty eye sockets" (171).

Love in ***Red Cavalry*** is not romantic meetings under the moon (they occur only in the later novella **"The Kiss"**), not decadently convoluted, capricious feelings but open, blunt passion, unbridled erotics. Sashka, the "lady of all the squadrons," copulates with another man almost before the eyes of her dying former partner.

Several hours later, that same man strikes her in the face for being in no hurry to send the dead man's mother "the orphan's share" (**"The Widow"**). The washerwoman Irina goes to sleep with the heavy-jowled cook Vasilii right in front of Galin, who loves her and "educates" her (the one who lectured about assassinated emperors) (**"Evening"**).

As it moves back into epic perspective, the last war becomes history. But at the same time history becomes another of its victims, crushed in the millstones of the belligerent sides. One feels pity and compassion not only for people but also for the shattered legend.

According to Babel', "the burning history of the outskirts" is molded by the proximity of several tribes. "The Jews here threaded the gain of the Russian muzhik² to the Polish pan, and the Czech colonist to the Lodz factory" (121). Lying peacefully in the cemetery in Kozin are four generations spanning 300 years. And today, people still go to the synagogue; they argue about Hassidism and celebrate the Sabbath. However, now all this is taking place against a different background.

> In Berestechko itself, the old order had been given an airing: but it was still firmly rooted here. . . .
>
> Berestechko reeks unredeemably even now, and a violent smell of rotten herrings emanates from all its inhabitants. The little town reeks on, awaiting a new era; but instead of human beings there go about mere shadows of frontier misfortunes.
>
> (122)

In **"Zamost'e,"** the narrator suddenly awakes out of a terrible dream in which eros and thanatos are irresistibly intertwined and intermixed, like milk and blood, only to find himself in another horror.

> In the stillness I could hear the far-off breath of groaning. The smoke of secret murder strayed around us.
>
> "Somebody is being killed." I said. "Who is it?"
>
> "The Poles are getting the wind up," the muzhik answered. "The Poles are killing the Jews."
>
> . . . The muzhik made me light a cigarette from his. "The Jews are to blame for everything on our side and on yours. There'll be mighty few of them left after the war. How many Jews are there in the whole world?"
>
> "Ten million," I answered, putting the bridle on my horse.
>
> "There'll only be 200,000 left," cried the muzhik.
>
> (178, 180)

From this Jewish milieu and culture come two noteworthy heretics. One, an old shopkeeper, like a character out of a Dickensian novel, dreams about a sweet revolution and an improbable International. "And I want an International of good people; I would like every soul to be taken into account and given first-category rations. There, soul, please eat and enjoy life's pleasures" (**"Ghedali,"** 32).

The other, a young man with the face of Spinoza, a rabbi's son and a Bolshevik, dies at some forgotten railway station near Rovno—the death of the last of the princes, the end of that Hassidic culture.

In *Red Cavalry,* the Polish element is as multidimensional and multifaceted. The church is an ever present landmark: "White churches gleamed in the distance, like buckwheat fields. . . . It was almost midday when I had finished and was free at last. I went up to the window and saw the Berestechk temple—white and mighty. It was gleaming in the warm sunlight like a china tower" (148). The Poles (like the Cossacks) "cut up the Jews." But the Poles also include slaughtered prisoners, and meaninglessly proud shliakhta,³ and the old bell-ringer fearlessly defending his temple.

The Polish tribe, too, has its heretic. Pan Apolek, a strange wandering painter, is one of the few in the *Red Cavalry* world who creates rather than destroys. He works to order but does not sell himself. Like the painters of the Renaissance, he joins the mundane with the celestial; he transfers down-to-earth life to icons, transforming sinners into saints. He cherishes his own apocrypha—of Christ pitying the unfortunate Deborah, who had borne his son, whom "the priests concealed."

In the argument about Apolek's art, despite its jocular style, some sentiments extremely important to Babel' slip out.

> "He has made saints of you in your lifetime," cried the Vicar of Dubno and Novokonstantinov in answer to the crowd's defense of Apolek. "He has surrounded you with the unspeakable attributes of holiness—you—thrice fallen into the sin of disobedience, distillers of brandy in secret, merciless usurers, makers of false weights and merchants of your own daughters' innocence."
>
> "Your holiness," then said limping Vitol'd, a buyer-up of stolen goods and the keeper of the cemetery, "who will tell the ignorant people about the things in which the all-merciful Lord God sees truth? And isn't there more truth in the pictures of Pan Apolek who satisfies our pride than in your words so full of blame and aristocratic wrath?"
>
> (55)

The question of the "buyer-up of stolen goods" is rhetorical. It is apparent where the truth lies in this dialogue about painting and morality. Apolek seems to be the only apostle in the bloody flow of life racing somewhere. It is not for nothing that, along with the "naïve and colorful" portrait icons, the narrator gives him (this time in the novella **"U sviatogo Valenta"** [**"In St. Valentine's Church"**]) a painting with a spark of genius.

At that instant the velvet curtain beside the altar swayed, shook and slipped to one side. A niche was revealed in the blue depth of which, against a background of cloud-furried sky, ran a bearded figure in a Polish great coat of orange—barefooted, with torn and bleeding mouth. A hoarse cry pierced our ears then. I saw that the man in the orange coat was being followed by hatred and overtaken by his pursuers. He put out a hand to ward off the coming blow, and blood flowed from that hand in a purple stream. . . . The figure in the niche was none other than that of Jesus Christ—the most extraordinary image of God I have ever seen in my life.

(152-53)

Apolek's icon is the Savior seeking liberation from a world where nothing can be changed. The wandering painter's art is not Catholic (although the icon hangs in a church), just as Ghedali's International is not Judaism. It is simply Christianity, the gospel of the street—of Socrates, of Skovoroda, of an as yet unknown preacher from Judea.

A disciple of Apolek is what the narrator would be—and is.

The wise and beautiful life of Pan Apolek went to my head like an old wine. In Novograd-Volynsk, among the ruins of a town swiftly brought to confusion, fate threw before my feet a New Testament that had lain concealed from the world. Hallowed with ingenuousness, I made a vow then to follow Pan Apolek's example. And the sweetness of meditated rancor, the bitter scorn I felt for the dogs and swine of mankind, the fire of silent and intoxicating revenge—all this I sacrificed to my new vow.

(48)

The narrator's "I" bonds the fragmentary epos of *Red Cavalry.* It is, of course, not biographical, although Babel''s *Red Cavalry* pseudonym is mentioned in the novellas several times.

Babel''s status—a staff official of "commander" rank, with his own orderly, sufficiently independent of the rank and file, and with a modicum of influence—has nothing in common with the status of the "bespectacled," wretched Kirill Liutov, a stranger to the Cossack crowd seeking to ingratiate himself with them.

(V. Kovskii)

But neither is there some concocted biography or prescribed image of Babel''s central figure. The narrator *is there,* but he is legendary, elusive, faceless, like Homer or Boian,[4] whose strings "twanged the glory" of eleventh-century centaurs. Instead of a biography, the narrator has a system of signatory details and reactions, which are, moreover, shifting and contradictory. He may be a Russian or a Jew, a newspaperman or a rear convoy officer with an orderly, a bungler and dreamer, or a quite able and tenacious cavalryman.

These images, masks, and transformations are united, it seems, by one key metonymic detail.

I handed him a paper whereby I was to be attached to the staff of the division.

"Put it down in the Order of the Day," said the Comdiv, "put him down for every satisfaction save that of the front. Can you read and write?"

"Yes, I can read and write," I replied, envying the flower and iron of that youthfulness. "I graduated in law from St. Petersburg University."

"Oh, you are one of the *Kinderbalsams,*"[5] he laughed. "Specs on your nose. What a nasty little object! They've sent you along without any enquiries; and this is a hot place for specs."

("My First Goose," 35)

Opposite the moon, on the bank of a sleeping pond, I was sitting—spectacled, with boils on my neck and bandages on my legs.

("Evening")

Red Cavalry is a book about a *Kinderbalsam* in specs in a redskin land. He is a person from the outside, an observer, and a witness attempting, as the poet said, "to flow like a drop with the masses," but organically incapable of this. The world dream blinding the eyes of other cavalrymen and blending with pogroms, pillage, a flippant attitude toward the lives of others and one's own death is not, it seems, alien to him. He keeps trying to appear as one of them, to get rid of his "moral specs." But the most he can do is wring the neck of a goose or frighten old women with a gun. He cannot shoot a dying man at the latter's own request and goes into "the unforgettable attack near Chesniki" with an unloaded weapon: "The Poles go for me, and I don't go for them."

It is as though the narrator has stumbled into the Red Cavalry from out of the nineteenth century. He is related to Tolstoy's Pierre (also bespectacled) or Garshin's heroes who went to war "to suffer with the people," to present their chests to bullets but not punch holes in others.

But this paradoxical situation—side-by-side, but not together—helps the hero to understand both Sashka's meekness and Akinfiev's frenzy, thoughts of the Hassids, and the gospel of Apolek.

Babel''s hero is split in more important ways than Russian-Jew or correspondent-staff worker. He is also a centaur: a participant in the Red Cavalry campaign and at the same time an epic viewer and painter of it. To an artist, it is good to be a viewer from the outside.

There is no air in the book's novella tales. The science of hate blinds the characters. In their eyes the world is transformed into a black-white empty space that just has to be overcome. "Then we began to pursue General Denikin, and killed thousands of them and drove them into the Black Sea" (**"A Letter,"** 14). "We were wiping out the *shliakhta* up beyond Belaia Tserkov'. We were wiping them out and making a clean job of it so that even the trees went and bent" (**"Konkin,"** 113).

Italy to Sidorov, who is dreaming to kill its king, is sunshine and bananas. The narrator of that same novella, **"Italian Sunshine,"** sees the real Italian landscape in the devastated town on the Zbruch River.

> The singed town—columns broken and dug into the earth, the malevolent, crooked, little fingers of old women—seemed to me raised up aloft into the air, as snug and chimerical as dream-visions. The crude brightness of the moon flowed over it with inexhaustible force. The damp mould of the ruins flowered like the marble of opera seats. And I waited with an uneasy mind for Romeo to appear from the clouds—a Romeo in satin and singing of love—while a dismal electrician in the wings keeps a finger on the switch of the moon.
>
> (23)

The true romanticist is not the boring ideological killer Sidorov, but the narrator, who is thus able to visualize the scene after the battle.

The opera comparison in **"Italian Sunshine"** is not accidental. In his story **"Probuzhdenie"** [**"Awakening"**] Babel recalls a rebuke of his Odessa acquaintance and critic of his first stories: "Your landscapes look like descriptions of stage settings." Nevertheless, the luxurious, colorful, blazing, decorative qualities of Babel''s landscapes are retained in **Red Cavalry.** Babel''s epic characters are natural precisely on such a stage, which, incidentally, they themselves do not notice. The art of seeing the world belongs to the narrator.

In his early essay, "Odessa" (1916), Babel asks rhetorically: "If one thinks about it, will one not find that there never has been a truly joyous, shining description of sunlight in Russian literature?" "The literary Messiah, whom people have been awaiting for so long and so fruitlessly," he goes on to predict, "will come from there: from sunlit steppes surrounded by sea."

And then he appears a decade later, to see the sun, at a most unsuitable time of civil discord and bloody campaigns.

> Yesterday was the first day of slaughter at Brody. Having lost our way on the blue earth we had no knowledge of it, not I nor my friend Afon'ka Bida. . . . The rye was tall, the sun resplendent, and the soul, all undeserving of those blazing, winged skies, longed for drawn-out tortures."
>
> (**"The Road to Brody"**)

> Andriushka . . . unbuttoned the old man's trousers, shook him slightly, and began to pull them off the dying man. . . . The sun came out of the clouds at that

moment and impetuously surrounded Andriushka's horse, its lively pace and the devil-may-care swing of its docked tail.
>
> (**"Squadron Commander Trunov"**)

Babel''s sunsets and nights, moons, stars, and simply the details of his surrounding world are just as original, vividly picturesque, as though lit up with theater lights, and sharp as a sudden gunshot.

> Night flew toward me on mettlesome horses. The whole universe responded with vociferations from the transport wagons, and on the earth, girdled about with shrill sounds, the roads disappeared. Stars crept forth out of the fresh womb of night, and deserted villages blazed on the horizon.
>
> (**"Two Ivans"**)

Iurii Olesha, author of *Zavist'* [*Envy*], whom Babel in a later interview called a fellow Odessite and a writer of "the Odessa, southern Russian school," "in his old age . . . opened a metaphor shop." Babel' would have been a must in this imaginary shop, featured in the most prominent places. The goods in **Red Cavalry** number in the hundreds. Metaphors (more strictly speaking tropes: comparisons, hyperboles, etc.) flash in every point of the text and not just illuminate the plot space but acquire independent value of their own.

The world of people crushed by suffering and blinded by hate is colorless. God's world, even mutilated by war, is amazing and stunning. Far from despoiling it, blood, urine, and tears accentuate its poetry and beauty.

The most famous aphorism from Viktor Shklovskii's "critical romance" about Babel' (1924), on the whole a very penetrating piece, has been: "The meaning of Babel''s method is that he speaks in one and the same voice of stars and gonorrhea." This is one-sided and inaccurate. What is remarkable in **Red Cavalry,** among other things, is the range of intonations, the architectonic structure of the book. The matter-of-fact tone of speech about horrible things, which had taken aback contemporaries (some saw it as deliberate aestheticism) melds with the style of a military report or protocol, of a comic story, of lofty rhetoric and the exalted lyricism of the "poem in prose."

The fragmentary epic of **Red Cavalry** stands at an intersection of stylistic experiments of the twenties: from the verbal blizzards of Pil'niak to the bare simplicity of Dobychin, from the everyday life tales of Zoshchenko to the philosophical incorrectness of Platonov.

The book begins and ends with a road. **"Crossing the Zbruch"** presents almost all significant motifs. The three concluding novellas are the finale: They close the story lines and develop the summary formulae-aphorisms.

"Posle boia" ["After the battle"] is based on a dispute with Akinfiev, who just cannot understand "them as get muddled in the fight and don't put no cartridges in the pistols." The final formula stresses—retroactively—the principal quality of the bespectacled Kinderbalsam: his paradoxical pacifism and irrational "Molokanism."[6]

> The village was swimming and swelling, and muddy clay was oozing from its dismal wounds. The first star glimmered above me and fell into the clouds. The rain lashed the willows and spent itself. Evening flew into the sky like a flock of birds, and darkness crowned me with its watery wreath. I felt all my strength ebbing away, and bent beneath the funeral garland, continued on my way, imploring fate to grant me the simplest of proficiencies—the ability to kill my fellow men.

In "Pesnia" ["The song"], Sashka Koniaev, alias Sashka the Christ, sings a Kuban' song reminiscent of either an old romance or a new Yesenin. The simple tune transforms people: The narrator stops threatening the old landlady with a revolver and tries to go to sleep with good thoughts, the old woman herself reflects that she is a woman dreaming of her bit of serendipitous happiness. "Those songs are indispensable to us. No one can see an end to the war, and Sashka the Christ, our squadron's singer, is not yet ripe for death" (207).

In "Syn rabbi" ["The rabbi's son"], the narrator, for the first time in the *Red Cavalry* world, discovers his double. In "My First Goose," the narrator mentions the manuscripts and tattered old clothes that had fallen out of his trunk. In the last novella there is a similar situation, but here the narrator is collecting "the scattered belongings of the Red Army soldier Bratslavsky" that had fallen out of the dying man's case.

> His things were strewn about pell-mell—mandates of the propagandist and memorandum books of the Jewish poet; the portraits of Lenin and Maimonides lay side by side: the knotted iron of Lenin's skull beside the dull silk of the portraits of Maimonides. A lock of woman's hair lay in a book, the Resolutions of the Party's Sixth Congress, and the margins of communist leaflets were crowded with crooked lines of Hebrew verse. They fell upon me in a mean, depressing rain—pages of the Song of Songs and those revolver cartridges.
>
> (212)

The rabbi's son manages to do what the narrator was never able to do: to meld Russian and Jewish, literature and revolution, a lock of woman's hair and party resolutions. Perhaps that is why he dies?!

> He died before we reached Rovno. He—that last of the princes—died amid his poetry, phylacteries, and coarse linen leggings. We buried him at some forgotten station or other. And I, who can scarcely contain the tempests of my imagination within this primeval body of mine, was there beside my brother when he breathed his last.
>
> (212)

Brother—the final word of the novella, the cycle, the book. Some try to ascribe it religious meaning, seeing the narrator's "kinship" to Jewishness or his "affinity" to the Hassidic wise men. But the thing is that, within the structure of the book built according to the laws of "the closeness and unity of the poetic line," this episode and this definition also rhyme with each other.

In "Two Ivans," a novella about unrecognized Russian doubles, the pacifist deacon and his torturer Ankifiev, the earlier quoted naturalistic scene with the body of the dead Pole covered with urine is followed by a connotational blow, another of Babel's formulas. "With the Commander-in Chief Pilsudsky's proclamation, I wiped away the smelly liquid from the skull of my unknown brother, and went on, bent beneath the weight of the saddle" (171).

The narrator's brother is not only the rabbi's son, Red Army man Bratslavsky, but also the unknown dead enemy (no one has yet suspected the narrator of being of Polish descent). Similarly, he lists as friends the meek Sashka the Christ, the raving lover of horses, Savitsky, the reckless Afon'ka Bida.

It was not Babel' who said: And all ye are brethren (Matthew 23:8). But he essentially talks about the same thing. The narrator's exuberant imagination seeks to found an "International of Good Men" in the world of *Red Cavalry*. The trouble is that good people, as Bulgakov's Ieshua says, do not know of their goodness or brotherhood.

> "Pan comrade, the International is eaten with—"
>
> "It's eaten with gunpowder," I answered the old man, "and flavored with the best blood."
>
> (32)

And one more good man who, not suspecting how he would be ridiculed many years later, wrote a review (or signed someone else's).

> Citizen Babel' was unable to see the great upheavals of class struggle, it was alien and objectionable to him, but he does, however, see, with the passion of a sick sadist, the quivering breasts of a Cossack woman conjured up in his imagination, her bare thighs, and so on. He sees the world "as a meadow crossed by naked women, stallions, and mares." Indeed, with such an imagination, one can only write slander about the Red Cavalry.

Budennyi may have been a good military leader, but he was a bad, biased, and ill-tempered reader.

> We were both of us rocked by the same passions. Both of us looked upon the world as a meadow in May—a meadow crossed by women and horses.
>
> ("The Story of a Horse")

The dispute with Budennyi did not erupt because the renowned cavalryman knew nothing about poetry (although, indeed, he did not). What was worse is that he wanted to write a different myth into history, a different picture of the actions, roles, and objectives of his troops and their political commissar. The system, consolidated by the iron hand of that commissar, gave the powers that be a monopoly on creating myths, on describing events, past and current. Only talented appointees had the right of such description. Babel's talent was of a different, unearthly origin. That is why he perished.

They say that history is written by the winners. No, alas, no. (E. Pomianovskii)

Translator's Notes

Translation © 2001 M. E. Sharpe, Inc., from the Russian text © 1999 Igor' Sukhikh. "O zvezdakh, krovi, liudiakh, loshadiakh," *Zvezda* 12 (1999): 222-32. Translated by Vladimir Talmy.

"Konarmiia" is a contraction of "Konnaia armiia," that is, "Cavalry Army." *Red Cavalry* is the title of the English translation of the book by Nadia Helstein, published (and copyrighted) in 1929 by Alfred A. Knopf. The translations of all quotes from *Konarmiia* in this article, as well as the titles of the respective novellas, have been taken from this translation. I have, however, ventured to correct several apparent mistranslations, as well as to adapt name transliterations to the current accepted Library of Congress standard. Page references to this edition will follow each citation in parentheses.—Trans.

1. The term *Pan,* in Polish, means "gentleman," "owner," or "landlord" and is used as a common address for "Mister." In Russian, depending on the context, *Pan* may be used simply as an address to or among Poles or, in a somewhat derogatory sense, as denoting Poles in general.

2. *Muzhik,* a Russian peasant, may also refer colloquially to any man.

3. *Shliakhta* is the term for Polish small-landed gentry; in Russian, it is also a derogatory reference to Poles in general.

4. Boian is the legendary bard of Russian legends and *bylinas.*

5. *Kinderbalsam* is derogatory slang for students.

6. Molokanism refers to the Molokan Christian religious sect that originated in Russia.

FURTHER READING

Criticism

Bojanowska, Edyta J. "*E Pluribus Unum*: Isaac Babel's *Red Cavalry* as a Story Cycle." *Russian Review* 59 (July 2000): 371-89.

    Identifies the unifying thematic and stylistic elements of the stories in *Red Cavalry.*

Borenstein, Eliot. "Isaak Babel: Dead Fathers and Sons." In *Men without Women: Masculinity and Revolution in Russian Fiction, 1917-1929,* pp. 73-124. Durham, N.C.: Duke University Press, 2000.

    Considers masculinity as a key theme of *Red Cavalry.*

Danow, David K. "A Poetics of Inversion: The Non-Dialogic Aspect in Isaac Babel's *Red Cavalry.*" *Modern Language Review* 86, no. 4 (October 1991): 939-53.

    Discusses the lack of verbal communication in *Red Cavalry,* contending that "this is a world in which a dialogic response, were it offered, would yet prove of no avail."

Erlich, Victor. "Color and Line: The Art of Isaac Babel." In *Modernism and Revolution: Russian Literature in Transition,* pp. 145-62. Cambridge, Mass.: Harvard University Press, 1994.

    Elucidates the defining characteristics of *Red Cavalry.*

Hetenyi, Zsuzsa. "The Visible Idea: Babel's Modelling Imagery." *Canadian Slavonic Papers* 36, nos. 1-2 (March-June 1994): 55-67.

    Maintains that by "collating Babel's diary with the stories of his *Red Cavalry* one can discover some important connections" that illustrate the way in which Babel creates imagery.

Schreurs, Marc. "Two Forms of Montage in Babel's *Konarmija.*" *Russian Literature* 31, no. 2 (April 1987): 243-92.

    Describes the narrative structure of *Red Cavalry* in terms of montage.

——. *Procedures of Montage in Isaak Babel's* Red Cavalry. Amsterdam: Rodopi, 1989, 215 p.

    Full-length study of Babel's use of montage techniques in *Red Cavalry.*

Sicher, Efraim. *Style and Structure in the Prose of Isaak Babel.* Columbus, Ohio: Slavica Publishers, 1985, 140 p.

    Stylistic analysis of *Red Cavalry.*

————. "The 'Jewish Cossack': Isaac Babel in the First Red Cavalry." In *Studies in Contemporary Jewry IV: Jews and the European Crisis, 1914-21,* edited by Jonathan Frankel, pp. 113-34. Oxford: Oxford University Press, 1988.

Utilizes new material from Babel's *1920 Diary* to illuminate the author's experiences during the Soviet-Polish War, which were the basis for the stories in *Red Cavalry.*

————. "Babel's 'Shy Star': Reference, Inter-reference and Interference." *New Zealand Slavonic Journal* 36 (2002): 259-75.

Explores intertextuality in "Crossing the Zbruck."

Stine, Peter. "Isaac Babel and Violence." *Modern Fiction Studies* 30, no. 2 (summer 1984): 237-55.

Explores the role of violence in Babel's work, particularly the stories in *Red Cavalry.*

Van Baak, J. J. *The Place of Space in Narrative: A Semiotic Approach to the Problem of Literary Space: With an Analysis of the Role of Space in I. E. Babel's* Konarmija. Amsterdam: Rodopi, 1983, 276 p.

Full-length analysis of the role of space in *Red Cavalry.*

Van der Eng, Jan. "The Pointed Conclusion as Story Finale and Cyclic Element in *Red Cavalry.*" In *Language and Literary Theory: In Honor of Ladislav Matejka,* edited by Benjamin A. Stolz, I. R. Titunik, and Lubomir Dolezel, pp. 585-94. Ann Arbor: University of Michigan Press, 1984.

Underscores the role of the endings in the stories of *Red Cavalry,* asserting that "it sheds an unexpected light on the thematic essence of the complex of internal associative connections."

————. "Types of Inner Tales in *Red Cavalry.*" In *Text and Context: Essays to Honor Nils Åke Nilsson,* edited by Peter Alberg Jensen, et al., pp. 128-38. Stockholm: Almqvist & Wiksell, 1987.

Discusses the characteristics of the inner tale in *Red Cavalry,* as well as "their relevance for the narrative form in which they are embedded as well as their function for the cycle as the encompassing whole."

Additional coverage of Babel's life and career is contained in the following sources published by Thomson Gale: *Contemporary Authors,* Vols. 104, 155; *Contemporary Authors New Revision Series,* Vol. 113; *Dictionary of Literary Biography,* Vol. 272; *Encyclopedia of World Literature in the 20th Century,* Ed. 3; *European Writers,* Vol. 11; *Literature Resource Center; Major 20th-Century Writers,* Ed. 1; *Reference Guide to Short Fiction,* Ed. 2; *Reference Guide to World Literature,* Eds. 2, 3; *Short Stories for Students,* Vol. 10; *Short Story Criticism,* Vol. 16; *Twayne's World Authors;* and *Twentieth-Century Literary Criticism,* Vols. 2, 13.

Mavis Gallant
1922-

(Born Mavis de Trafford Young) Canadian short story writer, novelist, critic, playwright, and essayist.

The following entry presents criticism of Gallant's short fiction from 1990 through 2003. For earlier criticism of Gallant's short fiction, see *SSC*, Volume 5.

INTRODUCTION

Regarded as an important contemporary fiction writer, Gallant is particularly admired for her finely crafted short stories, most of which have been published in the *New Yorker*. A Canadian who has lived most of her adult life in France, Gallant often depicts the plight of alienated people in unfamiliar and indifferent environments. Populated by alienated expatriates and disillusioned souls, Gallant's stories offer insight into the contemporary human experience in Europe and North America, exposing the ironies of human nature that balance comedy and tragedy. Her fiction often conveys a sense of ambiguity about the past and its effects on the present, and routinely presents narrative conflicts that reflect the prevalent attitudes of postwar society.

BIOGRAPHICAL INFORMATION

Gallant was born on August 11, 1922, in Montreal, Canada. She experienced a difficult childhood, and themes of alienation and loneliness surface frequently in her stories. When she was ten years old, her father died and her mother soon remarried. Over the next eight years, Gallant attended seventeen different schools, completing her education at a New York City high school after she was sent there to live with a guardian. She subsequently returned to Montreal during World War II, and briefly worked at the National Film Board before she became a feature reporter for the *Montreal Standard* in 1944. While working for the *Standard,* Gallant began to publish short stories in a number of Canadian literary magazines. In 1950 she moved to Paris and became a full-time writer. Since that time, she has resided in Paris, although she has retained her Canadian citizenship. Her stories began appearing in the *New Yorker,* which has continuously published her stories since 1951. Over the next three decades, she published several collections of these stories, such as *The Other Paris* (1956), *My Heart Is Broken* (1964), *The Pegnitz*

Junction (1973), and *From the Fifteenth District* (1979). In 1981 Gallant published *Home Truths,* which was awarded the Governor General's Award, Canada's most prestigious literary prize. The following year her play *What Is to Be Done?* premiered at Toronto's Tarragon Theatre. She stayed in Canada for a time, accepting an appointment as writer-in-residence at the University of Toronto in 1983 and 1984, but eventually returned to Paris. In 2002 Gallant received the Literary Grand Prix Award at the Blue Metropolis International Literary Festival in Montreal.

MAJOR WORKS OF SHORT FICTION

Most of Gallant's short stories were initially published in the *New Yorker,* and then published in book form. Her first collection of stories, *The Other Paris,* explores the theme of dislocation, particularly as experienced by Americans and Canadians in Europe, and emphasizes the ways society affects individuals. In the title story, for instance, a young American woman travels to Paris anticipating romance and adventure, but finds instead a somber postwar ennui. *My Heart Is Broken,* an anthology of several stories and a novella, examines the despair of a variety of exiles who inhabit a series of rundown hotels in Europe. In a similar vein, *From the Fifteenth District* centers on a group of North American expatriates in World War II Europe. Another recurrent theme of Gallant's fiction involves exploring the individuality of the Canadian character amid a confusing and challenging outside world. Delineating the lives of young Canadians at home and abroad at different moments of the twentieth century, *Home Truths* concludes with a sequence of six "Montreal stories," which approximate the upheaval and rejection Gallant experienced as a child and adolescent in Montreal between World War I and World War II. *In Transit* (1988) consists of stories previously published in the 1950s and 1960s, separated into three sections that alternately focus on parents and children, adolescents, and preadolescent youngsters. Half of the eleven stories in *Across the Bridge* (1993) recount moments in the lives of the fictional Carette family in prewar and postwar Montreal, and the other half trace their fortunes as expatriates in Paris. *The Collected Stories of Mavis Gallant* (1996) presents a vast selection of Gallant's fiction encompassing her entire career. *Paris Stories* (2002) collects a variety of Gallant's best-known stories set in Paris, including "The Moslem Wife," "In Plain Sight," "Grippes and Poche," and "The Ice Wagon Going down the Street."

CRITICAL RECEPTION

Gallant's reputation developed after years of relative critical neglect, especially in her native Canada, and she is now recognized as one of Canada's best short story writers. In the late 1980s critical attention to her work increased as commentators began to recognize her command of the English language, skillful use of narrative forms, and her deft character studies. Her fiction has been compared to that of Anton Chekhov, Katherine Anne Porter, Henry James, Virginia Woolf, and Joseph Conrad. Although some critics have complained that her fiction is relentlessly pessimistic and emotionally cold, others have lauded her work for its understated irony, precise attention to detail, and penetrating insight into the human condition. Moreover, several critics have commended the objectivity of Gallant's perceptions of twentieth-century world history, particularly her views of French anti-Semitism and the Fascist movement. Commentators have explored the link between Gallant's interest in art and her fiction, and have underscored the role of the narrator in her stories. Themes of betrayal, abandonment, loss, memory, cultural identity, and alienation have been viewed as central to her short fiction. Critics have also examined the significance of her expa-

triate perspective with respect to definitions of the Canadian character.

PRINCIPAL WORKS

Short Fiction

The Other Paris 1956
My Heart Is Broken (short stories and novel) 1964; also published as *An Unmarried Man's Summer,* 1965
The Pegnitz Junction (novella and short stories) 1973
The End of the World and Other Stories 1974
From the Fifteenth District (novella and short stories) 1979
Home Truths: Selected Canadian Stories 1981
Overhead in a Balloon: Stories of Paris 1985
In Transit 1988
Across the Bridge 1993
The Moslem Wife and Other Stories 1993
The Collected Stories of Mavis Gallant 1996; published in Canada and the United Kingdom as *The Selected Stories of Mavis Gallant*
Paris Stories 2002
Varieties of Exile: Stories 2003

Other Major Works

Green Water, Green Sky (novel) 1959
A Fairly Good Time (novel) 1970
What Is to Be Done? (play) 1982
Paris Notebooks: Essays and Reviews (essays and criticism) 1986

CRITICISM

Ronald Hatch (essay date winter 1990)

SOURCE: Hatch, Ronald. "Mavis Gallant and the Fascism of Everyday Life." *Essays on Canadian Writing,* no. 42 (winter 1990): 9-40.

[*In the following essay, Hatch regards several of Gallant's short stories as her attempt to understand and confront the dangers of fascism.*]

Mavis Gallant has commented that the most difficult yet necessary task of the postwar period is to reach an understanding of Fascism ("An Interview" 39-41). Although she treats this issue directly in relatively few of her stories, her fiction as a whole presents aspects of human nature that indicate the vulnerability of individuals and societies to potentially fascistic systems of thought. The crucial event leading to her concern with fascism may well have occurred while Gallant was a reporter for the Montreal *Standard* at the end of the war, and was shown the first pictures to be released of the concentration camps. Her reaction was disbelief. In an interview with Geoff Hancock, she recalls saying to her editor: "We're dreaming. This isn't real. We're in a nightmare" ("An Interview" 39). Gallant was asked to write the captions for the pictures and a short covering article: "Now, imagine being twenty-two," she says,

> being the intensely left-wing political romantic I was, passionately anti-fascist, having believed that a new kind of civilization was going to grow out of the ruins of the war—out of victory over fascism—and having to write *the explanation* of something I did not myself understand.
>
> ("An Interview" 39)

For Gallant, the major question was how a culture as rich and brilliant as Germany's could fall to such depths. To obtain an answer, she felt it essential to ask the Germans. Yet when she mentioned this in her newspaper copy, she found that for the first time in her career with the *Standard* her material was rejected. In its place, the *Standard* used an article that "was a prototype for all the cliches we've been bludgeoned with ever since." When she asked why her copy had been rejected, she was told that the editors had thought her references to German culture absurd. One of her colleagues commented: "All the Germans are bastards and that's that." Yet as Gallant saw, such an attitude merely placed a label on an entire people and did not even begin to explain why the Germans had embraced fascism. As Gallant says, at this time: "The *why* was desperately important to people like myself who were twenty-two and had to live with this shambles" ("An Interview" 40).

In 1950, five years after the end of World War II, her interests and her decision to make her living as a fiction writer led Gallant to leave the Montreal *Standard* and go to Europe, where she travelled widely and lived for a time in many different countries—England, Spain, Austria, France—finally choosing Paris as her writing base. When Gallant left Canada, she already spoke French fluently and possessed a passing knowledge of German. In Spain, she quickly learned Spanish, her facility with languages allowing her to integrate quickly into European culture. Gallant discovered that being *in* a culture but not *of* it gave her the ideal perspective to explore the different social layerings of the postwar period. She found at once that the old European civilization had been shattered by the war and the experience

of fascism. The Yalta Conference had created, not one Europe, but two, with Germany divided and Poland abandoned. The end of World War II brought yet another conflict, the Cold War, and a period of affluence and consumer culture that was widely believed to be the millennium (Leuchtenburg 4-5). As Gallant quickly realized, neither the Cold War nor the new affluence created an atmosphere in which the analysis of fascism could take place as a precondition for human development.

In a different writer, Gallant's need to answer the "why" of fascism might well have led to fictional reconstructions of the 1920s and 1930s, historical documentary of the type recently undertaken by Sylvia Fraser about the Third Reich. But Gallant has always felt strongly that she must write about her own time, about what she has seen and experienced, for only in this way can she penetrate to the small but crucial moments in people's lives during which the relationship between thought and behaviour is made manifest. While acknowledging that the regimes of Mussolini and Hitler arose from specific economic and political conditions, she saw also that these dictatorships were made possible by a state of mind that allowed people to embrace fascist ideals. As Gallant has commented, while discussing her German stories of the 1960s, she did not want to write about "the historical causes of Fascism—just its small possibilities in people" ("An Interview" 41). Thus, when Gallant comes to portray actual Fascists, she does not isolate them as mutants outside the mainstream of humanity. Rather, she portrays how fascism can captivate ordinary people everywhere. Gallant's stories reveal that the "small possibilities" that brought the Fascists to power in the 1920s and 1930s were not peculiar to a few European states, but were, and still are, a powerful fact of Western consciousness.

Although Gallant does not tackle fascism head-on in her European stories of the 1950s, her interest in the interaction between the psychological and the social is already evident. The conservative impulse to reify the world into known and conventional patterns particularly fascinates her, for such conservatism denies the randomness and uncertainty of what Joan Didion has termed the "dailiness of life" (121). In **"The Other Paris,"** for example, Gallant portrays the young American, Carol, passionately searching for new directions. But Carol brings to Europe the surface optimism and affluence of the Eisenhower years, and adamantly refuses to see Paris in all its postwar economic chaos. While Carol wants a larger ideal to give shape and form to her energy, she identifies this ideal with a preconceived image of Paris: an artistic Montparnasse that died in the Depression.

Throughout **"The Other Paris,"** Gallant suggests that Carol's need for a sustaining vision can be met only by facing the chaotic reality of postwar Europe, with its rubble and refugees. The real beginning for both Europe and America rests with Carol's acknowledging "her unshared confusion" (30), and moving outwards to take account of the decay and loss. Yet, as Gallant shows, this proves too much for Carol, who takes refuge from the dissolution of Europe in marriage with a mindless American. Together they will at least be able to live self-sufficiently: "No one could point to them, or criticize them, or humiliate them by offering to help" (29). Self-sufficiency is by no means a bad ideal, as Gallant fully appreciates in her own life as an artist, but in Carol's case, the ideal becomes a means of ignoring or bypassing present experience. Carol is thrown back into an antiquated subjective universe, which demands that she forget her European experience or "remember it and describe it and finally believe it as it had never been at all" (30). Here the prose, with phrase layering upon phrase, replicates the layers of memory that isolate the individual from the present, creating a past that offers protection against a world without direction.

This sense of people erecting walls against the present appears also in **"A Day Like Any Other,"** which portrays a wealthy American family, the Kennedys, who have successfully insulated themselves from anything disturbing in the past or present. Mr. Kennedy lives in a series of European spas, searching for a cure for his nonexistent illness. His wife and two young daughters trail around Europe after him, Mrs. Kennedy living in a dreamworld of good marriages for her two children. The Kennedys have completely ignored the fact of Nazism and World War II by recreating the expatriate spa life of the late nineteenth and early twentieth centuries, the life captured in Ford Madox Ford's *The Good Soldier*. Yet this sheltered world, insulated from the present, is unwittingly disrupted when Mrs. Kennedy hires a Czechoslovakian "Volksdeutsch" as the children's new governess. By way of entertaining them, Frau Stengel tells the children stories about Hitler and the ungrateful Czechs.

The opening situation of **"A Day Like Any Other"** seems a classic case of weak liberalism about to be undermined by the darkness of fascism. Yet to portray Frau Stengel as a kind of fifth column within the home of the Kennedys would emphasize the effect of ideas and opinions, creating the kinds of situations in which intellectuals talk about their problems—something Gallant abhors. Gallant, in fact, chooses the opposite tack. Her portrait shows the Kennedy children enjoying Frau Stengel's Hitler stories, not because Hitler appeals to them, but because the repetitiveness of the stories provides the permanence they crave. The Kennedy girls even enjoy Frau Stengel's stories about little children "who had been killed in bombardments or separated forever from their parents" (226). Gallant points out that any system of ideas, any pattern of the mind, offers comfort so long as it can be sustained. But such worlds,

she suggests, inevitably break down when challenged by the onslaught of the changing present.

When this breakdown occurs in the relationship between Frau Stengel and the Kennedy children, the little girls are plunged into terror so great that they dare not speak of it. Gallant intensifies the effect by refusing to allow the reader into the children's minds, presenting only the evidence of their fear—they lie huddled together in bed, asleep, with the windows sealed against the terrors outside. They look to Mrs. Kennedy like "two question marks" (239). She can see the form of the questions embodied by the children, but not the terror concealed therein. So powerful are the mind-numbing patterns of her adult conventional thought, that she continues to interpret the children as symbols of innocence, and turns away from the questions they provoke about the security of her own mental constructs. The story's ending proves extraordinarily powerful. Gallant leaves us not only with the children's absolute fear, but also with their isolation from even the most fundamental source of reassurance—their mother. They are left alone with no hope, save the building of barricades against reality—the uncertain night.

These early stories about the innocent American abroad in Europe reflect how Gallant's fiction, in its largest dimension, explores an aspect of what Marx called "false consciousness," in which patterns of thought remain "alienated" from the individual's "social being" (Berger 6). These early stories express a continual battle between concept and percept, what a character thinks he knows about the world and what he actually perceives. Carol and the Kennedys employ conservative patterns of thought from an idealized past to fend off the shambles of postwar Europe. The Kennedy children, ignorant of the past, robbed of familiar patterns in the present, can only hide behind the flimsy shelter of blankets and curtains. These conservative impulses serve for self-protection, but at the price of sequestering individuals from the world. Moreover, both stories convey the fear that gives rise to the walls of convention, and indicate that the characters may well spend their lives searching for ever-stronger walls of custom to shut out that fear.

At the farthest boundary of the mind's conservative impulse lies fascism. Although fascism is often seen today as an event, or series of events, that occurred at a particular time in the past, it is far more insidious than that: it is conservatism of the mind that endeavours to resolve the confusion of everyday life by imposing a doctrine that gives total and unbreakable shape to all relationships. Gallant first offers a portrait of a Fascist in **"Señor Pinedo"** (1954), a story of postwar Spain that arose from her two-year stay in Madrid. It was not, however, until the early 1960s that she finally managed to overcome her repugnance for the German past, and travelled to Germany itself to begin her analysis in earnest. For Gallant it was particularly important to see Germany firsthand before she wrote about it, since she was convinced that she must understand the German motives for embracing fascism. She has commented that "the victims, the survivors that is, would probably not be able to tell us anything, except for the description of life at point zero." She felt convinced, however, that if she could penetrate the nuances of "every day living" in Germany, she would find "the origin of the worm—the worm that had destroyed the structure" ("An Interview" 39, 40).

Gallant has mentioned that the crucial events that finally allowed her to travel to Germany were "The colonial wars of the fifties and sixties." Living much of the time in France, Gallant had ready access to news of the wars in both Indochina and Algeria. These reports showed that the Nazis held no monopoly on barbarism, that "civilization was no barrier anywhere" ("An Interview" 40). Thus, when Gallant finally began visiting Germany after de Gaulle ended the Algerian War, it was possible for her to write about the German situation with some detachment.

As a result of her travels in Germany, Gallant realized that after the war a large proportion of the nation's people had chosen to forget Germany's past and begin life afresh. Even today it is possible to find Germans who fought in World War II behaving as if the Hitler period had never existed. According to such people, the way things are at present is the way they have always been. While this mass amnesia helped produce the German economic miracle of the 1950s and 1960s, since it allowed people to concentrate on rebuilding the nation, it also permitted unexorcized ghosts and demons from the time of the Third Reich to haunt the collective psyche. In stories such as **"The Latehomecomer,"** Gallant explores a virtual state of national schizophrenia by juxtaposing past and present, allowing the reader to watch as people in the present unwittingly renew past fascist forms.[1]

During the 1960s and 1970s, Gallant wrote nine stories centring on the German question. Since it is impossible to do justice to all nine in the space available, the two related stories, **"Ernst in Civilian Clothes"** and **"Willi"** (both published in 1963), have been chosen as paradigms.[2] These two stories hold particular interest because they deal with soldiers who served under the führer, and who must come to terms with their experience of having fought for the ideals of the Third Reich. **"Willi"** and **Ernst in Civilian Clothes** also offer us an excellent opportunity to study Gallant's evolving technique. **"Willi,"** the first of Gallant's German stories, rarely departs from the straightforward, linear style of her early European fiction. Although published less than a year after **"Willi,"** **"Ernst in Civilian Clothes"**

is an example of Gallant's most mature work; it shows us how the seemingly solid surfaces of the present are wormed into and convulsed by the German past.

Both stories develop the same basic situation: two German ex-soldiers, Willi and Ernst, find themselves, in the 1960s, living in France, rootless, and somehow unattached to the present. Taken prisoner at the end of the war, they do not return immediately to Germany, and do not, therefore, participate in the postwar "unlearning" of the fascist past.

The advantages of this "latehomecomer" situation to a writer involved in social exploration should be obvious.[3] As Gallant learned at the end of the war when she was a reporter for the Montreal *Standard,* most people saw fascism as brutish, repressive terror. Yet such a view makes it virtually impossible to understand why a large proportion of the German population would flock to the fascist cause. In **"Willi,"** however, Gallant portrays events from the point of view of a "latehomecomer" who has kept his old national socialist ideals alive. Looking through Willi's eyes, the reader learns with some astonishment that it is possible to prefer the Third Reich to the new federal republic. The French keep Willi a prisoner of war until 1948. On his return to Germany, he grows increasingly contemptuous of his countrymen for relinquishing all ideals for the sake of affluence. One of his sisters has an American boyfriend, and over the years the entire family becomes as "happy as seals around a rich new brother-in-law, a builder in Stuttgart." Disgusted with Germany's new obsession with surfaces, Willi has returned to live in France: "He doesn't like the French better than he does the Germans; he just despises them less" (29).

Through Willi, Gallant brings out the features of fascism that made it so appealing to German youth in the 1930s. Willi has been, and still is, attracted to fascism because of its ideals of health, beauty, and loyalty—its belief that humanity should live for something beyond mere material gain.[4] Everything about Willi belies the conventional film version of the German soldier. A kind, gentle man, he has gone out of his way to help his friend Ernst, supplying him with a new suit of clothing and allowing Ernst to stay in his apartment. Gallant is not, of course, attempting to deny the repression and violence inherent in Nazism, but to show that any picture of the Third Reich that emphasizes only its brutality must be profoundly misleading. Such a picture fails to show how national socialism could attract the many idealistic young people, such as Willi, who thronged to its banner as a way of creating a better life. Willi finds that accepted opinion condemns the Third Reich and all it stood for, while applauding Germany's new economic success. Yet Willi finds life empty in a society lacking national socialist ideals. The new Germany, with its emphasis on money and success, appears to him as vulgarity and greed incarnate.

Having convinced the reader of the fascination of fascism for Willi, an idealistic young man, Gallant proceeds to show the effect of fascist idealism on his life. Realizing that most people learn about fascism through films, she portrays Willi in Paris working as a consultant, providing details about the German army for directors shooting French films about the war. Willi teaches the young extras, often German students, how to sing and march, how to wear their uniforms, how to be German in the old tradition. He approaches his film job with the same kind of zeal he gave to his soldiering. When the students do not take their jobs seriously, laughing and clowning, Willi shouts in exasperation: "When I think I was ready to die for *you!*" (29). The effect is a double exposure. We see Willi on the film set teaching students to act like good Nazis with all the zeal he formerly gave to being a good Nazi soldier himself. Then he did not question Hitler's ideal; now he does not question its applicability to the film. He never stops to think about the new generation's casual attitude to work, its tendency to turn jobs into play. He simply dismisses it as irresponsible. In fact, he enters into the illusion of the film. He is treating postwar German students, in Paris, as though they were recruits for the Third Reich's Wehrmacht. Willi's life, we come to realize, has been a perpetual training program to work on a film set. Willi can never be himself; he always *acts* for a larger end, never realizing that his life thereby becomes theatre: an abstraction from life.

Because Willi can devote himself equally well to the war effort and to the making of films, one might think that Gallant is hinting at opportunism. Yet, to assume that would be to miss the point. Willi still believes that national socialism stood for simple moral ideals. For Willi, those ideals were not propaganda, but truth. He still does not smoke or drink, and delights in recollecting the old days, when "health was glory and he was taught something decent about girls" (29). Yet this kind of abstract idealism leaves the individual separated from everyday events, and completely unable to deal with life. For example, Willi has never married. In fact he cannot even bring himself to talk about the subject openly: "He sometimes meets a girl and hopes something will come of it—he is still looking for that—but he has never been sure he had the right girl" (29). Willi does not say that he wants sex or romance or a companion or marriage or a home, but refers to the entire subject as "it" and "that." In Willi, Gallant gives a comic-pathetic turn to the quality of naïve heroism associated with sculpture and painting in the Third Reich.[5]

To demonstrate how such pristine idealism can be easily perverted, as it was into the actual violence of police arrests and torture in the Third Reich, Gallant shows us a further development in Willi's filmmaking. When an acting job as an SS officer becomes available, Willi obtains it for his friend Ernst. This is by no means easy, since Ernst is "brown-haired and slight"; he does not at all conform to the film image of a member of the German military elite. How, then, do image and reality coincide? At first only in a lie, for Willi gains the job for Ernst by falsely representing him as a former German officer.

Even after shooting for the film begins, image and reality refuse to converge. When Ernst is supposed to push the actor playing the part of the Jewish professor, he has so much respect for the idea of a professor that he apologizes with each shove. By confusing the film with reality, Ernst reveals himself as a genuinely kind, respectful person who would have great difficulty in hurting anyone: "Ernst has too much respect for the professor. Ernst wouldn't hurt a fly. Somebody must have hurt a fly once, or they wouldn't keep on making these movies. But it wasn't Willi or Ernst" (30). Only when Willi worries that Ernst will lose the job, and urges him on with the thought that a good performance might expedite his long-awaited pension, does Ernst take courage and give the actor playing the professor a hard push. In fact, the push proves so effective that the actor stumbles and drops the loaf of bread he carries as a prop. Suddenly the scene becomes real: the "professor" is startled, his "wife" cries out, and they both struggle to retrieve the bread, which has been dropped "on the dirty pavement" (30).

The incident has suddenly taken on reality because Ernst has finally managed to play his role properly. He has become capable of cruelty. Indeed, a disagreement ensues between the director and his staff over whether the scene may not be "overdone" (30). The quickness with which Ernst succeeds in playing an SS officer reveals what might have happened under national socialism had Ernst been compelled to do something his gentle nature rejected. While it is true that Willi encourages Ernst with the thought of his pension, this makes the scene even more similar to what happened under the Third Reich, where people such as Ernst quickly learned the conduct required to survive.

Although the film scene suggests the way in which gentle idealism can be twisted into brutality, Gallant does not end the story with Ernst's successful push. To do so would only be to suggest that human beings contain a hidden reservoir of animal instincts that flows out when the restraints of civilization are loosened. This is certainly a common enough explanation of fascism, and Gallant offers a glimpse of latent brutality in Ernst. But she goes a step further to show that the dehumanized conditions necessary for the unleashing of such brutality are implicit in the apparently pure ideals themselves.

As we saw earlier, Willi's idealism leads him to treat women as abstractions rather than as people. In the final scene, Gallant develops the consequences of this idea when she portrays Willi attempting to win a young woman. Still steeped in his fascist ideals, Willi wants the unnamed girl to personify virginal purity: "it is always the same girl, the one they told him once he was going to have to defend" (30). But the girl does not want to be treated as a figure of purity. When Willi arrives at her parents' house, she brings him "ice and whiskey on a tray." She is "proud to be entertaining a man," and clearly wants Willi to play the part of the worldly male. When Willi, who does not drink, proves unable to fulfil these expectations, the girl begins to sulk, and this leads Willi to ask a "stupid" question: "Don't you like me?" The question is not stupid in itself; the stupidity lies in its timing: "He always asks too soon, and the failure begins there." By showing his vulnerability, he lets the girl know that "she could be cruel" (30). Willi's idealism has failed to take account of the sexual politics involved in male-female relationships, the fact that sexuality involves power. His naïvety permits cruelty to surface.

What Gallant outlines briefly in **"Willi"** about sexual politics, she develops more fully in her later German stories, especially **"The Latehomecomer."** As Gallant sees it, the sexual and marital relations between men and women act as an engine of social relations in the larger political sphere. Women serve men, but expect in return a share in the benefits of male economic power and security. Men expect to find in women servants and paragons of virtue. Not only does this create a class structure that divides men and women, it also tends to polarize power and virtue. When the two forces become separated, people are left unable to deal with everyday events, except in terms of absolute ideals. The result is that power tends towards tyranny and virtue towards passivity, the ideal conditions for an authoritarian state.

Gallant underlines the role of power in sexuality when Willi inadvertently mentions that his brother-in-law "has a bathroom tiled" with "lapis lazuli." The cost of the precious stone so impresses the girl that she immediately assumes that anyone so rich must be a *"gangster"* (30, 31). This misconception makes Willi appear mysterious and dangerous to the girl, and thus romantically appealing. Once again, the situation becomes charged with energy, and Willi recognizes that he has been given "the upper hand" (31). The ex-Wehrmacht German has been given power, has been invited to act the part of a gangster. The incident shows the dialectic at the heart of an abstract idealism such as fascism. Where Willi wants the girl to be pure goodness, the girl wants Willi to embody darkness and evil; Gallant suggests that on one level, the search for absolute purity gives rise to its opposite—corruption. Were Willi to accept the power being offered to him as the sexual complement to his idealism, he would be well on his way to playing the part of tyrant in a personal relationship.

His rejection of power, however, contains implications that prove equally dangerous—if not more so, because they are more subtle and consistent with Willi's high-mindedness. When he discovers that the girl finds him attractive because of his supposed relation to a gangster, he simply rejects her. He remains faithful to his ideal, refusing to engage in the game of life: "He has waited so long he must be certain; he has waited too long to afford a mistake." Unable to make the ideal incarnate, Willi walks away from life altogether. Towards the story's conclusion, we are told: "He didn't see the girl again" (31).[6] The decent, comic-pathetic little hero is as unable to respond to real human relationships as the superficial, money-grabbing kin of whom he complains, or the ordinary postwar girl who can find him attractive only as a gangster.

The gangster reference points to the larger, more public dimension of the destructive compartmentalization attendant upon a conservative idealism such as Willi's. As Hannah Arendt argues in her study of Adolf Eichmann and "the banality of evil," people all too often oversimplify fascism when they claim that Eichmann was a brutal gangster (41-42). They miss the point of Eichmann's idealism, and fail to see that his idealism made it possible for him to detach himself from the world, thereby authorizing the deaths of millions. One cannot help seeing similarities between Eichmann's banal idealism and Willi's, although Gallant is not, of course, dealing with public figures such as Eichmann. Willi lacks the force of character to administer genocide. He is the "willee" rather than the "willer." But his actions indicate how events on the larger political field were made possible by the desire of ordinary people to see their lives, and those of others, in terms of ideals. Indeed, our witnessing the effects of fascist ideals in domestic situations where they do not trigger immediate moral revulsion allows us to see both their appeal and their hazards for people everywhere.

As Gallant's metaphor of the cinema reveals, the purity of Willi's need to see people in terms of ideals results in the transformation of people into celluloid abstractions. When people resist such a use, as inevitably they must, he cannot reevaluate the ideals; he cannot rise to the challenge by engaging in the give-and-take of ordinary relationships. Instead, he walks away from real life, all the while desperately wanting the ideal film to continue playing. He is profoundly disappointed and lonely, but only because those who are unworthy in his scheme of things cease to exist for him as real people as surely as did the victims of Hitler's "final solution." The ease with which all this occurs in everyday situations makes it evident that everyday life could in fact assume the features of cinematic nightmare, or holocaust, under the direction of a suitably demagogic leader. In the end, then, Willi's idealism, which appears positive on the surface, proves damaging to himself and, given the right circumstances, could be even more damaging to others.

Although Ernst plays a relatively small role in the story **"Willi,"** Gallant recognized the potential inherent in his chameleon character, and devoted her next-published German story, **"Ernst in Civilian Clothes,"** to his history. In doing so, she retains a minor role for Willi in **"Ernst in Civilian Clothes."** Yet the new story possesses a far more complex narrative structure, with the histories of Ernst and Willi crossing and recrossing, allowing Gallant to develop the two ex-soldiers as opposing poles of the same conservative impulse. With **"Ernst in Civilian Clothes,"** she also overcomes one of the main weaknesses of **"Willi."** Despite its theme of fascism in ordinary life, the linear narrative style of **"Willi"** distances the reader from the past, and leaves the impression that the fascist era is something that can now be discussed and labelled as over. Although **"Willi"** shows clearly enough the potential dangers that fascist idealism holds for society, by the story's end, the reader could be excused for believing that the Third Reich had been safely buried in history. In **"Ernst in Civilian Clothes,"** however, the narrative moves the reader continually between past and present, its fluidity deconstructing our normal sense of a present firmly situated in the here and now. Once the seemingly stable present crumbles, it becomes apparent that fascism cannot simply be seen as a series of events locked away in the past, but must be recognized, with frightening teleological immediacy, as a pattern of habits and assumptions that continue into the present. As Gallant shows, no one, not even the reader, can entirely escape the insidious influence of fascism's small possibilities in people.

Although the idea of deconstruction might seem to link Gallant to the American postmodernist fiction writers of the 1960s and 1970s, in fact Gallant never intrudes as narrator to break the illusion that the story is an objective record.[7] Her notion of demystification has more in common with the style of Continental writers, and in particular Bertolt Brecht's *Verfremdung* devices. As will be recalled, Brecht did not want his audience either to lose themselves in the reality behind the proscenium arch, or to remain completely detached, alienated. His audiences were meant to enjoy the alternative reality, but also to find it unfamiliar—unsettling—so that they might return, changed, to their daily lives. To achieve this double effect, Brecht created "a representation . . . which allows us to recognize its subject, but at the same time makes it seem unfamiliar" (88).

Gallant takes this idea of defamiliarization one stage further when she begins **"Ernst in Civilian Clothes"** by immersing both her principal character and the reader in a version of everyday life that appears altogether unfamiliar. Having been in the military, cut off from civilian life for some 30 years, Ernst now finds himself in no-man's-land, and must make his way over to the other side where daily life seems normal and familiar. Gallant begins with a filmic pan around one of Paris's more dilapidated apartment courtyards. Ernst opens a window onto a world that is *there* in all its physicality, but that lies out of reach, dislocated. Life behind the other windows is "implicit in its privacy." Ernst does not see neighbours, even people, but "Forms . . . poised at stove and table, before mirrors, insolently unconcerned with Ernst." The familiar has become abstract. Time has frozen: "the afternoon sky has not changed since he last glanced at it a day or two ago" (131). Like Willi in the earlier story, Ernst is also alienated. But where Willi clings to an idealist identity, Ernst's identity "dissolve[s]" in existential experience. Gallant's metaphors of solidity give way to the fluid: Ernst's trouser bottoms "slide to his calf" when he sits down, and he remains tenuously "afloat" in the stream of events (132). Homeless, he lives in Willi's room, wearing clothes borrowed for him by Willi. The only things that make him seem "anchored" are his military boots, which have been "unsuccessfully camouflaged" to look civilian (132). Ernst is clearly unsettled, and the effect on the reader is likewise unsettling.

From the story's outset, Gallant establishes the unease of a military presence masquerading in civilian dress, and thus leads the reader to look beneath the surfaces of everyday life. As the story unrolls, we learn that Ernst has lived virtually his entire life in the military: first in the Hitler Jugend, then the German Army, and finally the French foreign legion. The military, which gave structure to his life, has suddenly dismissed him, and he finds himself in a watery present where objects lack their normal solidity and outlines. In Martin Heidegger's term, he is *geworfen,* or thrown, into the present.

Gallant has commented that she began the story after learning that the French foreign legion had, in the interest of economy, discharged a large number of its men at the end of the Algerian War (personal interview).[8] This move was disastrous for most of the legionnaires, since it left them homeless. In Ernst's case, the legion fails even to supply the promised pension. As Gallant saw the situation, it was outrageously shabby treatment on France's part. Yet as she began to develop Ernst, the ex-German soldier, it became evident that the telling of his story could reveal not only the callousness of the legion (which figures as one of many betrayals), but could also open up the present for the reader, revealing its sources in a dark and monstrous past. Instead of seeing the present as something organically whole, ineluctably given, Ernst, the man of dissolved identity, sees things disjointedly as he emerges from one reality—the military—into another—civilian life. His perspective acts as a solvent upon the surfaces of the seemingly solid postwar world.

To emphasize the extent to which Ernst stands outside the reality assumed by civilian society, Gallant underlines the metaphysical implications of his dilemma as an ex-legionnaire. He possesses no self as such, except that given by his identity papers:

> The document has it that he is Ernst Zimmermann, born in 1927, in Mainz. If he were to lose that paper, he would not expect any normal policeman to accept his word of honor. He is not likely to forget his own name, but he could, if cornered, forget the connection between an uncertified name and himself. Fortunately, his identification is given substance by a round purple stamp on which one can read *Préfecture de Police*.
>
> (132-33)

Having as his only "substance" the purple police stamp, and finding it easy to forget the connections between his name and himself, Ernst, a latehomecomer, discovers not only society but his own self to be alien and unpredictable. In a sense, then, **"Ernst in Civilian Clothes"** emerges as an ironic version of the conventional bildungsroman. Ernst begins with no identity of his own save that stamped on him by society. From this point he must create a new self by learning about the world. Yet Gallant gives a savage twist to the genre when she portrays Ernst, not as an intense and sensitive youth, but as an ex-soldier who wants only to learn the rules of the game in order to survive. As such, he stands in direct contrast to puritan, idealist Willi.

What Ernst does, in a rather stumbling way, throughout the few hours covered in the story, reflects what all of Europe did after 1945, when it took upon itself the task of rebuilding civilization and finding a new rationale for itself. But Ernst's search for a new self in the early 1960s does not merely reflect the route taken by Europe in 1945, it also offers a critique of that route. Released unwillingly from the military in 1963, 18 years after the end of World War II, Ernst finds a new society already intact, one that he must try to join. Yet every step he takes to answer the question "What is Ernst?" leads to the conclusion that the social world is precariously hollow and unable to give him substance.

In reconstructing himself as a civilian, Ernst must first decide on a nationality. Normally, of course, nationality is a given, but when Ernst reflects on his nationality he faces the same problem faced by Europeans in 1945 when boundaries shifted: "He does not know if he is German or Austrian. His mother was Austrian and his stepfather was German. He was born before Austria became Germany, but when he was taken prisoner by the Americans in April, 1945, Austria and Germany were one" (133). Ernst's confusion reminds us that what now appear to be stable, enduring boundaries are of very recent making. More than that, however, as he attempts to fulfil his need to choose a nation, the inherent absurdity of nationalism in the postwar situation is revealed:

> He looks at the railway posters with which Willi has decorated the room, and in a resolution that must bear a date (January 28, 1963) he decides, My Country. A new patriotism, drained from the Legion, flows over a field of daffodils, the casino at Baden-Baden, a gingerbread house, part of the harbor at Hamburg, and a couple of sea gulls.
>
> (133)

In pledging allegiance to vapid railway posters, Ernst brings out the lack of substance in German nationalism. After the war, almost everyone agreed that nationalism was an evil. The very name national socialism made it impossible to speak of nationalism in positive terms. Ashamed of their past, most Germans declared themselves finished with nationalism. By the time Ernst leaves the legion in 1963, moreover, Germany has been split into the Federal Republic and the German Democratic Republic, with the West Germans refusing to admit the East's separate political reality, and being forced to build their own national identity from innocuous images.[9]

When Ernst says to himself "My Country," he sees the nation's heraldry in terms of a "field of daffodils" resplendent with touristic images, such as Bavarian houses, and even "a couple of sea gulls"—perhaps an unwitting recognition of the scavenging impulse that has gone into creating the new national identity. Thus, in choosing such a nation, Ernst gains not substance, but pretty images served up for commercial purposes. Its reduction to slick tourism does not, however, make nationalism any the less important—or dangerous. If Ernst makes the wrong choice he could find himself in jeopardy: "Austrians are not allowed to join the Foreign Legion. If he were Austrian now and tried to live in Austria, he might be in serious trouble" (133). As Ernst discovers, postwar nationalism may offer no real substance but it still carries all the punitive divisiveness of former nationalisms.

The search for employment proves as unhelpful as the search for nationalism in providing Ernst with a solid social structure of identity. In **"Willi,"** Gallant introduces the idea of a work ethic without moral value. In **"Ernst in Civilian Clothes,"** she develops this idea further, through the character of Willi's brother-in-law, the vulgar capitalist, when she has Willi write to him to obtain a job for Ernst. Naturally enough, Willi gives assurances that Ernst has not deserted, that his papers are in order. But in the 1960s, Germany's economic miracle is in full bloom, and Willi's brother-in-law, a builder, needs all the workers he can obtain. He replies that "even if Ernst is a deserter he will take him on" (133).[10] Gallant suggests here that in the booming 1960s, Germany finds it unnecessary to search the past for moral certitude. Bottom-line materialism brooks no unsettling questions. Everyone in Germany has begun again, bringing the nation riches, the implication being that Ernst should forget about his wartime service to Germany and France, and take whatever shape the economic climate demands.[11] (The recent case of Kurt Waldheim, former secretary-general of the United Nations, testifies to the accuracy of Gallant's insight.)

As can be seen, the assumptions behind Ernst's first job offer are not conducive to a sense of security and a solid identity. The brother-in-law's letter perplexes Ernst: "What use are papers if the first person you deal with as a civilian does not ask to see even copies of them?" (133). An economic system that does not ask any questions during a period of prosperity is not likely to offer aid and comfort when the prosperity ends. The situation described differs little from that of the 1920s, a point Gallant underlines when she mentions that Ernst "looks shabby and unemployed, like the pictures of men in German street crowds before the Hitler time" (135). In fact, the main thing that joining the Hitler Jugend meant to him and his family was "a great saving in clothes" (135). While Germany wants to forget its past, Ernst's very presence reminds one of the lack of individual security and firm public direction that, after 1929, led Germans to flock to the promises of national socialism.

Ernst's late return to civilian life, his dismissal from the legion with no profession, no skills—"nothing" (135)—offers a fugitive's perspective on the state of modern Europe and the plight of all Europeans who, for one reason or another, lost their place in the order of things after the Second World War. By setting the story on the rue de Lille, Gallant revisits with heightened intensity the broad social base established in some of her earlier stories, such as **"The Other Paris"** and **"Autumn Day."** **"Ernst in Civilian Clothes"** includes not only the two German ex-soldiers, who have been left homeless after the war, but also the French poor who are virtually prisoners in their own country. Ironically, their lives resemble those of Willi and Ernst, the enemy war veterans. Indeed, the story's setting suggests that parts of Paris are more like prisoner-of-war camps than the havens of love and laughter suggested by sentimental clichés. It is a hard winter, "the coldest since 1880," and the poor are to be given "fifty kilos of free coal" as well as some free gas for cooking and heating "until March 31st" (142). That the poor receive free coal and gas says something about the government's largess, but more about the economic plight of the have-nots.[12] The poor also have trouble getting food, and Willi finds that "The only vegetables on public sale that morning were frozen Brussels sprouts" (140)—sprouts being one of the common wartime foodstuffs.

Through the lives of Ernst and Willi, Gallant brings out the vast difference between high and low cultures, illuminating some of the irreducible ambiguities of postwar existence, where Willi's neighbour can first complain about the lack of food, and then invite a friend down to watch *"L'Homme du xxe Siècle"* on television (138). In the course of the story, we see more and more clearly the wide gap between the culture of France and the actual living conditions of many of the people. More important still is Gallant's perception that the people themselves do not recognize the differences. Strangely enough, the poor even manage to identify with the image of twentieth-century man produced by high culture, and do not see that the difficulties of their own lives contradict such media images. The Germans, one is reminded, looked to Hitler's version of the Superman as a means of escaping their difficulties.

As has been noted, Gallant's technique extends the deconstruction of conventional views from the present into the past. This allows the reader to reexamine assumptions about World War II. By the 1960s, World War II has, for most people, settled into memory, with fascist Germany seen as an aberration. But as Ernst sits idly in Willi's Paris apartment waiting to return to Germany, he finds the past surfacing in image and anecdote to confute such assumptions. For example, when Ernst and Willi are captured by the armies of liberation, they are told they are uniquely evil, that they will have to pay for the rest of their lives. Their guards tell them: "You have lost the war. You are not ordinary prisoners. You may never go home again" (141). In other words, the liberators assume the Germans will be kept as conscript workers forever. Willi "says to this day that the Americans sold their prisoners at one thousand five hundred francs a head." Although such sales were not officially sanctioned, they still occurred, the Americans wanting the money, the French wanting the workers.[13] "Ernst finds such suppositions taxing" (134), and chooses not to think about them, for, if they are true, then the allies bought and sold Germans just as the Germans bought and sold Jews. In this respect, **"Ernst in Civilian Clothes"** reminds one of Joseph Heller's *Catch-22,* in which the character of Milo Minderbinder is used to dismantle comfortable assumptions about the United States's moral superiority in World War II.

Gallant's deconstruction may be less flamboyant than Heller's, but it is also more extensive, since it forces the reader to see the war as continuing into the present. Officially the war ended in 1945, but Ernst is finally demobbed only in the 1960s, and during this interval he has been fighting continuously—for France. From Ernst's standpoint, it matters little which nation he chooses: "He has fought for Germany and for France and, according to what he has been told each time, for civilization" (135). For the reader, it comes as a shock to find France's colonial wars placed in the same category as Germany's war. The popular wisdom maintains that the Germans were evil and the French good. Yet Ernst's experience in fighting for both Germany and France provides a different set of contours to modern history. Both the Germans and the French told their soldiers that their wars were "for civilization." In times of war, such slogans often seem to make perfectly good sense. But Ernst, attempting to find a place for himself in the civilization for which he has fought, shows that whether or not one ends on the winning side of any given war, civilization does not extend very far among the disadvantaged.

Ernst's sudden appearance in civilian clothes also brings to light the processes by which people distance themselves from, and rewrite the past in order to make their present safe. Ernst discovers, while reading a newspaper, that it is the twentieth anniversary of the end of the struggle for Stalingrad. The newspaper "is full of it," with the battle being treated in such a way that "it seems a defeat all around, and a man with a dull memory, like Ernst, can easily think that France and Germany fought on the same side twenty years ago" (143). The battle for Stalingrad was of course a major defeat for Germany, a victory for the Russians, and a crucial turning point in the war. In 1963, however, in the middle of the Cold War, the West is no longer allied to Russia, but to Germany. In order to bring the past into line with the present, French newspapers distort history so that the Soviets as well as the Germans appear to have lost the battle. Whether by conscious distortion or not, the past is rewritten to bring it into accord with what the journalists think constitutes the present.[14] The grip of the present proves so strong that the general populace, many of whom lived through the war, willingly accept public distortion of their own experience.

Because Ernst does not yet exist as part of the communally established present, his mind can bring to the surface a wholly different image of Stalingrad to disprove the accepted interpretation: "On an uncrowded screen a line of ghosts shuffles in snow, limps through the triumphant city, and a water cart cleans the pavement their feet have touched" (144). Gallant does not say whether Ernst was present at Stalingrad (this is unlikely, given his age), and in fact the image seems to hang in the air, a glimpse into Europe's collective unconscious. Indeed, Gallant's refusal to offer a logical explanation for the appearance of Ernst's image of Stalingrad gives it a kind of visionary validity. The image simply appears when Ernst hears a song sung over the radio by Charles Aznavour, and is moved by it. Aznavour's love song, dwelling as the genre will on the inextricable mingling of pain and joy, provides the emotional trigger for this evocative image of Stalingrad. The beauty and power of the image shatter the newspaper's prosy revisionism. In place of "defeat all around" at Stalingrad, we have the almost sacramental moment of linked joy and suffering as the Russians cleanse their city of limping German ghosts. The image of the real past demands to be dealt with.

However, even though Ernst continually causes us, as readers, to reorient ourselves both to the present and the past, Gallant never allows her central character to become an ordering consciousness for the story. The image of Stalingrad may surface, but Ernst cannot use it to develop a historical narrative. Embodying the principle of radical change, Ernst survives by continually forgetting the past. For example, Willi has procured Ernst's civilian clothes and expects him to return them when Ernst begins working in Germany. But Ernst will forget everything: "His debts and obligations dissolve in his tears. Ernst's warm tears, his good health, and his poor memory are what keep him afloat" (132). Ernst can know things about the past, but his character does not allow him to organize such knowledge or see it as important. Ernst has "met young girls in Paris who think Dien Bien Phu was a French victory, and he has let them go on thinking it, because it is of no importance. Ernst was in Indo-China and knows it was a defeat" (144). Since Ernst's priority remains daily survival on an ad hoc basis, he proves incapable of shaping his experiences into a coherent historical picture.

Through Ernst, Gallant dramatizes the principle of extreme relativism that characterizes much of the post-Nietzschean age.[15] In one sense, he can be thought of as embodying the inchoate impulse of life to manifest itself in protean forms. As he copes with the present, various ways of ordering the world—through nationalism and the work ethic, or in a complete disjunction from the past—offer themselves as structuring principles. Their very number, however, breaks down the correctness of any particular view, and betrays their origins in ideology or propaganda.

In this chaos, Ernst's friend Willi continues to exemplify the conservative impulse to turn patterns of the mind into objective truths. In small, he echoes the central Hitlerian abuse of Nietzsche's notion of the *Übermensch*. Where Ernst is swamped with sensations, Willi attempts to turn lived experience into a kind of absolute Apollonian order: "Willi is always reading about the last war" and continually collects "evidence" in a series of scrapbooks. But no matter how hard he tries, Willi cannot arrive at a final judgement. He must wait for an authority, "the lucid, the wide-awake, and above all the rational person who will come out of the past and say with authority, 'This was true,' and 'This was not'" (143). Yet even as Willi waits in the present for the supreme judge to arrive, Gallant reveals the folly of such assumptions about history through the disjunctions of her story line. With no warning to the reader, Gallant suddenly announces that the story's one set of "attested facts"—the place and date of Ernst's birth as given on his identity papers—is false. Ernst was not born in Mainz as his papers indicate, but in the Voralberg. He has forgotten his exact age, and may be "either thirty-four or thirty-six." "Only his mother, if she is still living, and still cares, could make the essential corrections" (134). With such reversals, the narrative line convincingly undermines Willi's attempt to find absolute truths that exist independently of the biases inherent in any historical system.[16]

Throughout the course of the story, the reader has been urged to look behind such things as Ernst's purple police stamp to find the genuine crucible of present-day experience. In Ernst's case, it proves necessary to replace empirical and positivistic assumptions with a mythic vision:

> During one of the long, inexplicable halts on the mysterious voyage, where arrival and travelling were equally dreaded, another lad in man's uniform, standing crushed against Ernst, said, "We're in Mainz." "Well?" "Mainz is finished. There's nothing left." "How do you know? We can't see out," said Ernst. "There is nothing left anywhere for us," said the boy. "My father says this is the Apocalypse." What an idiot, Ernst felt; but later on, when he was asked where he came from, he said, without hesitating, and without remembering why, "Mainz."
>
> (134)

Having repressed the implications of what it means to name Mainz as his place of birth, Ernst carries with him a past that he fails to understand, perhaps chooses deliberately not to understand. He accepts the city of Mainz as mere geography, when it actually represents the Apocalypse. Consequently, he carries with him "attested facts" imbued with a meaning about which he knows nothing.

At about the same time Gallant published **"Ernst in Civilian Clothes,"** Theodor Adorno cautioned that West Germany, the Bundesrepublik, would never possess its own future if it continued to accept superficial assumptions about its origins: "Aufgearbeitet wäre die Vergangenheit erst dann, wenn die Ursachen des Vergangenen beseitigt wären" (29). Adorno argues that not until Germany begins to understand the causes of the past will the past become accessible and the nation achieve maturity. Where the Willies of the world assume that such an understanding of the past will be a straightforward search for facts, from a position of neutrality, Gallant shows that all positions in the present are irrevocably involved with, and tainted by, the fascism that is supposedly under investigation.

Because of the story's continual process of deconstruction, the reader often feels understandably disturbed by its atmosphere of hidden menace. In the postwar years, many travellers to Germany commented that the landscape itself seemed haunted by the ghosts of fascism. Gallant herself, as has been mentioned, found it impossible to travel in Germany for many years after the war, because of her feelings of repugnance for German fas-

cism. In this regard, Ernst, as a soldier masquerading in civilian clothes, evokes brilliantly the sense of a wartime spirit only partially transformed in the present. Monstrous shapes appear to lurk about him, and many of his comments and actions are charged with the menace of an unexorcized past. One has the impression that a terrible revelation is at hand. This feeling appears to be confirmed when Ernst reflects that, since the time he put on his Hitler Jugend uniform at age seven, he can recall only two occasions when he wore civilian clothes: when he was confirmed, and when he was "created a Werewolf" (135). This brief reference to a werewolf immediately conjures up images of animality, of a man transformed into a wolf. When Gallant then mentions that Ernst has followed a mother and child who live in a neighbouring apartment and take afternoon strolls together in the Jardin des Tuileries, the reader probably expects the worst. Ernst's reasoning is brutally pragmatic and wholly sexual: "Ernst followed this woman because she was fit for his attention. He would have sought a meeting somewhere, but the weather was against it" (138). Given the story's implication that it contains a hidden mystery about the dark past of fascism, it appears that Ernst will now appear as Nazi beast.

Yet even in the earlier story, **"Willi,"** Gallant has shown the assumptions behind such a view to be simplistic. The implication here is that Ernst, as a latehomecomer, brings his animality from the Nazi past into the present, which is assumed to be entirely civilized. Gallant allows the reader to make these conventional assumptions and then undermines them completely. Ernst's pursuit of the mother and child on their afternoon walk appears at first as a journey into the darkest period of the past, with Ernst as the werewolf at the centre of the labyrinth. The trees in the park metamorphose into statues; the "smoke of the blue charcoal fire was darker than the sky"; a "brave old maniac of a woman" rises out of "a sea of feeding pigeons" (136). Yet when the revelation arrives, Ernst does not himself metamorphose into a werewolf from the past. Instead, all of Paris in the present is transformed:

> The mother and child are engulfed and nearly trampled suddenly by released civil servants running away from their offices behind the Gare d'Orsay. They run as if there were lions behind them. It has never been as cold as this in Paris. . . . There are two policemen here to protect them, and there are traffic lights to be obeyed, but every person and every thing is submerged by the dark and the cold and the torrent of motorcars and a fear like a fear of lions.
>
> (137)

Where one expected to find only the particular instance of a woman and child fleeing before Ernst, one discovers all of Paris in flight. The image of darkness has been transferred from an individual to an entire society.

The ordinary restraints of a civil society, policemen, and traffic lights, have proven insufficient to protect the people from immersion in darkness and fear—"a fear like a fear of lions."

Through her image of flight, Gallant reveals the dark, hidden side of contemporary life, which so resembles the period during the 1930s when the fear of hidden forces caused people to flee to the apparent safety of national socialism. In literal terms, the scene shows Paris in the 1960s terrorized by uncontrolled automobile traffic, the lion rampant being the logo of the Peugeot automobile. The lions also recall the lions of the Roman spectacles, the implication being that Paris citizens feel themselves victims, trapped and overwhelmed by the modern world. The flight, the fear, proves most effective in evoking the violent and exploitative side of supposedly civilized French society.

That this image of public fear should surface even while Ernst as werewolf stalks the woman, appears altogether appropriate. Yet Gallant once again forces the reader to look behind the apparent reality of the situation. Far from infusing the vision of nightmare with any notion of individual viciousness or evil, Ernst remains indifferent to the darkness. When he grows tired of watching, he simply leaves the "child and the woman trembling on the curb," and returns to Willi's apartment (137). In Ernst we see no hatred, no fear, no emotion of any kind. He does not speculate about the situation; he simply immerses himself in it. In this case, he actually enters the traffic, and becomes part of it. He "threads his way across, against the light" (137). His attitude—that it does not matter, that it is of no importance—embodies powerfully the sense that everything has been reduced to a posture of survival. For Ernst it no longer makes sense to attempt to bestow meaning on the present.

Ernst's refusal of meaning, or at least indifference to it, will seem to many even more monstrous than the kind of violence and brutality that might earlier have been thought to be a part of Ernst's supposed werewolf personality. Humankind, the philosophers have repeatedly told us, achieves its humanity by imbuing the raw stratum of existence with meaning, not by immersing itself in it, uncaringly. Yet at this crucial moment, Gallant opens a window onto Ernst's werewolf past, enlarging and clarifying the very meaning of the word. She reveals that Ernst is not uncaring because he is a monster, but because monstrous things happened to him in his wartime youth. In a sense Ernst is a monster, for he "lay on the ground vomiting grass, bark, and other foods he had eaten" (142). But he is also a frightened adolescent who, at the end of the war, attempts to return to his mother:

> He walked all one night to the town where his mother and stepfather were. The door was locked, because the forced-labor camps were open now and ghosts in rags

were abroad and people were frightened of them. His mother opened the door a crack when she recognized the Werewolf's voice (but not his face or his disguise) and she said, "You can't stay here." There was a smell of burning. They were burning his stepfather's S.S. uniform in the cellar. Ernst's mother kissed him, but he had already turned away. The missed embrace was a salute to the frightening night, and she shut the door on her son and went back to her husband. Even if she had offered him food, he could not have swallowed. His throat closed on his breath. He could not swallow his own spit. He cannot now remember his own age or what she was like. He is either thirty-four or thirty-six, and born in Mainz.

(142-43)

As the past comes into focus, it becomes apparent that Ernst is not the mythical werewolf of medieval times, but a former member of a guerrilla force, the Werewolves, organized by Himmler at the end of the war when defeat was certain. Armed young boys were told to put on civilian clothes, destroy their identification papers, and then sabotage the approaching allied armies. A Werewolf he might be, but at age 16 Ernst follows his human instincts to return to his mother for help. Ironically, his mother and stepfather are too deeply implicated in the SS, and too frightened, to help him. Being left with no regiment, uniform, papers, or parents, Ernst is effectively robbed of everything that might give his world form. In choosing to live for the present only, intent upon fulfilling his animal needs for food, shelter, and sex, Ernst behaves as honestly as possible in the aftermath of his apocalypse.

Gallant's introduction of material about the Werewolves illustrates, through the story line, how easy it has become—even for the reader—to accept propagandistic legends about the war as truth. It is comforting to think that Nazis were literally capable of becoming wild animals, for if that is true, then civilized people cannot become Nazis. This type of thinking did in fact occur during and immediately after the end of the war. The need to explain away the evil enemy was so great that Nazi propaganda was accepted at face value. H. R. Trevor-Roper mentions that "The usurpation of Radio Werewolf by Goebbels is responsible for many of the popular misconceptions about the Werewolves . . ." (46). Clearly the propaganda was believed because it fulfilled existing expectations about Nazi soldiers.

Near the story's end, Gallant gives a final twist to her development of the Werewolf material as illustration of the process by which the complexity of past and present is reduced to a single barbaric image. Having allowed readers to dupe themselves into thinking Nazi soldiers were man-beasts, Gallant returns to the subject (permitting embarrassed readers some comfort) by showing a supposed authority on the subject making the same error. In leafing through one of Willi's scrapbooks about the war, Ernst finds an article by an "eminent author" in which "it is claimed that young Werewolves were animals. Their training had lowered the barrier between wolves and men. Witnesses heard them howling in the night" (145). Recognizing that this information is false, Ernst smiles, but Gallant notes that such a smile on the face of a German ex-soldier will simply be taken as further proof of the existence of Werewolves:

> He grins, suddenly, reading, without knowing he has shown his teeth. If he were seen at this moment, an element of folklore would begin to seep through Europe, where history becomes folklore in a generation: "On the rue de Lille, a man of either thirty-six or thirty-four, masquerading in civilian clothes, became a wolf." He reads: "Witnesses saw them eating babies and tearing live chickens apart."
>
> (145)

Taking their cue from eminent authorities and propagandists, the general public continues to manufacture horror stories about Werewolves, turning history into folklore before our eyes.

To the reader newly humbled by Gallant's stratagems, Ernst may still appear dangerous, but no more dangerous than the ordinary people who misinterpret the past to keep the present safe. Ernst, we realize, has been seeking security ever since he was made a Werewolf. He seeks it, not because he is a monster, but because, when his officers ordered him to become a Werewolf in civilian clothes, he lost his identity, lost everything that would entitle him to be treated as a prisoner of war. Now that he is again in civilian clothes, this time in Paris, he experiences the unsettling realization that those civilian clothes still offer him no form and meaning. France and Germany are once again civilized, as that term is commonly understood, but so-called civilization still regards itself as able to dismiss people such as Ernst who were called on to fight for its survival. That Ernst could fight for the Third Reich and present-day France and be left destitute by both indicates that the entire concept of civilization is suspect. It is no longer enough to ask why civilization, in its traditional forms of philosophy, art, and religion, failed to hold fast against the Nazis. Gallant now asks if civilization itself is not the culprit.

To this end, Gallant turns inwards to everyday family life in Paris. Through walls thin as paper, Ernst overhears everything that occurs in the neighbouring apartment, and learns that the daily ritual itself causes violence. Family life begins ordinarily enough in the morning, with the husband going off to work, the mother preparing the meals, and the child leaving for school. However, as the daily cycle continues, a tone of aggression soon creeps into the mother's voice. No particular problem appears, but love has clearly been replaced by a sense of imprisonment in the daily round of shopping, cooking, and child care. By noon, the endless boredom of this routine has the mother screaming at the child, demanding that he obey. By afternoon the beatings have begun:

> In the evening the voice climbs still higher. "You will see, when your father comes home!" It is a bird shrieking. Whatever the child has done or said is so monstrously disobedient that she cannot wait for the father to arrive. She has to chase the child and catch him before she can beat him. There is the noise of running, a chair knocked down, something like marbles, perhaps the chestnuts, rolling on the floor. "You *will* obey me!" It is a promise of the future now. The caught child screams. If the house were burning, if there were lions on the stairs, he could not scream more. All round the court the neighbours stay well away from their windows. It is no one's concern. When his mother beats him, the child calls for help, and calls *"Maman."* His true mother will surely arrive and take him away from his mother transformed. Who else can he appeal to? It makes sense. Ernst has heard grown men call for their mothers.
>
> (138-39)

Caught in a terrifying situation where his own mother has turned against him, the child has no recourse but to appeal to the very person beating him. It is nonsense but, as Ernst admits, it also makes sense, for the child has no one else. The alternative is to stop crying for help altogether, accept the mother's unjust authority, and become totally obedient. This is Ernst's own solution: "He did not learn a trade in the Foreign Legion, but he did learn to obey" (139). One is reminded here of the Kennedy children in **"A Day Like Any Other,"** left by their mother to their individual nightmares of eternal retribution.

In **"Ernst in Civilian Clothes,"** the child's crying could conceivably draw help from Ernst or one of the neighbours, or from society as a whole, but everyone around assumes the rightness of such punishment. Ernst shows no compassion; his experience in the legion makes it easy for him to rationalize the situation: "He knows about submission and punishment and justice and power. He knows what the child does not know—that the screaming will stop, that everything ends" (139). While Ernst's response may be that of the so-called realist, in fact Gallant questions the conventional wisdom that says "everything ends" when, at the story's conclusion, she portrays Ernst during one of his recurrent dreams—a soldier making a search of a flooded cellar:

> There is another victim in the cellar, calling *"Mutti,"* and it is his duty to find him and rescue him and drag him up to the light of day. He wades forward in the dark, and knows, in sleep, where it is no help to him, that the voice is his own.
>
> (147)

The parallel between Ernst and the small boy reveals that everything does *not* end, and that ordinary, civilized people carry the atmosphere or spirit of their society inside themselves to the ends of their lives. Ernst's disastrous life had its beginnings in circumstances similar to those of the unfortunate French boy. In the process of growing up, Ernst has repressed his need for Mutti's protection, but it still manifests itself in dreams and in his fear of a world without authority. In Gallant's depiction, the family becomes what Erich Fromm has called the *"psychological agent of society,"* teaching children lifelong attitudes that assure the permanence of authoritarianism (245). Gallant suggests that, without a change in the power structure of the conventional family, individuals will continue to mature by creating organizations like the ones Ernst willingly joins—the Hitler Jugend, the Wehrmacht, and the French Foreign Legion. Whether this cycle results in ordinary hopeless domestic woe, or the horrors perpetrated by the Nazis, may well be a matter of time and circumstance.

While it is possible to conclude on a large social scale that nothing ends, that the past always informs the present, on the smaller scale the individual must of course make decisions, must move into the future. Even Ernst must begin to give himself shape, and, in the final lines of the story, Gallant shows Ernst making the crucial decision: "He will believe only what *he* knows. It is a great decision in an important day. Life begins with facts: he is Ernst Zimmermann, ex-Legionnaire" (147). It is a brave boast, reminiscent of Sartre in its existential quality, but the entire story has shown the extent to which Ernst remains unwittingly defined by larger forces. Moreover, only a few lines before, Ernst announces that if everyone is lying, "he will invent his own truth" (147). Which of the alternatives are we to take as correct? Perhaps both. Gallant implies that it will be the lot of people such as Ernst, who imagine they can make a wholly fresh start by scraping away all the lies and uncertainties of their culture, to continue contradicting themselves. Ernst remains both the soldier searching for the child and the child himself. In fact, even as he makes his grand decision to be himself, Gallant allows us to overhear, in the last line of the story, "the child beaten by his mother" calling "*Maman, Maman*" (147). The reader hears the connection between "Mutti" and "Maman," but Ernst cannot. Ironically and pathetically, Ernst's striving to become an adult who believes only the facts leaves him in the condition of the child crying for protection.

It is a grim picture, not only of the fascism in everyday life, but of the difficulty of avoiding such oppression and beginning anew. Neither Willi in his absolutism nor Ernst in his relativism appears to offer a solution. Yet the story itself presents a third kind of intelligence, which goes beyond that of Ernst and Willi. As has been seen, **"Ernst in Civilian Clothes"** is by no means entirely nihilistic. Images such as those of Stalingrad and the Werewolf break through the veil of unknowing to connect past and present. In Gallant's narrative schema, the reader exists for moments in both the past and the present, and therefore perceives the past as it continues to exist unrecognized in the present—a perception for the most part unavailable to, or denied by the characters in the stories. Gallant's purpose is not to undermine the present with accounts of dark atrocities, but to make the past a part of the present, something real that must be declared and taken into account as individuals prepare to create the future. Her stories present themselves as archaeological encounters in which the seemingly fresh, ahistorical present is gradually stripped away to reveal layer upon layer of unrecognized past experience, all of which, Gallant suggests, recreates itself in daily life unless recognized and exposed.

This essay has considered only a few of Gallant's stories that depict the subversive influence of everyday fascism, a theme that has continued to interest her. Much of her recent collection, *Overhead in a Balloon: Stories of Paris* (1985), portrays the sense of disarray arising from a resurgence of right-wing politics in contemporary French society. Although these more recent stories indicate the need for basic reforms in the social structure, the solutions offered by her characters prove comically conservative and inadequate. The sense of a historical cycle from World War II to the present is brilliantly rendered, particularly in the four stories centering on Edouard and Magdalena, where Gallant shows how the mind turns away from individual and social reconstruction to pursue the trappings of power. Gallant leaves us with a picture of Western individuals refusing to look beyond their own constructions, imprisoned by their own minds.

Notes

1. "The Latehomecomer" appeared in the *New Yorker,* 8 July 1974—too late to be included in *The Pegnitz Junction.* It was collected in *From the Fifteenth District* (1979).

2. "Willi" remains uncollected. It appeared in the *New Yorker* (1963). Gallant collected "Ernst in Civilian Clothes" in *The Pegnitz Junction* (1973).

3. Stories about the "latehomecomer," or *Spätheimkehrer,* form an important minor genre in German fiction. Wolfgang Borchert's *Draussen vor der Tür* is one of the better known.

4. Susan Sontag offers additional insights into the appeal of fascism in "Fascinating Fascism."

5. For further information on the art of this period, see Berthold Hinz (156 ff.).

6. This struggle between *Geist* and *Welt* appears as a common theme in late nineteenth- and early twentieth-century German literature (Hamburger 87).

7. The term *deconstruction* is, nevertheless, worth retaining in connection with Gallant's fiction, since it points to her technique of unfolding apparently transparent ideas and language to reveal their highly ambiguous natures once the assumptions of a given cultural base stand revealed.

8. For further information on the moral impact of the Algerian war, see Dorothy Pickles (215).

9. Even now, many young Germans complain that they do not know what it means to be German.

10. One recalls that the industrialists in the early 1930s were willing to use anyone to help them gain their ends. Their most notorious employee was Hitler himself.

11. Ralf Dahrendorf quotes approvingly Schumpeter's phrase about capitalism in describing the whole of modern German society as "bathed in an economic light" (56).

12. John Ardagh describes the problems, many of which were economic, that led to the revolts of 1968 (31-95).

13. Information on this delicate subject of the sale of prisoners of war by Americans is difficult to find. One of the few articles on the subject is Arthur L. Smith, Jr.'s.

14. French radio and television are government controlled. Unlike most North American newspapers, which present their biases under the guise of objective reporting, French newspapers do not attempt neutral factual reporting, most articles being written from an openly editorial point of view.

15. It is not so well known that Nietzsche strongly opposed the growing nationalism and militarism in Germany at the end of the nineteenth century. See *The Gay Science* (160-62; sec. 104). For further information, see Erich Heller.

16. Compare Hayden White's arguments in "The Historical Text as Literary Artifact."

Works Cited

Adorno, Theodor. *Erziehung zur Mündigkeit*. Frankfurt: Suhrkamp, 1963.

Ardagh, John. *The New France: A Society in Transition 1945-1977*. 3rd. ed. Harmondsworth, Eng.: Penguin, 1977.

Arendt, Hannah. *Eichmann in Jerusalem: A Report on the Banality of Evil*. Rev. ed. New York: Viking, 1965.

Berger, Peter L., and Thomas Luckmann. *The Social Construction of Reality: A Treatise in the Sociology of Knowledge*. Garden City, NJ: Anchor-Doubleday, 1967.

Brecht, Bertolt. "A Short Organum for the Theatre." *Playwrights on Playwriting: The Meaning and Making of Modern Drama from Ibsen to Ionesco*. Trans. John Willett. Ed. Toby Cole. New York: Hill, 1960. 72-105.

Dahrendorf, Ralf. "The New Germanies: Restoration, Revolution, Reconstruction" *Encounter* Apr. 1964: 50-58.

Didion, Joan. "Doris Lessing." *The White Album*. New York: Washington Square-Pocket Books, 1980. 119-25.

Fromm, Erich. *The Fear of Freedom*. 1942. London: Routledge, 1960.

Gallant, Mavis. "A Day Like Any Other." Gallant, *The Other Paris*. 217-40.

———. "Ernst in Civilian Clothes." *The Pegnitz Junction: A Novella and Five Short Stories*. New York: Random, 1973. 131-47.

———. "An Interview with Mavis Gallant." With Geoff Hancock. *A Special Issue on Mavis Gallant*. Ed. Hancock. Spec. issue of *Canadian Fiction Magazine* 28 (1978): 18-67.

———. "The Latehomecomer." *From the Fifteenth District: A Novella and Eight Short Stories*. Toronto: Macmillan, 1979. 117-38.

———. *The Other Paris*. Boston: Houghton, 1956.

———. "The Other Paris." Gallant, *The Other Paris*. 1-30.

———. Personal interview. Nov. 1979.

———. "Señor Pinedo." Gallant, *The Other Paris*. 199-216.

———. "Willi." *New Yorker* 5 Jan. 1963: 29-31.

Hamburger, Michael. *From Prophecy to Exorcism: The Premises of Modern German Literature*. London: Longmans, 1965.

Heller, Erich. "The Importance of Nietzsche: On the Modern German Mind." *Encounter* Apr. 1964: 59-66.

Hinz, Berthold. *Art in the Third Reich*. Trans. Robert Kimber and Rita Kimber. New York: Pantheon, 1979.

Leuchtenburg, William E. *A Troubled Feast: American Society Since 1945*. Rev. ed. Boston: Little, 1983.

Nietzsche, Friedrich. *The Gay Science*. Trans. Walter Kaufmann. New York: Vintage-Random, 1974.

Pickles, Dorothy. *The Fifth French Republic: Institutions and Politics*. 1960. London: Methuen, 1965.

Smith, Arthur L., Jr. "Die deutschen Kriegsgefangenen und Frankreich, 1945-1949." Ed. K. D. Bracker and H. P. Schwarz. *Vierteljahrshefte für Zeitgeschichte* 32 (1984): 103-21.

Sontag, Susan. "Fascinating Fascism." *Under the Sign of Saturn.* New York: Farrar, 1980. 71-105.

Trevor-Roper, H. R. *The Last Days of Hitler.* New York: Macmillan, 1947.

White, Hayden. "The Historical Text as Literary Artifact." *The Writing of History: Literary Form and Historical Understanding.* Ed. Robert H. Canary and Henry Kozicki. Madison: U of Wisconsin P, 1978. 41-62.

Charlotte Sturgess (essay date 1990)

SOURCE: Sturgess, Charlotte. "The Art of the Narrator in Mavis Gallant's Short Stories." *Etudes Canadiennes/ Canadian Studies,* no. 29 (1990): 213-22.

[*In the following essay, Sturgess examines the role of the narrator in Gallant's short stories.*]

Shifts in focus a certain vocal polyphony, a narration working through fragmentary accumulation, are ways in which contemporary Canadian stories work to revise their national story. Through displacement they seek to find a new space "within" and "without" the colonized territory. The paradox of a "source" to be found at once at the centre of, and in rupture with the heritage, is traced as a revision of borders, transgression of rights, an interrelation of dissonant themes. As Coral Ann Howells says of contemporary women's fiction:

> Most of them look like realistic fictions registering the surface details of daily life, yet the conventions of realism are frequently disrupted by shifts into fantasy or moments of vision so that they become split-level discourses when alternative ways of seeing are contained within the same fictional structure.[1]

In the context of split-level discourses, I see Mavis Gallant's fiction as tracing the design of self-division and rupture, involving concepts of "within" and "without" and play on the source and direction of voice. The form of her narrative is not exploded fragmentary discourse of overt dissent. It is rupture narrativised as a fundamental break-down in communication, which, in the process of story, reflects its own oppositions and self-divisions. We register this communication gap at all levels; socially, between the rootless cosmopolitan and his environment, culturally, between the French and English-speaking communities in her stories, individually, between husband and wife or parent and child. Cutting through these categories to present another form of division is that of public versus private authority or "truth," and between the past and the present as it also represents a form of authority and truth.[2] The disunity translates as a discrepancy between what "could be" and what, in reality, "is."

Mavis Gallant's voice sounds from an experimental position firmly rooted in the "city." The site varies from story to story, and with it the social mores of the group under scrutiny. Yet the concepts of duality and multiplicity, of an essential breach of communication are informed and inform through the "city." She renders an assumption of the cosmopolis not only as the space of representation in her stories, but as the locus of the individual consciousness. For Mavis Gallant's characters act within circumscribed limits of self-enclosure and self-absorption conterminous with a negative, although perhaps accurate appraisal of city life. The pervading aura of loss and abandon, of a sense of community become mere fantasy, accompanies her travellers to the Riviera as well as Paris, on winding train journeys as well as in Montreal. The combination of a specifically Canadian heritage and a cosmopolitan experience are where her narratives "come from" in a fundamental sense. It is the way this experience is voiced through the narrator's play of form that I wish to examine. Through a position of apparent detachment, of overwhelming yet elusive authority, the narrator voices the problem of form itself. Cultural, historical and individual crises of identity are thus subordinated to the necessary form of story. By inscribing shifts and breaks, confidence and betrayal, narrative will and anti-narrative contention, this voice works to reveal what "is" and offers no solution, Within this form of story her characters are destined to occupy space rather than to act within it. They are not only ineffectual as agents of their own destiny, but are accorded very little narrative space in which to record their presence.

By denying her characters access to direct voice, the narrator refuses them self-determination. Thus relieved of intent and purpose, they serve more to underscore the multiple codes governing their existence than to convince in their own right. These codes are both the stultifying ones of tradition and social necessity represented in the stories, and also the codes of fictional convention. For the inconsistency of the represented world which foregrounds the artificial structure of society also reveals the artifice of fiction. The question of narrative voice becomes then, as in much post-colonial fiction, the cross-roads of two realities, the text's and ours, no longer sharply defined. The mode of the short story is the privileged arena for this crossing of borders as its form favours voice as questioning, transgressive device rather than as a function of plot.[3] The disbelief anchored at the core of the narrative is the final cause of a narrator who frustrates our will as readers to be guided and reassured, in sum to be "centred" within the comfort of her vocal management. Forcing us to admit multiple perspectives of reading, she points to the narrative past as a shifting zone of individual perspective, she creates disbelief in a single authoritative voice of fiction and also of our reality.

In the words of Barthes, as an "impoverished narrative or myth,"[4] this past in its disbelief renders Mavis Gallant's voice her status as a Canadian writer. As she says herself she is an "expatriate" and not an "expatriot."

Whilst Mavis Gallant uses a poetics of temporal cohesion within her stories, for the narratives move through clearly-defined chronological space towards closure, the meanderings of the narrator present a sub-text of defiance. Her way of creating space both within the minds of her characters and within the expanded moment which is a hall-mark of Gallant's method, imposes the immediate seizure of voice over time.[5] For if it is the narrator who relates the sequential episodes of chronology, it is the same who slides in and out of the characters' minds, blending her voice with theirs. This defusing of the characters' capacity to think, speak and move through time, renders them as static zones of consciousness through which we hear, above all, the echo of voice. Positing the stance of objective by-stander, the narrator does not plunge us into the figural consciousness by a psychological commentary which could establish depth. She rather violates their space by permeation, establishing a network of conflicting perspectives from behind their façade. Narratorial commentary thus becomes a way of precluding insight whilst feigning to deliver it. Masking the transition between figural thoughts and narrative focus this manipulation of voice produces what Dorrit Cohn calls "the seamless junction between narrated monologues and their narrative context."[6] "Narrated monologues" are for Cohn the specifically non-verbal rendering of the mental workings of a character's mind through the narrator in free indirect style. This she opposes to free indirect speech which translates, through the narrator, a character's spoken discourse. As she says, the narrated monologue implies a whole realm of consciousness of which only a small part is opened to the reader. The narrator's frequent forays into non-verbalized spaces of consciousness, as she entwines her narrative thread with that of a character's thoughts, reveals the frequent use of this technique. It serves to highlight the way the characters do not accede to autonomous expression. The relation between thought and speech remains problematical, as does the definition of the source of voice. It confers a twilight quality on the narration, suspended on the brink of verbalization and forefronting the illimited zone of consciousness beyond. In the light of voice and perspective, of multiple and singular, of the narrator communicating with us the readers, I would like to look at the story **"Voices Lost in Snow."** It is the fourth narrative in the Linnet Muir cycle, a first-person account of childhood set in Montreal. The first passage reveals the extent of discontinuity between voices of the past and those of the present:

> Halfway between our two great wars, parents whose own early years had been shaped with Edwardian firmness were apt to lend a tone of finality to quite simple

remarks: "Because I say so" was the answer to "Why?" and a child's response to "What did I just tell you?" could seldom be anything but "Not to"—not to say, do, touch, remove, go out, argue, reject, eat, pick up, open, shout, appear to be cross. Dark riddles filled the corners of life because no enlightment was thought required. Asking questions was "being tiresome," while persistent curiosity got one nowhere, at least nowhere of interest. How much has changed? Observe the drift of words descending from adult to child—the fall of personal questions, observation, unnecessary instructions. Before long the listener seems blanketed. He must hear the voice as authority muffled, a hum through snow. The tone has changed—it may be coaxing, even plaintive—but the words have barely altered. They still claim the ancient right-of-way through a young life.[7]

This opening to the story which only declares an autobiographical narrator from the second paragraph on, begins in the didactic mode of an observer of a socio/cultural state of affairs. We the readers are addressed to witness and take heed of elements presented with the authority of a disinterested yet knowledgeable voice of her time. From behind this voice relating the generation gap and its problems is the voice of the implicated narrator, the adult experienced subject to her own inexperienced childhood. This subjective interest appears with: "not to say, do, touch, remove, go out, argue, reject, eat, pick up, open, shout, appear to sulk, appear to be cross." The focus has deepened, the voice has changed, we are no longer in the domain of the general but of the particular. The register has altered with the injection of emotive responses. Yet ambivalence reigns for the indirect way of transposing the speech act creates a focus centred on the very act of telling as the adult voice of the past reverberates through the consciousness of the child listening, and reaches us intact through the channel of the narrator. At such moments where the voice act imposes on narration, the temporality of "then" and "now" dissolves. Chronology, for all that it is clearly defined, collapses into the fundamental issue of voice. Source and direction are baffled in the process as the slide from an impersonal narration to a particular experience ends in this multiple focus. Just as our sympathy is aroused by the "dark riddles of the past" which we equate with the narrator's former experience, the subsequent use of impersonal "one" would take us back to the arena of collective experience with the automatic distancing this implies. It is at this juncture that the focus shifts from past experience to us for the narrator asks us directly "How much has changed?" Yet instead of an insight into the narrator's present situation our focus is directed to an imagistic sequence of voices drifting and falling like snow. The attraction of metaphor works to deliver the language from its realistic premises, we are caught in the atemporal image of the snow-drift and simultaneously in the flow of social commentary. Once again the voice of subjective experience is decentered, we as listeners are drawn into the scene of this suspended language which seems to include us as the audience which is "blanketed."[8] Thus from one sentence to the next we register split-levels of discourse, indefinite and multiple focusing which freezes the narration in the very act of giving voice. Not knowing where to locate the narrator's sympathy and faced with narration caught in its network of opposing terms, we are left suspended at the scene of the conflict.

The second paragraph plunges us into the past, the mode of narration changing to the present of dialogue and the narrator takes on the role of an experienced "I" who comments the inexperience of the child. Through the interweaving of direct voices from the past and the commentary of the narrator, an anecdote is recounted, an anecdote about misunderstanding. An interesting facet of this passage is that we learn in very few lines information on Linnet's family which, narrated in this fashion, does not function diegetically to "explain," but remains subordinated to the story-power of the anecdote. This digression into anecdote created within the main narrative thread, links characters together naturally, in the interest of story-telling. It is one way of segmenting the narrative into separate meaningful comments whilst still contributing to the chronological flow of narrative. In Mavis Gallant's stories we rarely have the impression of being told about people as they move through an elaborate universe. Yet in fact there are always a lot of fictional elements brought into play to construct this universe. Grandmothers, godmothers, disappearing uncles comprise a chain of chronology but they tend to be either disembodied voices of the past, brought to the surface for a moment, as in the anecdote, or we merely hear of their existence. This creates an open, exposed narrative as though what is to be seen and heard at any point in the chain will be equal to the sum of the whole. Paragraphs end on notes of incomprehension suggesting incompletion, and these breaks in understanding are the cause of self-division in the narrative. Or otherwise they end in a "home truth" as a comment which ends and dismisses a particular chapter of understanding. This also encloses the passage and implies a limit. To give a few examples from **"Voices Lost in Snow"**:

> As soon as I was old enough to understand from my reading of myths and legends that this journey was a pursuit of darkness, its terminal point a sunless underworld, the dream vanished.[9]

> I don't know where my father spent his waking life: just elsewhere.[10]

> She was the daughter of such a sensible, truthful, pessimistic woman—pessimistic in the way women become when they settle for what actually exists.[11]

> I had no way of knowing that "city" one day would also mean drab, filthy, flat, or that city blocks could turn into dull squares without mystery.[12]

These foreclosures seem to preclude narrative continuity, they are always marking limits on what can or will be said or understood. Just as voices are destined to be lost, they are only retrieved in patchwork recollection or relived event; theirs are "the only authentic voices" Linnet possesses. I think this is the thematized avowal of a central issue in Mavis Gallant's stories. They are concerned with voice just as they are concerned with the absence of voices adequate to the task of voicing this concern. The issue becomes one of "how" to find voice rather than "what" to tell. As such they participate in "the quest for language and narrative (which) coexists with the narrative of quest" as a Canadian phenomenon.[13]

As Lorna Irvine says: "Mavis Gallant pits loss against narrative sequence, showing how the ego struggles to master plot."[14] This loss at the centre is reflected in the narrator's self-effacement from the centre of her story which demands a simulation of absence. Within the finely-constructed convention of an absence of narrative authority, the narrator's voice is opaque. It comes to us as emotionless and guarded, screening and draining the fictional world of colour. Her role is not to draw us towards a "centre," be it psychological discovery, or even a centre divined through suggestion and hiatus. Gaps are not covering solutions or complete knowledge, or pointing to a truth beyond but they do suggest the potentiality of voice, just as they register its failure to sound out. I would like, finally, to look at a third-person narrative called "Virus X" which is also in the *Home Truths* collection. It is about two Canadians girls, Vera and Lottie, who meet up in Paris in radically differing circumstances. Vera has been shipped abroad after an unwanted pregnancy and is trapped in a rootless lifestyle of no return and little future. Lottie has come over on a scholarship towards a doctoral thesis on the assimilation of ethnic minorities in society. Rapidly her cultural certainties begin to fall apart as she is subjected to the pull and sway of Vera-induced bohemia. She gradually becomes aware, through the shattering of her neat, academic "assimilation" theory, of her own German roots and their importance. Vera comes from a Ukrainian background and knows at first-hand what being an undesirable immigrant means. It is the meeting of these opposed attitudes and expectations shown through shifting and split focuses that is interesting. Also the multiple layering of culture, and therefore voice, within a Canadian reality. I have chosen two passages to illustrate this play of form.

The first one is a scene in a restaurant in Paris where Lottie meets Vera for the first time since they were at school together in Canada:

> 'Une jeune fille très élégante,' the frizzy redhead down at the desk remarked. Lottie had to smile at that. No one here could know that Vera was only a girl from Winnipeg who had flunked out of high school and, on a suspicion of pregnancy, been shipped abroad to an exile without glamour. Some of the men in her family called themselves Rodney, and at least one was in poli-

tics. End syllables had been dropped from the name in any case, to make it less specifically Ukrainian. Vera had big hands and feet, a slouching walk, a head of blond steel wool. The nose was large, the eyes green and small. She played rough basket-ball, but also used to be seen downtown, Sunday-dressed, wearing ankle-strap shoes. Vera had made falsies out of a bra and gym socks—there were boys could vouch for it. In cooking class it turned out that she thought creamed carrots were made with real cream. She didn't know what white sauce was because they had never eaten at home. That spoke volumes for the sort of home it must be.[15]

An ironic shift in appraisal leads us into Lottie's thoughts, but once again the voice of social disapprobation collides with what we could take to be Lottie's reflections. Vera's affairs are the object of smalltown gossip which we divine through the murmurs of scandalized community. Yet it is a disinterested narrator who describes Vera until: "Vera had made falsies out of a bra and gym socks—there were boys could vouch for it," projects us into the realm of schoolgirl gossip. It would seem to take us back into the past, into the whispered confidences of the prim Lottie. Finally we have the crashing denunciation of the whole of Vera's family in their ignorance of "creamed carrots." They are dismissed to the margins of Canadian society by the self-righteous voice of the town which in fact narrates a dialogue. One between a perplexed Vera and the cooking instructor as the former justifies not knowing how to make "white sauce."

Cultural prejudice, the plural voice of the town wielding singular authority, and the personal rendering of experience are channeled across rifts in understanding. Lottie and Vera appear to be positioned at opposing poles of Canadian experience, addressing each other in codes of mutual misunderstanding. Yet one of the strengths of this story is the way Lottie's flawed heritage reveals itself the equal of Vera's but at a more subconscious level.

This preoccupation with identity and origins is explicited in a passage in which Vera describes Al, a Polish boyfriend who should be joining her in Strasbourg:

> Lottie looked at a round face and enormous dark eyes with fixed staring pupils. He seemed drugged or startled. "His eyes are blue," said Vera. "They look dark with that fancy lighting. I've been out to the refugee college, asking around. He's got it all wrong. It's only a dorm. They go to the university for classes. It sounded funny in the first place, teaching Slav lit to Slavs. May be he's found something else to do. Or not to do, more like it. He's got in with some Poles who live outside Paris and do weaving. They may also have prayer and patriotic evenings. "Right wing Bohemia," said Vera, looking down her large nose, "lives in the country and weaves its own skirts. *You* know." Over Lottie's cringing mind crept the fear that Vera might be

some sort of radical. Ukrainians were extreme one way or the other. You would have to know which of the Uke papers Vera's parents subscribed to, and even that wouldn't help unless you could read the language. "Get this," said Vera, and, adopting a manner Lottie assumed must be Al's, she read aloud, 'You cannot imagine what a change it is for me—yesterday *le grand luxe* in Roma, today here. But I must say, even though I have the palate of a gourmet, I find nothing wrong with the cooking.'[16]

The world evoked here spans five cultures from Slav Lit. to polish weaving in Paris, through Ukrainian politics to Canadian ideology. It ends on a foray through Italian tastes in luxury to Parisian tastes in cooking. This multilayered discourse is refracted through the prism of Lottie's cliché-ridden ideas, just as the absent Pole, Al, is interpreted through Vera. The languages and cultures hold no weight, are not elaborated in terms of fictional reality. They represent arbitrary markers on a map of Paris, as much part of the landscape as the gastronomical restaurants. Through Vera and Lottie they interact within a Canadian reality, they are "set" in Paris as it were, and resound within the world of the two girls, participating in their conflicts of views.

We seem to be confronted with a dilemma of perspective within the terms of Lottie and Vera's conflicting views. Lottie has adhered to a Canadian, even if small-minded and bigoted, sense of self. She has done so at the expense of an erased German heritage. Vera has turned her back on the possibility of a sense of self within her Ukrainian-Canadian context. The very idea of culture and identity is a matter of discourse, a game of names with no real significance. For Vera, Slav Lit. classes, Polish weaving and Right-Wing Bohemia are part of a vast anecdote. Vera can assimilate in any surroundings except her own; Lottie has to actively refuse all other space except the narrow path carved out at home. Voices of the past are lost or they impede progress, creating discontinuity of vital understanding. Voices of the present reverberate with the echo of these lost references. They come to us the readers through narrative registering absence through presence. The desire to speak makes itself heard in muffled tones, through a narratorial channel of disguise. A narrator willed to transparency in her opacity. Broken lines of genealogy, of fractured society, of the flawed individual, take root in the space of the narrator's effaced presence. By refusing the centre, her voice is all the more apt to carry, to influence by subterfuge, to create duality and deny this duality. By creating a paradox of reading, that of being nowhere in particular and everywhere at once, the narrator becomes the sign of voice itself, embodying the fictional gift of silent speech.

Notes

1. Coral Ann Howells, *Private and Fictional Words* (London: Methuen, 1987), p. 13.

2. For an analysis of voice opposing "public" to "private," see Michel Fabre, "Orphans's Progress, Reader's Progress, Le "on dit" et le non-dit chez Mavis Gallant," *Recherches Anglaises et Américaines* (Strasbourg), XVI (1983) pp. 57-67.

3. See Barbara Godard, "Stretching the Story: The Canadian Story Cycle," Paper given at the conference on the Short Story organized by the "Centre de Recherches sur la nouvelle anglaise," The Sorbonne, Paris, February 1988.

4. Roland Barthes in Barbara Godard, *ibid.* p. 12.

5. Joseph Frank, "Spatial Form in Modern Literature," *Sewanee Review,* 53 (Spring, 1945).

6. Dorrit Cohn, *Transparent Minds: Narrative Modes for Presenting Consciousness in Fiction* (Princeton, New Jersey: Princeton University Press, 1978).

7. Mavis Gallant, "Voices Lost in Snow" in *Home Truths* (Toronto: Macmillan, 1987), p. 282.

8. Analysis of the image and reader's role: Clare Hanson, "A Poetics of Short Fiction," *Re-reading the Short Story* (London: Macmillan, 1989), pp. 22-33.

9. Gallant, p. 284.

10. Gallant, p. 285.

11. Gallant, p. 286.

12. Gallant, p. 292.

13. Godard, p. 11.

14. Lorna Irvine, "Starting from the Beginning Every Time," *A Mazing Space: Writing Canadian Women Writing,* Ed: Shirley Neuman and Smaro Kamboureli (Edmonton, Alberta: Longspoon Press, 1986), p. 249.

15. Mavis Gallant, "Virus X" in *Home Truths,* p. 176.

16. Gallant, *ibid.,* pp 201-202.

Herbert Grabes (essay date 1990)

SOURCE: Grabes, Herbert. "Creating to Dissect: Strategies of Character Portrayal and Evaluation in Short Stories by Margaret Laurence, Alice Munro and Mavis Gallant." In *Modes of Narrative: Approaches to American, Canadian, and British Fiction,* edited by Reingard M. Nischik and Barbara Korte, pp. 119-28. Würzburg, Germany: Konigshausen and Neumann, 1990.

[*In the following essay, Grabes discusses Gallant's strategies for creating character portrayals in her story "Acceptance of Their Ways" and contrasts them with those of Alice Munro's "Who Do You Think You Are?" and Margaret Laurence's "To Set Our House in Order."*]

Let me begin with a few theoretical presuppositions. The first one is a restatement of Chatman's position that "a viable theory of character should preserve openness and treat characters as autonomous beings, not as mere plot functions."[1] Considering the illusionary power of literary characters, it may seem unnecessary to say this, but in most structuralist narratology 'character' has been unduly reduced to mere attributes connected with a plot,[2] to 'actants,'[3] to a stable link between a plot function and predicates,[4] or to an 'agent' in the plot line.[5]

The second presupposition is that fictional characters are imaginary constructs residing in the mind of the reader. This means that they are psychic phenomena formed by the reader in analogy to real-life characters, with the difference that their creation is not based on the open context of our experience of life but on the distinct and restricted information derived from the reading of one particular fictional text. This implies that the same categories for subsuming masses of detail (such as type, stereotype, individual, character trait, habit, mood, action, thinking, feeling) are active in the creation of fictional characters as in our perception of real-life characters. What is also active in both is the whole range of analytic categories (such as character development versus stable core, or consciousness versus the unconscious) and of evaluative categories (such as right or wrong, good or bad, innocent or guilty). The analogy further implies that with any one reader the same idiosyncratic model of character formation—referred to by psychologists as the 'implied theory of personality' ("implizite Persönlichkeitstheorie"[6])—is the basis for both real-life and fictional characters.

The third presupposition is that the specific condition under which the illusion of fictional characters is formed allows for a more rigid analysis of character formation, character analysis and evaluation than is the case with real-life characters. The reason is that the quantity and quality of information motivating and guiding the creation of the mental entity known as a 'fictional character' is strictly limited by the specific literary text, and that the particular selection of information provided or withheld, as well as its sequence and possible recurrence, makes it possible to observe more closely the strategies of constructing, analysing and evaluating characters.

That the *selection* of information pertaining to the formation of character is all-important hardly needs any further comment. One might just mention here that in fiction the information giving process is far less restricted than in life: whereas we can know about other people's feelings or thoughts only by means of inference from their words and deeds, to the omniscient narrator and his audience any character is, indeed, an open book.

The significance of the particular *sequence* of information for the building of fictional characters is much less obvious and has so far received more attention from psychologists than from narratologists. In an earlier paper on this particular matter,[7] I tried to show why the psychological investigation of "impression formation"[8] and the "primacy effect"[9] is of particular importance for the study of literary characters. Although information pertaining to a particular character is only received successively during the process of reading, we very early on create an illusion, on very scanty evidence, of a fairly complete person and work from this assumption while taking in further information. While we are reading, we are under the mistaken impression that the characters are already there and that we are simply getting to know more and more about them, whereas we are really just imagining them under the guidance of the text we are reading. And the same illusion makes us believe that we may analyse them, may get beneath the surface of their appearance, while in fact we are creating this depth from the sequence of the analytic or evaluative comments we are gradually taking in.

That finally *recurrence* deserves our special attention derives from the fact that recurrent information confirms earlier "impression formation" and is the basis for the illusion of stable character traits. Again there is a close analogy with the formation of our notion of real-life characters, at least if we are ready to share Jacques Lacan's view that the individuality and unity of any person consists in his or her "automatisme de répétition"[10] (Freud's "Wiederholungszwang"). Thus we have good reason to look closely at what an author has a fictional character repeatedly do or say (or not do and keep silent about).

As fictional characters are powerful illusions which capture the attention of the reader of fiction, close observation of the strategies of character construction, character analysis, and character evaluation may indeed reveal a great deal of the peculiarity and attractiveness of particular narratives as well as the particular style of their authors. I would like to demonstrate this by looking at the character portrayal in three short stories by Margaret Laurence, Alice Munro, and Mavis Gallant.

The text of Margaret Laurence's story "To Set Our House in Order" motivates the reader to imagine no fewer than nine characters, though in varying degrees. As to the quantity of information, Grandmother MacLeod and the first-person narrator Vanessa stand out clearly as the main characters, whereas others like Vanessa's baby brother, her dead uncle Roderick or the physician Dr Cates are only mentioned a few times and seem to consist of not much more than a name. But quantity of information alone is not a reliable measure of importance. It is true, of course, that Vanessa is all-important because as the narrator she is ever present: all information about the other characters is filtered through her consciousness. On the other hand, scarcity of information and physical absence do not necessarily signify diminished importance. As the story unfolds, it is the yet unborn baby that first compels the narrator's and the reader's attention, and it soon becomes clear that the whole story is delimited by the coming into the world of the narrator's baby brother. Even the very first sentence indicates that the "order" topicalized in the title of the story is disturbed by the baby even before its birth ("When the baby was almost ready to be born, something went wrong"[11]), and even when it is still absent it keeps the other characters constantly fearing that even more may go wrong, that the child and its mother may die. The mother, too, is mainly absent, and information about her is very scanty; but, again, she becomes all-important through the constant fear of the narrator and the other characters around her that she may die, that her temporary absence from home caused by the birth of the baby may become a permanent one.

As to the selection of information, the only inside view of a character we receive is that of the narrator-agent Vanessa, and this view is limited throughout to the scope of a ten-year-old girl's experience of the events as they are remembered and told by the narrating "I." This view includes the evaluation of all the other characters. However, the last sentence of the story ("I felt that whatever God might love in this world, it was certainly not order," p. 257), in conjunction with the title, which is taken from Grandmother MacLeod's maxim "God loves Order—he wants each one of us to set our house in order" (p. 248), makes it clear that the narrator has selected all the information—including that on the characters—to prove a point.

This is also the reason why Grandmother MacLeod is the figure that looms largest in the story. She, "steel-spined despite her apparent fragility" (p. 244), and someone who "did not believe in the existence of fear, or if she did, she never let on" (p. 245), she is clearly the antagonist of the fear-driven Vanessa and the other characters around her. Not able or willing to take note of the deteriorating situation during the Depression, or of the worries of a child fearing for her mother's life and those of a husband fearing for his wife's, she continues dressing and acting as a lady, refusing to help but insisting that the house be kept immaculate. She has nothing more important on her mind than selecting "two dozen lace-bordered handkerchiefs of pure Irish linen" (p. 250) from a Robinson & Cleaver catalogue while her daughter-in-law is about to have a Caesarean. If despite this she does not appear a total monster, it is owing to some additional information indicating that her hungry allegiance to the unchanging rigidity of material order—including the fixed principles of her dead father—constitutes a defense mechanism, a strategy to escape the threat of chaos and avoid the painful feeling of loss, whose intensity might kill her. When she bullies her son Ewen to name his new-born baby after her dead son Roderick, Vanessa remembers what she told her before: "*When your Uncle Roderick got killed, I thought I would die. But I didn't die*" (p. 254).

A repetition of this kind brings up the question of recurrence and its functions. Recurrence in this story is used throughout to lend identity to otherwise not fully developed characters. The mother repeatedly appears as weak and timid, the father constantly tries to hide his fear from Vanessa and gives in to the tyranny of Grandmother MacLeod, whereas her aunt Edna keeps ironising the tyrant's aristocratic pretensions.

Sequentiality of information is—except in the case of the narrator—not used for creating an impression of change in character but only for purposes of plot function and the addition of information. The baby that causes all the disturbance and fear is mentioned at the beginning and then again towards the end of the story, hardly ever in between. The same holds true for the mother. Their roles are dictated by plot alone, as is the case with Dr Cates, who is mentioned very briefly only twice. Sequentiality of information in the case of Grandmother MacLeod means only the addition of more of the same, with the effect that she appears as someone incapable of change. Sequentiality suggests change, however, in the case of Vanessa, whose initially quite specific fear of the loss of her mother has developed towards the end into an all-encompassing existential insecurity, a feeling that order cannot be the principle of a world in which so much may go wrong. The reason is that it is not until then that Vanessa and the reader learn how much more has already gone wrong than just the baby's fetal position: that her kind father as a boy not only damaged his brother Roderick's eye with an air rifle, but also gave up his youthful wish to go into the merchant marine and see the world when he decided to become a doctor after Roderick's early death in the Great War; that the imposing exterior of Grandfather MacLeod conceals a tragedy, for it turns out that the successful doctor would much rather have been a classical scholar; that the soldier's death of Uncle Roderick was not at all as heroic as her father's merciful lie made Grandmother MacLeod believe; and that Grandmother MacLeod betrays her hidden insecurity as soon as the name of her son Roderick is mentioned. All this is clearly put in to strengthen Vanessa's growing conviction "that whatever God might love in this world, it was certainly not order" (p. 257).

· · · · ·

Alice Munro's story "Who Do You Think You Are?" is in some ways similar to Margaret Laurence's "To Set Our House in Order": This story, too, is a story largely consisting of childhood memories. As with Vanessa in Laurence's story, the fact that Rose is the central char-

acter is not founded so much on sheer quantity of information as on perspective—we actually hear more about the "village idiot" Milton Homer. "Who Do You Think You Are?" is a third-person narrative, the perspective is limited to the recalling, analysing and evaluating mind of Rose, who thus acts as a 'reflector' and a third-person centre of consciousness. This implies that all information about the other six characters mentioned in the story is filtered through her mind, and the selection of information is an indication of her predilections.

This selection is clearly biased in favour of one character, Milton Homer, and to a lesser degree it favours the characters directly connected with him: his imitator Ralph Gillespie and the aunts who take care of him, Hattie and Mattie Homer. Brian, who at the beginning of the story gives the motivation for Rose's recollections ("There were some things Rose and her brother Brian could safely talk about, without running aground on principles or statements of position, and one of them was Milton Homer"[12]), seems soon to be forgotten. In fact, Rose is so much carried away by *her* imitation of Milton Homer that at one point in the story Brian laughingly says "Now that's enough," and his wife Phoebe tries to stop her before she rouses Brian's impatience. But these interruptions are of no avail; Rose goes on and on with her stories of Milton Homer and the people associated with him.

There must therefore be strong reasons for her obsessive selection, and we find them when we consider the quality and recurrence of the information selected. What accounts for Milton Homer's deviant, partly funny, partly outrageous and indecent behaviour, which is the object of Rose's roaming memory, is less a lack of intelligence than a total lack of any restraint:

> What was missing was a sense of precaution, Rose thought now. Social inhibition, though there was no such name for it at that time. Whatever it is that ordinary people lose when they are drunk, Milton Homer never had, or might have chosen not to have—and this is what interests Rose—at some early point in life.
>
> (p. 303)

It becomes clear that Milton Homer pays for this freedom from any social or moral restraint by being ostracized: he may run around the yards, but the doors of the houses remain closed to him. Later, when we hear that Rose is having an affair with a married man, we get an inkling of why she is interested in the possibility that Milton Homer's behaviour may nevertheless have been the result of a deliberate choice, and we also begin to understand why she does not want to discuss principles with her brother.

But there are other reasons for her obsessively selective memory. One is decidedly her craze for imitation. First we hear that Rose, in her brother's living room, revels in imitating Milton Homer (p. 300), and when asked how she can remember him so well she answers "'I didn't see him do it. What I saw was Ralph Gillespie *doing* Milton Homer'" (p. 301). A little later she points out that Milton Homer himself "was a mimic of ferocious gifts and terrible energy" (p. 302), and further towards the end of the story we learn that Ralph Gillespie had become obsessed with imitation: "Ralph don't know when to stop. He Milton Homer'd himself right out of a job" (p. 312). It is no wonder that Rose, who also does not know when to stop imitating, and very likely for that reason has become an actress, "felt his life, close, closer than the lives of men she'd loved, one slot over from her own" (p. 316).

This remark is the conclusion of the story, and while pointing out Rose's shift of concentration from Milton Homer to Ralph Gillespie and back to herself, we have touched on the question of sequence. In Alice Munro's story memory covers a much greater time span, and thus sequentiality of information can be used more easily to convey changes in the characters. We learn, for instance, that Milton Homer has become quieter with age, that Flo used to change her social contacts at an increasing rate before Rose finally had to take her to the County Home, that Ralph Gillespie never fully recovered from an accident in the navy and finally died. But these changes remain ephemeral in comparison to the change that memory brings about in Rose. First she reverts to the theme of Milton Homer only in order to avoid a clash of principles when talking with her brother Brian. Then this theme gains a striking autonomy, bringing Rose to realize her own interest in the possibility of deliberate social estrangement as a means of achieving freedom from social inhibition. Moving on to Milton Homer's aunts Hattie and Mattie, who with their Methodist morality embody the social inhibition he so totally lacks, Rose remembers that it was Hattie who asked her the disturbing question "Who do you think you are?", a question intended at the time merely as a reproach for thinking that she was "better than other people just because you can learn poems" (p. 306), but now revealing its much broader existential significance. As it was in Hattie's English class that Ralph Gillespie made Rose notice the literary implications of Milton Homer's name, her attention then becomes focussed on him as the "boy who specialized in Milton Homer imitations" (p. 308). The recollection of her last encounter with him leads Rose back to her present situation, including an unsatisfactory love affair, and her urge to conceal her intimate feelings from Brian and Phoebe. Thus the whole sequence of information on various characters is above all designed to effect a heightened self-knowledge in Rose, enabling her to find in the final recognition of her closeness to Ralph at least an approximate answer to the central question "Who do you think you are?".

. . . . .

As against the similarities of character portrayal in the two stories considered so far, the strategies of creating and dissecting character in Mavis Gallant's **"Acceptance of Their Ways"** look remarkably different. The story portrays an after-dinner conversation between three English women in a boarding house on the Italian Riviera, with the leave-taking of one of them the following morning as a coda. To this extent, there is a similarity to Alice Munro's story, which is delimited by Rose's talk in her brother Brian's living room. But a significant difference, if not the decisive one, lies in the choice of perspective. Whereas in Laurence's and Munro's stories characterisation is consistently filtered through the restricted consciousness of a narrator-agent or a reflector, in **"Acceptance of Their Ways"** we have both a 'reflector' in one of the three women, Lily Littel, and, in addition to this, an omniscient narrator. And it is this combination that is largely responsible for the continuous and ruthless dissecting of character which is the most prominent feature of this story.

As to the selection of information, there are only three characters and information is distributed much more evenly than in the stories previously discussed. Although we learn most about Lily Littel due to her additional role as a reflector, there is no really minor character. The quantity of information on each character is, in fact, quite remarkable; the story consists almost purely of character portrayal. Also remarkable is the quality of information. For all three characters it ranges from outward appearance, manners, and verbal expression to private thoughts, basic values, and deep convictions, from recognisable moods to the most hidden fears and desires. The result is a rare transparency of character, brought about for the two other women by Lily Littel's acute observations and ruthless analyses, and for Lily by an omniscient narrator who is just as merciless and devastatingly ironic.

The three characters we are thus induced to imagine are two 'gentlewomen,' the hostess Mrs Freeport and her old friend Mrs Garnett, and Lily Littel, a social climber who tries very hard to become like them and is therefore ready to accept their ways however odd they may seem to be. Though paired in that way, Mrs Freeport and Mrs Garnett are conceived as differently as two characters can be, the former domineering to the point of being sadistic, the latter rather submissive, but capricious. Both are also sentimental, which Lily, who can be both submissive and vengeful at the same time, is decidedly not.

These basic character traits are revealed through recurrent verbal and nonverbal behaviour as well as, in the case of Lily, through information directly presented by the omniscient narrator. The most obvious use of recurrence is, however, the repeated pointing out of the amazing contradictions within each character, especially in

Lily Littel, contradictions that often border on, and sometimes attain, the quality of paradox. Much of this contradictory behaviour could be classified as 'hypocrisy,' a form of behaviour traditionally attributed to the English upper classes, and there is ample evidence that the narrator uses Lily Littel's endeavours to emulate just this quality as a scathingly satirical device.

Mrs Freeport, who unsuccessfully runs a boarding-house, is so poor that she cannot even afford decent food for her guests and herself, but she keeps displaying her superiority and treats a paying guest like Lily like a servant. Always wanting to be in command, she turns out to be utterly dependent on those she tries to subject, alternatively insulting them and craving their friendship.

Mrs Garnett, an elderly widow of moderate financial and intellectual means, still likes to see herself as "the victim of the effects of her worrying beauty—a torment to shoe clerks and bus conductors,"[13] as the sentence, taking a decidedly ironic turn, continues. Considering herself to be badly treated by her friend Vanessa Freeport, she has nevertheless been coming back again and again for years, and though she speaks in a soft martyred tone of voice, she is vengeful enough to first persuade Mrs Freeport to prepare an Italian farewell dinner and then not to touch it at all.

But Lily Littel, though seemingly their disciple, in fact surpasses her models by far in her deliberately double-faced stance. She only stays on the Italian side of the border because she unfortunately cannot afford "the coarse and grubby gaiety of the French Riviera" (p. 203). She puts up with Mrs Freeport's condescending manner because she craves respectability and can punish her hostess from time to time by allegedly visiting her sister but in fact resorting to a hotel in Nice, where she ritually takes to the bottle. Ruthless in her desire to get on in the world, she is ready to suppress her true self, which is allowed to emerge only when she is drunk. "If Lily had settled for this bleached existence, it was explained by a sentence scrawled over a page of her locked diary: 'I live with gentlewomen now'" (pp. 205f.).

There is no evidence of change in any of the three double-faced characters. The sequence of information in this story simply involves the addition of more and more weaknesses of a similar kind and therefore rules out even the possibility of change. As is usually the case with satirical writing, the characters seem to be created only in order to be viciously dissected. Mavis Gallant's scalpel continuously touches to the quick. Watch it touching Lily Littel: "An excellent cook, she had dreamed of being a poisoner, but decided to leave that for the loonies; it was no real way to get on" (p. 205). In comparison the strategies of character portrayal

in Laurence's and Munro's stories appear rather tame and benevolent.

. . . . .

A comparison of character portrayal in the three stories makes evident that the narrative perspective strongly influences the range and quality of information. With a narrator-agent as in Laurence's story or a third-person centre of consciousness as in Munro's, inside views are necessarily restricted to the character of the narrator, whereas in Gallant's story they are deliberately limited to the character of Lily. Conversely, outside views are more or less restricted to the other characters in the first two stories and easily provided for all three in **"Acceptance of Their Ways."** But it is the very effective combination of the two that marks the increased potential of the omniscient narrator in that story. Looking at Lily and inside her, this narrator can say about Lily: "Her eyes, which were a washy blue, were tolerably kind when she was plotting mischief" (pp. 203f.).

As to the selection of information, it becomes obvious that with a larger number of characters in a short story we get a hierarchy of plenitude. Irrespective of the total number of characters, attention would appear to be focussed on not more than two or three: in Laurence's story on Grandmother MacLeod and Vanessa, in Munro's on Milton Homer, Ralph Gillespie and Rose, in Gallant's on all three women.

A comparison also shows that recurrence can be put to various uses. With Laurence it serves to give identity to the less fully developed characters; with Munro it emphasizes those traits in the fuller characters, Milton Homer and Ralph Gillespie, that are significant for Rose's self-knowledge; with Gallant it substantiates the profiles of the three characters, their differences and the mutual hypocrisy that is being satirized.

As far as the use of sequentiality is concerned, there is also some variety. In "To Set Our House in Order" it produces the impression of both change of character and unwillingness to change; in "Who Do You Think You Are?" it mainly indicates a change in self-awareness; and in **"Acceptance of Their Ways"** it brings out the impossibility of change and the narrator's preference for dissecting.

Character evaluation is largely implied in the strategies already mentioned, but something remains to be pointed out. In Laurence's and Munro's stories evaluation is linked to the narrator-agent and the reflector respectively; if evaluations of other characters are presented, these are re-evaluated by the narrator-agent and reflector. In Gallant's story the impression is created that it is mainly Lily who evaluates the two other women, their mutual evaluating included, but Lily herself is, as we have seen, continually at the mercy of the omniscient narrator's evaluating faculty. And evaluating is what this narrator likes to do—as does Lily.

Notes

1. Seymour Chatman, *Story and Discourse: Narrative Structure in Fiction and Film* (Ithaca/London: Cornell Univ. Press, 1978), p. 119.

2. Claude Bremond, *Logique de récit,* Poétique (Paris: Seuil, 1973).

3. A. J. Greimas, *Sémantique structurale: recherche de méthode,* Langue et langage (Paris: Larousse, 1966).

4. Tzvetan Todorov, *Poétique de la prose* (rev. ed., Paris: Seuil, 1973).

5. Teun A. van Dijk, "Philosophy of Action and Theory of Narrative," *Poetics,* 5 (1976), 287-338 (paper issued from a seminar held at the University of Amsterdam in 1974).

6. Cf. Jürgen Jahnke, *Interpersonale Wahrnehmung* (Stuttgart etc.: Kohlhammer, 1975).

7. Herbert Grabes, "Wie aus Sätzen Personen werden . . . : Über die Erforschung literarischer Figuren," *Poetica,* 10 (1978), 405-28.

8. Cf. S. E. Ash, "Forming Impressions of Personality," *Journal of Abnormal and Social Psychology,* 41 (1946), 258-90; Abraham S. Luchins, "Forming Impressions of Personality: A Critique," *Journal of Abnormal and Social Psychology,* 43 (1948), 318-25; Erving Goffman, "The Presentation of Self in Everyday Life," in Stephan P. Spitzer (ed.), *The Sociology of Personality: An Enduring Problem in Psychology* (New York etc.: Van Nostrand Reinhold, 1969), pp. 94-108.

9. Cf. Norman H. Anderson/Alfred A. Barrios, "Primacy Effects in Personality Impression Formation," in Clyde Hendrick/Russell A. Jones (eds.), *The Nature of Theory and Research in Social Psychology* (New York/London: Academic Press, 1972), pp. 210-18.

10. Cf. "Le seminaire sur 'La Lettre volée'" in *Écrits* (Paris: Seuil, 1966), pp. 11-61, here p. 11.

11. "To Set Our House in Order," in Wayne Grady (ed.), *The Penguin Book of Canadian Short Stories* (Markham, Ontario, etc.: Penguin, 1980), pp. 243-57, here p. 243; page numbers in the text refer to this edition.

12. "Who Do You Think You Are?", in Wayne Grady (ed.), *The Penguin Book of Canadian Short Stories,* pp. 299-316, here p. 299; page numbers in the text refer to this edition.

13. "Acceptance of Their Ways," in Alec Lucas (ed.), *Great Canadian Short Stories* (New York: Dell, 1971), pp. 203-11, here p. 205; page numbers in the text refer to this edition.

Lesley D. Clement (essay date September 1992)

SOURCE: Clement, Lesley D. "Mavis Gallant's Apprenticeship Stories, 1944-1950: Breaking the Frame." *English Studies in Canada* 18, no. 4 (September 1992): 317-34.

[*In the following essay, Clement surveys Gallant's early short fiction, maintaining that "the exposure to painterly forms and techniques that she experienced can be observed in the evolution of a visually powerful and evocative style within those short stories she wrote during her apprenticeship years."*]

In his 1977 interview with Mavis Gallant, Geoff Hancock, remarking on the visual quality of her stories, conjectured that Gallant "might [have] liked to have been a painter at one time." To this observation Gallant replied that she often imagines how she would respond to a scene were she recreating it on canvas (55). The daughter of Stewart Young, an artist whom she has described as having "an incredible sense of vocation" but "no talent," and as painting "like a provincial, minor late-impressionist" (Corbeil 21), Mavis Gallant embarked on her chosen vocation as a writer of fiction while working as a journalist in Montreal from 1944 to 1950. This was a period when Quebec art, breaking the stranglehold that Paris's academies and Ontario's Group of Seven had exercised over Canada's art scene, was discovering its own force as an essential medium for a unique culture. The articles Gallant wrote for *Harper's Bazaar* and the Montreal *Standard* describing the cultural *milieu* of Montreal during the 1940s reveal her fascination with this local art scene, particularly with the changes that Quebec art of the 1940s was undergoing. Gallant never embraced any of the aesthetic principles espoused and practised by the various factions that became prominent during this period; however, the exposure to painterly forms and techniques that she experienced can be observed in the evolution of a visually powerful and evocative style within those short stories she wrote during her apprenticeship years.

Gallant's framing of stories such as **"Good Morning and Goodbye," "Three Brick Walls," "Thank You for the Lovely Tea," "Jorinda and Jorindel,"** and **"Up North,"** all written or first drafted during this apprenticeship period, resembles the modernist tendency to enclose characters in a suspended or caught moment. This tendency is more characteristic of Joyce in *Dubliners* and Eliot in "The Love Song of J. Alfred Prufrock" than of Chekhov and Mansfield, two writers Gallant has acknowledged reading "enormously" when she was young (Martens 169). But already these early stories provide evidence of other elements borrowed from the visual arts—colour, light and dark, line, composition, and, ultimately, fluidity—elements that, through structure, perspective, and metaphor, would find full expression in her 1959 novel, *Green Water, Green Sky,*[1] and eventually become a trademark of Gallant's style. Like modern painters and writers before her, Gallant experimented with techniques borrowed from Cubist, Surrealist, and Kinetic art to attain fragmentation, distortion, and mobility; consequently, these apprenticeship stories become increasingly analogous to visual compositions attempting to break free from their spatial and temporal frames.

In a 1988 interview with Linda Leith, Gallant conveys the vibrancy of the Montreal life she experienced during the 1940s when she was establishing herself, first as a journalist, and then as a writer of fiction:

> Montreal was a city in transition. All the old conservative dead weight was still there, and of course French Canada was still locked, but there were elements breaking out, and that was what was so exciting. I'm thinking of the painters particularly, and in a city that size you tend to all know one another, the bohemia.
>
> (4)

As a journalist, Gallant usually chose subjects on which to report, rather than having them assigned to her (Baele C1). Although covering a great diversity of subjects for her Montreal *Standard* articles, Gallant gravitated toward those cultural stories involving current topics and issues from the arts. Short pieces include sketches of local personalities such as Eldon Grier, who held fresco painting classes at Montreal's Art Association; Mary Filer, a nurse who gained celebrity in Montreal with her annual painting of Nativity scenes on the city's Neurological Institute windows; and Dr. George Hall, a collector of early Canadian art.[2] Some of Gallant's feature stories for the *Standard Magazine* are of broader interest: for example, "Art Hoaxes that Baffle the Highbrow Critics" (23 July 1949: 17) and "Art for the Family Pocketbook" (6 Nov. 1948: 5+). The articles that best reveal Gallant's insight into the changes that Quebec art of the 1940s was undergoing are a *Harper's Bazaar* article, "Above the Crowd in French Canada" (July 1946: 58+), and two Montreal *Standard Magazine* articles, "An Art Curator and His Critics" (12 June 1948: 3+) and "Success Story of a Canadian Artist" (29 April 1950: 18-19).

In the first of these three articles, Gallant's intimate acquaintance with the local Montreal art scene is demonstrated in her selection of the new painters Robert La Palme, Jacques de Tonnancour, and Paul-Emile Borduas and the lately discovered "primitive" Marie Bouchard as worthy of note. Moreover, her description of Alfred Pellan's influence in freeing "his pupils of their inhibitions about color, form and subject matter" (128) anticipates what art historians now recognize as being an important catalyst of the radical transformations that Quebec and Canadian art underwent. With the return of Alfred Pellan to Montreal in 1940 from fourteen years in Paris, where he had been exposed to the Cubism of Léger, Picasso, and Miró, and the Surrealism of Ernst and the later Picasso and Miró, and his subsequent appointment, in June 1943, to a position at Montreal's École des Beaux-Arts, Quebec artists experienced a more intensive immersion into the techniques and forms of earlier European movements than they had yet received.

The invigorating controversies that ensued from the formation of two Montreal groups—the Prisme d'Yeux that formed around Pellan and the more stridently radical Automatistes that formed around Borduas—and the publications of their manifestoes in February and August of 1948 provided a fertile environment for the young Mavis Gallant. These controversies also formed the background for the problems that Robert Tyler Davis, director of Montreal's Art Association, had with the annual spring show, problems that Gallant describes in the second of these articles, "An Art Curator and His Critics." In terms of her own art, however, Gallant has never committed herself to the aspects of Surrealism and Abstract Expressionism that Borduas's Automatistes introduced into Canadian art; therefore, Pellan's Prisme d'Yeux group is much closer in spirit to the direction Gallant's art would take, particularly in her adherence to representationalism, even when incorporating surrealistic elements, and in her insistence that, as an artist, she should not be expected to establish any theoretical or ideological alliances (Hancock 42, 45; Martens 178-79).

The third of the articles mentioned above, a feature story on Goodridge Roberts, indicates that while Gallant probably knew members of Borduas's Automatistes only by reputation, she knew some of the Prisme d'Yeux group and its allies through friendship. She was acquainted with Philip Surrey, art editor of the Montreal *Standard,* from whom she originally obtained her job; as well, an editorial note (2) preceding this article on Goodridge Roberts states that Gallant had known Roberts since she was nineteen years old—for eight or nine years, therefore. Gallant's two-page article on Roberts is an intimate portrait of his childhood, early training and career as an artist, and present lifestyle. That Gallant knew not only Roberts well, but also his paintings, is further demonstrated when, in her introduction to *The War Brides,* Gallant tells an anecdote of travelling, as a reporter, on a train in New Brunswick, interviewing war brides on their reaction to the new land.[3] Gallant confesses:

> Nearly every aspect of the Canadian landscape struck me as moving and poetic then, for reasons that were

historical or literary or had something to do with Canadian painting and which were at a remove from the land itself: a field was not a field—it was a Goodridge Roberts. I foolishly expected a reaction tuned to mine.

(157)

During this time that Mavis Gallant was working for the Montreal *Standard,* she began writing and publishing fiction. By the time she left for Europe, in the fall of 1950, she had had four stories published in Montreal magazines: **"Good Morning and Goodbye"** and **"Three Brick Walls"** in Patrick Anderson's *Preview;* **"A Wonderful Country"** in the *Standard Magazine;* and **"The Flowers of Spring"** in *Northern Review.* Her two *Preview* stories, the first stories she published, form a diptych: **"Good Morning and Goodbye"** narrates the final hours of a young Jewish-German refugee, Paul, with his adoptive Canadian family, the Trennans; **"Three Brick Walls"** focusses on Paul's first hours in the city as he undergoes a new experience—freedom. These stories anticipate a predominant theme in Gallant's canon—the displaced person—Paul being displaced in terms of language, nationality, culture, and stage of life as he is poised on the brink of adulthood. Most pertinently, this diptych also illustrates that, although framing her stories as modernist writers before her had done, Gallant already possessed those pictorial and concrete qualities of style that would enable her to avoid what one reviewer condescendingly describes as her stagnation in "the fag-end of modernism" (Bilan 326).

That the first story is very much a story locked in a temporal frame analogous to the spatial frame of a painting is immediately suggested by the title, these two greetings—"good morning" and "goodbye"—marking the beginning and the end of Paul's contact with the Trennans on this final day with them. But the pattern of Paul's life extends beyond that involving the Trennan family, the family's pattern having grown around him after he "fumblingly" fit into their life. Because Paul is about to leave, his life stands in what Gallant refers to as "the vacuum that lies between the patterns in a life" (2). The opening lines of the story, describing a scene as perceived by Paul, convey a sense of his displacement. Paul opens his eyes, remembers that the day is the occasion of an end and a beginning, and turns his head to view a scene outside of himself: "the sun and the green leaves at the window, and the transparent shadow of one leaf above another." This static picture, given depth because of the shadows, reinforces the sense developed later that Paul's life with the Trennans is but a pattern superimposed on the pattern his life took before he arrived in Canada. The next sentence briefly shatters the static image when it becomes kinetic: "The trees moved in the wind and the shadow moved to the edge of the leaf and back again" (1). Paul's life, about to change, is a broken pattern awaiting the formation of a new pattern.

The second paragraph continues to describe the scene outside the window and so to reflect the situation in which Paul presently finds himself. By fitting into a pattern of life in this new country, Paul has suffered a fragmentation of his sense of self:

> He lay there and looked at the leaves and the crooked pieces of blue between them, and thought "I, Paul, am going away again." He had changed his name to Paul because the other sounded too German, and every morning for a long time he had said "I, Paul, today will do thus and so." In this way he had become one with the name. It had finally divided him into two separate people; one here, and one almost lost, on the other side of an ocean.

(1)

Gallant uses colours as well as shapes and framing devices to compose this picture: green has blue in it but is a distinct colour, just as the new Paul in a new land has emerged from this shadowy blue past.

Paul relies on images because the language that the Trennans speak is foreign to him. Unable to communicate his ideas, moods, and desires through words and phrases, he attempts on one occasion "to share and explain a great burden which was so overwhelmingly his own" by showing them the image of the large red "J" stamped on each page of his passport (1). Paul strives to communicate this burden, groping but not finding the English words to do so: "This is in my life, a certain thing" (2). While the Trennan family articulates "[e]very headache, each anger, every reaction," analysing them by breaking them down "into words and phrases and exclamations" (1), Paul has no way to break his feelings and moods down and thus to control them. So the large red "J" controls Paul's life despite his assumption of a new name in a new land. The Trennan family thinks that what Paul is feeling is shame (2), but he actually wishes to convey how this red "J" circumscribes and controls his life.

The Trennans are able to interlock the various patterns in their life into a continuous pattern, but for Paul the pattern of life with the Trennans is sliced from the new unknown pattern, quite literally, by the train that runs "in front of them, loudly and dustily" (3). The first part of Paul's story leaves this young man in a vacuum, the space between the patterns, as he experiences a sensation of freedom on the journey to the city.

In **"Three Brick Walls,"** Paul's story is resumed on Paul's first evening in the city. That Paul will not find freedom but simply replace one imprisoning pattern for another is immediately established by the parallelism between the opening scenes of the two stories. The sunlight and the transparent shadows of the leaves have been replaced by more concrete, hard-edged images: "his room faced a brick wall. There was a narrow street between the window and the wall, and a lamp post, and a small twisted tree." Paul has not yet fit into the pattern of this cramped brown and green room: against the rectangular and rectilinear shapes of the furniture and the striped seersucker bedspread, the key lies "slant-wise" on the bureau: "he was not yet aware that it belonged to him, and could be used" to fit into the pattern (4).

Feeling "absolutely completely unrestrained and free," Paul takes the key from the bureau and leaves the greens and browns of his room to enter "a grey evening in a grey city." Paul's room is on a street, "no longer than one block, and bounded on three sides by brick," where there are no children, Paul himself having been propelled into adulthood. He has become one of those Prufrockian citizens of the modern world, one of those "people who poked repetitive keys into the doorways and climbed the stairs inside[,] . . . those who have nothing of themselves outside lying around loose." Paul has already begun to sink into the street's pattern, gaining a sense of security from the "anonymity of the street" and discovering that "the three brick walls stood for shelter" (4). But because he is still in that vacuum—that point of freedom between two patterns—Paul ventures out of the imprisoning walls through the block's one open side.

On the street beyond there is no pattern, but rather a chaos of sounds and lights. Pyramids of apples and oranges, and coloured signs and posters, bombard him in their unpatterned and unstructured randomness. Entering a lunch room, Paul is forced to walk down a long tunnel-like stretch where he orders an unwanted sandwich and a cup of tea from a grotesque figure behind the counter. This surrealistic, nightmarish scene continues after Paul leaves the lunch room, when he ponders the vulnerability of a brightly lit ticket office that is open to converging crowds from all sides. Growing alarmed, even fearful, as he realizes that he himself is vulnerable to the contact he so wants to avoid, Paul escapes to his room, where he bends his arms, leans on the shutters, and trembles "with a sweet loneliness which required no people." From the safety of the frame—the walls protect him from the city, the ledge of his window from the street itself—he can become part of, but not be forced to make contact with, the "mass of people, a safe mass, without form" (6). This is the freedom he has sought. Believing himself to be free, he has learned to use one of those "repetitive keys" for immuring himself in a dull but safe cell. He has joined the Prufrocks of the modern world, those "lonely men in shirt-sleeves, leaning out of windows" ("The Love Song of J. Alfred Prufrock" line 72), these windows framing their languid subjects and thus enclosing them in both space and time.

Although this pair of stories was the first fiction Gallant published, she drafted several other stories during this

apprenticeship stage of her writing career, one even earlier. In her introduction to *Home Truths,* Gallant indicates that **"Thank You for the Lovely Tea"** (*New Yorker* 9 June 1956) was originally written when she was eighteen, and **"Jorinda and Jorindel"** (*New Yorker* 19 Sept. 1959) and **"Up North"** (*New Yorker* 21 Nov. 1959) during the forties while working on the Montreal *Standard* (xix). The greater sophistication of structure, perspective, and metaphor attained in these stories over that in the *Preview* pair suggests that the revisions for the *New Yorker* must have been extensive.[4] The traces of fragmentation, distortion, and mobility that were observed in the two earlier *Preview* stories increasingly resemble techniques used in Cubist paintings that stretch the two-dimensional spatial frame, creating a greater sense of the third dimension, depth, and even of the fourth, time.

It is particularly with regard to perspective and the effects of perspective on structure that **"Thank You for the Lovely Tea"** and Gallant's first *New Yorker* story, **"Madeline's Birthday,"** seem the creation of a more seasoned writer, one who has gained a more confident sense of her own unique style, than the writer of the *Preview* stories and the *Northern Review* story, **"The Flowers of Spring."** In the latter stories, Gallant adheres so steadily and consistently to the modernist ideal of a self-effacing narrative perspective that, despite the attempt to achieve the illusion of third and fourth dimensions through painterly metaphors and diptych structure in the *Preview* stories, the overall effect is flat. One of the aspects of Gallant's style, however, that will become a trademark of her stories and that can be noted as early as **"Thank You for the Lovely Tea"** and **"Madeline's Birthday"** is the sense of plurality that Gallant achieves by exposing her characters in their given situations to a number of different angles. As Gallant remarked to Michel Fabre in a July 1988 interview, "The events and characters in fiction are like works of art in a museum. You see them from different angles, you move round and around. You don't stand at the same place" (101). Gallant is specifically referring to the narrator, the transmitter, in this passage, but the "you" could as aptly refer to the audience, the receiver. Gallant always retains so tenacious a grip on perspective that the narrative voice unobtrusively but unwaveringly guides the reader in and around and through these events and characters as they are perceived from different angles; nevertheless, in her most satisfying because most challenging stories, a few angles—a few gaps of indeterminacy—always remain, revealed but unexplored, for the curious reader to view alone after the tour has drawn to an end.[5]

Thus, although she later experimented with alternative voices, Gallant arrived at a characteristic aspect of her style early in her writing career. Gallant's rare use of first-person perspective sometimes results in what Janice Kulyk Keefer calls "a curious awkwardness," not in the writer's transmitting, but in the reader's receiving of a story: "One's reading of these texts is vexed by a question that points to the unpersuasiveness of Gallant's choice of narrative mode: *why* is this person telling us his or her story in the first place?" (63). First-person narration seems appropriate in Gallant's *Standard Magazine* story, **"A Wonderful Country,"** largely because, as with the more mature Linnet Muir stories, the shifting perspective of the first-person voice is justified by the reflexive elements as we see the incipient writer of fiction beginning to emerge.⁶ The first-person narrator, a junior assistant in a real estate office, whose responsibility it is to find accommodation for refugees, is acquiring one of the qualities that, according to Gallant, is necessary for the development of a writer—the ability to empathize, and thus to achieve an authorial perspective that is one neither of distance nor of complete identification (Fabre 96-97; Martens 168, 172-73; Monroe). The arid, flat scene of **"A Wonderful Country"**—a brick duplex fronted by a yellow lawn on a street "still and flat, edged with telephone poles" (4)—would seem suitable for Gallant's characteristic third-person detachment. Gallant instead filters the story through a narrator who finds herself unable to maintain the professional distance she desires. She reluctantly draws closer as she observes the couple who are renting their home, and her attitude toward the couple's suburban lifestyle becomes less patronizing than it was at first. The narrator's professional distance also breaks down as she views the Hungarian refugee from a variety of vantage points, including that of the suburban couple, who sees him as "foreign and ridiculous," an attitude that counters, without negating, her earlier wish to have "made more effort to know him" and so to have attained a harmony of scene that was lacking (8).

With the merging of detached third-person narration and shifting perspectives in **"Thank You for the Lovely Tea,"** a characteristic element of Gallant's style is first achieved: a controlling voice that rarely comments but simply records the fragmented perspectives, in this case five, that her voice comprises. Of least importance to this story is the perspective of the new headmistress, who knows little more of her school's pupils than what the files tell her. While ostensibly broad-minded and open to change, she maintains professional distance by adhering to protocol when dealing with the pupils and receiving guests connected with the girls' lives outside the school's structure (6-7, 16); thus, the headmistress never becomes more involved than a detached, even voyeuristic, observer.

The story itself is composed of the perspectives of and on four figures: the three pupils—Ruth Cook, May Watson, and Helen McDonnell—and the mistress of Ruth's divorced father, Mrs. Holland, who takes the girls to tea. Mrs. Holland has not had the discipline of a school such as theirs, so knows little of perspective and proportion, two lessons the girls have been practising earlier this day. Consequently, Mrs. Holland can never appear more than "smart but smudged, as if paint had spilled over the outline of a drawing" (3). Helen, like Mrs. Holland a "natural victim" (15), has found a place in the school's structure after having been "uprooted . . . from her warm, rowdy, half-literate family" (11), but any threat of change shifts the perspective, making her nebulous position in the composition vulnerable. Her successful withstanding of May's goads at tea, however, signals that she has learned and now subscribes to those lessons on perspective and proportion. Like Paul of the *Preview* stories, who finds his freedom in the prison of his room, Helen's "dearest wish was to wear this uniform as long as she could, to stay on at the school forever, to melt, with no intervening gap, from the students' dining hall to the staff sitting room" (12).

May, Mrs. Holland observes, appears "quite strung up about something, but held in by training, by discipline" (14). This outing to the tearoom has brought back the image of her twin sister, from whom she has been parted so that they may develop separate identities. The image is resurrected at first by May's own reflection in the car's window (9), and then by memories at the tearoom, where she and her sister used to come on special occasions (11). When this undisciplined image from the past superimposes itself on her own emerging self-image, May loses her disciplined sense of perspective and proportion and attempts to make Helen lose hers. She still remains slightly vertiginous after returning to the school at the end of the day's outing. In contrast, Ruth is simply left wondering "if she would ever care enough about anyone to make all the mistakes those around her had made during the rainy-day tea with Mrs. Holland" (16). Throughout the day Ruth demonstrates the "patience and self-control" required to give the composition a sense of structure: when the art teacher points out that the horizon line is too low in her picture, Ruth adjusts the size and position of the flowerpots to attain perspective and proportion (3-4), just as later she keeps herself and the situation in check so as not to become a victim of the "mental and emotional spirals" that Mrs. Holland intuits just before May baits Helen (15). As Mrs. Holland recedes from the picture at the story's end, Ruth, like Paul, is framed by an upstairs window, shut off from any contacts that would disrupt the proportion and perspective of the structured composition.

"Thank You for the Lovely Tea," itself a well-composed picture harmonizing the different perspectives of the five characters on one another and the day's events, contains slight chinks that permit another perspective—that of the reader—which the steady uniplanar perspective of **"Good Morning and Goodbye,"** **"Three Brick Walls,"** and **"The Flowers of Spring,"** and the reflexive readjustments of perspective in **"A**

Wonderful Country," discourage. In **"Thank You for the Lovely Tea"** and many stories to follow, Gallant provides the reader with what Wolfgang Iser refers to as "a bundle of multiple viewpoints, the center of which is continuously shifted," permitting "new gaps to arise in the text," and also "a cutting—montage—or segmenting technique," permitting "relatively great freedom with respect to the concatenation of their [the stories'] textual patterns with one another in the reading process" ("Indeterminacy" 20-22). The narrative voice of **"Thank You for the Lovely Tea"** embraces the various perspectives of the characters' interactions as the scene shifts from the enclosed structures of the well-regulated school, Mrs. Holland's car, and the "oval tearoom newly done up with chrome and onyx" (13), back to the school, and thus guides the reader through space and time and keeps tight control over any interstices or diversions from the main route. Meanwhile, however, the reader is developing a certain agility in comprehending the "mental and emotional spirals" of all the characters. This agility becomes essential to the reading process when the seemingly neat pairing of the characters as vulnerable or strong, victim or victor, begins to break down, and when seemingly distinct outlines begin to blur, particularly when the characters take on identities outside the context of the depicted structures: the girls' home environments, Mrs. Holland's relations with Ruth's father and with Ruth herself. Ruth and Helen remain enclosed within the tightly structured composition, which the rules of perspective and proportion govern, and so outside the chaotic emotional experiences they spurn; May and Mrs. Holland, because attempting to be both inside and outside the composition, find themselves in a shifting uncertain terrain; but the reader, guided by the story's controlling voice in and around and out of the composition, moves freely within the recesses exposed but unexplored. "[F]iction, like painting," says Gallant in the introduction to **Home Truths,** "consists entirely of more than meets the eye; otherwise it is not worth a second's consideration" (xii).

Parallels can be drawn between Gallant's experimentation with fragmented perspective and the Cubist experimentation earlier in the century that so influenced Quebec painters of the 1940s. Cubists rejected perspective in its traditional sense of attempting to attain realism through three-dimensional optical effects. Nevertheless, their enclosing (although not always harmonizing) of fragmented forms within the whole composition, and the potential for viewers to bring their own perspectives, particularly when familiar objects are the source of fragmentation (although again this not necessarily resulting in harmony or completion), indicate that the Cubists did not ignore perspective, but rather "exploit[ed] it for new effects" (Gombich 455-56).[7]

But like Alfred Pellan and the Prisme d'Yeux group,[8] and unlike Paul-Emile Borduas and the Automatistes,

Gallant never committed herself to the surrealistic elements that transformed the Cubism of the Automatistes from a figurative to an abstract form of art. Gallant's own writing process, which she has on several occasions described as involving many stages of revision (for example, Fabre 99-100), contrasts with the automatic spontaneity attempted by many Surrealists, including Borduas's aptly named followers. Moreover, Gallant's suspicion of dreams and dream analysis and her ultimate rejection of them as a worthwhile subject of art[9] again dissociate her from the Surrealists. **"Jorinda and Jorindel"** goes beyond the distortions of **"Three Brick Walls"** in incorporating surrealistic elements into the text. But, as in the more complex **"Thank You for the Lovely Tea,"** Gallant requires a perspective from the reader, in this case one that entails the reader's recognition of her rejection of purportedly archetypal symbols from dream, fairy tale, Jungian psychology, and fantasy literature, symbols that promise escape but bring only entrapment.

The linked elements of dream and fairy tale form a frame for the story, which begins with the drunken exclamation of a house guest, "I've got it!" (that is, she has learned a Charleston dance step), merging with Irmgard's dream of the witch who has captured Jorinda and is attempting to capture Jorindel and change him into a bird. The dishevelled hair of Irmgard and the guest, Mrs. Bloodworth (17-18), associates both of them with the witch from the Brothers Grimm's **"Jorinda and Joringel,"** who first paralyses anyone coming near her castle and then, if the visitor is a fair maiden, changes her into a bird, puts her into a basket, and adds the victim to her collection.[10] Immediately, therefore, the reader is guided to question whether the young Irmgard with "her thumb in her mouth" (17) is an archetypal naïf with the imaginative capacity to break the frame of confining reality. Is Irmgard perhaps both jailer witch and jailed Jorinda?

Because two images frequently deemed archetypal symbols of potential spiritual awareness and rebirth—water and mirror—are integrated into the text, this irony is reinforced. Irmgard has thrice denied the "innocent" Freddy a place in her life to make room for the more worldly Bradley, the second denial eliciting the vertiginous sensation of coasting downhill on her bicycle and losing control (23). She now attempts to recall Freddy into her life, but he insists that if their friendship is to be renewed, it must be on his terms, and so he invites Irmgard to swim at a public beach, forbidden to Irmgard because reputedly polluted. While this may allude to Jung's water, "the commonest symbol for the unconscious," "spirit that has become unconscious," particularly that water reached through descent—"earthy and tangible . . . the fluid of the instinct-driven body, blood and the flowing of blood"—Irmgard's "descent into the depths" is not followed by the expected ascent (Jung

302-03). Just as the witch paralyses Jorindel and prevents the transformed Jorinda from flying away by putting her in a basket, so the water in which Irmgard swims is not a Jungian "mirror of the water" into which she descends and "risks a confrontation" by exposing her real self (Jung 304). Instead, witnessing the nakedness of Freddy, Irmgard escapes him by saying miserably, "I think my mother wants me now" (26). The mirror is provided not by the water but rather by her "stockbroker" cousin Bradley (21, 24) and, after he leaves, by her mother (25, 27).

Even with the re-introduction of the dream at the end of the story and the allusion to Lewis Carroll's fantasy, *Alice in Wonderland,* the irony continues. Irmgard may dream that Freddy—or is it Bradley or herself? she is not sure—has been snatched by a sinister force from the woods (28), but the commonplace reality of the situation is clear: Freddy has been sent back to the orphan asylum in Montreal, and Bradley has returned to his family in Boston. As Irmgard recalls her dream of the night before and attempts to understand and explain it, her mother becomes Carroll's Queen of Hearts, with her love of rules, especially at croquet, by vetoing dreams at breakfast (28). Unlike Alice, who confronts symbolic characters and situations in surrealistic dreamscapes reached through, first, descent into the underworld after falling down the rabbit hole and crossing a sea of tears, and, later, entrance into a world behind the looking glass, Irmgard looks not to the unconscious, not to the spirit or imagination, but to the rules of an adult world, to fix her place. Although the child Irmgard is not as crusted over with social conventions and skills as the adolescent Ruth Cook, neither girl has the potential for imaginative excursions into an unconscious or spiritual terrain. From "I've got it" to the polluted beach to "no dreams at breakfast," Irmgard's experience is not that of the private world of surrealistic fantasies but rather that of the public world of ordinary reality. Likewise, the reader's experience of a third and fourth dimension is attained not through any textual descent and confrontation with archetypal symbols from the unconscious, but rather through a discovery of the ironic integration of surrealistic elements into the story.

From the essentially two-dimensional *Preview* stories to the three- and four-dimensional **"Thank You for the Lovely Tea"** and **"Jorinda and Jorindel,"** these dimensions being attained primarily through the reader's perspective that attempts to pierce the Surrealist distortions and to harmonize or complete the Cubist fragmentation, Gallant's stories create the impression of compositions straining to break free from their frames. In **"Up North"** can be observed Gallant's first sustained achievement of the fourth dimension through kinetic effects other than those attained through reader response.

Gallant's successful integration of formal kinetic effects into this and later stories is markedly unlike the optical

tricks and dabbling in mixed media to which *avant-garde* artists—visual and literary—have resorted throughout the century. Early in the century, there were Naum Gabo's vibrating wires, what he called *Kinetic Constructions*; these were succeeded by various experiments with lights, motors, suspended structures (mobiles), and symbolic and optical games to create movement or the illusion of movement. Among literary artists, similar strategies have been employed: visual symbols and illustrations, varied typescript and colour of print, and pages left unbound for each reader to shuffle at will. Apart from the Russian Constructivists of the 1920s, the most radical experimentation with kinetic effects in both modern visual and post-modern literary art has been undertaken by French and American practitioners and their followers. Until recently, concern with kinetic effects had no revolutionary effect on Canadian art, perhaps because of the dominant strain of what Paul Duval has termed "High Realism." With Kinetic Art, "it is not essential that the work itself should move," since the kinetic effects "can be produced by the spectator moving in front of the work or by the spectator handling and manipulating the work"; nevertheless, Kinetic Art involves not simply the representation of movement but a concern "with movement itself, with movement as an integral part of the work" (Barrett 211). As with her incorporation of all visual and concrete elements into her narratives, with her creation of a sense of movement, Gallant eschews *avant-garde* tactics, instead exploiting the possibilities within the written word. As the Prisme d'Yeux group's manifesto of 1948 insisted on "pure painting," so too Gallant adheres to pure language. W. J. Keith, in *A Sense of Style,* forcefully declares this fidelity to her chosen medium: "Unlike some of her more conspicuous but perhaps less talented contemporaries, Gallant has never lost faith in the adequacy, the power, and even the glory of language" (115).

In **"Up North,"** Gallant again makes use of Cubist fragmentation, as the perspective shifts between Dennis and Roy McLaughlin, and of Surrealist distortion, in Dennis's vision of little men. The whole composition is set in motion when the characters experience what will become another trademark of Gallant's style—the disorientation created through travel, particularly by train. Two of the previous stories prepare for this motif. At the end of **"Good Morning and Goodbye,"** Paul is left revelling in the sense of freedom he experiences on the train, a "vacuum that lies between the patterns in a life" (2). In **"Thank You for the Lovely Tea,"** Ruth Cook, fearful of such a vacuum and the freedom it bodes, immediately transforms the car, which carries the group from the structure of the school to the structure of the department store's elevator and tearoom, into another imprisoning structure. She does so first, by insinuating that Mrs. Holland has eaten a piece of chocolate Ruth has left in her father's car (8-9), and then, by dismissing the doubts and fears Mrs. Holland has had about a trip to California taken in this car with Ruth's father, and so "reducing the trip . . . to a simple, unimportant outing involving two elderly people, long past love" (10). It is, however, in the window of this moving car and later in the moving elevator that May recalls her twin sister, a memory that incites her cruelty to Helen and results in her own suffering for this cruelty. Those who are more able to protect themselves—Paul, Ruth, Helen, and potentially Irmgard—remain static, framed in windows or posing by their reflectors. Those who are prone to being natural victims—Mrs. Holland, May, and Dennis—are unable to find solace within a static structure or pattern, because they are vulnerable to the haunting of ghosts, memories of unreconciled or inexplicable experiences from their past. In the case of Dennis, his ghosts acquire not just a private, but a historical, dimension.

Unlike Irmgard, whose potential ghost emerges during the course of the narrative, which is therefore told in the present tense, Dennis's own past fades into and is absorbed by the present: "When they woke up in the train, their bed was black with soot and there was soot in his Mum's blondie hair. They were miles north of Montreal, which had, already, sunk beneath his remembrance." This brief, bleak description, clearly from the perspective of the young boy himself, is followed by Dennis's description of the ghosts: "'D'you know what I sor in the night? . . . Well, the train must of stopped, see, and some little men with bundles on their backs got on. Other men was holding lanterns. They were all little. They were all talking French'" (49-50). While his mother accuses him of fantasy—"'You and your bloody elves'"—Dennis has a clear vision of his ghosts: "'They was people.'" And it is toward one of these ghosts, Dennis's father, a "mythical, towering, half-remembered figure," that "they were now travelling to join up north" (50).

As the train lumbers northward, Dennis's disorientation develops. The soot and the dark spun a thread back to an England of factories and air-raids, but now, stopped at a station, Dennis observes "a swamp with bristling black rushes, red as ink" and an "autumn sunrise; cold, red," which are "so strange to him, so singular, that he could not have said an hour later which feature of the scene was in the foreground or to the left or right" (51). From this point, the northward travel is accompanied by the cold brightening of the day. At first, Dennis is able to see his own face and those of his mother and McLaughlin, "remote and bodiless," reflected in the train window. Like a Cubist or Surrealist composition of transparent overlaid images, Dennis observes, behind these reflected faces, the light from the train windows falling "in pale squares on the upturned vanishing faces and on the little trees" outside the train. But as they pass "into an unchanging landscape of swamp and

bracken and stunted trees," and as the lights inside the train are extinguished, Dennis loses the image of himself and those around him (51-52).

The sense of Dennis's disorientation is reinforced by the story's structure when, on several occasions, the scene is shown not from Dennis's perspective, but from that of a passenger, Roy McLaughlin. At first McLaughlin dismisses mother and son in his reductive "Limey bride" and "Pest" (50), but he begins to have difficulties fixing his image of Dennis when, first, he wonders if the father has Indian blood (52-53), and then when he realizes that Dennis's ghosts belong to an unwritten history of which the young boy could have no knowledge: ghosts of the unemployed sent up north from the cities to get them off relief during the depression years (54).

Both Dennis and McLaughlin are thrown into vertigo when they reach a junction at which they must change trains. McLaughlin has made himself vulnerable by feeling responsibility and compassion (54). It is, however, with Dennis's fear and determination not to leave the train that **"Up North"** ends. For Dennis, the journey by train, which began with images connecting him to the past, has propelled him into new uncharted experiences. "You'll be seeing plenty of everything now," says McLaughlin in the closing sentence of the story (55). From the description given of this land and its people, the reader fills in the bleak and even brutalizing nature of these experiences. Whereas when the reader takes leave of Ruth Cook and the German refugee, Paul, they are framed by the structure of a window, and of Irmgard when she is standing by her mother's chair, looking to the reflection the mother will return, Dennis—to an even greater degree than May—is left in a state of vertigo, "clinging to the train, to air; to anything," and screaming, "I never saw *any*thing!" (55). Although it is the responsive reader who brings Dennis's vertigo to an end for him, the story's binary fragmentation of perspective and its fixing of Dennis within his own surrealistic historical vision lead the reader to one conclusion: Dennis's "anything" is a nothing that will ultimately cancel out Dennis's humanity. The starkness of the style and tenor of the only insights given Dennis's mother would seem to confirm this reading: "It's not proper country. . . . It's bare"; "It's the train whistle. It's so sad. It gets him down" (54). With his "little jacket" and "Tweedledum cap on his head," Dennis has been rushed "on this train into an existence where his clothes would be too good for him" (53). It is an existence made all the more terrifying because, like the red "J" that circumscribes Paul's life, Dennis's little men allude to a history as yet unwritten and hence reduced to a vertiginous, surrealistic, fragmented image, which does not yet harmoniously cohere with any charted reality.

The binary perspective of **"Up North"** may seem to limit the plurality of interpretative possibilities and, therefore, may appear less sophisticated than those stories that, beginning with **"Thank You for the Lovely Tea,"** embrace a number of perspectives and invite others from the reader. But this perspective reinforces other visual techniques integrated into the story: when the train has stopped, the characters experience vertigo; the sharply defined light and dark demarcating inside and outside the train have, by journey's end, been inverted and diffused; the few colours—the red and then blue of the sky—have been expunged. "It was quite day now; their faces were plain and clear, as if drawn without shading on white paper" (54).

In his essay, "The Reading Process," Wolfgang Iser suggests that "with a literary text we can only picture things which are not there; the written part of the text gives us the knowledge, but it is the unwritten part that gives us the opportunity to picture things; indeed without the elements of indeterminacy, the gaps in the text, we should not be able to use our imagination" (283). Gallant locks many of her apprenticeship stories in the frame of a fixed perspective or suspended moment, with characters paralysed through cowardice and inertia into inaction and non-being; nevertheless, her experimentation with painterly techniques and forms creates fragmentation, distortion, and mobility, and thus stories that strain to break the frames enclosing them. In these stories of her apprenticeship period, Gallant hones those formal qualities that provide visual signals for readers to compose into pictures with colour and light and shading, shape and texture and fluidity. By the time she left Montreal for Europe in 1950, Gallant's fiction exhibited those formal kinetic properties, produced through structure, perspective, and metaphor, that mark the breaking free of her style from frames that could well have enervated her art.

Notes

1. See my article, "Artistry in Mavis Gallant's *Green Water, Green Sky*: The Composition of Structure, Pattern, and Gyre," in *Canadian Literature* 129 (1991): 57-73, on the success of *Green Water, Green Sky* in breaking the frame.

2. "Fresco Class," *Rotogravure* 9 Nov. 1946: 12-13; "Window Artist," *Standard Review* 31 Jan. 1948: 3; "Family Doctor," *Standard Magazine* 4 Sept. 1948: 4, 22.

3. The *Standard* article that was the outcome of this trip was probably "These Are the First Impressions the War Brides Formed of Canada," *Rotogravure* 13 Oct. 1945: 4+.

4. Only in the case of "Up North" does it seem, from Gallant's comments in this introduction to *Home Truths*, that few revisions were actually undertaken: "I typed 'Up North' about eight years later, almost as I found it. Some pages had the

wobbly look of having been written in a train, and I probably started it during a journey very like the one described while on assignment for *The Standard*" (xix). The outcome of this assignment could have been one of several articles, the most likely being "Land Auction," *Photonews,* 12 Aug. 1950: 8-11, on St. Felicien, in northern Quebec. In a recent interview with Pleuke Boyce for *Books in Canada,* "Image and Memory" (Jan./Feb. 1990: 29-31), Gallant explains that although "Thank You for the Lovely Tea" was written "very early," the "finished version," the "complete story," was made "years later," and that it is mainly the dialogue that remains from the original (29).

5. The concept of "gaps" or "spaces" of indeterminacy, as developed by European phenomenologist Roman Ingarden and reception theorist Wolfgang Iser, is a useful one in this context and will be alluded to in the following discussions of "Thank You for the Lovely Tea," "Jorinda and Jorindel," and "Up North." An analysis of this relationship between narrative voice and reader response is one of the tasks undertaken by Janice Kulyk Keefer in *Reading Mavis Gallant,* especially in her third chapter, "Narrative Voice and Structure."

6. As with the Linnet Muir stories, this story draws on Gallant's experiences in Montreal during the 1940s. According to Judith Skelton Grant's biographical sketch in *Mavis Gallant and Her Works* (Toronto: ECW, n.d.), Gallant worked for a short time in the forties for a Montreal real estate firm (2).

7. The nature of these effects is developed in E. H. Gombrich's *Art and Illusion: A Study in the Psychology of Pictorial Representation* (Princeton: Princeton UP, 1972), when he argues that "[c]ubism . . . is the most radical attempt to stamp out ambiguity and to enforce one reading of the picture—that of a man-made construction, a colored canvas" (281), and that "[t]he function of representational clues in cubist paintings . . . is to narrow down the range of possible interpretations till we are forced to accept the flat pattern with all its tensions" (286). This conclusion has been disputed by Mark Roskill in *The Interpretations of Cubism* (Philadelphia: Art Alliance, 1985), 176-81, particularly this idea of a Cubist painting becoming in itself the only reading possible. This controversy relates to one of the challenges that Janice Kulyk Keefer sets herself in *Reading Mavis Gallant*: ". . . one of the aspects of her work with which I shall attempt to come to terms is the 'silencing effect' of her authoritative tone and incisive diction, which can turn every narrative statement into a pronouncement *ex cathedra*" (viii). It is again in Chapter 3 that Keefer most fully ad-

dresses this issue; she illustrates there the way the openness of Gallant's language counters the tendency to closure in the reductive world about which she writes.

8. Paul Duval, *Four Decades: The Canadian Group of Painters and Their Contemporaries, 1930-1970* (Toronto: Clarke, 1972), reports the following comment made by Alfred Pellan: "I embrace the surrealism of André Masson, Klee and Miró. But for Dali and Tanguy—those clever magicians—I have no respect. . . . The subconscious is only a part of the painting problem. Surrealism has added to the richness of the artist's raw material. That material should still be filtered through the conscious mind. The painter should be like a fisherman who keeps some fish and throws the rest back. Then, of course, the fish should be carefully mounted" (113).

9. Although fascinated by the phenomenon of dreams, Gallant's suspicion of them as a worthwhile subject for art can be detected in two *Standard Magazine* articles, "Freud or Double Talk?" (29 Mar. 1947: 3, 14) and "Dreams" (30 Oct. 1948: 5, 11), in which she questions the value and reliability of symbolic analysis of images in dreams. It is not surprising, therefore, that Gallant's later interest in Surrealism, as demonstrated in her *New York Times Book Review* article (28 May 1972: 4+), "Paris Letter: The Unsuccessful Surrealist," and in her comments on this article in her interview with Hancock (51), is as a political rather than a viable artistic movement. Nor is it surprising that in her 1982 CBC radio interview with Susan Leslie, although admitting "there is something about dreams that is curious," and relating a dream she had of Lucy Dreyfus, Gallant claims that she no longer reads Jungian dream analysis, preferring to "coast along with improbabilities" and "the idea of mystery."

10. In her *Standard Magazine* article, "Give the Kid a Gory Story" (29 June 1946: 9, 15), a passage depicting this scene was selected by Gallant "at random from standard fairy tale classics on the market" as having a particularly "Poe-like horror" (15).

Works Cited

Baele, Nancy. "A Canadian at Home in Paris." *The Ottawa Citizen* 27 Feb. 1988: C1, C10.

Barrett, Cyril. "Kinetic Art." *Concepts of Modern Art.* Ed. Tony Richardson and Nikos Stangos. New York: Harper, 1974. 211-23.

Bilan, R. P. Rev. of *From the Fifteenth District*, by Mavis Gallant. *University of Toronto Quarterly* 49 (Summer 1980): 326-27.

Corbeil, Carole. "Home Truths with a Touch of Gallant Wit." *The Globe and Mail* 7 Nov. 1981: X21.

Duval, Paul. *High Realism in Canada.* Toronto: Clarke, 1974.

Eliot, T. S. "The Love Song of J. Alfred Prufrock." *Collected Poems 1909-1962.* London: Faber, 1963. 13-17.

Fabre, Michel. "An Interview with Mavis Gallant." *Commonwealth* 11.2 (1989): 95-103.

Gallant, Mavis. "The Flowers of Spring." *Northern Review* June-July 1950: 31-39.

———. "Good Morning and Goodbye." *Preview* Dec. 1944: 1-3.

———. *Green Water, Green Sky.* Boston: Houghton, 1959.

———. Introduction. *Home Truths.* Toronto: Macmillan, 1982. xi-xxii.

———. Introduction. *The War Brides.* Ed. Joyce Hibbert. PMA, 1978. Rpt. as "Introduction to *The War Brides.*" *Paris Notebooks.* Toronto: Macmillan, 1988. 153-60.

———. "Jorinda and Jorindel." *Home Truths.* 17-28.

———. "Madeline's Birthday." *New Yorker* 1 Sept. 1951: 20-24.

———. "Thank You for the Lovely Tea." *Home Truths.* 2-16.

———. "Three Brick Walls." *Preview* Dec. 1944: 4-6.

———. "Up North." *Home Truths.* 49-55.

———. "A Wonderful Country." *Standard Magazine* 14 Dec. 1946: 4, 8.

Gombich, E. H. *The Story of Art.* 12th ed. London: Phaidon, 1972.

Hancock, Geoff. "An Interview with Mavis Gallant." *Canadian Fiction Magazine* 28 (1978): 18-67.

Iser, Wolfgang. "Indeterminacy and the Reader's Response in Prose Fiction." *Aspects of Narrative: Selected Papers from the English Institute.* Ed. J. Hillis Miller. New York: Columbia UP, 1971. 1-45.

———. "The Reading Process." *The Implied Reader: Patterns of Communication in Prose Fiction from Bunyan to Beckett.* Baltimore: Johns Hopkins UP, 1974. 274-94.

Jung, C. G. *The Basic Writings of C. G. Jung.* Ed. Violet Staub de Laszlo. New York: Modern Library-Random, 1959.

Keefer, Janice Kulyk. *Reading Mavis Gallant.* Toronto: Oxford UP, 1989.

Keith, W. J. *A Sense of Style: Studies in the Art of Fiction in English-Speaking Canada.* Toronto: ECW, 1989.

Leith, Linda. "Remembering Montreal in the 40s: A Conversation with Mavis Gallant." *Border/Lines* 13 (1988): 4-5.

Leslie, Susan. Interview. *Audience.* CBC FM. 6 Feb. 1982.

Martens, Debra. "An Interview with Mavis Gallant." *Rubicon* 4 (1984-85): 150-82.

Monroe, Pat. Interview. *The Afternoon Show.* CBC, Vancouver. 17 Feb. 1984.

Karen Smythe (essay date 1992)

SOURCE: Smythe, Karen. "The 'Home Truth' about *Home Truths*: Gallant's Ironic Introduction." In *Double Talking: Essays on Verbal and Visual Ironies in Canadian Contemporary Art and Literature,* edited by Linda Hutcheon, pp. 106-14. Toronto: ECW Press, 1992.

[*In the following essay, Smythe argues that "the ironic introduction to* Home Truths *is the perfect vehicle for Gallant's resistance to a limited and limiting definition of herself as a Canadian writer."*]

Mavis Gallant has come to be known as one of the ironists supreme in Canadian letters. Her fiction is characterized by detached narrators and an ironic tone, producing the effect of what one critic has called "something rather chilling" (Rooke 267). I would argue, however, that Gallant uses irony not only as a distancing technique for her own voice or as a subversive strategy that challenges forms and values, but also as a strategy that invites readers to enter into a participatory relation with the text. It is these latter two uses of irony that make Gallant's writing both sophisticated and challenging to the reader of Canadian fiction, as critics are beginning to note. The study of irony in Gallant's fiction is fast becoming a commonplace. But rather than try to place Gallant's irony in a Canadian context, I would like to approach her ironic comments *about* the critical tendency toward contextualizing Canadian literature in a nationalistic framework.

Gallant included "An Introduction," twelve pages of paracritical prose, in one of her more recent books, ***Home Truths: Selected Canadian Stories.*** I call this preface "paracritical" because it is written as commentary on the text, but is something other than criticism. Such prefaces seem to provide an introduction to the work, and when included in the text, especially when they precede the fiction (making them para*textual* as well), they provide tacit and/or explicit suggestions for interpreting that text. But Gallant's preface subverts this convention by refusing to offer specific interpretations; rather, she tells us, in introducing her "Canadian Stories," how *not* to read.

What is unusual about Gallant's preface is that instead of merely guiding our reading of her "Canadian" stories, she is defending her identity and her poetics from potential detractors. The introduction itself, then, is an example of "structural irony" defined as a sustained use of some structural feature in a text to produce "duplicity of meaning" (Appendix 2, 33). The preface stands structurally to suggest alternate readings of the proclaimed "Canadian Stories." Taken literally, the subtitle of the collection, "Selected Canadian Stories," would seem to suggest that Gallant adheres to a nationalistic aesthetic, one that she might explain in the introduction. Yet Gallant uses the forum of the preface ironically to declare that "where his work is concerned, the writer, like any other artist, owes no more and no less to his compatriots than to people at large" (xiii). Her remarks, then, ensure that the fiction they preface will not be reduced to a single reading as "Canadian Stories"; Gallant thereby discourages critics/readers from what Robert Kroetsch calls "recourse to an easy version of national definition" ("Beyond Nationalism" vii).

With the inclusion of the subtitle, it would seem that Gallant is guilty of "domestic embellishment" (xii), which is, she says, demanded of "Canadian writers, though only when their work is concerned with Canada and Canadians." The titular use (in both senses) of nationality in the description of her fiction ensures not only that the market is targeted, but also that the critical reception and interpretation of the stories is at least partially predetermined as well. But it would appear that the subtitle was not Gallant's invention at all. In her limited discussion of it, Gallant implicitly refutes the idea that it reflects a nationalistic intention on *her* part. She raises the issue of nationalism explicitly, immediately after citing the phrase "Canadian stories," and in doing so she alerts us to the paradoxical use of the subtitle of her collection: "What I am calling, most clumsily, the national sense of self is quite separate from nationalism, which I distrust and reject absolutely, and even patriotism, so often used as a stick to beat people with" (xv). Her resistance to the nationalist label of literature is written into her preface, which indicates that the subtitle—the interpretive interference—is in her view a structurally ironic addition.

Assuming then that "Selected Canadian Stories" was a marketing idea that promised greater sales and wider readership (which would, no doubt, be welcomed by Gallant herself) the introduction Gallant provides serves to resist this label and to demonstrate the anti-nationalistic stance of the author.[1] Gallant's ironic preface allows her to play the publishing game and to criticize its political implications at the same time. She uses the example of Canadian painting (which is clearly a displacement for the art of writing) to indicate her feelings about nationalistically inclined Canadian criticism: "A Montreal collector once told me that he bought Canadian paintings in order to have a unifying theme in the decoration of his house. It means—if anything so silly can have a meaning—that art is neutral adornment, a slightly superior brand of chintz, and that Canadian painters, because they are Canadian, work from a single vision" (xi). She quickly adds that "To dissent would lead into hostile territory" (xi). Her vocabulary is telling: even as she withdraws from a discussion of nationally oriented criticism, she has made her point.

The title itself, *Home Truths,* refers to an ironic type of idiom: "home truths" are painful facts, consisting of the contradiction between what *is* and what *should be* (Ross 86), between some kind of discomfort and the presumed comfort of "home." Gallant may have wanted this title to play against the subtitle ironically. The "truth" is that there is no consensus as to what constitutes, precisely, a "Canadian" story (much less a collection of stories). "Home" may be "Canada," but the only "Truths" are "Stories," Canadian or otherwise.

Gallant uses a subversive subtext to justify her stance as a Canadian "who has failed to 'paint Canadian'" (xii). While her preface might seem conventional on the surface—it seems briefly to describe the meaning of some of the stories (**"Saturday," "Jorinda and Jorindel," "Up North," "Thank You for the Lovely Tea,"** and the Linnet Muir stories)—it is also inherently ironic, and as Gallant says of fiction in general, it "consists entirely of more than meets the eye" (xii). She uses the genre of the prefatory introduction to undercut its own intentions, and subtextually ridicules the very form that she employs, as well as the content expected of her: "[i]t is as if a reassuring interpretation, a list of characteristics—the more rigid and confining the better—needed to be drawn up and offered for ratification" (xiii), she says of the "national identity" crisis. But Gallant refuses to confine herself or her fiction to any such definition, and those readers of her introduction who seek reassuring interpretations of the stories of *Home Truths* from the author herself are disappointed.

In fact, Gallant works *against* both "domestic" readings of her fiction and autobiographical interpretations, as well as the privileging of authorial intention in criticism of her work. In the preface, the *literal* reader—and Gallant claims that Canadians are indeed "very literal readers" (Hancock 51-52)—is directed to commit the biographical fallacy twice: once in reference to the life of the nation, and once in reference to the life of the author. For example, the kind of information Gallant includes in the preface might seem to promote biographi-

cal readings of the stories. Writing about the formal creative process, she divulges autobiographical information which has been included in the *content* of the stories:

> At the same time—I suppose about then—there began to be restored in some underground river of the mind a lost Montreal. An image of Sherbrooke Street, at night, with the soft gaslight and leaf shadows on the sidewalk—so far back in childhood that it is more a sensation than a picture—was the starting point. . . . The character I called Linnet Muir is not an exact reflection. I saw her as quite another person, but it would be untrue to say that I invented everything. I can vouch for the city: my Montreal is as accurate as memory can make it.
>
> (xxii)

Clearly the parallels between the author's life and the character in the quasi-autobiographical fiction exist and are even acknowledged openly by the writer. It would seem, then, that with the preface in place the biographical fallacy is encouraged.

However, it becomes obvious that the preface has a double meaning: it is being used ironically, as a tool to ward against such biographical readings. Gallant inserts an explicit disclaimer with respect to the autobiographical: "I am convinced that there is virtually no connection between mood and composition. 'How I've fooled them!' Colette once said of critics who saw in one of her novels the mirror of her own life" (xx). The tension between the "personal" surface content of the introduction and the explicit rejection of that content works toward the development of a parodic preface, as does the tension between the expected explication of the stories and the defensive, political tone. These different intentions force the reader to interpret the introduction, to decipher the distance between what is said (or not said) and what is meant—to read it ironically, in other words. The double meaning is generated from a surface commentary on the creative process, which is played against a subtextual criticism of that self-commentary. This doubling first defines the preface paracritically, and then redefines and subverts it metacritically.

The use of an explicit disclaimer is one marker for this reading of the preface. If Gallant is the kind of writer Kroetsch typifies as "slightly uneasy, somewhat exhausted . . . reluctantly paying attention" to criticism of their texts ("Beyond Nationalism" v), she is also, ironically, uneasy in her role as self-critic. Her prefatorial persona is as complex as her fictional one(s): it also requires a reading, an analysis of roles, and a differentiation among voices. With one voice, Gallant interprets the stories, while with another she de-privileges her own opinions; she reluctantly offers an introduction, only to take it away from the reader, and thus prevent a reductive approach. She discredits her own paracritical comments by describing her poor memory of the origins of her own stories:

Except for purely professional reasons, such as the writing of this introduction, I do not read my own work after it is in print. I had remembered **"Jorinda and Jorindel"** completely differently: I thought it was a story about a summer weekend party of adults and that the children were only incidental. . . . The span between the germ of an idea and its maturation can be very long indeed. . . . By the time I finally read the work in proof, its origin has sunk out of recollection.

(xix-xx)

With the embedded disclaimer, Gallant is able to offer remarks about the stories which make us question both the validity of those comments, *and* the putative intention of the preface.

In 1981, Gallant was not as popular with Canadian audiences as she should have been, as she is at pains to point out in her introduction: "I often have the feeling with Canadian readers that I am on trial" (xii). This kind of language is prevalent in the entire piece: she refers to questions asked by Canadians as an "interrogation," the tone of which "suggests something more antagonistic than simple curiosity"; she feels she is accused of having "concealed intentions," of "perpetrat-[ing] a fraud," of "committ[ing] an act of intellectual deception, evidence of which will turn up in the work itself" (xii). Ironically, *Home Truths: Selected Canadian Stories* won Gallant the 1981 Governor General's Award for fiction. Apparently the judges, too, were "very literal readers" of the qualified title of the collection. But if Gallant felt that she was on trial, then the subtitle, as well as her self-commentary in the introduction, can hardly be taken at face value.

Rather, Gallant's prefatory remarks constitute a form of "deconstructive [irony] . . . a kind of critical ironic stance that works to distance, undermine, unmask, relativize, destabilize. . . . This is primarily a form of critique which can at times border on the defensive . . ." (Appendix 1, 30). In effect, Gallant *has* been "on trial" for being a traitor to "Canadian Literature," since her work does not easily fall into what have become "Canadian" categories of theme and style. Gallant has not been as successful in terms of popularity and attention as other, perhaps less sophisticated writers (Margaret Atwood and Margaret Laurence, for example), writers whose work is easily recognizable as fitting the "Canadian" mould. Gallant's is in some ways "an alien sound" amongst other Canadian literature, to paraphrase her anecdote about feeling marginalized at the age of ten by her classmates, who "hated" her because she was bilingual (xvii).

Consequently, a tone of resentfulness is evident in her comments about Canadian art and about questions (or "interrogations") that she has received about her own fiction. In this context her focus on the Dreyfus case, which might seem incongruous with the rest of the in-

troduction (it is located in the midst of her explanation of the Linnet stories), is easily understood: she identifies with a man who, though patriotic (to a dangerous extreme), was labelled as a traitor and unfairly exiled for political reasons. Mentioning the case in the preface also serves to emphasize that Gallant's interests are not limited to those defined as "Canadian."

Gallant's prefatory introduction is defensive both of the integrity of her work and of her citizenship, as the epigraph indicates: "Only personal independence matters (Boris Pasternak)." Despite her surface silence on the subject, she is critical of the criteria apparently used for judging a "Canadian" work (namely that it be written in and/or about Canada, and contain pre-determined "Canadian" characteristics). The use of irony allows her to disseminate multiple messages (personal and political) to at least three separate audiences—the consumer market, the critical market, and the "unbiased" reader of irony—within a fairly conventional prefatorial form.

In order to interpret the preface, then, and uncover its ironic intent and content, the reader needs to place Gallant in the context of the Canadian literary scene—to locate "home," geographically and politically.[2] This raises the general question of whether or not irony is always intended, and is coded into a work, or if it is incorporated into the work by the reader whose ideas and biases are brought to it. If it is intended, if irony consists of speech coded for the *cognoscenti,* then it too is targeting an audience at the level of language, just as a preface might target an audience at the level of content. In order to decode ironic discourse, the content must first be contextualized by the reader, and this turns irony into a collaborative effort.

Gallant's preface might be seen as an intimate exchange between reader and writer, and the inherent ironies would then be verbal and structural wedges that attempt to open up critical space rather than close it down. Clearly she could have used the introduction to "Canadianize" her work, to make her readers feel "at home" in a gesture of authorial good will. Instead, she makes her introduction ironic, unsettling reader expectation. Gallant writes that, while she has sometimes "felt more at odds in Canada than anywhere else . . . [,] no writer calls a truce" (xiv). And since irony is a tool used for defamiliarization, not reconciliation, the ironic introduction to *Home Truths* is the perfect vehicle for Gallant's resistance to a limited and limiting definition of herself as a Canadian writer.

Notes

1. Gallant's *Overhead in a Balloon* is subtitled "Stories of Paris," but does not include an introduction, nor offer an explanation of the subtitle beyond the fact that the stories are *set* in Paris. Not

all of the stories in *Home Truths* are set in Canada; nor do they deal with "Canadian" issues per se. This comparison would reinforce the interpretation that the preface in *Home Truths* is being put to ironic ends.

2. It should be noted that Gallant's manuscript as submitted to the editors (now with her other papers at the Thomas Fisher Rare Book Library, University of Toronto) does not differ greatly from the published introduction. Minor changes in syntax are marked in dark black ink, but there is little evidence that the author's ideas were either solicited or emended by the Canadian publisher. Thus while the subtitle may be attributable to Macmillan's staff, it would seem that the preface itself is a product of Gallant's intention.

Karen E. Smythe (essay date 1992)

SOURCE: Smythe, Karen E. "Gallant's Sad Stories." In *Figuring Grief: Gallant, Munro, and the Poetics of Elegy,* pp. 22-60. Montreal: McGill-Queen's University Press, 1992.

[*In the following excerpt, Smythe addresses the defining characteristics of Gallant's short fiction, asserting that "Gallant's narrative strategies invite our empathic participation in the texts."*]

Though Mavis Gallant's fiction has received a great deal of critical attention in the last ten or twelve years, much of that criticism has been limited to noting Gallant's main themes: W. J. Keith states that "the concept of abandonment or betrayal" is central,[1] and Janice Kulyk Keefer and Neil K. Besner focus on the role that memory plays in her characters' and narrators' worlds. But few have attempted to relate the form of Gallant's fictions to their content. A special issue of *Essays on Canadian Writing*—the "Mavis Gallant Issue"—was published recently, and therein several articles explore structural and rhetorical facets of Gallant's work. Heather Murray insists that it is "the story rather than plot, the *way of telling* rather than what is told," that characterizes Gallant's narrative mode, a mode that demonstrates a "betrayal of generic expectations";[2] E. D. Blodgett, too, comments on the relation between Gallant's strategies and themes: "[Gallant] is an author who appears to know precisely, amid what often are no more than the fragments of a life, where to direct her reader, in such a way that even the *sense of loss* that *dépaysement* gathers in is *part of the plan*."[3]

Gallant's plan is, in very basic terms, to present the reader with segments of contemporary life as seen from her distinctly ironic perspective. In her oft-quoted brief essay "What Is Style?" Gallant writes: "Style is insepa-

rable from structure, part of the conformation of whatever the author has to say. What he says—this is what fiction is about—is that something is taking place and that nothing lasts. Against the sustained tick of a watch, fiction takes the measure of a life, a season, a look exchanged, the turning point, desire as brief as a dream, the grief and terror that after childhood we cease to express. The lie, the look, the grief are without permanence. The watch continues to tick where the story stops."[4] Gallant does present us with measures of lives, with experiences of "grief and terror," and her fiction *represents* or *figures* this grief in a form that is self-conscious about its own language and structure.

Gallant's narrative strategies invite our empathic participation in the texts. J. Brooks Bouson, in *The Empathic Reader: A Study of Narcissistic Character and the Drama of the Self,* discusses the reader's empathic experience in theoretical terms: "At once affective and cognitive, the empathic event involves a dynamic interplay between objective and subjective, conscious and unconscious, the verbalizable and the unverbalizable . . . Empathic reading also makes us aware of our affective and collusive involvements with literature, . . . and of the ways in which we may act out our own self-dramas when we interpret literary works."[5] The reader is invited to experience in Gallant's fiction what might be called "mimpathy," a philosophic term that combines concepts of mimesis and empathy and refers to the acting-out of "our own self-dramas" when we interpret the suffering of a literary character.

The conditions of mimpathy require that this suffering "must already be given in some form before it is possible for anyone to become a fellow sufferer. Pity and sympathy as experienced are always subsequent to the already apprehended and understood experience of another person who is pitied."[6] Gallant portrays characters as they experience the apprehended "after-*affects*" of loss (rather than portraying the actual experience of loss), and so induces readers to understand that experience for themselves in the course of mimpathic involvement, in giving form to that experience outside of the story's frame of reference. This representation of grief necessitates by definition an elegiac form, and in this Gallant's work shares several features with modernist predecessors. Critics such as Robertson Davies and Donald Jewison have commented on Gallant's "modernist mode";[7] Ronald Hatch compares **"The Other Paris"** to *Dubliners,* for instance, and Elmer Borklund makes a similar comparison: "These anti-romantic glimpses of dislocation and despair are rendered in deliberately hard, dry prose, reminiscent, like their subject matter, of Joyce's *Dubliners*."[8] Lorna Irvine compares Gallant's fiction in general to that of Joseph Conrad.[9] But a thus-far unnoted similarity between Gallant and writers such as Woolf, Joyce, and even Conrad is that both Gallant and these modernists write using an elegiac perspective.

Gallant's world-view is quite close to that of Woolf, who wondered whether "'sadness' . . . is . . . essential to the modern view."[10] In an interview with Janice Kulyk Keefer, Gallant discusses the relation between art and reality and states that "one is cheated in art"; "there's nothing pretty about [reality]. You know, there's pretty-sad and ugly-sad. Art is essentially a cheat . . . being a displacement."[11] In this statement she denotes reality as "ugly-sad," while art *about* sadness produces a displacement of the ugliness and takes the form of "pretty-sad." In Gallant's view a mood of sadness might be said to dominate both contemporary reality and contemporary art—her own included.

Gallant's fiction, though contemporary, is not part of any post-modern agenda. Instead, with her social/moral realism, her focus on the past and on the *interpretation* of the past in the present, Gallant would be better described as a late modernist. Alan Wilde suggests that "late modernism interposes a space of transition, a necessary bridge between more spacious and self-conscious experimental movements";[12] he also states that "reading appearances correctly is, in fact, the project of late modernism." As a late modernist Gallant is concerned not only with issues of representation but indeed with the project of reading—with reading memory and the past, and with reading responsibly. Her work is usually less formally experimental than that of her modernist predecessors, and it questions the kind of perceptions and representations of the past that a modernist aesthetic tends to produce. The paradigmatic models of modernist fiction-elegies provided by Woolf and Joyce, I have argued, have been adapted by late-modern writers such as Gallant who aim to rewrite modernity—to "work through" modernism by confronting and challenging various of its tenets, usually in a more realistic narrative mode.[13]

Gallant's fiction-elegy employs strategies of "displacement" such as irony, allegory, and metonymy. Themes of loss, betrayal, death, and grief are presented in terms of these strategies, which, adopting Julia Kristeva's terminology, could be called "elegiac modalities of *significance*."[14] Kristeva uses the French term *significance* to refer to "the work performed in language . . . that enables a text to signify what representative and communicative speech does not say."[15] Modalities of *significance* are necessary in literature since, as Kristeva writes, "representations proper to affects, and notably sadness," are "insufficiently stabilized to coagulate into signs, verbal or otherwise, actuated by the primary processes of displacement and condensation."[16] The work that Gallant's fiction performs in this way is the work of mourning, though this agenda is understated due to verbal displacements and condensations of affective response.

It is not only the understated that is of great significance in Gallant's work; what is not said, and what is unsayable, are crucial clues in reading her elegiac fiction as well. Wolfgang Iser's theory of literature as staging is particularly apt with reference to the unsayable in Gallant's elegiac fiction and fiction-elegies: "The recurrence of particular worlds in the literary text has always taken place on the prior understanding that it is a mode of enacting what is not there."[17] Gallant's prose makes use of the necessary conventions of elegy—what Iser would categorize as the "repertoire of the text," which create the appropriate conditions of the performance[18]—yet in terms of providing generic clues for the reader these elegiac conventions are very often obscured by the use of ironic allegories and alinear plot construction. As Heather Murray argues, it is the "way of telling" that dominates Gallant's stories, and it is the process of elegizing—the work (verb), not only the work (noun) of mourning—that structures the texts.

In other words, the reader's reconstruction of the textual, loss-dominated reality is made more difficult in Gallant's fiction than in fiction by Woolf, for instance. Though her fiction-elegies can be seen to derive from a modernist paradigm, the conventions of the genre are not often foregrounded as they are in the works of Woolf and early Joyce fiction-elegies, or even those of Munro. Hence the reader's paradigm, the model of mourning induced and produced upon reading Gallant's texts, is less explicitly directed by the author. We are, however, given contextual clues and markers of irony that assist us in the interpretative and reconstructive act, an act that Iser describes as a "staging" of oneself and that is "the means whereby representation is transferred from text to reader."[19] Just as Gallant selects from the modernist paradigm of fiction-elegy and then combines her selection syntagmatically into a new paradigm, the reader uses the new paradigm to select and construct a parallel paradigm of elegy. Iser argues that fictions are extensions of human beings and that "literature figures as a paradigmatic instance of this process [of world-making] because it is relieved of the pragmatic dimension so essential to real-life situations."[20] The reader's para-paradigm, so to speak, is a product of reading Gallant's (paradigmatic) text, of reading other elegies, and of personal experience of loss.

In his recent theory of fiction Michael Riffaterre refers to "mental frames of reference" to which the reader has access when reading. He states that these frames "are not just habits of thought; they constitute potential ministories, ready to unfold when needed and ready for reference when alluded to."[21] Such mental frames of reference contribute to the para-paradigm that, I am suggesting, the reader produces upon reading fiction-elegy. The active role that Riffaterre depicts for the reader of fiction in general is emphasized to a greater extent in the very structure and nature of fiction-elegy.

In my modernist examples the reader is situated within the frames of the fiction; in Gallant's versions the reader is directed less explicitly to participate in the construction of a textual model of mourning, though Gallant, using detached ironic narration, does insist on this participation and also on identification with the situations and emotions of her characters—if only to disagree with or to reject them.

Constance Rooke claims that "the lure to character/reader identification is much less in Gallant's fiction than in Laurence's or Munro's, partly because the character/author bond is so much weaker";[22] however, I would suggest that a consequence of a "weak" character/author bond is that the *reader*/author bond is strengthened. Gallant's narratorial distance is used as a trope of elegy, one that often tends to replace the modernist method of frame construction that leads the reader to the central experience of the text (think of the reader/Peter/Clarissa/Septimus framework in *Mrs Dalloway*, for instance). The Gallantian narrators' textual distance from the story presents the reader with the independent perspective of the narrating survivor figure, which points to emotional and intellectual reactions, thereby authorizing the reader to appropriate or derive those reactions from or against the suggestive circumstances of the narrative. Thus the trope of distance is both displacing and deictic.

Despite Rooke's claim that there is "something chilling in Gallant," a fairly common evaluation, there is an emotional range in Gallant's fiction that has not received due attention. The narratorial detachment, which could be mistaken for a modernist's aesthetic of impersonality, tends to disguise this affective aspect of her work; she does not often render emotional realism at the immediate point of crisis, but rather depicts the after-*a*ffects of experience, a displaced form of affect. Paul Ricoeur writes of the "capacity of metaphor to provide untranslatable information . . . [and] to yield some true insight about reality"[23]—and Gallant's texts are in this sense extended metaphors, allegories of remembering that provide what Ricoeur would call "models for reading reality in a new way."

The word "model" is of extreme importance in theorizing elegy. Jerome Bruner argues that a "mental model" of events patterned over time underlies all narrative,[24] but the genre of elegy—which has a particular function, a pragmatic function in its depiction of and insistence upon the reader's experience of grief—is a model in a particular way. For elegy to work, the reader must "place [his/her] own thoughts and feelings at the disposal of what representation seeks to make present in us," as Iser writes of the relationship between reader and text.[25] The emotions evoked for the reader who reconstructs a fiction-elegy are not the same feelings of grief and consolation as one has in actual life. The induced feelings are *modelled* on such authentic experiences of emotion, but as Ricoeur states, these literary feelings "are negative, suspensive experiences in relation to the literal emotions of everyday life. When we read, we do not literally feel fear or anger. Just as poetic language denies the first-order reference of descriptive discourse to ordinary objects of our concern, [modelled] feelings deny the first-order feelings which tie us to these first-order objects of reference."[26] This structure, which is divided or "split" between indirect representations of reality and models for reading reality (155), provides us with a point of entry into the elegiac text.

Gallant's narratorial distance creates this space or split between the structures of mourning. The text holds back emotion and resolutions, and provides a model of working through "real-life" confrontations with grief using an indirect form of guidance. Riffaterre provides a pragmatic explanation of the relationship between reading a text and applying it to "real life": "Narrative truth is thus a linguistic phenomenon; since it is experience through enactment by reading, it is a performative event in which participation on the reader's part can only serve to hammer the text's plausibility into his experience."[27] In this sense the narrative engenders a scene of transference, asking leading questions and giving no direct answers. Interestingly, Freud describes the psychoanalytic transference process as "a piece of real experience, but one which has been made possible by especially favourable conditions."[28] Gallant's stories construct analogous pieces of real experience. They are coded texts that create the possibility of a transferential model of reading, then: the reader, in the role of Freud's patient, is "led along the familiar paths to the awakening of the memories."[29] But the reader is also shown the *un*familiar, the strange. Ronald Hatch compares Gallant's strategy to a Brechtian *Verfremdung* (estrangement) device, and states that the reader of her fiction, like the audience of a Brecht play, "might return, changed" to daily life after engaging with her work.[30]

In the psychoanalytic model presented here, the text is not read as a patient; nor is Gallant. Instead, the text is the authoritative analyst and provides stories for the reader, the receptive analysand who must reconstruct and interpret the elegies by working through them. To extend the analogy, this model works Socratically, since the analyst (text), as Peter Brooks writes, "must help the analysand [reader] construct a narrative discourse whose syntax and rhetoric are more plausible, more convincing, more adequate to give an account of the story of the past than those that are originally presented, in symptomatic form, by the analysand."[31] Generally, the reader/analysand uses the text of story/self for the purpose of self-interpretation, which is the "event" of reading; in fiction-elegy, transference more specifically assists the reader to heighten awareness *of* and to grieve *for* communal and/or personal losses. This transference, which elicits interpretation, is invited by the text.[32] In Gallant's work the narratorial detachment invites the reader to enter into the transference relation; the invitation is reinforced by the use of irony, since it constructs double meanings that must be deciphered in context.

Ronald Schleifer suggests that irony is "the rhetorical trope that figures death: like the idea of death—like the very 'ideas' language gives rise to—irony is a material (linguistic) fact that creates 'immaterial' effects."[33] Irony has the potential to make the past present, then, as well as to create an *awareness* of loss and responsibility, as in the case of Gallant's fiction-elegy. Irony as trope is important in revisionist elegy such as Gallant's, in which the decorum of mourning is upheld but also is breached. Irony both constructs and disrupts meanings, and provides the distance required by the elegist and reader to construct the model of mourning, to locate oneself at a distance from the loss, *and* to critique the very model that the text represents on personal and cultural levels. Thus the reader's transferential reconstruction of the model of mourning in reading Gallant is most often *not* a duplication or re-presentation, but a revision.

Transference is both an activity involving reader and text, a rhetorical persuasion, and a *figuration,* a "mode of expression," as Cynthia Chase states, because it is in the process of transforming literary tropes during the act of reading that meaning and (variations on) consolation are produced. The former characteristic of transference is performative, and it obscures the latter characteristic—the figurative—with its "rhetorical designs upon the reader."[34] In modernist fiction-elegy, the tropological quality of transference is dominant; we seek consolation as a product, and the elegists within the fictions (Lily Briscoe, Stephen Dedalus) find such consolation in art, symbols, words in and of themselves. In late modernist fiction-elegy, however, it is the performative quality of transference that is emphasized by the authors; though the word "transference" is etymologically related to metaphor (*metaphorein,* to transfer), a particular *kind* of metaphor is used to figure the performative: metonymy. As Chase explains, "th[is] system of tropes [i.e., the "production of signs as action"] is fundamentally metonymic, a matter of *contiguity* between ideational representatives or signifiers."[35] Like the analytic aim to "'destroy' . . . persisting persuasion," Gallant's fiction-elegy aims to "destroy" a lack of consciousness about personal and public conditions of loss, and her realistic (metonymic) style serves to question metaphoric, tropological consolations—constructed fictions—that we too easily adopt for ourselves.

The reader's scene of transferential reconstruction is an activity that Peter Brooks calls "plotting"[36]—is a matter of "finding the right sequence of events, putting to-

gether the revelatory plot" (35). This readerly activity is heightened in reading Gallant's fiction-elegy, since Gallant's style of plot tends to be alinear and achronological—her narrators and characters are often exploring the past through memory. In fiction-elegy there is almost always a progression within the plot, a movement towards a revelation; for Woolf and Joyce that revelation provides consolation for character and reader alike. However, as Iser writes, "the greater the emphasis on compensation [in a literary text], the more dated the solution will appear to future generations of readers";[37] it is perhaps for this reason that the modernists' figuration of consolation in their fiction-elegies required revision in the first place, and that the late modern texts tend to raise more questions than they answer. Thus progression for the characters or narrators in Gallant's fiction-elegies is stunted; for the reader the progression is towards a consciousness of the character/narrator limitations as well as of a diminishment of personal and cultural values, both within the story and in society.

The transference produces consciousness, not consolation, and clarification, not obvious compensation, in Gallant's contemporary version of catharsis. For the reader (again, the analysand, not the analyst) the process of plotting (with the goal of anagnorisis) is an enactment of the work of mourning. The reader's plotting involves a sorting out of the temporal movements made by the texts. Keefer notes that "Gallant's fictive structures are dual: the backward spirals that give her characters access to memory are intersected by the forward hurtle of time."[38] It is to this forward hurtle or progression, to the "sustained tick of a watch,"[39] that the reader must become acclimatized, but Gallant places "hurdles" in the way of conventional consolation. The reading process involves metonymic transference (the work of mourning) as well as metaphoric transference (the transfer of meaning).

Gallant has described metaphorically the act of writing; she sees a story "build[ing] around its centre, rather like a snail."[40] This image is reminiscent of Woolf's description of "the house of fiction": "Dissatisfied the writer [Woolf] may have been; but her dissatisfaction was primarily with nature for giving an idea, without providing a house for it to live in . . . the idea started as the oyster starts or the snail to secrete a house for itself."[41] But where Woolf's metaphoric fiction-elegy consists of (or houses) fragmented forms that represent multiple perspectives on reality (which, in capturing reality, have potential for consolation in aesthetic form), Gallant's metonymic fiction-elegy figures fragmented lives and societies and resists tropological consolation.[42] For Gallant, memory is accessible but it is only partial and selective, and it has dubious recuperative powers.

"I don't think the story should be a fragment. A short story is not just something snatched out of a larger fiction," Gallant states in an interview.[43] Even her segmented longer works consist not of fragments but of syntagmatically connected fictions (*Green Water, Green Sky* and *A Fairly Good Time* are examples). For Gallant, "content, meaning, intention and form must make up a whole, and must above all have a reason to be."[44] She revises the experimentalist, fragmentary, and symbolic narrative of modernist writing, then; for Gallant, the "whole" short story is not a fragment of a larger possibility but an independent narrative, precisely (though not chronologically) plotted. It is often this use of plot as trope in connection to the themes of loss and abandonment that connotes the elegiac in Gallant's work, such that the reader "plots" the work of mourning.

While W. J. Keith (surprisingly) states that Gallant's work "does not have any obvious thematic preoccupations," he also notes in a contradictory manner that "we come to realize that she continually concerns herself with human beings as they are affected by change and especially war."[45] One of her obvious preoccupations is with the occupation of Europe during the Second World War and with human responses to the multiple crises and losses that it entailed. With what could be called her social/moral realism Gallant confronts many of the issues surrounding these events, and is indeed as Keith states, an "excellent analyst" who depicts "mid-twentieth-century spiritual *malaise*" (158).

PLOTTING THE PAST: SAMPLING
THE EARLY STORIES

The plots of Gallant's stories provide the reader with the repertoire of elegy: plot and story (*sjužet*) order the *fabula*, but Gallant's order is not one that satisfies the reader's idea of what reality *should* be like; instead of resolving tensions and consoling for losses, Gallant represents *dis*order, and the reader's habit of "reading for the plot" is disrupted, disturbed, forced to become a "plotting for the reading."

Peter Brooks believes that "plot is the internal logic of the discourse of mortality";[46] in a sense, this has been my argument for the proliferation of modern and late modern fiction-elegy, which is occasional only in that death is always an event: plot in fiction allows writers to explore psychological reactions to both death and loss, and it provides a structure for the narration of the work of mourning, which is, paradoxically, an act of narrativization itself. As Ricoeur suggests, plot has "a connecting function between an event or events and the story. A story is *made out of* events to the extent that plot *makes events into* a story. The plot, therefore, places us at the crossing point of temporality and narrativity."[47] In Gallant's stories "event" often is memory itself. This variation on the *fabula* does not eliminate plot, but it complicates its temporality.

Gallant's first collection, ***The Other Paris*** (1956), is admittedly less elegy-oriented than her later work. Two stories in ***The Other Paris,*** however, are early versions of the paradigmatic fiction-elegies in the first and third person that she later would write, **"Wing's Chips"** and **"About Geneva."** The former is a pseudo-autobiographical anecdote in which the adult narrator recalls a childhood summer. She recreates details based on "the picture in [her] memory" of the town that she lived in with her father.[48] The narrator, then, attempts to *read* her ekphrastic mental picture for its accuracy and truth. Though most details are recalled "with remarkable clarity" (142), she cannot remember the name of the town that she lived in with her father, and this paradoxical situation immediately provides us with a clue to the story's agenda: the forgetting of such a detail from childhood indicates an avoidance of what Freud would classify as "strong and often distressing affects" and suggests a loss or betrayal that the narrator must "work through" (or in terms of think-act theory, "think through") using narrative re-enactment. In analysis, "the process that should lead to the reproduction of the missing name has been so to speak *displaced*."[49] By analogy, as readers we begin to replace the process, to figure or construct a *fabula* from this plot, which is a "textual generator" in Riffaterre's terms.[50] Thus the reading of the fiction-elegy involves an initial *de*construction—what Jacques Derrida calls a form of "memory work" in itself[51]—before the model of mourning can be (re)constructed.

The elegiac repertoire of **"Wing's Chips"** includes the following: references to a harsh landscape (141); an "untended garden, in which only sunflowers and a few perennials survived" (142); the emotional detachment of the father, which implies parental neglect and a corresponding sense of abandonment in the child (145); unresolved affect, which becomes evident to the narrator only "years later" (147); emphasis on the artistic talents of the father, talents that are inherited by the narrating story-teller in displaced form as literary skills (150); and a semi-aesthetic object that stands as "proof" of her father's existence and identity (151).

It is the arrangement of these conventions or conditions of the performative text that is foregrounded, rather than the conventions themselves. The narrator explicitly draws attention to the fact that past events are not the same as remembered events. Her *father*'s narrative—which is an undeveloped plot embedded in the plot proper, and which serves as an inner frame of the fiction-elegy—is about "the England of his boyhood" (144) and is his conversational autobiography. Recalling pastoral-like details that he might have told her, his daughter thinks: "This was probably not at all what he said, but it was the image I retained—a landscape flickering and flooded with light, like the old silents at the cinema" (144). The tale is like a parable for the reader, advising us not to believe the story as told, for the events are likely different from the image retained and narrated as history. Her mental construction of a landscape "flooded with light" is quite fictive, then, though significantly the father's narrative has been translated by the child into a nearly ekphrastic, *wordless* visual image, one that represents a temporary closeness with her father and seemingly consoles the (now) narrating adult. But the consolation inherent in the symbolic version of the past is unsatisfactory, since it is not only fictional but knowingly false, and this is what the adult narrator comes to understand. Thus the narrator also questions the validity of such a trope of consolation. This is evident in the very fact that she consciously rewrites her past with the intent of a more accurate recovery, adjusting "the picture in [her] memory" in the process (141).

This conscious rewriting of the past is analogous to the reader's interpretive act, wherein the *fabula* is transcribed into another mental landscape. The words **"Wing's Chips"** both title the story and provide a clue to the meaning of the revelatory moment at the end of the narrative—they are the words on a sign painted by the girl's father, one that is a great source of pride for her. The sign is a metonymic sign of her father in that he produced it with his own hands, and it figuratively denotes her father; but it also displays the now forgotten name of the town where, we are told, the specific past summer in question was lived. Though the narrator looked at the sign every day of that summer and is able to recall minute details of other events—even of the colours of the sign, and the shape of the letters her father painted (150)—she cannot re-place the displaced name. The absent name on the consoling sign metaphorically denotes the void in the relationship with her father, and the metaphoric absence (via neglect and, later, death) of the man himself. It names him *in absentia,* and therefore names a lack as well. The sign, with the unnamed town in "P.Q.," is therefore contrasted with the landscape "flooded with light" as two different ways of figuring the past; the metaphoric sign is also a product of the narrator's memory, of the past reconstructed, but it contains the seeds of its own deconstruction—of memory work—within itself, and is therefore the more evocative way of figuring loss.

Derrida writes that "deconstruction is not an operation that supervenes *afterwards,* from the outside, one fine day; it is always already at work in the work; . . . the disruptive force of deconstruction is always already contained within the architecture of the work."[52] In reading fiction-elegy, the structure of which contains a "deconstructive" code, the reader is directed to reconstruct his/her own version of events in a reconstructive process such as that Riffaterre describes as "mentally rebuilding or hypothesizing a pretransformation text."[53] The reader, I am suggesting, subsequently transcribes the pretransformation text (acquired in reading Gallant's paradigmatic story) to a post-transformation text,

or perhaps a para-transformation text, as a useful model of mourning. Here consolation is found not in the form of symbolic signs but in the *formation* of signs; it is not the sign that reads **"Wing's Chips"** that leads the narrator to an affirmation of pride in her father, but the reconstruction of her past—a reconstruction that is admittedly never complete or completely accurate.

Thus the rejection of the symbol as a fictively "true" trope of consolation is another way that Gallant revises modernist tropes of elegy. Lily Briscoe's painting of Mrs Ramsay, for example, is a symbol, and consolation is found therein, not in the seemingly frustrating *process* of painting. Gallant seems to question the emotional validity of such a figure for the purposes of consolation, as she emphasizes the importance of signs—like the sign that says **"Wing's Chips"**—for memory work. But there are different kinds of signs, and different kinds of memory to consider in this context. The link between types of signs and types of memory is of interest to Paul de Man, whose interpretation of Hegel's concepts of sign and symbol leads him to suggest that since art is "of the past" and its paradigm is "thought rather than perception, the [temporal] sign rather than the [atemporal] symbol, writing rather than painting or music, it will also be memorization [*Gedachtnis*] rather than recollection [*Errinnerung*]."[54] In **"Wing's Chips"** the adult narrator does not recollect, nor use deluding symbolic recollection (as her father seems to have done), but she signifies her past, her father, and her loss in the metonymic act of telling.

"Wing's Chips" is a precursor story to Gallant's first-person fiction-elegies such as the Linnet Muir sequence in *Home Truths.*[55] **"About Geneva"** is a second story in *The Other Paris* that suggests an elegiac structure that recurs in Gallant's later third-person stories. The plot in this story consists of the attempt by the unnamed mother and "Granny" to extract the truth about the two children's visit with their father, who is living in Geneva with another woman. The broken-home scenario is presented *in medias res,* and the visit is over when the story begins. The events in the *fabula* consist of dialogue and mental reconstructions of the trip and of the past by the boy Colin, his sister Ursula, and their unhappy mother.

Neil Besner notes that "Geneva's appearance announces several realities,"[56] and indeed we are asked to consider the different versions of the reconstructed scene. The mother thinks, with reference to the children's accounts of the visit, "Which of them can one believe?" (198); the reader too must take this question into consideration. This issue of truth in story is, I have suggested, one of the central concerns in Gallant's fiction-elegy; the potential for a limited consolation depends directly on the capacity of a representation, constructed in memory, to embody a fictive truth. Colin's sudden statement early in the story, "I fed the swans,"[57] encapsulates the experience for him by evoking a fixed scene: "There, he had told about Geneva . . . As he said it, the image became static: a gray sky, a gray lake, and a swan wonderfully turning upside down with the black rubber feet showing above the water. His father was not in the picture at all; neither was *she*. But Geneva was fixed for the rest of his life: gray, lake, swan" (196). Colin's declarative statement is a think-act that evokes this fixed scene in his mind, one that denotes his own emotional reality.[58] The static and false image functions as a symbol, one that leaves out the figure of the father and, though inadequate, is used by Colin to reconstruct his recent trip to Geneva.

Ursula's reconstruction is also produced by a verbal act, but one of a different order. She is writing a play based on autobiographical details of her father's lover, who is from Russia (and who suggested the name and the plot of the play; the woman is called "the original Tatiana" by Ursula's mother [197]), and in speaking the one line written thus far—"The Grand Duke enters and sees Tatiana all in gold" (194)—she produces a fable out of the *fabula* of the trip. Emotional reality, it seems, is too difficult to confront, and the distance of the fiction (in the form of an imaginary play) from reality is somewhat consoling for Ursula. The thought of a literal production of the play makes her cry, though (195), since the gap between the reality of the painful visit and the fiction she has constructed is thereby dramatized. Thus the mythological translation of reality is also shown to be an inadequate figuration of the past for the work of mourning.

With these different versions of the story Gallant condenses the (pre-transformation) plot of **"About Geneva"** into an allegory of plotting. In other words, the reader must consider the subtextual story of the visit and the portrayal of that visit by Colin and Ursula, and then assess the elements of the story proper, plotting them into a plausible subtextual paradigm. This transferential reading process is exemplified when Colin's mother interprets what she thinks is the authoritative version of events—Colin's version. Since "Colin seemed to carry the story of the visit with him" (197), his mother sees her son as an extension of the man who left her: "She thought of her husband, and how odd it was that only a few hours before Colin had been with him. She touched the back of his neck. 'Don't,' he said. Frowning, concentrating, he hung up his tooth brush. 'I told about Geneva.'" (197). The boy seems to understand his mother's need for a reminder of her husband, and offers his image to her again. Her version of the story becomes changed in the transference; the think-act "He had fed swans," which is appropriated from Colin's "I fed the swans," becomes actualized as a mental construction: "She saw sunshine, a blue lake, and the boats Granny had described, heaped with coloured cushions" (197).

Thus Colin's symbol is transformed by his mother's reading into yet another symbol, one that represents not reality but her imagined version of the scene.

Because Colin's fiction is both possible and plausible, his mother temporarily believes the boy's representation (translated to her own vision) to be true, whereas Ursula's "one simple act of creating Tatiana and the Grand Duke" served to remove her "from the ranks of reliable witnesses" (197). But Colin's symbol is no more "true" than Ursula's drama, something that their mother cannot perceive. The ekphrastic image once actualized in her own mind, like the play, is seemingly unrelated to a reality external to the image-as-text, and is therefore not fictionally truthful or consoling. This revelation at the end of the story, though not a consolation, does indicate to the reader what a more useful model of mourning might entail: verbal versions of past events told in terms of signs, not symbols, would seem to provide a fictional truth.

Keefer paraphrases Frank Kermode and applies his ideas to Gallant, stating that "individual works of fiction cannot be too consoling, or they will not satisfy the reader's demand for 'complicity with reality.'"[59] The "effect of Gallant's vision," she suggests, "is not tragically cathartic but ironically disturbing" (46). I am arguing, however, that Gallant's fiction—elegiac, not tragic—directs the reader towards the construction of a parallel paradigm that simultaneously resists tropological consolation *and* encourages consciousness of tropological structures, and of the relation between memory and truth, language and fiction—even if, or rather *because* the characters in her stories do not arrive at this model themselves. Thus the reader is not only "disturbed" and abandoned, as Keefer suggests, but is stimulated *by* the disturbing events and characters to become actively involved in the rebuilding of the fiction-elegy. Character limitations, then, often can *move* the reader to move *beyond* disturbance.

Another early third-person story that demonstrates a failure of consolation for the *character* is **"An Emergency Case"** (1957), not collected until *In Transit* was published (1988). Again the significant events of the story have happened before the story begins: a little boy, Oliver, has been in a car accident with his parents, who did not survive. In hospital Oliver is talked *at* by several adults, though they fail to talk *with* him about his experience and loss. The doctor "had told Oliver that Oliver's parents were now in Heaven" (53), but this meaningless information is not retained by the traumatized child. The story portrays Oliver's emotional denial and the adult's emotional deficiencies. His lack of grief is a defence mechanism, or "the omission of affect" that often accompanies delayed mourning.[60] This omission is apparent in the story proper also; since the adults who surround the child have failed to grasp the boy's emotional condition, it is not rendered by the narrative voice either. Keefer's reference to the boy as "the unlikeable Oliver"[61] indicates, I think, a misreading of an intensely emotional story; if any of the characters are "unlikeable," the health-care workers might be.

The adults' inability to deal with the malaise of the mourner endows the narrative with a strategic coldness, one that has often been mistaken for authorial disinterest. Gallant's story demonstrates that the parent's death "hasn't been properly explained" to the child, as his adult roommate concludes (41). Details have been withheld from the boy, and narrative details have also been held back from the reader in a semi-Hemingwayesque style of narration. We must interpret the sparse storyline and construct a parallel fiction from our version of the *fabula,* just as Oliver must read the signs given him: "The taking away of the toys, the unscheduled attempt to wash him suggested that something unusual was about to take place. It could only mean his mother" (41). In this literalization and reversal of the Freudian "fort/da" scene, Oliver expects the signs that represent his mother—toys—to be replaced with his actual mother. To him they do not signify loss, then, but presence and retrieval. Gallant contextualizes Oliver's misinterpretation of absence for the reader, who is led to conclude that the "absence-of-grief" syndrome has induced the boy to invent not a consoling construct but one that will re-enact only the experience of loss: his mother will not replace the toys but will be repeatedly lost to the child. The absence of toys does not symbolize the mother's presence, as Oliver believes, but is a figure of loss, as the reader perceives. Our plotting of the story, like Oliver's, is anticipatory ("something unusual was about to take place," he thinks), but we are directed to construct a model of psychological response and to become empathically involved with Oliver, in contrast to the adults in the story, who seem oblivious of the needs of the child.

The title story of *The End of the World and Other Stories* (1974) invites a similar anticipatory participation. In this first-person story (the narrator's name is William), the triggering event—William's father's death—has already occurred, but this monologue is an effort to narrate emotional response, to plot not only the after-affects of loss but the fore-affects as well. The first words that the speaker announces are "I never like to leave Canada, because I'm disappointed every time";[62] the subsequent statement "I had to leave Canada to be with my father when he died" (89) provides the reader with the implied information that being with his father is a disappointment, his death a double loss. Reader expectations of an emotionally charged scene are first constructed, then dismantled. The narrator, too, is disappointed: "I had expected to get here in time for his last words, which ought to have been 'I'm sorry' . . . But my father never confided in me" (90). In order to

forgive his father, and to experience a memorable emotional bond with him before his death, William needs his father to apologize, to perform a consoling speech-act.

Instead, he is the one to perform a verbal service for his father: he "swear[s]" to him that he has tuberculosis, assuring him—promising him—that he will be cured (94). Since the man is dying, such a speech-act, though infelicitous under other circumstances, is not unsuccessful—the conditions of the promise are not expected to be fulfilled but are psychologically necessary none the less. Since the act is a lie, however, his father's statement "I knew you wouldn't lie to me" indicates to the speaker and the reader that the emotional bond created in the speech-act, the recognition his father has given him, is a fiction. The role of the narrator soon subsumes the importance of the father's role in this story, which follows a pattern of elegiac romance; the narrator-elegist quests for knowledge about himself and the world, though this knowledge is denied in the speech-acts exchanged between the two men.

The speech-act that his father does provide (he *thanks* his son for the reassurance) is not the one William desires. This surprise, then—not the death of the father—is what seems "like the end of the world" (94) to William. The exchange of lies has shattered William's imagined "world," his hoped-for consolation; what he had "thought [he] wanted to hear" was a speech-act that would have maintained his perspective on his father, the one he had constructed in his mind over the years. The disappointment in not having the long-imagined play performed becomes an experience of an unexpected, doubled loss. Again Gallant emphasizes the danger and fictive nature of conventional, romanticized expectations of consolation. She disrupts the reader's expectations of elegiac consolation in her fiction-elegies; but the end of one world is also the beginning of another, and her stories have the effect of heightening the reader's awareness of the stories we tell ourselves, and of the importance of their telling.

In *My Heart Is Broken* (1964) the majority of the stories are about adults who are orphaned or abandoned—common Gallantian themes. The characters aim to secure fictive consolations that will allow an acceptance of the ways of the world, to paraphrase one story in the collection.[63] The title of the collection implies that loss and grief are central concerns, and the fiction does portray characters confronting these experiences. Bernice Schrank compares this collection to *Dubliners,* stating that "*My Heart is Broken* invites analysis as a unified whole . . . the stories collectively illustrate various permutations of genteel angst and lower-class anomy."[64] The narratives possess the power to move the reader (as rhetoric is intended to do) both emotionally and intellectually. They also focus attention (often critically) on the ways in which characters figure their grief or construct consoling fictions for themselves. Besner notes of this collection that the reader is invited "to discern characters as frames or forms, as manners or idioms of perception,"[65] but while frames are evident in narratological terms, the emotional import of the stories certainly suggests that the characters are more powerfully present than the terms "forms" and "idioms of perception" would suggest. When confronted with loss in the outermost frame of the fiction-elegies, we are moved to re-evaluate both the values portrayed in the fiction and in our own lives, a re-evaluation that is not required of the reader by Woolf, and not often by Joyce either. Gallant's late modern fiction-elegy is less accepting of characters' fictive consolations and more meta-evaluative, then—it implicates the reader in what might be called an "ethics of grieving."

In **"Bernadette"** the ironically named Robbie Knight is a failed playwright, a frustrated artist-figure who is re-reading his literary influences[66] and mourning not only his lost youth but, eventually, lost love in his marriage as well. He is not moved to action by reading, however; the "only result of his [reading] project was a feeling of loss . . . He felt only that he and Nora had missed something, and that he ought to tell her so" (25). Robbie's ineffectualness in life (and in reading literature, suggests Schrank),[67] and in dealing with loss, is contrasted to pregnant Bernadette's vitality; the contrast is also between Robbie's perception of a rural working-class lifestyle as idyllic and Bernadette's memories of what her life was really like. Her memories are think-acts that, once "set in motion, brought up the image" of her home life (27). While Robbie mourns the death of his dreams, Bernadette's (non)mourning for the predicted future death of her unborn child becomes the story-within-the-story. Bernadette's story displaces Robbie's self-elegy, and shows its relative insignificance, thereby calling the Knights' values into question.

Nora Knight resembles an unsuccessful Mrs Dalloway whose "party had gone wrong" (32); her failure became "a symbol of the end" of her world (37). Nora is also a failed reader, one who pieces together a plausible story from events and conversations but mistakenly accuses her husband of impregnating Bernadette. Readers are positioned outside of Bernadette's naïve frame of reference and must evaluate her ideas of life, death, and religious consolation as well as those of the Knights. The reader contrasts these opposing models and reconstructs an alternative view or frame outside of the narrative text. Though Bernadette does not read the books given her by the Knights (or any others), she does go to the movies, and it is in the cinema that she experiences a "comforting dark" protection (41) as a spectator of events: "She did not identify herself with the heroine, but with the people looking on" (41), we are told. For Bernadette, detachment allows her to accept and even

to welcome the predicted death of her yet unborn child. Since we, too, are an audience, we are implicated in this protected spectatorship. Bernadette's adoption of conventional religious consolation for the imagined death of her baby is metaphorically aligned with her escapism at the movies: neither requires her to *think,* and Gallant indeed is making a moral judgment about Bernadette's "destructive placidity," as Schrank notes (67), forcing the reader to think.

In **"The Moabitess"** the protagonist, immediately identified in the first words of the story as "elderly Miss Horeham,"[68] is preparing for her own death. Her aversion to sexual activity, what she calls "that side of life" (43), provides a clue to the reader that her lifelong virginity is perhaps related to a misguided reading of the biblical line "A virtuous [hence virginal] woman is a crown to her husband" (50). This choice has placed her in the position of spectator, and our perspective as spectator-of-the-spectator aligns us with her narrow "vision of life" (47), where her eyes are the "centre of the house, of the world" (54). In reading the story we are presented with the memory of her father. The mention of his death makes her "stutter so . . . that the others thought she would choke" (45). The fiction-elegy psychonarrates her alternating feelings of hatred and love for "Mr Percy Horeham, who had irresponsibly departed from life in 1946 and left his maiden daughter not a penny" (46). Here Gallant condenses the history of Miss Horeham and that of her father to a single paragraph, which is a think-act wherein Miss Horeham performs a wish that her father die a second death, "another annihilation after death" (46).

Like Mr Horeham's locked box under his bed, containing the money for which his daughter had to beg, Miss Horeham constructs her own locked box of fictive memories—an atemporal construct that David O'Rourke identifies as an "idyllic past" under lock and key in the present.[69] This crypt-like box consoles her for her deprivations, despite the fact that it contains only meaningless items that she has endowed with value. She even calls a stone thrown at her a "gift"; her misinterpretation of this abuse is analogous to her attitude towards her father's treatment of her, indicating that she is collecting her pain and translating her wounds into pleasure. In biblical law (in the Book of Matthew) stones are thrown as a form of punishment; the act also functions as an accusation of some kind of sexual sin, such as prostitution. To accuse is to label, to name. The protagonist's name, Miss Horeham, is appropriate then—despite the fact that she remains sexually inactive as an adult—because incestuous activity is suggested throughout the story.

Other items in her box that have symbolic significance are her father's butterfly collection, stored in a glass box (52), and the letters her father wrote to her when she was a schoolgirl (53), addressed in a subtly amorous tone. She reads the words written by a now-dead man and, putting on a scarf, enters a fantasy world that solaces her. She experiences an epiphany, wherein she actually sees her younger self in the mirror in the role of Ruth, remembering "how they had acted out the glorious [biblical] stories" of love and lust (53). The acting out "had all been harmless and a secret, and gave them the feeling that something rich was being lived" (53); the *think*-acting out of what she "acted out" with her father now provides Miss Horeham with a secretive pleasure, though clearly the reader evaluates the questionable morality of the originating act as well as the validity of the consolation attributed to its memory.

Her revealed hatred of her father causes the reader to contrast the consoling memory with the implied reality of Miss Horeham's past, and empathy is thereby stirred for the somewhat irritating old woman. Her fictions are, for her, necessary; but the story structure, which is also box-like, places the reader at the outer frame and allows us to evaluate her mental construction as one that reflects "love of established order" (49) and not true memory. Her epiphany occurs in her invented "small, clear field of light" (52), which is like a spotlight projected on the stage and emphasizes her role as actress, artificer, as well as the reader's role as artificer in reconstructing the story. The reader detects embedded works of mourning for Miss Horeham's past life with her father and for the life unlived *because* of that past. Gallant spotlights the fictionality of memory in this story, and by exposing a woman's secret self-vision she critiques the limited perspective produced by a veiled or boxed-in view of the past. The cost of the illusion of control over the past and life itself—the cost of the crypt—is life itself.

Peter Frazier is another character in *My Heart Is Broken* who creates illusory compensations at great cost to himself and others.[70] Described as one of the "peacock parents" (247), Peter enacts a work of mourning in **"The Ice Wagon Going down the Street"** by denying loss with distorted memory. The narrator asserts that "peacocks love no one. They wander about the parked cars looking elderly, bad-tempered, mournful and lost,"[71] which Peter certainly is. Peter is the dominant focalizer in the story, and the narrative begins and ends with Peter remembering a woman named Agnes Brusen. "Remembering the past" is a Sunday pastime for him and his wife Sheilah (246), and they speak names of people "as if they were magic," as if they could resurrect them. The Fraziers live in, rather than learn from, the past. Though he keeps the name Agnes a secret from his wife (272), Peter thinks of her when he remembers the past. The story opens and closes in the present tense, though throughout Peter's thoughts move back and forth

in past time, narratologically indicating his (and Sheilah's) hollow repetition of the past. It is Peter's use of the past that is called into question by Gallant.

The story proper is about the Fraziers' loss of social stature and of the feeling of being in love; but perhaps more importantly it is about the recuperative power of memory, about significant moments of solitude and of union with another. The image of Agnes as a child watching the ice wagon is one of privacy and beauty; it provides epiphanies for both herself and for Peter, to whom she describes it (267). Peter *sees* the scene, and actually hallucinates a transferential epiphany: "He thinks of the ice wagon going down the street. He sees something he has never seen in his life—a Western town that belongs to Agnes. Here is Agnes . . . Nothing moves except the shadows and the ice wagon and the changing amber of the child's eyes. The child is Peter . . . He is there" (273).

Peter uses Agnes's name as a charm that triggers an epiphanic moment. Derrida writes that the proper name remains after death, that "in calling or naming someone while he is alive, we know that his name can survive him and *already survives him*; the name begins during his life to get along without him, speaking and bearing his death each time it is inscribed . . . if at my friend's death I retain only the memory and the name, the memory in the name, . . . this defect or default reveals the structure of the name and its immense power as well: it is in advance "in memory of."[72] The name "Agnes Brusen" has this mnemonic power for Peter; the structure of the name-as-sign is symbolic, just as the name "Frazier," to Peter (and to Peter alone), is symbolic of power and prestige. In **"The Ice Wagon Going down the Street"** Gallant is depicting the process of epiphany, not just describing the epiphanic moment. She contrasts two different uses of memory in this allegory of grieving: distorting and disabling memory-as-symbol of the past—the Frazier's model of escape—versus memory as truthful fiction—Agnes's model of meaning.

Peter sees Agnes's epiphany and appropriates it, incapable as he is of having his own. His vision is an imaginative act that parallels the reader's, since Agnes's telling allows him to reconstruct her story and to interpret its significance. O'Rourke states that "ironically," Peter "does nothing with this epiphany" (106); but Peter does change because of this experience. The conversation that they have is of love and of death; the ice melts between them, so to speak, as they confide in one another about highly personal issues. The think-act Peter later performs brings him to a recognition of a potentially valuable vision of the past and of his emotions towards Agnes—but he does not act on this recognition. Though he returns to "a true Sunday morning" (273), he has identified the fictive truth of his constructed life with

Sheilah and has seen, perhaps, the inadequacy of the Balenciaga dress as a talisman (248). He begins to think of Sheilah and his father as a couple in terms of their similar superficial values. He has also invoked Agnes with the think-act, since she speaks the last words of the story, reminding the reader of the peacock analogy: "Agnes says to herself somewhere, Peter is lost" (273).

Though "Peter [literally] lost Agnes" (273), he retains her unspoken name as his talisman and constructs a version of her from "the puzzle he pieces together" (272). The name functions as a prosopopoetic trope, but its ultimate effectiveness is dubious—not because the metaphoric vision of the moving ice wagon is invalid but because it is so easily appropriated and then rejected by Peter. Peter's reconstruction of Agnes, of the image of the ice wagon, and of the prairie paradise is paradigmatic of the reader's involvement in the fiction-elegy, and clearly a reconstruction of another person's story—or of an author's story—will not substitute for an individual's interpretation of his or her own experience. But the glimpse of meaning that Peter gets is a glimpse that the reader, too, gets in the act of reading fiction-elegy; it is a glimpse that Gallant urges us to hang on to.

A HAUNTED HOUSE: ITS IMAGE
ON THE MIRROR

"Its Image on the Mirror" in *My Heart Is Broken* is subtitled "A Short Novel," and like Gallant's lengthier novels it can be read as an extended (and sequential) fiction-elegy wherein a female protagonist mourns for multiple losses.[73] Besner writes that one of its central themes is "the act and the art of remembering": "Showing that the processes through which memory asserts its truths are always significant," he states of the collection, "these stories invite readers to consider inventions, recollections, and recreations of the past by attending to the forms of the stories Gallant's narrators tell."[74] Jean Price, the narrator-elegist, mourns her dead brother and the "equally lost" sister[75] whom, she thinks, has abandoned her. She also mourns her lost "unlived self," as Donald Jewison notes.[76] The plot-trigger of the story is the sale of the house where Jean grew up with her brother Frank and sister Isobel. The dramatic-monologue form establishes the reader in the role of listener (and eavesdropper), as an audience that is given "misleading impressions" and edited or "corrected thought[s]."[77]

Though John Moss claims that Jean's "reason for speaking is never apparent,"[78] the telling is its own *raison d'être*. Jean's narrative is a prolonged, performative work of mourning, occasioned by the sale of the house and the incomplete mourning for her brother. Through it she confronts "the problem of [her] sister" (62) and seeks some understanding of her self, life, and death. The narrative has the basic structure of elegiac romance,

wherein the narrator ostensibly narrates the biography of a dead or lost hero-figure, yet the biographical story is a thin disguise for the autobiography of the narrator who survives the hero and wishes to adopt the hero's identity for his/her own. Such autobiography is specifically confessional in nature. Besner notes that the novella is "both a report and a confession. Jean reports her memories as confessions: through changes in the way she calls up the past . . . she comes to a fuller way of making sense of herself and of history."[79] The monologuic **"Its Image on the Mirror"** is an apostrophic confession to Isa, who is Jean's imagined confess*or*; but Isa will not speak to Jean "out of her own death," or even in Jean's dreams (97), and little is learned of this elusive sister by Jean or by the reader. Ironically, though, what Jean confesses is that by telling the tale she hopes to create a "dead-and-buried Isobel" (62) who could no longer threaten her sense of self within the family or with her husband Tom. Thus Jean's *use* of memory and story-telling is called into question by Gallant, since Jean is presented as a character with emotional limitations that she does not completely recognize; at least Jean does not *confess* to having the knowledge of herself that Gallant allows the reader to have.

Telling the story is a way of burying the past and of forcing "life to begin," something for which Jean "had waited years" (63). Confession, writes Dennis Foster, is a representation of "an attempt to understand the terms and the limits by which the people are defined, both as they listen to the confessions of others and as they recount their own transgressions"; "the importance of confession, and of the language of fault in general, lies in its power to interpret."[80] But in Jean's confession there is a sense that her story is not only a delayed reaction to her losses but a reaction that *perpetuates* delay and postpones a direct confrontation with herself. The flashbacks and achronology also work to subvert plot progression, to stop time and problematize the textual position of potentially epiphanic revelations. The successful burial of the past in Jean's aesthetic terms would create a kind of mental *crypt,* which, writes Derrida, is "not a natural place, but the striking history of an artifice, an *architecture,* an artifact: of a place *comprehended* within another but rigorously separate from it, isolated from general space by partitions, an enclosure, an enclave . . . the crypt constructs another, more inward, forum like a closed rostrum or speaker's box, a *safe*: sealed, and thus internal to itself, a secret interior within the public square."[81] Jean's stated intent is to seal the past into its grave, to detach herself from it and to hide it within herself-as-house in an effort to make her life "safe" from the threat of Isa.

But Gallant's fiction-elegy "works" in spite of Jean's cryptographic goal because it is the "mode of narration that is responsible for the especial effect of this story and Gallant's other fiction," as Heather Murray argues.[82] Jean (s)crypts her past in front of the reader's eyes, and the reader uses what Derrida calls "the break-in technique that will allow us to penetrate into a crypt (it consists of locating the crack or the lock, choosing the angle of a partition, and forcing entry)."[83] The potential for the success of any method of mourning is limited by the capacity of the scribe or "scripter" to comprehend and to act on that comprehension—the latter being a dead-end for Jean, of course. But the efficacy of fiction-elegy depends upon the inducement of comprehension on the part of the reader, a goal which Gallant is able to achieve—despite her character's detached nature in this novella—by including characteristics of intelligence and signs of emotional suffering beneath her surface control of self and story.

Jean draws attention to her role as story-teller and elegist: "I am the only person who can tell the truth about anything now, because I am, in a sense, the survivor," she thinks (141). The story is about "vocabularies and grammars, and also about formal truths and fictional truths," notes Besner,[84] and Jean's (s)crypting is contrasted to Gallant's method of scripting the past. As the survivor the elegist stages a response to loss and grief and works through mourning in the act of staging, of writing. Jean's work is silent, though, and the entire fiction is in effect a think-act composition, since expression of emotion for Jean is nearly impossible. The Duncan family all suffered from "a fear of the open heart" (89), and even though the text is a work of mourning, Jean would never admit it as such—rather, she ironically claims at the end that the entire "story could wait" and that she "might never tell it" (153) to her husband, who knows few details about Isa's past or her relationship with Jean.

In claiming that "there is something in waiting for the final word," Jean is repeating her life-pattern of waiting, which turns her life into a kind of death. In this sense Jean is incapable of achieving the consolation that comes with acting on revelation. As Keefer writes, the telling of the story has no cathartic effect on Jean but leads only to a "passively ironic recognition" of her death-in-life condition.[85] Her reconstruction of memories is somewhat mechanical in that her think-acts produce not active emotion but tableaux, similar to her "last sight of the house at Allenton," which she compares to "those crowded religious paintings that tell a story" (57). Jean's memories do tell a story, but rather than producing a consoling fiction-elegy they often produce "discrete still-lifes," as Besner refers to them.[86]

Besner states that "Jean approaches her memories in a manner similar to the way in which readers approach fiction,"[87] as if they are not real, not her own. Though such detachment is a necessary part of the mourning process, Jean's approach to memories is undercut by

Gallant, in that her methodology of memory and mourning is clearly so inadequate and stilted that we, as readers, can construct other versions that work. The reader becomes empathically involved while Jean remains emotionally reticent, paradoxically silent within her own retrospective discursiveness.

The Allenton house becomes a prosopopoetic figure that contains all deaths and losses for Jean: "Even before the house was sold . . . it began to die . . . Ghosts moved in the deserted rooms, opening drawers, tweaking curtains aside. We never saw the ghosts, but we knew they were there. We were unable to account for them: no one had lived here but our family, and none of us had died in Allenton" (59)—none except Jean's emotional self, that is. Since a ghost watched Jean watching herself in the glass on one occasion (60), at least one of those unaccountable spectres is Jean's lost version of herself, the one that had dreams of a possible love that might surpass what she finds in her real life. Gallant's characteristic contrast between romantic and realistic world-views is not a simple opposition, as this story makes clear; within the "real" the use of the imagination and memory is crucial to the construction of a fictional truth. Jean's rejection of the imaginative in life does not allow her to see the difference between life and illusion, as she believes; it identifies her instead as someone who sees life in terms of simple oppositions rather than a complex mixture of fact and fiction, and as someone who—because of this perspective—is doomed to a mournful, cryptic existence rather than a celebratory one.

A salvational crypt such as Jean's paradoxically "allow[s] death to take no place in life," as Derrida claims of such "sepulchre[s]."[88] Her insistence on "waking" and "return[ing] to life" (155) is, Gallant suggests, an insistence on permanent mourning, on endless waking. The elegiac markers are evident in this story from the start. The first mention of Jean's brother is made almost parenthetically, in relation to an anecdote about "poor Isobel" (61). It is Isa's near-death (threatened by a kidney ailment) that is narrated first, its significance established through a long digression that also describes her marriage to Alfredo. Isobel is perceived by Jean, who can't "figure" her (out), as a real ghost, returning from the dead as she "tricked [the family] by not dying" (62). She definitely haunts Jean, who tries to live Isa's life vicariously (she even marries Tom, who proposed to Isa first), and Jean only partially exorcises her past. Her expectation of "true justice," of achieving revenge for the past by building a family with Tom (77), backfires as Isobel remains unimpressed, and "thankful she had escaped" (77).

Frank escapes the narrow world of Allenton first through service in the war, then by dying. His death is mentioned only parenthetically in the second part of the novel, with variants on the phrase "dead brother" preceding his name, such as "our dead brother Frank" (71) and "my dead brother's daughter" (73). Frank's death is the explicit cause for grief in section five, though Jean here admits that she "scarcely mourned" him, and "ought to pay for [her] indifference" (129): "I withdrew from my brother's death into a living country of wrangles and arrangements and sharing taxis . . . Although I speak now of his death, his death did not occur" (129). Speaking now of his death is her acknowledgment of that death as well as a version of delayed mourning. Her memory of the family scene reveals her mind performing this belated work: "the panes went black and reflected us: Isobel reading, our mother erect by the door, our father mourning and small. We were in a lighted cage. We could be seen from the street" (131). But Jean remains a spectator to her memories, which are sealed off, hidden in her safe.

The narration digresses to provide a trace of Frank; though "the ghost in the Allenton house cannot be Frank's," since "he left no trace" at all (131), Jean narrates a few days he spent with her and Isa to provide a sense of his presence, to invent a ghost and, with words, to replace the missing trace of her brother. But she also *dis*places that ghost, and focuses yet again on Isa's ghost and her capacity for love, which is so elusive to Jean that she can only be "warmed by the sudden presence of love" that she "could sense but not capture" (136).

What Jean perceives as a need for revenge on her sister is alternately a need for consolation, a need that is almost fulfilled: "I felt, that afternoon, the closest feeling I have to happiness. It is a sensation of contentment because everyone round me is doing the right thing. The pattern is whole" (75). However, this "pattern" seems to represent a negative, complacent, and mechanistic condition, and because Jean's use of memory and its translation to narrative are similarly attempts at making the pattern whole, but not necessarily true, the work of mourning is not completed. Her stifled, falsely ordered point of view produces instead an endless cycle of grief, as cyclical as Tom's unthought-out need to repeat his "parent's cycle—family into family: the interlocking circles" (79). Jean's recollection of the line Davy Sullivan quoted from *Anna Karenina*—"happy families are all the same" (79)—is, for the reader, ironic; the rest of Tolstoy's sentence, "each unhappy family is unhappy in its own way," is, of course, more apt. The most that the unhappy Duncan and Price families can say, as Jean does, is "we were still alive" (81).

Jean's comment about survival is juxtaposed with the start of the third section, which provides details about Frank's childhood and character. The information Jean gives contradicts her statement later in the text that she "had never known him" (145). Frank is a sign of ab-

sence for Jean, not only through his own death but even in his relationship to Isa when alive: she had written her name in his childhood books, thereby erasing his identity and ensuring the presence of her own. Jean's mother says "poor Frank" and "poor Isa" as if both offspring had been killed. Jean, reading these books to her children, notes that their inheritance from her will be "the assurance that there are no magic solutions" (84). Here Jean's displayed resistance to the imagination and her emotional limitations become evident; fairy tales, to her, are not imaginative stories but "stupid and a bore" (85). Her outspoken rejection of story suggests to the reader why Jean has had difficulty recovering from her past; but the telling of this story contradicts that absolute rejection, and its effect is potentially positive.

The reading of these books recalls memories for Jean of living "on the edge of [Isa's] life" (86), of putting herself in Isa's place, "adopting her credulousness, and even her memories, [which] I saw, could be made mine" (84). This adoption—typical of the narrator of an elegiac romance—had been part of her earlier effort to repair the wound of losing her sister's affection, a wound that affected her to the point where she referred to herself in the third person: "Isobel's sister, Jean Price, sits down, crosses her ankles, clasps her hands, smiles" (95). Jean cannot be consoled for the separation from her sister or from her entrance into the real world and her exit from the world of love and dreams.

Reading the childhood books provokes memory-digressions about Isobel, not of Frank, even though it is his absence that is the ostensible occasion for this narrative segment. Isobel's affair with Alec Campbell remains at the heart of Jean's grief: the real love she witnessed between the couple was a sight that awakened anguish in Jean (100), and still does. The story of her own marriage, described in part four, is eclipsed by Isobel, who, even there, "was center of things" (106). In this first-person story the autobiographical alternates with the biographical in a narrative of denial, delay, and waiting for mourning rather than a performance to that end. The act of waiting is implicitly compared to the act of dying: "The feeling [in Montreal] was of waiting, as the feeling in Allenton, years later, was of death" (108). Jean's life in Montreal is a stagnant one, and she is metaphorically dead in that she is waiting for her life to begin; but she is responsible for the state of emotional suspension she finds herself in, since it is Jean who is preventing herself from living by sealing herself off into a safe world.

In the last section of the story Gallant links the themes of life and death, biography and elegy by connecting Frank's death to Isa's first pregnancy (which was aborted). Isa confesses to Jean in Frank's empty bedroom, where Jean is to sleep (148); she has become Isa's confessor, taking Frank's place as she stands in for his ghost. The epiphanic moment for Jean occurs when Isa explains her ideas about love, which seem "astonishing and greatly intimate," and paradoxically cause her to understand "the inevitability of dying" (151). The union that Jean feels with Isa is the only possible consolation for her. Without it, she thinks, "we might as well die" (153). Jean's memory of this emotion remains in the present, and it is narrated in the present tense as she thinks of the scene: "There remains Isobel, then, cheek on hand, a little tired" (152). But Isa's rejection of Jean's hand signifies the return of death, of stagnation and the cold: "winter was still here and might never come to an end" (154).

In other words, Jean's life continues to be a survival, but little more:

> I suspected, then, sitting in Frank's unhaunted room, that all of us, save my brother, were obliged to survive. We had slipped into our winter as trustingly as every night we fell asleep. We woke from dreams of love remembered, a house recovered and lost, a climate imagined, a journey never made; we woke dreaming our mothers had died in childbirth and heard ourselves saying, "then there is no one left but me!" We would waken thinking the earth must stop, now, so that we could be shed from it like snow. I knew, that night, we would not be shed, but would remain, because that was the way it was. We would survive, and waking—because there was no help for it—forget our dreams and return to life.
>
> (155)

That there is "no help" for Jean is due to her refusal to risk, to question, to dream of real love, and to complete the narrative work of mourning by performing it as a reconstruction rather than as a record. She decides to believe of Isa's love affair with Alec that "a union of that sort was too fantastic to exist" (98); but while Besner suggests that Jean's conclusion demonstrates that "survivors must wake up to history" (87), Jean's awakening is merely a reinforcement of her mournful perspective on life. The rejection of the purely romantic for the purely realistic is not a revelation of the kind that allows a truthful awareness of self and world, and Jean's perceptions and interpretations have not been corrected in the course of her performance. Gallant's fiction-elegy suggests that a different *kind* of awakening than Jean's is required—that the reader must take the risk advised to the "fellow-wanderer" in the epigraph from Yeats's "The Shadowy Waters": to "mix ourselves into a dream / Not in its image on the mirror!"—for "beyond the world," there are possibilities for love and for life of which Jean cannot allow herself even to dream.

Notes

1. Keith, *A Sense of Style,* 101.
2. Murray, "Canada, Canonicity, the Uncanny," 114, 119; emphasis mine.
3. Blodgett, "Heresy and Other Arts," 4; emphasis mine.
4. Gallant, "What Is Style?" in *Paris Notebooks,* 177.
5. Bouson, *The Empathic Reader,* 171.
6. Dagobert, *Dictionary of Philosophy.*
7. Donald Jewison, "Speaking of Mirrors," 94; Robertson Davies, "The Novels of Mavis Gallant," 69.
8. Borklund, "Mavis Gallant," 324.
9. Ronald Hatch, "The Three Stages of Mavis Gallant's Short Fiction," 94; Lorna Irvine, "Starting from the Beginning Every Time," 246.
10. Woolf, *Diary,* 2:56.
11. Keefer, *Reading Mavis Gallant,* 207. Keefer's quote is from her (unpublished) interview with Gallant, conducted in Paris, June 1987, and quoted in her "Mavis Gallant: A Profile," 205. The emendation and the ellipses are Keefer's.
12. Wilde, *Horizons of Assent,* 120-1, 109.
13. As used by Freud in "Remembering, Repeating and Working-Through," 1914, the phrase "working-through" implies a "work of remembering" through an "acting out" (151). Late modern writers "work through" modernism via repetition with a difference.
14. Kristeva, "On the Melancholic Imaginary," 107.
15. Roudiez, introduction to Kristeva's *Desire in Language,* 18.
16. Kristeva, "On the Melancholy Imaginary," 108.
17. Iser, *Prospecting,* 282.
18. Iser, "The Reality of Fiction," 21.
19. Iser, *Prospecting,* 244.
20. Ibid., 270.
21. Riffaterre, *Fictional Truth,* 4.
22. Rooke, "Fear of the Open Heart," 267.
23. Ricoeur, "The Metaphorical Process as Cognition," 141, 155.
24. Bruner, "The Narrative Construction of Reality," 6.
25. Iser, *Prospecting,* 244.
26. Ricoeur, "The Metaphorical Process," 155.
27. Riffaterre, *Fictional Truth,* xiv.

28. Freud, "Remembering, Repeating, Working-Through," 154. Freud also indicates that transference is a "first-order" experience of reality, and *not* a representation, by insisting that transference could not successfully destroy neuroses "*in absentia* or *in effigie*." See "The Dynamics of Transference," 108.

29. Freud, "Remembering," 154-5.

30. Hatch, "Mavis Gallant and the Fascism of Everyday Life," 21. Though Hatch's comparison is interesting, Gallant's aesthetic and political stances are, of course, vastly different from those of Brecht.

31. Brooks, "The Idea of a Psychoanalytic Literary Criticism," 10.

32. See Peter Brooks, "Psychoanalytic Constructions and Narrative Meanings," 57.

33. Schleifer, *Rhetoric and Death*, 58.

34. Chase, "'Transference' as Trope," 214.

35. Ibid., 217.

36. Brooks, *Reading for the Plot*, 35.

37. Iser, *Prospecting*, 247.

38. Keefer, *Reading Mavis Gallant*, 163.

39. Gallant, "What is Style?" 177.

40. Hancock, "An Interview with Mavis Gallant," 45.

41. Woolf, introduction to *Mrs Dalloway*, vii-viii.

42. Munro, too, describes the structure of fiction as a house that "presents what is outside in a new way." See "What Is Real?" 224.

43. Hancock, "An Interview with Mavis Gallant," 48.

44. Gallant, "What Is Style?" 177.

45. Keith, *Canadian Literature in English*, 158.

46. Brooks, *Reading for the Plot*, 22.

47. Ricoeur, "Narrative Time," 167.

48. Gallant, "Wing's Chips," in *The Other Paris*, 141.

49. Freud, *The Psychopathology of Everyday Life*, 22, 2.

50. Riffaterre, *Fictional Truth*, 20.

51. Derrida, *Memoires for Paul de Man*, 73.

52. Ibid., 73.

53. Riffaterre, *Fictional Truth*, xv.

54. De Man, "Sign and Symbol in Hegel's *Aesthetics*," 773.

55. Similarly, "Rose" (Dec. 1960), an uncollected story, prefigures these continuing concerns with childhood, betrayal, memory, and recovery, which are explicitly thematized in the story. Interestingly, the protagonist of "Rose" is named Irmgard, as is the child in "Jorinda and Jorindel," a later story (Sept. 1959), collected in *Home Truths* (1981).

56. Besner, *The Light of the Imagination*, 24.

57. Gallant, "About Geneva," in *The Other Paris*, 196.

58. Freud's thesis, which equates writing with fantasy, is similar to this theory of think-act evocation: "Mental work is linked to some current impression, some provoking occasion in the present which has been able to arouse one of the subject's major wishes." See "Creative Writers and Day-Dreaming," 147.

59. Keefer, *Reading Mavis Gallant*, 46.

60. Deutsch, "Absence of Grief," 228.

61. Keefer, *Reading Mavis Gallant*, 109.

62. Gallant, "The End of the World," in *The End of the World and Other Stories*, 88.

63. Helmut Bonheim comments that in "Acceptance of their Ways" (Jan. 1960) the "ratio of story to discourse time gives Gallant's narrative a distinctly modernist flavour." Bonheim states that the technique of alternating perception and apperception is "that of James Joyce" in *Ulysses*. Gallant uses the technique to a greater extent in her longer fictions. See Bonheim's "The Aporias of Lily Little," 75.

64. Schrank, "Popular Culture," 57.

65. Besner, *The Light of the Imagination*, 27.

66. Gallant, "Bernadette," in *My Heart Is Broken*, 24.

67. Schrank, "Popular Culture," 61.

68. Gallant, "The Moabitess," in *My Heart Is Broken*, 42.

69. O'Rourke, "Exiles in Time," 101.

70. The story was also published in *Home Truths*, 1981.

71. Gallant, "The Ice Wagon Going down the Street," in *My Heart Is Broken*, 256.

72. Derrida, *Memoires*, 49.

73. Peter Stevens claims that "a full revelation" is not possible for the reader of Gallant's novels "until all the pieces can be placed together when the reader reaches the last page" ("Perils of Compassion," 68); but it is doubtful whether the reader indeed reaches a "full revelation" even then.

74. Besner, *The Light of the Imagination,* 27.

75. Gallant, "Its Image on the Mirror" in *My Heart Is Broken,* 60.

76. Jewison, "Speaking of Mirrors," 103.

77. Gallant, "Its Image on the Mirror," 101, 103.

78. Moss, *A Reader's Guide,* 84.

79. Besner, *The Light,* 29.

80. Foster, *Confession and Complicity,* 7, 16.

81. Derrida, *"Fors,"* 67-68.

82. Murray, "Canada, Canonicity, and the Uncanny," 115.

83. Derrida, *"Fors,"* 68.

84. Besner, *The Light of the Imagination,* 38.

85. Keefer, *Reading Mavis Gallant,* 63.

86. Besner, *The Light of the Imagination,* 31.

87. Ibid., 37.

88. Derrida, *"Fors,"* 78.

Works Cited

Besner, Neil. *The Light of the Imagination: Mavis Gallant's Fiction.* Vancouver: University of British Columbia Press 1988.

Blodgett, E. D. "Heresy and Other Arts: A Measure of Mavis Gallant's Fiction." *Essays on Canadian Writing* 42 (Winter 1990): 1-8.

Bonheim, Helmut. "The Aporias of Lily Littel: Mavis Gallant's 'Acceptance of Their Ways.'" *Ariel* 18, no. 4 (Oct. 1987): 67-78.

Bouson, J. Brooks. *The Empathetic Reader: A Study of the Narcissistic Character and the Drama of the Self.* Amherst: University of Massachusetts Press 1989.

Brook, Peter. *Reading for the Plot: Design and Intention in Narrative.* New York: Alfred A. Knopf 1984.

———. "Psychoanalytic Constructions and Narrative Meanings." *Paragraph: The Journal of Modern Critical Theory Group* 7 (1986): 53-76.

———. "The Idea of a Psychoanalytic Literary Criticism." In *Discourse in Psychoanalysis and Literature,* ed. Shlomith Rimmon-Kenan. London: Methuen 1987. 1-18.

Bruner, Jerome. "The Narrative Construction of Reality." *Critical Inquiry* 18, no. 1 (Autumn 1991): 1-21.

Chase, Cynthia. "'Transference' as Trope and Persuasion." *Discourse in Psychoanalysis and Literature,* ed. Shlomith Rimmon-Kenan. London: Methuen 1987. 211-32.

de Man, Paul. "Sign and Symbol in Hegel's *Aesthetics.*" *Critical Inquiry* 18, no. 4 (Summer 1982): 761-75.

Derrida, Jacques. *"Fors:* The Anglish Words of Nocolas Abraham and Maria Torok."*Georgia Review* 31, no. 1 (1977): 64-116.

———. *Memoires for Paul de Man.* Trans. Cecile Lindsay, Jonathan Culler, Eduardo Cadava. New York: Columbia University Press 1986.

Deutsch, Helen. "Absence of Grief." *Psychoanalytic Quarterly* 6 (1937): 12-22.

Dictionary of Philosophy. Ed. Dagobert D. Runes. Totowa: Littlefield, Adams, and Co. 1968.

Foster, Dennis A. *Confession and Complicity in Narrative.* Cambridge: Cambridge University Press 1987.

Freud, Sigmund. *The Complete Psychological Works of Sigmund Freud.* Ed. James Strachey. 24 vols. London: Hogarth Press 1953. Vol. 6, *The Psychopathology of Everyday Life* (1901). Vol. 8, *Jokes and Their Relation to the Unconscious* (1905). Vol. 9, "Creative Writers and Daydreaming" (1908), 141-54. Vol. 12, "The Dynamics of Transference" (1912), 97-108; and "Remembering, Repeating, and Working-Through" (1914), 145-56. Vol. 17, "The Uncanny," 217-56.

Gallant, Mavis. *The Other Paris.* Boston: Houghton Mifflin 1956.

———. *My Heart Is Broken.* New York: Random House 1964.

———. *The End of the World and Other Stories.* Toronto: McClelland and Steward 1974.

———. *Home Truths: Selected Canadian Stories.* Toronto: Macmillan of Canada 1981.

———. "What Is Style?" *Paris Notebooks: Essays and Reviews.* Toronto: Macmillan of Canada 1986. 176-79.

Hancock, Geoff. "An Interview with Mavis Gallant." *Canadian Fiction Magazine* 28 (1978):19-67.

Hatch, Ronald B. "The Three Stages of Mavis Gallant's Short Fiction." *Canadian Fiction Magazine* 28 (1978): 92-114.

———. "Mavis Gallant and the Fascism of Everyday Life." *Essays on Canadian Writing* 42 (Winter 1990): 9-40.

Iser, Wolfgang. "The Reality of Fiction: A Functionalist Approach to Literature." *New Literary History* 7, no. 1 (Autumn 1975): 7-38.

———. *Prospecting: From Reader Response to Literary Anthropology.* Baltimore: Johns Hopkins University Press 1989.

Jewison, Donald B. "Speaking of Mirrors: Imagery and Narration in Two Novellas by Mavis Gallant." *Studies in Canadian Literature* 10, no. 1-2 (1985): 94-109.

Keefer, Janice Kulyk. "Mavis Gallant: A Profile." In *The Macmillan Anthology* I, ed. John Metcalf and Leon Rooke. Toronto: Macmillan of Canada 1988. 193-215.

————. *Reading Mavis Gallant.* Toronto: Oxford University Press 1989.

Keith, W. J. *Canadian Literature in English.* London: Longman 1985.

————. *A Sense of Style: Studies in the Art of Fiction in English-Speaking Canada.* Toronto: ECW Press 1989.

Kristeva, Julia. "On the Melancholic Imaginary." Trans. Louise Burchill. In *Discourse in Psychoanalysis and Literature,* ed. Shlomith Rimmon-Kenan. New York: Methuen 1987. 104-23.

Moss, John. *A Reader's Guide to the Canadian Novel.* Toronto: McClelland and Stewart 1981.

Munro, Alice. "What Is Real?" In *Making It New,* ed. John Metcalf. Toronto: Methuen 1982. 223-6.

Murray, Heather. "'Its Image on the Mirror': Canada, Canonicity, The Uncanny." *Essays on Canadian Writing* 42 (Winter 1990): 102-30.

O'Rourke, David. "Exiles in Time: Gallant's *My Heart Is Broken.*" *Canadian Literature* 93 (1982): 98-107.

Ricoeur, Paul. "The Metaphorical Process as Cognition, Imagination, and Feeling." *On Metaphor.* Ed. Sheldon Sacks. Chicago: University of Chicago Press 1979. 141-57.

————. "Narrative Time." *On Narrative.* Ed. W. J. T. Mitchell. Chicago: University of Chicago Press 1980. 165-86.

Rifaterre, Michael. *Fictional Truth.* Baltimore: Johns Hopkins University Press 1990.

Rooke, Constance. "Fear of the Open Heart." In *A Mazing Space,* ed. Smaro Kamboureli and Shirley Neuman. Edmonton: Longspoon/NeWest Press 1986. 256-69.

Roudiez, Leon S. Introduction to *Desire in Language* by Julia Kristeva. Trans. Leon S. Roudiez. New York: Columbia University Press 1980. 1-22.

Schleifer, Ronald. *Rhetoric and Death: The Language of Modernism and Postmodernist Discourse Theory.* Urbana: University of Illinois Press 1990.

Shrank, Bernice. "Popular Culture and Political Consciousness in Mavis Gallant's *My Heart Is Broken.*" *Essays on Canadian Writing* 42 (Winter 1990): 57-71.

Stevens, Peter. "Perils of Compassion." *Canadian Literature* 56 (1973): 61-70.

Wilde, Alan. *Horizons of Assent: Modernism, Post-Modernism and the Ironic Imagination.* Baltimore: Johns Hopkins University Press 1981.

Woolf, Virginia. *Mrs Dalloway.* New York: Harcourt, Brace and Co. 1925.

————. *The Diary of Virginia Woolf.* Ed. Anne Oliver Bell. 5 vols. London: Hogarth Press 1977-84.

Danielle Schaub (essay date summer 1993)

SOURCE: Schaub, Danielle. "Spatial Patterns of Oppression in Mavis Gallant's Linnet Muir Sequence."[1] *Studies in Canadian Literature* 18, no. 2 (summer 1993): 132-55.

[*In the following essay, Schaub addresses the ways in which spatial patterns affect memory in Gallant's* Home Truths.]

A wealth of references to spatial constituents charges the atmosphere of Mavis Gallant's Linnet Muir sequence [in] **Home Truths** (**HT** 217-330).[2] As those stories are the sublimated product of memory,[3] numerous crucial images call on spatial polarities.[4] These terms combined with other stylistic devices expose local cultural phenomena with precision: laying out the stories' fictional landscape amounts to determining what Linnet, the protagonist/narrator, senses as the social, religious and cultural limitations imposed on all the characters. This reality emerges from her recollections of her life in Montreal as a child and then as a late teenager, that is, in the nineteen-twenties and forties.[5] A fictionalised projection of Gallant at the time (**HT** xxii), Linnet gives a rather grim picture of her compatriots and their outlook on life, as if time had not erased the memory of the frustrations she (and thus Gallant too) experienced in her youth. Significantly, Linnet perceives the space in which the characters move as shrunken, a concomitant of the local cultural, social and religious oppressiveness: definitely not overwhelmed by nostalgia, Gallant resorts to spatially laden language to throw an ironic light on those restrictions.[6]

In the representation of the city, which is "not so much . . . a physical location as a psychological state" (Jarrett 174), the spatial references are coloured with numerous undertones. The emotional coloration of spatial elements plays a considerable role in the (re)constructions of locations. For instance, while in New York, Linnet is longing for a heavily distorted Montreal:

> My memory of Montreal took shape while I was there. It was not a jumble of rooms . . . , but the faithful record of the true survivor. I retained, I rebuilt a superior civilization. In that drowned world, Sherbrooke Street seemed to be glittering and white; the vision of a house upon that street was so painful that I was obliged to banish it from the memorial. The small hot rooms of a summer cottage became enormous and cool. If I say that Cleopatra floated down the Chateauguay River,

that the Winter Palace was stormed on Sherbrooke Street, that Trafalgar was fought on Lake St. Louis, I mean it naturally; they were the natural backgrounds of my exile and fidelity.

(*HT* 223)

Linnet could not describe more clearly how memory works, how its beautifying process involves spatial changes: "small" becomes "enormous," "hot" becomes "cool,"[7] a "drowned world" seems "glittering and white," and movement renders common places magical. The initial verb "took shape" even points to spatial invention/spatial memory. Once actual comparison cannot challenge it, memory embellishes the remembered object, place or person and even sets out to negate the existence of "the jumble of rooms" in which the Muirs used to live, and opposes to it the pretended faithfulness of real memory—the memory generating positive reminiscences. In comparison with the clarity of perception *du vécu hic et nunc*—that is, of the present experience—the past becomes a "drowned world" whose haziness alters and modifies things for the better; by referring to her expanding memory, Linnet makes Montreal look small. Similarly, the achromatic purity ("glittering and white") of the recollection imparts Linnet's will to forget the stronger chromatic, unpleasant, components of her past. Actual evidence of modification backs up the argument: houses—essential components of the urban landscape—are obliterated. Yet they "[bear] the essence of the notion of home" (Bachelard 5), which amounts to bringing a sheltering and reassuring warmth. That she equates her remembrances with a memorial evokes a parallel between them and funeral orations where defects, weaknesses and shortcomings are left unmentioned and/or beautified (*HT* 6). The long balanced sentence (*HT* 7-8) at the end punctuates the earnest yet illusory perception of the past as do the initial phrases "*seemed to be*" and "*became enormous.*" The first dramatic section (*HT* 7) with its periodic structure paralleling three "that" clauses of pure geographic fantasy postpones the main idea and stresses its importance: no harm is meant; imagination is allowed licence. The second section (*HT* 8), a shorter and thus more powerful main clause, restates the first one in objective, explanatory, abstract terms and no longer in spatial visual images: "exile" and "fidelity" merge to sharpen the nostalgic yearning for an otherwise disillusioned world.

> Montreal, in memory, was a leafy citadel where I knew every tree. . . . Sherbrooke Street had been the dream street, pure white. . . . It was a moat I was not allowed to cross alone; it was lined with gigantic spreading trees through which light fell like a rain of coins.
>
> (*HT* 235)

The sense of space and nature present in the description marks the magic quality of Linnet's recollection, its expansion into myth. Glittering colours, magnitude, veg-

etation—these transform remembrances for the better. Memory's actual counterpart, it appears from the next quotation, lacks grandeur, indeed might as well not exist:

> One day, standing at a corner, waiting for the light to change, I understood that the Sherbrooke Street of my exile—my Mecca, my Jerusalem—was. . . . *only* this. The limitless green where in a perpetual spring I had been taken to play was the campus of McGill University. A house, whose beauty had brought tears to my sleep . . . was a narrow stone thing with a shop on the ground floor and offices above. . . . Through the bare panes of what might have been the sitting room, with its private window seats, I saw neon striplighting along a ceiling. Reality, as always, was narrow and dull.
>
> (*HT* 235-236)

Linnet exposes the shock of disillusionment by humorously contrasting the sordid reality with the magnificent picture of her memory equated with mystic places of worship. Boundless expanse in unchanging propitious weather materialises as grounds which the reader soon recognises as bounded and exposed to harsh weather. The magnificent house capable of moving Linnet to extreme emotions turns out to be an unqualifiable building, at the most cramped and unpoetic. Crude artificial lighting replaces warm and comfortable decorations. Only bleakness prevails as marked by the repetition of the adjective "narrow." The accumulation of confining terms related to the actual setting serving as a basis for memories is striking. The contrast between the "aesthetically comfortable" (*HT* 292) character of her recollections and the spatial discovery that the word city means "drab, filthy, flat, or that city blocks could turn into dull squares without mystery" (*HT* 292) shakes Linnet with dismay, as the cumulative disparaging adjectives emphasise.

The same correction of reality marks Linnet's memory of Dr. Chauchard's house. The only one to grasp her sensitivity and grant her marked favours, Dr. Chauchard is the person closest to her except for an old *bonne* (also a French-Canadian of a good old Québécois family, who has fallen on hard times).

> The house he came to remained for a long time enormous in my memory, though the few like it still standing—"still living," I nearly say—are narrow, with thin, steep staircases and close, high-ceilinged rooms.
>
> (*HT* 302)

The description of her recollection and of the actual house again shows how selective—and even corrective—memory is. This confrontation of remembrance and its object confers fluidity to the perception of culture. What is and what might ideally be—the difference between the adult's perception of space and the child's naturally deformed remembrance of it[8]—thus alternatively evoked, produce the undulating motion of self-enquiry. Significantly, the above quotation also discloses a spatial reality, namely that Montreal's architecture in part illustrates the harsh principles of Presbyterianism. Some areas still display houses with Scottish characteristics like Chauchard's: "narrow, with thin, steep staircases and close, high-ceilinged rooms, [they are] the work of Edinburgh architects and [date] from when Montreal was a Scottish city" (*HT* 302). Their narrowness and height convey the imperative that people should follow the narrow path and look upwards "to open [their] eyes unto the heavens" (Knox 4: 294) so as to be "delivered from all fear, all torment and all temptation" (Knox 2: 109). As they are given no space to expand either physically or spiritually, they have neither free choice nor freedom to exist (Sartre, 73-102).

In **"Between Zero and One"** (*HT* 238-260), the prevalent restrictions on emotional freedom, perceived by the narrator and protagonist if not by the other characters, are reflected in the topographical details. The decor in which the action—or rather inaction—takes place is described in spatial terms of restrictive psychological impact. Linnet makes revealing comments on the atmosphere at work:

> I remember a day of dark spring snowstorms, ourselves reflected on the black windows, the pools of warm light here and there, the green-shaded lamps, the dramatic hiss and gurgle of the radiators that always sounded like the background to some emotional outburst, the sudden slackening at the end of the afternoon when every molecule of oxygen in the room had turned into poison.
>
> (*HT* 240)

The protagonist's associative memory has lost none of the irritating sounds, smells, colours and heat. Rather than offering comfort in contrast to the unfavourable climate, the interior locale Linnet describes seems to reproduce it. In spite of occasional patches of shaded light, the pictures evoke a dark, stifling atmosphere punctuated by the infuriating noises of the radiators. These depressing images piled up in the loose sentence echo the characters' frustrations with their meaningless lives. When—if at all—will an "emotional outburst" liberate them? One can hardly imagine their lives without the slow moving lift, a symbol for the exiguity, smallness, and limitedness of their world:

> I climbed to the office in a slow reassuring elevator with iron grille doors, sharing it with inexpressive women and men—clearly the trodden-on. No matter how familiar our faces became, we never spoke. The only sound, apart from the creaking cable, was the gasping and choking of a poor man who had been gassed at the Somme and whose lungs were said to be in shreds. He had an old man's pale eyes and wore a high stiff collar and stared straight before him, like everyone else.
>
> (*HT* 246)

Imprisoned in life as in the lift with an iron fence preventing emotions from coming out, the characters follow the path society designated them. Linnet makes fun of the normative rules that dictate the slow pace of the flock. Communication between people who have not been formally introduced is impossible. The only person who departs from the norm is the gassed veteran from the First World War but then his is a message of oppression, a cry for emotional and physical freedom. However, apart from his gasp for air and his choking which may be seen as an incapacity rather than as a symptom of restricting social norms, he conforms. His collar is stiff and the look on his face is as blank as a fish's. Clearly, real communication cannot exist among citizens abiding by the local inhibitions which religion exacerbates. Whatever they do, they are overcome with their sense of sin, for man is "never able to fulfil the works of the Law in perfection" (Knox 2: 107) so that they live in the terror of God, in the terror of the "plagues to fall upon [them] in particular for [their] grievous offences" (Knox 4: 295).[9] Bearing the stamp of imported pre-war British behavioural patterns, the characters have typically cool, shy and repressed attitudes registered in the physical background.

With the subtle collage of random memories from her past life and extra-temporal reflections on cultural issues, Linnet evokes a provincial world where emotions, rather than having a positive effect on mores, have to be repressed. As soon as she mentions crossing the border between the United States and Canada, spatial and human barrenness strike the reader: Linnet discovers "a curiously *empty* country, where the faces of people [give] nothing away" (*HT* 222; emphasis added). It soon appears, from the accumulation of comments in passing, that "'like' and 'don't like' [are such] heavy emotional statements" (*HT* 229) that Canadians keep "their reactions, like their lovemaking, *in the dark*" (*HT* 230; emphasis added). The confinement in the dark of their shameful and unavowed self marks the national repression, predominant in all fields. Questioning her country's ban on spontaneous responses, Linnet eventually discloses the ironic advantages of composure, in a detached voice rather like that of an anthropologist assessing the value of social behaviour in some far-off country:

> Now, of course there is much to be said on the other side: people who do not display what they feel have practical advantages [1]. They can go away to be killed as if they didn't mind [2]; they can see their sons off to war without a blink [3]. Their upbringing is intended for a crisis [4]. When it comes, they behave themselves [5]. But it is murder in everyday life—truly murder [6]. The dead of heart and spirit litter the landscape [7]. Still, keeping a straight face makes life tolerable under stress [8]. It makes *public life* tolerable—that is all I am saying [9]; because in private people still got drunk, went after each other with bottles and knives . . . [10].
>
> (*HT* 227-228; numbers between brackets added).

The initial balanced sentence [1] considers the impact of countenance in abstract terms and concedes it a beneficial function. The examples of advantages emphasized by the loose structures of sentences [2] and the verbs of motion show the tip of the iceberg: they assert with insistence the importance of the façade and relegate feelings to a dark corner. The next purposefully short simple sentence [3] sets out a theorem that the narrator subsequently proves by reducing it to the absurd [4-8]. By first delaying and preparing the way for the main thought, namely the ability to behave in cold blood, the next periodic sentence [5] alerts the reader to the assumed importance of repressed emotional responses. However, the following statement [6] brings the reduction to the real crisis: murder. (Playing the momentary crisis against murder in everyday life ironically punctuates the ridiculous attachment to apathy). The resulting waste invades the emotional landscape: a purely spatial image [7] involving no motion whatsoever ("litter the landscape") enhances the climactic message. But then, as if to tease the reader somewhat more, Linnet praises impassiveness [8]: it "makes life tolerable under stress." The concession, though, is short-lived: it is immediately corrected and restricted to the italicised public life [9]. And the correction reinforced in the re-statement [10] suddenly echoes a different voice. Linnet gets involved and recollects violent—and thus energetic—scenes of private lives, which annihilates the hypothetical value of restraint and denounces it.

And indeed the numerous references to behavioural responses interspersed here and there cynically show the negative effect self-control has on human beings. Most of the characters are about to lose their sanity from frustration and repression:

> . . . the winter tunnels, the sudden darkness that April day, the years he'd had of this long green room, the knowledge that he would die and be buried "Assistant Chief Engineer Grade II" without having overtaken Chief Engineer McCreery had simply snapped the twig, the frail matchstick in the head that is all we have to keep us sensible.
>
> (*HT* 240)

The cumulative spatial descriptions of depressing restrictive impact pave the way for the final metaphor pointing to the precariousness of people's psychological balance. Linnet equates repression with the dark winter weather whose spatiality is made palpable through the tunnel image. Further comments of spatial impact prove that her colleagues' psychological imbalance results from their education and its success in "[making them] invisible to [themselves]" (*HT* 243). Adults thus live in a "world of falsehood and evasion" (*HT* 229) where everything is "hushed, muffled, disguised" (*HT* 230). The overwhelming anger resulting from the age-old-inflicted

"deprivation of the senses, mortification of mind and body" (*HT* 245) is anything but surprising. "Easily angry, easily offended" (*HT* 247), married women are especially prone to be bitter. These, the reader is told, keep "[yelling]—to husbands, to children, to dogs, to postmen, to a neighbor's child" (*HT* 263). The epitome of what restriction and lack of opening both privately and professionally do to people is to be found in Mrs. Ireland, one of Linnet's colleagues. Named after the battered wife of England—the normative ruler whose inhibiting repression causes discontent—she is a battered wife too.[10] In spite of all her degrees, she does not know any better than to explode in wrath at any moment. One can but appreciate the double pun contained in her name—an evocation of a fragile psychological and political landscape—and understand the sarcastic criticism of the still pervasive constraining British norms.

Linnet's recollection of the population whether it evokes past or present situations deforms the picture derisively. She repeatedly ridicules the emptiness of her compatriots' lives in spatial terms that incidentally determine the difference between men and women:

> When I was young I thought that men had small lives of their own creation. I could not see why, born enfranchised, without the obstacles and constraints attendant on women, they set such close limits for themselves and why, once the limits had been reached, they seemed so taken aback. . . . There was a space of life I used to call "between Zero and One" and then came a long mystery. I supposed that men came up to their wall, their terminal point, quite a long way after One.
>
> (*HT* 238)

The images conjured up in this passage evidently reveal what Linnet thinks of the people around her. A posteriori, the vague reference to age intimates that the narrator is considerably removed from her childhood and teens. Indeed, it points to the distance between the time when Linnet, the protagonist, perceives facts and the time when Linnet, the narrator, relates them. From the start men's lives are shown as exiguous of their own volition. Linnet's incomprehension of such a narrow choice—their "close limits"—is marked by the opposition between men being "born enfranchised" and "the obstacles and constraints attendant on women." Spatial polarities thus immediately allude to the inequality of the sexes as well as to her puzzlement over the men's surprise at being limited. Life is also considered in terms of space and numbers, but the latter leave so little scope that it suggests how little Linnet expects from life. She cannot decode the "long mystery" after One either for her age, or for her sex. And yet, ironically, men do not seem to go beyond One, at least if one considers what the male characters do with their lives:

> Why didn't they move, walk, stretch, run? Each of them seemed to inhabit an invisible square; the square was shared with my desk, my graph, my elastic bands.

The contents of the square were tested each morning. . . . Sometimes one glimpsed another world, like
an extra room ("It was my daughter made me lunch today"—said with a shrug, lest it be taken for boasting)
or a wish outdistanced, reduced, shrunken, trailing
somewhere in the mind: "I often wanted. . . ."

(*HT* 246-247)

The initial question and its asyndeton enhance the lack
of scope characteristic of men's lives: the succession of
negated and non-coordinated verbs of motion reduces
their range to virtually nothing. And indeed the next
comment defines their world as "an invisible square"
whose confines are reminiscent of nests through the latter's association with "primal images" that "bring out
the primitiveness" (Bachelard 91) in man. The men's
careful checking of their belongings each morning is indeed not far from a bird's feverish struggle to build a
perfect nest for itself and its next of kin. The irony,
though, lies in the totally selfish character of the en-
deavour stressed by the italicised first-person possessive
pronoun. However an opening seems to lead onto another secret room, one whose existence is immediately
denied for fear of revealing one's feelings. Emotions
cannot come to the fore as obviously reflected in the
meaningless content of the reported speech: it simply
reveals an insignificant scene in the life of a supposedly
free man. Further confirmation of the negative character
attributed to emotions appears in the comparison of this
other world to "a wish outdistanced, reduced, shrunken,
trailing somewhere in the mind," namely to a micro-
scopic hidden corner of one's heart signalled by the
past participles of spatial contraction.

If men lead limited lives, women enjoy even less scope.[11]
As Linnet caustically remarks, their opportunities are
painfully restricted because of the "obstacles and constraints" hampering them. Theirs is the constricted space
"between Zero and One," as marked by the space allo-
cated to them:

A few girls equipped with rackety typewriters and adding machines sat grouped at the far end of the room,
separated from the men by a balustrade. I was the first
woman ever permitted to work on the men's side of the
fence. A pigeon among the cats was how it sometimes
felt.

(*HT* 242)

The secretaries' remote location in the room and the
physical separation between them and the men stress
the hopelessness of their banishment. The strikingly
short sentence with the reversed cliché stressing the
foray into the animal world appropriately conveys Linnet's feeling of entrapment in a world that does not
grant women any rights. Further descriptions of their
situation in "the darkest part, away from the window"
(*HT* 255) spatially confirm the minimal respect granted
them. Linnet resents the separation and equates it to

women being "penned in like sheep" (*HT* 226) or
"parked like third-class immigrants" (*HT* 255)—two
phrases proclaiming the spatial constraints imposed on
them and her revulsion at their degraded status. Men so
deeply resent the uniqueness of Linnet's position "on
the men's side of the fence" that they cannot refrain
from venting their feelings: she repeatedly hears, "if it
hadn't been for the god-damned war we would never
have hired even one of the god-damned women" (*HT*
317). Linnet goes on to disclose that even outside work,
"where women were concerned men were satisfied with
next to nothing. If every woman was a situation, she
was somehow always the same situation, and what was
expected from the woman—the situation—was so limited it was insulting" (*HT* 262). Considering the nonexistent respect for women at work, their humiliating
reduction to an abstract concept of unchanging nature is
anything but surprising.

The variations on the theme "a pigeon among the cats"
illustrate "that there are two races, those who tread on
people's lives, and the others" (*HT* 244). Thus Linnet's
first appearance at work arouses her male colleagues'
resentment against her presence:

And so, in an ambience of doubt, apprehension, foreboding, incipient danger, and plain hostility, for the
first time in the history of the office a girl was allowed
to sit with the men. And it was here, at the desk facing
Bertie Knox's, on the only uncomfortable chair in the
room, that I felt for the first time that almost palpable
atmosphere of sexual curiosity, sexual resentment, and
sexual fear that the presence of a woman can create
where she is not wanted. If part of the resentment vanished when it became clear that I did not know what I
was doing, the feeling that women were "trouble" never
disappeared.

(*HT* 243-244)

In this passage, the succession of periodic sentences increases the weight of the final main clauses whose of-
fensiveness echoes the hostile male discourse. As she
sits opposite Bertie Knox, the fictional counterpart of
John Knox whose teachings established "the divinely
ordained superiority of men over women" (Ridley 270),
the spatial confrontation takes on a further dimension:[12]
religion confirms the inferiority of women and justifies
male contempt. The piling up of feelings with overlapping meanings also makes for a tangible perception of
the atmosphere, so much so that the reader shudders
from revolt: the cumulative pinning down of male antagonism to women reinforces its extent, indeed univer-
salizes it.

Worse still, women discriminate too. Battered as she is,
Mrs. Ireland does not seek support from other women;
she makes their situation worse:

"Girl?" She [Mrs. Ireland] could never keep her voice
down, ever. "There'll not be a girl in this office again,
if I have a say. Girls make me sick, sore, and weary."

I thought about that for a long time. I had believed it was only because of the men that girls were parked like third-class immigrants at the far end of the room—the darkest part, away from the windows—with the indignity of being watched by Supervisor, whose sole function was just that. But there, up on the life raft, stepping on girls' fingers, was Mrs. Ireland, too. If that was so, why didn't Mrs. Ireland get along with the men, and why did they positively and openly hate her . . . ?

(*HT* 255)

Mrs. Ireland's rejection of "girls" (the commonly masculine derogatory term for women) and the double metaphor ("life raft" and "stepping on girls' fingers") enhance the secretaries' hopeless exclusion from professional recognition. Mrs. Ireland's revulsion paralleled with male arrogance only reinforces the abominable reality made palpable through the relegation to obscure and remote areas. The first metaphor concerning Mrs. Ireland's position "up on the life raft" spatially proclaims the universality of the age-old discrimination—whether women come first or last. The puzzling question as to why the men do not esteem Mrs. Ireland, their equal in intelligence and education—if not their superior—confirms the inequality, indeed poses its inescapability. As to the second image showing Mrs. Ireland fighting for her own survival, it just confines all the more women's, not to say "girls'", scope for responsible action.

No more welcome than women, children live in a confined atmosphere. Their situation is so undesirable that Linnet sums up her own experiences as those undergone in the "prison of childhood" (*HT* 225): parents—or rather adults in general—are inflexibly strict with children, as if to punish them for some primeval sin linked with their actual birth.[13]

> Halfway between our two great wars, parents whose own early years had been shaped with Edwardian firmness were apt to lend a tone of finality to quite simple remarks: "Because I say so" was the answer to "Why?," and a child's response to "What did I just tell you?" could seldom be anything but "Not to"—not to say, do, touch, remove, go out, argue, reject, eat, pick up, open, shout, appear to sulk, appear to be cross. Dark riddles filled the corners of life because no enlightenment was thought required. Asking questions was "being tiresome," while persistent curiosity got one nowhere, at least nowhere of interest.

(*HT* 282)

Translated in visual images, the detached sociological comment on educational methods derides the rigid reality of children's lives. No perspective is granted to children; the adults' final retorts allow no opening. Repressive threats and orders mar relations for good, for children cannot be themselves nor move about freely. Any natural instinct has to be curbed: the series of jux-

taposed prohibited actions highlights the overwhelming ban on spontaneous reactions. Overpowered, children do not even have a little bright corner to hide in: they are brought up in total darkness, with no possible escape nor enlightening discovery. Parents' answer to their children's need to know the reason for a decision "seems to speak out of the lights, the stones, the snow; out of the crucial second when inner and outer forces join, and the environment becomes part of the enemy too" (*HT* 293). Far from abating the children's wretchedness, the spatial analogy and the enmity of outer space exposes their predicament more acutely.

Exiled in the twenties, children cannot aspire to a better position in the forties:

> How much has changed? Observe the drift of words descending from adult to child—the fall of personal questions, observations, unnecessary instructions. Before long the listener seems blanketed. He must hear the voice as authority muffled, a hum through snow. The tone has changed—it may be coaxing, even plaintive—but the words have barely altered. They still claim the ancient right-of-way through a young life.

(*HT* 282)

Invited to participate in the sociological enquiry, the reader soon discovers that adults still use their hierarchical authority (like God's in paradise) to sentence children to life imprisonment. The apposition of drifting words and its asyndeton render the forcefulness with which adults exert their power: interestingly expressed in terms of space (the "drift of words *descending*" and the "*fall* of questions"), their control announces further cosmic imagery involving heaven and hell.[14] No longer addressed directly, the reader visualizes, indeed physically experiences, the "drift of words" as blanketing. The drowned out voice of authority thus aptly evokes an insignificant change: authoritarian vigour has withdrawn in favour of luring and lament.[15] But the content of the discourse remains the same; parental prerogative cannot be done away with—a mocking hint at the universally abusive character of education.

Under the adverse circumstances, children feel miserable. Linnet indirectly reports her own helplessness in the description of the time lapse *entre chien et loup*:

> There was one sunken hour on January afternoons, just before the street lamps were lighted, that was the gray of true wretchedness, as if one's heart and stomach had turned into the same dull, cottony stuff as the sky; it was attached to a feeling of loss, of helpless sadness, unknown to children in other latitudes.

(*HT* 311)

Equated with the distressing atmosphere of winter twilight, children's despair becomes an inescapable fact; the more so as the loose sentence echoes their neglect and the emptiness of their lives: they experience their inner space—"one's heart and stomach"—as equally revolting as their outer space—"the dull, cottony stuff [of] the sky." However, the source of Linnet's injured, indeed repressed, sensitivity, her depressing lot bears fruit. Drop by drop, she filters her emotions as if through "the cottony stuff of the sky," the spatial symbol of her unhappiness that will eventually engender her art.[16] Her childhood experiences indeed contribute to the pervading spatial imagery of her stories: her visual rendering of emotions colours the narration of her past anxieties. Another cause for anguish, Linnet's childhood excursions to town with her father are remembered in terms of space:

> These Saturdays have turned into one whitish afternoon, a windless snowfall, a steep street. Two persons descend the street, stepping carefully. The child, reminded every day to keep her hands still, gesticulates wildly—there is the flash of a red mitten. I will never overtake this pair. Their voices are lost in snow.
>
> (*HT* 283)

Memory turns numerous outings into one, assimilating them all with one spatial perception; achromatic, without a breath of air but enough snow to drown voices, it characteristically takes the walkers downward, for it recalls unpleasant moments. The red mitten flashing in the white surrounding—a striking colour in the otherwise white, thus emotionless, landscape—stresses the child's vitality confirmed by her erratic movements. But this image belongs to the past and cannot be retraced: time has changed the data—the father no longer is; the child has grown into an adult. Their voices, like their figures, are drowned in snow: past events belong to an inaccessible time where spatial and temporal components merge in haziness. The excursions often take the pair to a doctor or a teacher with whom the child stays while the father runs errands or pays visits to friends. The subsequent meetings at the station traumatize the child for fear she should be late and miss both her father and the train. Her dreams after her father's death clearly translate her obsessive anxiety in spatial terms:

> . . . after his death, which would not be long in coming, I would dream that someone important had taken a train without me. My route to the meeting place—deviated, betrayed by stopped clocks—was always downhill. As soon as I was old enough to understand from my reading of myths and legends that this journey was a pursuit of darkness, its terminal point a sunless underworld, the dream vanished.
>
> (*HT* 284)

Darkness, abandonment, deviation, obstacles, declivity, all these dominate Linnet's dreams and pave the route of childhood, another descent into hell.

Movement is evoked throughout the sequence since Linnet moves back and forth between the past and the present as the shift in tenses implies. Her past experiences—almost forgotten or at least removed from her—weigh on her in such a way that returning home is like embarking on a "journey into a new life and a past dream" (*HT* 228): movement thus translates her eagerness to plunge into life. She even has "a sensation of loud, ruthless power, like an enormous waterfall. The past, the part [she] would rather not have lived, [becomes] small and remote, a dark pinpoint" (*HT* 225). Life and its opportunities lie ahead: the energetic spatial simile expresses her hope for a better future. The past and its unpleasant reality disappear: reduced to nought, they cease to have an impact on her. "A gate shut on a part of [her] life" (*HT* 221), she moves on with optimism. Thus in the stream of life with its inevitable hardships, she is heard saying: "Sink or swim? Of course I swam" (226), thereby extending the preceding water imagery with the implicit determination to overcome adversity.

> My life was my own revolution—the tyrants deposed, the constitution wrenched from unwilling hands; I was, all by myself, the liberated crowd setting the palace on fire; I was the flags, the trees, the bannered windows, the flower-decked trains. The singing and the skyrockets of the 1848 [revolution] I so trustingly believed would emerge out of the war were me, no one but me; and, as in the lyrical first days of any revolution, as in the first days of any love affair, there wasn't the whisper of a voice to tell me, "You might compromise."
>
> (*HT* 225-226)

Suggestive of the intense determination with which she fights, the extended metaphor and its spatial components leave no doubt about Linnet's designs. The first section in the enumeration announces her will to change, indeed to purge the country of its despots in charge of wielding antiquated, yet cherished, dogmas. The second one symbolises the individual character of her enterprise while the third one pays tribute to her freedom, authenticity, openness and evolution. "The singing and the skyrockets" proclaim her acute happiness while the parallel between love and revolution rejects concessions. In short, the passage confirms her firm intention to change things and not to let narrow-minded dicta undermine her self-confidence.

The rigidity with which everything is set comes out even in art. Like other countries with split-up communities, the titles of art works are "identified in two languages" (*HT* 299), even when they do not call for translation. The physical presence on paper of both titles ridicules the immutable refusal to make an effort, a cold refusal to understand the other group. Unfortunately such limitations take away the poetical breath of any writer:

> I could write without hearing anyone, but poetry was leaving me. It was not an abrupt removal but like a recurring tide whose high-water mark recedes inch by inch. Presently I was deep inland and the sea was gone.
>
> (*HT* 248)

An echo to the set of rules imposed on journalists flowing from a dried up "intellectual bath" (***HT*** 320-321), the sea imagery aptly conveys Linnet's progressively declining literary inspiration. It also reverberates with James Joyce's imagery: inland, poetic inspiration perishes as paralysis prevails; at sea, paralysis is defeated by new, and unconstraining, horizons. Freedom of thought and lyric creativeness can only be restored through the rhythmic rocking of the waves. But originality is not looked for in Canada: Linnet's audition with Miss Urn, whose name recalls Keats' ode and its celebration of beauty in static art (Jarrett 177n4), ironically illustrates Canada's attachment to old values:

> Miss Urn received me in a small room of a dingy office suite on St. Catherine Street. We sat down on opposite sides of a table. I was rendered shy by her bearing, which had a headmistress quality, and perplexed by her accent—it was the voice any North American actor will pick up after six months of looking for work in the West End, but I did not know that.

> (***HT*** 250)

The small space in which the audition takes place mirrors the narrow-mindedness of artistic demand. The location in town reminds the readers of prudish maidens venerating St. Catherine in the hope of finding a husband while the actual street exhibiting sex shops calls for a further comic comparison. The stress put on the spatial opposition that separates Miss Urn and Linnet also marks a contrast in their outlook. Free of taboo and open to novelty, Linnet reads a passage of Thornton Wilder's *The Skin of Our Teeth*. Her choice of a play then on show in New York is a first offence. That it is a "self-conscious" play,[17] and therefore a challenge, rules it out in the eyes of Miss Urn, who favours Dodie Smith's unthreatening, cosy family play *Dear Octopus*. To make matters worse, Linnet on her different wave length misreads the second play as she mistakes it for a parody. Genuine creativity is thus annihilated since bigotry and intolerance control art.

Open-mindedness definitely does not distinguish WASP Canadians. Strictly adhering to British norms, they have also adopted their model's imperialist attitudes. Whatever is not English is met with contempt and rejection as not "part of the Empire and the Crown" (***HT*** 245). In a sardonic mood, Linnet defines their insularism in opposition to her parents' innovative approach:

> This overlapping in one room of French and English, of Catholic and Protestant—my parents' way of being, and so to me life itself—was as unlikely, as unnatural to the Montreal climate as a school of tropical fish. Only later would I discover that most other people simply floated in mossy little ponds labelled "French and Catholic" or "English and Protestant," never wondering what it might be like to step ashore; or wondering, perhaps, but weighing up the danger. To be out of a pond is to be in unmapped territory. The earth might be flat; you could fall over the edge quite easily.

> (***HT*** 305)

The comparison of bilingual, and at the same time bi-confessional, groups in Montreal to "a school of tropical fish" spatially establishes that the "two tribes [know] nothing whatsoever about each other" (***HT*** 245). The localization of each community in "mossy little ponds" extends the piscatorial and spatial simile. That they are labelled accordingly merely evidences the local ossification and fear of assimilation. The latter prevents any one of them from edging through the tangles of moss towards the other pond. The previously spatially laden image is further expanded upon in geographical terms. The passage implies that, frightened to be left on their own, they seek the security of the label of the group. Floating rather than following a definite course, the spatial equivalent of "being" rather than "existing" (Sartre 73-102), they cannot possibly consider opening themselves up, for their attachment to the community confers assurance, if not arrogance, on them and a feeling of superiority recalling their forefathers' when they landed in Canada.

In a country characterized by its "national pigheadedness" (***HT*** 261), outsiders have no access to real citizenship. Immigrants are easy to spot for origins can never be discarded in a society abiding by strict normative rules. Immigrants are so badly received that if a Canadian woman of old stock marries an immigrant she had better keep her maiden name, at least if she wants to succeed professionally. As Linnet explains: "in Canada you [are] also whatever your father [happened] to be, which in my case [is] English" (***HT*** 220). Accents of course can betray one's origins; Linnet herself shows how it functions in Canada:

> I can see every face, hear every syllable, which evoked, for me, a street, a suburb, a kind of schooling. I could just hear out of someone saying to me, "Say, Linnet, couja just gimme a hand here, please?" born here, born in Glasgow; immigrated early, late; raised in Montreal, no, farther west.

> (***HT*** 239)

Linnet directs her wit at her own ability to localize people's origins by their accents and to pin them down to a type of education, area or even street. As in all rural and provincial communities, it is of the utmost significance to know if one really belongs, what landmarks one can claim. Once part and parcel of the community, it is essential to safeguard its cohesion and specificity by protecting it against intruders.

To make matters worse some people cultivate their "foreignness." Linnet remembers her father refusing the process of cultural integration out of pride of his origins, just as many British citizens living in the colonies. And indeed, after years of residence in Canada, this Englishman by birth dies more British than Canadian. But what is true for him should not necessarily hold for his offspring. Nevertheless, owing to the system, Linnet is considered an immigrant on two counts for her return also turns her into a newcomer for those long established. Significantly, at the beginning of **"In Youth Is Pleasure,"** Linnet reveals that her father's "death turned [her] life into a helpless migration" (*HT* 219), a spatial image involving reductive movement. Thus both his birth and death contribute to isolate her from others and to take her on the road paved by outcasts. She ends up "being an outsider in her own home" (Howells 102) for she "[has] neither the wealth nor the influence a provincial society requires to make a passport valid" (*HT* 232).

Similarly, the remittance man (a Briton banished young for some obscure disgrace[18]) Linnet meets one summer and observes in an attempt to understand her own reality, retains his Britishness till death.[19] Initially cut off from all his ties, he ends up totally isolated, for he "was raised to behave well in situations that might never occur, trained to become a genteel poor on continents where even the concept of genteel poverty never existed" (*HT* 269). To her, he is "a curio cabinet" (*HT* 275) from which she takes everything out "piece by piece, [examines] the objects [and sets] them down" (*HT* 275) once she has understood what it contains. She points out that remittance men are "like children, perpetually on their way to a harsh school . . . [who are] sent 'home' to childhoods of secret grieving among strangers" (*HT* 269). This spatial metaphor curiously echoes her own experience: she was sent to a convent at the age of four "where Jansenist discipline still had a foot on the neck of the twentieth century and where, as an added enchantment, [she] was certain not to hear a word of English" (*HT* 299; emphasis added). She too was totally cut off from her milieu and had to live by the rules of a world she could not relate to. Like the remittance man who "would never live in England, not as it is now" (*HT* 275) she feels "apart from everyone, isolated" (*HT* 280). So when she hears that he died during the war she rejoices that he will never "be forced to relive his own past" (*HT* 280). One inevitably wonders how he could for he had no identity, therefore no past can be ascribed to him. This is made explicit when Linnet discovers the story she once wrote (although she does not remember when) about the remittance man's mysterious friend—"a man from *somewhere* living *elsewhere*" (*HT* 281; emphasis added).[20] He is thus positively different from the remittance man—but also, as the vague localizers imply, a fiction, an abstraction without real substance, indeed a man from nowhere living nowhere. The other immigrants she meets are equally trapped. They try to integrate by applying for citizenship, changing their names and eating cornflakes, but in vain. At any time, they may be reminded of their alien origins: they cannot shun the effects of xenophobia.[21]

To escape from such a stifling and incomprehensible atmosphere, Linnet turns to writing. "Anything [she cannot] decipher [she turns] into fiction, which [is] a way of untangling knots" (*HT* 261), the complex knots of her identity. To the reader's delight her suffering is transformed into art, the art revealed in the stories she casually narrates and defines through an extended spatial metaphor: "every day is a new parcel one unwraps, layer on layer of tissue paper covering bits of crystal, scraps of words in a foreign language, pure white stones" (*HT* 248). She filters, drop by drop, her recollections and reveals the jewels of her art. The reader follows her meandering path as she is looking for herself in others and opening the secret drawer of one character after another. But soon she is seen shutting it again promptly: she feels that she should not "[look] inside a drawer that [does] not belong to [her]" (*HT* 234), nor "[put] life through a sieve" (*HT* 281). Why she should not is in fact echoed by her recognition of the local smallness, the limits of an art bred by suggestions and inhibitions, and her latent awareness concerning her own self. Once she has grasped the emptiness of the immigrants' reality she is no longer interested in them because they can teach her nothing new. By then no one can serve her as a model to understand who or what she really is; she is another, different from others. For throughout her quest, she intuitively senses that in the end she will only find "another variety of exile" (*HT* 281).[22]

Estranged within her family, her hometown, her country, her sole remedy is writing. Generated by her need to understand herself and anchored in her re-discovery of her native Montreal, her prose eventually discloses the multiple facets of her culture. It emerges from the three layers of memory and historical time involved in her narration: twice removed from her childhood, Linnet, the narrator, looks back on the memories of her childhood as a teenager. This contributes to the detachment with which she can extract the numerous components of Canadian culture whose spatial reflection plays an important role in delineating local limitations. Concerned with aspects of the three dimensions, the spatial polarities used divide the world essentially into high and low, up and down, above and below or beneath, leaving those related to length and width in the background, with sometimes a reference to lengthy routes or processes. The up/down polarity and its related expressions evoke images of survival and decline and as such enhance the cultural pressures. Often linked with Linnet's attitude to life, the concept "up" and its equivalents by and large imply endurance and vital force or refer to an imaginary or utopian reality, whereas the concept "down" and its corresponding phrases, associated with obtuse behaviour and drabness, point to dissolution and annihilation. Movement contrasts mobility with immobility, going up with going down, floating with drowning, ascending with falling: lack of movement is characteristic of restrained Canadians, while movement and water imagery stress Linnet's free response and willingness to live unhampered. Similarly, colours typify Linnet's lively and affective response, so that the achromatic black, white and grey seem to invade the landscape of emotional repression. Finally, Gallantian polarities involving measures and proportions comprise oppositions such as exiguous and vast, small and big, narrow and wide, close and far, limited and limitless, enclosed and open, fenced in and unfenced. Contrary to the first concept of this binary opposition evidencing the local constriction and narrow-mindedness, the second concept reinforces Linnet's desire to question dogmas, to live freely and fully. In short, the positive polarity of each spatial binary opposition refers to either Linnet's desire to keep body and soul together or to an imaginary/utopian reality; on the other hand, the negative one emphasizes either the latter's real dull counterpart or Linnet's fellow citizens' compliance with the local intolerance. It thus appears from the spatial imagery that any group—be it social, political, religious or linguistic—refuses to accept any intrusion, let alone admit the worth of a custom, attitude or belief different from the age-old approved norm. Gallant's consistent use of spatial polarities tinged with irony confirms that what she explained about Montreal in an interview holds for her fictional Canada at large: "All those small worlds of race and language and religion and class, all shut away from one another. A series of airtight compartments" (Hancock 25). Enslaved by their blind obedience to social and religious rules, Gallant's Canadians can neither live nor let live. Those with scope flee from the place, as Mavis Gallant herself did in her twenties; the others stay behind and succumb to the weight of obligations and frustration. Their deep-rooted restraint and repression inherited from the first immigrants hamper communication and estranges them from themselves. Irreversibly inhibited, they have no future ahead: their bleak lives and their disappointing perspectives offer no outlet nor compensation. In the end, the spatial and achromatic illustration of the dryness, isolation and displacement at the heart of Gallant's Canadian experience derisively appears in all its oppressive and alienating reality.

Notes

1. I am most indebted to the Israel Association for Canadian Studies without whose research grant this paper would not have seen the light.

2. All references to the Linnet Muir sequence are incorporated into the text of the article using the abbreviation *HT.*

3. Bachelard's theories and Proust's experiments have shown that, besides being time-bound, memory is an essentially spatially laden component of spiritual life.

4. Weisgerber's book, *L'espace romanesque,* on which this study is based, offers a clear introduction to spatial analysis while abundantly illustrating the forms spatial components can take in fiction. He pays attention to and stresses the binary oppositions of the adverbs, prepositions, adjectives, nouns, verbs . . . that convey spatial realities. Other critics, like Bachelard, Ingarden, Lotman, Maatje, Matoré, Meyer and Spoerri have also significantly contributed to make readers aware of the existence of space in fiction, but do not offer a specific approach. In his book *The Linguistic Moment,* J. Hillis Miller also discusses space, but he restricts his study to "spatial images for time" (xvii).

5. One should emphasise that the stories set in Canada are *pré-Révolution Tranquille,* that is, a period unshaken by the cultural changes non-British or Western European immigrants have brought about. Not out of dishonesty, but out of a lack of assimilated first-hand experience, Gallant's picture of Canada thus overlooks the new multi-cultural nature of Canadian society, particularly in cities like Montreal, Toronto and Vancouver (Janice Kulyk Keefer, letter dated 27 July 1991). Personal conversations with Mavis Gallant make it obvious that she still sees Canada as it was—or almost—when she left the country in 1950. Needless to say, that does not detract from the stories' worth; but one should be aware of the standpoint chosen.

6. An echo to the Muir sequence, the other Canadian stories also disclose the pervading stranglehold through their narrator's and/or characters' perception of the setting in which the action takes place. Like Linnet, they come to use what Matoré calls "the vocabulary of spatialized psychism" (90) to convey their outlook on life and the local limitations.

7. Weisgerber includes temperatures, sounds, smells and lighting in the qualitative categories that contribute to the perception of space, though they are not strictly speaking spatial elements (18).

8. One should remember Piaget's remarks that a child's awareness of space differs strikingly from the adult's: overwhelmed by what he/she senses as the enormous dimensions of the adult world, the child may well remember a radically strained environment.

9. Echoing Calvin's theories that "there will never be plentitude or perfection" (Calvin 28), Knox' confirm God's "perpetual condemnation" (Knox 3: 166) of man. According to them, "if we say we have no sin, (even after we are regenerated), we deceive ourselves, and the verity of God is not

into us" (Knox 2: 107). For "no man on earth (Jesus Christ excepted) has given, gives or shall give in work that obedience to the Law which the Law requires" (Knox 2: 108).

10. Her appearance too partakes of the general restraint: she keeps her hair braided in an attempt to control it, just as she constantly wears a scarf to conceal an aspect of her private life, namely the bruises resulting from the violence her husband exerts on her.

11. My article "Squeezed 'Between Zero and One': Feminine Space in Mavis Gallant's *Home Truths*" gives ampler information about the opportunities of women.

12. Knox claimed that since "no animal [is] prepared to be ruled by his female" (Ridley 270), why should man be? So "to reign over man can never be the right to woman" (Percy 218).

13. For an overview of the limitations attendant on the lives of children in Gallant's fiction at large, see Kulyk Keefer's chapter on "The Prison of Childhood" (89-118).

14. These comprise the "descent into hell" (*HT* 284) which Linnet experiences as she anxiously walks to meet her father (see p. 16) and the "fall over the edge" (*HT* 305) of the earth which monolingual Montrealers fear should they try to establish contact with the other linguistic community (see pp. 18-19).

15. Linnet further uses an eloquent image to define parental voices: "being constantly observed and corrected was like having a fly buzzing around one's plate" (*HT* 284). But adult conversations deal with "shut-in velvet-draped unaired low-voice problems" (*HT* 293), a spatial image whose palpable quality cannot escape anyone. Charlotte Sturgess (217-218) gives an interesting interpretation of the voices heard in the two quotations concerning parental attitudes towards children.

16. The spatial component of artistic creation will be further discussed on pp. 17-18 and 21-22.

17. Self-conscious plays are self-reflexive (Scholes 100), thus trying to lay bare their potential. Like metafictional novels or stories (Gass 25), they "systematically [draw] attention to [their] status as an artefact in order to pose questions about the relationship between fiction and reality" (Waugh 2).

18. The cause of the banishment—or rather "the romantic crime" (*HT* 271)—is often "just the inability to sit for an examination, to stay at a university, to handle an allowance, to gain a toehold in any profession, or even to decide what he wanted to do—an ineptitude so maddening to live with

that the Father preferred to shell out forever rather than watch his heir fall apart before his eyes" (*HT* 271).

19. Linnet's comments revealingly confirm his origins. "Frank Cairns was stamped, labelled, ticketed by his tie (club? regiment? school?); by his voice, manner, haircut, suit; by the impression he gave of being stranded in a jungle, waiting for a rescue party—from England, of course" (*HT* 265).

20. This calls to mind Linnet's comment on her father: "He was seldom present. I don't know where my father spent his waking life: just elsewhere" (*HT* 285), longing for his birthplace.

21. My article on "Mavis Gallant's Montreal: A Harbour for Immigrants?" offers further views on immigrants and the space allotted to them in Canadian culture.

22. Her awareness echoes Coral Ann Howells' reflection about Gallant's collection of Canadian stories: "the most disturbing home truth of all is that the condition of being dispossessed is as common in Canada as it is among Canadians abroad" (94).

Works Cited

Alter, Robert Martin. *Partial Magic. The Self-Conscious Genre.* Berkeley: U of California P, 1975.

Bachelard, Gaston. *The Poetics of Space.* Trans. Maria Jolas. Boston: Beacon, 1969.

Calvin, Jean. *Calvin: Theological Treatises.* Ed. and trans. J. K. S. Reid. The Library of Christian Classics: Ichtus Edition. Philadelphia: Westminster, 1954.

Gallant, Mavis. *Home Truths: Selected Canadian Stories.* Laurentian Library 71. Toronto: Macmillan, 1981.

Gass, William. "Philosophy and the Form of Fiction." *Fiction and the Figures of Life.* New York: Knopf, 1970: 3-26.

Hancock, Geoffrey. "An Interview with Mavis Gallant." *Canadian Fiction Magazine,* no. 28 (1978): 18-67.

Howells, Coral Ann. *Private and Fictional Words: Canadian Women Novelists of the 1970s and 1980s.* London: Methuen, 1987.

Ingarden, Roman. *Das Literariche Kunstwerk.* Tübingen: Niemeyer, 1960.

Jarrett, Mary. "The presentation of Montreal in Mavis Gallant's 'Between Zero and One' and of Toronto in Margaret Atwood's *Cat's Eye.*" *Canadian Studies* (Talence) 29 (1990): 173-181.

Knox, John. *The Works of John Knox.* Ed. David Laing. 4 vols. Edinburgh: Bannatyne.

Kulyk Keefer, Janice. *Reading Mavis Gallant.* Toronto: Oxford UP, 1989.

Lotman, Jurij. *The Structure of the Artistic Text.* Trans. Gail Lenhoff and Ronald Vroon. Ann Harbor, Michigan: Michigan Slavic Contributions, 1977.

Maatje, Frank C. *Der Doppelroman: Eine literatursystematische Studie über duplikative Erzählstrukturen.* Groningen: J. B. Wolters, 1964.

————. "Literaire-ruimtebenadering." *Forum der letteren* 6.1 (1965): 1-16.

————. *Literatuurwetenschap: Grondslagen van een theorie van het literaire werk.* Utrecht: A. Oosthoeck, 1970.

Matoré, Georges. *L'espace humain: L'expression de l'espace dans la vie, la pensée et l'art contemporains.* Sciences et techniques humaines 2. Paris: La Colombe, 1962.

Meyer, Herman. "Raumgestaltung und Raumsymbolik in der Erzählkunst." *Studium generale* 10. 10 (1957): 620-630.

Miller, J. Hillis. *The Linguistic Moment: From Wordsworth to Stevens.* Princeton, N.J.: Princeton UP, 1985.

Sartre, Jean-Paul. *Being and Nothingness: An Essay on Phenomenological Ontology.* Trans. Hazel E. Barnes. London: Routledge, 1958.

Schaub, Danielle. "Mavis Gallant's Montreal: A Harbour for Immigrants?" *Canadian Studies* (Talence) 29 (1990): 195-201.

————. "Squeezed 'Between Zero and One': Feminine Space in Mavis Gallant's *Home Truths.*" *Recherches anglaises et américaines* 22 (1989): 53-59.

Scholes, Robert. "Metafiction," *Iowa Review* 1 (Fall 1970): 100-115.

Spoerri, Théophile. "Eléments d'une critique constructive." *Trivium* 8.3 (1950): 165-187.

Sturgess, Charlotte. "The Art of the Narrator in Mavis Gallant's Short Stories." *Canadian Studies* (Talence) 29 (1990): 213-222.

Waugh, Patricia. *Metafiction: The Theory and Practice of Self-Conscious Fiction.* London: Routledge (New Accents), 1984.

Weisgerber, Jean. *L'espace romanesque.* Lausanne: L'Age de l'Homme, 1978.

Diane Simmons (essay date 1993)

SOURCE: Simmons, Diane. "Remittance Men: Exile and Identity in the Short Fiction of Mavis Gallant." In *Canadian Women Writing Fiction,* edited by Mickey Pearlman, pp. 28-40. Jackson: University Press of Mississippi, 1993.

[*In the following essay, Simmons examines the figure of the Remittance Man in Gallant's short fiction.*]

In a semi-autobiographical series of stories in Mavis Gallant's **Home Truths,** the nineteen-year-old Linnet Muir returns to Montreal after a childhood spent, from the age of four, in a series of Canadian and American boarding schools. After probing various mysteries about her family and her past, such as the circumstances of her father's death, Linnet will, like Gallant, leave Canada permanently for France.

Linnet's investigations among her father's friends—she has broken with her mother—produce several versions of her father's death, and the girl soon decides that, whatever the actual events, "he had died of homesickness; sickness for England was the consumption, the gun, everything" (**Home Truths,** 235). Then, on a commuter train, she meets Frank Cairns, a remittance man, and in studying him, the young Linnet seems to find a key that unlocks the mystery of her father's life and her own.

The Remittance Man, Gallant writes, was a peculiarly British institution through which young people, usually sons, were sent away to live lives of puzzled exile, never quite understanding what had been their crime:

> Like all superfluous and marginal persons, remittance men were characters in a plot. The plot . . . described a powerful father's taking umbrage at his son's misconduct and ordering him out of the country. . . . Hordes of young men who had somehow offended their parents were shipped out. . . . Banished young, as a rule, the remittance man . . . drifted for the rest of his life, never quite sounding or looking like anyone around him, seldom raising a family or pursuing an occupation . . . remote, dreamy, bored. . . . They were like children waiting for the school vacation so they could go home, except that at home nobody wanted them: the nursery had been turned into a billiards room and Nanny dismissed.
>
> (266-68)

In characterizing the Remittance Man, Gallant describes not only Linnet's English-exiled father, lost to his child and himself, not only the child Linnet, exiled at an unusually young age to a particularly strict religious school by non-religious parents, but also something she sees in the Canadian personality. Here, everyone seems to feel a sense of loss; it is a country of children pushed from some all-but-forgotten nest: "I've never been in a country where there was so much gap between reality and dream," Gallant said of Canada in an interview. "The people's lives don't match up to what they seem to think they were and the people invent things or they invent backgrounds or they invent families. . . . In Europe, you can't invent because everyone knows too much" (quoted in [Neil K. Besner, *The Light of Imagination: Mavis Gallant's Fiction.* (Vancouver: University of British Columbia Press, 1988)], 8).

The Remittance Man also seems to provide a model for the array of characters, usually Canadian or English but sometimes Central European, who have been transplanted to the Paris or Riviera of Gallant's short stories. All are versions of the Remittance Man, for all, though we may not be shown the reasons, are adrift, not quite connecting with the life going on around them. All seem to have suffered some early loss, and, by choosing to live abroad, they are only acting out their inner sense of exile. Life abroad is Gallant's pervasive metaphor, not only for exile but also for the self-exile that inevitably follows. Paradoxically, life abroad also is seen by Gallant's characters as holding out the hope of a cure, at least for the symptoms of self-exile. In a foreign place, connection can be replaced by romance; identity can be replaced by a role that is necessarily simplified for foreign consumption. The unlucky among Gallant's characters are cured of their yearning for connection and identity; they find a role and disappear into it. The lucky may be forced, for a moment, to see themselves in their full infirmity; in this moment, though fleeting, they find home.

In Gallant's boarding-school story, **"Thank-you for the Lovely Tea,"** included in the "At Home" section of *Home Truths,* Gallant goes even further than in the avowedly autobiographical Linnet Muir section to get to the source of self-exile. Here we see in its infancy the loss of the places and relationships that allow one to know oneself. In the story, three young girls leave school for a few hours to take tea with Mrs. Holland, the mistress of Ruth's father. The girls have suffered different types of loss: May has been separated from her identical twin, who has been sent to another school thousands of miles away; Helen has been torn from a large, warm, crude family by a relative who wants to make her a lady; Ruth's mother, for unknown reasons, has gone to live in another country and Ruth has been sent to school.

At tea, Mrs. Holland's tense insecurity rocks the girls' emotional boat, and their responses show how self-exile works at an early age. May, lost from her twin and mirror, is lost from herself. With no self to refer to, she imitates Ruth, whether in the choice of ice cream or her example of cruelty to Helen, even though it is much more painful to be the torturer than to be the victim. Helen, who has been trained to despise her crude family, desires only to stay in the controlled boarding-school world forever, even though her reverence for the school's stiff gentility makes her the butt of the other girls' jokes. She can't imagine facing life as an adult because she perceives the limbo into which she has been cast; she can never go back to being like her family, but also knows she will never really be a "lady" like the girls with more refined backgrounds. Ruth demonstrates the third and most chilling response. While the others, despite their defenses, blunder against their real feelings of loss during the tense tea, Ruth does not, for already she has learned to banish the suffering self by banishing all feeling. Afterwards she wonders if she

would "ever care enough about anyone to make all the mistakes those around her had made" (*HT,* 16).

In **"The Other Paris,"** the title piece of Gallant's first short-story collection, published in 1956, we see a young North American woman a few years older than the Ruth in **"Thank-you for the Lovely Tea,"** but one who has not yet learned how to make herself invulnerable to the desire for some kind of feeling. At twenty-two, Carol Frazier is working in an American governmental agency in post-World War II Paris, and has just become engaged to marry her boss, Howard Mitchell. Carol is not in love with Howard and feels this to be a problem, but is certain she would be if only she could find the romantically picturesque Paris of films and songs. She believes that if she "spoke to the right person, or opened the right door, or turned down an unexpected street, the city would reveal itself and she would fall in love" (*The Other Paris,* 9).

Though she is young and "romantic," Carol has already unconsciously given up any claim to real connection or deep feeling, hoping only that charming scenes might allow her to manufacture a mood resembling love and happiness. But cold and dreary postwar Paris does not oblige. Rain obscures the sunrise from the steps of Sacré-Coeur, Christmas carols on the Place Vendôme are a crass media event, and a private concert to which Carol and Howard have been invited is a crashing failure as part of the ceiling comes loose, faulty wiring causes lights to flash off and on, and Carol is snubbed by her hosts, faded aristocrats who are not, after all, particularly picturesque.

Finally, and by accident, Carol does "turn down an unexpected street," finding herself in the impoverished and dirty room where her coworker, Odile, carries on an entirely uncharming affair with the refugee Felix, a boy much younger than Odile, closer in age to Carol herself. And suddenly Carol does feel something, moved by the love Felix and Odile have for one another, an emotion so authentic it does not need to be charming or even appropriate to survive. Suddenly, Carol imagines a powerful love, being loved herself, not by Felix, certainly not by Howard, but by "some other man, some wonderful person who did not exist." For a moment she feels as if she has "at last opened the right door," but quickly she retreats (*OP,* 28). A true Remittance Man, Carol cannot want love, she recognizes in this moment, only romance, and what she has just experienced must be scorned out of existence: "That such a vision could come from Felix and Odile was impossible. . . . she remembered in time what Felix was—a hopeless parasite. And Odile was silly and immoral and old enough to know better" (*OP,* 29). She decides to forget the real, troubling, fantasy-challenging Paris, to remember instead "the Paris of films." She will also, it is clear, forget her momentary "vision" of love and settle for a marriage that has, after all, begun in Paris and "would sound romantic and interesting, more and more so as time passed" (*OP*, 30).

In **"The Remission,"** a story in Gallant's 1979 collection, *From the Fifteenth District*, Alec Webb, upon learning that he has an incurable disease, leaves England with his wife and children to die on the French Riviera. Here he goes into a three-year remission, and both illness and remission represent another "variety of exile."

Like the father in the Linnet Muir stories, Alec is a father who is there but not there, who can "see his children, but only barely." Cut off from adult responsibility by illness and exile, he had "left [them] behind" (*From the Fifteenth District*, 90). He cannot see his children because he has become a child again himself, aimless, of the moment, utterly unable to comprehend responsibility to others or self. Only romance moves him. For him, the momentary cure is not a romantic French scene, but a dream of lost England, as in the midst of a medical "crisis" he appears fully dressed—though having substituted a scarf for a tie—to watch the coronation of Elizabeth II on television.

Alec's condition is mirrored by the entire English colony; though they are not literally ill, all exist in a limbo similar to Alec's remission. Cut off from adult responsibility, they play at life, acting out parts. When they do have ailments, the local doctor notes, they are "nursery ailments; what his patients really wanted was to be tucked up next to a nursery fire and fed warm bread-and-milk" (*FD*, 82). They all have a story of themselves, a role they play, which, like Alec's illness, explains their existence in simple terms. The caricature of this is Wilkinson, who literally plays the role of an Englishman in films set on the Riviera. He plays "the chap with the strong blue eyes and ginger mustache . . . who flashed on for a second, just long enough to show there was an Englishman in the room," and who is good with a line such as "Don't underestimate Rommel" (*FD*, 95, 99).

The others, too, have invented roles for themselves, repeating their lines over and over. Mr. Cranefield is a writer of romance novels that repeat the story of the same imaginary blond couple. On his table are framed pictures of the young man and woman, actually illustrations cut from magazines, which are his models. "I keep them there," he says, "so that I never make a mistake" (*FD*, 87). There, too, is Mrs. Massie, who greets every newcomer with a gift of her *Flora's Gardening Encyclopaedia* (her name is not, of course, Flora) and the information, "It is by way of being a classic. Seventeen editions. I do all the typing myself" (*FD*, 107). And there is Major Lamprey, whose story is that he intends "to die fighting on my own doorstep" (*FD*, 112) no matter who invades the Riviera.

Alec's wife, Barbara, also finds release on the Riviera from adult responsibilities, as she ceases to function as a parent and takes on a new, simpler role as Wilkinson's lover. It is as if, having moved up in English society by marrying Alec, Barbara now sees that a pretend upper-class Englishman is even better than a real upper-class Englishman.

While characters in many of Gallant's stories are offered the chance to break out of their roles—though they seldom take that opportunity—that does not happen here. **"The Remission"** is not really about the adults, but about the children and how they are formed. Here we see both the hopeless end and the near-hopeless beginning of the life of exile that obsesses Gallant's work. The children are deserted not only by their parents, who are lost in their own childish dreams, but also by the other adults who are equally useless in their vague offers of help, possible typing jobs, pocket money from gardening, or advice: "You will grow up you know" (103). As exile produces adults who cannot act as adults, it also produces children who cannot act as children. As the adults slough off responsibility for fantasy, the children are crushed by the need to find something to tell them who they are. They cling to their one useful memory of their father, his warning that it is dangerous to smoke in bed. "'Death is empty without God,' one of the children shrills at the funeral. 'Where did that come from?' everyone asks. 'Had he heard it? Read it? Was he performing? No one knew'" (*FD*, 111). Their mother is only an embarrassment, and they study her "as if measuring everything she still had to mean in their lives" (*FD*, 102). As if aware that they have been stunted, the children now "talk as if they are still eleven or twelve when Alec had stopped seeing them grow," and to others they look like "imitations of English children—loud, humorless, dutiful, clear" (*FD*, 103). Slowly the children begin to lose identifying characteristics. They no longer look much alike, or like their parents. They stop fighting, stop speaking to each other, barely seem to know each other. Though the details of these children's exile are different from Ruth's in **"Thank-you for the Lovely Tea,"** the result is the same. Banished young from adult concern, they are miniature versions of the Remittance Man. Until the children can invent roles for themselves, they are defined by nothing but loss, and the only way to banish the suffering is not to feel. At fourteen, Molly knows "there was no freedom but to cease to love" (103).

In her collection *Overhead in a Balloon*, 1979, Gallant no longer sees Europe through the eyes of romantic North Americans or British. The Paris of these stories is seen rather "through the imaginations of native or long-time Parisians [who] see Paris as the centre and the circumference of the universe." This is a Paris in which "old buildings are being demolished, trees cut down, whole blocks gutted to make way for parkades or shopping centres" (*LI* [*Light of Imagination*], 140). The politics of the seventies and eighties also infuses the stories and, in **"Speck's Idea,"** art dealer Sandor Speck loses one gallery to demolition when his block is replaced by a parking garage. Another gallery is bombed by Basque separatists who mistake his gallery for a travel agency exploiting their country.

But though we now have a more sophisticated and knowledgeable view of Paris, it is still the city of dreams, still holding out the promise of an answer, a cure. In Speck's Paris, there will always be an audience for lectures on such topics as "the secrets of Greenland," because "in no other capital city does the population wait more trustfully for the mystery to be solved, the conspiracy laid bare" (*Overhead in a Balloon,* 12). And even longtime residents like Sandor Speck cannot help glimpsing Paris as a movie set in a "French film designed for export . . . the lights . . . reflected, quivering, in European-looking puddles" (*OB,* 5).

Sandor Speck is both a native Parisian and another variety of exile, the second generation in France of a family coming from somewhere in central Europe. Even if he is on his native soil, we still recognize him as a Remittance Man, a "character in a plot" he must work to invent. As Carol Frazier believes love will follow if she can contact romantic and picturesque Paris, Sandor Speck—whose failures in marriage have caused him to all but give up on love in its ordinary form—believes he will feel secure if he can connect himself to wealthy and powerful Paris. Thus, he moves his gallery to an exorbitantly expensive building and seeks out opportunities to rub elbows with the prominent. Though Speck is more sophisticated than Carol, he is not much more successful at inducing Paris to provide the settings he believes will allow him to manufacture the feelings he needs. The "upper class hush" of his expensive neighborhood is continually shattered by left-wing attacks on a right-wing bookstore, and the sirens of ambulance and police. And his exalted neighbors, counts and princes, are "spiteful, quarrelsome, and avaricious" (*OB,* 1), even more disappointing than the aristocrats who snub Carol.

Speck does not maneuver Paris into the proper settings much better than does Carol, yet he is more practiced at manipulating his love life, which, after the breakup of his last marriage, appears to be subsumed by art. He is in search of an unknown painter who will give the art industry the "revitalization" editorials are calling for, and will benefit his finances and reputation. Much as Mr. Cranefield of **"The Remission"** lovingly depicts the perfect blond couple in romance after romance, Speck sits down with a pencil and pad to draw up specifications for the perfect French artist:

> A French painter, circa 1864-1949, forgotten now except by a handful of devoted connoisseurs. Populist yet

refined, local but universal, he would send rays, beacons, into the thickening night of the West, just as Speck's gallery shone bravely into the dark street.

$$(OB, 8)$$

The artist's politics must be drawn with painstaking precision. Should the artist have been a member of the Resistance? The Resistance is no longer chic; its youngest members are in their seventies. But what about state-subsidized museums, where Resistance work would be prized, possibly even required? Speck solves the problem by writing: "1941—Conversations with Albert Camus" (*OB,* 9). As Speck lists on his pad all the characteristics of the perfect artist, only one little thing is missing, a person who can be made to embody these characteristics, the artist himself, "the tiny, enduring wheel set deep in the clanking, churning machinery of the art trade" (*OB,* 14).

Speck happens to hear of an obscure, long-dead artist named Hubert Cruche ("Don't get rid of the Cruches," Speck advises the acquaintance who mentions his collection of the artist's work), and Speck sets out to the Paris suburbs to court the painter's widow. He approaches her, as he always approaches artists' widows, through a "subtle approximation of courtship" (*OB,* 18), winning her to his will by listening to her accounts of life with the great man and of her own vital importance to his work, as he pretends to eat the sickening sweets she adores. He plays his role, never forgetting his mission, to take possession of the Cruche paintings she owns and, most importantly, to appropriate the myth of the artist, which he will then rework into the myth he needs. Indeed, Speck's attempt to win the widow and her dead husband, his mixing of "courtship" and "bargain hunting," serves as a metaphor for the attempt to love, or find something resembling love, in much of Gallant's work. And while Carol Frazier and even Barbara Webb, the adulterous wife of **"The Remission,"** are still romantics, Speck knows himself to be more advanced, a bit of a whore: "It was true that his feeling for art stopped short of love; it had to. The great cocottes of history had shown similar prudence." He is a whore for the obvious financial reasons but also, as probably is the case with most whores, as with remittance men, he does not dare feel: "For what if he were to allow passion for painting to set alight his common sense? How would he be able to live, then, knowing that the ultimate fate of art was to die of anemia in safe-deposit vaults?" (*OB,* 29). And how to love if love, too, is always locked away to die?

But Speck's manipulations crash to a halt as the artist's Saskatchewan-born widow, Lydia, not only fails to respond to Speck's "pseudo courtship" in the expected way but also seems to see through his manipulations with bewildering ease. Deprived of the role he relies on, Speck is suddenly naked and vulnerable. The ridiculous old widow in her shabby house now appears "as a tough little pagan figure, with a goddess's gift for reading men's lives." As Carol, exposed to the passionate Felix, has a sudden vision of being loved, Speck has "a quick vision of himself clasping her knees and sobbing out the betrayal of his marriage" (*OB*, 24), the last thing in the world he meant to include in his assault on the widow.

Indeed, Speck has met his match. Far from being charmed and manipulated, Lydia seems to take Speck's approach as an opportunity to arrange a contest between him and an Italian art dealer, the prize being Lydia, her paintings, and the myth of Hubert Cruche. Speck responds by "falling back on the most useless of all lover's arguments . . . 'I was there first'" (*OB*, 41).

In the end, after seeming to favor the Italian, Lydia comes back to Speck and allows him to mount the first Cruche show. The show will then proceed to Milan, where, hyped by the prestige of a Paris opening, Lydia's paintings will probably sell for a great deal of money. Speck sees that his choices had been arranged for him, either to go second and to seem to be taking crumbs, or to go first and set up the fortunes of his rival. He elects to go first.

Speck is thoroughly defeated by Lydia and knows it. Still he is granted a moment of uplift at the end of the story, an uncommon event in Gallant's work. The weather improves, there's a cab at the cab stand as he returns from Lydia's suburb by bus (having wrecked his Bentley upon hearing about his rival), and he "seemed to have passed a mysterious series of tests, and to have been admitted to some new society, the purpose of which he did not yet understand. He was a saner, stronger, wiser person" than he had been before (*OB*, 47). He decides to sign his own catalog introduction to the Cruche show, rather than ghosting it for some important person as he had intended.

The tests Speck has passed are similar to those undergone by many of Gallant's adult characters. He has been given the dangerous opportunity to see through his own pretenses to the real self beneath. When this danger presents itself to Carol Frazier she flees, preferring a life of empty illusion to catching a glimpse of her desire for and fear of connection. Speck emerges, however, as from the wreck of his Bentley, battered but alive, and feels an immense if fleeting sense of relief. He is, after all, unlike Carol, momentarily alive. And he has formed a real, if tawdry, connection, finding with Lydia "a patch of landscape they held in common—a domain reserved for the winning, collecting, and sharing out of profits, a territory where believer and skeptic, dupe and embezzler, the loving and the faithless could walk hand in hand" (*OB* 46). This is not much of a connection, and it is steeped in irony. But it is something, and more than Speck had before he met Lydia.

Lydia's secret weapon, that which allows her to wreck Speck's sophisticated and practiced charade, seems to be the bleak power she derives from her childhood in Saskatchewan. Speck, as he recognizes, has been both "defeated" and paradoxically, albeit briefly, saved by a "landscape," the "cold oblong" of a province (*OB*, 43). Similarly, in **"The Ice Wagon Going Down the Street,"** a story collected in the "Canadians Abroad" section of **Home Truths,** the urbane, lost Peter Frazier is momentarily ripped out of his self- and life-denying pretenses by Agnes Brusen, a plain little woman, "poor quality really" from a small town in Saskatchewan (*HT,* 129). It is as if in Gallant's world pretense will spring up given the slightest nourishment of culture or sophistication. While it may be true, as Gallant says, that "in Europe you can't invent because everyone knows too much," this does not stop her characters from going to Europe and devoting themselves to the attempt. Integrity, ironically, seems to be nurtured in those cold and barren Canadian landscapes where buds of pretense, along with almost everything else, freeze on the vine.

In **"The Ice Wagon Going Down the Street"** Peter Frazier is doing the postwar "international thing," but not very successfully. He is a true Remittance Man, living on the crumbs of a fortune which was made by his great-grandfather, a Scottish immigrant to Canada, guarded by his grandfather, and used up by his father. Like the British abroad in **"The Remission,"** Peter is cut off from the wealth and prominence that is the only birthright he can imagine, and he tries to reinvent himself by playing a role. He poses as the devil-may-care son of a wealthy and powerful family, entirely unable to take the ordinary struggles of life seriously, living as if his work were a "pastime, and his real life a secret so splendid he could share it with no one except himself" (*HT,* 115). He has married Sheilah, a flashy woman of a poor background, one who supports Peter's view of himself as "a peacock" and does what she must to lure opportunity their way as Peter dreams his life.

Banished from his birthright, Peter is banished again, this time from the Canadian society of Paris. Having made an ass of himself at an important wedding—he is only beginning to grasp that he must be a little careful—his connections fail him. He is shipped out to glamourless Geneva, where he makes a faint pretense of working at a clerk's job while he and Sheilah await their next opportunity. His superior in this job is a young Canadian woman, Agnes Brusen, whose education and career is the product of great sacrifice by her Norwegian immigrant family. Though Peter finds her unattractive, boring, even ridiculous—she cannot begin to function at one of Sheilah's mock-elegant little dinners—he is also afraid of her. In her, he recognizes his own proud, ambitious, fervent immigrant ancestors, feels the "charge of moral certainty round her, the belief in work, the faith in undertakings." And in her presence, he glimpses himself as the played-out end of the line. She is at the beginning, and she seems to say to him, "You can begin, but not begin again" (*HT,* 118).

Nothing much happens between Peter and Agnes. Unused to alcohol, she gets drunk at a party, and Peter is ordered by the hostess, a woman he now understands he must cultivate, to take her home. Lonely and frightened, sickened by the swinishness of the supposedly refined and educated world her family has sacrificed so much for her to reach, she clings to him briefly and tells him *her* story, how, as a child in a big family, she would get up early on a summer morning to watch the ice wagon going down the street. In such a moment, she tells him, "it's you, you, once in your life alone in the universe. You think you know everything that can happen. Nothing is ever like that again" (*HT,* 132). And that is really all. Peter returns home, where Sheilah is just coming in all aglow, having apparently seduced a man she met at the party and thereby secured Peter the promise of a job in Ceylon.

Nothing happens. But for the rest of Peter's life, as he and Sheilah knock around the world, "always on the fringe of disaster, the fringe of a fortune," still viewing themselves as "peacocks," he thinks of Agnes almost as if they had once been lovers. Like Peter, Agnes is also in exile, lonely and lost. Unlike Peter, she has a little shred of home to hold onto, a moment when the self was felt, that gives her an integrity Peter has never had. She shares this with him, and sometimes throughout the years he allows himself to use it, to feel how it would be to have a self:

> Nothing moves except the shadows and the ice wagon and the changing amber of the child's eyes. The child is Peter. He has seen the grain of the cement sidewalk and the grass in the cracks, and the dust, and the dandelions at the edge of the road. He is there. He has taken the morning that belongs to Agnes, he is up before the others, and he knows everything. There is nothing he doesn't know.
>
> (*HT,* 134)

This knowledge does not have much to do with the life Peter must live. In real life as he knows it, morning is all about "dimness and headache and remorse and regrets" (*HT,* 134). In real life, Peter doesn't know what he would do with Agnes's morning. Finally, self-knowledge and the integrity that comes with it is as bleak and barren as a slab of sidewalk in a dusty Saskatchewan town. Gallant's characters don't want it at this price. But in cherishing Agnes and her morning, Peter, one of the lucky in Gallant's world, is able at least to know what has been lost.

Writings by Mavis Gallant

The Other Paris. Cambridge, Mass.: Houghton Mifflin, 1956; London: André Deutsch, 1957; reprint, Freeport, N.Y.: Books for Libraries Press, 1970. Includes "The

Other Paris," "Autumn Day," "Poor Franzi," "Going Ashore," "The Picnic," "The Deceptions of Marie-Blanche," "Wing's Chips," "The Legacy," "One Morning in June," "About Geneva," "Señor Pinedo," and "A Day Like Any Other."

From the Fifteenth District: A Novella and Eight Short Stories. New York: Random House, 1979; London: Jonathan Cape, 1980. Includes "The Four Seasons," "The Moslem Wife," "The Remission," "The Latecomer," "Baum, Gabriel, 1935-( )," "From the Fifteenth District," "Potter," "His Mother," and "Irina."

Home Truths: Selected Canadian Stories. Toronto: Macmillan, 1981; New York: Random House, 1985. Introduction by Mavis Gallant. Includes "Thank You for the Lovely Tea," "Jorinda and Jorindel," "Saturday," "Up North," "Orphan's Progress," "The Prodigal Parent," "In the Tunnel," "The Ice Wagon Going Down the Street," "Bonaventure," "Virus X," "In Youth Is Pleasure," "Between Zero and One," "Varieties of Exile," "Voices Lost in Snow," "The Doctor," and "With a Capital T."

Overhead in a Balloon: Stories of Paris. Toronto: Macmillan, 1986; New York: W. W. Norton, 1988. Includes "Speck's Idea," "Overhead in a Balloon," "Luc and His Father," "A Painful Affair," "Larry," "A Flying Start," "Grippes and Poche," "A Recollection," "Rue de Lille," "On the Colonel's Child," "Lena" and "The Assembly."

Lesley D. Clement (essay date spring 1994)

SOURCE: Clement, Lesley D. "Mavis Gallant's Stories of the 1950's: Learning to Look." *The American Review of Canadian Studies* 24, no. 1 (spring 1994): 57-72.

[*In the following essay, Clement contends that the stories Gallant wrote during the 1950s provide insight into her coherent and vivid imagery and "are particularly good guides for readers learning to see her fiction and hence read it responsively."*]

At a static moment in **"The Picnic,"** one of the first stories Mavis Gallant wrote after arriving in France in 1950-1951,[1] a photographic image is developed of a harmonious scene in which the grande dame of a "typical" French town is surrounded by five attentive American children (117-118).[2] This is a precisely rendered composition, similar to those that the camera will capture throughout the day to serve as visual evidence in an American magazine that the picnic is "a symbol of unity between two nations" (106); nevertheless, this photographic image is, as Gallant describes in another story from the fifties, **"The Other Paris,"** "a coherent picture, accurate but untrue" (30). Desiring images of consistency, coherence, and harmony so that this picnic will become a significant symbol, participants and observers trust the seen and dismiss the unseen—those tensions and failures that Paula Marshall, wife of the major organizing this picnic, intuits will lead to "fresh misunderstandings and further scandals" (120-121). Responsive readers of this story receive Paula's "sudden prophetic vision of the day ahead" (120) as conveying greater truth than those accurate snapshots that will be used for morale and propaganda.

But how are we, as readers, to respond to Gallant's fiction and not be, as so many of her characters are, lulled, paralyzed, or even victimized by falsifying images? If we are to read Gallant's fiction responsively, not subjectively or arbitrarily but affectively and effectively, achieving the aesthetic response that Wolfgang Iser defines as "the fulfillment of that which has been prestructured by the language of the text,"[3] our reading process must become a visualizing process. Just as many of the characters in Gallant's early stories are given opportunities for learning to look,[4] so too readers of Gallant may respond to signals in her texts that show us not simply how to *read* her fiction but how to *see* it.

In the stories written or drafted during the 1940s, Gallant was already encouraging and developing her readers' responsiveness by occasionally opening up, but leaving unexplored, angles of perception—what Iser denominates "gaps of indeterminacy" or "structured blanks" that "stimulate the process of ideation to be performed by the reader on terms set by the text" (*AR,* 169). To this end, Gallant experimented with techniques borrowed from cubist, surrealist, and kinetic art and so attained fragmentation, distortion, and mobility in her attempts to break from the frames in which she was inclined to place her characters and enclose her readers' perspectives. By the publication of her first novel, *Green Water, Green Sky,* Gallant successfully broke the frame in her continued use of techniques from the visual arts that, through structure, perspective, and metaphor, create a kinetic medium for characters and readers alike.[5] The stories that Gallant wrote and published in the intervening years, during the 1950s, are particularly good guides for readers learning to see her fiction and hence read it responsively.

Iser argues that whereas the static photographic image may simply reproduce an existing object and thus exclude observers of this image from a composition they passively see but do not actively create, the literary image, while governed by the schemata of the text, requires a reader to assemble these schemata and therefore to constitute the multiple meanings of the text (*AR,* 135-142). Unlike much modern and postmodern fiction, in which the multiplication of gaps "is intimately connected to the ever greater precision of representation" and in which the gaps arising "out of the overprecision

of representation cause the reader to become more and more disoriented" (*AR,* 206-207), in Gallant's fiction, the disorientation that may result from the high degree of indeterminacy created by an almost overwhelming number of precisely defined images is tempered by the controlling perspective that embraces all the other perspectives recorded in the course of the narrative. While Gallant's characters often experience extreme disorientation, occasionally even vertigo, because they are unable to fix an image of self within any context or environment, Gallant's readers rarely experience more disorientation than that stimulated by the fluctuating or mercurial effect produced as the focus shifts from one perspective to another, leaving hollow gaps to be bridged.[6]

Responsive readers of Gallant may not be able to compose static pictures in which all parts are structured into a harmonious and coherent whole. They can, however, assemble the details of the stories, which Gallant herself has delineated using techniques borrowed from the visual arts—color, light and dark, perspective, proportion, framing, and ultimately fluidity—into open compositions permitting a plurality of interpretative perspectives. In such early stories as **"One Morning in June," "Poor Franzi," "About Geneva," "Going Ashore,"** and **"Autumn Day,"** Gallant offers responsive readers insights into viewing her stories as multidimensional compositions.

If read in terms of simply the first two of the four textual perspectives that Iser identifies as prestructuring aesthetic response—character and plot-line (the other two being narrator and reader)—Gallant's **"One Morning in June"** and **"Poor Franzi"** are static and hence closed pictures. Characters remain suspended within a two-dimensional plane, even though characters have equal opportunities as readers to break this frame by developing faculties of perception and response that open into a third dimension, depth, and a fourth, movement. In each of these stories, the progress of a relationship between two central characters rests upon their ability to shatter the flat surface although, as is so often the case in Gallant's early fiction, **"The Other Paris"** being the most notable example, the shattering of this surface may mean discontinuance of the relationship. Characters, therefore, opt consciously or unconsciously to remain secure within the frame rather than risk challenging the deceiving images that keep the frame in place. As the central characters attempt to observe each other, both **"One Morning in June"** and **"Poor Franzi"** develop this internal structure of perception. Like the concentric circles of an op art painting that achieve an illusion of depth and movement, the textual perspectives created from the perceptions of the couples are encircled by the perceptions of observers or potential observers in the text. If, in turn, these concentric circles radiated out through, first, the narrator's perspective and, then, a multitude of readers' perspectives, the resulting composition, as with an op art painting, would be an illusive tour de force and remain very much a closed structure. Gallant has always eschewed such gimmicks, trusting to the potential of language to create texts eliciting visual responses that open up a range of interpretative possibilities.

In **"One Morning in June,"** the situation, which rests with the presently "paralyzed . . . tremulous movement of friendship" (173) between two young Americans, Barbara and Mike, staying in Menton, a resort town in the south of France, is traced along the parallel lines of their two perspectives. Not only are the lines parallel, but the segments devoted to each perspective are roughly proportionate. These structural features underscore the eventual inability of either character to achieve a multidimensional composition with oblique and therefore converging lines and with proportions adjusted to attain a sense of foreground and background. Although the situation in **"Poor Franzi"** is presented from a more distanced vantage point but within a more specifically defined political context than that of **"One Morning in June,"** it is developed similarly and reinforced by the myopia of Elizabeth (57, 66, 68) and the disturbingly unfocused gaze of Franzi (58), an uncaring and potentially cruel opportunist whose callous attitude towards others may be attributed to the displacement he and his family have undergone during the fluctuations of Austria's political situation. Since readers of these two stories cannot look to the characters themselves for paradigms of perception, they must bridge the gaps in the stories to assemble what and why these characters fail to see.

The failures of Mike, in **"One Morning in June,"** are of particular interest because he is just finishing a year in France, which his parents have financed to allow him to discover and test his talents as an artist. Mike's self-absorption as he dwells on his own imperfections and envies what he falsely perceives others to possess is largely responsible for hindering his piercing through surface appearances. But the controlling perspective of the narrator constantly invites readers to break the flat plane, in which these characters seem content to remain becalmed, by spiralling into the past, while leaving the characters suspended in the present, to provide historical dimensions of the characters and their present environment.

Mike, we learn in one of these spirals, has spent an unproductive winter since he has yet to develop the mechanics of perspective and proportion, color and shading. His paintings are "flat, empty, and the color of cement," and although at first he blames the sunless Paris winter, he later sees that "its gray contained every shade in a beam of light, but this effect he was unable to reproduce" (178).[7] Menton proves a better source of

inspiration for Mike than Paris because, with its soft colors, it can be more easily rendered into the kind of pictures that will appeal to his parents, eagerly awaiting his "winter's harvest" (178). But like the artist who has taught Mike in Paris and advised him to come to Menton, remembered "as a paradise of lemon ice and sunshine" (179), Mike creates images that are accurate but untrue. Ignoring the "shelled, battered, and shabby" Menton, which Barbara's aunt perceives, Mike paints "with the speed and method of Barbara's aunt producing a pair of Argyle socks" and renders "with fidelity the blue of the sea, the pink and white of the crumbling villas, and the red of the geraniums," as "flushed and accurate as a Technicolor still" (179-181). While he applies paint to canvas, Barbara produces her own "Technicolor still," snapping a picture to place alongside all her other "Souvenirs de France"—an "image of Mike looking rapt and destined, his eyes secretively shadowed, high above the sea" (182).

This scene excellently demonstrates Iser's discussion of the kinetic effect created by gaps of indeterminacy during the reading process: "Thus every moment of reading is a dialectic of pretension and retention, conveying a future horizon yet to be occupied, along with a past (and continually fading) horizon already filled; the wandering viewpoint carves its passage through both at the same time and leaves them to merge together in the wake" (*AR,* 112). Reading retrospectively, we recognize that Barbara has simply reproduced an image of her preconceived image of Mike and art in general. Just as Mike has preconceived images of Barbara with reference to her financial and social status, Barbara views Mike as gaining independence and purpose through his calling as an artist. But Mike, like the central character in Gallant's earliest published story, "Good Morning and Goodbye," is in "the vacuum that lies between the patterns in a life" (2); in fact, this whole year seems a vacuum as Mike awaits someone to propel him into a new pattern (178, 182). This reading is tempered, if not actually in Iser's term "negated" (*AR,* 212-231), by the protensive nature of the reading process in that Barbara forgets "once more to wind her film" (182). Perhaps Barbara has, after all, accidentally caught a true image—Mike suspended in a vacuum between two photographic images—although not an exact one. Or perhaps her photograph will reflect the third dimension, created by superimposed images, which neither she nor Mike can perceive. Retrospectively, we realize the significance of the surrealistic description of the snapshots Barbara has mounted in her album: "ghostly buildings floated on the surface of the Seine, and the steps of the Sacré-Coeur, transparent, encumbered the grass at Versailles" (175). In terms of character and plot-line, however, this "future horizon" is never "occupied." Barbara may achieve an illusion of depth through her double exposures that Mike never achieves in his paintings, but it is the reader who truly experiences the third and fourth dimensions that Iser describes being created "in the time-flow of the reading process" as "past and present continually converge in the present moment, and the synthesizing operations of the wandering viewpoint enable the text to pass through the reader's mind as an ever-expanding network of connections" (*AR*, 116).

Because Mike and Barbara, Elizabeth and Franzi, are at the center, within the frame, they are unable to attain the distance necessary to develop a multidimensional composition through perspective, proportion, and gradations of color and light. They resemble that kind of reader that Iser identifies as least responsive because most "committed" to preestablished attitudes and perspectives (*AR*, 201-202). In contrast, argues Iser, responsive readers can experience the text as a "living event" only through "the emergence of a third dimension, which comes into being through [their] continual oscillation between involvement and observation" (*AR*, 128).[8] Gallant's readers are thus guided to reject as models those characters who are so self-absorbed that their readings of characters and situations break down into a series of "glances" rather than becoming a meaningful and productive visualizing process gained through disinterested participation. But the onlookers, or potential onlookers, in Gallant's stories are equally incapable as the central characters of viewing the scene from multiple perspectives: for instance, the "fat man taking his dog for a run" and the aunt in **"One Morning in June"** (180, 188-189) and the family of Americans, the Wrights, and their English companion, Miss Mewling, in **"Poor Franzi."** All are as myopic as Elizabeth in viewing "the landscape that none of them knew": "Behind the solid peaks were softer shapes, shifting and elusive: she could not have said if they were clouds or mountains. But then, she thought, no one can, unless they have better eyes than mine, and know the country very well" (68; see **"One Morning in June"** 187-188).

In each story, the "better eyes" must be those of readers who, guided by the narrator through time and space, attain, if not a "ringside seat" (Keefer, 22), then a fluid vantage point where involvement and observation, identification and detachment, past and future may converge. In each story, therefore, we are guided to create a composition with color and shading, perspective and proportion. In **"About Geneva,"** however, a third dimension, depth, is prestructured not simply through the textual perspectives of narrator and reader, as in **"One Morning in June"** and **"Poor Franzi,"** but as well through those of character and plot-line.

If in **"One Morning in June"** readers are granted a perspective from several rows behind the "ringside seats," and in **"Poor Franzi"** from the front-row balcony, then in **"About Geneva"** the readers' perspective, as the story opens, is from the rear benches. In the

background is Granny, framed by the door of her Nice apartment, looking "small, lonely, and patient"; in the foreground, implied rather than described, is the taxi bringing Ursula and Colin back from the airport, after a two-week visit in Geneva with their father and his new lover, and the children's mother (190). This tableau shifts to another in the sitting room as the observer is ushered slightly closer, but our perspective, as in **"One Morning in June"** and **"Poor Franzi,"** remains that of an outsider looking in; unlike these stories, however, it is focused on one main character—the unnamed mother. The other members of this family gain interest because they provide signals for the mother as she attempts to read the relationships within the Geneva composition and, through this reading, to build a narrative of "why her husband had left her" (198). The mother makes it all the more imperative to read from the visual signals because she has warned Granny that there should "be no direct questions, no remarks" (192).

So the situation rests with the mother's striving to compose not simply a harmonious picture in which all details cohere but a multifaceted one that can reveal to her the unseen reasons for her husband's past conduct to her, a composition, therefore, with both depth and movement. Ursula, who has come back with the opening line of a play she has begun to write in Geneva, provides the image that might transport the mother into the past where explanations are to be found—"'The Grand Duke enters and sees Tatiana all in gold'"— particularly because of Tatiana's associations with the father's lover (194-195). For Ursula, Tatiana merely provides an exotic diversion from the drab Nice environment (195) and her own dowdy image (196). The mother realizes, "Everything about the trip, in the end, would crystallize around Tatiana and the Grand Duke," but because Ursula has for the moment taken over the role of Tatiana, as the dramatic present tense of the image confirms, there is nothing this potentially revealing image can tell her about the past (196). And by fictionalizing her Geneva experience and having thus "removed herself from the ranks of reliable witnesses" (197), Ursula cannot provide her mother with the image she now needs.

Seven-year-old Colin's image of Geneva is more useful, not for what it pictures but for what it does not picture. Because Ursula's image is so personal and immediate, it pictures too much, and the mother cannot use it to assemble a narrative of why her husband has left her. As Iser says of the literary text, "we can only picture things which are not there; the written part of the text gives us the knowledge, but it is the unwritten part that gives us the opportunity to picture things . . ." (*Implied Reader*, 283). "'I fed the swans,' Colin suddenly shouted." Having articulated the image, Colin closes what has been an open, fluid image: "As he said it, the image became static: a gray sky, a gray lake, and a swan wonderfully turning upside down with the black rubber feet showing above the water. His father was not in the picture at all; neither was *she*. But Geneva was fixed for the rest of his life: gray, lake, swan" (196). Geneva now being fixed and therefore drained of imaginative potential, Colin begins to "invent" a new story of being sick on the plane (196-197).

Because the mother cannot use Ursula's Tatiana, it is Colin's image—without color, perspective, or proportion—that becomes the catalyst, not for a multifaceted narrative attaining its temporal element through the fourth dimension, movement, but simply a three-dimensional composition attaining depth through the overlaying of images. Granny dismisses the children's images because she already has a remembered image that blocks reception and hence perception of any other: "white water birds, a parasol, a boat heaped with colored cushions" (192). Superimposing the exotic colors from Granny's image (reinforced by the golden Tatiana) onto Colin's image of feeding the swans, the mother creates a composition that reflects, if not an exact image of Geneva, a truthful image that incorporates her response:

> She saw sunshine, a blue lake, and the boats Granny had described, heaped with colored cushions. She saw her husband and someone else (probably in white, she thought, ridiculously bouffant, the origin of Tatiana). . . . Colin seemed to carry the story of the visit with him, and she felt the faintest stirrings of envy, the resentfulness of the spectator, the loved one left behind.
>
> (197)

Envy and resentment bring her too close and, paradoxically, relegate her to a position of observer on the rear benches. She has progressed beyond the perspectives of Mike and Barbara, Elizabeth and Franzi, in breaking the two-dimensional frame by composing a three-dimensional picture that synthesizes the family members' various images of Geneva. Now, however, the feelings of envy and resentment paralyze her at the crossroads, perceiving but unable to partake in the "wandering viewpoint" that, Iser argues (*Implied Reader* 279; *AR,* 20-22, 108-111), actuates the potentially kinetic elements of the reading process by setting observer and observed in motion. And so, the story concludes, "nothing had come back from the trip but her own feelings of longing and envy, the longing and envy she felt at night, seeing, at a crossroad or over a bridge, the lighted windows of a train sweep by" (198).

Geneva must remain for the mother forever unvisited, in Iser's sense a "fading horizon," but with no new horizon to take its place and therefore no story to tell. But for twelve-year-old Emma Ellenger, the central figure in **"Going Ashore,"** as one port of call fades on the receding horizon, on an emerging horizon looms a new destination. In contrast to her mother, who is "happy, or at least not always *un*happy, in a limited area of the ship—the bar, the beauty salon, and her own cabin" because within these confines able to avoid her past failures and dismal future prospects, all of which signify her fading beauty, Emma has no fear of being "adrift on an ocean whose immenseness [her mother] could not begin to grasp" (74-75). Emma is given room to maneuver as she develops the skills of seeing that will enable her to survive once the ship has put her and her mother on shore permanently. With the focus on Emma, rather than on the mother, **"Going Ashore"** is the first of Gallant's stories to achieve multiple dimensions through all its textual perspectives—those of reader, narrator, character, and plot-line.

The protensive and retrospective narrative line of **"Going Ashore,"** which traces Emma's hopes and reservations that this cruise will produce the miracle to form a meaningful mother-daughter relationship, provides a sense of continuity between the ports of call and the past, present, and future time frames. Originally, Emma has "caught" this feeling of an impending miracle from her otherwise world-weary mother (77-78); she even at times has caught her mother's Prufrockian despair as when, in response to her mother's asking why they have come on this voyage, Emma's voice echoes the voice in Eliot's poem that conveys a sense of the futility of language to break barriers and communicate. "'I don't know. I don't know why we came at all'" (78; see "The Love Song of J. Alfred Prufrock," lines 96-98, 106-110). But Emma is to her mother as this voice is to Prufrock. "Answers and explanations belonged to another language, one she had still to acquire" (79). The fluid composition Emma achieves as the images of Tangier and Gibraltar converge will help her acquire this language.

As the story opens, the concrete, accurate image of Tangier, "humped and yellowish, speckled with houses, under a wintry sky," has begun to meld with the hazy, invented image of "North Africa [as] an imaginary place, half desert, half jungle," the blended image being circumscribed from the vantage point of the porthole (79-80). In Tangier itself, however, this image is almost submerged by the real thing (83). In clinging to, first, the image of Eddy within her Tangier composition and, then, the tiger she purchases, Emma never succumbs to her mother's flat, because totally introspective, perspective. Freed from her porthole perspective, she has not felt compelled, as has her mother, to don those reflective sunglasses that her mother uses to narrow her vision (85) or to deflect distorted images she wishes to ignore (86), and without which Emma's mother experiences incapacitating vulnerability (93). For Emma, the real Tangier is a disappointment, but her imaginative responsiveness enables her to retain some of her original sense of anticipation as they rush downhill to where the launch awaits to take them back to the ship and the day spins itself "out in reverse" (93) like a film being rewound.

For her unresponsive mother, Tangier has, mercifully, disappeared forever, but for Emma, what had been a protensive view of Tangier, a future horizon, has moved through the present to become a retrospective view, a memory, and so seems "different again, exotic and remote, with the ring of lights around the shore, the city night sounds drifting over the harbor." Emma is not oblivious to the inaccuracy of this image, recognizing that "the café, the clock in the square, the shop where they had bought the bracelet, had nothing to do with the Tangier she had imagined or this present view from the ship" (99), just as she ultimately responds to the chipped, fake tiger not as a magical talisman capable of granting wishes nor as a source of despair and cynicism once its real nature is exposed but as simply something "she had loved . . . for an afternoon" (102). The tiger, her symbol of Africa, will not be forgotten but will be an image on a receding horizon as she embraces the past and the future that make up the dynamic present moment:

> Africa was over, this was something else. The cabin grew steadily lighter. . . . She could see the gulls swooping and soaring, and something on the horizon—a shape, a rock, a whole continent untouched and unexplored. A tide of newness came in with the salty air: she thought of new land, new dresses, clean, untouched, unworn. A new life. She knelt, patient, holding the curtain, waiting to see the approach to shore.
>
> (103)

In her imaginative responsiveness and openness to life, which enable her to conjoin inner and outer perspectives and prevent self-absorption, and in her resiliency to disappointment, which prevents the extremes of cynicism and sentimentality and enables her to embrace life's flux, young Emma Ellenger stands out as a character with "better eyes" than those of most characters who people Gallant's early fiction. But can this imagination, openness, and resiliency withstand the transition from cruise ship to shore, from youthfulness to maturity, from an ahistorical to a historical milieu? Are Gallant's characters able to retain the perceptiveness, even the clairvoyance, of their childhood in a world in which their developing social attitudes confront not a tabula rasa but a slate intricately etched with historical significance? Gallant's stories of the 1950s explore these questions time and time again, and statistically, those characters who suffer from myopia, tunnel vision, eye strain, or blindness outnumber those with healthy eyes and good to excellent vision. Another story very much concerned with seeing and not seeing, for example, is **"The Moabitess,"** set in a shabby French *pension* off season, and highlighting the pathetic figure of Miss Horeham, who having nursed her father for many years is now

left practically destitute. Like Emma's mother, but without the aid of reflective sunglasses, Miss Horeham has developed "a small, particular field of vision, as if her eye were eternally pressed to a knothole" (***My Heart is Broken,*** 45). She uses this perspective to escape such surrealistic scenes as the argument between Mr. Wynn and Mr. Oxley by narrowing her focus to one image: that of herself transformed into the exotic Biblical Ruth with treasures from her trunk, mostly discards departing residents have given her.

"The Other Paris," "The Picnic," "A Day Like Any Other," "Señor Pinedo," "Bernadette," and **"The Old Place,"** like much of Gallant's later fiction, all foreground the personal narratives of the characters within a broader historical background than these other early stories, with the exception of **"Poor Franzi"**; nevertheless, they are all equally concerned with exploring the characters' inability to see clearly. This purblindness usually arises from the blocking of unwanted images by sentimentalized, picturesque, or exotic images that can be assembled into recognizable and harmonious compositions. In **"Señor Pinedo,"** set in Franco's Madrid, the first-person narrator visually renders the silence following horror in a surrealistic description of the courtyard in which a young boy has been crushed by an elevator: with its "harsh division of light and shadow" as in the arena of a bull ring, the sunlit faces become "white and expressionless, with that curious Oriental blankness that sometimes envelops the whole arena during moments of greatest emotion" (213). The surrealism of this scene is reproduced at the end in the inability of the narrator, as an outsider, to read the silence of Señor Pinedo's audience listening to this civil servant espouse "the truth and good faith of the movement to which he had devoted his life": "as I could not see his listeners' faces, I could not have said whether the silence was owing to respect, delight, apathy, or a sudden fury of some other emotion so great that only silence could contain it" (216). Another characteristic Gallant motif—memory—is integrated into the visualizing component of the reading process explored in **"The Old Place."** Dennis and Charlotte, the adult children of memory-obsessed parents, reject their parents' history, for Dennis' mother composed from remembered images of an idyllic Dutchess County garden and for Charlotte's father from those of horrific Nazi concentration camps, as "a cult of images, not of feelings." Photographs are simply "squares of silence" (72, 80), and Dennis and Charlotte prefer squares of their own creation—colorless, shadeless, flat lifestyles in which no associations, no fixed and fixating images, will emerge to demand allegiance.

None of these characters successfully learns to look, all opting instead for two-dimensional perspectives. In Gallant's stories of the fifties, however, there is one adult character who may serve as a paradigm for readers learning to look—the first-person narrator of **"Autumn Day,"** Cecilia Rowe. Depicting the three-month period following her reunion with her husband in Salzburg, where he has been posted with the Army of Occupation, Cecilia becomes the focus of a story tracing her transition from immaturity to maturity, from an introverted two-dimensional perspective to an extroverted multidimensional perspective, and hence from impercipience to percipience. The narrative of Cissy's transition is played out against the background of an Austrian populace in transition, a period of reflection and rebuilding. As Cissy clings to her girlish attire and mannerisms, Herr Enrich, the owner of the farmhouse where Cissy and her husband board, clings to a time before the war when he took in a different calibre of boarders (34).

The greatest gap of indeterminacy opened up in this story is that between Cissy's three-month transition period and the rendering of these three months into a narrative eight years later. The mature Cecilia looks back with understanding, not cynicism, at the naive self-consciousness of her nineteen-year-old self, a product of an ideology disseminated through glossy magazines, romance novels, and Hollywood movies. From this perspective, she traces the changes Cissy underwent to turn poses into "real feelings" essential to establish a "real marriage" (33). These changes correspond to the changes that occur as Cissy's "Herbsttag," a melancholic and sentimental composition, is transformed into **"Autumn Day,"** a narrative that incorporates grotesque, even frightening elements. Images of a frozen yellow-and-brown bird (41-42), the flashing gold teeth of a paranoid boarder (42-44), and the rouged and then blushing cheeks of a woman accused by Cissy's friend of an affair (45) filter through the flat gray shadows of the composition in garish surrealistic splashes of color. As these images are then played out in reverse (49-51), the two-dimensional frame is shattered and a polygonal, chromatic narrative emerges.

After being forced for the first time to see herself not at the center of the composition but "as if I had been a spectator all along" (49-50) and then witnessing a revealing image of her husband in the mirror (51), Cecilia traces the modulations of acceptance, desperation, and fortitude through which Cissy passes as she crosses from poses to real feelings, from girlhood to womanhood, from impercipience to percipience. Even Cecilia's summation, focused entirely on the personal narrative, with the historical dimension recalled only through the allusion to a "frontier," captures the sense that fluctuation, not sequence, best characterizes the direction of her life (52-53).

Cecilia has delivered her reading of the "too much" (53) that had happened during three months at the Salzburg farmhouse. But what of the eight years that have followed? The immediacy of the restrained desperation of Cecilia's closing words—"But we're not safe yet, I thought, looking at my husband—this stranger, mute, helpless, fumbling, enclosed. . . . But we'll be all right. Take my word for it. We'll be all right" (53)—leaves these eight years a truly indeterminate gap and **"Autumn Day"** a truly open, multifaceted composition. At most it can be said that Cecilia Rowe develops into a character with "better eyes" than those characters in Gallant's early fiction who insist on closing gaps with images that cohere into a harmonious composition reflecting the prevailing ideology.

As Cecilia Rowe establishes a perspective of eight years that permits her to revisit her emergence from girlhood to womanhood, but as she keeps this perspective fluid to explore the transition in terms of past, present, and future and the constant "wavering" (52) through these dimensions, so too readers of Gallant, although approaching her fiction from the perspective of their own dispositions, cannot remain passively gazing from one fixed position. Gallant has said of multiple textual perspectives, "The events and characters in fiction are like works of art in a museum. You see them from different angles, you move round and around. You don't stand at the same place" (Fabre 101). Having moved "round and around" and having necessarily participated in the protensive and retrospective flux of the reading process, readers can then begin to read the unseen through the seen. "Fiction, like painting," says Gallant in her introduction to **Home Truths,** "consists entirely of more than meets the eye; otherwise it is not worth a second's consideration" (xii).

But to begin, readers need to ascertain what it is that meets the eye. Demanding an accurate picture, one that conforms to a familiar ideology, many of Gallant's characters narrow or restrict the focus of their perspective so that a harmonious composition, in which all images cohere, emerges. These characters resemble those readers of Joyce's *Ulysses* whom Iser describes, in his essay "Indeterminacy and the Readers' Response in Prose Fiction," as "annoyed by all these gaps, which arise in fact through the overprecision of presentation," an annoyance that Iser views as "a confession" that "we prefer to be pinned down by texts, forgoing our own judgment" and that "we obviously expect literature to present us with a world that has been cleared of contradictions" (40). Gallant's readers can learn to look at her fiction with eyes that permit kinetic, multidimensional compositions to emerge from the gaps between the vividly etched images her stories provide. Although these images do not always cohere and may, therefore, create unsettling reading experiences because of their mercurial effects, the most rewarding of Mavis Gallant's early stories reveal an artistry that generates aesthetic responses dependent on a close reading through a vivid visualizing of her texts.

Notes

1. Mavis Gallant has made a notation on the typescript of "The Picnic," located in the Mavis Gallant Collection (Manuscript Collection 189, box 1) of the Thomas Fisher Rare Book Library, University of Toronto, that this story, originally entitled "Before the Battle," was one of the first stories she wrote in France, 1950-1951.

2. Unless otherwise specified, all references to Gallant's fiction cited parenthetically are from short stories in *The Other Paris* (Toronto: Macmillan, 1986).

3. *The Act of Reading* (1978, 21). Hereafter cited parenthetically as *AR*. To avoid problems of subjectivity and arbitrariness (discussed by Iser *AR*, 21-27) and to highlight the textual sources of the visual responses, I will be following the example of Iser in my discussion of reader response. Although Iser has been criticized by such theorists as Terry Eagleton for telling "us less how to read than what happens anyway when we do so" and therefore for running "the risk of leaving everything exactly as it was" ("Rituals," 294), by which he means leaving everything within the "liberal humanist" tradition (*Literary Theory* 1983, 78-86), it seems to me that Iser's approach permits close textual analysis while accounting for the reader in the text, both valuable pursuits of literary criticism.

4. This phrase, which I have used in my title, is borrowed from the title of a useful handbook by Joshua C. Taylor, *Learning to Look: A Handbook for the Visual Arts* (Chicago: University of Chicago Press, 1957).

5. See my articles, "Artistry in Mavis Gallant's *Green Water, Green Sky*: The Composition of Structure, Pattern, and Gyre," *Canadian Literature* 129 (1991): 57-73, and "Mavis Gallant's Apprenticeship Stories, 1944-1950: Breaking the Frame," *English Studies in Canada* 18 (1992): 317-334.

6. Two possible exceptions to these generalizations are "Pegnitz Junction," in *The Pegnitz Junction* (New York: Random House, 1973), and "The Assembly," in *Overhead in a Balloon* (Toronto: Macmillan, 1985).

7. In an aptly entitled article published in the 4 October 1987 issue of *New York Times Magazine,* "Paris When It Shimmers," Gallant captures in language what Mike fails to capture in paint. Her opening and closing descriptions (19, 47) are particularly evocative of the different grays that Paris winters produce.

8. Gallant has remarked in several interviews (Baele, C10; Boyce, 30-31; Hancock, 28, 45, 58) that many of her stories are inspired by scenes she has remembered or observed and then herself responded to by filling in the indeterminate gaps, so building a vividly detailed fictional composition that is more real for her than the memory of the original. Consequently, Gallant has defined a position similar to that of Iser on the reader as essential for herself as creative writer: the writer bridges the gaps of indeterminate characters and situations she has observed as her readers must bridge those gaps in her texts (Fabre, 96-97; Martens, 168, 172-173; Monroe).

Works Cited

Baele, Nancy. "A Canadian at Home in Paris." Interview with Mavis Gallant. *Ottawa Citizen* (27 February 1988): C1, C10.

Boyce, Pleuke. "Image and Memory." Interview with Mavis Gallant. *Books in Canada* (January/February 1990): 29-31.

Eagleton, Terry. *Literary Theory: An Introduction.* Oxford: Basil Blackwell, 1983.

———. "Rituals of Reconciliation." Review of *Prospecting: From Reader Response to Literary Anthropology,* by Wolfgang Iser. *Times Literary Supplement* (16-22 March 1990): 294.

Eliot, T. S. "The Love Song of J. Alfred Prufrock." In *The Complete Poems and Plays of T. S. Eliot,* 13-17. London: Faber, 1969.

Fabre, Michel. "An Interview with Mavis Gallant." *Commonwealth* 11, no. 2 (Spring 1989): 95-103.

Gallant, Mavis. "About Geneva." *Charm* (June 1955): 94+. Rpt. in *The Other Paris,* 190-198. Toronto: Macmillan, 1986.

———. "Autumn Day." *New Yorker* (29 October 1955): 31-38. Rpt. in *The Other Paris,* 31-53. Toronto: Macmillan, 1986.

———. "Bernadette." *New Yorker* (12 January 1957): 22-24. Rpt. in *My Heart is Broken,* 14-41. Toronto: General Publishing, 1982.

———. "A Day Like Any Other." *New Yorker* (7 November 1953): 37-44. Rpt. in *The Other Paris,* 217-240. Toronto: Macmillan, 1986.

———. "Going Ashore." *New Yorker* (18 December 1954): 32+. Rpt. in *The Other Paris,* 69-103. Toronto: Macmillan, 1986.

———. "Good Morning and Goodbye." *Preview* (December 1944): 1-3.

———. *Green Water, Green Sky.* 1959. Rpt. Toronto: Macmillan, 1983.

———. "An Introduction." *Home Truths,* xi-xxii. Toronto: Macmillan, 1982.

————. "The Moabitess." *New Yorker* (2 November 1957): 42-46. Rpt. in *My Heart is Broken,* 42-54. Toronto: General Publishing, 1982.

————. "The Old Place." *Texas Quarterly* 1, no. 2 (Spring 1958): 66-80.

————. "One Morning in June." *New Yorker* (7 June 1952): 27-52. Rpt. in *The Other Paris,* 173-189. Toronto: Macmillan, 1986.

————. "The Other Paris." *New Yorker* (11 April 1953): 27-36. Rpt. in *The Other Paris,* 1-30. Toronto: Macmillan, 1986.

————. "The Picnic." *New Yorker* (9 August 1952): 23-28. Rpt. in *The Other Paris,* 104-121. Toronto: Macmillan, 1986.

————. "Poor Franzi." *Harper's Bazaar* (October 1954): 153+. Rpt. in *The Other Paris,* 54-68. Toronto: Macmillan, 1986.

————. "Señor Pinedo." *New Yorker* (9 January 1954): 23-28. Rpt. in *The Other Paris,* 199-216. Toronto: Macmillan, 1986.

Hancock, Geoff. "An Interview with Mavis Gallant." *Canadian Fiction Magazine* 28 (1978): 18-67.

Iser, Wolfgang. *The Act of Reading: A Theory of Aesthetic Response.* Baltimore: John Hopkins University Press, 1978.

————. *The Implied Reader: Patterns of Communication in Prose Fiction from Bunyan to Beckett.* Baltimore: John Hopkins University Press, 1974.

————. "Indeterminacy and the Reader's Response in Prose Fiction." In *Aspects of Narrative: Selected Papers from the English Institute,* 1-45. Edited by J. Hillis Miller. New York: Columbia University Press, 1971.

Keefer, Janice Kulyk. *Reading Mavis Gallant.* Toronto: Oxford University Press, 1989.

Martens, Debra. "An Interview with Mavis Gallant." *Rubicon* 4 (Winter 1984-1985): 151-182.

Monroe, Pat. "Interview with Mavis Gallant." *The Afternoon Show.* CBC, Vancouver, 17 February 1984.

Judith Farr (review date 8 February 1997)

SOURCE: Farr, Judith. Review of *The Collected Stories of Mavis Gallant,* by Mavis Gallant. *America* 176, no. 4 (8 February 1997): 33-4.

[*In the following favorable evaluation of* The Collected Stories of Mavis Gallant, *Farr emphasizes the role of language and communication in Gallant's short stories.*]

I first read Mavis Gallant when I was 16, studying French while boarding for the summer in the Woodmont section of Montreal with a dignified Anglophone lady. Over tea each afternoon, this woman complained that "English Quebec" was being overwhelmed by "foreign speakers," often pausing to address her maid, a Québecoise, in an accurate but brutally inflected French that seemed to say "I disdain this language but am forced to use it." One day, while reading Gallant's acutely observant story **"The Fenton Child,"** I overheard two children chattering together. One spoke French, the other English. But their identical sing-song cadences, composing a kind of patois bred of amity and necessity, made me suddenly realize the multiple significances in Gallant's tale. Like so many of the stories in her **Collected Stories,** this one was ordered by the theme of communication and, indeed, of communions—failed or achieved—through language.

Gallant's **Collected Stories** is a 900-page volume that gathers together selections from eight books written from the 1930's to the 1990's. Although each story is memorably distinct, the fictional world Gallant creates has recognizable characteristics that have remained the same throughout six decades. Her characters mostly inhabit European or Canadian cities, where they are for various reasons not quite at home and where perils, great and small, await them—in a false lover's smile, from a parent's treachery, with the disillusionments caused by the bright expectations of Christmas or vacation time or changes in state such as marriage. In this fragile world of shifting accents, polyglot speakers and people with or without passports, language and its uses assume vital importance.

Thus, in that early story **"The Fenton Child,"** as in her other fictions of Montreal, Paris, Italy, Switzerland and the rest, Gallant seizes on those divisions, hostilities, unions and affections stimulated or even produced by speech. Her story's fictional character—the plucky teenage Nora, with her French-speaking Catholic mother and English, instinctively Protestant father—has been, she claims, equally "raised in two languages." That is, like Mavis Gallant herself, Nora has been equally exposed to the two cultural currents that nourish, divide or unite the citizens of Montreal. Vulnerable as Nora is, lied to and kept in the dark (like so many of Gallant's poignant servant girls), she *listens* for truth in the nuances of French or English diction used by the devious adults who hire her to tend a horribly neglected baby. The baby, son of a mysterious brief liaison between an English father and a French Canadian mother, has been exiled to a foundling hospital and comes "home" at the story's end. But Nora recognizes in his speechless wails the metaphor of lasting alienation.

At the heart of **"The Fenton Child"** is the silence of the child's mother and foster-mother, a withholding of communication that results from suffering and hatred and in turn creates deprivation and sorrow. This silence that casts out love is, like language in all its forms and deficits, a metaphor in Gallant's *oeuvre,* one that, as she declares in her Preface, was shaped by her "regional beginnings"—"wholly Quebec," "English . . . with a strong current of French," that "left me with two systems of behavior, divided by syntax and tradition" and steadily enriched and complicated her imagination.

This imagination creates through definition. A dry, almost repellent prosaicism often shapes Gallant's fictive atmospheres, corresponding to her character's limitations. The reader gets used to careful notations of "linoleum-covered floors on which scatter rugs slipped and slid underfoot," of "white lateral blinds," and "cardboard suitcase[s] with . . . rope strap[s]." Such unsentimental realism, however, can also yield to moments of near-poetic description: "The girls took no notice of the Colonel. He was invisible to them, wiped out of being by a curtain pulled over the inner eye." Sometimes it leads to philosophy: "The illusion of love was a blight imposed by the film industry." Often, it ushers in the comic: "Her teeth are like leaves in winter"; "Berthe couldn't hand her a teaspoon without receiving a shock, like a small silver bullet. Her sister believed the current was generated by a chemical change that occurred as she flew out of Fort Lauderdale."

But almost invariably it is by means of language—its uses and disuse, how it is regarded, learned, avoided or even transcended—that we approach Gallant's troubled, travelled but never serenely urbane men, women and children. So the Nora of **"The Fenton Child"** discovers a man's egoism by his mispronunciation of the English *th.* "You'd like him," his shallow lover tells Piotr in the brilliantly specific **"Potter,"** "he speaks three different languages." The peculiarity of the Colonel's wife in **"New Year's Eve,"** suggested by the observation that "she could not read any Russian and would not try," is summarized by the fact that she has stopped talking to the Colonel altogether after their daughter's death. The Colonel, on the other hand, one of Gallant's sad, well-intentioned strivers, is "able to learn the structure of any language." That is, in "the heart of [his] isolation," he tries to *understand*: people, situations, the past and present, himself.

Though it results in a sort of dulled or sometimes desperate knowledge, urbanity—or at least living in different places—does not often lead to happiness in Gallant's fiction. Those of her heroes who endure preserve the living memory of their roots. This gives them a humanity that sustains them as well as others. Like young Carmela in **"The Four Seasons,"** "mute and watchful" among "the powerful and strange," Gallant's heroes instinctively retain the pleasure in nature, in sheer existence, that is proof against the world's blows. Others, like the poor, dying, middle-aged Piotr, are able to find

a sort of "slow happiness, like water rising" from giving "tenderness" where it is needed. So—following out the theme of communication and communion—we are told of him that Laurie "could not pronounce 'Piotr' and never tried; she said Peter, Prater, Potter, and Otter and he answered to all. Why not? He loved her."

That both speech and silence can be forms of love in these *Collected Stories* seems itself metaphoric of the supreme value of words to a writer as clear-eyed and assured as Mavis Gallant. In the capaciousness of this volume, to which the author invites us to turn as to a house that can be entered and left as we like, there is a largesse of sympathy that recalls both fluent speech and compassionate silence.

Danielle Schaub (essay date 1998)

SOURCE: Schaub, Danielle. "Text and Image: *Overhead in a Balloon.*" In *Mavis Gallant,* pp. 119-39. New York: Twayne Publishers, 1998.

[*In the following essay, Schaub offers a thematic and stylistic overview of the stories in* Overheard in a Balloon, *emphasizing the way the stories explore the "interaction between text and image."*]

Overhead in a Balloon, Gallant's collection of Parisian stories, explores the mentality of her adoptive fellow citizens in the late seventies and early eighties with the sharpness of the best introduced social critic. From an insider's perspective, Gallant exposes the pettiness and superficiality of the artistic and literary world (patrons and creators alike) as well as of the petite bourgeoisie, the upper-middle class, and the impoverished aristocrats. Several of the stories are linked by the recurrence of certain characters: **"Speck's Idea"** and **"Overhead in a Balloon"** both stage Sandor Speck, the curator of an art gallery, and his assistant, Walter Obermauer; **"Larry," "A Painful Affair," "A Flying Start,"** and **"Grippes and Poche"** all allude to a famous American patron of the arts, Miss Pugh, and the last three refer to the rivalry of a French writer and his English counterpart for the favors of Miss Pugh; **"A Recollection," "Rue de Lille," "The Colonel's Child,"** and **"Lena"** deal with the first and second wives of a literary broadcaster whose recollections are convincingly told in the first person owing to the true feelings or fascination he had, or has, for both. Standing apart are two stories concerned with further established citizens: **"Luc and His Father"** reveals a son's failure to follow his father's model, and therefore career, by failing the entrance exam securing admission to one of the *Grandes Ecoles*; and **"The Assembly"** reports the prejudiced discussion of flat owners in a building after one of them has been molested. The stories prove Gallant's familiarity with French letters, art, architecture, mores, and prejudice over changing demography (most of which appears in *The Paris Notebooks*).[1]

With its emphasis on the world of art, *Overhead in a Balloon* lends itself to a discussion of the interaction between text and image, and the extra interpretative dimension that interrelation affords. An avid visitor of museums and galleries, Gallant often discloses her appreciation for art (though not for the artistic clique) through descriptions of, and allusions to, paintings and photographs, but she surpasses herself here as she captures the world of culture.[2] **"Speck's Idea"** and the title story, more than half of the book, highlight the value and purpose of art in Paris and represent art works that have an impact on the textual interpretation. But several of the other stories not directly concerned with art describe the visual in the decor, such as **"Luc and His Father," "Larry,"** and **"A Flying Start,"** for instance.

Gallant's awareness of the problems posed by the representation of images in fiction and their potential as a source of irony goes back to her years as a journalist and finds an echo in Linnet's ironical consideration of the caption for a picture portraying a bear and a boy eating a bun: "There is no trick to it. You just repeat what the picture has told you like this: 'Boy eats bun as bear looks on.' The reason why anything has to go under the picture at all is that a reader might wonder, 'Is that a bear looking on?' It looks like a bear, but that is not enough for saying so" (*HT* [*Home Truths*], 318). As Barthes would say, Linnet's comment on the picture "is a matter of a denoted description of the image."[3] But she goes beyond a mere denotation; she also takes the image's reception into account. Without any attempt at theorizing, she pinpoints the "terror of uncertain signs" (Barthes 1977, 39), which makes the presence of the linguistic message necessary. In other words, she emphasizes the taming effect of captions, leaving no freedom of interpretation to the readers, who, in this case, are not endowed with perceptiveness or, as Barthes would have it, needs the "*anchorage* of all the possible (denoted) meanings of the object" (39). Linnet goes on thinking about the mechanics of captions: "You have a space to fill in which the words must come out even. The space may be tight; in that case, you can remove 'as' and substitute a comma, though that makes the kind of terse statement to which your reader is apt to reply, 'So what?' Most of the time, the Truth with a Capital T is a matter of elongation: 'Blond boy eats small bun as large bear looks on'" (*HT,* 318). Both compression and expansion of the caption change the impact of the picture. Compression, in that it takes away the links between the various denoted elements of the composition, reduces the "anchorage," whereas expansion, that is, the exact pinning down of characteristics, increases it. The irony of the passage here lies in the use of "Truth with a Capital T" in relation to the

caption that leaves the field least open to interpretation, that "appears to duplicate the image" (Barthes 1977, 26). Linnet's exposition of the problems of representation calls to mind Barthes's question: "Does the image duplicate certain of the informations [*sic*] given in the text by a phenomenon of redundancy or does the text add a fresh information to the image?" (33).

By specifically narrowing the scope of interpretation, the linguistic message suits the needs of society, "concerned to tame the Photograph, to temper the madness which keeps threatening to explode in the face of whoever looks at it."[4] The overqualifying caption, the elongating text, nullifies the potential effect of the image, prevents the image from affecting the readers in any personal way. The reductive quality of the linguistic sign directs the readers' attention to harmless concepts. As Barthes says, one "means of taming the Photograph is to generalize, to gregarize, banalize it until it is no longer confronted by any image in relation to which it can mark itself, assert its special character, its scandal, its madness" (Barthes 1981, 118).

As Linnet goes on discussing unscrupulous, lyric, or crazy captions, she further prolongs Barthes's observations. Rules obliquely emerge from the presentation of various plausible reactions to rejectable types of linguistic text. The implication is that the person in charge of "what goes under the pictures" (*HT,* 318) should not elicit reactions from the readers. The neutral, yet all-embracing, text suits the demand: "[I]t is not the business of 'reader' to draw conclusions. Our subscribers are not dreamers or smart alecks; when they see a situation in a picture, they want that situation confirmed" (320). For, as Barthes says, "when generalized, [the image] completely de-realizes the human world of conflicts and desires, under cover of illustrating it" (Barthes 1981, 118). Told "to admire a contribution to pictorial journalism" (*HT,* 320) in the back issues of *Life,* Linnet decides to rephrase the caption: "Boy eats bun as bear looks on. Note fur on bear" (320). The tautological addition to the already reductive text ridicules the task of the caption writer and of the readers. As Barthes would have it, the readers can only "subject [the Photograph's] spectacle to the civilized code of perfect illusions" delimited by the text, rather than "[confronting] in it the wakening of intractable reality" (Barthes 1981, 119).

Gallant's attitude to the first pictures of concentration camps falls within Barthes's second option, that of allowing the photograph to open up new vistas and to display reality in its true light. Asked to write the captions and a text of 750 words, Gallant decided that "there must be no descriptive words in this, no adjectives. Nothing like 'horror,' 'horrifying' because what the pictures are saying is stronger and louder" (iHancock, 39). What she sensed then is that "the Photograph is an extended, loaded evidence—as if it caricatured not the figure of what it represents (quite the converse) but its very existence" (Barthes 1981, 115). What actually came out in the special issue was a severely tampered-with version of Gallant's captions, full of "adverbs and adjectives smothering the real issue, and the covering article, which was short, was a prototype for all the cliches we've been bludgeoned with ever since" (iHancock, 40). When she inquired about the reasons for the alterations, she heard: "Culture! Our readers never went to high school and you're talking about culture? All the Germans are bastards and that's that" (40).⁵ This reaction definitely reduces the pictures to some almost innocuous images of the concentration camps, indeed denies the universal lure of fascism. The text and the captions thus minimize a terrifying reality. But Gallant rejected, and still rejects, the lie: "But that wasn't that and it still isn't" (40). To her, the travestied version reads like the following dichotomy: the picture tells a story; the text smothers it. The text should enhance the photographic message, not tone it down; it should reflect, not limit nor distort, the message.

Gallant's early career as a journalist undoubtedly awakened her perception of the complex relationship between picture and text. Her fiction gives examples of double layers of text: Linnet Muir reveals that in Canada, as in other countries with split-up communities, the titles of art works are "identified in two languages" (*HT,* 299), even when they do not call for translation. Behind the doubly printed text, and the accompanying comment to the effect that a house "had on display landmarks identified in two languages . . . as if the engraver had known they would find their way to a wall in Montreal" (299), lies the ironic smile of the bilingual speaker. The physical presence of both titles, not only on the engravings, but specifically on the printed page in Gallant's book, ridicules the flat refusal to open one's mind to others, the cold refusal to understand others, even where no misunderstanding can exist.⁶

Descriptions of, or allusions to, images abound in Gallant's fiction and journalism.⁷ Her story **"In the Tunnel"** re-presents a painting of Judas, after he hangs himself, and several paintings of Jesus in an abandoned chapel somewhere on the Riviera. As Mary Condé rightly notes, the painting of Judas "controls the narrative," "drawing together the story's themes of politics, nationality and cruelty."⁸ The idea of punishment pervades the whole story, securing an inescapable link between text and image, the more so as the biblical reference inherent in the painting adds another layer of contextuality.⁹

Another example of pictorial control of the narrative can be found in **"Bonaventure."** Several engravings adorn the walls of the pavilion in which the protagonist, Douglas Ramsay, is put up: once again, the story is centered on the punishment of Judas as well as on the last photograph of the late artist Moser, looking "like a famous picture of Freud going into exile" (*HT,* 145). The visual reflects the insidious acts and words of Katherine Moser, the artist's widow, for in the narrative past and present, she is seen subjecting all around her to the idea of punishment. To mention but two key instances, Katherine imposed a severe diet in the countryside on Moser, who abhorred both healthy food and nature, and she inflicts on Douglas Ramsay exhausting excursions to force him to enjoy nature (which he equally abhors) and art. As Douglas realizes while visiting an exhibition of impressionist paintings (164) that, owing to ill health, the painters were dependent on their wives, Katherine snaps back that he had better rest, reproducing the pattern of relationship she had with her late husband. In fact, she mimics the overprotectiveness of the painters' wives and also reenacts the sacrifice of Douglas's mother, who looks after her invalid husband, a situation that plagues Ramsay.

Only when faced with the prospect of being left alone with Katherine "at the chalet [with] the incomprehensible language of birds, and the cat with its savage nature, and the cannibal magpies, the cannibal jays" (*HT,* 166) for a whole month does Ramsay manage to break the spell of punishment. At the pension to which he escapes from Katherine, he finds in a drawer a forgotten sketch "of a naked and faceless woman wearing a pearl necklace" (169). A reminder of the "headless statue of an adolescent girl . . . [with] small breasts, slightly down-pointed" (164), which delighted him as an incarnation of Anne, Katherine's adolescent daughter, the drawing seems to anticipate Ramsay's final discovery: perhaps he was mistaken; perhaps he needs the nursing of a woman, whose identity has yet to be determined, as suggested by the featureless face on the drawing.

With the presence of Judas etched indelibly in the readers' memories, the text reflects the image, stressing the similarity between Ramsay and his spiritual father (the late Moser), between Ramsay and his biological father (spiritually dead owing to his wife's equation of chastisement with justice). The final words provide evidence that Ramsay's attempt to disclaim heredity, both biological and spiritual, has failed: he too will be trapped—indeed he has been all along—in a retributive system in which he cannot have the upper hand. The images in the text thus reverberate with punishment and retribution, two ideas that the text illustrates at different levels.

In other stories, oil paintings, photographs, and posters impress a sense of duty and obligation. In **"Thank You for the Lovely Tea,"** for instance, oil portraits of dignitaries and donors adorn the walls of the Catholic convent school where Ruth is a boarder, and a photograph of the late king and queen hangs in her classroom, powerful reminders of the school's cultural, ethical, and religious values that turn the place into a prison. On an outing, beyond the reach of the system's stern-looking representatives—both living and pictorially represented—Ruth and her friends can revel in harassing her father's lover.

Conversely, one could argue that in **"Luc and His Father,"** the oil portraits of public servants, a photograph of his father's graduating class, and a picture of his mother overwhelm Luc, a French youth, so much so that they exert a negative influence on him. The Jesuits who run the "examination factory . . . able to jostle any student, even the dreamiest, into a respectable institute for higher learning" see through him and warn his parents that they should see to his lack of adjustment.[10] Reflecting her husband's manly talk to Luc, the mother replaces the photograph of her husband's graduating class with a framed poster of Che Guevara, bought on the advice of a salesman according to whom Che Guevara "had no political significance . . . had become manly, decorative kitsch" (**OB** [*Overhead in a Balloon*], 78). Ironically, the father objects to the photograph of Hitler tacked near his son's bed because "he [does] not want Luc quite that manly" (79).

Trying to escape his stifling background, Luc takes a fancy to a young woman he has met at political meetings. In the long run, the politically correct Jesuit counselor—he wears "a small crucifix on one lapel and a Solidarnosc badge on the other" (**OB,** 82)—having read his letters—equally correct in such an overbearing institution—manages to ruin Luc's chance of escaping his milieu, which is after all based on false values. Back home, after hearing of his girlfriend's engagement to a cousin, Luc receives one more pictorial message; another picture of his mother adorns his desk, "a charming one taken at the time of her engagement. She wore, already, the gold earrings. . . . Her expression was smiling, confident but untried" (98). The implication of the text leaves no doubt about the intended message; the photograph highlights Luc's parents' socially correct—though perhaps unhappy—choice of each other, emphasizing Luc's incorrect, hence unsuccessful, choice. A clear sign of wealth, the gold earrings, his mother's "talisman" (97), confirm the rightfulness of Luc's parents' claim, crowned by the smile. The radiance of the smile displays no sign of life's inscriptions, no unpleasant subtext of trying experiences (like her son's failure, for instance).

The last scene—the father's tête-à-tête with his son—stages the father's final attempt at taking Luc back on to the right path while disclosing the old man's melancholy perception of his son's romance. Showing his determination to forgo such foolish thoughts, he turns to his wife's picture. By stating, "I always admired that picture of your mother" (**OB,** 100), that is, by setting a model, he annihilates any hopes he might have cherished for a spontaneous, fully gratifying relationship for his son, indeed for humanity at large.

In **"Larry,"** another father, the elder Pugh, checks on his son, the title character, during a short visit in Paris and takes that opportunity to advise him about marriage, in spite of his own erring married life. After a failed attempt as a sculptor, Larry looks after a large, opulent house in the Huitième Arrondissement for the summer. In the course of the conversation, Larry's father announces his intention to bequeath a portrait of himself to his son. Larry's remembrance of the painting—"[his father] appeared to be elegant and reliable, the way things and people are always said to have been when one looks back at them" (**OB,** 116)—points to its unreliability, indeed reflects a general tendency in the story itself. The narrative reveals everyone's unreliability, starting with the rich landlords, who pilfer from hotels, then Larry, who breaks into their liquor cabinet, and finally his father, whose "sudden inclinations" (114) pass before morals or his family's interest. Just after the narrative voice reports that "shutters [are] bolted, curtains drawn on the streets with art names: Murillo, Rembrandt, Van Dyck [*sic*]" (113), as if art were reduced to names, the father expresses his views of art: "I suppose you found out there wasn't much to art in the long run" (113). With its indirect allusion to the ill-valued worth of art, the statement reinforces the unreliability of the portrait; it is further confirmed by Larry's memory of the mark left when the father, walking out on his wife, took the painting off the wall—"a blank place on the wall" (117), probably the truest image of him. The father's worthlessness is incidentally substantiated by the allusion to the allowance his rich daughter and art benefactress, Maggie, pays him "to keep away" (113). Larry, who envies his half-sister's wealth, is outraged that she should leave her fortune to an arts foundation when he, the would-be artist, could benefit from her support.

"A Flying Start" gives a good picture of the maneuvers performed by other would-be artists to win the favors of Miss Mary Margaret Pugh, an American patron of the arts and the Maggie of the previous short story. Most of the story consists of a section of the memoir that the French author Henri Grippes writes to recapture with questionable reliability the period when his English rival, Victor Prism, was the protégé of Miss Pugh. Recalling Prism's hesitant steps to be admitted by his patron, Grippes focuses on the impression that "an oil painting of the martyrdom of Saint Sebastian" (**OB,** 124) made on Prism: "He thought of mile upon mile of museum portraits—young men, young saints pierced with arrows, with nothing to protect them from the staring of women but a coat of varnish" (124). Often represented as a beautiful youth wounded by arrows, the Roman martyr sentenced to be shot to death by archers for converting many soldiers in his cohort appears in the foreground virtually naked, as in Antonello's painting.

The compelling observation of the painting results from Prism's projection in the pierced naked body of his own vulnerability, not to say ordeal, when braving Miss Pugh's analytical stare. Ever so often ill at ease with his pretended vocation, Prism cannot avoid catching a glimpse of the painting, a reminder of his predicament. Prism's obsession with the painting finds its *mise en abyme* in his unfinished novel staging his alter ego as the male character and Miss Pugh as the female character: "Christopher seemed to leave a trail of sawdust. There were arrow wounds everywhere. He did not know what other people thought and felt about anything, but he could sense to a fine degree how they thought and felt about him. He lived on the feelings he aroused, sought acquaintances among those in whom these feelings were not actively hostile" (125). Prism's plight comes to an end when another mental vision of "museum rooms full of portraits of St. Sebastian, with nothing for protection but a thin coat of varnish" (128) makes him think of the two schools of art conservation. Reviewing the claims of both—the one refusing to restore the original color, the other restoring it whether or not the painter had originally taken fading into account—he has a flash, draws "a blank sheet toward him" (128), the symbol of a new start, and writes: "Are we to take for granted that the artist thinks he knows what he is doing?" (128). Grippes notes that "at that moment, Prism the critic was born" (128). The juxtaposition of Prism's question and Grippes's statement no doubt conveys Gallant's sarcastic view of the literary critic whose sudden vision gives him or her a new vocation, but without the tools.

Funnily enough, Prism secures the favors of Miss Pugh when, asked to give an opinion of Picasso, he represents Picasso in a picture of the mind that helps him focus his anger at the unconceited yet frightfully rich painter whose money he could put to better use. Reminiscent of Larry's feelings toward his half-sister, the young man's anger causes Miss Pugh to compare her half-brother to Picasso, not for his artistic talent but for his looks, which sentences him to sisterly oblivion. Ironically, Prism's visualization of the artist, rather than his works of art, deprives the question of its metonymy and art of its value.

The slippage from art to artists finds its reflection in **"A Painful Affair"**; Miss Pugh does "not believe in art, only in artists" (***OB,*** 109). Miss Pugh's devotion to art is thus questioned, the more so as she considers that "in art deception is a rule" (125). The irony, though, lies in the contemptible controversy that separates her two protégés at the time of the commemoration of her centenary, proving that she should not have believed in artists either. Further evidence lies in the appraisal of her belongings that gives them "an aura of sham" (106); no matter what convictions Miss Pugh held, she was exposed to deception over and over again.

Deceit also flourishes in **"Speck's Idea"** and **"Overhead in a Balloon,"** two stories that highlight ways in which art is consumed, used, disposed of, and discussed in an illusory manner.[11] **"Speck's Idea"** concerns the title character's attempt to bring fame to his name and his art gallery. **"Overhead in a Balloon"** stars Speck's Swiss assistant, Walter Obermauer, in his peregrination through life, religion, and art. In both stories, text and image weave a web of meaning where the image, consisting of real or fictitious paintings, book covers, and films, reflects the message of the story, which in turn conveys the characters' attitude to pictorial creation, and to art in general. By merging with, and in, the text, images and the imaginary create a meaningful network that throws light on the reception of art in both stories, and on the selfishness of human endeavor.

In **"Speck's Idea,"** an initial picture of human and political desolation finds its textual counterpart in an imaginary article foretelling many ills if all carry on ignoring the situation. Prompted by this imaginary article, Dr. Sandor Speck, an art dealer seeking prominence and prosperity, looks for ways of bringing about a new era. He then conceives an abstract image without forms or hues by conceptualizing an exhibition based on the invention, on the intellectual creation, of the work and life of an artist—likely to catch on—whose existence he has yet to trace. In other words, the text is based on the presentation of images or paintings that may or may not exist. He eventually decides to display ideal culture—or at least what he believes it to be—by exhibiting the works of a mediocre painter. The text, however, shows that this painter's re-presentation to the world does not really aim to boost a new, more dignified culture, but rather to promote an unsuccessful art dealer. The whole point of the story, evidently, is to make fun of the mercantile art world and of the production of culture in a politically and financially minded society, as comes out through the numerous paintings, drawings, and decorations depicted. The actors of this *théâtre de dupes* are the artists who produce indifferent works and the consumers who believe they are buying art objects. In between stands the illusionist, Sandor Speck, who tricks artists about what they do, and their customers about what they buy.

At the core of the story lies the basic question of authenticity and validity of both text and image in and beyond the fictional world. The creation of the imaginary artist originates in an authenticated text within the text. The "disturbing article in *Le Monde*" is presented with exact references between parentheses—"(front page, lower middle, turn to page 26)" (***OB,*** 8)—that confer on it a real character. A sign presumably from the real world, yet belonging to the fictional realm by its very presence in the story, the article, written "by a man who never [takes] up his pen unless civilisation [is] in danger" (8), is meant to unsettle its readers—and supposedly the story's readers too—by mirroring the contemporary decline of society:

> Its title, "Redemption Through Art—Last Hope for the West?," had been followed by other disturbing questions: When would the merchants and dealers, compared rather unfairly to money-changers driven from the temple, face up to their responsibility as the tattered century declined? Must the flowering gardens of Western European culture wilt and die along with the decadent political systems, the exhausted parliaments, the shambling elections, the tired liberal impulses? What of the man in the street, too modest and confused to mention his cravings? Was he not gasping for one remedy and only one—artistic renovation? And where was this to come from? "In the words of Shakespr," the article concluded, supposedly in English, "That is the qustn [*sic*]."
>
> (*OB*, 8)

The picture raised by the successive questions displays culture—fictional or actual, the readers may wonder—as endangered by the commercial and political strongholds that cannot take in values of a different nature. The content of the article curiously recalls a historical harangue: on 15 March 1848, Sándor Petöfi, a Hungarian poet, became a national hero by addressing a crowd in Budapest and preconizing a revolution, indeed calling to arms to save the world and humanity.[12] The provoking questions result in Speck's immediate reaction, ironically so, for by hitting on the idea of the ideal artist agreeable to all, he falls back on the very characteristics abused by the columnist. Indeed, by devising an all-purpose figure, he sticks to philistinism and mercantilism. But then the columnist's mutilation of Shakespeare's name and a famous line from *Hamlet* reveals his own incapacity to safeguard the world's cultural heritage. This inevitably raises doubts about the identity of the writer: it could easily be Sandor Speck himself, the modern transposition and homonym, at least where his first name is concerned, of the historical figure whose discourse is echoed in less violent, but nonetheless culturally equivalent, words. The problem of the article's authenticity and the identity of its author thus remains unsolved.

Remaining on precarious foundations, Speck then starts elaborating on the life of the "savior," inventing a series of data, which raise problems of choice over the appropriate representation. A discussion with a Lodge brother eventually leads him to dig out of oblivion a second-rate painter by the name of Hubert Cruche. His surname, an aptronym, immediately creates a multiple image in the minds of the readers; *une cruche* in French means a jug, jugful, or "fool." The first meaning alludes to his life being filled up with convenient data pouring from Speck's mind; the second stands for his work being poured out on to the market to satiate humanity's thirst for a renewed cultural message; and the third hints at his being cheated on two levels (an unsuspect-

ing cuckold, he never questioned the motives behind the sale of all his production for a period of 16 years to his wife's lover; and posthumously he is used by Speck, who tries to gain personal recognition through him). His first name, Hubert, *le patron des chasseurs,* even suggests that without benefiting from it, he offers protection to the East European hunter Speck.

The analogy between Speck and a hunter is further clarified by the existence and name change of another fictional character, namely the protagonist of John Marlyn's *Under the Ribs of Death.*[13] This immigrant novel, published in 1957, shows how, in a vain attempt to integrate, Sandor Hunyadi changes his name to Alex Hunter. The parallel highlights Speck's fruitless endeavor and the ultimate reality that he too is a broken man. Apart from being a hunter, Speck also turns out to be a shopkeeper whose small-town mentality finds a reflection in his aptronym: it is appropriate that *Speck* means bacon in German, since Sandor Speck is the "butcher" of art. Incidentally, taken literally as a very small piece, mark, or spot, the name of Speck would reinforce the futility of the art dealer's enterprise, its worthless achievement. Alternatively, taken as an abbreviation, the name would suggest that the man embodies speculation without being able to assimilate cultural and ideological data.[14]

Traces of culture, displayed in paintings, books, and art objects, show that the cultural patrimony has an illusory quality. Nonexistence schools of art, such as the Tirana School, are disclosed (*OB*, 3); blatantly fake paintings appear in galleries (3, 7, 35); souvenirs and other consumers' objects no longer refer to traditional values but to other, new, equally conventional ones—the Pompidou Art Centre instead of the Eiffel Tower, for instance (44); trivial letters marked by royal stamps are more attractive than real art (28). All these take characters and readers alike into a realm of meanness and decadence.

In such a context, Speck can safely adopt, and persist in, a purely mercantile attitude. His approach to art encompasses only commercial, speculative concerns: "He knew one thing—art had sunk low on the scale of consumer necessities. To mop up a few back bills, he was showing part of his own collection—his last-ditch old-age-security reserve. He clasped his hands behind his neck, staring at a Vlaminck India ink on his desk. It had been certified genuine by an expert now serving a jail sentence in Zurich" (*OB*, 35). Art becomes merely a commodity to be sold in order to make a living. The oxymoronic disclosure about the "genuine" Vlaminck adds to the debasement of aesthetic values. Other allusions to dubious transactions (7, 14) reveal that where money is concerned, Speck does not shrink from any criminal offense, be it faking (7, 14) or stealing (3, 14) a painting, or even making something up from start to finish such as an art school or even a painter (3, 8-11).

Besides, his recollections of the parting argument he had with his second wife confirm Speck's commercial approach: "In her summing-up of his moral nature, a compendium that had preceded her ringing 'Fascist's, Henriette had declared that Speck appraising an artist's work made her think of a real-estate loan officer examining Chartres Cathedral for leaks. It was true that his feeling for art stopped short of love; it had to. . . . For what if he were to allow passion for painting to set alight his common sense? How would he be able to live then, knowing that the ultimate fate of art was to die of anemia in safe-deposit vaults?" (29). The comparison with an estate agency loan officer establishes the real nature of Speck's job. He does not, in the least, care about the artistic quality of what he sells; only budget matters concern him. The two questions hinting at an unlikely weakness caused by genuine enjoyment prove to what extent art has sunk low, not "on the scale of consumer necessities" as Speck would have it, but at a more elevated, disinterested level where art is appreciated for its own sake rather than tucked away for fear of robbers in search of marketable goods.

Because speculators have invaded the market, Lydia Cruche, the painter's widow, acts as a shrewd business-woman, flinching at no stratagem available to raise the value of her inheritance. Rather than being a *cruche,* she takes after Croesus, king of Lydia, and cleverly tricks Speck into supporting her own financial hopes. Calling to mind two real artist widows, Lydia Cruche behaves like a leech sucking its prey's blood. Like Magritte's wife, she makes sure that all her husband's works will sell well, as she has already shown that over a period of 16 years she could manage to secure just that. Alternatively, like Utrillo's wife, who kept her husband as if on a leash because of his addiction to alcohol, Lydia is a tough opponent in financial transactions. By pretending to be a Japhethite, a member of a sect rejecting the graven image as creation rivaling God, and thus regarding artists as impostors, she feigns a lack of interest in a retrospective of her husband's works—in other words, she refuses the kind of meat Speck offers her, the better to chew afterward. Eventually, by calling on the services of an Italian dealer, she manages to put Speck in a weaker position—the hunter thus gets hunted by the very wife of the hunters' patron saint.

Of course, Speck suffers from the ups and downs of his enterprise. An art dealer, he expresses his emotions through visual images taken from books, films, and paintings and through mental images. Visual references to the landscape (*OB,* 5, 46) offer a transposition of his feelings, at times also compared with actual paintings (23, 43, 45). Even films or cartoons (5, 46) reflect some emotional state of mind, and a series of pictures evoking Parisian society and emerging from Speck's imagination, perception, or recollection (12-13) clarify his moods. An unexpected source of pictures, his emotions

add up to the overall artistic parody. On leaving Lydia Cruche after his defeat and the wreck of his car, Speck has to take a bus back to central Paris. While waiting for the bus, he equates "the dark shopping center with its windows shining for no one" to "a Magritte vision of fear" (45), a metonymy that reflects Speck's feeling of betrayal. His feelings, expressed through imaginary or real artistic images whose source is made clear by description or allusion, contribute to the visual qualities of the text.

Similarly, political ideas are rendered through images. Although camouflaged under the innocent sounding name of Amandine—a name redolent of sweets or exquisite chocolates—the shop opposite Speck's gallery conveys a clear political message. The pictures, book covers, and other pieces on show clearly indicate that the shop owner favors the French fascist movement called Jeune Europe:[15] "On the cover of one volume, Uncle Sam shook hands with the Russian Bear over prostrate Europe, depicted as a maiden in a dead faint. A drawing of a spider on a field of banknotes (twelve hundred francs with frame, nine hundred without) jostled the image of a crablike hand clawing away at the map of France" (*OB,* 6). These sarcastic attacks on American hegemony, the power of the Soviet Union, and the greed of Jewish bankers were the usual fare of wartime German propaganda. At this stage, the readers may share the amused contempt of the implied author—not to say of the author herself—for such views, as the bookseller's name, Chassepoule (hen chaser), seems to point to his trivial pursuit.

As for Speck, he does not question such fascist ideals, for he refuses to take positions or to get involved. In fact, when he looks for a location for his art gallery, he looks for a "safe place" (*OB,* 1-2) politically. However, though he remains neutral, he does not altogether abstain from thinking of the multilateral political reception of his invented painter, thereby giving another poor picture of artistic endeavor: "Left, Right, and Center would unite on a single theme: how the taste of two full generations had been corrupted by foreign speculation, cosmopolitan decadence, and the cultural imperialism of the Anglo-Saxon hegemony" (9). Out of commercial motives, Speck struggles for everybody's agreement, which stresses the weakness of his political arguments. As Janice Kulyk Keefer remarks, "French politics is a crazy salad" (1989, 186) of contradictory positions, and its blatant leanings toward nationalism bear a strong resemblance to World War II right-wing opinions. The same applies to Speck's imaginary show, for which he dreams of enjoying everybody's approval, though he cannot avoid expressing his preference:

> He could see the structure of the show, the sketchbooks and letters in glass cases. It might be worthwhile lacquering the walls black, concentrating strong spots on

the correspondence, which straddled half a century, from Degas to Cocteau. The scrawl posted by Drieu la Rochelle just before his suicide would be particularly effective on black. Céline was good; all that crowd was back in vogue now. He might use the early photo of Céline in regimental dress uniform with a splendid helmet. Of course, there would be word from the Left, too, with postcards from Jean Jaurès, Léon Blum, and Paul Éluard, and a jaunty get-well message from Louis Aragon and Elsa.

(OB, 10)

The emphasis laid on people championing extreme right-wing ideas is inescapable: three sentences are devoted to Drieu La Rochelle—a man of letters who was to be executed by firing squad after World War II for collaborating with the Germans—and to Céline, whose major anti-Semitic and pro-German writings during the war earned him public condemnation and incarceration in Denmark. Only one sentence is devoted to left-wingers: the pooh-poohing way Speck speaks about them proves that he adds them as an afterthought to please everyone. In fact, the readers feel that he rather agrees with fascist ideas, especially in the light of the insult proffered by his wife on leaving him and his own disparaging remark to Lydia Cruche after she has tricked him into accepting her demands.

In the end, however, the readers wonder who has tricked whom, for Sandor Speck expresses his triumph in two powerful images in which the landscape reflects his elated mood and where the cartoon picture he imagines visually proclaims his victory as the hunter taming the wife of the hunters' patron saint and Speck's second wife, too: "He opened his eyes and saw rain clouds over Paris glowing with light—the urban aurora. It seemed to Speck that he was entering a better weather zone, leaving behind the gray, indefinite mist in which the souls of discarded lovers are said to wander. He welcomed this new and brassy radiation. He saw himself at the center of a shadeless drawing, hero of a sort of cartoon strip, subduing Lydia, taming Henriette" (*OB*, 46). Although this picture clearly establishes Speck's confidence, it still raises doubts as to the real intentions of Lydia Cruche, who could change her mind once again. For in the courting game on which Speck has embarked, no one knows who will get the upper hand, as the people involved in it have radically different interests.

In **"Overhead in a Balloon,"** the paintings displayed by the text also illustrate an aspect of French culture, namely the general decline of upper-class Parisian society as further exemplified by the experiences of Walter, a lonely art gallery assistant. As he befriends a mediocre French painter with a chain-link name—the distinctive token of nobility—and eventually moves into the flat of the painter's family, Walter is confronted by the way in which French aristocracy establishes and main-

tains—or rather cripples—human relationships. This unfortunate situation, reflected in the paintings of his new friend "Aymeric Something Something de Something de Saint-Régis" (*OB*, 59), is a source of daily, though unconscious, suffering. Walter is indeed unable to decode Aymeric's paintings, even though they suggestively disclose the social behavior of the French aristocracy, and by extension of his own family too: "Now he painted country houses. Usually he showed the front with the white shutters and all the ivy, and a stretch of lawn with white chairs and a teapot and cups, and some scattered pages of *Le Figaro*—the only newspaper, often the only anything, his patrons read. He had a hairline touch and could reproduce *Le Figaro*'s social calendar, in which he cleverly embedded his client's name and his own. Some patrons kept a large magnifying glass on a table under the picture, so that guests, peering respectfully, could appreciate their host's permanent place in art" (49-50). The description "poses the problem of representation within the represented universe of the narrative . . . by embedding one Art form, that of the picture, within another, the narrative."[16] The embedding functions on different levels: it reflects, as Sturgess argues, the characters' environmental subordination (47), but it also mirrors their superficiality. While depicting done-up country houses, Aymeric confines his attention to their conventional facades and external signs of wealth, much in accordance with the accepted conduct of his family, whose affected politeness conceals their real nature and inclinations. Moreover, the actual presence of the patron's name and his own on the reproduction of *Le Figaro* textually and pictorially announces their eagerness to be publicized. Beyond mere publicity stands the ultimate necessity to bridge the gap left by their shallow and empty lives. The image of the magnifying glass to decipher the represented text metaphorically confirms the pressing need to inflate the values of the bourgeois patrons encoded—a meaningless endeavor that does not fool those capable of interpreting the signs. Aymeric's minuscule signature on his paintings—a combination of the pictorial and the scriptural—finds a verbal echo in the reference to his voice, which is described as a "signature that [requires] a magnifying glass; what he [has] to say [is] clear but a kind of secret" (52). The analogy offers a symbolic reinforcement of the aristocracy's ambiguous need to be seen, yet not ostentatiously.

Besides reflecting the characters' shallowness, the description of Aymeric's painting mirrors the story's structuring process, evidencing metafictional self-reflexiveness. The painting actually reveals what Gallant does when devising her story: she too shows the facade, the surface of things, its hotchpotch of disconnected details and her characters' lack of culture and obsession with fame and moving in the best circles. Her ironic vision "overhead in a balloon" gives the story her stamp as well as ridicules her characters, whose names are embedded in the description of a kind of vanity fair. The visual thus mirrors the organizational principle of the text, adding a further layer of complexity.

Further textual and visual intermingling occurs in the description of the inflated picture story about the art gallery: "It happened that one of the Paris Sunday supplements had published a picture story on Walter's gallery, with captions that laid stress on the establishment's boldness, vitality, visibility, international connections, and financial vigor. The supplement had cost Walter's employer a packet, and Walter was not surprised that one of the photographs showed him close to collapse, leaning for support against the wall safe in his private office" (*OB,* 50). The fictitious magazine article combines both modes of representation, whose fictional description ridicules the undertaking by verbally stressing the paradoxical message of weakness hidden in the pictures. Pictorial and scriptural presentations thus work at cross purposes, thereby adding an extra ironic layer of meaning. The irony culminates in the insight into the financial burden of the enterprise, whose foreseeable disappointing outcome manifests itself as only Aymeric, prompted by his gullibility, pays an eager visit to the gallery. He imagines the place as packed with anxious buyers: "The accompanying article described mobbed openings, private viewings to which the police were summoned to keep order, and potential buyers lined up outside in below-freezing weather, bursting in the minute the doors were opened to grab everything off the walls. The name of the painter hardly mattered; the gallery's reputation was enough" (50).

But his actual experience as sole visitor affords a contrast to this illusion, not only in terms of numbers but also in terms of the outcome: "Aymeric showed courteous amazement when he heard just how much a show of that kind would cost. The uncultured talk about money was the gallery's way of refusing him, though a clause in the rejection seemed to say that something might still be feasible, in some distant off-season, provided that Aymeric was willing to buy all his own work" (*OB,* 51). In spite of the basic differences between these two pictures—the one imaginary, the other real (as real as fiction can be)—both evoke financial transactions and a purely materialistic approach to art. Some artists are businessmen whose talent ceases to be of aesthetic value: they and others alike take a purely pecuniary interest in art. The comparisons of Aymeric to Degas and Picasso—implicit in one case, explicit in the other—can therefore not be qualitative; denoting a purely matter-of-fact concern, the analogies only establish a parallel to Degas for not being married and to Picasso for having added his mother's maiden name to his own. No artistic similarity can be discerned. All neglect quality; money rules all. At least both text and image convey this idea.

Other textual and visual elements confirm this view while stressing the loss on the human level. For instance, Aymeric's assumption "that a show, a sort of retrospective of lawns and *Figaros,* would bring fresh patronage, perhaps even from abroad" (*OB,* 50) highlights the artist's greed. On the other hand, such a retrospective would imply a vast collection of quasi duplicates—a reflection of French superficiality and ostentation. With these sets of doubles, triples, and quadruples, Gallant brings out in bold a peculiar aspect of art, namely that when artists have a good subject matter, they sometimes paint it over and over again—as exemplified by modern painters (such as Monet, Cézanne, Magritte, and Munch, to mention but a few) and ancient painters alike. In addition, yet another set of images comes to mind with the reference to the kind of country houses Aymeric is "called in to immortalize" (50): "a done-up village bakery, a barn refurbished and brightened with yellow awnings 'Dallas' had lately made so popular" (50). The allusion to *Dallas,* with its flashy ranches and mansions, not to mention the characters' decadent lifestyle, reinforces the mercantile perception of art and the deterioration of human relations it seems to involve.

The allusion to the film is far from coincidental, for the family watches the serial in semireligious silence on a television set with a display of buttons that act as so many barriers to true communication. A *mise en abyme* in an admittedly different genre—that of the New World—the serial illustrates the nature of relationships within the family circle.[17] Robert, Aymeric's cousin, even goes so far as to announce his wedding in the middle of an episode, as if he were talking about a trivial fact. This recalls similar utterances in *Dallas:* Robert's announcement taking place in front of "a bright, silent screen" (67)—the image of failed communication—echoes the hollowness of human relations conveyed by the television show. Robert's careless attitude to human relations is further visually exemplified in his finger drawings of the flat and its new boundaries once he has decided to evict Walter: "'We will have to rearrange the space,' said Robert. He traced lines with his finger on the polished table and, with the palm of his hand, wiped something out" (70). A symbolic and ephemeral picture of exclusion, the drawing signifies the annihilation of human emotions and the need of living space; anyway, it cannot appeal to anyone from an aesthetic point of view. As such it recalls Robert's attitude when he conducts an explanatory session on the extended family's dreams: in godlike fashion, Robert decides what they mean, often offering a pessimistic interpretation of the animals and violent scenes that people Walter's dreams. The sacred interpretation is based on clues taken from a Bible-like book, whose text and images Robert uses to achieve his ends—instead of offering comfort to others.

Since art and religion no longer fulfill their function, they can neither offer visions of a better world nor bring comfort to souls in want of an ideal. Barthes sees a connection between the images that invade the world and human discontent: "What characterizes the so-called advanced societies is that they today consume images and no longer, like those of the past, beliefs; they are therefore more liberal, less fanatical, but also more 'false' (less 'authentic')—something we translate, in ordinary consciousness, by the avowal of an impression of nauseated boredom, as if the universalized image were producing a world that is without difference (indifferent), from which can rise, here and there, only the cry of anarchisms, marginalisms, and individualisms" (Barthes 1981, 118-19). Thus the mystically inclined Walter looks for a spiritual message in art, but in vain. His constant attempts at harmonizing art and faith lead him to the gradual discovery of their incompatibility: "Immersion in art had kept him from spiritual knowledge. What he had mistaken for God's beckoning had been a dabbing in colors, sentiment cut loose and set afloat by the sight of a stained-glass window. Years before, when he was still training Walter, his employer had sent him to museums, with a list of things to examine and ponder. God is in art, Walter had decided; then, God *is* art. Today, he understood: art is God's enemy. God hates art, the trifling rival creation" (*OB*, 60). Since Walter searches for an absolute in art but cannot find it there, he ends up expressing his aversion forcefully—somehow earnestly echoing Lydia Cruche's pretended rejection of the graven image, therefore bringing to mind other layers of textual and visual reverberations. A Puritan rejecting works of art, he reminds the readers of some Calvinists who objected to the worship of the holy images and destroyed them: "Virtually anything portrayed as art turned his stomach. There was hardly anything he could look at without feeling sick" (66).

An expression of his religious inclination, his physical disgust for visual arts also points to his inability to cope with life. Since most objects, beings, and situations have their reflection in art, nothing he ever witnesses or takes part in can ever please him. At some stage, in a discussion with Aymeric, he discriminates between art and Aymeric's paintings: "'I hate art, too,' said Walter. 'Oh, I don't mean that I hate what you do. That, at least, has some meaning—it lets people see how they imagine they live'" (*OB*, 54). Walter's feeling of repulsion raises an interesting issue, namely that of art and its meaning. Art, according to him, has lost its significance. However, Walter finds Aymeric's superficial and idyllic picture of society meaningful—an arresting paradox if one considers that "Fine art is that in which the hand, the head, and the heart of man go together."[18] Besides, the picture Aymeric gives of society goes against Walter's profound wish to establish proper relations with others. His artistic delusion results from his desperate need to belong. Ironically, the human warmth he

erroneously seeks in his adoptive family turns out to be a profit-making enterprise for the family and a devastating source of worries for Walter. The misreading of Aymeric's paintings thus suggests that Walter is a prey to the glamorous message French aristocracy conveys in art. A pedestrian character, Walter takes everything at its face value. Contrary to the expected reliability inherent in his Swiss citizenship, Walter Obermauer is a dropout who cannot adjust to the necessities of life. As his name indicates, he is the upper wall without retaining wall, ready to collapse at any excess of weight.

An exponent of materialistic society, Walter shows signs of a spiritual corruption whose origin can be traced to a purely mercantile approach to culture. Built in a slapdash fashion by contractors in search of money, the cultural edifice on which art rests offers no safe ground. Gallant underscores its devastating loss of significance through images reflecting aesthetic degradation.[19] The quest for beauty has been replaced by the mercantile operations of would-be artists and art dealers. In Paris, apparently, the middle ground between weak-willed artists and a gullible public is held by unscrupulous people, who fix the rules of the game as arbitrarily as the ministers of the most exotic religious faiths.

Unlike postmodern photography, which "defamiliarises the images that surround us" "through a demystifying use of irony," the paintings, drawings, and photographs represented in Gallant's fiction are not necessarily ironical in themselves.[20] They become so owing to the interaction between text and image. The irony thereby created is multiple, one mode of representation reflecting the other almost ad infinitum, obviously depending on the readers' ability to see further layers of interrelation. As written texts and images do not have only one interpretation, superimposed decoding adds to their riches. Their multiple readings enhance the ironic impact of representation, the visual reflecting the textual, and vice versa. Because Gallant describes and refers to images that tend to present a rigid message of retribution and punishment, or to reveal ungratifying relationships and unacceptable views, she emphasizes and derides the selfishness of human endeavor conveyed in her stories. Emerging from the interaction between text and image, the characters' innate talent for destruction reduces constructive ideals to nothing. By reinforcing the message of the text on which the image is superimposed, the visual enhances the readers' awareness of the self-inflicted, and therefore ineluctable, human degradation prevailing in Gallant's work.

Notes

1. Witness her essay on Marguerite Yourcenar, and her reviews of books by or about Giraudoux, Simone de Beauvoir, Colette, Simenon. Witness also her 1968 *Paris Notebooks*: from an external ob-

server's standpoint, she describes the *évènements de Mai 68,* conveying the uproar caused by the students' revolt and the illusion that it would bring about drastic changes to French society. Also with full knowledge, she recounts the Gabrielle Russier case—the affair of a teacher with one of her pupils that ended up with preventive detention, a partial trial, unemployment, and suicide—highlighting the gendered, social, and racist bias of the French legal system.

2. Neil Besner mentions Gallant's recurrent reference "to paintings, to pictures, and to characters watching them" ("A Broken Dialogue: History and Memory in Mavis Gallant's Short Fiction," *Essays in Canadian Writing* 33 [Fall 1986]: 95). Her appreciation also manifests itself through the careful pictures she creates as she describes places and people. For a discussion of the way Gallant exploits techniques from the visual arts, see the articles of Lesley D. Clement: "Artistry in Mavis Gallant's *Green Water, Green Sky*: The Composition of Structure, Pattern, and Gyre." *Canadian Literature* 129 (Summer 1991): 57-73; "Mavis Gallant's Apprenticeship Stories 1944-1950: Breaking the Frame," *English Studies in Canada* 18 (1992): 317-34; "Mavis Gallant's Stories of the 1950s: Learning to Look," *American Review of Canadian Studies* 24, no. 1 (Spring 1994): 57-73.

3. Roland Barthes, *Image, Music, Text,* trans. Stephen Heath (New York: Noonday Press, 1977), 39; hereafter cited in the text as Barthes 1977.

4. Roland Barthes, *Camera Lucida: Reflections on Photography,* trans. Richard Howard (New York: Noonday Press, 1981), 117; hereafter cited in the text as Barthes 1981.

5. Ironically, the man who said these words echoed Goebbels, Hitler's minister for propaganda, who is credited with saying: "When I hear the word Culture, I take out my gun."

6. The titles of the engravings are "Le Petit Palais—The Petit Palais; Place Vendôme—Place Vendôme; Rue de la Paix—Rue de la Paix" (*Home Truths: Selected Canadian Stories* [Toronto: Macmillan, 1981; reprint, New York: Random House, 1981], 299; hereafter cited in the text as *HT*).

7. Besides social topics, Gallant often chose to cover cultural and artistic subjects in her articles. Among those dealing with art, see "Above the Crowd in French Canada," *Harper's Bazaar,* July 1946, 58-59, 128-129; "Fresco Class," *The Standard,* Section Rotogravure, 9 November 1946, 12-13; "An Art Curator and His Critics," *Standard Magazine,* 12 June 1948, 3, 16, 22; "Art for the Family Pocket," *Standard Magazine,* 6 November 1948, 5, 22; "Success Story of a Canadian Artist," *Standard Magazine,* 29 April 1950, 18-19.

8. Mary Condé, "The Chapel Paintings in Mavis Gallant's 'In the Tunnel,'" in *Image et récit: Littérature(s) et arts visuels du Canada,* ed. Jean-Michel Lacroix, Simone Vauthier, and Héliane Venture (Paris: Presse de la Sorbonne Nouvelle, 1993), 98, 110.

9. Umberto Eco, *La Production des signes* (Paris: Librairie Générale Française, 1992), 72-79. See Condé's fine analysis for a further discussion of the various ways in which text and image intersect.

10. Mavis Gallant, *Overhead in a Balloon: Stories of Paris* (Toronto: Macmillan, 1985), 73; hereafter cited in the text as *OB*.

11. As Neil Besner rightly points out, the common concern with art is not the only aspect that links these two stories. Indeed, they both focus in different degrees on Sandor Speck, an art dealer, and his assistant, Walter: Gallant examines their place in French society and their political and ideological response to the situation they are confronted with (*The Light of Imagination: Mavis Gallant's Fiction.* Vancouver: University of British Columbia Press, 1988, 141).

12. I am indebted to Wolfgang Hochbruck for drawing my attention to the similarity in discourse. See Sándor Petőfi's poem "Magyars, Rise, Your Country Calls You!" in *Petőfi by Himself,* trans. Watson Kirkconnell (Budapest: Corvina Press, 1973), 29-32.

13. John Marlyn, *Under the Ribs of Death* (Toronto: McClelland and Stewart, 1957). Again, my thanks go to Wolfgang Hochbruck for reminding me of the name change in the earlier novel, allowing me to exploit the interpretation of the aptronym to the full.

14. Charlotte Sturgess makes such a point in an unpublished paper entitled "Pictorial Representation and Narrative in Mavis Gallant's 'Speck's Idea'" read in Strasbourg in May 1991.

15. Ronald Hatch rightly remarks that "Speck's Idea" "portrays the sense of disarray arising from a resurgence of right-wing politics in contemporary French society" ("Mavis Gallant and the Fascism of Everyday Life," *Essays in Canadian Writing* 42 [Winter 1990]: 37).

16. Charlotte Sturgess, "Narrative Strategies in 'Overhead in a Balloon,'" *Journal of the Short Story in English* 12 (Spring 1989): 47; hereafter cited in the text.

17. *Mise en abyme* refers to self-duplication within the finished work, such as a painting within the painting, representing the latter, or a story within

the story, mirroring the latter. The work within the work need not be a certified copy; it may summarize, schematize, transpose, or even announce in different ways what it represents. See Lucien Dällenbach, *Le Récit spéculaire* (Paris: Seuils, 1977); Jean Ricardou, *Le Nouveau roman* (Paris: Seuils, 1978), 47-65; Linda Hutcheon, *Narcissistic Narrative: The Metafictional Paradox* (London: Routledge, 1980), 53-56.

18. John Ruskin, *The Two Paths: Being Lectures on Art and Its Application to Decoration and Manufacture* (London: George Allen, 1900), Lecture 2, 57.

19. Her views on writers are not any less critical. Witness her satirical descriptions of Prism and Grippes. In "A Flying Start," Prism attempts to write a novel about himself and his benefactress, rejects the idea, and instantly becomes a literary critic. Grippes, on the other hand, does write, but he only produces mediocre novels about reactionary, provincial young men inspired by his tax collector, Poche, whose figure he changes slightly for the purpose of each new novel, following right-wing ideology dictating linear plots whose end can only be death (148). When Poche disappears, so does his inspiration, and Grippes starts clinging to an image from his past, the figure of a religious woman in gray whom he cannot summon to his imagination "because to depict life is to attract its ill-fortune" (146). Like Poche cornering him with his tax forms, Grippes would like to corner the woman to discover how to use her as a character. Both lifelikeness and pure creativity escape him altogether.

20. Linda Hutcheon, *Splitting Ironies: Contemporary Canadian Ironies* (Toronto: Oxford University Press, 1991), 113.

Mary Condé (essay date spring 1999)

SOURCE: Condé, Mary. "'Pichipoi' in Mavis Gallant's 'Malcolm and Bea.'" *Journal of the Short Story in English/Les Cahiers de la Nouvelle*, no. 32 (spring 1999): 77-86.

[*In the following essay, Condé explores Gallant's treatment of memory, history, and identity in her story "Malcolm and Bea."*]

Mavis Gallant is a writer profoundly influenced by the Holocaust, by "the first pictures of death camps" which, she wrote in 1972, "stopped a whole generation in its tracks" (Gallant 1972 196). In her "Paris Notebook" of the student riots of 1968 she records the seventeen-

year-old Barbara's remark that the German students who are being deported are needed: ". . . *Oui, nous avons besoin des allemands.*" Gallant comments,

> Her mother, who spent the war years in a concentration camp, says nothing. I feel as if I were watching two screens simultaneously.

(Gallant 1968 15)

In a review of Günter Grass from 1973 she recalls that he

> had been a prisoner of war at 17, and the Americans had forced him to look at Dachau: it is something he mentions when he is interviewed. Occasionally he will say that he broke with his youthful past at that moment; in this book he says he did not believe what he saw. Probably both are true.

(Gallant 1973 205)

In her observations on these two seventeen-year-olds we sense the same engagement with the managing of memories which is central to the story **"Malcolm and Bea"**.

Gallant is also constantly alert in her journalism to French anti-Semitism (e.g. Gallant 1968 33, 45, 66, 89, 1983 239). She observes in parenthesis in a review that

> (The persistent French fantasy about Jewish ears might be worth an anthropologist's attention: they are supposed to stick out, like President Kennedy's, or to be set low on the head, like those of Pope John XXIII, or to have attached earlobes, like Virginia Woolf's.)

(Gallant 1973 146)

In another parenthesis, in another review, she says of 1985, that

> (the most popular radio station in France is occupied for much of its daytime broadcasting by a teller of scatological and racist jokes. Jews, a constant butt, do not complain, because, apparently, they do not wish to be seen as spoilsports.)

(Gallant 1985 182)

She wrote in a review of 1976:

> The respectability of French anti-Semitism is its longest taproot. The educated and intelligent Robert Brasillach wrote, with pride, "Anti-Semitism is not a German invention, it is French tradition." Every country breeds a virus of racist jokes for amusement; a strain circulating in France for about a year now has been based on puns to do with deportation—this in a city where ghosts of deported children haunt the railway stations; ghosts visible, alas, to fewer and fewer of the living.

(Gallant 1976 218)

'Malcolm and Bea', a story originally published in *The New Yorker* on 23 March 1968, included in Gallant's 1988 collection *In Transit*, but omitted from her recent

Selected Stories, is permeated with references to nationality and race. In the first paragraph the Englishman Malcolm Armitage, in France with NATO, places children at play as American, and he himself is placed as 'not French' (77). He once, before he learnt not to tease her, asked his Canadian wife "'Who do you hate most, Bea? The English, the French, or the Americans?'" (78) Bea lies in telling Malcolm that her mother was French-Canadian, rather than Native Canadian (86). His friend Leonard Baum self-pityingly tells Malcolm that ". . . My life today makes no more sense than a sweeper's in India. . . ." (89) Leonard's wife Verna, reproaching Malcolm and Bea for what she perceives as their incompetence, says to them with the sublime irrelevance and lack of irony so typical of Gallant's characters,

> . . . If intelligent young parents like you two can't do the right things, what can you expect from people like the Congolese? I don't mean that racially. . . .
>
> (92)

It seems clear that the Baums themselves are Jewish, although this is never made explicit; in a story from 1979, **'Baum, Gabriel, 1935- ( )'**, which has some analogies with **'Malcolm and Bea'**, Gabriel Baum's parents are presumed murdered in concentration camps in 1943 (Gallant 1997 455). Since her marriage Verna Baum has converted to Catholicism, and they are described as 'a raggle-taggle international family' (88), moving from country to country with Leonard's various postings. It is Leonard Baum who first proposes 'Pichipoi' as a controlling idea in human life, and thus for Gallant's story, by telling Malcolm that one of the statements in his own projected obituary would be 'All his life he thought he was going to Pichipoi.'

Leonard asks Malcolm if he knows what Pichipoi means, and Malcolm thinks to himself:

> I know about Pichipoi. It was the name of an unknown place. The Jews in Paris invented it. It was their destination, but it was a place that might not be any worse than the present. Some of them thought it might even be better, because no one had come back yet to say it was worse. They couldn't imagine it. It was half magic. Sometimes in their transit camps they'd say, "Let's get to Pichipoi and get it over with."
>
> (89)

Malcolm and Leonard, two men oppressed by unsatisfactory marriages, are at this point in a tunnel in a traffic jam, on their way back to the temporary homes in a foreign country they are about to leave for temporary homes in two other foreign countries. Malcolm at first explicitly rejects any connection between Leonard, and by association himself, and the Jews who thought about Pichipoi, although this explicit rejection may of course suggest the seduction of such a connection. Malcolm reasons with himself, first, that Leonard was not in France at the time of the deportation of the Jews, but 'must have been in Canada, in college.' Secondly, 'Leonard is still in control of his life.' Thirdly, although he is miserable because his girlfriend has tried to kill herself, because his name is now known to the police, because he has to go home to face his wife, and because he is being forced to leave France because 'the French have kicked us out and they hate us', his future is not going to get any worse. Fourthly, Malcolm feels that Leonard should not say 'Pichipoi' since it is a word that is, after all, 'entirely magic' because children invented it. Malcolm concludes his thoughts:

> It is a sacred word. But it was such a long time ago, as long ago as the Children's Crusade. Leonard is generous; he knows he is presuming. He is on sacred ground, with his shoes on. They were on their way to dying. If every person thought his life was a deportation, that he had no say in where he was going, or what would happen once he got there, the air would be filled with invisible trains and we would collide in our dreams.
>
> (89)

Malcolm is thinking here, as from time to time he narrates, in the first person. It is one of Gallant's achievements as a storyteller that the shifts from first to third person in her narratives brilliantly suggest the illogical and self-interested interpolations of individuals into a clear and rational discourse on history. Malcolm makes sensible distinctions between Leonard's situation and the situation of the beleaguered Jews in wartime Paris, but his consoling aside to himself that

> it was such a long time ago, as long ago as the Children's Crusade

shows how faint to his perceptions are the ghosts of deported French children haunting the railway stations. That doomed assault on Jerusalem had tragic consequences for thousands of children, but it took place in 1212. To consign the deported French children to the same shadowy realms of the past indicates, ironically enough, the same abnegation of responsibility as Malcolm's historically accurate assessment that he himself would have been "what—four, five? Roy's age?" (89) Debórah Dwork, in her study *Children With A Star: Jewish Youth in Nazi Europe* (1991) claims that the focus of all the histories of the Holocaust, written over a period of almost fifty years, is adults: "Children are conspicuously, glaringly, and screamingly silently absent" (Dwork 253). This is not true of **"Malcolm and Bea"**, for Malcolm's attitude to his small stepson Roy is one of the moral touchstones of the story. Roy himself, however, is remarkably silent as a character, and remains an enigma to his stepfather.

Leonard never explicitly defines what "Pichipoi" means to him, and Malcolm's analysis of the word is significantly different from that of most historians. Annette

Wieviorka records that the first convoy of Jews left Drancy for Auschwitz on 27 March 1942, and that it was in an infirmary, around September 1942, that some Jewish children came up with the word "Pichipoi", which was then adopted by all deportees. She explains that

> Originally, it designated an imaginary place in Yiddish folklore and a popular children's rhyme. Made up from the Polish words *pich* ("drink") and *poi* ("give the livestock water"), this fantastic hamlet came to stand for their last hope.
>
> (Wieviorka 137)

She goes on to quote from Georges Wellers' documentary account *De Drancy à Auschwitz* (1946):

> In the camp at Drancy, Pichipoi represented the unknown place where you were being sent, where things would be better and easier,
>
> (Wellers 68)

and from André Schwarz-Bart's novel *The Last of the Just* (1973):

> So it was that at Drancy a belief was current in a distant kingdom called Pichipoi, where the Jews, guided by the staves of their blond shepherds, would be permitted to graze industriously on the grass of a fresh start.
>
> (Schwarz-Bart 351)

Schwarz-Bart makes it clear that their real destination was literally incredible to the Jews (Schwarz-Bart 395-396), and that "Pichipoi", despite its disquieting overtones of Jews as animals, however kindly treated, is emphatically a good place. Malcolm defines it, in far more pessimistic terms, as "a place that might not be any worse than the present".

Another word which has resonance for the concentration camps is "Canada", the name given to the storehouses in which the property stolen from the prisoners as they arrived was collected (Höss 95, Vrba 266). Bea is reading *Montcalm and Wolfe*, Parkman's nineteenth-century history of her country, a choice which suggests that she, like Malcolm, has little investment in contemporary history, and she tells Malcolm that she has got up to the part about Canada being the prey of jackals (78). This is near the beginning of the second volume, so that unless Bea is merely being provocative, she is an assiduous reader; Parkman remarks of the mid-eighteenth century that "Canada was the prey of official jackals" (Parkman II 19). The connections between the two Canadas here, both standing for theft on a colossal scale, suggest another potential identification with the Jews.

Malcolm's judgement that in using a word which children invented Leonard "is on sacred ground, with his shoes on" is curiously linked to the "sacred grass" of

the story's opening sentence, the grass between the apartment blocks, the "holy grass" on which the American wives stand in bare feet drinking coffee and on which the American children play. The *gardien*, "a bad-tempered old man in a dirty collar" (78), futilely blows his whistle to drive both groups off, and is goaded into rage by the American wives, "furiously whistling, like a lifeguard who for some reason was unable to launch a boat", and literally dancing with rage (90). The sacredness of the ground here is clearly nothing more than a bureaucratic figment, monitored by a figure who is not only impotent but ridiculous. It is also curious that the terms Malcolm uses of the Jewish children, that they were on their way to dying, and that they had no say in where they were going, are applicable to himself. By the end of the story, too, as Janice Kulyk Keefer has pointed out, Malcolm "makes his own appropriation" of "Pichipoi" (Keefer 170). Denying its specific historical association, he identifies its real meaning as being alone, as each person being flung separately into a room without windows (94).

Karen Smythe has identified Gallant's project as a writer as the presentation of "segments of contemporary life as seen from her distinctly ironic perspective" (Smythe 22), and Neil Besner has spoken of her "stories in which memory makes history into home" (Besner 93) in **"Malcolm and Bea"** Gallant shows how contemporary life and the memory of history are self-indulgently merged by characters in search of the stability of home. Bea, who sometimes describes "a house and a garden and a set of parents" in her past (81) as if Malcolm had never seen the reality, has, after all, nothing intrinsic to do with the plight of eighteenth-century Canada. When she tells Malcolm she has read *Montcalm and Wolfe* up to the part where it says Canada was the prey of jackals,

> she looks as if *he* were the jackal, because he was born in England. She looks as if she had access to historical information Malcolm will never understand.
>
> (78)

This ludicrous version of historical information as privileged memory is matched by a darkly comic moment of forgetfulness when Leonard Baum, declaiming about his responsibilities to his family, despite his possession of a mistress, cannot remember his own wife's name (88). Similarly, Bea, planning a hypothetical separation from Malcolm, says to him, "'All right, you take Roy, I'll keep Ruth'", forgetting that Roy is not Malcolm's child (81). Roy himself, at the end of the story, is absorbed not in his own memories, but the "Kodachrome holiday memories" (91) of the Baums.

Memory is demonstrated as arbitrary, both in terms of the characters' own lives and in the relevance they attach to historical events; for this reason Gallant assigns the same notion of sacred ground to the idea of doomed

Jewish children and to a pointless and often broken rule. The word "Pichipoi" itself is remembered inaccurately by Malcolm, and used, first by Leonard and then by himself, to express a self-pitying view of what are relatively safe and affluent lives.

There is a parallel here with Bea's treatment of her son Roy. She is alert to what he should not watch on television, exclaiming angrily, "'The goddamn mother's died. Roy shouldn't be looking at that'" (93), but at the same time quite capable of telling the child that she brought the wrong baby home from hospital:

> "I had a lovely boy but some other mother got him. They gave me Roy by mistake."
>
> (79)

She will protect Roy only against fictional but not real cruelty, just as Malcolm will engage with "Pichipoi" only on a sentimental level. It is the horror of the story **"Baum, Gabriel, 1935-( )"** that Gabriel Baum acquires "a variety of victim experiences":

> Gabriel had been shot, stoned, drowned, suffocated, and marked off for hanging; had been insulted and betrayed; had been shoved aboard trains and dragged out of them; had been flung from the back of a truck with such accidental violence that he had broken his collarbone.
>
> (Gallant 1997 462)

The horror here is that Gabriel is acting out all the possibilities of his parents' death on film, for an audience, "some eating their dinner" (Gallant 1997 462).

In **"Malcolm and Bea"** Leonard Baum has discarded his Jewish identity, just as Bea has decided not to trust Malcolm (86) and has discarded her Native Canadian identity. But Leonard resumes a kind of ersatz Hollywood identity as a Jew by appropriating "Pichipoi" in the midst of his torrent of clichés about his life. Malcolm, a more sympathetic character than Leonard, who partly narrates the story and in doing so establishes himself in control of some of its ironies, comes a little closer to a consideration of what the word really connotes, but ultimately shows that the ghosts of deported children haunting the railway stations are invisible to him too. His reflection on Leonard's use of the word "Pichipoi", that

> If every person thought his life was a deportation, that he had no say in where he was going, or what would happen once he got there, the air would be filled with invisible trains and we would collide in our dreams,
>
> (89)

suggests, finally, that the air is indeed filled with invisible trains. The warring aspirations of the married couples could certainly be aptly described as collisions in dreams, but they are colluding in their denial of a real and atrocious suffering.

The fact that **"Malcolm and Bea"** was not reprinted in Gallant's recent *Selected Stories* may indicate that she is now dissatisfied with it (Gallant 1997 XVIII), but it is a fine and very disturbing story. When *In Transit* was published in Britain, a critic commented on all the stories in the collection that

> Children here do not share a secret language or code; left clinging to the spars of adult wreckage they enjoy no such luxury as a common cause.
>
> (Wordsworth 13)

In **"Malcolm and Bea"** the secret meaning of "Pichipoi" is cracked open, and then utterly degraded.

Works Cited

Besner, Neil K. *The Light of Imagination: Mavis Gallant's Fiction.* (Vancouver: U of British Columbia P, 1988).

Dwork, Debórah. *Children With A Star: Jewish Youth in Nazi Europe.* (New Haven and London: Yale UP, 1991).

Gallant, Mavis.

JOURNALISM

'The Events in May: A Paris Notebook—I' (first published in *The New Yorker,* 14 September 1968) in Mavis Gallant, *Paris Notebooks: Essays & Reviews* (Toronto: Macmillan of Canada, 1986), 9-49.

"The Events in May: A Paris Notebook—II" (first published in *The New Yorker,* 21 September 1968), *Paris Notebooks,* 50-95.

Review of *Jean Giraudoux: The Writer and His Work* by Georges Lemaitre (New York: Frederick Ungar, 1971) and *Lying Woman* by Jean Giraudoux, translated by Richard Howard (New York: Winter House, 1971) (first published in *The New York Times Book Review,* 30 January 1972), Paris Notebooks, 195-199.

"Paul Léautaud, 1872-1956" (first published in *The New York Times Book Review,* 9 September 1973), *Paris Notebooks,* 142-152.

Review of *From the Diary of a Snail* by Günter Grass, translated by Ralph Manheim (New York: Harcourt Brace Jovanovich, 1973) (first published in *The New York Times Book Review,* 30 September 1973), *Paris Notebooks* 204-207.

Review of *Céline* by Patrick McCarthy (New York: Viking, 1976) (first published in *The New York Times Book Review,* 18 July 1976), *Paris Notebooks,* 215-221.

Review of *The French* by Theodore Zeldin (New York: Pantheon Books, 1983) (first published in *The New York Times Book Review,* 20 March 1983), *Paris Notebooks,* 236-241.

"Limpid Pessimist: Marguerite Yourcenar" (first published in *The New York Review of Books*, 5 December 1985), *Paris Notebooks*, 180-191.

FICTION

"Malcolm and Bea" (first published in *The New Yorker,* 23 March 1968), *In Transit* (Ottawa: Penguin Books Canada, 1988), 77-95.

"Baum, Gabriel, 1935-( )" (first published 1979), 452-472.

Höss, Rudolf. *Autobiography*. Translated by Constantine FitzGibbon. *KL Auschwitz Seen By the SS* (first published 1970) with foreword by Jerzy Rawicz. (Owiecim: Auschwitz-Birkenau State Museum, 1997) 27-101.

Keefer, Janice Kulyk. *Reading Mavis Gallant*. (Toronto, New York and Oxford: Oxford UP, 1989).

Merler, Grazia. *Mavis Gallant: Narrative Patterns and Devices*. (Ottawa: Tecumseh P, 1978).

Parkman, Francis. *Montcalm and Wolfe* (first published 1884), 2 vols., with introduction by Thomas Seccombe. (London: J. M. Dent and New York: E. P. Dutton, 1908).

Schwarz-Bart, André. *The Last of the Just* (first published as *Le dernier des Justes,* Paris: Editions du Seuil, 1959). Translated by Stephen Becker. (New York: Atheneum, 1960).

Smythe, Karen E. *Figuring Grief: Gallant, Munro, and the Poetics of Elegy*. (Montreal and Kingston, London and Buffalo: McGill-Queen's UP, 1992).

Vrba, Rudolf. "Majdanek." Translated by Michael Jacobs and Laurence Weinbaum. *London Has Been Informed . . . Reports by Auschwitz Escapees*. Ed. Henryk Owiebocki. (Owiecim: Auschwitz-Birkenau State Museum, 1997). 256-273.

Wellers, Georges. *De Drancy à Auschwitz*. (Paris: Editions du Centre, 1946).

Wieviorka, Annette. "Jewish Identity in the First Accounts by Extermination Camp Survivors from France." Translated by Françoise Rosset. *Yale French Studies 85, Discourses of Jewish Identity in Twentieth-Century France*. Ed. Alan Astro. (New Haven: Yale UP, 1994). 135-151.

Wordsworth, Christopher. "New Fiction." *The Guardian*, 22 February 1990. 13.

Pilar Somacarrera (essay date autumn 2000)

SOURCE: Somacarrera, Pilar. "Genre Transgressions and Auto/Biography in Mavis Gallant's 'When We Were

Nearly Young.'" *Journal of the Short Story in English/ Les Cahiers de la Nouvelle*, no. 35 (autumn 2000): 69-84.

[*In the following essay, Somacarrera asserts that "When We Were Nearly Young" transgresses the genre of short fiction, contending that the piece blends "narrative, essay, journalistic piece, memoir and autobiography."*]

As Claire Obaldia points out, the intensive concern with generic studies in recent times has clearly shown that despite—or perhaps because of—the striking progress in this field, the question of "genre" remains one of the most difficult in literary theory (1). Aristotle made taxonomy the very praxis of poetics, aiming to find the "essential quality" of each genre. Recent critical directions, however, argue that literary texts are composed of heterogeneous and often contradictory generic strands and discourses.[1] This breaking of the boundaries of genre is a pervasive tendency in Canadian literature in English, which, as Belén Martín has observed, has been associated with Canada's liberation from British and American imperialism and with its search for a literary identity (63). Experimentation with genre is present in works such as Alice Munro's *Lives of Girls and Women*, which stands at the borderline between the collection of short stories and the novel, and John Glassco's *Memoirs of Montparnasse,* combining aspects of journal, diary, sketchbook and travel narrative. Critical attention has been paid to the blurring of genres in these and other Canadian writers. For example, the critical volume edited by K. P. Stich *Reflections. Autobiography and Canadian Literature,* contains one essay which analyses Glassco's book and two dedicated to Munro's fiction.[2]

In Mavis Gallant, however, the issue of genre has been relatively neglected, especially if compared with other aspects of her fiction, such as style, themes, narrative techniques, irony and the importance of historical and social issues, which have received more critical attention.[3] Her story **"When We Were Nearly Young"**, about four young people living in the postwar Madrid of the early fifties, is an example of the layering and mixing of genres I have just referred to. It stands in a borderline territory between narrative, essay, journalistic piece, memoir and autobiography. Although Gallant does not admit being conscious of generic constraints in her works, she has practised all the genres I have listed before. She is primarily a writer of short fiction, as illustrated by her eleven collections of short stories, but she is also a fine writer of essays, as she has demonstrated in *The Paris Notebooks: Essays and Reviews*. In this article I will analyse **"When We Were Nearly Young"** with a view to showing how it transgresses the genres of the short story, autobiography and essay. This genre transgression is an essential component in the representation of the narrative "I". Generic analysis also provides insight into the tone of the story, which is very intimate and very detached at the same time, and not always as "dispassionate and critically calculating" as Kulyk Keefer describes it (*Reading*, 166). In fact, **"When We Were Nearly Young"** contains glimpses of an intensely personal voice absent in **"Señor Pinedo"**, Gallant's other story about Spain. Because the story contains much documentary information about the Madrid of the early fifties, it is easy to think of it as a mere reportage, but, as I will try to demonstrate, it is really concerned with a failed attempt on the narrator's part to capture her Self through the Spanish background.

As a short story, **"When We Were Nearly Young"** presents some peculiarities that deviate from the traditional form of this genre. As Tamas Dobozy observes, Gallant blasts away assumptions delimiting the organization of experience offered by the traditional short story (86). It lacks a sense of trajectory and the abrupt ending breaks the reader's expectations of closure and finality. There is a not a chronological structure but, rather, a succession of habitual actions. This is typical of Gallant's stories, which never follow a linear pattern but, rather, in the author's words, "build around their centre, rather like a snail" ("What Is Style?" 45). Plot is reduced to a minimum, and some crucial information like the narrator's professional activity in Madrid is missing. The traditional conventions governing short stories like "totality" and "unity of effect" are also absent, since the story is a collage of different tableaux which sometimes are not even connected. In addition, as in much of Gallant's fiction, character is not posited at prime but, rather, the characters are symbolic of Gallant's impressions about the passivity of the Spaniards. When asked about Spanish people in the fifties in a recent interview,[4] she answered "they were slow, slow. They walked slowly, they weren't quick". This is reproduced quite literally in the story:

> The difference between them and any three broke people anywhere was a certain passiveness, as though everything had been dealt with in advance. . . . When we walked together, their steps slowed in rhythm, as if they had all three been struck with the same reluctance to go on.

(188)[5]

Given the fact that the story is largely based on autobiographical material, as the author herself has acknowledged in the recent interview I have just referred to, the most problematic aspect of the story is the relationship between the narrator and the writer. As Janice Kulyk Keefer points out, unlike other Canadian writers like Mordecai Richler or Norman Levine, Gallant has rejected any form of autobiographical fiction (*Reading* 8), and she has insisted that the "I" in the story is not her:

> The stories I wrote about Spain are fiction but they are based on fact. But it is not factual fact, as I'm telling you now. Because if I wrote a story about Málaga as it was, it would be based on that, but I would not be in it. I might say "I", but it wouldn't be *I, me*.

(Somacarrera interview)

Gallant's zeal to make a clear distinction between herself as an author and the narrator of her story becomes irrelevant in view of poststructuralist literary theories which consider that all writing is autobiographical, and that all autobiographies are fictive. Shirley Neuman says the following in her chapter about "Life Writing" in the *Literary History of Canada*:

> Perhaps the blurring of generic distinctions is simply the logical consequence of Cocteau's observation, made many years ago, that every word we write is part of our self-portrait, an observation reformulated and quoted by Eli Mandel as epigraph to *Life Sentence* (1981): "When autobiography ceases to be, I shall write from the point of view of a Brazilian general". Certainly that position that all writing is autobiographical has found justification in and has also partly been impelled by post-structuralist theories which call into question the unity of the speaking/writing subject as well as the referentiality of language.

(335)

David Williams uses the term "fictional autobiography" to refer to these first person narratives about a life (176), but the term that best defines Gallant's story is auto/biography,[6] which is frequently used in postmodern literary criticism to refer to narratives about women's lives based on memories from youth and childhood whose narrators are fictional, but share many characteristics of the writer and her experiences. Although Danielle Schaub claims that readers gain no insight from the knowledge that Gallant experienced personally what she describes in **"When We Were Nearly Young"** (1), this information is essential in order to assign the story to the genre of auto/biography, since, as Liz Stanley observes, auto/biography is more properly to be seen as an artful construction within a narrative that more often than not employs a variety of methods which imply referentiality (128). Auto/biography also collects into it social science and other apparently objective ways of producing and using life stories of different kinds. The narrative "I" in **"When We Were Nearly Young"** remains a fictional character, but goes through the same personal experiences in Madrid as Gallant did. However, as Donna Stanton has it, the main issue in auto/biographical writing is not the referentiality, but the "graphing" of the "auto", that is, the creation of a textual self: "the excision of bio from autobiography is designed to bracket the traditional emphasis on the narration of "a life" and that notion's facile presumption of referentiality (vii). Sherrill Grace adds that any writer's autobiographical 'I' is a fiction, a creation and a discourse (189). Grace's words about Margaret Atwood's autobiographical writing can be transcribed to Gallant's story: Gallant's autobiographical "I" has little directly to do with "Mavis Gallant", but a great deal to do with the practices of autobiography. It is significant, for example, that the four characters in the story are writing their diaries, that is, they are engaged in life-writing practices ("We began keeping diaries at about the same time" 188).

Although **"When We Were Nearly Young"** is a *fictional* biography of an "I", it features several characteristics of autobiography, as defined in classical theories about this genre. One of the main characteristics of autobiography is, following Roy Pascal, a search for one's inner standing (*selbstbesinnung*) (182). It is an effort to capture the Self, or in Hegel's claim, to know the self through consciousness. Georges Gusdorf observes that autobiography is typical of a society that fosters the "the curiosity of the individual about himself, the wonder he feels about the mystery of his own destiny" (31). The narrator announces at the beginning of the story that she is engaged in a quest for self-knowledge and for her destiny: "I thought these signs . . . would tell me what direction my life was going to take" (184). Later in the story, she confesses that she went to Madrid to make sense of her life:

> My own character seemed to me ill defined; I believed that this was unfortunate and unique. I thought that if I set myself against a background into which I could not possibly merge that some outline would present itself.
>
> (189)

Two other features of autobiography are also present in the story: the sense of distance and what Philip Lejeune calls the retrospective view (25). Georges Gusdorf has written: "Autobiography . . . requires a man to take distance in order to reconstitute himself in the focus of his special unity and identity across time" (35). This is precisely what the narrator of **"When We Were Nearly Young"** was aiming at when she went to Madrid, as she herself admits in the previous quotation from the story. As for the retrospective view, it is clear from the outset of the narrative: "In Madrid, nine years ago, we lived on the thought of money" (184). The nine years that went by between the actual events of the story and the time of the narration determine the presentation of things, since the story is pervaded by the sense, which is typical of autobiography, that the person who remembers the past is no longer the same she was in the past.

In autobiography the past is subsumed under a vision from the present, and the inevitable passing of time performs ironic twists in linguistic categories, as with the adjective "New" when applied to Pablo, one of the narrator's Spanish friends:

> He was one of the New Spaniards—part of the first generation grown to maturity under Franco. He was the

generation they were so proud of in the newspapers. But he must be—he is—well over thirty now, and no longer new.
>
> (185)

In fact, the narrator of **"When We Were Nearly Young"** is poignantly aware of the working of memory and language on the events of the past: "Eventually, they were caught, for me, not by time but by the freezing of memory. And when I looked in the diary I had kept during that period, all I could find was descriptions of the weather" (191). The closing paragraph thus broaches Gallant's typical concern with memory's apprehension of time past. In Liz Stanley's words this is an explicit textual recognition that the "past" is indeed past and thus essentially unrecoverable (61). The story closes on the irresolvable displacement of memory by the equalizing force of language. Memories in **"When We Were Nearly Young"** never have an enlightening role:

> I have never been back to Madrid. My memories are of squares and monuments, of things that are free or cheap. I see us huddled in coats, gloved and scarved, fighting the icy wind, pushing along to the ten-peseta place. In another memory it is so hot we can scarcely force ourselves to the park, where we will sit under elm trees and look at newspapers.
>
> (188)

The narrator of **"When We Were Nearly Young"** makes an effort to retrieve the memories of her time in Madrid, but what she remembers is a faded reflection of what she experienced there, as her memories about her life in Madrid are rather trivial.

According to Gusdorf, autobiography also responds to the more or less anguished restlessness of the person who is growing older and wonders whether his or her life has been lived in vain and wasted (36). As its title indicates, **"When We Were Nearly Young"** is a story about the transitory nature of youth, reflected in the characters' obsession about getting to be thirty. Gallant herself has referred to this critical age:

> In your thirties, you were supposed to have cruised your whole life, people got married young . . . Thirty is like a landmark and, of course, thirty is not eighteen. So there was a slice of life, to me, that went between seventeen and twenty-two, about, and that was one slice, then you went from twenty-two to thirty. And thirty was like a wall. If you were going to do something important, you had better do it before that age.
>
> (Somacarrera interview)

These words are echoed by the narrator when she refers to this stage of her life:

> He made us so afraid of being thirty that even poor Pilar was alarmed, although she had eight years of grace. I was frightened of it, too. I was not by any means in first youth, and I could not say that the shape of my life was a mystery.
>
> (189)

As the title of the story indicates, the narrator and her friends are still young but already too old to continue living aimlessly.

"When We Were Nearly Young" is about an episode in a woman's life. Sherrill Grace has also observed that when the Subject writing autobiographically is female, as in **"When We Were Nearly Young"**, the assumptions and codes of the genre shift dramatically (191). The female model for autobiography, instead of positing a separate, discrete Self, stresses interdependence, community and identification *with* rather than *against*. This is illustrated in the story by the frequent use of the first person plural narrator "We" instead of "I", a practice which is reflected in the title of the story. This use transcribes the narrator's identification with her Spanish friends in **"When We Were Nearly Young"**, which is set up from the beginning of the story, when the protagonist recounts that, like them, she was always waiting for money:

> In Madrid, nine years ago, we lived on the thought of money. Our friendships were nourished with talk of money we expected to have, and what we intended to do when it came. . . . The thing we had in common was that we were all waiting for money.
>
> (84)

In fact, Neil Besner considers the companionship between the four "nearly young" people the main focus of the story (*Light* 21). The narrator and her friends shared hunger ("We were always vaguely hungry" (186), financial difficulties ("We came to a financial crisis about the same moment" 190), and seemed to lead parallel lives, as is suggested by the following parallelistic structures: "I dreamed of food. Pilar dreamed of things chasing her, and Pablo dreamed of me and Carlos dreamed he was on the top of the mountain preaching to multitudes" (190).

The story lacks a teleological Self, centred and developing towards a goal, which is also typical of female autobiography. The "I" of **"When We Were Nearly Young"** is, in fact, quite the opposite from this, as she seems rather disoriented and waiting for a goal in life: "In those days I was always looking for signs . . . I thought these signs would tell me what direction my life was going to take and what might happen from now on" (185). The perception of time in the story is also very personal, an aspect which also relates it to autobiographical narratives written by women:

> Time was like water dropping—Madrid time. [. . .] and I was afraid of the movement of time, at once too quick and too slow [. . .] I had chosen the very city where time dropped, a drop from the roof of a cave, one drop at a time.
>
> (189-90)

The slow passing of time which the narrator associates with Madrid is, in fact, related to the narrator's own waiting for money, "her waiting for time to drop into the pool" (191). As Anna Belford Ulanov points out, feminine time is always personal, and that influences her global perception of the world and time, which usually comes as a sudden enlightment, as opposed to masculine exposition, which is irrational, progressive and logic (177,169). In fact, in Gallant's narratives, according to Janice Kulyk Keefer, time becomes the principal hero or villain ("Strange" 724).

Insomuch as the story is close to autobiography, it is also close to the essay. The essay as conceived by Montaigne, is often full of autobiographical content, and, according to Graham Good, it is based, more than any other form except the diary, on the individual's self-experience (8). Because of its liminal status between the narrative and the essay, **"When We Were Nearly Young"** has been included in an anthology of Canadian essays,[7] a fact which has led Neil Besner to raise questions about the genre of this text:

> Is this work a report, an essay masquerading as a story? Or is it a story masquerading as a reflection, a memoir? Could it be both? How to distinguish, on what grounds? The presence or absence of documentary reference? The status of the narrator as reporter or story-teller? Which aspects of focus or style?
>
> ("A Broken Dialogue", 89-90)

Douglas Malcom annotated the story as "a humorous essay about waiting for money in Madrid", but also cited it as a short story contributed to *The New Yorker* (119,121). The documentary reference is definitely a component of the story, since much of the socio-economical information is based on facts, such as the atmosphere of material deprivation in the Spain of the fifties.

In order to determine to what extent **"When We Were Nearly Young"** is, using Besner's words, "an essay masquerading as a story", I will draw on recent criticism about this genre, by Graham Good and Claire Obaldia. These two critics emphasize formlessness as one of the essay's main characteristics. The essay, adds Good, does not aim at system at all and is specifically unorganized (1). Obaldia says the following about the asystematic nature of this genre:

> Rather than progressing in a linear and planned fashion, the essay develops around a number of topics which offer themselves along the way. And this sauntering from one topic to the next together with the way in which each topic is informally "tried out" suggests a tentativeness, a looseness, in short a randomness which seems to elude the unifying conception.
>
> (2)

At the textual level, this lack of organization is reflected in the lack of coherence between paragraphs, or even inside a paragraph. In fact, in **"When We Were Nearly Young"**, it is easy to disagree with the author's paragraphing: for example, the second paragraph of the story contains three different topics which could have made three different paragraphs. Obaldia's analysis of the essay's developing "around a number of topics which offer themselves along the way," describes a technique which is often used in Gallant's story:

> We began keeping diaries at about the same time. I don't remember who started it. Carlos's was secret. Pilar asked how to spell words. Pablo told everything before he wrote it down. It was a strange occupation, considering the ages we were, but we hadn't enough to think about. Poverty is not a goad but a paralysis. I have never been back to Madrid. My memories are of squares and monuments . . .
>
> (188)

Thought in the essay stays close to its objects and shares their space and atmosphere. The connections between thoughts in this genre are often made through things, rather than being linked directly in a continuous argument. In the passage I have just quoted, the narrator rambles from her reference to her and her friends' diaries to their situation of paralysis, and finally makes an incursion into the present.

According to Good's description, the essay presupposes an independent observer, a specific object and a sympathetic reader (4). This is exactly what Gallant did when she was in Spain. In the interview I held with her, she emphasises how she "was on her own" in the country and how much "she wanted to see the Spanish reality" by herself. An essay also presupposes a language capable of rendering and communicating observation, whether physical or mental (Good 4). The physical sensations recounted in **"When We Were Nearly Young"** are many, like the narrator's hunger and the smells and tastes of the Spanish restaurants. Mental observations also abound. To quote but an example, these are the narrator's thoughts when her friend Pilar pretended that she lived at the Museo Romántico:

> I say "boys" because I never thought of them as men. I am by the window, with my back turned. I disapprove, and it shows. I feel like a prig. I tip the painted blind, just to see the street and be reassured by a tram going by. It *is* the twentieth century.
>
> (187)

The uncertainty and disorientation at the outset of the story are also typical of an essay. The narrator is waiting for money, but she doesn't know exactly how much money she will receive: "Every day I went to the Central Post Office, and I made the rounds of the banks and the travel agencies, where letters and money could come. I was not certain how much it might be" (184).

Finally, the sense of transitoriness and provisionality which informs the story is also characteristic of the essay as defined by Good:

> Self and object define each other, but momentarily . . . The essay makes claim to truth, but not permanent truth. Its truths are particular, of the here and now. . . . The essay offers knowledge of the moment, not more . . . The essayist's truths are "for me" and "for now", personal and provisional.
>
> (4)

I have already mentioned how the narrator's impressions of Madrid are entirely provisional and they, in fact, vanish with time, as the ending of the story endorses. The beginning also emphasises this sense of the moment, of concrete time and place: "In Madrid, nine years ago, we lived on the thought of money. Our friendships were nourished with talk of money we expected to have, and what we intended to do when it came" (184). As Danielle Schaub argues, the openings of Gallant's stories direct the reader to their very core (140). If she had gone back to Madrid five years later, her experience would have been completely different. The cynical first sentence refuses pretense of heartfelt feelings, announces the shallow basis for the friendship which dissolves once the protagonist-narrator does receive some money. Another characteristic of the essay, as noted by Claire Obaldia, is to examine an idea from different angles (3), in a kind of dialogical approach, choosing arguments for and against. Gallant uses this procedure when discussing stereotypes about Spanish people: "Were they typical Spaniards? I don't know what a typical Spaniard is. They didn't dance or play the guitar. Truth and death and pyromania did not lurk in their dark eyes; at least I never saw it" (188).

However, **"When We Were Nearly Young"** does not meet one of the main demands of the essay. According to Claire Obaldia, the essay's essential quality is persuasion (5). A typical essay, therefore, would have allowed for a straightforward criticism of Franco's Spain, in order to persuade the reader of the Spanish dictatorship's faults, but Gallant does not want to persuade us of anything, she just presents things as they are. When I interviewed her, she admitted that "she didn't go to Spain to preach or to talk about politics but, rather, to see" (Somacarrera interview).[8] The words *Franco* and *dictatorship* are mentioned in the story, but only in an elusive commentary: "There was the Spanish situation, of course, and I had certainly given a lot of thought to it before coming to Spain, but now that I was here and down and out I scarcely noticed it" (190).

As Marcus Billson declares, "genres are essentially contracts between a writer and his audience" (260). However in the case of **"When We Were Nearly Young"**, Gallant's indications about how to read the story seem to be at odds with the generic features that emerge from a close reading of the text. Mavis Gallant insists that we should read **"When We Were Nearly Young"** as mere fiction. She also testifies to the "shifting" or instinctive nature of her aesthetic: "I've never read [my work] as something with a pattern. I can't help you there." (Hancock 24). When asked whether she was conscious about the essay-like quality of **"When We Were Nearly Young"**, she responded that "she couldn't really judge it herself" (Somacarrera interview). However, it becomes evident from my analysis that in **"When We Were Nearly Young"**, Gallant plays with the readers' and the critics' expectations and subverts generic constraints, following Barthes' definition of Text:

> The Text doesn't come to a stop with literature; it cannot be apprehended as part of a hierarchy or even a simple division of genres. What constitutes the Text is [. . .] its subversive force with regard to old classifications.

(75)

Gallant's story is not only characterized by its subversive resistance to classifications, but also by its liminality, as defined by the layering and mixing of different genres presented in my analysis. As a short story, it fits Current-García and Patrick's definition, when they say that the logic of this genre is the complex logic of mental and emotional experience, such as associative linkings, personal memories and fear and faith, rationalized reasons for behaviour and subsurface thinking that goes on (99-100).

At its outset, **"When We Were Nearly Young"** follows the principles of classical autobiography, as established by Gusdorf and Lejeune, in that it is a story about the search for one's Self with a sense of distance and retrospective view dealing with the restlessness of growing older. Gallant's preoccupation with the unreliability of memory, present not only in this story but throughout her work, is also one of the main concerns of autobiography. However, the story does not completely follow the principles of this genre, as defined by Gusdorf. The search for the Self which is typical of autobiography gives way to disorientation, a disorientation which the narrator shares with her Spanish friends. Gusdorf also observes that an autobiography aims at finding a coherent and complete expression of a destiny (35). However, **"When We Were Nearly Young"** is not coherent, as it lacks a plot and consists in a series of comments about the narrator's state of mind and her motivations for going to Spain, together with her disorganized impressions about the country and her friends. It cannot be considered a complete account of a life, but, rather, a fragment. If autobiography is the diagramme of a destiny, this story would be just a sketch of a destiny, a sketch that leaves all the questions about the protagonist's future unsolved. The "I" wonders what direction her life is going to take, but she finds no answer.

Insomuch as the story has a first person fictional narrator who tells a story which is based on personal experience, the text is auto/biographical, following the tradi-

tion of many narratives by Canadian women writers, such as Alice Munro or Margaret Laurence. The story's auto/biographical elements and its reflective tone also link it to the essay, a genre which Claire Obaldia defines as marginal and a-generic (3). Auto/biography and essay share their reliance on provisional impressions, their dialogic nature and the lack of a teleological self. The asystematic nature of the essay fits what Tamas Dobozy calls the "anarchic aesthetic" of Gallant's early and later stories (65), and so does the essay's sense of transitoriness and provisionality. The story lacks, however, the persuasive dimension of the essay, since Gallant's aim is not to criticize Franco's Spain, but, rather, to record a turning point in the narrator's life.

I hope to have demonstrated that Gallant does draw on the genres of auto/biography and essay, a-generic and problematic as they intrinsically are, and undermines them at the same time. Her generic choices, conscious or unconscious as they may be, are related to the very transgression of these genres and play a crucial role in the codification of the meaning of the story. One of the main stylistic features of Gallant's work is, in Tamas Dobozy's words, disjuncture (65). In the case of **"When We Were Nearly Young"**, since the text does not contain the full fictional account of a narrator's life, but just of an episode in her life, the short story is the adequate genre to present this fragmented and partial vision of the mystery of an "I"'s destiny. Indeed, it is well known that the short story has been Gallant's most frequent and obvious generic choice throughout her career because it provides her with an adequate form for the disjunction of her stories. That critics have found reminiscences of an essay in the story is also understandable, since the word *essay* comes from the French *essai* and *essayer*, to attempt, to experiment, to try out, and the text clearly has a tentative and loose structure. However, it is not an essay "about waiting for money in Madrid", as Douglas Malcom claims (119), but, rather, an essay about a life in a turning point. The documentary references about Madrid become a mere background which does not make any sense if they are not read in connection to the "I". The squalor of the Madrid of the fifties is the squalor of her own disoriented Self. The truth about facts is ultimately subordinated to the truth about the "I". Therefore, if I had to answer Besner's question about whether the narrator is a reporter or storyteller, I would reply that she is an auto/biographer, since generic analysis reveals that the story is not really about the Spain of the fifties, but about a failed attempt of an "I" to capture her Self.

Notes

1. Frederic Jameson in *The Political Unconscious: Narrative as a Socially Symbolic Act* argues that the inevitable layering and mixing of several genres in any text obviates the "typologizing abuses" of traditional genre theory (175).

2. See Timothy Dow Adams, "The Geography of Genre in John Glassco's *Memoirs of Montparnasse*"; Robert Thacker, "'So Shocking a Veredict in Real Life': Autobiography in Alice Munro's Stories", and Charles Hanly, "Autobiography in Alice Munro's Story 'Fits'".

3. About Gallant's use of irony, see Barbara Godard, "Modalities of the Edge: Towards a Semiotics of Irony: The Case of Mavis Gallant"; about her style and themes, George Woodcock, "Memory, Imagination, Artifice: The Late Short Fiction of Mavis Gallant"; and about her use of history, Janice Kulyk Keefer, "Mavis Gallant and the Angel of History".

4. "An Interview with Mavis Gallant" by Pilar Somacarrera, in *Atlantis,* Journal of the Spanish Association of Anglo-American Studies (XXII, 1, June 2000, forthcoming). This interview focuses on Gallant's stay in Spain and the two stories she wrote about this country. It will be referred to as "Somacarrera interview" in the text of the article.

5. All references to "When We Were Nearly Young" are from Mavis Gallant, *Selected Stories.* London, Blomsbury, 1997, and will be incorporated into the text of the article.

6. As Liz Stanley points out, the term auto/biography refuses any easy distinction between biography and autobiography, and recognises, instead, their symbiosis (127).

7. William H. New, *Modern Canadian Essays.* Toronto: Macmillan, 1976.

8. "Señor Pinedo", her other story about Spain, however, does include some oblique and understated criticism about Franco's dictatorship.

Works Cited

Barthes, Roland. "From Work to Text." *Textual Strategies: Perspectives in Post-Structuralist Criticism.* Ed. Josué V. Harari. Ithaca, New York: Cornell U P, 1979. 73-81.

Belford Ulanov, Anna. *The Feminine in Jungian Psychology and in Christian Theology.* Evanston: Northwestern University Press, 1971.

Besner, Neil. "A Broken Dialogue: History and Memory in Mavis Gallant's Short Fiction". *Essays on Canadian Writing* 33, (Fall 1986): 89-99.

———. *The Light of the Imagination. Mavis Gallant's Fiction.* Vancouver: University of British Columbia Press, 1988.

Billson, Marcus. "The Memoir: New Perspectives on a Forgotten Genre". *Genre* 10.2 (Summer 1977): 259-82.

Current-García, Eugene and Walton R. Patrick. *What is the Short Story.* Chicago, Scott-Foresman, 1961.

Dobozy, Tamas. "'Designed Anarchy' in Mavis Gallant's *The Moslem Wife and Other Stories*". *Canadian Literature* 158 (autumn 1998): 65-88.

Dow Adams, Timothy. "The Geography of Genre in John Glassco's *Memoirs of Montparnasse*". *Reflections. Autobiography and Canadian Literature.* Ed. Stich. Ottawa: U of Ottawa P, 1988. 15-25.

Gallant, Mavis. "What Is Style?". *The Paris Notebooks. Essays and Reviews.* Toronto: Macmillan, 1988. 176-179.

———. *Selected Stories.* Bloomsbury: London, 1997.

Godard, Barbara. "Modalities of the Edge: Towards a Semiotics of Irony: The Case of Mavis Gallant", *Essays on Canadian Writing* 42 (winter 1990): 72-101.

Good, Graham. *The Observing Self. Rediscovering the Essay.* New York: Routledge, 1988.

Grace, Sherrill. "Gender as Genre: Atwood's Autobiographical 'I'". *Margaret Atwood. Language and Subjectivity.* Ed. Nicholson. New York: St. Martin's Press. 189-303.

Gusdorf, Georges. "Conditions and Limits of Autobiography". *Autobiography: Essays Theoretical and Critical.* Ed. Olney Princeton: Princeton U P. 28-48.

Hancock, George. "An Interview with Mavis Gallant". *Canadian Fiction Magazine* 28 (1978): 19-67.

Hanly, Charles. "Autobiography in Alice Munro's Story 'Fits'". *Reflections. Autobiography and Canadian Literature.* Ed. Stich. Ottawa: U of Ottawa P, 1988. 163-174.

Jameson, Frederic. *The Political Unconscious: Narrative as a Socially Symbolic Act.* Ithaca: Cornell U P, 1981.

Kulyk Keefer, Janice. "Strange Fashions of Forsaking: Criticism and the Fiction of Mavis Gallant". *Dalhousie Review* 64:4, (1984-85): 721-735.

———. "Mavis Gallant and the Angel of History", *University of Toronto Quarterly* 55 (1986): 282-301.

———. *Reading Mavis Gallant.* Oxford: Oxford University Press, 1989.

Lejeune, Philippe. *Le pacte autobiographique.* Paris: Seuil, 1975.

Malcom, Douglas. "An Annotated Bibliography of Works By and About Mavis Gallant". *Canadian Fiction Magazine* 28 (1978): 110-125.

Martín, Belén. *Género literario/género femenino. Veinte años del ciclo de cuentos en Canadá.* Oviedo: RKO, 1999.

Neuman, Shirley. "Life-Writing". *Literary History of Canada* vol. IV. Ed. W. H. New. Toronto. U of Toronto P, 1990. 333-370.

New, W. H. (ed.) *Modern Canadian Essays.* Toronto: Macmillan, 1976.

Obaldia, Claire. *The Essayistic Spirit. Literature, Modern Criticism and the Essay.* Oxford: Clarendon Press, 1995.

Pascal, Roy. *Design and Truth in Autobiography.* Cambridge: Cambridge U P, 1960.

Schaub, Danielle. *Mavis Gallant.* Boston: Twayne Publishers, 1998.

Somacarrera, Pilar. "An Interview with Mavis Gallant". *Atlantis* (Journal of the Spanish Association of Anglo-American Studies), XXII (1) (June 2000, forthcoming).

Stanley, Liz. *The Auto/Biographical I,* Manchester, Manchester U P, 1992.

Stanton, Donna (ed.) *The Female Autograph: Theory and Practice of Autobiography from the 10th to the 20th Century.* Chicago: U of Chicago P, 1984.

Stich, K. P. *Reflections. Autobiography and Canadian Literature.* Ottawa: U of Ottawa P, 1988.

Thacker, Robert. "'So Shocking a Veredict in Real Life': Autobiography in Alice Munro's Stories", *Reflections. Autobiography and Canadian Literature.* Ed. Stich. Ottawa: U of Ottawa P, 1988. 153-161.

Williams, David. *Confessional Fictions: A Portrait of the Artist in the Canadian Novel.* Toronto: Toronto U P, 1991.

Woodcock, George. "Memory, Imagination, Artifice: The Late Short Fiction of Mavis Gallant". *Canadian Fiction Magazine* 28 (1978): 74-91.

Lesley D. Clement (essay date 2000)

SOURCE: Clement, Lesley D. "Towards an Illumination of Gallant's Late Fiction." In *Learning to Look: A Visual Response to Mavis Gallant's Fiction,* pp. 230-48. Montreal: McGill-Queen's University Press, 2000.

[*In the following essay, Clement traces Gallant's development as a short story writer, focusing on the stylistic aspects and thematic concerns of her later work.*]

Speaking generally of "the metaphysic that informs Gallant's vision of reality," Janice Keefer concludes that "Gallant's way of seeing is at the furthest possible remove from that of the visionary"; nowhere, Keefer contends, are there "the consolations of form, the artist's role as priest of the imagination, and the proposi-

tion that art can somehow order and make meaningful the chaos of experience."[1] Gallant's canon provides few examples of vision and illumination in the conventional sense: an artist's revelation of the unseen or elucidation of the opaque by infusing the raw material of art with a spiritual or intellectual light that kindles or sparks in the reader an intensified responsiveness and thus more enlightened outlook on life. In Gallant's earliest fiction, published in the 1940s and 1950s, characters through whom the narrative is told or reflected tend to be too myopic because too self-absorbed to acquire a perspective and sense of proportion to discern the gap between subject and object, preconception and reality; nevertheless, Gallant's readers, alert to her fiction's visual cues, are provided with fluid and multiple perspectives that permit them to bridge these gaps and so gain insight that the characters fail to attain. Gallant's fiction of the 1960s and early 1970s exposes the effects of the characters' purblindness, chiefly the dehumanization consequent upon the imposition of pattern or shape by those too incapacitated by narrow circumstances or maimed psyche to escape "the consolation of form" to which Keefer refers; thus, as with the earliest fiction, insight or illumination, while available to Gallant's responsive readers, is often closed to the characters. With the expansion of Gallant's palette as she represents her world and simultaneously celebrates and parodies it, especially in her stories of the mid and late 1970s, moments of illumination multiply for characters and readers alike. This illumination, fluid and open, resembles the impact of parody described by Linda Hutcheon: "With parody—as with any form of reproduction—the notion of the original as rare, single, and valuable (in aesthetic or commercial terms) is called into question. This does not mean that art has lost its meaning and purpose, but that it will inevitably have a new and different significance. In other words, parody works to foreground the *politics* of representation . . . post-modernist parody is a value-problematizing, de-naturalizing form of acknowledging the history (and through irony, the politics) of representations."[2]

In a world grown dark through the reductiveness caused by materialism and commercialism, traditional light effects connoting inspiration and enlightenment are inappropriate. This is apparent in the outbreaks of violence that punctuate Gallant's stories during a three-year period at the end of the 1970s and beginning of the 1980s—from the time of **"Speck's Idea"** (19 Nov. 1979) to **"Grippes and Poche"** (29 Nov. 1982)—and that then recur in stories of the 1990s such as **"In Plain Sight"** (25 Oct. 1993) and **"Scarves, Beads, Sandals"** (20 and 27 Feb. 1995). Only a writer who has guided her readers to look—and see—among even the palest and darkest and greyest shades will provide illumination and discover light in the black madness of the contemporary world and psyche. Gallant's most recent achievements re-create her world with the perspective, density, shading, coloration, and occasional muted and splintered light effects that not simply reflect and double but also refract and multiply the original.

VIOLENCE IN A COLOURLESS, STRUCTURED
WORLD: 1979-1982

Violence is particularly evident in the group of four stories anthologized in *Overhead in a Balloon*—"A Painful Affair," "Larry," "A Flying Start," and "Grippes and Poche"[3]—tied together loosely through the character of Henri Grippes, a French novelist living in Paris, and in a sequel to this quartet, **"In Plain Sight,"** that is included in *The Selected Stories of Mavis Gallant.* "Grippes and Poche," the most substantial of the five stories, focuses on the relationship Grippes develops with O. Poche, a tax controller who summons Grippes to query his financial statements and becomes his muse for a series of novels Grippes publishes in the 1960s and 1970s. Passing time is marked by the changing colour of the file folders in which Grippes's financial records are kept in Poche's office. When Grippes is first summoned to Poche's "windowless, brown-painted cubicle," France is five years into de Gaulle's presidency; Grippes's as yet meagre record is enclosed in "a duncolored folder" (130). Time passes: "The duncolored Gaullist-era jacket on Grippes' file had worn out long ago and been replaced, in 1969, by a cover in cool banker's green. Green presently made way for a shiny black-and-white marbled effect, reflecting the mood of opulence of the early seventies. Called in for his annual springtime confession, Grippes remarked about the folder: 'Culture seems to have taken a decisive turn'" (139). Later in the 1970s the black-and-white folder is replaced by one in "a pretty peach mottled shade" that darkens and fails to stand up to Grippes's annual reviews: "It was the heyday of the Giscardian period, when it seemed more important to keep the buttons polished than to watch where the regiment was heading" (140). At the story's end, with a Socialist government in power, Grippes "wonder[s] about the new file cover. Pink? Too fragile—look what had happened with the mottled peach. Strong denim blue, the shade standing for *giovinezza* and workers' overalls? It was no time for a joke, not even a private one" (147).

Ironically, the file folders in the tax office provide the colour in these stories about Paris, and the essentially colourless but structured Poche provides the inspiration for Grippes's series of novels. The novels emerge as Grippes becomes aware of "shadowy outlines behind a frosted-glass pane" and then admits these incarnations of Poche; these shadows are "turned into young men, each bringing his own name and address, his native region of France portrayed on color postcards, and an index of information" (136). Being shadows, they fail to illuminate present or future but instead represent Grippes's reactionary response and avoidance of the

contemporary world, "a slice of French writing about life as it had been carved up and served a generation before" (137). Years earlier Grippes has been deterred from moving to London by Victor Prism's obviously exaggerated but still "strange and terrifying account of gang wars, with pimps and blackmailers shot dead on the steps of the National Gallery" (103). Now Grippes is confronted with equally terrifying scenes of violence that at least partially explain his failure to confront contemporary life.

Grippes's "illumination," like Speck's, occurs one winter evening, but what seems imminent now is the final sunset rather than the brazen dawn of the earlier *Overhead in a Balloon* stories: "he crossed Boulevard du Montparnasse just as the lights went on—the urban moonrise. The street was a dream street, faces flat white in the winter mist. It seemed to Grippes that he had crossed over to the nineteen-eighties, had only just noticed the new decade. In a recess between two glassed-in sidewalk cafés, four plainclothes cops were beating up a pair of pickpockets." Grippes justifies not writing about "real life" with the argument that "to depict life is to attract its ill-fortune," but he then decides that there is a greater authority than the violence he has just witnessed: "Four gun-bearing young men in jeans and leather jackets were not final authority; final authority was something written, the printed word, even when the word was mistaken. The simplest final authority in Grippes' life had been O. Poche and a book of rules" (146-7). And so Grippes finds himself faced with a void, unable to find anything in today's world about which to write. "The frosted-glass door was reverting to dull white; there were fewer shadows for Grippes to let in"; ultimately Grippes faces "a flat-white glass door" (145-6). Grippes thinks he has found a new muse, a woman he has seen praying in a "rebel church . . . where services were still conducted in Latin," but she "moved off in a gray blur" with "a streaming window between them Grippes could not wipe clean" (148-9). To avoid fear and obsession, harbingers of madness, Grippes retreats further into the past for his subjects and inspiration; as he moves from white to grey, the black "madness" of his landscape and inscape threatens (149-50).

A change in government brings no changes to this landscape but simply hands the reins of power over to the more aggressive faction of the moment. **"In Plain Sight"** demonstrates Grippes's disillusion when the Left is given its chance to incarnate the principles to which it had been clinging for over five decades. These principles have taken the shape of "Utopia rising out of calm waters, like Atlantis emerging, dripping wet and full of promise" with "spires and gleaming windows, the marble pavements and year-round unchanging sunrise." For Grippes this image disappears when "a computerized portrait of François Mitterrand, first Socialist president of the Fifth Republic, had unrolled on the television screen, in the manner of a window blind. Grippes . . . had voted for a short list of principles, not their incarnation."[4] When they have the potential to be realized, Grippes's principles assume a new form: "Utopia was a forsaken city now, bone-dry, the color of scorched newsprint. Desiccated, relinquished, it announced a plaintive message" (878). Grippes writes well into the night an article entitled "Utopia Our Way," which he keeps "as cloudy and imprecise as his native talent could make it. Visions of perfection emerge and fade but the written word remains to trip the author who runs too fast for his time or lopes alongside at not quite the required pace" (880). Grippes is of the second variety of writer. His reconstruction of Utopia is as an imagined cinema of bygone days with leg-room, clean floors, ice cream "sold by a motherly vendor, [which] tasted of real vanilla," and audiences that applauded indiscriminately. The once "capacious theater" has "been cut into eight small places, each the size of a cabin in a medium-haul jet." Grippes's article concludes with confidence "that a drastic change, risen from the very depths of an ancient culture, would soon restore intelligible speech" (881).

Grippes's domestic problems are no less banal than his politics. Public and private are eerie reflections of one another. He is haunted by Mme Parfaire (to polish, to perfect), who wishes to play wife, mother, servant, and muse to him. Her only rival seems to be Mme Obier, who dresses "in layers of fuzzy black." For others Mme Obier may be one of "the floating shreds of his past," but for Grippes "she was the fragment of a rich cultural past," the past "of the sixties, when her flowing auburn hair and purple tights had drawn cheers in the Coupole." It is little wonder that Grippes, shadowing his older women friends across "the line to a final zone of muddle, mistakes, and confused expectations" (870-1), discovers that his resources and inspiration are growing dim. The story concludes: "his goddess is a victim of the times, hard up for currency and short of ideas, ideas of divine origin in particular. She scarcely knows how to eke out the century. Meanwhile, she hangs on to 'Residents are again . . . ,' hoping (just as Grippes does) that it amounts to the equivalent of the folding money every careful city dweller keeps on hand for muggers" (887).

Alternative images connoting inspiration in **"In Plain Sight"** offset these final allusions to devalued currency and testy notices penned to fellow tenants. "As an inventor of a great number of imaginary events Grippes knows that the reflection of reality is no more than just that; it is as flat and mute as a mirror. Better to sound plausible than merely in touch with facts" (885). What provides Grippes with the inspiration to forge links between past and present, personal and public, memory and history, inner and outer, imagination and fact, is an inexplicable two-toned siren, which for older Parisians "has the tone and pitch of a newsreel soundtrack. They think, Before the war, and remember things in black-and-white." This siren interweaves with Grippes's sleeping dreams and thus keeps his "rare bursts of political optimism in perspective . . . with a mixture of dread and unaccountable nostalgia: the best possible mixture for a writer's psyche" (868). Depending solely on verbal memory stimulated by the garishness of his immediate surroundings—clouds that have "soaked up the lights of Montparnasse and gave them back as a reddish glow," moths that "beat about inside the red shade" of his desk lamp—Grippes finds himself plagiarizing words he has heard and read (881-2). He finally digs into his remembered past and recreates a visual image, rather than a verbal account, that has the immediacy and originality to blend imagination and fact and so to illuminate and validate the narrative it sparks. Grippes begins to shade in a drawing he has been sketching of "a tall Renault, all right angles, built in the thirties, still driven in the early forties by black-market operators and the police. He shaded it black and put inside three plainclothes inspectors" (882). The drawing becomes mobile in his memory as the car approaches his grandparents' farm and, after young Henri has inadvertently betrayed his grandfather, as it leaves with his handcuffed grandfather. The young Henri has given the police the clue they need to the whereabouts of his grandfather's contraband money when he suggests that they look "in the dark and in plain sight" (883).

With his structured men and pious women Grippes has avoided the dark and thus the light that the abysses of memory and history might shed on his life in contemporary Paris. In **"Grippes and Poche"** Grippes's series of novels inspired by Poche has earned him acclaim and popularity with readers of every type: "The shoreline of the eighties, barely in sight, was ready to welcome Grippes, who had re-established the male as hero, whose left-wing heartbeat could be heard, loyally thumping, behind the armor of his right-wing traditional prose" (*Overhead in a Balloon,* 141-2). Later, when Poche has deserted him as muse, and Grippes is considering whether the pious woman he has seen praying will be his next, he wonders if "he could get away with dealing with her from a distance. All that was really needed for a sturdy right-wing novel was its pessimistic rhythm: and then, and then, and then, and death. Grippes had that rhythm" (148). Now, years later, in **"In Plain Sight"** the siren's two tones split rather than mesh, and Grippes still favours the linear form: "He could hear two distinct tones and saw them as lines across the sky: a shrill humming—a straight, thin path—and a lower note that rose and dipped and finally descended in a slow spiral, like a plane shot down . . . the somewhat deeper note fell away quite soon; the other, more piercing cry streamed on and on, and gradually vanished in the bright day" (*Selected Stories,* 885-6).

In "these leaden times" (876) Grippes has failed to discern the spiralling silver plane, preferring the linear movement that he thinks connects past to present to future . . . and death. For Grippes the siren remains "a long ribbon of sound [that] unwinds in his sleep," and he cannot capture the image on paper. He cannot transpose visual to verbal: "Everything is gray-on-gray—pavement, windows, doorways, faces, clothes—under an opaque white sky. A child turns toward the camera—toward Grippes, the unmoving witness. Then, from a level still deeper than the source of the scene rises an assurance that lets him go on sleeping: None of this is real." The call goes unheeded. Although he associates the air-raid siren with his war years on the farm with his grandparents and in Paris after his betrayal of his grandfather, he cannot trace how or why he makes this association: "it still belongs to black-and-white adventures—in a habitual dream, perhaps to peace of a kind" (874). The image of the "silvery plane" (874, 875), also associated with the air-raid siren, is from "the slow, steady swindle of history and experience" (882) that he denies: it is from the war films he saw in his youth, "the best historical evidence his waking mind can muster" (874), and the sites of films being shot in contemporary Paris in which "a silvery plane . . . follows its own clear-cut shadow over the heart of Paris" to incite the "authentic" appearance of "panic in the streets" (875).

For Grippes, the silvery, downward-spiralling plane remains simply a metaphor to describe the lower tone of the siren. The only effect that an awareness of the greys has on him is to make him wary of donning his newly cleaned, apple-green plastic jacket "acquired a whole generation ago. The jacket might seem too decorative for these leaden times—it is the remnant of a more frivolous decade . . . but it is not shabby. Shabbiness arouses contempt in the world outlook of a goon. It brings on the sharp edge of the knife" (876). As the bohemian auburn hair and purple tights of Mme Obier are of the past, so too the apple-green jacket; he instead seriously considers the option of the "rose velvet" middle-class respectability of Mme Parfaire, which would not only provide him with well-cooked meals and vigilant caretaking but also "stop the downward spiral of her dreams," which implicate him in sinister intrusions on her life (878, 886).

In contrast, Gallant's muse continues to spark the imagination, and Gallant herself to illuminate life around her—past and present, history and contemporary events—material that while perhaps "in the dark" is also "in plain sight." Nor has she, as Grippes, mired in a "sturdy right-wing" prose rhythm of "and then, and then, and then, and death," reached a stalemate. Instead, she has caught the movement of the silvery plane, not just plummeting but levelling off, rising, dipping, looping. Emulating the movement of a plane rather than the restricted linear movement of the hot-air balloon, her muse has inspired her to reflect and refract the world around her with the perspective, density, shading, coloration, and illumination, however subdued and fragmented, essential to escape flat reproductions that fail to be plausible.

"Visions of Perfection" Illuminated

While reflecting and refracting contemporary scenes and issues, **"Speck's Idea"** and **"Overhead in a Balloon"** parody the metaphoric conception of the illuminative function and significance of art, and hence its visionary potential. When Speck considers the structure of his spring show, his first thought is that "it might be worthwhile lacquering the walls black, concentrating strong spots on the correspondence, which straddled half a century, from Degas to Cocteau."[5] This correspondence is as much an invention as the artist to whom it is addressed: "Populist yet refined, local but universal, he would send rays, beacons, into the thickening night of the West, just as Speck's gallery shone bravely into the dark street" (8). In Cruche, Speck thinks he has found the artist to give lustre to "the comforting lights of the gallery" (7), but Speck's lights are eclipsed by the derrick lights, shop windows, and brassy radiation of commerce and industry more powerful than his small gallery. For Walter art is a rival to religion as a form of creation, "a dabbling in colors, sentiment cut loose and set afloat by the sight of a stained-glass window" (60). In a world in which "we have stopped trusting our feelings" and "been shown not only the smile but the teeth" (9), the gleaming white animal smile of Lydia Cruche emerging victorious out of the dark with her battered black umbrella raised as a trophy (44-5) could well ensure the failure of art to guide, sustain, or illuminate.

With the more delicate, mellow tones of the Magdalena quartet, the only lights that seem to blaze are those of the checkpoint when the train is brought to a stop; however, once these are seen to be "dull and brown,"[6] other lights, mostly artificial, to compensate for the lack of natural light, are perceived as providing the consolation of companionship and community: Magdalena with her "sunny hair" (154) and "sunny" nature (157); the harsh yellow star that stands out "on top of some folded silk things the color of the palest edge of sunrise" (156); Édouard and Juliette's L-shaped apartment, so dark that "the lights [were] turned on all day in winter," and their studies, from which they "could look out and see the comforting glow of each other's working life, a lamp behind a window" (162-3). Édouard thinks art to be antithetical to these lights and sense of community. As Magdalena and Édouard part at Marseilles, he inserts a book of poetry between them because "poetry is meant for one reader only. Magdalena, gazing tenderly down from the compartment window, must have seen just the shape of the poem on the page. I turned away from the slant of morning sunlight—not away from her . . . I stuck to our promise and never once raised my eyes. At the same time, I saw everything—the shade of her white hatbrim aslant on her face, her hand with the wedding ring" (160).

Édouard prefers to move in shadows, given the damage he has inflicted on the lives of the two women he loves and the exposure that full light might impart. When Juliette learns that Édouard has seen Magdalena several times more than the once he admits to, she scrutinizes him closely, as she would the American novels she translates, and has one of her "unexpected visions. Just now, it was as if three walls of the court outside had been bombed flat. Through a bright new gap she saw straight through to my first marriage. We—my first wife and I—postured in the distance, like characters in fiction" (165). Appropriately Édouard makes documentary television series, having given up any aspirations he had as a young man to write novels about characters who fail to recognize that they are "all dead . . . in a special Hell, made to measure" (171): "Because I can't wrench life around to make it fit some fantasy. Because I don't know how to make life sound worse or better, or how to make it sound true" (174). He instead enters his own Hell made to measure, the life of "one of those uneasy, shadowy couples, perpetually waiting for a third person to die or divorce" (181). Only after Juliette dies does he brave "the flat, shadeless light of [the suburban] line . . . said to attract violent crime" (177) to visit his now infirm "poor, mad, true, and only wife," Magdalena, but he still spurns the illumination that her "pure love" might spark (187). In contrast, Juliette has sought and discovered "a different coloration to her manner, a glaze of independence, as though she had been exposed to a new kind of sun," when, after travelling alone to America, she returns and demands an interview with Magdalena (181). This interview may bring nothing but her recognition and acceptance that "those who outlasted jeopardy had to be covered" (165), but this "chink of light"[7] sustains her and confers on her a certain dignity in her sacrifices and disappointments.

The same stoicism and moderation, which come with hardship and experience, and therefore the same mellow colours and flickering lights emerging from darkness, whiteness, and greyness, pervade *Across the Bridge*. The opening quartet—**"1933," "The Chosen Husband," "From Cloud to Cloud,"** and **"Florida"**[8]—is typical. The final two stories are dominated by the relationship between Raymond and the Carette sisters, Marie and Berthe, Raymond's mother and aunt respectively. Raymond, the perpetual adolescent decked out in his silver and white cowboy suit, still clings to "the summer of 1969, for the ease with which he jumped from cloud to cloud" with a mother and aunt who doted on him: "Berthe thinks of how easy it must have been for Raymond to leave, with the sun

freshly risen, slanting along side streets, here and there front steps sluiced and dark, the sky not yet a burning glass . . . When she and Marie ransacked the house on Boulevard Pie IX, looking for clues, imagining he'd left a letter, left some love, they kept the shades drawn, as if there were another presence in the rooms, tired of daylight" (41). This other presence is that of Marie's deceased husband, Louis, the intricate arrangements leading to their marriage being the subject of **"The Chosen Husband."** Raymond's last memories of his father are of him "dying of emphysema, upright in the white-painted wicker chair, in blazing forbidden sunlight." Louis spends his last days with "gaze upturned . . . as if . . . seeking divine assistance," staring "at a moon in sunlight, pale and transparent—a memory of dozens of other waning moons" (34). Raymond, attracted by a recruitment advertisement on television picturing "a swaying carpet of jungle green, filmed from a helicopter," has enlisted to fight in the war in Vietnam (39). Father and son both are burnt out from this futile seeking of something of significance in barren landscapes.

In **"Florida"** Marie and Berthe also seek something of significance through their gaiety and symbols of affluence. Marie dresses for a paltry Christmas dinner at Raymond's latest seedy Florida motel venture in her hibiscus-patterned chiffon and her red sandals, and boasts of Berthe's red and gold Christmas tree and of her sister's purchasing power: Berthe buys her own fur coats, the latest "a mink coat (pastel, fully let out)" (46-8). Marie returns from Florida "dressed in a new outfit of some sherbet tone—strawberry, lemon-peach—with everything matching, sometimes even her hair" (43). Little has changed since, as young women in **"The Chosen Husband,"** Marie and Berthe dressed alike in marine blues, reds, and whites (13-14, 21, 22, 28). Only on the day that Louis comes to propose marriage is Marie dressed in colours of mourning—she wears Berthe's mauve and black kimono with a mauve chiffon scarf over Berthe's aluminium curlers—but she immediately changes into "Berthe's white sharkskin sundress and jacket and toeless suède shoes" (27). Like garish splashes of colour on a neutral background, these women fail to find "grounding," and Marie absorbs and then transmits to Berthe "silvery shocks"—"like a small silver bullet"—every time she visits Florida (51, 44, 43). Even the "paper-white narcissi on Marie's dressing table, a welcome-home present [from Berthe] reflected on and on in the three mirrors . . . absorbed a charge and hurled it back" (44).

In contrast with the representatives of these later generations is Mme Carette, mother of Berthe and Marie, portrayed in **"1933"** and **"The Chosen Husband"** in mauves and dove greys—"the colors of half-mourning" (5, 14)—shades that blend with the "whitish stone" of the houses with front steps "painted pearl-gray, to match the building stone" in the respectable part of Montreal where they live (13, 16): "She wore the neutral shades of half-mourning, the whitish grays of Rue Saint-Hubert, as though everything had to be used up—even remnants of grief" (21). Mme Carette is attired in the colours that best complement the black and white snapshots in which her image is captured and the memory she ultimately will become, the only "eternal" life she may attain: "The wedding party walked in a procession down the steps and around the corner: another impression in black-and-white. The August pavement burned under the women's thin soles . . . Three yellow leaves fell—white, in a photograph" (30). Berthe, the spinster aunt, is both inside and outside this picture, as she will be both inside and outside the new family that forms when Marie leaves to live with her husband in a different part of town: "Berthe saw the street as if she were bent over the box camera, trying to keep the frame straight. It was an important picture, like a precise instrument of measurement" (31).

"Forain" (24 June 1991) depicts a similar failure of bright lights and colours to blend with or complement the "leaden" tones of a world poised between darkness and light. Blaise Forain (he is French, although his surname might suggest otherwise), publisher of translations of East European literature, has a premonition of the final "blaze" his company will likely experience since "the destruction of the Wall—radiant paradigm—had all but demolished Forain" (123). He has just attended the funeral of the brightest light in the "Blaise Editions" firmament, Adam Tremski: "Every light in the city was ablaze in the dark rain. Seen through rivulets on a window, the least promising streets showed glitter and well-being . . . Suddenly, although he had not really forgotten them, Forain remembered the manuscripts he had snatched back from Halina . . . What if there were only a little, very little, left to be composed? . . . Filling gaps was a question of style and logic, and could just as well take place after translation" (128-9). Forain goes ahead with his publication of Tremski's text, and despite his doubts about the translated and edited version, "a posthumous novel-length manuscript of Tremski's was almost ready for the printer, with a last chapter knitted up from fragments he had left trailing" (130). The gaps have been filled by translator, editor, and reader, but since the revisions depend solely on "style and logic," we are left to wonder how faithful Forain has remained to Tremski, to what degree the text illuminates the novel *The Cherry Orchard,* "with a moody description of curses and fistfights as imported workers try to install a satellite dish in the garden," that Forain himself has considered writing (124-5).

Among the stories of *Overhead in a Balloon* and *Across the Bridge,* **"A State of Affairs"** (23 Dec. 1991) emerges as the one most closely approximating the balancing of celebration and parody of Gallant's stories of

the mid- and late 1970s. The story excels in its effective use of second person to augment Gallant's characteristic third-person narration; the reader is therefore more directly addressed as inside and outside, unseen and seen, dark and light are threaded into ever-changing positions and relationships. The perspective is flexible and fluid, unlike **"The Concert Party"** (25 Jan. 1988) and **"Mlle Dias de Corta"** (28 Dec. 1992 and 4 Jan. 1993), in which the effect of second-person narration is solely absurd. In **"The Concert Party"** the narrator, Steve Burnet, assumes a second-person perspective to address Harry Lapwing, a man he dislikes: "I thought that if I could not keep my feelings cordial I might at least try to flatten them out, and I remembered advice my Aunt Elspeth had given me: 'Put yourself in the other fellow's place, Steve. It saves wear.'"[9] Steve's experiment is unsuccessful: the "you" is capricious and obtrusive, and Harry Lapwing is as distasteful to Steve (and reader) as when the experiment began. All the "flattening" has succeeded in doing is bringing out Steve's old grudges and peevishness.

In **"Mlle Dias de Corta,"** the drawing of the reader into the text is parodied as, throughout the story, the narrator addresses an actress who once boarded with her and who has become pregnant and then been abandoned by the narrator's son. The narrator has been prompted to write to this woman when, after many years, she sees her on a television commercial: "The shot of your face at the oven door, seen as though the viewer were actually in the oven, seemed to me original and clever. (Anny said she had seen the same device in a commercial about refrigerators.) I wondered if the oven was a convenient height or if you were crouched on the floor" (155). In both examples the narrators' literalness in interpreting the world through other eyes flattens, frames, and eventually skews perspective and proportion. As Steve, in **"The Concert Party,"** switches back from second to first person, he concedes: "In plain terms, this is not a recollection but the memory of one, riddled with mistakes of false time and with hindsight" (35). Once again, the concept that art has illuminative potential is parodied.

In contrast, the beautifully balanced proportions and modulated shifts of **"A State of Affairs"** complement the lucid perspective that illuminates M Wroblewski's "state of affairs," so avoiding the ludicrous perspectives that mar these other two stories. In the opening pages of **"A State of Affairs,"** "you" is introduced simply to reinforce the narrator's appeal to readers to put themselves in the scene and imagine or see the contemporary "state of affairs" as Wroblewski perceives it. As the story shifts gently and gradually into the mind of Wroblewski, the "you" embraces both reader and Wroblewski's correspondent, an old friend who has remained in Warsaw. The scenes shift more and more inwards after Wroblewski has received a long letter from his friend that tells of a death threat he has received in response to his talking on radio of his wartime ghetto experiences. His friend attributes this hatred to human nature: "On that score, nothing has changed . . . It is in the brain, blood, and bone. I don't mean this for you. You were always different." Wroblewski takes his friend's comment as "a compliment, yes, but no one wants to be singled out, tested, examined, decreed an exception" (132), and so his anecdotes and observations become an argument to convince his friend that there is hope of redemption and salvation through the goodness of human nature. "He had been holding silent conversations with no one in particular for some time. Then the letter came and he began addressing his friend. He avoids certain words, such as 'problem,' 'difficulty,' 'catastrophe,' and says instead, 'A state of affairs'" (139).

When, at the end of the story, the narrative shifts entirely to Wroblewski's monologue, the positions of reader and Warsaw correspondent completely overlap. We have been drawn into the "state of affairs" of this man who apologizes for being "boringly optimistic," even though he recognizes that there are distorted minds responsible for death threats and shouts of "Hitler lives!" This story is of a survivor to a survivor, and when Wroblewski ends with "I may have more to tell you tomorrow. In the meantime, I send you God's favor" (147), we feel that although, like his wife, he may be advancing to senility, it is not dementia, and that his optimism and blessings are warranted. Lucid and responsive, sane yet aware of the potential for madness, poised between light and dark, the perspective is quintessentially Gallant.

Two versions of dawn in the story illuminate a reading of the light effects, particularly as associated with this theme of sanity and madness. The first comes with reference to Wroblewski's wife, Magda, who has lost all track of time and place: "She is poised on the moment between dark and light, when the last dream of dawn is shredding rapidly and awareness of morning has barely caught hold. She lives that split second all day long" (134). As Magda sinks further and further into memories of the past, her dawn is an extension of the night and the dreams it produces. In contrast, the second version of dawn is that of Wroblewski himself, who, recognizing the banality of evil and suffering, fears neither past nor present: "Shreds of episodes shrugged off, left behind, strewed the roads. Only someone pledged to gray dawns would turn back to examine them. You might as well collect every letter you see lying stained in a gutter and call the assortment an autobiography" (136).

What, then, are the "chinks of light" in which Wroblewski expresses confidence (132)? What are these chinks of light that illuminate the grey dawn rather than recede into the blackness of night and madness? Wrob-

lewski depends on these chinks of light because he lives in a bureaucratic world whose acts of charity are a parody of giving and receiving: the mayor's boxes of Christmas chocolates distributed to the elderly, dutifully collected despite their being unwanted and so staggeringly large that they are impossible to store (137); or the revocation of the television tax of a man who has simply "filed an affidavit" declaring his penury, "here, in Paris, where every resident is supposed to be accounted for; where the entire life of every authorized immigrant is lodged inside a computer or crammed between the cardboard covers of a dossier held together with frayed cotton tape" (138).

Moreover, Wroblewski lives in a world whose colours he no longer recognizes. The coloured snapshots of relatives in Canberra that he receives from his wife's niece are of total strangers, and so he files them in large brown envelopes (131). When he receives a letter from "a Mme Carole Fournier, of Customers' Counselling Service" at his bank offering him a cash credit of fifteen thousand francs, he sees the gift as "a bright balloon with a long string attached. The string could be passed from hand to hand—to the bank and back. He saw himself holding fast to the string" (141-2). This balloon and string, he discovers, he is too old to receive. At the bank, he is in a red, white, and blue world that excludes him as much as does the termination of the Nansen passports, which until recently had entitled Wroblewski and other Polish political refugees to reside in France for nearly fifty years (139). On the "cerulean surface" of the bank's computer screen, he can read facts about himself: "Her computer, like all those he had noticed in the bank, had a screen of azure. It suggested the infinite." The red plastic rims of Mme Fournier's glasses match the two red combs in her hair. Her office is "a white cubicle with a large window and no door" and "white lateral blinds at the window." Outside the bank is a familiar world, but inside the colours complement the interrogation rather than the welcome that the letter implied he would receive (143). In contrast are the inviting white awning and umbrellas at a favourite neighbourhood café, the Atelier in Montparnasse, reminding him of "the South, when Nice and Monaco were still within his means and not too crowded . . . He can retrace every step of their holiday round . . . a change into spotless, pressed clothes—cream and ivory tones for Magda, beige or lightweight navy for him. An apéritif under a white awning" (136). The comfortable familiarity of this memory again contrasts with a recent excursion his doctor has ordered him to take after he has "had a dizzy spell in the street and had to enter a private art gallery and ask to sit down. (They were not very nice about it.)" Wroblewski has gone to Saint-Malo, "alone in a wet season." He has visited Chateaubriand's grave, on which Sartre had urinated and "from the edge of the grave took the measure of the ocean": "He left the grave and the sea and started back to the walled city. He thought of other violations and of the filth that can wash over quiet lives. In the dark afternoon the lighted windows seemed exclusive, like careless snubs" (142).

In Saint-Malo there is no pretence of Wroblewski's being anything but an outsider, whereas the bank has trifled with its customers' desire to be special, part of an exclusive circle or club. Wroblewski, enticed by the deceptively affable tone, thinks that the cash credit might prove useful to his wife after he has died and before the will is settled. When he first approaches Customers' Counselling Service, he continues to feel welcome, as Carole Fournier's "profile reminded him of an actress, Elzbieta Barszczewska. When Barszczewska died, in her white wedding dress, at the end of a film called *The Leper,* the whole of Warsaw went into mourning" (143). As the cordial and gracious atmosphere turns into that of an interrogation, Wroblewski and Mme Fournier, understanding that the system has made them both dupes, refuse to let the system undermine their humanity and dignity. Mme Fournier, "touch[ing] her talisman, Gemini, as if it really could allow her a double life: one with vexations and one without," apologizes to Wroblewski and tells him he should not worry about "the problem" of his death. Nor is Wroblewski a comic figure in the silly charade the bank has inflicted upon him: "He adjusted his hat at a jaunty angle. Everything he had on that day looked new, even the silk ascot, gray with a small pattern of yellow, bought by Magda at Arnys, on the Rue de Sèvres—oh, fifteen years before. Nothing was frayed or faded. He never seemed to wear anything out" (146).

Wroblewski does not ignore the darkness that threatens, nor does he attempt to ward it off in dignified but meaningless poses and gestures. He is only too aware of "the dark riddle of the man and the death letter" that his Warsaw friend has received (133), the "violations and . . . the filth that can wash over quiet lives" (142), the darkness towards which his wife's mind is drifting, and his own "problem" of impending death. He cannot fail to be reminded of this darkness with the tower of Montparnasse shadowing the neighbourhood in which he lives and the cafés he frequents. His courage to confront the tower sustains him, a quality nourished by his cultural experiences, confused as some of his memories of names and dates of these may be. It does not matter whether it was the announcement of the death of President de Gaulle or President Georges Pompidou that, on his sixty-sixth birthday, brought to a close a performance of *Ondine* in which Isabelle Adjani (perhaps) played her first important part. "It is history," and what remains is the collective gasp of the audience (144). The movie in which Barszczewska starred may not have stirred all Warsaw to mourn, but the memory still connects Wroblewski to a city that he has long departed.

At the end of the story he writes to his friend: "Please take good care of yourself. Your letters are precious to me. We have so many memories. Do you remember *The Leper,* and the scene where she dies at her own wedding? She was much more beautiful than Garbo or Dietrich—don't you think?" (147) Even if his friends, the Polish political refugees in Paris, have had their Nansen passports revoked and are now "stateless," some have and can still make their small contributions. Of the three people Wroblewski mentions (all aged between eighty-one and eighty-eight), only a "former critic of East European literature" has "at some point [fallen] into a depression and [given] up bothering with letters." An engraver "who still works in an unheated studio on the far side of Montmartre" converses with Wroblewski about the best strategy to take to counteract this new "state of affairs." A third, an artist, has given Wroblewski the greatest gift of all. She "once modelled a strong, stunning likeness of Magda. She could not afford to have it cast, and the original got broken or was lost—he can't remember. It was through a work of art that he understood his wife's beauty. Until then he had been proud of her charm and distinction. He liked to watch her at the piano; he watched more than he listened, perhaps" (139-40).

Wroblewski is not himself an artist, nor has he made any direct contribution to the arts—before retiring, he taught French at the Polish high school—but he has developed an artist's ability to see beauty, "chinks of light," in a world where the sordid and banal threaten to close the gaps and extinguish the light. The first "evidence" that Wroblewski presents to his friend of a world where redemption is possible is the conjectured small gesture of the owner of Chez Marcel, who "would remember them, offer free glasses of cognac with their coffee: jovial, generous, welcoming—One Europe, One World." Even in the Atelier, which opened in the 1980s but which Wroblewski thinks of as "the new place"— "It seems to have been in Montparnasse forever"—has newspapers "on wooden holders, in the old way" and patient, usually courteous waiters (132-3). The Montparnasse tower, unlike the azure or cerulean computer screens suggesting infinity but spawning only facts, reflects and re-creates a landscape that can be imaginatively grasped: "Across the street the mirrored walls of the building that now rises above the Coupole reflect an Île-de-France sky: watered blue with a thin screen of clouds." Wroblewski imagines his friend confronting him with assembled memories that contradict his reading of this re-created scene: "His friend in Warsaw is completely alert, with an amazing memory of events, sorted out, in sequence. If he were here, at this moment, he would find a historical context for everything: the new building and its mirrors . . . Who, after hearing the voice of an old man over the radio, could sit down and compose a threat? . . . his friend might say: I have seen his face, which is lean and elegant. What do you still hope for? What can you still expect? So much for your chinks of light" (133).

Wroblewski holds fast simultaneously to the world around him and to his vision of it. He confronts the darkness of the looming black tower—itself as powerless as the blue computer screen, itself simply a reflection—and finds colour and light and life as images flow pass and are caught and multiplied in its black mirrored surfaces: "I will go out and meet you, or the thought of you, which never quits me now. I will read the news and you can tell me what it means. We will look at those mirrored walls across the boulevard and judge the day by colors: pale gold, gray, white-and-blue. A sheet of black glass means nothing: it is not a cloud or the sky. Let me explain. Give me time. From that distance, the dark has no power. It has no life of its own. It is a reflection" (147).

CONCLUSION: A VISUALIZATION AND CELEBRATION OF THE UNSEEN

In the preface to *Encounters: Essays on Literature and the Visual Arts* (1971), one of the first successful collections "to explore the encounters between literature and the visual arts," John Dixon Hunt, arguing against a formulaic approach to these encounters, observes that while all the essays in the collection "provide literary texts with visual analogues that illuminate their creative or cultural origins and meanings," each essay "determines its own method and comparativist criteria."[10] The next step, Hunt believes, will be "assessing the procedures and results of such case histories" so that "the critical possibilities of any larger scheme of relationships between art and literature [can] begin to emerge."[11] The dangers inherent in critical approaches that draw parallels between literature and the visual arts—"at their least successful there emerges a rather arbitrary series of *correspondences,* almost a parlour game of analogies in which the two forms are shuffled for more intriguing juxtapositions"—are equally formidable even with writers who have been directly influenced by the visual arts, Hunt warns.[12] Yet he encourages critics to pursue these lines of investigation: "just because it is difficult to isolate clearly how a writer has used structures learnt from the visual arts or how words may be deployed in place of images it seems no reason to shirk what can be for several literary works and events a crucial encounter with the visual arts."[13]

Over a decade later James Heffernan edited *Space, Time, Image, Sign: Essays on Literature and the Visual Arts* (1987), a collection of essays growing out of a conference held at Dartmouth College in 1984 that was mandated "not simply to make specific comparisons across the borderline between the arts, but to scrutinize the borderline itself, to raise explicitly theoretical questions about the complex relations between images and texts."

As a theoretical text, this collection was to establish "new principles of comparison" between the pictorial and literary arts and so augment previous "juxtapositional or periodic" studies of the relation between the sister arts, studies that "have analyzed the way in which a particular picture resembles, recalls, or influences a particular text that is juxtaposed with it, or . . . have tried to explain how a given set of pictures and texts together define a particular historical period."[14] With this and similar works that have followed these two pioneer collections of essays, critics have reached no consensus on theoretical principles on which to base comparisons between literary and visual arts,[15] and so we are left with the text, with the picture.

Martin Jay's essay "Vision in Context: Reflections and Refractions" (1996) begins with the observation: "The model of 'reading texts,' which served productively as the master metaphor for postobjectivist interpretations of many different phenomena, is now giving way to models of spectatorship and visuality, which refuse to be redescribed in entirely linguistic terms."[16] An examination of Gallant's fiction contributes substantially to the ongoing theoretical debates about "the complex relations between images and texts." Gallant's early fiction challenges the traditional distinction between the visual arts as spatial and the literary arts as temporal.[17] Later, we see her fiction challenging the boundaries that critics have erected between the visual arts, thought dependent on ocular perception of the external world, and the literary arts, thought dependent on mental conception of an inner world. Throughout, the greatest challenge that Gallant's fiction issues to those who would erect boundaries between the sister arts is a great strength: a style that makes visible the invisible through gaps and absences in texts that stimulate the reader-spectator's imagination; a style that inspires us to picture things not there but that are prestructured by the language of the text. Wolfgang Iser writes: "Communication in literature . . . is a process set in motion and regulated not by a given code but by a mutually restrictive and magnifying interaction between the explicit and the implicit, between revelation and concealment. What is concealed spurs the reader into action, but this action is also controlled by what is revealed; the explicit in its turn is transformed when the implicit has been brought to light."[18]

Arthur Danto paraphrases Paul Klee's observation "that art does not render the visible but renders visible, which means that we see by means of art something not to be seen in other ways, something in effect that must be made visible," and concludes that "art attains here the level of thought, and the artwork is a thought given a kind of sensuous embodiment."[19] Gallant expresses a similar point when, in the preface to her *Selected Stories,* she contemplates "the shock of change" that often instigates the "impulse to write" and contributes to "the stubbornness needed to keep going": "Probably, it means a jolt that unbolts the door between perception and imagination and leaves it ajar for life, or that fuses memory and language and waking dreams. Some writers may just simply come into the world with overlapping vision of things seen and things as they might be seen" (xiv-xv). Throughout the five decades of her writing career, the visual properties of Gallant's style have evolved from what Woodcock describes as her ability to create an "impeccable verbal texture and [a] marvellous painterly surface of the scene imagined through the translucent veil of words, the kind of surface that derives from a close and highly visual sense of the interrelationship of sharply observed detail."[20]

From her earliest explorations of displacement and the disparity between perception and reality, through her later explorations of memory and history, to her more recent explorations of the role of culture in a contemporary world where commercialism and madness threaten to extinguish the potential for illumination and enlightenment, Mavis Gallant has exercised powers of envisaging and rendering the world—"things seen and things as they might be seen"—parallel to the ways that the artist sees and re-creates it. She challenges her readers to look and respond through allusions, analogies, and structures suggesting the lines, shapes, and colours that confer on her fiction the perspective, proportion, density, and fluidity to illuminate the printed page. Engaged in these visual properties of Gallant's fiction, we acquire a heightened percipience of the manifold richness of worlds and lives that may otherwise have been relegated to the unseen and unsung.

Notes

1. Keefer, *Reading Mavis Gallant,* 22.

2. Hutcheon, *The Politics of Postmodernism,* 93-4.

3. The *New Yorker* publication dates for these four stories are as follows: "A Painful Affair" (16 Mar. 1981), "Larry" (16 Nov. 1981), "A Flying Start" (13 Sept. 1982), and "Grippes and Poche" (29 Nov. 1982). All references to these stories are from Gallant, *Overhead in a Balloon.*

4. Gallant, *Selected Stories,* 877.

5. Gallant, *Overhead in a Balloon,* 10.

6. Ibid., 155.

7. The phrase "chinks of light," from "A State of Affairs" (*Across the Bridge,* 132, 133), will be found in several passages quoted later in this chapter. Unless otherwise indicated, all further references, given in textual parentheses, are to *Across the Bridge.*

8. "1933" was published as "Déclassé" in *Mademoiselle* (Feb. 1987). The remaining three were pub-

lished in the *New Yorker:* "The Chosen Husband" (15 Apr. 1985), "From Cloud to Cloud" (8 July 1985), and "Florida" (26 Aug. 1985).

9. Gallant, "The Concert Party," 32.

10. Hunt, ed., preface to *Encounters,* 7, 9-10.

11. Ibid., 9.

12. Ibid., 9-10.

13. Ibid., 10.

14. Heffernan, ed., preface to *Space, Time, Image, Sign,* xiii.

15. Ibid., xiv. The editors' preface to *Word and Visual Imagination,* ed. Höltgen, Daly, and Lottes, remarks that "the relationship between word and visual imagination, or word and image, is a topic that continues to excite considerable interest. This interest manifests itself in conferences, journals and publications" (5), which are then duly mentioned (5-7). Although the studies in this particular collection attempt "to illuminate the variety of literary experience through the interaction of the verbal and visual in given works," they "may be regarded as case histories of different modes of interaction of the verbal and visual": "In the search for answers we cannot readily apply models deriving from either linguistics or communications theory as though they were monolithic systems" (7-8).

16. Jay, "Vision in Context," *Vision in Context,* ed. Brennan and Jay, 3.

17. In his foreword to *Spatial Form in Narrative,* ed. Smitten and Daghistany (1981), Joseph Frank writes: "Critical ideas are even more notoriously short-lived than most of the literature that gives rise to them; but the stubborn longevity of my youthfully audacious conjectures seems to indicate that they managed to hit on something central to the modern (and even postmodern) situation of literature in our time" (11).

18. Iser, *The Act of Reading,* 168-9.

19. Danto, "Description and the Phenomenology of Perception," *Visual Theory,* ed. Bryson, Holly, and Moxey, 211.

20. Woodcock, "Memory, Imagination, Artifice," 74.

Works Cited

Works by Mavis Gallant

Overhead in a Balloon: Stories of Paris. Toronto: Macmillan 1985.

Across the Bridge: New Stories. Toronto: McClelland and Stewart 1993.

The Selected Stories of Mavis Gallant. Toronto: Mc-Clelland and Stewart 1996.

SECONDARY SOURCES

Danto, Arthur C. "Description and the Phenomenology of Perception." In *Visual Theory: Painting and Interpretation,* ed. Norman Bryson, Michael Ann Holly, and Keith Moxey. Cambridge: Polity Press, 1991.

Heffernan, James A. W., ed. *Space, Time, Image, Sign: Essays on Literature and the Visual Arts.* New York: Peter Lang 1987.

Höltgen, Karl Josef, Peter M. Daly, and Wolfgang Lottes, eds. *Word and Visual Imagination: Studies in the Interaction of English Literature and the Visual Imagination.* Erlangen: Univ.-Bibliotek Erlangen-Nürnberg 1988.

Hunt, John Dixon, ed. *Encounters: Essasys on Literature and the Visual Arts.* London: Studio Vista 1971.

Hutcheon, Linda. *The Politics of Postmodernism.* London: Routledge 1989.

Iser, Wolfgang. *The Act of Reading: A Theory of Aesthetic Response.* Baltimore: Johns Hopkins University Press 1978.

Jay, Martin. "Vision in Context: Reflections and Refractions." In *Vision in Context: Historical and Contemporary Perspectives on Sight,* ed. Teresa Brennan and Martin Jay. New York: Routledge 1996.

Keefer, Janice Kulyk. *Reading Mavis Gallant.* Toronto: Oxford University Press 1989.

Smitten, Jeffrey R., and Ann Daghistany, eds. *Spatial Form in Narrative.* Ithaca: Cornell University Press 1981.

Woodcock, George. "Memory, Imagination, Artifice: The Late Short Fiction of Mavis Gallant." *Canadian Fiction Magazine* 28 (1978): 74-91.

Janice Kulyk Keefer (essay date 2002)

SOURCE: Keefer, Janice Kulyk. "'Radiant Paradigms and Chinks of Light': Mavis Gallant's Polish Émigrés in Paris." In *Varieties of Exile: New Essays on Mavis Gallant,* edited by Nicole Côté and Peter Sabor, pp. 37-48. New York: Peter Lang, 2002.

[*In the following essay, Keefer assesses "Forain" and "A State of Affairs" as literary achievements.*]

"If we are moved by a story, it has meant something, perhaps something important to us; if we are not moved, then it is, as story, meaningless" (Geddes, 817). I've adapted this remark of T. S. Eliot to remind us that

whatever our theoretical orientation or critical practice, we must be passionate readers—resistant, yes, but also responsive to what complex literary texts have to offer us, attentive to the terms they work within. It behooves us, in other words, to be moved by what we read, and what we choose to write upon.

"Forain" and **"A State of Affairs,"** two of Mavis Gallant's more recent stories, seem to me to be among the most moving works in her oeuvre—moving precisely because of the obliquity with which she approaches the inherently elegiac nature of her subject: the last remnants of the Polish émigré community in Paris—those émigrés who arrived, that is, in the decade following the end of World War II. Perhaps I find these texts particularly moving because of my own "Polish connection," or perhaps it is because of the tenderness with which Gallant describes the love between husband and wife in both stories, and the attention she pays to what Irving Layton, in his elegy for Keine Lazarovitch, has called "the inescapable lousiness of growing old" (Geddes, 210). At any rate, I hope to offer you a reading of **"Forain"** and **"A State of Affairs"** that will illuminate how these stories mean and how they move us.

The fictive worlds Gallant creates in these texts are structurally complex, ironically charged, historically engaged, and the prose through which those worlds unfold is, as always, beautifully intelligent. **"Forain"** and **"A State of Affairs"** are in some ways mirror images of each other, with the important difference that the former is told from the point of view of Blaise Forain, a dubious Parisian publisher of Eastern European literature in translation, while the latter is given us from the perspective of Mr Wroblewski, an elderly Polish émigré, whose occasionally mistaken perceptions, not always reliable memories, and fictionalizing desires make him in some ways as problematic a focalizer as Blaise Forain.

"Forain" opens on a leaden winter day, with the funeral of Adam Tremski, a Polish Jew who has perished of "mortal grief" (*Selected Stories,* 637) at the death, not long before his own, of his wife Barbara. Mr Wroblewski, of **"A State of Affairs"**—the phrase is his euphemism for words like "problem," "difficulty," "catastrophe" (648)—is in precarious health and his wife Magda is afflicted by Alzheimer's, though the disease is never named as such. Both Tremski and Wroblewski are historically marked men: Wroblewski, though not Jewish, survived internment at Dachau—what Tremski went though during the war is alluded to by a charcoal portrait of him done in June 1945: "a face that had come through: only just" (638). Barbara, who left her Polish officer husband for life with the seedy, entropic Tremski, rescuing him from his hopeless incapacity for business, and Magda, a former musician and teacher, are women of exemplary intelligence and beauty: stunning in their youth, they retain their attractiveness and elegance in old age. Their husbands deserve them, *tout court*: they possess an integrity and selflessness that make them two of the most sympathetic men in Gallant's oeuvre. When Tremski falls apart after Barbara's death, becoming incapable of shaving or putting his false teeth in; when Mr Wroblewski lies to a friend in Warsaw about the conversation on Schubert he's just held with the minimally capable Magda, it breaks your heart. The marriages between Adam and Barbara, Maciek and Magda are defined by mutual love, loyalty, and respect—qualities rare enough to find between the numerous husbands and wives depicted in Gallant's fiction.

"All that is personal soon rots; it must be packed in ice or salt," or so Yeats advises us (*Selected Poetry*, XX). Masterful touches of ice and salt are provided in **"Forain"** and **"A State of Affairs"** in ways which bring to mind Nabokov's use of irony and satire to camouflage the outright tenderness with which, for example, he represents Krug's wife and child in *Bend Sinister*, or his own wife and child in *Speak Memory*. In her exposure of the unscrupulousness of a publisher more concerned with the profit than with the poetic motive, and her introduction, into the lives of the Wroblewskis, of a bank official who first offers and then withdraws a vital service which would have eased Mr Wroblewski's mind regarding his invalid wife, Gallant deflects our attention from the pathos of the émigrés to the complexities and ironies of the contexts—social, cultural, historical—in which that pathos achieves such memorable expression.

Elegy, in other words, goes hand in hand with exposure, with the utterly deft critique of social forms and values that has always distinguished not only Gallant's fiction, but also her early journalism, and the essays and narratives collected in *Paris Notebooks*. Thus in **"Forain,"** our glimpse of the generation of old, post-war Polish émigrés, in mourning not only for lost friends "but for all the broken ties and old, unwilling journeys" (627) is supplemented by a succinct, caustic view of the new, post-Wall generation of mobile or migrant Poles who come to Paris not to escape persecution, but to lead more exciting, and more materially rewarding lives. The "thin, pretty girl, part of the recent, non-political emigration" who comes to work for Forain's company has no compunctions about faking the last chapter of Tremski's unfinished manuscript, or about "spreading the story that Forain had been the lover of Barbara" (641). However wittily presented, these falsifications of Tremski's manuscript and of Barbara's memory bring to mind that signal act of desecration referred to in **"A State of Affairs"**—Sartre's urinating on Chateaubriand's grave at St-Malo.

The "filth that can wash over quiet lives," the "violations" of ordinary human decency (650) are linked by Gallant not only to Sartre's clownish gesture, and, more

chillingly, to the anti-semitism which still erupts in Warsaw, but also to the surveillance and harassment of immigrants in contemporary Paris, immigrants without the cachet of the Polish émigrés, with their Nansen passports. In **"Forain,"** Gallant gives us a glimpse of "lines of immigrants standing along the north side of central police headquarters" with "Algerians in a separate queue" (638). She singles out the Portuguese taxi driver intimidated by Forain at the end of the story, and the waiter who cheats Forain of his wine at a café—a young, clumsy man with "coarse fair hair: foreign, probably working without papers, in the shadow of the most powerful police in France" (638). The xenophobia of the French, the plight of the involuntarily "displaced and dispossessed" (629) to which Gallant has drawn our attention for the past forty years or more—that these issues find a place in **"Forain"** bears witness to the inclusiveness of Gallant's vision, the rigorous nature of her sympathy, which refuses to restrict itself to whatever is in moral fashion. In **"A State of Affairs,"** we are reminded that "In Paris [. . .] the entire life of every immigrant is lodged inside a computer or crammed between the cardboard covers of a dossier held together with frayed cotton tape" (647). This kind of scrutiny is presumably an advance upon conditions "in the old days," when refusal of applications for French citizenship by people like the Wroblewskis "was so consistent that one was discouraged at the outset" from applying (649). Though Marie-Louise, sent by the city's social services to help care for the helpless Magda, has automatic French citizenship due to her birth in Martinique, what Gallant emphasizes as a donnée of contemporary Parisian life is the radical insecurity that afflicts the lives of migrants, whether from Poland or Algeria. As Gallant presents it in **"Forain"** and **"A State of Affairs,"** Paris is a city of highly selective light, of corporate castles and child beggars.

. . . . .

Among the new wave of arrivals from Lech Walesa's Poland, **"Forain"** shows us, are scholars seeking out their displaced compatriots in order to chronicle and evaluate what has ceased to be lived experience and become "history": "Scholars who looked dismayingly youthful, speaking the same language, but with a new, jarring vocabulary [. . .] taping reminiscences, copying old letters" (628). Yet their subjects, instead of feeling gratitude at this validation of their lives, are not impressed: "History turned out to be a plodding science. What most émigrés settled for now was the haphazard accuracy of a memory like Tremski's" (629).

Adam Tremski, of course, is Gallant's invention. He is the most distinguished of Forain's "flock" (634) of East and Central European émigré writers—unlike the others, he could have found a better publisher, just as he could have moved up from the shabby, standard-issue émigré apartment he still occupied at his death. Nevertheless he does not join "the leviathan prophets, the booming novelists, the great mentors and tireless definers" lionized in the West (634), but remains in the company of those "self-effacing, flat-broke writers who [had] asked only to be read, believing they had something to say that was crucial to the West, that might even goad it into action" (637). Gallant doesn't spare these ingenuous, unworldly writers any irony: we learn that even the intelligent Tremski believed that a "great new war would leave central Europe untouched. The liberating missiles would sail across without ruffling the topmost leaf of a poplar tree." Ingenuousness, however, is matched by a wry embrace of sauve-qui-peut: "As for the contenders, well, perhaps their time was up" (637).

Gallant is especially perceptive about the plight of those writers, who, much to Blaise Forain's chagrin, continue long past 1989 to write "stories in which Socialist incoherence was matched by Western irrelevance" (636). Though these accounts of the "East-West dilemma" may be of historical value, their critique of 'the Way of the West' still valid, they are unmarketable, and thus unpublishable. Besides, even in the heyday of the Cold War, most Western readers and not been able to keep straight the names of Forain's various writers, and reviewers had rarely mentioned their work. Now the barbarism of the French reading public (635) is aggravated by the no less barbaric dictates of the Market Economy, for which money and memory have become interdependent. When the Berlin Wall came down, we learn, it brought with it the fortunes, such as they were, of Blaise Editions, causing an irreversible and catastrophic decline in sales. Whereas the Wall can be "hammered to still smaller pieces and sold all over the world," the work of Forain's authors can't. The satiric edge of Gallant's humour makes the situation more rather than less emphatic, as analogies are drawn between the (presumed) End of Communism and Vatican II's axing of the traditional Mass, so that publishers of prayer books in Latin and of "subtle and allusive stud[ies] of corruption in Minsk," circa 1973 (636), stand side by side in bankruptcy court. As for the members of Forain's flock, they would seem destined for the fate of double disappearance, their manuscripts rotting unread as they themselves die off.

Blaise Forain is one of the more hapless and engaging of Gallant's rogues: initially, at least, it is his honesty that quiets our unease at the way he operates. If he is "unreliable" (634) about paying his flock of writers their dues, it is not to get rich at their expense. He has "next to no money," we are told, and is "in continual debt to printers and banks" (634); quite sensibly, he needs to turn a profit—equally sensibly, he would prefer to be given the cash spent by Central and European embassies on gold medals and lavish receptions to mark the cultural service he has rendered to the "other Eu-

rope." If it is a question of medals or money, there is no question—despite the fiction in government circles that "trade and literature are supposed to have no connection" (635). But at certain points after Tremski's death, we are made aware of how the publisher is compromising his already-fraught integrity. Not only does Forain toy with the idea of effectively cannibalizing the lives and work of his "flock" to produce a "sly, quiet novel teasingly based on" [Chekhov's *The Cherry Orchard*] and set in the new, unified Germany (636), but a year after Tremski's death, Forain persuades himself that the man who'd made him his literary executor would have approved of the last chapter of an unfinished manuscript being "knitted up from fragments he had left trailing" (641). But even worse than Forain's publishing of Tremski's adulterated manuscript is his shift of allegiance from the Tremskis to the writer's stepdaughter, the crassly resentful, unintelligent Halima. When he catches himself in this act of disloyalty, Forain promises himself, head bowed as if in prayer, that "he would keep in mind things as they once were, not as they seemed to him now" (641)—a crucial task, one would think, for someone who "wanted every work he published to survive in collective memory, even when the paper it was printed on had been pulped, burned in the city's vast incinerators or lay moldering at the bottom of the Seine" (635). Forain's pious gesture at the end of this story, however, only leads him to "make a fool of himself to no purpose" (641), becoming a confrère of Halina's father who had fought a "war for nothing" (632).

. . . . .

The problematic role played in **"Forain"** by the preserver, disseminator, and adulterator of Tremski's work is transformed in **"A State of Affairs"** to the less complex intervention of a Fournier, rather than a Forain—the bank employee who summons Mr Wroblewski to her office to present him with a gift far more useful than the Christmas chocolates distributed to the elderly every year by the Mayor of Paris. This gift is a cash reserve from which he can draw, at times of need, without paying interest. The soul of courtesy, Mr Wroblewski undergoes an interview with Carole Fournier, explaining how important this cash reserve will be for his wife, should he predecease her. But when Mme Fournier learns Mr Wroblewski's age, and calculates the cost to him of undergoing the medical examinations the bank would demand of him, she withdraws the offer. Perhaps the émigré's only gain from the interview is a memory triggered by the sight of Carole Fournier's profile—the memory of Elzbieta Barszczewska, a wildly popular Polish actress of the interwar years. This incident seems trivial compared to the fact exposed at the end of the interview—that Mr Wroblewski's greatest problem is his own inevitable and impending death (654). And yet, on the story's final page, it is to Barszczewska that Wroblewski alludes in the poignantly deceptive letter he composes to his friend in Warsaw, summoning the shared memories of their youth.

Carole Fournier is, of course, a far less important and malign presence than Blaise Forain, but her embarrassment and panic at Mr Wroblewski's allusion to the fact of mortality have a particular significance. For Fournier is the product of an age in which azure computer screens, not God, "sugges[t] the infinite" (651), and where the mirror-glass of office towers masquerade as the sky. The information age, and the age of market values, Gallant seems to suggest, are anathema to both the preservation of memory and the consciousness of history: the antithesis to the computer screen in Fournier's office is, of course, the exchange of letters between Mr Wroblewski and his friend in Warsaw—the "dead" letters, too, which Magda writes, letters which, we are told, would be perfectly apropos if they'd been written forty-five years ago.

Mr Wroblewski's persistent connection to his unnamed correspondent in Warsaw—the thought of whom, he confesses, never quits him (654), is the trace, in this story, of that "angel of history" which haunts so much of Gallant's fiction—memory not as nostalgia, or passive reflection of the past, but as the painfully active desire to "stay in place, resurrect the dead and reconstruct the wreckage" (Lichtheim, 12). The memory of Mr Wroblewski's Warsaw friend is "completely alert" (643), so that the hate mail and death threat he receives after speaking in a radio broadcast of his experiences in the Warsaw ghetto reconfirm his earlier experiences of Polish anti-semitism as something bred in "the brain, blood and bone" (642). Mr Wroblewski's own memory—and conscience—is alert enough to catch, in his friend's disclaimer—"I don't mean this for you. You were always different" (642)—a distressing echo of what Wroblewski himself may have said to this same friend some fifty years ago, when the vilification of Jews was rampant in Poland: "Naturally you are completely different: I'm talking about all the others" (643).

That an elderly man should be sent a death threat for recalling to public memory horrific events and the shameful prejudices which contributed to those events is "the dark riddle" (63) woven into **"A State of Affairs,"** one which grimly counterpoints the donnée of the story—an elderly man's impending death "in a foreign city" (631). And it is no accident that the collective amnesia which has seized hold of post-Wall Europe—if not entrenched long before—is foregrounded in **"Forain."** Barbara's daughter from her first marriage is unable or unwilling to convey the importance of Tremski's work to her French husband, or to their twelve-year-old daughter. Unlike Magda Wroblewski, whom memory has abandoned except in cruelly selective ways, Halina chooses not to know, and not to remember. She is not alone, of course, as we learn from one of the story's more devastating aperçus:

> It was remarkable, Tremski had said, the way literate people, reasonably well travelled and educated, comfortably off, could live adequate lives without wanting to know what had gone before or happened elsewhere.
>
> (630)

Among the literate are journalists who substitute "a few names, a date looked up, a notion of geography" (631) for a sustained form of historical consciousness.

Any such consciousness is, of course, dependent on memory, which, as Gallant's oeuvre has so convincingly shown, is notoriously capricious or unreliable, and yet which remains crucial to the preservation of human decency and dignity. Memory is dependent, in **"Forain"** and **"A State of Affairs,"** on the material as well as the imagined: the Nansen passports Mr Wroblewski is so apprehensive about surrendering to the State, the 1950s apartment Tremski refuses to quit: "two rooms on a court, windowless kitchen, splintered floors, unheatable bathroom, no elevator, intimidating landlord" (628). Tremski's attachment to the physical traces of the past is his way of keeping faith with memory. It seems entirely fitting that Forain's prayer for the repose of Tremski's soul comes in the form of a mental inventory of the contents of the writer's apartment. There is something unbearably poignant about this list of objects soon to vanish—layers of coats on pegs, boots and umbrellas, unread newspapers and journals, shelves of books and empty or overflowing files, and photographs of friends from the 50s and 60s. The unopened crates and boxes littering the place remind us of Tremski's essential homelessness, that he never seemed really to have moved into this apartment where he lived for some forty years (640). The table that serves for both writing and eating, the narrow couch that doubles as Halina's bed, the window providing "the sort of view that prisoners see" (637)—all of these remind me of the dismally cramped apartments one finds in former Soviet bloc countries, and in which all too many people are still compelled to live out their lives.

In **"A State of Affairs,"** the equivalent of, or counter to, Tremski's apartment, is the bust of Magda made by an impoverished émigré sculptor. Because the work was never cast, no trace of the likeness remains, for the original was lost or broken long ago. The absence of this material record of Magda's youth is especially devastating to Mr Wroblewski, since it was through this work of art, we learn, that he first came to understand his wife's beauty (648). But it's not just the loss of the distant past, but the erasure, as well, of the immediate past that Mr Wroblewski finds so distressing—the unexplained cutting down, for example, of a stand of trees in his neighbourhood, an absence which, ironically, the otherwise oblivious Magda points out to him.

In this context, then, the demolition of the Berlin Wall becomes especially significant. Hateful as it was, the wall offered what Forain calls a "radiant paradigm," whereby the world could be divided, with Manichean neatness, into good and evil, truth and lies, the desirable and the abominable. With the disappearance of the Wall, more is lost than Blaise Forain's solvency: the paradigm it offered may have been fictive, but it formed a focus for that moral discourse Auden describes in "September 1, 1939"—those "ironic points of light" that "Flash out wherever the Just/Exchange their messages" (*Selected Poems*, 89)—the kind of discourse Tremski and his fellow émigré writers helped to sustain.

In **"A State of Affairs,"** that "radiant paradigm" has shrunk to mere "chinks of light" (643)—what Mr Wroblewski would like to show his Jewish friend to displace the "dark riddle" of racial hatred. Were this friend able to travel to Paris, Mr Wroblewski believes, he would encounter the "jovial, generous, welcoming" mood of "One Europe, One World" (643), a Europe in which no one will suffer for being thought a stranger, a foreigner, an outsider. In Mr Wroblewski's fantasies, the two elderly men would sit together in a Montparnasse café to discuss "the news and [. . .] what it means" in a world that can be judged by something as innocuous as the colours reflected by the glassed office buildings: "pale gold, gray, white and blue" (654). It is not difficult to construe what Mr Wroblewski's friend, given his "amazing memory of events," his ability to supply a "historical context for everything" (643), would make of such "chinks of light" as the new Europe affords. The endings of **"Forain"** and **"A State of Affairs"** offer ironic parallels between the deceptions and disloyalty practiced by Blaise Forain towards Adam Tremski, and the heartbreaking lies told by Mr Wroblewski to his Warsaw friend about Magda's fine health and his own unruffled state of mind.

. . . . .

"In the end it was always a poem that ran through the mind—not a string of dates."

(629)

The poem that runs through **"Forain"** and **"A State of Affairs"** is an elegy for the "displaced and dispossessed" (628). I would like to end this paper by looking at the imagery of darkness and light through which this poem comes to haunt Gallant's prose, and to move us towards a perception of our own moral riddles, our own mortality.

Most of the mourners at Adam Tremski's funeral are elderly Polish émigrés, some of whom have "migrated to high-rise apartments in the outer suburbs, to deeper loneliness and cheaper rents" (630).

Some had spent all these years in France without social security or health insurance, either for want of means or because they had never found their feet in the right sort of employment. Possibly they believed that a long life was in itself full payment for a safe old age. Should the end turn out to be costly and prolonged, then, please, allow us to dream and float in the thickest, deepest darkness, unaware of the inconvenience and clerical work we may cause.

(632-3)

That "thickest, deepest darkness"—a dearly-earned oblivion—makes the "glitter and well-being" (640) of material prosperity in Paris more than a little suspect: though "Every light in the city [may be] ablaze in the dark rain" (640), we can infer that to most émigrés these "lighted windows see[m] exclusive, like careless snubs" (651). In **"A State of Affairs"**, we learn how the Wroblewskis have put behind them the "gray dawns" of emigrant neediness, the begging—but not the crawling—for "enough to eat, relief from pain, a passport, employment" (646). Yet between the azure computer screen of Carole Fournier and the mirror facade of the Montparnasse tower, "a sheet of black glass [that] means nothing" (654), what is there for them to choose?

Writing to his friend, Mr Wroblewski tries to disarm the "dark riddle" that continues to plague them both: "From that distance," he urges, "the dark has no power. It has no life of its own. It is a reflection" (654). In Paris together they will "exchange visions through the afternoon and into the evening, with the lights inside the café growing brighter and brighter as the trees outside become part of the night" (644). Mr Wroblewski's visionary fantasy is comparable to his wife's delusion that there is a musician playing Schubert all night long in the neighbouring apartment. And yet the limbo in which Magda's loss of memory has stranded her is a constant warning to her husband: "She is poised on the moment between dark and light, when the last dream of dawn is shredding rapidly and awareness of morning has barely caught hold. She lives that split second all day long" (644). For both their sakes, Mr. Wroblewski must "hold to his side of the frontier between sleeping and waking" (647) for as long as he can.

Given so much darkness—the anxiety and despair of these émigrés' old age, their poverty or financial worries—and given the suspect glitter of the city's lights, what do they offer us, those ironic illuminations Gallant presents to us—the radiant paradigm of the Berlin Wall, the chinks of light proffered by the New Europe? Perhaps it is only the lessons we can draw from them, if we are capable of doing so—that the radiance stemmed from an untenable simplification of moral possibilities, and the chinks of light from self-protective blindness: that reality, with or without quotation marks, is far more complex, ambiguous, paradoxical than we can bear to admit. We can remember here those qualities of contradiction and irresolution that distinguished Adam Tremski, a Jew who may have been "a true convert" to Catholicism, or "just a writer who sometimes sounded like one," a man who "could claim one thing and its opposite in the same sentence" (629). We can also remember the consoling truth devised by Mr Wroblewski at the end of **"A State of Affairs"**: "A sheet of black glass means nothing: it is not a cloud or the sky" (654).

Perhaps these lessons—what we remember of what has moved us—give us light enough to see by: just.

Bibliography

Gallant, Mavis. *The Paris Notebooks. Essays and Reviews by Mavis Gallant.* Toronto: Macmillan, 1968 and 1986.

———. *The Selected Stories of Mavis Gallant.* Toronto: McClelland and Stewart, 1996.

Yeats, W. B. *Selected Poetry,* ed. Timothy Webb. London: Penguin, 1991.

Barbara Gabriel (essay date fall 2003)

SOURCE: Gabriel, Barbara. "The Wounds of Memory: Mavis Gallant's 'Baum, Gabriel (1935-),' National Trauma, and Postwar French Cinema." *Essays on Canadian Writing,* no. 80 (fall 2003): 189-216.

[*In the following essay, Gabriel uses the tropes of French cinema and national trauma in order to explore issues of memory and history in Gallant's "Baum, Gabriel, 1935-( )."*]

. . . I already am quite rich with significant dates.

—Sigmund Freud, letter to Wilhelm Fliess, 30 May 1896

While history and memory have long been seen as central to the fictional landscape of Mavis Gallant, what has largely been overlooked is the extent to which their twinning is reflected in seismic shifts in the field of historiography itself. The growing interest in the writing of collective memory provides one important index of this new turn within a constellation of concerns that becomes even more complex when it is folded into the problems posed by national trauma. Nearly all of the literature of trauma since Freud agrees that events unassimilable to immediate experience are marked by repression and belatedness. Yet can there be such a thing as *national* trauma? If so, then how can we connect it to the more sedimented practices of communal memory that constitute the thinking around "nation"? The French historiographic turn to history as memory operates in a line of inheritance from the *Annales* historians to figures such as Maurice Halbwachs and Jacques Le Goff, but it is the concept of *lieux de memoires* posed famously by Pierre Nora in his monumental seven-volume

study that may be most productive for thinking through the notion of national trauma. Nora argues that France's memory of itself is stitched up at a range of "sites" or "places" that are, at once, physical and symbolic. My own sense, following this lead, is that national trauma is most productively understood as a *blessure de memoire,* not so much a collectivity of individual wounds, in short, as a tear in the phantasmatic of "nation." What it shares with more traditional notions of trauma are the temporal delays and displacements that register its arrival as historical event.

The comic surface of Gallant's **"Baum, Gabriel (1935-)"** belies the complex issues of national memory and traumatic history played out through the two central characters of this major short fiction. The title figure, whose dates are laid out at the start like an unfinished tombstone, will soon enough be the last of the Baums, a personal inheritance of loss traced against the historical cataclysm of the European Holocaust. In turn, his best friend, Dieter Pohle, is a young German who lives out the troubling of memory and history of the immediate postwar generation. The two make their living as actors in Paris, alternately taking up their historical roles and changing places by performing in films about the Second World War that proliferated in the 1960s and 1970s in France.

On the face of it, this is a history at a comic second remove, a narrative in which the historical roles of the villains and victims of history have already been effaced from living memory. What seems to take its place is a male buddy movie about two exiles down and out in Paris, chronicling their shared girlfriends and acting jobs, along with the vagaries of day-to-day existence. Yet a closer look at the cinematic backdrop of this story tells us that the past has not been forgotten, after all, and that there is another kind of national history as well as another kind of archive at stake in this complex fiction. These films themselves occupied an important role in the construction of French popular memory of the war, ranging from a wave of resistance films designed to cover France's historical complicity under Marechal Petain in Vichy to the films of the 1970s that, following Marcel Ophuls's breakthrough documentary, *The Sorrow and the Pity* (1969), provoked a more critical confrontation with the collaborationist regime of wartime France.

My reading of **"Baum, Gabriel (1935-)"** at the coordinates of national trauma and French cinema will recover the extent to which Gallant—long understood as a writer attentive to both memory and history—was writing history as resurgent memory at the precise moment when this historiographic shift was emerging in postwar France. In fact, while the challenges posed by an enlarged understanding of history are at the centre of her fiction, in the cinematic intertext of **"Baum, Gab-**

riel (1935-)," they write this coming to memory in terms of the very medium that broke through the wave of national repression. Given her own early years as a film reviewer as well as a journalist for the Montreal *Standard,* along with her description in the preface to **The Selected Stories of Mavis Gallant** of her own fiction typically beginning in a rush of images like "unedited film" (xvii), this alertness to the cultural site that provoked French anamnesis about its wartime collaboration is hardly surprising. Yet, as always in Gallant, this play on history and memory, dispersed over a range of comic as well as tragic tonalities, charts a fictional landscape in which to remember *forgetting* is to enter an intensely ethical field.

. . . . .

[I]t was not until May that the last of the Baums tried on his uniform.

—Mavis Gallant, **"Baum, Gabriel (1935-)"** (466)

On the face of it, the comic surface of the story tests the limits of representation around the historical event that has frequently been regarded as posing a crisis of the incommensurable.[1] Yet, long before Italian director Robert Begnini ventured a comedy of the death camps, both Chaplin and Brecht had turned to comedy to lampoon the figure of Hitler himself, while Isaac Bashevis Singer had woven a threnody of loss and pain through characters who are both death-haunted Holocaust survivors and caught up in the erotic farce of love triangles. Like Singer, Gallant refuses the generic demands of history as melodrama in favour of layered character and event. Where she departs from the Nobel prize-winning writer's own frameworks is in unrelenting attention to the stubborn particulars of history.

The structure of **"Baum, Gabriel (1935-)"** is explicitly that of Brechtian tableau, with each episode both setting up and sometimes ironizing events unfolding decade by decade. As an actor himself, Gabriel plays a Brechtian season that alternates *Mother Courage* and *The Caucasian Chalk Circle* for an "audience of schoolchildren and factory workers brought in by the busload, apparently against their will" (455). It is an aside that points up some of the self-delusions of the contemporary French left, but, like nearly all of the allusions in the story, it also has a precise historical referent, this time in ideological debates about popular culture and education in France that had been inaugurated at the time of the Popular Front government of the 1930s (Rigby 39-67). The opening tableau, entitled "Uncle August," establishes some of the central contours of the story in its account of Gabriel's meeting with his only surviving relative. Unlike his father and mother, Uncle August "had got out of Europe in plenty of time," his sidestepping of destiny of a piece with his commercial adroitness as a man who "owned garages in Rosario and Santa Fe and commercial real estate in Buenos Aires" (452). With his pre-First World War German manners, his old-fashioned British clothes, and his Swiss watch and luggage, he is "a tight, unyielding remainder of the European shipwreck" (453).

The turn of phrase sums up what is usually regarded as Gallant's preeminent theme: the changing maps and borders as well as the torn-up human rubble of the long Second World War, whose consequences spiral forward to the collapse of the Berlin wall in the stories of **Across the Bridge.** The label on the brandy bottle that August stares at evokes "cities whose names have been swept off the map: Breslau 1884, Dantzig 1897, St. Petersburg 1901" (453). Yet what Gallant understands is that this Uncle August, with his tattered remains of a life firmly tucked into place as identity, adheres all the more strongly to the waning belief system of the old order. Face to face with his only surviving relative, he bullies him with questions about his legitimacy, when and where his parents were married, in a counterpointing of bourgeois morality with historical catastrophe that propels the former into the no-man's-land of the absurd. Soon enough, Gabriel will receive word from Argentina about this uncle's death. What follows is a memorial in his head whose image in marble he silently inscribes:

Various Baums: Gone

Father: 1909-1943 (probably)

Mother: 1912-1943 (probably)

Uncle: 1899-1977

Gabriel B: 1935-

(455)

Against the casual comedy of Uncle August, this memorial tucked away "where it could not be lost or stolen" returns us to the dark undercurrents of history (456). As a character, Gabriel seems to be curiously devoid of affect. He spends his days with other out-of-work actors in a Montparnasse *bar-tabac* awaiting calls for television appearances as an extra, just as his theatre performances consisted of five or six lines of play text. Yet this minor actor, who is equally a bit player in history, also lives out his life at a second remove. He will soon meet up with a Bavarian fellow actor of the same age, Dieter Pohle, sharing casual acting assignments that culminate in the two friends playing out their historical roles as German and Jew in French films about the Second World War. What they also have in common is a habit of treating the women in their lives with casual abandon, less cads than inured to the affective content of relationships altogether. Yet this pale imitation of a life masks more turbulent emotions that ripple up from the past. Bereft of a language for his situation, Gabriel somatizes trauma in his body in symptomatic complaints that surface during his uncle's interrogations about the past.

This buried history as psychoanalytic case history is by no means unique in Gallant. Since her earliest fiction, categories of repression and displacement have been staged in narratives whose realist surfaces are frequently broken up by lacunae, creating puzzle pictures that, on closer inspection, mime unconscious processes.[2] For the orphaned Gabriel, the neon lights of La Meduse glow warmly in the polluted winter fog, "the lights of home" (455). Yet the full intensity of this historical scar is rendered only obliquely. Gabriel is drawn to the German girl Liselotte "as to a blurred reflection, a face half-recalled" (456). As in Gallant's play text, *What Is to Be Done?*, women are sidelined in triangulated relations that cover up the intensity of intermale bonds. Yet even this layer of social comedy cannot mute the inchoate despair of Gabriel's inner life. Numbed by the cataclysm that turned him into history's orphan, Gabriel imagines that everyone's life is "like a half-worked crossword puzzle" (456). As in the classic psychoanalytic account, that which cannot be remembered is condemned to be repeated as Gabriel finds himself irresistibly drawn to Liselotte, a dimly recalled image from the past. Embarked "on the au-pair adventure, pursuing spiritual cleanness through culture, she could be seen afternoons in the Parc Monceau reading books of verse . . ." (457). He had "promised the child-Gabriel he would never marry a German, but it was not that simple; in a way she did not seem German enough" (457).

Half hidden in the folds of this tragicomic text is a narrative of the death in life of the trauma survivor. Like witnesses of Hiroshima, Holocaust survivors experience the dulled memory of what is inadmissible to consciousness. In his study of Hiroshima, historian and psychologist Robert Jay Lifton enlarged the very notion of "survivor."[3] As in the case of observers of shell shock in the Great War, the earliest scene of an enlarged institutional discourse of psychic trauma in the twentieth century, it became clear that wounding extended far beyond those who were physically injured. In the end, Lifton turned to the term *hibakusha*, a direct translation from the Japanese, meaning "explosion-affected person" (qtd. in Higgins 34). All of Gabriel's relations are marked by the penumbra of loss and numbing that is his historical inheritance. Like his fellow "bachelor orphans" who share his hangout, Gabriel clings to the *bar-tabac*, La Meduse, as a surrogate home, but this stability turns out to be illusory when the establishment changes commercial hands and posts a sign after the Yom Kippur War that "Owing to the Economic Situation no One may Sit for more than Thirty Minutes over a Single Order" (463). Dieter remarks matter-of-factly: "That sign was the end of life as we knew it in the sixties" (463). In the same way, Gabriel's relationship with Liselotte ends in an emotional draw when she gives up on Paris and returns home to Germany. Throughout the story, Gabriel can only inhabit the borrowed clothes of others' lives; as he stands at the grey platform to see her off,

the "train was blurred, as if he were looking at it through Liselotte's tears" (458). In the final tableau, the whole fragile architecture of his existence comes crashing down when Dieter announces that he has bought a bakery in his native town and is going home to the Bavarian countryside. In a cartoon rendering of Gabriel's response to this impending loss, the green of the park turns to a "dull color, as if thunderous clouds had gathered low in the sky" (470). Yet, when Dieter tells Gabriel of the room set aside for him, he is once more recalled to life: "The greens emerged again, fresh and bright. He saw the room that could be his. . . . He saw, in a lime press, sheets strewn with lavender. His clothes hung up or folded. His breakfast on a white tablecloth, under a lime tree. A basket of warm bread, another of boiled eggs. Dieter's wife putting her hand on the white coffee pot to see if it was still hot enough for Gabriel" (470).

In the oscillation between the comic and the tragic that marks the whole of the story, the deliberate ironies of the way in which this shared male fantasy depends on women quickly give way to the shadowy drama of the past. His childhood trauma revives in the form of the younger Gabriel, who thrashes around in his heart "outraged and jealous," saying, "Think about empty rooms, letters left behind, cold railway stations washed down with disinfectant, dark glaciers of time" (470). As in **"The Four Seasons,"** which opens *From the Fifteenth District,* time operates on more than one plane in the text. Against the precise chronological unfolding of public history is the indeterminate movement backward and forward between past and present, inner and outer time. Also conspicuously at stake is the layered meld of conscious and unconscious processes. All of the traumatic vectors of Gabriel's life, in which personal history merges seamlessly with catastrophic European history, are allotted to the "younger" Gabriel and surface unbidden at unpredictable intervals as the renewed experience of loss and abandonment.

In his own evolving work around traumatic neuroses, Freud moved from a thinking of neurosis as stalled memory to a model in which the symptom itself is a mode of memory (Wollheim 36). It is this bodily archive that is replayed persistently in **"Baum, Gabriel (1935-)"** in a mode of memorializing that is out of place as well as out of time. While Gabriel is strangely silent in the intrusive interview with his only surviving relative, what cannot be spoken is registered somatically:

> He suffered from only two complaints, which he had never mentioned. The first had to do with his breathing, which did not proceed automatically, like other people's. Sometimes, feeling strange and ill, he would realize that heart and lungs were suspended on a stopped, held breath. Nothing disastrous had come of this. His second complaint was that he seemed to be

haunted, or inhabited, by a child—a small, invisible version of himself, a Gabriel whose mauled pride he was called on to salve, whose claims against life he was forced to meet with whatever thin means time provided, whose scores he had rashly promised to settle before realizing that debt and payment never interlock. His uncle's amazing question and the remark that followed it awoke the wild child, who began to hammer on Gabriel's heart.

(453)

In Adorno's resonant phrase to describe his own postwar exile, Gabriel's is a "damaged life." Yet clues for the recovery of this selfhood torn asunder are dispersed throughout the story, traced in disjunctive fragments in which past and present collide. Each tableau unfolds in chronological sequence, dates and events only gradually making sense of a history that will soon point us back to an even earlier archaeological layer. "Uncle August" is dated at the start of the 1960s, when Gabriel is twenty-five, and it follows on the heels of his service in Algeria, presumably during 1958 and 1959; the third episode, "The Interview," is dated as 1965, when Gabriel is thirty; the date of the fourth episode, "Unsettling Rumors," can be determined from the Yom Kippur War, fixing it precisely in 1973. The final tableau, "The Surrender," is set in 1978, only one year before publication of the story in the *New Yorker* and its appearance in the same year in the short-story collection *From the Fifteenth District.* Throughout the story, this careful attention to the concreteness of events and even dates operates in relation to another kind of time, one that complicates history by introducing the model of a different memory archive.

Gabriel's interview with his uncle introduces the most important of the facts that we must piece together. In the exchange that follows his uncle's attempts to establish his legitimacy, what emerges, instead, is information critical to both Gabriel's own life history and the national history being played out on a decade-by-decade canvas. Gabriel responds to his uncle's question about when he last saw his parents by replying that he was eight years old. Given the date of his birth, stated in the title of the story, we can place this event in 1943, the same year as his parents' probable death in his imaginary family memorial. He had been left with a neighbour who had told him that "they'd be back": they were in "Marseilles. We were supposed to be from Alsace, but their French sounded wrong. People noticed I wasn't going to school. Someone reported them" (454). It is a story that would be retold in another version in cinematic form a decade later in Louis Malle's film *Au revoir les enfants* (1987), in which a young Jewish boy is hidden in Lyon during the Vichy years while his parents are taken off to the death camps. In Malle's film, it is the child himself who is denounced and taken away, while in Gallant's story the young Gabriel survives but is propelled into all future time with the hauntings of a survivor. Yet the full import of this scene of trauma at the age of eight, a moment when his neighbour's well-intentioned promise is broken by the arc of history, is fully apparent only in the final tableau of the story.

"The Surrender" brings together all the strands of private and public history, past and present, in the layered ironies that characterize Gallant's major fiction. Dieter tells Gabriel about a thirteen-hour television film project about the occupation, to be launched in the spring and calling for a Nabokovian cast of characters who will include "a coal-miner, an anti-Semitic aristocrat, a Communist militant, a peasant with a droll Provencal accent, a long-faced Protestant intellectual, and a priest in doubt about his vocation. Three Jews will be discovered to have jumped or fallen with them: one aged rabbi, one black-market operator, and one anything" (465). Once more, comedy and tragedy blur each other's outlines as this post-Holocaust man without qualities lives out his historical inheritance in mimed gestures. "'The one anything will be me'," Gabriel decided, helping himself to chestnuts. He saw, without Dieter's needing to describe them, the glaring lights, the dogs straining at their leashes, the guards running and blowing whistles, the stalled train, a rainstorm, perhaps" (465). Yet the ironies intensify when Dieter tells Gabriel that, at forty-three years of age (fixing this episode in 1978), he is "the wrong age to play a Jew" (465). His advice to his friend is meant to "bridge this stage of his occupation career by becoming a surrendering officer" (466). The moral chiaroscuro demanded of the drama will now be satisfied by a rescripted history that calls for a humane, idealistic Wehrmaht officer, played by Gabriel, as opposed to the "not so good" SS officer acted by Dietrich (466). Although Gabriel appears to register no response to this new "surrender," the story tunnels in once more to its centre as case history:

> Gabriel was breathing at a good rhythm—and not too shallow—not too fast. An infinity of surrenders had preceded this one, in color and in black-and-white, with music and without. A long trail of application forms and Employment questionnaires had led Gabriel here: "Baum, Gabriel, b. 1935, Germany, nat. French, mil. serv. obl. fulf." (Actually, for some years now his date of birth had rendered the assurance about military service unnecessary.) Country words ran meanwhile in his head. He thought, Dense thickets, lizards and snakes, a thrush's egg, a bee, lichen, wild berries, dark thorny leaves, pale mushrooms. Each word carried its own fragrance.

(470)

What follows this stabilizing fantasy of a home in the myth-idyll of his German friend's own dream of *heimat* is a scene of Dieter's temporary collapse, Volkswagen buses waiting to pick up the actors, and a final, overwhelming irony. In the closing line of the story, Dieter sighs and, in terms that confirm his total inability to understand his friend's own kingdom of loss, remarks off-handedly, "my father lived to be ninety" (412).

. . . . .

> It was around this time, when French editorial alarm about the morally destructive aspect of Western prosperity was at its most feverish, that a man calling himself Briseglace wandered into the bar and began asking all the aliens and strangers there if they were glad to be poor.
>
> —Mavis Gallant, **"Baum, Gabriel (1935-)"** (459)

Still marking time in 1965, Gabriel, now thirty, looks for news about his Algerian pension and learns about "Western consumer society and the moral wounds that were being inflicted through full employment" (459). Once more, a whole cultural moment is invoked: that of the left anarchism of the Situationists and Guy Debord's *The Society of the Spectacle.* Within three short years, fuelled by an often fragile coalition of workers and students, this new mood would erupt in the barricades of Paris in 1968. Yet who is this journalist who comes to interview the inhabitants of La Meduse and turns up a life of Gabriel for the magazine *Paris-Match* in impoverished outlines that contrast with Gallant's own complex layering of character and event? Like all of her characters, he is precisely imagined in terms of time and place, these coordinates merging not so much to provide background as to create the very field of force in which he exists: "his stained fingers and cheap cigarettes, his pessimism and his boldness and his belief in the moral advantages of penury all came straight from the Latin quarter of the 1940s. He was the Occupation; he was the Liberation, too. The films that Dieter and Gabriel played in grew like common weeds from the heart of whatever young man he once had been" (460). His name is Briseglace, literally "broken mirror," and what is momentarily shattered by his facile rendering of the personal trauma of a young German Jewish child in Vichy, France, is Gabriel's own fragile identity Yet, if Briseglace's cynical journalism stands in sharp counterpoint to the range and complexity of **"Baum, Gabriel (1935-)"** itself, it also returns us to the problems of representation and trauma raised at the outset: not only to the Brechtian distancing produced by the unfolding tableau structure of the story but also to the delicate equipoise of comic and tragic elements. Stylistically, it is a high-wire act that demands a reader's careful attention to sudden shifts in tone and modulation, moving unexpectedly from a burlesquing of traumatic history to the gradual burrowing under the skin of a character who cannot escape the melancholy of its burden.

Once again, the text spirals outward from individual trauma to the half-hidden national trauma in its folds. In a remarkable confluence of figures, it is the same metonym of "broken mirror" central to Henri Rousso's

The Vichy Syndrome: History and Memory in France since 1944 (1991), the highly influential analysis of France's coming to memory around its wartime collaboration, which first appeared in French in 1990, over a decade after Gallant's story. Rousso uses the term to describe a stage in the unfolding of the effaced memory of a nation, but the common trope draws the line tightly between two registers of trauma as well as two kinds of case history in ways particularly productive for reading **"Baum, Gabriel (1935-)."**

What does Rousso mean by a Vichy "syndrome," and how can this jagged chronology of memory and history help us to read Gallant's story? The very name of the Institut d'Histoire du Temps Present where Rousso worked with his fellow French historians is instructive in its explicit understanding of the past as an excavation of the present—an archaeological figure that also returns us to Freud. Rousso's study is widely regarded as the first comprehensive mapping of the most "dramatic and traumatic episode of contemporary French history—the period between France's fall in June . . . 1940 and the liberation four years later, when the Vichy regime and De Gaulle's Free French competed for legitimacy, and collaborationists and resisters fought each other without mercy" (Hoffman vii). Yet it is equally an attempt to confront the way in which the postliberationist French only gradually awakened to the buried memories and events of that period, exploding consolatory myths promulgated by De Gaulle himself. With great deliberateness, the leader of the Free French in London returned to Paris and a hero's welcome to declare in a famous speech that the city had been "freed by itself, freed by its own people with the support of the armies of France, with the cooperation of the whole of France, of the France which fights, of the only France, of the true France, of the eternal France" (qtd. in Bosworth 112). The deliberate fictions proclaimed in this speech of 15 August 1944 were consciously designed to restore a certain fantasy of nationhood, one in which the glory of the French state with its mythos of being the bearer of Enlightenment liberation remained intact.[4] To Georges Bideaut, then De Gaulle's ally, though he would later become his bitterest enemy, he laid out the grand design of this postwar era even more transparently: "Vichy was always and has remained null and void; *it did not happen*" (Bosworth 112; emphasis added).

The troping of a "true France" echoes both the French right of Action Francaise and the opposing battle lines of left and right from the time of the Dreyfus affair through the occupation (Ungar 154). Indeed, one of the most enduring themes in recent French history writing is the pattern of recurrence and return in an ongoing national drama.[5] Yet, if such a model increasingly transforms our understanding of the way in which history is both experienced and written, it has even more relevance to understanding moments of national trauma. I have been arguing for a reading of national trauma as contingent on a particular notion of the nation-state. In recent years, we have become increasingly familiar with the understanding of "nation" as a constellation of historical discourses and representations, performatively instituted as well as bound up with relations of power and desire. Yet this is also a formation that serves an important mirroring function for the stability of the subject, in a relay of identifications that contributes to the fiction of coherence. When the mirror shatters, what is broken is not merely the phantasmatic of nation (whose ontological status must, in any event, always be put into question) but also the very ground of dailiness.[6]

For over twenty years now, Gallant has been researching and writing a study of the Dreyfus affair, whose political divisions constitute an ongoing fault line in France's collective memory of itself since the historical caesura of the French Revolution, the mythic event at the centre of the nation's history. When these disparate visions erupted once more in the anarchic social revolution of Paris in 1968, the dispatches to the *New Yorker* magazine describing "the events of May," in a widely read, two-part eyewitness account that provided America with its day-by-day window on the national drama, were written by a Canadian writer living in Paris, Mavis Gallant.

The relationship of the fiction to this active social witnessing, in a society where intellectual and cultural life are saturated by politics and history, has never been sufficiently explored. A closer look at **"Baum, Gabriel (1935-)"** confirms that Gallant's pervasive fusing of history and memory is more than a highly personal and idiosyncratic twinning in the fiction. Rather, it takes place within a pervasive postwar coming to memory as well as shifts in the history of writing history itself. Folded back into this wider cultural field, her work presents itself as operating in a European field of memory work that emerged in the late 1960s and continues in the present as a veritable memory industry of films, literature, art, memorials, and museums. This attention to the vicissitudes of public as well as private memory in Gallant follows the international catastrophes of the Second World War through to the twists and turns of Eastern Europe, following the fall of the Berlin Wall, in a number of her late short stories. After arriving in Paris in the early 1950s, she had a ringside seat to the intersections of history and collective memory occurring at such diverse sites as fiction, newspapers and popular media, trials, the discipline of historiography itself, and—critical to the story that I am telling—the institution of cinema.

The reason for this is clear enough. In the recent revisioning of memory and history, history *as* memory, Vichy France has been widely regarded as the locus

classicus and model case. In the years that followed the Second World War, French society was rocked by this succession of scandals, debates, trials, and media and film events revisioning the *années noires* that were part of the fabric of the daily life of any French citizen who read the newspaper or watched television. For intellectuals and artists, these events were markers of an encounter with history that was as much ethical as political, sparking ongoing wars of recrimination and defence. Rousso himself makes the case for the continuity of the Fourth Republic and the De Gaulle period of the Fifth Republic. It was May 1968 that broke up the myth forever, a moment when the young generation confronted both the pieties and the silences of their parents' generation. It was no coincidence, Rousso reminds us, that Marcel Ophuls and the other makers of *The Sorrow and the Pity* were "sixty-eighters" (viii). Yet, if it is too simple to construct a divide of "cowards or stinkers," to invoke the opposition famously thrown up by Sartre, a moral reckoning with historical reality was long overdue (Rousso ix). It came in slow stages, inching toward a covered-over past in ways echoed by Gallant's remarkably prescient story "Virus X," which uncannily predates Rousso's own medical trope for historical amnesia—this time within an even more explicit individual psychoanalytic case history.

Rousso's national case history is marked by four phases. The earliest, which extends from 1944 to 1954, is described as a stage of unfinished mourning. In language drawn from the influential work of Alexander Mitscherlich and Margarete Mitscherlich-Nielsen to describe Germany's response to its own traumatic past, Rousso sketches a period making almost no serious engagement with the unresolved contradictions of wartime. Although the liberation had scored deep divisions around purging and amnesty in the body politic, the majority of the population anticipated that time would repair the rifts. The years 1954-71 are characterized by a second phase of extended repression, mobilized by a new myth-history whose principal antagonists were collaborators and resistant militants. Rousso exposes this "resistantialist" (the spelling is instructive) myth, which replaced historical "resistants" with the comforting legend of a unified national resistance. Following 1968, when Gallant was the American intellectual's window on the "Red Spring" (*le printemps rouge*), the repressed memory of Vichy returned to shatter the past, which became like the shards of a "broken mirror." The third phase is marked by the appearance of Ophuls's breakthrough documentary, *The Sorrow and the Pity* (1969).

It is widely agreed by historians of the period that only in the past twenty-five years has a more accurate picture of the 1940-44 occupation and the *État Francais* at Vichy emerged. The assumption that traumatic experience is recorded only belatedly belongs to Freud. The first time around, it is both an event and a nonevent, with the equivocal status of an occurrence, in his own words, that is *"non-arrivée"* (qtd. in Wollheim 33). The complex range of disguises and subterfuges by means of which it is registered at even the individual level already poses a series of questions about the ontology of experience, displacement, and screen memories. When we proceed to the question of national case history, we are in even more problematic and overdetermined terrain. Here contested memories are invested with the schisms of history that belong not only to the realm of unevenly situated experience but also to political ideology, to painful memories that shut down in a protective economy of the subject, but equally to public memory coaxed into shape and configured with great deliberateness—as was the case with Gaullist France in the postwar period. Here Freud's earlier theories of the work of psychic censorship as analogous to the literal erasures of the political censor are even more apposite. It was not until the end of 1973 that a reform in archive law provided access to some of the documents previously hidden away, prompting a spurt of thesis writing, notably at the Institut d'Histoire du Temps Present, where Rousso held his post (Bosworth 113). What did it take, then, for this effaced material to be restored to national consciousness, and what is at stake in this coming to social memory?

De Gaulle had not been the only master forger of history in the postwar period. In Milan Kundera's *The Book of Laughter and Forgetting,* the narrator recounts attempts by Gustav Husak to efface the Czech past after the 1968 Soviet overthrow of the reformist Alexander Dubcek regime. No fewer than 145 historians were dismissed from their positions at research institutions and universities. Among them was Milan Hubl, who later told Kundera that the first step in liquidating a people is to efface their memory: "Destroy its books, its culture, its history. Then have someone write new books, manufacture a new culture, invent a new history. Before long the nation will begin to forget what it is and what it was. The world around it will forget even faster" (159).

While the self-conscious turn to the metahistorical dimension of history writing has been readily absorbed into literary criticism because of its attentiveness to the rhetoric of the text, Gallant's own crossing of history with private and public memory has more in common with even more recent shifts in historiography. As Saul Friedlander suggests, "when historical consciousness tends towards a static, monumental representation of the past, it stands at the gates of collective memory" (qtd. in Ungar 20). In turn, the opening up of the historical record to include new and different histories that demand shifts in what achieves evidentiary status also has ethical implications. Lynn Hunt has suggested that we think of history as an "ethical and political practice rather than an epistemology with a clear ontological status" (19). In this context, a case can be made for the

Second World War's importance in the West in inaugurating the moral shock that put new pressure on the writing of history. John Bosworth argues that, for more than a generation, the politics and culture of society after society have been underpinned by "rival histories" of the Second World War (4). Equally clear, he suggests, is that the long Second World War, Auschwitz, and Hiroshima posed grand-scale ethical issues, which did not begin to lose their force as proper names for moral shock until the end of the twentieth century. With the collapse of already fragile Western humanist frameworks, the task ahead was to find what could be recovered in the ruins of traditional ethics (Gabriel). It is within this wider historical crisis of meaning and value that **"Baum, Gabriel (1935-)"** and nearly all of Gallant's major fiction belong.

· · · · ·

> Gabriel had been shot, stoned, drowned, suffocated, and marked off by hanging; had been insulted and betrayed; had been shoved aboard trains and dragged out of them; had been flung from the back of a truck with such accidental violence that he had broken his collarbone. His demise, seen by millions of people, some eating their dinner, was still needed to give a push to the old dishonorable plot—told ever more simple now, like a fable—while Dieter's fate was still part of its moral.

> On this repeated game of death and consequences Dieter's seniority depended. He told Gabriel that the French would be bored with entertainment based on the Occupation by about 1982. . . .

> —Mavis Gallant, **"Baum, Gabriel (1935-)"** (462)

In many ways, **"Baum, Gabriel (1935-)"** is a model text for talking about Gallant's writing of history and memory, the way in which past and present merge in a doubled time that indexes historical event in and through characters situated in an exact social field. Yet what is the status of historical reference in this fiction, the line between what I am suggesting has been read as merely "noise" and what needs to be recovered as "information"? Even more to the point, what is the status of the "date" in such a flow of references? While a date might be seen as offering up a truth claim of sorts, mooring us in a putative "real" of history, the issues at stake are also more complicated—and never more so than in the framework of traumatic narratives.[7]

To acknowledge this more complex and overdetermined archive is not to abandon responsibility to the events of the past but to layer our understanding of how history is represented, retrieved, and experienced across private and public memories. In the case of **"Baum, Gabriel (1935-),"** dates repeatedly return us to events in France's national history, even as they expand our knowledge of the story's title figure, orphaned in 1943 in Marseille. Even these seemingly incidental details in the thread of a fictional narrative return us to the ethical imperatives of history. *Why Marseille? And why 1943?*

Almost certainly, Gallant had in mind a dramatic moment in the unfolding history of France in the Second World War, following the collapse of the political and territorial distinctions between occupied and unoccupied zones. In the wake of the Allies landing in North Africa on 8 November 1942, German forces moved across the line to occupy southern cities such as Marseille. While the complex relationship between the Germans and the French authorities remains an integral part of this story (one brought to renewed public consciousness by the assassination in June 1993 of Vichy police chief Rene Bousquet, only weeks before he was scheduled to come to trial), two events merged in Marseille in 1943.[8] Violent resistance by certain sectors of the civilian population contributed to the razing of the Old Port of Marseille in January 1943. This event merged with a massive roundup throughout Marseille known as Operation Tiger, in which thousands of Jews were arrested and sent to camps in France that were way stations to the death camps of Poland. In their study *Vichy France and the Jews,* Michael Marrus and Robert Paxton describe Drancy, the most important of these camps for transports from the unoccupied zone, as a virtual "antechamber to Auschwitz" (252).

As with the haunting of Netta Asher in **"The Moslem Wife"** and the capture of Dr. Chaffee in **"The Four Seasons,"** then, Gabriel's own family narrative stages a dark drama of the Second World War in which even the smallest geographical reference or date is rendered with precision. Yet this fidelity to event—its virtual *unhiding,* given its moment in France's slow passage to Vichy memory—is also vastly complicated at another level by the overdeterminations that attend traumatic history. Questions of representation also become, willy-nilly, problems of chronology, in ways that are productive in thinking about Gallant's fiction as a whole.

To those readers who had followed her work over the years, the publication of her selected stories was a welcome but disorienting event. The familiar arrangements of the fiction in landmark volumes such as *From the Fifteenth District, Home Truths,* and *Overhead in the Balloon* were now exposed as entirely arbitrary. The new and rather unusual fictional ordering was a decade-by-decade framework, moving from the 1930s to the 1990s, according to the time in which the fiction was set. Yet this flagging of chronology also immediately presents a new set of problems. Stories such as **"The Moslem Wife"** and **"The Four Seasons"** are set in the 1940s but were not published until the 1970s. What does this tell us about the conditions of production and reception of historical events or their relationship to social memory in particular times and places? More radical yet are the issues that attend the belatedness of traumatic memories and histories. **"Baum, Gabriel (1935-)," even where it is set in the Paris of the present (concluding in the year prior to its publication), is cen-

tred on a character whose whole family was wiped out in the death camps. Is this a story, then, of the late 1970s or of the 1940s, and how can we separate past from present in a present-past that is both individual and national? What is the relationship of the title to that distilled scene hidden in the folds of the narrative in freeze-frame: a Jewish German boy of eight, hidden in 1943 in Marseille by a neighbour who tells him that his mother and father will be "back," but whom he will never see again?

When Gallant arrived in Paris in 1951, she encountered a nation whose public memory of its wartime past had gone underground. Yet, almost alone in the decade that unfolded, at least one French filmmaker, Alain Resnais, returned insistently to themes of memory and history, working in the folds and interstices of official censorship to evoke a traumatic national past. This first stage of coming to Second World War conscience and memory at the site of cinema in France is worth taking seriously for an understanding of Gallant's historical context. "When people ask me what books have influenced me, I don't always know. Maybe it's film as much as anything. I was absolutely fascinated with the German cinema for a time in the 1970s and, of course, the French have always been passionate about film. It was just part of the air I breathed when I first came to Paris" (Gallant, interview). Even before Gallant arrived in France in the 1950s, she had a long-standing interest in cinema. Her first job after returning from New York to Montreal was with the National Film Board, while during her final two years as a journalist for the Montreal *Standard* in 1949 and 1950, she often wrote film reviews. One of the most striking things about the preface to *The Selected Stories of Mavis Gallant* is the frequency to which Gallant alludes to figures of film to capture her writing process. When she recounts her early career as a journalist in the era of photo features, she describes these stories as "something like miniature scripts; I always saw the pictures as stills from a film" (xiv). Later, when she turns to fiction and her characteristic mode of composition, the cinematic analogies are even more insistent: "The first flash of fiction arrives without words. It consists of a fixed image, like a slide or (closer still) a freeze frame . . ." (xvi). The characters arrive with a full set of characteristics, including age, nationality, profession, well-defined attitudes, and a "private centre of gravity":

> Over the next several days I take down long passages of dialogue. Whole scenes then follow, complete in themselves but like disconnected parts of a film. . . . Finally (I am describing a long and complex process as simply as I can), the story will seem to be entire, in the sense that nearly everything needed has been written. It is entire but unreadable. Nothing fits. A close analogy would be an unedited film. The first frame may have dissolved into sound and motion. . . .

> (xvii)

While the intensely visual nature of Gallant's prose has been remarked on, what has been left out of this picture is the degree to which many of the formal characteristics of her mature fiction are drawn from cinema. Abrupt transitions as well as gaps in the narrative at times mimic the deliberate breaking up of continuity editing of the *Nouvelle Vague* generation of filmmakers whose cinematic innovations were closely connected, in turn, to experimental French fiction of the period (Higgins 1-18). These links frequently extended to active collaborative work in films such as *Hiroshima mon amour,* whose script was cowritten by Alain Resnais and Marguerite Duras. The traumatic witnessing characteristic of Resnais's cinema finds its counterpart in the message written on the wall by the Aristo in the made-for-television film about the occupation in **"Baum, Gabriel (1935-)"**: "MY FRIENDS REMEMBERED" (470). Resnais's deliberate indeterminacies and layering of past and present-past provided a radical formal grammar for unconscious experience that was, at the same time, moored in the ethical demands of historical memory and responsibility. Gallant herself has said in an interview with me, "Who could miss Resnais in those days?" By 1955, this leading director of the French New Wave had produced a searing documentary of the concentration camps, *Night and Fog,* which had a profound impact on viewers throughout Europe, not least of all on an emerging generation of new filmmakers in Germany (Margarethe von Trotta would later reprise a scene from *Night and Fog* in her own *Marianne and Juliane* of 1981). Working as a journalist for the Montreal *Standard* during the war, Gallant had been asked to write captions for the first photographs of the death camps to emerge in the West. She took the nightmare pictures home and told her editors that she refused to find words for this world at degree zero. Within a few years, still preoccupied with what had happened, "the *why* of it," she travelled to Germany to find "the origin of the worm" (Gallant, interview with Hancock 40). Over a decade later, the German stories of **The Pegnitz Junction** finally emerged, fictions that posed memory as ethical work in ways that resonate with the urgent question of the concentration camp survivor and novelist Jean Cayrol's voice-over in Resnais's *Night and Fog*: "who is responsible?"

Gilles Deleuze has observed that Resnais "has only one cinematographic subject, body or actor: he who returns from the dead" (qtd. in Greene 32). No doubt, the French philosopher has in mind, among others, a line of tragic characters that includes the Japanese survivor of Hiroshima and his French actress-lover, haunted by the death of her German lover during Vichy in *Hiroshima mon amour* (1959), and the young man, Bernard, who cannot forget the torture that he witnessed as an ex-soldier in the colonial wars in Algeria in *Muriel* (1963). Framed in this way, these characters and the cinematic universes that they inhabit constitute important acts of moral witnessing in a cinema of history and memory whose preoccupations frequently parallel those of Gallant's fiction. Gabriel Baum is not alone as a survivor of traumatic history in her stories. The traumatic event that closes the story of a contemporary French right-wing family in **"Luc and His Father"** in *Overhead in a Balloon* (its intensities deliberately ironized and almost buried in the text as an unheard confessional on the father's wedding night) unravels the ongoing nightmare of French torture in Algeria in ways that directly recall the ex-soldier Bernard in *Muriel*. Both Christine in the title novella of *The Pegnitz Junction* and Thomas in *The Latehomecomer* journey to memory and responsibility in postwar Germany, shadowed by the ghosts of the past. Finally, Netta Asher in **"The Moslem Wife"** is haunted and changed forever by the traumatic witnessing of partisans hanged in a doorway in the south of wartime France. All of these characters are *hikabushi* in ways that cross Lifton's observations about Hiroshima survivors with Resnais's own Japanese Noh drama-like travellers mediating the worlds of the dead and the living.

As we have seen, this anamnesis was slow in coming in France in the postwar period. It emerged not only through a series of complex twists and turns but also at a wide range of cultural sites. Yet no element of Gallant's story is more attentive to the "places" of French rememory than the central dramatic irony of the fiction: one in which the two central characters act out their historical roles in French films of the 1960s and 1970s, thereby staging and foregrounding the very medium that historians agree was central to the recovery of Vichy memory—and in the decades in which this memory was unfolding.

Marcel Ophuls's film *The Sorrow and the Pity* is widely agreed to be the breakthrough event in the resurgent French memory of Vichy. Shot in 1968-69 as a film designed for television, it was bought by twenty-seven countries, even as the state-owned French television network itself refused to show it. It finally opened in 1971 in a small theatre in the Latin Quarter before moving to a larger film house on the Champs-Elysées. As Naomi Greene suggests, *The Sorrow and the Pity* is concerned as much with "the very process of memory" as with the facts of the Vichy era itself (71). The town of Clermont-Ferrand at the centre of the documentary is cited in deliberate *hommage* to Ophuls's film in Gallant's story "Virus X" as the female protagonist confronts her own repressed historical memory in a personal case history that once more mirrors the painful national coming to memories of the Second World War: "the newspaper finally mentioned an epidemic grippe that was surging through Europe. The symptoms resembled those of pneumonia. The popular name for it was Virus X. There had been two new deaths in Clermont-Ferrand. *Why do they always tell about what happened in Clermont-Ferrand?"* (**Home Truths** 206; emphasis added).

The picture that emerges in Ophuls's documentary is that of an occupied people characterized not by the spirit of resistance and unity held up by De Gaulle's consolatory mirror but "by daily fears and small acts of cowardice, by active and passive collaboration. We begin to see the deep-seated attitudes that encouraged collaboration—attitudes that made France, as we are reminded several times, the only European country to actively collaborate. Witnesses may deny the widespread enthusiasm that was felt for Petain, but newsreel clips repeatedly show us the cheering crowds that hailed the *Marechal* wherever he went" (Greene 71). This more sobering reading of the reality of the Vichy years is implicitly staged in **"Baum, Gabriel (1935-)."** When the thirteen-hour television project about the occupation is filmed in the streets of Paris in the late 1970s, a crowd gathers, "drawn by the lights and the equipment and the sight of the soldiers in German uniform. Some asked if they might be photographed with them; this often happened when a film of that kind was made in the streets" (469). Gabriel is left to observe that no one ever asked to have a picture taken with him when he was playing a "wretched, desperate victim" (469). But it is an earlier surreal sequence that makes the point about French collaboration with the Germans even more succinctly. As an elderly couple edge up to the two actors in German officer uniform, the woman asks "in German, in a low voice, *'What are you doing here?'"* (469; emphasis added).

The 1970s in France witnessed a resurgence of Vichy memory, fuelled by those, such as Ophuls, who belonged to the generation of 1968. The anti-authoritarian spirit of the student rebellions combined with historiographic shifts and relaxed censorship to create the conditions of possibility for a confrontation with the buried past, one that began to peter out by the 1980s in ways that retrospectively make Dieter's offhand remark ("He told Gabriel that the French would be bored by films about the Occupation by about 1982") remarkably prescient. By contrast, the 1970s witnessed a veritable explosion of Second World War memory that came to be called *la mode retro*: "a forties revival visible in worlds as diverse as fashion, historical scholarship, journalism, and, most visibly, cinema. Between 1974 and 1978 some forty-five films dealing with World War II were shot—more than in the course of the entire previous decade. In 1976 alone, *la mode retro* set its stamp on eleven films, 7 percent of France's total output" (Greene 65).

Over two decades, cinema became a central cultural site for memory in a contest of meaning that is exemplary of the stakes of social memory and history, inten-

sified by the framework of national trauma. Yet even the key films engaged in this recovery of buried history tell less a story of moral progress than one of constant mediation and negotiation with the traumatic archive. Arguably, even Gallant's distilled ironic scene in the streets where Dieter and Gabriel act out their occupation film in German uniforms to welcoming Parisians offers less salve to the national wound than the two films by Louis Malle that bookended *la mode retro: Lacombe Lucien* (1974), which ranked sixth at the box office and was seen by over a quarter of a million people within three weeks of its Paris release, and *Au revoir les enfants,* both of which, in the end, "soften or erase the most troubling zones of the past" (Greene 73, 91).[9]

Gallant's own writing of the wounds of memory in **"Baum, Gabriel (1935-)"** is staged at the site of both individual and national trauma in a present-past that complicates both time and history. Gabriel's question about the occupation film ("Who's there at the end?" 470) belongs to the out-of-work actor surveying a screenplay as his meal ticket, but, like almost everything else in Gallant's story, it also resounds with the death-haunted ironies of the survivor. In the final analysis, this drama of recurrence and return, with its dissonant music played out on a field of childhood trauma as well as repressed national memory, recalls the Marx of "The Eighteenth Brumaire of Louis Bonaparte" as much as Freud: history and its personages happen *"the first time as tragedy, the second as farce"* (594; emphasis added). What makes these complex tonalities even more compelling as traumatic witnessing in Gallant's fiction is that they never flinch from history's ethical demand.

Notes

1. Studies of both the Holocaust and Hiroshima almost routinely begin with the crisis of representation posed by traumatic narratives. Hiroshima provides a particularly poignant figure for the problem of witnessing in that many of those present at the cataclysm actually went blind (Maclear 4). Holocaust representation, whether in literature, film, or eyewitness accounts, persistently addresses the problem of describing the incommensurable (see, e.g., Avisar; Felman and Laub; Friedlander; LaCapra; and Langer). Yet it is important to note that this problem is equally pervasive in the art and cultural practices concerned with these traumas, whether it is post-Hiroshima Butto dance, the multimedia art of Vera Frenkel, the sculpture of Rachel Whiteread, or the writing of Beckett and Blanchot. In the last two cases, an interesting new problematic emerges, that of the relationship of post-Mallarmean high modernism with its suspicion of the referent and the crisis of representation

posed by the ethical problems of modernity. The question of reference is also at the heart of recent writing around trauma. See Ruth Leys's critique of the work of Cathy Caruth in her *Trauma: A Genealogy* (2000), particularly the final chapter, "The Pathos of the Literal: Trauma and the Crisis of Representation."

2. Stories such as "In the Tunnel," "Virus X," and "An Alien Flower" are only a few of the fictions that model themselves on the deep history inaugurated by Breuer and emerged as the more fully theorized psychoanalytic case histories of Freud. Gallant's complicated and ambivalent relationship to psychoanalysis remains another story, but her understanding of its basic tenets almost certainly informs her prescient reading of the unfolding national case histories of Germany and France in the postwar period. Maier's *The Unmasterable Past: History, Holocaust, and German National Identity*, whose title is drawn from Adorno, captures the ethical as well as the epistemological crisis that belongs to Germany in the postwar period.

3. The title character of Gallant's story is not a Holocaust survivor in the sense that the term is normally deployed: one who has survived the death camps personally. Nor is he a second-generation "survivor": one who bears the traumatic scarring of parents who have emerged from the concentration camps. Yet his unconscious is riddled with images drawn directly from the camp as though he had witnessed them personally. When he is acting in his role as a victim-Jew, he sees, "*without Dieter's needing to describe them,* the glaring lights, the dogs straining at their leashes, the guards running and blowing whistles, the stalled train" (emphasis added). In contrast, the title of Gallant's story "Pitchipoi" is based on the fantasy name that Jewish children gave to an Auschwitz that they could *not* imagine.

4. I am distilling here what might be a more comprehensive theorizing of the nation as fetish within a logic of castration and disavowal that belongs to Lacanian theory. In this sense, the nation is a mirror that is also a *misrecognition,* offering an image of wholeness and plenitude that is necessarily a stabilizing fiction. French historian Jules Michelet not only invokes a rhetoric of wholeness to describe the nation ("All other histories are mutilated; only ours is complete") but also does so in gendered tropes ("a true milky way") that may be worth reading more fully (qtd. in Greene 13). The figure of amputation frequently invoked to de-

scribe the lost territories of Alsace-Lorraine to Germany also supports my model of the nation as fetish object in instructive ways.

5. Studies of French history persistently note the way in which the epochal social divisions that followed the French Revolution repeat themselves in historical moments of crisis as diverse as the period of Louis Napoleon, the Dreyfus affair, the Popular Front, Vichy, and the student rebellions of 1968. As Robert Paxton notes, France is both always entering a new battle and restaging the old one. The American historian's pioneering study of Vichy France is widely regarded as having inaugurated a "Copernican revolution" in the history of the period (Jackson 10). First published in English in 1973, spawning a whole new generation of Vichy historiography, it preceded the appearance of "Baum, Gabriel (1935-)" in the *New Yorker* by less than six years, a time line that reminds us of Gallant's remarkable alertness to historical shifts. It also underlines the importance of placing her preoccupations with history and memory in the cauldron of Vichy coming to memory.

6. Recent studies of "nation" share the understanding of its mythic (Barthes) imaginary (Anderson) or "narrated" status (Bhabha). The reading of nation as a *phantasmatic* or imaginary formation of the subject has the advantage of reminding us that subjects do not so much belong to nations *as nations belong to subjects.* I stress the fetishistic character of the work that this formation does to remind us that it never succeeds in covering over an originary loss—hence the hysterical rhetoric from Michelet to De Gaulle around both the greatness and the "wholeness" of the French nation. It is this self-mirroring that is once more under attack in both a newly heterogeneous population of transnationals who are "others" and the threat of integration into the new Europe (see Silverman). Gallant explored the threat of this other/double in her first published story, "The Other Paris."

7. In the Germany of the 1970s, this work of memory taking place at a wide range of cultural sites, which included literature, film, painting, museums, and memorials, became known as *trauerarbeit,* and it included the work of new German filmmakers such as Fassbinder, Wenders, and Herzog, whom Gallant watched with great interest in the 1970s. A survey of museums and memorials created in the past few years alone provides evidence of a remarkable awakening to the ethical demand of memory: Daniel Libeskind's Holocaust memorial in Berlin and Rachel Whiteread's Holocaust

memorial in Vienna's Judenplatz, the new Terror-Haus in Budapest (whose stagings of Communist tyranny belong to still contested national memories), ongoing debates about memorializing the space of the twin towers felled on 9/11. At the same time, Africa's only memorial to the ravages of AIDS is decimated populations and imploding nations: evidence of the ongoing asymmetry of power in the struggle for memory even as official histories are broken up by alternative narratives.

8. My abbreviated telling here is drawn from Ryan. The events that shadow Gabriel's life and provide the ethical intensities as well as ironies of Gallant's story are dramatically expanded in Ryan: "The entire endeavor at the Old Port . . . cannot really be separated from Operation Tiger, the roundup of Jews. . . . [T]he new German presence in Marseilles guaranteed that foreign Jews who had escaped the dragnet of the previous summer would be hunted. In the Old Port operation it was plain that French Jews were in peril, too" (190). See also Marrus and Paxton 307, 308. In a nuanced account that explores the differences between both zones as well as organized and individual acts of rescue and solidarity, Julian Jackson nevertheless concludes that, "If one compares Vichy's role in the Final Solution to that of other semi-independent governments in Nazi Europe, there are few others who offered as much help as Vichy" (362).

9. In this regard, the cinema actually viewed by the French during the occupation is of interest (see Bazin). Andre Bazin's famous "realism" (widely read as an "idealism") typically operates to secure the notion of a national imaginary.

Works Cited

Adorno, Theodor. *Minima Moralia: Reflections from Damaged Life.* Trans. E. F. Jephcott. London: Verso, 1981.

Anderson, Benedict. *Imagined Communities: Reflections on the Origin and Spread of Nationalism.* London: Verso, 1983.

Avisar, Ilan. *Screening the Holocaust: Cinema's Images of the Unimaginable.* Bloomington: U of Indiana P, 1988.

Barthes, Roland. *Mythologies.* Paris: Seuil, 1970.

Bazin, Andre. *French Cinema of the Occupation and Resistance: The Birth of an Aesthetic.* New York: Ungar, 1981.

Bhabha, Homi K. *Nation and Narration.* New York: Routledge, 1990.

Bosworth, R. J. B. *Explaining Auschwitz and Hiroshima: History Writing and the Second World War 1945-1990.* London: Routledge, 1993.

Brecht, Bertolt. *The Resistible Rise of Arturo Ui.* London: Methuen, 1981.

Debord, Guy. *The Society of the Spectacle.* Detroit: Black and Red, 1977.

Felman, Shoshana, and Dori Laub, eds. *Testimony: Crises of Witnessing in Literature, Psychoanalysis, and History.* New York: Routledge, 1992.

Freud, Sigmund. *The Complete Letters of Sigmund Freud to Wilhelm Fliess 1887-1904.* Ed. Jeffrey Moussaieff Masson. Cambridge, MA: Belknap, 1985.

Friedlander, Saul. *Probing the Limits of Representation: Nazism and the "Final Solution."* Cambridge, MA: Harvard UP, 1992.

Gabriel, Barbara. "The Ethics of Memory." *Postmodernism and the Ethical Subject.* Ed. Barbara Gabriel and Suzan Ilcan. Montreal: McGill-Queen's UP, forthcoming.

Gallant, Mavis. "Baum, Gabriel (1935-)." Gallant, *Selected Stories* 452-72.

———. "The Events of May: A Paris Notebook—I and II." *Paris Notebooks: Essays and Reviews.* New York: Random House, 1986. 9-95.

———. *From the Fifteenth District.* Toronto: McClelland, 1979.

———. *Home Truths.* Toronto: McClelland, 1981.

———. Interview with Barbara Gabriel. Paris, 1986.

———. Interview with Geoff Hancock. *Canadian Fiction Magazine* 28 (1978): 18-67.

———. *Overhead in a Balloon.* Toronto: McClelland, 1986.

———. *The Pegnitz Junction.* Toronto: McClelland, 1973.

———. Preface. Gallant, *Selected Stories* x-lx.

———. *The Selected Stories of Mavis Gallant.* Toronto: McClelland, 1996.

———. *What Is to Be Done?* Montreal: Quadrant, 1983.

Greene, Naomi. *Landscapes of Loss: The National Past in Postwar French Cinema.* Princeton: Princeton UP, 1999.

Halbwachs, Maurice. *On Collective Memory.* Ed. Lewis A. Coser. Chicago: U of Chicago P, 1992.

Higgins, Lynne. *New Novel, New Wave, New Politics: Fiction and the Representation of History in Postwar France.* Lincoln: U of Nebraska P, 1996.

Hunt, Lynne. "History as Gesture: Or, The Scandal of History." *Consequences of Theory.* Ed. Jonathan Arac and Barbara Johnson. Baltimore: Johns Hopkins UP, 1990. 91-107.

Jackson, Julian. *The Dark Years: Vichy France, 1940-44.* Oxford: Oxford UP, 2002.

Kundera, Milan. *The Book of Laughter and Forgetting.* Trans. Michael Henry Heim. New York: Penguin, 1981.

Langer, Lawrence. *The Holocaust and the Literary Imagination.* New Haven: Yale UP, 1975.

LaCapra, Dominick. *Writing History, Writing Trauma.* Baltimore: Johns Hopkins UP, 2001.

Leys, Ruth. *Trauma: A Genealogy.* Chicago: U of Chicago P, 2000.

Le Goff, Jacques. *History and Memory.* Paris: Gallimard, 1988.

Maclear, Kyo. *Beclouded Visions: Hiroshima-Nagasaki and the Art of Witness.* Albany: State U of New York P, 1991.

Maier, Charles S. *The Unmasterable Past: History, Holocaust, and German National Identity.* Cambridge, MA: Harvard UP, 1990.

Marrus, Michael R., and Robert O. Paxton. *Vichy France and the Jews.* Stanford: Stanford UP, 1981.

Marx, Karl. "The Eighteenth Brumaire of Louis Bonaparte." *The Marx-Engels Reader.* Ed. Robert C. Tucker. 2nd ed. New York: Norton, 1978. 594-617.

Mitscherlich, Alexander, and Margarete Mitscherlich-Nielsen. *The Inability to Mourn: Principles of Collective Behaviour.* Trans. Beverly R. Placzek. New York: Grove, 1975.

Nora, Pierre. *Places of Memory.* Paris: Gallimard, 1984-93.

Paxton, Robert. *Vichy France: Old Guard and New Order, 1940-44.* New York: Norton, 1975.

"Phantasy (or Fantasy)." *The Language of Psychoanalysis.* Ed. Jean Laplanche and Jean-Bertrand Pontalis. London: Karmac, 1996. 314-19.

Rousso, Henri. *The Vichy Syndrome: History and Memory in France since 1944.* Trans. Arthur Goldhammer. Cambridge, MA: Harvard UP, 1991.

Rigby, Brian. *Popular Culture in Modern France: A Study of Cultural Discourse.* London: Routledge,1991.

Ryan, Donna F. *The Holocaust and the Jews of Marseilles: The Enforcement of Anti-Semitic Policies in Vichy France.* Urbana: U of Illinois P, 1996.

Silverman, Maxim. *Deconstructing the Nation: Immigration, Racism, and Citizenship in Modern France.* New York: Routledge, 1992.

Singer, Isaac Bashevis. *Enemies: A Love Story.* Trans. Alizan Shevrin and Elizabeth Shub. New York: Farrar, 1972.

Ungar, Steven. *Scandal and Aftereffect: Blanchot and France since 1930.* Minneapolis: U of Minnesota P, 1995.

Wollheim, Richard. *Freud.* London: Fontana, 1991.

FURTHER READING

Criticism

Baele, Nancy. "A Climate of Mind." *Canadian Forum* 75, no. 858 (April 1997): 35-7.
　Offers a laudatory review of *The Selected Stories of Mavis Gallant,* asserting that Gallant "stands among the best writers of the century, the equal of Nabokov."

Bell, Millicent. "Fiction Chronicle." *Partisan Review* 64, no. 3 (1997): 414-27.
　Elucidates the influence of history on the subject matter and organization of the stories in *The Collected Stories of Mavis Gallant.*

Bell, Pearl K. "Rara Mavis." *New Republic* 215, no. 22 (25 November 1996): 42-5.
　Identifies exile as a key theme in Gallant's *Collected Stories.*

Betts, Doris. Review of *Across the Bridge,* by Mavis Gallant. *America* 170, no. 8 (5 March 1994): 28.
　Positive review of *Across the Bridge.*

Condé, Mary. "The Chapel Paintings in Mavis Gallant's 'In the Tunnel.'" In *Image et Récit: Littérature(s) et Arts Visuels du Canada,* edited by Jean-Michel Lacroix, Simone Vauthier, and Héliane Ventura, pp. 97-110. Paris: Presses de la Sorbonne Nouvelle, 1993.
　Underscores the significance of the painting of Judas in "In the Tunnel."

———. "Mavis Gallant and the Politics of Cruelty." *Yearbook of English Studies* 31 (2001): 168-81.
　Explores Gallant's treatment of anti-Semitism and the dangers of fascism in her stories "Malcolm and Bea" and "In the Tunnel."

Dobozy, Tamas. "Designed Anarchy" in Mavis Gallant's *The Moslem Wife and Other Stories.*" *Canadian Literature,* no. 158 (autumn 1998): 65-88.

Analyzes Gallant's anarchic aesthetic in the stories of *The Moslem Wife and Other Stories.*

Dvorak, Marta. "Mavis Gallant's Fiction: Taking the (Rhetorical) Measure of the Turning Point." In *Varieties of Exile: New Essays on Mavis Gallant,* edited by Nicole Côté and Peter Sabor, pp. 63-74. New York: Peter Lang, 2002.

Examines Gallant's narrative process in the stories of *Home Truths.*

Furman, Laura. "Stories of Mavis Gallant." *Saturday Night* 111, no. 8 (October 1996): 109-14.

Overview of Gallant's life and literary interests.

Gabriel, Barbara. "Gallant Language." *Canadian Forum* 72, no. 827 (March 1994): 38-40.

Explicates Gallant's use of language in the stories of *Home Truths.*

Gallant, Mavis and David Finkle. "Mavis Gallant: An Oeuvre Extraordinaire." *Publishers Weekly* 243, no. 41 (7 October 1996): 46-7.

Interview in which Gallant discusses her creative process, her relationship with her literary editors, and the publication of her *Collected Stories.*

Gardam, Jane. "The Language of Her Imagination." *Spectator* 278, no. 8805 (3 May 1997): 42-3.

Finds *The Selected Stories of Mavis Gallant* to be an enjoyable yet exhausting read.

Greenstein, Michael. "How They Write Us: Accepting and Excepting 'The Jew' in Canadian Fiction." *Shofar* 20, no. 2 (winter 2002): 5-39.

Considers the depiction of Jewish characters in the work of several female Canadian authors, including Gallant.

Ingham, David. "The Poetics of Dislocation." *Books in Canada* 31, no. 3 (May 2002): 19-20.

Contends that the 2002 rerelease of *Home Truths* shows that the collection holds up well over time.

Keefer, Janice Kulyk. "Bridges and Chasms: Multiculturalism and Mavis Gallant's 'Virus X.'" *World Literature Written in English* 31, no. 2 (1991): 100-11.

Explores Gallant's depiction of multiculturalism in "Virus X."

Krauss, Jennifer. "Family Secrets." *New Republic* 210, no. 13 (28 March 1994): 43-5.

Surveys the major thematic concerns of *Across the Bridge.*

Mathews, Lawrence. "Ghosts and Saints: Notes on Mavis Gallant's *From the Fifteenth District.*" *Essays on Canadian Writing,* no. 42 (winter 1990): 154-72.

Maintains that readers may discern saints and ghosts in *From the Fifteenth District.*

Murray, Heather. "'Its Image on the Mirror': Canada, Canonicity, the Uncanny." *Essays on Canadian Writing,* no. 42 (winter 1990): 102-30.

Discusses Gallant as a Canadian writer.

Prose, Francine. "Unknown Master: The Fictions of Mavis Gallant." *Harper's Magazine* 306, no. 1835 (April 2003): 88-92.

Lauds Gallant's *Paris Stories* as cerebral yet deeply affecting.

Schaub, Danielle. "Structural Patterns of Alienation and Disjunction: Mavis Gallant's Firmly-Structured Stories." *Canadian Literature,* no. 136 (spring 1993): 45-59.

Stylistic examination of three Gallant stories, asserting that the firmly structured tales convey "patterns of fragmentation, disconnection, or alienation."

Schrank, Bernice. "Popular Culture and Political Consciousness in Mavis Gallant's *My Heart is Broken.*" *Essays on Canadian Writing,* no. 42 (winter 1990): 57-71.

Investigates the references to books and movies in the stories of *My Heart is Broken* and maintains that "the stories collectively illustrate various permutations of genteel angst and lower-class anomy."

Smythe, Karen. "The Silent Cry: Empathy and Elegy in Mavis Gallant's Novels." *Studies in Canadian Literature* 15, no. 2 (spring 1990): 116-35.

Argues that Gallant's longer fictions enable the reader to develop an empathetic attachment that Gallant does not allow in her short stories.

Ware, Tracy. Review of *Across the Bridge,* by Mavis Gallant. *Studies in Short Fiction* 32, no. 2 (spring 1995): 239-40.

Regards *Across the Bridge* to be one of Gallant's best works of short fiction.

Whitfield, Agnès. "(Dis)playing Différance: *Across the Bridge* by Mavis Gallant." In *Varieties of Exile: New Essays on Mavis Gallant,* edited by Nicole Côté and Peter Sabor, pp. 49-62. New York: Peter Lang Publishing, Inc., 2002.

Aims to "weave together two previously separate

strands in critical studies of Mavis Gallant's writing: on the one hand, the demonstrated importance of deferral at various levels in her writing; and, on the other, the singularly complex and paradoxical inter-linguistic and intercultural context from which she writers as an expatriate author."

Wilkshire, Claire. "'Voice is Everything': Reading Mavis Gallant's 'The Pegnitz Junction.'" *University of Toronto Quarterly* 69, no. 4 (fall 1994): 891-916.

Claims that the polyphony of "The Pegnitz Junction" makes it "one of Gallant's most intricate and densely textured fictions."

Additional coverage of Gallant's life and career is contained in the following sources published by Thomson Gale: *Contemporary Authors,* **Vols. 69-72;** *Contemporary Authors New Revision Series,* **Vols. 29, 69, 117;** *Contemporary Canadian Authors,* **Vol. 1;** *Contemporary Literary Criticism,* **Vols. 7, 18, 38, 172;** *Contemporary Novelists,* **Ed. 7;** *Dictionary of Literary Biography,* **Vol. 53;** *DISCovering Authors: Canadian Edition*; *DISCovering Authors: Most-studied Authors*; *Encyclopedia of World Literature in the 20th Century,* **Ed. 3;** *Literature Resource Center; Major 20th-Century Writers,* **Eds. 1, 2;** *Reference Guide to English Literature,* **Ed. 2;** *Reference Guide to Short Fiction,* **Ed. 2; and** *Short Story Criticism,* **Vol. 5.**

Olive Senior
1941-

(Full name Olive Marjorie Senior) Jamaican short story writer, poet, and nonfiction writer.

INTRODUCTION

Senior is regarded as a distinctive voice in West Indian literature. Critics have praised her reproduction of authentic Jamaican Creole in her written work, as well as her insightful exploration of such issues as identity, cultural nationalism, class stratification, and the oppressive impact of religion on women and the poor. Her portraits of the lives of Jamaican children and women struggling to transcend ethnic, class, and gender roles are viewed as notable literary achievements of West Indian fiction.

BIOGRAPHICAL INFORMATION

Senior was born December 23, 1941, in western Jamaica, in an isolated area known for its hilly, limestone terrain. This early environment figures prominently in her poetry and fiction. As a child she attended Montego Bay High School for Girls, where she excelled in her studies and founded a school literary magazine. During this time she also began to contribute articles for *The Daily Gleaner,* the major newspaper on the island. After high school Senior traveled to Wales briefly to study journalism, and then she attended Carleton University, in Ottawa, Canada. She received her B.A. degree in journalism from Carleton in 1967. Around this time she began to write her first short stories. In 1980 several of her poems appeared in the influential poetry collection *Jamaica Women.* She worked as a freelance writer and researcher as well as an editor of the influential periodical *Jamaica Journal* from 1982 to 1989. Senior has been a guest lecturer and writer-in-residence in both the Caribbean and North America. She has received several prestigious awards for her work, including the Institute of Jamaica Centenary Medal in 1980, the Commonwealth Writers Prize in 1987, the Silver Musgrave Medal for Literature in 1989, and the F. G. Bressani Literary Prize for poetry in 1994. She makes her home in Toronto, Canada, but spends much of her time in Kingston, Jamaica.

MAJOR WORKS OF SHORT FICTION

Many of Senior's stories are concerned with issues of ethnicity and identity. *Summer Lightning and Other Stories* (1986), Senior's first collection of short fiction,

is comprised of ten short stories set in rural Jamaican communities, utilizes Jamaican Creole, and focuses on the perspective of poor, rural children. In "Ballad," a young schoolgirl, Lenora, is reproached by her teacher for writing a eulogy on the local harlot, Miss Rilla. Told Miss Rilla is not an appropriate subject for her admiration, Lenora disagrees and describes her identification with Miss Rilla's alienation from the community and refusal to submit to oppressive societal expectations. Several stories, such as "Bright Thursdays," concern the alienation that results from moving children from home to home, usually in search of financial security and social mobility. Senior's second collection, *Arrival of the Snake-Woman and Other Stories* (1989), is viewed as a more expansive book that switches the focus of the stories to more urban, middle-class settings. Reviewers note that she also experiments with the stories in the collection and utilizes standard English more than Jamaican Creole. In the title story, a mysterious, exotic Indian woman causes much disruption among the women of a small Jamaican village. Over time the woman overcomes the alienation of being the outsider and gains the trust and friendship of the other women. Reviewers argue that the story signifies the resistance to change and the fear of outsiders and nonconformity in isolated West Indian communities. In "Two Grandmothers," a young girl juxtaposes the worlds of her two grandmothers through a series of monologues: Grandmother Del lives in rural poverty but is blessed with a generous and caring community; Grandmother Elaine lives in affluence in the city but lacks the camaraderie of a close community of friends and neighbors. Senior's most recent collection, *Discerner of Hearts* (1995), includes nine stories that once again focus on female characters who struggle to transcend a rigid hierarchal class structure. These stories are set in Jamaica and in various times from the colonial period to the present day.

CRITICAL RECEPTION

Critics commend Senior's short fiction as insightful and humorous and identify the strength of her writing as the creation of richly detailed portrayals of Jamaican community life. Some view these depictions as a form of cultural nationalism and an affirmation of the value of the rural, small-town experience. Senior's use of language is a recurring topic of critical interest; reviewers consider her utilization of Jamaican Creole and oral storytelling traditions as powerful narrative devices. In particular, her well-crafted use of Standard English and Jamaican Creole denotes issues of hierarchy and class stratification in Jamaican society. Senior's stories are also noted for their interplay between tradition and modernity as well as their sensitive representations of the female experience from a woman's perspective. Themes of alienation, displacement, child abuse, racial discrimination, colonial victimization, and the search for personal and cultural identities have been named as the key motifs of Senior's short fiction. Lauded for her rich depiction of Jamaican culture and her insight into the human condition, Senior is regarded as a major figure in the development of Jamaican literature.

PRINCIPAL WORKS

Short Fiction

Summer Lightning and Other Stories 1986
Arrival of the Snake-Woman and Other Stories 1989
Discerner of Hearts 1995

Other Major Works

The Message Is Change: A Perspective on the 1972 General Elections (nonfiction) 1972

A-Z of Jamaican Heritage (nonfiction) 1984
Talking of Trees (poetry) 1986
Working Miracles: Women's Lives in the English-speaking Caribbean (nonfiction) 1991
Gardening in the Tropics (poetry) 1994

CRITICISM

Evelyn O'Callaghan (essay date spring 1988)

SOURCE: O'Callaghan, Evelyn. "Feminist Consciousness: European/American Theory, Jamaican Stories." *Journal of Caribbean Studies* 6, no. 2 (spring 1988): 143-62.

[*In the following essay, O'Callaghan considers the political orientation of contemporary West Indian women's fiction through an examination of four short story collections written by Jamaican female authors, including Senior's* Summer Lightning.]

The impetus for this paper was a desire to explore the political orientation of contemporary West Indian women's fiction. Four recently published collections of short stories by Jamaican women seemed a manageable starting point for a preliminary investigation: Olive Senior's ***Summer Lightning***;[1] Hazel Campbell's *Woman's Tongue*;[2] The Sistren Collective's *Lionheart Gal*;[3] and Opal Palmer Adisa's *Bake Face and Other Guava Stories*.[4] Inevitably, a theoretical "clearing the decks" has made comprehensive textual analysis impossible given the restrictions of such an essay, so I'd like to start by briefly generalizing about the scope and content of each book.

Summer Lightning's ten stories of rural Jamaican community life are, in my opinion, the finest of the collections. The majority of tales feature a female character, but the dominant perspective is that of the child, and it is evocation of the child's world, an often mysterious jumble of magic and horror, that is Senior's main achievement. The stories deal with threats from the external world, whether physical or emotional, and the half-understood and painful conflicts within.

Each story is fitted with a narrative language integrated into the dominant point of view; often, narrative language is the speaker's language and spans the Jamaican creole continuum, stretching its resources to the full. The first two pages alone utilize Biblical pronouncement, modern technological jargon, Rastafarian apocalyptic imagery and the proverbial style of folk wisdom, in the utterance of Bro. Justice. In addition, the sociolinguistic patterning of speech events is accurately observed—the "double conversation" (8) is one example. No concessions are made to the foreign reader in the way of parenthesized explanations or glosses.

Senior subtly exposes the repressiveness and self-sacrifice at the core of conventional morality as it has been applied to women, and the spiritual and emotional deformities which result. Only Bekkah, in **"Do Angels Wear Brassieres,"** has the inner resources to challenge the stultifying restrictions imposed by authority on the girl-child; Ma Bell, in **"Country of the One Eye God,"** representing the final phase of life, emerges as a victim whose complicity in her oppression is largely the result of a false value system inculcated by traditional religion.

Most of the stories, then, at once portray an almost idyllic community organically connected to the Jamaican landscape *and* reveal the frightening inadequacies in the society for the nurturing of the maturing individual.

Woman's Tongue contains eight stories, two of which are not up to the overall standard: the attempt to invoke a mysterious extra-physical force at work in the love affair of "The Painting" seems to me rather strained, and the final political allegory/fairy tale works on the didactic level at the expense of the literary—although this may well be the author's intention. The other well-written stories work together to form a medley of women's voices, telling their stories of artistic creation, spiritual renewal or disillusionment, the breakup of marriage and the pain of exploitative relationships.

Like Senior, Hazel Campbell has an unfaltering ear for Jamaican speech and, since her scope is wider (urban and rural; middle class and poor; the suburb, the slum and the seaside resort are all depicted), she has ample scope for capturing its rich variety, unimpeded by irritating translations or embedded information. By and large, the narrative employs West Indian English reportage, but even her "best 'pop-style' language" (1) is uniquely Jamaican, and in the excellent "Miss Girlie" creole and standard are woven into a seamless medium.

As in *Lionheart Gal,* women's reality in the contemporary Jamaica of supermarket shortages, the "parallel economy" and constant financial hardship is not a pleasant one. Without hectoring, Campbell reiterates the point that a social philosophy which stresses only material advancement has a negative effect on personal relationships. A quiet irony at Ivan's expense ("Miss Girlie") indicts his warped values and the insensitive logic by which he proposes to make Girlie "proud so till!" by using the money he gains from prostituting her to "set her up" in a comfortable life-style.

A straitlaced Christianity—one in which the merit of salvation "had probably less to do with a concern for her soul and more for the protection of her virginity" (23)—is partly responsible for the instillation of submissiveness in these women, all "dutiful wives." But the unhealthy relationship between the sexes more often comes down to a failure of communication and an inability to question stereotypical roles. A hint, however, that this is not an unalterable state of affairs occurs at the end of "The Thursday Wife" where "patient Mary" thinks that perhaps she will no longer be able to "accommodate" her husband's behaviour (42).

Opal Palmer Adisa's collection of "Guava Stories" (so-called, I presume, because they are to be like the Black peasant women who form their subject matter—"smooth outside and sweeter inside") consists of four stories set in rural and village Jamaica. They are told in matter-of-fact standard English with occasional lyrical splashes, and some intrusive explanation for the foreign reader (the constitution of Solomon Gundy, 98), but the dialogue is for the most part a credible representation of Jamaican Creole.

At times, the author attempts to make a story carry more weight than it is able to: "Widows Walk," for example, where the motif of rivalry between human woman and West African sea-goddess is the ground for several incidences of supernatural vision and premonition which aren't fully integrated into the protagonist's emotional dilemma, and which lead to anticipation of a resolution very different from the rather flat ending we get.

However, most of the stories, particularly "Bake Face," skilfully expose the social and emotional perplexities faced by these women and their strategies for coping (or not) with their men, children and earning a livelihood. As Barbara Christian asserts in her salutory introduction, the web of female relationships is a vital force in this coping process, and the stories are all from the woman's viewpoint.

Lionheart Gal is, as Honour Ford Smith introduces it, a collection of fifteen accounts of ways in which the women of the Sistren Theatre Collective have "come to terms with difficulties in their personal lives" as they move "from girlhood to adulthood, country to city, isolated individual experiences to a more politicised collective awareness" (xiii). The "plot" then isn't so different from the other books: what is striking, however, is the way the raw (and I use this adjective deliberately) material comes across in the women's own testimonies, in the nearest scribal equivalent to orature I have read for a while. Of course, the uncompromising use of Jamaican Creole as the reader's only access to a direct encounter with these characters and their self-perceptions is a major factor in this immediacy.

There are more stories here, rounded out by a wealth of incidental detail which cumulatively reflects Jamaica, now and in the recent past, and what it means to working-class women, in this case brought together by the emergency employment (crash) programme of the 1970s. Barbara Christian's observation about Adisa's female characters being neither overt rebels nor content earth mothers (x) applies here, too, despite Ford Smith's initial attempt to fit the testimonies into a neat double-legacy paradigm of Nanny/nanny role models (xiv).

The dominant impression is of the "toughness" of these women's lives, and like Defoe's Moll Flanders, there is little energy left over from "hustling" for the basics in an exploitative system to devote to romantic illusions. Indeed, as Ford Smith puts it, "sexual relationships between men and women are often characterised by the tedious playing out of a power struggle ritualised by trade-offs of money and sex" (xvii).

Yet these testimonies are so animated, so dramatic, so filled with humour and "spunks" that it is pure condescension to react with pity; over and over, one senses the aptness of the title, *Lionheart Gal.*

I have used the Sistren stories largely as a control, to test the applicability of political ideology as it informs the more "crafted" fictions. However, a brief digression is necessary here to rebut the anticipated complaints that *Lionheart Gal* is "merely" autobiography.

Conventionally, it is almost a given that women's writing (cross-culturally) contains autobiographical/confessional elements, and criticism has paid close attention to these—often with unpleasant consequences for the writer.[5] Lorna Goodison, another Jamaican writer, has acknowledged the autobiographical charge: "I have had people telling me that they [her poems] were too private. Somebody actually said that reading my work is like looking through a keyhole. . . ."[6] However, she claims, the truth of a particular feeling in a poem is more than an individual response, but speaks to (and for) the reader's experience also. Since the experiences of the Sistren women do likewise, and have been shaped and transformed in the text—by the editor, by the Collective, and by individual story-tellers (a process clearly delineated in the Introduction, xxvi-xxx), I felt justified in writing about *Lionheart Gal* as I read it: a collection of fascinating stories.

In any case, critical resistance to autobiography as literature is minimal in studies of Black and Third World writing: according to Selwyn Cudjoe, the genre has a long history in Afro-American writing. Since the objective accounts of much diasporic narrative were patently untrue, it was left to personal accounts to convey the reality.[7] However, he distinguishes between the personal in the sense of egotistic subjectivity, and the collective personal: autobiography "is presumed generally to be of service to the group. It is never meant to glorify the exploits of the individual, and the concerns of the collective predominate. One's personal experiences are assumed to be an authentic expression of the society . . ." (10).

Finally, Mark McWatt convincingly argues that the tradition of the autobiographical novel is well-established in West Indian literature, and that the critic must come to terms with the "ultrafictional" experience (the truth behind the fiction) as part of the reading experience.[8] In addition, he suggests, "reality, the truth of actual experience, aspires to the shape and condition of fiction in order to be rescued from irrelevance and to participate in the power and permanence of art" (10). In that the long-unheard women of the Sistren Collective have chosen to articulate their (selected, edited, rewritten, "fictionalized") realities in a relatively permanent published form, they are making a political statement of intent to be heard in the public forum, and the collection of stories is thus extremely relevant to the topic under discussion.

One feature common to the collections is the sounding of the personal note, the attention to emotional response, particularly in close relationships. Perhaps this is a specifically female concern; certainly, several of the contributors to *Black Women Writers at Work* are of this opinion.[9] Not that male writers do not treat relationships as complex and significant, but these tend to be confrontational ones outside the male-female/domestic/community context in which women writers set their fiction; further, as Toni Cade Bambara puts it, Black women writers "are less likely to skirt the feeling place, to finesse with language, to camouflage emotions" (19).

Feminist theory, however, maintains the integral and necessary relation of the private and the public, the personal and the economic. According to Terry Eagleton, feminism does not recognise a distinction between questions of the human subject and questions of political struggle.[10] The clarification of this vital issue is one of the achievements of the Sistren Collective, as we hear in "Foxy and di Macca Palace War": "After we done talk ah get to feel dat di little day-to-day tings dat happen to we as women, is politics too. For instance, if yuh tek yuh pickney to hospital and it die in yuh hand— dat is politics. . . . If yuh man box yuh down, dat is politics. But plenty politicians don't tink dose tings have anyting to do wid politics" (*Lionheart Gal*, 253). Indeed Cornelia Butler Flora makes the case for female participation in the political process necessitating bringing "the female world . . . into public view—[and] that the public arena be expanded to include 'private' issues."[11] The achievement of this, she feels, is in fact a radical move since "the role of the state changes, male privilege within and outside the home is challenged, and the contradictions of patriarchy and capitalism are heightened" (557).

So, if one accepts the above, these stories in bringing the personal (private, emotional issues) into the public arena (literature) are making a contribution to feminist politics and are thus best analyzed by feminist literary criticism.

Which feminist literary theory, though? Well, a preliminary survey of recent American and European approaches seems to me to reveal five general orientations, although I am greatly simplifying here and, obviously, several approaches may be used in textual application.

The first focuses on *images of women* as they appear in literature, usually by men, and tries to ascertain whether such images take women's social and individual reality into account. I would include here aesthetic representations of women by female writers in what Showalter calls the "feminine stage":[12] that is, the phase in literary production where women internalize standards of the dominant (male) tradition in their work, including traditional views on social roles.

Generally, this approach seeks to explain the ideological bases which inform the (largely negative) images of women, and to illuminate the power conflict, largely resolved in favour of male dominance, that has led to the promotion of such stereotypes. Its methodology subordinates "literary" to political concerns and as such relates to Elaine Fido's definition of feminist (as opposed to womanist) criticism which deals with the writers' "understanding of the power relations in their experiential world."[13] Of course, it also explains their *lack* of understanding of such power relations where they uncritically adopt male stereotypes.

Since these Caribbean writers are *not* in the "feminine stage," such an orientation does not apply, although one can find stereotypical or limited presentations of women in West Indian literature by men.[14] But since sociological studies[15] have indicated that cross-cultural self-conceptions of men and women appear to be more dramatic than contrasts between those who share the same socio-cultural system, *is* it, in fact, possible to decide which stereotypes of women are negative?

For example, the "clinging mother" in Adisa's story, "Me Man Angel," who "after nine children . . . still felt hollow, unfulfilled" (61) and who channels all her devouring and possessive love into an almost sexual relationship with her sickly nephew, could indeed be perceived as a negative stereotype. But this would ignore the equally extraordinary responses of her husband, children and community to the angel-child, because of his vulnerability and singular (androgynous?) ability to demonstrate affection towards all sexes and age-groups.

Full motherhood, in the Jamaican context, is almost sacred.[16] And since Perry, in Adisa's story, is clearly portrayed as the community's child, drawing out "motherly" virtues of tenderness, generosity and unselfishness in everyone, then Denise's "excessive" devotion is no more than he deserves.

Another approach, which focuses on the woman writer, attempts to *recuperate a female tradition,* to prove, as in Showalter's title, that female authors have "a literature of their own." Usually, an exhaustive historical survey of women writers is used to demonstrate the existence of a hidden literary tradition. This is seen as a preferable alternative to the assimilation of women's art, like other minority art, into the canon—which, as Joanna Russ points out, "will thereby be more complete, but fundamentally unchanged."[17]

Instead, it attempts to define the consequences of the patriarchal order for female literary production (or to explain the *lack* of it) in the specific contexts (social, legal and so on) of woman's status in her society, and involves analysis of the psychological and imaginative strategies of female creativity. This means re-examining existing critical evaluation of women writers which ignore such factors since, as Cheri Register has shown, critics have tended to take the normative viewpoint as masculine and so judge female authors in terms of their conformity to sub-category status—hence generalizations about "the lady novelist" and the narrow/peripheral range of her experience.[18] Feminist critics question the supposed objectivity of such a tradition, and elaborate the contexts in which women *actually* wrote.

Attempts to discover early West Indian women writers are still in progress, so it is difficult to identify a female literary tradition into which these stories can be fitted. Indeed, they can be seen as part of the ongoing development of such a tradition. Perhaps this critical approach may help to illuminate why a female literary tradition has only recently emerged. However, since British and White American women writers, at least up to the 1950s, were primarily middle-class and university educated, it may not be feasible to take generalizations about their conditions and their strategies as bases for analyzing the emergence of a Caribbean "literature of their own."

Further, in the West Indian situation, admission of women writers into such a canon as exists has not been problematic since this canon is *not* an attempt to shore up the status quo, eschewing any deviant or subversive minority art. In fact, a large proportion of Caribbean fiction actively critiques the exclusivist establishment of Western literary tradition. Indeed, it might be asked whether Caribbean or women writers desire assimilation into the traditional canon.

A third direction in feminist literary theory, which concentrates on female characteristics in language and form, is that of the *New French Feminists*. As far as I can make out, these critics build on existing psychoanalytic theory, especially Jacques Lacan's model of the symbolic order as that of "the Law," the male order of culture and civilization and, of course, language.[19]

Since this symbolic order is in fact the patriarchal sexual and social order of society, feminist criticism views assimilation into it as induction into oppression. However, for the girl-child the entry is only partial, and she retains easier access to the pre-Oedipal patterns which are repressed in the symbolic order. These patterns (what Julia Kristeva calls the semiotic, the other side of language, and what I take to mean the underpinnings of language which correspond to the unruly, unhindered flow of bodily drives in the infant) are bound up with the child's contact with the mother's body and thus closely connected with femininity.

The French Feminists develop from this semiotic a theory of woman's language—écriture féminine—which is vitally linked to female sexuality. As a force *within* normal discourse concerned with the bodily and material qualities of language, with creative excess rather than precise meaning, with fluidity, plurality, diffusion, sensuousness and open-endedness, such impulses serve as a means of undermining normal discourse, and thus, the symbolic order.

So feminist writers are seen to be protesting their marginalization by phallocentric culture and language, by finding their own language, that which articulates their sexuality, or in Heléne Cixous's phrase, "writes the body." Such an approach relates to Fido's categorization of "womanist" criticism which concentrates on how writers "reflect the richness and complexity of woman's particular relation to sensuous experience" (9) as seen "in the very structures of language" (12) and literary form they utilize.

The trouble with the semiotic, given its fluid, open-ended, anarchic characteristics, is that it is impossible to codify and thus to comment on. However, I have a few initial reservations about this approach. Firstly, it can be taken to imply that women's use of language, at its most feminine, is *anti*-rational, *anti*-phallocentric, *anti*-system. To an extent, this suggests some kind of female essence, one that values difference from the male norm as a criterion. I feel this logic to be limited.

Again, one might question whether there is a specifically female way of using language, something I am not yet convinced of. There are certain linguistic and stylistic similarities in the short stories examined here, but are they specifically feminine traits?

Finally, if entrance into the symbolic order involves language acquisition, does this apply to all languages? Are West Indian Creoles also vehicles of the symbolic

order, or is it possible to say that they originated partly outside the confines of rigid civilization and culture as it was imposed by colonialism? Some of Harris's criticism suggests that the West Indian writer's (authentic) use of his/her language has subversive potential equal to that of écriture féminine.

However, close attention to the specifics of the woman writer's use of language and to the encoded revelations of the unconscious in this language, perhaps implicitly suggesting subtle subversion of the natural order of an authority, is an approach that proves useful for some of the stories; for example, Senior's **"Love Orange."**

Barely contained within chronology, this short piece is a timid foray into the "dark tunnel of my childhood" (15), a mind-realm where, perhaps, the boundaries between unconscious drives and the real are less clearly delineated.

Two symbols predominate: the orange (round, complete, organic, native, enclosed potential, positive) and the mutilated doll (unsymmetrical—"half a face and a finger missing"—man-made, stridently female in "billowing dress and petticoats," imported, and associated with nausea, fear and death).

For the child, the world which waits outside (adult sexuality?) is a threat to be warded off by rituals and talismans, although it intrudes in dream and vision, and it is to these we might look for elucidation. If the major symbols "write the body" and encode unconscious desires, the story might be read as an ambivalent desire for wholeness through giving love ("commitment") while dreading the vulnerability such giving entails for a woman (love is imaged as finite and exhaustible, like the orange). Giving (love/sexual submission) promises a new birth out of the "dark, silent house" (15), the "dark tunnel" (13); but it also involves dissection (of the orange/self), mutilation (the doll) and a kind of death: a violation, glimpsed as the nauseating "doll crawling into my hand and nestling there and I would run into the garden and be sick" (12).

To avoid the issue, the child buries the doll and resolves to trust her "orange" only to "one who could return no more" (14) and thus be unable to change and reject her. Incipient womanhood, sexuality, the ability to give fully, are tied to morbidity, and when the child *makes* the (misunderstood) giving gesture, her last protective stronghold crumbles, as do the bones of her hand smashed in the car door (15), to which she responds with numbness.

Movement between real and imaginary is imperceptible, as fluid as the story's structure, and certainly the externalization of body/self in sensuous objects is part of the linguistic strategy which, along with the incompleteness of the narrative (and persona), may place the piece within the realm that the French feminists outline. However, I want to stress that this is a rather *forced* reading. I have totally ignored the significance of the doll's European-ness, its China-blue eyes (linked with the sky/an all-seeing, revengeful God), and its (presumably) white, deformed plaster limbs: these details might be central to a West Indian critic's interpretation.

Black Feminist Criticism is another fairly recent direction in feminist theory, and focuses the preceding concerns onto Black women. Criticism following this directive points out Black experience as it shapes literary expression, and addresses the warping of literary images of Black women by racism. It traces the strategies women writers have used to counter these obstacles, by celebrating positive images or by subverting stereotyped ideals.[20]

This is Barbara Christian's methodology in *Black Women Novelists,*[21] where she traces the development of a Black female tradition of writers *and* critically examines the portrayal of various images of women in the light of contemporary thinking about race and gender. Significantly, she draws attention to ultimately destructive myths of "strong Black women" such as the matriarch of the 1950s and 60s who is in fact a variation of the nineteenth century "mammy" figure.

What is innovative about this critical approach is a concentration on the Black perspective; but I feel this has been part of most West Indian literary criticism, including that of women's fiction, for some time now. One reservation, however, is that Black feminist criticism, in published form anyway, is overwhelmingly Afro-*American* and certain generalizations about that context may not apply in the Caribbean.

Occasionally, this criticism may contain inaccuracies about the very different cultural orientations of Black people worldwide. An example in Barbara Christian's otherwise excellent study is a reference to West Indian immigrants to the United States being "different from other European immigrants, however, in that their land had never been truly theirs . . ." (81). It is difficult to see how German Jews had more claim to their land than Black Jamaicans had to theirs. Perhaps the claim results from her view of the West Indian's "hybrid culture, based on their African origins but very much affected by the British system that held them in bondage" (81), which seems a rather negative view of the creative processes involved in creolization.

Finally, I have utilized the umbrella term *prescriptive feminist criticism* for the approach which outlines, and evaluates according to, criteria for "good" or "authentic" women's literature. This approach includes all types

of criticism which lay down a norm of what feminist writing should say/do. Marxist-feminist writers like Adrienne Rich might serve as an example, since they appear to feel that women's literature should dedicate itself to the forging of a new consciousness of oppression by developing cultural myths of women in struggle and women in revolution. Such an agenda postulates a female audience and the writer's implicit aim of challenging sexism in language and culture with an ultimate utopian end—a transformed society.

Literature then is seen as serving the cause of liberation by, for example, promoting sisterhood, raising consciousness, and so on. Josephine Donovan, in her "Afterward" to *Feminist Literary Criticism,* concludes that "[t]he feminist critic maintains, in short, that there are truths and probabilities about the female experience that form a criterion against which to judge the authenticity of a literary statement about women" (77). She herself does not say what these are but rather calls for refining what is meant by women's reality/perspective (a kind of feminist epistemology) in order to specify this criterion.

The problem with any prescriptive approach is *who* determines the criteria for "good"; here, it is the cause of feminist liberation—but which feminists? The notion of "authenticity" is also problematic. If this is taken to mean the realistic portrayal of female experience and consciousness, it still presupposes a qualified judge of *what* is realistic. It does not seem possible to me to make universal statements about the truth of "woman's experience" or "woman's perspective" outside the cultural contexts of that experience or perspective. Even within the short stories mentioned, so many different experiences are conveyed. Doreen's life (in "The Emancipation of a Household Slave," *Lionheart Gal*) is a "hustle. Di main focus was weh and weh fi do fi get money" (103); so is that of "Miss Girlie" (*Woman's Tongue*). But Doreen's growth of self-assertion is for her own approbation (107-8) while Girlie's assumption of strength goes hand-in-hand with acquiescence in her own exploitation: "She would have to be strong. No more weeping. She would do the things her man wanted her to do. Help him to get the things he wanted even though it meant heartache for her" (56). Clearly, Girlie's choice cannot be seen as serving the cause of liberation, but is it thus less "authentic" than Doreen's?

And, of course, prescriptive criticism sidetracks the issue of prioritizing affiliations, for instance racial solidarity over feminist, as illustrated in a comment by Gwendolyn Brooks in *Black Women Writers at Work*: "Yes, black women have got some problems with black men and vice versa, but these are family matters. At no time must we allow whites, males or females, to convince us that we should split . . . It's another divisive tactic" (47).

The main difficulty I have with European and American feminist theory is the rather limited conception of "difference" which underpins much of their ideology. It is based on a gender-linked dichotomy pointed out by Simone de Beauvoir in the early days of feminist thinking: the normative sex is masculine and "neutral" truth has in fact been equated with the masculine perspective, so that when we read "x is true of all of us" what is really meant is that "x is true of all men." Men are the first, authentic sex and women the second, deviant sex.

Since the symbolic order is patriarchal and the only means of articulation is through the symbolic order, women's consciousness is shaped by and expressed in a language embodying a masculine perception of the world. The second sex sees the world, including herself, through male spectacles and can only "speak from within patriarchal discourse rather than from a source exterior to phallocentric symbolic forms."[22] Clearly, within the normative and perceptual order of this culture of which women writers are both a part *and* from which they are excluded,[23] literary self-expression will be problematic, since "feminine" is a kind of subcategory, conjuring up simply the opposite of what language allocates to the masculine/normative; so concepts such as subjective, irrational, physical and so on are feminine determinants.

To pretend that these differences do not exist, that women are not really different from men and art is "universal," is clearly absurd, no matter how well-intentioned such a view is to promote equality.

Some feminist aesthetic theory has moved on to make a positive of difference: rather than viewing it as a matter of deficiency, inferiority, loss, the feminine can be considered as a negation of the phallic and thus the privileged carrier of alternative vision. Thus, qualities antithetical to dominant male characteristics are stressed (receptivity versus productivity, sensitivity versus rationality) as a way of subverting the patriarchal order and its traditional (masculinist) criteria of art.

But in such a line of thinking, differentiation becomes "mere inversion,"[24] continuing what Showalter (13) calls the "dependency of opposition"[25] and discourse about "women's art" leads to grouping *all* artists together on the basis of being women and to prescriptive views on what they are/should be, in opposition to the male norm. And despite condemnation of the assumption of *one* female reality based on fixed ideas about the "nature of woman," some feminists do try to replace one set of "objective" standards with another programmatic set (focusing on opposition) in literary theory.[26]

The danger of such prescription (based on difference from the male) is that it can obscure differences *within* the feminist community; indeed, as Bronwyn Levy re-

minds us, matters like class- and race-based oppression are *not* little differences easily overcome if women unite.[27] In fact, the very notion of "otherness" that forms the matrix for this approach takes on new significance in cultures that have experienced colonialism. The connection has been observed between women's writing as a political act in the anti-patriarchal struggle, and Third World writing as a political act in the anti-colonial struggle.[28] But for the female Third World writer, the situation is unique, for if she is other (inferior) to men, and Third World literature is also other (inferior) to that of "the Great Tradition," then she is the other other.

My point is that certain rigid presuppositions in feminist aesthetics which do not take into sufficient account other differences (cultural and racial, say) within the community of women, make wholesale acceptance of feminist literary analyses rather difficult in the Caribbean context where varying priorities in women's writing cannot be trimmed to fit any neat paradigm of committed "women's art."

I would like to end by suggesting that there is not *one* political orientation in the work of West Indian women writers, but several; and by illustrating three of these which predominate in the short story collections.

THE FEMINIST ORIENTATION

In that all the writers represent female experience from the woman's perspective and create complex and credible images of women involved in some kind of power struggle, they are fulfilling a feminist agenda.

Lionheart Gal is clearly motivated by a feminist orientation—indeed, the book's conceptual framework was an attempt to answer questions dealing with women's awareness of their oppression *as women* (xxvii). Certainly, they are also oppressed by race/class hierarchical assumptions, but their stories are expressions of the *female* perspective on this experience.

The first story, "Rebel Pickney," begins with the statement, "All my life me live in fear," (3) and the accounts that follow outline the reasons for such a condition. In childhood, adult socialization is often synonymous with brutality: Betty, the "rebel pickney" tells us, "My faada no believe inna no discipline at all, but murderation. Just pure beating" (5); Senior's stories bear out this elevation of cruelty into a philosophy: "All the same right is right and there is only one right way to bring up a child and that is by bus' ass pardon my french Miss Mary but hard things call for hard words. That child should be be getting blows from the day she born" (***Summer Lightning,*** 69).

Adolescence is accompanied by sexual initiation, but ignorant of the workings of their own bodies ("Me no know what pregnant mean. Dem always a tell yuh seh baby drop out a sky, and come inna plane and all dem something deh" (22). With men always ready to use sweet-talk or force, motherhood is premature, often un-welcome, and the cause of familial and social sanctions. It also puts a stop to education: "dem boy pickney . . . dem go round and breed off woman an is not dem a feel it. Dem can go a school same way, but di gal dem haffi stop from school" (23). Without skill training, young mothers must either face underpayment and ex-ploitation in the labour market, or the insecurity of de-pendence on a man who then has the right to control her life and body.

Significantly, however, these stories chart the women's tactics for dealing with such situations, their processes of asserting independence and attempting autonomy. An early disadvantage is seen to be the discouragement in girls of enquiry: "I grew up thinking it was wrong to ask questions" (115). Clearly, through Sistren, these women *have* come to question the inevitability of the patterning of their lives as a first step in liberation, al-though it is important to remember that this is by no means true of others outside the Collective. Further, these women feel a responsibility, as Doreen puts it, to help other women to learn from her "grass roots reality on stage" that "black people are not born to be poor and exploited" (108). They attempt then, to paraphrase Ntozake Shange, to shatter the silence of foremothers, to expose the lies and the myths about what it is like to be a grown woman.[29]

Campbell's stories also seem to have a feminist per-spective, not so much in the lauding of women's strength under duress, but in pointing up the toll taken by their adoption of the submissive role in male/female interaction. Jamaican men appear fairly negatively here. Peter ("The Painting") is a weak individual who over-extends himself climbing the social ladder and then runs off, leaving his dependent wife to shoulder the consequences. Bertie ("The Thursday Wife") feels safe in his philandering because at home his well trained "Mary, patient Mary, . . . through all the years had never even questioned him when many other women would have made a stink" (42). Ivan actively terrorizes Girlie into selling herself for his American dollars, and Mrs. Telfer in "Supermarket Blues" is not much better off: "She would ask Ralph for more money and he would shout at her, yelling that she was asking for more and more money and bringing less and less into the house" (64).

These women's complicity (despite potential or actual financial self-sufficiency) in the assumption that they are their men's possessions and servants, fulfilled in sacrificing for them and catering to every whim (Bertie "had even threatened to box her because she hadn't ironed his merinos" [37]), and the failure of communi-cation between the sexes (also featured in Adisa's title

story) make for an indictment of gender relations that gathers force as the stories progress. The only hope for improvement lies in the anger and the querying of the situation that *Woman's Tongue* surely provokes in the reader.

CULTURAL NATIONALISM

In accurately rendering the "Jamaicanness" of women's lives, the writers make a contribution to West Indian lit-erature by furthering the claim that the region has a dy-namic and complex cultural life of its own. Lorna Goodison, in praising West Indian writers like Earl Lovelace for stressing the positives of Caribbean cul-tural achievement, repudiates the literary stance of be-wailing our lack: "It seems to me pointless to spend so much time washing down the corpse and dressing it, when officially you don't dead yet."[30]

Certainly, Hazel Campbell conveys a sense of a living culture, "a mixing of old customs and new ways" (71), as, for example, in "Easter Sunday Morning," where African-derived obeah rituals and the arcane mysteries of herbal healing come into exciting contact with the orthodox Anglican church and its parson with "a mod-ern scientific mind" (75). In Adisa's *Bake Face,* the em-phasis is on the continuity of African heritage in the lives of Jamaican peasants. Old goddesses, Oshun and Yemoja, retain power and must be pacified (114); old rituals to counteract obeah and spirit possession are uti-lized regularly (for example, by "Miss Maud, the com-munity myalist" [51-2]); and signs, omens and portents are acknowledged as important.

Adisa's collection, it seems to me, deliberately sets out to establish the existence of an alternative Jamaican culture to that imposed by imperial Britain. This is a political orientation followed by other Jamaican women writers such as Erna Brodber, who has stressed the need for recording oral history,[31] an account of the past handed down via ancestors rather than textbooks. In-deed, she has followed her own advice in *Jane and Louisa Will Soon Come Home* (1980).

Similarly, Michelle Cliff (like Adisa, Jamaican-born, now living in the United States) holds the view that "to write as a complete Caribbean woman" necessitates a reclamation of the "African part of ourselves" as well as utilizing ancestral art forms and language (Jamaican Creole or, as she calls it, *patois*).[32] For Cliff, this delib-erate counterbalancing is crucial for "a writer coming from a culture of colonialism" (13) and has politically influenced the direction her writing has taken.

Olive Senior's *Summer Lightning* can also be seen as partially motivated by cultural nationalism in that the stories not only value the way of life of rural communi-ties, emphasizing the role of older women as the memory of the tribe (16) but actively condemn the logic that teaches contempt for one's origins as an inevitable part of progress and modernity. This is the point of **"Ascot."** But typically, she ensures that no easy moral is drawn: in **"Real Old Time T'ing,"** townie Patricia's search "for her roots" is translated into greedy acquisition of antiques and junk alike merely for the sake of having, while the narrator/community voice unknowingly reflects an equal lack of connection to (symbols of) the past when she explains that "people glad to get rid of all the ol' bruck furniture they have around. They want to go and trust plastic living room chair and aluminum dinette set down at Mr. V. Store" (61).

Comprehension of Jamaica's colonial trauma (Prudence in *Lionheart Gal* is able to connect the lack of father/daughter relationship with the devaluation of family life during slavery [111]), and an acknowledgement of the creole culture which has emerged through time's transformation suggests an implicit orientation towards advocating cultural sovereignty in these texts. Cliff has noted the role of creole languages in this task (13), and *Lionheart Gal* refers to the sterility of the creative imagination when offered only foreign channels of expression (184). In consolidating the literary potential of the Jamaican Creole continuum, these writers are challenging the hegemony not only of the "Queen's English," but of any outward-looking value system.

CRITIQUE OF RACE/CLASS HIERARCHY

Finally, any concern with origins (and indeed, with the nature of womanhood) in the Caribbean will be inextricably bound up with race/class concerns (the two being virtually synonymous in Jamaican society for some time), as is evident, for instance, in "Grandma's Estate" (*Lionheart Gal*).

Campbell's racial observations are matter-of-fact and unobtrusive; without being told, we fit her characters into their race/class bracket, and there is little stridency in the casual references to White people as parsimonious employers or gullible tourists to be milked. Different attitudes to people, depending on their position in the hierarchy (to Miss Maud and Mrs. Telfer by supermarket staff, for example), are wryly observed but never questioned. Campbell presents the facts and leaves the reader to judge.

Adisa, by contrast, is quick to call attention to race and stresses "Blackness" as the norm of physical beauty: Richard ("Duppy Get Her") is ashamed of his "red nega" colouring and "wanted to be purple-dark like the rest of them" (46). This contradicts the criteria internalized by Doreen, who notices that teachers favour "di tall hair fair skin pickney dem . . . Me did waan be like dem. Di whole heapa cussing bout how me black and ugly, only boots me now to say me a no notten" (*Lionheart Gal*, 99).

In that these women writers tell of and address themselves to Jamaicans, the vast majority of whom are non-white, they are fulfilling Gwendolyn Brooks's directive: "I know that the Black emphasis must be not *against white* but *FOR Black.*"[33] But Olive Senior's stories, which frequently undermine the positive portrayal of the Jamaican peasantry by implicit criticism of the debilitating internalization of race/class prejudices, seem to me more informed by a race/class critique than the others.

Throughout **Summer Lightning,** the niceties of this hierarchy are adhered to by the decent, strict elite among the community: your race/class determines how and from which entrance you are admitted to a house (1), a Black labourer who turns Rasta is seen as losing the respect which his middle-class employers consider their due (6); self-worth is imaged in terms of possession of a certain life style, that is: "a big house with heavy mahogany furniture and many rooms, fixed mealtimes, a mother and father who were married to each other and lived together in the same house . . . who would send you to school with the proper clothes . . ." (**"Bright Thursdays,"** 36).

Inevitably, social standing is linked with race: "brown skin with straight hair" is superior to "dark skin but almost straight hair," which is superior to black, and so on. One *can* rise socially, through education or money, but this involves adopting the values of the "clear" middle class who fear the encroachment of the Black masses into their territory and who, like Miss Christie, have nothing but contempt for the likes of the "uppity black gal" who "seduced" her son to "raise her colour" (40).

Social mobility, then, involves repudiating all previous connections for a life of imitation and conformity. In this, *all* classes are in agreement and here is the rub of Senior's indictment. That Myrtle, in **"Bright Thursdays,"** should be seduced by "a young man of high estate . . . [who] had come visiting the Wheelers where Myrtle was a young servant" (38), and that the resultant child is neither acknowledged nor supported by him or his family, can be explained in the social context. But that Myrtle should raise her daughter to admire, imitate and aspire to the ways of those "of high estate," at the cost of alienation from her own class and colour, is untenable.

The stories, then, vitiate the values informing the rural peasantry's desire to keep up appearances (16), to associate only with "good" families (18) and their tendency to denigrate their own people and their own race: "everybody know this country going to the dog these days for is pure black people children they pushing to send high school. Anybody ever hear you can educate monkey?" (**"Ballad,"** 109-10). Further, by depicting the confusion, self-doubt and fragmentation which such contradictions wreak on the child's psyche—Lenore, Laura, the narrator of **"Confirmation Day"**—such attitudes assume evil proportions and lessen the stature of the older women in the community who instil racism and snobbery along with manners and morals.

Perhaps this brief survey of political directions in the work of Caribbean women writers indicates the complex social visions which inform their stories, and the inapplicability to them of literary criticism linked to a particular political programme. In writing about responses to her own work, Audre Lord notes that: "Black writers . . . who step outside the pale of what black writers are supposed to be, are condemned to silences in black literary circles that are as total and destructive as any imposed by racism."[34] Her point is that any insistence on a unilateral definition of "blackness," however motivated, spells trouble for creativity: "In the mistaken belief that unity must mean sameness, differences within the black community . . . were sometimes mislabeled, oversimplified, and repressed" (102).

I have attempted to point out similar problems for Caribbean women's writing when an over-rigid concept of feminist theory is applied. I hold, with Lord, "that difference is a reason for celebration and growth" (103) and therefore, instead of pursuing a linear analysis of political orientation in the works of these writers, it might be more apt to use the crossroads model elaborated by Fido[35] and Tate,[36] and to situate each work at a point where its place on the continuums of political direction intersect. I have chosen to illustrate three such scales: more or less concern with feminist politics; more or less concern with protesting negative assumptions about race; and more or less concern with the promotion of creole cultural forms unique to the region.

As Fido points out in "Crossroads," "[w]omen writers in the third world have a complex series of possibilities to realise in their work, if they choose to effect full consciousness of their situation." It is their skill that they do so, and ours as critics to draw attention also to the differences of orientation within and between their works.

Notes

1. Published, Kingston and Port-of-Spain: Longman Caribbean, 1986. All page references to this edition.

2. Published, Kingston, Jamaica: Savacou, 1985. All page references to this edition.

3. Published, London: The Women's Press, 1986. All page references to this edition.

4. Published, Berkeley: Kelsey St. Press, 1986. All page references to this edition.

5. See Sigrid Weigel, "Double Focus: On the History of Women's Writing," *Feminist Aesthetics,* ed. Gisela Ecker (London: The Women's Press, 1985) 66: "As far as women are concerned, no distinction is made between the *writer* and the *person.*" Elaine Showalter, in *A Literature of their Own: British Women Novelists from Brönte to Lessing* (London: Virago, 1978) 303, demonstrates this in her account of the distress of Sylvia Plath's mother at the publication of *The Bell Jar.*

6. Lorna Goodison, interviewed by Nadi Edwards, November 18, 1984, part one, *Pathways: A Journal of Creative Writing,* 2,4 (December 1984) 9.

7. Selwyn R. Cudjoe, essay on Maya Angelou, *Black Women Writers (1950-1980): A Critical Evaluation,* ed. Mari Evans (Garden City, New York: Anchor Books, 1984). Toni Morrison (*Black Women Writers [1950-1980]* 339) seems to agree with Cudjoe that the "autobiographical form is classic in Black American or Afro-American literature because it provided an instance in which a writer could be representative. . . ."

8. Mark McWatt, "Beyond the Novel: Prolegomena to Any Future Theory of West Indian Fiction," paper to Sixth Annual Conference on West Indian Literature, University of the West Indies, St. Augustine (May 1986) 7-9.

9. *Black Women Writers at Work,* ed. Claudia Tate (New York: Continuum, 1983). See, for example, comments by Ntozake Shange (151-52), Kristin Hunter (85) and Sonia Sanchez (143).

10. Terry Eagleton, *Literary Theory: An Introduction* (Oxford: Basil Blackwell, 1983) 215.

11. Cornelia Butler Flora, "From Sex Roles to Patriarchy: Recent Developments in the Sociology of Women—A Review Essay," *The Sociological Quarterly,* 23 (Autumn 1982) 557.

12. Showalter (1978,13) has defined three stages through which most literary subcultures pass in relation to the dominant one: imitation and internalization of the dominant tradition's modes and standards; protests against these standards and values, and advocacy of minority rights and values; self-discovery, a turning inward freed from some of the "dependency of opposition" in the search for identity. Applied to women's writing, these three stages are the *Feminine, Feminist* and *Female* phases.

13. Elaine Fido, "Feminist and Womanist Discourses: West Indian/American Lesbian Writers," paper to Sixth Annual Conference on West Indian Literature, Univ. of the West Indies, St. Augustine (May 1986) 9.

14. Random examples are deLisser's manipulative, materialistic Black middle-class women, and some of Lamming's mother figures—not to mention Naipaul's "sluts." Women may also figure as simply catalysts or symbols in a plot featuring the hero's development—Lovelace's Sylvia (*The Dragon Can't Dance,* 1979) and Harris's Catalena (*The Secret Ladder,* 1963). And women may be minimized to the point of near invisibility, as Rhonda Cobham claims of Jamaican nationalist literature and the "typical West Indian novel," in "Women in Jamaican Literature 1900-1950," *Out of the Kumbla: Womanist Perspectives on Caribbean Literature,* ed. Carole Boyce Davies and Elaine Savory Fido (Trenton, New Jersey: African World Press, in press).

15. Edwardo Almeida Acosta and María Eugenia Sánchez de Almeida, "Psychological Factors Affecting Change in Women's Roles and Status: A Cross-Cultural Study," *International Journal of Psychology,* 18 (1983) 27.

16. See, for example, Olive Senior's "Ballad": "God ordain all women to have children and if women don't have children she no better than mule because God curse is on her" (113).

17. Joanna Russ, *How to Suppress Women's Writing* (London: The Women's Press, 1984) 110.

18. Cheri Register, "American Feminist Literary Criticism: A Bibliographical Introduction," *Feminist Literary Criticism: Explorations in Theory,* ed. Josephine Donovan (Lexington: Univ. Press of Kentucky, 1975) 8-11.

19. As Terry Eagleton explains it (*Literary Theory,* 163-71, 187-91) Lacan holds that the child in the pre-Oedipal stage is involved in a close, libidinal relationship with another body, usually the mother's. Enter the father, who signifies the "wider familial and social network" into which the child must be assimilated. However, this socialization involves division from the mother's body, and desire (love for her body that, in this wider network, is incestuous) is driven underground into the unconscious. Thus, entrance into the symbolic order is accompanied by the dawn of gender awareness and the repression of pre-Oedipal bonds.

20. However, consider the angry reaction within the Black community that greeted Ntozake Shange's *for colored girls* due to its treatment of Black women's emotional vulnerability at a period when only positive images were encouraged by the Black media. The film version of Alice Walker's *The Color Purple* has elicited similar responses regarding its portrayal of Black men.

21. Barbara Christian, *Black Women Novelists: The Development of a Tradition, 1892-1976* (Westport, CT: Greenwood Press, 1980).

22. Gisela Ecker, "Introduction," *Feminist Aesthetics,* 21.

23. See Terry Eagleton, *Literary Theory,* 190 and Sigrid Weigel, "Double Focus," 61.

24. See Silvia Bovenschen, "Is There a Feminine Aesthetic?", *Feminist Aesthetics,* 35. Consider also Sigrid Weigel's comment in the same collection: "The utopia of woman as an 'authentic' sex does not mean—to reverse patriarchal relations—claiming to be the only or the superior sex, rather it demands that woman is no longer defined in relation to man. Instead, she sees and experiences herself as autonomous and considers her relations with herself and with others as her own and not as deviant" (79).

25. In a slightly different context, Barbara Christian shows the dangers that arise in literature from this dependency of opposition. In *Black Women Novelists* she contends that Black women writing in the 1920s and attempting to refute earlier, negative images of women, fell into the trap of *reacting to* White society's view of Blacks.

26. For example, Heide Gottner-Abendroth, "Nine Principles of a Matriarchal Aesthetic," *Feminist Aesthetics,* 81-94.

27. Bronwyn Levy, "Women Experiment Down Under: Reading the Difference," *A Double Colonization: Colonial and Post-Colonial Women's Writing,* ed. Kirsten Holst Peterson and Anna Rutherford (Aarhus: Dangaroo Press, 1986) 169-86.

28. Lorna Goodison, interviewed by Nadi Edwards, part two, *Pathways,* 3,5 (Dec. 1985) 10.

29. Ntozake Shange, *Black Women Writers at Work,* 162.

30. Lorna Goodison, interviewed by Nadi Edwards, part two, 6.

31. Erna Brodber, interviewed by Evelyn O'Callaghan, April 7, 1982.

32. Michelle Cliff, *The Land of Look Behind: Prose and Poetry* (New York: Firebrand, 1985) 14.

33. Gwendolyn Brooks, *Black Women Writers at Work,* 78.

34. Audre Lord, *Black Women Writers at Work,* 101.

35. Elaine Fido, "Crossroads: Textures of Reality in the Poetry of Lorna Goodison, Christine Craig, Olive Senior and Esther Phillips," *Out of the Kumbla* (in press).

36. Claudia Tate, *Black Women Writers at Work,* xvi.

Liz Gerschel (review date April 1988)

SOURCE: Gerschel, Liz. "Caribbean Childhoods." *Third World Quarterly* 10, no. 2 (April 1988): 995-98.

[*In the following review, Gerschel praises the well-crafted stories in* Summer Lightning, *concluding that it is "an outstanding collection by an extremely talented writer."*]

One of the best books published in 1987 was undoubtedly Olive Senior's ***Summer Lightning and Other Stories.*** Told in dynamic and powerful language, this perceptive, humorous and poignant first collection reflects the author's own experience of life in rural Jamaica, and the inter-related and often conflicting worlds of children and adults. Although over the last few years there has been increasing interest in the works of black American women writers, the literary strengths of Caribbean woman have not received the same attention. This is a pity, as there is no lack of good writing by women from the Caribbean.

A significant and promising development has occurred, however, with the establishment by the Commonwealth Foundation in December 1987 of a new prize 'to reward and encourage the upsurge of new Commonwealth writing and ensure that writers of merit reach a wider audience outside their country of origin'. The first Commonwealth Writers' Prize was awarded to Olive Senior for *Summer Lightning,* after she was runner-up to the Canadian, Margaret Atwood, in the Caribbean and Canada region. (The other three regions are Africa, Eurasia and Southeast Asia and the South Pacific.)

Olive Senior's superbly crafted stories draw heavily on her own experience of growing up in the intensity and warmth of a village where everybody knows your present business and your past history. Her strength as a writer lies in her power to recreate that world, its people, their relationships and their language. Her characters are instantly recognisable to anyone familiar with rural Jamaica, but could equally well be met anywhere. They are real people, caught between the everyday world and the world of the imagination, with lasting ties and confusing emotions. Many of her stories are extremely funny and she often uses humour for ironic social comment, as in the story, **'Ascot'**, about a young man who 'reach far' beyond the village in which he was born and returns with his white wife for a visit, during which he patronises his friends, lies, ignores his mother and, despite all this, is still seen as a sort of hero. In the beautifully structured and very funny, **'Real old time t'ing'**, the children returning to the village are themselves middle-aged, and Olive Senior carefully contrasts the old style of village life with town-influenced 'progress'.

It is a characteristic of her writing that she weaves an imaginative awareness of underlying dreams and fears into the story of a particular event. Time and again she returns to the theme of conflicting needs between generations, and in particular to the child isolated and lonely in an adult world only half-understood. In such a world, the child is an innocent and powerless outsider, only half-aware of the sexual complexities of the surrounding adult relationships and often a victim of adult distrusts and jealousies. Olive Senior's skill in capturing the intensity and confusion of a child's emotions carries the reader along, evoking recognition of half-forgotten memories; in many of the stories, she presents the adult world from the child's point of view, painfully contrasting the innocence and vividness of childhood loves, fears and longings with the often brutal insensitivity of the adult world. In **'The boy who loved ice-cream'**, the unhappiness of the child habitually afraid of his father's inexplicable moods is sublimated in his longing for imagined and as yet never-tasted ice-cream, 'the one bright constant in a world of changeable adults'. As the story unfolds, the narrative viewpoint switches from child to father and back, culminating in a rush of words as the climax of the story is reached and the boy is literally swept away in the fury of his father's jealous pain.

Poignancy marks many of the stories. In **'Love Orange'**, Olive Senior creates a memorable image as a child's desire to give and receive love is misunderstood by the adults around her:

> Love, I thought, was like an orange, a fixed and sharply defined amount, limited, finite. Each person had this amount of love to distribute . . . That is why I preferred to live with my grandparents then since they had fewer people to love than my parents and so my portion of their love-orange would be larger.

When her grandmother is dying, the child's supreme gift of her 'whole orange' is rejected: this is a story about deaths, real and spiritual, in a child's world.

The title story, too, explores a lonely child's need for love and understanding. His faith in the power of adults to look after him contrasts strongly with the lack of understanding of his fears and his needs shown by the 'respectable' aunt and uncle with whom he lives. This contrast ironically makes him dependent on and vulnerable to less 'respectable' men, a Rastafarian gardener and a strange summer visitor.

In many of the stories, Olive Senior seems to be questioning the relationship between 'respectability' and humanity. The back-biting hypocrisy and lack of love of the church-going characters in **'Ballad'** is contrasted with the generous spirit of Miss Rilla ('not fit person to write composition about'), now dead, but in the child-narrator's imagination 'just keeping everybody up in Heaven laughing and because she look so pretty like Missis Queen when she dress up, they ask her to wear her red dress to brighten up Heaven even though everybody suppose to wear white'. It is a longer story than the others, the characters' history of romance and death is more fully developed (combining the European and Caribbean idea of the ballad) and the bittersweet feelings of adolescent friendship and loss are sensitively and strongly drawn. But in Olive Senior's stories, as in real life, comedy and tragedy are juxtaposed. **'Do angels wear brassieres?'** is the hilarious story of a confident and mischievous little girl questioning mealy-mouthed morality in general and the visiting Bishop in particular; it is full of creative energy and is likely to have you laughing aloud as Olive Senior follows the tradition of Samuel Selvon and others in turning spoken Creole to literary purpose.

Olive Senior's powerful use of the full range of Jamaican Creole is an exciting feature of this collection, and one which impressed the judges from the Commonwealth Foundation panel. She chooses and controls her language with sensitivity, strength and humour, telling some stories in a form nearest to standard English and others in a broad dialect form rich with proverbs and expressions (which, although not difficult to understand, might be more accessible to some readers were a brief glossary to be included—publishers please take note). Creole is a dynamic and precise linguistic tool which is here not confined to use in dialogue, but which also serves to create dramatically effective narrative, both for humorous effect and for serious purpose. In her choice of register, her manipulation of narrative viewpoint and the overall sharp vibrancy of her writing, Olive Senior demands and excites the reader's attention. The judges commented on the very high standard of the submissions for this first Commonwealth Writers' Prize; in awarding it to Olive Senior for *Summer Lightning* they have chosen an outstanding collection by an extremely talented writer.

Olive Senior and Charles H. Rowell (interview date summer 1988)

SOURCE: Senior, Olive, and Charles H. Rowell. "An Interview with Olive Senior." *Callaloo* 11, no. 3 (summer 1988): 480-90.

[*In the following interview, Senior discusses the major influences on her writing, the function of her creative work, and the implications of being a Jamaican writer.*]

The following interview was conducted through the mails during the period of March-May, 1988, between Charlottesville, Virginia, U.S.A., and Kingston, Jamaica, West Indies, two months following my meeting and talking with Olive Senior in Jamaica.

—C. H. R.

[*Rowell*]: *If you had to assess your past in terms of your relationships with the arts, what would you say* *are the probable forces, experiences, or individuals that motivated you to become and shaped you as a writer—a poet and a fictionist?*

[Senior]: I didn't grow up influenced by what I suppose you would call "the arts." I was born and grew up in rural Jamaica and my early childhood was far removed in space and time from any substantive external contacts and influences. My major influence then was the oral tradition—storytelling, "hot" preaching, praying and testifying (for religious influence was strong), concerts, "tea-meetings," and so on. Later came formal exposure to "English" literature in high school, encouraged by a succession of teachers who were, I suppose, delighted to find a student who was so avaricious for books, so seduced as I was by words well crafted. I also from earliest childhood had a very strong visual sense which was nurtured by studying art and things like art history in high school—at one time I wanted to be a painter; and I have always had an intense curiosity about the natural world, natural phenomena, though I can't say I really applied myself very much to the sciences. But these three elements—word, vision, nature—have remained important to me.

Of course not to be overlooked as a profound influence in determining what I have become are the socio-psychological elements of my childhood which made me extremely introverted and introspective, which caused me to create imaginary universes as an escape from the realities of everyday existence, to perceive (subconsciously then of course), books, knowledge as embodied in the word, as a key to personal affirmation and power. For there is absolutely nothing literary in my family background or social heritage.

I don't know what *motivated* me to become a writer other than a passion for the written word, for books. My teachers encouraged me to write, to be sure, because I suppose I showed early promise of skill, but "to write" is a far different thing from being "a writer." There were many examples in Jamaica of people who "wrote"—i.e., poems and stories which were published in the newspapers and various periodicals—though I don't think I knew any of them; in fact I didn't know of any Jamaican who was a *writer* in the sense of having that as a vocation. So even though all my life I have wanted "to write," it is only the last few years that I have come to acknowledge myself and to be acknowledged as a "writer"—i.e., a person who, theoretically at any rate, could devote all one's time to that activity.

I suppose I and the whole concept of writing in Jamaica have matured together; to be a writer is probably for the first time being acknowledged as a legitimate field of endeavor though—unlike other fields—it attracts few or no social, emotional or financial rewards. In 1972 when I was writing my first book—a commissioned work on the 1972 general election—a middle-class lady asked me what I was doing with myself. I told her I was writing a book. She said, "A book?" and roared with laughter. After that book was published to good critical and public reception, an old school mate saw me and asked what I was doing with myself. I said, "Writing." She dismissed that instantly. "Writing?" she said, as if I had said whoring. "So when are you going to settle down and have children?"

Times and attitudes have changed—somewhat. Or maybe it's only my own perceptions that have changed. People's reactions to **Summer Lightning** and my other work, to my winning the Commonwealth Writers Prize, demonstrate an increasing recognition that what people like myself are doing is considered worthy of acknowledgement. But in a society whose base has become so intensely materialistic, where the majority of the people spend their lives confronting the issues of sheer *survival,* it is also regarded as something irrelevant, eccentric, foolhardy, quixotic. You somehow get the feeling that the society at large would be far more impressed if you were using your "brains" to make money and so display some of those trappings of success held so dear. I can't imagine too many children out there—of whatever class—being encouraged to take their writing talents seriously. And yet children of today at least have what those of my generation did not have—some highly visible writers—men and women—as role models.

Of course, in my childhood those West Indians who were writers were those who had chosen exile—only Vic Reid so far as I know stayed at home, and for a long time he was making a living as a journalist anyway. So when it came time for me to choose what I wanted to do in life, I chose journalism—"writing" was essentially something that one did for the *Gleaner* (our daily newspaper), from time to time trying a little short story, a little poem "on the side," while dreaming, waiting for the opportunity to tackle the big one—the novel.

I am on far more certain ground when I look at the forces that have shaped me as a writer. The fact that I grew up in a backward village with no laid-on entertainment, no media, forced us to create drama—poetry, tragedy, comedy—out of our everyday existence. Life and Art were the same thing. My childhood imbued me with a sense of the drama, magic and mystery inherent in all human transactions, in the forces beyond our knowing, in the natural world itself. It is the fragments of these dramas, mysteries, enigmas of everyday life that I am reconstructing in my work—**"Arrival of the Snake-Woman"** is a good example of this.

Yet I was also racially and socially a child of mixed worlds, socialized unwittingly and simultaneously into both—worlds which embodied the polarizations of race and class, yet which at bottom could not be separated.

For what cemented us was the process of creolization; some embraced and acknowledged it, some repudiated it, but repudiation was never entirely possible because over everything was the colonial superstructure and *they* determined everything. *They* not only controlled the economy, our lives, *they* also set the social rules (a situation I have tried to come to grips with, even marginally, in **"View from the Terrace"**). Moving between these two worlds, I felt displaced, as if I belonged to neither (now I *know* I belong to both). But all of this made me very conscious as a child of living two modes of existence—one private, sorrowful, introspective. The other was fundamentally social: if your birth, life events, and safe passage to the next world were so dependent on other people, on "community," on the support and goodwill of others, how could you afford to be anti-social? The constant tug between private aloofness and community and social sharing has shaped my personality, my world-view and my work. So too have the contradictions inherent in race and class, in poverty and wealth, power and powerlessness, European values versus indigenous values rooted in Africa, to which I was exposed and the way in which these contradictions were manifested in the *word,* in the politics inherent in the spoken word versus the written, in Jamaican creole versus the language of the Bible, Shakespeare—and the schoolroom.

The kind of existence I lived as a child also made me aware that individual consciousness was somehow important in the mundane scheme of things, yet individual life was infinitesimally small in a larger and incomprehensible universe; in the pull and push of history. Perhaps this is why I am so concerned with the struggle of individuals to affirm themselves, to create self-identity out of chaotic personal and social history.

Do you find the writing of the two forms—the poem and the short story—require two different facets of your aesthetic sensibility?

I think not. I don't think there is that much difference in my poems and my stories—apart from the length and complexity, of course. I am in both forms telling stories, exploring consciousness. I can't always decide on what form what I want to say will take. I have started out to write stories that have ended up as poems and had ideas for poems that have ended up as stories. If there is a difference it is that in my poems I am more explicitly political than in my stories.

Why do you write poems and short stories? (I don't raise that as a silly or flippant question.) And what do you want your creative work to do? Do you view your reader as having a public function?

Do you mean why do I write at all? Because I am not committed to writing only stories or poems or anything in particular, you know.

Why do I write? Because the imperative to do so has been the strongest single force in my life and though I have been sidetracked by many, many muses, abused this one and wished it away, anxious always about the exacting nature of the commitment, I think it has finally claimed me. I have finally accepted the fact that, yes, writing is what I am supposed to do with my life; it is the way I affirm myself.

I am not sure that I can answer the other parts of your question as straightforwardly as you have asked them. And I confess that I don't know what you mean by readers having a "public function," though I do believe readers have a function, which I will discuss later.

From the very start, I have been very conscious of craft. *Simplicity* and *restraint* are the two disciplines that I consciously try to impose on my work (both poetry and prose). Simplicity because I want the work to be accessible though I hope it will also reverberate with complex meanings. I think everything I write operates on at least two levels—sometimes more. I am highly conscious of writing to be read—aloud if you wish—of transposing to the page some of the storyteller's art—so the flow, the rhythm of everything is carefully worked.

I suppose it helps that my entire professional life has been spent either as a journalist or an editor—both crafts that teach you to impose a rigid discipline on written expression. "Write tight" is the reporter's maxim. So I cut, edit, rewrite, reduce my work, purge it of "fat" so that the stories, the poems, can achieve a simplicity in the telling. I don't always succeed of course, but that is my intention.

At the same time, I objectively impose restraint on the content, attempt to suppress raw emotion as much as possible, no matter how deeply felt, or to express it obliquely. Thus the objective stance of the writer plays a key role, as does the subjective interpretation on the part of the reader.

For what you see on the page is only part of the story. The inexplicable, the part not expressed, the part withheld is the part that you the reader will have to supply from your emotional and imaginative stock, the part that will enable the work to resonate. So that in **"Arrival of the Snake-Woman,"** for instance, although I tell so much about everybody, everything else, the story doesn't answer the fundamental questions about the "Snake-Woman" herself, questions about her interior life that are posed at the end of the work.

I believe it's my job as a writer not to say it all, for I am only one-half of the equation—reader-writer—and that the work becomes complete only when it is read, when the reader enters the world I have created. I therefore tend to leave a lot of my work open-ended, as so many of the stories of *Summer Lightning* are.

For isn't the concept of certainty boring? I myself believe we are all part of the social forces that exist long before we are born, during our lifetimes, after we are gone; forces that shape our destinies. We therefore live at all times within a configuration of possibilities. So in my created world, there are no saints, no villains, no absolute good, no absolute evil. While I personally abhor violence, exploitation of any sort, in my work I am willing to explore the forces that shape the life of the exploiter as much as the exploited, the violent as much as the victim. The man in **"View from the Terrace,"** for instance, is not a sympathetic character, but an exploration of his life is important to us because he—people like him—has played a significant role in shaping and perpetuating certain attitudes in our society, even as he himself is a victim of his class background and of the colonial structure. Ultimately, we are all nothing more—or less—than children of the universe.

Thus I try hard not to be judgmental. Nor am I interested in teaching specific lessons. I am trying to find a way of apprehending reality and presenting it so that for the reader there can be that moment of recognition, of saying "yes," to a world that is familiar yet new.

But, also, I write because as a human being, as a Jamaican with a strong commitment to my homeland, I want to reaffirm those parts of our heritage that have been misplaced, misappropriated, subsumed, submerged, never acknowledged fully as the source of our strength; I want people to know that "literature" can be created out of the fabric of our everyday lives, that our stories are as worth telling as those of Shakespeare—or the creators of *Dallas*.

Summer Lightning *is grounded in place and folk (vernacular) voices. Will you talk about the collection of stories? How is your forthcoming volume,* **Arrival of the Snake-Woman,** *different from the first?*

Summer Lightning is rooted in rural Jamaica, set mainly in the forties and fifties (the period of my growing up) with the exception of one story (**"Country of the One-Eye God"**) which is obviously of the seventies—and probably even more relevant to the eighties. I believe *Summer Lightning* to be a true expression of everyday life in the part of the world I describe, i.e., deep rural Jamaica, in terms of the behaviors, beliefs, practices narrated and the language used. The stories in *Summer Lightning* are told largely from a child's perspective and express some of the powerlessness, frustrations and lack of understanding by the adult world, the alienation I myself felt as a child. It is probably because I have (unwittingly) expressed some universal truths that, despite its narrow setting, *Summer Lightning* has managed to strike a responsive chord in people all over the world, people whose cultures are entirely foreign to the one I describe.

Though both books share many elements in common, *Arrival of the Snake-Woman* is more complex in themes, wider in scope and more experimental in form. *Summer Lightning* is tightly focussed on one world—that of rural Jamaica at a particular point in time; *Arrival* is more expansive. The stories span a time period from the closing days of slavery (1830s) to the present. While the consciousness in *Summer Lightning* is mainly that of the child, the stories in *Arrival* are also told from the point of view of adults (males and females) as well as children of different races and classes. The experiences described are urban as well as rural; in short, while *Summer Lightning* focussed mainly on the peasantry, in *Arrival* I am beginning to explore the lives of the rising black and brown bourgeoisie.

In *Arrival* I am also experimenting—tentatively—with magical realism. I believe it is a form well suited to our societies as it enables us artistically to fuse the mundane with the other world which lurks not too far beyond our everyday existence—the magical, spiritual, whatever you choose to call it. For me, writing, literature, is inextricably fused with magic. Though most of my writing is in a realistic vein, I am conscious at all times of other possibilities lurking just beyond consciousness, of the great ineffable mystery that lies at the core of each life, at the heart of every story.

In recent years I have been very much affected by the work of Latin American writers—particularly Jorge Amado, Gabriel Garcia Marquez and Mario Vargas Llosa—and I believe their example is helping me to shape the work that I am writing now.

Your poems and stories assume, as does the work of other new Caribbean writers, a voice of certainty or self-assurance. That is, unlike the previous generations of Caribbean writers, you don't concern yourself with public battles against colonialism and white racism. You don't focus on public issues; you concentrate on the interior lives of your characters.

I am not sure I entirely agree with some of what you are saying here. I don't know that the subject matter of Caribbean literature has changed substantively over the years—there are common threads running through the literature from the forties and fifties which are still there in the work that is being produced today—that is, the search for an identity both personal and national, the exploration of issues of race and class, that is, the subtleties of race and class, the encounter with race . . . and not just battles with "white racism" per se; the attempt to affirm indigenous culture, and so on.

What has changed, I agree, is the form, the way in which some of us are exploring these issues; for instance, the fact that Caribbean women writers have now

come to the fore is opening up to us a completely new approach to the topic of the Caribbean mother—one of our great literary preoccupations—and of our relationship with that mother. It is also, I believe, personalizing the socio-political issues.

It is true that I don't focus on public issues, but that doesn't mean that I do not share in the social and political preoccupations. In fact, I would say that a very strong sociopolitical consciousness informs all my work. I believe that I am dealing with fundamentally the same issues as before—the impact of colonialism, forms of racism, issues of justice, notions of power/powerlessness. But for me, the human being, the individual life, is the primary focus of everything, so all experience tends to be filtered through a particular consciousness. The most creative act for me as a writer is to assume that consciousness and give it expression. I am entering people's lives and recreating their autobiographies. Although my concerns are explicitly existential, I am nevertheless highly conscious of the socio-political environment, the *context* in which we operate.

You have been writing creatively for a while now. Why did you delay in publishing your creative works in book form? Your books are recent publications. Why?

Perhaps this goes back to my notion of the configuration of possibilities—or the possibility of configuration. Perhaps the books came out when I was ready for publication. Meaning that I did try to get *Summer Lightning* published before it was taken by Longman—without success, but I am not sure I was really trying very hard. It came to be published at the time it was for two main reasons. First, metropolitan publishers had once again decided to show some interest in Caribbean literature and were actively searching for material. I also feel that I have benefited from the tremendous resurgence of interest in the English-speaking world in the genre of short fiction. A few years ago, publishers didn't want to *know* if you were into poems and short stories. Everyone kept saying, "Let us know when you have a novel." I think that the success of *Summer Lightning* has come when I am ready for it; had it happened a few years back I would have been psychologically unable to cope with the sudden public interest not only in the work but—something I had not anticipated—in the writer.

What are the effects of your small local audience and the absence of large presses on contemporary writing in Jamaica? That is, what are the effects on you and other Jamaican writers who did not go into exile, who remain at home in Jamaica?

The principal effect is that we are entirely dependent on metropolitan publishers and all that it entails—though obviously so are the writers in exile. It does mean though that the perceived marketability outside your own country of what you write is what determines publication. Nowadays metropolitan publishers are more accepting of the language in which we write; my publisher never suggested any changes at all to **Summer Lightning** but in earlier days it meant that writers had to make concessions, compromises to suit foreign tastes. And of course being here far from the mainstream means that it is difficult for us to get our work published at all. So far as I know the Caribbean writers who are getting published in the United States are those who are based there.

In Jamaica there is generally an absence of outlets for our work—including periodicals. There are no grants, prizes, etc., offered. So to stay at home and write is a considerable act of faith. None of us can devote our full creative energies to writing because we all have to earn a living by other means. This is probably why so few people are writing longer fiction; it is difficult to find the time/head space to sustain that kind of effort. It's really here a case of the strongest surviving—many writers of talent over the years have simply ceased writing, have never fulfilled their potential; there is also little encouragement for young writers to persevere. But, yet, enough people surface and hang in there year after year to make the scene an almost lively one.

There are some good things about staying at home. For one thing we don't have the same identity crisis, the same sense of alienation from both our homeland and a host country that writers in exile seem to have. We seem to have a stronger sense of being rooted, a greater confidence in having a sense of *place* for even in cussing it we affirm that the place belongs to us. There is the opportunity for continued renewal of the vital parts of the self through daily contact with *our* world, no matter how trying at times we find that world.

Will you talk about your work as editor and publisher and how you are helping to solve the problem of publication outlets for writers and other artists in Jamaica? You are editor of Jamaica Journal *and managing director of Institute of Jamaica Publications. What are your objectives for the two projects?*

I regret that we are not doing very much to "solve" the problem since our own resources are so limited. But we are trying. We are committed to publishing works on Jamaican culture in the broadest sense—e.g., history, science and the arts; to provide the necessary support for the work of the Institute of Jamaica by assisting other divisions with their publications, by undertaking joint ventures with these divisions and by developing marketable items such as prints, posters, postcards with a cultural theme. We are trying to produce work of international quality and at the same time generate funds to sustain our efforts. We are something new for Ja-

maica—an institution that deals with culture but which we run as a business, for that's the only way we can survive.

We publish a limited number of book titles each year, and, though our latest effort—*From Our Yard*—is a poetry anthology, we are not concentrating at this time on literary work though we hope to do more as our finances improve.

Jamaica Journal is not so much an outlet for creative work as for the product of researchers and scholars and visual artists. We tend to publish the work of established writers only and seem to have been concentrating on poetry—probably because we get more high-quality poetry submitted than prose. *Jamaica Journal* is internationally recognized as an authoritative source of information on Jamaican culture, but even more important to us is the vital role we see ourselves playing in helping Jamaicans to know more about themselves.

The more I talk with Caribbean writers of different language groups (e.g., Francophone, Anglophone, Dutch and Hispanic), the more I discover how separated you, in the Caribbean, are from one another; and we in the U.S.A. from you. (In the Caribbean you, of course, know more about us than we know about you.) That is a major problem. Will you talk about it and its historical and contemporary implications?

What can I say? The fragmentation of the Caribbean was historically determined by European penetration and conquest—and we have never managed to transcend these boundaries. The situation is getting worse, because each of our territories is now being subjected to a new form of cultural imperialism that is not only inhibiting the possibility of developing our own natural cultures but of developing a pan-Caribbean culture. Despite all the rhetoric about Caribbean economic integration, a new center-periphery system is evolving which is based in Washington and a new cultural system is evolving located somewhere between Dallas and Hollywood.

I think there is an intense desire on the part of creative artists, writers of the Caribbean to get together, to share, because we have more in common than we have separating us. But how do we operationalize that? Carifesta (Caribbean Arts Festival) was conceived as a vehicle for bringing us all together, and for two or three times did that beautifully, but Carifesta seems to have foundered—temporarily we hope.

You recently won the Commonwealth Writers Prize. What is the Commonwealth Writers Prize? What does winning it mean to you personally?

The Commonwealth Writers Prize was established by three British organizations—the Commonwealth Foundation, the Royal Over-Seas League and the Book

Trust—and was awarded for the first time in 1987 when *Summer Lightning* won. According to the organizers, one of the aims is to bring to a wider public the works of authors of merit in their own countries. Works of fiction—novels, plays and short stories are eligible; works have to have been published within a certain time period and are submitted by publishers. For purposes of judging, the Commonwealth is divided into four regions: Africa; the Caribbean and Canada; Eurasia; and South-east Asia and the Pacific. Two winners from each region go on to the final judging in London by a different panel of judges.

Winning the prize has meant a validation of my faith in myself as a writer and has given me and *Summer Lightning* the kind of publicity and exposure I would not have had otherwise.

There are numerous excellent contemporary poets and fiction writers living in or exiled from Jamaica. Will you talk about contemporary Jamaican literature and the present literary scene in Jamaica, especially in Kingston?

The literary scene fills me alternately with hope and despair. Despair because as a writer and publisher I live in a society which seems basically unresponsive to literature; hope because we still manage to publish, to be published, to interest business firms in supporting what we do, to buy books to donate to schools which cannot afford to purchase their own, and so on. Despair because there are so few outlets for our work and hope because so much of it is still being produced. Despair because our bookselling industry seems to be getting more and more "commercial" i.e., with less and less interest in promoting indigenous material; hope because there are a few exceptions, for example, in the last year or so at least two young people have taken the bold step of starting their own bookshops, and seem to care about writers and writing.

The literary scene has changed dramatically in the last few decades. Far more people are being professional about pursuing writing as a craft rather than as a "hobby." It's an area in which the impact of the University of the West Indies has undoubtedly been felt—so many of our established writers are graduates of the university or teach there; university teachers such as Mervyn Morris, Edward Baugh, Edward Brathwaite and John Hearne have encouraged many young writers on-campus and off. West Indian literature has assumed a rightful place in the university curriculum (and that of the schools) and this must help to stimulate writing; so must the development of a body of West Indian literary criticism.

For many years the literary excitement seemed to be centered around poetry, and several fine poets emerged at about the same time. Some of them like Mervyn

Morris, Edward Baugh, Anthony McNeill remained in Jamaica and Dennis Scott (now at Yale) was also at home until recently. Lorna Goodison has now emerged as a tremendously exciting poet—like Anthony McNeil, someone whose life is dedicated to poetry—and her third collection should be out soon. Of course "Miss Lou"—Louise Bennett, who has popularized the writing and performance of poetry in Jamaican dialect—has a special place in our hearts; she is constantly invoked as an inspiration to young writers, especially the "dub" or performance poets who emerged in the seventies—poets like Mutabaruka, Oku Onoura and Mikey Smith (who died tragically). The dub poets with their uncompromising lyrics and reggae rhythms have added a new dimension to poetry and indeed have initiated a reconsideration of what we should classify as "literature."

There are many other talented poets in Jamaica who are more "mainstream" in their approach—of these Velma Pollard, Gloria Escoffery and Pam Mordecai are about to have their first volumes published, though their work is already well known.

On the whole, it is the women writers who are displaying the most versatility—many write poems and prose with equal facility. In addition to her volume of poems, Velma Pollard is about to have a book of prose published; Christine Craig, who is known as a fine poet, writes good stories; I believe Lorna Goodison has been experimenting with prose; and Erna Brodber (better known for prose) also writes poetry.

The prose scene has not been as lively as that of poetry—or drama. Jamaica has never really produced many fiction writers; only three novelists have lived and worked here in recent times—Neville Dawes, John Hearne and Vic Reid. Neville died some years back, and Vic died last year, leaving behind among other things, an interesting autobiography he was working on—written in verse! (Part of it was published in *Jamaica Journal*.)

Since Sylvia Wynter's *The Hills of Hebron* was published in the 1960s, we hadn't produced a new local novelist until Erna Brodber whose *Jane and Louisa* came out in 1980 to critical acclaim for her experimental narrative style. Erna keeps on writing—her new novel should appear shortly. Another published prose writer is Hazel D. Campbell who has had two collections of stories published. Three Jamaican writers resident abroad have been attracting some attention recently—Michelle Cliff and Opal Palmer Adisa in the U.S.A. and Merle Collins in the U.K. Conversely, one Jamaican resident in the U.S.A., Anthony Winkler, has had his two humorous, bawdy novels first published by a Jamaican publisher.

Drama is currently a very lively area of the arts—at the center of a controversy about how far artists should pander to public tastes. There are so-called playwrights of the "give the public what it wants" school offering explicit sex, abuse of women, four-letter-words and coarse humor who seem to make a good living from staging their plays to full houses at makeshift "little theatres" all over the island. Serious playwrights have a much harder time getting an audience—and their plays therefore hardly get produced, except for Trevor Rhone whose finely-wrought works are now Jamaican classics which are being studied in schools.

A lot of creative writing talent goes into two other popular ventures—one is the well established annual national pantomime, a highly popular traditional fare woven around a humorous and topical script, original music and spirited dancing. The other is radio dramatic serials in dialect—to which many of us become addicted. Barbara Gloudon is a witty writer who is a stalwart of many pantomimes and who currently has a popular new radio serial going. Elaine Perkins is the other queen of home-grown radio drama. The fact that radio is by far the most popular medium of communication in Jamaica suggests that radio drama is among the most popular of literary endeavours and a medium for shaping literary tastes.

Finally, we have all been empowered over the last decade by the work of Sistren, a group of mainly working-class women who have developed and sustained a theatrical collective since 1973. They have crafted fine plays out of the everyday lives of women like themselves and their own life-stories have now been turned into a book—*Lionheart Gal* (edited by Honor Ford-Smith). *Lionheart Gal* is almost a paradigm of the Jamaican literary experience right now—the insistence on the right to use our own language, to speak with our own voices, a literature that is being written from the inside out instead of from the outside looking in, which describes much of our literary history.

Of course all of this literary activity is taking place in direct competition with the products of the metropole that are in the bookshops, on the airwaves and via VCRs, satellite dishes and our own television station which feeds a steady diet of the most popular of American TV soaps.

There isn't a literary scene in terms of salons, meetings or organizations. Some of the writers happen to be friends and meet frequently; with others, our paths never seem to cross, despite the smallness of the society and the fact that most writers seem to be based in Kingston.

And yet we are very conscious of each other. Knowing that there are others like us is sometimes enough to sustain us.

Velma Pollard (essay date summer 1988)

SOURCE: Pollard, Velma. "An Introduction to the Poetry and Fiction of Olive Senior." *Callaloo* 11, no. 3 (summer 1988): 540-45.

[*In the following essay, Pollard surveys the key thematic concerns in Senior's short stories and poetry.*]

Short stories and poems by Olive Senior have been appearing in journals and anthologies in Jamaica and overseas for more than a decade. It was not however till December 1985 that the first complete volume reached the bookstands—a collection of poems, *Talking of Trees,* published by Calabash Press, Jamaica. A few months later (early 1986), a collection of short stories, *Summer Lightning and other stories,* now in its second printing, was published by Longman, U.K. This paper discusses the more common themes in Senior's prose and poetry and comments briefly on their treatment.

Senior's short stories and poetry are the work of a creative talent of great sensitivity which expresses tremendous understanding of the human condition, particularly that of poor people both rural and urban. The attempt to slot her writing into a particular genre immediately gives one an uncomfortable feeling. For the work is knit together by a common landscape and a recurring concern for humanity. Both poetry and prose bring the country paths of Senior's childhood and the urban experiences of her young womanhood into focus. The themes of both concern the experiences of people in these environments who represent different points along a scale of social and financial privilege.

The point of view preferred, particularly in the prose published so far, is the child's eye view, complete with all the wonder and confusion implied by the lines quoted at the beginning of this section. The stories presented here, like the stories in *Summer Lightning,* reflect that preference.

The child's eye view is not childlike. It is a clear vision through which the irrationalities of adults, the inequities in society and from time to time the redeeming features in the environment, are expressed. The exploitation of the child's vision allows Senior space for the imaginative forays her readers find most engaging, and for the dramatic presentation of human foibles seen from the point of view of the little person looking and feeling from under. Rutherford's comment in her review of the collection *Summer Lightning,* is to the point:

> One of Olive Senior's great gifts is her ability to enable us to enter imaginatively into the mind of the child. We feel the child's loneliness, the desperate attempts to comprehend seemingly incomprehensible situations. . . .
>
> (114)

Rahim makes a somewhat similar observation:

> Senior's power seems to lie in her presentation of child-
> hood in relation to the questions of faith and inno-
> cence.
>
> (35)

The narrative voice in fact records children's reactions
to phenomena, to their own condition, and perhaps more
critically, to the adults with whom they interact. "Bright
Thursdays" for example describes a small girl's discomfort as she adjusts to the strange and demanding
formality in the upper-class home of a newly acquired
guardian (an unacknowledged grandmother), after the
easy casualness of life with a working-class mother
who had in fact been a servant to a member of the family. In **"Ballad"** the child eulogizes her favorite adult,
Miss Rilla, a woman of whose life-style her step-mother
heartily disapproves and on whom she expects God to
exact punishment. In **"Confirmation Day"** the young
candidate is perplexed by the symbolism of the Angli-
can communion into which she is being inducted, is no
less perplexed by the memory of another more dramatic
induction (by water in the village river) into a less sophisticated flock, and finally rejects what both have to
offer in the supreme indictment of the Christian religion
"I'd rather be a child of someone else, being a child of
god is too frightening. . . ."

Religion and adult attitudes and behavior receive the
harshest implied judgment from Senior. These are the
areas of greatest confusion for the children in these fascinating stories. In **"Bright Thursdays"** the Christian
God is as threatening and illogical as the requirements
of the domestic situation in which the heroine Laura
finds herself. Mealtime in the new home is one of the
major trials of the child's life. It takes place at "The
Table" in the "Dining Room" where three people huddle
together at one end of a table which could easily accommodate twelve. Over it hang beribboned and be-
whiskered grandparents looking down from oval picture
frames. She fears the clouds on the way to school in
this environment for they

> reminded her of the pictures she used to get in Sunday
> School showing Jesus coming to earth again, floating
> down on one of these fat white clouds . . . these pic-
> tures only served to remind her that she was a sinner
> and that God would one day soon appear out of the sky
> flashing fire and brimstone to judge and condemn her.

"Do Angels Wear Brassieres?" tells of one child's
bold attempt to deal with trying adults and with menacing Christianity in one fell swoop. The stage is well set
in the opening lines:

> Beccka down on her knees ending her goodnight
> prayers and Cherry telling her softly, "And ask God to
> bless Auntie Mary." Beccka vex that anybody could in-

terrupt her private conversation with God so, say loud
loud, "No. Not praying for nobody that tek weh mi
best glassy eye marble."

By the end of that story the child Beccka has outsmarted
and won the respect (perhaps even the fear) of the Archdeacon visiting the house and has thrown the entire
adult household into confusion.

Beccka comes closer than any of Senior's children to
expressing the intense rebelliousness against adult control so frequently felt by children. The above quotation
from it, taken with the following extract from Senior's
interview with Anna Rutherford, suggests something almost autobiographical about the spirit of this piece if
not the tale itself:

> I had this tremendous sense from a very early age, of
> being in constant rebellion, of my relationships with
> adults as being one of struggle against them. I felt that
> my freedom was being compromised and taken away
> from me in most of my encounters with adults. . . .
>
> (15)

In the fiction even the child's relationship with God is
threatened with adult control. But the child can be victorious there: "Beccka just stick out her tongue at the
world, wink at God . . . kiss her mother and get into
bed." In the real world the child is not so lucky. The interview extract above continues: "a lot of this rebellion
was not overt, it was internalized or expressed in oblique ways. . . ." In the fiction the author can be generous. One adult, Mr. O'Connor, passes the test set by
the child. He is not ignorant and frightened in the same
way as Auntie Mary who cannot understand why a child
should want to know about reproduction, for example.
To the hardest of the questions he is asked—"Do Angels wear brassieres?"—he gives a satisfactory answer.
Rahim comments on the lighthearted humor of this story
but points out that "it brings to the surface the negative
qualities of a way of life regulated by a fear of God."
The comment may in fact be applied to several of the
stories.

The grandest indictment of religion, and indeed of adult
behavior, comes certainly in **"The Arrival of the
Snake-Woman,"** reproduced here. The uncompromising nature of fundamentalist religion is shamelessly exposed in the attitude of the parson-cum-emergency-
doctor to the heathen Miss Coolie and her ailing baby.
The child narrator is paralyzed in his inability to come
to terms with the contrast between notions of Christian
charity preached in church—the love of man to man—
and the manifestation of hate implicit in the Parson's
behavior. The artist in Senior is reacting to attitudes she
as a person has always found reprehensible. Note this
statement from the interview quoted above:

> A very restricted, narrow, kind of Christianity com-
> bined with poverty is, I think, a ruthless combination,

in that they both attack the spirit, they are both anti-life, they are both anti-freedom, soul-destroying as far as I am concerned.

But poverty in the prose fiction receives less harsh censure than religion and adult control. It is frequently accompanied by positive values of love and community feeling. It is rural poverty in close knit societies where people take care of each other and where the land provides at least subsistence. The starkness of real need is described in the poetry where urban poverty is treated. In the city the human spirit buckles under circumstances it cannot overcome and even friendship is useless. "The Scavenger," for example, describes the city dump as the John Crow, the local vulture, sees it. There is no food for him there, nothing beside pieces of carcass. Needy humans have scoured it before him:

> . . . hardly any food kind on
> dump Brother Festus and his tribe
> no grab dat already?

"City Poem," perhaps the most poignant of all, records the story of urban renewal as told by a victim:

> Wen de bulldoza come a back-a-wall
> we jus pick up all we have an all
> we have is children an we leave
> Mavis doan wan leave Mavis aksin
> why why why A seh Mavis
> move fus aks question las
> de ting out dere biggern yu
> an it caan talk
> so Mavis move to but is like
> she leave all sense behin. Fram dat
> all Mavis good fah is aksin
> why

The existential question "why" is put into the mouth of the newly homeless friend Mavis, whose wits have left her. The indictment of society lies in the fact that there is no answer for Mavis. The bulldozer, the symbol of the planners who take no account of the needs of the poor, masterminds events that affect their lives:

> "de ting out dere biggern yu . . ."

Other thematic interests in Senior's work include historical matters reflecting Senior's personal research into the history of the Jamaican people at home and in countries to which they have migrated, especially Panama. Of the poems reproduced here, "Nansi Tory" is concerned with the Afro-Jamaican, the man who did not return to Africa; "Searching for my Grandfather" is about the Jamaican who did not return from Panama. **"The Arrival of the Snake-Woman"** explores the Jamaican situation in which ex-African and ex-Asian strive to find a place in the post-colonial society.

The village is a microcosm of Jamaica. Senior gives a believable description of the integration of a post-emancipation immigrant into a rural village. Through the child's eye the author reveals early attitudes of the races to each other, the garbled versions of history available to the unlettered poor and the interplay of Afro-Caribbean religion and American evangelism. Without implying any evaluation, the author allows the haphazard pattern of Jamaican family life and of community living to become part of the reader's consciousness.

In this as in other stories Senior treats important concerns with the sometimes humorous, sometimes ironic voice which makes the necessary point without the tedium which might so easily attend it. The Indian woman's arrival into the village, for example, comes very soon after the parson's warning against the specific temptation identified in the Biblical passage: "The daughters of Zion are haughty, and walk with stretched forth necks and wanton eyes, walking and mincing as they go, and making a tinkling with their feet." And indeed Miss Coolie's multiple bangles were likely to make a tinkling sound. Her sari, draped about her from head to foot, might cause her to walk with mincing steps. No wonder the young boy thought the two things might be related.

The adult Auntie Mary in **"Do Angels Wear Brassieres?"** complains to her friend about the precociousness of her grandniece and so exposes the disadvantages of the situation in which a child brought up by foolish and ignorant adults lives.

> "Guess what she asks me the other day nuh?—if me know how worms reproduce."
>
> "Say what maam?"
>
> "As Jesus is me judge. Me big woman she come and ask that. Reproduce I say. Yes Auntie Mary she say as if I stupid. When the man worm and the lady worm come together they have baby. You know how it happen?—Is so she ask me."
>
> "What you saying maam? Jesus of Nazareth!"
>
> "Yes, please. That is what the child ask me. Lightning come strike me dead if is lie I lie. In my own house. My own sister pickney. So help me I was so frighten that pickney could so impertinent that right away a headache strike me like autoclaps. . . ."

Senior's effectiveness lies partly in the precision with which she reproduces the speech of the characters. In her writing she exploits fully the complex Jamaican speech community, making use of the flexibility the different codes allow. There are stereotypes of language and class easily recognizable in these works. Auntie Mary, for example, is funny and distressing partly because she is so real. The imaginative child who tries to dispel her loneliness in "See the Tiki Tiki Scatter" is engaging because we can hear her voice as she dramatizes her grandmother's song:

> Oh burr-EAK the NEWS to MOTH-er
> And TELL her that I LOVE-er

And TELL her NOT to WAIT for MEEE
FOR I'M NOT COMING HOOOOOOME.

Her isolation becomes pitiful when the attempt to fraternize with Peggy the maid is thwarted by the finality
of Peggy's words, spoken in a code which contrasts
with that of the narrative voice and increases the gulf
between them: "No. No white people back yaso. Go
weh. Back to yu big house." The fit of theme, character
and language is impeccable. And this is equally true of
the verse. Note for example the tale of the bulldozer's
action told by the victim (quoted above), and compare
with it the lines spoken by the middle-class observer
who happens to pass through the ghetto:

> (And if you taught me to speak
> with your words would I touch
> could I reach beyond the collapse
> of garbage cans in hungry streets?)

Senior prevents the authorial voice from becoming intrusive. Always the narrator uses the speech style of the
characters. Look again at the opening lines of **"Do Angels Wear Brassieres?"** quoted earlier, and indeed at
most of the excerpts in this piece. This aspect of Senior's work appears unselfconscious on the page. However she is aware of the value of the voice and conscious of the effectiveness of its use. Note the following
statement from the interview with Rutherford:

> I am more and more concerned that my characters
> should speak directly to the reader and therefore I am
> dealing almost purely in narrative, in letting people tell
> their own story. . . .

Olive Senior is a talent not to be taken lightly. Few
writers are able to combine social comment with such a
deep understanding of human nature and such a linguistic facility. Her extensive research into aspects of Jamaican history and social context, and her fine eye for
detail as she lives and moves around Jamaica, arm her
with "facts" which she transforms into prose and poetry.

CRITICAL RECEPTION

Any comment on the critical reception of Senior's literary output would be premature at this time. It is enough
to say that local and foreign newspapers and journals
have published favorable reviews of both the poetry
and the prose collections. The Commonwealth Writers
Prize, which she was awarded recently, speaks for itself
as a mark of the appreciation of a panel of highly regarded literary minds. As her work becomes more well-
known, critical articles will no doubt appear in literary
journals and are likely to substantiate the claims made
by this commentary.

HONORS AND AWARDS

Over the years Senior has won several prizes for submissions of poetry and short stories to the Jamaican Annual Literary Competition. She is a recipient of the Ja-

maica Centenary Medal for creative writing offered by
the Institute of Jamaica. Last year (1987) she received
the Jamaica Press Association award for "Editorial Excellence."

The prestigious Commonwealth Writers Prize, awarded
for the collection *Summer Lightning and other stories,*
adds an international dimension to the reception of Senior's work and is the crowning point of an already distinguished career.

Velma Pollard (essay date 1992)

SOURCE: Pollard, Velma. "Mothertongue Voices in the
Writing of Olive Senior and Lorna Goodison." In *Moth-
erlands: Black Women's Writing from Africa, the Caribbean and South Asia,* edited by Susheila Nasta, pp.
238-53. New Brunswick, N.J.: Rutgers University Press,
1992.

[*In the following essay, Pollard analyzes the language
of Senior's stories and Lorna Goodison's verse in order
to investigate how the two authors "use the complex
language situation" of the West Indies "to their advantage in the act of creating, particularly in terms of
character identification."*]

Jean D'Costa, Jamaican linguist and foremost Caribbean writer of children's novels, contends that the West
Indian writer who wishes to satisfy himself, his local
audience and his foreign audience, must evolve a 'literary dialect' which not only satisfies both these audiences but also is an authentic representation of the 'language culture' of his community.[1] And Garth St Omer,
one of the better known of the West Indian novelists,
comments on the dilemma of the post-colonial writer
who must not only represent the society honestly but
must be understood by all in the society.[2] Both these
writers are addressing a situation that is the context of
this discussion on Mothertongue. The tension between
the ability to use a number of overlapping codes and
the necessity to be understood not only within the society but by the reader outside of it is a constant part of
the Caribbean writer's reality as s/he creates in prose or
in poetry.

This essay looks at the language of the prose of Olive
Senior and the poetry of Lorna Goodison to see how
this, and other linguistic tensions are resolved in the
writing of these two women who have achieved national and international recognition. It notes how they
use the complex language situation to their advantage
in the act of creating, particularly in terms of character
identification.

A brief description of what D'Costa refers to as a 'poly-
dialectal continuum with a creole base', is in order. The
official language of Jamaica is Standard Jamaican En-

glish (SJE), a dialect of English as accessible to English speakers the world over as Standard American or Standard Australian English. It is the language of the school and of all the official organisations of the society. The majority of Jamaicans, however, speak Jamaican Creole (JC), a Creole of English lexicon which everyone in the speech community understands. Because of the lexical relationship between the two languages most Creole speakers regard themselves as English speakers. There is, in addition, a code introduced by the Rastafari, a socio-religious group, and adopted by other speakers, particularly the young. This code, Dread Talk (DT), has been described as an example of lexical expansion within a Creole system,[3] in this case Jamaican Creole. The grammatical structures of the code are, with few exceptions, the same as those of JC. The lexical items, however, taken originally from English, the source of most Jamaican words, have been subjected to a number of word-making processes drastic enough to give some words new sounds and others new meanings.

Most educated speakers in the society switch from one to the other of the codes described above, with no difficulty at all, as the discourse situation demands. Uneducated speakers tend to speak JC regularly and to attempt to switch to SJE only when they perceive the social situation to require it.

Because language and social class, in the stereotypical descriptions of these, are closely aligned, creative writers are able to use the codes to identify prototypical characters and attitudes. This is not to suggest a particular self-consciousness in the production of literary writing, for I believe that what we will look at is a reproduction of natural speech. What the artists have done is to select to write about situations requiring the use of the different codes available to speakers. It is precisely because the natural language of the people in the community is reproduced, that we are able to discuss language as it functions within the speech community, using as evidence texts from the writing we are about to examine.

OLIVE SENIOR

While all the stories in Olive Senior's two collections[4] might serve as a kind of laboratory for examining Jamaican speech, it might be useful to examine the speech behaviour of the characters presented in one story in detail, and then flesh out the comments possible with references from others. We will look at **'Real Old Time T'ing'** from the earlier collection, largely because the content of the tale forces the author to have characters switch from one code to the next, thus offering us good examples of how the language operates in the real-life situation.

An ageing father, recently made a widower, finds himself up against a social-climbing daughter who wants him to build a new house bigger than the one in which

he had raised their family of nine. Patricia, the nouveau riche, is introduced by the narrator who obviously does not intend this character to be a favourite with the reader. Examine the tone of the lines which begin the piece and introduce Patricia to the reader: 'Is the one name Patricia did start up bout how Papa Sterling need a new house . . .'

When Patricia eventually enters the stage her language is immediately perceived to be different from the narrator's. JC is the language of the teller of the tale. Patricia attempts to speak SJE:

> But hear the one Patricia she—this one Sunday she did drive down with the pickney dem. The husband didnt come:
>
> 'Poppa, this place really just too bad. The children shame to come here. We have to do something about it.'

The JC plural 'pickney dem' in the narrator's language is replaced in Patricia's by the SJE translation: 'the children'. Note also the JC past tense 'did drive down' (not to be confused with the emphatic 'did' possible to SJE) where English would prefer 'drove' or 'had driven'. The attitude to Patricia is made clear in the idiomatic 'the one Patricia she' a turn of phrase reserved for deep disdain.

Patricia considers herself a speaker of SJE but her English retains the tell-tale signs of late or incomplete acquisition, its style typical of the speech of someone newly arrived at her current station in life. One expects 'the children are ashamed to come here', for example, where Patricia uses the JC 'the children shame . . .'

The father in the story is a JC speaker who controls SJE well enough to use it for effect. He pretends confusion when his daughter makes the suggestion that his house is too small:

> Too small? How yu mean gal? Doan is seven of you raise in this house. Plus yu mother alive then and me make nine. Nine of we live here. And now yu all gone and yu mother dead leaving me one and you telling me this house that I build with my very hands too small. Child you are speaking to me in parables.
>
> (p. 55)

Note that the last of the sentences in the extract above is in English and is in distinct contrast to what comes before. Papa has switched to English to allow the daughter to see the ridiculousness of her suggestion. He is being sarcastic. What his daughter says is quite clear. It is no parable but it is so illogical that there must be something not immediately obvious to him.

The JC used in the passages above is not pure or broad Creole which is, in any case, an abstraction for analysis by linguists. In terms of D'Costa's description, it lies somewhere along a continuum between JC and SJE. The non-JC speaker, while rare in the Jamaican community, is not shut out: and the foreign reader who understands English can make sense of it.

Let us look at the grammatical features of that part of the discourse, not found in English: The verb 'to be' does not always appear in JC where SJE would expect it, as in the chunk: 'now you—all gone and you mother—dead'. The verbs are not always marked to indicate past time where this is the time of the activity. See, for example, in '. . . this house that I BUILD with my very hands . . .'. The subject pronoun 'we' is used in the object position as in '. . . Nine of we live here . . .'.

The language with all its nuances, is clear to the Jamaican reader, and the essential sense can be gleaned by the foreign reader even if some of the finer points might be missed.

Miss Myrtella, who aspires to Papa's hand, is a caricature of someone who knows the virtue of English as a status marker. She talks with her mouth 'curl round the words', and is afflicted with an exaggerated case of the added 'H'. Note the following report:

> 'Ho Cousin Orris,' she call out. Horace is Papa Sterling first name. 'Oi dont know wot to do hit his so howful to be ha woman holl holone him this worl Cousin Orris.'

While the dropping and adding of 'H' (as in '[H]am and [H]eggs') is common in Jamaican speech, the sustained adding exemplified in the excerpt above signals the speaker's intention to produce fine English.

Miss Myrtella has other attributes of the class Patricia wants to belong to. She wears good clothes; she knows about (green) tea (as 'opposed perhaps to folk drinks like mint and fever grass) and she sticks out her little finger while drinking from a cup. The two women are competitors. Miss Myrtella's arrival challenges Patricia's monopoly on these things. Patricia says maliciously that Miss Myrtella has no class and, among other things, 'can't speak properly', where 'properly' signifies English. The reader knows that Patricia herself has some difficulty with the language, although she has fewer problems than Miss Myrtella. But their competition serves only to underscore the point made earlier, that many Jamaicans who perceive themselves to be speakers of English are not.

While the use of language to identify character is most highly developed in this story, perhaps because its themes are class and society, it is also carefully matched with character in all the other stories. In the story **'Ascot'**, in the same collection, the written rather than

the spoken word helps the reader note the development of the hero. Compare the following letters sent home to his mother from America as Ascot moves up in the world:

> Dear Ma wel i am her in New York is big plase and they have plenty car I am going to get one yr loving son Ascot.

> Dear mother wel here I am in Connecticut. Connecticut is Big plais. I driveing car two year now but is not wite yr loving son Ascot.

> Dear Mother Chicago is Big plais I drivein wite car for a wite man but he don make me where wite is blak unform so I mite leave yr loving son Ascot.

With each letter the language is more grammatically close to English, the sentences longer. (The amount of money sent home also increases with each letter.) When Ascot actually returns home on a visit, we note the change in his oral expression as well. The last record of his speech before migration runs: 'Laaad Mass Jackie is nuh me do it sah', as he defends himself from the charge of banana theft. When we meet him again he greets everybody and introduces his wife, '. . . this is my wife Anthea', language being only one of the markers of this man's social development.

Constantly language marks off territory in an unobtrusive but precise way. This continues in Senior's second collection of short stories, although the language is consistently closer to English as the characters are closer to the middle and upper levels of the society. Note, however, the broad JC used as the maid in **'See the Tiki-Tiki Scatter'** rejects the granddaughter of the house with these words: 'No, no white people back yaso . . . Go weh. Back to yu big house' (p. 85). The word 'yaso', which translates as 'here' or more precisely 'in this place', signals a purer, broader level of JC than Senior commonly uses. The language of the helper in a household is likely to be far from English. People in the Big House speak English. People in all the big houses in the stories speak English.

In another story from that collection, **'Two Grandmothers'**, the narrator, their granddaughter in common, interacts with two women from different social worlds. Language is one of the measures of identification of these worlds. The narrator, recently back from holidaying with her father's mother, reports to her own mother:

> Mummy can you believe that everyone in church remembered me? And they said: 'WAT-A-WAY-YU-GROW' and 'HOW IS YU DAADIE?' and 'HOW IS YU MAAMIE?' till I was tired.

Her personal and instructive comment is:

> Mummy, that is the way they talk, you know, just like Richie and the gardener next door. 'WAT-A-WAY-YU-GROW.' They dont speak properly the way we do, you know.

(p. 70)

The narrative voice in Senior's stories depends entirely on the identity of the narrator. In those instances, however, where the language is a version of JC, it is the turn of phrase, the idiom, more than the differences in grammar or lexicon, which signal its use. The non-JC speaker is unlikely to have difficulty understanding the words. Note the opening gambit of perhaps the most popular story of the collection *Summer Lighting*, '**Do Angels Wear Brassières?**':

> Beccka down on her knees ending her goodnight prayers and Cherry telling her softly, 'And ask God to bless Auntie Mary.' Beccka vex that anybody could interrupt her private conversation with God so, say loud loud, 'no. Not praying for nobody that tek weh mi best glassy eye marble.'
>
> (p. 67)

or the righteous indignation of Aunt Mary at the kind of question Beccka chooses to ask her, whether she knew 'how worms reproduce':

> 'Yes, please. That is what the child ask me. Lightning come strike me dead if is lie I lie. In my own house. My own sister pickney. So help me I was so frighten that pickney could so impertinent that right away a headache strike me like autoclaps . . .'
>
> (p. 69)

Mothertongue, certainly for a writer like Senior, is a number of speech codes: the broad JC of the maid in '**See the Tiki-Tiki Scatter**', the English of the middle and upper classes, the hyper-corrected forms sometimes used by the aspirants to competence in English, the barely non-standard forms which make up the relaxed speech of many educated Jamaicans or the mixture of all these as the educated speaker switches from one code to the other, responding to situation or trying for effect. Because she is true to the characters she creates, and because she creates characters across the social boundaries, Senior exposes the reader to a very wide range of possibilities within the continuum between JC and SJE. Any study of this artist's language must take account of this range.

Concerning voice in her work, Senior, in an interview with Anna Rutherford, makes the following revealing statement:

> To me the sound of the voice is extremely important. I try to utilize the voice a great deal in my work and more and more find that what is happening is that the voice is taking over. In other words I am more and more concerned that my characters should speak directly to the reader and therefore I am dealing almost purely in narrative, in letting people tell their own story.[5]

They tell it each in her/his own mothertongue.

Lorna Goodison

Although poetry and good prose share many features, there are several differences, not the least of which is the terseness of the poetic form. An examination of mothertongue in poetry, in this case Lorna Goodison's poetry, is qualitatively different from the exercise just performed on Senior's prose.

Pamela Mordecai and Edward Baugh have both commented on Goodison's ability to slide from one to the other code of the Jamaican speech community. Mordecai notes the significance of the effective use of code-sliding as part of the 'mix-up' that is Jamaican culture.[6] Baugh's more detailed description praises her skill at, *inter alia*, 'interweaving erudite literary allusion with the earthiness of traditional speech'.[7] The idea of interweaving runs close to the present description which uses the term 'overlapping' to describe one feature of Goodison's style.

Two related features are here identified: one grammatical, the other lexical. In the one, two or three codes are made to overlap within the same line or poem: in the other the occasional JC item is woven into a poem whose fabric is undoubtedly SJE. The fact that all the codes in the Jamaican speech community are English-related facilitates the effectiveness of Goodison's strategies. If one of the codes were French-related, as is the situation in St Lucia, for example, the procedure would not be possible.

Baugh, in his study, looks at the poem 'Poui' from the second collection *I am Becoming My Mother*[8] and shows how, by using JC verb forms in the first and last lines ('She don't put out for just anyone / . . . and she don't even notice'), the poet gives a JC flavour to a poem written almost entirely in SJE. In Goodison's hand the occasional JC item is like yeast in its effect on the mass of the poem. The content is accessible to JC and non-JC speaker alike, the language can be claimed by both.

Another poem from the series in which 'Poui' appears, 'Shame Mi Lady', furnishes a good example of both grammatical and lexical overlap operating within the same three lines. In order to receive the force of the strategy the reader has to be able not only to recognise but to produce JC because intonation is important. Let us examine the lines. The poet compares herself with the shrub whose name is the title of the poem:

> now, if I can find favour (me with my bold face)
> you bashful you shy you innocent lady
> must/bound to find absolution/grace
>
> (p. 14)

The 'you' of the second line is emphatic in English and is opposed to 'I' in the line above. But another reading is possible. The 'you' can be pronounced with a short 'u' in which case it becomes a JC pronoun with the accompanying predicate adjective 'bashful'. The utterance 'yu bashful' thus translates to English 'you are bashful'.

The line then contains three sentences describing the lady and the sense must wait on the next line. That next line admits both JC and SJE, giving the reader the choice between the JC 'must (and) bound' of emphatic obligation, and the English 'must'. There are lexical sleights which depend only partly on intonation for their point. 'Bold face', for example, can be one Creole term, with the stress on 'bold', meaning 'fearless' bordering on rude, or two English words with equal stress, the one qualifying the other. In the same line a pun on 'favour' is also hinted at. The SJE meaning is dominant but lurking behind it is the kind of JC sentence, 'you face favour . . .', for which the listener is expected to supply some animal considered daring in folk parlance, 'favour' being in JC a verb meaning 'resemble'.

The poem 'My Will' has 46 lines. Among them there is only one instance of linguistic overlap. But the single word does have the effect of including JC among the vehicles of expression. The poet is leaving in her will a number of positive attributes and behaviours she wishes on her son. Included is the following: 'May you never know hungry' (p. 19). The uninitiated may well pass that over as an error and replace 'hungry' with the English 'hunger'. But what it is, is the JC predicate adjective 'hungry' in a sentence that might read 'may you never hungry' and might translate to SJE 'may you never be hungry'.

Later in the same poem Goodison, wishing for the boy none of the dangerous commodity, gold, translates the Creole 'bold face' explained above, to English '. . . its face is too bold'. The initiated will immediately hear 'it too bold face'. And so here again JC and SJE are interwoven or overlap in the same utterance, this time only by inference. At this level the notions depend entirely on the listener's knowledge. The national community may hear two voices, the international community, one.

The rendering of complex behaviours and the sound of complex voices in a single statement by the deft manipulation of lexicon and syntax of the different codes is, I believe, Goodison's major contribution to Caribbean literature.

Perhaps the most daring use of this strategy is in the poem 'Ocho Rios II' from the earliest collection *Tamarind Season*.[9] In this poem it is necessary to express emotions felt by all Jamaicans. Speakers of JC, SJE and of the code of Rastafari are represented. The scene is set in Ocho Rios, the second largest tourist city of Jamaica. The poem begins with discourse by a Rastafarian who enters the stage soliloquising: 'Today I again I forward to the sea'. The form 'again' recognises both the habit of the Rasta man and the existence of an earlier poem 'Ocho Rios I', analysed in detail by Mordecai in the study cited above. The first person pronoun used initially might be either JC or Dread Talk (DT), but its

repetition in the sentence with overtones of the first person alternative, 'I and I', available only to DT, identifies the speaker as a Rasta man. The choice of verb reinforces this interpretation. For while 'forward' adequately describes the act of walking, it is not used in this way in SJE or in JC. It is, however, a commonplace in DT. The first movement of the poem continues:

> . . . to the build-up beach where a faithful few
> lie rigid, submit to the smite of the sun.
> Today I bless you from the sore chambers of my
> temples.

These lines are written in SJE except for one area of possible grammatical overlap with DT. The reader may now recognise it in the last line. The first person pronoun 'I', because of the repetition performed in the first line, may be identified as either DT or SJE. The presence of the Rasta man is maintained by the use of DT. SJE indicates that the sentiment expressed is shared by the larger Jamaica.

An examination of an additional stanza, one again involving the sentiments of all Jamaica, serves to reinforce the point. It is the third movement of the poem in which Jamaica blesses the tourist and apologises to him for inclement weather:

> Bless you with a benediction of green rain, no feel no
> way
> its not that the land of the sea and the sun has failed,
> is so rain stay.
> You see man need rain for food to grow
> so if is your tan, or my yam fi grow? is just so.
>
> P.S thanks for coming anyway.

> (p. 53)

In the first of these lines the double negative introduces the aside which marks the switch from English to JC, 'no feel no way'. In the next line the explanation 'is so rain stay' is JC. It is the voice of the peasant farmer for whom 'green rain' which ruins the tourist's tan is a blessing. It brings green lushness and productivity to the plants which are his source of income. He apologises for what might seem to the tourist to be a selfish preference; rain over sun. Note that JC used here can be understood (I believe) by the English-speaking foreigner who might himself have rendered it 'that is how rain is'.

All the speakers identify with the sentiments of the next two lines but it is the voice of the Rasta man that articulates it. What seems to be the impersonal 'man' in SJE is in fact the multifunctional pronoun of DT sometimes represented by its variants, 'the man', 'I-man', 'the I'. It is followed by the unmarked verb of JC and of DT. The next line continues with the voice of the peasant farmer in JC, to be followed by the polished

English of the tourist board representative thanking the disappointed tourist for choosing Jamaica for his holiday. In each case it is language that identifies the different actors in this dramatic piece; and the voices of characters identify their place in the society, the sectors of the society they represent, enhancing the word pictures which they accompany. It is in this example that Goodison's use of the languages of the society in poetry resembles most Senior's use of it in prose.

Dread Talk, the code of Rastafari, features very strongly in the poem above. Elsewhere in Goodison the Rasta man, through his words, is constantly acknowledged as part of the Jamaican manscape. Sometimes it is necessary to repeat an idea already expressed in SJE, to accommodate this code. The repetition, however, is not obtrusive because the words are different. Note for example the following from 'Ceremony for the Banishment of the King of Swords' from the collection *Heart-ease*:[10] '. . . go through this again so you can penetrate it . . .' (p. 53) To 'penetrate' in SJE means to go through in a very literal sense. In DT, however, it means to 'understand'. The sentence really means 'go through that again so you can understand it'. What is important for the purposes of this paper is the extent to which Goodison seems to have internalised the multilingual nature of the speech community.

Another example is found in 'A Rosary of Your Names' from this same collection. God is worshipped here in a litany of fine words:

> Your names are infinity
> light and possibility
> and right
> and blessed
> and upfull

(p. 58)

'Upfull' is a DT word whose meaning includes both 'right' and 'blessed'. And, although it is not an English word, its sound is so much in accord with the words around it that the ear accustomed to English does not reject it.

The final example of this use is the last stanza of the poem 'Heartease I', in which the poet puns on the sound of the pronoun 'I' and so includes one strong symbol from the Rastafarian belief system articulated in the words of the code: the sound which is shared by the first person pronoun mentioned before, and the organ of sight:

> Believe, believe
> and believe this
> the eye know how far
> Heartease is

(p. 33)

'The-I' is an alternative to 'I-man' and 'I-and-I'. It is the Rastafarian sound of the 'ego'. It is also the sound which describes the organ of sight. 'Seeing' is very important to the Rastafari, its opposite 'blindness' is a hallmark of non-believers. Again one might easily think Goodison is employing non-standard English and needs to correct the verb to 'knows'. But the sentence is: 'I know how far Heartease is'. Choosing to write 'eye' instead of 'I' concedes that the reader will take the former for granted but needs to be pointed to the latter. Goodison is generalising a sentiment. The narrator knows how far away from the present reality Heartease is, as do we all, especially the Rasta man who is particularly far from ease in the society in which he is the oppressed (downpressed). Here is clever artistry that goes beyond the simple pun and describes a multiple consciousness in what seems on the surface to be a single mode of expression.

One challenge Goodison has more than adequately met is the representation of the complex Jamaican language situation within the terse form that is poetry.

CONCLUSION

Mothertongue as it is traditionally defined, is one-dimensional. It is that one language the individual first acquires and learns to use in communicating with other people. To operate effectively in the Jamaican situation however, and in situations similar to it, is to master at least two codes. Mothertongue in the Jamaican situation might usefully be thought of as 'language' rather than 'a language'. Indeed, recent research into Caribbean language has certainly begun to consider acquisition in these terms.[11]

This brief incursion into the use of language by two creative writers points to the intricacy of the patterns people in the Jamaican and similar speech situations continually make. The exercise also responds in part to the concerns articulated by D'Costa and St Omer and referred to at the beginning of this essay. Both local and foreign readers are accommodated by these two artists; although admittedly, one group, for whom this complexity of codes is Mothertongue, responds to each text on more levels than the other.

Notes

1. Jean D'Costa, 'The West Indian Novelist and Language: a Search for a Literary Medium' In *Studies in Caribbean Language,* ed. Lawrence Carrington et al., University of the West Indies, St Augustine 1983.

2. Garth St Omer, *The Colonial Novel,* a Ph.D. dissertation, Princeton University, 1975: published by University Microfilms, Ann Arbor, Michigan.

3. For a description of this speech see Velma Pollard, 'Dread Talk: the Speech of the Rastafari of Jamaica', *Caribbean Quarterly* vol. 26, no. 4, 1982.

4. Olive Senior, *Summer Lightning and Other Stories,* Longman, Harlow, 1986; and *Arrival of the Snake-Woman and Other Stories,* Longman, Harlow, 1989. All page references in the text are to these editions.

5. Anna Rutherford, 'Olive Senior Interview' in *Kunapipi* vol. viii, no. 2, 1986.

6. Pamela Mordecai, 'Wooing with Words: Some Comments on the Poetry of Lorna Goodison', *Jamaica Journal* no. 45, 1981, pp. 38-40.

7. Edward Baugh, 'Goodison on the Road to Heartease', *Journal of West Indian Literature* vol. 1, no. 1, 1986, p. 20.

8. Lorna Goodison, '*I Am Becoming My Mother,* New Beacon Books, London, 1986.

9. Lorna Goodison, *Tamarind Season,* The Institute of Jamaica, Kingston 1980.

10. Lorna Goodison, *Heartease,* New Beacon Books London, 1988.

11. See Lawrence D Carrington, 'Acquiring Language In a Creole Setting', *Papers and Reports on Child Language Development,* no. 28, Stanford University, California, 1989.

Ameena Gafoor (essay date winter 1993)

SOURCE: Gafoor, Ameena. "The Image of the Indo-Caribbean Woman in Olive Senior's 'The Arrival of the Snake-Woman.'" *Callaloo* 16, no. 1 (winter 1993): 34-43.

[*In the following essay, Gafoor elucidates Senior's depiction of the Caribbean female experience in her story "The Arrival of the Snake-Woman," contending that the story "seems to present a culmination of all the phases of readjustment and accommodation inherent in migration and displacement."*]

This paper looks at the portrayal of the Indian woman in the contemporary literature of the anglophone Caribbean. It attempts to examine the processes of readjustment and accommodation, acculturation, interculturation and indigenization in its attempt to explore Indo-Caribbean female experience: the psychosocial and spiritual growth and the quest for identity within the context of the Indian diaspora in the Caribbean. It explores the Indian woman's claim to a place as home in the multiracial, multicultural Caribbean *vis à vis* a tradi-tion of colonial discourse which privileges European possession of the "discovered" lands of the New World while several culturally discrete groups, displaced by colonialism and indentureship, jostle for ontological space and identity in the colonial social reality. The dominant transplanted group in the Caribbean can be seen to have a protest registered against disinheritance and dispossession in Caliban's now famous words of anger hurled at Prospero: "this island's mine, by Sycorax my mother" in Shakespeare's political allegory *The Tempest.*

Many West Indian authors have portrayed various aspects of Indo-Caribbean female experience[1] and I have chosen to examine Olive Senior's short story, **"The Arrival of the Snake-Woman"**[2] because it seems to present a culmination of all the phases of readjustment and accommodation inherent in migration and displacement. It starts at the beginning of the process with the woman as an alien and works its way through the alienation and isolation of the exile, colonial victimization and racial exclusion to the conscious decision to integrate culturally and also to address the issue of her tentative hold on land and home. This paper also reveals that this short story is counter-discursive: it depicts resistance to the colonial power base and questions the centre/margin paradigm of dominant discourse in a manner which characterizes post-colonial writing. Ashcroft, Griffiths, and Tiffin address themselves in *The Empire Writes Back* (Routledge, 1989) to the question of the dismantling of the power hierarchy entrenched in colonial texts, the abrogation of European power and its false premises, the reappropriation of indigenous cultural forms and the recognition that hybridity and syncreticity are the most viable means to recuperation and selfhood in the semiotics of postcolonial writing and, although Senior's short story is not itself a rewriting of a colonial text, it is newer writing which intervenes in and resists dominant discourse about the *other.* It relates how the Indo-Caribbean woman manages in the colonial minefield.

Senior's short story depicts a plural society in what is unmistakably colonial Jamaica, the temporal setting estimated at the first half of the twentieth century. At its heart, the work portrays racial antagonisms, cultural differences, alienation, exclusion, powerlessness, subjection, and conformity, all of which have come to characterize the construction of the colonial world. The text can be read as an interrogation of patriarchal morality, as an imaginative document of the Indian female immigrant experience in a tangled web of human relationships, or as a story of adolescence and growing up in the multicultural prism as the adult male narrator, Ishmael, recaptures his boyhood and adolescent struggles of grappling with the ambiguities and ambivalences, confusions and contradictions of the adult world around him. The most crucial issues in regional literature have been race, class, and identity—not unnaturally so considering the multi-racial, multicultural nature of our social reality—and these issues have impacted significantly in this short story.

The story unfolds as follows: SonSon, a Jamaican creole with two other "babymothers" to his credit, wins Miss Coolie in a capricious straw-drawing game. (The historical parallel between this act and European capriciousness in the disembarking of forced labor at this island or that, and afterwards the uncertainty of indentured labourers about their destination, cannot be missed: the element of choice entirely absent, rendering the alien a victim of an unchosen destiny, washed up at ports of exile on unchosen shores). In the rural Jamaican village, Miss Coolie is a figure marginalised both by the dominant creole culture and by the minority European ruling culture; she is a stranger, an outcast, on the fringe. Hers is the existential dilemma of what Todorov identifies as the "discovery *self* makes of the *other*."³ The precise circumstances of Miss Coolie's transfer to the rural village in the mountains of Jamaica remain a mystery but one can assume that she has walked away from her own fold of racial and cultural cohesion, first in India and now in Montego Bay, and has no cultural support system around her.

This character is haunted by the specters of gender and race. Shunned by the existing creole society who, because she is the "other" woman, brand her as a "temptress" and a "witch" and ostracized by the white status quo which labels her as a "heathen . . . the epitome of sin . . . the devil incarnate" for her stubborn resistance to Christianity, Miss Coolie lives in isolation and loneliness, excluded from the "benevolence" of colonialism. Her son, seriously ill, is refused medical aid by the Church because she is deemed a pagan heathen. She decisively saddles her donkey and makes the arduous journey over the mountains to reach the hospital. After this hurdle, she is threatened with the exclusion of her son from colonial education, from "the magic that was contained in black and white squiggles on paper . . . the true source of power" (23). Reality for the colonial is constructed by the white world and rigidly defined by *writing* and *paper* and Miss Coolie (coming from a scribal culture) is not intimidated by this. She readily understands the *power* of writing and concedes that formal education is the only means of re-empowerment, of subverting the status quo, of acquiring writing and *paper* and reappropriating the land (and landscape) from the whites. This knowledge crucially informs her decision to accept Christianity and immerse herself into the creolization process. She realizes that compromise is inevitable for survival. On one of the few occasions when this usually reticent woman breaks her silence, she announces with certainty that her son would go to school and become a lawyer: "Then he will get *paper* for the land. For everybody. Then white man can't come and

tek it weh" (note the colonial's metonymic use of *paper* for title document). But the narrator (now a reflecting adult) states: "*I didn't know that Miss Coolie knew about these concerns*" (36, my emphasis). Clearly, Miss Coolie is a subversive figure, her submission to the alien religion arising out of the sheer necessity to undertake a role (to write herself into Parson's script) in order to survive and to test her will to rise above her colonized, marginalised, victimized condition.

The narrator's admission of his unawareness is important in the presentation of this character because what makes this short story most interesting in the exploration of Indian female experience is its objective perception. Although this is a very personal representation of Miss Coolie by Ish, it is not a subjective apprehension of reality. The author, a mixed creole woman, through the authority of a male adult creole narrating voice recapturing his adolescence, attempts to textualise the experience of an Indian woman. There are many instances in the story when the narrator confesses that he is enthralled by her presence, unsure of her intentions or puzzled by the logic of her existence; he is astounded by many of her actions and equally disillusioned by society's reactions to her. It is as if they inhabit two juxtaposed worlds in the village. Ishmael's account of Miss Coolie is gentle and sympathetic; she forms the "centre of his consciousness" since he is drawn to her by the magic and mystery of her alienness, but the effect of his unawareness is ironic. This short story best exemplifies the complexity of being an Indian woman in the multiracial situation in the Caribbean. Ultimately, this is a story of how society sees Miss Coolie, and I suspect this technique (of the objective narrator who has not been granted omniscience) has something to do with Miss Coolie ultimately appearing comfortable in visible material wealth. She has been given a stereotypical role and although most of the other short stories in this collection are clearly feminist, I suggest that this depiction is symptomatic of the ironic racial relationship in Caribbean societies where cultural differences remain esoteric, more so considering the temporal setting of this work.

Miss Coolie's outer reality corresponds with stereotypes of the acquisitive and usurious Indian shopkeeper,⁴ the exotic, mysterious sexual object associated with romantic ideas of the eastern charm and grace, the resourceful mother and dutiful wife. Her sexuality has been exploited, for although SonSon has many other women, the *idea* of her attracted him; he desired her "from the way their body so neat and trim and they move their hip when they walk just like a snake and they don't wear no proper clothes just these thin little clothes-wrap, thinner than cobweb you can see every line of their body when they walk" (2-3). Her sexuality earns her the devalued labels of "witch" and "temptress" while her race earns her that of "heathen." The text depicts her as the dutiful, resourceful and patient wife and mother with the irresponsible, largely absent but doting Caribbean husband who thrives in the romantic relationship. And Miss Coolie herself is said to fancy a creole man because: "These coolie-woman like nayga-man . . . for the coolie man is the wussest man in the whole world. If they have a wife and she just say 'kemps!'—he quick fe chop off her head" (3). Thus, even the Indian man is portrayed as a stereotype of the cutlass-wielding wife-murderer and an unconscionable interloper.

However, these images are false and limiting and make Miss Coolie a problematic figure. Contrary to the surface impression, Miss Coolie explodes the myth of Indian stereotypes in this work. The text is replete with evidence of her struggle for survival and identity in the polyglot social milieu and her challenge to the status quo. One suspects that one of her main reasons for capitulation to Christianity was a desire to transcend the dilemma of homelessness and displacement, to own land and consolidate her unchosen destiny. Duddy Kravitz's grandfather, in the eponymous Canadian novel by Mordecai Richler best asserts the immigrant's will to counter homelessness and identity thus: "A man without land is nobody." Through her ingenuity and resourcefulness, Miss Coolie shows society that there are *alternatives* to colonial confinement and repression, that the marginalised can be liberated to take her place in the centre of the text, for the narrator acknowledges that "her coming by some mysterious and still ill-defined process was helping me to see that there were other paths, that there were alternatives beyond the pure and narrow path, to the Heaven of Parson Bedlow or the road to Hell that everyone said was Moses's" (11-12). Miss Coolie shows the creole villagers that distance is no obstacle in a crisis when all the while they are quite content to live or die quietly over the mountains, their fate in Parson's hands. She inspires Ish with hope that it is possible for blacks to aspire to be doctors. She shows them that *paper* could be obtained for the land to overcome dispossession by the whites in the future. She teaches them not to accept society with all its flaws and its false base by her example of a faith in the ability of *self* (a humanistic position). Her "alienness insulated" her (to borrow Naipaul's phrase) from the contradictions of the racial *mêlée*. She literally and metaphorically starts "a fire in the dead hearth," and effects an alteration of the configuration of society constructed by Europe with its binary notions of good and evil synonymous with white and black, and its apocalyptic vision of corresponding Heaven and Hell—"a radical division into paired opposites," and what Frantz Fanon sees as the product of a "manichaeism delerium."[5]

Miss Collie's "foreignness" or "otherness" and the fact that she has "traveled" are assets rather than reasons for victimization. The narrator recognizes: "she also had from the start an understanding of the world that the rest of us lacked, a pragmatic drive that allowed her to dispassionately weigh alternatives, make her decisions and act, while we still floundered around in a confused tangle of emotions, family ties, custom and superstition" (43-44). And as for her "heathenness," he reflects: "in any event I had begun to wonder if she was real Heathen after all, she was so good and kind to me, so hard-working, so totally serene and uncomplaining in the face of her loneliness and adversity" (11). The role of the Indian woman in this work is as the bringer of a fresh consciousness to the fossilized (four hundred-year old) apathy and resignation pervading a rural Jamaica enclosed and insulated by the mountains; but, most importantly, her connection with the creole society in her everyday relationships saves her from becoming a casualty of colonialism and the scapegoat of a society which sees her as *other.*

Miss Coolie has effected a rewriting of the Garden of Eden myth. The snake in the Garden of Eden tempted the Mother of mankind with knowledge which brought awareness of sexuality, shame, guilt and the pain and penalty of mortality. This "snake" woman, this "temptress," brings knowledge which serves to awaken the peasantry, initiate social change and create awareness of alternatives. Senior even subverts the Genesis myth where God had told Adam that the ground would be cursed—"in toil you shall eat of it"—for, as if by her wizardry, Miss Coolie is able to grow a range of foods other than the hard-to-grow crops, without the usual laboriousness and with a single-mindedness that reminds the reader of the pleasure of husbandry among the two "gardeners" in the pre-fall state of innocence. The reader cannot help but be encouraged by Miss Coolie's ingenuity, her thriftiness and creativity for all her "outrageous and barbaric" ways (which are ascribed to her but which the reader never encounters). In time, Miss Coolie frees herself from the margins and footnotes of Parson's script; she owns the property and occupies centre space "at Top Rock where the old-time white people used to live, a house built to last of solid mahogany and cedar shingles but which over the years had fallen into *decay* . . . Miss Coolie has restored it, added to it" (43). However, this liberation or alteration of colonial hegemony is ambiguous, for Miss Coolie has offered an alternative discourse but, instead of exploring an alternative avenue to self-actualization, is seen to have built upon the decadence and ruins of colonialism a further compromise, encroaching upon it, taking possession of it and *altering* it.[6] Yet the fact remains that she refuses to limit her possibility for life to the narrow confines constructed by colonialism, and abrogates the laws and logic of a repressive colonialism by her subversive actions, seeking an epistemological and ontological alternative—alternative ways of knowing and being.

Miss Coolie's conscious decision to convert to Christianity and plunge radically into the acculturation process, to cease resistance to creolization, her casting off of the old self of "outsider and outcast" in order to become a new self that is accepted by society, her psychosocial and spiritual growth thereafter deserve some further examination. Near the end of his tale, the adolescent narrator, always viewing Miss Coolie's dilemma with a pristine understanding and sympathy, reflects: "Long afterwards I realized that Miss Coolie must have taken the decision to join the Church while she was down in the Bay (at the hospital), must have spent the time there *giving thought to their new life, the way ahead and how best she could deal with the situation that faced her*" (39, my emphasis). In this instance, one can assume that the journey motif has facilitated, not self-discovery, but a plan for reprieve and recuperation from the assaults of colonialism whereby she discards her "heathen clothes and bangles," changes to European styles, joins the Christian church and submits to the parameters of colonial/new world morality. She pits herself to the new role with the same passion and vigor with which she had resisted it. The question of her creolization is settled in this symbolic image where Miss Coolie joins the creole women on their long trek to market "as they came *to the point where Miss Coolie's track joined the main path,* there she was with her loaded donkey, *and as she fell in with them* in the darkness, *she looked no different* from the black and mulatto women of the district carrying their goods to market" (39, my emphasis). Earlier, the narrator recalls that her baptism was a "turning point" in her life "for it marked the stage when she began to firmly control her own destiny . . . It was as if she herself had decided to accept totally the life into which she had been thrust, to become fully a part of the district, to cast off the mantle of outsider and outcast" (39).

But after all is said and done, Miss Coolie—having made comfortable provision for her family—*reverts* to her saris, her heathen bangles and rings and her red spot on her forehead; she gives all her daughters Indian names and rejects the Church once the government school is established. I am tempted to agree with Ashcroft, Griffiths and Tiffin about the inevitability of hybridity[7] in multicultural societies, and disagree with Birbalsingh's statement that "the process . . . of creolization involves the gradual adoption of Caribbean manners while relinquishing Indian customs in pursuit of social recognition and acceptance."[8] Indeed, the last image in the work is the reflection of the Ganges in her eyes (even Ish and, by extension, society see this) even after she has invested a lifetime of energy and struggle on Caribbean soil.

To continue on the question of creolization and indigenization, the cross-cultural imagination has projected through its narrator an awareness of the loss that comes with alienation, made all the more distressing by a language barrier: "faraway and sorrowful" eyes (6). He "never knew whether she spoke so little because she was naturally very reticent or whether she never really felt comfortable speaking English, or whether in her early years of hardship, isolation and exile she had got into the habit of not speaking" (7); again, looking at a map of India, "her eyes immediately filled with tears and she turned away from the mortar and wiped her eyes on the edge of the sari and went hurriedly on with her pounding" (10). But the more subtle spiritual loss that is engendered in compromise is never depicted in the text (indeed there is no explanation for the sudden reversion to eastern customs after a seemingly successful creolization). Thus, the narration takes a huge psychological leap and offers an ambivalent conclusion—one which glosses over the cultural underpinnings: "It was as if, crossing over the mountains to start a new life, or perhaps even earlier when she crossed the sea, she had *left behind all that reminded her of the old, shed her identity and her history,* became transformed into whatever we would make of her, our Miss Coolie" (6-7, my emphasis). This, again, is the conclusion of an objective perception for, while to the narrator she has creolized completely, the author still has her in the image of the capitalist Indian money-lender on the hill, complete in sari. I find this problematic or perhaps this is the kind of ambivalence which characterizes perceptions of the Indo-Caribbean woman.

My thesis is that there is no radical or automatic turning point, no "shedding of the old identity," as perceived by the narrator. There is, most likely, the submersion of the old cultural identity in the cultural displacement, a yielding involved in the process of readjustment and accommodation, in the need not to be ostracized as *other,* a spiritual compromise involved in suppressing that old identity—an ironic gap of which the narrator is unaware. The sense of triumph at the end of the work over his mother-in-law's visible material progress as an indication of successful readjustment and integration is society's reading of the Indo-Caribbean woman, the same ironic sense of triumph in Parson's jubilant singing as Miss Coolie enters the Church and submits to its "civilizing" influence. My theory is that while the narrator "dissembled" with Parson in order to reach his goals (for he is totally disgusted by Parson's morality and confesses that Parson made liars out of them all), Miss Coolie compromised by immersing herself into the creolization process but without losing her Indian world view and the psychological imprint of having been born an Indian (and *this* is the *essence* of the indigenization process).

Therefore, the denouement of the work can be seen as revealing the author's anxiety over assimilation and racial integration:

Her arrival represented a loosening of bonds that had previously bound her, that bind all of us to our homes. Cut free from her past, she was thus free of the duties and obligations that tie us so tightly to one another, sometimes in a stranglehold. She became a free agent with the flexibility that enabled her to soar above our world which was still structured around her faith in the bisi nuts . . . Miss Coolie, in short, is our embodiment of the spirit of the new age, an age in which sentiment has been replaced by pragmatism and superstition by materialism.

(44)

This paper argues for Miss Coolie's identity, for the perseverance of her elemental self in the creolization process, because selfhood is constructed on difference and individuality and, as Jean Baker Miller confirms, "growth requires engagement with difference and with people embodying that difference."[9] I would pause at the idea that this character has shed her old self. Such "pragmatism" *might* be truer of a later generation of Indians born in the Caribbean where the ideology of nationalism might work to blur cultural differences and foster a sense of oneness. This idea has been commented on by the writer, Sam Selvon.[10] The missing link (the gap of unawareness) in this work is a blurring over the notion that identity is not derived through absorption, but through an acceptance of difference from whence Miss Coolie's certainty is derived.

Furthermore, there is ample evidence of Miss Coolie's inventiveness, subversiveness, her connectedness with society, to reaffirm her sense of self that the material success and its visibility seem merely incidental and not the means of validation of self. I feel that the strength of the work lies in the silences of this subversive figure (silence as resistance to dominant discourse) just as the strength of the narrative technique lies in the "grey" areas in the narrator's consciousness—that is, the sense of wonderment and puzzlement of the creole child of the stranger beside him. Michael Anthony's short story "Enchanted Alley" depicts another young creole male protagonist who experiences a similar sense of wonderment at the exotic in the foods and dress of Indians in another island setting, and this seems to be an element of the cross-cultural imagination and of the multicultural reality.

I rather like to agree with the Indian psychiatrist, Kakar,[11] who proffers (to paraphrase) that Indians carry with them a template of their ancestry, a coherent and consistent world image of values and beliefs, and the self-conscious efforts of Hindus to repudiate it are by and large futile. Jung confirms this cultural and psychic attachment to the cultural matrix with his theory of the "collective unconscious."[12] Miss Coolie's re/version (a re-writing of the colonial script) to the saris is an attempt at subversion (an alternative script) of what Erna Brodber, in her *Myal,* calls the "spirit thievery" although

an insight into Indian rituals is not given by Senior but has been observed in contemporary (post-colonial) works (in addition to *Myal*) where the reappropriation of a semiotic of culture (repressed and devalued cultural persistences) as a route to the reclamation of self through a subjective or omniscient narrator has been useful. (Some examples of this technique are Shinebourne's *Last English Plantation* and Ralph Ellison *Invisible Man*). Our narrator sees only the external packaging not the inner reality; he does not perceive the psychic struggle to preserve the authentic self under the many overlays acquired in the indigenization process; so he assumes a state of total assimilation, "cut free from the bonds of the past." In the village, there is a strong sense of dependence on prolific African rituals and communality and, again, the lack of consciousness of parallel Indian rituals and customs could very well lead to the conclusion that the Indo-Caribbean character has been inevitably subsumed by the dominant creole culture. Again one might be tempted to conclude that Miss Coolie is a problematic figure, having all the elements of the struggle for selfhood but derailed and shunted onto the stereotypical line, for all her struggle to survive within the barbed fence of racial and colonial contradictions, her ultimate triumph is the acquisition of wealth (materialism) instead of the reappropriation of her submerged and devalued cultural forms (spirituality). Note that at the very end of the work, even as an adult, the narrator is still in the dark: "And Miss Coolie now. *I will always wonder about her. For I find her still as great a mystery* as when she came as our snake-woman, so little of herself has she revealed. Has she found happiness . . . ? Does she accept without regret . . . ?" (45, my emphasis).

Sylvia Winter makes a distinction between creolization and indigenization: "Whilst the creolization process represents a more or less 'false assimilation' in which the dominated people adopt elements from the dominant . . . in order to obtain prestige and status, the 'indigenisation' process represents the more *secretive process* by which the dominated culture survives; and resists" (my emphasis).[13] But Braithwaite feels that there is no such cultural synthesis as urged by Wynter and by Ashcroft, Griffiths and Tiffin above:

> The whole argument really rests on an understanding of core culture . . . At the moment it seems to me, it would be impossible to claim that Indians and ex-Africans in the Caribbean, even in Trinidad, share a common culture and that this culture is central to the region and to their own sensibilities. The culture of the region, in my view, shows essential differences expressed in personal and group attitudes, behavior and perception. Integration and national understanding are far more likely to have real meaning if they are based upon knowledge of these differences.[14]

Yet, implicit in this work is the conviction that Miss Coolie has unobtrusively and imperceptibly been participating in an acculturation process but without abandoning her inherent Indianness. The Indian woman character has grown certain of herself, has disrupted the obstructing paradigms of the status quo, has freed herself from the margins of invisibility, has connected with creole society; she is a celebration of female cultural strength, *enhancing and being enhanced by* the creole reality and, by these struggles, merits a claim to ontological space in the new lands to which she was originally brought by the colonizer and, later, to new lands of the village, ironically, by the colonized SonSon.

Finally, Dutch economist J. S. Furnivall's assessment of the polyglot societies of the Caribbean and the nature of togetherness, in the first half of the twentieth century when this story is set, is interesting: "The plural society owes its existence to external facts; it is a union of disparate parts, and lacks a common social will. There is a medley of people who mix but do not combine. The different sections of the community lie side by side, but separately, within the same political unit."[15] And recall the narrator's apprehension of the intended union when Miss Coolie, bludgeoned into acceptance of Christianity, decides to be baptized: the description of the "image of Parson and Miss Coolie together was still too disturbing to me, a violent image even," tells of the racial and cultural chasms created by colonization. The meeting of two entities so diametrically opposed to each other seems to the young narrator as catastrophic as the collision of two worlds but Miss Coolie, in her ability to readjust and accommodate to the social reality as evidenced in Senior's short story, has exploded the theory of the discrete, unchangeable nature of the plural society.

A creole identity then is not a totalizing, monolithic construct but the process of creolization is an accommodating, protean ontological space where human relationships grow despite polarized theories so that Edward Said's words about exile would be appropriate for the writer, critic and subject of the texts alike: "Exile, far from being the fate of those nearly forgotten unfortunates who have been dispossessed and expatriated, becomes something closer to a norm, an experience of crossing boundaries and charting new territories in defiance of the classic canonic enclosures, however much the loss and sadness of exile may also need acknowledgement and registering."[16]

Notes

I would like to thank Ken Ramchand who inspired me to investigate the experience of the Indo-Caribbean woman in yet another text.

1. For example, Harold Ladoo, *No Pain Like This Body* (Toronto: Anansi Press, 1972), Edgar Mittleholzer, *Corentyne Thunder* (London: Eyre & Spottiswoode, 1941), Ismith Khan, *The Jumbie Bird* (London: Longman, 1961), to name a very few.

2. In *The Arrival of the Snake-Woman and Other Stories* (Longman, 1989). All further references to the text are noted in the body of the paper.

3. Tzvetan Todorov, *The Conquest of America,* trans. Richard Howard (New York: Harper Row, 1984), 3.

4. It may be instructive to note that Earl Lovelace in *The Dragon Can't Dance* (Longman, 1979) depicts an Indo-Caribbean male character who is known in society by the stereotypical label of "channa boy."

5. Ashcroft, Griffiths and Tiffin, *The Empire Writes Back* (London: Routledge, 1989), 124-25.

6. Caribbean critic, Michael Gilkes, has remarked (in conversation) that flowers are now growing out of the ruins of an old sugar mill, perhaps a symbol of life and rebirth springing from the decadence and ruin of colonialism. Perhaps Senior should not be faulted for this image.

7. Ashcroft, Griffiths and Tiffin, 180.

8. Frank Birbalsingh, *Passion and Exile* (Hansib, 1988), 75.

9. Jean Baker Miller, *Towards a New Psychology of Women* (Boston: Beacon Press, 1976), 13.

10. Sam Selvon, "Three into One Can't Go—East Indian, Trinidadian and West Indian," in *India in the Caribbean,* eds. David Dabydeen and Brinsley Samaroo (Hansib, 1987), 13-24.

11. Sudhir Kakar, *The Inner World: A Psychoanalytic Study of Childhood and Society in India,* 2nd ed. (Delhi: Oxford University Press, 1986).

12. Read, Fordham, and Adler, eds, *The Collected Works of Carl G. Jung: The Archetypes and the Collective Unconscious,* trans. R. F. C. Hull (Pantheon Books, 1959).

13. Sylvia Winter, "Jonkonnu in Jamaica," *Jamaica Journal* (June 1970), 39.

14. Edward Braithwaite, *Contradictory Omens* (Mona, Jamaica: Savacou Publications, 1974), 48.

15. Furnivall, *Colonial Policy and Practice* (Cambridge University Press, 1948), quoted in Paul Singh, "Socialism in a Plural Society: A Pamphlet" (London: Fabian Research Series 30, 1972).

16. Edward Said, "Figures, Configurations, Transfigurations" (Keynote Address to 1989 ACLALS Conference), in *From Commonwealth to Post-Colonial,* ed. Anna Rutherford (Coventry: Dangaroo Press, 1992), 15.

Richard F. Patteson (essay date January 1993)

SOURCE: Patteson, Richard F. "The Fiction of Olive Senior: Traditional Society and the Wider World." *ARIEL* 24, no. 1 (January 1993): 13-33.

[*In the following essay, Patteson regards Senior as a dominant voice in the development of a postcolonial West Indian literature and delineates the defining characteristics of the stories comprising* Summer Lightning *and* The Arrival of the Snake-Woman.]

In his foreword to Michel de Certeau's *Heterologies,* Wlad Godzich points out that in many parts of the world the old colonial order has been supplanted by a "neo-colonialism of center and periphery" in which the "former colonial powers together with other economically dominant nations constitute the core whereas the former colonies form the periphery. The latter admits of measurement in relation to the core as an index of its degree of development, where it is of course implicit that the core's own development is normative and somehow 'natural'" (xi-xii). Nowhere is this more true than in the Caribbean where, as Olive Senior has put it, "a new center-periphery system is evolving which is based in Washington and a new cultural system is evolving located somewhere between Dallas and Hollywood" ("Interview" 487). The problems inherent in the literary expression of cultural identity come into particularly sharp focus in the twelve nations of the English-speaking Caribbean because the lingering pull of the old colonial power, Britain, is so forcefully augmented by the looming presence of the United States. To a certain extent, Caribbean writers have little choice but to define themselves within the "empowered" or "dominant" discourse of the West. They may adopt a different point of view (and often a political stance at least mildly critical of the West), but their linguistic medium, their genres, and even their audience tend to be primarily Western.

Senior succeeds, to a greater degree than most, in finding a voice that is, through the frequent use of Jamaican English and a shrewd reliance on the devices of oral storytelling, somewhat different from standard forms of European discourse. Although she has published only two volumes of short stories, she has already established herself as one of the more talented artists currently working in that genre and a major force in the development of a postcolonial West Indian literature. Senior's astute deployment of Jamaican Creole in dialogue within stories narrated in standard Jamaican English[1] does not mark her originality or significance. This is an old, reliable device employed by many writers from both the Caribbean and elsewhere. Moreover, inasmuch as those fragments of dialect are subsumed into and dominated by the language of the narrator, a colonial situation, with regard to the two forms of discourse, still prevails. The language of narration in effect works as a corrective, reducing the dialect language to the status of a variation on a norm and thus marginalizing it.

But this situation does not obtain when writers tell stories entirely in Jamaican English or some other creole dialect, as V. S. Reid and Samuel Selvon (among others) have done. Some of the difficulties inherent in such a project are formidable. Kenneth Ramchand observes that "few West Indian authors reproduce dialect precisely in their works" but calls Reid's efforts in *New Day* "a convincing extension of the familiar" (*West Indian* 99-100). And Selvon, speaking of *Moses Ascending,* says, "I experimented . . . with using both this [modified dialect] and an archaic form of English which is not spoken anywhere today." Moses' language in that novel is, in Ramchand's words, also a kind of "successful invention"—successful because it evokes real creole speech but remains intelligible to a wider audience. The exclusive use of "pure" dialect, Selvon argues, "would have been obscure and difficult to understand." He goes on to say that "Standard English or 'proper English' is also used as a part of [West Indian] dialect in certain phrases or words" (Selvon 60-61). When that happens, parts of the formerly dominant language are themselves subsumed into a new vernacular. As Ramchand has written more recently, "[o]nce there came into existence a class of West Indians who combined Standard and dialect in their linguistic competence, the two registers became open to influence from each other" ("West Indian" 105). This is the point at which Senior enters the picture.

Clearly, the search for an authentic voice for the expression of the "matter" of the West Indies has been in progress for decades, and Senior owes a considerable debt to distinguished predecessors and older contemporaries like Selvon, Reid, and John Hearne. In several of the stories in her first book, **Summer Lightning,** a version of vernacular Jamaican speech—and one not so obviously "invented" as Reid's or Selvon's—is the norm rather than the deviation. Senior's importance as a writer does not rest exclusively upon those stories, but they are among her best, and her bold placement of them alongside ones narrated in standard English is a signal confirmation of her status as a leading postcolonial writer. The dialect stories in a sense validate the others, and the polyphonous voice that emerges moves from one form of discourse to another with facility and commanding assurance. The most immediate effect gained is one of intense verisimilitude, for Senior's prodigious mastery of the varieties of English speech in Jamaica, the "continuum" of Jamaican English, is a brilliant reflection of the linguistic versatility in daily life that is a hallmark of Caribbean creole culture. On a deeper level, the medley of discourses that constitutes her two short story collections represents the countercolonization of a language once associated with hegemonic authority.

Yet even though Senior accomplishes this linguistic feat, she is still the product of a society whose educational, economic, religious, and political institutions are predominantly European in origin and character. And the genre itself—the written fictional story created for its own effect—if not entirely a European or American invention, is at least intimately connected with that cultural matrix. Wilson Harris, along with many others, has roundly criticized the Anglophone Caribbean's most celebrated man of letters, V. S. Naipaul, for his allegiance in his early novels to what Ramchand calls "the mainstream tradition of the English nineteenth-century novel" (*West Indian* 9). Naipaul and others like him, Harris insists, employ "a 'coherency' based on the English social model to describe a native world" (45). Harris decries the use of that literary form to render "invalid" the native world and to pander to the wider audience outside the Caribbean by supporting Western notions of superiority. But surely (whatever one may think of Naipaul) Senior's fiction does not aim for or achieve such an effect. Her studies of family relationships, while as conventionally realistic as Naipaul's fiction, are actually subtle attacks on systems of power dynamics analogous to those underlying colonialism itself. And, moreover, her tales owe as much to a tradition of oral storytelling in Africa as to the genre developed by Poe, Chekhov, and deMaupassant. Reflecting on her childhood, Senior has remarked: "My major influence then was the oral tradition. . . . Later came formal exposure to 'English' literature in high school" ("Interview" 480). The single word "later" speaks volumes about the subordination of the written and the "formal" to the oral and the vernacular in the genesis of Senior's stories, and their final manifestation as works of literature is still marked by a spoken quality, a sense of a personality telling the story, that emerges from and vitalizes the written text.

I

Senior herself has offered the most succinct description of her fictional world. The stories of *Summer Lightning,* she says, focus on the Jamaica of her childhood and emphasize the problems and perspectives of poor rural children, while those in *Arrival of the Snake-Woman* are more expansive, involving characters "of different races and classes," rich and poor, in both rural and urban settings. But both collections are explorations of Jamaican experience and identity within a larger network of competing cultures. "I want people to know," she states, "that 'literature' can be created out of the fabric of our everyday lives, that our stories are as worth telling as those of Shakespeare—or the creators of *Dallas*" ("Interview" 484). An awareness of that enveloping, sometimes corrosive larger culture is never very far in the background of Senior's stories precisely because the problematic relationship between the isolated, enclosed societies of the West Indies and the wider world is such a pervasive fact of Caribbean life.

It is striking how insistently that wider world encroaches upon the rural and traditional in Senior's fiction. The collision occasionally occurs when an outsider appears in a rural village (as in **"Arrival of the Snake-Woman"**) and initiates a process of change that may or may not be beneficial.[2] More common is the plot involving the return of a native who has been altered in some important way by exposure to the outside world. Several times in *Summer Lightning* Senior employs variations on this formula. In **"Ascot,"** for instance, a pretentious ne'er-do-well comes back to the village of his birth after several years spent in the United States drifting from one job to another. Since boyhood his ambition has been "to dress up in white clothes and drive a big white car" (29). When he appears at the house of Lily, the story's narrator, and her parents, he is indeed dressed in white and driving a white rental car. He is also accompanied by an American wife who is "just finishing up her Master Degree" (32). All agree that Ascot has come up in the world, but his financial and social successes have not been matched by moral growth. At first he attempts to convince his wife that he is a member of Lily's more prosperous family; when that ruse fails, he repeatedly slights and insults his mother, Miss Clemmie, and her younger, darker children. Ascot, whose features are largely Caucasian, has always conceived of himself as belonging to the larger, white world. And although maintaining that self-image necessitates the humiliation of his own mother, Miss Clemmie remains intensely proud of him. The other neighbors in the district are quite impressed as well, when they hear about Ascot, but Lily confides to the reader at the end that "is only me one Miss Clemmie did tell how there was not a bite to eat in the house that day and Ascot never even leave her a farthing" (35). Lily's disapproval, as well as that of her outraged father, casts a cloud over Miss Clemmie's parental pride, strongly suggesting that too casual an adoption of the materialistic and racist values of the West is a high price to pay for Western prosperity.

"Real Old Time T'ing" displays the contrast between traditional values and outside corruption less starkly. Like **"Ascot,"** this story is told entirely in Jamaican English, the narrator here being an unidentified member of the community. Her commentary on the action and sardonic asides dramatically enhance the spoken quality of the tale, linking it firmly to an oral tradition that predates the "short story" by many centuries. The comic plot has to do with one Papa Sterling and his upwardly mobile daughter Patricia who, having married a successful Kingston lawyer, decides that her father needs a new house, "for it look bad how [he] living in this old board house it dont even have sanitary convenience" (54). Much of the story's considerable humor, derives from Patricia's conflict with Papa Sterling's third cousin, Miss Myrtella, who has lived in England and speaks with a "foreign" accent. One of the funniest effects in the story is the narrator's effort to mimic Miss Myrtella's British English through her own Jamaican dialect. Miss Myrtella has also acquired, along with her accent, a number of antiques, and when Patricia, who is intent on "finding her roots" (54) by buying all the "old time ting" she can find, offers to purchase some of them, Miss Myrtella responds acidly, "'You seem to forget that this his my ouse. Hit his not ha store you know." Patricia is so annoyed that she "grab up her handbag and flounce out of the house" (62). Some time later Papa Sterling's new home is finished, and Miss Myrtella, whom Patricia did not invite to the housewarming party, shows up anyway as Papa's new bride. Patricia, however, swallows her pride and kisses her new stepmother, realizing that she now stands to inherit "all kind of old time ting" (66).

Patricia's acquisitiveness is a less serious offense than Ascot's egotistical pretense and crass ambition, and her greed is, after all, balanced by her generosity (albeit self-serving) to Papa Sterling. In **"Ascot"** people can get hurt when the modern and traditional collide, but **"Real Old Time T'ing,"** with its gentle mixture of old and new, urban and rural, England and Jamaica, implies that such things can and perhaps must coexist in the construction of a distinctive creole culture. Only rarely does Senior present Western influence as an unalloyed evil, or even as a factor wholly extraneous to Caribbean experience. Although she clearly recognizes the destructive potential in headlong assimilation of Western (especially American) ways, she also implicitly acknowledges the interpenetration of the cosmopolitan and the insular as an essential element in the process of creolization.

Growing up "racially and socially a child of mixed worlds, socialized unwittingly and simultaneously into both," Senior recalls that those worlds "embodied the polarizations of race and class" but "at bottom could not be separated." The process, she readily admits, leaves a substantial measure of alienation in its wake, and she speaks eloquently of the conflicts that she and other West Indians have endured—"contradictions inherent in race and class, in poverty and wealth, power and powerlessness, European values versus indigenous values rooted in Africa." Those contradictions, Senior perceived early in life, "were manifested in the *word*, in the politics inherent in the spoken word versus the written, in Jamaican creole versus the language of the Bible, Shakespeare—and the schoolroom" ("Interview" 481-82). The sense of displacement that can accompany creolization as a new culture gradually, often painfully,

emerges is the dramatic impetus of many of Senior's stories, and clearly her command of voice is one of her most effective means of transcending and transforming that sort of anomy.

Other such strategies in Senior's fiction have more to do with the architecture of family relationships than with language, but they, too, bear directly on the connections between power and identity and often have distinctly political implications. One of the most frequently recurring of these is the imaging of childhood alienation as both a product of and a metaphor for the displacements of colonialism. Senior, who herself grew up with relatives, maintains that the stories in *Summer Lightning* told from a child's perspective "express some of the powerlessness, frustrations and lack of understanding by the adult world . . . I myself felt as a child" ("Interview" 484).[3] But her tales of childhood, in *Arrival of the Snake-Woman* as well as in *Summer Lightning,* are more than autobiographical. In many of these stories children live with people who are not their natural parents (or occasionally with parents who are distant and uncaring). More often than not, as in **"Summer Lightning"** or **"Bright Thursdays,"** the child's real parents are less well off financially, less educated, or less "cultivated" than the surrogate family. Frequently, too, the child or her natural mother is a dark-skinned Jamaican whereas the adoptive family is light-skinned or even white. In almost all cases, authentic parents or parental figures are for some reason absent or placed at a distance from the child. The foster parents are suffocatingly present, but they embody different (more European) values and exercise a kind of authority closely associated with the schoolroom and the established church. Senior's stories are not simple allegories, however. It is far less useful to see family relationships as a disguise for colonial politics in her work than to understand both structures as analogous, and sometimes interrelated, systems of power dynamics.

Examples of these and similar configurations are not hard to find in Senior. In **"Bright Thursdays,"** a young girl named Laura lives with her affluent grandparents in "a big house with heavy mahogany furniture" (36). Laura is the illegitimate child of their son and a servant girl who is both poor and black. The story's pronounced preoccupation with skin colour emanates from Myrtle, Laura's mother, who earlier tried to "improve" her complexion by rubbing cocoa butter into it, and from the grandmother, Miss Christie, who is acutely embarrassed by the dark little child she has agreed to raise. Laura herself is embarrassed and alienated not only by her skin colour but by the difficulty she faces in learning and remembering "the social graces that Miss Christie had inculcated in her." When her father arrives for a visit from abroad (like Ascot, with an American wife in tow), she suffers "a two-fold anxiety: not to let her mother down to Miss Christie, and not to let Miss

Christie down in front of this white woman from the United States . . ." (52). But Laura's greatest desire is that her father "attend her, acknowledge her, love her" (52). Instead, he first ignores her, then angrily dismisses her as "the bloody little bastard" (53). With that Laura silently declares herself "an orphan," and the clouds, which she has always associated with her fears and insecurities, seem to disappear. This conclusion is very similar to that of **"Confirmation Day,"** in which another little girl declares her independence from a patriarchal god who sits in judgement among the clouds: "I know instinctively that not the reeds in the river nor the wine nor the blood of Christ nor the Book of Common Prayer can conquer me. And not a single cloud of god in that sky" (84).[4] In both stories liberation from authority figures and the ideologies they embody—the deconstruction of repressive cultural and psychological codes—is an essential prerequisite for the construction of an adult identity—whether for an individual or for a society as a whole.

The novella **"Ballad,"** the longest and best story in *Summer Lightning,* is an elegiac reminiscence of a woman who has been a positive and necessary force in the life of the narrator, a girl named Lenora. The account is a self-consciously "told" story. At one point Lenora even addresses her audience directly, and throughout, the language is her natural creole speech. But more importantly, this *telling* is a substitute for the composition about Miss Rilla that Lenora has been forbidden by her teacher to *write*. Miss Rilla, it seems, is not considered a "fit" subject by the guardians of polite society—at least not a fit subject for the written discourse that encodes that society's ideologies and values. It is appropriate that the battle lines are drawn in this way at the beginning and that Lenora instinctively turns to the tradition of oral storytelling for her tribute, because in the process of finding that authentic voice to describe Miss Rilla, she discovers herself as well.

Miss Rilla, more forcefully than Myrtle in **"Bright Thursdays,"** is the embodiment of traditional, rural Jamaica and its values. Throughout the telling of her "ballad," Lenora grapples her way toward a recognition that this woman, who is scorned by her family and her teacher, is her true spiritual mother. Lenora lives with her father and MeMa, her stepmother, but she gets no affection from them. Speaking of MeMa, she says, "I know that she dont love me like her own children but that Miss Rilla love me because she dont have no other children to love" (102). And whereas Lenora's home life is filled with violence and abuse (as is that of everyone she knows), Miss Rilla and the man with whom she lives, Poppa D, are "nice to one another" (118). In objective terms, the conduct of the churchgoing, "respectable" members of the community is no more exemplary than that of Miss Rilla, but she has had a number of men in her life, and one of them, years before,

shot and killed another. This scandal looms in her background and fixes her forever in the community's eyes as a "bad" woman. MeMa and her friends "talk about the wicked thing that Miss Rilla do and how she is harlot" (113). To Lenora she is something else entirely. Even very early in the story she has enough understanding of the importance of the relationship to describe her friend's death like this: "O Lord. No more laughing. No more big gold earring. No more Miss Rilla gizada [a coconut tart] to cool down me temper when MeMa beat me. All the sweetness done" (104).

In **"Ballad,"** the conventional, restrictive values of the community are transmitted through two institutions of largely European origin: the schoolroom and the church. At school Lenora is one of her teacher's favorites, but after Miss Rilla's death she finds it hard to concentrate on her studies, and her schoolwork suffers. MeMa beats her, telling her that the teacher only likes her because she is darker than MeMa's own children "and everybody saying how black man time come now and they all sticking together" (109). And she adds that "everybody know this country going to the dog these days for is pure black people children they pushing to send high school. Anybody every hear you can educate monkey?" (109-10). MeMa, who has earlier denounced Lenora's friend Blue Boy as "pure Coromantee nigger" (101),[5] is fearful that the old order, in which light-skinned Jamaicans like herself and her children enjoyed social dominance, might be passing. Both Teacher and MeMa, in different ways, represent the establishment, although Teacher, with his more democratic notions about education, is certainly the more sympathetic of the two. What has kept Lenora going, however, has not been Teacher's encouragement but that of Miss Rilla, who wanted her to stay in school to liberate herself from the familiar cycle of pregnancy and male domination.

The established church is not attacked quite so directly in **"Ballad"** as in some of Senior's other stories, but Lenora does move clearly away from revealed religion as she reflects on Miss Rilla's ostracism by the society that practices it. Earlier in the story, Lenora has expressed concern about Miss Rilla's fate, saying: "And sometime I not so sure that she really gone to Heaven at all since from the time I know her she never even go to church" (115). But by the time she comes to the end of her journey of self-discovery, she is able to reject any belief system that excludes the only real mother she has ever had. As for Miss Rilla "down there burning in hell fire," she boldly asserts, "I dont believe that at all. I believe that Miss Rilla laughing so much that Saint Peter take her in just to brighten up Heaven" (134). Having previously lamented that with Miss Rilla's passing, there is "nobody to tell me nothing" (112), she finally wishes only to be like Miss Rilla in life and to join her after death.

In many of Senior's stories that foreground a child's rebellion against repressive adult/colonial values, there is in the background a loving mother (or mother surrogate, like Miss Rilla) whose effect on the child is potentially more positive. The "true" mother in these situations is almost invariably blacker and less formally educated than the people who actually raise the children, but she often possesses a wisdom and generosity of spirit that the adoptive parents lack. Even the bewildered and spurned Miss Clemmie in **"Ascot"** has much to teach (if her son would only learn) about forgiveness and love. Senior has commented that "the topic of the Caribbean mother . . . and of our relationship to that mother" has become one of the "great literary preoccupations" of the region ("Interview" 485). Senior consistently stresses the importance of the mother and identifies her with a valuable, nurturing mother *culture,* and the empowerment of the mother figure, subtly and a bit hesitantly in *Summer Lightning* but explicitly and forcefully in *Arrival of the Snake-Woman,* can be seen as a virtual paradigm of decolonization.

II

The major themes of *Summer Lightning*—the search for personal and cultural identities, the nurturing role of the West Indian mother in creole society, the problematic and complex relationships between traditional ways and the wider world—are continued and expanded in *Arrival of the Snake-Woman.* **"The View from the Terrace"** takes up the question of identity most directly, focusing as it does on the lifelong struggle of its protagonist, Mr. Barton, to associate himself with what Senior has called "the colonial superstructure" that "determined everything" ("Interview" 481-82). From early childhood Barton has longed for "a world that somehow seemed rooted on its axis" (96) and finds it in the literature of "daffodils and the downs and snow and damsels in distress" (96)—the imagined world of England. Cultivated by teachers and "a succession of English bosses . . . who appreciated . . . his liking for things 'civilised,' i.e. English" (96), he develops a distaste for black people (although he is himself darker than his first wife) and a deep-seated discomfort for his native country.[6] But trips to Europe make him aware that he is not really English, either, and his second marriage, to an "incredibly vulgar" (105) white Englishwoman, ends in divorce.

Barton is, moreover, estranged from all three of his children. One son has moved to Canada, married a white woman, and "lost all interest in the West Indies" (98-99); another has been cut off by his father for marrying "a coal black girl" (99); and Barton's daughter cannot be forgiven for having once been involved in radical politics. Even in his relations with his children Barton is caught between identification with the islands and the African heritage on the one hand and defection to the

world of Europe and North America on the other. Toward the end of his life Barton, alone except for his servant Marcus, builds a house on a secluded hillside and is distressed, though intrigued, when a black woman with several children puts a hut on the opposing slope. As the years pass, the number of children increases. His inability to accept this alien presence on "*his* hill" (90), or even to comprehend who the woman is and what she represents, epitomizes the central dilemma of his own life, and shortly after being informed by Marcus that the woman's children have been fathered by several men, including Marcus himself, Mr. Barton dies—evidently of shock. The woman's shack, however, after being washed away in a rainstorm, is rebuilt, and she returns to the hillside to continue to raise her family. That continuity, based firmly upon a traditional, rural, African-rooted culture, stands in stark contrast to Barton's isolation. The view from his terrace is the future, and the image that lingers after the story ends is that of the two houses—the one filled with life (the woman's name is Miss Vie), the other, a grand but desiccated shell, awkward and out of place.

The idea of home—where it is, what it is—is never very far from the centre of Senior's attention. Barton's "European" house in **"The View from the Terrace"** is divided from Miss Vie's "Jamaican" hut by a deep ravine; in **"The Tenantry of Birds"** Senior attempts to bridge that gulf, bringing the two kinds of homes, with all their iconic associations, together. The "tenantry" of the title is a "rather bedraggled" (46), somewhat wild-looking bird tree growing in an otherwise very formal, English garden belonging to a wealthy Kingston couple. For the wife, the tree represents a small part of the countryside where she spent many pleasant summers as a child. For her husband Philip, a university professor and political activist, the tree is an "unsightly" (47) excrescence which he would like to cut down. Nolene, the wife, is particularly fond of watching "the star boarders . . . the pecharies" drive out the "rough, uncouth, chattering and uncaring" (46-47) kling-klings when they attempt to take over. This detail provides the story with its governing metaphor and Nolene with the example she later needs to take similar action of her own. As Philip becomes more involved in politics (and acquires a black mistress), the marriage disintegrates. He sends Nolene to Miami with their children "for safety's sake" (56), as he puts it. One of the most delicate points Senior makes is that Philip, who like his wife is a light-skinned Jamaican of the privileged social class, does not immerse himself in island politics because of any innate sensitivity to island culture. His political activity is motivated more by ambition and ego than by sympathetic understanding; and his behaviour toward his wife is closely akin to that of master to servant—or of colonial power to colony.

The story explores several sets of oppositions—city and country, artifice and nature, the modern and the traditional—but Senior does not reconcile them in the easiest or most obvious way, by reconciling Nolene and Philip. Instead, she has Nolene return from Miami and reclaim the house. But the formal garden will have to go: "She would plant a new garden. First she would find the gardener and tell him never to touch the bird tree. It was *her* tree and *her* house and she was staying. *He* could move out" (61). To reassure herself she recites a spell that she and her cousins used to call out deep within the Jamaican countryside (to chase away wasps), and she laughs "at the craziness of it. The power" (61). "Power" is the key word here, for the inner strength Nolene draws on to expel the domineering, exploitative, and faithless husband—her colonial master—and seize the house as a home for her children is explicitly linked to the folk ways of rural Jamaica. The story's conclusion is strongly positive. The house, like Barton's, is a "European" structure in modern Kingston, but it will have a garden evocative of the countryside, and it will be presided over by a mother who has reached into her past and found a core of values to sustain her.[7]

"Lily, Lily" is an interlocking web of familiar Senior paradigms, with particular emphasis on the empowered mother as a source of both strength and liberation. One Lily of the story's title is a little girl born out of wedlock and brought up by prosperous relatives, the DaSilvas, who raise her as their own child after she is given up by her mother, Mrs. DaSilva's cousin of the same name. In the course of time young Lily, sexually abused by her "father," flees to the home of her "Aunt Lily." As in several other Senior stories, a child finds herself in a foster home, under an authority that misuses its power, and without the ability to free herself easily or claim her real heritage. When Lily finally comes under the protection of her natural mother, she is liberated not just from the danger of physical abuse but also from the restrictions placed upon women by the society of that day. Lily agrees to send her daughter back to the DaSilvas only on the condition that the girl be allowed to go to St. Catherine's, a school formerly restricted to whites, so that she may "get out of that house" and just as significantly reap the full benefits of "the very process of change that is sweeping the world" (141). The elder Lily has herself quietly grown in learning, sophistication, and ambition during the years since her daughter was born. As the story closes she is preparing to leave Jamaica temporarily for Panama to "seize the opportunities opening up elsewhere" and learn "new ways of seeing, of doing" (141-42). For Lily, interaction with the wider world promises to be a strengthening, constructive experience rather than the morally and culturally debilitating one it is for many of Senior's characters.

The narrative method of **"Lily, Lily"** distinguishes it from all of Senior's other fiction. The point of view is multiple. Emmeline Greenfield, a local gossip, begins the tale in a long monologue spoken to a visiting friend. This section provides background information from a member of the community whose knowledge is as partial as her prejudice is blatant. Other parts of the story are relayed through an omniscient narrator, the consciousness of young Lily, the perspective of Mrs. DaSilva, and most important, a letter from the elder Lily to the DaSilvas. It is in this letter that Senior scores her most potent political points. If Emmeline Greenfield's and Lucy DaSilva's accounts are "official" versions of the events that take place (the versions authorized by a community that places social status above all else), Lily's letter is the impassioned, personal version—and the true one.

Nowhere in Senior's fiction is the protean power of discourse to alter reality more vividly enacted. Lily's letter, openly didactic, frequently strident, always polemical, is a rhetorical trumpet blast that brings the DaSilvas to their knees. Declaring that *she* will make the decisions concerning Lily's future (and will expose Mr. DaSilva's crimes if he or his wife should oppose her), she criticizes the limitations imposed on women by society; she denounces "male betrayal" as well as the "things called 'status,' 'power,' 'respectability'" (139); and she heaps scorn on "the people who rule" Jamaica, "the Governor and the clique surrounding him at Kings House" (141)—all male figures, of course, and all, in the early years of this century, English. The corrupt patriarchal family structure that Lily undermines when she forces the DaSilvas to obey her wishes is as much a product of the colonial sociopolitical system as a microcosmic model of it. The way to liberation from this kind of oppression is exhibited by Lily both through the example of her conduct and through her warning to Mrs. DaSilva to place her responsibilities as a mother above those "as a wife and social arbiter" (143). The inherent power of motherhood in this story extends far beyond protection, however, or even nurturing. Lily's gift to her daughter—and to herself—has to do also with intellectual and moral growth, the freedom to be a whole person, and the means to define and shape one's own future.

The ideas explicitly articulated by Lily in her letter to the DaSilvas—ideas about growth, freedom, and a new society—are woven so delicately into the fabric of **"Arrival of the Snake-Woman"** that their presence is hardly detectable, but this novella is nonetheless Senior's most eloquent meditation on the birth of modern Jamaica out of the island's exposure, for better or worse, to the wider world. The story is actually told, or rather written down, shortly after the turn of the century, but most of it takes place in "the old days" (45), when the narrator, a physician, was a small boy growing up in an isolated rural community. The plot hinges on the coming of an Indian woman, Miss Coolie, to the village, her initial ostracism by most of its inhabitants, and her profoundly constructive effect on them over the years. When Miss Coolie first arrives, she is shunned by the people of Mount Rose largely because she refuses to be baptized in Parson Bedlow's church, causing the Parson to brand her a "Whore of Babylon" (10). She is gradually accepted by most of the villagers, however, and in time she does join the church so that her young son Biya can attend Bedlow's school. Later she opens a small shop in her house, expands it as business grows, and becomes "the most prosperous citizen in the district" (42-43)—eventually even living "at Top House where the old time white people, then Parson Bedlow, used to live" (43). More than a quietly satisfying Horatio Alger story, **"Arrival of the Snake-Woman"** is a moving exploration of cultural convergence in which a shift in power relations among people of African, European, and Indian ancestry signals the emergence of a modern creole society.

The story opens in a time when slavery is still a living memory—at least to Papa Dias, the oldest man in the community, and Mother Miracle, whose father "was one of the old masters" (16). These elderly figures are the bearers of an African tradition that still, many years after emancipation,[8] holds sway in rural areas like Mount Rose. Papa Dias, who is also of mixed African and European descent, is "a man of *knowledge*" who can do "*workings*" and "divine fate from throwing bisi the way his old Oyo[9] grandfather had taught him," and some say he can "summon Shango god of thunder" (15-16). Mother Miracle's magic is more mundane. She conducts services in her yard, "reading" people's illnesses and treating them with bush medicine and "holy water" (19).

Parson Bedlow and his wife Miss Rita are the first white people to come back into the district since "the old-time" whites "died off or moved away" (12) after slavery ended. The arrival of these new authority figures is announced, amusingly, through a bit of pre-Columbian technology—a man blowing on a conch shell. What Parson Bedlow represents, with his fire-and-brimstone fundamentalism, is nothing less than the establishment of a neocolonial power structure. The villagers are surprised that the Parson has not come to take their land, but the hegemony he intends to impose is more insidious as well as more through. The first words of "this strange white man" are, "My children, Let Us Pray" (14), and he immediately proceeds to gather the people into the protective custody of the ultimate patriarchal authority, with himself, installed at Top House, as chief deputy and warden. Gradually, the Parson's "preaching about devils and idolaters and false prophets and miracle workers" (20) has its desired effect, and the influence of Papa Dias and Mother Miracle wanes. But what really

binds the people to Parson Bedlow and Miss Rita is "the book-learning" that they pass on "to the children in the little schoolhouse which they built," for no one wants to give up "the magic . . . contained in black and white squiggles on paper" (23). It is important to note that Papa Dias, too, knows "how to write things down in a book" (15), and this, along with his Oyo knowledge has been a major source of his influence. Senior herself, speaking of her childhood, has called "knowledge as embodied in the word . . . a key to personal affirmation and power" ("Interview" 480). Throughout the story, this emphasis on writing and the role of the writer in asserting such power is a subtle but significant subtext. Ironically, the knowledge that provides Bedlow with his hold over the villagers in the short term may ultimately provide them with the means to define themselves and create their own society.

The attitude of Ishmael, the narrator, toward Miss Coolie is crucial to the development of the story. From the beginning, when his cousin SonSon brings the "Snake-Woman" to the district as his wife, Ishmael stands in awe of her. Because he has already learned "all about India and the Ganges and the Heathen" (3) in Parson Bedlow's school, Ishmael sees her as a romantic figure, evocative of a world far beyond his remote village. He strikes up a friendship with her (greatly displeasing his mother, who is afraid of alienating the Parson) and remains loyal to her all his life, even marrying one of her daughters. When Miss Coolie becomes "the chief demon in Parson Bedlow's pantheon" (10), Ishmael refuses to turn against her—and she, in turn, provides him with a motivation for remaining healthily skeptical toward the Parson. Matters come to a head for Ishmael when young Biya becomes seriously ill and Parson Bedlow, who administers modern medicines to the community, will not treat him. Miss Coolie has to take the child on donkey back to the nearest hospital—a "day and night journey for a man and so lonely no one ever went alone" (30). Biya survives, but the event leaves Ishmael unable "to reconcile Parson's preaching about charity and love and the ministry of Jesus . . . with his behavior to Miss Coolie and Biya" (32). He vows to reject Parson, "his life, his world, his book learning" (32). In the end, Ishmael does not reject everything that Parson represents—but it is Miss Coolie (like the beloved Miss Rilla in **"Ballad"**) who insists that he go back to school and become a doctor.

Miss Coolie's eventual baptism, far from signaling her defeat by Parson Bedlow, marks her emergence as a free person—the stage when she begins "to control her own destiny." As Ishmael puts it: "It was as if she herself had decided to accept totally the life into which she had been thrust, to become fully a part of the district, to cast off the mantle of outsider and outcast" (39). But her conversion is ambivalent. Later in life, when she is prosperous and her children are grown, she reverts to wearing saris and bangles. By this time Parson Bedlow is long gone and Miss Coolie is the matriarch of the community, free to be both Jamaican and Indian.

A similar ambivalence colours Ishmael's thoughts as he brings his story to a close. He realizes that Miss Coolie brought to Mount Rose "an understanding of the world that the rest of us lacked" (43). Freed from her own past, she has acquired a "flexibility" that enabled her to transform herself from a passive outsider to a shaping force within the community. But, as always in Senior's fiction, such "flexibility" has its negative side. "Miss Coolie," Ishmael reluctantly concludes, "is our embodiment of the spirit of the new age, an age in which sentiment has been replaced by pragmatism and superstition by materialism" (44). Ishmael lives in the city so that his own children "will not have to go through the pains of adjustment" (42) that he did when he first left Mount Rose, but he returns "home" occasionally to visit Miss Coolie and her family, which, through his marriage, has become his own. When he does return, he admits to himself that he still feels "halfway between the old world . . . and the new, unable to shake off the old strictures . . . not feeling, like Miss Coolie, at ease enough to shift fully into the relentless present" (44-45).

For Ishmael, living in a world increasing removed from Oyo grandfathers and bush medicines, telling his story is a way of establishing and comprehending who he is. "And this," he reflects, "is why I sometimes sit and write down the things that happened in the old days, so that my children will be able to see clearly where we are coming from, should they ever need signposts" (45). **"Arrival of the Snake-Woman"** takes place in the later years of the nineteenth century, when rural Jamaica's exposure to a wider world was just beginning. Today, the age of colonialism is over, but the "new center-periphery system" is a reality. It would be naive to think that the process of cultural convergence will stop (what culture, after all, is not in some sense "creole"?); but it would be needlessly cynical to assume that the process must end in the obliteration or absorption of one culture by another. That is why the problem of voice is so important and the role of the writer, so essential. Like the Caribbean mother in Senior's stories, the writer must both nurture and liberate. If Ishmael's story is a "signpost," pointing the way not just forward to a complex future but also back to the wisdom of the ancestors and the sound of the conch, so is Senior's fiction. As she herself has put it, "I want to reaffirm those parts of our heritage that have been misplaced, misappropriated, subsumed, submerged, never acknowledged fully as the source of our strength" ("Interview" 484).

Notes

1. It should be pointed out that standard English as spoken in Jamaica differs somewhat from that spoken in Britain (even though the two are mutually intelligible), just as there are differences among standard American, British, and Canadian speech.

2. A prototypical example of this plot device is found in Lovelace's *The Schoolmaster,* where "progress" associated with education or knowledge is presented in Miltonic terms as corruption.

3. Pollard makes several perceptive observations on Senior's criticism of received authority.

4. This sentiment is also expressed in Senior's "Ancestral Poem": "One day I did not pray. / A gloss of sunlight through / the leaves betrayed me so / abstracted me from rituals. / And discarded prayers and / disproven myths / confirmed me freedom." See Mordecai and Morris 78.

5. "The place of origin of many of the slaves brought to Jamaica in the late seventeenth and early eighteenth centuries. . . . in Jamaica, those who escaped and joined the Maroons came to dominate them and gained a reputation for fierceness." See Cassidy and LePage, *Dictionary of Jamaican English.* The Coromantee territory was located in present-day Ghana.

6. Senior has made the point that "the exploration of race and class, that is, the subtleties of race and class, the encounter with race" is a major theme in Caribbean literature but that it is by no means limited to "battles with 'white racism' per se." This is clearly the case in her own fiction. See "Interview" 485.

7. Another story in *Snake-Woman,* "The Two Grandmothers," moves toward quite a different kind of ending, as its narrator, growing up with a light-skinned, wealthy, cosmopolitan grandmother and a dark, poorer one who lives in the country, ultimately opts for the life of wealth, glamour, and modernity epitomized by her favorite television program—*Dallas.*

8. The abolition of slavery throughout the British Empire took full effect in 1838.

9. The Oyo state, located in present-day Nigeria, was a powerful kingdom during the seventeenth and early eighteenth centuries.

Works Cited

Cassidy, Frederick and R. B. LePage, eds. *Dictionary of Jamaican English.* London: Cambridge UP, 1980.

Godzich, Wlad. Foreword. *Heterologies: Discourse on the Other.* By Michel de Certeau. Minneapolis: U of Minnesota P, 1986. vii-xxi.

Harris, Wilson. "The Unresolved Constitution." *Caribbean Quarterly* 14.1-2 (1968): 43-47.

Lovelace, Earl. *The Schoolmaster.* London: Heinemann, 1983.

Mordecai, Pamela and Mervyn Morris, eds. *Jamaica Woman: An Anthology of Poems.* London: Heinemann, 1978.

Pollard, Velma. "An Introduction to the Poetry and Fiction of Olive Senior." *Callaloo* 11.3 (1988): 540-46.

Ramchand, Kenneth. "West Indian Literary History." *Callaloo* 11.1 (1988): 95-100.

———. *The West Indian Novel and Its Background.* London: Heinemann, 1983.

Selvon, Samuel. "Samuel Selvon Talking: A Conversation with Kenneth Ramchand." *Canadian Literature* 95 (1982): 56-64.

Senior, Olive. *Arrival of the Snake-Woman and Other Stories.* London: Longman, 1989.

———. "An Interview with Olive Senior." By Charles H. Rowell. *Callaloo* 11.3 (1988): 480-90.

———. *Summer Lightning and Other Stories.* London: Longman, 1986.

John Thieme (essay date 1994)

SOURCE: Thieme, John. "'Mixed Worlds': Olive Senior's *Summer Lightning*." *Kunapipi* 16, no. 2 (1994): 90-5.

[*In the following essay, Thieme finds several of the stories in* Summer Lightning *to be autobiographical in nature and focused on the issue of identity.*]

Superficially the bulk of the stories in Olive Senior's *Summer Lightning* (1986) are primarily naturalistic accounts of a particular experience of growing up in rural Jamaica in the 1940's and 1950's. The stories repeatedly construct a situation in which a child-protagonist, usually a girl, has been displaced from the peasant home of her early youth and relocated in a middle-class household. Senior has said that this situation replicates the experience of her own youth,[1] which involved a similar movement between houses and made her socially, as well as racially, 'a child of mixed worlds, socialized unwittingly and simultaneously into both',[2] and the reader who knows this, even if s/he is anxious to avoid seeing the text simply as a fictionalized transcription of aspects of the author's own experience, may well be tempted to assume that its range is narrowly circumscribed by the particular nature of this situation represented. In fact, although the stories of *Summer Lightning* do work extremely well as naturalistic accounts of Jamaican rural life and owe much to their being rooted in concrete particularities, the predicament of the displaced child pro-

vides a medium for commenting on central conflicts of the society more generally. The accounts of ways in which children are socialized open up windows on issues of class, race, religion, education, gender, sexuality, language and migration.

Frequently the child who acts as the pivotal point of a particular story, whether as a first- or third-person centre of consciousness, is initiated into knowledge about the behavioural imperatives of the society, discovers that these are by no means monolithic and becomes involved in making some kind of tacit choice between its discrepant codes. In **'Bright Thursdays'** the protagonist Laura, the child of an extra-marital liaison between a dark-skinned countrywoman and a fair-skinned 'young man of high estate'[3] who has since been shipped off to the United States, is sent by her mother to live in the household of her middle-class paternal grandparents with the injunction to 'let them know you have broughtuptcy' (p. 36). Unfortunately Laura finds that any 'broughtuptcy' she does have still leaves her a misfit in her new environment, where a meal instead of being 'something as natural as breathing is a ritual, something for which you prepared yourself by washing your hands and combing your hair and straightening your dress before approaching the Table' (p. 37), and is left feeling that there is 'no space allotted for her' (p. 37). Arguably the story, like the majority of the pieces in *Summer Lightning* is about the attempt to claim a space for oneself or, as Senior has put it herself, 'to create self-identity out of chaotic personal and social history'.[4]

Laura's sense of insecurity in her new social world is figured most strikingly in her response to clouds she observes as she waits for the bus that takes her to school. She associates these with pictures of Jesus she has seen in Sunday School, in which he is represented as descending to earth on a white cloud. Having had the notion that he is a God of judgement and punishment instilled into her through the church, the pictures make her feel that she is a sinner about to be visited by such a God, who will 'one day soon appear out of the sky flashing fire and brimstone to judge her' (p. 46). So her reaction to the clouds can be read as an expression of her guilt-ridden feelings of social inferiority and sense that she will be judged by some patriarchal authority figure. In the denouement, her father returns to Jamaica for a visit with his white American wife. Laura sees him as a rescuer-figure who will release her both from her fear of clouds and the uncertainty that surrounds her Thursdays, a day that she has always felt either 'turned out to be very good or very bad' (p. 36). However, on his return, her father proves to have no real interest in her at all—he is neither a deliverer nor a patriarchal God of judgement—and she receives rather more attention from his wife. The obvious conclusion, that fathers are not knights in shining armour who come to rescue latter-day Rapunzels from the misery of everyday life and that, if Laura is to achieve any kind of self-affirmation, it will be through her own endeavours, is reinforced at the very end of **'Bright Thursdays',** when she overhears her father refer to her as a 'bloody little bastard' (p. 53). In a second she makes herself an 'orphan' (p. 53), thereby renouncing any loyalties she has previously felt towards the middle-class world, and dissipating the threatening clouds. This makes explicit what has been implicit throughout: that what she has taken to be some kind of malevolent force in the natural world is in fact a product of her own particular psycho-social conditioning. Her decision to 'orphan' herself emancipates her both from the middle-class social aspirations inculcated in her by her mother and from the guilt-ridden sensibility induced in her by a branch of the Christian religion[5] that reinforces the society's class and colour hierarchies. She is left a free agent to find the space that she has hitherto felt 'Life' has not allotted her. **'Bright Thursdays'** is typical of *Summer Lightning* in its skill in depicting areas of major social conflict through nuances and for the subtle way in which it exposes how the socially constructed has been naturalized.

The stories encompass a broad range of Jamaican social experience and span the whole range of the linguistic continuum[6] with an easy movement between different tonal registers and between Creole and Standard English in the narrative voices employed. Class snobberies are at the centre of **'Real Old Time T'ing'**; **'Ascot'** is concerned with migration abroad and the different responses the metropolitan success of the trickster-hero elicits in those who have remained behind; **'Country of the One Eye God',** the one story set in a later period—the 1970's—dramatizes conflicts between generations and rural and urban value-systems, particularly in the area of religion. And religion is also to the fore in **'Confirmation Day',** a first-person account of a girl's fearful response to becoming 'a child of god' (p. 81) which uses the clouds metaphor of **'Bright Thursdays'** in an almost identical way, and **'Do Angels Wear Brassieres',** in which the precocious Beccka, a more socially confident child-protagonist than Laura, subversively refashions God in her own image as 'a big fat anansi in the corner of the roof'[7] and, completely uncowed by the judgemental aspects of the respectable brand of local Christianity that instil fear into Laura, envisages a gossipy neighbour who calls her 'the devil own pickney' (p. 68) being punished in the after-life: 'Fat Katie will get her comeuppance on Judgement Day for she wont able to run quick enough to join the heavenly hosts' (p. 70). The witty and irreverential tone is quite different from that of **'Bright Thursdays'** and the comic use of Jamaican Creole perfectly complements the 'force-ripe' (p. 69) Beccka's capacity to function as a satirist of social hypocrisy, particularly when she pits her biblical knowledge against that of a visiting archdeacon, asking him a series of riddles that culminates in the question

that give the fiction its memorable title. Again the dominant thrust of the story is anti-middle class and, although its touch is light, it can be read as an attack on the way in which children are socialized into 'respectable' values (values which have their origins in the colonial culture) with a resultant loss of spontaneity and a positive response to the society's folk culture. All of these stories involve a dialogue between different areas of Jamaican social experience and in the two finest pieces, **'Ballad'** and the title-story, the child-protagonist makes a choice between adult role models who represent the supposedly opposed worlds of the island's middle-class and folk cultures. **'Ballad',** a sustained linguistic *tour de force* narrated in a 'mesolect' form of Jamaican Creole and incorporating forms closer to 'basilect'[8] in its dialogue, juxtaposes the two cultures on the level of discourse, as is clear from its opening words:

> Teacher ask me to write composition about The Most unforgettable Character I Ever Meet and I write three page about Miss Rilla and Teacher tear it up and say that Miss Rilla not fit person to write composition about and right way I feel bad . . .[9]

(p. 100)

Miss Rilla is 'not a fit subject' for scribal discourse in the context of the educational curriculum of the late colonial period, but the text itself opposes this view by instating her as the subject of the 'ballad' it foregrounds itself as being. Gradually it reveals why Miss Rilla has been seen to be beyond both social and literary pales. As a 'scarlet woman' who has had a succession of lovers, some of them younger than herself and one of whom has been killed in a fight over her, she has infringed the sexual taboos of the society and not surprisingly this has stirred up the jealousy of 'respectable' women like the narrator Lenora's step-mother. However, on a more general level, Miss Rilla can be seen to embody the vibrancy of the oral, folk culture and a joy in life which transgresses the codes of the middle-class society in a more radically disruptive way. At several points Lenora speculates on whether Miss Rilla will be admitted into Heaven and by the end she decides she probably will be:

> . . . if there is no forgiveness it mean that Miss Rilla is down there burning in hell fire. But I tell you already that I dont believe that at all. I believe that Miss Rilla laughing so much that Saint Peter take her in just to brighten up Heaven.[10]

(p. 134)

Earlier Lenora has been encouraged to study hard so that she can go on to high school and perhaps become a teacher, but the story ends with her expressing doubts as to whether she wishes to pursue this middle-class ideal and plumping instead for the folk values represented by Miss Rilla. In **'Summer Lightning'** a lonely boy living in the middle-class household of his aunt and uncle takes refuge in a garden room of indeterminate identity and which he thinks of as his 'secret room, a place where he could hide during thunderstorms' (p. 1). Alienated from his snobbish aunt and his uncle, the boy finds his affections are fought over the Rastafarian Brother Justice and a mysterious man who comes to stay in the house for a few weeks each year 'for his "nerves"' (p. 1). The atmosphere is laden with menace and what Senior has referred to as 'the drama, magic, and mystery inherent in all human transactions'.[11] Like the boy, the reader has to decode ambiguous signifiers. Mysteries surround the nature of the strange man, the garden room and summer lightning. Equally enigmatic are his uncle's box-level, which is associated with memory and perception, and an ivory elephant which he is given by the 'man' with an instruction to turn it towards the door for luck, a gnomic piece of advice since the garden room in which he keeps it has three doors. As the story develops, the boy is drawn to the man's company and spends less time with his former friend Brother Justice, a figure of whom his aunt disapproves since his conversion to Rastafari has led to his deserting the 'respect for them which had been inculcated in men like him for centuries' (p. 6). Brother Justice, who has been disturbed many years before by the man's 'watching him the way he should be watching a woman' (p. 7), reacts by telling the aunt to look after the boy. The story reaches its climax with summer lightning flashing outside and the boy feeling threatened as, 'through a film like that covering the eye of the spirit level' (p. 10), he sees the man approaching him. The open-ended narrative breaks off here, leaving what happens next and the issue of whether the man *is* a child molester unresolved.[12] All the major symbols are, however, reinvoked in the closing paragraphs and there is resolution of another kind, as the boy makes *his* social choice by seizing the ivory elephant and pointing it towards the garden door through which he feels sure Brother Justice will now come; he is no longer unsure as to where 'good luck' lies and consciously chooses the social outsider over the threatening middle-class character. And the narrative also clarifies the significance of the garden room. Immediately before the final incident the boy has felt that if the man ever touches him, 'everything—Bro. Justice, the room, the magic world, even the order of the aunt and uncle's life that he both loved and despised—would be lost to him for ever' (p. 9). The room and the things he associates with it are his childhood, to which he now clings desperately in the face of adult behaviour that threatens an end to innocence.

Notes

1. Unpublished talk, University of North London, 8 May 1990.

2. Charles H. Rowell, 'An Interview with Olive Senior', *Callaloo,* 11, 3 (1988), 481. Subsequent references cite 'Rowell'.

3. *Summer Lightning* (London: Longman, 1986), p. 38. Subsequent references are to this edition and are cited in the text.

4. Rowell, p. 482.

5. Ostensibly the Anglican church, the state church of Jamaica. In her entry on the church in her *A-Z of Jamaican Heritage* (Kingston: Heinemann/Gleaner Co., 1983) p. 6, Senior comments: 'The Church of England was the church of the ruling class and planters and therefore supported the institution of slavery.'

6. David DeCamp, 'Social and Geographic Factors in Jamaican Dialects', in R. B. Le Page, ed., *Creole Language Studies* (London: Macmillan, 1961), p. 82, expresses the linguistic situation in Jamaica as follows: 'Nearly all the speakers of English in Jamaica could be arranged in a sort of linguistic continuum, ranging from the speech of the most backward peasant or labourer all the way to that of the well-educated urban professional. Each speaker represents not a single point but a span of this continuum, for he is usually able to adjust his speech upward or downward for some distance along it.'

7. Anansi (or Anancy) is a spiderman-trickster figure of the Akan peoples of West Africa, brought to the Caribbean by the slaves of the Middle Passage. As Senior notes in her *A-Z of Jamaican Heritage,* p. 5, he 'personifies the qualities of survival' in the face of colonial oppression. Anansi stories are among the most popular form of folk tales in Jamaica. Cf. Edward Kamau Brathwaite's representation of the subversive potential of the Anansi figure in 'Ananse', *The Arrivants,* pp. 165-7.

8. 'Basilect' is a term used to refer to that segment of the linguistic continuum that is assumed to be 'furthest' from Standard English; 'acrolect' that which is assumed to be closest; and 'mesolect' refers to all the intermediate varieties of the Creole. See Derek Bickerton, *Dynamics of a Creole System* (Cambridge: Cambridge UP, 1975), p. 24.

9. The essay-topic suggests the metropolitan model of the *Reader's Digest*'s 'My Most Unforgettable Character' feature. Cf. similar passages in V. S. Naipaul's *A House for Mr. Biswas* (Harmondsworth: Penguin, 1969), pp. 356-7; and Jamaica Kincaid, *Annie John* (London: Picador, 1985), pp. 38-45.

10. Cf. Beccka's imagined version of Fat Katie's 'comeuppance' on Judgement day, quoted above.

11. Rowell, p. 481.

12. Senior says, Rowell, p. 483: '. . . what you see on the page is only part of the story. The inexplicable, the part not expressed, the part withheld is the part that you the reader will have to supply from your emotional and imaginative stock . . . I believe it's my job as a writer not to say it all, for I am only one half of the equation—reader-writer—and that the work becomes complete only when it is read, when the reader enters the world I have created. I therefore tend to leave a lot of my work open-ended.'

Michael Thorpe (review date spring 1996)

SOURCE: Thorpe, Michael. Review of *Discerner of Hearts,* by Olive Senior. *World Literature Today* 70, no. 2 (spring 1996): 455.

[*In the following review, Thorpe provides a favorable evaluation of* Discerner of Hearts.]

The nine stories in Olive Senior's collection *Discerner of Hearts* are set in Jamaica, from the colonial period to the present day. Unfortunately, they are not chronologically arranged, so that **"Zig Zag,"** which clearly, like the opening title story, is pre-Independence, comes at the end, after **"The Cho Choo Vine,"** which glances at Rastafarianism. In most, black is not yet beautiful and white is the index of social advantage. Taken together, the collection, regardless of chronology, reflects a constricted society whose relationships are overdetermined by class and color; caste-power, or the lack of it, is constantly felt.

The viewpoint, with one exception, is female, in first or third person. At the center are two monologues which subtly blend Jamaican patois with Standard English. In **"You Think I Mad, Miss?"** Francina Mytella Jones goes from car to car in the street, begging to the accompaniment of a fractured litany of her betrayed life, while in **"Swimming in the Ba'Ma Grass"** Miss Lyn utters a poignant elegy for a husband murdered by a trigger-happy policeman, who is the law. These stories and the collection as a whole need a glossary for the less-initiated reader, and one wonders why this publishing house, which has provided glossaries for writers from similar linguistic backgrounds (e.g., M. G. Vassanji and Shyam Selvadurai), omits one in this case. The meaning of such words as fassing, susu, and buckra pickney are not always deducible from context.

Most of the stories use a Standard narrative mainly, in the third person, except for the child's subjective viewpoint of **"The Case Against the Queen,"** carefully differentiating the patois of servants and the less-educated—those whom the servant Cissy, in the title story, realizes "needed to be so careful, to live good in the world, for there was nothing else between them and the night." In this story, although the daughter of the house, Theresa, belongs to that class whom "nothing seemed to threaten," she desires to reach out and empathize with her family's fearfully superstitious servant. In **"Zig Zag"** Sadie, the daughter of a shabby genteel white family, also reaches out to the servant Desrine and her numerous progeny in the bush, but she can do little; her equivocal status is pointed up when her mother deplores her "looking so black" from staying out in the sun. However, being white or light-skinned is a depreciating asset, an outmoded recipe for success in the world.

Old colonial caste gives way before the new materialism. The black servant's son, newly returned with "his Panama strut, his American accent," can aspire to Brid, his mother's poor white employer's daughter, and she in her innermost heart desires him. This story, and others, ends with a defining moment of self-realization; the inner life, often suppressed, emerges uppermost. The reader ponders this and what it implies or promises. With **"The Lizardy Man and His Lady"** we witness from the traumatized standpoint of children and servants the deadly, contemporary "big big" world of "coke and the crack and all them sinting."

The publisher's blurb describes Olive Senior as "one of the most exciting talents writing in Canada today"; writing and published in Canada, yes, and this fortunately gains her an international audience—but hers is a Jamaican, not (yet) a Canadian voice.

Barbara Lalla (essay date 1996)

SOURCE: Lalla, Barbara. "Leavings." In *Defining Jamaican Fiction: Marronage and the Discourse of Survival,* pp. 104-14. Tuscaloosa: University of Alabama Press, 1996.

[*In the following excerpt, Lalla views "Country of the One-Eyed God" as "a study in marronage because it is a tale of leaving and being left and consequently of the cold logic behind seemingly irrational violence."*]

Marronage results from fragmentation internal to the Jamaican setting and from a tension between local and imperial cultures.[1] The growth of a national consciousness sensitizes local writers to separation of communities within the island and to the consequences of abandonment as some Jamaicans select voluntary exile and others are left behind. Moreover, beyond the connection between the dispossessed woman and the deprived child lies a chain effect that links the abandoned child to the violently resentful and demanding youth and eventually to the adult as predator. The gathering hostility of Icy Barton ("I killed you totally in my heart," Thomas 159) diffuses as she reunites with her mother, but this outcome does not hold true for all children whose mothers leave "to go to foreign" (Senior, **"Country of the One-Eye God"** 21). Senior explores the end result of metamorphosis from such childhood in a consciousness tormented simultaneously by exclusion and claustrophobia.

Through the exploration of altered perspective, current Jamaican fiction reviews entrenched Caribbean visions of alienation by considering the aborted, the miscarried, the dropped-and-left child that strikes back by turning on society or on the family that is society's microcosm.[2] Senior's **"Country of the One-Eye God"** (*Summer Lightning*) conveys a terrifying vision of the reject turned monster. It is a study in marronage because it is a tale of leaving and being left and consequently of the cold logic behind seemingly irrational violence. In Senior's tale, as in Thomas's, abandonment prompts resentment. In **"Country of the One-Eye God"** this resentment has social repercussions.

This short story, like any literature in a multicultural context, explores Otherness as a dialectic of interaction and rift between unlikes. Senior presents cultural confrontation with linguistic consequences in a physical context that at first understates cultural distinctions but gradually articulates them as part of the text's meaning. Here, as in other areas of this analysis, meaning is taken as being, at least to some extent, both socially and culturally determined. (David Birch relates culture-dependent meaning to the prioritizing of parole, 131-33.)

Ma B and Jacko are originally of one culture; the links of kinship and village background, the nurture of grandson by grandmother are emphasized. Yet their confrontation reveals profound cultural schism both at the heart of the community and in the bosom of the family. From the context of Ma B's culture, Jacko is a monster who has turned his back on his home community for an essentially unknown way of life.

In addition, Jacko has found himself on the shearing edge of separating communities and is part of a wider social fragmentation. The separating communities are partially defined by semantic variation between cultural groups. It is essential to the argument that follows to recognize that Jamaican society at present is divided not merely into classes that are economically divided but, even among the most deprived, separated by worldview. To distinguish these views as rural versus urban or as young versus old would be to oversimplify the dichotomy, because the rift is produced by several intersecting distinctions likely to vary from one set of individuals to another.

In the multidimensional space of Jamaican society, Jacko has located himself quite differently from Ma Bell. Each of his utterances functions as an act of identity by which he locates himself in this space. One of the clashing cultures is characteristically old, conservative, spiritual, and inward turned in its orientation to the community; the other is young, radical, disillusioned, fragmenting, and out directed. These different orientations produce in Ma Bell and Jacko distinctly different meanings for terms they would seem to have in common. This dichotomy in lexical meaning is important because the semantic drift intensifies the gap between these groups and reflects the alienation of focal characters of the narrative from each other.

DISTANCE

In **"Country of the One-Eye God,"** Senior introduces the theme of ruptured communication from her opening line. Ma Bell is isolated from her family. News of the grandson whom Ma Bell raised comes to her indirectly, incompletely, and disjointedly. An electronic rather than a human medium confirms and completes this news, and the electronic medium is itself of foreign source—the radio originates from the United States. At this point in the narrative most of Ma Bell's dialogue is with the Lord, but it is one-sided; she talks to a God who appears to be deaf. Her links with children and grandchildren abroad are practically nonexistent, consisting of a letter "once in a blue moon." From Jacko himself, since he left home two years before, she "never hear one living word." All communication lines between Jacko and others represented or mentioned in the tale are ruptured. He is distanced from members of the family who have become part of foreign progressive culture and from those that remain in rural conservative culture, and he is out of touch with the urban youth-gang culture with which he has affiliated himself. Ma Bell exists in a closed network that supports little variation in behavior. She is closely constrained by norms and shows a high degree of conformity in her speech (cf. Milroy 155, 178, 184). The break in communication is not to be attributed only to the physical remoteness between her rural location and the urban setting to which her grandson has shifted. The explanation cannot be completed solely by reference to a sort of time warp produced as one community changes faster than another. Her actual encounter with Jacko demonstrates that the rift goes deeper.

The problem with Jacko is in fact a series of cleavages that merge to produce a massive personality flaw. Senior does not present him as a lunatic but as a horrifying mix of desperation and coldly deliberate criminality. She links these characteristics to psychological damage resulting from abandonment. Jacko's departure from normal behavior relates to the rupture of his earliest and most essential links: it begins in the silence of his parents. The magnetic pull of North American culture and the related fragmentation of traditional Jamaican ties is an undertone throughout the text and becomes explicit in Jacko's embittered outcry: "Look how long I wait for them to send for me. . . . Next year never did came for me" (21). Ma Bell's old-fashioned upbringing—talk and chastisement—has only hardened his resentment. Now his needs narrow and crystalize to material survival: "Me no need no more talk any more. Just give me di money" (21).

Communication failure becomes apparent as the turn-taking of normal conversation breaks down in various dialogues. Her muttering of personal needs and commitments for which she has approportioned small sums of money meet with no response. Her threat to bawl to the neighbors is equally meaningless to him, except as grim justice for the discipline she meted out in his earlier years. He ridicules her dialogue with God as useless effort of "rag tag and bobtail" to communicate with "high and mighty" (24). To Jacko, any attempt to cross this gap—the ultimate class barrier—between God and the Jamaican poor is ludicrous. As he raises the gun, her pleadings to him fall on deaf ears even as he dismisses her prayers to God as useless. It is clear that much of the action rests on aborted communication, and the structure of the text is a composite of discourses, almost all broken in some way.

The dialogue between Ma B and Jacko deteriorates to pleading on one side and demanding on the other, and cultural lesion between the speakers limits their mutual intelligibility. Apart from this dialogue, the text contains other embedded discourse such as fragmented news and one-sided dialogue with God. The breakdown in communication between Jacko and Ma Bell is a function of cultural distance. The elderly speaker with expectations of respect and family loyalty, accustomed to being addressed as "Ma Bell" even by her seventy-year-old nephew, is faced first with Jacko's "cold detachment" and absence of greeting and kinship title. She refers to herself as his "old gran"; he never addresses her as such. He calls her "old lady" and eventually "Ma B," but by that time he has also distanced and generalized her with the generic label, "unno old woman."

Nonverbal communication reveals similar breakdowns. Through such gestures as his grasping for the rum, Jacko displays a lack of manners that renders his words meaningless to Ma Bell. His offensive reaction (JC *suckteeth*) at the name of Jesus and sprawling back in her best chair, his searching of her most private garments, his sneering laughter at the notion of Judgment Day, and his obscenity render the gun in her face unsurprising. Seen against the conventions of nonverbal communication normative to Ma Bell's culture, the irrationality of violence is an almost logical development of his incomprehensible rudeness. Maureen Warner-Lewis ("Mask") throws useful light on the relationship of vio-

lence and evil to normative values with reference to this text. At the same time, Ma Bell's act of closing her eyes in prayer is empty of significance to Jacko. He is secure in his own isolation by silence that her prayers will be inaudible to God and the gunshot unnoticed by her neighbors.

A gulf yawns between Jacko's concept of civilization as foreign (versus the local experience of those "that turndown back here," 21) and Ma B's concept of civilization as respectability (versus the revelation of wildness in the kin turned stranger). Ma B perceives civilization as a world of orderly routine, versus a world "all catacorner and moving off course" (19).

The unbridgeable distance of the youth turned monster emerges in the imagery that dehumanizes him beginning with his initial scratching on the door through his metamorphosis to hairy stranger and dismissal of his comrades in laconic comment, "fren a dawg." This recategorization of Jacko's group from human to bestial has been foreshadowed earlier in the text through such traditional images of evil as the viper. The recategorization to nonhuman becomes overt in the *dawg* metaphor. *Dawg* in Jamaican Creole usage carries overwhelmingly negative associations in contrast to positive connotations of *dog* in usage by metropolitan English-speaking communities. Negative connotations of savagery are compounded by the metaphor of him wolfing down his food (20).

Jacko's stature grows from simply being a strange child, to one who is "bull buck and duppy conqueror" elsewhere but a boy to Ma B, to a huge and threatening presence. Jacko's recategorization from human to nonhuman is a transformation foreshadowed in her early recognition of evil distilled into the boy so that, as she complains to Jacob, they "that dont do nobody nothing bring children into the world and before them old enough to spit, is animal them turn" (18). A field of lexical items thus reduces Jacko's humanity and entails his growing inhumanity. Indeed, by the time Jacko has completed his path of destruction through her house and turned on her person, her trust in his common humanity and in their kinship is hopelessly frail: "God, he is my very blood. He wouldn't really kill me? Eh, God?" (25).

Throughout the text, lexical items appear to carry separate meanings for the two consciousnesses that confront each other without understanding. This is particularly true where a word includes the semantic component of affirming or negating distance, for the conflicting cultures in the text differ in their notions of spatial organization. Crucial to meaning is the distance of the deserted boy from his parents. But distance also affects other perceptions, like that of *foreign*. Ma Bell's orientation to *foreign* is different from Jacko's. She is aware of incoming news or rare letters from loved ones; he is turned outward: "I haffe leave. . . . Look how long I wait for them to send for me" (21). Unlike Ma B, Jacko sees both her and himself as castoffs, "turn down back here," and he is prepared to murder his way out. He plans for *foreign* with money and passport; Ma Bell plans too, but for a different journey. She looks forward to her flamboyant exit in a splendor of white satin, with the neighbors oohing and aahing. Her ultimate departure is planned in conformity to her community's norms. Between her commitment to respectability and his disregard for opinion yawns a fearful distance in values ("Ma Bell shrank away," 20).

The entire action of the narrative spans no more than a day, perhaps even a few hours, from the radio broadcast to the actual encounter with Jacko. However, the narrative expands by implicature through embedded reflections on the past, as in Ma B's family history and Jacko's bitter memories. Senior similarly embeds in the narrative dark hints of the future, implicit in Ma B's premonitions and in the manifold suggestions of burial, particularly in references to the burial money itself, "that is my future" (25). At the same time, the development of Jacko over his nineteen years into a vast physical threat is compressed into a fleeting sensation. Ma B notices that "he had a presence that forced even his grandmother to look away. She shivered and knew that someone had walked over her grave. In the pale light, Ma Bell suddenly wondered how such a little boy could suddenly grow so huge as to fill all the spaces in the room. She felt shrivelled and light, compressed into the interstices of space by his nearness" (22-23).

Material values dominate Jacko's worldview as spiritual values dominate Ma Bell's, and his material presence is an imprisoning nearness like the circle of the kitchen, which tightens around them after the search. The nearness is intensely physical, highlighting their emotional distance. The claustrophobia intensifies through images of entrapment and through the impression of Jacko expanding as the action progresses while Ma Bell shrinks. The relationship between Ma B and Jacko becomes a cord that tightens to strangulation point, so the metaphor of the cord transforms through semantic drift from a binding thread of kinship to a tightening of the heart with fear, eventually becoming a noose that traps and strangles. The encroachment on the grandmother's space is an important feature of Jacko's nonverbal communication of aggression. The closer he moves toward her physically the further he advances toward stripping her of the burial money and sending her out of the world as poor and naked as she came in.

Leaving

The problem of how each will leave is the issue that defines both Ma Bell's and Jacko's thinking and action throughout, and related terms proliferate in the text: *jail*

breaker, left home, last grandchild had left, tek off, runway, run away, shrank away, a haffe leave, leave? Go where, far, passport, go to foreign, walk way leave me, to run, lef it, never leave this place alive, sent off, leave, leave that way, leave this world, go into the next world.

Socioculturally separate groups speaking what appears to be the same language may, in certain situations, be unintelligible to each other. What appears to be formally the same word may differ semantically from group to group or may be semantically loaded in one group and practically meaningless in the other. In **"Country of the One-Eye God,"** the word *leave* has different implications for Ma Bell and Jacko.

An essential and shared semantic dimension of the word *leave* is mobility in a direction away from the location of the speaker at the time of utterance. But the ideological orientations of Ma Bell and Jacko are quite differently indicated by deictic terms of spatial reference. Within the narrow and highly specific universe of the short story, the focal characters distinguish *in/out, up/down,* and *far/near* in relation to quite different values. For Ma Bell, for example, *up/down* in a social context has connotations of respectability, economically defined but also strongly bound to notions of morality. For Jacko, *up/down* is socially defined purely in monetary terms, not surprisingly, because his early desertion by his parents has been explained to him as resting squarely on monetary considerations ("They could never afford to send for me," 21).

Similarly, *in/out* has acquired for Jacko, with his different value system, associations of imprisonment and escape that are not apparent in Ma Bell's speech for the greater part of the text. The same value differences affect other terms crucial to the text, such as *family* and *stranger,* in which notions such as *in* or *out* are inherent. The concept of *family* in the conservative culture includes associations of warmth, loyalty, and above all respect, whereas in the underworld youth-gang culture the right to demand monetary support may override all. This mutates Jacko to a stranger in the eyes of Ma Bell and leaves her in a state of bewilderment because, at the same time, she recognizes him as her blood.

With such different perceptions, it is not surprising that other crucial terms, such as *foreign,* should be differently loaded in the usage of the two main characters. To Ma Bell, to have gone foreign and succeeded is a social achievement in its widest sense, one that a breath of scandal may well destroy. However, pride and shame are emotions motivated quite differently in the cultures of "old gran" and "bull buck." For the youth, to go foreign is to escape. For Ma Bell, *foreign* is "over there"; for Jacko, *foreign* is out and (materially) up. For Jacko, the alternative to *foreign* is to be "turn down back here" and to be forever in, buried alive.

Not surprisingly, the different orientations of Ma B and Jacko produce varying understandings of *dead,* as they do of *leave. Dead* for Jacko is final. In his view, Ma Bell will soon "dead and lef" the money; the concept of burial money is not one he can possibly grasp. For Ma Bell, *dead* is not a terminal concept. Apart from her vision of attending her own glorious funeral, Ma Bell's religious convictions include certainty of an afterlife. She advises Jacko to surrender himself to an almost certain death sentence and directs him to Jesus for help with an optimism directed beyond death—"is not too late." But the problem is that, for Jacko, God (if he exists) is located *up* as oppressive authority, as unjust distributor of wealth, and out of the location of the speaker. In this framework, God has not only deserted but also ridicules those who are "poor and turn down." God's *up* is not the same for Jacko as for Ma Bell. Jacko's *up/down* orientation is causally related to secret shame. For Jacko, pride is stimulated by material acquisition and by recognition of physical power, whereas for Ma Bell this type of achievement can produce only "duppy conqueror." Thus, she is proud to have brought up children who could "go foreign" even if they have subsequently forgotten her, provided they retain respectability. Jacko's undying shame is to have been left behind.

Indeed, to Ma Bell and to Jacko, *leaving* can hardly mean the same thing. Ma Bell orders him to "just know you place" from an entirely different spatial organization. Jacko lost his place as a young child, never subsequently found it, and has no concept of Ma Bell's sense of security in place. Other contrasting categorizations (of what is appropriate to *bwoy* as distinct from *big man,* of what constitutes practical help, of the meaning of *talk* itself) are so disparate that the grandmother and grandson speak to each other about leaving from entirely separate perspectives. It is not surprising that his speech is vanity to her and that hers is foolishness to him (20-21). Moreover, an important dichotomy in the text is that between stasis and change, as is reinforced by their contrasting meanings to Ma B and Jacko. To Ma B, stasis is order and calm, whereas change intimates a world "cata-corner and moving off course"; change is dissolution. But to Jacko, escape lies only through change, and stasis is old, empty, and forgotten as the turned-down pot. His present desperation, articulated in "a haffe leave," is indistinguishable from his initial abandonment and unchangeable status as deserted child. The sentence, "a haffe leave," is syntactically ambiguous, for it carries implications of past tense and passive voice as well as nonpast and active meanings. In the Creole, Jacko's resentment at having been left and his desperation to leave fuse in a single output that marks neither tense nor voice.

So for Jacko *leave* is an absolute term, taking the subject permanently away and completely out of a *down*

situation. In his expectation, to *leave* (active meaning) is to escape; in his tragic experience, to *leave* (Creole unmarked passive sense, "be left") is to be deserted. His alienation and thus his character as outcast are defined both by passive suffering (rejection, having been left) and by active intention (escape, need to leave). For Ma Bell the term raises questions of where, of how far. It does not automatically imply *foreign.* Her grandson had left the neighborhood but not the island, and she plans for the time when she too will leave, but in style—the memorable exit in satin and polished wood with silver handles. Of course, she can only leave through an agency outside of herself, at God's summons and borne by twelve strong men. Jacko takes the business of leaving into his own hands. He rejects stasis. This urgency and this disregard for others are aspects of his badness to Ma Bell, for whom leaving must be orderly and must not incur inconvenience or injury to others. Because Jacko considers himself to have been dumped by family, society, and God, he feels justified in leaving at his own convenience.

These differences are tied to their varying perceptions of material security. For Jacko, the money is a way out, the way to foreign. For Ma Bell, it is a provision for respectability when the time comes for her to "leave this world." Jacko says she "soon dead and lef" the money anyway, not recognizing that where for him it is a means of leaving, for her it is a means of leaving respectably. Of course, he turns out to be right in a grim sense because his intervention will separate her from the hope of this respectable departure.

The money thus becomes a snare for Ma Bell. It will bring her death without providing the stylish exit. Physically and emotionally stripped, she will leave as poor and naked as she came. Jacko will leave her as "poor and turn down" as he himself was left. The strange child with the "right hand of falsehood," the child "whose mouth speaketh vanity," does not "lift up his head" like the others she has raised. He lifts up his hand, with the gun. By this time the ruptured dialogue has fragmented completely. Her pleading is meaningless to Jacko, her threats empty, and her prayers useless. His demand has placed her in an impossible dilemma, to relinquish the burial money which is her future or to cling to it, die, and be stripped.

The gun does not go off in the text, and what is not in the text can be semantically as important as what is. The gaps define for the reader the boundaries of Ma Bell's experience. Thus, although readers have information hidden from characters other than Ma Bell (such as the location of the money), they cannot be audience to the gunshot because they are tied to her perspective, subject to her capacity to report. There is no certainty of the gunshot; there can be no such closure. And readers must to some extent be bounded by Ma Bell's experience to experience adequately the Otherness of Jacko. In any case, real history is open ended, and closure is a strategy of traditional fiction and so vulnerable to exposure as a lie. Senior's open-ended tale conveys two tragedies. One is Jacko's failed search for identity through escape to *foreign*; the other is Ma B's tragic underestimation of the repercussions associated with betrayal and abandonment. The composite tragedy hinges on a mutual misunderstanding. Neither comprehends what *leaving* means to the other.

Although the reader's perspective is tied to Ma Bell's, the reader shares with the writer experiences external to the text. This is social information associated with the individual's total network of linguistic categorizations. Readers make judgments unconfined by the horizons of the particular character whose point of view defines the discourse. At least to some extent, linguistic orientation independently defines judgments of the focal character. In analyzing the differences between Ma Bell's language and Jacko's, it is almost impossible to avoid imposing values implied by use of language, by categorizations. Readers' analyses are thus a weighing and balancing of ideologically loaded structures and meanings that may vary in the different cultures that interact in the text and in their own idiolects. This choice between ideologically loaded meanings, informed by matters extrinsic to the text (for example, other comparable texts or social situations) renders reading a political act. The evolving background of experience means that readers provide the sequel to the action, but they do so only while recognizing that from Ma Bell's point of view, the gun is the end of the story.

The reader is thus not autonomous, not free to a degree suggestive of bardicide (brilliantly dissected by Levin), but integrated into the communication process by the writer to complete the speaker/message/hearer requirements of discourse. The writer manipulates reader interpretation through the placement of gaps, through the exploitation of semantic drift in the usage of words by different characters. The writer also manipulates the reader by intertextuality through which the reader's attention is drawn to relevant extrinsic experiences, which include clearly identifiable allusions such as biblical references as well as more universal, archetypal imagery, such as that of blood. Ma Bell's usage early associates blood with kinship and closeness, but her later usage destabilizes this positive sense of the term. She uses it with her earlier meaning (that is, the speaker/character's meaning remains unchanged) but in a context of impending violence that evokes in the reader a consciousness of the negative associations of blood. Thus, there is plurality of textual meaning as distinct from the character's meaning. The semantic drift of the evolving metaphor introduces blood, like the cord im-

age earlier discussed, as a kinship bond, but in the end the image of the raised gun and her identification of her assailant as her "very blood" cumulatively suggest murder.

Figurative language is ideologically loaded in **"Country of the One-Eye God."** In the text, culturally defined metaphors convey socially determined meaning, as in the recurrent *turned-down* reference. The turned-down pot with its implications of emptiness and disuse is made more poignant in Jacko's speech by the fact that the term *pot* itself is never articulated, leaving the reader open to other implications of the phrase *turned-down* and reinforcing reader sensitivity to Jacko's sense of rejection and desertion.

Ma Bell's rural cottage reflects Jamaica in microcosm, and events in the story parallel patterns of history. Generations of discipline by preaching and chastisement on the one hand and marginalization on the other conclude in colonial schizophrenia. Colonial disappointment at being left hardens into a desperation to leave; yearning sharpens into demand and pain into violence. Parallel to the continuing attraction of the foreign metropolis runs a gravitational pull of Kingston that lures rural youth to urban homelessness, frustration, and crime. Shattered family ties thus recall not only the unraveling imperial-colonial relationship but the torn fabric of Jamaica's internal history. Society's inability to support all its children forces some into a dehumanizing struggle for survival that unleashes almost apocalyptic chaos.

"Country of the One-Eye God" lends itself to current critical interpretation of the literary text as inherently political, as a revision of a history yet in progress and so as a network of unfinished meanings. The text denies closure not only because of all that is left unstated in its ending but also because tensions between contrasting cultures and culture-defined meanings interfere on surface with the coherence of the text. So do unanswered questions in the dialogue, responses that appear not to fit the comments that triggered them, lexis shifting semantically with context. But this apparent incoherence is itself profoundly meaningful, highlighting through the communication gaps rifts widening in a society of disintegrating values, a society drawn by the relentless attraction of *foreign* even as it increasingly entraps the "poor one that turn down back here." Thus, semantic inconsistency within the society of conflicting cultures produces a surface incoherence, but this surface incoherence, through semantic drift, actually reinforces through congruence the deeper coherence of the text, the paradigmatic relations between consistent webs of meaning in each of the conflicting cultures, of Ma B and Jacko. In these conflicting cultures, the flaws of different generations intersect in a fragmentation of society that is intensified by social conditions.

Senior articulates her characters' sense of a widespread social malaise through biblical apocalyptic imagery to convey a traditional Jamaican insistence that there is "evil, evil, evil in the land" (18). This is not a native evil, inherent in the land, but a new savagery induced by economic hardship ("is the hard times breeding them tough pickney," 18). Indeed, economic considerations underlie Jacko's motherlessness and influence his denial of the old gran's authority and of all other authority. The end, foreshadowed in the beginning, demonstrates that the gun is Jacko's tragedy as well as Ma Bell's, an ambiguity conveyed in the phrase *their destruction*: "It predick you know Ma B. As the Good Book say Job Thirtieth Verse Twelve upon my right hand rise the youth they push away my feet and raise up against me the ways of their destruction" (19). The text conveys fragmentation of values and dissolution of communication lines in a situation where a culture has split and where its conventional and radical offshoots intersect again tragically.

Where *Myal* portrayed marronage in the indigenous consciousness confronted with colonial or neocolonial power, **"Country of the One-Eye God"** demonstrates the growing rift between radical and conservative consciousnesses within Jamaican society. This plural perspective propels the reader beyond Ma Bell's limited point of view to an understanding of what it means to be the leavings of a society.

Notes

1. The material in this section of chapter 4 is based largely on a paper titled "Intercultural Communication in 'Country of the One-Eye God,'" first presented at the Conference on West Indian Literature, the University of Guyana, 1992, and used here with permission of *Carib: Journal of the West Indian Association of Commonwealth Literature and Language Studies.*

2. Earlier Jamaican literature celebrated the quests of innumerable small waifs and strays. Left untended following the ravages of an epidemic and fearful of being sent to a labor camp, Jean D'Costa's children of *Escape to Last Man's Peak* search for a locus at which to establish an alternative free community in the mountains. Namba Roy's "sparrows" find that they have exchanged the physical marronage in the mountains where they were born for marronage that is social and psychological (*No Black Sparrows*).

Works Cited

Birch, David. *Language, Literature, and Critical Practice: Ways of Analysing Text.* London: Routledge, 1989.

Levin, Richard. "The Poetics and Politics of Bardicide." *PMLA* 105 (May 1990): 491-504.

Milroy, Leslie. *Language and Social Networks.* Oxford: Basil Blackwell, 1980.

Senior, Olive. *Arrival of the Snake-Woman and Other Stories.* London: Longman Caribbean, 1989.

———. *Summer Lightning.* London: Longman Caribbean, 1986.

Warner-Lewis, Maureen. "Mask of the Devil: Perverse Artistic Energy in Caribbean Literature." Paper presented at the tenth annual conference on West Indian Literature, University of the West Indies, St. Augustine, Trinidad, 1991.

Miki Flockemann (essay date May 1998)

SOURCE: Flockemann, Miki. "Asian Diasporas, Contending Identities and New Configurations: Stories by Agnes Sam and Olive Senior." *English in Africa* 25, no. 1 (May 1998): 71-86.

[*In the following essay, Flockemann compares the treatment of ethnic and cultural identity in Senior's "Arrival of the Snake-Woman" and Agnes Sam's "Jesus is Indian."*]

> Her arrival represented a loosening of the bonds that had previously bound her, that bind all of us to our homes. Cut free from her past, she was thus free of the duties and obligations that tie us so tightly to one another, sometimes in a stranglehold.
>
> —Olive Senior, **"Arrival of the Snake-Woman"** (1989, 44)

> "I am cut off from India. I am cut off from South Africa. I am not rooted anywhere. . . . I am not part of the Asian community; I am not part of the British community and I have never really been part of the exiled community. My interests are in Africa. I am African."
>
> —Agnes Sam, Interview (Myburg 1991, 4)

In the introductory section to his *Southern African Literatures* (1995), Michael Chapman notes the need for a comparative study of Southern African literatures across genre, language and geographic boundaries within Africa as part of a broader process of democratisation (1995, 10). However, one detects in his concluding remarks some apprehension at the possible stifling of a distinctly South African accent in the "currently fashionable cultural diffusion" of a "'black Atlantic' creolisation of Africa and the West" (1995, 429). What then of South African writers whose works express cultural affiliations not only with Africa and the West, and who write from an exile not enforced but chosen?

Rather than enter into the already extensive debate around the project of writing a Southern African literary history,[1] I intend extending the scope of comparison in order to sharpen rather than "stifle the 'South African' accent" (Chapman 1995, 429). The aim here is to show that the work of a writer of Indian descent like Agnes Sam, who calls herself an African and maintains her South African accent, can usefully be compared with a writer situated in the diaspora, like Olive Senior, a West Indian of African descent. Discussion will focus on the two title stories from Sam's *Jesus is Indian and Other Stories* (1990), and Senior's ***Arrival of the Snake-Woman and Other Stories*** (1989). Instead of resulting in "cultural diffusion," such a comparison will demonstrate how, despite their different geopolitical contexts, Sam and Senior use representations of "Asianness" to destabilise dominant discourses of identity in ways that have implications for the processes of democratisation referred to by Chapman. This is not to suggest an "authentic" South East Asian or Indian identity within the South African or Afro-Caribbean contexts. As Shamiel Jeppie points out in his discussion of recent attempts to project or re-claim an ethnic Malay (or Malaysian) identity for Cape Muslims, the dynamic and ambivalent aspects of identity become particularly evident during a "liminal moment" such as "the end of the old and the inauguration of the 'new' South Africa." Jeppie reminds us that identity "needs constant restatement, there are always others to be displaced. This fact alone makes identity part of the political field" (1996, 87; see also Fakier, 1996).

It is interesting to speculate why Sam's *Jesus is Indian,* which was published while she was in exile in the UK, has not received the same critical attention locally as Zoë Wicomb's *You Can't Get Lost in Cape Town* (1990), since both explore issues of "minority" identity and exile as well as the coming to consciousness of the child/woman. Sam, however, uses a variety of narrative perspectives and locations whereas Wicomb's is a more coherently organised short story cycle. Wicomb's stories also deal in a more familiar and direct way with the politics of identity and the "in-betweenness" of coloured experience, whereas the experiences described by Sam are complicated by an "alternative" Indian (but Catholic, not Hindu) identity which tends to be subsumed in the oppositional black/white discourses.[2] More recently a number of studies concerned with South African Indians have appeared. For instance, commenting on the scant scholarship on the history of Indian women in South Africa during the early years of indenture, Devarashanam Govinden draws on her own family history in an attempt to redress this absence. According to Govinden, such transnational projects of reclaiming past histories will play an important role in foregrounding "contradictions in our projects of nation-building," particularly in the context of the relationship between gender and colonialism (1997, 2).[3]

In Olive Senior's **"Arrival of the Snake-Woman,"** the recollections of the boy Ishmael are used describe the impact of the arrival of an outsider, Miss Coolie, on a Jamaican village at the end of last century. Even before her arrival Ishmael is half in love with and half terrified of the "heathen" woman from India with "snake-like hips" (3) who has chosen to cross the mountains to be SonSon's new wife and who, in the process, becomes the catalyst for changes that transform the rural community. From school Ishmael "knew all about India and the Ganges and the Heathens who lived there" (3), but the community's prejudices become evident when SonSon's friend Moses describes the "coolies" as the "wut-lessess [most worthless] set of people," particularly the men, for coming all the way from India and then being willing "to work in de cane fe nutten" (3). The women are something else though, says Moses, "their body so neat and trim and they move their hip when they walk just like a snake and they don't wear proper clothes . . . yu can see every line of their body when they walk" (3). When Ishmael first sees the snake-woman his "heart somersaulted" (5) at the sight of her framed in the doorway of SonSon's house, with her gold bracelets and necklaces—complete with nose ring (the sure mark of a heathen)—her garment "like bits and pieces of spider's web" (5). However, the exoticism of the snake-woman is complicated by the ambivalent markers of her hair and skin: Ishmael notices that while her hair is as straight as the white parson's wife's, her skin "was as dark as ours" (5).

The system of Indian indentured labour referred to in Senior's story has echoes in the South African indentured labour system described in Agnes Sam's introduction to *Jesus is Indian* when she describes how the importation of Indian labour frustrated Zulu attempts to bring about the failure of the sugar-cane economy. Sam notes that Indian women were essential to the processes of adaptation to the new conditions and bore the brunt of the discriminatory labour practices, often having to mediate between their own cultural value systems and the demands of plantation managers. Interestingly, she quotes a description of the Indian woman as exotic object of colonial desire in the *Natal Mercury* of 1860 which echoes Moses' description of the "coolie women" in Jamaica, ". . . the women, with their flashing eyes, with their half-covered bodies, evidently beings of a different race and kind to anything we have seen yet" (Sam 1989, 10).

While for Olive Senior "Miss Coolie" represents the cultural outsider as catalyst, Agnes Sam's work is concerned with the Asian woman as "cultural insider." Writing from exile in Britain in 1989, Agnes Sam says:

> South African Indians like myself have lost mother tongue, family name, religion, culture, history, and historical links with India. Cut off from India, apartheid has further separated us from the other communities in South Africa, thereby exacerbating our isolation.

> (Sam 1990, 11)

Unlike Agnes Sam, many South African Indians do see themselves as part of a cohesive group, and are generally perceived as such by other South Africans. However, Sam's reference to a sense of "rootlessness" quoted in the epigraph can be compared to Olive Senior's description of moving between two very different households while growing up in rural Jamaica. According to Senior, this resulted in "pretty much being shifted between two extremes of a continuum based on race, colour and class" (author's note to *Arrival of the Snake-Woman*). Significantly, her title story has been described as "a moving exploration of cultural convergence in which a shift in power relations among people of African, European and Indian ancestry signals the emergence of a modern creole society" (Patteson 1993, 28).

Despite similar histories of displacement and colonialism, however, the concept of creolisation has a far more problematic history in the South African than in the Caribbean context.[4] Wilmot James describes coming across references in the State Archives to a proposition couched in the language of "a manual for dog breeders" for "mongrelising" the Indian community in South Africa. This plan (rejected by Eben Donges for being "impractical") was the brainchild of one of the architects of apartheid, Jan Raats. Raats "had a particularly dastardly plan for the Indians," says James, for, "like many Nationalists of the time he regretted that the repatriation of Indians was not possible because their cultural distinctiveness and community cohesion were a threat to apartheid." To this end, Raats proposed that "the Indian community would become 'mongrelised' by actively allowing African blood to enter the Indian breeding pool" (James 1996). Obviously this reference to "mongrelisation" has a very different ideological history to the Caribbean experience of cultural creolisation as imbricated within the processes of modernity. Nevertheless, the concept of a creole continuum which involves a non-hierarchical relationship between a variety of cultural influences has some bearing on the two stories by Agnes Sam and Olive Senior, especially in the light of Patteson's reference to the "emergence of a modern creole society" represented by Senior's **"Arrival of the Snake-Woman."**

As Sam points out, her work has been neglected in the country of her birth for a number of reasons, and I will argue that re-reading these stories in the context of post-election South Africa offers scope for a fresh look at some of the debates around the emergent South African nationhood and identity in this currently fluid political field (see Jeppie 1996, 87; Crehan 1997). In considering how "Indian-ness" is constructed as unsettling dominant discourses of identity, Senior's **"Arrival of the Snake-Woman"** should be read against a pragmatic cultural creolisation in the Caribbean, while in the South African context the Population Registration Act (1950) catered for a separate "Indian" racial classification as distinct from "Cape" and "Other Coloureds." One can, however, detect a shift from representing Asian women as "in-between," perceived as not-quite white, and not-quite black, to re-claiming their cultural "difference." As mentioned earlier, this does not posit an "authentic" Indian identity, but, rather, offers a challenge to the totalising systems of both apartheid and patriarchy by refusing to co-operate with hegemonic naming systems.

This shift becomes evident when comparing "Jesus is Indian" with a story by another South African of Indian descent, namely Jayapraga Reddy's "Friends" (1987). Referring to the way "race stratifications are reinforced by internal stratifications in oppressed communities themselves," Annemarie van Niekerk describes "Friends" as an "excellent fictional illustration of the practical operation of overlapping and interacting power hierarchies" in the way that the chain of oppression is maintained through the "co-operation" of oppressed peoples (1992, 38). However, in Reddy's story, the Indian child Asha can hardly be described as "co-operative"; instead, Asha is caught up in a complex hegemony of desire when she and her friend Phumza, the daughter of the woman employed by Asha's mother, become involved in a fight over the possession of a "large lifelike doll with a blue dress and golden hair" (Reddy 1987, 109). The doll is associated with values that result in the girls' exclusion from the dominant culture, but is at the same time an object of desire for both the Indian and the African child: "She [Phumza] was drawn irresistibly towards it" (109). When Asha recognises in Phumza's eyes the "unspoken yearning" indicative of the insidious power of hegemonic culture, she "felt something stir and uncoil within" (109), and viciously tramples the doll in inarticulate rage, just as she wishes she could smash the television screen that appears to have such a powerful control over her mother who evades responsibility for her life by compulsively watching soap operas. Situated within the apartheid dichotomy of black and white, European and African, Reddy's "Friends" illustrates the familiar class/race/gender nexus when Phumza learns the lesson of "the unfairness of it all" (111). Despite her apparent friendship with Asha, the battle over the doll has mapped out her future as distinct from Asha's: "Reluctantly she relinquished her hold [on the doll]. She turned and followed her mother to the washing line" (111). The television screen and the washing line here each exert their respective class-based hold over the two mothers, Indian employer and African employee.

Reddy's story reflects a common trope, namely the child's gendered rite of passage into a given South African class/race hierarchy. However, instead of the crude conflict depicted in "Friends," a different direction is offered in Sam's *Jesus is Indian* which deals with the relationships between women and across generations in a range of South African contexts. Sam is at pains in her introduction to her collection to show that the history of Indians in South Africa is not just a story of conquest (1989, 2). She achieves this by focusing on choices that do not appear possible to Reddy's Phumza and Asha. In her introduction Sam comments on the way South African Indians have been "excluded from South African history,"[5] and it is a matter of concern, says Sam, that such a marginalised group "becomes an easily identifiable scapegoat" because they are placed "as a buffer between whites and Africans" (1989, 9). The apparent contradiction in Sam's claim quoted in the epigraph to this article, "I am an African," despite her sense of "rootlessness," and belonging neither to an Asian nor to an exiled community in Britain, develops into a counter-discourse to the master narrative of apartheid. "Indian-ness," instead of being perceived as a "buffer" or a marker of marginalisation, becomes an enabling position that offers what Caroline Rooney in a review of Sam's collection suggests are explorations of the past and present histories in anticipation of "new configurations in the future" (1990, 6).

The first two stories in Sam's collection use the narrative perspective of a child and are set in the present, whereas the final stories are about a lost childhood, set in the past; this suggests that these stories should be read in relation to one another. "High Heels," the first story, uses the disingenuous voice of a small child, Ruthie, to weave together two motifs, each involving a test. The first test is provided by her friend Lindiwe's taunt that she must earn the right to be of an age to wear high heels by entering the "secret room" that Ruthie has discovered in her home. When Ruthie completes her part of the bargain by crossing the threshold into what turns out to be a secret Hindu prayer room situated within a Christian household, Lindiwe challenges her to a second test, to explain what the secret means—and why the room must be kept secret. The "meaning" of the secret Hindu prayer room within the Catholic house that Ruthie fails to grasp at this stage emerges as a trope running through the collection as a whole, and this establishes a dialogue between the present and the past. For instance, the second last story, "The Story Teller" is presented as oral history that has "come down to us with slight changes when told by different members of the family" (125), and relates the tale of children who are "shanghaied" from India by being tricked onto a ship carrying indentured labourers to South Africa (as Sam suspects her own grandfather was). The last story, "And They Christened It Indenture," traces the gradual resistance of Indians to this form of "slavery by another name" as well as Christianity's endorsement of the indentured labour system; this then provides a meaning for the "secret" Ruthie failed to grasp in the first story.

While *Jesus is Indian* is apparently not composed as a typical South African short fiction cycle with its empha-sis on a distinctive region and community (as defined by Sue Marais 1995), it is nevertheless interesting to look at the collection in the context of such short fiction cycles. After all, in her introduction Sam identifies the theme running through her collection as the figure of Ruth (from the Book of Ruth 1.16), "the epitome of the migrant wife [who] is still willing to adapt" (13). Similarly, it is useful to read these stories in relation to other short fiction produced by South African women during the 1980s, particularly in view of the increasing popularity of fictional autobiography (see Daymond 1996). At the same time, as Sam points out, one should be wary of assuming that black women generally write autobiographically (Sam 1988, 73; see also Wicomb 1993). Just as the West imposed an identity on the Orient, says Neloufer de Mel, the hegemony of a patriarchal literary establishment and tradition has given women writers a particular space—that of autobiography and domestic life (1995, 244). However, drawing on the debate concerning identity formation between Edward Said and Aijaz Ahmed, who warns that identities "should not be seen in purely Manichean terms as polarities which contaminate but never enablingly inform each other" (quoted in De Mel 1995, 244), De Mel claims that far from being constrained by this "categorising," women writers as gendered subjects have made "creative use of the space conceded to them" (1995, 244). The fact that the first two stories in *Jesus is Indian* are told from the perspective of a child seems significant in terms of the way "new" South African writing uses recollections of childhood to explore South African subjectivities from a variety of perspectives, informed in interesting ways by the writers' own race/class/gender positions.[6] It will become evident that, while Sam is concerned with the absence of Indians from South African history, her stories which deal with childhood, though written in the 1980s, ultimately address the future South African society of the 1990s.

Like "High Heels," the narrative voice in "Jesus is Indian" is situated inside a child's consciousness, though the narrator here, perhaps appropriately (mis)named Angelina, is slightly older than "baby girl" Ruthie. Two narrative strands are interwoven in "Jesus is Indian": the first—indicated by the use of parentheses—records the thoughts and feelings going through Angelina's mind under the stern surveillance of Sister Bonaventura in her Catholic school. This is interspersed with dialogue as the "cheeky" Angelina as pupil-narrator fires uncomfortable questions at Sister in the classroom, while at home her Hama (mother) complains that, "these electric light children know too much" (29), whenever Angelina challenges traditional expectations. Then there is the story Angelina herself is writing—indicated by italics—which deals with relationships between her mother and older sister, Honey, as well as Honey's transition into young womanhood. A number of motifs are introduced in the first paragraph when Angelina reflects:

> (Who invented school? Who said little children must sit still in a desk pretending they wide awake when they dreaming of comics and swings and stealing fruit from Mrs Mumble?)
>
> (Me, I'm not a good girl, but I'm even praying for the bell to ring, frighten even to look at Sonnyboy standing behind Sister, moving every way Sister moves and making monkey faces behind her back. You know me, once I start to laugh, I won't never stop.)
>
> (24)

One could argue that when Angelina claims that she is "not a good girl" she is accepting the judgement passed upon her failure to conform to the demands of both Catholic education and Indian tradition. At the same time, her question, "Who invented school?" challenges one of the very authorities that she is forced to obey, as well as indicating her awareness of the pretence involved in this. The mimicry of the "monkey faces" which Sonnyboy enacts behind Sister's back as well as the threat of ensuing laughter serve to disrupt the colonial educational system in which Angelina is forced to excise Hindu words from her story, and to re-name her mother for the convenience of Sister who refuses to recognise the language of her pupils: "Sister say she never come to learn. She come to teach!" (28). In addition, Sister attempts to censor references in Angelina's story to the emerging sexuality of Honey. After a brief expulsion from the school Angelina is allowed to return, but offers a final challenge to Sister Bonaventura, "Hama say Jesus is Indian because Jesus wear dhoti and Jesus can understand our language" (33). Angelina's claim that she will never use an English name for her Hama is prompted by Hama saying:

> *"What* that sister know? Hey? Don't Jesus wear a dhoti like Ghandi? Don't Hama talk to Jesus in our language? Don't Jesus answer all Hama's prayers? Don't Honey get a rich husband? You so clever, what you think that means? Hey? You electric light children and you don't know? Jesus is Indian. You go to school and tell that sister."
>
> (33)

Although Hama effectively turns the tables on Sister Bonaventura by appropriating Christianity, but on Indian terms, Angelina's challenge raises a number of questions. Should we see this as merely an amusing but naive rebellion against an authority figure, or are we being invited to see the apparently disingenuous account as offering "new configurations of the future"? According to Caroline Rooney one can read this in different ways, namely, either as "expressive of a desire

for syncretism, as a metaphoric equation, or as a teasing, deliberately provocative contradiction" (1990, 6). While I am not suggesting a conflation of the fictional Angelina with Agnes Sam, it is nevertheless significant, in view of Rooney's comment, that in interviews Agnes Sam has stressed the importance of speaking and writing in her own accent and voice, and in a style that is not dictated by publishers' perceptions of what and how black women write (Sam 1988, 74). One can thus safely argue that "Jesus is Indian" represents an example of what De Mel refers to as the "creative use of the space conceded" (1995, 244). A comment on Olive Senior's stories, which explore similar challenges to authority figures (parents and teachers) and the ideologies embodied by them, is pertinent to Angelina's (and Hama's) challenge in "Jesus is Indian." As Patteson puts it, such apparently naive defiance involves "the deconstruction of repressive cultural and psychological codes [which are] an essential prerequisite for the construction of an adult identity—whether for an individual or for a society as a whole" (1993, 21), and the complex analogies between familial and colonial relationships explored by both Senior and Sam should be viewed in this light.

As mentioned previously, *Jesus is Indian* is not typical of the South African short fiction cycle with its emphasis on a cohesive region, community and identity in the face of apartheid dislocations. Unlike these "composed cycles," Sam's stories, a number of which were previously published elsewhere, are set in different locations, sometimes undefined, and use a variety of narrative voices and fictional styles, ranging from realism to parable and oral story-telling traditions. However, the "new strand developing in the genre" identified by Marais (1995) can also apply to Sam's collection, particularly in relation to the self-reflexivity of "Jesus is Indian" in which the processes of story-writing are integral to the challenge that Angelina offers to Sister Bonaventura. According to Marais:

> These works are more radical than the cycles mentioned earlier since they not only set out to expose the fictionality of the grand myth of apartheid as a "master narrative," but also self-consciously meditate on their *own* (re-) presentations of South African reality as discursive constructs.
>
> (1995, 32)

Earlier it was suggested that when the stories in Sam's collection are read as part of a "discursive continuum" (Rooney 1990, 6) provided by Sam's introduction and the last story, "And They Christened It Indenture," a dialectical relationship is established between the different stories. Moreover, re-reading "Jesus is Indian" in the post-election context appears to confirm Rooney's suggestion that the understanding introduced by Angelina's "interrogation" of adult taboos is a "deferred one," and one "which the reader may only reach at the end of the book" (1990, 6). Each story, read in this context, offers scope for a more complex, richer interpretation, than if read individually.

In her discussion of short fiction written by South African women in the 1980s, Margaret Daymond refers to the development of two different traditions which are embodied in the work of Bessie Head, on the one hand, and Nadine Gordimer on the other; namely, "the traditional tale telling of black communities and modernism's short story" (1996, 193). These comments are interesting in view of some of the criticisms of Sam's occasional lack of verisimilitude. For instance, referring to the "unevenness" in Sam's writing, Sally-Ann Murray says that "Sam is a realist writer who paradoxically has a healthy distrust of the conventions of storytelling—fact often slips into fiction and vice versa, so as to tell a larger story of life within and *without* a particular community" (1991, 187). Murray says that while Sam avoids essentialising or universalising her women, readers might want "more concrete evidence of the effects of the environment," though the dust cover claims that the stories are "set among the Indians of South Africa . . . the larger story seems to apply to Indians as minorities in the West" (Murray 1991, 187). Rooney, however, asks whether the lack of contextual grounding is not a deliberate strategy "to make us experience for ourselves the lack of access to 'secret rooms'" (1990, 6). This "risks a certain whimsicality," yet, as Rooney rightly says, the stories do not intend to give information, but to ask questions (1990, 6).

Looking at Sam's work in relation to the two paradigms referred to by Daymond—that is, tale-telling, as in Sam's "The Story Teller," and her modernist-style "Child and Dove"—it becomes evident that Sam moves easily between these two paradigms. Sam describes how three of her stories (including "Child and Dove") are associated with a European work of art: "I had in mind an African exile wandering through the galleries in Europe and reminded of situations at home." She refers to her unpublished experimental novel *What Passing Bells* as "impressionistic, its form suggestive of a fractured society . . . its purpose was to frustrate the reader's need for continuity," and angrily questions the assumption that "a black woman experimenting with language and form has no business in writing" (Sam 1988, 75). A similar concern with the experimental use of language is evident in Patteson's comments on Olive Senior's "command of voice" as a way of "transcending and transforming . . . the sense of displacement that can accompany creolization into a new culture" (1993, 19). According to Patteson, Senior is aware of contradictions manifested in language; "in the politics inherent in the spoken word versus the written, in Jamaican creole versus the language of the Bible, Shakespeare—and the schoolroom" (interview, quoted in Patteson 1993, 19). Instead of unevenness, then, it might be more appropriate to see the variety of styles and voices adopted in Sam's stories in relation to Senior's similar use of a "medley of discourses" which "represent the countercolonization of a language once associated with hegemonic authority" (Patteson 1993, 15).

In a review of the work of Farida Karodia, another exiled South African of Indian descent, Lauretta Ngcobo criticises Karodia's "honest" first novel, *Daughters of the Twilight,* because "it portrays life in the seams of South Africa rather than in the mainstream" (1988, 306). However, this emphasis on the "seams" rather than the "mainstream" seems relevant to Sam's impatience (expressed during a writers' forum) with the emphasis on the overtly political rather than the more intimate processes of subject formation and the choices that are available.[7] Daymond also stresses the question of choice, seeing it as a feature distinguishing writing by black and white women of the last decade. While black writers in the 1980s were generally engaged in sociopolitical realism rather than in tale-telling, says Daymond, "their writing can still be distinguished from Gordimer's example in the way they tend to give importance to the ordinary choices made by women in their daily lives" (Daymond 1995, 199). Referring to Gcina Mhlophe's much-anthologised autobiographical story, "The Toilet," which describes how she became a writer in defiance of her ideological and physical exclusion from South African society, Daymond says: "It is a long step from a woman's writing a story to a people's attaining freedom, but this glimpse of a woman's spirited choice, even of the capacity to imagine it, represents an inner strength which promises its external equivalent" (1996, 204). Such choices and the powerful subtext provided by the self-reflexivity of the process of writing are also evident in "Jesus is Indian" where Angelina decides to complete her essay and continue with English despite the fact that she hates school, because she recognises that the alternative would be to succumb to the equally constraining demands of Indian tradition: "I rather go to school than stay at home and do cooking and housework with Hama" (30).

Unlike "Jesus is Indian," in which Angelina's "storywriting" offers imagined choices and "new configurations" for the future, in Olive Senior's story Ishmael uses his story to make sense of his past and of a changing, modern Jamaica: "And this is why I sometimes sit and write down the things that happened in the old days, so that my children will be able to see clearly where we are coming from, should they ever need signposts" (45). In the two stories by Senior and Sam, "Asian-ness" is shown as destabilising both the dominant and the traditional social structures. The position of the migrant woman, far from resulting in marginalisation within her community, is seen as a force for introducing changes, which are, however, in the case of

Miss Coolie, not always positive. When her son Biya does not respond to traditional healers and the parson refuses to treat her dying child because she is a "heathen," Miss Coolie decides to undertake on her own the hazardous journey to the Bay to see a medical doctor. This decision results in a liberation of sorts for Miss Coolie, who now "began to firmly control her own destiny" (39). On her return she converts to Christianity, as this is the only way to ensure that her son will have access to education, but once the government school has been established, she returns to her Hindu faith.

This pragmatism identifies Miss Coolie as "the embodiment of the spirit of the new age" (44); her rupture from her country of birth provides her from the start "with an understanding of the world that the rest of us lacked" (43). Insisting that Ishmael continue his schooling despite his gradual disillusionment with Christianity after witnessing the parson's treatment of her, Miss Coolie tells him, "you don't know nothing bout world" (34). Her "knowledge" enables her to "become a free agent," to "do business" with whomsoever she pleases, and in the process, she acquires the most prestigious property, Top House, which formerly belonged to the "old-time white people." However, while the "new age" brings the medical expertise that can cure her son Biya and enable him to become a lawyer and return the title deeds of the land to the community, it (or Miss Coolie) also introduces the community to "butter instead of coconut oil, to sweet-smelling salts, powders and pomades, toothpaste instead of chewstick, healing oil and liniment for our pains . . . boots and shoes, hair-straightening combs and skin bleaches, the first sewing machine" (40). In both cases, "new configurations" of the future for Angelina and the "new age" of a modern creole society for Ishmael and Miss Coolie come as the result of an encounter between Asian-ness and dominant and/or traditional values. This also entails loss, however, and for Ishmael, Miss Coolie always remains "a mystery." He wonders whether she has accepted her new life without regret: "I can never be sure, for there is the evidence of the saris, the red dot, the Indian names. And sometimes, when I look into her eyes, I can still see the Ganges" (45). Comparing the creolisation and "cultural convergence" suggested in Olive Senior's Jamaican story with Sam's South African stories suggests the possibility for similar pragmatic cultural creolisations in the South African context as we move away from discourses of identity based on apartheid oppositions and engage with the tricky discourses of an apparently "new" nationhood.

In light of this it is interesting to note how another voice from the Asian diaspora, that of Shirley Geok-lin Lim, eloquently describes how it was the intersection of Confucianism and Catholicism which she encountered while growing up in Malaysia that enabled her to imagine a possible non-patriarchal social structure. Referring to herself as an "already multiply colonized subject," Lim says these oppressions do not come from a hegemonic centre: "Instead, I see a colonial subject as the cultural site for the contradictions inherent in the intersections of multiple conserving circles of authority" (1993, 244). One is reminded here of Angelina challenging Sister Bonaventura's censorship of her writing at school, but also hiding under the kitchen table at home when her mother tries to beat her with a feather-duster for her un-Indian behaviour. But Sam's story does not merely pose Angelina as a "site of contradictions," a Catholic Indian (like Sam herself); rather, Angelina's resilience offers alternatives not possible to either her mother or Sister Bonaventura, precisely because she is able to negotiate a position between both English-speaking Catholicism and Indian-ness. Describing herself as situated in the cross-ways between Confucianism, Malay feudalism, Roman Catholicism and British colonialism, Shirley Lim emphasises the effects of a multilogical rather than monological environment in which none of these cultural systems on their own "offered a girl-child a stable, established, supporting society." However, "Each system, oppressive alone, became interrogative and subversive in the matrix of multiculturalism" (1993, 246). Given the problematic status of multiculturalism in the South African context with its apartheid legacy of separate but unequal development and the inequitable power dynamics involved in this, Lim's comment recalls the debate between Said and Ahmed referred to earlier which suggested the possibility of identities which do not contaminate, but "enablingly inform each other" (De Mel 1995, 244). Looked at this way, the different values and beliefs encountered by the Asian woman in the diaspora do not "co-exist in parallel structures but [react] on each other, calling into question their differences" (Lim 1993, 246). A similar point is made by Samir Dayal who argues the need to theorise ethnicity, race, class, gender and nation more explicitly and strongly with reference to "diaspora":

> Cultural difference is a theoretically useful concept not primarily because it points to the discreteness of one culture from another but because it reminds of the *constitutiveness* of difference. That is to say, among other things, that sovereignty is denied to the subject, and organic self-identity and self-sufficiency are denied to a culture as such.
>
> (1996, 54)

Clearly, Lim's account of the way "points of escape" are offered at the intersection of different cultural systems could be useful for the renewed focus on the politics of identity in the South African context, and will no doubt strike a chord with many caught between conflicting systems of value and knowledge during this time of transition and returned exiles. Despite the continuing movement of dispossessed peoples, refugees and illegal immigrants throughout Asia, Africa, Europe and the Americas, Sam suggests that it is possible that migration is not only the reaction of a victim, but can be the enactment of choice. As she claims rather provocatively in her introduction to *Jesus is Indian,* for the woman in modern and post-modern society, migration need no longer emphasise the migrant woman's "chattle nature"; instead, she says, "it can signal our independence and status as individuals" (13) when migration is a choice, not merely a historical necessity.

Notes

1. For detailed engagement with the parameters of Chapman's project see Leon de Kock (1997) and Stewart Crehan (1997). See also Johannes A. Smit et al., ed. (1996).

2. The dust cover of Ronnie Govender's recently published prize-winning collection *At the Edge and Other Cato Manor Stories* claims that during the 1960s Govender was the first to "ventur[e] to explore the lives, tragedies and patois of the Indian community" (Arcadia: Manx Publishers, 1996).

3. Quoted by kind permission of the author, who is also working on images of social and cultural history in Jayapraga Reddy's unpublished autobiography "The Unbending Reed."

4. This is suggested by Chapman's reservations about "black Atlantic" creolisation and cultural diffusions referred to at the beginning of this article. See also Samir Dayal's interesting discussion on "Diaspora and Double Consciousness" in relation to Carol Boyce Davies's discussion of both the transformative and resistant aspects of Afro-diasporic culture in which she "rejects concepts of hybridity and syncretism in favour of repetition and re-memory" (Dayal 1996).

5. In her introduction Sam objects to the minimal coverage devoted to Indian peasants in Colin Bundy's *The Rise and Fall of the South African Peasantry,* seeing it as a further example of the exclusion of Indians from South African history (9). It is interesting to note that in keeping with recent re-writings of South African history for the school curriculum, a popular history like the *Reader's Digest Illustrated History of South Africa* (updated 1992, with Bundy as advisor) perhaps prematurely sub-titled "The Real Story," devotes a chapter to Indian indentured labour, titled "No more than units of labour." Commenting on the way bigotry and discrimination were increasingly "written into the law," the article quotes a Bengali newspaper which claimed that, "The only difference between Negro slavery and coolie emigration is that the former was open slavery and the latter is slavery in disguise" (225), echoing the point

made by Sam in her last story which frames the collection, "And They Christened It Indenture."

6. See Flockemann (1998).

7. Hosted by the *Mail & Guardian,* "Transforming South Africa: The Power of Imaginative Writing." Cape Town, Sept. 1995. To illustrate her point, Sam read from the first story in her collection, "High Heels."

Works Cited

Chapman, Michael. 1995. *Southern African Literatures.* London and New York: Longman.

Crehan, Stewart. 1997. "1994 and All That: Re-writing South African Literary History." *Pretexts* 6.1: 101-112.

Dayal, Samir. 1996. "Diaspora and Double Consciousness." *The Journal of Midwest Modern Language Association* 29.1: 46-62.

Daymond, Margaret. 1996. "Gender and 'History': 1980s South African Women's Stories in English." *Ariel* 27.1: 191-215.

De Mel, Neloufer. 1995. "Women as Gendered Subject and other Discourses in Contemporary Sri Lankan Fiction in English." *Into the Nineties, Post-Colonial Women's Writing.* Ed. Anna Rutherford, Lars Jensen, Shirley Chew. Aarhus: Dangaroo.

De Kock, Leon. 1997. "An Impossible History." *English in Africa* 24.1 (1997): 103-117.

Fakier, Yazeed. 1996. "A Debate Coloured by Race." *Cape Times* 4 Dec.: 8.

Flockemann, Miki. 1998. "'If I were her': Fictions of Development from Cape Town, Canada and the Caribbean." *Journal of Literary Studies* (Autumn 1998) [forthcoming].

Geok-lin Lim, Shirley. 1993. "Asians in Anglo-American Feminism: Reciprocity and Resistance." *Changing Subjects, The Making of Feminist Literary Criticism.* Ed. Gayle Greene and Coppelia Kahn. London and New York: Routledge.

Govinden, Davarashanam. 1997. "The Indentured Experience—Indian Women in Colonial Natal." Unpublished conference paper. Gender and Colonialism Conference. University of the Western Cape, Jan. 13-15.

James, Wilmot. 1997. "Apartheid's Death Machines." *Cape Times* 11 Nov.: 1.

Jeppie, Shamil. 1996. "Commemorations and Identities: The 1994 Tercentenary of Islam in South Africa." *Islam and the Question of Minorities.* Ed. Tamara Sonn. Atlanta, GA: Scholar's Press.

Marais, Sue. 1995. "Getting Lost in Cape Town: Spatial and Temporal Dislocation in the South African Short Fiction Cycle." *English in Africa* 22.2: 29-44.

Murray, Sally-Ann. 1991. "Telling Stories." *Current Writing* 3.1: 184-192

Myburg, Marietjie. 1991. "The Loneliness of the Long Distance Writer." *Daily Dispatch: In Focus.* 19 Feb.: 4.

Ngcobo, Lauretta. 1988. "Apartheid South Africa: Through Women's Eyes." *Third World Quarterly* 10.1: 299-306.

Patteson, Richard. 1993. "The Fiction of Olive Senior, Traditional Society and the Wider World." *Ariel* 24.1: 13-35.

Reddy, Jayapraga. 1987. "Friends." *On the Fringe of Dreamtime and Other Stories.* Johannesburg: Skotaville.

Rooney, Caroline. 1990. "Living Histories." *Southern African Review of Books* Feb/May: 6.

Sam, Agnes. 1988. "South Africa: Guest of Honour Amongst the Uninvited Newcomers to England's Great Tradition." *Let it be Told: Essays by Black Women in Britain.* Ed. Lauretta Ngcobo. London: Virago.

———. 1994 (1989). *Jesus is Indian and Other Stories.* London: Heinemann Educational.

Saunders, Christopher, ed. 1992. *The Illustrated History of South Africa: The Real Story.* Cape Town: Readers Digest.

Senior, Olive. 1989. *Arrival of the Snake-Woman.* Trinidad and Jamaica: Longman.

Smit, Johannes A., Johan van Wyk, and Jean-Philippe Wade. 1996. *Rethinking South African Literary History.* Durban: Y Press.

Van Niekerk, Annemarie. 1992. "Aspects of Race, Class and Gender in Jayapraga Reddy's *On the Fringe of Dreamtime and Other Stories. Unisa English Studies* 30.2: 35-40.

Wicomb, Zoë. 1993. *Between the Lines: Interviews with Nadine Gordimer, Menan du Plessis, Zoë Wicomb and Lauretta Ngcobo.* Ed. Eva Hunter and Craig MacKenzie. Grahamstown: NELM. 79-98.

Barbara Lalla (essay date October 1998)

SOURCE: Lalla, Barbara. "Registering Woman: Senior's Zig-zag Discourse and Code-Switching in Jamaican Narrative." *ARIEL* 29, no. 4 (October 1998): 83-98.

[*In the following essay, Lalla traces the changing language in Senior's story "Zig-zag," arguing that "the shifting experiences and perspectives of the child protagonist emerge through a multifaceted and shifting discourse."*]

The traumatic process of becoming a woman, in the setting of a brown, rural, middle-class Jamaican family, is a dominant factor in shaping the language of Olive

Senior's short story **"Zig-zag,"** in *Discerner of Hearts.* Jamaican Creole, Standard English, and intermediate varieties of these comprise Jamaican discourse, and **"Zig-zag"** shifts between the codes and intersects scribal discourse with suggestions of orality. Through these shifts, **"Zig-zag"** traces the emotional upheavals of its central character, Sadie, one of two daughters in a household fraught with tensions about mixed roots.

Sadie's sister, Muffet, is older, fairer, better behaved, admired, and inevitably politely spoken. Her father is withdrawn, obsessed with mysterious, apparently intellectual work that no one can actually define but that we naturally associate with written and therefore Standard English. The household reflects the language continuum of the larger society. Her mother clings anxiously to the acrolect, harassed by every threat of social betrayal, hedged in by the very boundaries she lays down for the protection of the family—social boundaries with linguistic dimensions. The mother is nervous about the future of the girls and the education on which this depends—an education that displays itself through language which is a dimension of the behavior that she assesses. She is anxious about how they will turn out, frantic lest Sadie "turn-down."

A maid, Desrine, has parallel concerns about her children, especially Manuela, whom Sadie meets at Desrine's house and later at her own. Desrine, whose language is firmly located in the Creole, is not occupied by implications of code choice. However, she is anxious enough about her daughter's education to suppress the girl's speech. Manuela's language behaviour involves significant silences. When Sadie meets her on the road to Desrine's house, Manuela is silent to the children of her own community. At Sadie's home, she suppresses her socially stigmatized speech unless alone with Sadie.

Sadie is torn between the varying form and content of conflicting codes. She is fascinated by the folk wisdom and African background of Desrine, and by the physical vitality of Manuela that contrasts with the intellectual development expected of Sadie herself. However, their communication is cut short once Manuela becomes pregnant. This break in communication does not resolve the linguistic complexities of Sadie's situation. Muffet leaves for an education in town. Desrine prepares to leave the job so that she can care for Manuela's child, even as Desrine's mother cared for Desrine's children. Sadie is left to consider her options for development. The shifting experiences and perspectives of the child protagonist emerge through a multifaceted and shifting discourse. One dimension of complexity in the language situation of these characters is that of confrontation between codes; another related dimension is that of confrontation between oral and scribal discourse, the oral discourse utilizing a structure governed by the operation of memory.

The short story is framed as a recollection of developing feminine consciousness, as a resurfacing of intimate experiences from the past, with all the immediacy with which these experiences flash into the mind. The delivery of these recollections is characterized by orality. Mary Chamberlain tells us that "oral sources are different from conventional sources precisely because they deal with perception and subjectivity" and she suggests that this is not a limitation but achieves a "different credibility" (95). Chamberlain associates the definition of the individual with properties of memory, and indeed Sadie's view of herself is based on her recollections of her experiences—recollections that are her own construction. At the same time, Chamberlain notes that memory manifests elements of shared consciousness and is also associated with a process of social production, so memory is both subjective and collective (96, 101). A further insight of Chamberlain, relevant to the account of Sadie's development, is that memory is multi-layered and multifaceted, for memories change and distort under social and cultural influences (106). The narrator of **"Zig-Zag"** recollects the developing consciousness of the girl in a voice that echoes the girl's voice. Literary, scribal usage blurs into the style of an oral delivery.

Gordon Rohlehr has described the language situation in which Caribbean writers currently operate as an *oral/ scribal continuum,*[1] and this is a helpful concept to apply to any analysis of Senior's language. Also useful is Edward Kamau Brathwaite's concept of *nation language,* a dimension of Caribbean language especially allied to the African aspect of Caribbean experience, associated with folk culture and derived, originally, as a strategy for survival and for preservation of culture (21-25; see also Torres-Saillant 129-31). However, Senior's writing profits best from a combination of these concepts, a vision of *nation language* that embraces not only the Creole but the local versions of Standard English that continually interface with the Creole. **"Zig-zag"** presents a situation in which the girl's life-as-it-should-be is laid out before her like a text already written, but in which life-as-it-is surfaces and interrupts this text, like a subtext in which the Creole setting intercepts the official and standard one. In a sense Sadie's inquisitive and incorrigible view continually rewrites the text that has been prepared for her. This effect is largely achieved by movement between codes, between the official language and the Creole.

Another dimension to the structure of the tale lies in the fact that even as the text unfolds, intercepted by subtext, this unfolding is the subject of recollection. The narrator looks back at events moving forward, events not presented in chronological order but in an order based on causal relationships between the events and the development of an adolescent feminine consciousness. The brown girl becomes increasingly aware of

tangled roots, conveyed in the entanglement of language codes, and through metaphor—the stubborn roots of the water hyacinth and the dangerously curly strands of her own hair. Through recurrent combing and plaiting, her mother and others about her struggle to bring these roots under control, to repress the wildness inherent in Sadie and burgeoning in sexual curiosity. As the narrative shifts between Standard English and Creole, the dialectic of plaiting and loosening hair parallels a dialectic of repressed sexuality and self-expression:

> Then she realised her hair was loose and she had to plait it back.
>
> But when she touched it, she found that her hair was totally out of control now, had turned into a wild animal. A *leggo beas!*

(214)

The time frame of the narrative is complex for a number of reasons. The time of narration (the point from which the narrator recalls events, retrospectively) is located well beyond the story and is stable. However, the time of the narrated (the movement of events forward, prospectively) is discontinuous. The inherent retrospectivity of the narration surfaces from time to time through the prospectivity of the time movement to hint at disturbing events already past but not yet revealed. Embedded in the main third-person narrative is one in first person, Sadie's embedded story of a journey to Desrine's house. This embedded narrative implicates a psychological journey to a more African past than Sadie is allowed to articulate. In a sense, the embedded story parallels Sadie's dream at the end of the tale—with a crucial difference. In her dream, Sadie is no longer the centre of attention to the other participants, but has become invisible and peripheral.

The tools for accomplishing such effects of intersecting retrospectivity and prospectivity are tense (which is concerned with location in time of the event) and aspect (which is non-deictic, involving distribution of time within the event). However, in Caribbean literary discourse, switches between Standard English and Creole (which mark tense and aspect quite differently) interrupt retrospectivity. The switch to the Creole unmarked verb (which is Past and Perfective[2]) facilitates parallel but contrasting time references, for this unmarked form in the Creole is identical to the Narrative Present of Standard English discourse. Sadie's account of her journey has all the immediacy of an oral performance because of a shift to first person and to present tense in Standard English discourse. At the same time retrospectivity is not lost, because of the significance of the unmarked verb in the Creole voice: "From they scream out, 'Mama come!' the children, except for Manuela, never say another word" (165).

It is essential to note that the movement between codes is a fundamental aspect of the Caribbean setting and of Caribbean characterization. Code switching in Caribbean literary discourse is an essential strategy for perspectival shift on the ideological plane. In Olive Senior's fiction, political implications of code shifting include those of gender. Senior conveys the subtle changes in the developing girl child by exploiting the complex language situation of the Caribbean in which language codes of different status (for example, Standard English and Creole) coexist with each other and with a range of intermediate varieties.

Perspective, or point-of-view, may be perceptual or conceptual. Spatio-temporal perspective is essentially perceptual. It is equivalent, as Fowler points out, to viewing position in the visual arts, an angle from which the object of representation is seen (127). Ideological perspective involves a mental rather than physical stance, an attitude to the object represented. Senior's narrative conveys an inside view hinged to the mental stance of a developing girl child in rural Jamaica—a child whose family situation prescribes the use of Standard English but demands full comprehension and inevitable use, at times, of Jamaican Creole. The dialogue varies widely between a Jamaican variety of Standard English and the Jamaican Creole.

Sadie's narrative is, for the most part, Standard English, but is colloquial. The opening sentence is passive, a structure not marked in the Creole, but progresses toward the colloquial phrasal verb *dressed up,* then to the yet more informal *mashed up.* Standard English word choice and morphology persist however in terms like *imprinted.* The orality of the narrative is marked by merged and fragmented sentences, comma splices, abbreviations, and informal phrasal verbs like *knocking about.* Orality is further marked by creole intrusions ("Sadie . . . faasing in everything" 155). These are brief but effective, sometimes conveying phonological differences from the official language but, more often, marking lexical or syntactic differences without losing the comprehension of the non-creole reader, for Senior installs such terms in a context that illuminates them, or installs them close to Standard English near-synonyms. The fact is that the central consciousness controls the full and fluid continuum not only between Standard and Creole but between formal (literary) language of the educated and the oral tradition to which she is exposed. Indeed, she is particularly exposed to the oral tradition as a girl closely tied to domestic affairs of the house and to the maid, Desrine.

Sadie's speech is counter discursive, often questioning rather than declarative and, especially, questioning the definitions of others:

"What's a queendom?"

"A country ruled over by a queen."

(158)

Indeed Senior conveys Sadie's perspective through a wide range of syntactic choices, for example, by thematic adjustments like passivization. Passivization (as in the example above) effects focus on the action rather than the agent and reflects the speaker's weighting of events. Senior manifests Sadie's perspective on the ideological plane through other categories such as transitivity (indicating the nature of her participation in the process that the clause expresses) and modality (indicating, for example, the girls's commitment to the truth of the utterance):[3]

Muffet said no, they had to choose a foreign name. Why? Asked Sadie.

Because foreign is elegant and written about in books, said Muffet.

(157)

Muffet articulates the prescribed view, marking obligation and coercion by the phrase *had to.* Sadie questions this prescription and Muffet responds with the passive, *is written about,* that establishes an action for which no agent is necessary, a universe in which the predominance of *foreign* is established and self-evident.

In addition to manipulating the sentence structure of Standard English, Senior poignantly conveys ideological perspective through the selection of a code not traditionally associated with literary discourse. Code-switching from Standard to Creole effects perspectival shift by highlighting points of view traditionally regarded as peripheral. Sadie, marginalized at home, becomes central at Desrine's house, as "bakra pickney," and Desrine's daughter, Manuela, is mainly responsible for this, because association with Sadie raises Manuela's status. At Desrine's house, when Sadie is not visiting, Manuela is central as the fairest. Yet Manuela marginalizes Sadie at Sadie's own home if Muffet is with them, because Muffet is fairer than Sadie and committed to acceptable behavior. Language is a significant aspect of behavior in the developing girls.

The complex linguistic background is a crucial dimension of Senior's Caribbean setting and of her characterization. The subdued, refined voices confront loud undisciplined outbursts. Muffet sneers politely,

Who ever heard of a granadilla? I have! Sadie shouted. . . .

Heh heh heh! She would cackle, as loud and careless as a market woman.

(157-58)

Sadie's loudness is associated by others with the vulgarity of a Creole speaker, even when she does not actually produce Creole speech. In any case, she is frequently associated with unmentionable creole terms, like *baggy,* whether she actually articulates them or whether they occur as part of the narrative that conveys her perspective. Sadie moves with awkward enthusiasm through a setting fissured by communication gulfs of various dimensions.

Senior recognizes communication gulfs based on spatial and ideological dimensions. She reflects, in Desrine's complaint, the gulf between those "clear slap a England" and those in rural Jamaica. But this spatial gulf is mirrored by a social gulf between the educated and the uneducated—a gulf widened or narrowed by racial features:

> Backra pickney can stay in school for them parents can afford it. Stay as long as they like. Till them all grow beard. But is not so for black people. . . . Well, me can't quarrel with King or Queen as the case may be, for is clear a England them live so them can't know how hard nayga have fe work out them soul-case so find food for pickney here, much less find school fee. Clear slap a England, you nuh see it, Sadie? Bucknam Palace. So how them must know what a gwan here? Governor na send and tell them. Governor na send and tell them one living thing. You nuh see it?
>
> (176)

The creole setting is one of zig-zag paths to avoid these chasms, the route between Sadie's and Desrine's house, the boundary between classes and races, the unspoken routes through Sadie's sociohistorical background, the shameful roots of her too curly hair. (Her comb is of metaphorical significance to her mother; it is the key to the future.) Sadie's colloquial Standard English speech, intercepted by Creole outbursts is yet another zig-zag path between the gulfs.

In selecting codes for her particular purposes, the author reflects attitudes to language which have changed considerably in the Caribbean over the past two centuries. As a result, code-shifting has increased in ease, frequency, and acceptability, raising the issue of what narratologists term *legibility,* the degree to which a text can be read with comprehension (Prince, *Narratology* 132-43). A conspicuous achievement of Senior is the legibility of her texts for a wide and varied readership, despite the prominence of orality in her delivery. For early writers, who included Creole to indicate the distance of their subjects and the incomprehensibility of their setting, legibility was not so important a requirement.[4] However, for writers who code-shift in order to signal a perspectival shift, legibility is crucial. Many of Senior's readers are not Creole speakers in the first place, and their involvement with these texts places them in what might loosely be compared to a type of contact situation. The Caribbean writer must therefore take steps to preserve intelligibility while shifting perspective in this way.

The Caribbean writer must balance the demands of authenticity (what Toolan calls the "faithful record effect" [31]) against the need to preserve universal comprehen-sion. Senior's writing addresses this need: in representing a centre of consciousness who is a bilingual Creole and Standard English speaker, she chooses Sadie, the child in between.

The girl protagonist departs from established language attitudes in **"Zig-zag."** Sadie's place (in terms of class, race, and gender) is rigidly defined. Her problem is partially summed up in Muffet's rebuke: "Have you ever seen a princess with a natty head?" (159) Her assumption of a higher class is play-acting, and she gets tired of playing the lady, a role tied to affectation of formal Standard English:

> Sometimes, though, Sadie got tired of being a princess and all the pretending, of the speaky-spokey life it entailed, for Muffet said princesses had to speak properly at all times.
>
> (161)

Sadie injects Creole into her dialogue sometimes for shock value, sometimes to establish expertise in local mysteries. Gradually the view of real women as princesses is exploded to a view of princesses as unreal. Reality lies in the domestic world that real people inhabit, the world steeped in African survivals that are "true-true." Senior conveys Sadie's double vision through co-existing codes that are associated with different registers. The movement between codes reflects the growing girl's shifting perspective.

The Standard English/Creole relationship is both subtle and complex in the discourse of **"Zig-Zag."** The lexis is distinctively Caribbean although the vast majority of Caribbean English/Creole words are derived from English. Senior interferes little with Standard spelling. However, one process of lexical development in the Caribbean has been phonological change radical enough to make many creole words of English origin unrecognizable to the non-creole speaker. In many cases, this allows both a Standard and Creole *reading* of the same word. By rendering a Creole sentence in Standard English orthography, Senior presents an easily digestible Standard vocabulary leaving the Standard English reader who knows little or no Creole to deal more easily with the unfamiliar syntax ("Is look a look down"). But the Creole speaker naturally retains oral (creole) pronunciation, pronouncing *worse* as [wus] in the sentence, "Desrine's mouth would long out worse than ever." Similarly, processes known in Standard English but more frequent in Creole, like reduplication, produce Creole words or phrases composed of parts familiar in the Standard. ("How she can get through her business if him a call-call her all the time?") Additionally, the Creole voice emerges through lexical preferences, like *lick* for *blow.* (Manuela would "rub wherever it was that the lick fell.")

Legibility also rests on the ability of Creole words to shift word class and to function in a wider variety of ways than in the Standard. Thus Sadie is referred to as *faasing* in everything.[5] This multifunctionality is closely linked to the flexionless patterns of characteristically analytic Creole sentence structure. This too has contributed to the expansion of Creole lexicon by freeing words to operate in sentence positions and with syntactic functions that are closed to them in the international language. Again, Senior exploits this characteristically Creole process to produce the faithful record effect—the impression of Creole speech based on a few features. Her Creole is representational enough to produce the impression, but not consistent enough to threaten comprehension. (See Slembrouck 109-19 on verbatim records.) By rearranging words familiar in Standard English, and recategorizing them to function differently in the sentence, she distinguishes the Creole from International English within the literary discourse without rendering the discourse unintelligible to non-Creole speakers: "the bolder ones would malice her off for being bad-minded and poor-show-great" (167). The movement between codes reflects an alternation of world views that becomes explicit in references to language attitudes. Language attitudes that emerge in the novel are gender related, because the cultivation of a lady is associated with the encouragement of Standard English usage rather than Creole. Particularly discouraged would be those elements in which the African element is most obvious, like *yabba, guzu, duppy,* and *su-su.*

Words of non-English origin are relatively few in the Creole in any case. They are rare in Senior's text. Indeed, these tend not to be recognized as real words, associated as they are with the African cultural past. This in turn is dismissed as "wickedness of heathenism" (177)—a type of knowledge that is improper in a developing lady. Sadie's "boldness" shocks the girls she is supposed to mix with in school rather than the "natty-head children." The "natty-head children" are cursed by everyone (including Desrine) because their parents are "bungo people with no ambition" (162), and because they are children who behave "as if they [are] the worst kind of cuffee" (168).

These are the children who are expected to grow into *ol' nayga.* Far more familiar than words of non-English origin are non-English phrases composed of English components. Not every term in the Creole has an identifiable corresponding term in Standard English (anisomorphism), and in Senior's discourse, the term *ol' nayga* has no corresponding Standard English term, although both *old* and *negro* are English words. The term is located in the same semantic field as *worthless,* and is not the sum of *old* and *of African descent.* In some texts, the semantic reinterpretation of such terms is open-ended. Winkler's *The Painted Canoe* reflects amelioration of the term, *old negar,* first used traditionally, as a term of abuse. The phrase eventually becomes a slogan of solidarity in the novel. Zachariah embraces

it in an effort to preserve identity by affirming self-worth. The phrase becomes a watch word and at last a recurrent battle-cry, "Old negar not easy to kill."

The amelioration of such terms comes about through socio-historical forces. Most recently, boundaries of acceptability have blurred not only with growing nationalism but with the widening attraction of black youth culture, which has focused on the ghetto experience. In specific contexts, Black English *nigger* has become an address for signifying intimacy, or at least common ground, but the provision is that part of this commonality must be racial. (*Nigger* is *not* a form of address that can be safely and generally employed by white speakers to black addressees.) This semantic transformation is by no means complete or universal. The choice between acceptance and non-acceptance is situationally constrained. In *The Painted Canoe* Zachariah accepts as positive the designation of *negar* when he returns to land, but his wife, Carina, resents it (224). Their situations differ in the separate experiences that constitute different contexts and impose separate meaning on the term for different characters. In **"Zig-zag,"** there is no amelioration of *ol' nayga.* The setting of a brown middle class household in the early to mid-twentieth century does not accommodate this type of semantic change, especially where a developing girl is concerned. Attitudes associated with *ol' nayga.* are gender sensitive.

Language attitudes in **"Zig-zag,"** as in other Caribbean texts, are important to the underlying propositions of the text that together compose the Caribbean setting.[6] The Caribbean setting is denied by Muffet, who dismisses it as unreal. Real language, like real hyacinths, comes from England. Sadie favors shared terms (like *pastures*) rather than terms that have little local currency (like *meadows*). Sadie's selection of the regional variant of international English or of the Creole is situationally constrained. At times, she violates these constraints with the impropriety of certain outbursts, the counter-discourse of a rebellious girl child. At other times the counter-discourse is not articulated by the character but is implicated through code-switching by the narrative voice that transmits her thoughts and the thoughts of others with whom she communicates closely. Several of these take the form of proverbs, of shared, inherited wisdom framed in conventional formulae: "Duppy know who to frighten" (167); "Water more than flour" (169, 75); "What is fe you can't be un-fe you" (170); "Cockroach have no business inna fowl roos" (182).

Yet even in these essentially Creole utterances, Standard English features intrude. Nation language must encompass other codes besides the Creole to facilitate the code-switching necessary to perspectival shift in this central consciousness. Sadie's situation demonstrates the pressure of a textualized language on an essentially oral language. "Foreign is elegant and written about in books," insists Muffet (157). So the presentation of Sadie's development is conveyed by Senior in Rohlehr's oral/scribal continuum.

Sadie's discourse is heterogeneous because it permits and at times demands Creole even as it continues to require Standard English competence. The mixing that occurs is neither random nor unchecked, as this would eventually result in an undifferentiated medium (see Devonish). Undifferentiation would suit no one, as it would merely deplete the total richness of a discourse with so much potential for sensitive manipulation of codes. Between the options available, writers make choices linked to a number of factors, including internal setting but also constrained by external factors such as the writer's dependence on cross-cultural readership.

The heterogeneity of Caribbean language separates its literary discourse from other literature in English, and helps to undermine presuppositions of established British texts. Nevertheless, the creole consciousness not only reflects the postcolonial Caribbean but fosters the intertextuality of Caribbean and "imperial" texts. The discourse structure of the postcolonial text facilitates subtexts that convey alternative, conflicting or outlandish visions as aspects of characterization in the developing girl. Sadie's point of view anchors the discourse in a local creole consciousness but it also establishes the ideological dislocation of this central consciousness. Senior manipulates Sadie's heterogeneous discourse in such a way as to represent (legibly) codes which are so different as to be mutually unintelligible to the uninitiated.

Senior's literary discourse prompts a different approach to what critics have understood as *nation language,* for Caribbean literary critics have used the phrase to refer almost exclusively to a code that is obviously Creole. However, *nation language* must—in an unprejudiced view—include discourse other than Creole. It must also cover discourse in which lexical items that are (deceptively) identical in form to English convey indigenous epistemes. This is of course especially true where the similarity exists only in writing, where any creole speaker *mentally* pronounces the word so differently from its international counterpart as to render the Creole unintelligible to the non-Creole speaker. The literary discourse in this way becomes a form of Caribbean language which empowers the Creole by controlling the imperial, written code even as it implicitly conveys the sound and meaning of oral Creole. Indeed, part of *nation language* must surely be this secret encoding of Creole epistemes under guise of conformity and with all the advantages of International comprehensibility.[7]

In **"Zig-zag,"** such linguistic transgression constitutes a resistance not only to inhibitions of class and of race

but of gender. A major distinction between Sadie and Muffet is Sadie's *faasness* set against Muffet's *shame.* Sadie's boldness demonstrates itself in aspects of her language—stridency, volubility, lack of inhibition regarding topic or word choice, and Creole preferences. As the narrator retells the events of a period in Sadie's life (retrospective discourse), the narrative reveals this period as one in which Sadie begins to plot her life—to rediscover her background and to speculate on her future—even as events unfold about her (prospective discourse). In the process she represses and then recalls uncomfortable incidents, recollections by Sadie partly encoded in Creole, embedded within the stream of recollections that is the narrative.

The language of memory, Chamberlain reminds us, is "the means by which tradition is transmitted, the means by which structure and values are internalized, passed on and inherited" (108). Sadie's memories become shaped by the anxieties and memories of her mother and Desrine. This is the period in which Sadie first becomes aware of essential criteria for her development, and it is the period in which she finds conflicting influences confronting each other. She is torn between foreign and local values, between the security of straight hair and the threat of *natty* hair. She must develop the *speakey/spokey* voice of a woman with social ambitions or articulate her own local composite of English and Creole. She must integrate the enlightenment associated with a sound British-based education with the earthy folk-wisdom tested by experience among women like Desrine. She must express or repress her developing sexual awareness by cultivating an attitude of *faasness* or of *shame.* Senior constructs the developing girl's counter-discourse out of an interplay between the codes as Sadie's expression forces its way through repression.

Sadie must choose between a reality that has been artificially constructed for her to grow towards and a reality that *is* real, but that has been dismissed as illusion. She must choose first between the princess and the woman who has to live in a Caribbean society. She chooses the woman, but this woman may be constructed in a number of ways. One option is Muffet's choice—wife, mother, and professional, on the *foreign* model—speakey/spokey. Another option is the sterile educated woman imaged in one of her teachers, whom the children dismiss as a mule. A final option appears to be what members of Sadie's class would dismiss as *ol'nayga.* Black women like Desrine struggle forward with their own pretensions and ambitions, mainly for their children, but they are caught in the vicious circle of work and reproduction. For them, the only way out seems to be through camouflage (hand-me-down dresses and hair-straight) or by frustrating their capacities to give life. The question of woman's power over her own body is raised by Desrine: "you want me was to dash them weh before they born and turn my body into graveyard?" (196). However, the only alternative she seems able to put forward denies her power, leaving her trapped in a cycle of child-bearing and drudgery. This is the attitude associated with *ol' nayga*.

Senior characterizes the developing middle-class girl in the rural Caribbean essentially through her language behavior, which is counter-discursive and transgressive: "How can I send you to you Aunt Min with you hair looking like bush? . . . You don't practise speaking properly" (216). The threat of entrapment by the suppressed African side of her background is conveyed by meshing the metaphor of hair with references to Creole usage—an entanglement of twisted roots that separate her both from her sexually precocious black playmate and from the prim, tightly plaited, and somehow sterile propriety of society's ideal girl. Sadie must choose between *shame* and *faasness*. Senior conveys the language behaviour of the transgressive brown girl mainly through oral features in the narrative—a code-shifting that now lies at the heart of nation language in literary discourse.[8]

Notes

1. "A continuum exists between a living oral tradition, and a growing scribal one in the West Indies. It relates to the continuum which exists between the various West Indian Creoles and Standard English. Most West Indian writers seem to enter this continuum at several points" (68).

2. The verb phrase in Caribbean English-based Creole has been extensively discussed; for a thorough treatment of this, see Winford 65.

3. Simpson discusses and builds on models by Fowler and others (46-118).

4. Representative writing of eighteenth- to nineteenth-century British authors who selected Caribbean settings is accessible in D'Costa and Lalla.

5. Accompanying shifts of meaning frequently occur but because the resulting word resembles a known word in the official language, in both form and meaning, the sense of familiarity is preserved and legibility (real or apparent) is maintained.

6. Prince defines setting in terms of underlying propositions (*Narratology* 73).

7. Lalla 1996 explores the emergence of a national literary discourse.

8. This article is a revised version of a paper presented at the International Conference of Caribbean Women Writers and Scholars, Florida International University, 26-27 Apr. 1996.

Works Cited

Brathwaite, Edward. "English in the Caribbean: Notes on Nation Language and Poetry." *English Literature:*

Opening up the Canon. Ed. Leslie A. Fiedler and Houston A. Baker. Baltimore: Johns Hopkins UP, 1981. 15-53.

Chamberlain, Mary. "Gender and Memory: Oral History and Women's History." *Engendering History: Caribbean Women in Historical Perspective.* Ed. Verene Shepherd, Bridget Brereton, and Barbara Bailey. Kingston: Ian Randle Publications; London: James Currey, 1995. 54-68.

D'Costa, Jean, and Barbara Lalla. *Voices in Exile: Jamaican Texts of the Eighteenth and Nineteenth Centuries.* Tuscaloosa: U of Alabama P, 1989.

Devonish, Hubert. "On the Existence of Autonomous Language Varieties in 'Creole Continuum Situations.'" Biennial Conference of the Society for Caribbean Linguistics, Cave Hill, Barbados, 1992.

Fowler, Roger. *Linguistic Criticism.* Oxford: Oxford UP, 1986.

Lalla, Barbara. *Defining Jamaican Fiction: Marronage and the Discourse of Survival.* Tuscaloosa: U of Alabama P, 1996.

Prince, Gerald. *Dictionary of Narratology.* Lincoln: U of Nebraska P, 1987.

———. *Narratology: The Form and Functioning of Discourse.* Berlin: Mouton, 1982.

Rohlehr, Gordon. "History as Absurdity." *My Strangled City and Other Essays.* Port of Spain: Longman Trinidad, 1992, 17-51.

Senior, Olive. *Discerner of Hearts and Other Stories.* Toronto: McClelland and Stewart, 1995.

Simpson, Paul. *Language, Ideology and Point of View.* London: Routledge, 1993.

Slembrouck, Stef. "The Parliamentary Hansard 'Verbatim' Report: the Written Construction of Spoken Discourse," *Language and Literature* 1:2 (1992): 109-19.

Toolan, Michael. "Significations of Representing Dialect," *Language and Literature* 1:1 (1992): 24-96.

Torres-Saillant, Silvio. *Caribbean Poetics: Toward an Aesthetic of West Indian Literature.* Cambridge: Cambridge UP, 1997.

Winford, Donald. *Predication in Caribbean English Creoles.* Amsterdam: John Publishing, 1993.

Winkler, Anthony. *The Painted Canoe.* Kingston: Kingston Publishers, 1983.

Velma Pollard (essay date 1998)

SOURCE: Pollard, Velma. "Images of Women in the Short Stories of Olive Senior." In *The Woman, the*

Writer and Caribbean Society, edited by Helen Pyne-Timothy, pp. 118-25. Los Angeles: Center for Afro-American Studies Publications, 1998.

[*In the following essay, Pollard considers the depiction of women in Senior's short stories.*]

At a time when our societies are fighting silent and not so silent battles for recognition of women's efforts inside and outside of the family milieu, this [essay] looks at some modern Caribbean writing and discusses the image of women portrayed there. I believe that the discussion will support the argument that Caribbean fiction, inspired as it is by Caribbean reality, has had no difficulty in describing women who play positive leadership roles, taking their rightful place. It suggests further that, where Caribbean fiction is part of the school's curriculum, there need be no fear that the next generation will be unaware of women's contribution to the building of our nations.

This chapter will review texts from two collections of short stories by Olive Senior, *Summer Lightning* and *The Arrival of the Snake-Woman.*[1] Senior's texts have been chosen for several reasons: They are well-written; they are as suitable for general reading as for school and university study; they treat the lives of people at different social levels in the society, as well as the interaction between people from different levels. To enjoy Senior's short stories, one only has to be able to read, for even when she treats themes that might be considered adult, Senior writes from a child's point of view, and so the work is suitable for general consumption. Senior depicts both urban and rural settings, as well as a variety of situations. To Caribbean readers, her images are local and accessible in every sense. In other words, her credibility, in the mind of the average Caribbean audience, is likely to be very high.

Emphasis in the chapter will be less on Senior's fine writing style and the skill with which she handles the different linguistic codes in use in Jamaica than on the characters she develops within each story. Regrettably, not all the stories can be touched on in a chapter as brief as this. In those that are mentioned, the focus will be on the unobtrusive strength of the various women characters as they operate in different situations.

Of ten stories in the collection *Summer Lightning,* only the title story can be said *not* to have an important female character. It may be that the artist, because of her own gender, looks at the female contribution to situations, which enables us to consider the work in the way I have suggested.

"Love Orange" is about a small girl's encounter with death and the emotions aroused by this encounter. She tries to give her best gift, an orange, to each of two dying old people, offering it as a symbol of her love and affection. The gesture does not work in either case, most ruefully in the case of a grandmother who should have appreciated the assurance of the child's love. It is a hard but necessary lesson this young woman learns: A gift must find acceptance with the receiver not merely the giver.

Noteworthy is the absence of any male other than Grandpa in the story. He appears once, on the way to the funeral of the first person to whom the child tries to give the orange, and is disposed of in one sentence: "My grandfather stepped high in the shiny black shoes and a shiny black suit ahead of her" (p. 13). *Her* refers to the grandmother, who is a chief character.

"Country of the One-Eyed God" treats a prototypical grandmother, a women who raises the child of her migrant offspring. But this boy forsakes his grandmother for "bad company" and eventually is sought by the police. He returns home to try to rob his grandmother of her savings and to go off again. She refuses to give up her money, and we are left to infer from the ending that he kills her. This grandmother is strong and sacrificing. She is also a casualty of the cruel social economic environment in which she lives.

The grandmother knows and accepts that she has had few of this world's goods in life and that she is likely to have as little in death if she does not take the situation into her own hands. So she saves enough for a beautiful coffin, to take her out of this world in a style her life could not afford her. The irony is that she loses her life in an attempt to defend the money.

Among the terrible things the villain tells his grandmother in their ritual discussion is that her god is a one-eyed god, who responds to/sees only one class in the society. The old woman's faith cannot accept this formulation, and she begins to look for examples as counterproof. The reader is left to ponder it.

The grandmother here is hard-working and prayerful. The villain is a young man who will not even allow her a decent death. Depicting a tragic death after a poverty-filled life for a brave woman, Senior illustrates for us one of the terrible truths of modern society, that the aged poor may not even die in peace.

"Ascot" is about the progress of a young man from village scrounger to returning resident complete with wife (with master's degree). What is interesting here is that a woman character in the story recognizes his success and even allows him to carry out the farce that hers, the best house in the district, is his "birth house." At the end, Senior portrays the boy's mother: Although he ignores her, brings her no money, and openly snubs her,

her husband, and their children, she has no word of re-proof for him. She is only proud he could come back to display his success and by implication hers.

"Bright Thursdays" looks at a small girl taken from the frugal home of her mother and placed in the aristo-cratic home of the parents of a father who has never ac-knowledged her existence. Here again Senior uses the opportunity to highlight a woman's compassion. When the child's mother takes a chance and dares to throw her daughter on the mercy of the grandparents, the grandmother, although she has the same feelings about the matter as her husband, unbends and finds a way to accept the child. Note the interchange between the couple as she introduces the topic obliquely:

> "Well, just look at the two of us. Look how many chil-dren and grandchildren we have, and not a one to keep our company."
>
> "Hm, so life stay. Once your children go to town, coun-try too lonely for them after that."
>
> "I suppose so, but it would really be nice to have a young person about the house. . . ."
>
> (*Summer Lightning,* p. 42)

Later she picks up the topic again:

> "But, Dolphie, why we don't get Myrtle's little girl here?"
>
> "What! And rake up that old thing again? You must be mad."
>
> "But nobody has to know who she is."
>
> (p. 43)

The narrator's comment runs: "They argued on and off for weeks, then finally they decided to invite the child to stay for a week or two" (p. 43). That week or two lasted for years, at least until the end of the tale.

The most critically acclaimed story in this collection is **"Do Angels Wear Brassieres?"** Beccka, a mischievous young girl, brings a high-ranking official of the Angli-can church, the Archdeacon, to his knees. From her store of biblical information, she tricks him with such questions as what is the smallest insect in the Bible. His answer, "the widow's mite," must yield to hers, "the wicked flee." He is mercifully saved from having to an-swer the title question by a domestic accident in which Beccka's guardian and grand-aunt, Auntie Marry, hear-ing the question put to Archdeacon, stops so suddenly in her fright and embarrassment that Cherry, coming up behind her, spills a pitcher of drink.

The story implies that bright children suffer a disadvan-tage when they are brought up by ignorant adults, such as Auntie Mary. Beccka's dialog with the Archdeacon, prematurely ended by the accident, is exactly the kind

Auntie Mary had feared she might have, based on ear-lier conversations in which the child had terrified her. Note the following extract from a conversation between Auntie Mary and a friend, Miss Katie. Beccka is the subject under discussion:

> "Guess what she asked me the other day, nuh?—if me know how worms reproduce."
>
> "Say what, ma'am?"
>
> "As Jesus is me judge. Me big woman she come and ask that. Reproduce I say. Yes, Auntie Mary, as if I stu-pid. When the man worm and the lady worm come to-gether and they have baby. You know how it hap-pen?—I so she ask me."
>
> "What you saying, ma'am? Jesus of Nazareth!"
>
> "Yes, please. That is what the child ask me."
>
> (*Summer Lightning,* p. 69)

The young girl in the story is bright and confident, al-though those are hardly the adjectives used by her grand-aunt to describe her. She prefers terms like *facety* (aggressive) and *force-ripe* (precocious). But these very traits are the ones the girl needs to be a successful per-son, an outstanding woman. She has an inquisitive mind and an active imagination. This character obviously has the author's approval.

Miss Rilla, the heroine of **"Ballad,"** is by any standards the best-drawn female in the collection. She is the topic chosen by the narrator when the teacher asks her to write about the most unforgettable character she ever met. The narrator is not allowed to do so, because her teacher, like the rest of polite society as represented by MeMa, the mother or guardian in the story, frowns on Miss Rilla. People believe her to be somewhat free with her physical favors. The narrator does not try to defend Miss Rilla from such accusations. In fact, she describes an incident suggesting that the accusations might be true, at least with regard to one young man. The narra-tor even allows us to hear a story about the murder of one of Miss Rilla's lovers by another in that number, a tragedy that occurred before the narrator was born. But the narrator makes Miss Rilla so loving and physiologi-cally whole that her influence on a little girl can only be good. Witness her behavior to the child one trying morning:

> "Hi, you little crying child with the red head. Come here. What you crying for?" [Miss Rilla asks].
>
> . . . I learn when she ask question, she don't want no answer for she using her apron to wipe my eye and when she done, I get a good look at her. I did think Miss Rilla was a gypsy woman though I never in my life see no gypsy but that is how she look. To Gawd! and me eye water done quick for she gone inside the house . . . and she came back out with a plate full of gizada that big and juicy and hot, and quick, I forgot 'bout beating and eye water.
>
> (*Summer Lightning,* p. 104)

That is a measure of the kind of woman Miss Rilla is. Miss Rilla dies quite suddenly, while sitting in a market truck on her way to Kingston. The narrator's loss is irreparable, her grief immeasurable.

"Ballad" is the final story in *Summer Lightning.* The final statement of **"Ballad"** is, therefore, the closing statement of the book. What we are left with at the end is the following: "And sometimes I get down on my knee and pray for the Lord to come and take me so I can see for myself where Miss Rilla gone to."

By contrast, the most remarkable woman in Senior's *The Arrival of the Snake-Woman* is the first and title story, the longest of seven stories in the collection.

The snake woman is the prototypical East Indian indentured servant, whose contribution to Jamaican population and culture came after the emancipation of Negro slaves. The story is about the integration into a small hill village society of a woman who is appropriately named Miss Coolie but who the boy narrator thinks of as a snake woman because of her svelte shape and sinuous walk. She is brought to the village by the man who wins her in a straw lottery (the boys draw straws to see who can entice her to leave the coast and come live with him in the village). For most of the story, Miss Coolie is an outcast, thanks to the attitude encouraged by a Christian person who reads a passage from the Bible to show that the arrival of a temptress fitting Miss Coolie's description had been prophesied: "The daughters of Zion are haughty, and walk with stretched fork necks and wanton eyes, walking and mincing as they go, and making a tinkling with their feet" (p. 5). Miss Coolie's gait and the jewels on her ankles make her the obvious object of description.

Miss Coolie's story is one of courageous integration and of driving ambition. She envisions her son becoming a lawyer who will get title to the land on which all the district people live, and although this seems like a distant dream, it comes true. Her daughter marries the narrator, who she foresees will do well. He becomes a doctor.

Unobtrusively, Senior goes about displacing the negative myths folklore has woven around people who came indentured from the East. Miss Coolie might be thought of as someone who obtains money by unfair means to make her dreams come true. However, when the narrator leaves to further his education, she gives him a heavy gold bangle that he is never to sell but to use as surety for loans if he is ever in need: "Ish, never sell this. Keep it and any time you need money go and pawn it. But never sell" (p. 43). He has to use it several times over the years. A black woman's son learns that shrewdness, not thievery, is part of what the Asians use to gain financial advantage. The instrument for this important message is a woman.

In **"The Tenantry of Birds,"** Senior looks at the plight of a typical middle-class wife of the 1970s, when political and social awareness dictated the class of academic man. Typically, the woman protagonist is replaced by a keen leftist-oriented research assistant. But by the time the story ends, this woman has changed from long-suffering wife to militant woman, not in the political but the personal sense. Invited by her husband to sue for divorce and return to Miami to live with her mother while he continues to occupy the marital home with his politically militant girlfriend, she decides to stay:

> Finally she came to her decision. She thought, to hell with it! She would throw out the crotons and the anthuriums, the gerberas and the ixorias, she would plant a new garden.

> *(The Arrival,* p. 61)

This woman had been inspired by different families of birds who made their home in her special tree, peccaries, kling-klings, and mockingbirds: They clearly knew who they were. The story ends with a description of the woman's joy in having overcome her troubles, with the final words: "the power." I have no reason to believe the author was conscious of it, but the word *empowerment* so common in women's nonfiction of this decade is what comes to me when I read the ending.

In **"The Two Grandmothers,"** Senior depicts the different worlds of two women in Jamaican society. They share a granddaughter, through whose eyes we see them, and she reports their implied attitudes toward each other. Grandmother Del, the father's mother, is, in the eyes of grandmother Elaine, the mother's mother, "a country bumpkin in the deepest waters" (p. 65), while grandmother Elaine represents much that is considered evil in Grandma Del's house. She whistles, wears makeup, and is admired by men. Senior uses devices similar to those employed in **"Bright Thursdays"** of the earlier collection. In both these stories, a child links two households. Senior uses the child's eye to show us women whose class consciousness is shown in some subtle and some not-so-subtle ways. Disdain for the foreign cousins who are "white" eventually causes the granddaughter in this story to think through her own situation and try to arrive at her own value system.

"Lily, Lily" is the final story in *The Arrival of the Snake-Woman.* Additional foibles and prejudices of middle-class Jamaica are set out for our inspection. The vehicle is the beautiful Lily, more beautiful than she should be, given the appearance of her parents, who are good-looking but certainly not good-looking enough and surely not white enough to have produced her, so the gossip mongers think. In the research about her true parentage, bits of history and fiction put together, we see society at its worst. Pride, ambition, and incest are among the themes to receive attention. But the most interesting commentary is found in the development of the character of Lily's real mother, her Aunt Lily. This woman makes tremendous psychological and philosophical leaps as the story unfolds, from a heart-broken pregnant seventeen year old to a confidant woman. Like the wife in the **"Tenantry of Birds,"** by the end of the story, Aunt Lily intends to control her life. She announces that she has the outrage to create her own wings and fly.

Senior is not a feminist in the narrower definitions of that term, but the honesty with which she identifies the strengths of the various women she draws suggests that a broad definition of the term would have to include her. Like several female writers from the Caribbean, Senior provides positive images of woman, positive female role models for emulation and ratification.

Note

1. Olive Senior, *Summer Lightning* (Harlow: Longman Caribbean, 1986), and *The Arrival of the Snake-Woman* (Harlow: Longman Caribbean, 1989). The same editions are used in all subsequent references to these works. Page numbers of quotations are provided in text.

Kathleen J. Renk (essay date 1999)

SOURCE: Renk, Kathleen J. "Reinscribing the Garden: Female Tricksters at the Crossroads." In *Caribbean Shadows and Victorian Ghosts: Woman's Writing and Decolonization*, pp. 121-50. Charlottesville: University Press of Virginia, 1999.

[*In the following excerpt, Renk discusses the protagonist of "Arrival of the Snake-Woman" as a trickster figure.*]

According to Ramabai Espinet, Mama Glo is a "benign and powerful" figure in Trinidadian folklore represented as a combination of a woman and a watersnake (48). In Espinet's poem "Mama Glo," this figure is presented as the harbinger of the "womanvoice" that "breaks the ascendancy darkness with crystal light." Mama Glo, like Kincaid's Lucy and Senior's snake-woman, is a female trickster who reinvests the "demonic" mythic characteristics of the snake and the female derived from the garden myth. Drawing on the positive representation of the snake as the rainbow serpent god, Da in Dahomean myth, the god whose figure "shapes" the globe,[1] and African Caribbean representations of the trickster, these characterizations reverse the demonization of the "exotic," evil female in the garden myth while expressing alternative modes of being that make possible a reseeing and reshaping of the Caribbean and, beyond that, the world.

Set in colonial Trinidad, Senior's **"Arrival of the Snake-Woman"** presents a female trickster figure alienated from locals. The snake-woman, whose East Indian name is unknown, has been taken by Son-Son, the narrator's cousin, as his wife. Son-Son and Cephas learn about the "snake-women" from Moses, who was "married" to one "four months of the year," until he came home to Geraldine. Moses relates that they are called snake-women "from the way their body so neat and trim and they move their hip when they walk just like a snake and they don't wear no proper clothes just these thin little clothes-wrap, thinner than cobweb, yu can see every line of their body when they walk."[2] And he goes on to state that these snake-women are the "coolie-women" imported from India when "slavey-days end" and black people no longer wanted to work the cane "for them little scrumps a-pay" (3).

For the African Caribbeans the snake-woman embodies sexual desire; she is the perfumed Orient, the enticing and alluring feminine being. And to Ish, the young narrator, she represents something between species. He sees her as a cross between a woman and a snake, "half-snake, half-woman" (3). A sexual figure who transgresses species, she is also the alluring and mesmerizing exotic who represents "heathen" ways. Even before she arrives in the village, Ish and the men are attracted to her because she represents the antithesis of the good, Christian woman. They have been told by Parson Bedlow that the people of India are "heathens" who have refused to accept Christianity, and like the idolators in the Old Testament, the East Indians seem to worship gold; they adorn themselves with gold trinkets, bangles, and earrings. Moses has told the men and Ish that the snake-woman wears "gold bangles all the way up her arms and her ankles, gold earrings in her ears, gold chains around her neck, gold rings on her fingers and—a sure sign of heathenness, a gold ring in her nose." But Ish does not care about this "heathenness." Even though Ish is afraid of what the snake-woman represents, he is "already half in love" with her before she arrives (4).

As Ameena Gafoor points out, Miss Coolie, the snake-woman, "has effected a rewriting of the Garden of Eden myth" in which the snake "tempted the Mother of mankind with knowledge" that brought about humanity's downfall. Gafoor states that the snake-woman, who is the "'temptress,' brings knowledge which serves to awaken the peasantry, initiate social change, and create awareness of alternatives" (37). Although Gafoor recognizes the subversive nature of the snake-woman, she does not recognize how the snake-woman draws on the trickster figure and her "cross-species" nature to realize these alternative modes of being a Caribbean woman.

The snake-woman, who wears "saris as light as Anansi web" (9), is "magical." She arrives without their seeing, stands "framed in the doorway" (5), and Ish sees her black eyes that are "so faraway and sorrowful" that he feels that he is "looking deep into the Ganges" (6). Like the trickster figure Legba, who stands at the crossroads where humanity and the gods meet,[3] the snake-woman "framed in the doorway" becomes the threshold for transformation while also serving as a nexus between colonized women and men.

When the snake-woman first arrives, she is shunned by all the natives except Ish, who attempts to ignore the Parson's demonization of her. And because she refuses to convert to Christianity, the Parson refuses her son, Biya, treatment at the medical clinic. Parson Bedlow shouts: "Get that woman out of here! We cannot have her here! Unclean!" (29).

But the snake-woman demonstrates the self-sufficiency and resourcefulness of some women who have experienced alienation and demonization. She takes a donkey and travels alone with her child to seek medical care, and it is at the clinic that she finds that new worlds are opening up for people of color. When she returns, she counsels Ish, her guide and friend, to become a doctor and help other people who cannot receive treatment, "people like Biya and me," and she also suggests that Biya will grow up to be a lawyer so that he can help people get "paper for the land" (36).

From this experience Ish recognizes the snake-woman's courage, tenacity, and willfulness and also sees that there are "other paths . . . alternatives beyond the pure and narrow path to Heaven" (11-12). Through her adherence to her cultural system, she has also shown Ish that there is more than one way to live and be "saved" and more than one way to "become" Caribbean.

The snake-woman also transforms the assumptions the men and women of the village make about other colonized people. Although she is first considered a heathen by the natives, and the women dislike her because she is married to Son-Son, the father of some of their children, her presence and womanhood force them to recognize their commonalities.

When the snake-woman is about to give birth to Biya, she sends Ish for help and the women begin to change toward her, "for a baby after all, made all women the same." The women bring her gifts of "dukuno, bammies, plantain, and sugarhead," and Nana seemingly embraces the snake-woman by practicing native African-based rituals during Miss Coolie's postpartum period. "Nana allowed no one to see Miss Coolie and the child for nine days, nor fresh air nor sun to touch them; during that time they had to be in the darkness of the room together, for that was the only way to protect the frail new soul from evil spirits passing" (26).

Ish also recognizes the connections between the snake-woman and the women of the island. Even from the beginning he sees that the "snake-woman's skin was as dark as ours" (5), and after she converts so that Biya can attend the Parson's school, the only school in the area, Ish sees that "she looked no different from the black and mulatto women of the district carrying their goods to market" (39). Ish, transformed by his friendship with the snake-woman—"my own life was shaped by Miss Coolie's coming"—recognizes that Miss Coolie and the people of the district share common experiences. All of them have lived their lives as lower-class colonials, all have been British subjects, and all long for their real "homes," either the home before the African diaspora or the land of the Ganges. When Ish shows Miss Coolie the map of the world, "where our tiny island and India were located so far apart and then a map of India itself, like our island coloured red" she turns and "[wipes] her eyes with the edge of her Sari" (10). She tacitly recognizes their common experience of colonial subjectivity while also demonstrating that she continues to feel a desire for her native home and an ambivalence about her place in the Caribbean world.

After the government school opens, Miss Coolie takes her children out of the Parson's school and resumes her own customs; she wears her bangles and saris, gives her daughters Indian names, and places red dots on their foreheads. We see that her home is still an aspect of her being and her way of knowing when Ish states that "sometimes when I look into her eyes, I can still see the Ganges" (45).

By pointing out the common characteristics shared by the Indian Caribbean and African Caribbean women, by attributing the trickster nature to Miss Coolie, and by showing how Miss Coolie effects a transformation of consciousness among African Caribbean people, Senior advances an alliance that begins to break down divisions between groups that share the Caribbean world. Although Miss Coolie does not reshape the way the outside world views the Caribbean, she effects an internal change that draws groups together. In contrast, Kincaid's trickster Lucy begins to reshape the placement of the Caribbean in the world and in the mind of the "decolonized" person.

Notes

1. Thompson, 176.

2. Senior, *Arrival of the Snake-Woman and Other Stories*, 2-3.

3. Marks, 60.

Bibliography

Espinet, Rambai, ed. *Creation Fire: A Cafra Anthology of Caribbean Women's Poetry.* Toronto: Sistervision, 1990.

Gafoor, Ameena. "The Image of the Indo-Caribbean Woman in Olive Senior's 'The Arrival of the Snake-woman.'" *Callaloo* 16, no. 1 (1993): 34-43.

Marks, Herbert. "Voodoo in Haiti." In *Afro-Caribbean Religion,* ed. Brian Gates, 58-66. London: Ward Lock Educational, 1980.

Senior, Olive. *Arrival of the Snake-Woman and Other Stories.* Essex: Longman, 1989.

Thompson, Robert Faris. *Flash of the Spirit.* New York: Vintage, 1984.

FURTHER READING

Criticism

Beittel, Mark, and Giovanna Covi. "Talking of Households: Olive Senior's Postcolonial Identities." In *Nationalism vs. Internationalism: (Inter)National Dimensions of Literatures in English,* edited by Wolfgang Zach and Ken L. Goodwin, pp. 389-97. Tubingen, Germany: Stauffenburg, 1996.
    Explores Senior's treatment of family dynamics in her works.

Donnell, Alison. "The Short Fiction of Olive Senior." In *Caribbean Women Writers: Fiction in English,* pp. 117-43. New York: St. Martin's Press, 1999.
    Offers a thematic and stylistic overview of Senior's short fiction.

Goddard, Horace I. Review of *Discerner of Hearts and Other Stories,* by Olive Senior. *Kola* 12, no. 1 (winter 2000): 61-2.
    Favorable evaluation of *Discerner of Hearts.*

Morgan, Paula. "East/West Indian/Woman/Other: At the Crossroads of Gender and Ethnicity." *MaComère* 3 (2000): 107-22.
    Examines the portrayal of women in *Arrival of the Snake-Woman,* contending that "Senior raises salient issues that are being negotiated even today."

Renk, Kathleen J. "The Holy Family in the Colonial Garden." In *Caribbean Shadows and Victorian Ghosts: Woman's Writing and Decolonization,* pp. 80-3. Charlottesville: University Press of Virginia, 1999.
    Elucidates the troubled father-daughter relationship at the heart of Senior's story "Bright Thursdays."

Senior, Olive, and Kwame Dawes. "Olive Senior." In *Talk Yuh Talk: Interviews with Anglophone Caribbean Poets,* edited by Kwame Dawes, pp. 73-85. Charlottesville: University Press of Virginia, 2001.
    Senior discusses the major themes of her poetry and fiction, her preference for writing poetry, and the major influences on her work.

Senior, Olive, and Marlies Glaser. "'A Shared Culture': An Interview with Olive Senior." *Matatu,* no. 12 (1994): 77-84.
    Senior reflects on her use of oral and scribal traditions, her recollections of Jamaican village life, and the political aspects of her work.

Thompson-Deloatch, Thelma B. "Conflicting Concepts of Time and Space: Narrative Technique in Selected Short Fiction of Olive Senior." *MaComère* 3 (2000): 141-52.
    Argues that *Summer Lightning* incorporates "conflicting concepts of time, place, and space as a unifying motif."

Additional coverage of Senior's life and career is contained in the following sources published by Thomson Gale: *Black Writers,* **Ed. 3;** *Contemporary Authors,* **Vol. 154;** *Contemporary Authors New Revision Series,* **Vols. 86, 126;** *Contemporary Novelists,* **Ed. 7;** *Contemporary Poets,* **Ed. 7;** *Contemporary Women Poets;* *Dictionary of Literary Biography,* **Vol. 157;** *Encyclopedia of World Literature in the 20th Century,* **Ed. 3;** *Literature Resource Center,* **and** *Reference Guide to Short Fiction,* **Ed. 2.**

How to Use This Index

> **Calvino, Italo**
> 1923-1985 .... CLC **5, 8, 11, 22, 33, 39,**
> **73; SSC 3, 48**

list all author entries in the following Gale Literary Criticism series:

AAL = *Asian American Literature*
BG = *The Beat Generation: A Gale Critical Companion*
BLC = *Black Literature Criticism*
BLCS = *Black Literature Criticism Supplement*
CLC = *Contemporary Literary Criticism*
CLR = *Children's Literature Review*
CMLC = *Classical and Medieval Literature Criticism*
DC = *Drama Criticism*
HLC = *Hispanic Literature Criticism*
HLCS = *Hispanic Literature Criticism Supplement*
HR = *Harlem Renaissance: A Gale Critical Companion*
LC = *Literature Criticism from 1400 to 1800*
NCLC = *Nineteenth-Century Literature Criticism*
NNAL = *Native North American Literature*
PC = *Poetry Criticism*
SSC = *Short Story Criticism*
TCLC = *Twentieth-Century Literary Criticism*
WLC = *World Literature Criticism, 1500 to the Present*
WLCS = *World Literature Criticism Supplement*

The cross-references

> See also CA 85-88, 116; CANR 23, 61;
> DAM NOV; DLB 196; EW 13; MTCW 1, 2;
> RGSF 2; RGWL 2; SFW 4; SSFS 12

list all author entries in the following Gale biographical and literary sources:

AAYA = *Authors & Artists for Young Adults*
AFAW = *African American Writers*
AFW = *African Writers*
AITN = *Authors in the News*
AMW = *American Writers*
AMWR = *American Writers Retrospective Supplement*
AMWS = *American Writers Supplement*
ANW = *American Nature Writers*
AW = *Ancient Writers*
BEST = *Bestsellers*
BPFB = *Beacham's Encyclopedia of Popular Fiction: Biography and Resources*
BRW = *British Writers*
BRWS = *British Writers Supplement*
BW = *Black Writers*
BYA = *Beacham's Guide to Literature for Young Adults*
CA = *Contemporary Authors*
CAAS = *Contemporary Authors Autobiography Series*
CABS = *Contemporary Authors Bibliographical Series*
CAD = *Contemporary American Dramatists*
CANR = *Contemporary Authors New Revision Series*
CAP = *Contemporary Authors Permanent Series*
CBD = *Contemporary British Dramatists*
CCA = *Contemporary Canadian Authors*
CD = *Contemporary Dramatists*
CDALB = *Concise Dictionary of American Literary Biography*
CDALBS = *Concise Dictionary of American Literary Biography Supplement*
CDBLB = *Concise Dictionary of British Literary Biography*

CMW = *St. James Guide to Crime & Mystery Writers*

CN = *Contemporary Novelists*

CP = *Contemporary Poets*

CPW = *Contemporary Popular Writers*

CSW = *Contemporary Southern Writers*

CWD = *Contemporary Women Dramatists*

CWP = *Contemporary Women Poets*

CWRI = *St. James Guide to Children's Writers*

CWW = *Contemporary World Writers*

DA = *DISCovering Authors*

DA3 = *DISCovering Authors 3.0*

DAB = *DISCovering Authors: British Edition*

DAC = *DISCovering Authors: Canadian Edition*

DAM = *DISCovering Authors: Modules*

   DRAM: *Dramatists Module;* **MST:** *Most-studied Authors Module;*

   MULT: *Multicultural Authors Module;* **NOV:** *Novelists Module;*

   POET: *Poets Module;* **POP:** *Popular Fiction and Genre Authors Module*

DFS = *Drama for Students*

DLB = *Dictionary of Literary Biography*

DLBD = *Dictionary of Literary Biography Documentary Series*

DLBY = *Dictionary of Literary Biography Yearbook*

DNFS = *Literature of Developing Nations for Students*

EFS = *Epics for Students*

EXPN = *Exploring Novels*

EXPP = *Exploring Poetry*

EXPS = *Exploring Short Stories*

EW = *European Writers*

FANT = *St. James Guide to Fantasy Writers*

FW = *Feminist Writers*

GFL = *Guide to French Literature,* Beginnings to 1789, 1798 to the Present

GLL = *Gay and Lesbian Literature*

HGG = *St. James Guide to Horror, Ghost & Gothic Writers*

HW = *Hispanic Writers*

IDFW = *International Dictionary of Films and Filmmakers: Writers and Production Artists*

IDTP = *International Dictionary of Theatre: Playwrights*

LAIT = *Literature and Its Times*

LAW = *Latin American Writers*

JRDA = *Junior DISCovering Authors*

MAICYA = *Major Authors and Illustrators for Children and Young Adults*

MAICYAS = *Major Authors and Illustrators for Children and Young Adults Supplement*

MAWW = *Modern American Women Writers*

MJW = *Modern Japanese Writers*

MTCW = *Major 20th-Century Writers*

NCFS = *Nonfiction Classics for Students*

NFS = *Novels for Students*

PAB = *Poets: American and British*

PFS = *Poetry for Students*

RGAL = *Reference Guide to American Literature*

RGEL = *Reference Guide to English Literature*

RGSF = *Reference Guide to Short Fiction*

RGWL = *Reference Guide to World Literature*

RHW = *Twentieth-Century Romance and Historical Writers*

SAAS = *Something about the Author Autobiography Series*

SATA = *Something about the Author*

SFW = *St. James Guide to Science Fiction Writers*

SSFS = *Short Stories for Students*

TCWW = *Twentieth-Century Western Writers*

WLIT = *World Literature and Its Times*

WP = *World Poets*

YABC = *Yesterday's Authors of Books for Children*

YAW = *St. James Guide to Young Adult Writers*

Literary Criticism Series
Cumulative Author Index

20/1631
See Upward, Allen

A/C Cross
See Lawrence, T(homas) E(dward)

Abasiyanik, Sait Faik 1906-1954
See Sait Faik
See also CA 123

Abbey, Edward 1927-1989 .... **CLC 36, 59**
See also AMWS 13; ANW; CA 45-48; 128; CANR 2, 41, 131; DA3; DLB 256, 275; LATS 1:2; MTCW 2; TCWW 2

Abbott, Edwin A. 1838-1926 .... **TCLC 139**
See also DLB 178

Abbott, Lee K(ittredge) 1947- .... **CLC 48**
See also CA 124; CANR 51, 101; DLB 130

Abe, Kobo 1924-1993 ...... **CLC 8, 22, 53, 81; SSC 61; TCLC 131**
See also CA 65-68; 140; CANR 24, 60; DAM NOV; DFS 14; DLB 182; EWL 3; MJW; MTCW 1, 2; RGWL 3; SFW 4

Abe Kobo
See Abe, Kobo

Abelard, Peter c. 1079-c. 1142 ...... **CMLC 11**
See also DLB 115, 208

Abell, Kjeld 1901-1961 .... **CLC 15**
See also CA 191; 111; DLB 214; EWL 3

Abercrombie, Lascelles
1881-1938 .... **TCLC 141**
See also CA 112; DLB 19; RGEL 2

Abish, Walter 1931- .... **CLC 22; SSC 44**
See also CA 101; CANR 37, 114; CN 7; DLB 130, 227

Abrahams, Peter (Henry) 1919- .... **CLC 4**
See also AFW; BW 1; CA 57-60; CANR 26, 125; CDWLB 3; CN 7; DLB 117, 225; EWL 3; MTCW 1, 2; RGEL 2; WLIT 2

Abrams, M(eyer) H(oward) 1912- ... **CLC 24**
See also CA 57-60; CANR 13, 33; DLB 67

Abse, Dannie 1923- .... **CLC 7, 29; PC 41**
See also CA 53-56; CAAS 1; CANR 4, 46, 74, 124; CBD; CP 7; DAB; DAM POET; DLB 27, 245; MTCW 1

Abutsu 1222(?)-1283 .... **CMLC 46**
See Abutsu-ni

Abutsu-ni
See Abutsu
See also DLB 203

Achebe, (Albert) Chinua(lumogu)
1930- ..... **BLC 1; CLC 1, 3, 5, 7, 11, 26, 51, 75, 127, 152; WLC**
See also AAYA 15; AFW; BPFB 1; BRWC 2; BW 2, 3; CA 1-4R; CANR 6, 26, 47, 124; CDWLB 3; CLR 20; CN 7; CP 7; CWRI 5; DA; DA3; DAB; DAC; DAM MST, MULT, NOV; DLB 117; DNFS 1; EWL 3; EXPN; EXPS; LAIT 2; LATS

1:2; MAICYA 1, 2; MTCW 1, 2; NFS 2; RGEL 2; RGSF 2; SATA 38, 40; SATA-Brief 38; SSFS 3, 13; TWA; WLIT 2; WWE 1

Acker, Kathy 1948-1997 .... **CLC 45, 111**
See also AMWS 12; CA 117; 122; 162; CANR 55; CN 7

Ackroyd, Peter 1949- .... **CLC 34, 52, 140**
See also BRWS 6; CA 123; 127; CANR 51, 74, 99, 132; CN 7; DLB 155, 231; HGG; INT CA-127; MTCW 1; RHW; SATA 153; SUFW 2

Acorn, Milton 1923-1986 .... **CLC 15**
See also CA 103; CCA 1; DAC; DLB 53; INT CA-103

Adamov, Arthur 1908-1970 .... **CLC 4, 25**
See also CA 17-18; 25-28R; CAP 2; DAM DRAM; EWL 3; GFL 1789 to the Present; MTCW 1; RGWL 2, 3

Adams, Alice (Boyd) 1926-1999 .. **CLC 6, 13, 46; SSC 24**
See also CA 81-84; 179; CANR 26, 53, 75, 88; CN 7; CSW; DLB 234; DLBY 1986; INT CANR-26; MTCW 1, 2; SSFS 14

Adams, Andy 1859-1935 .... **TCLC 56**
See also TCWW 2; YABC 1

Adams, (Henry) Brooks
1848-1927 .... **TCLC 80**
See also CA 123; 193; DLB 47

Adams, Douglas (Noel) 1952-2001 .. **CLC 27, 60**
See also AAYA 4, 33; BEST 89:3; BYA 14; CA 106; 197; CANR 34, 64, 124; CPW; DA3; DAM POP; DLB 261; DLBY 1983; JRDA; MTCW 1; NFS 7; SATA 116; SATA-Obit 128; SFW 4

Adams, Francis 1862-1893 .... **NCLC 33**

Adams, Henry (Brooks)
1838-1918 .... **TCLC 4, 52**
See also AMW; CA 104; 133; CANR 77; DA; DAB; DAC; DAM MST; DLB 12, 47, 189, 284; EWL 3; MTCW 1; NCFS 1; RGAL 4; TUS

Adams, John 1735-1826 .... **NCLC 106**
See also DLB 31, 183

Adams, Richard (George) 1920- ... **CLC 4, 5, 18**
See also AAYA 16; AITN 1, 2; BPFB 1; BYA 5; CA 49-52; CANR 3, 35, 128; CLR 20; CN 7; DAM NOV; DLB 261; FANT; JRDA; LAIT 5; MAICYA 1, 2; MTCW 1, 2; NFS 11; SATA 7, 69; YAW

Adamson, Joy(-Friederike Victoria)
1910-1980 .... **CLC 17**
See also CA 69-72; 93-96; CANR 22; MTCW 1; SATA 11; SATA-Obit 22

Adcock, Fleur 1934- .... **CLC 41**
See also CA 25-28R; 182; CAAE 182; CAAS 23; CANR 11, 34, 69, 101; CP 7; CWP; DLB 40; FW; WWE 1

Addams, Charles (Samuel)
1912-1988 .... **CLC 30**
See also CA 61-64; 126; CANR 12, 79

Addams, (Laura) Jane 1860-1935 . **TCLC 76**
See also AMWS 1; CA 194; DLB 303; FW

Addison, Joseph 1672-1719 .... **LC 18**
See also BRW 3; CDBLB 1660-1789; DLB 101; RGEL 2; WLIT 3

Adler, Alfred (F.) 1870-1937 .... **TCLC 61**
See also CA 119; 159

Adler, C(arole) S(chwerdtfeger)
1932- .... **CLC 35**
See also AAYA 4, 41; CA 89-92; CANR 19, 40, 101; CLR 78; JRDA; MAICYA 1, 2; SAAS 15; SATA 26, 63, 102, 126; YAW

Adler, Renata 1938- .... **CLC 8, 31**
See also CA 49-52; CANR 95; CN 7; MTCW 1

Adorno, Theodor W(iesengrund)
1903-1969 .... **TCLC 111**
See also CA 89-92; 25-28R; CANR 89; DLB 242; EWL 3

Ady, Endre 1877-1919 .... **TCLC 11**
See also CA 107; CDWLB 4; DLB 215; EW 9; EWL 3

A.E. .... **TCLC 3, 10**
See Russell, George William
See also DLB 19

Aelfric c. 955-c. 1010 .... **CMLC 46**
See also DLB 146

Aeschines c. 390B.C.-c. 320B.C. .... **CMLC 47**
See also DLB 176

Aeschylus 525(?)B.C.-456(?)B.C. .. **CMLC 11, 51; DC 8; WLCS**
See also AW 1; CDWLB 1; DA; DAB; DAC; DAM DRAM, MST; DFS 5, 10; DLB 176; LMFS 1; RGWL 2, 3; TWA

Aesop 620(?)B.C.-560(?)B.C. .... **CMLC 24**
See also CLR 14; MAICYA 1, 2; SATA 64

Affable Hawk
See MacCarthy, Sir (Charles Otto) Desmond

Africa, Ben
See Bosman, Herman Charles

Afton, Effie
See Harper, Frances Ellen Watkins

Agapida, Fray Antonio
See Irving, Washington

Agee, James (Rufus) 1909-1955 ...... **TCLC 1, 19**
See also AAYA 44; AITN 1; AMW; CA 108; 148; CANR 131; CDALB 1941-1968; DAM NOV; DLB 2, 26, 152; DLBY 1989; EWL 3; LAIT 3; LATS 1:2; MTCW 1; RGAL 4; TUS

Aghill, Gordon
See Silverberg, Robert

Agnon, S(hmuel) Y(osef Halevi)
1888-1970 .... **CLC 4, 8, 14; SSC 30; TCLC 151**
See also CA 17-18; 25-28R; CANR 60, 102; CAP 2; EWL 3; MTCW 1, 2; RGSF 2; RGWL 2, 3

Agrippa von Nettesheim, Henry Cornelius
1486-1535 .... **LC 27**

Aguilera Malta, Demetrio
1909-1981 .... **HLCS 1**
See also CA 111; 124; CANR 87; DAM MULT, NOV; DLB 145; EWL 3; HW 1; RGWL 3

Agustini, Delmira 1886-1914 .... **HLCS 1**
See also CA 166; DLB 290; HW 1, 2; LAW

Aherne, Owen
See Cassill, R(onald) V(erlin)

Ai 1947- .... **CLC 4, 14, 69**
See also CA 85-88; CAAS 13; CANR 70; DLB 120; PFS 16

Aickman, Robert (Fordyce)
1914-1981 .... **CLC 57**
See also CA 5-8R; CANR 3, 72, 100; DLB 261; HGG; SUFW 1, 2

Aidoo, (Christina) Ama Ata
1942- .... **BLCS; CLC 177**
See also AFW; BW 1; CA 101; CANR 62; CD 5; CDWLB 3; CN 7; CWD; CWP; DLB 117; DNFS 1, 2; EWL 3; FW; WLIT 2

Aiken, Conrad (Potter) 1889-1973 .... **CLC 1, 3, 5, 10, 52; PC 26; SSC 9**
See also AMW; CA 5-8R; 45-48; CANR 4, 60; CDALB 1929-1941; DAM NOV, POET; DLB 9, 45, 102; EWL 3; EXPS; HGG; MTCW 1, 2; RGAL 4; RGSF 2; SATA 3, 30; SSFS 8; TUS

Aiken, Joan (Delano) 1924-2004 ...... **CLC 35**
See also AAYA 1, 25; CA 9-12R; 182; 223; CAAE 182; CANR 4, 23, 34, 64, 121; CLR 1, 19, 90; DLB 161; FANT; HGG; JRDA; MAICYA 1, 2; MTCW 1; RHW; SAAS 1; SATA 2, 30, 73; SATA-Essay 109; SATA-Obit 152; SUFW 2; WYA; YAW

Ainsworth, William Harrison
1805-1882 .... **NCLC 13**
See also DLB 21; HGG; RGEL 2; SATA 24; SUFW 1

Aitmatov, Chingiz (Torekulovich)
1928- .... **CLC 71**
See Aytmatov, Chingiz
See also CA 103; CANR 38; CWW 2; DLB 302; MTCW 1; RGSF 2; SATA 56

Akers, Floyd
See Baum, L(yman) Frank

Akhmadulina, Bella Akhatovna
1937- .... **CLC 53; PC 43**
See also CA 65-68; CWP; CWW 2; DAM POET; EWL 3

Akhmatova, Anna 1888-1966 ..... **CLC 11, 25, 64, 126; PC 2, 55**
See also CA 19-20; 25-28R; CANR 35; CAP 1; DA3; DAM POET; DLB 295; EW 10; EWL 3; MTCW 1, 2; PFS 18; RGWL 2, 3

Aksakov, Sergei Timofeyvich
1791-1859 .... **NCLC 2**
See also DLB 198

Aksenov, Sergei (Pavlovich)
See Aksyonov, Vassily (Pavlovich)
See also CWW 2

Aksenov, Vassily
See Aksyonov, Vassily (Pavlovich)

Akst, Daniel 1956- .... **CLC 109**
See also CA 161; CANR 110

Aksyonov, Vassily (Pavlovich)
1932- .... **CLC 22, 37, 101**
See Aksenov, Vasilii (Pavlovich)
See also CA 53-56; CANR 12, 48, 77; DLB 302; EWL 3

Akutagawa Ryunosuke 1892-1927 ... **SSC 44; TCLC 16**
See also CA 117; 154; DLB 180; EWL 3; MJW; RGSF 2; RGWL 2, 3

Alabaster, William 1568-1640 .... **LC 90**
See also DLB 132; RGEL 2

Alain 1868-1951 .... **TCLC 41**
See also CA 163; EWL 3; GFL 1789 to the Present

Alain de Lille c. 1116-c. 1203 .... **CMLC 53**
See also DLB 208

Alain-Fournier .... **TCLC 6**
See Fournier, Henri-Alban
See also DLB 65; EWL 3; GFL 1789 to the Present; RGWL 2, 3

Al-Amin, Jamil Abdullah 1943- .... **BLC 1**
See also BW 1, 3; CA 112; 125; CANR 82; DAM MULT

Alanus de Insluis
See Alain de Lille

Alarcon, Pedro Antonio de
1833-1891 .... **NCLC 1; SSC 64**

Alas (y Urena), Leopoldo (Enrique Garcia)
1852-1901 .... **TCLC 29**
See also CA 113; 131; HW 1; RGSF 2

Albee, Edward (Franklin) (III)
1928- ... **CLC 1, 2, 3, 5, 9, 11, 13, 25, 53, 86, 113; DC 11; WLC**
See also AAYA 51; AITN 1; AMW; CA 5-8R; CABS 3; CAD; CANR 8, 54, 74, 124; CD 5; CDALB 1941-1968; DA; DA3; DAB; DAC; DAM DRAM, MST; DFS 2, 3, 8, 10, 13, 14; DLB 7, 266; EWL 3; INT CANR-8; LAIT 4; LMFS 2; MTCW 1, 2; RGAL 4; TUS

Alberti (Merello), Rafael
See Alberti, Rafael
See also CWW 2

Alberti, Rafael 1902-1999 .... **CLC 7**
See Alberti (Merello), Rafael
See also CA 85-88; 185; CANR 81; DLB 108; EWL 3; HW 2; RGWL 2, 3

Albert the Great 1193(?)-1280 ...... **CMLC 16**
See also DLB 115

Alcaeus c. 620B.C.- .... **CMLC 65**
See also DLB 176

Alcala-Galiano, Juan Valera y
See Valera y Alcala-Galiano, Juan

Alcayaga, Lucila Godoy
See Godoy Alcayaga, Lucila

Alcott, Amos Bronson 1799-1888 .... **NCLC 1**
See also DLB 1, 223

Alcott, Louisa May 1832-1888 . **NCLC 6, 58, 83; SSC 27; WLC**
See also AAYA 20; AMWS 1; BPFB 1; BYA 2; CDALB 1865-1917; CLR 1, 38; DA; DA3; DAB; DAC; DAM MST, NOV; DLB 1, 42, 79, 223, 239, 242; DLBD 14; FW; JRDA; LAIT 2; MAICYA 1, 2; NFS 12; RGAL 4; SATA 100; TUS; WCH; WYA; YABC 1; YAW

Alcuin c. 730-804 .... **CMLC 69**
See also DLB 148

Aldanov, M. A.
See Aldanov, Mark (Alexandrovich)

Aldanov, Mark (Alexandrovich)
1886(?)-1957 .... **TCLC 23**
See also CA 118; 181

Aldington, Richard 1892-1962 .... **CLC 49**
See also CA 85-88; CANR 45; DLB 20, 36, 100, 149; LMFS 2; RGEL 2

Aldiss, Brian W(ilson) 1925- . **CLC 5, 14, 40; SSC 36**
See also AAYA 42; CA 5-8R, 190; CAAE 190; CAAS 2; CANR 5, 28, 64, 121; CN 7; DAM NOV; DLB 14, 261, 271; MTCW 1, 2; SATA 34; SFW 4

Aldrich, Bess Streeter
1881-1954 .... **TCLC 125**
See also CLR 70

Alegria, Claribel
See Alegria, Claribel (Joy)
See also CWW 2; DLB 145, 283

Alegria, Claribel (Joy) 1924- .... **CLC 75; HLCS 1; PC 26**
See Alegria, Claribel
See also CA 131; CAAS 15; CANR 66, 94, 134; DAM MULT; EWL 3; HW 1; MTCW 1; PFS 21

Alegria, Fernando 1918- .... **CLC 57**
See also CA 9-12R; CANR 5, 32, 72; EWL 3; HW 1, 2

Aleichem, Sholom .... **SSC 33; TCLC 1, 35**
See Rabinovitch, Sholem
See also TWA

Aleixandre, Vicente 1898-1984 .... **HLCS 1; TCLC 113**
See also CANR 81; DLB 108; EWL 3; HW 2; RGWL 2, 3

Aleman, Mateo 1547-1615(?) .... **LC 81**

Alencon, Marguerite d'
See de Navarre, Marguerite

Alepoudelis, Odysseus
See Elytis, Odysseus
See also CWW 2

Aleshkovsky, Joseph 1929-
See Aleshkovsky, Yuz
See also CA 121; 128

Aleshkovsky, Yuz .... **CLC 44**
See Aleshkovsky, Joseph

Alexander, Lloyd (Chudley) 1924- ... **CLC 35**
See also AAYA 1, 27; BPFB 1; BYA 5, 6, 7, 9, 10, 11; CA 1-4R; CANR 1, 24, 38, 55, 113; CLR 1, 5, 48; CWRI 5; DLB 52; FANT; JRDA; MAICYA 1, 2; MAICYAS 1; MTCW 1; SAAS 19; SATA 3, 49, 81, 129, 135; SUFW; TUS; WYA; YAW

Alexander, Meena 1951- .... **CLC 121**
See also CA 115; CANR 38, 70; CP 7; CWP; FW

Alexander, Samuel 1859-1938 .... **TCLC 77**

Alexie, Sherman (Joseph, Jr.)
1966- .... **CLC 96, 154; NNAL; PC 53**
See also AAYA 28; BYA 15; CA 138; CANR 65, 95, 133; DA3; DAM MULT; DLB 175, 206, 278; LATS 1:2; MTCW 1; NFS 17; SSFS 18

al-Farabi 870(?)-950 .... **CMLC 58**
See also DLB 115

Alfau, Felipe 1902-1999 .... **CLC 66**
See also CA 137

Alfieri, Vittorio 1749-1803 .... **NCLC 101**
See also EW 4; RGWL 2, 3

Alfred, Jean Gaston
See Ponge, Francis

Alger, Horatio, Jr. 1832-1899 .... **NCLC 8, 83**
See also CLR 87; DLB 42; LAIT 2; RGAL 4; SATA 16; TUS

Al-Ghazali, Muhammad ibn Muhammad
1058-1111 .... **CMLC 50**
See also DLB 115

Algren, Nelson 1909-1981 ..... **CLC 4, 10, 33; SSC 33**
See also AMWS 9; BPFB 1; CA 13-16R; 103; CANR 20, 61; CDALB 1941-1968; DLB 9; DLBY 1981, 1982, 2000; EWL 3; MTCW 1, 2; RGAL 4; RGSF 2

al-Hariri, al-Qasim ibn 'Ali Abu Muhammad al-Basri
1054-1122 .... **CMLC 63**
See also RGWL 3

Ali, Ahmed 1908-1998 .... **CLC 69**
See also CA 25-28R; CANR 15, 34; EWL 3

Ali, Tariq 1943- .... **CLC 173**
See also CA 25-28R; CANR 10, 99

Alighieri, Dante
See Dante

Allan, John B.
See Westlake, Donald E(dwin)

Allan, Sidney
See Hartmann, Sadakichi

Allan, Sydney
See Hartmann, Sadakichi

Allard, Janet .... **CLC 59**

Allen, Edward 1948- .... **CLC 59**

Allen, Fred 1894-1956 .... **TCLC 87**

Allen, Paula Gunn 1939- ..... **CLC 84; NNAL**
See also AMWS 4; CA 112; 143; CANR 63, 130; CWP; DA3; DAM MULT; DLB 175; FW; MTCW 1; RGAL 4

Allen, Roland
See Ayckbourn, Alan

Allen, Sarah A.
See Hopkins, Pauline Elizabeth

Allen, Sidney H.
See Hartmann, Sadakichi

Allen, Woody 1935- .... **CLC 16, 52, 195**
See also AAYA 10, 51; CA 33-36R; CANR 27, 38, 63, 128; DAM POP; DLB 44; MTCW 1

Allende, Isabel 1942- ... **CLC 39, 57, 97, 170; HLC 1; SSC 65; WLCS**
See also AAYA 18; CA 125; 130; CANR 51, 74, 129; CDWLB 3; CLR 99; CWW 2; DA3; DAM MULT, NOV; DLB 145; DNFS 1; EWL 3; FW; HW 1, 2; INT CA-130; LAIT 5; LAWS 1; LMFS 2; MTCW 1, 2; NCFS 1; NFS 6, 18; RGSF 2; RGWL 3; SSFS 11, 16; WLIT 1

Alleyn, Ellen
See Rossetti, Christina (Georgina)

Alleyne, Carla D. .... **CLC 65**

Allingham, Margery (Louise)
1904-1966 .... **CLC 19**
See also CA 5-8R; 25-28R; CANR 4, 58; CMW 4; DLB 77; MSW; MTCW 1, 2

Allingham, William 1824-1889 ...... **NCLC 25**
See also DLB 35; RGEL 2

Allison, Dorothy E. 1949- .... **CLC 78, 153**
See also AAYA 53; CA 140; CANR 66, 107; CSW; DA3; FW; MTCW 1; NFS 11; RGAL 4

Alloula, Malek .... **CLC 65**

Allston, Washington 1779-1843 .... **NCLC 2**
See also DLB 1, 235

Almedingen, E. M. .... **CLC 12**
See Almedingen, Martha Edith von
See also SATA 3

Almedingen, Martha Edith von 1898-1971
See Almedingen, E. M.
See also CA 1-4R; CANR 1

Almodovar, Pedro 1949(?)- .... **CLC 114; HLCS 1**
See also CA 133; CANR 72; HW 2

Almqvist, Carl Jonas Love
1793-1866 .... **NCLC 42**

al-Mutanabbi, Ahmad ibn al-Husayn Abu al-Tayyib al-Jufi al-Kindi
915-965 .... **CMLC 66**
See also RGWL 3

Alonso, Damaso 1898-1990 .... **CLC 14**
See also CA 110; 131; 130; CANR 72; DLB 108; EWL 3; HW 1, 2

Alov
See Gogol, Nikolai (Vasilyevich)

al'Sadaawi, Nawal
See El Saadawi, Nawal
See also FW

Al Siddik
See Rolfe, Frederick (William Serafino Austin Lewis Mary)
See also GLL 1; RGEL 2

Alta 1942- .... **CLC 19**
See also CA 57-60

Alter, Robert B(ernard) 1935- .... **CLC 34**
See also CA 49-52; CANR 1, 47, 100

Alther, Lisa 1944- .... **CLC 7, 41**
See also BPFB 1; CA 65-68; CAAS 30; CANR 12, 30, 51; CN 7; CSW; GLL 2; MTCW 1

Althusser, L.
See Althusser, Louis

Althusser, Louis 1918-1990 .... **CLC 106**
See also CA 131; 132; CANR 102; DLB 242

Altman, Robert 1925- .... **CLC 16, 116**
See also CA 73-76; CANR 43

Alurista .... **HLCS 1**
See Urista (Heredia), Alberto (Baltazar)
See also DLB 82; LLW 1

Alvarez, A(lfred) 1929- .... **CLC 5, 13**
See also CA 1-4R; CANR 3, 33, 63, 101, 134; CN 7; CP 7; DLB 14, 40

Alvarez, Alejandro Rodriguez 1903-1965
See Casona, Alejandro
See also CA 131; 93-96; HW 1

Alvarez, Julia 1950- .... **CLC 93; HLCS 1**
See also AAYA 25; AMWS 7; CA 147; CANR 69, 101, 133; DA3; DLB 282; LATS 1:2; LLW 1; MTCW 1; NFS 5, 9; SATA 129; WLIT 1

Alvaro, Corrado 1896-1956 .... **TCLC 60**
See also CA 163; DLB 264; EWL 3

Amado, Jorge 1912-2001 ... **CLC 13, 40, 106; HLC 1**
See also CA 77-80; 201; CANR 35, 74; CWW 2; DAM MULT, NOV; DLB 113, 307; EWL 3; HW 2; LAW; LAWS 1; MTCW 1, 2; RGWL 2, 3; TWA; WLIT 1

Ambler, Eric 1909-1998 .... **CLC 4, 6, 9**
See also BRWS 4; CA 9-12R; 171; CANR 7, 38, 74; CMW 4; CN 7; DLB 77; MSW; MTCW 1, 2; TEA

Ambrose, Stephen E(dward)
1936-2002 .... **CLC 145**
See also AAYA 44; CA 1-4R; 209; CANR 3, 43, 57, 83, 105; NCFS 2; SATA 40, 138

Amichai, Yehuda 1924-2000 .. **CLC 9, 22, 57, 116; PC 38**
See also CA 85-88; 189; CANR 46, 60, 99, 132; CWW 2; EWL 3; MTCW 1

Amichai, Yehudah
See Amichai, Yehuda

Amiel, Henri Frederic 1821-1881 .... **NCLC 4**
See also DLB 217

Amis, Kingsley (William)
1922-1995 ...... **CLC 1, 2, 3, 5, 8, 13, 40, 44, 129**
See also AITN 2; BPFB 1; BRWS 2; CA 9-12R; 150; CANR 8, 28, 54; CDBLB 1945-1960; CN 7; CP 7; DA; DA3; DAB; DAC; DAM MST, NOV; DLB 15, 27, 100, 139; DLBY 1996; EWL 3; HGG; INT CANR-8; MTCW 1, 2; RGEL 2; RGSF 2; SFW 4

Amis, Martin (Louis) 1949- .... **CLC 4, 9, 38, 62, 101**
See also BEST 90:3; BRWS 4; CA 65-68; CANR 8, 27, 54, 73, 95, 132; CN 7; DA3; DLB 14, 194; EWL 3; INT CANR-27; MTCW 1

Ammianus Marcellinus c. 330-c. 395 .... **CMLC 60**
See also AW 2; DLB 211

Ammons, A(rchie) R(andolph)
1926-2001 ...... **CLC 2, 3, 5, 8, 9, 25, 57, 108; PC 16**
See also AITN 1; AMWS 7; CA 9-12R; 193; CANR 6, 36, 51, 73, 107; CP 7; CSW; DAM POET; DLB 5, 165; EWL 3; MTCW 1, 2; PFS 19; RGAL 4

Amo, Tauraatua i
See Adams, Henry (Brooks)

Amory, Thomas 1691(?)-1788 .... **LC 48**
See also DLB 39

Anand, Mulk Raj 1905-2004 ...... **CLC 23, 93**
See also CA 65-68; CANR 32, 64; CN 7; DAM NOV; EWL 3; MTCW 1, 2; RGSF 2

Anatol
See Schnitzler, Arthur

Anaximander c. 611B.C.-c. 546B.C. .... **CMLC 22**

Anaya, Rudolfo A(lfonso) 1937- ...... **CLC 23, 148; HLC 1**
See also AAYA 20; BYA 13; CA 45-48; CAAS 4; CANR 1, 32, 51, 124; CN 7; DAM MULT, NOV; DLB 82, 206, 278; HW 1; LAIT 4; LLW 1; MTCW 1, 2; NFS 12; RGAL 4; RGSF 2; WLIT 1

Andersen, Hans Christian
1805-1875 .... **NCLC 7, 79; SSC 6, 56; WLC**
See also AAYA 57; CLR 6; DA; DA3; DAB; DAC; DAM MST, POP; EW 6; MAICYA 1, 2; RGSF 2; RGWL 2, 3; SATA 100; TWA; WCH; YABC 1

Anderson, C. Farley
See Mencken, H(enry) L(ouis); Nathan, George Jean

Anderson, Jessica (Margaret) Queale
1916- .... **CLC 37**
See also CA 9-12R; CANR 4, 62; CN 7

Anderson, Jon (Victor) 1940- .... **CLC 9**
See also CA 25-28R; CANR 20; DAM POET

Anderson, Lindsay (Gordon)
1923-1994 .... **CLC 20**
See also CA 125; 128; 146; CANR 77

Anderson, Maxwell 1888-1959 .... **TCLC 2, 144**
See also CA 105; 152; DAM DRAM; DFS 16, 20; DLB 7, 228; MTCW 2; RGAL 4

Anderson, Poul (William)
1926-2001 .... **CLC 15**
See also AAYA 5, 34; BPFB 1; BYA 6, 8, 9; CA 1-4R; 181; 199; CAAE 181; CAAS 2; CANR 2, 15, 34, 64, 110; CLR 58; DLB 8; FANT; INT CANR-15; MTCW 1, 2; SATA 90; SATA-Brief 39; SATA-Essay 106; SCFW 2; SFW 4; SUFW 1, 2

Anderson, Robert (Woodruff)
1917- .... **CLC 23**
See also AITN 1; CA 21-24R; CANR 32; DAM DRAM; DLB 7; LAIT 5

Anderson, Roberta Joan
See Mitchell, Joni

Anderson, Sherwood 1876-1941 .. **SSC 1, 46; TCLC 1, 10, 24, 123; WLC**
See also AAYA 30; AMW; AMWC 2; BPFB 1; CA 104; 121; CANR 61; CDALB 1917-1929; DA; DA3; DAB; DAC; DAM MST, NOV; DLB 4, 9, 86; DLBD 1; EWL 3; EXPS; GLL 2; MTCW 1, 2; NFS 4; RGAL 4; RGSF 2; SSFS 4, 10, 11; TUS

Andier, Pierre
See Desnos, Robert

Andouard
See Giraudoux, Jean(-Hippolyte)

Andrade, Carlos Drummond de ..... **CLC 18**
See Drummond de Andrade, Carlos
See also EWL 3; RGWL 2, 3
Andrade, Mario de .... **TCLC 43**
See de Andrade, Mario
See also DLB 307; EWL 3; LAW; RGWL
2, 3; WLIT 1
Andreae, Johann V(alentin)
1586-1654 .... **LC 32**
See also DLB 164
Andreas Capellanus fl. c. 1185- .... **CMLC 45**
See also DLB 208
Andreas-Salome, Lou 1861-1937 ... **TCLC 56**
See also CA 178; DLB 66
Andreev, Leonid
See Andreyev, Leonid (Nikolaevich)
See also DLB 295; EWL 3
Andress, Lesley
See Sanders, Lawrence
Andrewes, Lancelot 1555-1626 .... **LC 5**
See also DLB 151, 172
Andrews, Cicily Fairfield
See West, Rebecca
Andrews, Elton V.
See Pohl, Frederik
Andreyev, Leonid (Nikolaevich)
1871-1919 .... **TCLC 3**
See Andreev, Leonid
See also CA 104; 185
Andric, Ivo 1892-1975 .... **CLC 8; SSC 36;
TCLC 135**
See also CA 81-84; 57-60; CANR 43, 60;
CDWLB 4; DLB 147; EW 11; EWL 3;
MTCW 1; RGSF 2; RGWL 2, 3
Androvar
See Prado (Calvo), Pedro
Angelique, Pierre
See Bataille, Georges
Angell, Roger 1920- .... **CLC 26**
See also CA 57-60; CANR 13, 44, 70; DLB
171, 185
Angelou, Maya 1928- ... **BLC 1; CLC 12, 35,
64, 77, 155; PC 32; WLCS**
See also AAYA 7, 20; AMWS 4; BPFB 1;
BW 2, 3; BYA 2; CA 65-68; CANR 19,
42, 65, 111, 133; CDALBS; CLR 53; CP
7; CPW; CSW; CWP; DA; DA3; DAB;
DAC; DAM MST, MULT, POET, POP;
DLB 38; EWL 3; EXPN; EXPP; LAIT 4;
MAICYA 2; MAICYAS 1; MAWW;
MTCW 1, 2; NCFS 2; NFS 2; PFS 2, 3;
RGAL 4; SATA 49, 136; WYA; YAW
Angouleme, Marguerite d'
See de Navarre, Marguerite
Anna Comnena 1083-1153 .... **CMLC 25**
Annensky, Innokentii Fedorovich
See Annensky, Innokenty (Fyodorovich)
See also DLB 295
Annensky, Innokenty (Fyodorovich)
1856-1909 .... **TCLC 14**
See also CA 110; 155; EWL 3
Annunzio, Gabriele d'
See D'Annunzio, Gabriele
Anodos
See Coleridge, Mary E(lizabeth)
Anon, Charles Robert
See Pessoa, Fernando (Antonio Nogueira)
Anouilh, Jean (Marie Lucien Pierre)
1910-1987 . **CLC 1, 3, 8, 13, 40, 50; DC
8, 21**
See also CA 17-20R; 123; CANR 32; DAM
DRAM; DFS 9, 10, 19; EW 13; EWL 3;
GFL 1789 to the Present; MTCW 1, 2;
RGWL 2, 3; TWA
Anselm of Canterbury
1033(?)-1109 .... **CMLC 67**
See also DLB 115
Anthony, Florence
See Ai

Anthony, John
See Ciardi, John (Anthony)
Anthony, Peter
See Shaffer, Anthony (Joshua); Shaffer, Peter (Levin)
Anthony, Piers 1934- .... **CLC 35**
See also AAYA 11, 48; BYA 7; CA 200;
CAAE 200; CANR 28, 56, 73, 102, 133;
CPW; DAM POP; DLB 8; FANT; MAICYA 2; MAICYAS 1; SAAS
22; SATA 84, 129; SATA-Essay 129; SFW
4; SUFW 1, 2; YAW
Anthony, Susan B(rownell)
1820-1906 .... **TCLC 84**
See also CA 211; FW
Antiphon c. 480B.C.-c. 411B.C. .... **CMLC 55**
Antoine, Marc
See Proust, (Valentin-Louis-George-Eugene)
Marcel
Antoninus, Brother
See Everson, William (Oliver)
Antonioni, Michelangelo 1912- .... **CLC 20,
144**
See also CA 73-76; CANR 45, 77
Antschel, Paul 1920-1970
See Celan, Paul
See also CA 85-88; CANR 33, 61; MTCW
1; PFS 21
Anwar, Chairil 1922-1949 .... **TCLC 22**
See Chairil Anwar
See also CA 121; 219; RGWL 3
Anzaldua, Gloria (Evanjelina)
1942-2004 .... **HLCS 1**
See also CA 175; 227; CSW; CWP; DLB
122; FW; LLW 1; RGAL 4; SATA-Obit
154
Apess, William 1798-1839(?) .... **NCLC 73;
NNAL**
See also DAM MULT; DLB 175, 243
Apollinaire, Guillaume 1880-1918 .... **PC 7;
TCLC 3, 8, 51**
See Kostrowitzki, Wilhelm Apollinaris de
See also CA 152; DAM POET; DLB 258;
EW 9; EWL 3; GFL 1789 to the Present;
MTCW 1; RGWL 2, 3; TWA; WP
Apollonius of Rhodes
See Apollonius Rhodius
See also AW 1; RGWL 2, 3
Apollonius Rhodius c. 300B.C.-c.
220B.C. .... **CMLC 28**
See Apollonius of Rhodes
See also DLB 176
Appelfeld, Aharon 1932- ... **CLC 23, 47; SSC
42**
See also CA 112; 133; CANR 86; CWW 2;
DLB 299; EWL 3; RGSF 2
Apple, Max (Isaac) 1941- .... **CLC 9, 33; SSC
50**
See also CA 81-84; CANR 19, 54; DLB
130
Appleman, Philip (Dean) 1926- .... **CLC 51**
See also CA 13-16R; CAAS 18; CANR 6,
29, 56
Appleton, Lawrence
See Lovecraft, H(oward) P(hillips)
Apteryx
See Eliot, T(homas) S(tearns)
Apuleius, (Lucius Madaurensis)
125(?)-175(?) .... **CMLC 1**
See also AW 2; CDWLB 1; DLB 211;
RGWL 2, 3; SUFW
Aquin, Hubert 1929-1977 .... **CLC 15**
See also CA 105; DLB 53; EWL 3
Aquinas, Thomas 1224(?)-1274 ..... **CMLC 33**
See also DLB 115; EW 1; TWA

Aragon, Louis 1897-1982 .... **CLC 3, 22;
TCLC 123**
See also CA 69-72; 108; CANR 28, 71;
DAM NOV, POET; DLB 72, 258; EW 11;
EWL 3; GFL 1789 to the Present; GLL 2;
LMFS 2; MTCW 1, 2; RGWL 2, 3
Arany, Janos 1817-1882 .... **NCLC 34**
Aranyos, Kakay 1847-1910
See Mikszath, Kalman
Aratus of Soli c. 315B.C.-c.
240B.C. .... **CMLC 64**
See also DLB 176
Arbuthnot, John 1667-1735 .... **LC 1**
See also DLB 101
Archer, Herbert Winslow
See Mencken, H(enry) L(ouis)
Archer, Jeffrey (Howard) 1940- .... **CLC 28**
See also AAYA 16; BEST 89:3; BPFB 1;
CA 77-80; CANR 22, 52, 95; CPW; DA3;
DAM POP; INT CANR-22
Archer, Jules 1915- .... **CLC 12**
See also CA 9-12R; CANR 6, 69; SAAS 5;
SATA 4, 85
Archer, Lee
See Ellison, Harlan (Jay)
Archilochus c. 7th cent. B.C.- .... **CMLC 44**
See also DLB 176
Arden, John 1930- .... **CLC 6, 13, 15**
See also BRWS 2; CA 13-16R; CAAS 4;
CANR 31, 65, 67, 124; CBD; CD 5;
DAM DRAM; DFS 9; DLB 13, 245;
EWL 3; MTCW 1
Arenas, Reinaldo 1943-1990 .. **CLC 41; HLC
1**
See also CA 124; 128; 133; CANR 73, 106;
DAM MULT; DLB 145; EWL 3; GLL 2;
HW 1; LAW; LAWS 1; MTCW 1; RGSF
2; RGWL 3; WLIT 1
Arendt, Hannah 1906-1975 .... **CLC 66, 98**
See also CA 17-20R; 61-64; CANR 26, 60;
DLB 242; MTCW 1, 2
Aretino, Pietro 1492-1556 .... **LC 12**
See also RGWL 2, 3
Arghezi, Tudor .... **CLC 80**
See Theodorescu, Ion N.
See also CA 167; CDWLB 4; DLB 220;
EWL 3
Arguedas, Jose Maria 1911-1969 .... **CLC 10,
18; HLCS 1; TCLC 147**
See also CA 89-92; CANR 73; DLB 113;
EWL 3; HW 1; LAW; RGWL 2, 3; WLIT
1
Argueta, Manlio 1936- .... **CLC 31**
See also CA 131; CANR 73; CWW 2; DLB
145; EWL 3; HW 1; RGWL 3
Arias, Ron(ald Francis) 1941- .... **HLC 1**
See also CA 131; CANR 81; DAM MULT;
DLB 82; HW 1, 2; MTCW 2
Ariosto, Ludovico 1474-1533 ... **LC 6, 87; PC
42**
See also EW 2; RGWL 2, 3
Aristides
See Epstein, Joseph
Aristophanes 450B.C.-385B.C. .... **CMLC 4,
51; DC 2; WLCS**
See also AW 1; CDWLB 1; DA; DA3;
DAB; DAC; DAM DRAM, MST; DFS
10; DLB 176; LMFS 1; RGWL 2, 3; TWA
Aristotle 384B.C.-322B.C. .... **CMLC 31;
WLCS**
See also AW 1; CDWLB 1; DA; DA3;
DAB; DAC; DAM MST; DLB 176;
RGWL 2, 3; TWA
Arlt, Roberto (Godofredo Christophersen)
1900-1942 .... **HLC 1; TCLC 29**
See also CA 123; 131; CANR 67; DAM
MULT; DLB 305; EWL 3; HW 1, 2; LAW

Armah, Ayi Kwei 1939- . **BLC 1; CLC 5, 33, 136**
See also AFW; BRWS 10; BW 1; CA 61-64; CANR 21, 64; CDWLB 3; CN 7; DAM MULT, POET; DLB 117; EWL 3; MTCW 1; WLIT 2

Armatrading, Joan 1950- .... **CLC 17**
See also CA 114; 186

Armitage, Frank
See Carpenter, John (Howard)

Armstrong, Jeannette (C.) 1948- .... **NNAL**
See also CA 149; CCA 1; CN 7; DAC; SATA 102

Arnette, Robert
See Silverberg, Robert

Arnim, Achim von (Ludwig Joachim von Arnim) 1781-1831 ..... **NCLC 5; SSC 29**
See also DLB 90

Arnim, Bettina von 1785-1859 ...... **NCLC 38, 123**
See also DLB 90; RGWL 2, 3

Arnold, Matthew 1822-1888 ..... **NCLC 6, 29, 89, 126; PC 5; WLC**
See also BRW 5; CDBLB 1832-1890; DA; DAB; DAC; DAM MST, POET; DLB 32, 57; EXPP; PAB; PFS 2; TEA; WP

Arnold, Thomas 1795-1842 .... **NCLC 18**
See also DLB 55

Arnow, Harriette (Louisa) Simpson 1908-1986 .... **CLC 2, 7, 18**
See also BPFB 1; CA 9-12R; 118; CANR 14; DLB 6; FW; MTCW 1, 2; RHW; SATA 42; SATA-Obit 47

Arouet, Francois-Marie
See Voltaire

Arp, Hans
See Arp, Jean

Arp, Jean 1887-1966 .... **CLC 5; TCLC 115**
See also CA 81-84; 25-28R; CANR 42, 77; EW 10

Arrabal
See Arrabal, Fernando

Arrabal, Fernando 1932- ... **CLC 2, 9, 18, 58**
See Arrabal (Teran), Fernando
See also CA 9-12R; CANR 15; EWL 3; LMFS 2

Arrabal (Teran), Fernando 1932-
See Arrabal, Fernando
See also CWW 2

Arreola, Juan Jose 1918-2001 .... **CLC 147; HLC 1; SSC 38**
See also CA 113; 131; 200; CANR 81; CWW 2; DAM MULT; DLB 113; DNFS 2; EWL 3; HW 1, 2; LAW; RGSF 2

Arrian c. 89(?)-c. 155(?) .... **CMLC 43**
See also DLB 176

Arrick, Fran .... **CLC 30**
See Gaberman, Judie Angell
See also BYA 6

Arrley, Richmond
See Delany, Samuel R(ay), Jr.

Artaud, Antonin (Marie Joseph) 1896-1948 .... **DC 14; TCLC 3, 36**
See also CA 104; 149; DA3; DAM DRAM; DLB 258; EW 11; EWL 3; GFL 1789 to the Present; MTCW 1; RGWL 2, 3

Arthur, Ruth M(abel) 1905-1979 ..... **CLC 12**
See also CA 9-12R; 85-88; CANR 4; CWRI 5; SATA 7, 26

Artsybashev, Mikhail (Petrovich) 1878-1927 .... **TCLC 31**
See also CA 170; DLB 295

Arundel, Honor (Morfydd) 1919-1973 .... **CLC 17**
See also CA 21-22; 41-44R; CAP 2; CLR 35; CWRI 5; SATA 4; SATA-Obit 24

Arzner, Dorothy 1900-1979 .... **CLC 98**

Asch, Sholem 1880-1957 .... **TCLC 3**
See also CA 105; EWL 3; GLL 2

Ascham, Roger 1516(?)-1568 .... **LC 101**
See also DLB 236

Ash, Shalom
See Asch, Sholem

Ashbery, John (Lawrence) 1927- .. **CLC 2, 3, 4, 6, 9, 13, 15, 25, 41, 77, 125; PC 26**
See Berry, Jonas
See also AMWS 3; CA 5-8R; CANR 9, 37, 66, 102, 132; CP 7; DA3; DAM POET; DLB 5, 165; DLBY 1981; EWL 3; INT CANR-9; MTCW 1, 2; PAB; PFS 11; RGAL 4; WP

Ashdown, Clifford
See Freeman, R(ichard) Austin

Ashe, Gordon
See Creasey, John

Ashton-Warner, Sylvia (Constance) 1908-1984 .... **CLC 19**
See also CA 69-72; 112; CANR 29; MTCW 1, 2

Asimov, Isaac 1920-1992 ..... **CLC 1, 3, 9, 19, 26, 76, 92**
See also AAYA 13; BEST 90:2; BPFB 1; BYA 4, 6, 7, 9; CA 1-4R; 137; CANR 2, 19, 36, 60, 125; CLR 12, 79; CMW 4; CPW; DA3; DAM POP; DLB 8; DLBY 1992; INT CANR-19; JRDA; LAIT 5; LMFS 2; MAICYA 1, 2; MTCW 1, 2; RGAL 4; SATA 1, 26, 74; SCFW 2; SFW 4; SSFS 17; TUS; YAW

Askew, Anne 1521(?)-1546 .... **LC 81**
See also DLB 136

Assis, Joaquim Maria Machado de
See Machado de Assis, Joaquim Maria

Astell, Mary 1666-1731 .... **LC 68**
See also DLB 252; FW

Astley, Thea (Beatrice May) 1925-2004 .... **CLC 41**
See also CA 65-68; 229; CANR 11, 43, 78; CN 7; DLB 289; EWL 3

Astley, William 1855-1911
See Warung, Price

Aston, James
See White, T(erence) H(anbury)

Asturias, Miguel Angel 1899-1974 .... **CLC 3, 8, 13; HLC 1**
See also CA 25-28; 49-52; CANR 32; CAP 2; CDWLB 3; DA3; DAM MULT, NOV; DLB 113, 290; EWL 3; HW 1; LAW; LMFS 2; MTCW 1, 2; RGWL 2, 3; WLIT 1

Atares, Carlos Saura
See Saura (Atares), Carlos

Athanasius c. 295-c. 373 .... **CMLC 48**

Atheling, William
See Pound, Ezra (Weston Loomis)

Atheling, William, Jr.
See Blish, James (Benjamin)

Atherton, Gertrude (Franklin Horn) 1857-1948 .... **TCLC 2**
See also CA 104; 155; DLB 9, 78, 186; HGG; RGAL 4; SUFW 1; TCWW 2

Atherton, Lucius
See Masters, Edgar Lee

Atkins, Jack
See Harris, Mark

Atkinson, Kate 1951- .... **CLC 99**
See also CA 166; CANR 101; DLB 267

Attaway, William (Alexander) 1911-1986 .... **BLC 1; CLC 92**
See also BW 2, 3; CA 143; CANR 82; DAM MULT; DLB 76

Atticus
See Fleming, Ian (Lancaster); Wilson, (Thomas) Woodrow

Atwood, Margaret (Eleanor) 1939- ... **CLC 2, 3, 4, 8, 13, 15, 25, 44, 84, 135; PC 8; SSC 2, 46; WLC**
See also AAYA 12, 47; AMWS 13; BEST 89:2; BPFB 1; CA 49-52; CANR 3, 24, 33, 59, 95, 133; CN 7; CP 7; CPW; CWP; DA; DA3; DAB; DAC; DAM MST, NOV, POET; DLB 53, 251; EWL 3; EXPN; FW; INT CANR-24; LAIT 5; MTCW 1, 2; NFS 4, 12, 13, 14, 19; PFS 7; RGSF 2; SATA 50; SSFS 3, 13; TWA; WWE 1; YAW

Aubigny, Pierre d'
See Mencken, H(enry) L(ouis)

Aubin, Penelope 1685-1731(?) .... **LC 9**
See also DLB 39

Auchincloss, Louis (Stanton) 1917- .. **CLC 4, 6, 9, 18, 45; SSC 22**
See also AMWS 4; CA 1-4R; CANR 6, 29, 55, 87, 130; CN 7; DAM NOV; DLB 2, 244; DLBY 1980; EWL 3; INT CANR-29; MTCW 1; RGAL 4

Auden, W(ystan) H(ugh) 1907-1973 . **CLC 1, 2, 3, 4, 6, 9, 11, 14, 43, 123; PC 1; WLC**
See also AAYA 18; AMWS 2; BRW 7; BRWR 1; CA 9-12R; 45-48; CANR 5, 61, 105; CDBLB 1914-1945; DA; DA3; DAB; DAC; DAM DRAM, MST, POET; DLB 10, 20; EWL 3; EXPP; MTCW 1, 2; PAB; PFS 1, 3, 4, 10; TUS; WP

Audiberti, Jacques 1899-1965 .... **CLC 38**
See also CA 25-28R; DAM DRAM; EWL 3

Audubon, John James 1785-1851 . **NCLC 47**
See also ANW; DLB 248

Auel, Jean M(arie) 1936- .... **CLC 31, 107**
See also AAYA 7, 51; BEST 90:4; BPFB 1; CA 103; CANR 21, 64, 115; CPW; DA3; DAM POP; INT CANR-21; NFS 11; RHW; SATA 91

Auerbach, Erich 1892-1957 .... **TCLC 43**
See also CA 118; 155; EWL 3

Augier, Emile 1820-1889 .... **NCLC 31**
See also DLB 192; GFL 1789 to the Present

August, John
See De Voto, Bernard (Augustine)

Augustine, St. 354-430 .... **CMLC 6; WLCS**
See also DA; DA3; DAB; DAC; DAM MST; DLB 115; EW 1; RGWL 2, 3

Aunt Belinda
See Braddon, Mary Elizabeth

Aunt Weedy
See Alcott, Louisa May

Aurelius
See Bourne, Randolph S(illiman)

Aurelius, Marcus 121-180 .... **CMLC 45**
See Marcus Aurelius
See also RGWL 2, 3

Aurobindo, Sri
See Ghose, Aurabinda

Aurobindo Ghose
See Ghose, Aurabinda

Austen, Jane 1775-1817 ...... **NCLC 1, 13, 19, 33, 51, 81, 95, 119; WLC**
See also AAYA 19; BRW 4; BRWC 1; BRWR 2; BYA 3; CDBLB 1789-1832; DA; DA3; DAB; DAC; DAM MST, NOV; DLB 116; EXPN; LAIT 2; LATS 1:1; LMFS 1; NFS 1, 14, 18, 20; TEA; WLIT 3; WYAS 1

Auster, Paul 1947- .... **CLC 47, 131**
See also AMWS 12; CA 69-72; CANR 23, 52, 75, 129; CMW 4; CN 7; DA3; DLB 227; MTCW 1; SUFW 2

Austin, Frank
See Faust, Frederick (Schiller)
See also TCWW 2

Austin, Mary (Hunter) 1868-1934 . **TCLC 25**
See Stairs, Gordon
See also ANW; CA 109; 178; DLB 9, 78, 206, 221, 275; FW; TCWW 2

Averroes 1126-1198 .... **CMLC 7**
See also DLB 115

Avicenna 980-1037 .... **CMLC 16**
See also DLB 115

Avison, Margaret (Kirkland) 1918- .. **CLC 2, 4, 97**
See also CA 17-20R; CANR 134; CP 7; DAC; DAM POET; DLB 53; MTCW 1

Axton, David
See Koontz, Dean R(ay)

Ayckbourn, Alan 1939- ...... **CLC 5, 8, 18, 33, 74; DC 13**
See also BRWS 5; CA 21-24R; CANR 31, 59, 118; CBD; CD 5; DAB; DAM DRAM; DFS 7; DLB 13, 245; EWL 3; MTCW 1, 2

Aydy, Catherine
See Tennant, Emma (Christina)

Ayme, Marcel (Andre) 1902-1967 ... **CLC 11; SSC 41**
See also CA 89-92; CANR 67; CLR 25; DLB 72; EW 12; EWL 3; GFL 1789 to the Present; RGSF 2; RGWL 2, 3; SATA 91

Ayrton, Michael 1921-1975 .... **CLC 7**
See also CA 5-8R; 61-64; CANR 9, 21

Aytmatov, Chingiz
See Aitmatov, Chingiz (Torekulovich)
See also EWL 3

Azorin .... **CLC 11**
See Martinez Ruiz, Jose
See also EW 9; EWL 3

Azuela, Mariano 1873-1952 .. **HLC 1; TCLC 3, 145**
See also CA 104; 131; CANR 81; DAM MULT; EWL 3; HW 1, 2; LAW; MTCW 1, 2

Ba, Mariama 1929-1981 .... **BLCS**
See also AFW; BW 2; CA 141; CANR 87; DNFS 2; WLIT 2

Baastad, Babbis Friis
See Friis-Baastad, Babbis Ellinor

Bab
See Gilbert, W(illiam) S(chwenck)

Babbis, Eleanor
See Friis-Baastad, Babbis Ellinor

Babel, Isaac
See Babel, Isaak (Emmanuilovich)
See also EW 11; SSFS 10

Babel, Isaak (Emmanuilovich) 1894-1941(?) .. **SSC 16, 78; TCLC 2, 13**
See Babel, Isaac
See also CA 104; 155; CANR 113; DLB 272; EWL 3; MTCW 1; RGSF 2; RGWL 2, 3; TWA

Babits, Mihaly 1883-1941 .... **TCLC 14**
See also CA 114; CDWLB 4; DLB 215; EWL 3

Babur 1483-1530 .... **LC 18**

Babylas 1898-1962
See Ghelderode, Michel de

Baca, Jimmy Santiago 1952- . **HLC 1; PC 41**
See also CA 131; CANR 81, 90; CP 7; DAM MULT; DLB 122; HW 1, 2; LLW 1

Baca, Jose Santiago
See Baca, Jimmy Santiago

Bacchelli, Riccardo 1891-1985 .... **CLC 19**
See also CA 29-32R; 117; DLB 264; EWL 3

Bach, Richard (David) 1936- .... **CLC 14**
See also AITN 1; BEST 89:2; BPFB 1; BYA 5; CA 9-12R; CANR 18, 93; CPW; DAM NOV, POP; FANT; MTCW 1; SATA 13

Bache, Benjamin Franklin 1769-1798 .... **LC 74**
See also DLB 43

Bachelard, Gaston 1884-1962 ...... **TCLC 128**
See also CA 97-100; 89-92; DLB 296; GFL 1789 to the Present

Bachman, Richard
See King, Stephen (Edwin)

Bachmann, Ingeborg 1926-1973 .... **CLC 69**
See also CA 93-96; 45-48; CANR 69; DLB 85; EWL 3; RGWL 2, 3

Bacon, Francis 1561-1626 .... **LC 18, 32**
See also BRW 1; CDBLB Before 1660; DLB 151, 236, 252; RGEL 2; TEA

Bacon, Roger 1214(?)-1294 .... **CMLC 14**
See also DLB 115

Bacovia, George 1881-1957 .... **TCLC 24**
See Vasiliu, Gheorghe
See also CDWLB 4; DLB 220; EWL 3

Badanes, Jerome 1937-1995 .... **CLC 59**

Bagehot, Walter 1826-1877 .... **NCLC 10**
See also DLB 55

Bagnold, Enid 1889-1981 .... **CLC 25**
See also BYA 2; CA 5-8R; 103; CANR 5, 40; CBD; CWD; CWRI 5; DAM DRAM; DLB 13, 160, 191, 245; FW; MAICYA 1, 2; RGEL 2; SATA 1, 25

Bagritsky, Eduard .... **TCLC 60**
See Dzyubin, Eduard Georgievich

Bagrjana, Elisaveta
See Belcheva, Elisaveta Lyubomirova

Bagryana, Elisaveta .... **CLC 10**
See Belcheva, Elisaveta Lyubomirova
See also CA 178; CDWLB 4; DLB 147; EWL 3

Bailey, Paul 1937- .... **CLC 45**
See also CA 21-24R; CANR 16, 62, 124; CN 7; DLB 14, 271; GLL 2

Baillie, Joanna 1762-1851 .... **NCLC 71**
See also DLB 93; RGEL 2

Bainbridge, Beryl (Margaret) 1934- . **CLC 4, 5, 8, 10, 14, 18, 22, 62, 130**
See also BRWS 6; CA 21-24R; CANR 24, 55, 75, 88, 128; CN 7; DAM NOV; DLB 14, 231; EWL 3; MTCW 1, 2

Baker, Carlos (Heard) 1909-1987 .... **TCLC 119**
See also CA 5-8R; 122; CANR 3, 63; DLB 103

Baker, Elliott 1922- .... **CLC 8**
See also CA 45-48; CANR 2, 63; CN 7

Baker, Jean H. .... **TCLC 3, 10**
See Russell, George William

Baker, Nicholson 1957- .... **CLC 61, 165**
See also AMWS 13; CA 135; CANR 63, 120; CN 7; CPW; DA3; DAM POP; DLB 227

Baker, Ray Stannard 1870-1946 .... **TCLC 47**
See also CA 118

Baker, Russell (Wayne) 1925- .... **CLC 31**
See also BEST 89:4; CA 57-60; CANR 11, 41, 59; MTCW 1, 2

Bakhtin, M.
See Bakhtin, Mikhail Mikhailovich

Bakhtin, M. M.
See Bakhtin, Mikhail Mikhailovich

Bakhtin, Mikhail
See Bakhtin, Mikhail Mikhailovich

Bakhtin, Mikhail Mikhailovich 1895-1975 .... **CLC 83**
See also CA 128; 113; DLB 242; EWL 3

Bakshi, Ralph 1938(?)- .... **CLC 26**
See also CA 112; 138; IDFW 3

Bakunin, Mikhail (Alexandrovich) 1814-1876 .... **NCLC 25, 58**
See also DLB 277

Baldwin, James (Arthur) 1924-1987 . **BLC 1; CLC 1, 2, 3, 4, 5, 8, 13, 15, 17, 42, 50, 67, 90, 127; DC 1; SSC 10, 33; WLC**
See also AAYA 4, 34; AFAW 1, 2; AMWR 2; AMWS 1; BPFB 1; BW 1; CA 1-4R; 124; CABS 1; CAD; CANR 3, 24; CDALB 1941-1968; CPW; DA; DA3; DAB; DAC; DAM MST, MULT, NOV, POP; DFS 11, 15; DLB 2, 7, 33, 249, 278; DLBY 1987; EWL 3; EXPS; LAIT 5; MTCW 1, 2; NCFS 4; NFS 4; RGAL 4; RGSF 2; SATA 9; SATA-Obit 54; SSFS 2, 18; TUS

Bale, John 1495-1563 .... **LC 62**
See also DLB 132; RGEL 2; TEA

Ball, Hugo 1886-1927 .... **TCLC 104**

Ballard, J(ames) G(raham) 1930- . **CLC 3, 6, 14, 36, 137; SSC 1, 53**
See also AAYA 3, 52; BRWS 5; CA 5-8R; CANR 15, 39, 65, 107, 133; CN 7; DA3; DAM NOV, POP; DLB 14, 207, 261; EWL 3; HGG; MTCW 1, 2; NFS 8; RGEL 2; RGSF 2; SATA 93; SFW 4

Balmont, Konstantin (Dmitriyevich) 1867-1943 .... **TCLC 11**
See also CA 109; 155; DLB 295; EWL 3

Baltausis, Vincas 1847-1910
See Mikszath, Kalman

Balzac, Honore de 1799-1850 ... **NCLC 5, 35, 53; SSC 5, 59; WLC**
See also DA; DA3; DAB; DAC; DAM MST, NOV; DLB 119; EW 5; GFL 1789 to the Present; LMFS 1; RGSF 2; RGWL 2, 3; SSFS 10; SUFW; TWA

Bambara, Toni Cade 1939-1995 .... **BLC 1; CLC 19, 88; SSC 35; TCLC 116; WLCS**
See also AAYA 5, 49; AFAW 2; AMWS 11; BW 2, 3; BYA 12, 14; CA 29-32R; 150; CANR 24, 49, 81; CDALBS; DA; DA3; DAC; DAM MST, MULT; DLB 38, 218; EXPS; MTCW 1, 2; RGAL 4; RGSF 2; SATA 112; SSFS 4, 7, 12

Bamdad, A.
See Shamlu, Ahmad

Bamdad, Alef
See Shamlu, Ahmad

Banat, D. R.
See Bradbury, Ray (Douglas)

Bancroft, Laura
See Baum, L(yman) Frank

Banim, John 1798-1842 .... **NCLC 13**
See also DLB 116, 158, 159; RGEL 2

Banim, Michael 1796-1874 .... **NCLC 13**
See also DLB 158, 159

Banjo, The
See Paterson, A(ndrew) B(arton)

Banks, Iain
See Banks, Iain M(enzies)

Banks, Iain M(enzies) 1954- .... **CLC 34**
See also CA 123; 128; CANR 61, 106; DLB 194, 261; EWL 3; HGG; INT CA-128; SFW 4

Banks, Lynne Reid .... **CLC 23**
See Reid Banks, Lynne
See also AAYA 6; BYA 7; CLR 86

Banks, Russell (Earl) 1940- .... **CLC 37, 72, 187; SSC 42**
See also AAYA 45; AMWS 5; CA 65-68; CAAS 15; CANR 19, 52, 73, 118; CN 7; DLB 130, 278; EWL 3; NFS 13

Banville, John 1945- .... **CLC 46, 118**
See also CA 117; 128; CANR 104; CN 7; DLB 14, 271; INT CA-128

Banville, Theodore (Faullain) de 1832-1891 .... **NCLC 9**
See also DLB 217; GFL 1789 to the Present

Baraka, Amiri 1934- .... **BLC 1; CLC 1, 2, 3, 5, 10, 14, 33, 115; DC 6; PC 4; WLCS**
See Jones, LeRoi
See also AFAW 1, 2; AMWS 2; BW 2, 3; CA 21-24R; CABS 3; CAD; CANR 27, 38, 61, 133; CD 5; CDALB 1941-1968; CP 7; CPW; DA; DA3; DAC; DAM MST, MULT, POET, POP; DFS 3, 11, 16; DLB 5, 7, 16, 38; DLBD 8; EWL 3; MTCW 1, 2; PFS 9; RGAL 4; TUS; WP

Baratynsky, Evgenii Abramovich
1800-1844 .... **NCLC 103**
See also DLB 205

Barbauld, Anna Laetitia
1743-1825 .... **NCLC 50**
See also DLB 107, 109, 142, 158; RGEL 2

Barbellion, W. N. P. .... **TCLC 24**
See Cummings, Bruce F(rederick)

Barber, Benjamin R. 1939- .... **CLC 141**
See also CA 29-32R; CANR 12, 32, 64, 119

Barbera, Jack (Vincent) 1945- .... **CLC 44**
See also CA 110; CANR 45

Barbey d'Aurevilly, Jules-Amedee
1808-1889 .... **NCLC 1; SSC 17**
See also DLB 119; GFL 1789 to the Present

Barbour, John c. 1316-1395 .... **CMLC 33**
See also DLB 146

Barbusse, Henri 1873-1935 .... **TCLC 5**
See also CA 105; 154; DLB 65; EWL 3; RGWL 2, 3

Barclay, Alexander c. 1475-1552 .... **LC 109**
See also DLB 132

Barclay, Bill
See Moorcock, Michael (John)

Barclay, William Ewert
See Moorcock, Michael (John)

Barea, Arturo 1897-1957 .... **TCLC 14**
See also CA 111; 201

Barfoot, Joan 1946- .... **CLC 18**
See also CA 105

Barham, Richard Harris
1788-1845 .... **NCLC 77**
See also DLB 159

Baring, Maurice 1874-1945 .... **TCLC 8**
See also CA 105; 168; DLB 34; HGG

Baring-Gould, Sabine 1834-1924 ... **TCLC 88**
See also DLB 156, 190

Barker, Clive 1952- .... **CLC 52; SSC 53**
See also AAYA 10, 54; BEST 90:3; BPFB 1; CA 121; 129; CANR 71, 111, 133; CPW; DA3; DAM POP; DLB 261; HGG; INT CA-129; MTCW 1, 2; SUFW 2

Barker, George Granville
1913-1991 .... **CLC 8, 48**
See also CA 9-12R; 135; CANR 7, 38; DAM POET; DLB 20; EWL 3; MTCW 1

Barker, Harley Granville
See Granville-Barker, Harley
See also DLB 10

Barker, Howard 1946- .... **CLC 37**
See also CA 102; CBD; CD 5; DLB 13, 233

Barker, Jane 1652-1732 .... **LC 42, 82**
See also DLB 39, 131

Barker, Pat(ricia) 1943- ...... **CLC 32, 94, 146**
See also BRWS 4; CA 117; 122; CANR 50, 101; CN 7; DLB 271; INT CA-122

Barlach, Ernst (Heinrich)
1870-1938 .... **TCLC 84**
See also CA 178; DLB 56, 118; EWL 3

Barlow, Joel 1754-1812 .... **NCLC 23**
See also AMWS 2; DLB 37; RGAL 4

Barnard, Mary (Ethel) 1909- .... **CLC 48**
See also CA 21-22; CAP 2

Barnes, Djuna 1892-1982 .... **CLC 3, 4, 8, 11, 29, 127; SSC 3**
See Steptoe, Lydia
See also AMWS 3; CA 9-12R; 107; CAD; CANR 16, 55; CWD; DLB 4, 9, 45; EWL 3; GLL 1; MTCW 1, 2; RGAL 4; TUS

Barnes, Jim 1933- .... **NNAL**
See also CA 108, 175; CAAE 175; CAAS 28; DLB 175

Barnes, Julian (Patrick) 1946- . **CLC 42, 141**
See also BRWS 4; CA 102; CANR 19, 54, 115; CN 7; DAB; DLB 194; DLBY 1993; EWL 3; MTCW 1

Barnes, Peter 1931-2004 .... **CLC 5, 56**
See also CA 65-68; CAAS 12; CANR 33, 34, 64, 113; CBD; CD 5; DFS 6; DLB 13, 233; MTCW 1

Barnes, William 1801-1886 .... **NCLC 75**
See also DLB 32

Baroja (y Nessi), Pio 1872-1956 .... **HLC 1; TCLC 8**
See also CA 104; EW 9

Baron, David
See Pinter, Harold

Baron Corvo
See Rolfe, Frederick (William Serafino Austin Lewis Mary)

Barondess, Sue K(aufman)
1926-1977 .... **CLC 8**
See Kaufman, Sue
See also CA 1-4R; 69-72; CANR 1

Baron de Teive
See Pessoa, Fernando (Antonio Nogueira)

Baroness Von S.
See Zangwill, Israel

Barres, (Auguste-)Maurice
1862-1923 .... **TCLC 47**
See also CA 164; DLB 123; GFL 1789 to the Present

Barreto, Afonso Henrique de Lima
See Lima Barreto, Afonso Henrique de

Barrett, Andrea 1954- .... **CLC 150**
See also CA 156; CANR 92

Barrett, Michele .... **CLC 65**

Barrett, (Roger) Syd 1946- .... **CLC 35**

Barrett, William (Christopher)
1913-1992 .... **CLC 27**
See also CA 13-16R; 139; CANR 11, 67; INT CANR-11

Barrie, J(ames) M(atthew)
1860-1937 .... **TCLC 2**
See also BRWS 3; BYA 4, 5; CA 104; 136; CANR 77; CDBLB 1890-1914; CLR 16; CWRI 5; DA3; DAB; DAM DRAM; DFS 7; DLB 10, 141, 156; EWL 3; FANT; MAICYA 1, 2; MTCW 1; SATA 100; SUFW; WCH; WLIT 4; YABC 1

Barrington, Michael
See Moorcock, Michael (John)

Barrol, Grady
See Bograd, Larry

Barry, Mike
See Malzberg, Barry N(athaniel)

Barry, Philip 1896-1949 .... **TCLC 11**
See also CA 109; 199; DFS 9; DLB 7, 228; RGAL 4

Bart, Andre Schwarz
See Schwarz-Bart, Andre

Barth, John (Simmons) 1930- ... **CLC 1, 2, 3, 5, 7, 9, 10, 14, 27, 51, 89; SSC 10**
See also AITN 1, 2; AMW; BPFB 1; CA 1-4R; CABS 1; CANR 5, 23, 49, 64, 113; CN 7; DAM NOV; DLB 2, 227; EWL 3; FANT; MTCW 1; RGAL 4; RGSF 2; RHW; SSFS 6; TUS

Barthelme, Donald 1931-1989 ... **CLC 1, 2, 3, 5, 6, 8, 13, 23, 46, 59, 115; SSC 2, 55**
See also AMWS 4; BPFB 1; CA 21-24R; 129; CANR 20, 58; DA3; DAM NOV; DLB 2, 234; DLBY 1980, 1989; EWL 3; FANT; LMFS 2; MTCW 1, 2; RGAL 4; RGSF 2; SATA 7; SATA-Obit 62; SSFS 17

Barthelme, Frederick 1943- ...... **CLC 36, 117**
See also AMWS 11; CA 114; 122; CANR 77; CN 7; CSW; DLB 244; DLBY 1985; EWL 3; INT CA-122

Barthes, Roland (Gerard)
1915-1980 .... **CLC 24, 83; TCLC 135**
See also CA 130; 97-100; CANR 66; DLB 296; EW 13; EWL 3; GFL 1789 to the Present; MTCW 1, 2; TWA

Bartram, William 1739-1823 .... **NCLC 145**
See also ANW; DLB 37

Barzun, Jacques (Martin) 1907- ..... **CLC 51, 145**
See also CA 61-64; CANR 22, 95

Bashevis, Isaac
See Singer, Isaac Bashevis

Bashkirtseff, Marie 1859-1884 .... **NCLC 27**

Basho, Matsuo
See Matsuo Basho
See also PFS 18; RGWL 2, 3; WP

Basil of Caesaria c. 330-379 .... **CMLC 35**

Basket, Raney
See Edgerton, Clyde (Carlyle)

Bass, Kingsley B., Jr.
See Bullins, Ed

Bass, Rick 1958- .... **CLC 79, 143; SSC 60**
See also ANW; CA 126; CANR 53, 93; CSW; DLB 212, 275

Bassani, Giorgio 1916-2000 .... **CLC 9**
See also CA 65-68; 190; CANR 33; CWW 2; DLB 128, 177, 299; EWL 3; MTCW 1; RGWL 2, 3

Bastian, Ann .... **CLC 70**

Bastos, Augusto (Antonio) Roa
See Roa Bastos, Augusto (Antonio)

Bataille, Georges 1897-1962 .... **CLC 29; TCLC 155**
See also CA 101; 89-92; EWL 3

Bates, H(erbert) E(rnest)
1905-1974 .... **CLC 46; SSC 10**
See also CA 93-96; 45-48; CANR 34; DA3; DAB; DAM POP; DLB 162, 191; EWL 3; EXPS; MTCW 1, 2; RGSF 2; SSFS 7

Bauchart
See Camus, Albert

Baudelaire, Charles 1821-1867 . **NCLC 6, 29, 55; PC 1; SSC 18; WLC**
See also DA; DA3; DAB; DAC; DAM MST, POET; DLB 217; EW 7; GFL 1789 to the Present; LMFS 2; PFS 21; RGWL 2, 3; TWA

Baudouin, Marcel
See Peguy, Charles (Pierre)

Baudouin, Pierre
See Peguy, Charles (Pierre)

Baudrillard, Jean 1929- .... **CLC 60**
See also DLB 296

Baum, L(yman) Frank 1856-1919 .. **TCLC 7, 132**
See also AAYA 46; BYA 16; CA 108; 133; CLR 15; CWRI 5; DLB 22; FANT; JRDA; MAICYA 1, 2; MTCW 1, 2; NFS 13; RGAL 4; SATA 18, 100; WCH

Baum, Louis F.
See Baum, L(yman) Frank

Baumbach, Jonathan 1933- .... **CLC 6, 23**
See also CA 13-16R; CAAS 5; CANR 12, 66; CN 7; DLBY 1980; INT CANR-12; MTCW 1

Bausch, Richard (Carl) 1945- .... **CLC 51**
See also AMWS 7; CA 101; CAAS 14;
CANR 43, 61, 87; CSW; DLB 130

Baxter, Charles (Morley) 1947- . **CLC 45, 78**
See also CA 57-60; CANR 40, 64, 104, 133;
CPW; DAM POP; DLB 130; MTCW 2

Baxter, George Owen
See Faust, Frederick (Schiller)

Baxter, James K(eir) 1926-1972 .... **CLC 14**
See also CA 77-80; EWL 3

Baxter, John
See Hunt, E(verette) Howard, (Jr.)

Bayer, Sylvia
See Glassco, John

Baynton, Barbara 1857-1929 .... **TCLC 57**
See also DLB 230; RGSF 2

Beagle, Peter S(oyer) 1939- .... **CLC 7, 104**
See also AAYA 47; BPFB 1; BYA 9, 10,
16; CA 9-12R; CANR 4, 51, 73, 110;
DA3; DLBY 1980; FANT; INT CANR-4;
MTCW 1; SATA 60, 130; SUFW 1, 2;
YAW

Bean, Normal
See Burroughs, Edgar Rice

Beard, Charles A(ustin)
1874-1948 .... **TCLC 15**
See also CA 115; 189; DLB 17; SATA 18

Beardsley, Aubrey 1872-1898 .... **NCLC 6**

Beattie, Ann 1947- ..... **CLC 8, 13, 18, 40, 63,
146; SSC 11**
See also AMWS 5; BEST 90:2; BPFB 1;
CA 81-84; CANR 53, 73, 128; CN 7;
CPW; DA3; DAM NOV; DLB 218,
278; DLBY 1982; EWL 3; MTCW 1, 2;
RGAL 4; RGSF 2; SSFS 9; TUS

Beattie, James 1735-1803 .... **NCLC 25**
See also DLB 109

Beauchamp, Kathleen Mansfield 1888-1923
See Mansfield, Katherine
See also CA 104; 134; DA; DA3; DAC;
DAM MST; MTCW 2; TEA

Beaumarchais, Pierre-Augustin Caron de
1732-1799 .... **DC 4; LC 61**
See also DAM DRAM; DFS 14, 16; EW 4;
GFL Beginnings to 1789; RGWL 2, 3

Beaumont, Francis 1584(?)-1616 .. **DC 6; LC
33**
See also BRW 2; CDBLB Before 1660;
DLB 58; TEA

Beauvoir, Simone (Lucie Ernestine Marie
Bertrand) de 1908-1986 .... **CLC 1, 2, 4,
8, 14, 31, 44, 50, 71, 124; SSC 35;
WLC**
See also BPFB 1; CA 9-12R; 118; CANR
28, 61; DA; DA3; DAB; DAC; DAM
MST, NOV; DLB 72; DLBY 1986; EW
12; EWL 3; FW; GFL 1789 to the Present;
LMFS 2; MTCW 1, 2; RGSF 2; RGWL
2, 3; TWA

Becker, Carl (Lotus) 1873-1945 ..... **TCLC 63**
See also CA 157; DLB 17

Becker, Jurek 1937-1997 .... **CLC 7, 19**
See also CA 85-88; 157; CANR 60, 117;
CWW 2; DLB 75, 299; EWL 3

Becker, Walter 1950- .... **CLC 26**

Beckett, Samuel (Barclay)
1906-1989 .. **CLC 1, 2, 3, 4, 6, 9, 10, 11,
14, 18, 29, 57, 59, 83; DC 22; SSC 16,
74; TCLC 145; WLC**
See also BRWC 2; BRWR 1; BRWS 1; CA
5-8R; 130; CANR 33, 61; CBD; CDBLB
1945-1960; DA; DA3; DAB; DAC; DAM
DRAM, MST, NOV; DFS 2, 7, 18; DLB
13, 15, 233; DLBY 1990; EWL 3; GFL
1789 to the Present; LATS 1:2; LMFS 2;
MTCW 1, 2; RGSF 2; RGWL 2, 3; SSFS
15; TEA; WLIT 4

Beckford, William 1760-1844 .... **NCLC 16**
See also BRW 3; DLB 39, 213; HGG;
LMFS 1; SUFW

Beckham, Barry (Earl) 1944- .... **BLC 1**
See also BW 1; CA 29-32R; CANR 26, 62;
CN 7; DAM MULT; DLB 33

Beckman, Gunnel 1910- .... **CLC 26**
See also CA 33-36R; CANR 15, 114; CLR
25; MAICYA 1, 2; SAAS 9; SATA 6

Becque, Henri 1837-1899 ... **DC 21; NCLC 3**
See also DLB 192; GFL 1789 to the Present

Becquer, Gustavo Adolfo
1836-1870 .... **HLCS 1; NCLC 106**
See also DAM MULT

Beddoes, Thomas Lovell 1803-1849 .. **DC 15;
NCLC 3**
See also DLB 96

Bede c. 673-735 .... **CMLC 20**
See also DLB 146; TEA

Bedford, Denton R. 1907-(?) .... **NNAL**

Bedford, Donald F.
See Fearing, Kenneth (Flexner)

Beecher, Catharine Esther
1800-1878 .... **NCLC 30**
See also DLB 1, 243

Beecher, John 1904-1980 .... **CLC 6**
See also AITN 1; CA 5-8R; 105; CANR 8

Beer, Johann 1655-1700 .... **LC 5**
See also DLB 168

Beer, Patricia 1924- .... **CLC 58**
See also CA 61-64; 183; CANR 13, 46; CP
7; CWP; DLB 40; FW

Beerbohm, Max
See Beerbohm, (Henry) Max(imilian)

Beerbohm, (Henry) Max(imilian)
1872-1956 .... **TCLC 1, 24**
See also BRWS 2; CA 104; 154; CANR 79;
DLB 34, 100; FANT

Beer-Hofmann, Richard
1866-1945 .... **TCLC 60**
See also CA 160; DLB 81

Beg, Shemus
See Stephens, James

Begiebing, Robert J(ohn) 1946- .... **CLC 70**
See also CA 122; CANR 40, 88

Begley, Louis 1933- .... **CLC 197**
See also CA 140; CANR 98; DLB 299

Behan, Brendan (Francis)
1923-1964 .... **CLC 1, 8, 11, 15, 79**
See also BRWS 2; CA 73-76; CANR 33,
121; CBD; CDBLB 1945-1960; DAM
DRAM; DFS 7; DLB 13, 233; EWL 3;
MTCW 1, 2

Behn, Aphra 1640(?)-1689 .. **DC 4; LC 1, 30,
42; PC 13; WLC**
See also BRWS 3; DA; DA3; DAB; DAC;
DAM DRAM, MST, NOV, POET; DFS
16; DLB 39, 80, 131; FW; TEA; WLIT 3

Behrman, S(amuel) N(athaniel)
1893-1973 .... **CLC 40**
See also CA 13-16; 45-48; CAD; CAP 1;
DLB 7, 44; IDFW 3; RGAL 4

Belasco, David 1853-1931 .... **TCLC 3**
See also CA 104; 168; DLB 7; RGAL 4

Belcheva, Elisaveta Lyubomirova
1893-1991 .... **CLC 10**
See Bagryana, Elisaveta

Beldone, Phil "Cheech"
See Ellison, Harlan (Jay)

Beleno
See Azuela, Mariano

Belinski, Vissarion Grigoryevich
1811-1848 .... **NCLC 5**
See also DLB 198

Belitt, Ben 1911- .... **CLC 22**
See also CA 13-16R; CAAS 4; CANR 7,
77; CP 7; DLB 5

Bell, Gertrude (Margaret Lowthian)
1868-1926 .... **TCLC 67**
See also CA 167; CANR 110; DLB 174

Bell, J. Freeman
See Zangwill, Israel

Bell, James Madison 1826-1902 .... **BLC 1;
TCLC 43**
See also BW 1; CA 122; 124; DAM MULT;
DLB 50

Bell, Madison Smartt 1957- ...... **CLC 41, 102**
See also AMWS 10; BPFB 1; CA 111, 183;
CAAE 183; CANR 28, 54, 73, 134; CN
7; CSW; DLB 218, 278; MTCW 1

Bell, Marvin (Hartley) 1937- .... **CLC 8, 31**
See also CA 21-24R; CAAS 14; CANR 59,
102; CP 7; DAM POET; DLB 5; MTCW
1

Bell, W. L. D.
See Mencken, H(enry) L(ouis)

Bellamy, Atwood C.
See Mencken, H(enry) L(ouis)

Bellamy, Edward 1850-1898 ..... **NCLC 4, 86,
147**
See also DLB 12; NFS 15; RGAL 4; SFW
4

Belli, Gioconda 1948- .... **HLCS 1**
See also CA 152; CWW 2; DLB 290; EWL
3; RGWL 3

Bellin, Edward J.
See Kuttner, Henry

Bello, Andres 1781-1865 .... **NCLC 131**
See also LAW

Belloc, (Joseph) Hilaire (Pierre Sebastien
Rene Swanton) 1870-1953 .... **PC 24;
TCLC 7, 18**
See also CA 106; 152; CLR 102; CWRI 5;
DAM POET; DLB 19, 100, 141, 174;
EWL 3; MTCW 1; SATA 112; WCH;
YABC 1

Belloc, Joseph Peter Rene Hilaire
See Belloc, (Joseph) Hilaire (Pierre Sebastien Rene Swanton)

Belloc, Joseph Pierre Rene Hilaire
See Belloc, (Joseph) Hilaire (Pierre Sebastien Rene Swanton)

Belloc, M. A.
See Lowndes, Marie Adelaide (Belloc)

Belloc-Lowndes, Mrs.
See Lowndes, Marie Adelaide (Belloc)

Bellow, Saul 1915- . **CLC 1, 2, 3, 6, 8, 10, 13,
15, 25, 33, 34, 63, 79, 190; SSC 14;
WLC**
See also AITN 2; AMW; AMWC 2; AMWR
2; BEST 89:3; BPFB 1; CA 5-8R; CABS
1; CANR 29, 53, 95, 132; CDALB 1941-
1968; CN 7; DA; DA3; DAB; DAC;
DAM MST, NOV, POP; DLB 2, 28, 299;
DLBD 3; DLBY 1982; EWL 3; MTCW
1, 2; NFS 4, 14; RGAL 4; RGSF 2; SSFS
12; TUS

Belser, Reimond Karel Maria de 1929-
See Ruyslinck, Ward
See also CA 152

Bely, Andrey .... **PC 11; TCLC 7**
See Bugayev, Boris Nikolayevich
See also DLB 295; EW 9; EWL 3; MTCW
1

Belyi, Andrei
See Bugayev, Boris Nikolayevich
See also RGWL 2, 3

Bembo, Pietro 1470-1547 .... **LC 79**
See also RGWL 2, 3

Benary, Margot
See Benary-Isbert, Margot

Benary-Isbert, Margot 1889-1979 .... **CLC 12**
See also CA 5-8R; 89-92; CANR 4, 72;
CLR 12; MAICYA 1, 2; SATA 2; SATA-
Obit 21

Benavente (y Martinez), Jacinto
1866-1954 .... **HLCS 1; TCLC 3**
See also CA 106; 131; CANR 81; DAM
DRAM, MULT; EWL 3; GLL 2; HW 1,
2; MTCW 1, 2

Benchley, Peter (Bradford) 1940- .. **CLC 4, 8**
See also AAYA 14; AITN 2; BPFB 1; CA
17-20R; CANR 12, 35, 66, 115; CPW;
DAM NOV, POP; HGG; MTCW 1, 2;
SATA 3, 89

Benchley, Robert (Charles)
1889-1945 .... **TCLC 1, 55**
See also CA 105; 153; DLB 11; RGAL 4

Benda, Julien 1867-1956 .... **TCLC 60**
See also CA 120; 154; GFL 1789 to the
Present

Benedict, Ruth (Fulton)
1887-1948 .... **TCLC 60**
See also CA 158; DLB 246

Benedikt, Michael 1935- .... **CLC 4, 14**
See also CA 13-16R; CANR 7; CP 7; DLB
5

Benet, Juan 1927-1993 .... **CLC 28**
See also CA 143; EWL 3

Benet, Stephen Vincent 1898-1943 ... **SSC 10;**
TCLC 7
See also AMWS 11; CA 104; 152; DA3;
DAM POET; DLB 4, 48, 102, 249, 284;
DLBY 1997; EWL 3; HGG; MTCW 1;
RGAL 4; RGSF 2; SUFW; WP; YABC 1

Benet, William Rose 1886-1950 ..... **TCLC 28**
See also CA 118; 152; DAM POET; DLB
45; RGAL 4

Benford, Gregory (Albert) 1941- ..... **CLC 52**
See also BPFB 1; CA 69-72, 175; CAAE
175; CAAS 27; CANR 12, 24, 49, 95,
134; CSW; DLBY 1982; SCFW 2; SFW
4

Bengtsson, Frans (Gunnar)
1894-1954 .... **TCLC 48**
See also CA 170; EWL 3

Benjamin, David
See Slavitt, David R(ytman)

Benjamin, Lois
See Gould, Lois

Benjamin, Walter 1892-1940 .... **TCLC 39**
See also CA 164; DLB 242; EW 11; EWL
3

Ben Jelloun, Tahar 1944-
See Jelloun, Tahar ben
See also CA 135; CWW 2; EWL 3; RGWL
3; WLIT 2

Benn, Gottfried 1886-1956 .. **PC 35; TCLC 3**
See also CA 106; 153; DLB 56; EWL 3;
RGWL 2, 3

Bennett, Alan 1934- .... **CLC 45, 77**
See also BRWS 8; CA 103; CANR 35, 55,
106; CBD; CD 5; DAB; DAM MST;
MTCW 1, 2

Bennett, (Enoch) Arnold
1867-1931 .... **TCLC 5, 20**
See also BRW 6; CA 106; 155; CDBLB
1890-1914; DLB 10, 34, 98, 135; EWL 3;
MTCW 2

Bennett, Elizabeth
See Mitchell, Margaret (Munnerlyn)

Bennett, George Harold 1930-
See Bennett, Hal
See also BW 1; CA 97-100; CANR 87

Bennett, Gwendolyn B. 1902-1981 .... **HR 2**
See also BW 1; CA 125; DLB 51; WP

Bennett, Hal .... **CLC 5**
See Bennett, George Harold
See also DLB 33

Bennett, Jay 1912- .... **CLC 35**
See also AAYA 10; CA 69-72; CANR 11,
42, 79; JRDA; SAAS 4; SATA 41, 87;
SATA-Brief 27; WYA; YAW

Bennett, Louise (Simone) 1919- .... **BLC 1;**
CLC 28
See also BW 2, 3; CA 151; CDWLB 3; CP
7; DAM MULT; DLB 117; EWL 3

Benson, A. C. 1862-1925 .... **TCLC 123**
See also DLB 98

Benson, E(dward) F(rederic)
1867-1940 .... **TCLC 27**
See also CA 114; 157; DLB 135, 153;
HGG; SUFW 1

Benson, Jackson J. 1930- .... **CLC 34**
See also CA 25-28R; DLB 111

Benson, Sally 1900-1972 .... **CLC 17**
See also CA 19-20; 37-40R; CAP 1; SATA
1, 35; SATA-Obit 27

Benson, Stella 1892-1933 .... **TCLC 17**
See also CA 117; 154, 155; DLB 36, 162;
FANT; TEA

Bentham, Jeremy 1748-1832 .... **NCLC 38**
See also DLB 107, 158, 252

Bentley, E(dmund) C(lerihew)
1875-1956 .... **TCLC 12**
See also CA 108; DLB 70; MSW

Bentley, Eric (Russell) 1916- .... **CLC 24**
See also CA 5-8R; CAD; CANR 6, 67;
CBD; CD 5; INT CANR-6

ben Uzair, Salem
See Horne, Richard Henry Hengist

Beranger, Pierre Jean de
1780-1857 .... **NCLC 34**

Berdyaev, Nicolas
See Berdyaev, Nikolai (Aleksandrovich)

Berdyaev, Nikolai (Aleksandrovich)
1874-1948 .... **TCLC 67**
See also CA 120; 157

Berdyayev, Nikolai (Aleksandrovich)
See Berdyaev, Nikolai (Aleksandrovich)

Berendt, John (Lawrence) 1939- ...... **CLC 86**
See also CA 146; CANR 75, 93; DA3;
MTCW 1

Beresford, J(ohn) D(avys)
1873-1947 .... **TCLC 81**
See also CA 112; 155; DLB 162, 178, 197;
SFW 4; SUFW 1

Bergelson, David (Rafailovich)
1884-1952 .... **TCLC 81**
See Bergelson, Dovid
See also CA 220

Bergelson, Dovid
See Bergelson, David (Rafailovich)
See also EWL 3

Berger, Colonel
See Malraux, (Georges-)Andre

Berger, John (Peter) 1926- .... **CLC 2, 19**
See also BRWS 4; CA 81-84; CANR 51,
78, 117; CN 7; DLB 14, 207

Berger, Melvin H. 1927- .... **CLC 12**
See also CA 5-8R; CANR 4; CLR 32;
SAAS 2; SATA 5, 88; SATA-Essay 124

Berger, Thomas (Louis) 1924- .. **CLC 3, 5, 8,**
11, 18, 38
See also BPFB 1; CA 1-4R; CANR 5, 28,
51, 128; CN 7; DAM NOV; DLB 2;
DLBY 1980; EWL 3; FANT; INT CANR-
28; MTCW 1, 2; RHW; TCWW 2

Bergman, (Ernst) Ingmar 1918- ...... **CLC 16,**
72
See also CA 81-84; CANR 33, 70; CWW
2; DLB 257; MTCW 2

Bergson, Henri(-Louis) 1859-1941 . **TCLC 32**
See also CA 164; EW 8; EWL 3; GFL 1789
to the Present

Bergstein, Eleanor 1938- .... **CLC 4**
See also CA 53-56; CANR 5

Berkeley, George 1685-1753 .... **LC 65**
See also DLB 31, 101, 252

Berkoff, Steven 1937- .... **CLC 56**
See also CA 104; CANR 72; CBD; CD 5

Berlin, Isaiah 1909-1997 .... **TCLC 105**
See also CA 85-88; 162

Bermant, Chaim (Icyk) 1929-1998 ... **CLC 40**
See also CA 57-60; CANR 6, 31, 57, 105;
CN 7

Bern, Victoria
See Fisher, M(ary) F(rances) K(ennedy)

Bernanos, (Paul Louis) Georges
1888-1948 .... **TCLC 3**
See also CA 104; 130; CANR 94; DLB 72;
EWL 3; GFL 1789 to the Present; RGWL
2, 3

Bernard, April 1956- .... **CLC 59**
See also CA 131

Bernard of Clairvaux 1090-1153 .. **CMLC 71**
See also DLB 208

Berne, Victoria
See Fisher, M(ary) F(rances) K(ennedy)

Bernhard, Thomas 1931-1989 ..... **CLC 3, 32,**
61; DC 14
See also CA 85-88; 127; CANR 32, 57; CD-
WLB 2; DLB 85, 124; EWL 3; MTCW 1;
RGWL 2, 3

Bernhardt, Sarah (Henriette Rosine)
1844-1923 .... **TCLC 75**
See also CA 157

Bernstein, Charles 1950- .... **CLC 142,**
See also CA 129; CAAS 24; CANR 90; CP
7; DLB 169

Bernstein, Ingrid
See Kirsch, Sarah

Berriault, Gina 1926-1999 .... **CLC 54, 109;**
SSC 30
See also CA 116; 129; 185; CANR 66; DLB
130; SSFS 7,11

Berrigan, Daniel 1921- .... **CLC 4**
See also CA 33-36R, 187; CAAE 187;
CAAS 1; CANR 11, 43, 78; CP 7; DLB 5

Berrigan, Edmund Joseph Michael, Jr.
1934-1983
See Berrigan, Ted
See also CA 61-64; 110; CANR 14, 102

Berrigan, Ted .... **CLC 37**
See Berrigan, Edmund Joseph Michael, Jr.
See also DLB 5, 169; WP

Berry, Charles Edward Anderson 1931-
See Berry, Chuck
See also CA 115

Berry, Chuck .... **CLC 17**
See Berry, Charles Edward Anderson

Berry, Jonas
See Ashbery, John (Lawrence)
See also GLL 1

Berry, Wendell (Erdman) 1934- ... **CLC 4, 6,**
8, 27, 46; PC 28
See also AITN 1; AMWS 10; ANW; CA
73-76; CANR 50, 73, 101, 132; CP 7;
CSW; DAM POET; DLB 5, 6, 234, 275;
MTCW 1

Berryman, John 1914-1972 ... **CLC 1, 2, 3, 4,**
6, 8, 10, 13, 25, 62
See also AMW; CA 13-16; 33-36R; CABS
2; CANR 35; CAP 1; CDALB 1941-1968;
DAM POET; DLB 48; EWL 3; MTCW 1,
2; PAB; RGAL 4; WP

Bertolucci, Bernardo 1940- ...... **CLC 16, 157**
See also CA 106; CANR 125

Berton, Pierre (Francis Demarigny)
1920-2004 .... **CLC 104**
See also CA 1-4R; CANR 2, 56; CPW;
DLB 68; SATA 99

Bertrand, Aloysius 1807-1841 .... **NCLC 31**
See Bertrand, Louis oAloysiusc

Bertrand, Louis oAloysiusc
See Bertrand, Aloysius
See also DLB 217

Bertran de Born c. 1140-1215 .... **CMLC 5**

Besant, Annie (Wood) 1847-1933 ..... **TCLC 9**
See also CA 105; 185

Bessie, Alvah 1904-1985 .... CLC 23
See also CA 5-8R; 116; CANR 2, 80; DLB
26
Bestuzhev, Aleksandr Aleksandrovich
1797-1837 .... NCLC 131
See also DLB 198
Bethlen, T. D.
See Silverberg, Robert
Beti, Mongo .... BLC 1; CLC 27
See Biyidi, Alexandre
See also AFW; CANR 79; DAM MULT;
EWL 3; WLIT 2
Betjeman, John 1906-1984 .... CLC 2, 6, 10,
34, 43
See also BRW 7; CA 9-12R; 112; CANR
33, 56; CDBLB 1945-1960; DA3; DAB;
DAM MST, POET; DLB 20; DLBY 1984;
EWL 3; MTCW 1, 2
Bettelheim, Bruno 1903-1990 .... CLC 79;
TCLC 143
See also CA 81-84; 131; CANR 23, 61;
DA3; MTCW 1, 2
Betti, Ugo 1892-1953 .... TCLC 5
See also CA 104; 155; EWL 3; RGWL 2, 3
Betts, Doris (Waugh) 1932- ..... CLC 3, 6, 28;
SSC 45
See also CA 13-16R; CANR 9, 66, 77; CN
7; CSW; DLB 218; DLBY 1982; INT
CANR-9; RGAL 4
Bevan, Alistair
See Roberts, Keith (John Kingston)
Bey, Pilaff
See Douglas, (George) Norman
Bialik, Chaim Nachman
1873-1934 .... TCLC 25
See also CA 170; EWL 3
Bickerstaff, Isaac
See Swift, Jonathan
Bidart, Frank 1939- .... CLC 33
See also CA 140; CANR 106; CP 7
Bienek, Horst 1930- .... CLC 7, 11
See also CA 73-76; DLB 75
Bierce, Ambrose (Gwinett)
1842-1914(?) ..... SSC 9, 72; TCLC 1, 7,
44; WLC
See also AAYA 55; AMW; BYA 11; CA
104; 139; CANR 78; CDALB 1865-1917;
DA; DA3; DAC; DAM MST; DLB 11,
12, 23, 71, 74, 186; EWL 3; EXPS; HGG;
LAIT 2; RGAL 4; RGSF 2; SSFS 9;
SUFW 1
Biggers, Earl Derr 1884-1933 .... TCLC 65
See also CA 108; 153; DLB 306
Billiken, Bud
See Motley, Willard (Francis)
Billings, Josh
See Shaw, Henry Wheeler
Billington, (Lady) Rachel (Mary)
1942- .... CLC 43
See also AITN 2; CA 33-36R; CANR 44;
CN 7
Binchy, Maeve 1940- .... CLC 153
See also BEST 90:1; BPFB 1; CA 127; 134;
CANR 50, 96, 134; CN 7; CPW; DA3;
DAM POP; INT CA-134; MTCW 1;
RHW
Binyon, T(imothy) J(ohn) 1936- .... CLC 34
See also CA 111; CANR 28
Bion 335B.C.-245B.C. .... CMLC 39
Bioy Casares, Adolfo 1914-1999 .... CLC 4, 8,
13, 88; HLC 1; SSC 17
See Casares, Adolfo Bioy; Miranda, Javier;
Sacastru, Martin
See also CA 29-32R; 177; CANR 19, 43,
66; CWW 2; DAM MULT; DLB 113;
EWL 3; HW 1, 2; LAW; MTCW 1, 2
Birch, Allison .... CLC 65
Bird, Cordwainer
See Ellison, Harlan (Jay)

Bird, Robert Montgomery
1806-1854 .... NCLC 1
See also DLB 202; RGAL 4
Birkerts, Sven 1951- .... CLC 116
See also CA 128; 133, 176; CAAE 176;
CAAS 29; INT CA-133
Birney, (Alfred) Earle 1904-1995 .. CLC 1, 4,
6, 11; PC 52
See also CA 1-4R; CANR 5, 20; CP 7;
DAC; DAM MST, POET; DLB 88;
MTCW 1; PFS 8; RGEL 2
Biruni, al 973-1048(?) .... CMLC 28
Bishop, Elizabeth 1911-1979 ..... CLC 1, 4, 9,
13, 15, 32; PC 3, 34; TCLC 121
See also AMWR 2; AMWS 1; CA 5-8R;
89-92; CABS 2; CANR 26, 61, 108;
CDALB 1968-1988; DA; DA3; DAC;
DAM MST, POET; DLB 5, 169; EWL 3;
GLL 2; MAWW; MTCW 1, 2; PAB; PFS
6, 12; RGAL 4; SATA-Obit 24; TUS; WP
Bishop, John 1935- .... CLC 10
See also CA 105
Bishop, John Peale 1892-1944 ..... TCLC 103
See also CA 107; 155; DLB 4, 9, 45; RGAL
4
Bissett, Bill 1939- .... CLC 18; PC 14
See also CA 69-72; CAAS 19; CANR 15;
CCA 1; CP 7; DLB 53; MTCW 1
Bissoondath, Neil (Devindra)
1955- .... CLC 120
See also CA 136; CANR 123; CN 7; DAC
Bitov, Andrei (Georgievich) 1937- ... CLC 57
See also CA 142; DLB 302
Biyidi, Alexandre 1932-
See Beti, Mongo
See also BW 1, 3; CA 114; 124; CANR 81;
DA3; MTCW 1, 2
Bjarme, Brynjolf
See Ibsen, Henrik (Johan)
Bjoernson, Bjoernstjerne (Martinius)
1832-1910 .... TCLC 7, 37
See also CA 104
Black, Robert
See Holdstock, Robert P.
Blackburn, Paul 1926-1971 .... CLC 9, 43
See also BG 2; CA 81-84; 33-36R; CANR
34; DLB 16; DLBY 1981
Black Elk 1863-1950 .... NNAL; TCLC 33
See also CA 144; DAM MULT; MTCW 1;
WP
Black Hawk 1767-1838 .... NNAL
Black Hobart
See Sanders, (James) Ed(ward)
Blacklin, Malcolm
See Chambers, Aidan
Blackmore, R(ichard) D(oddridge)
1825-1900 .... TCLC 27
See also CA 120; DLB 18; RGEL 2
Blackmur, R(ichard) P(almer)
1904-1965 .... CLC 2, 24
See also AMWS 2; CA 11-12; 25-28R;
CANR 71; CAP 1; DLB 63; EWL 3
Black Tarantula
See Acker, Kathy
Blackwood, Algernon (Henry)
1869-1951 .... TCLC 5
See also CA 105; 150; DLB 153, 156, 178;
HGG; SUFW 1
Blackwood, Caroline 1931-1996 .... CLC 6, 9,
100
See also BRWS 9; CA 85-88; 151; CANR
32, 61, 65; CN 7; DLB 14, 207; HGG;
MTCW 1
Blade, Alexander
See Hamilton, Edmond; Silverberg, Robert
Blaga, Lucian 1895-1961 .... CLC 75
See also CA 157; DLB 220; EWL 3

Blair, Eric (Arthur) 1903-1950 .... TCLC 123
See Orwell, George
See also CA 104; 132; DA; DA3; DAB;
DAC; DAM MST, NOV; MTCW 1, 2;
SATA 29
Blair, Hugh 1718-1800 .... NCLC 75
Blais, Marie-Claire 1939- .... CLC 2, 4, 6, 13,
22
See also CA 21-24R; CAAS 4; CANR 38,
75, 93; CWW 2; DAC; DAM MST; DLB
53; EWL 3; FW; MTCW 1, 2; TWA
Blaise, Clark 1940- .... CLC 29
See also AITN 2; CA 53-56; CAAS 3;
CANR 5, 66, 106; CN 7; DLB 53; RGSF
2
Blake, Fairley
See De Voto, Bernard (Augustine)
Blake, Nicholas
See Day Lewis, C(ecil)
See also DLB 77; MSW
Blake, Sterling
See Benford, Gregory (Albert)
Blake, William 1757-1827 . NCLC 13, 37, 57,
127; PC 12; WLC
See also AAYA 47; BRW 3; BRWR 1; CD-
BLB 1789-1832; CLR 52; DA; DA3;
DAB; DAC; DAM MST, POET; DLB 93,
163; EXPP; LATS 1:1; LMFS 1; MAI-
CYA 1, 2; PAB; PFS 2, 12; SATA 30;
TEA; WCH; WLIT 3; WP
Blanchot, Maurice 1907-2003 .... CLC 135
See also CA 117; 144; 213; DLB 72, 296;
EWL 3
Blasco Ibanez, Vicente 1867-1928 . TCLC 12
See also BPFB 1; CA 110; 131; CANR 81;
DA3; DAM NOV; EW 8; EWL 3; HW 1,
2; MTCW 1
Blatty, William Peter 1928- .... CLC 2
See also CA 5-8R; CANR 9, 124; DAM
POP; HGG
Bleeck, Oliver
See Thomas, Ross (Elmore)
Blessing, Lee 1949- .... CLC 54
See also CAD; CD 5
Blight, Rose
See Greer, Germaine
Blish, James (Benjamin) 1921-1975 . CLC 14
See also BPFB 1; CA 1-4R; 57-60; CANR
3; DLB 8; MTCW 1; SATA 66; SCFW 2;
SFW 4
Bliss, Frederick
See Card, Orson Scott
Bliss, Reginald
See Wells, H(erbert) G(eorge)
Blixen, Karen (Christentze Dinesen)
1885-1962
See Dinesen, Isak
See also CA 25-28; CANR 22, 50; CAP 2;
DA3; DLB 214; LMFS 1; MTCW 1, 2;
SATA 44; SSFS 20
Bloch, Robert (Albert) 1917-1994 .... CLC 33
See also AAYA 29; CA 5-8R, 179; 146;
CAAE 179; CAAS 20; CANR 5, 78;
DA3; DLB 44; HGG; INT CANR-5;
MTCW 1; SATA 12; SATA-Obit 82; SFW
4; SUFW 1, 2
Blok, Alexander (Alexandrovich)
1880-1921 .... PC 21; TCLC 5
See also CA 104; 183; DLB 295; EW 9;
EWL 3; LMFS 2; RGWL 2, 3
Blom, Jan
See Breytenbach, Breyten
Bloom, Harold 1930- .... CLC 24, 103
See also CA 13-16R; CANR 39, 75, 92,
133; DLB 67; EWL 3; MTCW 1; RGAL
4
Bloomfield, Aurelius
See Bourne, Randolph S(illiman)

Bloomfield, Robert 1766-1823 ..... **NCLC 145**
See also DLB 93

Blount, Roy (Alton), Jr. 1941- .... **CLC 38**
See also CA 53-56; CANR 10, 28, 61, 125;
CSW; INT CANR-28; MTCW 1, 2

Blowsnake, Sam 1875-(?) .... **NNAL**

Bloy, Leon 1846-1917 .... **TCLC 22**
See also CA 121; 183; DLB 123; GFL 1789
to the Present

Blue Cloud, Peter (Aroniawenrate)
1933- .... **NNAL**
See also CA 117; CANR 40; DAM MULT

Bluggage, Oranthy
See Alcott, Louisa May

Blume, Judy (Sussman) 1938- .... **CLC 12, 30**
See also AAYA 3, 26; BYA 1, 8, 12; CA 29-
32R; CANR 13, 37, 66, 124; CLR 2, 15,
69; CPW; DA3; DAM NOV, POP; DLB
52; JRDA; MAICYA 1, 2; MAICYAS 1;
MTCW 1, 2; SATA 2, 31, 79, 142; WYA;
YAW

Blunden, Edmund (Charles)
1896-1974 .... **CLC 2, 56**
See also BRW 6; CA 17-18; 45-48; CANR
54; CAP 2; DLB 20, 100, 155; MTCW 1;
PAB

Bly, Robert (Elwood) 1926- .... **CLC 1, 2, 5,
10, 15, 38, 128; PC 39**
See also AMWS 4; CA 5-8R; CANR 41,
73, 125; CP 7; DA3; DAM POET; DLB
5; EWL 3; MTCW 1, 2; PFS 6, 17; RGAL
4

Boas, Franz 1858-1942 .... **TCLC 56**
See also CA 115; 181

Bobette
See Simenon, Georges (Jacques Christian)

Boccaccio, Giovanni 1313-1375 ... **CMLC 13,
57; SSC 10**
See also EW 2; RGSF 2; RGWL 2, 3; TWA

Bochco, Steven 1943- .... **CLC 35**
See also AAYA 11; CA 124; 138

Bode, Sigmund
See O'Doherty, Brian

Bodel, Jean 1167(?)-1210 .... **CMLC 28**

Bodenheim, Maxwell 1892-1954 .... **TCLC 44**
See also CA 110; 187; DLB 9, 45; RGAL 4

Bodenheimer, Maxwell
See Bodenheim, Maxwell

Bodker, Cecil 1927-
See Bodker, Cecil

Bodker, Cecil 1927- .... **CLC 21**
See also CA 73-76; CANR 13, 44, 111;
CLR 23; MAICYA 1, 2; SATA 14, 133

Boell, Heinrich (Theodor)
1917-1985 ..... **CLC 2, 3, 6, 9, 11, 15, 27,
32, 72; SSC 23; WLC**
See Boll, Heinrich
See also CA 21-24R; 116; CANR 24; DA;
DA3; DAB; DAC; DAM MST, NOV;
DLB 69; DLBY 1985; MTCW 1, 2; SSFS
20; TWA

Boerne, Alfred
See Doeblin, Alfred

Boethius c. 480-c. 524 .... **CMLC 15**
See also DLB 115; RGWL 2, 3

Boff, Leonardo (Genezio Darci)
1938- .... **CLC 70; HLC 1**
See also CA 150; DAM MULT; HW 2

Bogan, Louise 1897-1970 .... **CLC 4, 39, 46,
93; PC 12**
See also AMWS 3; CA 73-76; 25-28R;
CANR 33, 82; DAM POET; DLB 45, 169;
EWL 3; MAWW; MTCW 1, 2; PFS 21;
RGAL 4

Bogarde, Dirk
See Van Den Bogarde, Derek Jules Gaspard
Ulric Niven
See also DLB 14

Bogosian, Eric 1953- .... **CLC 45, 141**
See also CA 138; CAD; CANR 102; CD 5

Bograd, Larry 1953- .... **CLC 35**
See also CA 93-96; CANR 57; SAAS 21;
SATA 33, 89; WYA

Boiardo, Matteo Maria 1441-1494 .... **LC 6**

Boileau-Despreaux, Nicolas 1636-1711 . **LC 3**
See also DLB 268; EW 3; GFL Beginnings
to 1789; RGWL 2, 3

Boissard, Maurice
See Leautaud, Paul

Bojer, Johan 1872-1959 .... **TCLC 64**
See also CA 189; EWL 3

Bok, Edward W(illiam)
1863-1930 .... **TCLC 101**
See also CA 217; DLB 91; DLBD 16

Boker, George Henry 1823-1890 . **NCLC 125**
See also RGAL 4

Boland, Eavan (Aisling) 1944- .. **CLC 40, 67,
113; PC 58**
See also BRWS 5; CA 143, 207; CAAE
207; CANR 61; CP 7; CWP; DAM POET;
DLB 40; FW; MTCW 2; PFS 12

Boll, Heinrich
See Boell, Heinrich (Theodor)
See also BPFB 1; CDWLB 2; EW 13; EWL
3; RGSF 2; RGWL 2, 3

Bolt, Lee
See Faust, Frederick (Schiller)

Bolt, Robert (Oxton) 1924-1995 .... **CLC 14**
See also CA 17-20R; 147; CANR 35, 67;
CBD; DAM DRAM; DFS 2; DLB 13,
233; EWL 3; LAIT 1; MTCW 1

Bombal, Maria Luisa 1910-1980 .... **HLCS 1;
SSC 37**
See also CA 127; CANR 72; EWL 3; HW
1; LAW; RGSF 2

Bombet, Louis-Alexandre-Cesar
See Stendhal

Bomkauf
See Kaufman, Bob (Garnell)

Bonaventura .... **NCLC 35**
See also DLB 90

Bond, Edward 1934- .... **CLC 4, 6, 13, 23**
See also AAYA 50; BRWS 1; CA 25-28R;
CANR 38, 67, 106; CBD; CD 5; DAM
DRAM; DFS 3, 8; DLB 13; EWL 3;
MTCW 1

Bonham, Frank 1914-1989 .... **CLC 12**
See also AAYA 1; BYA 1, 3; CA 9-12R;
CANR 4, 36; JRDA; MAICYA 1, 2;
SAAS 3; SATA 1, 49; SATA-Obit 62;
TCWW 2; YAW

Bonnefoy, Yves 1923- . **CLC 9, 15, 58; PC 58**
See also CA 85-88; CANR 33, 75, 97;
CWW 2; DAM MST, POET; DLB 258;
EWL 3; GFL 1789 to the Present; MTCW
1, 2

Bonner, Marita .... **HR 2**
See Occomy, Marita (Odette) Bonner

Bonnin, Gertrude 1876-1938 .... **NNAL**
See Zitkala-Sa
See also CA 150; DAM MULT

Bontemps, Arna(ud Wendell)
1902-1973 ..... **BLC 1; CLC 1, 18; HR 2**
See also BW 1; CA 1-4R; 41-44R; CANR
4, 35; CLR 6; CWRI 5; DA3; DAM
MULT, NOV, POET; DLB 48, 51; JRDA;
MAICYA 1, 2; MTCW 1, 2; SATA 2, 44;
SATA-Obit 24; WCH; WP

Boot, William
See Stoppard, Tom

Booth, Martin 1944-2004 .... **CLC 13**
See also CA 93-96; 188; 223; CAAE 188;
CAAS 2; CANR 92

Booth, Philip 1925- .... **CLC 23**
See also CA 5-8R; CANR 5, 88; CP 7;
DLBY 1982

Booth, Wayne C(layson) 1921- .... **CLC 24**
See also CA 1-4R; CAAS 5; CANR 3, 43,
117; DLB 67

Borchert, Wolfgang 1921-1947 .... **TCLC 5**
See also CA 104; 188; DLB 69, 124; EWL
3

Borel, Petrus 1809-1859 .... **NCLC 41**
See also DLB 119; GFL 1789 to the Present

Borges, Jorge Luis 1899-1986 ... **CLC 1, 2, 3,
4, 6, 8, 9, 10, 13, 19, 44, 48, 83; HLC 1;
PC 22, 32; SSC 4, 41; TCLC 109;
WLC**
See also AAYA 26; BPFB 1; CA 21-24R;
CANR 19, 33, 75, 105, 133; CDWLB 3;
DA; DA3; DAB; DAC; DAM MST,
MULT; DLB 113, 283; DLBY 1986;
DNFS 1, 2; EWL 3; HW 1, 2; LAW;
LMFS 2; MSW; MTCW 1, 2; RGSF 2;
RGWL 2, 3; SFW 4; SSFS 17; TWA;
WLIT 1

Borowski, Tadeusz 1922-1951 .... **SSC 48;
TCLC 9**
See also CA 106; 154; CDWLB 4; DLB
215; EWL 3; RGSF 2; RGWL 3; SSFS
13

Borrow, George (Henry)
1803-1881 .... **NCLC 9**
See also DLB 21, 55, 166

Bosch (Gavino), Juan 1909-2001 ..... **HLCS 1**
See also CA 151; 204; DAM MST, MULT;
DLB 145; HW 1, 2

Bosman, Herman Charles
1905-1951 .... **TCLC 49**
See Malan, Herman
See also CA 160; DLB 225; RGSF 2

Bosschere, Jean de 1878(?)-1953 ... **TCLC 19**
See also CA 115; 186

Boswell, James 1740-1795 ... **LC 4, 50; WLC**
See also BRW 3; CDBLB 1660-1789; DA;
DAB; DAC; DAM MST; DLB 104, 142;
TEA; WLIT 3

Bottomley, Gordon 1874-1948 ..... **TCLC 107**
See also CA 120; 192; DLB 10

Bottoms, David 1949- .... **CLC 53**
See also CA 105; CANR 22; CSW; DLB
120; DLBY 1983

Boucicault, Dion 1820-1890 .... **NCLC 41**

Boucolon, Maryse
See Conde, Maryse

Bourdieu, Pierre 1930-2002 .... **CLC 198**
See also CA 130; 204

Bourget, Paul (Charles Joseph)
1852-1935 .... **TCLC 12**
See also CA 107; 196; DLB 123; GFL 1789
to the Present

Bourjaily, Vance (Nye) 1922- .... **CLC 8, 62**
See also CA 1-4R; CAAS 1; CANR 2, 72;
CN 7; DLB 2, 143

Bourne, Randolph S(illiman)
1886-1918 .... **TCLC 16**
See also AMW; CA 117; 155; DLB 63

Bova, Ben(jamin William) 1932- ...... **CLC 45**
See also AAYA 16; CA 5-8R; CAAS 18;
CANR 11, 56, 94, 111; CLR 3, 96; DLBY
1981; INT CANR-11; MAICYA 1, 2;
MTCW 1; SATA 6, 68, 133; SFW 4

Bowen, Elizabeth (Dorothea Cole)
1899-1973 . **CLC 1, 3, 6, 11, 15, 22, 118;
SSC 3, 28, 66; TCLC 148**
See also BRWS 2; CA 17-18; 41-44R;
CANR 35, 105; CAP 2; CDBLB 1945-
1960; DA3; DAM NOV; DLB 15, 162;
EWL 3; EXPS; FW; HGG; MTCW 1, 2;
NFS 13; RGSF 2; SSFS 5; SUFW 1;
TEA; WLIT 4

Bowering, George 1935- .... **CLC 15, 47**
See also CA 21-24R; CAAS 16; CANR 10;
CP 7; DLB 53

Bowering, Marilyn R(uthe) 1949- .... **CLC 32**
See also CA 101; CANR 49; CP 7; CWP

Bowers, Edgar 1924-2000 .... **CLC 9**
See also CA 5-8R; 188; CANR 24; CP 7; CSW; DLB 5

Bowers, Mrs. J. Milton 1842-1914
See Bierce, Ambrose (Gwinett)

Bowie, David .... **CLC 17**
See Jones, David Robert

Bowles, Jane (Sydney) 1917-1973 ..... **CLC 3, 68**
See Bowles, Jane Auer
See also CA 19-20; 41-44R; CAP 2

Bowles, Jane Auer
See Bowles, Jane (Sydney)
See also EWL 3

Bowles, Paul (Frederick) 1910-1999 . **CLC 1, 2, 19, 53; SSC 3**
See also AMWS 4; CA 1-4R; 186; CAAS 1; CANR 1, 19, 50, 75; CN 7; DA3; DLB 5, 6, 218; EWL 3; MTCW 1, 2; RGAL 4; SSFS 17

Bowles, William Lisle 1762-1850 . **NCLC 103**
See also DLB 93

Box, Edgar
See Vidal, (Eugene Luther) Gore
See also GLL 1

Boyd, James 1888-1944 .... **TCLC 115**
See also CA 186; DLB 9; DLBD 16; RGAL 4; RHW

Boyd, Nancy
See Millay, Edna St. Vincent
See also GLL 1

Boyd, Thomas (Alexander)
1898-1935 .... **TCLC 111**
See also CA 111; 183; DLB 9; DLBD 16

Boyd, William 1952- .... **CLC 28, 53, 70**
See also CA 114; 120; CANR 51, 71, 131; CN 7; DLB 231

Boyesen, Hjalmar Hjorth
1848-1895 .... **NCLC 135**
See also DLB 12, 71; DLBD 13; RGAL 4

Boyle, Kay 1902-1992 .... **CLC 1, 5, 19, 58, 121; SSC 5**
See also CA 13-16R; 140; CAAS 1; CANR 29, 61, 110; DLB 4, 9, 48, 86; DLBY 1993; EWL 3; MTCW 1, 2; RGAL 4; RGSF 2; SSFS 10, 13, 14

Boyle, Mark
See Kienzle, William X(avier)

Boyle, Patrick 1905-1982 .... **CLC 19**
See also CA 127

Boyle, T. C.
See Boyle, T(homas) Coraghessan
See also AMWS 8

Boyle, T(homas) Coraghessan
1948- .... **CLC 36, 55, 90; SSC 16**
See Boyle, T. C.
See also AAYA 47; BEST 90:4; BPFB 1; CA 120; CANR 44, 76, 89, 132; CN 7; CPW; DA3; DAM POP; DLB 218, 278; DLBY 1986; EWL 3; MTCW 2; SSFS 13, 19

Boz
See Dickens, Charles (John Huffam)

Brackenridge, Hugh Henry
1748-1816 .... **NCLC 7**
See also DLB 11, 37; RGAL 4

Bradbury, Edward P.
See Moorcock, Michael (John)
See also MTCW 2

Bradbury, Malcolm (Stanley)
1932-2000 .... **CLC 32, 61**
See also CA 1-4R; CANR 1, 33, 91, 98; CN 7; DA3; DAM NOV; DLB 14, 207; EWL 3; MTCW 1, 2

Bradbury, Ray (Douglas) 1920- .... **CLC 1, 3, 10, 15, 42, 98; SSC 29, 53; WLC**
See also AAYA 15; AITN 1, 2; AMWS 4; BPFB 1; BYA 4, 5, 11; CA 1-4R; CANR 2, 30, 75, 125; CDALB 1968-1988; CN 7; CPW; DA; DA3; DAB; DAC; DAM MST, NOV, POP; DLB 2, 8; EXPN; EXPS; HGG; LAIT 3, 5; LATS 1:2; LMFS 2; MTCW 1, 2; NFS 1; RGAL 4; RGSF 2; SATA 11, 64, 123; SCFW 2; SFW 4; SSFS 1, 20; SUFW 1, 2; TUS; YAW

Braddon, Mary Elizabeth
1837-1915 .... **TCLC 111**
See also BRWS 8; CA 108; 179; CMW 4; DLB 18, 70, 156; HGG

Bradfield, Scott (Michael) 1955- .... **SSC 65**
See also CA 147; CANR 90; HGG; SUFW 2

Bradford, Gamaliel 1863-1932 .... **TCLC 36**
See also CA 160; DLB 17

Bradford, William 1590-1657 .... **LC 64**
See also DLB 24, 30; RGAL 4

Bradley, David (Henry), Jr. 1950- .... **BLC 1; CLC 23, 118**
See also BW 1, 3; CA 104; CANR 26, 81; CN 7; DAM MULT; DLB 33

Bradley, John Ed(mund, Jr.) 1958- . **CLC 55**
See also CA 139; CANR 99; CN 7; CSW

Bradley, Marion Zimmer
1930-1999 .... **CLC 30**
See Chapman, Lee; Dexter, John; Gardner, Miriam; Ives, Morgan; Rivers, Elfrida
See also AAYA 40; BPFB 1; CA 57-60; 185; CAAS 10; CANR 7, 31, 51, 75, 107; CPW; DA3; DAM POP; DLB 8; FANT; FW; MTCW 1, 2; SATA 90, 139; SATA-Obit 116; SFW 4; SUFW 2; YAW

Bradshaw, John 1933- .... **CLC 70**
See also CA 138; CANR 61

Bradstreet, Anne 1612(?)-1672 ...... **LC 4, 30; PC 10**
See also AMWS 1; CDALB 1640-1865; DA; DA3; DAC; DAM MST, POET; DLB 24; EXPP; FW; PFS 6; RGAL 4; TUS; WP

Brady, Joan 1939- .... **CLC 86**
See also CA 141

Bragg, Melvyn 1939- .... **CLC 10**
See also BEST 89:3; CA 57-60; CANR 10, 48, 89; CN 7; DLB 14, 271; RHW

Brahe, Tycho 1546-1601 .... **LC 45**
See also DLB 300

Braine, John (Gerard) 1922-1986 . **CLC 1, 3, 41**
See also CA 1-4R; 120; CANR 1, 33; CD-BLB 1945-1960; DLB 15; DLBY 1986; EWL 3; MTCW 1

Braithwaite, William Stanley (Beaumont)
1878-1962 .... **BLC 1; HR 2; PC 52**
See also BW 1; CA 125; DAM MULT; DLB 50, 54

Bramah, Ernest 1868-1942 .... **TCLC 72**
See also CA 156; CMW 4; DLB 70; FANT

Brammer, William 1930(?)-1978 ...... **CLC 31**
See also CA 77-80

Brancati, Vitaliano 1907-1954 .... **TCLC 12**
See also CA 109; DLB 264; EWL 3

Brancato, Robin F(idler) 1936- .... **CLC 35**
See also AAYA 9; BYA 6; CA 69-72; CANR 11, 45; CLR 32; JRDA; MAICYA 2; MAICYAS 1; SAAS 9; SATA 97; WYA; YAW

Brand, Dionne 1953- .... **CLC 192**
See also BW 2; CA 143; CWP

Brand, Max
See Faust, Frederick (Schiller)
See also BPFB 1; TCWW 2

Brand, Millen 1906-1980 .... **CLC 7**
See also CA 21-24R; 97-100; CANR 72

Branden, Barbara .... **CLC 44**
See also CA 148

Brandes, Georg (Morris Cohen)
1842-1927 .... **TCLC 10**
See also CA 105; 189; DLB 300

Brandys, Kazimierz 1916-2000 .... **CLC 62**
See also EWL 3

Branley, Franklyn M(ansfield)
1915-2002 .... **CLC 21**
See also CA 33-36R; 207; CANR 14, 39; CLR 13; MAICYA 1, 2; SAAS 16; SATA 4, 68, 136

Brant, Beth (E.) 1941- .... **NNAL**
See also CA 144; FW

Brathwaite, Edward Kamau
1930- .... **BLCS; CLC 11; PC 56**
See also BW 2, 3; CA 25-28R; CANR 11, 26, 47, 107; CDWLB 3; CP 7; DAM POET; DLB 125; EWL 3

Brathwaite, Kamau
See Brathwaite, Edward Kamau

Brautigan, Richard (Gary)
1935-1984 .... **CLC 1, 3, 5, 9, 12, 34, 42; TCLC 133**
See also BPFB 1; CA 53-56; 113; CANR 34; DA3; DAM NOV; DLB 2, 5, 206; DLBY 1980, 1984; FANT; MTCW 1; RGAL 4; SATA 56

Brave Bird, Mary .... **NNAL**
See Crow Dog, Mary (Ellen)

Braverman, Kate 1950- .... **CLC 67**
See also CA 89-92

Brecht, (Eugen) Bertolt (Friedrich)
1898-1956 ..... **DC 3; TCLC 1, 6, 13, 35; WLC**
See also CA 104; 133; CANR 62; CDWLB 2; DA; DA3; DAB; DAC; DAM DRAM, MST; DFS 4, 5, 9; DLB 56, 124; EW 11; EWL 3; IDTP; MTCW 1, 2; RGWL 2, 3; TWA

Brecht, Eugen Berthold Friedrich
See Brecht, (Eugen) Bertolt (Friedrich)

Bremer, Fredrika 1801-1865 .... **NCLC 11**
See also DLB 254

Brennan, Christopher John
1870-1932 .... **TCLC 17**
See also CA 117; 188; DLB 230; EWL 3

Brennan, Maeve 1917-1993 ... **CLC 5; TCLC 124**
See also CA 81-84; CANR 72, 100

Brent, Linda
See Jacobs, Harriet A(nn)

Brentano, Clemens (Maria)
1778-1842 .... **NCLC 1**
See also DLB 90; RGWL 2, 3

Brent of Bin Bin
See Franklin, (Stella Maria Sarah) Miles (Lampe)

Brenton, Howard 1942- .... **CLC 31**
See also CA 69-72; CANR 33, 67; CBD; CD 5; DLB 13; MTCW 1

Breslin, James 1930-
See Breslin, Jimmy
See also CA 73-76; CANR 31, 75; DAM NOV; MTCW 1, 2

Breslin, Jimmy .... **CLC 4, 43**
See Breslin, James
See also AITN 1; DLB 185; MTCW 2

Bresson, Robert 1901(?)-1999 .... **CLC 16**
See also CA 110; 187; CANR 49

Breton, Andre 1896-1966 .. **CLC 2, 9, 15, 54; PC 15**
See also CA 19-20; 25-28R; CANR 40, 60; CAP 2; DLB 65, 258; EW 11; EWL 3; GFL 1789 to the Present; LMFS 2; MTCW 1, 2; RGWL 2, 3; TWA; WP

Breytenbach, Breyten 1939(?)- .. **CLC 23, 37, 126**
See also CA 113; 129; CANR 61, 122; CWW 2; DAM POET; DLB 225; EWL 3

Bridgers, Sue Ellen 1942- .... **CLC 26**
See also AAYA 8, 49; BYA 7, 8; CA 65-68; CANR 11, 36; CLR 18; DLB 52; JRDA; MAICYA 1, 2; SAAS 1; SATA 22, 90; SATA-Essay 109; WYA; YAW

Bridges, Robert (Seymour)
1844-1930 .... **PC 28; TCLC 1**
See also BRW 6; CA 104; 152; CDBLB 1890-1914; DAM POET; DLB 19, 98

Bridie, James .... **TCLC 3**
See Mavor, Osborne Henry
See also DLB 10; EWL 3

Brin, David 1950- .... **CLC 34**
See also AAYA 21; CA 102; CANR 24, 70, 125, 127; INT CANR-24; SATA 65; SCFW 2; SFW 4

Brink, Andre (Philippus) 1935- . **CLC 18, 36, 106**
See also AFW; BRWS 6; CA 104; CANR 39, 62, 109, 133; CN 7; DLB 225; EWL 3; INT CA-103; LATS 1:2; MTCW 1, 2; WLIT 2

Brinsmead, H. F(ay)
See Brinsmead, H(esba) F(ay)

Brinsmead, H. F.
See Brinsmead, H(esba) F(ay)

Brinsmead, H(esba) F(ay) 1922- ...... **CLC 21**
See also CA 21-24R; CANR 10; CLR 47; CWRI 5; MAICYA 1, 2; SAAS 5; SATA 18, 78

Brittain, Vera (Mary) 1893(?)-1970 . **CLC 23**
See also BRWS 10; CA 13-16; 25-28R; CANR 58; CAP 1; DLB 191; FW; MTCW 1, 2

Broch, Hermann 1886-1951 .... **TCLC 20**
See also CA 117; 211; CDWLB 2; DLB 85, 124; EW 10; EWL 3; RGWL 2, 3

Brock, Rose
See Hansen, Joseph
See also GLL 1

Brod, Max 1884-1968 .... **TCLC 115**
See also CA 5-8R; 25-28R; CANR 7; DLB 81; EWL 3

Brodkey, Harold (Roy) 1930-1996 .. **CLC 56; TCLC 123**
See also CA 111; 151; CANR 71; CN 7; DLB 130

Brodsky, Iosif Alexandrovich 1940-1996
See Brodsky, Joseph
See also AITN 1; CA 41-44R; 151; CANR 37, 106; DA3; DAM POET; MTCW 1, 2; RGWL 2, 3

Brodsky, Joseph . **CLC 4, 6, 13, 36, 100; PC 9**
See Brodsky, Iosif Alexandrovich
See also AMWS 8; CWW 2; DLB 285; EWL 3; MTCW 1

Brodsky, Michael (Mark) 1948- .... **CLC 19**
See also CA 102; CANR 18, 41, 58; DLB 244

Brodzki, Bella ed. .... **CLC 65**

Brome, Richard 1590(?)-1652 .... **LC 61**
See also BRWS 10; DLB 58

Bromell, Henry 1947- .... **CLC 5**
See also CA 53-56; CANR 9, 115, 116

Bromfield, Louis (Brucker)
1896-1956 .... **TCLC 11**
See also CA 107; 155; DLB 4, 9, 86; RGAL 4; RHW

Broner, E(sther) M(asserman)
1930- .... **CLC 19**
See also CA 17-20R; CANR 8, 25, 72; CN 7; DLB 28

Bronk, William (M.) 1918-1999 .... **CLC 10**
See also CA 89-92; 177; CANR 23; CP 7; DLB 165

Bronstein, Lev Davidovich
See Trotsky, Leon

Bronte, Anne 1820-1849 ..... **NCLC 4, 71, 102**
See also BRW 5; BRWR 1; DA3; DLB 21, 199; TEA

Bronte, (Patrick) Branwell
1817-1848 .... **NCLC 109**

Bronte, Charlotte 1816-1855 ...... **NCLC 3, 8, 33, 58, 105; WLC**
See also AAYA 17; BRW 5; BRWC 2; BRWR 1; BYA 2; CDBLB 1832-1890; DA; DA3; DAB; DAC; DAM MST, NOV, DLB 21, 159, 199; EXPN; LAIT 2; NFS 4; TEA; WLIT 4

Bronte, Emily (Jane) 1818-1848 ... **NCLC 16, 35; PC 8; WLC**
See also AAYA 17; BPFB 1; BRW 5; BRWC 1; BRWR 1; BYA 3; CDBLB 1832-1890; DA; DA3; DAB; DAC; DAM MST, NOV, POET; DLB 21, 32, 199; EXPN; LAIT 1; TEA; WLIT 3

Brontes
See Bronte, Anne; Bronte, Charlotte; Bronte, Emily (Jane)

Brooke, Frances 1724-1789 .... **LC 6, 48**
See also DLB 39, 99

Brooke, Henry 1703(?)-1783 .... **LC 1**
See also DLB 39

Brooke, Rupert (Chawner)
1887-1915 ..... **PC 24; TCLC 2, 7; WLC**
See also BRWS 3; CA 104; 132; CANR 61; CDBLB 1914-1945; DA; DAB; DAC; DAM MST, POET; DLB 19, 216; EXPP; GLL 2; MTCW 1, 2; PFS 7; TEA

Brooke-Haven, P.
See Wodehouse, P(elham) G(renville)

Brooke-Rose, Christine 1926(?)- ..... **CLC 40, 184**
See also BRWS 4; CA 13-16R; CANR 58; 118; CN 7; DLB 14, 231; EWL 3; SFW 4

Brookner, Anita 1928- .. **CLC 32, 34, 51, 136**
See also BRWS 4; CA 114; 120; CANR 37, 56, 87, 130; CN 7; CPW; DA3; DAB; DAM POP; DLB 194; DLBY 1987; EWL 3; MTCW 1, 2; TEA

Brooks, Cleanth 1906-1994 . **CLC 24, 86, 110**
See also AMWS 14; CA 17-20R; 145; CANR 33, 35; CSW; DLB 63; DLBY 1994; EWL 3; INT CANR-35; MTCW 1, 2

Brooks, George
See Baum, L(yman) Frank

Brooks, Gwendolyn (Elizabeth)
1917-2000 ... **BLC 1; CLC 1, 2, 4, 5, 15, 49, 125; PC 7; WLC**
See also AAYA 20; AFAW 1, 2; AITN 1; AMWS 3; BW 2, 3; CA 1-4R; 190; CANR 1, 27, 52, 75, 132; CDALB 1941-1968; CLR 27; CP 7; CWP; DA; DA3; DAC; DAM MST, MULT, POET; DLB 5, 76, 165; MAWW; MTCW 1, 2; PFS 1, 2, 4, 6; RGAL 4; SATA 6; SATA-Obit 123; TUS; WP

Brooks, Mel .... **CLC 12**
See Kaminsky, Melvin
See also AAYA 13, 48; DLB 26

Brooks, Peter (Preston) 1938- .... **CLC 34**
See also CA 45-48; CANR 1, 107

Brooks, Van Wyck 1886-1963 .... **CLC 29**
See also AMW; CA 1-4R; CANR 6; DLB 45, 63, 103; TUS

Brophy, Brigid (Antonia)
1929-1995 .... **CLC 6, 11, 29, 105**
See also CA 5-8R; 149; CAAS 4; CANR 25, 53; CBD; CN 7; CWD; DA3; DLB 14, 271; EWL 3; MTCW 1, 2

Brosman, Catharine Savage 1934- ..... **CLC 9**
See also CA 61-64; CANR 21, 46

Brossard, Nicole 1943- .... **CLC 115, 169**
See also CA 122; CAAS 16; CCA 1; CWP; CWW 2; DLB 53; EWL 3; FW; GLL 2; RGWL 3

Brother Antoninus
See Everson, William (Oliver)

The Brothers Quay
See Quay, Stephen; Quay, Timothy

Broughton, T(homas) Alan 1936- ..... **CLC 19**
See also CA 45-48; CANR 2, 23, 48, 111

Broumas, Olga 1949- .... **CLC 10, 73**
See also CA 85-88; CANR 20, 69, 110; CP 7; CWP; GLL 2

Broun, Heywood 1888-1939 .... **TCLC 104**
See also DLB 29, 171

Brown, Alan 1950- .... **CLC 99**
See also CA 156

Brown, Charles Brockden
1771-1810 .... **NCLC 22, 74, 122**
See also AMWS 1; CDALB 1640-1865; DLB 37, 59, 73; FW; HGG; LMFS 1; RGAL 4; TUS

Brown, Christy 1932-1981 .... **CLC 63**
See also BYA 13; CA 105; 104; CANR 72; DLB 14

Brown, Claude 1937-2002 ... **BLC 1; CLC 30**
See also AAYA 7; BW 1, 3; CA 73-76; 205; CANR 81; DAM MULT

Brown, Dee (Alexander)
1908-2002 .... **CLC 18, 47**
See also AAYA 30; CA 13-16R; 212; CAAS 6; CANR 11, 45, 60; CPW; CSW; DA3; DAM POP; DLBY 1980; LAIT 2; MTCW 1, 2; NCFS 5; SATA 5, 110; SATA-Obit 141; TCWW 2

Brown, George
See Wertmueller, Lina

Brown, George Douglas
1869-1902 .... **TCLC 28**
See Douglas, George
See also CA 162

Brown, George Mackay 1921-1996 ... **CLC 5, 48, 100**
See also BRWS 6; CA 21-24R; 151; CAAS 6; CANR 12, 37, 67; CN 7; CP 7; DLB 14, 27, 139, 271; MTCW 1; RGSF 2; SATA 35

Brown, (William) Larry 1951-2004 . **CLC 73**
See also CA 130; 134; CANR 117; CSW; DLB 234; INT CA-134

Brown, Moses
See Barrett, William (Christopher)

Brown, Rita Mae 1944- .... **CLC 18, 43, 79**
See also BPFB 1; CA 45-48; CANR 2, 11, 35, 62, 95; CN 7; CPW; CSW; DA3; DAM NOV, POP; FW; INT CANR-11; MTCW 1, 2; NFS 9; RGAL 4; TUS

Brown, Roderick (Langmere) Haig-
See Haig-Brown, Roderick (Langmere)

Brown, Rosellen 1939- .... **CLC 32, 170**
See also CA 77-80; CAAS 10; CANR 14, 44, 98; CN 7

Brown, Sterling Allen 1901-1989 ...... **BLC 1; CLC 1, 23, 59; HR 2; PC 55**
See also AFAW 1, 2; BW 1, 3; CA 85-88; 127; CANR 26; DA3; DAM MULT, POET; DLB 48, 51, 63; MTCW 1, 2; RGAL 4; WP

Brown, Will
See Ainsworth, William Harrison

Brown, William Hill 1765-1793 .... **LC 93**
See also DLB 37

Brown, William Wells 1815-1884 ...... **BLC 1; DC 1; NCLC 2, 89**
See also DAM MULT; DLB 3, 50, 183, 248; RGAL 4

Browne, (Clyde) Jackson 1948(?)- ... **CLC 21**
See also CA 120

Browning, Elizabeth Barrett
1806-1861 ... **NCLC 1, 16, 61, 66; PC 6; WLC**
See also BRW 4; CDBLB 1832-1890; DA; DA3; DAB; DAC; DAM MST, POET; DLB 32, 199; EXPP; PAB; PFS 2, 16; TEA; WLIT 4; WP

Browning, Robert 1812-1889 . **NCLC 19, 79; PC 2, 61; WLCS**
See also BRW 4; BRWC 2; BRWR 2; CD-BLB 1832-1890; CLR 97; DA; DA3; DAB; DAC; DAM MST, POET; DLB 32, 163; EXPP; LATS 1:1; PAB; PFS 1, 15; RGEL 2; TEA; WLIT 4; WP; YABC 1

Browning, Tod 1882-1962 .... **CLC 16**
See also CA 141; 117

Brownmiller, Susan 1935- .... **CLC 159**
See also CA 103; CANR 35, 75; DAM NOV; FW; MTCW 1, 2

Brownson, Orestes Augustus
1803-1876 .... **NCLC 50**
See also DLB 1, 59, 73, 243

Bruccoli, Matthew J(oseph) 1931- ... **CLC 34**
See also CA 9-12R; CANR 7, 87; DLB 103

Bruce, Lenny .... **CLC 21**
See Schneider, Leonard Alfred

Bruchac, Joseph III 1942- .... **NNAL**
See also AAYA 19; CA 33-36R; CANR 13, 47, 75, 94; CLR 46; CWRI 5; DAM MULT; JRDA; MAICYA 2; MAICYAS 1; MTCW 1; SATA 42, 89, 131

Bruin, John
See Brutus, Dennis

Brulard, Henri
See Stendhal

Brulls, Christian
See Simenon, Georges (Jacques Christian)

Brunner, John (Kilian Houston)
1934-1995 .... **CLC 8, 10**
See also CA 1-4R; 149; CAAS 8; CANR 2, 37; CPW; DAM POP; DLB 261; MTCW 1, 2; SCFW 2; SFW 4

Bruno, Giordano 1548-1600 .... **LC 27**
See also RGWL 2, 3

Brutus, Dennis 1924- ... **BLC 1; CLC 43; PC 24**
See also AFW; BW 2, 3; CA 49-52; CAAS 14; CANR 2, 27, 42, 81; CDWLB 3; CP 7; DAM MULT, POET; DLB 117, 225; EWL 3

Bryan, C(ourtlandt) D(ixon) B(arnes)
1936- .... **CLC 29**
See also CA 73-76; CANR 13, 68; DLB 185; INT CANR-13

Bryan, Michael
See Moore, Brian
See also CCA 1

Bryan, William Jennings
1860-1925 .... **TCLC 99**
See also DLB 303

Bryant, William Cullen 1794-1878 . **NCLC 6, 46; PC 20**
See also AMWS 1; CDALB 1640-1865; DA; DAB; DAC; DAM MST, POET; DLB 3, 43, 59, 189, 250; EXPP; PAB; RGAL 4; TUS

Bryusov, Valery Yakovlevich
1873-1924 .... **TCLC 10**
See also CA 107; 155; EWL 3; SFW 4

Buchan, John 1875-1940 .... **TCLC 41**
See also CA 108; 145; CMW 4; DAB; DAM POP; DLB 34, 70, 156; HGG; MSW; MTCW 1; RGEL 2; RHW; YABC 2

Buchanan, George 1506-1582 .... **LC 4**
See also DLB 132

Buchanan, Robert 1841-1901 .... **TCLC 107**
See also CA 179; DLB 18, 35

Buchheim, Lothar-Guenther 1918- .... **CLC 6**
See also CA 85-88

Buchner, (Karl) Georg
1813-1837 .... **NCLC 26, 146**
See also CDWLB 2; DLB 133; EW 6; RGSF 2; RGWL 2, 3; TWA

Buchwald, Art(hur) 1925- .... **CLC 33**
See also AITN 1; CA 5-8R; CANR 21, 67, 107; MTCW 1, 2; SATA 10

Buck, Pearl S(ydenstricker)
1892-1973 .... **CLC 7, 11, 18, 127**
See also AAYA 42; AITN 1; AMWS 2; BPFB 1; CA 1-4R; 41-44R; CANR 1, 34; CDALBS; DA; DA3; DAB; DAC; DAM MST, NOV; DLB 9, 102; EWL 3; LAIT 3; MTCW 1, 2; RGAL 4; RHW; SATA 1, 25; TUS

Buckler, Ernest 1908-1984 .... **CLC 13**
See also CA 11-12; 114; CAP 1; CCA 1; DAC; DAM MST; DLB 68; SATA 47

Buckley, Christopher (Taylor)
1952- .... **CLC 165**
See also CA 139; CANR 119

Buckley, Vincent (Thomas)
1925-1988 .... **CLC 57**
See also CA 101; DLB 289

Buckley, William F(rank), Jr. 1925- . **CLC 7, 18, 37**
See also AITN 1; BPFB 1; CA 1-4R; CANR 1, 24, 53, 93, 133; CMW 4; CPW; DA3; DAM POP; DLB 137; DLBY 1980; INT CANR-24; MTCW 1, 2; TUS

Buechner, (Carl) Frederick 1926- . **CLC 2, 4, 6, 9**
See also AMWS 12; BPFB 1; CA 13-16R; CANR 11, 39, 64, 114; CN 7; DAM NOV; DLBY 1980; INT CANR-11; MTCW 1, 2

Buell, John (Edward) 1927- .... **CLC 10**
See also CA 1-4R; CANR 71; DLB 53

Buero Vallejo, Antonio 1916-2000 ... **CLC 15, 46, 139; DC 18**
See also CA 106; 189; CANR 24, 49, 75; CWW 2; DFS 11; EWL 3; HW 1; MTCW 1, 2

Bufalino, Gesualdo 1920-1996 .... **CLC 74**
See also CA 209; CWW 2; DLB 196

Bugayev, Boris Nikolayevich
1880-1934 .... **PC 11; TCLC 7**
See Bely, Andrey; Belyi, Andrei
See also CA 104; 165; MTCW 1

Bukowski, Charles 1920-1994 ... **CLC 2, 5, 9, 41, 82, 108; PC 18; SSC 45**
See also CA 17-20R; 144; CANR 40, 62, 105; CPW; DA3; DAM NOV, POET; DLB 5, 130, 169; EWL 3; MTCW 1, 2

Bulgakov, Mikhail (Afanas'evich)
1891-1940 ..... **SSC 18; TCLC 2, 16, 159**
See also BPFB 1; CA 105; 152; DAM DRAM, NOV; DLB 272; EWL 3; NFS 8; RGSF 2; RGWL 2, 3; SFW 4; TWA

Bulgya, Alexander Alexandrovich
1901-1956 .... **TCLC 53**
See Fadeev, Aleksandr Aleksandrovich; Fadeev, Alexandr Alexandrovich; Fadeyev, Alexander
See also CA 117; 181

Bullins, Ed 1935- ... **BLC 1; CLC 1, 5, 7; DC 6**
See also BW 2, 3; CA 49-52; CAAS 16; CAD; CANR 24, 46, 73, 134; CD 5; DAM DRAM, MULT; DLB 7, 38, 249; EWL 3; MTCW 1, 2; RGAL 4

Bulosan, Carlos 1911-1956 .... **AAL**
See also CA 216; RGAL 4

Bulwer-Lytton, Edward (George Earle Lytton) 1803-1873 .... **NCLC 1, 45**
See also DLB 21; RGEL 2; SFW 4; SUFW 1; TEA

Bunin, Ivan Alexeyevich 1870-1953 ... **SSC 5; TCLC 6**
See also CA 104; EWL 3; RGSF 2; RGWL 2, 3; TWA

Bunting, Basil 1900-1985 ...... **CLC 10, 39, 47**
See also BRWS 7; CA 53-56; 115; CANR 7; DAM POET; DLB 20; EWL 3; RGEL 2

Bunuel, Luis 1900-1983 ... **CLC 16, 80; HLC 1**
See also CA 101; 110; CANR 32, 77; DAM MULT; HW 1

Bunyan, John 1628-1688 ..... **LC 4, 69; WLC**
See also BRW 2; BYA 5; CDBLB 1660-1789; DA; DAB; DAC; DAM MST; DLB 39; RGEL 2; TEA; WCH; WLIT 3

Buravsky, Alexandr .... **CLC 59**

Burckhardt, Jacob (Christoph)
1818-1897 .... **NCLC 49**
See also EW 6

Burford, Eleanor
See Hibbert, Eleanor Alice Burford

Burgess, Anthony . **CLC 1, 2, 4, 5, 8, 10, 13, 15, 22, 40, 62, 81, 94**
See Wilson, John (Anthony) Burgess
See also AAYA 25; AITN 1; BRWS 1; CD-BLB 1960 to Present; DAB; DLB 14, 194, 261; DLBY 1998; EWL 3; MTCW 1; RGEL 2; RHW; SFW 4; YAW

Burke, Edmund 1729(?)-1797 .... **LC 7, 36; WLC**
See also BRW 3; DA; DA3; DAB; DAC; DAM MST; DLB 104, 252; RGEL 2; TEA

Burke, Kenneth (Duva) 1897-1993 ... **CLC 2, 24**
See also AMW; CA 5-8R; 143; CANR 39, 74; DLB 45, 63; EWL 3; MTCW 1, 2; RGAL 4

Burke, Leda
See Garnett, David

Burke, Ralph
See Silverberg, Robert

Burke, Thomas 1886-1945 .... **TCLC 63**
See also CA 113; 155; CMW 4; DLB 197

Burney, Fanny 1752-1840 .... **NCLC 12, 54, 107**
See also BRWS 3; DLB 39; NFS 16; RGEL 2; TEA

Burney, Frances
See Burney, Fanny

Burns, Robert 1759-1796 ... **LC 3, 29, 40; PC 6; WLC**
See also AAYA 51; BRW 3; CDBLB 1789-1832; DA; DA3; DAB; DAC; DAM MST, POET; DLB 109; EXPP; PAB; RGEL 2; TEA; WP

Burns, Tex
See L'Amour, Louis (Dearborn)
See also TCWW 2

Burnshaw, Stanley 1906- .... **CLC 3, 13, 44**
See also CA 9-12R; CP 7; DLB 48; DLBY 1997

Burr, Anne 1937- .... **CLC 6**
See also CA 25-28R

Burroughs, Edgar Rice 1875-1950 . **TCLC 2, 32**
See also AAYA 11; BPFB 1; BYA 4, 9; CA 104; 132; CANR 131; DA3; DAM NOV; DLB 8; FANT; MTCW 1, 2; RGAL 4; SATA 41; SCFW 2; SFW 4; TUS; YAW

Burroughs, William S(eward)
1914-1997 .. **CLC 1, 2, 5, 15, 22, 42, 75, 109; TCLC 121; WLC**
See Lee, William; Lee, Willy
See also AAYA 60; AITN 2; AMWS 3; BG 2; BPFB 1; CA 9-12R; 160; CANR 20, 52, 104; CN 7; CPW; DA; DA3; DAB;

DAC; DAM MST, NOV, POP; DLB 2, 8,
16, 152, 237; DLBY 1981, 1997; EWL 3;
HGG; LMFS 2; MTCW 1, 2; RGAL 4;
SFW 4

Burton, Sir Richard F(rancis)
1821-1890 .... **NCLC 42**
See also DLB 55, 166, 184

Burton, Robert 1577-1640 .... **LC 74**
See also DLB 151; RGEL 2

Buruma, Ian 1951- .... **CLC 163**
See also CA 128; CANR 65

Busch, Frederick 1941- ... **CLC 7, 10, 18, 47, 166**
See also CA 33-36R; CAAS 1; CANR 45,
73, 92; CN 7; DLB 6, 218

Bush, Barney (Furman) 1946- .... **NNAL**
See also CA 145

Bush, Ronald 1946- .... **CLC 34**
See also CA 136

Bustos, F(rancisco)
See Borges, Jorge Luis

Bustos Domecq, H(onorio)
See Bioy Casares, Adolfo; Borges, Jorge
Luis

Butler, Octavia E(stelle) 1947- .. **BLCS; CLC 38, 121**
See also AAYA 18, 48; AFAW 2; AMWS
13; BPFB 1; BW 2, 3; CA 73-76; CANR
12, 24, 38, 73; CLR 65; CPW; DA3;
DAM MULT, POP; DLB 33; LATS 1:2;
MTCW 1, 2; NFS 8; SATA 84; SCFW 2;
SFW 4; SSFS 6; YAW

Butler, Robert Olen, (Jr.) 1945- ...... **CLC 81, 162**
See also AMWS 12; BPFB 1; CA 112;
CANR 66; CSW; DAM POP; DLB 173;
INT CA-112; MTCW 1; SSFS 11

Butler, Samuel 1612-1680 .... **LC 16, 43**
See also DLB 101, 126; RGEL 2

Butler, Samuel 1835-1902 .... **TCLC 1, 33; WLC**
See also BRWS 2; CA 143; CDBLB 1890-
1914; DA; DA3; DAB; DAC; DAM MST,
NOV; DLB 18, 57, 174; RGEL 2; SFW 4;
TEA

Butler, Walter C.
See Faust, Frederick (Schiller)

Butor, Michel (Marie Francois)
1926- .... **CLC 1, 3, 8, 11, 15, 161**
See also CA 9-12R; CANR 33, 66; CWW
2; DLB 83; EW 13; EWL 3; GFL 1789 to
the Present; MTCW 1, 2

Butts, Mary 1890(?)-1937 .... **TCLC 77**
See also CA 148; DLB 240

Buxton, Ralph
See Silverstein, Alvin; Silverstein, Virginia
B(arbara Opshelor)

Buzo, Alex
See Buzo, Alexander (John)
See also DLB 289

Buzo, Alexander (John) 1944- .... **CLC 61**
See also CA 97-100; CANR 17, 39, 69; CD
5

Buzzati, Dino 1906-1972 .... **CLC 36**
See also CA 160; 33-36R; DLB 177; RGWL
2, 3; SFW 4

Byars, Betsy (Cromer) 1928- .... **CLC 35**
See also AAYA 19; BYA 3; CA 33-36R,
183; CAAE 183; CANR 18, 36, 57, 102;
CLR 1, 16, 72; DLB 52; INT CANR-18;
JRDA; MAICYA 1, 2; MAICYAS 1;
MTCW 1; SAAS 1; SATA 4, 46, 80;
SATA-Essay 108; WYA; YAW

Byatt, A(ntonia) S(usan Drabble)
1936- .... **CLC 19, 65, 136**
See also BPFB 1; BRWC 2; BRWS 4; CA
13-16R; CANR 13, 33, 50, 75, 96, 133;
DA3; DAM NOV, POP; DLB 14, 194;
EWL 3; MTCW 1, 2; RGSF 2; RHW;
TEA

Byrne, David 1952- .... **CLC 26**
See also CA 127

Byrne, John Keyes 1926-
See Leonard, Hugh
See also CA 102; CANR 78; INT CA-102

Byron, George Gordon (Noel)
1788-1824 ..... **DC 24; NCLC 2, 12, 109, 149; PC 16; WLC**
See also BRW 4; BRWC 2; CDBLB 1789-
1832; DA; DA3; DAB; DAC; DAM MST,
POET; DLB 96, 110; EXPP; LMFS 1;
PAB; PFS 1, 14; RGEL 2; TEA; WLIT 3;
WP

Byron, Robert 1905-1941 .... **TCLC 67**
See also CA 160; DLB 195

C. 3. 3.
See Wilde, Oscar (Fingal O'Flahertie Wills)

Caballero, Fernan 1796-1877 .... **NCLC 10**

Cabell, Branch
See Cabell, James Branch

Cabell, James Branch 1879-1958 .... **TCLC 6**
See also CA 105; 152; DLB 9, 78; FANT;
MTCW 1; RGAL 4; SUFW 1

Cabeza de Vaca, Alvar Nunez
1490-1557(?) .... **LC 61**

Cable, George Washington
1844-1925 .... **SSC 4; TCLC 4**
See also CA 104; 155; DLB 12, 74; DLBD
13; RGAL 4; TUS

Cabral de Melo Neto, Joao
1920-1999 .... **CLC 76**
See Melo Neto, Joao Cabral de
See also CA 151; DAM MULT; DLB 307;
LAW; LAWS 1

Cabrera Infante, G(uillermo) 1929- . **CLC 5, 25, 45, 120; HLC 1; SSC 39**
See also CA 85-88; CANR 29, 65, 110; CD-
WLB 3; CWW 2; DA3; DAM MULT;
DLB 113; EWL 3; HW 1, 2; LAW; LAWS
1; MTCW 1, 2; RGSF 2; WLIT 1

Cade, Toni
See Bambara, Toni Cade

Cadmus and Harmonia
See Buchan, John

Caedmon fl. 658-680 .... **CMLC 7**
See also DLB 146

Caeiro, Alberto
See Pessoa, Fernando (Antonio Nogueira)

Caesar, Julius .... **CMLC 47**
See Julius Caesar
See also AW 1; RGWL 2, 3

Cage, John (Milton, Jr.)
1912-1992 .... **CLC 41; PC 58**
See also CA 13-16R; 169; CANR 9, 78;
DLB 193; INT CANR-9

Cahan, Abraham 1860-1951 .... **TCLC 71**
See also CA 108; 154; DLB 9, 25, 28;
RGAL 4

Cain, G.
See Cabrera Infante, G(uillermo)

Cain, Guillermo
See Cabrera Infante, G(uillermo)

Cain, James M(allahan) 1892-1977 .. **CLC 3, 11, 28**
See also AITN 1; BPFB 1; CA 17-20R; 73-
76; CANR 8, 34, 61; CMW 4; DLB 226;
EWL 3; MSW; MTCW 1; RGAL 4

Caine, Hall 1853-1931 .... **TCLC 97**
See also RHW

Caine, Mark
See Raphael, Frederic (Michael)

Calasso, Roberto 1941- .... **CLC 81**
See also CA 143; CANR 89

Calderon de la Barca, Pedro
1600-1681 .... **DC 3; HLCS 1; LC 23**
See also EW 2; RGWL 2, 3; TWA

Caldwell, Erskine (Preston)
1903-1987 .... **CLC 1, 8, 14, 50, 60; SSC 19; TCLC 117**
See also AITN 1; AMW; BPFB 1; CA 1-4R;
121; CAAS 1; CANR 2, 33; DA3; DAM
NOV; DLB 9, 86; EWL 3; MTCW 1, 2;
RGAL 4; RGSF 2; TUS

Caldwell, (Janet Miriam) Taylor (Holland)
1900-1985 .... **CLC 2, 28, 39**
See also BPFB 1; CA 5-8R; 116; CANR 5;
DA3; DAM NOV, POP; DLBD 17; RHW

Calhoun, John Caldwell
1782-1850 .... **NCLC 15**
See also DLB 3, 248

Calisher, Hortense 1911- ..... **CLC 2, 4, 8, 38, 134; SSC 15**
See also CA 1-4R; CANR 1, 22, 117; CN
7; DA3; DAM NOV; DLB 2, 218; INT
CANR-22; MTCW 1, 2; RGAL 4; RGSF
2

Callaghan, Morley Edward
1903-1990 ..... **CLC 3, 14, 41, 65; TCLC 145**
See also CA 9-12R; 132; CANR 33, 73;
DAC; DAM MST; DLB 68; EWL 3;
MTCW 1, 2; RGEL 2; RGSF 2; SSFS 19

Callimachus c. 305B.C.-c.
240B.C. .... **CMLC 18**
See also AW 1; DLB 176; RGWL 2, 3

Calvin, Jean
See Calvin, John
See also GFL Beginnings to 1789

Calvin, John 1509-1564 .... **LC 37**
See Calvin, Jean

Calvino, Italo 1923-1985 .... **CLC 5, 8, 11, 22, 33, 39, 73; SSC 3, 48**
See also AAYA 58; CA 85-88; 116; CANR
23, 61, 132; DAM NOV; DLB 196; EW
13; EWL 3; MTCW 1, 2; RGSF 2; RGWL
2, 3; SFW 4; SSFS 12

Camara Laye
See Laye, Camara
See also EWL 3

Camden, William 1551-1623 .... **LC 77**
See also DLB 172

Cameron, Carey 1952- .... **CLC 59**
See also CA 135

Cameron, Peter 1959- .... **CLC 44**
See also AMWS 12; CA 125; CANR 50,
117; DLB 234; GLL 2

Camoens, Luis Vaz de 1524(?)-1580
See Camoes, Luis de
See also EW 2

Camoes, Luis de 1524(?)-1580 . **HLCS 1; LC 62; PC 31**
See Camoens, Luis Vaz de
See also DLB 287; RGWL 2, 3

Campana, Dino 1885-1932 .... **TCLC 20**
See also CA 117; DLB 114; EWL 3

Campanella, Tommaso 1568-1639 .... **LC 32**
See also RGWL 2, 3

Campbell, John W(ood, Jr.)
1910-1971 .... **CLC 32**
See also CA 21-22; 29-32R; CANR 34;
CAP 2; DLB 8; MTCW 1; SCFW; SFW 4

Campbell, Joseph 1904-1987 .... **CLC 69; TCLC 140**
See also AAYA 3; BEST 89:2; CA 1-4R;
124; CANR 3, 28, 61, 107; DA3; MTCW
1, 2

Campbell, Maria 1940- .... **CLC 85; NNAL**
See also CA 102; CANR 54; CCA 1; DAC

Campbell, (John) Ramsey 1946- ..... **CLC 42; SSC 19**
See also AAYA 51; CA 57-60; 228; CAAE
228; CANR 7, 102; DLB 261; HGG; INT
CANR-7; SUFW 1, 2

Campbell, (Ignatius) Roy (Dunnachie)
1901-1957 .... **TCLC 5**
See also AFW; CA 104; 155; DLB 20, 225;
EWL 3; MTCW 2; RGEL 2

Campbell, Thomas 1777-1844 .... **NCLC 19**
See also DLB 93, 144; RGEL 2

Campbell, Wilfred .... **TCLC 9**
See Campbell, William

Campbell, William 1858(?)-1918
See Campbell, Wilfred
See also CA 106; DLB 92

Campion, Jane 1954- .... **CLC 95**
See also AAYA 33; CA 138; CANR 87

Campion, Thomas 1567-1620 .... **LC 78**
See also CDBLB Before 1660; DAM POET;
DLB 58, 172; RGEL 2

Camus, Albert 1913-1960 ...... **CLC 1, 2, 4, 9,
11, 14, 32, 63, 69, 124; DC 2; SSC 9,
76; WLC**
See also AAYA 36; AFW; BPFB 1; CA 89-
92; CANR 131; DA; DA3; DAB; DAC;
DAM DRAM, MST, NOV; DLB 72; EW
13; EWL 3; EXPN; EXPS; GFL 1789 to
the Present; LATS 1:2; LMFS 2; MTCW
1, 2; NFS 6, 16; RGSF 2; RGWL 2, 3;
SSFS 4; TWA

Canby, Vincent 1924-2000 .... **CLC 13**
See also CA 81-84; 191

Cancale
See Desnos, Robert

Canetti, Elias 1905-1994 .. **CLC 3, 14, 25, 75,
86; TCLC 157**
See also CA 21-24R; 146; CANR 23, 61,
79; CDWLB 2; CWW 2; DA3; DLB 85,
124; EW 12; EWL 3; MTCW 1, 2; RGWL
2, 3; TWA

Canfield, Dorothea F.
See Fisher, Dorothy (Frances) Canfield

Canfield, Dorothea Frances
See Fisher, Dorothy (Frances) Canfield

Canfield, Dorothy
See Fisher, Dorothy (Frances) Canfield

Canin, Ethan 1960- .... **CLC 55; SSC 70**
See also CA 131; 135

Cankar, Ivan 1876-1918 .... **TCLC 105**
See also CDWLB 4; DLB 147; EWL 3

Cannon, Curt
See Hunter, Evan

Cao, Lan 1961- .... **CLC 109**
See also CA 165

Cape, Judith
See Page, P(atricia) K(athleen)
See also CCA 1

Capek, Karel 1890-1938 .... **DC 1; SSC 36;
TCLC 6, 37; WLC**
See also CA 104; 140; CDWLB 4; DA;
DA3; DAB; DAC; DAM DRAM, MST,
NOV; DFS 7, 11; DLB 215; EW 10; EWL
3; MTCW 1; RGSF 2; RGWL 2, 3; SCFW
2; SFW 4

Capote, Truman 1924-1984 . **CLC 1, 3, 8, 13,
19, 34, 38, 58; SSC 2, 47; WLC**
See also AMWS 3; BPFB 1; CA 5-8R; 113;
CANR 18, 62; CDALB 1941-1968; CPW;
DA; DA3; DAB; DAC; DAM MST, NOV,
POP; DLB 2, 185, 227; DLBY 1980,
1984; EWL 3; EXPS; GLL 1; LAIT 3;
MTCW 1, 2; NCFS 2; RGAL 4; RGSF 2;
SATA 91; SSFS 2; TUS

Capra, Frank 1897-1991 .... **CLC 16**
See also AAYA 52; CA 61-64; 135

Caputo, Philip 1941- .... **CLC 32**
See also AAYA 60; CA 73-76; CANR 40,
135; YAW

Caragiale, Ion Luca 1852-1912 ...... **TCLC 76**
See also CA 157

Card, Orson Scott 1951- .... **CLC 44, 47, 50**
See also AAYA 11, 42; BPFB 1; BYA 5, 8;
CA 102; CANR 27, 47, 73, 102, 106, 133;
CPW; DA3; DAM POP; FANT; INT
CANR-27; MTCW 1, 2; NFS 5; SATA
83, 127; SCFW 2; SFW 4; SUFW 2; YAW

Cardenal, Ernesto 1925- .... **CLC 31, 161;
HLC 1; PC 22**
See also CA 49-52; CANR 2, 32, 66; CWW
2; DAM MULT, POET; DLB 290; EWL
3; HW 1, 2; LAWS 1; MTCW 1, 2;
RGWL 2, 3

Cardinal, Marie 1929-2001 .... **CLC 189**
See also CA 177; CWW 2; DLB 83; FW

Cardozo, Benjamin N(athan)
1870-1938 .... **TCLC 65**
See also CA 117; 164

Carducci, Giosue (Alessandro Giuseppe)
1835-1907 .... **PC 46; TCLC 32**
See also CA 163; EW 7; RGWL 2, 3

Carew, Thomas 1595(?)-1640 . **LC 13; PC 29**
See also BRW 2; DLB 126; PAB; RGEL 2

Carey, Ernestine Gilbreth 1908- ...... **CLC 17**
See also CA 5-8R; CANR 71; SATA 2

Carey, Peter 1943- .... **CLC 40, 55, 96, 183**
See also CA 123; 127; CANR 53, 76, 117;
CN 7; DLB 289; EWL 3; INT CA-127;
MTCW 1, 2; RGSF 2; SATA 94

Carleton, William 1794-1869 .... **NCLC 3**
See also DLB 159; RGEL 2; RGSF 2

Carlisle, Henry (Coffin) 1926- .... **CLC 33**
See also CA 13-16R; CANR 15, 85

Carlsen, Chris
See Holdstock, Robert P.

Carlson, Ron(ald F.) 1947- .... **CLC 54**
See also CA 105, 189; CAAE 189; CANR
27; DLB 244

Carlyle, Thomas 1795-1881 ..... **NCLC 22, 70**
See also BRW 4; CDBLB 1789-1832; DA;
DAB; DAC; DAM MST; DLB 55, 144,
254; RGEL 2; TEA

Carman, (William) Bliss 1861-1929 ... **PC 34;
TCLC 7**
See also CA 104; 152; DAC; DLB 92;
RGEL 2

Carnegie, Dale 1888-1955 .... **TCLC 53**
See also CA 218

Carossa, Hans 1878-1956 .... **TCLC 48**
See also CA 170; DLB 66; EWL 3

Carpenter, Don(ald Richard)
1931-1995 .... **CLC 41**
See also CA 45-48; 149; CANR 1, 71

Carpenter, Edward 1844-1929 .... **TCLC 88**
See also CA 163; GLL 1

Carpenter, John (Howard) 1948- ... **CLC 161**
See also AAYA 2; CA 134; SATA 58

Carpenter, Johnny
See Carpenter, John (Howard)

Carpentier (y Valmont), Alejo
1904-1980 . **CLC 8, 11, 38, 110; HLC 1;
SSC 35**
See also CA 65-68; 97-100; CANR 11, 70;
CDWLB 3; DAM MULT; DLB 113; EWL
3; HW 1, 2; LAW; LMFS 2; RGSF 2;
RGWL 2, 3; WLIT 1

Carr, Caleb 1955- .... **CLC 86**
See also CA 147; CANR 73, 134; DA3

Carr, Emily 1871-1945 .... **TCLC 32**
See also CA 159; DLB 68; FW; GLL 2

Carr, John Dickson 1906-1977 .... **CLC 3**
See Fairbairn, Roger
See also CA 49-52; 69-72; CANR 3, 33,
60; CMW 4; DLB 306; MSW; MTCW 1,
2

Carr, Philippa
See Hibbert, Eleanor Alice Burford

Carr, Virginia Spencer 1929- .... **CLC 34**
See also CA 61-64; DLB 111

Carrere, Emmanuel 1957- .... **CLC 89**
See also CA 200

Carrier, Roch 1937- .... **CLC 13, 78**
See also CA 130; CANR 61; CCA 1; DAC;
DAM MST; DLB 53; SATA 105

Carroll, James Dennis
See Carroll, Jim

Carroll, James P. 1943(?)- .... **CLC 38**
See also CA 81-84; CANR 73; MTCW 1

Carroll, Jim 1951- .... **CLC 35, 143**
See also AAYA 17; CA 45-48; CANR 42,
115; NCFS 5

Carroll, Lewis ..... **NCLC 2, 53, 139; PC 18;
WLC**
See Dodgson, Charles L(utwidge)
See also AAYA 39; BRW 5; BYA 5, 13; CD-
BLB 1832-1890; CLR 2, 18; DLB 18,
163, 178; DLBY 1998; EXPN; EXPP;
FANT; JRDA; LAIT 1; NFS 7; PFS 11;
RGEL 2; SUFW 1; TEA; WCH

Carroll, Paul Vincent 1900-1968 ...... **CLC 10**
See also CA 9-12R; 25-28R; DLB 10; EWL
3; RGEL 2

Carruth, Hayden 1921- ..... **CLC 4, 7, 10, 18,
84; PC 10**
See also CA 9-12R; CANR 4, 38, 59, 110;
CP 7; DLB 5, 165; INT CANR-4; MTCW
1, 2; SATA 47

Carson, Anne 1950- .... **CLC 185**
See also AMWS 12; CA 203; DLB 193;
PFS 18

Carson, Rachel
See Carson, Rachel Louise
See also AAYA 49; DLB 275

Carson, Rachel Louise 1907-1964 .... **CLC 71**
See Carson, Rachel
See also AMWS 9; ANW; CA 77-80; CANR
35; DA3; DAM POP; FW; LAIT 4;
MTCW 1, 2; NCFS 1; SATA 23

Carter, Angela (Olive) 1940-1992 ...... **CLC 5,
41, 76; SSC 13; TCLC 139**
See also BRWS 3; CA 53-56; 136; CANR
12, 36, 61, 106; DA3; DLB 14, 207, 261;
EXPS; FANT; FW; MTCW 1, 2; RGSF 2;
SATA 66; SATA-Obit 70; SFW 4; SSFS
4, 12; SUFW 2; WLIT 4

Carter, Nick
See Smith, Martin Cruz

Carver, Raymond 1938-1988 ..... **CLC 22, 36,
53, 55, 126; PC 54; SSC 8, 51**
See also AAYA 44; AMWS 3; BPFB 1; CA
33-36R; 126; CANR 17, 34, 61, 103;
CPW; DA3; DAM NOV; DLB 130;
DLBY 1984, 1988; EWL 3; MTCW 1, 2;
PFS 17; RGAL 4; RGSF 2; SSFS 3, 6,
12, 13; TCWW 2; TUS

Cary, Elizabeth, Lady Falkland
1585-1639 .... **LC 30**

Cary, (Arthur) Joyce (Lunel)
1888-1957 .... **TCLC 1, 29**
See also BRW 7; CA 104; 164; CDBLB
1914-1945; DLB 15, 100; EWL 3; MTCW
2; RGEL 2; TEA

Casal, Julian del 1863-1893 .... **NCLC 131**
See also DLB 283; LAW

Casanova de Seingalt, Giovanni Jacopo
1725-1798 .... **LC 13**

Casares, Adolfo Bioy
See Bioy Casares, Adolfo
See also RGSF 2

Casas, Bartolome de las 1474-1566
See Las Casas, Bartolome de
See also WLIT 1

Casely-Hayford, J(oseph) E(phraim)
1866-1903 .... **BLC 1; TCLC 24**
See also BW 2; CA 123; 152; DAM MULT

Casey, John (Dudley) 1939- .... **CLC 59**
See also BEST 90:2; CA 69-72; CANR 23,
100

Casey, Michael 1947- .... **CLC 2**
See also CA 65-68; CANR 109; DLB 5
Casey, Patrick
See Thurman, Wallace (Henry)
Casey, Warren (Peter) 1935-1988 .... **CLC 12**
See also CA 101; 127; INT CA-101
Casona, Alejandro .... **CLC 49**
See Alvarez, Alejandro Rodriguez
See also EWL 3
Cassavetes, John 1929-1989 .... **CLC 20**
See also CA 85-88; 127; CANR 82
Cassian, Nina 1924- .... **PC 17**
See also CWP; CWW 2
Cassill, R(onald) V(erlin)
1919-2002 .... **CLC 4, 23**
See also CA 9-12R; 208; CAAS 1; CANR
7, 45; CN 7; DLB 6, 218; DLBY 2002
Cassiodorus, Flavius Magnus c. 490(?)-c.
583(?) .... **CMLC 43**
Cassirer, Ernst 1874-1945 .... **TCLC 61**
See also CA 157
Cassity, (Allen) Turner 1929- .... **CLC 6, 42**
See also CA 17-20R; 223; CAAE 223;
CAAS 8; CANR 11; CSW; DLB 105
Castaneda, Carlos (Cesar Aranha)
1931(?)-1998 .... **CLC 12, 119**
See also CA 25-28R; CANR 32, 66, 105;
DNFS 1; HW 1; MTCW 1
Castedo, Elena 1937- .... **CLC 65**
See also CA 132
Castedo-Ellerman, Elena
See Castedo, Elena
Castellanos, Rosario 1925-1974 .... **CLC 66;**
HLC 1; SSC 39, 68
See also CA 131; 53-56; CANR 58; CD-
WLB 3; DAM MULT; DLB 113, 290;
EWL 3; FW; HW 1; LAW; MTCW 1;
RGSF 2; RGWL 2, 3
Castelvetro, Lodovico 1505-1571 .... **LC 12**
Castiglione, Baldassare 1478-1529 ...... **LC 12**
See Castiglione, Baldesar
See also LMFS 1; RGWL 2, 3
Castiglione, Baldesar
See Castiglione, Baldassare
See also EW 2
Castillo, Ana (Hernandez Del)
1953- .... **CLC 151**
See also AAYA 42; CA 131; CANR 51, 86,
128; CWP; DLB 122, 227; DNFS 2; FW;
HW 1; LLW 1; PFS 21
Castle, Robert
See Hamilton, Edmond
Castro (Ruz), Fidel 1926(?)- .... **HLC 1**
See also CA 110; 129; CANR 81; DAM
MULT; HW 2
Castro, Guillen de 1569-1631 .... **LC 19**
Castro, Rosalia de 1837-1885 ... **NCLC 3, 78;**
PC 41
See also DAM MULT
Cather, Willa (Sibert) 1873-1947 . **SSC 2, 50;**
TCLC 1, 11, 31, 99, 132, 152; WLC
See also AAYA 24; AMW; AMWC 1;
AMWR 1; BPFB 1; CA 104; 128; CDALB
1865-1917; CLR 98; DA; DA3; DAB;
DAC; DAM MST, NOV; DLB 9, 54, 78,
256; DLBD 1; EWL 3; EXPN; EXPS;
LAIT 3; LATS 1:1; MAWW; MTCW 1,
2; NFS 2, 19; RGAL 4; RGSF 2; RHW;
SATA 30; SSFS 2, 7, 16; TCWW 2; TUS
Catherine II
See Catherine the Great
See also DLB 150
Catherine the Great 1729-1796 .... **LC 69**
See Catherine II
Cato, Marcus Porcius
234B.C.-149B.C. .... **CMLC 21**
See Cato the Elder
Cato, Marcus Porcius, the Elder
See Cato, Marcus Porcius

Cato the Elder
See Cato, Marcus Porcius
See also DLB 211
Catton, (Charles) Bruce 1899-1978 . **CLC 35**
See also AITN 1; CA 5-8R; 81-84; CANR
7, 74; DLB 17; SATA 2; SATA-Obit 24
Catullus c. 84B.C.-54B.C. .... **CMLC 18**
See also AW 2; CDWLB 1; DLB 211;
RGWL 2, 3
Cauldwell, Frank
See King, Francis (Henry)
Caunitz, William J. 1933-1996 .... **CLC 34**
See also BEST 89:3; CA 125; 130; 152;
CANR 73; INT CA-130
Causley, Charles (Stanley)
1917-2003 .... **CLC 7**
See also CA 9-12R; 223; CANR 5, 35, 94;
CLR 30; CWRI 5; DLB 27; MTCW 1;
SATA 3, 66; SATA-Obit 149
Caute, (John) David 1936- .... **CLC 29**
See also CA 1-4R; CAAS 4; CANR 1, 33,
64, 120; CBD; CD 5; CN 7; DAM NOV;
DLB 14, 231
Cavafy, C(onstantine) P(eter) .... **PC 36;**
TCLC 2, 7
See Kavafis, Konstantinos Petrou
See also CA 148; DA3; DAM POET; EW
8; EWL 3; MTCW 1; PFS 19; RGWL 2,
3; WP
Cavalcanti, Guido c. 1250-c.
1300 .... **CMLC 54**
See also RGWL 2, 3
Cavallo, Evelyn
See Spark, Muriel (Sarah)
Cavanna, Betty .... **CLC 12**
See Harrison, Elizabeth (Allen) Cavanna
See also JRDA; MAICYA 1; SAAS 4;
SATA 1, 30
Cavendish, Margaret Lucas
1623-1673 .... **LC 30**
See also DLB 131, 252, 281; RGEL 2
Caxton, William 1421(?)-1491(?) .... **LC 17**
See also DLB 170
Cayer, D. M.
See Duffy, Maureen
Cayrol, Jean 1911- .... **CLC 11**
See also CA 89-92; DLB 83; EWL 3
Cela (y Trulock), Camilo Jose
See Cela, Camilo Jose
See also CWW 2
Cela, Camilo Jose 1916-2002 .... **CLC 4, 13,**
59, 122; HLC 1; SSC 71
See Cela (y Trulock), Camilo Jose
See also BEST 90:2; CA 21-24R; 206;
CAAS 10; CANR 21, 32, 76; DAM
MULT; DLBY 1989; EW 13; EWL 3; HW
1; MTCW 1, 2; RGSF 2; RGWL 2, 3
Celan, Paul .... **CLC 10, 19, 53, 82; PC 10**
See Antschel, Paul
See also CDWLB 2; DLB 69; EWL 3;
RGWL 2, 3
Celine, Louis-Ferdinand .. **CLC 1, 3, 4, 7, 9,**
15, 47, 124
See Destouches, Louis-Ferdinand
See also DLB 72; EW 11; EWL 3; GFL
1789 to the Present; RGWL 2, 3
Cellini, Benvenuto 1500-1571 .... **LC 7**
Cendrars, Blaise .... **CLC 18, 106**
See Sauser-Hall, Frederic
See also DLB 258; EWL 3; GFL 1789 to
the Present; RGWL 2, 3; WP
Centlivre, Susanna 1669(?)-1723 .... **LC 65**
See also DLB 84; RGEL 2
Cernuda (y Bidon), Luis 1902-1963 . **CLC 54**
See also CA 131; 89-92; DAM POET; DLB
134; EWL 3; GLL 1; HW 1; RGWL 2, 3

Cervantes, Lorna Dee 1954- ..... **HLCS 1; PC**
35
See also CA 131; CANR 80; CWP; DLB
82; EXPP; HW 1; LLW 1
Cervantes (Saavedra), Miguel de
1547-1616 .... **HLCS; LC 6, 23, 93; SSC**
12; WLC
See also AAYA 56; BYA 1, 14; DA; DAB;
DAC; DAM MST, NOV; EW 2; LAIT 1;
LATS 1:1; LMFS 1; NFS 8; RGSF 2;
RGWL 2, 3; TWA
Cesaire, Aime (Fernand) 1913- .... **BLC 1;**
CLC 19, 32, 112; DC 22; PC 25
See also BW 2, 3; CA 65-68; CANR 24,
43, 81; CWW 2; DA3; DAM MULT,
POET; EWL 3; GFL 1789 to the Present;
MTCW 1, 2; WP
Chabon, Michael 1963- ... **CLC 55, 149; SSC**
59
See also AAYA 45; AMWS 11; CA 139;
CANR 57, 96, 127; DLB 278; SATA 145
Chabrol, Claude 1930- .... **CLC 16**
See also CA 110
Chairil Anwar
See Anwar, Chairil
See also EWL 3
Challans, Mary 1905-1983
See Renault, Mary
See also CA 81-84; 111; CANR 74; DA3;
MTCW 2; SATA 23; SATA-Obit 36; TEA
Challis, George
See Faust, Frederick (Schiller)
See also TCWW 2
Chambers, Aidan 1934- .... **CLC 35**
See also AAYA 27; CA 25-28R; CANR 12,
31, 58, 116; JRDA; MAICYA 1, 2; SAAS
12; SATA 1, 69, 108; WYA; YAW
Chambers, James 1948-
See Cliff, Jimmy
See also CA 124
Chambers, Jessie
See Lawrence, D(avid) H(erbert Richards)
See also GLL 1
Chambers, Robert W(illiam)
1865-1933 .... **TCLC 41**
See also CA 165; DLB 202; HGG; SATA
107; SUFW 1
Chambers, (David) Whittaker
1901-1961 .... **TCLC 129**
See also CA 89-92; DLB 303
Chamisso, Adelbert von
1781-1838 .... **NCLC 82**
See also DLB 90; RGWL 2, 3; SUFW 1
Chance, James T.
See Carpenter, John (Howard)
Chance, John T.
See Carpenter, John (Howard)
Chandler, Raymond (Thornton)
1888-1959 .... **SSC 23; TCLC 1, 7**
See also AAYA 25; AMWC 2; AMWS 4;
BPFB 1; CA 104; 129; CANR 60, 107;
CDALB 1929-1941; CMW 4; DA3; DLB
226, 253; DLBD 6; EWL 3; MSW;
MTCW 1, 2; NFS 17; RGAL 4; TUS
Chang, Diana 1934- .... **AAL**
See also CA 228; CWP; EXPP
Chang, Eileen 1921-1995 .... **AAL; SSC 28**
See Chang Ai-Ling; Zhang Ailing
See also CA 166
Chang, Jung 1952- .... **CLC 71**
See also CA 142
Chang Ai-Ling
See Chang, Eileen
See also EWL 3
Channing, William Ellery
1780-1842 .... **NCLC 17**
See also DLB 1, 59, 235; RGAL 4
Chao, Patricia 1955- .... **CLC 119**
See also CA 163

Chaplin, Charles Spencer
1889-1977 .... **CLC 16**
See Chaplin, Charlie
See also CA 81-84; 73-76

Chaplin, Charlie
See Chaplin, Charles Spencer
See also DLB 44

Chapman, George 1559(?)-1634 . **DC 19; LC 22**
See also BRW 1; DAM DRAM; DLB 62, 121; LMFS 1; RGEL 2

Chapman, Graham 1941-1989 .... **CLC 21**
See Monty Python
See also CA 116; 129; CANR 35, 95

Chapman, John Jay 1862-1933 .... **TCLC 7**
See also AMWS 14; CA 104; 191

Chapman, Lee
See Bradley, Marion Zimmer
See also GLL 1

Chapman, Walker
See Silverberg, Robert

Chappell, Fred (Davis) 1936- .... **CLC 40, 78, 162**
See also CA 5-8R, 198; CAAE 198; CAAS 4; CANR 8, 33, 67, 110; CN 7; CP 7; CSW; DLB 6, 105; HGG

Char, Rene(-Emile) 1907-1988 .... **CLC 9, 11, 14, 55; PC 56**
See also CA 13-16R; 124; CANR 32; DAM POET; DLB 258; EWL 3; GFL 1789 to the Present; MTCW 1, 2; RGWL 2, 3

Charby, Jay
See Ellison, Harlan (Jay)

Chardin, Pierre Teilhard de
See Teilhard de Chardin, (Marie Joseph) Pierre

Chariton fl. 1st cent. (?)- .... **CMLC 49**

Charlemagne 742-814 .... **CMLC 37**

Charles I 1600-1649 .... **LC 13**

Charriere, Isabelle de 1740-1805 .. **NCLC 66**

Chartier, Alain c. 1392-1430 .... **LC 94**
See also DLB 208

Chartier, Emile-Auguste
See Alain

Charyn, Jerome 1937- .... **CLC 5, 8, 18**
See also CA 5-8R; CAAS 1; CANR 7, 61, 101; CMW 4; CN 7; DLBY 1983; MTCW 1

Chase, Adam
See Marlowe, Stephen

Chase, Mary (Coyle) 1907-1981 .... **DC 1**
See also CA 77-80; 105; CAD; CWD; DFS 11; DLB 228; SATA 17; SATA-Obit 29

Chase, Mary Ellen 1887-1973 .... **CLC 2; TCLC 124**
See also CA 13-16; 41-44R; CAP 1; SATA 10

Chase, Nicholas
See Hyde, Anthony
See also CCA 1

Chateaubriand, Francois Rene de
1768-1848 .... **NCLC 3, 134**
See also DLB 119; EW 5; GFL 1789 to the Present; RGWL 2, 3; TWA

Chatterje, Sarat Chandra 1876-1936(?)
See Chatterji, Saratchandra
See also CA 109

Chatterji, Bankim Chandra
1838-1894 .... **NCLC 19**

Chatterji, Saratchandra .... **TCLC 13**
See Chatterje, Sarat Chandra
See also CA 186; EWL 3

Chatterton, Thomas 1752-1770 .... **LC 3, 54**
See also DAM POET; DLB 109; RGEL 2

Chatwin, (Charles) Bruce
1940-1989 .... **CLC 28, 57, 59**
See also AAYA 4; BEST 90:1; BRWS 4; CA 85-88; 127; CPW; DAM POP; DLB 194, 204; EWL 3

Chaucer, Daniel
See Ford, Ford Madox
See also RHW

Chaucer, Geoffrey 1340(?)-1400 .. **LC 17, 56; PC 19, 58; WLCS**
See also BRW 1; BRWC 1; BRWR 2; CD-BLB Before 1660; DA; DA3; DAB; DAC; DAM MST, POET; DLB 146; LAIT 1; PAB; PFS 14; RGEL 2; TEA; WLIT 3; WP

Chavez, Denise (Elia) 1948- .... **HLC 1**
See also CA 131; CANR 56, 81; DAM MULT; DLB 122; FW; HW 1, 2; LLW 1; MTCW 2

Chaviaras, Strates 1935-
See Haviaras, Stratis
See also CA 105

Chayefsky, Paddy .... **CLC 23**
See Chayefsky, Sidney
See also CAD; DLB 7, 44; DLBY 1981; RGAL 4

Chayefsky, Sidney 1923-1981
See Chayefsky, Paddy
See also CA 9-12R; 104; CANR 18; DAM DRAM

Chedid, Andree 1920- .... **CLC 47**
See also CA 145; CANR 95; EWL 3

Cheever, John 1912-1982 ..... **CLC 3, 7, 8, 11, 15, 25, 64; SSC 1, 38, 57; WLC**
See also AMWS 1; BPFB 1; CA 5-8R; 106; CABS 1; CANR 5, 27, 76; CDALB 1941-1968; CPW; DA; DA3; DAB; DAC; DAM MST, NOV, POP; DLB 2, 102, 227; DLBY 1980, 1982; EWL 3; EXPS; INT CANR-5; MTCW 1, 2; RGAL 4; RGSF 2; SSFS 2, 14; TUS

Cheever, Susan 1943- .... **CLC 18, 48**
See also CA 103; CANR 27, 51, 92; DLBY 1982; INT CANR-27

Chekhonte, Antosha
See Chekhov, Anton (Pavlovich)

Chekhov, Anton (Pavlovich)
1860-1904 ...... **DC 9; SSC 2, 28, 41, 51; TCLC 3, 10, 31, 55, 96; WLC**
See also BYA 14; CA 104; 124; DA; DA3; DAB; DAC; DAM DRAM, MST; DFS 1, 5, 10, 12; DLB 277; EW 7; EWL 3; EXPS; LAIT 3; LATS 1:1; RGSF 2; RGWL 2, 3; SATA 90; SSFS 5, 13, 14; TWA

Cheney, Lynne V. 1941- .... **CLC 70**
See also CA 89-92; CANR 58, 117; SATA 152

Chernyshevsky, Nikolai Gavrilovich
See Chernyshevsky, Nikolay Gavrilovich
See also DLB 238

Chernyshevsky, Nikolay Gavrilovich
1828-1889 .... **NCLC 1**
See Chernyshevsky, Nikolai Gavrilovich

Cherry, Carolyn Janice 1942-
See Cherryh, C. J.
See also CA 65-68; CANR 10

Cherryh, C. J. .... **CLC 35**
See Cherry, Carolyn Janice
See also AAYA 24; BPFB 1; DLBY 1980; FANT; SATA 93; SCFW 2; SFW 4; YAW

Chesnutt, Charles W(addell)
1858-1932 .... **BLC 1; SSC 7, 54; TCLC 5, 39**
See also AFAW 1, 2; AMWS 14; BW 1, 3; CA 106; 125; CANR 76; DAM MULT; DLB 12, 50, 78; EWL 3; MTCW 1, 2; RGAL 4; RGSF 2; SSFS 11

Chester, Alfred 1929(?)-1971 .... **CLC 49**
See also CA 196; 33-36R; DLB 130

Chesterton, G(ilbert) K(eith)
1874-1936 . **PC 28; SSC 1, 46; TCLC 1, 6, 64**
See also AAYA 57; BRW 6; CA 104; 132; CANR 73, 131; CDBLB 1914-1945;

CMW 4; DAM NOV, POET; DLB 10, 19, 34, 70, 98, 149, 178; EWL 3; FANT; MSW; MTCW 1, 2; RGEL 2; RGSF 2; SATA 27; SUFW 1

Chiang, Pin-chin 1904-1986
See Ding Ling
See also CA 118

Chief Joseph 1840-1904 .... **NNAL**
See also CA 152; DA3; DAM MULT

Chief Seattle 1786(?)-1866 .... **NNAL**
See also DA3; DAM MULT

Ch'ien, Chung-shu 1910-1998 .... **CLC 22**
See Qian Zhongshu
See also CA 130; CANR 73; MTCW 1, 2

Chikamatsu Monzaemon 1653-1724 ... **LC 66**
See also RGWL 2, 3

Child, L. Maria
See Child, Lydia Maria

Child, Lydia Maria 1802-1880 .. **NCLC 6, 73**
See also DLB 1, 74, 243; RGAL 4; SATA 67

Child, Mrs.
See Child, Lydia Maria

Child, Philip 1898-1978 .... **CLC 19, 68**
See also CA 13-14; CAP 1; DLB 68; RHW; SATA 47

Childers, (Robert) Erskine
1870-1922 .... **TCLC 65**
See also CA 113; 153; DLB 70

Childress, Alice 1920-1994 . **BLC 1; CLC 12, 15, 86, 96; DC 4; TCLC 116**
See also AAYA 8; BW 2, 3; BYA 2; CA 45-48; 146; CAD; CANR 3, 27, 50, 74; CLR 14; CWD; DA3; DAM DRAM, MULT, NOV; DFS 2, 8, 14; DLB 7, 38, 249; JRDA; LAIT 5; MAICYA 1, 2; MAIC-YAS 1; MTCW 1, 2; RGAL 4; SATA 7, 48, 81; TUS; WYA; YAW

Chin, Frank (Chew, Jr.) 1940- ...... **CLC 135; DC 7**
See also CA 33-36R; CANR 71; CD 5; DAM MULT; DLB 206; LAIT 5; RGAL 4

Chin, Marilyn (Mei Ling) 1955- .... **PC 40**
See also CA 129; CANR 70, 113; CWP

Chislett, (Margaret) Anne 1943- ...... **CLC 34**
See also CA 151

Chitty, Thomas Willes 1926- .... **CLC 11**
See Hinde, Thomas
See also CA 5-8R; CN 7

Chivers, Thomas Holley
1809-1858 .... **NCLC 49**
See also DLB 3, 248; RGAL 4

Choi, Susan 1969- .... **CLC 119**
See also CA 223

Chomette, Rene Lucien 1898-1981
See Clair, Rene
See also CA 103

Chomsky, (Avram) Noam 1928- ..... **CLC 132**
See also CA 17-20R; CANR 28, 62, 110, 132; DA3; DLB 246; MTCW 1, 2

Chona, Maria 1845(?)-1936 .... **NNAL**
See also CA 144

Chopin, Kate .... **SSC 8, 68; TCLC 127; WLCS**
See Chopin, Katherine
See also AAYA 33; AMWR 2; AMWS 1; BYA 11, 15; CDALB 1865-1917; DA; DAB; DLB 12, 78; EXPN; EXPS; FW; LAIT 3; MAWW; NFS 3; RGAL 4; RGSF 2; SSFS 17; TUS

Chopin, Katherine 1851-1904
See Chopin, Kate
See also CA 104; 122; DA3; DAC; DAM MST, NOV

Chretien de Troyes c. 12th cent. - . **CMLC 10**
See also DLB 208; EW 1; RGWL 2, 3; TWA

Christie
See Ichikawa, Kon

Christie, Agatha (Mary Clarissa)
1890-1976 .. **CLC 1, 6, 8, 12, 39, 48, 110**
See also AAYA 9; AITN 1, 2; BPFB 1;
BRWS 2; CA 17-20R; 61-64; CANR 10,
37, 108; CBD; CDBLB 1914-1945; CMW
4; CPW; CWD; DA3; DAB; DAC; DAM
NOV; DFS 2; DLB 13, 77, 245; MSW;
MTCW 1, 2; NFS 8; RGEL 2; RHW;
SATA 36; TEA; YAW

Christie, Philippa .... **CLC 21**
See Pearce, Philippa
See also BYA 5; CANR 109; CLR 9; DLB
161; MAICYA 1; SATA 1, 67, 129

Christine de Pizan 1365(?)-1431(?) .... **LC 9**
See also DLB 208; RGWL 2, 3

Chuang Tzu c. 369B.C.-c.
286B.C. .... **CMLC 57**

Chubb, Elmer
See Masters, Edgar Lee

Chulkov, Mikhail Dmitrievich
1743-1792 .... **LC 2**
See also DLB 150

Churchill, Caryl 1938- .... **CLC 31, 55, 157;**
DC 5
See Churchill, Chick
See also BRWS 4; CA 102; CANR 22, 46,
108; CBD; CWD; DFS 12, 16; DLB 13;
EWL 3; FW; MTCW 1; RGEL 2

Churchill, Charles 1731-1764 .... **LC 3**
See also DLB 109; RGEL 2

Churchill, Chick
See Churchill, Caryl
See also CD 5

Churchill, Sir Winston (Leonard Spencer)
1874-1965 .... **TCLC 113**
See also BRW 6; CA 97-100; CDBLB
1890-1914; DA3; DLB 100; DLBD 16;
LAIT 4; MTCW 1, 2

Chute, Carolyn 1947- .... **CLC 39**
See also CA 123; CANR 135

Ciardi, John (Anthony) 1916-1986 . **CLC 10,**
40, 44, 129
See also CA 5-8R; 118; CAAS 2; CANR 5,
33; CLR 19; CWRI 5; DAM POET; DLB
5; DLBY 1986; INT CANR-5; MAICYA
1, 2; MTCW 1, 2; RGAL 4; SAAS 26;
SATA 1, 65; SATA-Obit 46

Cibber, Colley 1671-1757 .... **LC 66**
See also DLB 84; RGEL 2

Cicero, Marcus Tullius
106B.C.-43B.C. .... **CMLC 3**
See also AW 1; CDWLB 1; DLB 211;
RGWL 2, 3

Cimino, Michael 1943- .... **CLC 16**
See also CA 105

Cioran, E(mil) M. 1911-1995 .... **CLC 64**
See also CA 25-28R; 149; CANR 91; DLB
220; EWL 3

Cisneros, Sandra 1954- .... **CLC 69, 118, 193;**
HLC 1; PC 52; SSC 32, 72
See also AAYA 9, 53; AMWS 7; CA 131;
CANR 64, 118; CWP; DA3; DAM MULT;
DLB 122, 152; EWL 3; EXPN; FW; HW
1, 2; LAIT 5; LATS 1:2; LLW 1; MAI-
CYA 2; MTCW 2; NFS 2; PFS 19; RGAL
4; RGSF 2; SSFS 3, 13; WLIT 1; YAW

Cixous, Helene 1937- .... **CLC 92**
See also CA 126; CANR 55, 123; CWW 2;
DLB 83, 242; EWL 3; FW; GLL 2;
MTCW 1, 2; TWA

Clair, Rene .... **CLC 20**
See Chomette, Rene Lucien

Clampitt, Amy 1920-1994 .... **CLC 32; PC 19**
See also AMWS 9; CA 110; 146; CANR
29, 79; DLB 105

Clancy, Thomas L., Jr. 1947-
See Clancy, Tom
See also CA 125; 131; CANR 62, 105;
DA3; INT CA-131; MTCW 1, 2

Clancy, Tom .... **CLC 45, 112**
See Clancy, Thomas L., Jr.
See also AAYA 9, 51; BEST 89:1, 90:1;
BPFB 1; BYA 10, 11; CANR 132; CMW
4; CPW; DAM NOV, POP; DLB 227

Clare, John 1793-1864 .. **NCLC 9, 86; PC 23**
See also DAB; DAM POET; DLB 55, 96;
RGEL 2

Clarin
See Alas (y Urena), Leopoldo (Enrique
Garcia)

Clark, Al C.
See Goines, Donald

Clark, (Robert) Brian 1932- .... **CLC 29**
See also CA 41-44R; CANR 67; CBD; CD
5

Clark, Curt
See Westlake, Donald E(dwin)

Clark, Eleanor 1913-1996 .... **CLC 5, 19**
See also CA 9-12R; 151; CANR 41; CN 7;
DLB 6

Clark, J. P.
See Clark Bekederemo, J(ohnson) P(epper)
See also CDWLB 3; DLB 117

Clark, John Pepper
See Clark Bekederemo, J(ohnson) P(epper)
See also AFW; CD 5; CP 7; RGEL 2

Clark, Kenneth (Mackenzie)
1903-1983 .... **TCLC 147**
See also CA 93-96; 109; CANR 36; MTCW
1, 2

Clark, M. R.
See Clark, Mavis Thorpe

Clark, Mavis Thorpe 1909-1999 ...... **CLC 12**
See also CA 57-60; CANR 8, 37, 107; CLR
30; CWRI 5; MAICYA 1, 2; SAAS 5;
SATA 8, 74

Clark, Walter Van Tilburg
1909-1971 .... **CLC 28**
See also CA 9-12R; 33-36R; CANR 63,
113; DLB 9, 206; LAIT 2; RGAL 4;
SATA 8

Clark Bekederemo, J(ohnson) P(epper)
1935- .... **BLC 1; CLC 38; DC 5**
See Clark, J. P.; Clark, John Pepper
See also BW 1; CA 65-68; CANR 16, 72;
DAM DRAM, MULT; DFS 13; EWL 3;
MTCW 1

Clarke, Arthur C(harles) 1917- .... **CLC 1, 4,**
13, 18, 35, 136; SSC 3
See also AAYA 4, 33; BPFB 1; BYA 13;
CA 1-4R; CANR 2, 28, 55, 74, 130; CN
7; CPW; DA3; DAM POP; DLB 261;
JRDA; LAIT 5; MAICYA 1, 2; MTCW 1,
2; SATA 13, 70, 115; SCFW; SFW 4;
SSFS 4, 18; YAW

Clarke, Austin 1896-1974 .... **CLC 6, 9**
See also CA 29-32; 49-52; CAP 2; DAM
POET; DLB 10, 20; EWL 3; RGEL 2

Clarke, Austin C(hesterfield) 1934- .. **BLC 1;**
CLC 8, 53; SSC 45
See also BW 1; CA 25-28R; CAAS 16;
CANR 14, 32, 68; CN 7; DAC; DAM
MULT; DLB 53, 125; DNFS 2; RGSF 2

Clarke, Gillian 1937- .... **CLC 61**
See also CA 106; CP 7; CWP; DLB 40

Clarke, Marcus (Andrew Hislop)
1846-1881 .... **NCLC 19**
See also DLB 230; RGEL 2; RGSF 2

Clarke, Shirley 1925-1997 .... **CLC 16**
See also CA 189

Clash, The
See Headon, (Nicky) Topper; Jones, Mick;
Simonon, Paul; Strummer, Joe

Claudel, Paul (Louis Charles Marie)
1868-1955 .... **TCLC 2, 10**
See also CA 104; 165; DLB 192, 258; EW
8; EWL 3; GFL 1789 to the Present;
RGWL 2, 3; TWA

Claudian 370(?)-404(?) .... **CMLC 46**
See also RGWL 2, 3

Claudius, Matthias 1740-1815 .... **NCLC 75**
See also DLB 97

Clavell, James (duMaresq)
1925-1994 .... **CLC 6, 25, 87**
See also BPFB 1; CA 25-28R; 146; CANR
26, 48; CPW; DA3; DAM NOV, POP;
MTCW 1, 2; NFS 10; RHW

Clayman, Gregory .... **CLC 65**

Cleaver, (Leroy) Eldridge
1935-1998 .... **BLC 1; CLC 30, 119**
See also BW 1, 3; CA 21-24R; 167; CANR
16, 75; DA3; DAM MULT; MTCW 2;
YAW

Cleese, John (Marwood) 1939- .... **CLC 21**
See Monty Python
See also CA 112; 116; CANR 35; MTCW 1

Cleishbotham, Jebediah
See Scott, Sir Walter

Cleland, John 1710-1789 .... **LC 2, 48**
See also DLB 39; RGEL 2

Clemens, Samuel Langhorne 1835-1910
See Twain, Mark
See also CA 104; 135; CDALB 1865-1917;
DA; DA3; DAB; DAC; DAM MST, NOV;
DLB 12, 23, 64, 74, 186, 189; JRDA;
LMFS 1; MAICYA 1, 2; NCFS 4; NFS
20; SATA 100; SSFS 16; YABC 2

Clement of Alexandria
150(?)-215(?) .... **CMLC 41**

Cleophil
See Congreve, William

Clerihew, E.
See Bentley, E(dmund) C(lerihew)

Clerk, N. W.
See Lewis, C(live) S(taples)

Cleveland, John 1613-1658 .... **LC 106**
See also DLB 126; RGEL 2

Cliff, Jimmy .... **CLC 21**
See Chambers, James
See also CA 193

Cliff, Michelle 1946- .... **BLCS; CLC 120**
See also BW 2; CA 116; CANR 39, 72; CD-
WLB 3; DLB 157; FW; GLL 2

Clifford, Lady Anne 1590-1676 .... **LC 76**
See also DLB 151

Clifton, (Thelma) Lucille 1936- .... **BLC 1;**
CLC 19, 66, 162; PC 17
See also AFAW 2; BW 2, 3; CA 49-52;
CANR 2, 24, 42, 76, 97; CLR 5; CP 7;
CSW; CWP; CWRI 5; DA3; DAM MULT,
POET; DLB 5, 41; EXPP; MAICYA 1, 2;
MTCW 1, 2; PFS 1, 14; SATA 20, 69,
128; WP

Clinton, Dirk
See Silverberg, Robert

Clough, Arthur Hugh 1819-1861 ... **NCLC 27**
See also BRW 5; DLB 32; RGEL 2

Clutha, Janet Paterson Frame 1924-2004
See Frame, Janet
See also CA 1-4R; 224; CANR 2, 36, 76,
135; MTCW 1, 2; SATA 119

Clyne, Terence
See Blatty, William Peter

Cobalt, Martin
See Mayne, William (James Carter)

Cobb, Irvin S(hrewsbury)
1876-1944 .... **TCLC 77**
See also CA 175; DLB 11, 25, 86

Cobbett, William 1763-1835 .... **NCLC 49**
See also DLB 43, 107, 158; RGEL 2

Coburn, D(onald) L(ee) 1938- .... **CLC 10**
See also CA 89-92

Cocteau, Jean (Maurice Eugene Clement)
1889-1963 ...... **CLC 1, 8, 15, 16, 43; DC 17; TCLC 119; WLC**
See also CA 25-28; CANR 40; CAP 2; DA; DA3; DAB; DAC; DAM DRAM, MST, NOV; DLB 65, 258; EW 10; EWL 3; GFL 1789 to the Present; MTCW 1, 2; RGWL 2, 3; TWA

Codrescu, Andrei 1946- .... **CLC 46, 121**
See also CA 33-36R; CAAS 19; CANR 13, 34, 53, 76, 125; DA3; DAM POET; MTCW 2

Coe, Max
See Bourne, Randolph S(illiman)

Coe, Tucker
See Westlake, Donald E(dwin)

Coen, Ethan 1958- .... **CLC 108**
See also AAYA 54; CA 126; CANR 85

Coen, Joel 1955- .... **CLC 108**
See also AAYA 54; CA 126; CANR 119

The Coen Brothers
See Coen, Ethan; Coen, Joel

Coetzee, J(ohn) M(axwell) 1940- ..... **CLC 23, 33, 66, 117, 161, 162**
See also AAYA 37; AFW; BRWS 6; CA 77-80; CANR 41, 54, 74, 114, 133; CN 7; DA3; DAM NOV; DLB 225; EWL 3; LMFS 2; MTCW 1, 2; WLIT 2; WWE 1

Coffey, Brian
See Koontz, Dean R(ay)

Coffin, Robert P(eter) Tristram
1892-1955 .... **TCLC 95**
See also CA 123; 169; DLB 45

Cohan, George M(ichael)
1878-1942 .... **TCLC 60**
See also CA 157; DLB 249; RGAL 4

Cohen, Arthur A(llen) 1928-1986 ...... **CLC 7, 31**
See also CA 1-4R; 120; CANR 1, 17, 42; DLB 28

Cohen, Leonard (Norman) 1934- ...... **CLC 3, 38**
See also CA 21-24R; CANR 14, 69; CN 7; CP 7; DAC; DAM MST; DLB 53; EWL 3; MTCW 1

Cohen, Matt(hew) 1942-1999 .... **CLC 19**
See also CA 61-64; 187; CAAS 18; CANR 40; CN 7; DAC; DLB 53

Cohen-Solal, Annie 19(?)- .... **CLC 50**

Colegate, Isabel 1931- .... **CLC 36**
See also CA 17-20R; CANR 8, 22, 74; CN 7; DLB 14, 231; INT CANR-22; MTCW 1

Coleman, Emmett
See Reed, Ishmael

Coleridge, Hartley 1796-1849 .... **NCLC 90**
See also DLB 96

Coleridge, M. E.
See Coleridge, Mary E(lizabeth)

Coleridge, Mary E(lizabeth)
1861-1907 .... **TCLC 73**
See also CA 116; 166; DLB 19, 98

Coleridge, Samuel Taylor
1772-1834 ...... **NCLC 9, 54, 99, 111; PC 11, 39; WLC**
See also BRW 4; BRWR 2; BYA 4; CDBLB 1789-1832; DA; DA3; DAB; DAC; DAM MST, POET; DLB 93, 107; EXPP; LATS 1:1; LMFS 1; PAB; PFS 4, 5; RGEL 2; TEA; WLIT 3; WP

Coleridge, Sara 1802-1852 .... **NCLC 31**
See also DLB 199

Coles, Don 1928- .... **CLC 46**
See also CA 115; CANR 38; CP 7

Coles, Robert (Martin) 1929- .... **CLC 108**
See also CA 45-48; CANR 3, 32, 66, 70, 135; INT CANR-32; SATA 23

Colette, (Sidonie-Gabrielle)
1873-1954 .... **SSC 10; TCLC 1, 5, 16**
See also Willy, Colette
See also CA 104; 131; DA3; DAM NOV; DLB 65; EW 9; EWL 3; GFL 1789 to the Present; MTCW 1, 2; RGWL 2, 3; TWA

Collett, (Jacobine) Camilla (Wergeland)
1813-1895 .... **NCLC 22**

Collier, Christopher 1930- .... **CLC 30**
See also AAYA 13; BYA 2; CA 33-36R; CANR 13, 33, 102; JRDA; MAICYA 1, 2; SATA 16, 70; WYA; YAW 1

Collier, James Lincoln 1928- .... **CLC 30**
See also AAYA 13; BYA 2; CA 9-12R; CANR 4, 33, 60, 102; CLR 3; DAM POP; JRDA; MAICYA 1, 2; SAAS 21; SATA 8, 70; WYA; YAW 1

Collier, Jeremy 1650-1726 .... **LC 6**

Collier, John 1901-1980 . **SSC 19; TCLC 127**
See also CA 65-68; 97-100; CANR 10; DLB 77, 255; FANT; SUFW 1

Collier, Mary 1690-1762 .... **LC 86**
See also DLB 95

Collingwood, R(obin) G(eorge)
1889(?)-1943 .... **TCLC 67**
See also CA 117; 155; DLB 262

Collins, Hunt
See Hunter, Evan

Collins, Linda 1931- .... **CLC 44**
See also CA 125

Collins, Tom
See Furphy, Joseph
See also RGEL 2

Collins, (William) Wilkie
1824-1889 .... **NCLC 1, 18, 93**
See also BRWS 6; CDBLB 1832-1890; CMW 4; DLB 18, 70, 159; MSW; RGEL 2; RGSF 2; SUFW 1; WLIT 4

Collins, William 1721-1759 .... **LC 4, 40**
See also BRW 3; DAM POET; DLB 109; RGEL 2

Collodi, Carlo .... **NCLC 54**
See Lorenzini, Carlo
See also CLR 5; WCH

Colman, George
See Glassco, John

Colman, George, the Elder
1732-1794 .... **LC 98**
See also RGEL 2

Colonna, Vittoria 1492-1547 .... **LC 71**
See also RGWL 2, 3

Colt, Winchester Remington
See Hubbard, L(afayette) Ron(ald)

Colter, Cyrus J. 1910-2002 .... **CLC 58**
See also BW 1; CA 65-68; 205; CANR 10, 66; CN 7; DLB 33

Colton, James
See Hansen, Joseph
See also GLL 1

Colum, Padraic 1881-1972 .... **CLC 28**
See also BYA 4; CA 73-76; 33-36R; CANR 35; CLR 36; CWRI 5; DLB 19; MAICYA 1, 2; MTCW 1; RGEL 2; SATA 15; WCH

Colvin, James
See Moorcock, Michael (John)

Colwin, Laurie (E.) 1944-1992 .... **CLC 5, 13, 23, 84**
See also CA 89-92; 139; CANR 20, 46; DLB 218; DLBY 1980; MTCW 1

Comfort, Alex(ander) 1920-2000 .... **CLC 7**
See also CA 1-4R; 190; CANR 1, 45; CP 7; DAM POP; MTCW 1

Comfort, Montgomery
See Campbell, (John) Ramsey

Compton-Burnett, I(vy)
1892(?)-1969 .... **CLC 1, 3, 10, 15, 34**
See also BRW 7; CA 1-4R; 25-28R; CANR 4; DAM NOV; DLB 36; EWL 3; MTCW 1; RGEL 2

Comstock, Anthony 1844-1915 ...... **TCLC 13**
See also CA 110; 169

Comte, Auguste 1798-1857 .... **NCLC 54**

Conan Doyle, Arthur
See Doyle, Sir Arthur Conan
See also BPFB 1; BYA 4, 5, 11

Conde (Abellan), Carmen
1901-1996 .... **HLCS 1**
See also CA 177; CWW 2; DLB 108; EWL 3; HW 2

Conde, Maryse 1937- ..... **BLCS; CLC 52, 92**
See also BW 2, 3; CA 110, 190; CAAE 190; CANR 30, 53, 76; CWW 2; DAM MULT; EWL 3; MTCW 1

Condillac, Etienne Bonnot de
1714-1780 .... **LC 26**

Condon, Richard (Thomas)
1915-1996 .... **CLC 4, 6, 8, 10, 45, 100**
See also BEST 90:3; BPFB 1; CA 1-4R; 151; CAAS 1; CANR 2, 23; CMW 4; CN 7; DAM NOV; INT CANR-23; MTCW 1, 2

Condorcet 1743-1794 .... **LC 104**
See also GFL Beginnings to 1789

Confucius 551B.C.-479B.C. .... **CMLC 19, 65; WLCS**
See also DA; DA3; DAB; DAC; DAM MST

Congreve, William 1670-1729 ... **DC 2; LC 5, 21; WLC**
See also BRW 2; CDBLB 1660-1789; DA; DAB; DAC; DAM DRAM, MST, POET; DFS 15; DLB 39, 84; RGEL 2; WLIT 3

Conley, Robert J(ackson) 1940- .... **NNAL**
See also CA 41-44R; CANR 15, 34, 45, 96; DAM MULT

Connell, Evan S(helby), Jr. 1924- . **CLC 4, 6, 45**
See also AAYA 7; AMWS 14; CA 1-4R; CAAS 2; CANR 2, 39, 76, 97; CN 7; DAM NOV; DLB 2; DLBY 1981; MTCW 1, 2

Connelly, Marc(us Cook) 1890-1980 . **CLC 7**
See also CA 85-88; 102; CANR 30; DFS 12; DLB 7; DLBY 1980; RGAL 4; SATA-Obit 25

Connor, Ralph .... **TCLC 31**
See Gordon, Charles William
See also DLB 92; TCWW 2

Conrad, Joseph 1857-1924 ..... **SSC 9, 67, 69, 71; TCLC 1, 6, 13, 25, 43, 57; WLC**
See also AAYA 26; BPFB 1; BRW 6; BRWC 1; BRWR 2; CA 104; 131; CANR 60; CDBLB 1890-1914; DA; DA3; DAB; DAC; DAM MST, NOV; DLB 10, 34, 98, 156; EWL 3; EXPN; EXPS; LAIT 2; LATS 1:1; LMFS 1; MTCW 1, 2; NFS 2, 16; RGEL 2; RGSF 2; SATA 27; SSFS 1, 12; TEA; WLIT 4

Conrad, Robert Arnold
See Hart, Moss

Conroy, (Donald) Pat(rick) 1945- ... **CLC 30, 74**
See also AAYA 8, 52; AITN 1; BPFB 1; CA 85-88; CANR 24, 53, 129; CPW; CSW; DA3; DAM NOV, POP; DLB 6; LAIT 5; MTCW 1, 2

Constant (de Rebecque), (Henri) Benjamin
1767-1830 .... **NCLC 6**
See also DLB 119; EW 4; GFL 1789 to the Present

Conway, Jill K(er) 1934- .... **CLC 152**
See also CA 130; CANR 94

Conybeare, Charles Augustus
See Eliot, T(homas) S(tearns)

Cook, Michael 1933-1994 .... **CLC 58**
See also CA 93-96; CANR 68; DLB 53

Cook, Robin 1940- .... **CLC 14**
    See also AAYA 32; BEST 90:2; BPFB 1;
    CA 108; 111; CANR 41, 90, 109; CPW;
    DA3; DAM POP; HGG; INT CA-111
Cook, Roy
    See Silverberg, Robert
Cooke, Elizabeth 1948- .... **CLC 55**
    See also CA 129
Cooke, John Esten 1830-1886 .... **NCLC 5**
    See also DLB 3, 248; RGAL 4
Cooke, John Estes
    See Baum, L(yman) Frank
Cooke, M. E.
    See Creasey, John
Cooke, Margaret
    See Creasey, John
Cooke, Rose Terry 1827-1892 ...... **NCLC 110**
    See also DLB 12, 74
Cook-Lynn, Elizabeth 1930- .... **CLC 93;**
        NNAL
    See also CA 133; DAM MULT; DLB 175
Cooney, Ray .... **CLC 62**
    See also CBD
Cooper, Anthony Ashley 1671-1713 .. **LC 107**
    See also DLB 101
Cooper, Douglas 1960- .... **CLC 86**
Cooper, Henry St. John
    See Creasey, John
Cooper, J(oan) California (?)- .... **CLC 56**
    See also AAYA 12; BW 1; CA 125; CANR
    55; DAM MULT; DLB 212
Cooper, James Fenimore
        1789-1851 .... **NCLC 1, 27, 54**
    See also AAYA 22; AMW; BPFB 1;
    CDALB 1640-1865; DA3; DLB 3, 183,
    250, 254; LAIT 1; NFS 9; RGAL 4; SATA
    19; TUS; WCH
Cooper, Susan Fenimore
        1813-1894 .... **NCLC 129**
    See also ANW; DLB 239, 254
Coover, Robert (Lowell) 1932- ..... **CLC 3, 7,**
        15, 32, 46, 87, 161; SSC 15
    See also AMWS 5; BPFB 1; CA 45-48;
    CANR 3, 37, 58, 115; CN 7; DAM NOV;
    DLB 2, 227; DLBY 1981; EWL 3;
    MTCW 1, 2; RGAL 4; RGSF 2
Copeland, Stewart (Armstrong)
        1952- .... **CLC 26**
Copernicus, Nicolaus 1473-1543 .... **LC 45**
Coppard, A(lfred) E(dgar)
        1878-1957 .... **SSC 21; TCLC 5**
    See also BRWS 8; CA 114; 167; DLB 162;
    EWL 3; HGG; RGEL 2; RGSF 2; SUFW
    1; YABC 1
Coppee, Francois 1842-1908 .... **TCLC 25**
    See also CA 170; DLB 217
Coppola, Francis Ford 1939- ... **CLC 16, 126**
    See also AAYA 39; CA 77-80; CANR 40,
    78; DLB 44
Copway, George 1818-1869 .... **NNAL**
    See also DAM MULT; DLB 175, 183
Corbiere, Tristan 1845-1875 .... **NCLC 43**
    See also DLB 217; GFL 1789 to the Present
Corcoran, Barbara (Asenath)
        1911- .... **CLC 17**
    See also AAYA 14; CA 21-24R, 191; CAAE
    191; CAAS 2; CANR 11, 28, 48; CLR
    50; DLB 52; JRDA; MAICYA 2; MAIC-
    YAS 1; RHW; SAAS 20; SATA 3, 77;
    SATA-Essay 125
Cordelier, Maurice
    See Giraudoux, Jean(-Hippolyte)
Corelli, Marie .... **TCLC 51**
    See Mackay, Mary
    See also DLB 34, 156; RGEL 2; SUFW 1
Corinna c. 225B.C.-c. 305B.C. ...... **CMLC 72**
Corman, Cid .... **CLC 9**
    See Corman, Sidney
    See also CAAS 2; DLB 5, 193

Corman, Sidney 1924-2004
    See Corman, Cid
    See also CA 85-88; 225; CANR 44; CP 7;
    DAM POET
Cormier, Robert (Edmund)
        1925-2000 .... **CLC 12, 30**
    See also AAYA 3, 19; BYA 1, 2, 6, 8, 9;
    CA 1-4R; CANR 5, 23, 76, 93; CDALB
    1968-1988; CLR 12, 55; DA; DAB; DAC;
    DAM MST, NOV; DLB 52; EXPN; INT
    CANR-23; JRDA; LAIT 5; MAICYA 1,
    2; MTCW 1, 2; NFS 2, 18; SATA 10, 45,
    83; SATA-Obit 122; WYA; YAW
Corn, Alfred (DeWitt III) 1943- .... **CLC 33**
    See also CA 179; CAAE 179; CAAS 25;
    CANR 44; CP 7; CSW; DLB 120, 282;
    DLBY 1980
Corneille, Pierre 1606-1684 ... **DC 21; LC 28**
    See also DAB; DAM MST; DLB 268; EW
    3; GFL Beginnings to 1789; RGWL 2, 3;
    TWA
Cornwell, David (John Moore)
        1931- .... **CLC 9, 15**
    See le Carre, John
    See also CA 5-8R; CANR 13, 33, 59, 107,
    132; DA3; DAM POP; MTCW 1, 2
Cornwell, Patricia (Daniels) 1956- . **CLC 155**
    See also AAYA 16, 56; BPFB 1; CA 134;
    CANR 53, 131; CMW 4; CPW; CSW;
    DAM POP; DLB 306; MSW; MTCW 1
Corso, (Nunzio) Gregory 1930-2001 . **CLC 1,**
        11; PC 33
    See also AMWS 12; BG 2; CA 5-8R; 193;
    CANR 41, 76, 132; CP 7; DA3; DLB 5,
    16, 237; LMFS 2; MTCW 1, 2; WP
Cortazar, Julio 1914-1984 .. **CLC 2, 3, 5, 10,**
        13, 15, 33, 34, 92; HLC 1; SSC 7, 76
    See also BPFB 1; CA 21-24R; CANR 12,
    32, 81; CDWLB 3; DA3; DAM MULT,
    NOV; DLB 113; EWL 3; EXPS; HW 1,
    2; LAW; MTCW 1, 2; RGSF 2; RGWL 2,
    3; SSFS 3, 20; TWA; WLIT 1
Cortes, Hernan 1485-1547 .... **LC 31**
Corvinus, Jakob
    See Raabe, Wilhelm (Karl)
Corwin, Cecil
    See Kornbluth, C(yril) M.
Cosic, Dobrica 1921- .... **CLC 14**
    See also CA 122; 138; CDWLB 4; CWW
    2; DLB 181; EWL 3
Costain, Thomas B(ertram)
        1885-1965 .... **CLC 30**
    See also BYA 3; CA 5-8R; 25-28R; DLB 9;
    RHW
Costantini, Humberto 1924(?)-1987 . **CLC 49**
    See also CA 131; 122; EWL 3; HW 1
Costello, Elvis 1954- .... **CLC 21**
    See also CA 204
Costenoble, Philostene
    See Ghelderode, Michel de
Cotes, Cecil V.
    See Duncan, Sara Jeannette
Cotter, Joseph Seamon Sr.
        1861-1949 .... **BLC 1; TCLC 28**
    See also BW 1; CA 124; DAM MULT; DLB
    50
Couch, Arthur Thomas Quiller
    See Quiller-Couch, Sir Arthur (Thomas)
Coulton, James
    See Hansen, Joseph
Couperus, Louis (Marie Anne)
        1863-1923 .... **TCLC 15**
    See also CA 115; EWL 3; RGWL 2, 3
Coupland, Douglas 1961- .... **CLC 85, 133**
    See also AAYA 34; CA 142; CANR 57, 90,
    130; CCA 1; CPW; DAC; DAM POP
Court, Wesli
    See Turco, Lewis (Putnam)

Courtenay, Bryce 1933- .... **CLC 59**
    See also CA 138; CPW
Courtney, Robert
    See Ellison, Harlan (Jay)
Cousteau, Jacques-Yves 1910-1997 .. **CLC 30**
    See also CA 65-68; 159; CANR 15, 67;
    MTCW 1; SATA 38, 98
Coventry, Francis 1725-1754 .... **LC 46**
Coverdale, Miles c. 1487-1569 .... **LC 77**
    See also DLB 167
Cowan, Peter (Walkinshaw)
        1914-2002 .... **SSC 28**
    See also CA 21-24R; CANR 9, 25, 50, 83;
    CN 7; DLB 260; RGSF 2
Coward, Noel (Peirce) 1899-1973 . **CLC 1, 9,**
        29, 51
    See also AITN 1; BRWS 2; CA 17-18; 41-
    44R; CANR 35, 132; CAP 2; CDBLB
    1914-1945; DA3; DAM DRAM; DFS 3,
    6; DLB 10, 245; EWL 3; IDFW 3, 4;
    MTCW 1, 2; RGEL 2; TEA
Cowley, Abraham 1618-1667 .... **LC 43**
    See also BRW 2; DLB 131, 151; PAB;
    RGEL 2
Cowley, Malcolm 1898-1989 .... **CLC 39**
    See also AMWS 2; CA 5-8R; 128; CANR
    3, 55; DLB 4, 48; DLBY 1981, 1989;
    EWL 3; MTCW 1, 2
Cowper, William 1731-1800 ..... **NCLC 8, 94;**
        PC 40
    See also BRW 3; DA3; DAM POET; DLB
    104, 109; RGEL 2
Cox, William Trevor 1928-
    See Trevor, William
    See also CA 9-12R; CANR 4, 37, 55, 76,
    102; DAM NOV; INT CANR-37; MTCW
    1, 2; TEA
Coyne, P. J.
    See Masters, Hilary
Cozzens, James Gould 1903-1978 . **CLC 1, 4,**
        11, 92
    See also AMW; BPFB 1; CA 9-12R; 81-84;
    CANR 19; CDALB 1941-1968; DLB 9,
    294; DLBD 2; DLBY 1984, 1997; EWL
    3; MTCW 1, 2; RGAL 4
Crabbe, George 1754-1832 .... **NCLC 26, 121**
    See also BRW 3; DLB 93; RGEL 2
Crace, Jim 1946- .... **CLC 157; SSC 61**
    See also CA 128; 135; CANR 55, 70, 123;
    CN 7; DLB 231; INT CA-135
Craddock, Charles Egbert
    See Murfree, Mary Noailles
Craig, A. A.
    See Anderson, Poul (William)
Craik, Mrs.
    See Craik, Dinah Maria (Mulock)
    See also RGEL 2
Craik, Dinah Maria (Mulock)
        1826-1887 .... **NCLC 38**
    See Craik, Mrs.; Mulock, Dinah Maria
    See also DLB 35, 163; MAICYA 1, 2;
    SATA 34
Cram, Ralph Adams 1863-1942 ..... **TCLC 45**
    See also CA 160
Cranch, Christopher Pearse
        1813-1892 .... **NCLC 115**
    See also DLB 1, 42, 243
Crane, (Harold) Hart 1899-1932 .... **PC 3;**
        TCLC 2, 5, 80; WLC
    See also AMW; AMWR 2; CA 104; 127;
    CDALB 1917-1929; DA; DA3; DAB;
    DAC; DAM MST, POET; DLB 4, 48;
    EWL 3; MTCW 1, 2; RGAL 4; TUS
Crane, R(onald) S(almon)
        1886-1967 .... **CLC 27**
    See also CA 85-88; DLB 63

Crane, Stephen (Townley)
1871-1900 ...... **SSC 7, 56, 70; TCLC 11, 17, 32; WLC**
See also AAYA 21; AMW; AMWC 1; BPFB 1; BYA 3; CA 109; 140; CANR 84; CDALB 1865-1917; DA; DA3; DAB; DAC; DAM MST, NOV, POET; DLB 12, 54, 78; EXPN; EXPS; LAIT 2; LMFS 2; NFS 4, 20; PFS 9; RGAL 4; RGSF 2; SSFS 4; TUS; WYA; YABC 2

Cranmer, Thomas 1489-1556 .... **LC 95**
See also DLB 132, 213

Cranshaw, Stanley
See Fisher, Dorothy (Frances) Canfield

Crase, Douglas 1944- .... **CLC 58**
See also CA 106

Crashaw, Richard 1612(?)-1649 .... **LC 24**
See also BRW 2; DLB 126; PAB; RGEL 2

Cratinus c. 519B.C.-c. 422B.C. ..... **CMLC 54**
See also LMFS 1

Craven, Margaret 1901-1980 .... **CLC 17**
See also BYA 2; CA 103; CCA 1; DAC; LAIT 5

Crawford, F(rancis) Marion
1854-1909 .... **TCLC 10**
See also CA 107; 168; DLB 71; HGG; RGAL 4; SUFW 1

Crawford, Isabella Valancy
1850-1887 .... **NCLC 12, 127**
See also DLB 92; RGEL 2

Crayon, Geoffrey
See Irving, Washington

Creasey, John 1908-1973 .... **CLC 11**
See Marric, J. J.
See also CA 5-8R; 41-44R; CANR 8, 59; CMW 4; DLB 77; MTCW 1

Crebillon, Claude Prosper Jolyot de (fils)
1707-1777 .... **LC 1, 28**
See also GFL Beginnings to 1789

Credo
See Creasey, John

Credo, Alvaro J. de
See Prado (Calvo), Pedro

Creeley, Robert (White) 1926- .. **CLC 1, 2, 4, 8, 11, 15, 36, 78**
See also AMWS 4; CA 1-4R; CAAS 10; CANR 23, 43, 89; CP 7; DA3; DAM POET; DLB 5, 16, 169; DLBD 17; EWL 3; MTCW 1, 2; PFS 21; RGAL 4; WP

Crevecoeur, Hector St. John de
See Crevecoeur, Michel Guillaume Jean de
See also ANW

Crevecoeur, Michel Guillaume Jean de
1735-1813 .... **NCLC 105**
See Crevecoeur, Hector St. John de
See also AMWS 1; DLB 37

Crevel, Rene 1900-1935 .... **TCLC 112**
See also GLL 2

Crews, Harry (Eugene) 1935- ..... **CLC 6, 23, 49**
See also AITN 1; AMWS 11; BPFB 1; CA 25-28R; CANR 20, 57; CN 7; CSW; DA3; DLB 6, 143, 185; MTCW 1, 2; RGAL 4

Crichton, (John) Michael 1942- .... **CLC 2, 6, 54, 90**
See also AAYA 10, 49; AITN 2; BPFB 1; CA 25-28R; CANR 13, 40, 54, 76, 127; CMW 4; CN 7; CPW; DA3; DAM NOV, POP; DLB 292; DLBY 1981; INT CANR-13; JRDA; MTCW 1, 2; SATA 9, 88; SFW 4; YAW

Crispin, Edmund .... **CLC 22**
See Montgomery, (Robert) Bruce
See also DLB 87; MSW

Cristofer, Michael 1945(?)- .... **CLC 28**
See also CA 110; 152; CAD; CD 5; DAM DRAM; DFS 15; DLB 7

Criton
See Alain

Croce, Benedetto 1866-1952 .... **TCLC 37**
See also CA 120; 155; EW 8; EWL 3

Crockett, David 1786-1836 .... **NCLC 8**
See also DLB 3, 11, 183, 248

Crockett, Davy
See Crockett, David

Crofts, Freeman Wills 1879-1957 .. **TCLC 55**
See also CA 115; 195; CMW 4; DLB 77; MSW

Croker, John Wilson 1780-1857 .... **NCLC 10**
See also DLB 110

Crommelynck, Fernand 1885-1970 .. **CLC 75**
See also CA 189; 89-92; EWL 3

Cromwell, Oliver 1599-1658 .... **LC 43**

Cronenberg, David 1943- .... **CLC 143**
See also CA 138; CCA 1

Cronin, A(rchibald) J(oseph)
1896-1981 .... **CLC 32**
See also BPFB 1; CA 1-4R; 102; CANR 5; DLB 191; SATA 47; SATA-Obit 25

Cross, Amanda
See Heilbrun, Carolyn G(old)
See also BPFB 1; CMW; CPW; DLB 306; MSW

Crothers, Rachel 1878-1958 .... **TCLC 19**
See also CA 113; 194; CAD; CWD; DLB 7, 266; RGAL 4

Croves, Hal
See Traven, B.

Crow Dog, Mary (Ellen) (?)- .... **CLC 93**
See Brave Bird, Mary
See also CA 154

Crowfield, Christopher
See Stowe, Harriet (Elizabeth) Beecher

Crowley, Aleister .... **TCLC 7**
See Crowley, Edward Alexander
See also GLL 1

Crowley, Edward Alexander 1875-1947
See Crowley, Aleister
See also CA 104; HGG

Crowley, John 1942- .... **CLC 57**
See also AAYA 57; BPFB 1; CA 61-64; CANR 43, 98; DLBY 1982; FANT; SATA 65, 140; SFW 4; SUFW 2

Crowne, John 1641-1712 .... **LC 104**
See also DLB 80; RGEL 2

Crud
See Crumb, R(obert)

Crumarums
See Crumb, R(obert)

Crumb, R(obert) 1943- .... **CLC 17**
See also CA 106; CANR 107

Crumbum
See Crumb, R(obert)

Crumski
See Crumb, R(obert)

Crum the Bum
See Crumb, R(obert)

Crunk
See Crumb, R(obert)

Crustt
See Crumb, R(obert)

Crutchfield, Les
See Trumbo, Dalton

Cruz, Victor Hernandez 1949- ... **HLC 1; PC 37**
See also BW 2; CA 65-68; CAAS 17; CANR 14, 32, 74, 132; CP 7; DAM MULT, POET; DLB 41; DNFS 1; EXPP; HW 1, 2; LLW 1; MTCW 1; PFS 16; WP

Cryer, Gretchen (Kiger) 1935- .... **CLC 21**
See also CA 114; 123

Csath, Geza 1887-1919 .... **TCLC 13**
See also CA 111

Cudlip, David R(ockwell) 1933- .... **CLC 34**
See also CA 177

Cullen, Countee 1903-1946 .... **BLC 1; HR 2; PC 20; TCLC 4, 37; WLCS**
See also AFAW 2; AMWS 4; BW 1; CA 108; 124; CDALB 1917-1929; DA; DA3; DAC; DAM MST, MULT, POET; DLB 4, 48, 51; EWL 3; EXPP; PFS 3; RGAL 4; SATA 18; WP

Culleton, Beatrice 1949- .... **NNAL**
See also CA 120; CANR 83; DAC

Cum, R.
See Crumb, R(obert)

Cummings, Bruce F(rederick) 1889-1919
See Barbellion, W. N. P.
See also CA 123

Cummings, E(dward) E(stlin)
1894-1962 .. **CLC 1, 3, 8, 12, 15, 68; PC 5; TCLC 137; WLC**
See also AAYA 41; AMW; CA 73-76; CANR 31; CDALB 1929-1941; DA; DA3; DAB; DAC; DAM MST, POET; DLB 4, 48; EWL 3; EXPP; MTCW 1, 2; PAB; PFS 1, 3, 12, 13, 19; RGAL 4; TUS; WP

Cummins, Maria Susanna
1827-1866 .... **NCLC 139**
See also DLB 42; YABC 1

Cunha, Euclides (Rodrigues Pimenta) da
1866-1909 .... **TCLC 24**
See also CA 123; 219; DLB 307; LAW; WLIT 1

Cunningham, E. V.
See Fast, Howard (Melvin)

Cunningham, J(ames) V(incent)
1911-1985 .... **CLC 3, 31**
See also CA 1-4R; 115; CANR 1, 72; DLB 5

Cunningham, Julia (Woolfolk)
1916- .... **CLC 12**
See also CA 9-12R; CANR 4, 19, 36; CWRI 5; JRDA; MAICYA 1, 2; SAAS 2; SATA 1, 26, 132

Cunningham, Michael 1952- .... **CLC 34**
See also CA 136; CANR 96; DLB 292; GLL 2

Cunninghame Graham, R. B.
See Cunninghame Graham, Robert (Gallnigad) Bontine

Cunninghame Graham, Robert (Gallnigad) Bontine 1852-1936 .... **TCLC 19**
See Graham, R(obert) B(ontine) Cunninghame
See also CA 119; 184

Curnow, (Thomas) Allen (Monro)
1911-2001 .... **PC 48**
See also CA 69-72; 202; CANR 48, 99; CP 7; EWL 3; RGEL 2

Currie, Ellen 19(?)- .... **CLC 44**

Curtin, Philip
See Lowndes, Marie Adelaide (Belloc)

Curtin, Phillip
See Lowndes, Marie Adelaide (Belloc)

Curtis, Price
See Ellison, Harlan (Jay)

Cusanus, Nicolaus 1401-1464 .... **LC 80**
See Nicholas of Cusa

Cutrate, Joe
See Spiegelman, Art

Cynewulf c. 770- .... **CMLC 23**
See also DLB 146; RGEL 2

Cyrano de Bergerac, Savinien de
1619-1655 .... **LC 65**
See also DLB 268; GFL Beginnings to 1789; RGWL 2, 3

Cyril of Alexandria c. 375-c. 430 . **CMLC 59**

Czaczkes, Shmuel Yosef Halevi
See Agnon, S(hmuel) Y(osef Halevi)

Dabrowska, Maria (Szumska)
1889-1965 .... **CLC 15**
See also CA 106; CDWLB 4; DLB 215;
EWL 3

Dabydeen, David 1955- .... **CLC 34**
See also BW 1; CA 125; CANR 56, 92; CN
7; CP 7

Dacey, Philip 1939- .... **CLC 51**
See also CA 37-40R; CAAS 17; CANR 14,
32, 64; CP 7; DLB 105

Dafydd ap Gwilym c. 1320-c. 1380 ..... **PC 56**

Dagerman, Stig (Halvard)
1923-1954 .... **TCLC 17**
See also CA 117; 155; DLB 259; EWL 3

D'Aguiar, Fred 1960- .... **CLC 145**
See also CA 148; CANR 83, 101; CP 7;
DLB 157; EWL 3

Dahl, Roald 1916-1990 .... **CLC 1, 6, 18, 79**
See also AAYA 15; BPFB 1; BRWS 4; BYA
5; CA 1-4R; 133; CANR 6, 32, 37, 62;
CLR 1, 7, 41; CPW; DA3; DAB; DAC;
DAM MST, NOV, POP; DLB 139, 255;
HGG; JRDA; MAICYA 1, 2; MTCW 1,
2; RGSF 2; SATA 1, 26, 73; SATA-Obit
65; SSFS 4; TEA; YAW

Dahlberg, Edward 1900-1977 .. **CLC 1, 7, 14**
See also CA 9-12R; 69-72; CANR 31, 62;
DLB 48; MTCW 1; RGAL 4

Daitch, Susan 1954- .... **CLC 103**
See also CA 161

Dale, Colin .... **TCLC 18**
See Lawrence, T(homas) E(dward)

Dale, George E.
See Asimov, Isaac

Dalton, Roque 1935-1975(?) ..... **HLCS 1; PC
36**
See also CA 176; DLB 283; HW 2

Daly, Elizabeth 1878-1967 .... **CLC 52**
See also CA 23-24; 25-28R; CANR 60;
CAP 2; CMW 4

Daly, Mary 1928- .... **CLC 173**
See also CA 25-28R; CANR 30, 62; FW;
GLL 1; MTCW 1

Daly, Maureen 1921- .... **CLC 17**
See also AAYA 5, 58; BYA 6; CANR 37,
83, 108; CLR 96; JRDA; MAICYA 1, 2;
SAAS 1; SATA 2, 129; WYA; YAW

Damas, Leon-Gontran 1912-1978 .... **CLC 84**
See also BW 1; CA 125; 73-76; EWL 3

Dana, Richard Henry Sr.
1787-1879 .... **NCLC 53**

Daniel, Samuel 1562(?)-1619 .... **LC 24**
See also DLB 62; RGEL 2

Daniels, Brett
See Adler, Renata

Dannay, Frederic 1905-1982 .... **CLC 11**
See Queen, Ellery
See also CA 1-4R; 107; CANR 1, 39; CMW
4; DAM POP; DLB 137; MTCW 1

D'Annunzio, Gabriele 1863-1938 ... **TCLC 6,
40**
See also CA 104; 155; EW 8; EWL 3;
RGWL 2, 3; TWA

Danois, N. le
See Gourmont, Remy(-Marie-Charles) de

Dante 1265-1321 .... **CMLC 3, 18, 39, 70; PC
21; WLCS**
See also DA; DA3; DAB; DAC; DAM
MST, POET; EFS 1; EW 1; LAIT 1;
RGWL 2, 3; TWA; WP

d'Antibes, Germain
See Simenon, Georges (Jacques Christian)

Danticat, Edwidge 1969- .... **CLC 94, 139**
See also AAYA 29; CA 152; 192; CAAE
192; CANR 73, 129; DNFS 1; EXPS;
LATS 1:2; MTCW 1; SSFS 1; YAW

Danvers, Dennis 1947- .... **CLC 70**

Danziger, Paula 1944-2004 .... **CLC 21**
See also AAYA 4, 36; BYA 6, 7, 14; CA
112; 115; 229; CANR 37, 132; CLR 20;
JRDA; MAICYA 1, 2; SATA 36, 63, 102,
149; SATA-Brief 30; WYA; YAW

Da Ponte, Lorenzo 1749-1838 .... **NCLC 50**

Dario, Ruben 1867-1916 .... **HLC 1; PC 15;
TCLC 4**
See also CA 131; CANR 81; DAM MULT;
DLB 290; EWL 3; HW 1, 2; LAW;
MTCW 1, 2; RGWL 2, 3

Darley, George 1795-1846 .... **NCLC 2**
See also DLB 96; RGEL 2

Darrow, Clarence (Seward)
1857-1938 .... **TCLC 81**
See also CA 164; DLB 303

Darwin, Charles 1809-1882 .... **NCLC 57**
See also BRWS 7; DLB 57, 166; LATS 1:1;
RGEL 2; TEA; WLIT 4

Darwin, Erasmus 1731-1802 .... **NCLC 106**
See also DLB 93; RGEL 2

Daryush, Elizabeth 1887-1977 ...... **CLC 6, 19**
See also CA 49-52; CANR 3, 81; DLB 20

Das, Kamala 1934- .... **CLC 191; PC 43**
See also CA 101; CANR 27, 59; CP 7;
CWP; FW

Dasgupta, Surendranath
1887-1952 .... **TCLC 81**
See also CA 157

**Dashwood, Edmee Elizabeth Monica de la
Pasture** 1890-1943
See Delafield, E. M.
See also CA 119; 154

da Silva, Antonio Jose
1705-1739 .... **NCLC 114**

Daudet, (Louis Marie) Alphonse
1840-1897 .... **NCLC 1**
See also DLB 123; GFL 1789 to the Present;
RGSF 2

d'Aulnoy, Marie-Catherine c.
1650-1705 .... **LC 100**

Daumal, Rene 1908-1944 .... **TCLC 14**
See also CA 114; EWL 3

Davenant, William 1606-1668 .... **LC 13**
See also DLB 58, 126; RGEL 2

Davenport, Guy (Mattison, Jr.)
1927-2005 .... **CLC 6, 14, 38; SSC 16**
See also CA 33-36R; CANR 23, 73; CN 7;
CSW; DLB 130

David, Robert
See Nezval, Vitezslav

Davidson, Avram (James) 1923-1993
See Queen, Ellery
See also CA 101; 171; CANR 26; DLB 8;
FANT; SFW 4; SUFW 1, 2

Davidson, Donald (Grady)
1893-1968 .... **CLC 2, 13, 19**
See also CA 5-8R; 25-28R; CANR 4, 84;
DLB 45

Davidson, Hugh
See Hamilton, Edmond

Davidson, John 1857-1909 .... **TCLC 24**
See also CA 118; 217; DLB 19; RGEL 2

Davidson, Sara 1943- .... **CLC 9**
See also CA 81-84; CANR 44, 68; DLB
185

Davie, Donald (Alfred) 1922-1995 .... **CLC 5,
8, 10, 31; PC 29**
See also BRWS 6; CA 1-4R; 149; CAAS 3;
CANR 1, 44; CP 7; DLB 27; MTCW 1;
RGEL 2

Davie, Elspeth 1919-1995 .... **SSC 52**
See also CA 120; 126; 150; DLB 139

Davies, Ray(mond Douglas) 1944- ... **CLC 21**
See also CA 116; 146; CANR 92

Davies, Rhys 1901-1978 .... **CLC 23**
See also CA 9-12R; 81-84; CANR 4; DLB
139, 191

Davies, (William) Robertson
1913-1995 .... **CLC 2, 7, 13, 25, 42, 75,
91; WLC**
See Marchbanks, Samuel
See also BEST 89:2; BPFB 1; CA 33-36R;
150; CANR 17, 42, 103; CN 7; CPW;
DA; DA3; DAB; DAC; DAM MST, NOV,
POP; DLB 68; EWL 3; HGG; INT CANR-
17; MTCW 1, 2; RGEL 2; TWA

Davies, Sir John 1569-1626 .... **LC 85**
See also DLB 172

Davies, Walter C.
See Kornbluth, C(yril) M.

Davies, William Henry 1871-1940 ... **TCLC 5**
See also CA 104; 179; DLB 19, 174; EWL
3; RGEL 2

Da Vinci, Leonardo 1452-1519 ..... **LC 12, 57,
60**
See also AAYA 40

Davis, Angela (Yvonne) 1944- .... **CLC 77**
See also BW 2, 3; CA 57-60; CANR 10,
81; CSW; DA3; DAM MULT; FW

Davis, B. Lynch
See Bioy Casares, Adolfo; Borges, Jorge
Luis

Davis, Frank Marshall 1905-1987 ...... **BLC 1**
See also BW 2, 3; CA 125; 123; CANR 42,
80; DAM MULT; DLB 51

Davis, Gordon
See Hunt, E(verette) Howard, (Jr.)

Davis, H(arold) L(enoir) 1896-1960 . **CLC 49**
See also ANW; CA 178; 89-92; DLB 9,
206; SATA 114

Davis, Rebecca (Blaine) Harding
1831-1910 .... **SSC 38; TCLC 6**
See also CA 104; 179; DLB 74, 239; FW;
NFS 14; RGAL 4; TUS

Davis, Richard Harding
1864-1916 .... **TCLC 24**
See also CA 114; 179; DLB 12, 23, 78, 79,
189; DLBD 13; RGAL 4

Davison, Frank Dalby 1893-1970 ..... **CLC 15**
See also CA 217; 116; DLB 260

Davison, Lawrence H.
See Lawrence, D(avid) H(erbert Richards)

Davison, Peter (Hubert) 1928- .... **CLC 28**
See also CA 9-12R; CAAS 4; CANR 3, 43,
84; CP 7; DLB 5

Davys, Mary 1674-1732 .... **LC 1, 46**
See also DLB 39

Dawson, (Guy) Fielding (Lewis)
1930-2002 .... **CLC 6**
See also CA 85-88; 202; CANR 108; DLB
130; DLBY 2002

Dawson, Peter
See Faust, Frederick (Schiller)
See also TCWW 2, 2

Day, Clarence (Shepard, Jr.)
1874-1935 .... **TCLC 25**
See also CA 108; 199; DLB 11

Day, John 1574(?)-1640(?) .... **LC 70**
See also DLB 62, 170; RGEL 2

Day, Thomas 1748-1789 .... **LC 1**
See also DLB 39; YABC 1

Day Lewis, C(ecil) 1904-1972 . **CLC 1, 6, 10;
PC 11**
See Blake, Nicholas
See also BRWS 3; CA 13-16; 33-36R;
CANR 34; CAP 1; CWRI 5; DAM POET;
DLB 15, 20; EWL 3; MTCW 1, 2; RGEL
2

Dazai Osamu .... **SSC 41; TCLC 11**
See Tsushima, Shuji
See also CA 164; DLB 182; EWL 3; MJW;
RGSF 2; RGWL 2, 3; TWA

de Andrade, Carlos Drummond
See Drummond de Andrade, Carlos

de Andrade, Mario 1892(?)-1945
 See Andrade, Mario de
 See also CA 178; HW 2
Deane, Norman
 See Creasey, John
Deane, Seamus (Francis) 1940- ...... **CLC 122**
 See also CA 118; CANR 42
de Beauvoir, Simone (Lucie Ernestine Marie Bertrand)
 See Beauvoir, Simone (Lucie Ernestine Marie Bertrand) de
de Beer, P.
 See Bosman, Herman Charles
de Brissac, Malcolm
 See Dickinson, Peter (Malcolm de Brissac)
de Campos, Alvaro
 See Pessoa, Fernando (Antonio Nogueira)
de Chardin, Pierre Teilhard
 See Teilhard de Chardin, (Marie Joseph) Pierre
Dee, John 1527-1608 .... **LC 20**
 See also DLB 136, 213
Deer, Sandra 1940- .... **CLC 45**
 See also CA 186
De Ferrari, Gabriella 1941- .... **CLC 65**
 See also CA 146
de Filippo, Eduardo 1900-1984 ... **TCLC 127**
 See also CA 132; 114; EWL 3; MTCW 1; RGWL 2, 3
Defoe, Daniel 1660(?)-1731 .... **LC 1, 42, 108; WLC**
 See also AAYA 27; BRW 3; BRWR 1; BYA 4; CDBLB 1660-1789; CLR 61; DA; DA3; DAB; DAC; DAM MST, NOV; DLB 39, 95, 101; JRDA; LAIT 1; LMFS 1; MAICYA 1, 2; NFS 9, 13; RGEL 2; SATA 22; TEA; WCH; WLIT 3
de Gourmont, Remy(-Marie-Charles)
 See Gourmont, Remy(-Marie-Charles) de
de Gournay, Marie le Jars 1566-1645 .... **LC 98**
 See also FW
de Hartog, Jan 1914-2002 .... **CLC 19**
 See also CA 1-4R; 210; CANR 1; DFS 12
de Hostos, E. M.
 See Hostos (y Bonilla), Eugenio Maria de
de Hostos, Eugenio M.
 See Hostos (y Bonilla), Eugenio Maria de
Deighton, Len .... **CLC 4, 7, 22, 46**
 See Deighton, Leonard Cyril
 See also AAYA 6; BEST 89:2; BPFB 1; CDBLB 1960 to Present; CMW 4; CN 7; CPW; DLB 87
Deighton, Leonard Cyril 1929-
 See Deighton, Len
 See also AAYA 57; CA 9-12R; CANR 19, 33, 68; DA3; DAM NOV, POP; MTCW 1, 2
Dekker, Thomas 1572(?)-1632 ..... **DC 12; LC 22**
 See also CDBLB Before 1660; DAM DRAM; DLB 62, 172; LMFS 1; RGEL 2
de Laclos, Pierre Ambroise Franois
 See Laclos, Pierre Ambroise Francois
Delacroix, (Ferdinand-Victor-)Eugene 1798-1863 .... **NCLC 133**
 See also EW 5
Delafield, E. M. .... **TCLC 61**
 See Dashwood, Edmee Elizabeth Monica de la Pasture
 See also DLB 34; RHW
de la Mare, Walter (John) 1873-1956 . **SSC 14; TCLC 4, 53; WLC**
 See also CA 163; CDBLB 1914-1945; CLR 23; CWRI 5; DA3; DAB; DAC; DAM MST, POET; DLB 19, 153, 162, 255, 284; EWL 3; EXPP; HGG; MAICYA 1, 2; MTCW 1; RGEL 2; RGSF 2; SATA 16; SUFW 1; TEA; WCH

de Lamartine, Alphonse (Marie Louis Prat)
 See Lamartine, Alphonse (Marie Louis Prat) de
Delaney, Franey
 See O'Hara, John (Henry)
Delaney, Shelagh 1939- .... **CLC 29**
 See also CA 17-20R; CANR 30, 67; CBD; CD 5; CDBLB 1960 to Present; CWD; DAM DRAM; DFS 7; DLB 13; MTCW 1
Delany, Martin Robison 1812-1885 .... **NCLC 93**
 See also DLB 50; RGAL 4
Delany, Mary (Granville Pendarves) 1700-1788 .... **LC 12**
Delany, Samuel R(ay), Jr. 1942- .... **BLC 1; CLC 8, 14, 38, 141**
 See also AAYA 24; AFAW 2; BPFB 1; BW 2, 3; CA 81-84; CANR 27, 43, 115, 116; CN 7; DAM MULT; DLB 8, 33; FANT; MTCW 1, 2; RGAL 4; SATA 92; SCFW; SFW 4; SUFW 2
De la Ramee, Marie Louise (Ouida) 1839-1908
 See Ouida
 See also CA 204; SATA 20
de la Roche, Mazo 1879-1961 .... **CLC 14**
 See also CA 85-88; CANR 30; DLB 68; RGEL 2; RHW; SATA 64
De La Salle, Innocent
 See Hartmann, Sadakichi
de Laureamont, Comte
 See Lautreamont
Delbanco, Nicholas (Franklin) 1942- .... **CLC 6, 13, 167**
 See also CA 17-20R, 189; CAAE 189; CAAS 2; CANR 29, 55, 116; DLB 6, 234
del Castillo, Michel 1933- .... **CLC 38**
 See also CA 109; CANR 77
Deledda, Grazia (Cosima) 1875(?)-1936 .... **TCLC 23**
 See also CA 123; 205; DLB 264; EWL 3; RGWL 2, 3
Deleuze, Gilles 1925-1995 .... **TCLC 116**
 See also DLB 296
Delgado, Abelardo (Lalo) B(arrientos) 1930-2004 .... **HLC 1**
 See also CA 131; CAAS 15; CANR 90; DAM MST, MULT; DLB 82; HW 1, 2
Delibes, Miguel .... **CLC 8, 18**
 See Delibes Setien, Miguel
 See also EWL 3
Delibes Setien, Miguel 1920-
 See Delibes, Miguel
 See also CA 45-48; CANR 1, 32; CWW 2; HW 1; MTCW 1
DeLillo, Don 1936- ..... **CLC 8, 10, 13, 27, 39, 54, 76, 143**
 See also AMWC 2; AMWS 6; BEST 89:1; BPFB 1; CA 81-84; CANR 21, 76, 92, 133; CN 7; CPW; DA3; DAM NOV, POP; DLB 6, 173; EWL 3; MTCW 1, 2; RGAL 4; TUS
de Lisser, H. G.
 See De Lisser, H(erbert) G(eorge)
 See also DLB 117
De Lisser, H(erbert) G(eorge) 1878-1944 .... **TCLC 12**
 See de Lisser, H. G.
 See also BW 2; CA 109; 152
Deloire, Pierre
 See Peguy, Charles (Pierre)
Deloney, Thomas 1543(?)-1600 .... **LC 41**
 See also DLB 167; RGEL 2
Deloria, Ella (Cara) 1889-1971(?) ..... **NNAL**
 See also CA 152; DAM MULT; DLB 175

Deloria, Vine (Victor), Jr. 1933- ...... **CLC 21, 122; NNAL**
 See also CA 53-56; CANR 5, 20, 48, 98; DAM MULT; DLB 175; MTCW 1; SATA 21
del Valle-Inclan, Ramon (Maria)
 See Valle-Inclan, Ramon (Maria) del
Del Vecchio, John M(ichael) 1947- .. **CLC 29**
 See also CA 110; DLBD 9
de Man, Paul (Adolph Michel) 1919-1983 .... **CLC 55**
 See also CA 128; 111; CANR 61; DLB 67; MTCW 1, 2
DeMarinis, Rick 1934- .... **CLC 54**
 See also CA 57-60, 184; CAAE 184; CAAS 24; CANR 9, 25, 50; DLB 218
de Maupassant, (Henri Rene Albert) Guy
 See Maupassant, (Henri Rene Albert) Guy de
Dembry, R. Emmet
 See Murfree, Mary Noailles
Demby, William 1922- .... **BLC 1; CLC 53**
 See also BW 1, 3; CA 81-84; CANR 81; DAM MULT; DLB 33
de Menton, Francisco
 See Chin, Frank (Chew, Jr.)
Demetrius of Phalerum c. 307B.C.- .... **CMLC 34**
Demijohn, Thom
 See Disch, Thomas M(ichael)
De Mille, James 1833-1880 .... **NCLC 123**
 See also DLB 99, 251
Deming, Richard 1915-1983
 See Queen, Ellery
 See also CA 9-12R; CANR 3, 94; SATA 24
Democritus c. 460B.C.-c. 370B.C. . **CMLC 47**
de Montaigne, Michel (Eyquem)
 See Montaigne, Michel (Eyquem) de
de Montherlant, Henry (Milon)
 See Montherlant, Henry (Milon) de
Demosthenes 384B.C.-322B.C. ...... **CMLC 13**
 See also AW 1; DLB 176; RGWL 2, 3
de Musset, (Louis Charles) Alfred
 See Musset, (Louis Charles) Alfred de
de Natale, Francine
 See Malzberg, Barry N(athaniel)
de Navarre, Marguerite 1492-1549 ..... **LC 61**
 See Marguerite d'Angouleme; Marguerite de Navarre
Denby, Edwin (Orr) 1903-1983 .... **CLC 48**
 See also CA 138; 110
de Nerval, Gerard
 See Nerval, Gerard de
Denham, John 1615-1669 .... **LC 73**
 See also DLB 58, 126; RGEL 2
Denis, Julio
 See Cortazar, Julio
Denmark, Harrison
 See Zelazny, Roger (Joseph)
Dennis, John 1658-1734 .... **LC 11**
 See also DLB 101; RGEL 2
Dennis, Nigel (Forbes) 1912-1989 ...... **CLC 8**
 See also CA 25-28R; 129; DLB 13, 15, 233; EWL 3; MTCW 1
Dent, Lester 1904-1959 .... **TCLC 72**
 See also CA 112; 161; CMW 4; DLB 306; SFW 4
De Palma, Brian (Russell) 1940- ...... **CLC 20**
 See also CA 109
De Quincey, Thomas 1785-1859 ..... **NCLC 4, 87**
 See also BRW 4; CDBLB 1789-1832; DLB 110, 144; RGEL 2
Deren, Eleanora 1908(?)-1961
 See Deren, Maya
 See also CA 192; 111
Deren, Maya .... **CLC 16, 102**
 See Deren, Eleanora

Derleth, August (William)
　　1909-1971 .... **CLC 31**
　　See also BPFB 1; BYA 9, 10; CA 1-4R; 29-
　　32R; CANR 4; CMW 4; DLB 9; DLBD
　　17; HGG; SATA 5; SUFW 1

Der Nister 1884-1950 .... **TCLC 56**
　　See Nister, Der

de Routisie, Albert
　　See Aragon, Louis

Derrida, Jacques 1930-2004 .... **CLC 24, 87**
　　See also CA 124; 127; CANR 76, 98, 133;
　　DLB 242; EWL 3; LMFS 2; MTCW 1;
　　TWA

Derry Down Derry
　　See Lear, Edward

Dersonnes, Jacques
　　See Simenon, Georges (Jacques Christian)

Desai, Anita 1937- .... **CLC 19, 37, 97, 175**
　　See also BRWS 5; CA 81-84; CANR 33,
　　53, 95, 133; CN 7; CWRI 5; DA3; DAB;
　　DAM NOV; DLB 271; DNFS 2; EWL 3;
　　FW; MTCW 1, 2; SATA 63, 126

Desai, Kiran 1971- .... **CLC 119**
　　See also BYA 16; CA 171; CANR 127

de Saint-Luc, Jean
　　See Glassco, John

de Saint Roman, Arnaud
　　See Aragon, Louis

Desbordes-Valmore, Marceline
　　　1786-1859 .... **NCLC 97**
　　See also DLB 217

Descartes, Rene 1596-1650 .... **LC 20, 35**
　　See also DLB 268; EW 3; GFL Beginnings
　　to 1789

Deschamps, Eustache 1340(?)-1404 .. **LC 103**
　　See also DLB 208

De Sica, Vittorio 1901(?)-1974 .... **CLC 20**
　　See also CA 117

Desnos, Robert 1900-1945 .... **TCLC 22**
　　See also CA 121; 151; CANR 107; DLB
　　258; EWL 3; LMFS 2

Destouches, Louis-Ferdinand
　　　1894-1961 .... **CLC 9, 15**
　　See Celine, Louis-Ferdinand
　　See also CA 85-88; CANR 28; MTCW 1

de Tolignac, Gaston
　　See Griffith, D(avid Lewelyn) W(ark)

Deutsch, Babette 1895-1982 .... **CLC 18**
　　See also BYA 3; CA 1-4R; 108; CANR 4,
　　79; DLB 45; SATA 1; SATA-Obit 33

Devenant, William 1606-1649 .... **LC 13**

Devkota, Laxmiprasad 1909-1959 . **TCLC 23**
　　See also CA 123

De Voto, Bernard (Augustine)
　　　1897-1955 .... **TCLC 29**
　　See also CA 113; 160; DLB 9, 256

De Vries, Peter 1910-1993 ..... **CLC 1, 2, 3, 7,
　　10, 28, 46**
　　See also CA 17-20R; 142; CANR 41; DAM
　　NOV; DLB 6; DLBY 1982; MTCW 1, 2

Dewey, John 1859-1952 .... **TCLC 95**
　　See also CA 114; 170; DLB 246, 270;
　　RGAL 4

Dexter, John
　　See Bradley, Marion Zimmer
　　See also GLL 1

Dexter, Martin
　　See Faust, Frederick (Schiller)
　　See also TCWW 2

Dexter, Pete 1943- .... **CLC 34, 55**
　　See also BEST 89:2; CA 127; 131; CANR
　　129; CPW; DAM POP; INT CA-131;
　　MTCW 1

Diamano, Silmang
　　See Senghor, Leopold Sedar

Diamond, Neil 1941- .... **CLC 30**
　　See also CA 108

Diaz del Castillo, Bernal
　　　1496-1584 .... **HLCS 1; LC 31**
　　See also LAW

di Bassetto, Corno
　　See Shaw, George Bernard

Dick, Philip K(indred) 1928-1982 ... **CLC 10,
　　30, 72; SSC 57**
　　See also AAYA 24; BPFB 1; BYA 11; CA
　　49-52; 106; CANR 2, 16, 132; CPW;
　　DA3; DAM NOV, POP; DLB 8; MTCW
　　1, 2; NFS 5; SCFW; SFW 4

Dickens, Charles (John Huffam)
　　　1812-1870 .... **NCLC 3, 8, 18, 26, 37, 50,
　　86, 105, 113; SSC 17, 49; WLC**
　　See also AAYA 23; BRW 5; BRWC 1, 2;
　　BYA 1, 2, 3, 13, 14; CDBLB 1832-1890;
　　CLR 95; CMW 4; DA; DA3; DAB; DAC;
　　DAM MST, NOV; DLB 21, 55, 70, 159,
　　166; EXPN; HGG; JRDA; LAIT 1, 2;
　　LATS 1:1; LMFS 1; MAICYA 1, 2; NFS
　　4, 5, 10, 14, 20; RGEL 2; RGSF 2; SATA
　　15; SUFW 1; TEA; WCH; WLIT 4; WYA

Dickey, James (Lafayette)
　　　1923-1997 .... **CLC 1, 2, 4, 7, 10, 15, 47,
　　109; PC 40; TCLC 151**
　　See also AAYA 50; AITN 1, 2; AMWS 4;
　　BPFB 1; CA 9-12R; 156; CABS 2; CANR
　　10, 48, 61, 105; CDALB 1968-1988; CP
　　7; CPW; CSW; DA3; DAM NOV, POET,
　　POP; DLB 5, 193; DLBD 7; DLBY 1982,
　　1993, 1996, 1997, 1998; EWL 3; INT
　　CANR-10; MTCW 1, 2; NFS 9; PFS 6,
　　11; RGAL 4; TUS

Dickey, William 1928-1994 .... **CLC 3, 28**
　　See also CA 9-12R; 145; CANR 24, 79;
　　DLB 5

Dickinson, Charles 1951- .... **CLC 49**
　　See also CA 128

Dickinson, Emily (Elizabeth)
　　　1830-1886 ... **NCLC 21, 77; PC 1; WLC**
　　See also AAYA 22; AMW; AMWR 1;
　　CDALB 1865-1917; DA; DA3; DAB;
　　DAC; DAM MST, POET; DLB 1, 243;
　　EXPP; MAWW; PAB; PFS 1, 2, 3, 4, 5,
　　6, 8, 10, 11, 13, 16; RGAL 4; SATA 29;
　　TUS; WP; WYA

Dickinson, Mrs. Herbert Ward
　　See Phelps, Elizabeth Stuart

Dickinson, Peter (Malcolm de Brissac)
　　　1927- .... **CLC 12, 35**
　　See also AAYA 9, 49; BYA 5; CA 41-44R;
　　CANR 31, 58, 88, 134; CLR 29; CMW 4;
　　DLB 87, 161, 276; JRDA; MAICYA 1, 2;
　　SATA 5, 62, 95, 150; SFW 4; WYA; YAW

Dickson, Carr
　　See Carr, John Dickson

Dickson, Carter
　　See Carr, John Dickson

Diderot, Denis 1713-1784 .... **LC 26**
　　See also EW 4; GFL Beginnings to 1789;
　　LMFS 1; RGWL 2, 3

Didion, Joan 1934- . **CLC 1, 3, 8, 14, 32, 129**
　　See also AITN 1; AMWS 4; CA 5-8R;
　　CANR 14, 52, 76, 125; CDALB 1968-
　　1988; CN 7; DA3; DAM NOV; DLB 2,
　　173, 185; DLBY 1981, 1986; EWL 3;
　　MAWW; MTCW 1, 2; NFS 3; RGAL 4;
　　TCWW 2; TUS

di Donato, Pietro 1911-1992 .... **TCLC 159**
　　See also CA 101; 136; DLB 9

Dietrich, Robert
　　See Hunt, E(verette) Howard, (Jr.)

Difusa, Pati
　　See Almodovar, Pedro

Dillard, Annie 1945- .... **CLC 9, 60, 115**
　　See also AAYA 6, 43; AMWS 6; ANW; CA
　　49-52; CANR 3, 43, 62, 90, 125; DA3;
　　DAM NOV; DLB 275, 278; DLBY 1980;
　　LAIT 4, 5; MTCW 1, 2; NCFS 1; RGAL
　　4; SATA 10, 140; TUS

Dillard, R(ichard) H(enry) W(ilde)
　　　1937- .... **CLC 5**
　　See also CA 21-24R; CAAS 7; CANR 10;
　　CP 7; CSW; DLB 5, 244

Dillon, Eilis 1920-1994 .... **CLC 17**
　　See also CA 9-12R, 182; 147; CAAE 182;
　　CAAS 3; CANR 4, 38, 78; CLR 26; MAI-
　　CYA 1, 2; MAICYAS 1; SATA 2, 74;
　　SATA-Essay 105; SATA-Obit 83; YAW

Dimont, Penelope
　　See Mortimer, Penelope (Ruth)

Dinesen, Isak ..... **CLC 10, 29, 95; SSC 7, 75**
　　See Blixen, Karen (Christentze Dinesen)
　　See also EW 10; EWL 3; EXPS; FW; HGG;
　　LAIT 3; MTCW 1; NCFS 2; NFS 9;
　　RGSF 2; RGWL 2, 3; SSFS 3, 6, 13;
　　WLIT 2

Ding Ling .... **CLC 68**
　　See Chiang, Pin-chin
　　See also RGWL 3

Diphusa, Patty
　　See Almodovar, Pedro

Disch, Thomas M(ichael) 1940- ... **CLC 7, 36**
　　See Disch, Tom
　　See also AAYA 17; BPFB 1; CA 21-24R;
　　CAAS 4; CANR 17, 36, 54, 89; CLR 18;
　　CP 7; DA3; DLB 8; HGG; MAICYA 1, 2;
　　MTCW 1, 2; SAAS 15; SATA 92; SCFW;
　　SFW 4; SUFW 2

Disch, Tom
　　See Disch, Thomas M(ichael)
　　See also DLB 282

d'Isly, Georges
　　See Simenon, Georges (Jacques Christian)

Disraeli, Benjamin 1804-1881 ... **NCLC 2, 39,
　　79**
　　See also BRW 4; DLB 21, 55; RGEL 2

Ditcum, Steve
　　See Crumb, R(obert)

Dixon, Paige
　　See Corcoran, Barbara (Asenath)

Dixon, Stephen 1936- .... **CLC 52; SSC 16**
　　See also AMWS 12; CA 89-92; CANR 17,
　　40, 54, 91; CN 7; DLB 130

Djebar, Assia 1936- .... **CLC 182**
　　See also CA 188; EWL 3; RGWL 3; WLIT
　　2

Doak, Annie
　　See Dillard, Annie

Dobell, Sydney Thompson
　　　1824-1874 .... **NCLC 43**
　　See also DLB 32; RGEL 2

Doblin, Alfred .... **TCLC 13**
　　See Doeblin, Alfred
　　See also CDWLB 2; EWL 3; RGWL 2, 3

Dobroliubov, Nikolai Aleksandrovich
　　See Dobrolyubov, Nikolai Alexandrovich
　　See also DLB 277

Dobrolyubov, Nikolai Alexandrovich
　　　1836-1861 .... **NCLC 5**
　　See Dobroliubov, Nikolai Aleksandrovich

Dobson, Austin 1840-1921 .... **TCLC 79**
　　See also DLB 35, 144

Dobyns, Stephen 1941- .... **CLC 37**
　　See also AMWS 13; CA 45-48; CANR 2,
　　18, 99; CMW 4; CP 7

Doctorow, E(dgar) L(aurence)
　　　1931- .... **CLC 6, 11, 15, 18, 37, 44, 65,
　　113**
　　See also AAYA 22; AITN 2; AMWS 4;
　　BEST 89:3; BPFB 1; CA 45-48; CANR
　　2, 33, 51, 76, 97, 133; CDALB 1968-
　　1988; CN 7; CPW; DA3; DAM NOV,
　　POP; DLB 2, 28, 173; DLBY 1980; EWL
　　3; LAIT 3; MTCW 1, 2; NFS 6; RGAL 4;
　　RHW; TUS

Dodgson, Charles L(utwidge) 1832-1898
See Carroll, Lewis
See also CLR 2; DA; DA3; DAB; DAC;
DAM MST, NOV, POET; MAICYA 1, 2;
SATA 100; YABC 2

Dodsley, Robert 1703-1764 .... **LC 97**
See also DLB 95; RGEL 2

Dodson, Owen (Vincent) 1914-1983 .. **BLC 1;
CLC 79**
See also BW 1; CA 65-68; 110; CANR 24;
DAM MULT; DLB 76

Doeblin, Alfred 1878-1957 .... **TCLC 13**
See Doblin, Alfred
See also CA 110; 141; DLB 66

Doerr, Harriet 1910-2002 .... **CLC 34**
See also CA 117; 122; 213; CANR 47; INT
CA-122; LATS 1:2

Domecq, H(onorio Bustos)
See Bioy Casares, Adolfo

Domecq, H(onorio) Bustos
See Bioy Casares, Adolfo; Borges, Jorge
Luis

Domini, Rey
See Lorde, Audre (Geraldine)
See also GLL 1

Dominique
See Proust, (Valentin-Louis-George-Eugene)
Marcel

Don, A
See Stephen, Sir Leslie

Donaldson, Stephen R(eeder)
1947- .... **CLC 46, 138**
See also AAYA 36; BPFB 1; CA 89-92;
CANR 13, 55, 99; CPW; DAM POP;
FANT; INT CANR-13; SATA 121; SFW
4; SUFW 1, 2

Donleavy, J(ames) P(atrick) 1926- .... **CLC 1,
4, 6, 10, 45**
See also AITN 2; BPFB 1; CA 9-12R;
CANR 24, 49, 62, 80, 124; CBD; CD 5;
CN 7; DLB 6, 173; INT CANR-24;
MTCW 1, 2; RGAL 4

Donnadieu, Marguerite
See Duras, Marguerite

Donne, John 1572-1631 ... **LC 10, 24, 91; PC
1, 43; WLC**
See also BRW 1; BRWC 1; BRWR 2; CD-
BLB Before 1660; DA; DAB; DAC;
DAM MST, POET; DLB 121, 151; EXPP;
PAB; PFS 2, 11; RGEL 3; TEA; WLIT 3;
WP

Donnell, David 1939(?)- .... **CLC 34**
See also CA 197

Donoghue, P. S.
See Hunt, E(verette) Howard, (Jr.)

Donoso (Yanez), Jose 1924-1996 ... **CLC 4, 8,
11, 32, 99; HLC 1; SSC 34; TCLC 133**
See also CA 81-84; 155; CANR 32, 73; CD-
WLB 3; CWW 2; DAM MULT; DLB 113;
EWL 3; HW 1, 2; LAW; LAWS 1; MTCW
1, 2; RGSF 2; WLIT 1

Donovan, John 1928-1992 .... **CLC 35**
See also AAYA 20; CA 97-100; 137; CLR
3; MAICYA 1, 2; SATA 72; SATA-Brief
29; YAW

Don Roberto
See Cunninghame Graham, Robert
(Gallnigad) Bontine

Doolittle, Hilda 1886-1961 . **CLC 3, 8, 14, 31,
34, 73; PC 5; WLC**
See H. D.
See also AMWS 1; CA 97-100; CANR 35,
131; DA; DAC; DAM MST, POET; DLB
4, 45; EWL 3; FW; GLL 1; LMFS 2;
MAWW; MTCW 1, 2; PFS 6; RGAL 4

Doppo, Kunikida .... **TCLC 99**
See Kunikida Doppo

Dorfman, Ariel 1942- .... **CLC 48, 77, 189;
HLC 1**
See also CA 124; 130; CANR 67, 70, 135;
CWW 2; DAM MULT; DFS 4; EWL 3;
HW 1, 2; INT CA-130; WLIT 1

Dorn, Edward (Merton)
1929-1999 .... **CLC 10, 18**
See also CA 93-96; 187; CANR 42, 79; CP
7; DLB 5; INT CA-93-96; WP

Dor-Ner, Zvi .... **CLC 70**

Dorris, Michael (Anthony)
1945-1997 .... **CLC 109; NNAL**
See also AAYA 20; BEST 90:1; BYA 12;
CA 102; 157; CANR 19, 46, 75; CLR 58;
DA3; DAM MULT, NOV; DLB 175;
LAIT 5; MTCW 2; NFS 3; RGAL 4;
SATA 75; SATA-Obit 94; TCWW 2; YAW

Dorris, Michael A.
See Dorris, Michael (Anthony)

Dorsan, Luc
See Simenon, Georges (Jacques Christian)

Dorsange, Jean
See Simenon, Georges (Jacques Christian)

Dorset
See Sackville, Thomas

Dos Passos, John (Roderigo)
1896-1970 ... **CLC 1, 4, 8, 11, 15, 25, 34,
82; WLC**
See also AMW; BPFB 1; CA 1-4R; 29-32R;
CANR 3; CDALB 1929-1941; DA; DA3;
DAB; DAC; DAM MST, NOV; DLB 4,
9, 274; DLBD 1, 15; DLBY 1996; EWL
3; MTCW 1, 2; NFS 14; RGAL 4; TUS

Dossage, Jean
See Simenon, Georges (Jacques Christian)

Dostoevsky, Fedor Mikhailovich
1821-1881 ... **NCLC 2, 7, 21, 33, 43, 119;
SSC 2, 33, 44; WLC**
See Dostoevsky, Fyodor
See also DA; DA3; DAB; DAC;
DAM MST, NOV; EW 7; EXPN; NFS 3,
8; RGSF 2; RGWL 2, 3; SSFS 8; TWA

Dostoevsky, Fyodor
See Dostoevsky, Fedor Mikhailovich
See also DLB 238; LATS 1:1; LMFS 1, 2

Doty, M. R.
See Doty, Mark (Alan)

Doty, Mark
See Doty, Mark (Alan)

Doty, Mark (Alan) 1953(?)- .... **CLC 176; PC
53**
See also AMWS 11; CA 161, 183; CAAE
183; CANR 110

Doty, Mark A.
See Doty, Mark (Alan)

Doughty, Charles M(ontagu)
1843-1926 .... **TCLC 27**
See also CA 115; 178; DLB 19, 57, 174

Douglas, Ellen .... **CLC 73**
See Haxton, Josephine Ayres; Williamson,
Ellen Douglas
See also CN 7; CSW; DLB 292

Douglas, Gavin 1475(?)-1522 .... **LC 20**
See also DLB 132; RGEL 2

Douglas, George
See Brown, George Douglas
See also RGEL 2

Douglas, Keith (Castellain)
1920-1944 .... **TCLC 40**
See also BRW 7; CA 160; DLB 27; EWL
3; PAB; RGEL 2

Douglas, Leonard
See Bradbury, Ray (Douglas)

Douglas, Michael
See Crichton, (John) Michael

Douglas, (George) Norman
1868-1952 .... **TCLC 68**
See also BRW 6; CA 119; 157; DLB 34,
195; RGEL 2

Douglas, William
See Brown, George Douglas

Douglass, Frederick 1817(?)-1895 ..... **BLC 1;
NCLC 7, 55, 141; WLC**
See also AAYA 48; AFAW 1, 2; AMWC 1;
AMWS 3; CDALB 1640-1865; DA; DA3;
DAC; DAM MST, MULT; DLB 1, 43, 50,
79, 243; FW; LAIT 2; NCFS 2; RGAL 4;
SATA 29

Dourado, (Waldomiro Freitas) Autran
1926- .... **CLC 23, 60**
See also CA 25-28R; 179; CANR 34, 81;
DLB 145, 307; HW 2

Dourado, Waldomiro Freitas Autran
See Dourado, (Waldomiro Freitas) Autran

Dove, Rita (Frances) 1952- . **BLCS; CLC 50,
81; PC 6**
See also AAYA 46; AMWS 4; BW 2; CA
109; CAAS 19; CANR 27, 42, 68, 76, 97,
132; CDALBS; CP 7; CSW; CWP; DA3;
DAM MULT, POET; DLB 120; EWL 3;
EXPP; MTCW 1; PFS 1, 15; RGAL 4

Doveglion
See Villa, Jose Garcia

Dowell, Coleman 1925-1985 .... **CLC 60**
See also CA 25-28R; 117; CANR 10; DLB
130; GLL 2

Dowson, Ernest (Christopher)
1867-1900 .... **TCLC 4**
See also CA 105; 150; DLB 19, 135; RGEL
2

Doyle, A. Conan
See Doyle, Sir Arthur Conan

Doyle, Sir Arthur Conan
1859-1930 .... **SSC 12; TCLC 7; WLC**
See Conan Doyle, Arthur
See also AAYA 14; BRWS 2; CA 104; 122;
CANR 131; CDBLB 1890-1914; CMW
4; DA; DA3; DAB; DAC; DAM MST,
NOV; DLB 18, 70, 156, 178; EXPS;
HGG; LAIT 2; MSW; MTCW 1, 2; RGEL
2; RGSF 2; RHW; SATA 24; SCFW 2;
SFW 4; SSFS 2; TEA; WCH; WLIT 4;
WYA; YAW

Doyle, Conan
See Doyle, Sir Arthur Conan

Doyle, John
See Graves, Robert (von Ranke)

Doyle, Roddy 1958(?)- .... **CLC 81, 178**
See also AAYA 14; BRWS 5; CA 143;
CANR 73, 128; CN 7; DA3; DLB 194

Doyle, Sir A. Conan
See Doyle, Sir Arthur Conan

Dr. A
See Asimov, Isaac; Silverstein, Alvin; Silverstein, Virginia B(arbara Opshelor)

Drabble, Margaret 1939- ...... **CLC 2, 3, 5, 8,
10, 22, 53, 129**
See also BRWS 4; CA 13-16R; CANR 18,
35, 63, 112, 131; CDBLB 1960 to Present;
CN 7; CPW; DA3; DAB; DAC; DAM
MST, NOV, POP; DLB 14, 155, 231;
EWL 3; FW; MTCW 1, 2; RGEL 2; SATA
48; TEA

Drakulic, Slavenka 1949- .... **CLC 173**
See also CA 144; CANR 92

Drakulic-Ilic, Slavenka
See Drakulic, Slavenka

Drapier, M. B.
See Swift, Jonathan

Drayham, James
See Mencken, H(enry) L(ouis)

Drayton, Michael 1563-1631 .... **LC 8**
See also DAM POET; DLB 121; RGEL 2

Dreadstone, Carl
See Campbell, (John) Ramsey

Dreiser, Theodore (Herman Albert)
1871-1945 .... **SSC 30; TCLC 10, 18, 35, 83; WLC**
See also AMW; AMWC 2; AMWR 2; BYA 15, 16; CA 106; 132; CDALB 1865-1917; DA; DA3; DAC; DAM MST, NOV; DLB 9, 12, 102, 137; DLBD 1; EWL 3; LAIT 2; LMFS 2; MTCW 1, 2; NFS 8, 17; RGAL 4; TUS

Drexler, Rosalyn 1926- .... **CLC 2, 6**
See also CA 81-84; CAD; CANR 68, 124; CD 5; CWD

Dreyer, Carl Theodor 1889-1968 ...... **CLC 16**
See also CA 116

Drieu la Rochelle, Pierre(-Eugene)
1893-1945 .... **TCLC 21**
See also CA 117; DLB 72; EWL 3; GFL 1789 to the Present

Drinkwater, John 1882-1937 .... **TCLC 57**
See also CA 109; 149; DLB 10, 19, 149; RGEL 2

Drop Shot
See Cable, George Washington

Droste-Hulshoff, Annette Freiin von
1797-1848 .... **NCLC 3, 133**
See also CDWLB 2; DLB 133; RGSF 2; RGWL 2, 3

Drummond, Walter
See Silverberg, Robert

Drummond, William Henry
1854-1907 .... **TCLC 25**
See also CA 160; DLB 92

Drummond de Andrade, Carlos
1902-1987 .... **CLC 18; TCLC 139**
See Andrade, Carlos Drummond de
See also CA 132; 123; DLB 307; LAW

Drummond of Hawthornden, William
1585-1649 .... **LC 83**
See also DLB 121, 213; RGEL 2

Drury, Allen (Stuart) 1918-1998 .... **CLC 37**
See also CA 57-60; 170; CANR 18, 52; CN 7; INT CANR-18

Druse, Eleanor
See King, Stephen (Edwin)

Dryden, John 1631-1700 ..... **DC 3; LC 3, 21; PC 25; WLC**
See also BRW 2; CDBLB 1660-1789; DA; DAB; DAC; DAM DRAM, MST, POET; DLB 80, 101, 131; EXPP; IDTP; LMFS 1; RGEL 2; TEA; WLIT 3

du Bellay, Joachim 1524-1560 .... **LC 92**
See also GFL Beginnings to 1789; RGWL 2, 3

Duberman, Martin (Bauml) 1930- ..... **CLC 8**
See also CA 1-4R; CAD; CANR 2, 63; CD 5

Dubie, Norman (Evans) 1945- .... **CLC 36**
See also CA 69-72; CANR 12, 115; CP 7; DLB 120; PFS 12

Du Bois, W(illiam) E(dward) B(urghardt)
1868-1963 ..... **BLC 1; CLC 1, 2, 13, 64, 96; HR 2; WLC**
See also AAYA 40; AFAW 1, 2; AMWC 1; AMWS 2; BW 1, 3; CA 85-88; CANR 34, 82, 132; CDALB 1865-1917; DA; DA3; DAC; DAM MST, NOV; DLB 47, 50, 91, 246, 284; EWL 3; EXPP; LAIT 2; LMFS 2; MTCW 1, 2; NCFS 1; PFS 13; RGAL 4; SATA 42

Dubus, Andre 1936-1999 ..... **CLC 13, 36, 97; SSC 15**
See also AMWS 7; CA 21-24R; 177; CANR 17; CN 7; CSW; DLB 130; INT CANR-17; RGAL 4; SSFS 10

Duca Minimo
See D'Annunzio, Gabriele

Ducharme, Rejean 1941- .... **CLC 74**
See also CA 165; DLB 60

du Chatelet, Emilie 1706-1749 .... **LC 96**

Duchen, Claire .... **CLC 65**

Duclos, Charles Pinot- 1704-1772 .... **LC 1**
See also GFL Beginnings to 1789

Dudek, Louis 1918-2001 .... **CLC 11, 19**
See also CA 45-48; 215; CAAS 14; CANR 1; CP 7; DLB 88

Duerrenmatt, Friedrich 1921-1990 ... **CLC 1, 4, 8, 11, 15, 43, 102**
See Durrenmatt, Friedrich
See also CA 17-20R; CANR 33; CMW 4; DAM DRAM; DLB 69, 124; MTCW 1, 2

Duffy, Bruce 1953(?)- .... **CLC 50**
See also CA 172

Duffy, Maureen 1933- .... **CLC 37**
See also CA 25-28R; CANR 33, 68; CBD; CN 7; CP 7; CWD; CWP; DFS 15; DLB 14; FW; MTCW 1

Du Fu
See Tu Fu
See also RGWL 2, 3

Dugan, Alan 1923-2003 .... **CLC 2, 6**
See also CA 81-84; 220; CANR 119; CP 7; DLB 5; PFS 10

du Gard, Roger Martin
See Martin du Gard, Roger

Duhamel, Georges 1884-1966 .... **CLC 8**
See also CA 81-84; 25-28R; CANR 35; DLB 65; EWL 3; GFL 1789 to the Present; MTCW 1

Dujardin, Edouard (Emile Louis)
1861-1949 .... **TCLC 13**
See also CA 109; DLB 123

Duke, Raoul
See Thompson, Hunter S(tockton)

Dulles, John Foster 1888-1959 .... **TCLC 72**
See also CA 115; 149

Dumas, Alexandre (pere)
1802-1870 .... **NCLC 11, 71; WLC**
See also AAYA 22; BYA 3; DA; DA3; DAB; DAC; DAM MST, NOV; DLB 119, 192; EW 6; GFL 1789 to the Present; LAIT 1, 2; NFS 14, 19; RGWL 2, 3; SATA 18; TWA; WCH

Dumas, Alexandre (fils) 1824-1895 ...... **DC 1; NCLC 9**
See also DLB 192; GFL 1789 to the Present; RGWL 2, 3

Dumas, Claudine
See Malzberg, Barry N(athaniel)

Dumas, Henry L. 1934-1968 .... **CLC 6, 62**
See also BW 1; CA 85-88; DLB 41; RGAL 4

du Maurier, Daphne 1907-1989 .. **CLC 6, 11, 59; SSC 18**
See also AAYA 37; BPFB 1; BRWS 3; CA 5-8R; 128; CANR 6, 55; CMW 4; CPW; DA3; DAB; DAC; DAM MST, POP; DLB 191; HGG; LAIT 3; MSW; MTCW 1, 2; NFS 12; RGEL 2; RGSF 2; RHW; SATA 27; SATA-Obit 60; SSFS 14, 16; TEA

Du Maurier, George 1834-1896 ..... **NCLC 86**
See also DLB 153, 178; RGEL 2

Dunbar, Paul Laurence 1872-1906 ... **BLC 1; PC 5; SSC 8; TCLC 2, 12; WLC**
See also AFAW 1, 2; AMWS 2; BW 1, 3; CA 104; 124; CANR 79; CDALB 1865-1917; DA; DA3; DAC; DAM MST, MULT, POET; DLB 50, 54, 78; EXPP; RGAL 4; SATA 34

Dunbar, William 1460(?)-1520(?) .... **LC 20**
See also BRWS 8; DLB 132, 146; RGEL 2

Dunbar-Nelson, Alice .... **HR 2**
See Nelson, Alice Ruth Moore Dunbar

Duncan, Dora Angela
See Duncan, Isadora

Duncan, Isadora 1877(?)-1927 .... **TCLC 68**
See also CA 118; 149

Duncan, Lois 1934- .... **CLC 26**
See also AAYA 4, 34; BYA 6, 8; CA 1-4R; CANR 2, 23, 36, 111; CLR 29; JRDA; MAICYA 1, 2; MAICYAS 1; SAAS 2; SATA 1, 36, 75, 133, 141; SATA-Essay 141; WYA; YAW

Duncan, Robert (Edward)
1919-1988 .... **CLC 1, 2, 4, 7, 15, 41, 55; PC 2**
See also BG 2; CA 9-12R; 124; CANR 28, 62; DAM POET; DLB 5, 16, 193; EWL 3; MTCW 1, 2; PFS 13; RGAL 4; WP

Duncan, Sara Jeannette
1861-1922 .... **TCLC 60**
See also CA 157; DLB 92

Dunlap, William 1766-1839 .... **NCLC 2**
See also DLB 30, 37, 59; RGAL 4

Dunn, Douglas (Eaglesham) 1942- .... **CLC 6, 40**
See also BRWS 10; CA 45-48; CANR 2, 33, 126; CP 7; DLB 40; MTCW 1

Dunn, Katherine (Karen) 1945- .... **CLC 71**
See also CA 33-36R; CANR 72; HGG; MTCW 1

Dunn, Stephen (Elliott) 1939- .... **CLC 36**
See also AMWS 11; CA 33-36R; CANR 12, 48, 53, 105; CP 7; DLB 105; PFS 21

Dunne, Finley Peter 1867-1936 ...... **TCLC 28**
See also CA 108; 178; DLB 11, 23; RGAL 4

Dunne, John Gregory 1932-2003 ..... **CLC 28**
See also CA 25-28R; 222; CANR 14, 50; CN 7; DLBY 1980

Dunsany, Lord .... **TCLC 2, 59**
See Dunsany, Edward John Moreton Drax Plunkett
See also DLB 77, 153, 156, 255; FANT; IDTP; RGEL 2; SFW 4; SUFW 1

Dunsany, Edward John Moreton Drax Plunkett 1878-1957
See Dunsany, Lord
See also CA 104; 148; DLB 10; MTCW 1

Duns Scotus, John 1266(?)-1308 ... **CMLC 59**
See also DLB 115

du Perry, Jean
See Simenon, Georges (Jacques Christian)

Durang, Christopher (Ferdinand)
1949- .... **CLC 27, 38**
See also CA 105; CAD; CANR 50, 76, 130; CD 5; MTCW 1

Duras, Marguerite 1914-1996 . **CLC 3, 6, 11, 20, 34, 40, 68, 100; SSC 40**
See also BPFB 1; CA 25-28R; 151; CANR 50; CWW 2; DLB 83; EWL 3; GFL 1789 to the Present; IDFW 4; MTCW 1, 2; RGWL 2, 3; TWA

Durban, (Rosa) Pam 1947- .... **CLC 39**
See also CA 123; CANR 98; CSW

Durcan, Paul 1944- .... **CLC 43, 70**
See also CA 134; CANR 123; CP 7; DAM POET; EWL 3

Durfey, Thomas 1653-1723 .... **LC 94**
See also DLB 80; RGEL 2

Durkheim, Emile 1858-1917 .... **TCLC 55**

Durrell, Lawrence (George)
1912-1990 .... **CLC 1, 4, 6, 8, 13, 27, 41**
See also BPFB 1; BRWS 1; CA 9-12R; 132; CANR 40, 77; CDBLB 1945-1960; DAM NOV; DLB 15, 27, 204; DLBY 1990; EWL 3; MTCW 1, 2; RGEL 2; SFW 4; TEA

Durrenmatt, Friedrich
See Duerrenmatt, Friedrich
See also CDWLB 2; EW 13; EWL 3; RGWL 2, 3

Dutt, Michael Madhusudan
1824-1873 .... **NCLC 118**

Dutt, Toru 1856-1877 .... **NCLC 29**
See also DLB 240

Dwight, Timothy 1752-1817 .... **NCLC 13**
See also DLB 37; RGAL 4

Dworkin, Andrea 1946- .... **CLC 43, 123**
See also CA 77-80; CAAS 21; CANR 16,
39, 76, 96; FW; GLL 1; INT CANR-16;
MTCW 1, 2

Dwyer, Deanna
See Koontz, Dean R(ay)

Dwyer, K. R.
See Koontz, Dean R(ay)

Dybek, Stuart 1942- .... **CLC 114; SSC 55**
See also CA 97-100; CANR 39; DLB 130

Dye, Richard
See De Voto, Bernard (Augustine)

Dyer, Geoff 1958- .... **CLC 149**
See also CA 125; CANR 88

Dyer, George 1755-1841 .... **NCLC 129**
See also DLB 93

Dylan, Bob 1941- .... **CLC 3, 4, 6, 12, 77; PC
37**
See also CA 41-44R; CANR 108; CP 7;
DLB 16

Dyson, John 1943- .... **CLC 70**
See also CA 144

Dzyubin, Eduard Georgievich 1895-1934
See Bagritsky, Eduard
See also CA 170

E. V. L.
See Lucas, E(dward) V(errall)

Eagleton, Terence (Francis) 1943- .. **CLC 63,
132**
See also CA 57-60; CANR 7, 23, 68, 115;
DLB 242; LMFS 2; MTCW 1, 2

Eagleton, Terry
See Eagleton, Terence (Francis)

Early, Jack
See Scoppettone, Sandra
See also GLL 1

East, Michael
See West, Morris L(anglo)

Eastaway, Edward
See Thomas, (Philip) Edward

Eastlake, William (Derry)
1917-1997 .... **CLC 8**
See also CA 5-8R; 158; CAAS 1; CANR 5,
63; CN 7; DLB 6, 206; INT CANR-5;
TCWW 2

Eastman, Charles A(lexander)
1858-1939 .... **NNAL; TCLC 55**
See also CA 179; CANR 91; DAM MULT;
DLB 175; YABC 1

Eaton, Edith Maude 1865-1914 .... **AAL**
See Far, Sui Sin
See also CA 154; DLB 221; FW

Eaton, (Lillie) Winnifred 1875-1954 .... **AAL**
See also CA 217; DLB 221; RGAL 4

Eberhart, Richard (Ghormley)
1904- .... **CLC 3, 11, 19, 56**
See also AMW; CA 1-4R; CANR 2, 125;
CDALB 1941-1968; CP 7; DAM POET;
DLB 48; MTCW 1; RGAL 4

Eberstadt, Fernanda 1960- .... **CLC 39**
See also CA 136; CANR 69, 128

**Echegaray (y Eizaguirre), Jose (Maria
Waldo)** 1832-1916 .... **HLCS 1; TCLC 4**
See also CA 104; CANR 32; EWL 3; HW
1; MTCW 1

Echeverria, (Jose) Esteban (Antonino)
1805-1851 .... **NCLC 18**
See also LAW

Echo
See Proust, (Valentin-Louis-George-Eugene)
Marcel

Eckert, Allan W. 1931- .... **CLC 17**
See also AAYA 18; BYA 2; CA 13-16R;
CANR 14, 45; INT CANR-14; MAICYA
2; MAICYAS 1; SAAS 21; SATA 29, 91;
SATA-Brief 27

Eckhart, Meister 1260(?)-1327(?) ... **CMLC 9**
See also DLB 115; LMFS 1

Eckmar, F. R.
See de Hartog, Jan

Eco, Umberto 1932- .... **CLC 28, 60, 142**
See also BEST 90:1; BPFB 1; CA 77-80;
CANR 12, 33, 55, 110, 131; CPW; CWW
2; DA3; DAM NOV, POP; DLB 196, 242;
EWL 3; MSW; MTCW 1, 2; RGWL 3

Eddison, E(ric) R(ucker)
1882-1945 .... **TCLC 15**
See also CA 109; 156; DLB 255; FANT;
SFW 4; SUFW 1

Eddy, Mary (Ann Morse) Baker
1821-1910 .... **TCLC 71**
See also CA 113; 174

Edel, (Joseph) Leon 1907-1997 .. **CLC 29, 34**
See also CA 1-4R; 161; CANR 1, 22, 112;
DLB 103; INT CANR-22

Eden, Emily 1797-1869 .... **NCLC 10**

Edgar, David 1948- .... **CLC 42**
See also CA 57-60; CANR 12, 61, 112;
CBD; CD 5; DAM DRAM; DFS 15; DLB
13, 233; MTCW 1

Edgerton, Clyde (Carlyle) 1944- ...... **CLC 39**
See also AAYA 17; CA 118; 134; CANR
64, 125; CSW; DLB 278; INT CA-134;
YAW

Edgeworth, Maria 1768-1849 .... **NCLC 1, 51**
See also BRWS 3; DLB 116, 159, 163; FW;
RGEL 2; SATA 21; TEA; WLIT 3

Edmonds, Paul
See Kuttner, Henry

Edmonds, Walter D(umaux)
1903-1998 .... **CLC 35**
See also BYA 2; CA 5-8R; CANR 2; CWRI
5; DLB 9; LAIT 1; MAICYA 1, 2; RHW;
SAAS 4; SATA 1, 27; SATA-Obit 99

Edmondson, Wallace
See Ellison, Harlan (Jay)

Edson, Margaret 1961- ...... **CLC 199; DC 24**
See also CA 190; DFS 13; DLB 266

Edson, Russell 1935- .... **CLC 13**
See also CA 33-36R; CANR 115; DLB 244;
WP

Edwards, Bronwen Elizabeth
See Rose, Wendy

Edwards, G(erald) B(asil)
1899-1976 .... **CLC 25**
See also CA 201; 110

Edwards, Gus 1939- .... **CLC 43**
See also CA 108; INT CA-108

Edwards, Jonathan 1703-1758 .... **LC 7, 54**
See also AMW; DA; DAC; DAM MST;
DLB 24, 270; RGAL 4; TUS

Edwards, Sarah Pierpont 1710-1758 .. **LC 87**
See also DLB 200

Efron, Marina Ivanovna Tsvetaeva
See Tsvetaeva (Efron), Marina (Ivanovna)

Egeria fl. 4th cent. - .... **CMLC 70**

Egoyan, Atom 1960- .... **CLC 151**
See also CA 157

Ehle, John (Marsden, Jr.) 1925- ...... **CLC 27**
See also CA 9-12R; CSW

Ehrenbourg, Ilya (Grigoryevich)
See Ehrenburg, Ilya (Grigoryevich)

Ehrenburg, Ilya (Grigoryevich)
1891-1967 .... **CLC 18, 34, 62**
See Erenburg, Il'ia Grigor'evich
See also CA 102; 25-28R; EWL 3

Ehrenburg, Ilyo (Grigoryevich)
See Ehrenburg, Ilya (Grigoryevich)

Ehrenreich, Barbara 1941- .... **CLC 110**
See also BEST 90:4; CA 73-76; CANR 16,
37, 62, 117; DLB 246; FW; MTCW 1, 2

Eich, Gunter
See Eich, Gunter
See also RGWL 2, 3

Eich, Gunter 1907-1972 .... **CLC 15**
See Eich, Gunter
See also CA 111; 93-96; DLB 69, 124;
EWL 3

Eichendorff, Joseph 1788-1857 .... **NCLC 8**
See also DLB 90; RGWL 2, 3

Eigner, Larry .... **CLC 9**
See Eigner, Laurence (Joel)
See also CAAS 23; DLB 5; WP

Eigner, Laurence (Joel) 1927-1996
See Eigner, Larry
See also CA 9-12R; 151; CANR 6, 84; CP
7; DLB 193

Eilhart von Oberge c. 1140-c.
1195 .... **CMLC 67**
See also DLB 148

Einhard c. 770-840 .... **CMLC 50**
See also DLB 148

Einstein, Albert 1879-1955 .... **TCLC 65**
See also CA 121; 133; MTCW 1, 2

Eiseley, Loren
See Eiseley, Loren Corey
See also DLB 275

Eiseley, Loren Corey 1907-1977 .... **CLC 7**
See Eiseley, Loren
See also AAYA 5; ANW; CA 1-4R; 73-76;
CANR 6; DLBD 17

Eisenstadt, Jill 1963- .... **CLC 50**
See also CA 140

Eisenstein, Sergei (Mikhailovich)
1898-1948 .... **TCLC 57**
See also CA 114; 149

Eisner, Simon
See Kornbluth, C(yril) M.

Ekeloef, (Bengt) Gunnar
1907-1968 .... **CLC 27; PC 23**
See Ekelof, (Bengt) Gunnar
See also CA 123; 25-28R; DAM POET

Ekelof, (Bengt) Gunnar 1907-1968
See Ekeloef, (Bengt) Gunnar
See also DLB 259; EW 12; EWL 3

Ekelund, Vilhelm 1880-1949 .... **TCLC 75**
See also CA 189; EWL 3

Ekwensi, C. O. D.
See Ekwensi, Cyprian (Odiatu Duaka)

Ekwensi, Cyprian (Odiatu Duaka)
1921- .... **BLC 1; CLC 4**
See also AFW; BW 2, 3; CA 29-32R;
CANR 18, 42, 74, 125; CDWLB 3; CN
7; CWRI 5; DAM MULT; DLB 117; EWL
3; MTCW 1, 2; RGEL 2; SATA 66; WLIT
2

Elaine .... **TCLC 18**
See Leverson, Ada Esther

El Crummo
See Crumb, R(obert)

Elder, Lonne III 1931-1996 ..... **BLC 1; DC 8**
See also BW 1, 3; CA 81-84; 152; CAD;
CANR 25; DAM MULT; DLB 7, 38, 44

Eleanor of Aquitaine 1122-1204 ... **CMLC 39**

Elia
See Lamb, Charles

Eliade, Mircea 1907-1986 .... **CLC 19**
See also CA 65-68; 119; CANR 30, 62; CD-
WLB 4; DLB 220; EWL 3; MTCW 1;
RGWL 3; SFW 4

Eliot, A. D.
See Jewett, (Theodora) Sarah Orne

Eliot, Alice
See Jewett, (Theodora) Sarah Orne

Eliot, Dan
See Silverberg, Robert

Eliot, George 1819-1880 ...... **NCLC 4, 13, 23,
41, 49, 89, 118; PC 20; SSC 72; WLC**
See Evans, Mary Ann
See also BRW 5; BRWC 1, 2; BRWR 2;
CDBLB 1832-1890; CN 7; CPW; DA;
DA3; DAB; DAC; DAM MST, NOV;
DLB 21, 35, 55; LATS 1:1; LMFS 1; NFS
17; RGEL 2; RGSF 2; SSFS 8; TEA;
WLIT 3

Eliot, John 1604-1690 .... **LC 5**
See also DLB 24
Eliot, T(homas) S(tearns)
1888-1965 ...... **CLC 1, 2, 3, 6, 9, 10, 13, 15, 24, 34, 41, 55, 57, 113; PC 5, 31; WLC**
See also AAYA 28; AMW; AMWC 1; AMWR 1; BRW 7; BRWR 2; CA 5-8R; 25-28R; CANR 41; CDALB 1929-1941; DA; DA3; DAB; DAC; DAM DRAM, MST, POET; DFS 4, 13; DLB 7, 10, 45, 63, 245; DLBY 1988; EWL 3; EXPP; LAIT 3; LATS 1:1; LMFS 2; MTCW 1, 2; NCFS 5; PAB; PFS 1, 7, 20; RGAL 4; RGEL 2; TUS; WLIT 4; WP
Elizabeth 1866-1941 .... **TCLC 41**
Elkin, Stanley L(awrence)
1930-1995 .. **CLC 4, 6, 9, 14, 27, 51, 91; SSC 12**
See also AMWS 6; BPFB 1; CA 9-12R; 148; CANR 8, 46; CN 7; CPW; DAM NOV, POP; DLB 2, 28, 218, 278; DLBY 1980; EWL 3; INT CANR-8; MTCW 1, 2; RGAL 4
Elledge, Scott .... **CLC 34**
Elliott, Don
See Silverberg, Robert
Elliott, George P(aul) 1918-1980 .... **CLC 2**
See also CA 1-4R; 97-100; CANR 2; DLB 244
Elliott, Janice 1931-1995 .... **CLC 47**
See also CA 13-16R; CANR 8, 29, 84; CN 7; DLB 14; SATA 119
Elliott, Sumner Locke 1917-1991 ..... **CLC 38**
See also CA 5-8R; 134; CANR 2, 21; DLB 289
Elliott, William
See Bradbury, Ray (Douglas)
Ellis, A. E. .... **CLC 7**
Ellis, Alice Thomas .... **CLC 40**
See Haycraft, Anna (Margaret)
See also DLB 194; MTCW 1
Ellis, Bret Easton 1964- ...... **CLC 39, 71, 117**
See also AAYA 2, 43; CA 118; 123; CANR 51, 74, 126; CN 7; CPW; DA3; DAM POP; DLB 292; HGG; INT CA-123; MTCW 1; NFS 11
Ellis, (Henry) Havelock
1859-1939 .... **TCLC 14**
See also CA 109; 169; DLB 190
Ellis, Landon
See Ellison, Harlan (Jay)
Ellis, Trey 1962- .... **CLC 55**
See also CA 146; CANR 92
Ellison, Harlan (Jay) 1934- ... **CLC 1, 13, 42, 139; SSC 14**
See also AAYA 29; BPFB 1; BYA 14; CA 5-8R; CANR 5, 46, 115; CPW; DAM POP; DLB 8; HGG; INT CANR-5; MTCW 1, 2; SCFW 4; SFW 4; SSFS 13, 14, 15; SUFW 1, 2
Ellison, Ralph (Waldo) 1914-1994 .... **BLC 1; CLC 1, 3, 11, 54, 86, 114; SSC 26; WLC**
See also AAYA 19; AFAW 1, 2; AMWC 2; AMWR 2; AMWS 2; BPFB 1; BW 1, 3; BYA 2; CA 9-12R; 145; CANR 24, 53; CDALB 1941-1968; CSW; DA; DA3; DAB; DAC; DAM MST, MULT, NOV; DLB 2, 76, 227; DLBY 1994; EWL 3; EXPN; EXPS; LAIT 4; MTCW 1, 2; NCFS 3; NFS 2; RGAL 4; RGSF 2; SSFS 1, 11; YAW
Ellmann, Lucy (Elizabeth) 1956- ..... **CLC 61**
See also CA 128
Ellmann, Richard (David)
1918-1987 .... **CLC 50**
See also BEST 89:2; CA 1-4R; 122; CANR 2, 28, 61; DLB 103; DLBY 1987; MTCW 1, 2

Elman, Richard (Martin)
1934-1997 .... **CLC 19**
See also CA 17-20R; 163; CAAS 3; CANR 47
Elron
See Hubbard, L(afayette) Ron(ald)
El Saadawi, Nawal 1931- .... **CLC 196**
See al'Sadaawi, Nawal; Sa'adawi, al-Nawal; Saadawi, Nawal El; Sa'dawi, Nawal al-
See also CA 118; CAAS 11; CANR 44, 92
Eluard, Paul .... **PC 38; TCLC 7, 41**
See Grindel, Eugene
See also EWL 3; GFL 1789 to the Present; RGWL 2, 3
Elyot, Thomas 1490(?)-1546 .... **LC 11**
See also DLB 136; RGEL 2
Elytis, Odysseus 1911-1996 .... **CLC 15, 49, 100; PC 21**
See Alepoudelis, Odysseus
See also CA 102; 151; CANR 94; CWW 2; DAM POET; EW 13; EWL 3; MTCW 1, 2; RGWL 2, 3
Emecheta, (Florence Onye) Buchi
1944- .... **BLC 2; CLC 14, 48, 128**
See also AFW; BW 2, 3; CA 81-84; CANR 27, 81, 126; CDWLB 3; CN 7; CWRI 5; DA3; DAM MULT; DLB 117; EWL 3; FW; MTCW 1, 2; NFS 12, 14; SATA 66; WLIT 2
Emerson, Mary Moody
1774-1863 .... **NCLC 66**
Emerson, Ralph Waldo 1803-1882 . **NCLC 1, 38, 98; PC 18; WLC**
See also AAYA 60; AMW; ANW; CDALB 1640-1865; DA; DA3; DAB; DAC; DAM MST, POET; DLB 1, 59, 73, 183, 223, 270; EXPP; LAIT 2; LMFS 1; NCFS 3; PFS 4, 17; RGAL 4; TUS; WP
Eminescu, Mihail 1850-1889 .. **NCLC 33, 131**
Empedocles 5th cent. B.C.- .... **CMLC 50**
See also DLB 176
Empson, William 1906-1984 ... **CLC 3, 8, 19, 33, 34**
See also BRWS 2; CA 17-20R; 112; CANR 31, 61; DLB 20; EWL 3; MTCW 1, 2; RGEL 2
Enchi, Fumiko (Ueda) 1905-1986 ..... **CLC 31**
See Enchi Fumiko
See also CA 129; 121; FW; MJW
Enchi Fumiko
See Enchi, Fumiko (Ueda)
See also DLB 182; EWL 3
Ende, Michael (Andreas Helmuth)
1929-1995 .... **CLC 31**
See also BYA 5; CA 118; 124; 149; CANR 36, 110; CLR 14; DLB 75; MAICYA 1, 2; MAICYAS 1; SATA 61, 130; SATA-Brief 42; SATA-Obit 86
Endo, Shusaku 1923-1996 ..... **CLC 7, 14, 19, 54, 99; SSC 48; TCLC 152**
See Endo Shusaku
See also CA 29-32R; 153; CANR 21, 54, 131; DA3; DAM NOV; MTCW 1, 2; RGSF 2; RGWL 2, 3
Endo Shusaku
See Endo, Shusaku
See also CWW 2; DLB 182; EWL 3
Engel, Marian 1933-1985 .... **CLC 36; TCLC 137**
See also CA 25-28R; CANR 12; DLB 53; FW; INT CANR-12
Engelhardt, Frederick
See Hubbard, L(afayette) Ron(ald)
Engels, Friedrich 1820-1895 .. **NCLC 85, 114**
See also DLB 129; LATS 1:1

Enright, D(ennis) J(oseph)
1920-2002 .... **CLC 4, 8, 31**
See also CA 1-4R; 211; CANR 1, 42, 83; CP 7; DLB 27; EWL 3; SATA 25; SATA-Obit 140
Enzensberger, Hans Magnus
1929- .... **CLC 43; PC 28**
See also CA 116; 119; CANR 103; CWW 2; EWL 3
Ephron, Nora 1941- .... **CLC 17, 31**
See also AAYA 35; AITN 2; CA 65-68; CANR 12, 39, 83
Epicurus 341B.C.-270B.C. .... **CMLC 21**
See also DLB 176
Epsilon
See Betjeman, John
Epstein, Daniel Mark 1948- .... **CLC 7**
See also CA 49-52; CANR 2, 53, 90
Epstein, Jacob 1956- .... **CLC 19**
See also CA 114
Epstein, Jean 1897-1953 .... **TCLC 92**
Epstein, Joseph 1937- .... **CLC 39**
See also AMWS 14; CA 112; 119; CANR 50, 65, 117
Epstein, Leslie 1938- .... **CLC 27**
See also AMWS 12; CA 73-76, 215; CAAE 215; CAAS 12; CANR 23, 69; DLB 299
Equiano, Olaudah 1745(?)-1797 . **BLC 2; LC 16**
See also AFAW 1, 2; CDWLB 3; DAM MULT; DLB 37, 50; WLIT 2
Erasmus, Desiderius 1469(?)-1536 ..... **LC 16, 93**
See also DLB 136; EW 2; LMFS 1; RGWL 2, 3; TWA
Erdman, Paul E(mil) 1932- .... **CLC 25**
See also AITN 1; CA 61-64; CANR 13, 43, 84
Erdrich, Louise 1954- .... **CLC 39, 54, 120, 176; NNAL; PC 52**
See also AAYA 10, 47; AMWS 4; BEST 89:1; BPFB 1; CA 114; CANR 41, 62, 118; CDALBS; CN 7; CP 7; CPW; CWP; DA3; DAM MULT, NOV, POP; DLB 152, 175, 206; EWL 3; EXPP; LAIT 5; LATS 1:2; MTCW 1; NFS 5; PFS 14; RGAL 4; SATA 94, 141; SSFS 14; TCWW 2
Erenburg, Ilya (Grigoryevich)
See Ehrenburg, Ilya (Grigoryevich)
Erickson, Stephen Michael 1950-
See Erickson, Steve
See also CA 129; SFW 4
Erickson, Steve .... **CLC 64**
See Erickson, Stephen Michael
See also CANR 60, 68; SUFW 2
Erickson, Walter
See Fast, Howard (Melvin)
Ericson, Walter
See Fast, Howard (Melvin)
Eriksson, Buntel
See Bergman, (Ernst) Ingmar
Eriugena, John Scottus c.
810-877 .... **CMLC 65**
See also DLB 115
Ernaux, Annie 1940- .... **CLC 88, 184**
See also CA 147; CANR 93; NCFS 3, 5
Erskine, John 1879-1951 .... **TCLC 84**
See also CA 112; 159; DLB 9, 102; FANT
Eschenbach, Wolfram von
See Wolfram von Eschenbach
See also RGWL 3
Eseki, Bruno
See Mphahlele, Ezekiel
Esenin, Sergei (Alexandrovich)
1895-1925 .... **TCLC 4**
See Yesenin, Sergey
See also CA 104; RGWL 2, 3

Eshleman, Clayton 1935- .... **CLC 7**
See also CA 33-36R, 212; CAAE 212; CAAS 6; CANR 93; CP 7; DLB 5

Espriella, Don Manuel Alvarez
See Southey, Robert

Espriu, Salvador 1913-1985 .... **CLC 9**
See also CA 154; 115; DLB 134; EWL 3

Espronceda, Jose de 1808-1842 ..... **NCLC 39**

Esquivel, Laura 1951(?)- ... **CLC 141; HLCS 1**
See also AAYA 29; CA 143; CANR 68, 113; DA3; DNFS 2; LAIT 3; LMFS 2; MTCW 1; NFS 5; WLIT 1

Esse, James
See Stephens, James

Esterbrook, Tom
See Hubbard, L(afayette) Ron(ald)

Estleman, Loren D. 1952- .... **CLC 48**
See also AAYA 27; CA 85-88; CANR 27, 74; CMW 4; CPW; DA3; DAM NOV, POP; DLB 226; INT CANR-27; MTCW 1, 2

Etherege, Sir George 1636-1692 . **DC 23; LC 78**
See also BRW 2; DAM DRAM; DLB 80; PAB; RGEL 2

Euclid 306B.C.-283B.C. .... **CMLC 25**

Eugenides, Jeffrey 1960(?)- .... **CLC 81**
See also AAYA 51; CA 144; CANR 120

Euripides c. 484B.C.-406B.C. .... **CMLC 23, 51; DC 4; WLCS**
See also AW 1; CDWLB 1; DA; DA3; DAB; DAC; DAM DRAM, MST; DFS 1, 4, 6; DLB 176; LAIT 1; LMFS 1; RGWL 2, 3

Evan, Evin
See Faust, Frederick (Schiller)

Evans, Caradoc 1878-1945 ... **SSC 43; TCLC 85**
See also DLB 162

Evans, Evan
See Faust, Frederick (Schiller)
See also TCWW 2

Evans, Marian
See Eliot, George

Evans, Mary Ann
See Eliot, George
See also NFS 20

Evarts, Esther
See Benson, Sally

Everett, Percival
See Everett, Percival L.
See also CSW

Everett, Percival L. 1956- .... **CLC 57**
See Everett, Percival
See also BW 2; CA 129; CANR 94, 134

Everson, R(onald) G(ilmour)
1903-1992 .... **CLC 27**
See also CA 17-20R; DLB 88

Everson, William (Oliver)
1912-1994 .... **CLC 1, 5, 14**
See also BG 2; CA 9-12R; 145; CANR 20; DLB 5, 16, 212; MTCW 1

Evtushenko, Evgenii Aleksandrovich
See Yevtushenko, Yevgeny (Alexandrovich)
See also CWW 2; RGWL 2, 3

Ewart, Gavin (Buchanan)
1916-1995 .... **CLC 13, 46**
See also BRWS 7; CA 89-92; 150; CANR 17, 46; CP 7; DLB 40; MTCW 1

Ewers, Hanns Heinz 1871-1943 ..... **TCLC 12**
See also CA 109; 149

Ewing, Frederick R.
See Sturgeon, Theodore (Hamilton)

Exley, Frederick (Earl) 1929-1992 .... **CLC 6, 11**
See also AITN 2; BPFB 1; CA 81-84; 138; CANR 117; DLB 143; DLBY 1981

Eynhardt, Guillermo
See Quiroga, Horacio (Sylvestre)

Ezekiel, Nissim (Moses) 1924-2004 .. **CLC 61**
See also CA 61-64; 223; CP 7; EWL 3

Ezekiel, Tish O'Dowd 1943- .... **CLC 34**
See also CA 129

Fadeev, Aleksandr Aleksandrovich
See Bulgya, Alexander Alexandrovich
See also DLB 272

Fadeev, Alexandr Alexandrovich
See Bulgya, Alexander Alexandrovich
See also EWL 3

Fadeyev, A.
See Bulgya, Alexander Alexandrovich

Fadeyev, Alexander .... **TCLC 53**
See Bulgya, Alexander Alexandrovich

Fagen, Donald 1948- .... **CLC 26**

Fainzilberg, Ilya Arnoldovich 1897-1937
See Ilf, Ilya
See also CA 120; 165

Fair, Ronald L. 1932- .... **CLC 18**
See also BW 1; CA 69-72; CANR 25; DLB 33

Fairbairn, Roger
See Carr, John Dickson

Fairbairns, Zoe (Ann) 1948- .... **CLC 32**
See also CA 103; CANR 21, 85; CN 7

Fairfield, Flora
See Alcott, Louisa May

Fairman, Paul W. 1916-1977
See Queen, Ellery
See also CA 114; SFW 4

Falco, Gian
See Papini, Giovanni

Falconer, James
See Kirkup, James

Falconer, Kenneth
See Kornbluth, C(yril) M.

Falkland, Samuel
See Heijermans, Herman

Fallaci, Oriana 1930- .... **CLC 11, 110**
See also CA 77-80; CANR 15, 58, 134; FW; MTCW 1

Faludi, Susan 1959- .... **CLC 140**
See also CA 138; CANR 126; FW; MTCW 1; NCFS 3

Faludy, George 1913- .... **CLC 42**
See also CA 21-24R

Faludy, Gyoergy
See Faludy, George

Fanon, Frantz 1925-1961 .... **BLC 2; CLC 74**
See also BW 1; CA 116; 89-92; DAM MULT; DLB 296; LMFS 2; WLIT 2

Fanshawe, Ann 1625-1680 .... **LC 11**

Fante, John (Thomas) 1911-1983 .... **CLC 60; SSC 65**
See also AMWS 11; CA 69-72; 109; CANR 23, 104; DLB 130; DLBY 1983

Far, Sui Sin .... **SSC 62**
See Eaton, Edith Maude
See also SSFS 4

Farah, Nuruddin 1945- ...... **BLC 2; CLC 53, 137**
See also AFW; BW 2, 3; CA 106; CANR 81; CDWLB 3; CN 7; DAM MULT; DLB 125; EWL 3; WLIT 2

Fargue, Leon-Paul 1876(?)-1947 .... **TCLC 11**
See also CA 109; CANR 107; DLB 258; EWL 3

Farigoule, Louis
See Romains, Jules

Farina, Richard 1936(?)-1966 .... **CLC 9**
See also CA 81-84; 25-28R

Farley, Walter (Lorimer)
1915-1989 .... **CLC 17**
See also AAYA 58; BYA 14; CA 17-20R; CANR 8, 29, 84; DLB 22; JRDA; MAICYA 1, 2; SATA 2, 43, 132; YAW

Farmer, Philip Jose 1918- .... **CLC 1, 19**
See also AAYA 28; BPFB 1; CA 1-4R; CANR 4, 35, 111; DLB 8; MTCW 1; SATA 93; SCFW 2; SFW 4

Farquhar, George 1677-1707 .... **LC 21**
See also BRW 2; DAM DRAM; DLB 84; RGEL 2

Farrell, J(ames) G(ordon)
1935-1979 .... **CLC 6**
See also CA 73-76; 89-92; CANR 36; DLB 14, 271; MTCW 1; RGEL 2; RHW; WLIT 4

Farrell, James T(homas) 1904-1979 . **CLC 1, 4, 8, 11, 66; SSC 28**
See also AMW; BPFB 1; CA 5-8R; 89-92; CANR 9, 61; DLB 4, 9, 86; DLBD 2; EWL 3; MTCW 1, 2; RGAL 4

Farrell, Warren (Thomas) 1943- ...... **CLC 70**
See also CA 146; CANR 120

Farren, Richard J.
See Betjeman, John

Farren, Richard M.
See Betjeman, John

Fassbinder, Rainer Werner
1946-1982 .... **CLC 20**
See also CA 93-96; 106; CANR 31

Fast, Howard (Melvin) 1914-2003 .. **CLC 23, 131**
See also AAYA 16; BPFB 1; CA 1-4R; 181; 214; CAAE 181; CAAS 18; CANR 1, 33, 54, 75, 98; CMW 4; CN 7; CPW; DAM NOV; DLB 9; INT CANR-33; LATS 1:1; MTCW 1; RHW; SATA 7; SATA-Essay 107; TCWW 2; YAW

Faulcon, Robert
See Holdstock, Robert P.

Faulkner, William (Cuthbert)
1897-1962 .... **CLC 1, 3, 6, 8, 9, 11, 14, 18, 28, 52, 68; SSC 1, 35, 42; TCLC 141; WLC**
See also AAYA 7; AMW; AMWR 1; BPFB 1; BYA 5, 15; CA 81-84; CANR 33; CDALB 1929-1941; DA; DA3; DAB; DAC; DAM MST, NOV; DLB 9, 11, 44, 102; DLBD 2; DLBY 1986, 1997; EWL 3; EXPN; EXPS; LAIT 2; LATS 1:1; LMFS 2; MTCW 1, 2; NFS 4, 8, 13; RGAL 4; RGSF 2; SSFS 2, 5, 6, 12; TUS

Fauset, Jessie Redmon
1882(?)-1961 .. **BLC 2; CLC 19, 54; HR 2**
See also AFAW 2; BW 1; CA 109; CANR 83; DAM MULT; DLB 51; FW; LMFS 2; MAWW

Faust, Frederick (Schiller)
1892-1944(?) .... **TCLC 49**
See Austin, Frank; Brand, Max; Challis, George; Dawson, Peter; Dexter, Martin; Evans, Evan; Frederick, John; Frost, Frederick; Manning, David; Silver, Nicholas
See also CA 108; 152; DAM POP; DLB 256; TUS

Faust, Irvin 1924- .... **CLC 8**
See also CA 33-36R; CANR 28, 67; CN 7; DLB 2, 28, 218, 278; DLBY 1980

Faustino, Domingo 1811-1888 ...... **NCLC 123**

Fawkes, Guy
See Benchley, Robert (Charles)

Fearing, Kenneth (Flexner)
1902-1961 .... **CLC 51**
See also CA 93-96; CANR 59; CMW 4; DLB 9; RGAL 4

Fecamps, Elise
See Creasey, John

Federman, Raymond 1928- .... **CLC 6, 47**
See also CA 17-20R, 208; CAAE 208; CAAS 8; CANR 10, 43, 83, 108; CN 7; DLBY 1980

Federspiel, J(uerg) F. 1931- .... **CLC 42**
See also CA 146

Feiffer, Jules (Ralph) 1929- ...... **CLC 2, 8, 64**
    See also AAYA 3; CA 17-20R; CAD; CANR 30, 59, 129; CD 5; DAM DRAM; DLB 7, 44; INT CANR-30; MTCW 1; SATA 8, 61, 111

Feige, Hermann Albert Otto Maximilian
    See Traven, B.

Feinberg, David B. 1956-1994 .... **CLC 59**
    See also CA 135; 147

Feinstein, Elaine 1930- .... **CLC 36**
    See also CA 69-72; CAAS 1; CANR 31, 68, 121; CN 7; CP 7; CWP; DLB 14, 40; MTCW 1

Feke, Gilbert David .... **CLC 65**

Feldman, Irving (Mordecai) 1928- ..... **CLC 7**
    See also CA 1-4R; CANR 1; CP 7; DLB 169

Felix-Tchicaya, Gerald
    See Tchicaya, Gerald Felix

Fellini, Federico 1920-1993 .... **CLC 16, 85**
    See also CA 65-68; 143; CANR 33

Felltham, Owen 1602(?)-1668 .... **LC 92**
    See also DLB 126, 151

Felsen, Henry Gregor 1916-1995 ..... **CLC 17**
    See also CA 1-4R; 180; CANR 1; SAAS 2; SATA 1

Felski, Rita .... **CLC 65**

Fenno, Jack
    See Calisher, Hortense

Fenollosa, Ernest (Francisco)
    1853-1908 .... **TCLC 91**

Fenton, James Martin 1949- .... **CLC 32**
    See also CA 102; CANR 108; CP 7; DLB 40; PFS 11

Ferber, Edna 1887-1968 .... **CLC 18, 93**
    See also AITN 1; CA 5-8R; 25-28R; CANR 68, 105; DLB 9, 28, 86, 266; MTCW 1, 2; RGAL 4; RHW; SATA 7; TCWW 2

Ferdowsi, Abu'l Qasem 940-1020 . **CMLC 43**
    See also RGWL 2, 3

Ferguson, Helen
    See Kavan, Anna

Ferguson, Niall 1964- .... **CLC 134**
    See also CA 190

Ferguson, Samuel 1810-1886 .... **NCLC 33**
    See also DLB 32; RGEL 2

Fergusson, Robert 1750-1774 .... **LC 29**
    See also DLB 109; RGEL 2

Ferling, Lawrence
    See Ferlinghetti, Lawrence (Monsanto)

Ferlinghetti, Lawrence (Monsanto)
    1919(?)- .... **CLC 2, 6, 10, 27, 111; PC 1**
    See also CA 5-8R; CANR 3, 41, 73, 125; CDALB 1941-1968; CP 7; DA3; DAM POET; DLB 5, 16; MTCW 1, 2; RGAL 4; WP

Fern, Fanny
    See Parton, Sara Payson Willis

Fernandez, Vicente Garcia Huidobro
    See Huidobro Fernandez, Vicente Garcia

Fernandez-Armesto, Felipe .... **CLC 70**

Fernandez de Lizardi, Jose Joaquin
    See Lizardi, Jose Joaquin Fernandez de

Ferre, Rosario 1938- ...... **CLC 139; HLCS 1; SSC 36**
    See also CA 131; CANR 55, 81, 134; CWW 2; DLB 145; EWL 3; HW 1, 2; LAWS 1; MTCW 1; WLIT 1

Ferrer, Gabriel (Francisco Victor) Miro
    See Miro (Ferrer), Gabriel (Francisco Victor)

Ferrier, Susan (Edmonstone)
    1782-1854 .... **NCLC 8**
    See also DLB 116; RGEL 2

Ferrigno, Robert 1948(?)- .... **CLC 65**
    See also CA 140; CANR 125

Ferron, Jacques 1921-1985 .... **CLC 94**
    See also CA 117; 129; CCA 1; DAC; DLB 60; EWL 3

Feuchtwanger, Lion 1884-1958 .... **TCLC 3**
    See also CA 104; 187; DLB 66; EWL 3

Feuerbach, Ludwig 1804-1872 ..... **NCLC 139**
    See also DLB 133

Feuillet, Octave 1821-1890 .... **NCLC 45**
    See also DLB 192

Feydeau, Georges (Leon Jules Marie)
    1862-1921 .... **TCLC 22**
    See also CA 113; 152; CANR 84; DAM DRAM; DLB 192; EWL 3; GFL 1789 to the Present; RGWL 2, 3

Fichte, Johann Gottlieb
    1762-1814 .... **NCLC 62**
    See also DLB 90

Ficino, Marsilio 1433-1499 .... **LC 12**
    See also LMFS 1

Fiedeler, Hans
    See Doeblin, Alfred

Fiedler, Leslie A(aron) 1917-2003 ..... **CLC 4, 13, 24**
    See also AMWS 13; CA 9-12R; 212; CANR 7, 63; CN 7; DLB 28, 67; EWL 3; MTCW 1, 2; RGAL 4; TUS

Field, Andrew 1938- .... **CLC 44**
    See also CA 97-100; CANR 25

Field, Eugene 1850-1895 .... **NCLC 3**
    See also DLB 23, 42, 140; DLBD 13; MAICYA 1, 2; RGAL 4; SATA 16

Field, Gans T.
    See Wellman, Manly Wade

Field, Michael 1915-1971 .... **TCLC 43**
    See also CA 29-32R

Field, Peter
    See Hobson, Laura Z(ametkin)
    See also TCWW 2

Fielding, Helen 1958- .... **CLC 146**
    See also CA 172; CANR 127; DLB 231

Fielding, Henry 1707-1754 .... **LC 1, 46, 85; WLC**
    See also BRW 3; BRWR 1; CDBLB 1660-1789; DA; DA3; DAB; DAC; DAM DRAM, MST, NOV; DLB 39, 84, 101; NFS 18; RGEL 2; TEA; WLIT 3

Fielding, Sarah 1710-1768 .... **LC 1, 44**
    See also DLB 39; RGEL 2; TEA

Fields, W. C. 1880-1946 .... **TCLC 80**
    See also DLB 44

Fierstein, Harvey (Forbes) 1954- ..... **CLC 33**
    See also CA 123; 129; CAD; CD 5; CPW; DA3; DAM DRAM, POP; DFS 6; DLB 266; GLL

Figes, Eva 1932- .... **CLC 31**
    See also CA 53-56; CANR 4, 44, 83; CN 7; DLB 14, 271; FW

Filippo, Eduardo de
    See de Filippo, Eduardo

Finch, Anne 1661-1720 .... **LC 3; PC 21**
    See also BRWS 9; DLB 95

Finch, Robert (Duer Claydon)
    1900-1995 .... **CLC 18**
    See also CA 57-60; CANR 9, 24, 49; CP 7; DLB 88

Findley, Timothy (Irving Frederick)
    1930-2002 .... **CLC 27, 102**
    See also CA 25-28R; 206; CANR 12, 42, 69, 109; CCA 1; CN 7; DAC; DAM MST; DLB 53; FANT; RHW

Fink, William
    See Mencken, H(enry) L(ouis)

Firbank, Louis 1942-
    See Reed, Lou
    See also CA 117

Firbank, (Arthur Annesley) Ronald
    1886-1926 .... **TCLC 1**
    See also BRWS 2; CA 104; 177; DLB 36; EWL 3; RGEL 2

Fish, Stanley
    See Fish, Stanley Eugene

Fish, Stanley E.
    See Fish, Stanley Eugene

Fish, Stanley Eugene 1938- .... **CLC 142**
    See also CA 112; 132; CANR 90; DLB 67

Fisher, Dorothy (Frances) Canfield
    1879-1958 .... **TCLC 87**
    See also CA 114; 136; CANR 80; CLR 71,; CWRI 5; DLB 9, 102, 284; MAICYA 1, 2; YABC 1

Fisher, M(ary) F(rances) K(ennedy)
    1908-1992 .... **CLC 76, 87**
    See also CA 77-80; 138; CANR 44; MTCW 1

Fisher, Roy 1930- .... **CLC 25**
    See also CA 81-84; CAAS 10; CANR 16; CP 7; DLB 40

Fisher, Rudolph 1897-1934 .... **BLC 2; HR 2; SSC 25; TCLC 11**
    See also BW 1, 3; CA 107; 124; CANR 80; DAM MULT; DLB 51, 102

Fisher, Vardis (Alvero) 1895-1968 .... **CLC 7; TCLC 140**
    See also CA 5-8R; 25-28R; CANR 68; DLB 9, 206; RGAL 4; TCWW 2

Fiske, Tarleton
    See Bloch, Robert (Albert)

Fitch, Clarke
    See Sinclair, Upton (Beall)

Fitch, John IV
    See Cormier, Robert (Edmund)

Fitzgerald, Captain Hugh
    See Baum, L(yman) Frank

FitzGerald, Edward 1809-1883 .... **NCLC 9**
    See also BRW 4; DLB 32; RGEL 2

Fitzgerald, F(rancis) Scott (Key)
    1896-1940 ... **SSC 6, 31, 75; TCLC 1, 6, 14, 28, 55, 157; WLC**
    See also AAYA 24; AITN 1; AMW; AMWC 2; AMWR 1; BPFB 1; CA 110; 123; CDALB 1917-1929; DA; DA3; DAB; DAC; DAM MST, NOV; DLB 4, 9, 86, 219, 273; DLBD 1, 15, 16; DLBY 1981, 1996; EWL 3; EXPN; EXPS; LAIT 3; MTCW 1, 2; NFS 2, 19, 20; RGAL 4; RGSF 2; SSFS 4, 15; TUS

Fitzgerald, Penelope 1916-2000 . **CLC 19, 51, 61, 143**
    See also BRWS 5; CA 85-88; 190; CAAS 10; CANR 56, 86, 131; CN 7; DLB 14, 194; EWL 3; MTCW 2

Fitzgerald, Robert (Stuart)
    1910-1985 .... **CLC 39**
    See also CA 1-4R; 114; CANR 1; DLBY 1980

FitzGerald, Robert D(avid)
    1902-1987 .... **CLC 19**
    See also CA 17-20R; DLB 260; RGEL 2

Fitzgerald, Zelda (Sayre)
    1900-1948 .... **TCLC 52**
    See also AMWS 9; CA 117; 126; DLBY 1984

Flanagan, Thomas (James Bonner)
    1923-2002 .... **CLC 25, 52**
    See also CA 108; 206; CANR 55; CN 7; DLBY 1980; INT CA-108; MTCW 1; RHW

Flaubert, Gustave 1821-1880 .... **NCLC 2, 10, 19, 62, 66, 135; SSC 11, 60; WLC**
    See also DA; DA3; DAB; DAC; DAM MST, NOV; DLB 119, 301; EW 7; EXPS; GFL 1789 to the Present; LAIT 2; LMFS 1; NFS 14; RGSF 2; RGWL 2, 3; SSFS 6; TWA

Flavius Josephus
    See Josephus, Flavius

Flecker, Herman Elroy
    See Flecker, (Herman) James Elroy

Flecker, (Herman) James Elroy
1884-1915 .... **TCLC 43**
See also CA 109; 150; DLB 10, 19; RGEL
2

Fleming, Ian (Lancaster) 1908-1964 . **CLC 3,
30**
See also AAYA 26; BPFB 1; CA 5-8R;
CANR 59; CDBLB 1945-1960; CMW 4;
CPW; DA3; DAM POP; DLB 87, 201;
MSW; MTCW 1, 2; RGEL 2; SATA 9;
TEA; YAW

Fleming, Thomas (James) 1927- ...... **CLC 37**
See also CA 5-8R; CANR 10, 102; INT
CANR-10; SATA 8

Fletcher, John 1579-1625 .... **DC 6; LC 33**
See also BRW 2; CDBLB Before 1660;
DLB 58; RGEL 2; TEA

Fletcher, John Gould 1886-1950 .... **TCLC 35**
See also CA 107; 167; DLB 4, 45; LMFS
2; RGAL 4

Fleur, Paul
See Pohl, Frederik

Flieg, Helmut
See Heym, Stefan

Flooglebuckle, Al
See Spiegelman, Art

Flora, Fletcher 1914-1969
See Queen, Ellery
See also CA 1-4R; CANR 3, 85

Flying Officer X
See Bates, H(erbert) E(rnest)

Fo, Dario 1926- .... **CLC 32, 109; DC 10**
See also CA 116; 128; CANR 68, 114, 134;
CWW 2; DA3; DAM DRAM; DLBY
1997; EWL 3; MTCW 1, 2

Fogarty, Jonathan Titulescu Esq.
See Farrell, James T(homas)

Follett, Ken(neth Martin) 1949- .... **CLC 18**
See also AAYA 6, 50; BEST 89:4; BPFB 1;
CA 81-84; CANR 13, 33, 54, 102; CMW
4; CPW; DA3; DAM NOV, POP; DLB
87; DLBY 1981; INT CANR-33; MTCW
1

Fondane, Benjamin 1898-1944 ..... **TCLC 159**

Fontane, Theodor 1819-1898 .... **NCLC 26**
See also CDWLB 2; DLB 129; EW 6;
RGWL 2, 3; TWA

Fontenot, Chester .... **CLC 65**

Fonvizin, Denis Ivanovich
1744(?)-1792 .... **LC 81**
See also DLB 150; RGWL 2, 3

Foote, Horton 1916- .... **CLC 51, 91**
See also CA 73-76; CAD; CANR 34, 51,
110; CD 5; CSW; DA3; DAM DRAM;
DFS 20; DLB 26, 266; EWL 3; INT
CANR-34

Foote, Mary Hallock 1847-1938 .. **TCLC 108**
See also DLB 186, 188, 202, 221

Foote, Samuel 1721-1777 .... **LC 106**
See also DLB 89; RGEL 2

Foote, Shelby 1916- .... **CLC 75**
See also AAYA 40; CA 5-8R; CANR 3, 45,
74, 131; CN 7; CPW; CSW; DA3; DAM
NOV, POP; DLB 2, 17; MTCW 2; RHW

Forbes, Cosmo
See Lewton, Val

Forbes, Esther 1891-1967 .... **CLC 12**
See also AAYA 17; BYA 2; CA 13-14; 25-
28R; CAP 1; CLR 27; DLB 22; JRDA;
MAICYA 1, 2; RHW; SATA 2, 100; YAW

Forche, Carolyn (Louise) 1950- .... **CLC 25,
83, 86; PC 10**
See also CA 109; 117; CANR 50, 74; CP 7;
CWP; DA3; DAM POET; DLB 5, 193;
INT CA-117; MTCW 1; PFS 18; RGAL 4

Ford, Elbur
See Hibbert, Eleanor Alice Burford

Ford, Ford Madox 1873-1939 ... **TCLC 1, 15,
39, 57**
See Chaucer, Daniel
See also BRW 6; CA 104; 132; CANR 74;
CDBLB 1914-1945; DA3; DAM NOV;
DLB 34, 98, 162; EWL 3; MTCW 1, 2;
RGEL 2; TEA

Ford, Henry 1863-1947 .... **TCLC 73**
See also CA 115; 148

Ford, Jack
See Ford, John

Ford, John 1586-1639 .... **DC 8; LC 68**
See also BRW 2; CDBLB Before 1660;
DA3; DAM DRAM; DFS 7; DLB 58;
IDTP; RGEL 2

Ford, John 1895-1973 .... **CLC 16**
See also CA 187; 45-48

Ford, Richard 1944- .... **CLC 46, 99**
See also AMWS 5; CA 69-72; CANR 11,
47, 86, 128; CN 7; CSW; DLB 227; EWL
3; MTCW 1; RGAL 4; RGSF 2

Ford, Webster
See Masters, Edgar Lee

Foreman, Richard 1937- .... **CLC 50**
See also CA 65-68; CAD; CANR 32, 63;
CD 5

Forester, C(ecil) S(cott) 1899-1966 . **CLC 35;
TCLC 152**
See also CA 73-76; 25-28R; CANR 83;
DLB 191; RGEL 2; RHW; SATA 13

Forez
See Mauriac, Francois (Charles)

Forman, James
See Forman, James D(ouglas)

Forman, James D(ouglas) 1932- .... **CLC 21**
See also AAYA 17; CA 9-12R; CANR 4,
19, 42; JRDA; MAICYA 1, 2; SATA 8,
70; YAW

Forman, Milos 1932- .... **CLC 164**
See also CA 109

Fornes, Maria Irene 1930- .... **CLC 39, 61,
187; DC 10; HLCS 1**
See also CA 25-28R; CAD; CANR 28, 81;
CD 5; CWD; DLB 7; HW 1, 2; INT
CANR-28; LLW 1; MTCW 1; RGAL 4

Forrest, Leon (Richard)
1937-1997 .... **BLCS; CLC 4**
See also AFAW 2; BW 2; CA 89-92; 162;
CAAS 7; CANR 25, 52, 87; CN 7; DLB
33

Forster, E(dward) M(organ)
1879-1970 ...... **CLC 1, 2, 3, 4, 9, 10, 13,
15, 22, 45, 77; SSC 27; TCLC 125;
WLC**
See also AAYA 2, 37; BRW 6; BRWR 2;
BYA 12; CA 13-14; 25-28R; CANR 45;
CAP 1; CDBLB 1914-1945; DA; DA3;
DAB; DAC; DAM MST, NOV; DLB 34,
98, 162, 178, 195; DLBD 10; EWL 3;
EXPN; LAIT 3; LMFS 1; MTCW 1, 2;
NCFS 1; NFS 3, 10, 11; RGEL 2; RGSF
2; SATA 57; SUFW 1; TEA; WLIT 4

Forster, John 1812-1876 .... **NCLC 11**
See also DLB 144, 184

Forster, Margaret 1938- .... **CLC 149**
See also CA 133; CANR 62, 115; CN 7;
DLB 155, 271

Forsyth, Frederick 1938- .... **CLC 2, 5, 36**
See also BEST 89:4; CA 85-88; CANR 38,
62, 115; CMW 4; CN 7; CPW; DAM
NOV, POP; DLB 87; MTCW 1, 2

Forten, Charlotte L. 1837-1914 .... **BLC 2;
TCLC 16**
See Grimke, Charlotte L(ottie) Forten
See also DLB 50, 239

Fortinbras
See Grieg, (Johan) Nordahl (Brun)

Foscolo, Ugo 1778-1827 .... **NCLC 8, 97**
See also EW 5

Fosse, Bob .... **CLC 20**
See Fosse, Robert Louis

Fosse, Robert Louis 1927-1987
See Fosse, Bob
See also CA 110; 123

Foster, Hannah Webster
1758-1840 .... **NCLC 99**
See also DLB 37, 200; RGAL 4

Foster, Stephen Collins
1826-1864 .... **NCLC 26**
See also RGAL 4

Foucault, Michel 1926-1984 . **CLC 31, 34, 69**
See also CA 105; 113; CANR 34; DLB 242;
EW 13; EWL 3; GFL 1789 to the Present;
GLL 1; LMFS 2; MTCW 1, 2; TWA

Fouque, Friedrich (Heinrich Karl) de la
Motte 1777-1843 .... **NCLC 2**
See also DLB 90; RGWL 2, 3; SUFW 1

Fourier, Charles 1772-1837 .... **NCLC 51**

Fournier, Henri-Alban 1886-1914
See Alain-Fournier
See also CA 104; 179

Fournier, Pierre 1916- .... **CLC 11**
See Gascar, Pierre
See also CA 89-92; CANR 16, 40

Fowles, John (Robert) 1926- . **CLC 1, 2, 3, 4,
6, 9, 10, 15, 33, 87; SSC 33**
See also BPFB 1; BRWS 1; CA 5-8R;
CANR 25, 71, 103; CDBLB 1960 to
Present; CN 7; DA3; DAB; DAC; DAM
MST; DLB 14, 139, 207; EWL 3; HGG;
MTCW 1, 2; RGEL 2; RHW; SATA 22;
TEA; WLIT 4

Fox, Paula 1923- .... **CLC 2, 8, 121**
See also AAYA 3, 37; BYA 3, 8; CA 73-76;
CANR 20, 36, 62, 105; CLR 1, 44, 96;
DLB 52; JRDA; MAICYA 1, 2; MTCW
1; NFS 12; SATA 17, 60, 120; WYA;
YAW

Fox, William Price (Jr.) 1926- .... **CLC 22**
See also CA 17-20R; CAAS 19; CANR 11;
CSW; DLB 2; DLBY 1981

Foxe, John 1517(?)-1587 .... **LC 14**
See also DLB 132

Frame, Janet .. **CLC 2, 3, 6, 22, 66, 96; SSC
29**
See Clutha, Janet Paterson Frame
See also CN 7; CWP; EWL 3; RGEL 2;
RGSF 2; TWA

France, Anatole .... **TCLC 9**
See Thibault, Jacques Anatole Francois
See also DLB 123; EWL 3; GFL 1789 to
the Present; MTCW 1; RGWL 2, 3;
SUFW 1

Francis, Claude .... **CLC 50**
See also CA 192

Francis, Richard Stanley 1920- ... **CLC 2, 22,
42, 102**
See also AAYA 5, 21; BEST 89:3; BPFB 1;
CA 5-8R; CANR 9, 42, 68, 100; CDBLB
1960 to Present; CMW 4; CN 7; DA3;
DAM POP; DLB 87; INT CANR-9;
MSW; MTCW 1, 2

Francis, Robert (Churchill)
1901-1987 .... **CLC 15; PC 34**
See also AMWS 9; CA 1-4R; 123; CANR
1; EXPP; PFS 12

Francis, Lord Jeffrey
See Jeffrey, Francis
See also DLB 107

Frank, Anne(lies Marie)
1929-1945 .... **TCLC 17; WLC**
See also AAYA 12; BYA 1; CA 113; 133;
CANR 68; CLR 101; DA; DA3; DAB;
DAC; DAM MST; LAIT 4; MAICYA 2;
MAICYAS 1; MTCW 1, 2; NCFS 2;
SATA 87; SATA-Brief 42; WYA; YAW

Frank, Bruno 1887-1945 .... **TCLC 81**
See also CA 189; DLB 118; EWL 3

Frank, Elizabeth 1945- .... **CLC 39**
See also CA 121; 126; CANR 78; INT CA-126

Frankl, Viktor E(mil) 1905-1997 ...... **CLC 93**
See also CA 65-68; 161

Franklin, Benjamin
See Hasek, Jaroslav (Matej Frantisek)

Franklin, Benjamin 1706-1790 .... **LC 25;
WLCS**
See also AMW; CDALB 1640-1865; DA;
DA3; DAB; DAC; DAM MST; DLB 24,
43, 73, 183; LAIT 1; RGAL 4; TUS

**Franklin, (Stella Maria Sarah) Miles
(Lampe)** 1879-1954 .... **TCLC 7**
See also CA 104; 164; DLB 230; FW;
MTCW 2; RGEL 2; TWA

Fraser, Antonia (Pakenham) 1932- . **CLC 32,
107**
See also AAYA 57; CA 85-88; CANR 44,
65, 119; CMW; DLB 276; MTCW 1, 2;
SATA-Brief 32

Fraser, George MacDonald 1925- ...... **CLC 7**
See also AAYA 48; CA 45-48, 180; CAAE
180; CANR 2, 48, 74; MTCW 1; RHW

Fraser, Sylvia 1935- .... **CLC 64**
See also CA 45-48; CANR 1, 16, 60; CCA
1

Frayn, Michael 1933- . **CLC 3, 7, 31, 47, 176**
See also BRWC 2; BRWS 7; CA 5-8R;
CANR 30, 69, 114, 133; CBD; CD 5; CN
7; DAM DRAM, NOV; DLB 13, 14, 194,
245; FANT; MTCW 1, 2; SFW 4

Fraze, Candida (Merrill) 1945- .... **CLC 50**
See also CA 126

Frazer, Andrew
See Marlowe, Stephen

Frazer, J(ames) G(eorge)
1854-1941 .... **TCLC 32**
See also BRWS 3; CA 118; NCFS 5

Frazer, Robert Caine
See Creasey, John

Frazer, Sir James George
See Frazer, J(ames) G(eorge)

Frazier, Charles 1950- .... **CLC 109**
See also AAYA 34; CA 161; CANR 126;
CSW; DLB 292

Frazier, Ian 1951- .... **CLC 46**
See also CA 130; CANR 54, 93

Frederic, Harold 1856-1898 .... **NCLC 10**
See also AMW; DLB 12, 23; DLBD 13;
RGAL 4

Frederick, John
See Faust, Frederick (Schiller)
See also TCWW 2

Frederick the Great 1712-1786 .... **LC 14**

Fredro, Aleksander 1793-1876 .... **NCLC 8**

Freeling, Nicolas 1927-2003 .... **CLC 38**
See also CA 49-52; 218; CAAS 12; CANR
1, 17, 50, 84; CMW 4; CN 7; DLB 87

Freeman, Douglas Southall
1886-1953 .... **TCLC 11**
See also CA 109; 195; DLB 17; DLBD 17

Freeman, Judith 1946- .... **CLC 55**
See also CA 148; CANR 120; DLB 256

Freeman, Mary E(leanor) Wilkins
1852-1930 .... **SSC 1, 47; TCLC 9**
See also CA 106; 177; DLB 12, 78, 221;
EXPS; FW; HGG; MAWW; RGAL 4;
RGSF 2; SSFS 4, 8; SUFW 1; TUS

Freeman, R(ichard) Austin
1862-1943 .... **TCLC 21**
See also CA 113; CANR 84; CMW 4; DLB
70

French, Albert 1943- .... **CLC 86**
See also BW 3; CA 167

French, Antonia
See Kureishi, Hanif

French, Marilyn 1929- .. **CLC 10, 18, 60, 177**
See also BPFB 1; CA 69-72; CANR 3, 31,
134; CN 7; CPW; DAM DRAM, NOV,
POP; FW; INT CANR-31; MTCW 1, 2

French, Paul
See Asimov, Isaac

Freneau, Philip Morin 1752-1832 .. **NCLC 1,
111**
See also AMWS 2; DLB 37, 43; RGAL 4

Freud, Sigmund 1856-1939 .... **TCLC 52**
See also CA 115; 133; CANR 69; DLB 296;
EW 8; EWL 3; LATS 1:1; MTCW 1, 2;
NCFS 3; TWA

Freytag, Gustav 1816-1895 .... **NCLC 109**
See also DLB 129

Friedan, Betty (Naomi) 1921- .... **CLC 74**
See also CA 65-68; CANR 18, 45, 74; DLB
246; FW; MTCW 1, 2; NCFS 5

Friedlander, Saul 1932- .... **CLC 90**
See also CA 117; 130; CANR 72

Friedman, B(ernard) H(arper)
1926- .... **CLC 7**
See also CA 1-4R; CANR 3, 48

Friedman, Bruce Jay 1930- ...... **CLC 3, 5, 56**
See also CA 9-12R; CAD; CANR 25, 52,
101; CD 5; CN 7; DLB 2, 28, 244; INT
CANR-25; SSFS 18

Friel, Brian 1929- .... **CLC 5, 42, 59, 115; DC
8; SSC 76**
See also BRWS 5; CA 21-24R; CANR 33,
69, 131; CBD; CD 5; DFS 11; DLB 13;
EWL 3; MTCW 1; RGEL 2; TEA

Friis-Baastad, Babbis Ellinor
1921-1970 .... **CLC 12**
See also CA 17-20R; 134; SATA 7

Frisch, Max (Rudolf) 1911-1991 ... **CLC 3, 9,
14, 18, 32, 44; TCLC 121**
See also CA 85-88; 134; CANR 32, 74; CD-
WLB 2; DAM DRAM, NOV; DLB 69,
124; EW 13; EWL 3; MTCW 1, 2; RGWL
2, 3

Fromentin, Eugene (Samuel Auguste)
1820-1876 .... **NCLC 10, 125**
See also DLB 123; GFL 1789 to the Present

Frost, Frederick
See Faust, Frederick (Schiller)
See also TCWW 2

Frost, Robert (Lee) 1874-1963 .. **CLC 1, 3, 4,
9, 10, 13, 15, 26, 34, 44; PC 1, 39;
WLC**
See also AAYA 21; AMW; AMWR 1; CA
89-92; CANR 33; CDALB 1917-1929;
CLR 67; DA; DA3; DAB; DAC; DAM
MST, POET; DLB 54, 284; DLBD 7;
EWL 3; EXPP; MTCW 1, 2; PAB; PFS 1,
2, 3, 4, 5, 6, 7, 10, 13; RGAL 4; SATA
14; TUS; WP; WYA

Froude, James Anthony
1818-1894 .... **NCLC 43**
See also DLB 18, 57, 144

Froy, Herald
See Waterhouse, Keith (Spencer)

Fry, Christopher 1907- .... **CLC 2, 10, 14**
See also BRWS 3; CA 17-20R; CAAS 23;
CANR 9, 30, 74, 132; CBD; CD 5; CP 7;
DAM DRAM; DLB 13; EWL 3; MTCW
1, 2; RGEL 2; SATA 66; TEA

Frye, (Herman) Northrop
1912-1991 .... **CLC 24, 70**
See also CA 5-8R; 133; CANR 8, 37; DLB
67, 68, 246; EWL 3; MTCW 1, 2; RGAL
4; TWA

Fuchs, Daniel 1909-1993 .... **CLC 8, 22**
See also CA 81-84; 142; CAAS 5; CANR
40; DLB 9, 26, 28; DLBY 1993

Fuchs, Daniel 1934- .... **CLC 34**
See also CA 37-40R; CANR 14, 48

Fuentes, Carlos 1928- .. **CLC 3, 8, 10, 13, 22,
41, 60, 113; HLC 1; SSC 24; WLC**
See also AAYA 4, 45; AITN 2; BPFB 1;
CA 69-72; CANR 10, 32, 68, 104; CD-
WLB 3; CWW 2; DA; DA3; DAB; DAC;
DAM MST, MULT, NOV; DLB 113;
DNFS 2; EWL 3; HW 1, 2; LAIT 3; LATS
1:2; LAW; LAWS 1; LMFS 2; MTCW 1,
2; NFS 8; RGSF 2; RGWL 2, 3; TWA;
WLIT 1

Fuentes, Gregorio Lopez y
See Lopez y Fuentes, Gregorio

Fuertes, Gloria 1918-1998 .... **PC 27**
See also CA 178; 180; DLB 108; HW 2;
SATA 115

Fugard, (Harold) Athol 1932- . **CLC 5, 9, 14,
25, 40, 80; DC 3**
See also AAYA 17; AFW; CA 85-88; CANR
32, 54, 118; CD 5; DAM DRAM; DFS 3,
6, 10; DLB 225; DNFS 1, 2; EWL 3;
LATS 1:2; MTCW 1; RGEL 2; WLIT 2

Fugard, Sheila 1932- .... **CLC 48**
See also CA 125

Fukuyama, Francis 1952- .... **CLC 131**
See also CA 140; CANR 72, 125

Fuller, Charles (H.), (Jr.) 1939- .... **BLC 2;
CLC 25; DC 1**
See also BW 2; CA 108; 112; CAD; CANR
87; CD 5; DAM DRAM, MULT; DFS 8;
DLB 38, 266; EWL 3; INT CA-112;
MTCW 1

Fuller, Henry Blake 1857-1929 .... **TCLC 103**
See also CA 108; 177; DLB 12; RGAL 4

Fuller, John (Leopold) 1937- .... **CLC 62**
See also CA 21-24R; CANR 9, 44; CP 7;
DLB 40

Fuller, Margaret
See Ossoli, Sarah Margaret (Fuller)
See also AMWS 2; DLB 183, 223, 239

Fuller, Roy (Broadbent) 1912-1991 ... **CLC 4,
28**
See also BRWS 7; CA 5-8R; 135; CAAS
10; CANR 53, 83; CWRI 5; DLB 15, 20;
EWL 3; RGEL 2; SATA 87

Fuller, Sarah Margaret
See Ossoli, Sarah Margaret (Fuller)

Fuller, Sarah Margaret
See Ossoli, Sarah Margaret (Fuller)
See also DLB 1, 59, 73

Fulton, Alice 1952- .... **CLC 52**
See also CA 116; CANR 57, 88; CP 7;
CWP; DLB 193

Furphy, Joseph 1843-1912 .... **TCLC 25**
See Collins, Tom
See also CA 163; DLB 230; EWL 3; RGEL
2

Fuson, Robert H(enderson) 1927- .... **CLC 70**
See also CA 89-92; CANR 103

Fussell, Paul 1924- .... **CLC 74**
See also BEST 90:1; CA 17-20R; CANR 8,
21, 35, 69, 135; INT CANR-21; MTCW
1, 2

Futabatei, Shimei 1864-1909 .... **TCLC 44**
See Futabatei Shimei
See also CA 162; MJW

Futabatei Shimei
See Futabatei, Shimei
See also DLB 180; EWL 3

Futrelle, Jacques 1875-1912 .... **TCLC 19**
See also CA 113; 155; CMW 4

Gaboriau, Emile 1835-1873 .... **NCLC 14**
See also CMW 4; MSW

Gadda, Carlo Emilio 1893-1973 ...... **CLC 11;
TCLC 144**
See also CA 89-92; DLB 177; EWL 3

Gaddis, William 1922-1998 ... **CLC 1, 3, 6, 8, 10, 19, 43, 86**
See also AMWS 4; BPFB 1; CA 17-20R; 172; CANR 21, 48; CN 7; DLB 2, 278; EWL 3; MTCW 1, 2; RGAL 4

Gaelique, Moruen le
See Jacob, (Cyprien-)Max

Gage, Walter
See Inge, William (Motter)

Gaiman, Neil (Richard) 1960- .... **CLC 195**
See also AAYA 19, 42; CA 133; CANR 81, 129; DLB 261; HGG; SATA 85, 146; SFW 4; SUFW 2

Gaines, Ernest J(ames) 1933- .. **BLC 2; CLC 3, 11, 18, 86, 181; SSC 68**
See also AAYA 18; AFAW 1, 2; AITN 1; BPFB 2; BW 2, 3; BYA 6; CA 9-12R; CANR 6, 24, 42, 75, 126; CDALB 1968-1988; CLR 62; CN 7; CSW; DA3; DAM MULT; DLB 2, 33, 152; DLBY 1980; EWL 3; EXPN; LAIT 5; LATS 1:2; MTCW 1, 2; NFS 5, 7, 16; RGAL 4; RGSF 2; RHW; SATA 86; SSFS 5; YAW

Gaitskill, Mary (Lawrence) 1954- .... **CLC 69**
See also CA 128; CANR 61; DLB 244

Gaius Suetonius Tranquillus
See Suetonius

Galdos, Benito Perez
See Perez Galdos, Benito
See also EW 7

Gale, Zona 1874-1938 .... **TCLC 7**
See also CA 105; 153; CANR 84; DAM DRAM; DFS 17; DLB 9, 78, 228; RGAL 4

Galeano, Eduardo (Hughes) 1940- . **CLC 72; HLCS 1**
See also CA 29-32R; CANR 13, 32, 100; HW 1

Galiano, Juan Valera y Alcala
See Valera y Alcala-Galiano, Juan

Galilei, Galileo 1564-1642 .... **LC 45**

Gallagher, Tess 1943- .... **CLC 18, 63; PC 9**
See also CA 106; CP 7; CWP; DAM POET; DLB 120, 212, 244; PFS 16

Gallant, Mavis 1922- ..... **CLC 7, 18, 38, 172; SSC 5, 78**
See also CA 69-72; CANR 29, 69, 117; CCA 1; CN 7; DAC; DAM MST; DLB 53; EWL 3; MTCW 1, 2; RGEL 2; RGSF 2

Gallant, Roy A(rthur) 1924- .... **CLC 17**
See also CA 5-8R; CANR 4, 29, 54, 117; CLR 30; MAICYA 1, 2; SATA 4, 68, 110

Gallico, Paul (William) 1897-1976 ... **CLC 2**
See also AITN 1; CA 5-8R; 69-72; CANR 23; DLB 9, 171; FANT; MAICYA 1, 2; SATA 13

Gallo, Max Louis 1932- .... **CLC 95**
See also CA 85-88

Gallois, Lucien
See Desnos, Robert

Gallup, Ralph
See Whitemore, Hugh (John)

Galsworthy, John 1867-1933 .... **SSC 22; TCLC 1, 45; WLC**
See also BRW 6; CA 104; 141; CANR 75; CDBLB 1890-1914; DA; DA3; DAB; DAC; DAM DRAM, MST, NOV; DLB 10, 34, 98, 162; DLBD 16; EWL 3; MTCW 1; RGEL 2; SSFS 3; TEA

Galt, John 1779-1839 .... **NCLC 1, 110**
See also DLB 99, 116, 159; RGEL 2; RGSF 2

Galvin, James 1951- .... **CLC 38**
See also CA 108; CANR 26

Gamboa, Federico 1864-1939 .... **TCLC 36**
See also CA 167; HW 2; LAW

Gandhi, M. K.
See Gandhi, Mohandas Karamchand

Gandhi, Mahatma
See Gandhi, Mohandas Karamchand

Gandhi, Mohandas Karamchand 1869-1948 .... **TCLC 59**
See also CA 121; 132; DA3; DAM MULT; MTCW 1, 2

Gann, Ernest Kellogg 1910-1991 ..... **CLC 23**
See also AITN 1; BPFB 2; CA 1-4R; 136; CANR 1, 83; RHW

Gao Xingjian 1940- .... **CLC 167**
See Xingjian, Gao

Garber, Eric 1943(?)-
See Holleran, Andrew
See also CANR 89

Garcia, Cristina 1958- .... **CLC 76**
See also AMWS 11; CA 141; CANR 73, 130; DLB 292; DNFS 1; EWL 3; HW 2; LLW 1

Garcia Lorca, Federico 1898-1936 ...... **DC 2; HLC 2; PC 3; TCLC 1, 7, 49; WLC**
See Lorca, Federico Garcia
See also AAYA 46; CA 104; 131; CANR 81; DA; DA3; DAB; DAC; DAM DRAM, MST, MULT, POET; DFS 4, 10; DLB 108; EWL 3; HW 1, 2; LATS 1:2; MTCW 1, 2; TWA

Garcia Marquez, Gabriel (Jose) 1928- .... **CLC 2, 3, 8, 10, 15, 27, 47, 55, 68, 170; HLC 1; SSC 8; WLC**
See also AAYA 3, 33; BEST 89:1, 90:4; BPFB 2; BYA 12, 16; CA 33-36R; CANR 10, 28, 50, 75, 82, 128; CDWLB 3; CPW; CWW 2; DA; DA3; DAB; DAC; DAM MST, MULT, NOV, POP; DLB 113; DNFS 1, 2; EWL 3; EXPN; EXPS; HW 1, 2; LAIT 2; LATS 1:2; LAW; LAWS 1; LMFS 2; MTCW 1, 2; NCFS 3; NFS 1, 5, 10; RGSF 2; RGWL 2, 3; SSFS 1, 6, 16; TWA; WLIT 1

Garcilaso de la Vega, El Inca 1503-1536 .... **HLCS 1**
See also LAW

Gard, Janice
See Latham, Jean Lee

Gard, Roger Martin du
See Martin du Gard, Roger

Gardam, Jane (Mary) 1928- .... **CLC 43**
See also CA 49-52; CANR 2, 18, 33, 54, 106; CLR 12; DLB 14, 161, 231; MAICYA 1, 2; MTCW 1; SAAS 9; SATA 39, 76, 130; SATA-Brief 28; YAW

Gardner, Herb(ert George) 1934-2003 .... **CLC 44**
See also CA 149; 220; CAD; CANR 119; CD 5; DFS 18, 20

Gardner, John (Champlin), Jr. 1933-1982 ... **CLC 2, 3, 5, 7, 8, 10, 18, 28, 34; SSC 7**
See also AAYA 45; AITN 1; AMWS 6; BPFB 2; CA 65-68; 107; CANR 33, 73; CDALBS; CPW; DA3; DAM NOV, POP; DLB 2; DLBY 1982; EWL 3; FANT; LATS 1:2; MTCW 1; NFS 3; RGAL 4; RGSF 2; SATA 40; SATA-Obit 31; SSFS 8

Gardner, John (Edmund) 1926- .... **CLC 30**
See also CA 103; CANR 15, 69, 127; CMW 4; CPW; DAM POP; MTCW 1

Gardner, Miriam
See Bradley, Marion Zimmer
See also GLL 1

Gardner, Noel
See Kuttner, Henry

Gardons, S. S.
See Snodgrass, W(illiam) D(e Witt)

Garfield, Leon 1921-1996 .... **CLC 12**
See also AAYA 8; BYA 1, 3; CA 17-20R; 152; CANR 38, 41, 78; CLR 21; DLB 161; JRDA; MAICYA 1, 2; MAICYAS 1; SATA 1, 32, 76; SATA-Obit 90; TEA; WYA; YAW

Garland, (Hannibal) Hamlin 1860-1940 .... **SSC 18; TCLC 3**
See also CA 104; DLB 12, 71, 78, 186; RGAL 4; RGSF 2; TCWW 2

Garneau, (Hector de) Saint-Denys 1912-1943 .... **TCLC 13**
See also CA 111; DLB 88

Garner, Alan 1934- .... **CLC 17**
See also AAYA 18; BYA 3, 5; CA 73-76, 178; CAAE 178; CANR 15, 64, 134; CLR 20; CPW; DAB; DAM POP; DLB 161, 261; FANT; MAICYA 1, 2; MTCW 1, 2; SATA 18, 69; SATA-Essay 108; SUFW 1, 2; YAW

Garner, Hugh 1913-1979 .... **CLC 13**
See Warwick, Jarvis
See also CA 69-72; CANR 31; CCA 1; DLB 68

Garnett, David 1892-1981 .... **CLC 3**
See also CA 5-8R; 103; CANR 17, 79; DLB 34; FANT; MTCW 2; RGEL 2; SFW 4; SUFW 1

Garos, Stephanie
See Katz, Steve

Garrett, George (Palmer) 1929- .. **CLC 3, 11, 51; SSC 30**
See also AMWS 7; BPFB 2; CA 1-4R, 202; CAAE 202; CAAS 5; CANR 1, 42, 67, 109; CN 7; CP 7; CSW; DLB 2, 5, 130, 152; DLBY 1983

Garrick, David 1717-1779 .... **LC 15**
See also DAM DRAM; DLB 84, 213; RGEL 2

Garrigue, Jean 1914-1972 .... **CLC 2, 8**
See also CA 5-8R; 37-40R; CANR 20

Garrison, Frederick
See Sinclair, Upton (Beall)

Garrison, William Lloyd 1805-1879 .... **NCLC 149**
See also CDALB 1640-1865; DLB 1, 43, 235

Garro, Elena 1920(?)-1998 .. **HLCS 1; TCLC 153**
See also CA 131; 169; CWW 2; DLB 145; EWL 3; HW 1; LAWS 1; WLIT 1

Garth, Will
See Hamilton, Edmond; Kuttner, Henry

Garvey, Marcus (Moziah, Jr.) 1887-1940 .... **BLC 2; HR 2; TCLC 41**
See also BW 1; CA 120; 124; CANR 79; DAM MULT

Gary, Romain .... **CLC 25**
See Kacew, Romain
See also DLB 83, 299

Gascar, Pierre .... **CLC 11**
See Fournier, Pierre
See also EWL 3

Gascoigne, George 1539-1577 .... **LC 108**
See also DLB 136; RGEL 2

Gascoyne, David (Emery) 1916-2001 .... **CLC 45**
See also CA 65-68; 200; CANR 10, 28, 54; CP 7; DLB 20; MTCW 1; RGEL 2

Gaskell, Elizabeth Cleghorn 1810-1865 .... **NCLC 5, 70, 97, 137; SSC 25**
See also BRW 5; CDBLB 1832-1890; DAB; DAM MST; DLB 21, 144, 159; RGEL 2; RGSF 2; TEA

Gass, William H(oward) 1924- . **CLC 1, 2, 8, 11, 15, 39, 132; SSC 12**
See also AMWS 6; CA 17-20R; CANR 30, 71, 100; CN 7; DLB 2, 227; EWL 3; MTCW 1, 2; RGAL 4

Gassendi, Pierre 1592-1655 .... **LC 54**
See also GFL Beginnings to 1789

Gasset, Jose Ortega y
See Ortega y Gasset, Jose

Gates, Henry Louis, Jr. 1950- ... **BLCS; CLC 65**
See also BW 2, 3; CA 109; CANR 25, 53, 75, 125; CSW; DA3; DAM MULT; DLB 67; EWL 3; MTCW 1; RGAL 4

Gautier, Theophile 1811-1872 .. **NCLC 1, 59; PC 18; SSC 20**
See also DAM POET; DLB 119; EW 6; GFL 1789 to the Present; RGWL 2, 3; SUFW; TWA

Gawsworth, John
See Bates, H(erbert) E(rnest)

Gay, John 1685-1732 .... **LC 49**
See also BRW 3; DAM DRAM; DLB 84, 95; RGEL 2; WLIT 3

Gay, Oliver
See Gogarty, Oliver St. John

Gay, Peter (Jack) 1923- .... **CLC 158**
See also CA 13-16R; CANR 18, 41, 77; INT CANR-18

Gaye, Marvin (Pentz, Jr.)
1939-1984 .... **CLC 26**
See also CA 195; 112

Gebler, Carlo (Ernest) 1954- .... **CLC 39**
See also CA 119; 133; CANR 96; DLB 271

Gee, Maggie (Mary) 1948- .... **CLC 57**
See also CA 130; CANR 125; CN 7; DLB 207

Gee, Maurice (Gough) 1931- .... **CLC 29**
See also AAYA 42; CA 97-100; CANR 67, 123; CLR 56; CN 7; CWRI 5; EWL 3; MAICYA 2; RGSF 2; SATA 46, 101

Geiogamah, Hanay 1945- .... **NNAL**
See also CA 153; DAM MULT; DLB 175

Gelbart, Larry (Simon) 1928- .... **CLC 21, 61**
See Gelbart, Larry
See also CA 73-76; CANR 45, 94

Gelbart, Larry 1928-
See Gelbart, Larry (Simon)
See also CAD; CD 5

Gelber, Jack 1932-2003 ...... **CLC 1, 6, 14, 79**
See also CA 1-4R; 216; CAD; CANR 2; DLB 7, 228

Gellhorn, Martha (Ellis)
1908-1998 .... **CLC 14, 60**
See also CA 77-80; 164; CANR 44; CN 7; DLBY 1982, 1998

Genet, Jean 1910-1986 .. **CLC 1, 2, 5, 10, 14, 44, 46; TCLC 128**
See also CA 13-16R; CANR 18; DA3; DAM DRAM; DFS 10; DLB 72; DLBY 1986; EW 13; EWL 3; GFL 1789 to the Present; GLL 1; LMFS 2; MTCW 1, 2; RGWL 2, 3; TWA

Gent, Peter 1942- .... **CLC 29**
See also AITN 1; CA 89-92; DLBY 1982

Gentile, Giovanni 1875-1944 .... **TCLC 96**
See also CA 119

Gentlewoman in New England, A
See Bradstreet, Anne

Gentlewoman in Those Parts, A
See Bradstreet, Anne

Geoffrey of Monmouth c.
1100-1155 .... **CMLC 44**
See also DLB 146; TEA

George, Jean
See George, Jean Craighead

George, Jean Craighead 1919- .... **CLC 35**
See also AAYA 8; BYA 2, 4; CA 5-8R; CANR 25; CLR 1; 80; DLB 52; JRDA; MAICYA 1, 2; SATA 2, 68, 124; WYA; YAW

George, Stefan (Anton) 1868-1933 . **TCLC 2, 14**
See also CA 104; 193; EW 8; EWL 3

Georges, Georges Martin
See Simenon, Georges (Jacques Christian)

Gerald of Wales c. 1146-c. 1223 ... **CMLC 60**

Gerhardi, William Alexander
See Gerhardie, William Alexander

Gerhardie, William Alexander
1895-1977 .... **CLC 5**
See also CA 25-28R; 73-76; CANR 18; DLB 36; RGEL 2

Gerson, Jean 1363-1429 .... **LC 77**
See also DLB 208

Gersonides 1288-1344 .... **CMLC 49**
See also DLB 115

Gerstler, Amy 1956- .... **CLC 70**
See also CA 146; CANR 99

Gertler, T. .... **CLC 34**
See also CA 116; 121

Gertsen, Aleksandr Ivanovich
See Herzen, Aleksandr Ivanovich

Ghalib .... **NCLC 39, 78**
See Ghalib, Asadullah Khan

Ghalib, Asadullah Khan 1797-1869
See Ghalib
See also DAM POET; RGWL 2, 3

Ghelderode, Michel de 1898-1962 ..... **CLC 6, 11; DC 15**
See also CA 85-88; CANR 40, 77; DAM DRAM; EW 11; EWL 3; TWA

Ghiselin, Brewster 1903-2001 .... **CLC 23**
See also CA 13-16R; CAAS 10; CANR 13; CP 7

Ghose, Aurabinda 1872-1950 .... **TCLC 63**
See Ghose, Aurobindo
See also CA 163

Ghose, Aurobindo
See Ghose, Aurabinda
See also EWL 3

Ghose, Zulfikar 1935- .... **CLC 42**
See also CA 65-68; CANR 67; CN 7; CP 7; EWL 3

Ghosh, Amitav 1956- .... **CLC 44, 153**
See also CA 147; CANR 80; CN 7; WWE 1

Giacosa, Giuseppe 1847-1906 .... **TCLC 7**
See also CA 104

Gibb, Lee
See Waterhouse, Keith (Spencer)

Gibbon, Edward 1737-1794 .... **LC 97**
See also BRW 3; DLB 104; RGEL 2

Gibbon, Lewis Grassic .... **TCLC 4**
See Mitchell, James Leslie
See also RGEL 2

Gibbons, Kaye 1960- .... **CLC 50, 88, 145**
See also AAYA 34; AMWS 10; CA 151; CANR 75, 127; CSW; DA3; DAM POP; DLB 292; MTCW 1; NFS 3; RGAL 4; SATA 117

Gibran, Kahlil 1883-1931 . **PC 9; TCLC 1, 9**
See also CA 104; 150; DA3; DAM POET, POP; EWL 3; MTCW 2

Gibran, Khalil
See Gibran, Kahlil

Gibson, William 1914- .... **CLC 23**
See also CA 9-12R; CAD 2; CANR 9, 42, 75, 125; CD 5; DA; DAB; DAC; DAM DRAM, MST; DFS 2; DLB 7; LAIT 2; MTCW 2; SATA 66; YAW

Gibson, William (Ford) 1948- ... **CLC 39, 63, 186, 192; SSC 52**
See also AAYA 12, 59; BPFB 2; CA 126; 133; CANR 52, 90, 106; CN 7; CPW; DA3; DAM POP; DLB 251; MTCW 2; SCFW 2; SFW 4

Gide, Andre (Paul Guillaume)
1869-1951 ..... **SSC 13; TCLC 5, 12, 36; WLC**
See also CA 104; 124; DA; DA3; DAB; DAC; DAM MST, NOV; DLB 65; EW 8; EWL 3; GFL 1789 to the Present; MTCW 1, 2; RGSF 2; RGWL 2, 3; TWA

Gifford, Barry (Colby) 1946- .... **CLC 34**
See also CA 65-68; CANR 9, 30, 40, 90

Gilbert, Frank
See De Voto, Bernard (Augustine)

Gilbert, W(illiam) S(chwenck)
1836-1911 .... **TCLC 3**
See also CA 104; 173; DAM DRAM, POET; RGEL 2; SATA 36

Gilbreth, Frank B(unker), Jr.
1911-2001 .... **CLC 17**
See also CA 9-12R; SATA 2

Gilchrist, Ellen (Louise) 1935- .. **CLC 34, 48, 143; SSC 14, 63**
See also BPFB 2; CA 113; 116; CANR 41, 61, 104; CN 7; CPW; CSW; DAM POP; DLB 130; EWL 3; EXPS; MTCW 1, 2; RGAL 4; RGSF 2; SSFS 9

Giles, Molly 1942- .... **CLC 39**
See also CA 126; CANR 98

Gill, Eric 1882-1940 .... **TCLC 85**
See Gill, (Arthur) Eric (Rowton Peter Joseph)

Gill, (Arthur) Eric (Rowton Peter Joseph)
1882-1940
See Gill, Eric
See also CA 120; DLB 98

Gill, Patrick
See Creasey, John

Gillette, Douglas .... **CLC 70**

Gilliam, Terry (Vance) 1940- .... **CLC 21, 141**
See Monty Python
See also AAYA 19, 59; CA 108; 113; CANR 35; INT CA-113

Gillian, Jerry
See Gilliam, Terry (Vance)

Gilliatt, Penelope (Ann Douglass)
1932-1993 .... **CLC 2, 10, 13, 53**
See also AITN 2; CA 13-16R; 141; CANR 49; DLB 14

Gilman, Charlotte (Anna) Perkins (Stetson)
1860-1935 ...... **SSC 13, 62; TCLC 9, 37, 117**
See also AMWS 11; BYA 11; CA 106; 150; DLB 221; EXPS; FW; HGG; LAIT 2; MAWW; MTCW 1; RGAL 4; RGSF 2; SFW 4; SSFS 1, 18

Gilmour, David 1946- .... **CLC 35**

Gilpin, William 1724-1804 .... **NCLC 30**

Gilray, J. D.
See Mencken, H(enry) L(ouis)

Gilroy, Frank D(aniel) 1925- .... **CLC 2**
See also CA 81-84; CAD; CANR 32, 64, 86; CD 5; DFS 17; DLB 7

Gilstrap, John 1957(?)- .... **CLC 99**
See also CA 160; CANR 101

Ginsberg, Allen 1926-1997 .... **CLC 1, 2, 3, 4, 6, 13, 36, 69, 109; PC 4, 47; TCLC 120; WLC**
See also AAYA 33; AITN 1; AMWC 1; AMWS 2; BG 2; CA 1-4R; 157; CANR 2, 41, 63, 95; CDALB 1941-1968; CP 7; DA; DA3; DAB; DAC; DAM MST, POET; DLB 5, 16, 169, 237; EWL 3; GLL 1; LMFS 2; MTCW 1, 2; PAB; PFS 5; RGAL 4; TUS; WP

Ginzburg, Eugenia .... **CLC 59**
See Ginzburg, Evgeniia

Ginzburg, Evgeniia 1904-1977
See Ginzburg, Eugenia
See also DLB 302

Ginzburg, Natalia 1916-1991 .... **CLC 5, 11, 54, 70; SSC 65; TCLC 156**
See also CA 85-88; 135; CANR 33; DFS 14; DLB 177; EW 13; EWL 3; MTCW 1, 2; RGWL 2, 3

Giono, Jean 1895-1970 .... **CLC 4, 11; TCLC 124**
  See also CA 45-48; 29-32R; CANR 2, 35; DLB 72; EWL 3; GFL 1789 to the Present; MTCW 1; RGWL 2, 3

Giovanni, Nikki 1943- ...... **BLC 2; CLC 2, 4, 19, 64, 117; PC 19; WLCS**
  See also AAYA 22; AITN 1; BW 2, 3; CA 29-32R; CAAS 6; CANR 18, 41, 60, 91, 130; CDALBS; CLR 6, 73; CP 7; CSW; CWP; CWRI 5; DA; DA3; DAB; DAC; DAM MST, MULT, POET; DLB 5, 41; EWL 3; EXPP; INT CANR-18; MAICYA 1, 2; MTCW 1, 2; PFS 17; RGAL 4; SATA 24, 107; TUS; YAW

Giovene, Andrea 1904-1998 .... **CLC 7**
  See also CA 85-88

Gippius, Zinaida (Nikolaevna) 1869-1945
  See Hippius, Zinaida (Nikolaevna)
  See also CA 106; 212

Giraudoux, Jean(-Hippolyte)
  1882-1944 .... **TCLC 2, 7**
  See also CA 104; 196; DAM DRAM; DLB 65; EW 9; EWL 3; GFL 1789 to the Present; RGWL 2, 3; TWA

Gironella, Jose Maria (Pous)
  1917-2003 .... **CLC 11**
  See also CA 101; 212; EWL 3; RGWL 2, 3

Gissing, George (Robert)
  1857-1903 .... **SSC 37; TCLC 3, 24, 47**
  See also BRW 5; CA 105; 167; DLB 18, 135, 184; RGEL 2; TEA

Giurlani, Aldo
  See Palazzeschi, Aldo

Gladkov, Fedor Vasil'evich
  See Gladkov, Fyodor (Vasilyevich)
  See also DLB 272

Gladkov, Fyodor (Vasilyevich)
  1883-1958 .... **TCLC 27**
  See Gladkov, Fedor Vasil'evich
  See also CA 170; EWL 3

Glancy, Diane 1941- .... **NNAL**
  See also CA 136, 225; CAAE 225; CAAS 24; CANR 87; DLB 175

Glanville, Brian (Lester) 1931- .... **CLC 6**
  See also CA 5-8R; CAAS 9; CANR 3, 70; CN 7; DLB 15, 139; SATA 42

Glasgow, Ellen (Anderson Gholson)
  1873-1945 .... **SSC 34; TCLC 2, 7**
  See also AMW; CA 104; 164; DLB 9, 12; MAWW; MTCW 2; RGAL 4; RHW; SSFS 9; TUS

Glaspell, Susan 1882(?)-1948 ..... **DC 10; SSC 41; TCLC 55**
  See also AMWS 3; CA 110; 154; DFS 8, 18; DLB 7, 9, 78, 228; MAWW; RGAL 4; SSFS 3; TCWW 2; TUS; YABC 2

Glassco, John 1909-1981 .... **CLC 9**
  See also CA 13-16R; 102; CANR 15; DLB 68

Glasscock, Amnesia
  See Steinbeck, John (Ernst)

Glasser, Ronald J. 1940(?)- .... **CLC 37**
  See also CA 209

Glassman, Joyce
  See Johnson, Joyce

Gleick, James (W.) 1954- .... **CLC 147**
  See also CA 131; 137; CANR 97; INT CA-137

Glendinning, Victoria 1937- .... **CLC 50**
  See also CA 120; 127; CANR 59, 89; DLB 155

Glissant, Edouard (Mathieu)
  1928- .... **CLC 10, 68**
  See also CA 153; CANR 111; CWW 2; DAM MULT; EWL 3; RGWL 3

Gloag, Julian 1930- .... **CLC 40**
  See also AITN 1; CA 65-68; CANR 10, 70; CN 7

Glowacki, Aleksander
  See Prus, Boleslaw

Gluck, Louise (Elisabeth) 1943- .. **CLC 7, 22, 44, 81, 160; PC 16**
  See also AMWS 5; CA 33-36R; CANR 40, 69, 108, 133; CP 7; CWP; DA3; DAM POET; DLB 5; MTCW 2; PFS 5, 15; RGAL 4

Glyn, Elinor 1864-1943 .... **TCLC 72**
  See also DLB 153; RHW

Gobineau, Joseph-Arthur
  1816-1882 .... **NCLC 17**
  See also DLB 123; GFL 1789 to the Present

Godard, Jean-Luc 1930- .... **CLC 20**
  See also CA 93-96

Godden, (Margaret) Rumer
  1907-1998 .... **CLC 53**
  See also AAYA 6; BPFB 2; BYA 2, 5; CA 5-8R; 172; CANR 4, 27, 36, 55, 80; CLR 20; CN 7; CWRI 5; DLB 161; MAICYA 1, 2; RHW; SAAS 12; SATA 3, 36; SATA-Obit 109; TEA

Godoy Alcayaga, Lucila 1899-1957 .. **HLC 2; PC 32; TCLC 2**
  See Mistral, Gabriela
  See also BW 2; CA 104; 131; CANR 81; DAM MULT; DNFS; HW 1, 2; MTCW 1, 2

Godwin, Gail (Kathleen) 1937- ..... **CLC 5, 8, 22, 31, 69, 125**
  See also BPFB 2; CA 29-32R; CANR 15, 43, 69, 132; CN 7; CPW; CSW; DA3; DAM POP; DLB 6, 234; INT CANR-15; MTCW 1, 2

Godwin, William 1756-1836 .. **NCLC 14, 130**
  See also CDBLB 1789-1832; CMW 4; DLB 39, 104, 142, 158, 163, 262; HGG; RGEL 2

Goebbels, Josef
  See Goebbels, (Paul) Joseph

Goebbels, (Paul) Joseph
  1897-1945 .... **TCLC 68**
  See also CA 115; 148

Goebbels, Joseph Paul
  See Goebbels, (Paul) Joseph

Goethe, Johann Wolfgang von
  1749-1832 .... **DC 20; NCLC 4, 22, 34, 90; PC 5; SSC 38; WLC**
  See also CDWLB 2; DA; DA3; DAB; DAC; DAM DRAM, MST, POET; DLB 94; EW 5; LATS 1; LMFS 1:1; RGWL 2, 3; TWA

Gogarty, Oliver St. John
  1878-1957 .... **TCLC 15**
  See also CA 109; 150; DLB 15, 19; RGEL 2

Gogol, Nikolai (Vasilyevich)
  1809-1852 .... **DC 1; NCLC 5, 15, 31; SSC 4, 29, 52; WLC**
  See also DA; DAB; DAC; DAM DRAM, MST; DFS 12; DLB 198; EW 6; EXPS; RGSF 2; RGWL 2, 3; SSFS 7; TWA

Goines, Donald 1937(?)-1974 ... **BLC 2; CLC 80**
  See also AITN 1; BW 1, 3; CA 124; 114; CANR 82; CMW 4; DA3; DAM MULT, POP; DLB 33

Gold, Herbert 1924- ... **CLC 4, 7, 14, 42, 152**
  See also CA 9-12R; CANR 17, 45, 125; CN 7; DLB 2; DLBY 1981

Goldbarth, Albert 1948- .... **CLC 5, 38**
  See also AMWS 12; CA 53-56; CANR 6, 40; CP 7; DLB 120

Goldberg, Anatol 1910-1982 .... **CLC 34**
  See also CA 131; 117

Goldemberg, Isaac 1945- .... **CLC 52**
  See also CA 69-72; CAAS 12; CANR 11, 32; EWL 3; HW 1; WLIT 1

Golding, Arthur 1536-1606 .... **LC 101**
  See also DLB 136

Golding, William (Gerald)
  1911-1993 ..... **CLC 1, 2, 3, 8, 10, 17, 27, 58, 81; WLC**
  See also AAYA 5, 44; BPFB 2; BRWR 1; BRWS 1; BYA 2; CA 5-8R; 141; CANR 13, 33, 54; CDBLB 1945-1960; CLR 94; DA; DA3; DAB; DAC; DAM MST, NOV; DLB 15, 100, 255; EWL 3; EXPN; HGG; LAIT 4; MTCW 1, 2; NFS 2; RGEL 2; RHW; SFW 4; TEA; WLIT 4; YAW

Goldman, Emma 1869-1940 .... **TCLC 13**
  See also CA 110; 150; DLB 221; FW; RGAL 4; TUS

Goldman, Francisco 1954- .... **CLC 76**
  See also CA 162

Goldman, William (W.) 1931- ...... **CLC 1, 48**
  See also BPFB 2; CA 9-12R; CANR 29, 69, 106; CN 7; DLB 44; FANT; IDFW 3, 4

Goldmann, Lucien 1913-1970 .... **CLC 24**
  See also CA 25-28; CAP 2

Goldoni, Carlo 1707-1793 .... **LC 4**
  See also DAM DRAM; EW 4; RGWL 2, 3

Goldsberry, Steven 1949- .... **CLC 34**
  See also CA 131

Goldsmith, Oliver 1730-1774 .... **DC 8; LC 2, 48; WLC**
  See also BRW 3; CDBLB 1660-1789; DA; DAB; DAC; DAM DRAM, MST, NOV, POET; DFS 1; DLB 39, 89, 104, 109, 142; IDTP; RGEL 2; SATA 26; TEA; WLIT 3

Goldsmith, Peter
  See Priestley, J(ohn) B(oynton)

Gombrowicz, Witold 1904-1969 .... **CLC 4, 7, 11, 49**
  See also CA 19-20; 25-28R; CANR 105; CAP 2; CDWLB 4; DAM DRAM; DLB 215; EW 12; EWL 3; RGWL 2, 3; TWA

Gomez de Avellaneda, Gertrudis
  1814-1873 .... **NCLC 111**
  See also LAW

Gomez de la Serna, Ramon
  1888-1963 .... **CLC 9**
  See also CA 153; 116; CANR 79; EWL 3; HW 1, 2

Goncharov, Ivan Alexandrovich
  1812-1891 .... **NCLC 1, 63**
  See also DLB 238; EW 6; RGWL 2, 3

Goncourt, Edmond (Louis Antoine Huot) de
  1822-1896 .... **NCLC 7**
  See also DLB 123; EW 7; GFL 1789 to the Present; RGWL 2, 3

Goncourt, Jules (Alfred Huot) de
  1830-1870 .... **NCLC 7**
  See also DLB 123; EW 7; GFL 1789 to the Present; RGWL 2, 3

Gongora (y Argote), Luis de
  1561-1627 .... **LC 72**
  See also RGWL 2, 3

Gontier, Fernande 19(?)- .... **CLC 50**

Gonzalez Martinez, Enrique
  See Gonzalez Martinez, Enrique
  See also DLB 290

Gonzalez Martinez, Enrique
  1871-1952 .... **TCLC 72**
  See Gonzalez Martinez, Enrique
  See also CA 166; CANR 81; EWL 3; HW 1, 2

Goodison, Lorna 1947- .... **PC 36**
  See also CA 142; CANR 88; CP 7; CWP; DLB 157; EWL 3

Goodman, Paul 1911-1972 ..... **CLC 1, 2, 4, 7**
  See also CA 19-20; 37-40R; CAD; CANR 34; CAP 2; DLB 130, 246; MTCW 1; RGAL 4

GoodWeather, Harley
  See King, Thomas

Googe, Barnabe 1540-1594 .... **LC 94**
  See also DLB 132; RGEL 2

Gordimer, Nadine 1923- ...... **CLC 3, 5, 7, 10, 18, 33, 51, 70, 123, 160, 161; SSC 17; WLCS**
See also AAYA 39; AFW; BRWS 2; CA 5-8R; CANR 3, 28, 56, 88, 131; CN 7; DA; DA3; DAB; DAC; DAM MST, NOV; DLB 225; EWL 3; EXPS; INT CANR-28; LATS 1:2; MTCW 1, 2; NFS 4; RGEL 2; RGSF 2; SSFS 2, 14, 19; TWA; WLIT 2; YAW

Gordon, Adam Lindsay
1833-1870 .... **NCLC 21**
See also DLB 230

Gordon, Caroline 1895-1981 . **CLC 6, 13, 29, 83; SSC 15**
See also AMW; CA 11-12; 103; CANR 36; CAP 1; DLB 4, 9, 102; DLBD 17; DLBY 1981; EWL 3; MTCW 1, 2; RGAL 4; RGSF 2

Gordon, Charles William 1860-1937
See Connor, Ralph
See also CA 109

Gordon, Mary (Catherine) 1949- .... **CLC 13, 22, 128; SSC 59**
See also AMWS 4; BPFB 2; CA 102; CANR 44, 92; CN 7; DLB 6; DLBY 1981; FW; INT CA-102; MTCW 1

Gordon, N. J.
See Bosman, Herman Charles

Gordon, Sol 1923- .... **CLC 26**
See also CA 53-56; CANR 4; SATA 11

Gordone, Charles 1925-1995 .. **CLC 1, 4; DC 8**
See also BW 1, 3; CA 93-96; 180; 150; CAAE 180; CAD; CANR 55; DAM DRAM; DLB 7; INT CA-93-96; MTCW 1

Gore, Catherine 1800-1861 .... **NCLC 65**
See also DLB 116; RGEL 2

Gorenko, Anna Andreevna
See Akhmatova, Anna

Gorky, Maxim .... **SSC 28; TCLC 8; WLC**
See Peshkov, Alexei Maximovich
See also DAB; DFS 9; DLB 295; EW 8; EWL 3; MTCW 2; TWA

Goryan, Sirak
See Saroyan, William

Gosse, Edmund (William)
1849-1928 .... **TCLC 28**
See also CA 117; DLB 57, 144, 184; RGEL 2

Gotlieb, Phyllis (Fay Bloom) 1926- .. **CLC 18**
See also CA 13-16R; CANR 7, 135; DLB 88, 251; SFW 4

Gottesman, S. D.
See Kornbluth, C(yril) M.; Pohl, Frederik

Gottfried von Strassburg fl. c.
1170-1215 .... **CMLC 10**
See also CDWLB 2; DLB 138; EW 1; RGWL 2, 3

Gotthelf, Jeremias 1797-1854 .... **NCLC 117**
See also DLB 133; RGWL 2, 3

Gottschalk, Laura Riding
See Jackson, Laura (Riding)

Gould, Lois 1932(?)-2002 .... **CLC 4, 10**
See also CA 77-80; 208; CANR 29; MTCW 1

Gould, Stephen Jay 1941-2002 .... **CLC 163**
See also AAYA 26; BEST 90:2; CA 77-80; 205; CANR 10, 27, 56, 75, 125; CPW; INT CANR-27; MTCW 1, 2

Gourmont, Remy(-Marie-Charles) de
1858-1915 .... **TCLC 17**
See also CA 109; 150; GFL 1789 to the Present; MTCW 2

Gournay, Marie le Jars de
See de Gournay, Marie le Jars

Govier, Katherine 1948- .... **CLC 51**
See also CA 101; CANR 18, 40, 128; CCA 1

Gower, John c. 1330-1408 .... **LC 76; PC 59**
See also BRW 1; DLB 146; RGEL 2

Goyen, (Charles) William
1915-1983 .... **CLC 5, 8, 14, 40**
See also AITN 2; CA 5-8R; 110; CANR 6, 71; DLB 2, 218; DLBY 1983; EWL 3; INT CANR-6

Goytisolo, Juan 1931- .... **CLC 5, 10, 23, 133; HLC 1**
See also CA 85-88; CANR 32, 61, 131; CWW 2; DAM MULT; EWL 3; GLL 2; HW 1, 2; MTCW 1, 2

Gozzano, Guido 1883-1916 .... **PC 10**
See also CA 154; DLB 114; EWL 3

Gozzi, (Conte) Carlo 1720-1806 .... **NCLC 23**

Grabbe, Christian Dietrich
1801-1836 .... **NCLC 2**
See also DLB 133; RGWL 2, 3

Grace, Patricia Frances 1937- .... **CLC 56**
See also CA 176; CANR 118; CN 7; EWL 3; RGSF 2

Gracian y Morales, Baltasar
1601-1658 .... **LC 15**

Gracq, Julien .... **CLC 11, 48**
See Poirier, Louis
See also CWW 2; DLB 83; GFL 1789 to the Present

Grade, Chaim 1910-1982 .... **CLC 10**
See also CA 93-96; 107; EWL 3

Graduate of Oxford, A
See Ruskin, John

Grafton, Garth
See Duncan, Sara Jeannette

Grafton, Sue 1940- .... **CLC 163**
See also AAYA 11, 49; BEST 90:3; CA 108; CANR 31, 55, 111, 134; CMW 4; CPW; CSW; DA3; DAM POP; DLB 226; FW; MSW

Graham, John
See Phillips, David Graham

Graham, Jorie 1951- .... **CLC 48, 118; PC 59**
See also CA 111; CANR 63, 118; CP 7; CWP; DLB 120; EWL 3; PFS 10, 17

Graham, R(obert) B(ontine) Cunninghame
See Cunninghame Graham, Robert (Gallnigad) Bontine
See also DLB 98, 135, 174; RGEL 2; RGSF 2

Graham, Robert
See Haldeman, Joe (William)

Graham, Tom
See Lewis, (Harry) Sinclair

Graham, W(illiam) S(idney)
1918-1986 .... **CLC 29**
See also BRWS 7; CA 73-76; 118; DLB 20; RGEL 2

Graham, Winston (Mawdsley)
1910-2003 .... **CLC 23**
See also CA 49-52; 218; CANR 2, 22, 45, 66; CMW 4; CN 7; DLB 77; RHW

Grahame, Kenneth 1859-1932 ...... **TCLC 64, 136**
See also BYA 5; CA 108; 136; CANR 80; CLR 5; CWRI 5; DA3; DAB; DLB 34, 141, 178; FANT; MAICYA 1, 2; MTCW 2; NFS 20; RGEL 2; SATA 100; TEA; WCH; YABC 1

Granger, Darius John
See Marlowe, Stephen

Granin, Daniil 1918- .... **CLC 59**
See also DLB 302

Granovsky, Timofei Nikolaevich
1813-1855 .... **NCLC 75**
See also DLB 198

Grant, Skeeter
See Spiegelman, Art

Granville-Barker, Harley
1877-1946 .... **TCLC 2**
See Barker, Harley Granville
See also CA 104; 204; DAM DRAM; RGEL 2

Granzotto, Gianni
See Granzotto, Giovanni Battista

Granzotto, Giovanni Battista
1914-1985 .... **CLC 70**
See also CA 166

Grass, Guenter (Wilhelm) 1927- ... **CLC 1, 2, 4, 6, 11, 15, 22, 32, 49, 88; WLC**
See Grass, Gunter (Wilhelm)
See also BPFB 2; CA 13-16R; CANR 20, 75, 93, 133; CDWLB 2; DA; DA3; DAB; DAC; DAM MST, NOV; DLB 75, 124; EW 13; EWL 3; MTCW 1, 2; RGWL 2, 3; TWA

Grass, Gunter (Wilhelm)
See Grass, Guenter (Wilhelm)
See also CWW 2

Gratton, Thomas
See Hulme, T(homas) E(rnest)

Grau, Shirley Ann 1929- .... **CLC 4, 9, 146; SSC 15**
See also CA 89-92; CANR 22, 69; CN 7; CSW; DLB 2, 218; INT CA-89-92; CANR-22; MTCW 1

Gravel, Fern
See Hall, James Norman

Graver, Elizabeth 1964- .... **CLC 70**
See also CA 135; CANR 71, 129

Graves, Richard Perceval
1895-1985 .... **CLC 44**
See also CA 65-68; CANR 9, 26, 51

Graves, Robert (von Ranke)
1895-1985 .. **CLC 1, 2, 6, 11, 39, 44, 45; PC 6**
See also BPFB 2; BRW 7; BYA 4; CA 5-8R; 117; CANR 5, 36; CDBLB 1914-1945; DA3; DAB; DAC; DAM MST, POET; DLB 20, 100, 191; DLBD 18; DLBY 1985; EWL 3; LATS 1:1; MTCW 1, 2; NCFS 2; RGEL 2; RHW; SATA 45; TEA

Graves, Valerie
See Bradley, Marion Zimmer

Gray, Alasdair (James) 1934- .... **CLC 41**
See also BRWS 9; CA 126; CANR 47, 69, 106; CN 7; DLB 194, 261; HGG; INT CA-126; MTCW 1, 2; RGSF 2; SUFW 2

Gray, Amlin 1946- .... **CLC 29**
See also CA 138

Gray, Francine du Plessix 1930- ..... **CLC 22, 153**
See also BEST 90:3; CA 61-64; CAAS 2; CANR 11, 33, 75, 81; DAM NOV; INT CANR-11; MTCW 1, 2

Gray, John (Henry) 1866-1934 ...... **TCLC 19**
See also CA 119; 162; RGEL 2

Gray, Simon (James Holliday)
1936- .... **CLC 9, 14, 36**
See also AITN 1; CA 21-24R; CAAS 3; CANR 32, 69; CD 5; DLB 13; EWL 3; MTCW 1; RGEL 2

Gray, Spalding 1941-2004 .... **CLC 49, 112; DC 7**
See also CA 128; 225; CAD; CANR 74; CD 5; CPW; DAM POP; MTCW 2

Gray, Thomas 1716-1771 .... **LC 4, 40; PC 2; WLC**
See also BRW 3; CDBLB 1660-1789; DA; DA3; DAB; DAC; DAM MST; DLB 109; EXPP; PAB; PFS 9; RGEL 2; TEA; WP

Grayson, David
See Baker, Ray Stannard

Grayson, Richard (A.) 1951- .... **CLC 38**
See also CA 85-88; 210; CAAE 210; CANR 14, 31, 57; DLB 234

Greeley, Andrew M(oran) 1928- ...... **CLC 28**
See also BPFB 2; CA 5-8R; CAAS 7;
CANR 7, 43, 69, 104; CMW 4; CPW;
DA3; DAM POP; MTCW 1, 2

Green, Anna Katharine
1846-1935 .... **TCLC 63**
See also CA 112; 159; CMW 4; DLB 202,
221; MSW

Green, Brian
See Card, Orson Scott

Green, Hannah
See Greenberg, Joanne (Goldenberg)

Green, Hannah 1927(?)-1996 .... **CLC 3**
See also CA 73-76; CANR 59, 93; NFS 10

Green, Henry .... **CLC 2, 13, 97**
See Yorke, Henry Vincent
See also BRWS 2; CA 175; DLB 15; EWL
3; RGEL 2

Green, Julien (Hartridge) 1900-1998
See Green, Julian
See also CA 21-24R; 169; CANR 33, 87;
CWW 2; DLB 4, 72; MTCW 1

Green, Julian .... **CLC 3, 11, 77**
See Green, Julien (Hartridge)
See also EWL 3; GFL 1789 to the Present;
MTCW 2

Green, Paul (Eliot) 1894-1981 .... **CLC 25**
See also AITN 1; CA 5-8R; 103; CANR 3;
DAM DRAM; DLB 7, 9, 249; DLBY
1981; RGAL 4

Greenaway, Peter 1942- .... **CLC 159**
See also CA 127

Greenberg, Ivan 1908-1973
See Rahv, Philip
See also CA 85-88

Greenberg, Joanne (Goldenberg)
1932- .... **CLC 7, 30**
See also AAYA 12; CA 5-8R; CANR 14,
32, 69; CN 7; SATA 25; YAW

Greenberg, Richard 1959(?)- .... **CLC 57**
See also CA 138; CAD; CD 5

Greenblatt, Stephen J(ay) 1943- ...... **CLC 70**
See also CA 49-52; CANR 115

Greene, Bette 1934- .... **CLC 30**
See also AAYA 7; BYA 3; CA 53-56; CANR
4; CLR 2; CWRI 5; JRDA; LAIT 4; MAI-
CYA 1, 2; NFS 10; SAAS 16; SATA 8,
102; WYA; YAW

Greene, Gael .... **CLC 8**
See also CA 13-16R; CANR 10

Greene, Graham (Henry)
1904-1991 .... **CLC 1, 3, 6, 9, 14, 18, 27,
37, 70, 72, 125; SSC 29; WLC**
See also AITN 2; BPFB 2; BRWR 2; BRWS
1; BYA 3; CA 13-16R; 133; CANR 35,
61, 131; CBD; CDBLB 1945-1960; CMW
4; DA; DA3; DAB; DAC; DAM MST,
NOV; DLB 13, 15, 77, 100, 162, 201,
204; DLBY 1991; EWL 3; MSW; MTCW
1, 2; NFS 16; RGEL 2; SATA 20; SSFS
14; TEA; WLIT 4

Greene, Robert 1558-1592 .... **LC 41**
See also BRWS 8; DLB 62, 167; IDTP;
RGEL 2; TEA

Greer, Germaine 1939- .... **CLC 131**
See also AITN 1; CA 81-84; CANR 33, 70,
115, 133; FW; MTCW 1, 2

Greer, Richard
See Silverberg, Robert

Gregor, Arthur 1923- .... **CLC 9**
See also CA 25-28R; CAAS 10; CANR 11;
CP 7; SATA 36

Gregor, Lee
See Pohl, Frederik

Gregory, Lady Isabella Augusta (Persse)
1852-1932 .... **TCLC 1**
See also BRW 6; CA 104; 184; DLB 10;
IDTP; RGEL 2

Gregory, J. Dennis
See Williams, John A(lfred)

Grekova, I. .... **CLC 59**
See Ventsel, Elena Sergeevna
See also CWW 2

Grendon, Stephen
See Derleth, August (William)

Grenville, Kate 1950- .... **CLC 61**
See also CA 118; CANR 53, 93

Grenville, Pelham
See Wodehouse, P(elham) G(renville)

Greve, Felix Paul (Berthold Friedrich)
1879-1948
See Grove, Frederick Philip
See also CA 104; 141, 175; CANR 79;
DAC; DAM MST

Greville, Fulke 1554-1628 .... **LC 79**
See also DLB 62, 172; RGEL 2

Grey, Lady Jane 1537-1554 .... **LC 93**
See also DLB 132

Grey, Zane 1872-1939 .... **TCLC 6**
See also BPFB 2; CA 104; 132; DA3; DAM
POP; DLB 9, 212; MTCW 1, 2; RGAL 4;
TCWW 2; TUS

Griboedov, Aleksandr Sergeevich
1795(?)-1829 .... **NCLC 129**
See also DLB 205; RGWL 2, 3

Grieg, (Johan) Nordahl (Brun)
1902-1943 .... **TCLC 10**
See also CA 107; 189; EWL 3

Grieve, C(hristopher) M(urray)
1892-1978 .... **CLC 11, 19**
See MacDiarmid, Hugh; Pteleon
See also CA 5-8R; 85-88; CANR 33, 107;
DAM POET; MTCW 1; RGEL 2

Griffin, Gerald 1803-1840 .... **NCLC 7**
See also DLB 159; RGEL 2

Griffin, John Howard 1920-1980 ..... **CLC 68**
See also AITN 1; CA 1-4R; 101; CANR 2

Griffin, Peter 1942- .... **CLC 39**
See also CA 136

Griffith, D(avid Lewelyn) W(ark)
1875(?)-1948 .... **TCLC 68**
See also CA 119; 150; CANR 80

Griffith, Lawrence
See Griffith, D(avid Lewelyn) W(ark)

Griffiths, Trevor 1935- .... **CLC 13, 52**
See also CA 97-100; CANR 45; CBD; CD
5; DLB 13, 245

Griggs, Sutton (Elbert)
1872-1930 .... **TCLC 77**
See also CA 123; 186; DLB 50

Grigson, Geoffrey (Edward Harvey)
1905-1985 .... **CLC 7, 39**
See also CA 25-28R; 118; CANR 20, 33;
DLB 27; MTCW 1, 2

Grile, Dod
See Bierce, Ambrose (Gwinett)

Grillparzer, Franz 1791-1872 .... **DC 14;
NCLC 1, 102; SSC 37**
See also CDWLB 2; DLB 133; EW 5;
RGWL 2, 3; TWA

Grimble, Reverend Charles James
See Eliot, T(homas) S(tearns)

Grimke, Angelina (Emily) Weld
1880-1958 .... **HR 2**
See Weld, Angelina (Emily) Grimke
See also BW 1; CA 124; DAM POET; DLB
50, 54

Grimke, Charlotte L(ottie) Forten
1837(?)-1914
See Forten, Charlotte L.
See also BW 1; CA 117; 124; DAM MULT,
POET

Grimm, Jacob Ludwig Karl
1785-1863 .... **NCLC 3, 77; SSC 36**
See also DLB 90; MAICYA 1, 2; RGSF 2;
RGWL 2, 3; SATA 22; WCH

Grimm, Wilhelm Karl 1786-1859 .. **NCLC 3,
77; SSC 36**
See also CDWLB 2; DLB 90; MAICYA 1,
2; RGSF 2; RGWL 2, 3; SATA 22; WCH

**Grimmelshausen, Hans Jakob Christoffel
von**
See Grimmelshausen, Johann Jakob Christoffel von
See also RGWL 2, 3

**Grimmelshausen, Johann Jakob Christoffel
von** 1621-1676 .... **LC 6**
See Grimmelshausen, Hans Jakob Christof-
fel von
See also CDWLB 2; DLB 168

Grindel, Eugene 1895-1952
See Eluard, Paul
See also CA 104; 193; LMFS 2

Grisham, John 1955- .... **CLC 84**
See also AAYA 14, 47; BPFB 2; CA 138;
CANR 47, 69, 114, 133; CMW 4; CN 7;
CPW; CSW; DA3; DAM POP; MSW;
MTCW 2

Grosseteste, Robert 1175(?)-1253 . **CMLC 62**
See also DLB 115

Grossman, David 1954- .... **CLC 67**
See also CA 138; CANR 114; CWW 2;
DLB 299; EWL 3

Grossman, Vasilii Semenovich
See Grossman, Vasily (Semenovich)
See also DLB 272

Grossman, Vasily (Semenovich)
1905-1964 .... **CLC 41**
See Grossman, Vasilii Semenovich
See also CA 124; 130; MTCW 1

Grove, Frederick Philip .... **TCLC 4**
See Greve, Felix Paul (Berthold Friedrich)
See also DLB 92; RGEL 2

Grubb
See Crumb, R(obert)

Grumbach, Doris (Isaac) 1918- . **CLC 13, 22,
64**
See also CA 5-8R; CAAS 2; CANR 9, 42,
70, 127; CN 7; INT CANR-9; MTCW 2

Grundtvig, Nicolai Frederik Severin
1783-1872 .... **NCLC 1**
See also DLB 300

Grunge
See Crumb, R(obert)

Grunwald, Lisa 1959- .... **CLC 44**
See also CA 120

Gryphius, Andreas 1616-1664 .... **LC 89**
See also CDWLB 2; DLB 164; RGWL 2, 3

Guare, John 1938- .... **CLC 8, 14, 29, 67; DC
20**
See also CA 73-76; CAD; CANR 21, 69,
118; CD 5; DAM DRAM; DFS 8, 13;
DLB 7, 249; EWL 3; MTCW 1, 2; RGAL
4

Guarini, Battista 1537-1612 .... **LC 102**

Gubar, Susan (David) 1944- .... **CLC 145**
See also CA 108; CANR 45, 70; FW;
MTCW 1; RGAL 4

Gudjonsson, Halldor Kiljan 1902-1998
See Halldor Laxness
See also CA 103; 164

Guenter, Erich
See Eich, Gunter

Guest, Barbara 1920- .... **CLC 34; PC 55**
See also BG 2; CA 25-28R; CANR 11, 44,
84; CP 7; CWP; DLB 5, 193

Guest, Edgar A(lbert) 1881-1959 ... **TCLC 95**
See also CA 112; 168

Guest, Judith (Ann) 1936- .... **CLC 8, 30**
See also AAYA 7; CA 77-80; CANR 15,
75; DA3; DAM NOV, POP; EXPN; INT
CANR-15; LAIT 5; MTCW 1, 2; NFS 1

Guevara, Che .... **CLC 87; HLC 1**
See Guevara (Serna), Ernesto

Guevara (Serna), Ernesto
1928-1967 .... **CLC 87; HLC 1**
See Guevara, Che
See also CA 127; 111; CANR 56; DAM
MULT; HW 1

Guicciardini, Francesco 1483-1540 ..... **LC 49**

Guild, Nicholas M. 1944- .... **CLC 33**
See also CA 93-96

Guillemin, Jacques
See Sartre, Jean-Paul

Guillen, Jorge 1893-1984 . **CLC 11; HLCS 1;
PC 35**
See also CA 89-92; 112; DAM MULT,
POET; DLB 108; EWL 3; HW 1; RGWL
2, 3

Guillen, Nicolas (Cristobal)
1902-1989 .... **BLC 2; CLC 48, 79; HLC
1; PC 23**
See also BW 2; CA 116; 125; 129; CANR
84; DAM MST, MULT, POET; DLB 283;
EWL 3; HW 1; LAW; RGWL 2, 3; WP

Guillen y Alvarez, Jorge
See Guillen, Jorge

Guillevic, (Eugene) 1907-1997 .... **CLC 33**
See also CA 93-96; CWW 2

Guillois
See Desnos, Robert

Guillois, Valentin
See Desnos, Robert

Guimaraes Rosa, Joao 1908-1967 .... **HLCS 2**
See Rosa, Joao Guimaraes
See also CA 175; LAW; RGSF 2; RGWL 2,
3

Guiney, Louise Imogen
1861-1920 .... **TCLC 41**
See also CA 160; DLB 54; RGAL 4

Guinizelli, Guido c. 1230-1276 ...... **CMLC 49**

Guiraldes, Ricardo (Guillermo)
1886-1927 .... **TCLC 39**
See also CA 131; EWL 3; HW 1; LAW;
MTCW 1

Gumilev, Nikolai (Stepanovich)
1886-1921 .... **TCLC 60**
See Gumilyov, Nikolay Stepanovich
See also CA 165; DLB 295

Gumilyov, Nikolay Stepanovich
See Gumilev, Nikolai (Stepanovich)
See also EWL 3

Gump, P. Q.
See Card, Orson Scott

Gunesekera, Romesh 1954- .... **CLC 91**
See also BRWS 10; CA 159; CN 7; DLB
267

Gunn, Bill .... **CLC 5**
See Gunn, William Harrison
See also DLB 38

Gunn, Thom(son William)
1929-2004 . **CLC 3, 6, 18, 32, 81; PC 26**
See also BRWS 4; CA 17-20R; 227; CANR
9, 33, 116; CDBLB 1960 to Present; CP
7; DAM POET; DLB 27; INT CANR-33;
MTCW 1; PFS 9; RGEL 2

Gunn, William Harrison 1934(?)-1989
See Gunn, Bill
See also AITN 1; BW 1, 3; CA 13-16R;
128; CANR 12, 25, 76

Gunn Allen, Paula
See Allen, Paula Gunn

Gunnars, Kristjana 1948- .... **CLC 69**
See also CA 113; CCA 1; CP 7; CWP; DLB
60

Gunter, Erich
See Eich, Gunter

Gurdjieff, G(eorgei) I(vanovich)
1877(?)-1949 .... **TCLC 71**
See also CA 157

Gurganus, Allan 1947- .... **CLC 70**
See also BEST 90:1; CA 135; CANR 114;
CN 7; CPW; CSW; DAM POP; GLL 1

Gurney, A. R.
See Gurney, A(lbert) R(amsdell), Jr.
See also DLB 266

Gurney, A(lbert) R(amsdell), Jr.
1930- .... **CLC 32, 50, 54**
See Gurney, A. R.
See also AMWS 5; CA 77-80; CAD; CANR
32, 64, 121; CD 5; DAM DRAM; EWL 3

Gurney, Ivor (Bertie) 1890-1937 ... **TCLC 33**
See also BRW 6; CA 167; DLBY 2002;
PAB; RGEL 2

Gurney, Peter
See Gurney, A(lbert) R(amsdell), Jr.

Guro, Elena (Genrikhovna)
1877-1913 .... **TCLC 56**
See also DLB 295

Gustafson, James M(oody) 1925- ... **CLC 100**
See also CA 25-28R; CANR 37

Gustafson, Ralph (Barker)
1909-1995 .... **CLC 36**
See also CA 21-24R; CANR 8, 45, 84; CP
7; DLB 88; RGEL 2

Gut, Gom
See Simenon, Georges (Jacques Christian)

Guterson, David 1956- .... **CLC 91**
See also CA 132; CANR 73, 126; DLB 292;
MTCW 2; NFS 13

Guthrie, A(lfred) B(ertram), Jr.
1901-1991 .... **CLC 23**
See also CA 57-60; 134; CANR 24; DLB 6,
212; SATA 62; SATA-Obit 67

Guthrie, Isobel
See Grieve, C(hristopher) M(urray)

Guthrie, Woodrow Wilson 1912-1967
See Guthrie, Woody
See also CA 113; 93-96

Guthrie, Woody .... **CLC 35**
See Guthrie, Woodrow Wilson
See also DLB 303; LAIT 3

Gutierrez Najera, Manuel
1859-1895 .... **HLCS 2; NCLC 133**
See also DLB 290; LAW

Guy, Rosa (Cuthbert) 1925- .... **CLC 26**
See also AAYA 4, 37; BW 2; CA 17-20R;
CANR 14, 34, 83; CLR 13; DLB 33;
DNFS 1; JRDA; MAICYA 1, 2; SATA 14,
62, 122; YAW

Gwendolyn
See Bennett, (Enoch) Arnold

H. D. .... **CLC 3, 8, 14, 31, 34, 73; PC 5**
See Doolittle, Hilda

H. de V.
See Buchan, John

Haavikko, Paavo Juhani 1931- .. **CLC 18, 34**
See also CA 106; CWW 2; EWL 3

Habbema, Koos
See Heijermans, Herman

Habermas, Juergen 1929- .... **CLC 104**
See also CA 109; CANR 85; DLB 242

Habermas, Jurgen
See Habermas, Juergen

Hacker, Marilyn 1942- ...... **CLC 5, 9, 23, 72,
91; PC 47**
See also CA 77-80; CANR 68, 129; CP 7;
CWP; DAM POET; DLB 120, 282; FW;
GLL 2; PFS 19

Hadewijch of Antwerp fl. 1250- ... **CMLC 61**
See also RGWL 3

Hadrian 76-138 .... **CMLC 52**

Haeckel, Ernst Heinrich (Philipp August)
1834-1919 .... **TCLC 83**
See also CA 157

Hafiz c. 1326-1389(?) .... **CMLC 34**
See also RGWL 2, 3

Hagedorn, Jessica T(arahata)
1949- .... **CLC 185**
See also CA 139; CANR 69; CWP; RGAL
4

Haggard, H(enry) Rider
1856-1925 .... **TCLC 11**
See also BRWS 3; BYA 4, 5; CA 108; 148;
CANR 112; DLB 70, 156, 174, 178;
FANT; LMFS 1; MTCW 2; RGEL 2;
RHW; SATA 16; SCFW; SFW 4; SUFW
1; WLIT 4

Hagiosy, L.
See Larbaud, Valery (Nicolas)

Hagiwara, Sakutaro 1886-1942 .... **PC 18;
TCLC 60**
See Hagiwara Sakutaro
See also CA 154; RGWL 3

Hagiwara Sakutaro
See Hagiwara, Sakutaro
See also EWL 3

Haig, Fenil
See Ford, Ford Madox

Haig-Brown, Roderick (Langmere)
1908-1976 .... **CLC 21**
See also CA 5-8R; 69-72; CANR 4, 38, 83;
CLR 31; CWRI 5; DLB 88; MAICYA 1,
2; SATA 12

Haight, Rip
See Carpenter, John (Howard)

Hailey, Arthur 1920- .... **CLC 5**
See also AITN 2; BEST 90:3; BPFB 2; CA
1-4R; CANR 2, 36, 75; CCA 1; CN 7;
CPW; DAM NOV, POP; DLB 88; DLBY
1982; MTCW 1, 2

Hailey, Elizabeth Forsythe 1938- ..... **CLC 40**
See also CA 93-96, 188; CAAE 188; CAAS
1; CANR 15, 48; INT CANR-15

Haines, John (Meade) 1924- .... **CLC 58**
See also AMWS 12; CA 17-20R; CANR
13, 34; CSW; DLB 5, 212

Hakluyt, Richard 1552-1616 .... **LC 31**
See also DLB 136; RGEL 2

Haldeman, Joe (William) 1943- .... **CLC 61**
See Graham, Robert
See also AAYA 38; CA 53-56, 179; CAAE
179; CAAS 25; CANR 6, 70, 72, 130;
DLB 8; INT CANR-6; SCFW 2; SFW 4

Hale, Janet Campbell 1947- .... **NNAL**
See also CA 49-52; CANR 45, 75; DAM
MULT; DLB 175; MTCW 2

Hale, Sarah Josepha (Buell)
1788-1879 .... **NCLC 75**
See also DLB 1, 42, 73, 243

Halevy, Elie 1870-1937 .... **TCLC 104**

Haley, Alex(ander Murray Palmer)
1921-1992 .... **BLC 2; CLC 8, 12, 76;
TCLC 147**
See also AAYA 26; BPFB 2; BW 2, 3; CA
77-80; 136; CANR 61; CDALBS; CPW;
CSW; DA; DA3; DAB; DAC; DAM MST,
MULT, POP; DLB 38; LAIT 5; MTCW
1, 2; NFS 9

Haliburton, Thomas Chandler
1796-1865 .... **NCLC 15, 149**
See also DLB 11, 99; RGEL 2; RGSF 2

Hall, Donald (Andrew, Jr.) 1928- ...... **CLC 1,
13, 37, 59, 151**
See also CA 5-8R; CAAS 7; CANR 2, 44,
64, 106, 133; CP 7; DAM POET; DLB 5;
MTCW 1; RGAL 4; SATA 23, 97

Hall, Frederic Sauser
See Sauser-Hall, Frederic

Hall, James
See Kuttner, Henry

Hall, James Norman 1887-1951 ..... **TCLC 23**
See also CA 123; 173; LAIT 1; RHW 1;
SATA 21

Hall, Joseph 1574-1656 .... **LC 91**
See also DLB 121, 151; RGEL 2

Hall, (Marguerite) Radclyffe
1880-1943 .... **TCLC 12**
See also BRWS 6; CA 110; 150; CANR 83;
DLB 191; MTCW 2; RGEL 2; RHW

Hall, Rodney 1935- .... **CLC 51**
  See also CA 109; CANR 69; CN 7; CP 7;
  DLB 289
Hallam, Arthur Henry
  1811-1833 .... **NCLC 110**
  See also DLB 32
Halldor Laxness .... **CLC 25**
  See Gudjonsson, Halldor Kiljan
  See also DLB 293; EW 12; EWL 3; RGWL
  2, 3
Halleck, Fitz-Greene 1790-1867 .... **NCLC 47**
  See also DLB 3, 250; RGAL 4
Halliday, Michael
  See Creasey, John
Halpern, Daniel 1945- .... **CLC 14**
  See also CA 33-36R; CANR 93; CP 7
Hamburger, Michael (Peter Leopold)
  1924- .... **CLC 5, 14**
  See also CA 5-8R, 196; CAAE 196; CAAS
  4; CANR 2, 47; CP 7; DLB 27
Hamill, Pete 1935- .... **CLC 10**
  See also CA 25-28R; CANR 18, 71, 127
Hamilton, Alexander
  1755(?)-1804 .... **NCLC 49**
  See also DLB 37
Hamilton, Clive
  See Lewis, C(live) S(taples)
Hamilton, Edmond 1904-1977 .... **CLC 1**
  See also CA 1-4R; CANR 3, 84; DLB 8;
  SATA 118; SFW 4
Hamilton, Eugene (Jacob) Lee
  See Lee-Hamilton, Eugene (Jacob)
Hamilton, Franklin
  See Silverberg, Robert
Hamilton, Gail
  See Corcoran, Barbara (Asenath)
Hamilton, (Robert) Ian 1938-2001 . **CLC 191**
  See also CA 106; 203; CANR 41, 67; CP 7;
  DLB 40, 155
Hamilton, Jane 1957- .... **CLC 179**
  See also CA 147; CANR 85, 128
Hamilton, Mollie
  See Kaye, M(ary) M(argaret)
Hamilton, (Anthony Walter) Patrick
  1904-1962 .... **CLC 51**
  See also CA 176; 113; DLB 10, 191
Hamilton, Virginia (Esther)
  1936-2002 .... **CLC 26**
  See also AAYA 2, 21; BW 2, 3; BYA 1, 2,
  8; CA 25-28R; 206; CANR 20, 37, 73,
  126; CLR 1, 11, 40; DAM MULT; DLB
  33, 52; DLBY 01; INT CANR-20; JRDA;
  LAIT 5; MAICYA 1, 2; MAICYAS 1;
  MTCW 1, 2; SATA 4, 56, 79, 123; SATA-
  Obit 132; WYA; YAW
Hammett, (Samuel) Dashiell
  1894-1961 .... **CLC 3, 5, 10, 19, 47; SSC
  17**
  See also AAYA 59; AITN 1; AMWS 4;
  BPFB 2; CA 81-84; CANR 42; CDALB
  1929-1941; CMW 4; DA3; DLB 226, 280;
  DLBD 6; DLBY 1996; EWL 3; LAIT 3;
  MSW; MTCW 1, 2; RGAL 4; RGSF 2;
  TUS
Hammon, Jupiter 1720(?)-1800(?) .... **BLC 2;
  NCLC 5; PC 16**
  See also DAM MULT, POET; DLB 31, 50
Hammond, Keith
  See Kuttner, Henry
Hamner, Earl (Henry), Jr. 1923- ...... **CLC 12**
  See also AITN 2; CA 73-76; DLB 6
Hampton, Christopher (James)
  1946- .... **CLC 4**
  See also CA 25-28R; CD 5; DLB 13;
  MTCW 1
Hamsun, Knut .... **TCLC 2, 14, 49, 151**
  See Pedersen, Knut
  See also DLB 297; EW 8; EWL 3; RGWL
  2, 3

Handke, Peter 1942- .... **CLC 5, 8, 10, 15, 38,
  134; DC 17**
  See also CA 77-80; CANR 33, 75, 104, 133;
  CWW 2; DAM DRAM, NOV; DLB 85,
  124; EWL 3; MTCW 1, 2; TWA
Handy, W(illiam) C(hristopher)
  1873-1958 .... **TCLC 97**
  See also BW 3; CA 121; 167
Hanley, James 1901-1985 ..... **CLC 3, 5, 8, 13**
  See also CA 73-76; 117; CANR 36; CBD;
  DLB 191; EWL 3; MTCW 1; RGEL 2
Hannah, Barry 1942- .... **CLC 23, 38, 90**
  See also BPFB 2; CA 108; 110; CANR 43,
  68, 113; CN 7; CSW; DLB 6, 234; INT
  CA-110; MTCW 1; RGSF 2
Hannon, Ezra
  See Hunter, Evan
Hansberry, Lorraine (Vivian)
  1930-1965 ... **BLC 2; CLC 17, 62; DC 2**
  See also AAYA 25; AFAW 1, 2; AMWS 4;
  BW 1, 3; CA 109; 25-28R; CABS 3;
  CAD; CANR 58; CDALB 1941-1968;
  CWD; DA; DA3; DAB; DAC; DAM
  DRAM, MST, MULT; DFS 2; DLB 7, 38;
  EWL 3; FW; LAIT 4; MTCW 1, 2; RGAL
  4; TUS
Hansen, Joseph 1923- .... **CLC 38**
  See Brock, Rose; Colton, James
  See also BPFB 2; CA 29-32R; CAAS 17;
  CANR 16, 44, 66, 125; CMW 4; DLB
  226; GLL 1; INT CANR-16
Hansen, Martin A(lfred)
  1909-1955 .... **TCLC 32**
  See also CA 167; DLB 214; EWL 3
Hansen and Philipson eds. .... **CLC 65**
Hanson, Kenneth O(stlin) 1922- .... **CLC 13**
  See also CA 53-56; CANR 7
Hardwick, Elizabeth (Bruce) 1916- . **CLC 13**
  See also AMWS 3; CA 5-8R; CANR 3, 32,
  70, 100; CN 7; CSW; DA3; DAM NOV;
  DLB 6; MAWW; MTCW 1, 2
Hardy, Thomas 1840-1928 .... **PC 8; SSC 2,
  60; TCLC 4, 10, 18, 32, 48, 53, 72, 143,
  153; WLC**
  See also BRW 6; BRWC 1, 2; BRWR 1;
  CA 104; 123; CDBLB 1890-1914; DA;
  DA3; DAB; DAC; DAM MST, NOV,
  POET; DLB 18, 19, 135, 284; EWL 3;
  EXPN; EXPP; LAIT 2; MTCW 1, 2; NFS
  3, 11, 15, 19; PFS 3, 4, 18; RGEL 2;
  RGSF 2; TEA; WLIT 4
Hare, David 1947- .... **CLC 29, 58, 136**
  See also BRWS 4; CA 97-100; CANR 39,
  91; CBD; CD 5; DFS 4, 7, 16; DLB 13;
  MTCW 1; TEA
Harewood, John
  See Van Druten, John (William)
Harford, Henry
  See Hudson, W(illiam) H(enry)
Hargrave, Leonie
  See Disch, Thomas M(ichael)
Hariri, Al- al-Qasim ibn 'Ali Abu
  Muhammad al-Basri
  See al-Hariri, al-Qasim ibn 'Ali Abu Mu-
  hammad al-Basri
Harjo, Joy 1951- ..... **CLC 83; NNAL; PC 27**
  See also AMWS 12; CA 114; CANR 35,
  67, 91, 129; CP 7; CWP; DAM MULT;
  DLB 120, 175; EWL 3; MTCW 2; PFS
  15; RGAL 4
Harlan, Louis R(udolph) 1922- .... **CLC 34**
  See also CA 21-24R; CANR 25, 55, 80
Harling, Robert 1951(?)- .... **CLC 53**
  See also CA 147
Harmon, William (Ruth) 1938- .... **CLC 38**
  See also CA 33-36R; CANR 14, 32, 35;
  SATA 65
Harper, F. E. W.
  See Harper, Frances Ellen Watkins

Harper, Frances E. W.
  See Harper, Frances Ellen Watkins
Harper, Frances E. Watkins
  See Harper, Frances Ellen Watkins
Harper, Frances Ellen
  See Harper, Frances Ellen Watkins
Harper, Frances Ellen Watkins
  1825-1911 ..... **BLC 2; PC 21; TCLC 14**
  See also AFAW 1, 2; BW 1, 3; CA 111; 125;
  CANR 79; DAM MULT, POET; DLB 50,
  221; MAWW; RGAL 4
Harper, Michael S(teven) 1938- ... **CLC 7, 22**
  See also AFAW 2; BW 1; CA 33-36R; 224;
  CAAE 224; CANR 24, 108; CP 7; DLB
  41; RGAL 4
Harper, Mrs. F. E. W.
  See Harper, Frances Ellen Watkins
Harpur, Charles 1813-1868 .... **NCLC 114**
  See also DLB 230; RGEL 2
Harris, Christie
  See Harris, Christie (Lucy) Irwin
Harris, Christie (Lucy) Irwin
  1907-2002 .... **CLC 12**
  See also CA 5-8R; CANR 6, 83; CLR 47;
  DLB 88; JRDA; MAICYA 1, 2; SAAS 10;
  SATA 6, 74; SATA-Essay 116
Harris, Frank 1856-1931 .... **TCLC 24**
  See also CA 109; 150; CANR 80; DLB 156,
  197; RGEL 2
Harris, George Washington
  1814-1869 .... **NCLC 23**
  See also DLB 3, 11, 248; RGAL 4
Harris, Joel Chandler 1848-1908 ..... **SSC 19;
  TCLC 2**
  See also CA 104; 137; CANR 80; CLR 49;
  DLB 11, 23, 42, 78, 91; LAIT 2; MAI-
  CYA 1, 2; RGSF 2; SATA 100; WCH;
  YABC 1
Harris, John (Wyndham Parkes Lucas)
  Beynon 1903-1969
  See Wyndham, John
  See also CA 102; 89-92; CANR 84; SATA
  118; SFW 4
Harris, MacDonald .... **CLC 9**
  See Heiney, Donald (William)
Harris, Mark 1922- .... **CLC 19**
  See also CA 5-8R; CAAS 3; CANR 2, 55,
  83; CN 7; DLB 2; DLBY 1980
Harris, Norman .... **CLC 65**
Harris, (Theodore) Wilson 1921- .... **CLC 25,
  159**
  See also BRWS 5; BW 2, 3; CA 65-68;
  CAAS 16; CANR 11, 27, 69, 114; CD-
  WLB 3; CN 7; CP 7; DLB 117; EWL 3;
  MTCW 1; RGEL 2
Harrison, Barbara Grizzuti
  1934-2002 .... **CLC 144**
  See also CA 77-80; 205; CANR 15, 48; INT
  CANR-15
Harrison, Elizabeth (Allen) Cavanna
  1909-2001
  See Cavanna, Betty
  See also CA 9-12R; 200; CANR 6, 27, 85,
  104, 121; MAICYA 2; SATA 142; YAW
Harrison, Harry (Max) 1925- .... **CLC 42**
  See also CA 1-4R; CANR 5, 21, 84; DLB
  8; SATA 4; SCFW 2; SFW 4
Harrison, James (Thomas) 1937- ...... **CLC 6,
  14, 33, 66, 143; SSC 19**
  See Harrison, Jim
  See also CA 13-16R; CANR 8, 51, 79; CN
  7; CP 7; DLBY 1982; INT CANR-8
Harrison, Jim
  See Harrison, James (Thomas)
  See also AMWS 8; RGAL 4; TCWW 2;
  TUS
Harrison, Kathryn 1961- .... **CLC 70, 151**
  See also CA 144; CANR 68, 122

Harrison, Tony 1937- .... **CLC 43, 129**
See also BRWS 5; CA 65-68; CANR 44, 98; CBD; CD 5; CP 7; DLB 40, 245; MTCW 1; RGEL 2

Harriss, Will(ard Irvin) 1922- .... **CLC 34**
See also CA 111

Hart, Ellis
See Ellison, Harlan (Jay)

Hart, Josephine 1942(?)- .... **CLC 70**
See also CA 138; CANR 70; CPW; DAM POP

Hart, Moss 1904-1961 .... **CLC 66**
See also CA 109; 89-92; CANR 84; DAM DRAM; DFS 1; DLB 7, 266; RGAL 4

Harte, (Francis) Bret(t)
1836(?)-1902 ... **SSC 8, 59; TCLC 1, 25; WLC**
See also AMWS 2; CA 104; 140; CANR 80; CDALB 1865-1917; DA; DA3; DAC; DAM MST; DLB 12, 64, 74, 79, 186; EXPS; LAIT 2; RGAL 4; RGSF 2; SATA 26; SSFS 3; TUS

Hartley, L(eslie) P(oles) 1895-1972 ... **CLC 2, 22**
See also BRWS 7; CA 45-48; 37-40R; CANR 33; DLB 15, 139; EWL 3; HGG; MTCW 1, 2; RGEL 2; RGSF 2; SUFW 1

Hartman, Geoffrey H. 1929- .... **CLC 27**
See also CA 117; 125; CANR 79; DLB 67

Hartmann, Sadakichi 1869-1944 ... **TCLC 73**
See also CA 157; DLB 54

Hartmann von Aue c. 1170-c.
1210 .... **CMLC 15**
See also CDWLB 2; DLB 138; RGWL 2, 3

Hartog, Jan de
See de Hartog, Jan

Haruf, Kent 1943- .... **CLC 34**
See also AAYA 44; CA 149; CANR 91, 131

Harvey, Caroline
See Trollope, Joanna

Harvey, Gabriel 1550(?)-1631 .... **LC 88**
See also DLB 167, 213, 281

Harwood, Ronald 1934- .... **CLC 32**
See also CA 1-4R; CANR 4, 55; CBD; CD 5; DAM DRAM, MST; DLB 13

Hasegawa Tatsunosuke
See Futabatei, Shimei

Hasek, Jaroslav (Matej Frantisek)
1883-1923 .... **SSC 69; TCLC 4**
See also CA 104; 129; CDWLB 4; DLB 215; EW 9; EWL 3; MTCW 1, 2; RGSF 2; RGWL 2, 3

Hass, Robert 1941- ... **CLC 18, 39, 99; PC 16**
See also AMWS 6; CA 111; CANR 30, 50, 71; CP 7; DLB 105, 206; EWL 3; RGAL 4; SATA 94

Hastings, Hudson
See Kuttner, Henry

Hastings, Selina .... **CLC 44**

Hathorne, John 1641-1717 .... **LC 38**

Hatteras, Amelia
See Mencken, H(enry) L(ouis)

Hatteras, Owen .... **TCLC 18**
See Mencken, H(enry) L(ouis); Nathan, George Jean

Hauptmann, Gerhart (Johann Robert)
1862-1946 .... **SSC 37; TCLC 4**
See also CA 104; 153; CDWLB 2; DAM DRAM; DLB 66, 118; EW 8; EWL 3; RGSF 2; RGWL 2, 3; TWA

Havel, Vaclav 1936- ..... **CLC 25, 58, 65, 123; DC 6**
See also CA 104; CANR 36, 63, 124; CD-WLB 4; CWW 2; DA3; DAM DRAM; DFS 10; DLB 232; EWL 3; LMFS 2; MTCW 1, 2; RGWL 3

Haviaras, Stratis .... **CLC 33**
See Chaviaras, Strates

Hawes, Stephen 1475(?)-1529(?) .... **LC 17**
See also DLB 132; RGEL 2

Hawkes, John (Clendennin Burne, Jr.)
1925-1998 .. **CLC 1, 2, 3, 4, 7, 9, 14, 15, 27, 49**
See also BPFB 2; CA 1-4R; 167; CANR 2, 47, 64; CN 7; DLB 2, 7, 227; DLBY 1980, 1998; EWL 3; MTCW 1, 2; RGAL 4

Hawking, S. W.
See Hawking, Stephen W(illiam)

Hawking, Stephen W(illiam) 1942- . **CLC 63, 105**
See also AAYA 13; BEST 89:1; CA 126; 129; CANR 48, 115; CPW; DA3; MTCW 2

Hawkins, Anthony Hope
See Hope, Anthony

Hawthorne, Julian 1846-1934 .... **TCLC 25**
See also CA 165; HGG

Hawthorne, Nathaniel 1804-1864 ... **NCLC 2, 10, 17, 23, 39, 79, 95; SSC 3, 29, 39; WLC**
See also AAYA 18; AMW; AMWC 1; AMWR 1; BPFB 2; BYA 3; CDALB 1640-1865; DA; DA3; DAB; DAC; DAM MST, NOV; DLB 1, 74, 183, 223, 269; EXPN; EXPS; HGG; LAIT 1; NFS 1, 20; RGAL 4; RGSF 2; SSFS 1, 7, 11, 15; SUFW 1; TUS; WCH; YABC 2

Haxton, Josephine Ayres 1921-
See Douglas, Ellen
See also CA 115; CANR 41, 83

Hayaseca y Eizaguirre, Jorge
See Echegaray (y Eizaguirre), Jose (Maria Waldo)

Hayashi, Fumiko 1904-1951 .... **TCLC 27**
See Hayashi Fumiko
See also CA 161

Hayashi Fumiko
See Hayashi, Fumiko
See also DLB 180; EWL 3

Haycraft, Anna (Margaret) 1932-
See Ellis, Alice Thomas
See also CA 122; CANR 85, 90; MTCW 2

Hayden, Robert E(arl) 1913-1980 ..... **BLC 2; CLC 5, 9, 14, 37; PC 6**
See also AFAW 2; AMWS 2; BW 1, 3; CA 69-72; 97-100; CABS 2; CANR 24, 75, 82; CDALB 1941-1968; DA; DAC; DAM MST, MULT, POET; DLB 5, 76; EWL 3; EXPP; MTCW 1, 2; PFS 1; RGAL 4; SATA 19; SATA-Obit 26; WP

Haydon, Benjamin Robert
1786-1846 .... **NCLC 146**
See also DLB 110

Hayek, F(riedrich) A(ugust von)
1899-1992 .... **TCLC 109**
See also CA 93-96; 137; CANR 20; MTCW 1, 2

Hayford, J(oseph) E(phraim) Casely
See Casely-Hayford, J(oseph) E(phraim)

Hayman, Ronald 1932- .... **CLC 44**
See also CA 25-28R; CANR 18, 50, 88; CD 5; DLB 155

Hayne, Paul Hamilton 1830-1886 . **NCLC 94**
See also DLB 3, 64, 79, 248; RGAL 4

Hays, Mary 1760-1843 .... **NCLC 114**
See also DLB 142, 158; RGEL 2

Haywood, Eliza (Fowler)
1693(?)-1756 .... **LC 1, 44**
See also DLB 39; RGEL 2

Hazlitt, William 1778-1830 ...... **NCLC 29, 82**
See also BRW 4; DLB 110, 158; RGEL 2; TEA

Hazzard, Shirley 1931- .... **CLC 18**
See also CA 9-12R; CANR 4, 70, 127; CN 7; DLB 289; DLBY 1982; MTCW 1

Head, Bessie 1937-1986 ...... **BLC 2; CLC 25, 67; SSC 52**
See also AFW; BW 2, 3; CA 29-32R; 119; CANR 25, 82; CDWLB 3; DA3; DAM MULT; DLB 117, 225; EWL 3; EXPS; FW; MTCW 1, 2; RGSF 2; SSFS 5, 13; WLIT 2; WWE 1

Headon, (Nicky) Topper 1956(?)- ..... **CLC 30**

Heaney, Seamus (Justin) 1939- ..... **CLC 5, 7, 14, 25, 37, 74, 91, 171; PC 18; WLCS**
See also BRWR 1; BRWS 2; CA 85-88; CANR 25, 48, 75, 91, 128; CDBLB 1960 to Present; CP 7; DA3; DAB; DAM POET; DLB 40; DLBY 1995; EWL 3; EXPP; MTCW 1, 2; PAB; PFS 2, 5, 8, 17; RGEL 2; TEA; WLIT 4

Hearn, (Patricio) Lafcadio (Tessima Carlos)
1850-1904 .... **TCLC 9**
See also CA 105; 166; DLB 12, 78, 189; HGG; RGAL 4

Hearne, Samuel 1745-1792 .... **LC 95**
See also DLB 99

Hearne, Vicki 1946-2001 .... **CLC 56**
See also CA 139; 201

Hearon, Shelby 1931- .... **CLC 63**
See also AITN 2; AMWS 8; CA 25-28R; CANR 18, 48, 103; CSW

Heat-Moon, William Least .... **CLC 29**
See Trogdon, William (Lewis)
See also AAYA 9

Hebbel, Friedrich 1813-1863 . **DC 21; NCLC 43**
See also CDWLB 2; DAM DRAM; DLB 129; EW 6; RGWL 2, 3

Hebert, Anne 1916-2000 .... **CLC 4, 13, 29**
See also CA 85-88; 187; CANR 69, 126; CCA 1; CWP; CWW 2; DA3; DAC; DAM MST, POET; DLB 68; EWL 3; GFL 1789 to the Present; MTCW 1, 2; PFS 20

Hecht, Anthony (Evan) 1923-2004 .... **CLC 8, 13, 19**
See also AMWS 10; CA 9-12R; CANR 6, 108; CP 7; DAM POET; DLB 5, 169; EWL 3; PFS 6; WP

Hecht, Ben 1894-1964 ..... **CLC 8; TCLC 101**
See also CA 85-88; DFS 9; DLB 7, 9, 25, 26, 28, 86; FANT; IDFW 3, 4; RGAL 4

Hedayat, Sadeq 1903-1951 .... **TCLC 21**
See also CA 120; EWL 3; RGSF 2

Hegel, Georg Wilhelm Friedrich
1770-1831 .... **NCLC 46**
See also DLB 90; TWA

Heidegger, Martin 1889-1976 .... **CLC 24**
See also CA 81-84; 65-68; CANR 34; DLB 296; MTCW 1, 2

Heidenstam, (Carl Gustaf) Verner von
1859-1940 .... **TCLC 5**
See also CA 104

Heidi Louise
See Erdrich, Louise

Heifner, Jack 1946- .... **CLC 11**
See also CA 105; CANR 47

Heijermans, Herman 1864-1924 .... **TCLC 24**
See also CA 123; EWL 3

Heilbrun, Carolyn G(old)
1926-2003 .... **CLC 25, 173**
See Cross, Amanda
See also CA 45-48; 220; CANR 1, 28, 58, 94; FW

Hein, Christoph 1944- .... **CLC 154**
See also CA 158; CANR 108; CDWLB 2; CWW 2; DLB 124

Heine, Heinrich 1797-1856 .... **NCLC 4, 54, 147; PC 25**
See also CDWLB 2; DLB 90; EW 5; RGWL 2, 3; TWA

Heinemann, Larry (Curtiss) 1944- .. **CLC 50**
See also CA 110; CAAS 21; CANR 31, 81; DLBD 9; INT CANR-31

Heiney, Donald (William) 1921-1993
See Harris, MacDonald
See also CA 1-4R; 142; CANR 3, 58; FANT

Heinlein, Robert A(nson) 1907-1988 . **CLC 1, 3, 8, 14, 26, 55; SSC 55**
See also AAYA 17; BPFB 2; BYA 4, 13; CA 1-4R; 125; CANR 1, 20, 53; CLR 75; CPW; DA3; DAM POP; DLB 8; EXPS; JRDA; LAIT 5; LMFS 2; MAICYA 1, 2; MTCW 1, 2; RGAL 4; SATA 9, 69; SATA-Obit 56; SCFW; SFW 4; SSFS 7; YAW

Helforth, John
See Doolittle, Hilda

Heliodorus fl. 3rd cent. - .... **CMLC 52**

Hellenhofferu, Vojtech Kapristian z
See Hasek, Jaroslav (Matej Frantisek)

Heller, Joseph 1923-1999 . **CLC 1, 3, 5, 8, 11, 36, 63; TCLC 131, 151; WLC**
See also AAYA 24; AITN 1; AMWS 4; BPFB 2; BYA 1; CA 5-8R; 187; CABS 1; CANR 8, 42, 66, 126; CN 7; CPW; DA; DA3; DAB; DAC; DAM MST, NOV, POP; DLB 2, 28, 227; DLBY 1980, 2002; EWL 3; EXPN; INT CANR-8; LAIT 4; MTCW 1, 2; NFS 1; RGAL 4; TUS; YAW

Hellman, Lillian (Florence)
1906-1984 .. **CLC 2, 4, 8, 14, 18, 34, 44, 52; DC 1; TCLC 119**
See also AAYA 47; AITN 1, 2; AMWS 1; CA 13-16R; 112; CAD; CANR 33; CWD; DA3; DAM DRAM; DFS 1, 3, 14; DLB 7, 228; DLBY 1984; EWL 3; FW; LAIT 3; MAWW; MTCW 1, 2; RGAL 4; TUS

Helprin, Mark 1947- .... **CLC 7, 10, 22, 32**
See also CA 81-84; CANR 47, 64, 124; CDALBS; CPW; DA3; DAM NOV, POP; DLBY 1985; FANT; MTCW 1, 2; SUFW 2

Helvetius, Claude-Adrien 1715-1771 .. **LC 26**

Helyar, Jane Penelope Josephine 1933-
See Poole, Josephine
See also CA 21-24R; CANR 10, 26; CWRI 5; SATA 82, 138; SATA-Essay 138

Hemans, Felicia 1793-1835 ...... **NCLC 29, 71**
See also DLB 96; RGEL 2

Hemingway, Ernest (Miller)
1899-1961 .... **CLC 1, 3, 6, 8, 10, 13, 19, 30, 34, 39, 41, 44, 50, 61, 80; SSC 1, 25, 36, 40, 63; TCLC 115; WLC**
See also AAYA 19; AMW; AMWC 1; AMWR 1; BPFB 2; BYA 2, 3, 13, 15; CA 77-80; CANR 34; CDALB 1917-1929; DA; DA3; DAB; DAC; DAM MST, NOV; DLB 4, 9, 102, 210, 308; DLBD 1, 15, 16; DLBY 1981, 1987, 1996, 1998; EWL 3; EXPN; EXPS; LAIT 3, 4; LATS 1:1; MTCW 1, 2; NFS 1, 5, 6, 14; RGAL 4; RGSF 2; SSFS 17; TUS; WYA

Hempel, Amy 1951- .... **CLC 39**
See also CA 118; 137; CANR 70; DA3; DLB 218; EXPS; MTCW 2; SSFS 2

Henderson, F. C.
See Mencken, H(enry) L(ouis)

Henderson, Sylvia
See Ashton-Warner, Sylvia (Constance)

Henderson, Zenna (Chlarson)
1917-1983 .... **SSC 29**
See also CA 1-4R; 133; CANR 1, 84; DLB 8; SATA 5; SFW 4

Henkin, Joshua .... **CLC 119**
See also CA 161

Henley, Beth .... **CLC 23; DC 6, 14**
See Henley, Elizabeth Becker
See also CABS 3; CAD; CD 5; CSW; CWD; DFS 2; DLBY 1986; FW

Henley, Elizabeth Becker 1952-
See Henley, Beth
See also CA 107; CANR 32, 73; DA3; DAM DRAM, MST; MTCW 1, 2

Henley, William Ernest 1849-1903 .. **TCLC 8**
See also CA 105; DLB 19; RGEL 2

Hennissart, Martha 1929-
See Lathen, Emma
See also CA 85-88; CANR 64

Henry VIII 1491-1547 .... **LC 10**
See also DLB 132

Henry, O. ..... **SSC 5, 49; TCLC 1, 19; WLC**
See Porter, William Sydney
See also AAYA 41; AMWS 2; EXPS; RGAL 4; RGSF 2; SSFS 2, 18

Henry, Patrick 1736-1799 .... **LC 25**
See also LAIT 1

Henryson, Robert 1430(?)-1506(?) ..... **LC 20, 110**
See also BRWS 7; DLB 146; RGEL 2

Henschke, Alfred
See Klabund

Henson, Lance 1944- .... **NNAL**
See also CA 146; DLB 175

Hentoff, Nat(han Irving) 1925- .... **CLC 26**
See also AAYA 4, 42; BYA 6; CA 1-4R; CAAS 6; CANR 5, 25, 77, 114; CLR 1, 52; INT CANR-25; JRDA; MAICYA 1, 2; SATA 42, 69, 133; SATA-Brief 27; WYA; YAW

Heppenstall, (John) Rayner
1911-1981 .... **CLC 10**
See also CA 1-4R; 103; CANR 29; EWL 3

Heraclitus c. 540B.C.-c. 450B.C. ... **CMLC 22**
See also DLB 176

Herbert, Frank (Patrick)
1920-1986 .... **CLC 12, 23, 35, 44, 85**
See also AAYA 21; BPFB 2; BYA 4, 14; CA 53-56; 118; CANR 5, 43; CDALBS; CPW; DAM POP; DLB 8; INT CANR-5; LAIT 5; MTCW 1, 2; NFS 17; SATA 9, 37; SATA-Obit 47; SCFW 2; SFW 4; YAW

Herbert, George 1593-1633 ...... **LC 24; PC 4**
See also BRW 2; BRWR 2; CDBLB Before 1660; DAB; DAM POET; DLB 126; EXPP; RGEL 2; TEA; WP

Herbert, Zbigniew 1924-1998 ..... **CLC 9, 43; PC 50**
See also CA 89-92; 169; CANR 36, 74; CDWLB 4; CWW 2; DAM POET; DLB 232; EWL 3; MTCW 1

Herbst, Josephine (Frey)
1897-1969 .... **CLC 34**
See also CA 5-8R; 25-28R; DLB 9

Herder, Johann Gottfried von
1744-1803 .... **NCLC 8**
See also DLB 97; EW 4; TWA

Heredia, Jose Maria 1803-1839 .... **HLCS 2**
See also LAW

Hergesheimer, Joseph 1880-1954 ... **TCLC 11**
See also CA 109; 194; DLB 102, 9; RGAL 4

Herlihy, James Leo 1927-1993 .... **CLC 6**
See also CA 1-4R; 143; CAD; CANR 2

Herman, William
See Bierce, Ambrose (Gwinett)

Hermogenes fl. c. 175- .... **CMLC 6**

Hernandez, Jose 1834-1886 .... **NCLC 17**
See also LAW; RGWL 2, 3; WLIT 1

Herodotus c. 484B.C.-c. 420B.C. .. **CMLC 17**
See also AW 1; CDWLB 1; DLB 176; RGWL 2, 3; TWA

Herrick, Robert 1591-1674 .... **LC 13; PC 9**
See also BRW 2; BRWC 2; DA; DAB; DAC; DAM MST, POP; DLB 126; EXPP; PFS 13; RGAL 4; RGEL 2; TEA; WP

Herring, Guilles
See Somerville, Edith Oenone

Herriot, James 1916-1995 .... **CLC 12**
See Wight, James Alfred
See also AAYA 1, 54; BPFB 2; CA 148; CANR 40; CLR 80; CPW; DAM POP; LAIT 3; MAICYA 2; MAICYAS 1; MTCW 2; SATA 86, 135; TEA; YAW

Herris, Violet
See Hunt, Violet

Herrmann, Dorothy 1941- .... **CLC 44**
See also CA 107

Herrmann, Taffy
See Herrmann, Dorothy

Hersey, John (Richard) 1914-1993 .... **CLC 1, 2, 7, 9, 40, 81, 97**
See also AAYA 29; BPFB 2; CA 17-20R; 140; CANR 33; CDALBS; CPW; DAM POP; DLB 6, 185, 278, 299; MTCW 1, 2; SATA 25; SATA-Obit 76; TUS

Herzen, Aleksandr Ivanovich
1812-1870 .... **NCLC 10, 61**
See Herzen, Alexander

Herzen, Alexander
See Herzen, Aleksandr Ivanovich
See also DLB 277

Herzl, Theodor 1860-1904 .... **TCLC 36**
See also CA 168

Herzog, Werner 1942- .... **CLC 16**
See also CA 89-92

Hesiod c. 8th cent. B.C.- .... **CMLC 5**
See also AW 1; DLB 176; RGWL 2, 3

Hesse, Hermann 1877-1962 ... **CLC 1, 2, 3, 6, 11, 17, 25, 69; SSC 9, 49; TCLC 148; WLC**
See also AAYA 43; BPFB 2; CA 17-18; CAP 2; CDWLB 2; DA; DA3; DAB; DAC; DAM MST, NOV; DLB 66; EW 9; EWL 3; EXPN; LAIT 1; MTCW 1, 2; NFS 6, 15; RGWL 2, 3; SATA 50; TWA

Hewes, Cady
See De Voto, Bernard (Augustine)

Heyen, William 1940- .... **CLC 13, 18**
See also CA 33-36R; 220; CAAE 220; CAAS 9; CANR 98; CP 7; DLB 5

Heyerdahl, Thor 1914-2002 .... **CLC 26**
See also CA 5-8R; 207; CANR 5, 22, 66, 73; LAIT 4; MTCW 1, 2; SATA 2, 52

Heym, Georg (Theodor Franz Arthur)
1887-1912 .... **TCLC 9**
See also CA 106; 181

Heym, Stefan 1913-2001 .... **CLC 41**
See also CA 9-12R; 203; CANR 4; CWW 2; DLB 69; EWL 3

Heyse, Paul (Johann Ludwig von)
1830-1914 .... **TCLC 8**
See also CA 104; 209; DLB 129

Heyward, (Edwin) DuBose
1885-1940 .... **HR 2; TCLC 59**
See also CA 108; 157; DLB 7, 9, 45, 249; SATA 21

Heywood, John 1497(?)-1580(?) .... **LC 65**
See also DLB 136; RGEL 2

Hibbert, Eleanor Alice Burford
1906-1993 .... **CLC 7**
See Holt, Victoria
See also BEST 90:4; CA 17-20R; 140; CANR 9, 28, 59; CMW 4; CPW; DAM POP; MTCW 2; RHW; SATA 2; SATA-Obit 74

Hichens, Robert (Smythe)
1864-1950 .... **TCLC 64**
See also CA 162; DLB 153; HGG; RHW; SUFW

Higgins, Aidan 1927- .... **SSC 68**
See also CA 9-12R; CANR 70, 115; CN 7; DLB 14

Higgins, George V(incent)
1939-1999 .... **CLC 4, 7, 10, 18**
See also BPFB 2; CA 77-80; 186; CAAS 5;
CANR 17, 51, 89, 96; CMW 4; CN 7;
DLB 2; DLBY 1981, 1998; INT CANR-
17; MSW; MTCW 1

Higginson, Thomas Wentworth
1823-1911 .... **TCLC 36**
See also CA 162; DLB 1, 64, 243

Higgonet, Margaret ed. .... **CLC 65**

Highet, Helen
See MacInnes, Helen (Clark)

Highsmith, (Mary) Patricia
1921-1995 .... **CLC 2, 4, 14, 42, 102**
See Morgan, Claire
See also AAYA 48; BRWS 5; CA 1-4R; 147;
CANR 1, 20, 48, 62, 108; CMW 4; CPW;
DA3; DAM NOV, POP; DLB 306; MSW;
MTCW 1, 2

Highwater, Jamake (Mamake)
1942(?)-2001 .... **CLC 12**
See also AAYA 7; BPFB 2; BYA 4; CA 65-
68; 199; CAAS 7; CANR 10, 34, 84; CLR
17; CWRI 5; DLB 52; DLBY 1985;
JRDA; MAICYA 1, 2; SATA 32, 69;
SATA-Brief 30

Highway, Tomson 1951- ...... **CLC 92; NNAL**
See also CA 151; CANR 75; CCA 1; CD 5;
DAC; DAM MULT; DFS 2; MTCW 2

Hijuelos, Oscar 1951- .... **CLC 65; HLC 1**
See also AAYA 25; AMWS 8; CA 123; CANR 50, 75, 125; CPW; DA3;
DAM MULT, POP; DLB 145; HW 1, 2;
LLW 1; MTCW 2; NFS 17; RGAL 4;
WLIT 1

Hikmet, Nazim 1902(?)-1963 .... **CLC 40**
See also CA 141; 93-96; EWL 3

Hildegard von Bingen 1098-1179 . **CMLC 20**
See also DLB 148

Hildesheimer, Wolfgang 1916-1991 .. **CLC 49**
See also CA 101; 135; DLB 69, 124; EWL
3

Hill, Geoffrey (William) 1932- ...... **CLC 5, 8,
18, 45**
See also BRWS 5; CA 81-84; CANR 21,
89; CDBLB 1960 to Present; CP 7; DAM
POET; DLB 40; EWL 3; MTCW 1; RGEL
2

Hill, George Roy 1921-2002 .... **CLC 26**
See also CA 110; 122; 213

Hill, John
See Koontz, Dean R(ay)

Hill, Susan (Elizabeth) 1942- ...... **CLC 4, 113**
See also CA 33-36R; CANR 29, 69, 129;
CN 7; DAB; DAM MST, NOV; DLB 14,
139; HGG; MTCW 1; RHW

Hillard, Asa G. III .... **CLC 70**

Hillerman, Tony 1925- .... **CLC 62, 170**
See also AAYA 40; BEST 89:1; BPFB 2;
CA 29-32R; CANR 21, 42, 65, 97, 134;
CMW 4; CPW; DA3; DAM POP; DLB
206, 306; MSW; RGAL 4; SATA 6;
TCWW 2; YAW

Hillesum, Etty 1914-1943 .... **TCLC 49**
See also CA 137

Hilliard, Noel (Harvey) 1929-1996 ... **CLC 15**
See also CA 9-12R; CANR 7, 69; CN 7

Hillis, Rick 1956- .... **CLC 66**
See also CA 134

Hilton, James 1900-1954 .... **TCLC 21**
See also CA 108; 169; DLB 34, 77; FANT;
SATA 34

Hilton, Walter (?)-1396 .... **CMLC 58**
See also DLB 146; RGEL 2

Himes, Chester (Bomar) 1909-1984 .. **BLC 2;
CLC 2, 4, 7, 18, 58, 108; TCLC 139**
See also AFAW 2; BPFB 2; BW 2; CA 25-
28R; 114; CANR 22, 89; CMW 4; DAM
MULT; DLB 2, 76, 143, 226; EWL 3;
MSW; MTCW 1, 2; RGAL 4

Hinde, Thomas .... **CLC 6, 11**
See Chitty, Thomas Willes
See also EWL 3

Hine, (William) Daryl 1936- .... **CLC 15**
See also CA 1-4R; CAAS 15; CANR 1, 20;
CP 7; DLB 60

Hinkson, Katharine Tynan
See Tynan, Katharine

Hinojosa(-Smith), Rolando (R.)
1929- .... **HLC 1**
See Hinojosa-Smith, Rolando
See also CA 131; CAAS 16; CANR 62;
DAM MULT; DLB 82; HW 1, 2; LLW 1;
MTCW 2; RGAL 4

Hinton, S(usan) E(loise) 1950- .. **CLC 30, 111**
See also AAYA 2, 33; BPFB 2; BYA 2, 3;
CA 81-84; CANR 32, 62, 92, 133;
CDALBS; CLR 3, 23; CPW; DA; DA3;
DAB; DAC; DAM MST, NOV; JRDA;
LAIT 5; MAICYA 1, 2; MTCW 1, 2; NFS
5, 9, 15, 16; SATA 19, 58, 115; WYA;
YAW

Hippius, Zinaida (Nikolaevna) .... **TCLC 9**
See Gippius, Zinaida (Nikolaevna)
See also DLB 295; EWL 3

Hiraoka, Kimitake 1925-1970
See Mishima, Yukio
See also CA 97-100; 29-32R; DA3; DAM
DRAM; GLL 1; MTCW 1, 2

Hirsch, E(ric) D(onald), Jr. 1928- ... **CLC 79**
See also CA 25-28R; CANR 27, 51; DLB
67; INT CANR-27; MTCW 1

Hirsch, Edward 1950- .... **CLC 31, 50**
See also CA 104; CANR 20, 42, 102; CP 7;
DLB 120

Hitchcock, Alfred (Joseph)
1899-1980 .... **CLC 16**
See also AAYA 22; CA 159; 97-100; SATA
27; SATA-Obit 24

Hitchens, Christopher (Eric)
1949- .... **CLC 157**
See also CA 152; CANR 89

Hitler, Adolf 1889-1945 .... **TCLC 53**
See also CA 117; 147

Hoagland, Edward 1932- .... **CLC 28**
See also ANW; CA 1-4R; CANR 2, 31, 57,
107; CN 7; DLB 6; SATA 51; TCWW 2

Hoban, Russell (Conwell) 1925- ... **CLC 7, 25**
See also BPFB 2; CA 5-8R; CANR 23, 37,
66, 114; CLR 3, 69; CN 7; CWRI 5; DAM
NOV; DLB 52; FANT; MAICYA 1, 2;
MTCW 1, 2; SATA 1, 40, 78, 136; SFW
4; SUFW 2

Hobbes, Thomas 1588-1679 .... **LC 36**
See also DLB 151, 252, 281; RGEL 2

Hobbs, Perry
See Blackmur, R(ichard) P(almer)

Hobson, Laura Z(ametkin)
1900-1986 .... **CLC 7, 25**
See Field, Peter
See also BPFB 2; CA 17-20R; 118; CANR
55; DLB 28; SATA 52

Hoccleve, Thomas c. 1368-c. 1437 ...... **LC 75**
See also DLB 146; RGEL 2

Hoch, Edward D(entinger) 1930-
See Queen, Ellery
See also CA 29-32R; CANR 11, 27, 51, 97;
CMW 4; DLB 306; SFW 4

Hochhuth, Rolf 1931- .... **CLC 4, 11, 18**
See also CA 5-8R; CANR 33, 75; CWW 2;
DAM DRAM; DLB 124; EWL 3; MTCW
1, 2

Hochman, Sandra 1936- .... **CLC 3, 8**
See also CA 5-8R; DLB 5

Hochwaelder, Fritz 1911-1986 .... **CLC 36**
See Hochwalder, Fritz
See also CA 29-32R; 120; CANR 42; DAM
DRAM; MTCW 1; RGWL 3

Hochwalder, Fritz
See Hochwaelder, Fritz
See also EWL 3; RGWL 2

Hocking, Mary (Eunice) 1921- .... **CLC 13**
See also CA 101; CANR 18, 40

Hodgins, Jack 1938- .... **CLC 23**
See also CA 93-96; CN 7; DLB 60

Hodgson, William Hope
1877(?)-1918 .... **TCLC 13**
See also CA 111; 164; CMW 4; DLB 70,
153, 156, 178; HGG; MTCW 2; SFW 4;
SUFW 1

Hoeg, Peter 1957- .... **CLC 95, 156**
See also CA 151; CANR 75; CMW 4; DA3;
DLB 214; EWL 3; MTCW 2; NFS 17;
RGWL 3; SSFS 18

Hoffman, Alice 1952- .... **CLC 51**
See also AAYA 37; AMWS 10; CA 77-80;
CANR 34, 66, 100; CN 7; CPW; DAM
NOV; DLB 292; MTCW 1, 2

Hoffman, Daniel (Gerard) 1923- . **CLC 6, 13,
23**
See also CA 1-4R; CANR 4; CP 7; DLB 5

Hoffman, Eva 1945- .... **CLC 182**
See also CA 132

Hoffman, Stanley 1944- .... **CLC 5**
See also CA 77-80

Hoffman, William 1925- .... **CLC 141**
See also CA 21-24R; CANR 9, 103; CSW;
DLB 234

Hoffman, William M(oses) 1939- ..... **CLC 40**
See Hoffman, William M.
See also CA 57-60; CANR 11, 71

Hoffmann, E(rnst) T(heodor) A(madeus)
1776-1822 .... **NCLC 2; SSC 13**
See also CDWLB 2; DLB 90; EW 5; RGSF
2; RGWL 2, 3; SATA 27; SUFW 1; WCH

Hofmann, Gert 1931- .... **CLC 54**
See also CA 128; EWL 3

Hofmannsthal, Hugo von 1874-1929 ... **DC 4;
TCLC 11**
See also CA 106; 153; CDWLB 2; DAM
DRAM; DFS 17; DLB 81, 118; EW 9;
EWL 3; RGWL 2, 3

Hogan, Linda 1947- ..... **CLC 73; NNAL; PC
35**
See also AMWS 4; ANW; BYA 12; CA 120,
226; CAAE 226; CANR 45, 73, 129;
CWP; DAM MULT; DLB 175; SATA
132; TCWW 2

Hogarth, Charles
See Creasey, John

Hogarth, Emmett
See Polonsky, Abraham (Lincoln)

Hogg, James 1770-1835 .... **NCLC 4, 109**
See also BRWS 10; DLB 93, 116, 159;
HGG; RGEL 2; SUFW 1

Holbach, Paul Henri Thiry Baron
1723-1789 .... **LC 14**

Holberg, Ludvig 1684-1754 .... **LC 6**
See also DLB 300; RGWL 2, 3

Holcroft, Thomas 1745-1809 .... **NCLC 85**
See also DLB 39, 89, 158; RGEL 2

Holden, Ursula 1921- .... **CLC 18**
See also CA 101; CAAS 8; CANR 22

Holderlin, (Johann Christian) Friedrich
1770-1843 .... **NCLC 16; PC 4**
See also CDWLB 2; DLB 90; EW 5; RGWL
2, 3

Holdstock, Robert
See Holdstock, Robert P.

Holdstock, Robert P. 1948- .... **CLC 39**
See also CA 131; CANR 81; DLB 261;
FANT; HGG; SFW 4; SUFW 2

Holinshed, Raphael fl. 1580- .... **LC 69**
See also DLB 167; RGEL 2

Holland, Isabelle (Christian)
1920-2002 .... **CLC 21**
See also AAYA 11; CA 21-24R; 205; CAAE
181; CANR 10, 25, 47; CLR 57; CWRI
5; JRDA; LAIT 4; MAICYA 1, 2; SATA
8, 70; SATA-Essay 103; SATA-Obit 132;
WYA

Holland, Marcus
See Caldwell, (Janet Miriam) Taylor
(Holland)

Hollander, John 1929- .... **CLC 2, 5, 8, 14**
See also CA 1-4R; CANR 1, 52; CP 7; DLB
5; SATA 13

Hollander, Paul
See Silverberg, Robert

Holleran, Andrew 1943(?)- .... **CLC 38**
See Garber, Eric
See also CA 144; GLL 1

Holley, Marietta 1836(?)-1926 .... **TCLC 99**
See also CA 118; DLB 11

Hollinghurst, Alan 1954- .... **CLC 55, 91**
See also BRWS 10; CA 114; CN 7; DLB
207; GLL 1

Hollis, Jim
See Summers, Hollis (Spurgeon, Jr.)

Holly, Buddy 1936-1959 .... **TCLC 65**
See also CA 213

Holmes, Gordon
See Shiel, M(atthew) P(hipps)

Holmes, John
See Souster, (Holmes) Raymond

Holmes, John Clellon 1926-1988 ...... **CLC 56**
See also BG 2; CA 9-12R; 125; CANR 4;
DLB 16, 237

Holmes, Oliver Wendell, Jr.
1841-1935 .... **TCLC 77**
See also CA 114; 186

Holmes, Oliver Wendell
1809-1894 .... **NCLC 14, 81**
See also AMWS 1; CDALB 1640-1865;
DLB 1, 189, 235; EXPP; RGAL 4; SATA
34

Holmes, Raymond
See Souster, (Holmes) Raymond

Holt, Victoria
See Hibbert, Eleanor Alice Burford
See also BPFB 2

Holub, Miroslav 1923-1998 .... **CLC 4**
See also CA 21-24R; 169; CANR 10; CD-
WLB 4; CWW 2; DLB 232; EWL 3;
RGWL 3

Holz, Detlev
See Benjamin, Walter

Homer c. 8th cent. B.C.- .... **CMLC 1, 16, 61;
PC 23; WLCS**
See also AW 1; CDWLB 1; DA; DA3;
DAB; DAC; DAM MST, POET; DLB
176; EFS 1; LAIT 1; LMFS 1; RGWL 2,
3; TWA; WP

Hongo, Garrett Kaoru 1951- .... **PC 23**
See also CA 133; CAAS 22; CP 7; DLB
120; EWL 3; EXPP; RGAL 4

Honig, Edwin 1919- .... **CLC 33**
See also CA 5-8R; CAAS 8; CANR 4, 45;
CP 7; DLB 5

Hood, Hugh (John Blagdon) 1928- . **CLC 15,
28; SSC 42**
See also CA 49-52; CAAS 17; CANR 1,
33, 87; CN 7; DLB 53; RGSF 2

Hood, Thomas 1799-1845 .... **NCLC 16**
See also BRW 4; DLB 96; RGEL 2

Hooker, (Peter) Jeremy 1941- .... **CLC 43**
See also CA 77-80; CANR 22; CP 7; DLB
40

Hooker, Richard 1554-1600 .... **LC 95**
See also BRW 1; DLB 132; RGEL 2

hooks, bell
See Watkins, Gloria Jean

Hope, A(lec) D(erwent) 1907-2000 .... **CLC 3,
51; PC 56**
See also BRWS 7; CA 21-24R; 188; CANR
33, 74; DLB 289; EWL 3; MTCW 1, 2;
PFS 8; RGEL 2

Hope, Anthony 1863-1933 .... **TCLC 83**
See also CA 157; DLB 153, 156; RGEL 2;
RHW

Hope, Brian
See Creasey, John

Hope, Christopher (David Tully)
1944- .... **CLC 52**
See also AFW; CA 106; CANR 47, 101;
CN 7; DLB 225; SATA 62

Hopkins, Gerard Manley
1844-1889 .... **NCLC 17; PC 15; WLC**
See also BRW 5; BRWR 2; CDBLB 1890-
1914; DA; DA3; DAB; DAC; DAM MST,
POET; DLB 35, 57; EXPP; PAB; RGEL
2; TEA; WP

Hopkins, John (Richard) 1931-1998 .. **CLC 4**
See also CA 85-88; 169; CBD; CD 5

Hopkins, Pauline Elizabeth
1859-1930 .... **BLC 2; TCLC 28**
See also AFAW 2; BW 2, 3; CA 141; CANR
82; DAM MULT; DLB 50

Hopkinson, Francis 1737-1791 .... **LC 25**
See also DLB 31; RGAL 4

Hopley-Woolrich, Cornell George 1903-1968
See Woolrich, Cornell
See also CA 13-14; CANR 58; CAP 1;
CMW 4; DLB 226; MTCW 2

Horace 65B.C.-8B.C. .... **CMLC 39; PC 46**
See also AW 2; CDWLB 1; DLB 211;
RGWL 2, 3

Horatio
See Proust, (Valentin-Louis-George-Eugene)
Marcel

**Horgan, Paul (George Vincent
O'Shaughnessy)** 1903-1995 .. **CLC 9, 53**
See also BPFB 2; CA 13-16R; 147; CANR
9, 35; DAM NOV; DLB 102, 212; DLBY
1985; INT CANR-9; MTCW 1, 2; SATA
13; SATA-Obit 84; TCWW 2

Horkheimer, Max 1895-1973 .... **TCLC 132**
See also CA 216; 41-44R; DLB 296

Horn, Peter
See Kuttner, Henry

Horne, Frank (Smith) 1899-1974 .... **HR 2**
See also BW 1; CA 125; 53-56; DLB 51;
WP

Horne, Richard Henry Hengist
1802(?)-1884 .... **NCLC 127**
See also DLB 32; SATA 29

Hornem, Horace Esq.
See Byron, George Gordon (Noel)

**Horney, Karen (Clementine Theodore
Danielsen)** 1885-1952 .... **TCLC 71**
See also CA 114; 165; DLB 246; FW

Hornung, E(rnest) W(illiam)
1866-1921 .... **TCLC 59**
See also CA 108; 160; CMW 4; DLB 70

Horovitz, Israel (Arthur) 1939- .... **CLC 56**
See also CA 33-36R; CAD; CANR 46, 59;
CD 5; DAM DRAM; DLB 7

Horton, George Moses
1797(?)-1883(?) .... **NCLC 87**
See also DLB 50

Horvath, odon von 1901-1938
See von Horvath, Odon
See also EWL 3

Horvath, Oedoen von -1938
See von Horvath, Odon

Horwitz, Julius 1920-1986 .... **CLC 14**
See also CA 9-12R; 119; CANR 12

Hospital, Janette Turner 1942- .... **CLC 42,
145**
See also CA 108; CANR 48; CN 7; DLBY
2002; RGSF 2

Hostos, E. M. de
See Hostos (y Bonilla), Eugenio Maria de

Hostos, Eugenio M. de
See Hostos (y Bonilla), Eugenio Maria de

Hostos, Eugenio Maria
See Hostos (y Bonilla), Eugenio Maria de

Hostos (y Bonilla), Eugenio Maria de
1839-1903 .... **TCLC 24**
See also CA 123; 131; HW 1

Houdini
See Lovecraft, H(oward) P(hillips)

Houellebecq, Michel 1958- .... **CLC 179**
See also CA 185

Hougan, Carolyn 1943- .... **CLC 34**
See also CA 139

Household, Geoffrey (Edward West)
1900-1988 .... **CLC 11**
See also CA 77-80; 126; CANR 58; CMW
4; DLB 87; SATA 14; SATA-Obit 59

Housman, A(lfred) E(dward)
1859-1936 .... **PC 2, 43; TCLC 1, 10;
WLCS**
See also BRW 6; CA 104; 125; DA; DA3;
DAB; DAC; DAM MST, POET; DLB 19,
284; EWL 3; EXPP; MTCW 1, 2; PAB;
PFS 4, 7; RGEL 2; TEA; WP

Housman, Laurence 1865-1959 .... **TCLC 7**
See also CA 106; 155; DLB 10; FANT;
RGEL 2; SATA 25

Houston, Jeanne (Toyo) Wakatsuki
1934- .... **AAL**
See also AAYA 49; CA 103; CAAS 16;
CANR 29, 123; LAIT 4; SATA 78

Howard, Elizabeth Jane 1923- ..... **CLC 7, 29**
See also CA 5-8R; CANR 8, 62; CN 7

Howard, Maureen 1930- .... **CLC 5, 14, 46,
151**
See also CA 53-56; CANR 31, 75; CN 7;
DLBY 1983; INT CANR-31; MTCW 1, 2

Howard, Richard 1929- .... **CLC 7, 10, 47**
See also AITN 1; CA 85-88; CANR 25, 80;
CP 7; DLB 5; INT CANR-25

Howard, Robert E(rvin)
1906-1936 .... **TCLC 8**
See also BPFB 2; BYA 5; CA 105; 157;
FANT; SUFW 1

Howard, Warren F.
See Pohl, Frederik

Howe, Fanny (Quincy) 1940- .... **CLC 47**
See also CA 117, 187; CAAE 187; CAAS
27; CANR 70, 116; CP 7; CWP; SATA-
Brief 52

Howe, Irving 1920-1993 .... **CLC 85**
See also AMWS 6; CA 9-12R; 141; CANR
21, 50; DLB 67; EWL 3; MTCW 1, 2

Howe, Julia Ward 1819-1910 .... **TCLC 21**
See also CA 117; 191; DLB 1, 189, 235;
FW

Howe, Susan 1937- .... **CLC 72, 152; PC 54**
See also AMWS 4; CA 160; CP 7; CWP;
DLB 120; FW; RGAL 4

Howe, Tina 1937- .... **CLC 48**
See also CA 109; CAD; CANR 125; CD 5;
CWD

Howell, James 1594(?)-1666 .... **LC 13**
See also DLB 151

Howells, W. D.
See Howells, William Dean

Howells, William D.
See Howells, William Dean

Howells, William Dean 1837-1920 ... **SSC 36;
TCLC 7, 17, 41**
See also AMW; CA 104; 134; CDALB
1865-1917; DLB 12, 64, 74, 79, 189;
LMFS 1; MTCW 2; RGAL 4; TUS

Howes, Barbara 1914-1996 .... **CLC 15**
See also CA 9-12R; 151; CAAS 3; CANR
53; CP 7; SATA 5

Hrabal, Bohumil 1914-1997 ...... **CLC 13, 67; TCLC 155**
  See also CA 106; 156; CAAS 12; CANR 57; CWW 2; DLB 232; EWL 3; RGSF 2

Hrotsvit of Gandersheim c. 935-c. 1000 .... **CMLC 29**
  See also DLB 148

Hsi, Chu 1130-1200 .... **CMLC 42**

Hsun, Lu
  See Lu Hsun

Hubbard, L(afayette) Ron(ald) 1911-1986 .... **CLC 43**
  See also CA 77-80; 118; CANR 52; CPW; DA3; DAM POP; FANT; MTCW 2; SFW 4

Huch, Ricarda (Octavia) 1864-1947 .... **TCLC 13**
  See also CA 111; 189; DLB 66; EWL 3

Huddle, David 1942- .... **CLC 49**
  See also CA 57-60; CAAS 20; CANR 89; DLB 130

Hudson, Jeffrey
  See Crichton, (John) Michael

Hudson, W(illiam) H(enry) 1841-1922 .... **TCLC 29**
  See also CA 115; 190; DLB 98, 153, 174; RGEL 2; SATA 35

Hueffer, Ford Madox
  See Ford, Ford Madox

Hughart, Barry 1934- .... **CLC 39**
  See also CA 137; FANT; SFW 4; SUFW 2

Hughes, Colin
  See Creasey, John

Hughes, David (John) 1930- .... **CLC 48**
  See also CA 116; 129; CN 7; DLB 14

Hughes, Edward James
  See Hughes, Ted
  See also DA3; DAM MST, POET

Hughes, (James Mercer) Langston 1902-1967 ..... **BLC 2; CLC 1, 5, 10, 15, 35, 44, 108; DC 3; HR 2; PC 1, 53; SSC 6; WLC**
  See also AAYA 12; AFAW 1, 2; AMWR 1; AMWS 1; BW 1, 3; CA 1-4R; 25-28R; CANR 1, 34, 82; CDALB 1929-1941; CLR 17; DA; DA3; DAB; DAC; DAM DRAM, MST, MULT, POET; DFS 6, 18; DLB 4, 7, 48, 51, 86, 228; EWL 3; EXPP; EXPS; JRDA; LAIT 3; LMFS 2; MAICYA 1, 2; MTCW 1, 2; PAB; PFS 1, 3, 6, 10, 15; RGAL 4; RGSF 2; SATA 4, 33; SSFS 4, 7; TUS; WCH; WP; YAW

Hughes, Richard (Arthur Warren) 1900-1976 .... **CLC 1, 11**
  See also CA 5-8R; 65-68; CANR 4; DAM NOV; DLB 15, 161; EWL 3; MTCW 1; RGEL 2; SATA 8; SATA-Obit 25

Hughes, Ted 1930-1998 . **CLC 2, 4, 9, 14, 37, 119; PC 7**
  See Hughes, Edward James
  See also BRWC 2; BRWR 2; BRWS 1; CA 1-4R; 171; CANR 1, 33, 66, 108; CLR 3; CP 7; DAB; DAC; DLB 40, 161; EWL 3; EXPP; MAICYA 1, 2; MTCW 1, 2; PAB; PFS 4, 19; RGEL 2; SATA 49; SATA-Brief 27; SATA-Obit 107; TEA; YAW

Hugo, Richard
  See Huch, Ricarda (Octavia)

Hugo, Richard F(ranklin) 1923-1982 .... **CLC 6, 18, 32**
  See also AMWS 6; CA 49-52; 108; CANR 3; DAM POET; DLB 5, 206; EWL 3; PFS 17; RGAL 4

Hugo, Victor (Marie) 1802-1885 .... **NCLC 3, 10, 21; PC 17; WLC**
  See also AAYA 28; DA; DA3; DAB; DAC; DAM DRAM, MST, NOV, POET; DLB 119, 192, 217; EFS 2; EW 6; EXPN; GFL 1789 to the Present; LAIT 1, 2; NFS 5, 20; RGWL 2, 3; SATA 47; TWA

Huidobro, Vicente
  See Huidobro Fernandez, Vicente Garcia
  See also DLB 283; EWL 3; LAW

Huidobro Fernandez, Vicente Garcia 1893-1948 .... **TCLC 31**
  See Huidobro, Vicente
  See also CA 131; HW 1

Hulme, Keri 1947- .... **CLC 39, 130**
  See also CA 125; CANR 69; CN 7; CP 7; CWP; EWL 3; FW; INT CA-125

Hulme, T(homas) E(rnest) 1883-1917 .... **TCLC 21**
  See also BRWS 6; CA 117; 203; DLB 19

Humboldt, Wilhelm von 1767-1835 .... **NCLC 134**
  See also DLB 90

Hume, David 1711-1776 .... **LC 7, 56**
  See also BRWS 3; DLB 104, 252; LMFS 1; TEA

Humphrey, William 1924-1997 .... **CLC 45**
  See also AMWS 9; CA 77-80; 160; CANR 68; CN 7; CSW; DLB 6, 212, 234, 278; TCWW 2

Humphreys, Emyr Owen 1919- .... **CLC 47**
  See also CA 5-8R; CANR 3, 24; CN 7; DLB 15

Humphreys, Josephine 1945- ..... **CLC 34, 57**
  See also CA 121; 127; CANR 97; CSW; DLB 292; INT CA-127

Huneker, James Gibbons 1860-1921 .... **TCLC 65**
  See also CA 193; DLB 71; RGAL 4

Hungerford, Hesba Fay
  See Brinsmead, H(esba) F(ay)

Hungerford, Pixie
  See Brinsmead, H(esba) F(ay)

Hunt, E(verette) Howard, (Jr.) 1918- .... **CLC 3**
  See also AITN 1; CA 45-48; CANR 2, 47, 103; CMW 4

Hunt, Francesca
  See Holland, Isabelle (Christian)

Hunt, Howard
  See Hunt, E(verette) Howard, (Jr.)

Hunt, Kyle
  See Creasey, John

Hunt, (James Henry) Leigh 1784-1859 .... **NCLC 1, 70**
  See also DAM POET; DLB 96, 110, 144; RGEL 2; TEA

Hunt, Marsha 1946- .... **CLC 70**
  See also BW 2, 3; CA 143; CANR 79

Hunt, Violet 1866(?)-1942 .... **TCLC 53**
  See also CA 184; DLB 162, 197

Hunter, E. Waldo
  See Sturgeon, Theodore (Hamilton)

Hunter, Evan 1926- .... **CLC 11, 31**
  See McBain, Ed
  See also AAYA 39; BPFB 2; CA 5-8R; CANR 5, 38, 62, 97; CMW 4; CN 7; CPW; DAM POP; DLB 306; DLBY 1982; INT CANR-5; MSW; MTCW 1; SATA 25; SFW 4

Hunter, Kristin
  See Lattany, Kristin (Elaine Eggleston) Hunter

Hunter, Mary
  See Austin, Mary (Hunter)

Hunter, Mollie 1922- .... **CLC 21**
  See McIlwraith, Maureen Mollie Hunter
  See also AAYA 13; BYA 6; CANR 37, 78; CLR 25; DLB 161; JRDA; MAICYA 1, 2; SAAS 7; SATA 54, 106, 139; SATA-Essay 139; WYA; YAW

Hunter, Robert (?)-1734 .... **LC 7**

Hurston, Zora Neale 1891-1960 .... **BLC 2; CLC 7, 30, 61; DC 12; HR 2; SSC 4; TCLC 121, 131; WLCS**
  See also AAYA 15; AFAW 1, 2; AMWS 6; BW 1, 3; BYA 12; CA 85-88; CANR 61; CDALBS; DA; DA3; DAC; DAM MST, MULT, NOV; DFS 6; DLB 51, 86; EWL 3; EXPN; EXPS; FW; LAIT 3; LATS 1:1; LMFS 2; MAWW; MTCW 1, 2; NFS 3; RGAL 4; RGSF 2; SSFS 1, 6, 11, 19; TUS; YAW

Husserl, E. G.
  See Husserl, Edmund (Gustav Albrecht)

Husserl, Edmund (Gustav Albrecht) 1859-1938 .... **TCLC 100**
  See also CA 116; 133; DLB 296

Huston, John (Marcellus) 1906-1987 .... **CLC 20**
  See also CA 73-76; 123; CANR 34; DLB 26

Hustvedt, Siri 1955- .... **CLC 76**
  See also CA 137

Hutten, Ulrich von 1488-1523 .... **LC 16**
  See also DLB 179

Huxley, Aldous (Leonard) 1894-1963 .... **CLC 1, 3, 4, 5, 8, 11, 18, 35, 79; SSC 39; WLC**
  See also AAYA 11; BPFB 2; BRW 7; CA 85-88; CANR 44, 79; CDBLB 1914-1945; DA; DA3; DAB; DAC; DAM MST, NOV; DLB 36, 100, 162, 195, 255; EWL 3; EXPN; LAIT 5; LMFS 2; MTCW 1, 2; NFS 6; RGEL 2; SATA 63; SCFW 2; SFW 4; TEA; YAW

Huxley, T(homas) H(enry) 1825-1895 .... **NCLC 67**
  See also DLB 57; TEA

Huysmans, Joris-Karl 1848-1907 ... **TCLC 7, 69**
  See also CA 104; 165; DLB 123; EW 7; GFL 1789 to the Present; LMFS 2; RGWL 2, 3

Hwang, David Henry 1957- .... **CLC 55, 196; DC 4, 23**
  See also CA 127; 132; CAD; CANR 76, 124; CD 5; DA3; DAM DRAM; DFS 11, 18; DLB 212, 228; INT CA-132; MTCW 2; RGAL 4

Hyde, Anthony 1946- .... **CLC 42**
  See Chase, Nicholas
  See also CA 136; CCA 1

Hyde, Margaret O(ldroyd) 1917- .... **CLC 21**
  See also CA 1-4R; CANR 1, 36; CLR 23; JRDA; MAICYA 1, 2; SAAS 8; SATA 1, 42, 76, 139

Hynes, James 1956(?)- .... **CLC 65**
  See also CA 164; CANR 105

Hypatia c. 370-415 .... **CMLC 35**

Ian, Janis 1951- .... **CLC 21**
  See also CA 105; 187

Ibanez, Vicente Blasco
  See Blasco Ibanez, Vicente

Ibarbourou, Juana de 1895(?)-1979 .... **HLCS 2**
  See also DLB 290; HW 1; LAW

Ibarguengoitia, Jorge 1928-1983 ..... **CLC 37; TCLC 148**
  See also CA 124; 113; EWL 3; HW 1

Ibn Battuta, Abu Abdalla 1304-1368(?) .... **CMLC 57**
  See also WLIT 2

Ibn Hazm 994-1064 .... **CMLC 64**

Ibsen, Henrik (Johan) 1828-1906 .... **DC 2; TCLC 2, 8, 16, 37, 52; WLC**
  See also AAYA 46; CA 104; 141; DA; DA3; DAB; DAC; DAM DRAM, MST; DFS 1, 6, 8, 10, 11, 15, 16; EW 7; LAIT 2; LATS 1:1; RGWL 2, 3

Ibuse, Masuji 1898-1993 .... **CLC 22**
See Ibuse Masuji
See also CA 127; 141; MJW; RGWL 3

Ibuse Masuji
See Ibuse, Masuji
See also CWW 2; DLB 180; EWL 3

Ichikawa, Kon 1915- .... **CLC 20**
See also CA 121

Ichiyo, Higuchi 1872-1896 .... **NCLC 49**
See also MJW

Idle, Eric 1943- .... **CLC 21**
See Monty Python
See also CA 116; CANR 35, 91

Idris, Yusuf 1927-1991 .... **SSC 74**
See also AFW; EWL 3; RGSF 2, 3; RGWL
3; WLIT 2

Ignatow, David 1914-1997 .... **CLC 4, 7, 14,
40; PC 34**
See also CA 9-12R; 162; CAAS 3; CANR
31, 57, 96; CP 7; DLB 5; EWL 3

Ignotus
See Strachey, (Giles) Lytton

Ihimaera, Witi (Tame) 1944- .... **CLC 46**
See also CA 77-80; CANR 130; CN 7;
RGSF 2; SATA 148

Ilf, Ilya .... **TCLC 21**
See Fainzilberg, Ilya Arnoldovich
See also EWL 3

Illyes, Gyula 1902-1983 .... **PC 16**
See also CA 114; 109; CDWLB 4; DLB
215; EWL 3; RGWL 2, 3

Imalayen, Fatima-Zohra
See Djebar, Assia

Immermann, Karl (Lebrecht)
1796-1840 .... **NCLC 4, 49**
See also DLB 133

Ince, Thomas H. 1882-1924 .... **TCLC 89**
See also IDFW 3, 4

Inchbald, Elizabeth 1753-1821 ...... **NCLC 62**
See also DLB 39, 89; RGEL 2

Inclan, Ramon (Maria) del Valle
See Valle-Inclan, Ramon (Maria) del

Infante, G(uillermo) Cabrera
See Cabrera Infante, G(uillermo)

Ingalls, Rachel (Holmes) 1940- .... **CLC 42**
See also CA 123; 127

Ingamells, Reginald Charles
See Ingamells, Rex

Ingamells, Rex 1913-1955 .... **TCLC 35**
See also CA 167; DLB 260

Inge, William (Motter) 1913-1973 ..... **CLC 1,
8, 19**
See also CA 9-12R; CDALB 1941-1968;
DA3; DAM DRAM; DFS 1, 3, 5, 8; DLB
7, 249; EWL 3; MTCW 1, 2; RGAL 4;
TUS

Ingelow, Jean 1820-1897 .... **NCLC 39, 107**
See also DLB 35, 163; FANT; SATA 33

Ingram, Willis J.
See Harris, Mark

Innaurato, Albert (F.) 1948(?)- ... **CLC 21, 60**
See also CA 115; 122; CAD; CANR 78;
CD 5; INT CA-122

Innes, Michael
See Stewart, J(ohn) I(nnes) M(ackintosh)
See also DLB 276; MSW

Innis, Harold Adams 1894-1952 .... **TCLC 77**
See also CA 181; DLB 88

Insluis, Alanus de
See Alain de Lille

Iola
See Wells-Barnett, Ida B(ell)

Ionesco, Eugene 1912-1994 ... **CLC 1, 4, 6, 9,
11, 15, 41, 86; DC 12; WLC**
See also CA 9-12R; 144; CANR 55, 132;
CWW 2; DA; DA3; DAB; DAC; DAM
DRAM, MST; DFS 4, 9; EW 13; EWL 3;
GFL 1789 to the Present; LMFS 2;
MTCW 1, 2; RGWL 2, 3; SATA 7; SATA-
Obit 79; TWA

Iqbal, Muhammad 1877-1938 .... **TCLC 28**
See also CA 215; EWL 3

Ireland, Patrick
See O'Doherty, Brian

Irenaeus St. 130- .... **CMLC 42**

Irigaray, Luce 1930- .... **CLC 164**
See also CA 154; CANR 121; FW

Iron, Ralph
See Schreiner, Olive (Emilie Albertina)

Irving, John (Winslow) 1942- ... **CLC 13, 23,
38, 112, 175**
See also AAYA 8; AMWS 6; BEST 89:3;
BPFB 2; CA 25-28R; CANR 28, 73, 112,
133; CN 7; CPW; DA3; DAM NOV, POP;
DLB 6, 278; DLBY 1982; EWL 3;
MTCW 1, 2; NFS 12, 14; RGAL 4; TUS

Irving, Washington 1783-1859 . **NCLC 2, 19,
95; SSC 2, 37; WLC**
See also AAYA 56; AMW; CDALB 1640-
1865; CLR 97; DA; DA3; DAB; DAC;
DAM MST; DLB 3, 11, 30, 59, 73, 74,
183, 186, 250, 254; EXPS; LAIT 1;
RGAL 4; RGSF 2; SSFS 1, 8, 16; SUFW
1; TUS; WCH; YABC 2

Irwin, P. K.
See Page, P(atricia) K(athleen)

Isaacs, Jorge Ricardo 1837-1895 ... **NCLC 70**
See also LAW

Isaacs, Susan 1943- .... **CLC 32**
See also BEST 89:1; BPFB 2; CA 89-92;
CANR 20, 41, 65, 112, 134; CPW; DA3;
DAM POP; INT CANR-20; MTCW 1, 2

Isherwood, Christopher (William Bradshaw)
1904-1986 .... **CLC 1, 9, 11, 14, 44; SSC
56**
See also AMWS 14; BRW 7; CA 13-16R;
117; CANR 35, 97, 133; DA3; DAM
DRAM, NOV; DLB 15, 195; DLBY 1986;
EWL 3; IDTP; MTCW 1, 2; RGAL 4;
RGEL 2; TUS; WLIT 4

Ishiguro, Kazuo 1954- .. **CLC 27, 56, 59, 110**
See also AAYA 58; BEST 90:2; BPFB 2;
BRWS 4; CA 120; CANR 49, 95, 133;
CN 7; DA3; DAM NOV; DLB 194; EWL
3; MTCW 1, 2; NFS 13; WLIT 4; WWE
1

Ishikawa, Hakuhin
See Ishikawa, Takuboku

Ishikawa, Takuboku 1886(?)-1912 ..... **PC 10;
TCLC 15**
See Ishikawa Takuboku
See also CA 113; 153; DAM POET

Iskander, Fazil (Abdulovich) 1929- .. **CLC 47**
See Iskander, Fazil' Abdulevich
See also CA 102; EWL 3

Iskander, Fazil' Abdulevich
See Iskander, Fazil (Abdulovich)
See also DLB 302

Isler, Alan (David) 1934- .... **CLC 91**
See also CA 156; CANR 105

Ivan IV 1530-1584 .... **LC 17**

Ivanov, Vyacheslav Ivanovich
1866-1949 .... **TCLC 33**
See also CA 122; EWL 3

Ivask, Ivar Vidrik 1927-1992 .... **CLC 14**
See also CA 37-40R; 139; CANR 24

Ives, Morgan
See Bradley, Marion Zimmer
See also GLL 1

Izumi Shikibu c. 973-c. 1034 .... **CMLC 33**

J. R. S.
See Gogarty, Oliver St. John

Jabran, Kahlil
See Gibran, Kahlil

Jabran, Khalil
See Gibran, Kahlil

Jackson, Daniel
See Wingrove, David (John)

Jackson, Helen Hunt 1830-1885 .... **NCLC 90**
See also DLB 42, 47, 186, 189; RGAL 4

Jackson, Jesse 1908-1983 .... **CLC 12**
See also BW 1; CA 25-28R; 109; CANR
27; CLR 28; CWRI 5; MAICYA 1, 2;
SATA 2, 29; SATA-Obit 48

Jackson, Laura (Riding) 1901-1991 .... **PC 44**
See Riding, Laura
See also CA 65-68; 135; CANR 28, 89;
DLB 48

Jackson, Sam
See Trumbo, Dalton

Jackson, Sara
See Wingrove, David (John)

Jackson, Shirley 1919-1965 . **CLC 11, 60, 87;
SSC 9, 39; WLC**
See also AAYA 9; AMWS 9; BPFB 2; CA
1-4R; 25-28R; CANR 4, 52; CDALB
1941-1968; DA; DA3; DAC; DAM MST;
DLB 6, 234; EXPS; HGG; LAIT 4;
MTCW 2; RGAL 4; RGSF 2; SATA 2;
SSFS 1; SUFW 1, 2

Jacob, (Cyprien-)Max 1876-1944 .... **TCLC 6**
See also CA 104; 193; DLB 258; EWL 3;
GFL 1789 to the Present; GLL 2; RGWL
2, 3

Jacobs, Harriet A(nn)
1813(?)-1897 .... **NCLC 67**
See also AFAW 1, 2; DLB 239; FW; LAIT
2; RGAL 4

Jacobs, Jim 1942- .... **CLC 12**
See also CA 97-100; INT CA-97-100

Jacobs, W(illiam) W(ymark)
1863-1943 .... **SSC 73; TCLC 22**
See also CA 121; 167; DLB 135; EXPS;
HGG; RGEL 2; RGSF 2; SSFS 2; SUFW
1

Jacobsen, Jens Peter 1847-1885 .... **NCLC 34**

Jacobsen, Josephine (Winder)
1908-2003 .... **CLC 48, 102**
See also CA 33-36R; 218; CAAS 18; CANR
23, 48; CCA 1; CP 7; DLB 244

Jacobson, Dan 1929- .... **CLC 4, 14**
See also AFW; CA 1-4R; CANR 2, 25, 66;
CN 7; DLB 14, 207, 225; EWL 3; MTCW
1; RGSF 2

Jacqueline
See Carpentier (y Valmont), Alejo

Jacques de Vitry c. 1160-1240 ...... **CMLC 63**
See also DLB 208

Jagger, Mick 1944- .... **CLC 17**

Jahiz, al- c. 780-c. 869 .... **CMLC 25**

Jakes, John (William) 1932- .... **CLC 29**
See also AAYA 32; BEST 89:4; BPFB 2;
CA 57-60, 214; CAAE 214; CANR 10,
43, 66, 111; CPW; CSW; DA3; DAM
NOV, POP; DLB 278; DLBY 1983;
FANT; INT CANR-10; MTCW 1, 2;
RHW; SATA 62; SFW 4; TCWW 2

James I 1394-1437 .... **LC 20**
See also RGEL 2

James, Andrew
See Kirkup, James

James, C(yril) L(ionel) R(obert)
1901-1989 .... **BLCS; CLC 33**
See also BW 2; CA 117; 125; 128; CANR
62; DLB 125; MTCW 1

James, Daniel (Lewis) 1911-1988
See Santiago, Danny
See also CA 174; 125

James, Dynely
See Mayne, William (James Carter)
James, Henry Sr. 1811-1882 .... NCLC 53
James, Henry 1843-1916 .... SSC 8, 32, 47;
TCLC 2, 11, 24, 40, 47, 64; WLC
See also AMW; AMWC 1; AMWR 1; BPFB
2; BRW 6; CA 104; 132; CDALB 1865-
1917; DA; DA3; DAB; DAC; DAM MST,
NOV; DLB 12, 71, 74, 189; DLBD 13;
EWL 3; EXPS; HGG; LAIT 2; MTCW 1,
2; NFS 12, 16, 19; RGAL 4; RGEL 2;
RGSF 2; SSFS 9; SUFW 1; TUS
James, M. R.
See James, Montague (Rhodes)
See also DLB 156, 201
James, Montague (Rhodes)
1862-1936 .... SSC 16; TCLC 6
See James, M. R.
See also CA 104; 203; HGG; RGEL 2;
RGSF 2; SUFW 1
James, P. D. .... CLC 18, 46, 122
See White, Phyllis Dorothy James
See also BEST 90:2; BPFB 2; BRWS 4;
CDBLB 1960 to Present; DLB 87, 276;
DLBD 17; MSW
James, Philip
See Moorcock, Michael (John)
James, Samuel
See Stephens, James
James, Seumas
See Stephens, James
James, Stephen
See Stephens, James
James, William 1842-1910 .... TCLC 15, 32
See also AMW; CA 109; 193; DLB 270,
284; NCFS 5; RGAL 4
Jameson, Anna 1794-1860 .... NCLC 43
See also DLB 99, 166
Jameson, Fredric (R.) 1934- .... CLC 142
See also CA 196; DLB 67; LMFS 2
James VI of Scotland 1566-1625 .... LC 109
See also DLB 151, 172
Jami, Nur al-Din 'Abd al-Rahman
1414-1492 .... LC 9
Jammes, Francis 1868-1938 .... TCLC 75
See also CA 198; EWL 3; GFL 1789 to the
Present
Jandl, Ernst 1925-2000 .... CLC 34
See also CA 200; EWL 3
Janowitz, Tama 1957- .... CLC 43, 145
See also CA 106; CANR 52, 89, 129; CN
7; CPW; DAM POP; DLB 292
Japrisot, Sebastien 1931- .... CLC 90
See Rossi, Jean-Baptiste
See also CMW 4; NFS 18
Jarrell, Randall 1914-1965 .... CLC 1, 2, 6, 9,
13, 49; PC 41
See also AMW; BYA 5; CA 5-8R; 25-28R;
CABS 2; CANR 6, 34; CDALB 1941-
1968; CLR 6; CWRI 5; DAM POET;
DLB 48, 52; EWL 3; EXPP; MAICYA 1,
2; MTCW 1, 2; PAB; PFS 2; RGAL 4;
SATA 7
Jarry, Alfred 1873-1907 .... SSC 20; TCLC 2,
14, 147
See also CA 104; 153; DA3; DAM DRAM;
DFS 8; DLB 192, 258; EW 9; EWL 3;
GFL 1789 to the Present; RGWL 2, 3;
TWA
Jarvis, E. K.
See Ellison, Harlan (Jay)
Jawien, Andrzej
See John Paul II, Pope
Jaynes, Roderick
See Coen, Ethan
Jeake, Samuel, Jr.
See Aiken, Conrad (Potter)

Jean Paul 1763-1825 .... NCLC 7
Jefferies, (John) Richard
1848-1887 .... NCLC 47
See also DLB 98, 141; RGEL 2; SATA 16;
SFW 4
Jeffers, (John) Robinson 1887-1962 .. CLC 2,
3, 11, 15, 54; PC 17; WLC
See also AMWS 2; CA 85-88; CANR 35;
CDALB 1917-1929; DA; DAC; DAM
MST, POET; DLB 45, 212; EWL 3;
MTCW 1, 2; PAB; PFS 3, 4; RGAL 4
Jefferson, Janet
See Mencken, H(enry) L(ouis)
Jefferson, Thomas 1743-1826 . NCLC 11, 103
See also AAYA 54; ANW; CDALB 1640-
1865; DA3; DLB 31, 183; LAIT 1; RGAL
4
Jeffrey, Francis 1773-1850 .... NCLC 33
See Francis, Lord Jeffrey
Jelakowitch, Ivan
See Heijermans, Herman
Jelinek, Elfriede 1946- .... CLC 169
See also CA 154; DLB 85; FW
Jellicoe, (Patricia) Ann 1927- .... CLC 27
See also CA 85-88; CBD; CD 5; CWD;
CWRI 5; DLB 13, 233; FW
Jelloun, Tahar ben 1944- .... CLC 180
See Ben Jelloun, Tahar
See also CA 162; CANR 100
Jemyma
See Holley, Marietta
Jen, Gish .... AAL; CLC 70, 198
See Jen, Lillian
See also AMWC 2
Jen, Lillian 1956(?)-
See Jen, Gish
See also CA 135; CANR 89, 130
Jenkins, (John) Robin 1912- .... CLC 52
See also CA 1-4R; CANR 1, 135; CN 7;
DLB 14, 271
Jennings, Elizabeth (Joan)
1926-2001 .... CLC 5, 14, 131
See also BRWS 5; CA 61-64; 200; CAAS
5; CANR 8, 39, 66, 127; CP 7; CWP;
DLB 27; EWL 3; MTCW 1; SATA 66
Jennings, Waylon 1937- .... CLC 21
Jensen, Johannes V(ilhelm)
1873-1950 .... TCLC 41
See also CA 170; DLB 214; EWL 3; RGWL
3
Jensen, Laura (Linnea) 1948- .... CLC 37
See also CA 103
Jerome, Saint 345-420 .... CMLC 30
See also RGWL 3
Jerome, Jerome K(lapka)
1859-1927 .... TCLC 23
See also CA 119; 177; DLB 10, 34, 135;
RGEL 2
Jerrold, Douglas William
1803-1857 .... NCLC 2
See also DLB 158, 159; RGEL 2
Jewett, (Theodora) Sarah Orne
1849-1909 .... SSC 6, 44; TCLC 1, 22
See also AMW; AMWC 2; AMWR 2; CA
108; 127; CANR 71; DLB 12, 74, 221;
EXPS; FW; MAWW; NFS 15; RGAL 4;
RGSF 2; SATA 15; SSFS 4
Jewsbury, Geraldine (Endsor)
1812-1880 .... NCLC 22
See also DLB 21
Jhabvala, Ruth Prawer 1927- . CLC 4, 8, 29,
94, 138
See also BRWS 5; CA 1-4R; CANR 2, 29,
51, 74, 91, 128; CN 7; DAB; DAM NOV;
DLB 139, 194; EWL 3; IDFW 3, 4; INT
CANR-29; MTCW 1, 2; RGSF 2; RGWL
2; RHW; TEA
Jibran, Kahlil
See Gibran, Kahlil

Jibran, Khalil
See Gibran, Kahlil
Jiles, Paulette 1943- .... CLC 13, 58
See also CA 101; CANR 70, 124; CWP
Jimenez (Mantecon), Juan Ramon
1881-1958 .... HLC 1; PC 7; TCLC 4
See also CA 104; 131; CANR 74; DAM
MULT, POET; DLB 134; EW 9; EWL 3;
HW 1; MTCW 1, 2; RGWL 2, 3
Jimenez, Ramon
See Jimenez (Mantecon), Juan Ramon
Jimenez Mantecon, Juan
See Jimenez (Mantecon), Juan Ramon
Jin, Ha .... CLC 109
See Jin, Xuefei
See also CA 152; DLB 244, 292; SSFS 17
Jin, Xuefei 1956-
See Jin, Ha
See also CANR 91, 130; SSFS 17
Joel, Billy .... CLC 26
See Joel, William Martin
Joel, William Martin 1949-
See Joel, Billy
See also CA 108
John, Saint 10(?)-100 .... CMLC 27, 63
John of Salisbury c. 1115-1180 ..... CMLC 63
John of the Cross, St. 1542-1591 .... LC 18
See also RGWL 2, 3
John Paul II, Pope 1920- .... CLC 128
See also CA 106; 133
Johnson, B(ryan) S(tanley William)
1933-1973 .... CLC 6, 9
See also CA 9-12R; 53-56; CANR 9; DLB
14, 40; EWL 3; RGEL 2
Johnson, Benjamin F., of Boone
See Riley, James Whitcomb
Johnson, Charles (Richard) 1948- .... BLC 2;
CLC 7, 51, 65, 163
See also AFAW 2; AMWS 6; BW 2, 3; CA
116; CAAS 18; CANR 42, 66, 82, 129;
CN 7; DAM MULT; DLB 33, 278;
MTCW 2; RGAL 4; SSFS 16
Johnson, Charles S(purgeon)
1893-1956 .... HR 3
See also BW 1, 3; CA 125; CANR 82; DLB
51, 91
Johnson, Denis 1949- . CLC 52, 160; SSC 56
See also CA 117; 121; CANR 71, 99; CN
7; DLB 120
Johnson, Diane 1934- .... CLC 5, 13, 48
See also BPFB 2; CA 41-44R; CANR 17,
40, 62, 95; CN 7; DLBY 1980; INT
CANR-17; MTCW 1
Johnson, E. Pauline 1861-1913 .... NNAL
See also CA 150; DAC; DAM MULT; DLB
92, 175
Johnson, Eyvind (Olof Verner)
1900-1976 .... CLC 14
See also CA 73-76; 69-72; CANR 34, 101;
DLB 259; EW 12; EWL 3
Johnson, Fenton 1888-1958 .... BLC 2
See also BW 1; CA 118; 124; DAM MULT;
DLB 45, 50
Johnson, Georgia Douglas (Camp)
1880-1966 .... HR 3
See also BW 1; CA 125; DLB 51, 249; WP
Johnson, Helene 1907-1995 .... HR 3
See also CA 181; DLB 51; WP
Johnson, J. R.
See James, C(yril) L(ionel) R(obert)
Johnson, James Weldon 1871-1938 .. BLC 2;
HR 3; PC 24; TCLC 3, 19
See also AFAW 1, 2; BW 1, 3; CA 104;
125; CANR 82; CDALB 1917-1929; CLR
32; DA3; DAM MULT, POET; DLB 51;
EWL 3; EXPP; LMFS 2; MTCW 1, 2;
PFS 1; RGAL 4; SATA 31; TUS
Johnson, Joyce 1935- .... CLC 58
See also BG 3; CA 125; 129; CANR 102

Johnson, Judith (Emlyn) 1936- .... **CLC 7, 15**
See Sherwin, Judith Johnson
See also CA 25-28R, 153; CANR 34

Johnson, Lionel (Pigot)
1867-1902 .... **TCLC 19**
See also CA 117; 209; DLB 19; RGEL 2

Johnson, Marguerite Annie
See Angelou, Maya

Johnson, Mel
See Malzberg, Barry N(athaniel)

Johnson, Pamela Hansford
1912-1981 .... **CLC 1, 7, 27**
See also CA 1-4R; 104; CANR 2, 28; DLB
15; MTCW 1, 2; RGEL 2

Johnson, Paul (Bede) 1928- .... **CLC 147**
See also BEST 89:4; CA 17-20R; CANR
34, 62, 100

Johnson, Robert .... **CLC 70**

Johnson, Robert 1911(?)-1938 .... **TCLC 69**
See also BW 3; CA 174

Johnson, Samuel 1709-1784 .... **LC 15, 52;
WLC**
See also BRW 3; BRWR 1; CDBLB 1660-
1789; DA; DAB; DAC; DAM MST; DLB
39, 95, 104, 142, 213; LMFS 1; RGEL 2;
TEA

Johnson, Uwe 1934-1984 .. **CLC 5, 10, 15, 40**
See also CA 1-4R; 112; CANR 1, 39; CD-
WLB 2; DLB 75; EWL 3; MTCW 1;
RGWL 2, 3

Johnston, Basil H. 1929- .... **NNAL**
See also CA 69-72; CANR 11, 28, 66;
DAC; DAM MULT; DLB 60

Johnston, George (Benson) 1913- .... **CLC 51**
See also CA 1-4R; CANR 5, 20; CP 7; DLB
88

Johnston, Jennifer (Prudence)
1930- .... **CLC 7, 150**
See also CA 85-88; CANR 92; CN 7; DLB
14

Joinville, Jean de 1224(?)-1317 ..... **CMLC 38**

Jolley, (Monica) Elizabeth 1923- ..... **CLC 46;
SSC 19**
See also CA 127; CAAS 13; CANR 59; CN
7; EWL 3; RGSF 2

Jones, Arthur Llewellyn 1863-1947
See Machen, Arthur
See also CA 104; 179; HGG

Jones, D(ouglas) G(ordon) 1929- ..... **CLC 10**
See also CA 29-32R; CANR 13, 90; CP 7;
DLB 53

Jones, David (Michael) 1895-1974 .... **CLC 2,
4, 7, 13, 42**
See also BRW 6; BRWS 7; CA 9-12R; 53-
56; CANR 28; CDBLB 1945-1960; DLB
20, 100; EWL 3; MTCW 1; PAB; RGEL
2

Jones, David Robert 1947-
See Bowie, David
See also CA 103; CANR 104

Jones, Diana Wynne 1934- .... **CLC 26**
See also AAYA 12; BYA 6, 7, 9, 11, 13, 16;
CA 49-52; CANR 4, 26, 56, 120; CLR
23; DLB 161; FANT; JRDA; MAICYA 1,
2; SAAS 7; SATA 9, 70, 108; SFW 4;
YAW

Jones, Edward P. 1950- .... **CLC 76**
See also BW 2, 3; CA 142; CANR 79, 134;
CSW

Jones, Gayl 1949- ..... **BLC 2; CLC 6, 9, 131**
See also AFAW 1, 2; BW 2, 3; CA 77-80;
CANR 27, 66, 122; CN 7; CSW; DA3;
DAM MULT; DLB 33, 278; MTCW 1, 2;
RGAL 4

Jones, James 1921-1977 ...... **CLC 1, 3, 10, 39**
See also AITN 1, 2; AMWS 11; BPFB 2;
CA 1-4R; 69-72; CANR 6; DLB 2, 143;
DLBD 17; DLBY 1998; EWL 3; MTCW
1; RGAL 4

Jones, John J.
See Lovecraft, H(oward) P(hillips)

Jones, LeRoi .... **CLC 1, 2, 3, 5, 10, 14**
See Baraka, Amiri
See also MTCW 2

Jones, Louis B. 1953- .... **CLC 65**
See also CA 141; CANR 73

Jones, Madison (Percy, Jr.) 1925- ...... **CLC 4**
See also CA 13-16R; CAAS 11; CANR 7,
54, 83; CN 7; CSW; DLB 152

Jones, Mervyn 1922- .... **CLC 10, 52**
See also CA 45-48; CAAS 5; CANR 1, 91;
CN 7; MTCW 1

Jones, Mick 1956(?)- .... **CLC 30**

Jones, Nettie (Pearl) 1941- .... **CLC 34**
See also BW 2; CA 137; CAAS 20; CANR
88

Jones, Peter 1802-1856 .... **NNAL**

Jones, Preston 1936-1979 .... **CLC 10**
See also CA 73-76; 89-92; DLB 7

Jones, Robert F(rancis) 1934-2003 .... **CLC 7**
See also CA 49-52; CANR 2, 61, 118

Jones, Rod 1953- .... **CLC 50**
See also CA 128

Jones, Terence Graham Parry
1942- .... **CLC 21**
See Jones, Terry; Monty Python
See also CA 112; 116; CANR 35, 93; INT
CA-116; SATA 127

Jones, Terry
See Jones, Terence Graham Parry
See also SATA 67; SATA-Brief 51

Jones, Thom (Douglas) 1945(?)- ..... **CLC 81;
SSC 56**
See also CA 157; CANR 88; DLB 244

Jong, Erica 1942- .... **CLC 4, 6, 8, 18, 83**
See also AITN 1; AMWS 5; BEST 90:2;
BPFB 2; CA 73-76; CANR 26, 52, 75,
132; CN 7; CP 7; CPW; DA3; DAM
NOV, POP; DLB 2, 5, 28, 152; FW; INT
CANR-26; MTCW 1, 2

Jonson, Ben(jamin) 1572(?)-1637 . **DC 4; LC
6, 33, 110; PC 17; WLC**
See also BRW 1; BRWC 1; BRWR 1; CD-
BLB Before 1660; DA; DAB; DAC;
DAM DRAM, MST, POET; DFS 4, 10;
DLB 62, 121; LMFS 1; RGEL 2; TEA;
WLIT 3

Jordan, June (Meyer)
1936-2002 .. **BLCS; CLC 5, 11, 23, 114;
PC 38**
See also AAYA 2; AFAW 1, 2; BW 2, 3;
CA 33-36R; 206; CANR 25, 70, 114; CLR
10; CP 7; CWP; DAM MULT, POET;
DLB 38; GLL 2; LAIT 5; MAICYA 1, 2;
MTCW 1; SATA 4, 136; YAW

Jordan, Neil (Patrick) 1950- .... **CLC 110**
See also CA 124; 130; CANR 54; CN 7;
GLL 2; INT CA-130

Jordan, Pat(rick M.) 1941- .... **CLC 37**
See also CA 33-36R; CANR 121

Jorgensen, Ivar
See Ellison, Harlan (Jay)

Jorgenson, Ivar
See Silverberg, Robert

Joseph, George Ghevarughese .... **CLC 70**

Josephson, Mary
See O'Doherty, Brian

Josephus, Flavius c. 37-100 .... **CMLC 13**
See also AW 2; DLB 176

Josiah Allen's Wife
See Holley, Marietta

Josipovici, Gabriel (David) 1940- ...... **CLC 6,
43, 153**
See also CA 37-40R; 224; CAAE 224;
CAAS 8; CANR 47, 84; CN 7; DLB 14

Joubert, Joseph 1754-1824 .... **NCLC 9**

Jouve, Pierre Jean 1887-1976 .... **CLC 47**
See also CA 65-68; DLB 258; EWL 3

Jovine, Francesco 1902-1950 .... **TCLC 79**
See also DLB 264; EWL 3

Joyce, James (Augustine Aloysius)
1882-1941 .... **DC 16; PC 22; SSC 3, 26,
44, 64; TCLC 3, 8, 16, 35, 52, 159;
WLC**
See also AAYA 42; BRW 7; BRWC 1;
BRWR 1; BYA 11, 13; CA 104; 126; CD-
BLB 1914-1945; DA; DA3; DAB; DAC;
DAM MST, NOV, POET; DLB 10, 19,
36, 162, 247; EWL 3; EXPN; EXPS;
LAIT 3; LMFS 1, 2; MTCW 1, 2; NFS 7;
RGSF 2; SSFS 1, 19; TEA; WLIT 4

Jozsef, Attila 1905-1937 .... **TCLC 22**
See also CA 116; CDWLB 4; DLB 215;
EWL 3

Juana Ines de la Cruz, Sor
1651(?)-1695 ...... **HLCS 1; LC 5; PC 24**
See also DLB 305; FW; LAW; RGWL 2, 3;
WLIT 1

Juana Inez de La Cruz, Sor
See Juana Ines de la Cruz, Sor

Judd, Cyril
See Kornbluth, C(yril) M.; Pohl, Frederik

Juenger, Ernst 1895-1998 .... **CLC 125**
See Junger, Ernst
See also CA 101; 167; CANR 21, 47, 106;
DLB 56

Julian of Norwich 1342(?)-1416(?) . **LC 6, 52**
See also DLB 146; LMFS 1

Julius Caesar 100B.C.-44B.C.
See Caesar, Julius
See also CDWLB 1; DLB 211

Junger, Ernst
See Juenger, Ernst
See also CDWLB 2; EWL 3; RGWL 2, 3

Junger, Sebastian 1962- .... **CLC 109**
See also AAYA 28; CA 165; CANR 130

Juniper, Alex
See Hospital, Janette Turner

Junius
See Luxemburg, Rosa

Just, Ward (Swift) 1935- .... **CLC 4, 27**
See also CA 25-28R; CANR 32, 87; CN 7;
INT CANR-32

Justice, Donald (Rodney)
1925-2004 .... **CLC 6, 19, 102**
See also AMWS 7; CA 5-8R; CANR 26,
54, 74, 121, 122; CP 7; CSW; DAM
POET; DLBY 1983; EWL 3; INT CANR-
26; MTCW 2; PFS 14

Juvenal c. 60-c. 130 .... **CMLC 8**
See also AW 2; CDWLB 1; DLB 211;
RGWL 2, 3

Juvenis
See Bourne, Randolph S(illiman)

K., Alice
See Knapp, Caroline

Kabakov, Sasha .... **CLC 59**

Kabir 1398(?)-1448(?) .... **LC 109; PC 56**
See also RGWL 2, 3

Kacew, Romain 1914-1980
See Gary, Romain
See also CA 108; 102

Kadare, Ismail 1936- .... **CLC 52, 190**
See also CA 161; EWL 3; RGWL 3

Kadohata, Cynthia 1956(?)- .... **CLC 59, 122**
See also CA 140; CANR 124

Kafka, Franz 1883-1924 ... **SSC 5, 29, 35, 60;
TCLC 2, 6, 13, 29, 47, 53, 112; WLC**
See also AAYA 31; BPFB 2; CA 105; 126;
CDWLB 2; DA; DA3; DAB; DAC; DAM
MST, NOV; DLB 81; EW 9; EWL 3;
EXPS; LATS 1:1; LMFS 2; MTCW 1, 2;
NFS 7; RGSF 2; RGWL 2, 3; SFW 4;
SSFS 3, 7, 12; TWA

Kahanovitsch, Pinkhes
See Der Nister

Kahn, Roger 1927- .... **CLC 30**
See also CA 25-28R; CANR 44, 69; DLB
171; SATA 37

Kain, Saul
See Sassoon, Siegfried (Lorraine)

Kaiser, Georg 1878-1945 .... **TCLC 9**
See also CA 106; 190; CDWLB 2; DLB
124; EWL 3; LMFS 2; RGWL 2, 3

Kaledin, Sergei .... **CLC 59**

Kaletski, Alexander 1946- .... **CLC 39**
See also CA 118; 143

Kalidasa fl. c. 400-455 .... **CMLC 9; PC 22**
See also RGWL 2, 3

Kallman, Chester (Simon)
1921-1975 .... **CLC 2**
See also CA 45-48; 53-56; CANR 3

Kaminsky, Melvin 1926-
See Brooks, Mel
See also CA 65-68; CANR 16

Kaminsky, Stuart M(elvin) 1934- ..... **CLC 59**
See also CA 73-76; CANR 29, 53, 89;
CMW 4

Kamo no Chomei 1153(?)-1216 .... **CMLC 66**
See also DLB 203

Kamo no Nagaakira
See Kamo no Chomei

Kandinsky, Wassily 1866-1944 .... **TCLC 92**
See also CA 118; 155

Kane, Francis
See Robbins, Harold

Kane, Henry 1918-
See Queen, Ellery
See also CA 156; CMW 4

Kane, Paul
See Simon, Paul (Frederick)

Kanin, Garson 1912-1999 .... **CLC 22**
See also AITN 1; CA 5-8R; 177; CAD;
CANR 7, 78; DLB 7; IDFW 3, 4

Kaniuk, Yoram 1930- .... **CLC 19**
See also CA 134; DLB 299

Kant, Immanuel 1724-1804 ..... **NCLC 27, 67**
See also DLB 94

Kantor, MacKinlay 1904-1977 .... **CLC 7**
See also CA 61-64; 73-76; CANR 60, 63;
DLB 9, 102; MTCW 2; RHW; TCWW 2

Kanze Motokiyo
See Zeami

Kaplan, David Michael 1946- .... **CLC 50**
See also CA 187

Kaplan, James 1951- .... **CLC 59**
See also CA 135; CANR 121

Karadzic, Vuk Stefanovic
1787-1864 .... **NCLC 115**
See also CDWLB 4; DLB 147

Karageorge, Michael
See Anderson, Poul (William)

Karamzin, Nikolai Mikhailovich
1766-1826 .... **NCLC 3**
See also DLB 150; RGSF 2

Karapanou, Margarita 1946- .... **CLC 13**
See also CA 101

Karinthy, Frigyes 1887-1938 .... **TCLC 47**
See also CA 170; DLB 215; EWL 3

Karl, Frederick R(obert)
1927-2004 .... **CLC 34**
See also CA 5-8R; 226; CANR 3, 44

Karr, Mary 1955- .... **CLC 188**
See also AMWS 11; CA 151; CANR 100;
NCFS 5

Kastel, Warren
See Silverberg, Robert

Kataev, Evgeny Petrovich 1903-1942
See Petrov, Evgeny
See also CA 120

Kataphusin
See Ruskin, John

Katz, Steve 1935- .... **CLC 47**
See also CA 25-28R; CAAS 14, 64; CANR
12; CN 7; DLBY 1983

Kauffman, Janet 1945- .... **CLC 42**
See also CA 117; CANR 43, 84; DLB 218;
DLBY 1986

Kaufman, Bob (Garnell) 1925-1986 . **CLC 49**
See also BG 3; BW 1; CA 41-44R; 118;
CANR 22; DLB 16, 41

Kaufman, George S. 1889-1961 ...... **CLC 38;
DC 17**
See also CA 108; 93-96; DAM DRAM;
DFS 1, 10; DLB 7; INT CA-108; MTCW
2; RGAL 4; TUS

Kaufman, Sue .... **CLC 3, 8**
See Barondess, Sue K(aufman)

Kavafis, Konstantinos Petrou 1863-1933
See Cavafy, C(onstantine) P(eter)
See also CA 104

Kavan, Anna 1901-1968 .... **CLC 5, 13, 82**
See also BRWS 7; CA 5-8R; CANR 6, 57;
DLB 255; MTCW 1; RGEL 2; SFW 4

Kavanagh, Dan
See Barnes, Julian (Patrick)

Kavanagh, Julie 1952- .... **CLC 119**
See also CA 163

Kavanagh, Patrick (Joseph)
1904-1967 .... **CLC 22; PC 33**
See also BRWS 7; CA 123; 25-28R; DLB
15, 20; EWL 3; MTCW 1; RGEL 2

Kawabata, Yasunari 1899-1972 ..... **CLC 2, 5,
9, 18, 107; SSC 17**
See Kawabata Yasunari
See also CA 93-96; 33-36R; CANR 88;
DAM MULT; MJW; MTCW 2; RGSF 2;
RGWL 2, 3

Kawabata Yasunari
See Kawabata, Yasunari
See also DLB 180; EWL 3

Kaye, M(ary) M(argaret)
1908-2004 .... **CLC 28**
See also CA 89-92; 223; CANR 24, 60, 102;
MTCW 1, 2; RHW; SATA 62; SATA-Obit
152

Kaye, Mollie
See Kaye, M(ary) M(argaret)

Kaye-Smith, Sheila 1887-1956 .... **TCLC 20**
See also CA 118; 203; DLB 36

Kaymor, Patrice Maguilene
See Senghor, Leopold Sedar

Kazakov, Iurii Pavlovich
See Kazakov, Yuri Pavlovich
See also DLB 302

Kazakov, Yuri Pavlovich 1927-1982 . **SSC 43**
See Kazakov, Iurii Pavlovich; Kazakov,
Yury
See also CA 5-8R; CANR 36; MTCW 1;
RGSF 2

Kazakov, Yury
See Kazakov, Yuri Pavlovich
See also EWL 3

Kazan, Elia 1909-2003 .... **CLC 6, 16, 63**
See also CA 21-24R; 220; CANR 32, 78

Kazantzakis, Nikos 1883(?)-1957 .... **TCLC 2,
5, 33**
See also BPFB 2; CA 105; 132; DA3; EW
9; EWL 3; MTCW 1, 2; RGWL 2, 3

Kazin, Alfred 1915-1998 ..... **CLC 34, 38, 119**
See also AMWS 8; CA 1-4R; CAAS 7;
CANR 1, 45, 79; DLB 67; EWL 3

Keane, Mary Nesta (Skrine) 1904-1996
See Keane, Molly
See also CA 108; 114; 151; CN 7; RHW

Keane, Molly .... **CLC 31**
See Keane, Mary Nesta (Skrine)
See also INT CA-114

Keates, Jonathan 1946(?)- .... **CLC 34**
See also CA 163; CANR 126

Keaton, Buster 1895-1966 .... **CLC 20**
See also CA 194

Keats, John 1795-1821 ...... **NCLC 8, 73, 121;
PC 1; WLC**
See also AAYA 58; BRW 4; BRWR 1; CD-
BLB 1789-1832; DA; DA3; DAB; DAC;
DAM MST, POET; DLB 96, 110; EXPP;
LMFS 1; PAB; PFS 1, 2, 3, 9, 17; RGEL
2; TEA; WLIT 3; WP

Keble, John 1792-1866 .... **NCLC 87**
See also DLB 32, 55; RGEL 2

Keene, Donald 1922- .... **CLC 34**
See also CA 1-4R; CANR 5, 119

Keillor, Garrison .... **CLC 40, 115**
See Keillor, Gary (Edward)
See also AAYA 2; BEST 89:3; BPFB 2;
DLBY 1987; EWL 3; SATA 58; TUS

Keillor, Gary (Edward) 1942-
See Keillor, Garrison
See also CA 111; 117; CANR 36, 59, 124;
CPW; DA3; DAM POP; MTCW 1, 2

Keith, Carlos
See Lewton, Val

Keith, Michael
See Hubbard, L(afayette) Ron(ald)

Keller, Gottfried 1819-1890 .... **NCLC 2; SSC
26**
See also CDWLB 2; DLB 129; EW; RGSF
2; RGWL 2, 3

Keller, Nora Okja 1965- .... **CLC 109**
See also CA 187

Kellerman, Jonathan 1949- .... **CLC 44**
See also AAYA 35; BEST 90:1; CA 106;
CANR 29, 51; CMW 4; CPW; DA3;
DAM POP; INT CANR-29

Kelley, William Melvin 1937- .... **CLC 22**
See also BW 1; CA 77-80; CANR 27, 83;
CN 7; DLB 33; EWL 3

Kellogg, Marjorie 1922- .... **CLC 2**
See also CA 81-84

Kellow, Kathleen
See Hibbert, Eleanor Alice Burford

Kelly, M(ilton) T(errence) 1947- ...... **CLC 55**
See also CA 97-100; CAAS 22; CANR 19,
43, 84; CN 7

Kelly, Robert 1935- .... **SSC 50**
See also CA 17-20R; CAAS 19; CANR 47;
CP 7; DLB 5, 130, 165

Kelman, James 1946- .... **CLC 58, 86**
See also BRWS 5; CA 148; CANR 85, 130;
CN 7; DLB 194; RGSF 2; WLIT 4

Kemal, Yasar
See Kemal, Yashar
See also CWW 2; EWL 3

Kemal, Yashar 1923(?)- .... **CLC 14, 29**
See also CA 89-92; CANR 44

Kemble, Fanny 1809-1893 .... **NCLC 18**
See also DLB 32

Kemelman, Harry 1908-1996 .... **CLC 2**
See also AITN 1; BPFB 2; CA 9-12R; 155;
CANR 6, 71; CMW 4; DLB 28

Kempe, Margery 1373(?)-1440(?) ... **LC 6, 56**
See also DLB 146; RGEL 2

Kempis, Thomas a 1380-1471 .... **LC 11**

Kendall, Henry 1839-1882 .... **NCLC 12**
See also DLB 230

Keneally, Thomas (Michael) 1935- ... **CLC 5,
8, 10, 14, 19, 27, 43, 117**
See also BRWS 4; CA 85-88; CANR 10,
50, 74, 130; CN 7; CPW; DA3; DAM
NOV; DLB 289, 299; EWL 3; MTCW 1,
2; NFS 17; RGEL 2; RHW

Kennedy, A(lison) L(ouise) 1965- ... **CLC 188**
See also CA 168; 213; CAAE 213; CANR
108; CD 5; CN 7; DLB 271; RGSF 2

Kennedy, Adrienne (Lita) 1931- .... **BLC 2;
CLC 66; DC 5**
See also AFAW 2; BW 2, 3; CA 103; CAAS
20; CABS 3; CANR 26, 53, 82; CD 5;
DAM MULT; DFS 9; DLB 38; FW

Kennedy, John Pendleton
1795-1870 .... **NCLC 2**
See also DLB 3, 248, 254; RGAL 4

Kennedy, Joseph Charles 1929-
See Kennedy, X. J.
See also CA 1-4R, 201; CAAE 201; CANR
4, 30, 40; CP 7; CWRI 5; MAICYA 2;
MAICYAS 1; SATA 14, 86, 130; SATA-
Essay 130

Kennedy, William 1928- ... **CLC 6, 28, 34, 53**
See also AAYA 1; AMWS 7; BPFB 2; CA
85-88; CANR 14, 31, 76, 134; CN 7;
DA3; DAM NOV; DLB 143; DLBY 1985;
EWL 3; INT CANR-31; MTCW 1, 2;
SATA 57

Kennedy, X. J. .... **CLC 8, 42**
See Kennedy, Joseph Charles
See also CAAS 9; CLR 27; DLB 5; SAAS
22

Kenny, Maurice (Francis) 1929- ..... **CLC 87;
NNAL**
See also CA 144; CAAS 22; DAM MULT;
DLB 175

Kent, Kelvin
See Kuttner, Henry

Kenton, Maxwell
See Southern, Terry

Kenyon, Jane 1947-1995 .... **PC 57**
See also AMWS 7; CA 118; 148; CANR
44, 69; CP 7; CWP; DLB 120; PFS 9, 17;
RGAL 4

Kenyon, Robert O.
See Kuttner, Henry

Kepler, Johannes 1571-1630 .... **LC 45**

Ker, Jill
See Conway, Jill K(er)

Kerkow, H. C.
See Lewton, Val

Kerouac, Jack 1922-1969 ...... **CLC 1, 2, 3, 5,
14, 29, 61; TCLC 117; WLC**
See Kerouac, Jean-Louis Lebris de
See also AAYA 25; AMWC 1; AMWS 3;
BG 3; BPFB 2; CDALB 1941-1968;
CPW; DLB 2, 16, 237; DLBD 3; DLBY
1995; EWL 3; GLL 1; LATS 1:2; LMFS
2; MTCW 2; NFS 8; RGAL 4; TUS; WP

Kerouac, Jean-Louis Lebris de 1922-1969
See Kerouac, Jack
See also AITN 1; CA 5-8R; 25-28R; CANR
26, 54, 95; DA; DA3; DAB; DAC; DAM
MST, NOV, POET, POP; MTCW 1, 2

Kerr, (Bridget) Jean (Collins)
1923(?)-2003 .... **CLC 22**
See also CA 5-8R; 212; CANR 7; INT
CANR-7

Kerr, M. E. .... **CLC 12, 35**
See Meaker, Marijane (Agnes)
See also AAYA 2, 23; BYA 1, 7, 8; CLR
29; SAAS 1; WYA

Kerr, Robert .... **CLC 55**

Kerrigan, (Thomas) Anthony 1918- .. **CLC 4,
6**
See also CA 49-52; CAAS 11; CANR 4

Kerry, Lois
See Duncan, Lois

Kesey, Ken (Elton) 1935-2001 ... **CLC 1, 3, 6,
11, 46, 64, 184; WLC**
See also AAYA 25; BG 3; BPFB 2; CA
1-4R; 204; CANR 22, 38, 66, 124;
CDALB 1968-1988; CN 7; CPW; DA;
DA3; DAB; DAC; DAM MST, NOV,
POP; DLB 2, 16, 206; EWL 3; EXPN;
LAIT 4; MTCW 1, 2; NFS 2; RGAL 4;
SATA 66; SATA-Obit 131; TUS; YAW

Kesselring, Joseph (Otto)
1902-1967 .... **CLC 45**
See also CA 150; DAM DRAM, MST; DFS
20

Kessler, Jascha (Frederick) 1929- ...... **CLC 4**
See also CA 17-20R; CANR 8, 48, 111

Kettelkamp, Larry (Dale) 1933- .... **CLC 12**
See also CA 29-32R; CANR 16; SAAS 3;
SATA 2

Key, Ellen (Karolina Sofia)
1849-1926 .... **TCLC 65**
See also DLB 259

Keyber, Conny
See Fielding, Henry

Keyes, Daniel 1927- .... **CLC 80**
See also AAYA 23; BYA 11; CA 17-20R,
181; CAAE 181; CANR 10, 26, 54, 74;
DA; DA3; DAC; DAM MST, NOV;
EXPN; LAIT 4; MTCW 2; NFS 2; SATA
37; SFW 4

Keynes, John Maynard
1883-1946 .... **TCLC 64**
See also CA 114; 162, 163; DLBD 10;
MTCW 2

Khanshendel, Chiron
See Rose, Wendy

Khayyam, Omar 1048-1131 ... **CMLC 11; PC
8**
See Omar Khayyam
See also DA3; DAM POET

Kherdian, David 1931- .... **CLC 6, 9**
See also AAYA 42; CA 21-24R, 192; CAAE
192; CAAS 2; CANR 39, 78; CLR 24;
JRDA; LAIT 3; MAICYA 1, 2; SATA 16,
74; SATA-Essay 125

Khlebnikov, Velimir .... **TCLC 20**
See Khlebnikov, Viktor Vladimirovich
See also DLB 295; EW 10; EWL 3; RGWL
2, 3

Khlebnikov, Viktor Vladimirovich 1885-1922
See Khlebnikov, Velimir
See also CA 117; 217

Khodasevich, Vladislav (Felitsianovich)
1886-1939 .... **TCLC 15**
See also CA 115; EWL 3

Kielland, Alexander Lange
1849-1906 .... **TCLC 5**
See also CA 104

Kiely, Benedict 1919- ... **CLC 23, 43; SSC 58**
See also CA 1-4R; CANR 2, 84; CN 7;
DLB 15

Kienzle, William X(avier)
1928-2001 .... **CLC 25**
See also CA 93-96; 203; CAAS 1; CANR
9, 31, 59, 111; CMW 4; DA3; DAM POP;
INT CANR-31; MSW; MTCW 1, 2

Kierkegaard, Soren 1813-1855 ..... **NCLC 34,
78, 125**
See also DLB 300; EW 6; LMFS 2; RGWL
3; TWA

Kieslowski, Krzysztof 1941-1996 .... **CLC 120**
See also CA 147; 151

Killens, John Oliver 1916-1987 .... **CLC 10**
See also BW 2; CA 77-80; 123; CAAS 2;
CANR 26; DLB 33; EWL 3

Killigrew, Anne 1660-1685 .... **LC 4, 73**
See also DLB 131

Killigrew, Thomas 1612-1683 .... **LC 57**
See also DLB 58; RGEL 2

Kim
See Simenon, Georges (Jacques Christian)

Kincaid, Jamaica 1949- ...... **BLC 2; CLC 43,
68, 137; SSC 72**
See also AAYA 13, 56; AFAW 2; AMWS 7;
BRWS 7; BW 2, 3; CA 125; CANR 47,
59, 95, 133; CDALBS; CDWLB 3; CLR
63; CN 7; DA3; DAM MULT, NOV; DLB

157, 227; DNFS 1; EWL 3; EXPS; FW;
LATS 1:2; LMFS 2; MTCW 2; NCFS 1;
NFS 3; SSFS 5, 7; TUS; WWE 1; YAW

King, Francis (Henry) 1923- .... **CLC 8, 53,
145**
See also CA 1-4R; CANR 1, 33, 86; CN 7;
DAM NOV; DLB 15, 139; MTCW 1

King, Kennedy
See Brown, George Douglas

King, Martin Luther, Jr. 1929-1968 . **BLC 2;
CLC 83; WLCS**
See also BW 2, 3; CA 25-28; CANR 27,
44; CAP 2; DA; DA3; DAB; DAC; DAM
MST, MULT; LAIT 5; LATS 1:2; MTCW
1, 2; SATA 14

King, Stephen (Edwin) 1947- .... **CLC 12, 26,
37, 61, 113; SSC 17, 55**
See also AAYA 1, 17; AMWS 5; BEST
90:1; BPFB 2; CA 61-64; CANR 1, 30,
52, 76, 119, 134; CPW; DA3; DAM NOV,
POP; DLB 143; DLBY 1980; HGG;
JRDA; LAIT 5; MTCW 1, 2; RGAL 4;
SATA 9, 55; SUFW 1, 2; WYAS 1; YAW

King, Steve
See King, Stephen (Edwin)

King, Thomas 1943- .... **CLC 89, 171; NNAL**
See also CA 144; CANR 95; CCA 1; CN 7;
DAC; DAM MULT; DLB 175; SATA 96

Kingman, Lee .... **CLC 17**
See Natti, (Mary) Lee
See also CWRI 5; SAAS 3; SATA 1, 67

Kingsley, Charles 1819-1875 .... **NCLC 35**
See also CLR 77; DLB 21, 32, 163, 178,
190; FANT; MAICYA 2; MAICYAS 1;
RGEL 2; WCH; YABC 2

Kingsley, Henry 1830-1876 .... **NCLC 107**
See also DLB 21, 230; RGEL 2

Kingsley, Sidney 1906-1995 .... **CLC 44**
See also CA 85-88; 147; CAD; DFS 14, 19;
DLB 7; RGAL 4

Kingsolver, Barbara 1955- . **CLC 55, 81, 130**
See also AAYA 15; AMWS 7; CA 129; 134;
CANR 60, 96, 133; CDALBS; CPW;
CSW; DA3; DAM POP; DLB 206; INT
CA-134; LAIT 5; MTCW 2; NFS 5, 10,
12; RGAL 4

Kingston, Maxine (Ting Ting) Hong
1940- .... **AAL; CLC 12, 19, 58, 121;
WLCS**
See also AAYA 8, 55; AMWS 5; BPFB 2;
CA 69-72; CANR 13, 38, 74, 87, 128;
CDALBS; CN 7; DA3; DAM MULT,
NOV; DLB 173, 212; DLBY 1980; EWL
3; FW; INT CANR-13; LAIT 5; MAWW;
MTCW 1, 2; NFS 6; RGAL 4; SATA 53;
SSFS 3

Kinnell, Galway 1927- ..... **CLC 1, 2, 3, 5, 13,
29, 129; PC 26**
See also AMWS 3; CA 9-12R; CANR 10,
34, 66, 116; CP 7; DLB 5; DLBY 1987;
EWL 3; INT CANR-34; MTCW 1, 2;
PAB; PFS 9; RGAL 4; WP

Kinsella, Thomas 1928- .... **CLC 4, 19, 138**
See also BRWS 5; CA 17-20R; CANR 15,
122; CP 7; DLB 27; EWL 3; MTCW 1, 2;
RGEL 2; TEA

Kinsella, W(illiam) P(atrick) 1935- . **CLC 27,
43, 166**
See also AAYA 7, 60; BPFB 2; CA 97-100,
222; CAAE 222; CAAS 7; CANR 21, 35,
66, 75, 129; CN 7; CPW; DAC; DAM
NOV, POP; FANT; INT CANR-21; LAIT
5; MTCW 1, 2; NFS 15; RGSF 2

Kinsey, Alfred C(harles)
1894-1956 .... **TCLC 91**
See also CA 115; 170; MTCW 2

Kipling, (Joseph) Rudyard 1865-1936 . **PC 3;
SSC 5, 54; TCLC 8, 17; WLC**
See also AAYA 32; BRW 6; BRWC 1, 2;
BYA 4; CA 105; 120; CANR 33; CDBLB
1890-1914; CLR 39, 65; CWRI 5; DA;

DA3; DAB; DAC; DAM MST, POET; DLB 19, 34, 141, 156; EWL 3; EXPS; FANT; LAIT 3; LMFS 1; MAICYA 1, 2; MTCW 1, 2; RGEL 2; RGSF 2; SATA 100; SFW 4; SSFS 8; SUFW 1; TEA; WCH; WLIT 4; YABC 2

Kirk, Russell (Amos) 1918-1994 .. **TCLC 119**
See also AITN 1; CA 1-4R; 145; CAAS 9; CANR 1, 20, 60; HGG; INT CANR-20; MTCW 1, 2

Kirkham, Dinah
See Card, Orson Scott

Kirkland, Caroline M. 1801-1864 . **NCLC 85**
See also DLB 3, 73, 74, 250, 254; DLBD 13

Kirkup, James 1918- .... **CLC 1**
See also CA 1-4R; CAAS 4; CANR 2; CP 7; DLB 27; SATA 12

Kirkwood, James 1930(?)-1989 .... **CLC 9**
See also AITN 2; CA 1-4R; 128; CANR 6, 40; GLL 2

Kirsch, Sarah 1935- .... **CLC 176**
See also CA 178; CWW 2; DLB 75; EWL 3

Kirshner, Sidney
See Kingsley, Sidney

Kis, Danilo 1935-1989 .... **CLC 57**
See also CA 109; 118; 129; CANR 61; CD-WLB 4; DLB 181; EWL 3; MTCW 1; RGSF 2; RGWL 2, 3

Kissinger, Henry A(lfred) 1923- ..... **CLC 137**
See also CA 1-4R; CANR 2, 33, 66, 109; MTCW 1

Kivi, Aleksis 1834-1872 .... **NCLC 30**

Kizer, Carolyn (Ashley) 1925- ... **CLC 15, 39, 80**
See also CA 65-68; CAAS 5; CANR 24, 70, 134; CP 7; CWP; DAM POET; DLB 5, 169; EWL 3; MTCW 2; PFS 18

Klabund 1890-1928 .... **TCLC 44**
See also CA 162; DLB 66

Klappert, Peter 1942- .... **CLC 57**
See also CA 33-36R; CSW; DLB 5

Klein, A(braham) M(oses)
1909-1972 .... **CLC 19**
See also CA 101; 37-40R; DAB; DAC; DAM MST; DLB 68; EWL 3; RGEL 2

Klein, Joe
See Klein, Joseph

Klein, Joseph 1946- .... **CLC 154**
See also CA 85-88; CANR 55

Klein, Norma 1938-1989 .... **CLC 30**
See also AAYA 2, 35; BPFB 2; BYA 6, 7, 8; CA 41-44R; 128; CANR 15, 37; CLR 2, 19; INT CANR-15; JRDA; MAICYA 1, 2; SAAS 1; SATA 7, 57; WYA; YAW

Klein, T(heodore) E(ibon) D(onald)
1947- .... **CLC 34**
See also CA 119; CANR 44, 75; HGG

Kleist, Heinrich von 1777-1811 ...... **NCLC 2, 37; SSC 22**
See also CDWLB 2; DAM DRAM; DLB 90; EW 5; RGSF 2; RGWL 2, 3

Klima, Ivan 1931- .... **CLC 56, 172**
See also CA 25-28R; CANR 17, 50, 91; CDWLB 4; CWW 2; DAM NOV; DLB 232; EWL 3; RGWL 3

Klimentev, Andrei Platonovich
See Klimentov, Andrei Platonovich

Klimentov, Andrei Platonovich
1899-1951 .... **SSC 42; TCLC 14**
See Platonov, Andrei Platonovich; Platonov, Andrey Platonovich
See also CA 108

Klinger, Friedrich Maximilian von
1752-1831 .... **NCLC 1**
See also DLB 94

Klingsor the Magician
See Hartmann, Sadakichi

Klopstock, Friedrich Gottlieb
1724-1803 .... **NCLC 11**
See also DLB 97; EW 4; RGWL 2, 3

Kluge, Alexander 1932- .... **SSC 61**
See also CA 81-84; DLB 75

Knapp, Caroline 1959-2002 .... **CLC 99**
See also CA 154; 207

Knebel, Fletcher 1911-1993 .... **CLC 14**
See also AITN 1; CA 1-4R; 140; CAAS 1; CANR 1, 36; SATA 36; SATA-Obit 75

Knickerbocker, Diedrich
See Irving, Washington

Knight, Etheridge 1931-1991 ... **BLC 2; CLC 40; PC 14**
See also BW 1, 3; CA 21-24R; 133; CANR 23, 82; DAM POET; DLB 41; MTCW 2; RGAL 4

Knight, Sarah Kemble 1666-1727 .... **LC 7**
See also DLB 24, 200

Knister, Raymond 1899-1932 .... **TCLC 56**
See also CA 186; DLB 68; RGEL 2

Knowles, John 1926-2001 ... **CLC 1, 4, 10, 26**
See also AAYA 10; AMWS 12; BPFB 2; BYA 3; CA 17-20R; 203; CANR 40, 74, 76, 132; CDALB 1968-1988; CLR 98; CN 7; DA; DAC; DAM MST, NOV; DLB 6; EXPN; MTCW 1, 2; NFS 2; RGAL 4; SATA 8, 89; SATA-Obit 134; YAW

Knox, Calvin M.
See Silverberg, Robert

Knox, John c. 1505-1572 .... **LC 37**
See also DLB 132

Knye, Cassandra
See Disch, Thomas M(ichael)

Koch, C(hristopher) J(ohn) 1932- .... **CLC 42**
See also CA 127; CANR 84; CN 7; DLB 289

Koch, Christopher
See Koch, C(hristopher) J(ohn)

Koch, Kenneth (Jay) 1925-2002 .... **CLC 5, 8, 44**
See also CA 1-4R; 207; CAD; CANR 6, 36, 57, 97, 131; CD 5; CP 7; DAM POET; DLB 5; INT CANR-36; MTCW 2; PFS 20; SATA 65; WP

Kochanowski, Jan 1530-1584 .... **LC 10**
See also RGWL 2, 3

Kock, Charles Paul de 1794-1871 . **NCLC 16**

Koda Rohan
See Koda Shigeyuki

Koda Rohan
See Koda Shigeyuki
See also DLB 180

Koda Shigeyuki 1867-1947 .... **TCLC 22**
See Koda Rohan
See also CA 121; 183

Koestler, Arthur 1905-1983 ... **CLC 1, 3, 6, 8, 15, 33**
See also BRWS 1; CA 1-4R; 109; CANR 1, 33; CDBLB 1945-1960; DLBY 1983; EWL 3; MTCW 1, 2; NFS 19; RGEL 2

Kogawa, Joy Nozomi 1935- .... **CLC 78, 129**
See also AAYA 47; CA 101; CANR 19, 62, 126; CN 7; CWP; DAC; DAM MST, MULT; FW; MTCW 2; NFS 3; SATA 99

Kohout, Pavel 1928- .... **CLC 13**
See also CA 45-48; CANR 3

Koizumi, Yakumo
See Hearn, (Patricio) Lafcadio (Tessima Carlos)

Kolmar, Gertrud 1894-1943 .... **TCLC 40**
See also CA 167; EWL 3

Komunyakaa, Yusef 1947- .. **BLCS; CLC 86, 94; PC 51**
See also AFAW 2; AMWS 13; CA 147; CANR 83; CP 7; CSW; DLB 120; EWL 3; PFS 5, 20; RGAL 4

Konrad, George
See Konrad, Gyorgy

Konrad, Gyorgy 1933- .... **CLC 4, 10, 73**
See also CA 85-88; CANR 97; CDWLB 4; CWW 2; DLB 232; EWL 3

Konwicki, Tadeusz 1926- .... **CLC 8, 28, 54, 117**
See also CA 101; CAAS 9; CANR 39, 59; CWW 2; DLB 232; EWL 3; IDFW 3; MTCW 1

Koontz, Dean R(ay) 1945- .... **CLC 78**
See also AAYA 9, 31; BEST 89:3, 90:2; CA 108; CANR 19, 36, 52, 95; CMW 4; CPW; DA3; DAM NOV, POP; DLB 292; HGG; MTCW 1; SATA 92; SFW 4; SUFW 2; YAW

Kopernik, Mikolaj
See Copernicus, Nicolaus

Kopit, Arthur (Lee) 1937- ...... **CLC 1, 18, 33**
See also AITN 1; CA 81-84; CABS 3; CD 5; DAM DRAM; DFS 7, 14; DLB 7; MTCW 1; RGAL 4

Kopitar, Jernej (Bartholomaus)
1780-1844 .... **NCLC 117**

Kops, Bernard 1926- .... **CLC 4**
See also CA 5-8R; CANR 84; CBD; CN 7; CP 7; DLB 13

Kornbluth, C(yril) M. 1923-1958 .... **TCLC 8**
See also CA 105; 160; DLB 8; SFW 4

Korolenko, V. G.
See Korolenko, Vladimir Galaktionovich

Korolenko, Vladimir
See Korolenko, Vladimir Galaktionovich

Korolenko, Vladimir G.
See Korolenko, Vladimir Galaktionovich

Korolenko, Vladimir Galaktionovich
1853-1921 .... **TCLC 22**
See also CA 121; DLB 277

Korzybski, Alfred (Habdank Skarbek)
1879-1950 .... **TCLC 61**
See also CA 123; 160

Kosinski, Jerzy (Nikodem)
1933-1991 .... **CLC 1, 2, 3, 6, 10, 15, 53, 70**
See also AMWS 7; BPFB 2; CA 17-20R; 134; CANR 9, 46; DA3; DAM NOV; DLB 2, 299; DLBY 1982; EWL 3; HGG; MTCW 1, 2; NFS 12; RGAL 4; TUS

Kostelanetz, Richard (Cory) 1940- .. **CLC 28**
See also CA 13-16R; CAAS 8; CANR 38, 77; CN 7; CP 7

Kostrowitzki, Wilhelm Apollinaris de
1880-1918
See Apollinaire, Guillaume
See also CA 104

Kotlowitz, Robert 1924- .... **CLC 4**
See also CA 33-36R; CANR 36

Kotzebue, August (Friedrich Ferdinand) von
1761-1819 .... **NCLC 25**
See also DLB 94

Kotzwinkle, William 1938- ..... **CLC 5, 14, 35**
See also BPFB 2; CA 45-48; CANR 3, 44, 84, 129; CLR 6; DLB 173; FANT; MAI-CYA 1, 2; SATA 24, 70, 146; SFW 4; SUFW 2; YAW

Kowna, Stancy
See Szymborska, Wislawa

Kozol, Jonathan 1936- .... **CLC 17**
See also AAYA 46; CA 61-64; CANR 16, 45, 96

Kozoll, Michael 1940(?)- .... **CLC 35**

Kramer, Kathryn 19(?)- .... **CLC 34**

Kramer, Larry 1935- .... **CLC 42; DC 8**
See also CA 124; 126; CANR 60, 132; DAM POP; DLB 249; GLL 1

Krasicki, Ignacy 1735-1801 .... **NCLC 8**

Krasinski, Zygmunt 1812-1859 .... **NCLC 4**
See also RGWL 2, 3

Kraus, Karl 1874-1936 .... **TCLC 5**
See also CA 104; 216; DLB 118; EWL 3

Kreve (Mickevicius), Vincas
1882-1954 .... **TCLC 27**
See also CA 170; DLB 220; EWL 3

Kristeva, Julia 1941- .... **CLC 77, 140**
See also CA 154; CANR 99; DLB 242;
EWL 3; FW; LMFS 2

Kristofferson, Kris 1936- .... **CLC 26**
See also CA 104

Krizanc, John 1956- .... **CLC 57**
See also CA 187

Krleza, Miroslav 1893-1981 .... **CLC 8, 114**
See also CA 97-100; 105; CANR 50; CD-
WLB 4; DLB 147; EW 11; RGWL 2, 3

Kroetsch, Robert 1927- .. **CLC 5, 23, 57, 132**
See also CA 17-20R; CANR 8, 38; CCA 1;
CN 7; CP 7; DAC; DAM POET; DLB 53;
MTCW 1

Kroetz, Franz
See Kroetz, Franz Xaver

Kroetz, Franz Xaver 1946- .... **CLC 41**
See also CA 130; CWW 2; EWL 3

Kroker, Arthur (W.) 1945- .... **CLC 77**
See also CA 161

Kropotkin, Peter (Aleksieevich)
1842-1921 .... **TCLC 36**
See Kropotkin, Petr Alekseevich
See also CA 119; 219

Kropotkin, Petr Alekseevich
See Kropotkin, Peter (Aleksieevich)
See also DLB 277

Krotkov, Yuri 1917-1981 .... **CLC 19**
See also CA 102

Krumb
See Crumb, R(obert)

Krumgold, Joseph (Quincy)
1908-1980 .... **CLC 12**
See also BYA 1, 2; CA 9-12R; 101; CANR
7; MAICYA 1, 2; SATA 1, 48; SATA-Obit
23; YAW

Krumwitz
See Crumb, R(obert)

Krutch, Joseph Wood 1893-1970 ..... **CLC 24**
See also ANW; CA 1-4R; 25-28R; CANR
4; DLB 63, 206, 275

Krutzch, Gus
See Eliot, T(homas) S(tearns)

Krylov, Ivan Andreevich
1768(?)-1844 .... **NCLC 1**
See also DLB 150

Kubin, Alfred (Leopold Isidor)
1877-1959 .... **TCLC 23**
See also CA 112; 149; CANR 104; DLB 81

Kubrick, Stanley 1928-1999 .... **CLC 16;
TCLC 112**
See also AAYA 30; CA 81-84; 177; CANR
33; DLB 26

Kumin, Maxine (Winokur) 1925- ..... **CLC 5,
13, 28, 164; PC 15**
See also AITN 2; AMWS 4; ANW; CA
1-4R; CAAS 8; CANR 1, 21, 69, 115; CP
7; CWP; DA3; DAM POET; DLB 5;
EWL 3; EXPP; MTCW 1, 2; PAB; PFS
18; SATA 12

Kundera, Milan 1929- . **CLC 4, 9, 19, 32, 68,
115, 135; SSC 24**
See also AAYA 2; BPFB 2; CA 85-88;
CANR 19, 52, 74; CDWLB 4; CWW 2;
DA3; DAM NOV; DLB 232; EW 13;
EWL 3; MTCW 1, 2; NFS 18; RGSF 2;
RGWL 3; SSFS 10

Kunene, Mazisi (Raymond) 1930- ... **CLC 85**
See also BW 1, 3; CA 125; CANR 81; CP
7; DLB 117

Kung, Hans .... **CLC 130**
See Kung, Hans

Kung, Hans 1928-
See Kung, Hans
See also CA 53-56; CANR 66, 134; MTCW
1, 2

Kunikida Doppo 1869(?)-1908
See Doppo, Kunikida
See also DLB 180; EWL 3

Kunitz, Stanley (Jasspon) 1905- .. **CLC 6, 11,
14, 148; PC 19**
See also AMWS 3; CA 41-44R; CANR 26,
57, 98; CP 7; DA3; DLB 48; INT CANR-
26; MTCW 1, 2; PFS 11; RGAL 4

Kunze, Reiner 1933- .... **CLC 10**
See also CA 93-96; CWW 2; DLB 75; EWL
3

Kuprin, Aleksander Ivanovich
1870-1938 .... **TCLC 5**
See Kuprin, Aleksandr Ivanovich; Kuprin,
Alexandr Ivanovich
See also CA 104; 182

Kuprin, Aleksandr Ivanovich
See Kuprin, Aleksander Ivanovich
See also DLB 295

Kuprin, Alexandr Ivanovich
See Kuprin, Aleksander Ivanovich
See also EWL 3

Kureishi, Hanif 1954(?)- .... **CLC 64, 135**
See also CA 139; CANR 113; CBD; CD 5;
CN 7; DLB 194, 245; GLL 2; IDFW 4;
WLIT 4; WWE 1

Kurosawa, Akira 1910-1998 ..... **CLC 16, 119**
See also AAYA 11; CA 101; 170; CANR
46; DAM MULT

Kushner, Tony 1956(?)- .... **CLC 81; DC 10**
See also AMWS 9; CA 144; CAD; CANR
74, 130; CD 5; DA3; DAM DRAM; DFS
5; DLB 228; EWL 3; GLL 1; LAIT 5;
MTCW 2; RGAL 4

Kuttner, Henry 1915-1958 .... **TCLC 10**
See also CA 107; 157; DLB 8; FANT;
SCFW 2; SFW 4

Kutty, Madhavi
See Das, Kamala

Kuzma, Greg 1944- .... **CLC 7**
See also CA 33-36R; CANR 70

Kuzmin, Mikhail (Alekseevich)
1872(?)-1936 .... **TCLC 40**
See also CA 170; DLB 295; EWL 3

Kyd, Thomas 1558-1594 .... **DC 3; LC 22**
See also BRW 1; DAM DRAM; DLB 62;
IDTP; LMFS 1; RGEL 2; TEA; WLIT 3

Kyprianos, Iossif
See Samarakis, Antonis

L. S.
See Stephen, Sir Leslie

Laȝamon
See Layamon
See also DLB 146

Labrunie, Gerard
See Nerval, Gerard de

La Bruyere, Jean de 1645-1696 .... **LC 17**
See also DLB 268; EW 3; GFL Beginnings
to 1789

Lacan, Jacques (Marie Emile)
1901-1981 .... **CLC 75**
See also CA 121; 104; DLB 296; EWL 3;
TWA

Laclos, Pierre Ambroise Francois
1741-1803 .... **NCLC 4, 87**
See also EW 4; GFL Beginnings to 1789;
RGWL 2, 3

Lacolere, Francois
See Aragon, Louis

La Colere, Francois
See Aragon, Louis

La Deshabilleuse
See Simenon, Georges (Jacques Christian)

Lady Gregory
See Gregory, Lady Isabella Augusta (Persse)

Lady of Quality, A
See Bagnold, Enid

**La Fayette, Marie-(Madelaine Pioche de la
Vergne)** 1634-1693 .... **LC 2**
See Lafayette, Marie-Madeleine
See also GFL Beginnings to 1789; RGWL
2, 3

Lafayette, Marie-Madeleine
See La Fayette, Marie-(Madelaine Pioche
de la Vergne)
See also DLB 268

Lafayette, Rene
See Hubbard, L(afayette) Ron(ald)

La Flesche, Francis 1857(?)-1932 ...... **NNAL**
See also CA 144; CANR 83; DLB 175

La Fontaine, Jean de 1621-1695 .... **LC 50**
See also DLB 268; EW 3; GFL Beginnings
to 1789; MAICYA 1, 2; RGWL 2, 3;
SATA 18

Laforgue, Jules 1860-1887 . **NCLC 5, 53; PC
14; SSC 20**
See also DLB 217; EW 7; GFL 1789 to the
Present; RGWL 2, 3

Lagerkvist, Paer (Fabian)
1891-1974 ..... **CLC 7, 10, 13, 54; TCLC
144**
See Lagerkvist, Par
See also CA 85-88; 49-52; DA3; DAM
DRAM, NOV; MTCW 1, 2; TWA

Lagerkvist, Par .... **SSC 12**
See Lagerkvist, Paer (Fabian)
See also DLB 259; EW 10; EWL 3; MTCW
2; RGSF 2; RGWL 2, 3

Lagerloef, Selma (Ottiliana Lovisa)
1858-1940 .... **TCLC 4, 36**
See Lagerlof, Selma (Ottiliana Lovisa)
See also CA 108; MTCW 2; SATA 15

Lagerlof, Selma (Ottiliana Lovisa)
See Lagerloef, Selma (Ottiliana Lovisa)
See also CLR 7; SATA 15

La Guma, (Justin) Alex(ander)
1925-1985 . **BLCS; CLC 19; TCLC 140**
See also AFW; BW 1, 3; CA 49-52; 118;
CANR 25, 81; CDWLB 3; DAM NOV;
DLB 117, 225; EWL 3; MTCW 1, 2;
WLIT 2; WWE 1

Laidlaw, A. K.
See Grieve, C(hristopher) M(urray)

Lainez, Manuel Mujica
See Mujica Lainez, Manuel
See also HW 1

Laing, R(onald) D(avid) 1927-1989 . **CLC 95**
See also CA 107; 129; CANR 34; MTCW 1

Laishley, Alex
See Booth, Martin

Lamartine, Alphonse (Marie Louis Prat) de
1790-1869 .... **NCLC 11; PC 16**
See also DAM POET; DLB 217; GFL 1789
to the Present; RGWL 2, 3

Lamb, Charles 1775-1834 ..... **NCLC 10, 113;
WLC**
See also BRW 4; CDBLB 1789-1832; DA;
DAB; DAC; DAM MST; DLB 93, 107,
163; RGEL 2; SATA 17; TEA

Lamb, Lady Caroline 1785-1828 ... **NCLC 38**
See also DLB 116

Lamb, Mary Ann 1764-1847 .... **NCLC 125**
See also DLB 163; SATA 17

Lame Deer 1903(?)-1976 .... **NNAL**
See also CA 69-72

Lamming, George (William) 1927- ... **BLC 2;
CLC 2, 4, 66, 144**
See also BW 2, 3; CA 85-88; CANR 26,
76; CDWLB 3; CN 7; DAM MULT; DLB
125; EWL 3; MTCW 1, 2; NFS 15; RGEL
2

L'Amour, Louis (Dearborn)
1908-1988 .... **CLC 25, 55**
See Burns, Tex; Mayo, Jim
See also AAYA 16; AITN 2; BEST 89:2;
BPFB 2; CA 1-4R; 125; CANR 3, 25, 40;
CPW; DA3; DAM NOV, POP; DLB 206;
DLBY 1980; MTCW 1, 2; RGAL 4

Lampedusa, Giuseppe (Tomasi) di
.... **TCLC 13**
See Tomasi di Lampedusa, Giuseppe
See also CA 164; EW 11; MTCW 2; RGWL 2, 3

Lampman, Archibald 1861-1899 ... **NCLC 25**
See also DLB 92; RGEL 2; TWA

Lancaster, Bruce 1896-1963 .... **CLC 36**
See also CA 9-10; CANR 70; CAP 1; SATA 9

Lanchester, John 1962- .... **CLC 99**
See also CA 194; DLB 267

Landau, Mark Alexandrovich
See Aldanov, Mark (Alexandrovich)

Landau-Aldanov, Mark Alexandrovich
See Aldanov, Mark (Alexandrovich)

Landis, Jerry
See Simon, Paul (Frederick)

Landis, John 1950- .... **CLC 26**
See also CA 112; 122; CANR 128

Landolfi, Tommaso 1908-1979 .... **CLC 11, 49**
See also CA 127; 117; DLB 177; EWL 3

Landon, Letitia Elizabeth
1802-1838 .... **NCLC 15**
See also DLB 96

Landor, Walter Savage
1775-1864 .... **NCLC 14**
See also BRW 4; DLB 93, 107; RGEL 2

Landwirth, Heinz 1927-
See Lind, Jakov
See also CA 9-12R; CANR 7

Lane, Patrick 1939- .... **CLC 25**
See also CA 97-100; CANR 54; CP 7; DAM POET; DLB 53; INT CA-97-100

Lang, Andrew 1844-1912 .... **TCLC 16**
See also CA 114; 137; CANR 85; CLR 101; DLB 98, 141, 184; FANT; MAICYA 1, 2; RGEL 2; SATA 16; WCH

Lang, Fritz 1890-1976 .... **CLC 20, 103**
See also CA 77-80; 69-72; CANR 30

Lange, John
See Crichton, (John) Michael

Langer, Elinor 1939- .... **CLC 34**
See also CA 121

Langland, William 1332(?)-1400(?) ..... **LC 19**
See also BRW 1; DA; DAB; DAC; DAM MST, POET; DLB 146; RGEL 2; TEA; WLIT 3

Langstaff, Launcelot
See Irving, Washington

Lanier, Sidney 1842-1881 . **NCLC 6, 118; PC 50**
See also AMWS 1; DAM POET; DLB 64; DLBD 13; EXPP; MAICYA 1; PFS 14; RGAL 4; SATA 18

Lanyer, Aemilia 1569-1645 .... **LC 10, 30, 83; PC 60**
See also DLB 121

Lao-Tzu
See Lao Tzu

Lao Tzu c. 6th cent. B.C.-3rd cent.
B.C. .... **CMLC 7**

Lapine, James (Elliot) 1949- .... **CLC 39**
See also CA 123; 130; CANR 54, 128; INT CA-130

Larbaud, Valery (Nicolas)
1881-1957 .... **TCLC 9**
See also CA 106; 152; EWL 3; GFL 1789 to the Present

Lardner, Ring
See Lardner, Ring(gold) W(ilmer)
See also BPFB 2; CDALB 1917-1929; DLB 11, 25, 86, 171; DLBD 16; RGAL 4; RGSF 2

Lardner, Ring W., Jr.
See Lardner, Ring(gold) W(ilmer)

Lardner, Ring(gold) W(ilmer)
1885-1933 .... **SSC 32; TCLC 2, 14**
See Lardner, Ring
See also AMW; CA 104; 131; MTCW 1, 2; TUS

Laredo, Betty
See Codrescu, Andrei

Larkin, Maia
See Wojciechowska, Maia (Teresa)

Larkin, Philip (Arthur) 1922-1985 ... **CLC 3, 5, 8, 9, 13, 18, 33, 39, 64; PC 21**
See also BRWS 1; CA 5-8R; 117; CANR 24, 62; CDBLB 1960 to Present; DA3; DAB; DAM MST, POET; DLB 27; EWL 3; MTCW 1, 2; PFS 3, 4, 12; RGEL 2

La Roche, Sophie von
1730-1807 .... **NCLC 121**
See also DLB 94

La Rochefoucauld, Francois
1613-1680 .... **LC 108**

Larra (y Sanchez de Castro), Mariano Jose de 1809-1837 .... **NCLC 17, 130**

Larsen, Eric 1941- .... **CLC 55**
See also CA 132

Larsen, Nella 1893(?)-1963 .... **BLC 2; CLC 37; HR 3**
See also AFAW 1, 2; BW 1; CA 125; CANR 83; DAM MULT; DLB 51; FW; LATS 1:1; LMFS 2

Larson, Charles R(aymond) 1938- ... **CLC 31**
See also CA 53-56; CANR 4, 121

Larson, Jonathan 1961-1996 .... **CLC 99**
See also AAYA 28; CA 156

La Sale, Antoine de c. 1386-1460(?) . **LC 104**
See also DLB 208

Las Casas, Bartolome de
1474-1566 .... **HLCS; LC 31**
See Casas, Bartolome de las
See also LAW

Lasch, Christopher 1932-1994 .... **CLC 102**
See also CA 73-76; 144; CANR 25, 118; DLB 246; MTCW 1, 2

Lasker-Schueler, Else 1869-1945 ... **TCLC 57**
See Lasker-Schuler, Else
See also CA 183; DLB 66, 124

Lasker-Schuler, Else
See Lasker-Schueler, Else
See also EWL 3

Laski, Harold J(oseph) 1893-1950 . **TCLC 79**
See also CA 188

Latham, Jean Lee 1902-1995 .... **CLC 12**
See also AITN 1; BYA 1; CA 5-8R; CANR 7, 84; CLR 50; MAICYA 1, 2; SATA 2, 68; YAW

Latham, Mavis
See Clark, Mavis Thorpe

Lathen, Emma .... **CLC 2**
See Hennissart, Martha; Latsis, Mary J(ane)
See also BPFB 2; CMW 4; DLB 306

Lathrop, Francis
See Leiber, Fritz (Reuter, Jr.)

Latsis, Mary J(ane) 1927-1997
See Lathen, Emma
See also CA 85-88; 162; CMW 4

Lattany, Kristin
See Lattany, Kristin (Elaine Eggleston) Hunter

Lattany, Kristin (Elaine Eggleston) Hunter
1931- .... **CLC 35**
See also AITN 1; BW 1; BYA 3; CA 13-16R; CANR 13, 108; CLR 3; CN 7; DLB 33; INT CANR-13; MAICYA 1, 2; SAAS 10; SATA 12, 132; YAW

Lattimore, Richmond (Alexander)
1906-1984 .... **CLC 3**
See also CA 1-4R; 112; CANR 1

Laughlin, James 1914-1997 .... **CLC 49**
See also CA 21-24R; 162; CAAS 22; CANR 9, 47; CP 7; DLB 48; DLBY 1996, 1997

Laurence, (Jean) Margaret (Wemyss)
1926-1987 . **CLC 3, 6, 13, 50, 62; SSC 7**
See also BYA 13; CA 5-8R; 121; CANR 33; DAC; DAM MST; DLB 53; EWL 3; FW; MTCW 1, 2; NFS 11; RGEL 2; RGSF 2; SATA-Obit 50; TCWW 2

Laurent, Antoine 1952- .... **CLC 50**

Lauscher, Hermann
See Hesse, Hermann

Lautreamont 1846-1870 .. **NCLC 12; SSC 14**
See Lautreamont, Isidore Lucien Ducasse
See also GFL 1789 to the Present; RGWL 2, 3

Lautreamont, Isidore Lucien Ducasse
See Lautreamont
See also DLB 217

Lavater, Johann Kaspar
1741-1801 .... **NCLC 142**
See also DLB 97

Laverty, Donald
See Blish, James (Benjamin)

Lavin, Mary 1912-1996 . **CLC 4, 18, 99; SSC 4, 67**
See also CA 9-12R; 151; CANR 33; CN 7; DLB 15; FW; MTCW 1; RGEL 2; RGSF 2

Lavond, Paul Dennis
See Kornbluth, C(yril) M.; Pohl, Frederik

Lawler, Ray
See Lawler, Raymond Evenor
See also DLB 289

Lawler, Raymond Evenor 1922- .... **CLC 58**
See Lawler, Ray
See also CA 103; CD 5; RGEL 2

Lawrence, D(avid) H(erbert Richards)
1885-1930 .... **PC 54; SSC 4, 19, 73; TCLC 2, 9, 16, 33, 48, 61, 93; WLC**
See Chambers, Jessie
See also BPFB 2; BRW 7; BRWR 2; CA 104; 121; CANR 131; CDBLB 1914-1945; DA; DA3; DAB; DAC; DAM MST, NOV, POET; DLB 10, 19, 36, 98, 162, 195; EWL 3; EXPP; EXPS; LAIT 2, 3; MTCW 1, 2; NFS 18; PFS 6; RGEL 2; RGSF 2; SSFS 2, 6; TEA; WLIT 4; WP

Lawrence, T(homas) E(dward)
1888-1935 .... **TCLC 18**
See Dale, Colin
See also BRWS 2; CA 115; 167; DLB 195

Lawrence of Arabia
See Lawrence, T(homas) E(dward)

Lawson, Henry (Archibald Hertzberg)
1867-1922 .... **SSC 18; TCLC 27**
See also CA 120; 181; DLB 230; RGEL 2; RGSF 2

Lawton, Dennis
See Faust, Frederick (Schiller)

Layamon fl. c. 1200- .... **CMLC 10**
See Laȝamon
See also DLB 146; RGEL 2

Laye, Camara 1928-1980 ..... **BLC 2; CLC 4, 38**
See Camara Laye
See also AFW; BW 1; CA 85-88; 97-100; CANR 25; DAM MULT; MTCW 1, 2; WLIT 2

Layton, Irving (Peter) 1912- .... **CLC 2, 15, 164**
See also CA 1-4R; CANR 2, 33, 43, 66, 129; CP 7; DAC; DAM MST, POET; DLB 88; EWL 3; MTCW 1, 2; PFS 12; RGEL 2

Lazarus, Emma 1849-1887 ...... **NCLC 8, 109**

Lazarus, Felix
See Cable, George Washington

Lazarus, Henry
See Slavitt, David R(ytman)

Lea, Joan
See Neufeld, John (Arthur)

Leacock, Stephen (Butler)
1869-1944 .... **SSC 39; TCLC 2**
See also CA 104; 141; CANR 80; DAC; DAM MST; DLB 92; EWL 3; MTCW 2; RGEL 2; RGSF 2

Lead, Jane Ward 1623-1704 .... **LC 72**
See also DLB 131

Leapor, Mary 1722-1746 .... **LC 80**
See also DLB 109

Lear, Edward 1812-1888 .... **NCLC 3**
See also AAYA 48; BRW 5; CLR 1, 75; DLB 32, 163, 166; MAICYA 1, 2; RGEL 2; SATA 18, 100; WCH; WP

Lear, Norman (Milton) 1922- .... **CLC 12**
See also CA 73-76

Leautaud, Paul 1872-1956 .... **TCLC 83**
See also CA 203; DLB 65; GFL 1789 to the Present

Leavis, F(rank) R(aymond)
1895-1978 .... **CLC 24**
See also BRW 7; CA 21-24R; 77-80; CANR 44; DLB 242; EWL 3; MTCW 1, 2; RGEL 2

Leavitt, David 1961- .... **CLC 34**
See also CA 116; 122; CANR 50, 62, 101, 134; CPW; DA3; DAM POP; DLB 130; GLL 1; INT CA-122; MTCW 2

Leblanc, Maurice (Marie Emile)
1864-1941 .... **TCLC 49**
See also CA 110; CMW 4

Lebowitz, Fran(ces Ann) 1951(?)- ... **CLC 11, 36**
See also CA 81-84; CANR 14, 60, 70; INT CANR-14; MTCW 1

Lebrecht, Peter
See Tieck, (Johann) Ludwig

le Carre, John .... **CLC 3, 5, 9, 15, 28**
See Cornwell, David (John Moore)
See also AAYA 42; BEST 89:4; BPFB 2; BRWS 2; CDBLB 1960 to Present; CMW 4; CN 7; CPW; DLB 87; EWL 3; MSW; MTCW 2; RGEL 2; TEA

Le Clezio, J(ean) M(arie) G(ustave)
1940- .... **CLC 31, 155**
See also CA 116; 128; CWW 2; DLB 83; EWL 3; GFL 1789 to the Present; RGSF 2

Leconte de Lisle, Charles-Marie-Rene
1818-1894 .... **NCLC 29**
See also DLB 217; EW 6; GFL 1789 to the Present

Le Coq, Monsieur
See Simenon, Georges (Jacques Christian)

Leduc, Violette 1907-1972 .... **CLC 22**
See also CA 13-14; 33-36R; CANR 69; CAP 1; EWL 3; GFL 1789 to the Present; GLL 1

Ledwidge, Francis 1887(?)-1917 .... **TCLC 23**
See also CA 123; 203; DLB 20

Lee, Andrea 1953- .... **BLC 2; CLC 36**
See also BW 1, 3; CA 125; CANR 82; DAM MULT

Lee, Andrew
See Auchincloss, Louis (Stanton)

Lee, Chang-rae 1965- .... **CLC 91**
See also CA 148; CANR 89; LATS 1:2

Lee, Don L. .... **CLC 2**
See Madhubuti, Haki R.

Lee, George W(ashington)
1894-1976 .... **BLC 2; CLC 52**
See also BW 1; CA 125; CANR 83; DAM MULT; DLB 51

Lee, (Nelle) Harper 1926- . **CLC 12, 60, 194; WLC**
See also AAYA 13; AMWS 8; BPFB 2; BYA 3; CA 13-16R; CANR 51, 128; CDALB 1941-1968; CSW; DA; DA3; DAB; DAC; DAM MST, NOV; DLB 6; EXPN; LAIT 3; MTCW 1, 2; NFS 2; SATA 11; WYA; YAW

Lee, Helen Elaine 1959(?)- .... **CLC 86**
See also CA 148

Lee, John .... **CLC 70**

Lee, Julian
See Latham, Jean Lee

Lee, Larry
See Lee, Lawrence

Lee, Laurie 1914-1997 .... **CLC 90**
See also CA 77-80; 158; CANR 33, 73; CP 7; CPW; DAB; DAM POP; DLB 27; MTCW 1; RGEL 2

Lee, Lawrence 1941-1990 .... **CLC 34**
See also CA 131; CANR 43

Lee, Li-Young 1957- .... **CLC 164; PC 24**
See also CA 153; CANR 118; CP 7; DLB 165; LMFS 2; PFS 11, 15, 17

Lee, Manfred B(ennington)
1905-1971 .... **CLC 11**
See Queen, Ellery
See also CA 1-4R; 29-32R; CANR 2; CMW 4; DLB 137

Lee, Nathaniel 1645(?)-1692 .... **LC 103**
See also DLB 80; RGEL 2

Lee, Shelton Jackson 1957(?)- .. **BLCS; CLC 105**
See Lee, Spike
See also BW 2, 3; CA 125; CANR 42; DAM MULT

Lee, Spike
See Lee, Shelton Jackson
See also AAYA 4, 29

Lee, Stan 1922- .... **CLC 17**
See also AAYA 5, 49; CA 108; 111; CANR 129; INT CA-111

Lee, Tanith 1947- .... **CLC 46**
See also AAYA 15; CA 37-40R; CANR 53, 102; DLB 261; FANT; SATA 8, 88, 134; SFW 4; SUFW 1, 2; YAW

Lee, Vernon .... **SSC 33; TCLC 5**
See Paget, Violet
See also DLB 57, 153, 156, 174, 178; GLL 1; SUFW 1

Lee, William
See Burroughs, William S(eward)
See also GLL 1

Lee, Willy
See Burroughs, William S(eward)
See also GLL 1

Lee-Hamilton, Eugene (Jacob)
1845-1907 .... **TCLC 22**
See also CA 117

Leet, Judith 1935- .... **CLC 11**
See also CA 187

Le Fanu, Joseph Sheridan
1814-1873 .... **NCLC 9, 58; SSC 14**
See also CMW 4; DA3; DAM POP; DLB 21, 70, 159, 178; HGG; RGEL 2; RGSF 2; SUFW 1

Leffland, Ella 1931- .... **CLC 19**
See also CA 29-32R; CANR 35, 78, 82; DLBY 1984; INT CANR-35; SATA 65

Leger, Alexis
See Leger, (Marie-Rene Auguste) Alexis Saint-Leger

Leger, (Marie-Rene Auguste) Alexis
Saint-Leger 1887-1975 .. **CLC 4, 11, 46; PC 23**
See Perse, Saint-John; Saint-John Perse
See also CA 13-16R; 61-64; CANR 43; DAM POET; MTCW 1

Leger, Saintleger
See Leger, (Marie-Rene Auguste) Alexis Saint-Leger

Le Guin, Ursula K(roeber) 1929- ..... **CLC 8, 13, 22, 45, 71, 136; SSC 12, 69**
See also AAYA 9, 27; AITN 1; BPFB 2; BYA 5, 8, 11, 14; CA 21-24R; CANR 9, 32, 52, 74, 132; CDALB 1968-1988; CLR 3, 28, 91; CN 7; CPW; DA3; DAB; DAC; DAM MST, POP; DLB 8, 52, 256, 275; EXPS; FANT; FW; INT CANR-32; JRDA; LAIT 5; MAICYA 1, 2; MTCW 1, 2; NFS 6, 9; SATA 4, 52, 99, 149; SCFW; SFW 4; SSFS 2; SUFW 1, 2; WYA; YAW

Lehmann, Rosamond (Nina)
1901-1990 .... **CLC 5**
See also CA 77-80; 118; CANR 8, 73; DLB 15; MTCW 2; RGEL 2; RHW

Leiber, Fritz (Reuter, Jr.)
1910-1992 .... **CLC 25**
See also BPFB 2; CA 45-48; 139; CANR 2, 40, 86; DLB 8; FANT; HGG; MTCW 1, 2; SATA 45; SATA-Obit 73; SCFW 2; SFW 4; SUFW 1, 2

Leibniz, Gottfried Wilhelm von
1646-1716 .... **LC 35**
See also DLB 168

Leimbach, Martha 1963-
See Leimbach, Marti
See also CA 130

Leimbach, Marti .... **CLC 65**
See Leimbach, Martha

Leino, Eino .... **TCLC 24**
See Lonnbohm, Armas Eino Leopold
See also EWL 3

Leiris, Michel (Julien) 1901-1990 ..... **CLC 61**
See also CA 119; 128; 132; EWL 3; GFL 1789 to the Present

Leithauser, Brad 1953- .... **CLC 27**
See also CA 107; CANR 27, 81; CP 7; DLB 120, 282

le Jars de Gournay, Marie
See de Gournay, Marie le Jars

Lelchuk, Alan 1938- .... **CLC 5**
See also CA 45-48; CAAS 20; CANR 1, 70; CN 7

Lem, Stanislaw 1921- ...... **CLC 8, 15, 40, 149**
See also CA 105; CAAS 1; CANR 32; CWW 2; MTCW 1; SCFW 2; SFW 4

Lemann, Nancy (Elise) 1956- .... **CLC 39**
See also CA 118; 136; CANR 121

Lemonnier, (Antoine Louis) Camille
1844-1913 .... **TCLC 22**
See also CA 121

Lenau, Nikolaus 1802-1850 .... **NCLC 16**

L'Engle, Madeleine (Camp Franklin)
1918- .... **CLC 12**
See also AAYA 28; AITN 2; BPFB 2; BYA 2, 4, 5, 7; CA 1-4R; CANR 3, 21, 39, 66, 107; CLR 1, 14, 57; CPW; CWRI 5; DA3; DAM POP; DLB 52; JRDA; MAICYA 1, 2; MTCW 1, 2; SAAS 15; SATA 1, 27, 75, 128; SFW 4; WYA; YAW

Lengyel, Jozsef 1896-1975 .... **CLC 7**
See also CA 85-88; 57-60; CANR 71; RGSF 2

Lenin 1870-1924
See Lenin, V. I.
See also CA 121; 168

Lenin, V. I. .... **TCLC 67**
See Lenin

Lennon, John (Ono) 1940-1980 .. **CLC 12, 35**
See also CA 102; SATA 114

Lennox, Charlotte Ramsay
1729(?)-1804 .... **NCLC 23, 134**
See also DLB 39; RGEL 2

Lentricchia, Frank, (Jr.) 1940- .... **CLC 34**
See also CA 25-28R; CANR 19, 106; DLB 246

Lenz, Gunter .... **CLC 65**
Lenz, Jakob Michael Reinhold
 1751-1792 .... **LC 100**
 See also DLB 94; RGWL 2, 3
Lenz, Siegfried 1926- .... **CLC 27; SSC 33**
 See also CA 89-92; CANR 80; CWW 2;
 DLB 75; EWL 3; RGSF 2; RGWL 2, 3
Leon, David
 See Jacob, (Cyprien-)Max
Leonard, Elmore (John, Jr.) 1925- . **CLC 28,
 34, 71, 120**
 See also AAYA 22, 59; AITN 1; BEST 89:1,
 90:4; BPFB 2; CA 81-84; CANR 12, 28,
 53, 76, 96, 133; CMW 4; CN 7; CPW;
 DA3; DAM POP; DLB 173, 226; INT
 CANR-28; MSW; MTCW 1, 2; RGAL 4;
 TCWW 2
Leonard, Hugh .... **CLC 19**
 See Byrne, John Keyes
 See also CBD; CD 5; DFS 13; DLB 13
Leonov, Leonid (Maximovich)
 1899-1994 .... **CLC 92**
 See Leonov, Leonid Maksimovich
 See also CA 129; CANR 74, 76; DAM
 NOV; EWL 3; MTCW 1, 2
Leonov, Leonid Maksimovich
 See Leonov, Leonid (Maximovich)
 See also DLB 272
Leopardi, (Conte) Giacomo
 1798-1837 .... **NCLC 22, 129; PC 37**
 See also EW 5; RGWL 2, 3; WP
Le Reveler
 See Artaud, Antonin (Marie Joseph)
Lerman, Eleanor 1952- .... **CLC 9**
 See also CA 85-88; CANR 69, 124
Lerman, Rhoda 1936- .... **CLC 56**
 See also CA 49-52; CANR 70
Lermontov, Mikhail Iur'evich
 See Lermontov, Mikhail Yuryevich
 See also DLB 205
Lermontov, Mikhail Yuryevich
 1814-1841 .... **NCLC 5, 47, 126; PC 18**
 See Lermontov, Mikhail Iur'evich
 See also EW 6; RGWL 2, 3; TWA
Leroux, Gaston 1868-1927 .... **TCLC 25**
 See also CA 108; 136; CANR 69; CMW 4;
 NFS 20; SATA 65
Lesage, Alain-Rene 1668-1747 .... **LC 2, 28**
 See also EW 3; GFL Beginnings to 1789;
 RGWL 2, 3
Leskov, N(ikolai) S(emenovich) 1831-1895
 See Leskov, Nikolai (Semyonovich)
Leskov, Nikolai (Semyonovich)
 1831-1895 .... **NCLC 25; SSC 34**
 See Leskov, Nikolai Semenovich
Leskov, Nikolai Semenovich
 See Leskov, Nikolai (Semyonovich)
 See also DLB 238
Lesser, Milton
 See Marlowe, Stephen
Lessing, Doris (May) 1919- ... **CLC 1, 2, 3, 6,
 10, 15, 22, 40, 94, 170; SSC 6, 61;
 WLCS**
 See also AAYA 57; AFW; BRWS 1; CA
 9-12R; CAAS 14; CANR 33, 54, 76, 122;
 CD 5; CDBLB 1960 to Present; CN 7;
 DA; DA3; DAB; DAC; DAM MST, NOV;
 DFS 20; DLB 15, 139; DLBY 1985; EWL
 3; EXPS; FW; LAIT 4; MTCW 1, 2;
 RGEL 2; RGSF 2; SFW 4; SSFS 1, 12,
 20; TEA; WLIT 2, 4
Lessing, Gotthold Ephraim 1729-1781 . **LC 8**
 See also CDWLB 2; DLB 97; EW 4; RGWL
 2, 3
Lester, Richard 1932- .... **CLC 20**
Levenson, Jay .... **CLC 70**
Lever, Charles (James)
 1806-1872 .... **NCLC 23**
 See also DLB 21; RGEL 2

Leverson, Ada Esther
 1862(?)-1933(?) .... **TCLC 18**
 See Elaine
 See also CA 117; 202; DLB 153; RGEL 2
Levertov, Denise 1923-1997 .. **CLC 1, 2, 3, 5,
 8, 15, 28, 66; PC 11**
 See also AMWS 3; CA 1-4R, 178; 163;
 CAAE 178; CAAS 19; CANR 3, 29, 50,
 108; CDALBS; CP 7; CWP; DAM POET;
 DLB 5, 165; EWL 3; EXPP; FW; INT
 CANR-29; MTCW 1, 2; PAB; PFS 7, 17;
 RGAL 4; TUS; WP
Levi, Carlo 1902-1975 .... **TCLC 125**
 See also CA 65-68; 53-56; CANR 10; EWL
 3; RGWL 2, 3
Levi, Jonathan .... **CLC 76**
 See also CA 197
Levi, Peter (Chad Tigar)
 1931-2000 .... **CLC 41**
 See also CA 5-8R; 187; CANR 34, 80; CP
 7; DLB 40
Levi, Primo 1919-1987 ...... **CLC 37, 50; SSC
 12; TCLC 109**
 See also CA 13-16R; 122; CANR 12, 33,
 61, 70, 132; DLB 177, 299; EWL 3;
 MTCW 1, 2; RGWL 2, 3
Levin, Ira 1929- .... **CLC 3, 6**
 See also CA 21-24R; CANR 17, 44, 74;
 CMW 4; CN 7; CPW; DA3; DAM POP;
 HGG; MTCW 1, 2; SATA 66; SFW 4
Levin, Meyer 1905-1981 .... **CLC 7**
 See also AITN 1; CA 9-12R; 104; CANR
 15; DAM POP; DLB 9, 28; DLBY 1981;
 SATA 21; SATA-Obit 27
Levine, Norman 1924- .... **CLC 54**
 See also CA 73-76; CAAS 23; CANR 14,
 70; DLB 88
Levine, Philip 1928- .. **CLC 2, 4, 5, 9, 14, 33,
 118; PC 22**
 See also AMWS 5; CA 9-12R; CANR 9,
 37, 52, 116; CP 7; DAM POET; DLB 5;
 EWL 3; PFS 8
Levinson, Deirdre 1931- .... **CLC 49**
 See also CA 73-76; CANR 70
Levi-Strauss, Claude 1908- .... **CLC 38**
 See also CA 1-4R; CANR 6, 32, 57; DLB
 242; EWL 3; GFL 1789 to the Present;
 MTCW 1, 2; TWA
Levitin, Sonia (Wolff) 1934- .... **CLC 17**
 See also AAYA 13, 48; CA 29-32R; CANR
 14, 32, 79; CLR 53; JRDA; MAICYA 1,
 2; SAAS 2; SATA 4, 68, 119, 131; SATA-
 Essay 131; YAW
Levon, O. U.
 See Kesey, Ken (Elton)
Levy, Amy 1861-1889 .... **NCLC 59**
 See also DLB 156, 240
Lewes, George Henry 1817-1878 ... **NCLC 25**
 See also DLB 55, 144
Lewis, Alun 1915-1944 .... **SSC 40; TCLC 3**
 See also BRW 7; CA 104; 188; DLB 20,
 162; PAB; RGEL 2
Lewis, C. Day
 See Day Lewis, C(ecil)
Lewis, C(live) S(taples) 1898-1963 .... **CLC 1,
 3, 6, 14, 27, 124; WLC**
 See also AAYA 3, 39; BPFB 2; BRWS 3;
 BYA 15, 16; CA 81-84; CANR 33, 71,
 132; CDBLB 1945-1960; CLR 3, 27;
 CWRI 5; DA; DA3; DAB; DAC; DAM
 MST, NOV, POP; DLB 15, 100, 160, 255;
 EWL 3; FANT; JRDA; LMFS 2; MAI-
 CYA 1, 2; MTCW 1, 2; RGEL 2; SATA
 13, 100; SCFW; SFW 4; SUFW 1; TEA;
 WCH; WYA; YAW
Lewis, Cecil Day
 See Day Lewis, C(ecil)

Lewis, Janet 1899-1998 .... **CLC 41**
 See Winters, Janet Lewis
 See also CA 9-12R; 172; CANR 29, 63;
 CAP 1; CN 7; DLBY 1987; RHW;
 TCWW 2
Lewis, Matthew Gregory
 1775-1818 .... **NCLC 11, 62**
 See also DLB 39, 158, 178; HGG; LMFS
 1; RGEL 2; SUFW
Lewis, (Harry) Sinclair 1885-1951 . **TCLC 4,
 13, 23, 39; WLC**
 See also AMW; AMWC 1; BPFB 2; CA
 104; 133; CANR 132; CDALB 1917-
 1929; DA; DA3; DAB; DAC; DAM MST,
 NOV; DLB 9, 102, 284; DLBD 1; EWL
 3; LAIT 3; MTCW 1, 2; NFS 15, 19;
 RGAL 4; TUS
Lewis, (Percy) Wyndham
 1884(?)-1957 .. **SSC 34; TCLC 2, 9, 104**
 See also BRW 7; CA 104; 157; DLB 15;
 EWL 3; FANT; MTCW 2; RGEL 2
Lewisohn, Ludwig 1883-1955 .... **TCLC 19**
 See also CA 107; 203; DLB 4, 9, 28, 102
Lewton, Val 1904-1951 .... **TCLC 76**
 See also CA 199; IDFW 3, 4
Leyner, Mark 1956- .... **CLC 92**
 See also CA 110; CANR 28, 53; DA3; DLB
 292; MTCW 2
Lezama Lima, Jose 1910-1976 .... **CLC 4, 10,
 101; HLCS 2**
 See also CA 77-80; CANR 71; DAM
 MULT; DLB 113, 283; EWL 3; HW 1, 2;
 LAW; RGWL 2, 3
L'Heureux, John (Clarke) 1934- ...... **CLC 52**
 See also CA 13-16R; CANR 23, 45, 88;
 DLB 244
Li Ch'ing-chao 1081(?)-1141(?) .... **CMLC 71**
Liddell, C. H.
 See Kuttner, Henry
Lie, Jonas (Lauritz Idemil)
 1833-1908(?) .... **TCLC 5**
 See also CA 115
Lieber, Joel 1937-1971 .... **CLC 6**
 See also CA 73-76; 29-32R
Lieber, Stanley Martin
 See Lee, Stan
Lieberman, Laurence (James)
 1935- .... **CLC 4, 36**
 See also CA 17-20R; CANR 8, 36, 89; CP
 7
Lieh Tzu fl. 7th cent. B.C.-5th cent.
 B.C. .... **CMLC 27**
Lieksman, Anders
 See Haavikko, Paavo Juhani
Li Fei-kan 1904-
 See Pa Chin
 See also CA 105; TWA
Lifton, Robert Jay 1926- .... **CLC 67**
 See also CA 17-20R; CANR 27, 78; INT
 CANR-27; SATA 66
Lightfoot, Gordon 1938- .... **CLC 26**
 See also CA 109
Lightman, Alan P(aige) 1948- .... **CLC 81**
 See also CA 141; CANR 63, 105
Ligotti, Thomas (Robert) 1953- ...... **CLC 44;
 SSC 16**
 See also CA 123; CANR 49, 135; HGG;
 SUFW 2
Li Ho 791-817 .... **PC 13**
Li Ju-chen c. 1763-c. 1830 .... **NCLC 137**
Lilar, Francoise
 See Mallet-Joris, Francoise
Liliencron, (Friedrich Adolf Axel) Detlev
 von 1844-1909 .... **TCLC 18**
 See also CA 117
Lille, Alain de
 See Alain de Lille

Lilly, William 1602-1681 .... LC 27
Lima, Jose Lezama
   See Lezama Lima, Jose
Lima Barreto, Afonso Henrique de
   1881-1922 .... TCLC 23
   See Lima Barreto, Afonso Henriques de
   See also CA 117; 181; LAW
Lima Barreto, Afonso Henriques de
   See Lima Barreto, Afonso Henrique de
   See also DLB 307
Limonov, Edward 1944- .... CLC 67
   See also CA 137
Lin, Frank
   See Atherton, Gertrude (Franklin Horn)
Lin, Yutang 1895-1976 .... TCLC 149
   See also CA 45-48; 65-68; CANR 2; RGAL
   4
Lincoln, Abraham 1809-1865 .... NCLC 18
   See also LAIT 2
Lind, Jakov .... CLC 1, 2, 4, 27, 82
   See Landwirth, Heinz
   See also CAAS 4; DLB 299; EWL 3
Lindbergh, Anne (Spencer) Morrow
   1906-2001 .... CLC 82
   See also BPFB 2; CA 17-20R; 193; CANR
   16, 73; DAM NOV; MTCW 1, 2; SATA-
   Obit 125; TUS
Lindsay, David 1878(?)-1945 .... TCLC 15
   See also CA 113; 187; DLB 255; FANT;
   SFW 4; SUFW 1
Lindsay, (Nicholas) Vachel
   1879-1931 .... PC 23; TCLC 17; WLC
   See also AMWS 1; CA 114; 135; CANR
   79; CDALB 1865-1917; DA; DA3; DAC;
   DAM MST, POET; DLB 54; EWL 3;
   EXPP; RGAL 4; SATA 40; WP
Linke-Poot
   See Doeblin, Alfred
Linney, Romulus 1930- .... CLC 51
   See also CA 1-4R; CAD; CANR 40, 44,
   79; CD 5; CSW; RGAL 4
Linton, Eliza Lynn 1822-1898 .... NCLC 41
   See also DLB 18
Li Po 701-763 .... CMLC 2; PC 29
   See also PFS 20; WP
Lipsius, Justus 1547-1606 .... LC 16
Lipsyte, Robert (Michael) 1938- ...... CLC 21
   See also AAYA 7, 45; CA 17-20R; CANR
   8, 57; CLR 23, 76; DA; DAC; DAM
   MST, NOV; JRDA; LAIT 5; MAICYA 1,
   2; SATA 5, 68, 113; WYA; YAW
Lish, Gordon (Jay) 1934- ... CLC 45; SSC 18
   See also CA 113; 117; CANR 79; DLB 130;
   INT CA-117
Lispector, Clarice 1925(?)-1977 .... CLC 43;
   HLCS 2; SSC 34
   See also CA 139; 116; CANR 71; CDWLB
   3; DLB 113, 307; DNFS 1; EWL 3; FW;
   HW 2; LAW; RGSF 2; RGWL 2, 3; WLIT
   1
Littell, Robert 1935(?)- .... CLC 42
   See also CA 109; 112; CANR 64, 115;
   CMW 4
Little, Malcolm 1925-1965
   See Malcolm X
   See also BW 1, 3; CA 125; 111; CANR 82;
   DA; DA3; DAB; DAC; DAM MST,
   MULT; MTCW 1, 2
Littlewit, Humphrey Gent.
   See Lovecraft, H(oward) P(hillips)
Litwos
   See Sienkiewicz, Henryk (Adam Alexander
   Pius)
Liu, E. 1857-1909 .... TCLC 15
   See also CA 115; 190

Lively, Penelope (Margaret) 1933- .. CLC 32,
   50
   See also BPFB 2; CA 41-44R; CANR 29,
   67, 79, 131; CLR 7; CN 7; CWRI 5;
   DAM NOV; DLB 14, 161, 207; FANT;
   JRDA; MAICYA 1, 2; MTCW 1, 2; SATA
   7, 60, 101; TEA
Livesay, Dorothy (Kathleen)
   1909-1996 .... CLC 4, 15, 79
   See also AITN 2; CA 25-28R; CAAS 8;
   CANR 36, 67; DAC; DAM MST, POET;
   DLB 68; FW; MTCW 1; RGEL 2; TWA
Livy c. 59B.C.-c. 12 .... CMLC 11
   See also AW 2; CDWLB 1; DLB 211;
   RGWL 2, 3
Lizardi, Jose Joaquin Fernandez de
   1776-1827 .... NCLC 30
   See also LAW
Llewellyn, Richard
   See Llewellyn Lloyd, Richard Dafydd Viv-
   ian
   See also DLB 15
Llewellyn Lloyd, Richard Dafydd Vivian
   1906-1983 .... CLC 7, 80
   See Llewellyn, Richard
   See also CA 53-56; 111; CANR 7, 71;
   SATA 11; SATA-Obit 37
Llosa, (Jorge) Mario (Pedro) Vargas
   See Vargas Llosa, (Jorge) Mario (Pedro)
   See also RGWL 3
Llosa, Mario Vargas
   See Vargas Llosa, (Jorge) Mario (Pedro)
Lloyd, Manda
   See Mander, (Mary) Jane
Lloyd Webber, Andrew 1948-
   See Webber, Andrew Lloyd
   See also AAYA 1, 38; CA 116; 149; DAM
   DRAM; SATA 56
Llull, Ramon c. 1235-c. 1316 .... CMLC 12
Lobb, Ebenezer
   See Upward, Allen
Locke, Alain (Le Roy)
   1886-1954 .... BLCS; HR 3; TCLC 43
   See also AMWS 14; BW 1, 3; CA 106; 124;
   CANR 79; DLB 51; LMFS 2; RGAL 4
Locke, John 1632-1704 .... LC 7, 35
   See also DLB 31, 101, 213, 252; RGEL 2;
   WLIT 3
Locke-Elliott, Sumner
   See Elliott, Sumner Locke
Lockhart, John Gibson 1794-1854 .. NCLC 6
   See also DLB 110, 116, 144
Lockridge, Ross (Franklin), Jr.
   1914-1948 .... TCLC 111
   See also CA 108; 145; CANR 79; DLB 143;
   DLBY 1980; RGAL 4; RHW
Lockwood, Robert
   See Johnson, Robert
Lodge, David (John) 1935- .... CLC 36, 141
   See also BEST 90:1; BRWS 4; CA 17-20R;
   CANR 19, 53, 92; CN 7; CPW; DAM
   POP; DLB 14, 194; EWL 3; INT CANR-
   19; MTCW 1, 2
Lodge, Thomas 1558-1625 .... LC 41
   See also DLB 172; RGEL 2
Loewinsohn, Ron(ald William)
   1937- .... CLC 52
   See also CA 25-28R; CANR 71
Logan, Jake
   See Smith, Martin Cruz
Logan, John (Burton) 1923-1987 .... CLC 5
   See also CA 77-80; 124; CANR 45; DLB 5
Lo Kuan-chung 1330(?)-1400(?) .... LC 12
Lombard, Nap
   See Johnson, Pamela Hansford

Lombard, Peter 1100(?)-1160(?) ... CMLC 72
London, Jack 1876-1916 .. SSC 4, 49; TCLC
   9, 15, 39; WLC
   See London, John Griffith
   See also AAYA 13; AITN 2; AMW; BPFB
   2; BYA 4, 13; CDALB 1865-1917; DLB
   8, 12, 78, 212; EWL 3; EXPS; LAIT 3;
   NFS 8; RGAL 4; RGSF 2; SATA 18; SFW
   4; SSFS 7; TCWW 2; TUS; WYA; YAW
London, John Griffith 1876-1916
   See London, Jack
   See also CA 110; 119; CANR 73; DA; DA3;
   DAB; DAC; DAM MST, NOV; JRDA;
   MAICYA 1, 2; MTCW 1, 2; NFS 19
Long, Emmett
   See Leonard, Elmore (John, Jr.)
Longbaugh, Harry
   See Goldman, William (W.)
Longfellow, Henry Wadsworth
   1807-1882 .... NCLC 2, 45, 101, 103; PC
   30; WLCS
   See also AMW; AMWR 2; CDALB 1640-
   1865; CLR 99; DA; DA3; DAB; DAC;
   DAM MST, POET; DLB 1, 59, 235;
   EXPP; PAB; PFS 2, 7, 17; RGAL 4;
   SATA 19; TUS; WP
Longinus c. 1st cent. - .... CMLC 27
   See also AW 2; DLB 176
Longley, Michael 1939- .... CLC 29
   See also BRWS 8; CA 102; CP 7; DLB 40
Longus fl. c. 2nd cent. - .... CMLC 7
Longway, A. Hugh
   See Lang, Andrew
Lonnbohm, Armas Eino Leopold 1878-1926
   See Leino, Eino
   See also CA 123
Lonnrot, Elias 1802-1884 .... NCLC 53
   See also EFS 1
Lonsdale, Roger ed. .... CLC 65
Lopate, Phillip 1943- .... CLC 29
   See also CA 97-100; CANR 88; DLBY
   1980; INT CA-97-100
Lopez, Barry (Holstun) 1945- .... CLC 70
   See also AAYA 9; ANW; CA 65-68; CANR
   7, 23, 47, 68, 92; DLB 256, 275; INT
   CANR-7, -23; MTCW 1; RGAL 4; SATA
   67
Lopez Portillo (y Pacheco), Jose
   1920-2004 .... CLC 46
   See also CA 129; 224; HW 1
Lopez y Fuentes, Gregorio
   1897(?)-1966 .... CLC 32
   See also CA 131; EWL 3; HW 1
Lorca, Federico Garcia
   See Garcia Lorca, Federico
   See also DFS 4; EW 11; PFS 20; RGWL 2,
   3; WP
Lord, Audre
   See Lorde, Audre (Geraldine)
   See also EWL 3
Lord, Bette Bao 1938- .... AAL; CLC 23
   See also BEST 90:3; BPFB 2; CA 107;
   CANR 41, 79; INT CA-107; SATA 58
Lord Auch
   See Bataille, Georges
Lord Brooke
   See Greville, Fulke
Lord Byron
   See Byron, George Gordon (Noel)
Lorde, Audre (Geraldine)
   1934-1992 .. BLC 2; CLC 18, 71; PC 12
   See Domini, Rey; Lord, Audre
   See also AFAW 1, 2; BW 1, 3; CA 25-28R;
   142; CANR 16, 26, 46, 82; DA3; DAM
   MULT, POET; DLB 41; FW; MTCW 1,
   2; PFS 16; RGAL 4
Lord Houghton
   See Milnes, Richard Monckton

Lord Jeffrey
See Jeffrey, Francis
Loreaux, Nichol .... **CLC 65**
Lorenzini, Carlo 1826-1890
See Collodi, Carlo
See also MAICYA 1, 2; SATA 29, 100
Lorenzo, Heberto Padilla
See Padilla (Lorenzo), Heberto
Loris
See Hofmannsthal, Hugo von
Loti, Pierre .... **TCLC 11**
See Viaud, (Louis Marie) Julien
See also DLB 123; GFL 1789 to the Present
Lou, Henri
See Andreas-Salome, Lou
Louie, David Wong 1954- .... **CLC 70**
See also CA 139; CANR 120
Louis, Adrian C. .... **NNAL**
See also CA 223
Louis, Father M.
See Merton, Thomas (James)
Louise, Heidi
See Erdrich, Louise
Lovecraft, H(oward) P(hillips)
1890-1937 .... **SSC 3, 52; TCLC 4, 22**
See also AAYA 14; BPFB 2; CA 104; 133;
CANR 106; DA3; DAM POP; HGG;
MTCW 1, 2; RGAL 4; SCFW; SFW 4;
SUFW
Lovelace, Earl 1935- .... **CLC 51**
See also BW 2; CA 77-80; CANR 41, 72,
114; CD 5; CDWLB 3; CN 7; DLB 125;
EWL 3; MTCW 1
Lovelace, Richard 1618-1657 .... **LC 24**
See also BRW 2; DLB 131; EXPP; PAB;
RGEL 2
Lowe, Pardee 1904- .... **AAL**
Lowell, Amy 1874-1925 ... **PC 13; TCLC 1, 8**
See also AAYA 57; AMW; CA 104; 151;
DAM POET; DLB 54, 140; EWL 3;
EXPP; LMFS 2; MAWW; MTCW 2;
RGAL 4; TUS
Lowell, James Russell 1819-1891 ... **NCLC 2,
90**
See also AMWS 1; CDALB 1640-1865;
DLB 1, 11, 64, 79, 189, 235; RGAL 4
Lowell, Robert (Traill Spence, Jr.)
1917-1977 .... **CLC 1, 2, 3, 4, 5, 8, 9, 11,
15, 37, 124; PC 3; WLC**
See also AMW; AMWC 2; AMWR 2; CA
9-12R; 73-76; CABS 2; CANR 26, 60;
CDALBS; DA; DA3; DAB; DAC; DAM
MST, NOV; DLB 5, 169; EWL 3; MTCW
1, 2; PAB; PFS 6, 7; RGAL 4; WP
Lowenthal, Michael (Francis)
1969- .... **CLC 119**
See also CA 150; CANR 115
Lowndes, Marie Adelaide (Belloc)
1868-1947 .... **TCLC 12**
See also CA 107; CMW 4; DLB 70; RHW
Lowry, (Clarence) Malcolm
1909-1957 .... **SSC 31; TCLC 6, 40**
See also BPFB 2; BRWS 3; CA 105; 131;
CANR 62, 105; CDBLB 1945-1960; DLB
15; EWL 3; MTCW 1, 2; RGEL 2
Lowry, Mina Gertrude 1882-1966
See Loy, Mina
See also CA 113
Loxsmith, John
See Brunner, John (Kilian Houston)
Loy, Mina .... **CLC 28; PC 16**
See Lowry, Mina Gertrude
See also DAM POET; DLB 4, 54; PFS 20
Loyson-Bridet
See Schwob, Marcel (Mayer Andre)
Lucan 39-65 .... **CMLC 33**
See also AW 2; DLB 211; EFS 2; RGWL 2,
3

Lucas, Craig 1951- .... **CLC 64**
See also CA 137; CAD; CANR 71, 109;
CD 5; GLL 2
Lucas, E(dward) V(errall)
1868-1938 .... **TCLC 73**
See also CA 176; DLB 98, 149, 153; SATA
20
Lucas, George 1944- .... **CLC 16**
See also AAYA 1, 23; CA 77-80; CANR
30; SATA 56
Lucas, Hans
See Godard, Jean-Luc
Lucas, Victoria
See Plath, Sylvia
Lucian c. 125-c. 180 .... **CMLC 32**
See also AW 2; DLB 176; RGWL 2, 3
Lucretius c. 94B.C.-c. 49B.C. .... **CMLC 48**
See also AW 2; CDWLB 1; DLB 211; EFS
2; RGWL 2, 3
Ludlam, Charles 1943-1987 .... **CLC 46, 50**
See also CA 85-88; 122; CAD; CANR 72,
86; DLB 266
Ludlum, Robert 1927-2001 .... **CLC 22, 43**
See also AAYA 10, 59; BEST 89:1, 90:3;
BPFB 2; CA 33-36R; 195; CANR 25, 41,
68, 105, 131; CMW 4; CPW; DA3; DAM
NOV, POP; DLBY 1982; MSW; MTCW
1, 2
Ludwig, Ken .... **CLC 60**
See also CA 195; CAD
Ludwig, Otto 1813-1865 .... **NCLC 4**
See also DLB 129
Lugones, Leopoldo 1874-1938 .... **HLCS 2;
TCLC 15**
See also CA 116; 131; CANR 104; DLB
283; EWL 3; HW 1; LAW
Lu Hsun .... **SSC 20; TCLC 3**
See Shu-Jen, Chou
See also EWL 3
Lukacs, George .... **CLC 24**
See Lukacs, Gyorgy (Szegeny von)
Lukacs, Gyorgy (Szegeny von) 1885-1971
See Lukacs, George
See also CA 101; 29-32R; CANR 62; CD-
WLB 4; DLB 215, 242; EW 10; EWL 3;
MTCW 2
Luke, Peter (Ambrose Cyprian)
1919-1995 .... **CLC 38**
See also CA 81-84; 147; CANR 72; CBD;
CD 5; DLB 13
Lunar, Dennis
See Mungo, Raymond
Lurie, Alison 1926- ..... **CLC 4, 5, 18, 39, 175**
See also BPFB 2; CA 1-4R; CANR 2, 17,
50, 88; CN 7; DLB 2; MTCW 1; SATA
46, 112
Lustig, Arnost 1926- .... **CLC 56**
See also AAYA 3; CA 69-72; CANR 47,
102; CWW 2; DLB 232, 299; EWL 3;
SATA 56
Luther, Martin 1483-1546 .... **LC 9, 37**
See also CDWLB 2; DLB 179; EW 2;
RGWL 2, 3
Luxemburg, Rosa 1870(?)-1919 ..... **TCLC 63**
See also CA 118
Luzi, Mario 1914- .... **CLC 13**
See also CA 61-64; CANR 9, 70; CWW 2;
DLB 128; EWL 3
L'vov, Arkady .... **CLC 59**
Lydgate, John c. 1370-1450(?) .... **LC 81**
See also BRW 1; DLB 146; RGEL 2
Lyly, John 1554(?)-1606 .... **DC 7; LC 41**
See also BRW 1; DAM DRAM; DLB 62,
167; RGEL 2
L'Ymagier
See Gourmont, Remy(-Marie-Charles) de
Lynch, B. Suarez
See Borges, Jorge Luis

Lynch, David (Keith) 1946- ...... **CLC 66, 162**
See also AAYA 55; CA 124; 129; CANR
111
Lynch, James
See Andreyev, Leonid (Nikolaevich)
Lyndsay, Sir David 1485-1555 .... **LC 20**
See also RGEL 2
Lynn, Kenneth S(chuyler)
1923-2001 .... **CLC 50**
See also CA 1-4R; 196; CANR 3, 27, 65
Lynx
See West, Rebecca
Lyons, Marcus
See Blish, James (Benjamin)
Lyotard, Jean-Francois
1924-1998 .... **TCLC 103**
See also DLB 242; EWL 3
Lyre, Pinchbeck
See Sassoon, Siegfried (Lorraine)
Lytle, Andrew (Nelson) 1902-1995 ... **CLC 22**
See also CA 9-12R; 150; CANR 70; CN 7;
CSW; DLB 6; DLBY 1995; RGAL 4;
RHW
Lyttelton, George 1709-1773 .... **LC 10**
See also RGEL 2
Lytton of Knebworth, Baron
See Bulwer-Lytton, Edward (George Earle
Lytton)
Maas, Peter 1929-2001 .... **CLC 29**
See also CA 93-96; 201; INT CA-93-96;
MTCW 2
Macaulay, Catherine 1731-1791 .... **LC 64**
See also DLB 104
Macaulay, (Emilie) Rose
1881(?)-1958 .... **TCLC 7, 44**
See also CA 104; DLB 36; EWL 3; RGEL
2; RHW
Macaulay, Thomas Babington
1800-1859 .... **NCLC 42**
See also BRW 4; CDBLB 1832-1890; DLB
32, 55; RGEL 2
MacBeth, George (Mann)
1932-1992 .... **CLC 2, 5, 9**
See also CA 25-28R; 136; CANR 61, 66;
DLB 40; MTCW 1; PFS 8; SATA 4;
SATA-Obit 70
MacCaig, Norman (Alexander)
1910-1996 .... **CLC 36**
See also BRWS 6; CA 9-12R; CANR 3, 34;
CP 7; DAB; DAM POET; DLB 27; EWL
3; RGEL 2
MacCarthy, Sir (Charles Otto) Desmond
1877-1952 .... **TCLC 36**
See also CA 167
MacDiarmid, Hugh .... **CLC 2, 4, 11, 19, 63;
PC 9**
See Grieve, C(hristopher) M(urray)
See also CDBLB 1945-1960; DLB 20;
EWL 3; RGEL 2
MacDonald, Anson
See Heinlein, Robert A(nson)
Macdonald, Cynthia 1928- .... **CLC 13, 19**
See also CA 49-52; CANR 4, 44; DLB 105
MacDonald, George 1824-1905 .... **TCLC 9,
113**
See also AAYA 57; BYA 5; CA 106; 137;
CANR 80; CLR 67; DLB 18, 163, 178;
FANT; MAICYA 1, 2; RGEL 2; SATA 33,
100; SFW 4; SUFW; WCH
Macdonald, John
See Millar, Kenneth
MacDonald, John D(ann)
1916-1986 .... **CLC 3, 27, 44**
See also BPFB 2; CA 1-4R; 121; CANR 1,
19, 60; CMW 4; CPW; DAM NOV, POP;
DLB 8, 306; DLBY 1986; MSW; MTCW
1, 2; SFW 4
Macdonald, John Ross
See Millar, Kenneth

Macdonald, Ross ..... **CLC 1, 2, 3, 14, 34, 41**
See Millar, Kenneth
See also AMWS 4; BPFB 2; DLBD 6;
MSW; RGAL 4

MacDougal, John
See Blish, James (Benjamin)

MacDougal, John
See Blish, James (Benjamin)

MacDowell, John
See Parks, Tim(othy Harold)

MacEwen, Gwendolyn (Margaret)
1941-1987 .... **CLC 13, 55**
See also CA 9-12R; 124; CANR 7, 22; DLB
53, 251; SATA 50; SATA-Obit 55

Macha, Karel Hynek 1810-1846 .... **NCLC 46**

Machado (y Ruiz), Antonio
1875-1939 .... **TCLC 3**
See also CA 104; 174; DLB 108; EW 9;
EWL 3; HW 2; RGWL 2, 3

Machado de Assis, Joaquim Maria
1839-1908 .... **BLC 2; HLCS 2; SSC 24;
TCLC 10**
See also CA 107; 153; CANR 91; DLB 307;
LAW; RGSF 2; RGWL 2, 3; TWA; WLIT
1

Machaut, Guillaume de c.
1300-1377 .... **CMLC 64**
See also DLB 208

Machen, Arthur .... **SSC 20; TCLC 4**
See Jones, Arthur Llewellyn
See also CA 179; DLB 156, 178; RGEL 2;
SUFW 1

Machiavelli, Niccolo 1469-1527 ... **DC 16; LC
8, 36; WLCS**
See also AAYA 58; DA; DAB; DAC; DAM
MST; EW 2; LAIT 1; LMFS 1; NFS 9;
RGWL 2, 3; TWA

MacInnes, Colin 1914-1976 .... **CLC 4, 23**
See also CA 69-72; 65-68; CANR 21; DLB
14; MTCW 1, 2; RGEL 2; RHW

MacInnes, Helen (Clark)
1907-1985 .... **CLC 27, 39**
See also BPFB 2; CA 1-4R; 117; CANR 1,
28, 58; CMW 4; CPW; DAM POP; DLB
87; MSW; MTCW 1, 2; SATA 22; SATA-
Obit 44

Mackay, Mary 1855-1924
See Corelli, Marie
See also CA 118; 177; FANT; RHW

Mackay, Shena 1944- .... **CLC 195**
See also CA 104; CANR 88; DLB 231

Mackenzie, Compton (Edward Montague)
1883-1972 .... **CLC 18; TCLC 116**
See also CA 21-22; 37-40R; CAP 2; DLB
34, 100; RGEL 2

Mackenzie, Henry 1745-1831 .... **NCLC 41**
See also DLB 39; RGEL 2

Mackey, Nathaniel (Ernest) 1947- .... **PC 49**
See also CA 153; CANR 114; CP 7; DLB
169

MacKinnon, Catharine A. 1946- .... **CLC 181**
See also CA 128; 132; CANR 73; FW;
MTCW 2

Mackintosh, Elizabeth 1896(?)-1952
See Tey, Josephine
See also CA 110; CMW 4

MacLaren, James
See Grieve, C(hristopher) M(urray)

Mac Laverty, Bernard 1942- .... **CLC 31**
See also CA 116; 118; CANR 43, 88; CN
7; DLB 267; INT CA-118; RGSF 2

MacLean, Alistair (Stuart)
1922(?)-1987 .... **CLC 3, 13, 50, 63**
See also CA 57-60; 121; CANR 28, 61;
CMW 4; CPW; DAM POP; DLB 276;
MTCW 1; SATA 23; SATA-Obit 50;
TCWW 2

Maclean, Norman (Fitzroy)
1902-1990 .... **CLC 78; SSC 13**
See also AMWS 14; CA 102; 132; CANR
49; CPW; DAM POP; DLB 206; TCWW
2

MacLeish, Archibald 1892-1982 ... **CLC 3, 8,
14, 68; PC 47**
See also AMW; CA 9-12R; 106; CAD;
CANR 33, 63; CDALBS; DAM POET;
DFS 15; DLB 4, 7, 45; DLBY 1982; EWL
3; EXPP; MTCW 1, 2; PAB; PFS 5;
RGAL 4; TUS

MacLennan, (John) Hugh
1907-1990 .... **CLC 2, 14, 92**
See also CA 5-8R; 142; CANR 33; DAC;
DAM MST; DLB 68; EWL 3; MTCW 1,
2; RGEL 2; TWA

MacLeod, Alistair 1936- .... **CLC 56, 165**
See also CA 123; CCA 1; DAC; DAM
MST; DLB 60; MTCW 2; RGSF 2

Macleod, Fiona
See Sharp, William
See also RGEL 2; SUFW

MacNeice, (Frederick) Louis
1907-1963 .... **CLC 1, 4, 10, 53; PC 61**
See also BRW 7; CA 85-88; CANR 61;
DAB; DAM POET; DLB 10, 20; EWL 3;
MTCW 1, 2; RGEL 2

MacNeill, Dand
See Fraser, George MacDonald

Macpherson, James 1736-1796 .... **LC 29**
See Ossian
See also BRWS 8; DLB 109; RGEL 2

Macpherson, (Jean) Jay 1931- .... **CLC 14**
See also CA 5-8R; CANR 90; CP 7; CWP;
DLB 53

Macrobius fl. 430- .... **CMLC 48**

MacShane, Frank 1927-1999 .... **CLC 39**
See also CA 9-12R; 186; CANR 3, 33; DLB
111

Macumber, Mari
See Sandoz, Mari(e Susette)

Madach, Imre 1823-1864 .... **NCLC 19**

Madden, (Jerry) David 1933- .... **CLC 5, 15**
See also CA 1-4R; CAAS 3; CANR 4, 45;
CN 7; CSW; DLB 6; MTCW 1

Maddern, Al(an)
See Ellison, Harlan (Jay)

Madhubuti, Haki R. 1942- ... **BLC 2; CLC 6,
73; PC 5**
See Lee, Don L.
See also BW 2, 3; CA 73-76; CANR 24,
51, 73; CP 7; CSW; DAM MULT, POET;
DLB 5, 41; DLBD 8; EWL 3; MTCW 2;
RGAL 4

Madison, James 1751-1836 .... **NCLC 126**
See also DLB 37

Maepenn, Hugh
See Kuttner, Henry

Maepenn, K. H.
See Kuttner, Henry

Maeterlinck, Maurice 1862-1949 ..... **TCLC 3**
See also CA 104; 136; CANR 80; DAM
DRAM; DLB 192; EW 8; EWL 3; GFL
1789 to the Present; LMFS 2; RGWL 2,
3; SATA 66; TWA

Maginn, William 1794-1842 .... **NCLC 8**
See also DLB 110, 159

Mahapatra, Jayanta 1928- .... **CLC 33**
See also CA 73-76; CAAS 9; CANR 15,
33, 66, 87; CP 7; DAM MULT

Mahfouz, Naguib (Abdel Aziz Al-Sabilgi)
1911(?)- .... **CLC 153; SSC 66**
See Mahfuz, Najib (Abdel Aziz al-Sabilgi)
See also AAYA 49; BEST 89:2; CA 128;
CANR 55, 101; DA3; DAM NOV;
MTCW 1, 2; RGWL 2, 3; SSFS 9

Mahfuz, Najib (Abdel Aziz al-Sabilgi)
.... **CLC 52, 55**
See Mahfouz, Naguib (Abdel Aziz Al-
Sabilgi)
See also AFW; CWW 2; DLBY 1988; EWL
3; RGSF 2; WLIT 2

Mahon, Derek 1941- .... **CLC 27; PC 60**
See also BRWS 6; CA 113; 128; CANR 88;
CP 7; DLB 40; EWL 3

Maiakovskii, Vladimir
See Mayakovski, Vladimir (Vladimirovich)
See also IDTP; RGWL 2, 3

Mailer, Norman (Kingsley) 1923- . **CLC 1, 2,
3, 4, 5, 8, 11, 14, 28, 39, 74, 111**
See also AAYA 31; AITN 2; AMW; AMWC
2; AMWR 2; BPFB 2; CA 9-12R; CABS
1; CANR 28, 74, 77, 130; CDALB 1968-
1988; CN 7; CPW; DA; DA3; DAB;
DAC; DAM MST, NOV; DLB 2, 16,
16, 28, 185, 278; DLBD 3; DLBY 1980,
1983; EWL 3; MTCW 1, 2; NFS 10;
RGAL 4; TUS

Maillet, Antonine 1929- .... **CLC 54, 118**
See also CA 115; 120; CANR 46, 74, 77,
134; CCA 1; CWW 2; DAC; DLB 60;
INT CA-120; MTCW 2

Mais, Roger 1905-1955 .... **TCLC 8**
See also BW 1, 3; CA 105; 124; CANR 82;
CDWLB 3; DLB 125; EWL 3; MTCW 1;
RGEL 2

Maistre, Joseph 1753-1821 .... **NCLC 37**
See also GFL 1789 to the Present

Maitland, Frederic William
1850-1906 .... **TCLC 65**

Maitland, Sara (Louise) 1950- .... **CLC 49**
See also CA 69-72; CANR 13, 59; DLB
271; FW

Major, Clarence 1936- ... **BLC 2; CLC 3, 19,
48**
See also AFAW 2; BW 2, 3; CA 21-24R;
CAAS 6; CANR 13, 25, 53, 82; CN 7;
CP 7; CSW; DAM MULT; DLB 33; EWL
3; MSW

Major, Kevin (Gerald) 1949- .... **CLC 26**
See also AAYA 16; CA 97-100; CANR 21,
38, 112; CLR 11; DAC; DLB 60; INT
CANR-21; JRDA; MAICYA 1, 2; MAIC-
YAS 1; SATA 32, 82, 134; WYA; YAW

Maki, James
See Ozu, Yasujiro

Makine, Andrei 1957- .... **CLC 198**
See also CA 176; CANR 103

Malabaila, Damiano
See Levi, Primo

Malamud, Bernard 1914-1986 .. **CLC 1, 2, 3,
5, 8, 9, 11, 18, 27, 44, 78, 85; SSC 15;
TCLC 129; WLC**
See also AAYA 16; AMWS 1; BPFB 2;
BYA 15; CA 5-8R; 118; CABS 1; CANR
28, 62, 114; CDALB 1941-1968; CPW;
DA; DA3; DAB; DAC; DAM MST, NOV,
POP; DLB 2, 28, 152; DLBY 1980, 1986;
EWL 3; EXPS; LAIT 4; LATS 1:1;
MTCW 1, 2; NFS 4, 9; RGAL 4; RGSF
2; SSFS 8, 13, 16; TUS

Malan, Herman
See Bosman, Herman Charles; Bosman,
Herman Charles

Malaparte, Curzio 1898-1957 .... **TCLC 52**
See also DLB 264

Malcolm, Dan
See Silverberg, Robert

Malcolm X .... **BLC 2; CLC 82, 117; WLCS**
See Little, Malcolm
See also LAIT 5; NCFS 3

Malherbe, Francois de 1555-1628 .... **LC 5**
See also GFL Beginnings to 1789

Mallarme, Stephane 1842-1898 ...... **NCLC 4, 41; PC 4**
See also DAM POET; DLB 217; EW 7; GFL 1789 to the Present; LMFS 2; RGWL 2, 3; TWA

Mallet-Joris, Francoise 1930- .... **CLC 11**
See also CA 65-68; CANR 17; CWW 2; DLB 83; EWL 3; GFL 1789 to the Present

Malley, Ern
See McAuley, James Phillip

Mallon, Thomas 1951- .... **CLC 172**
See also CA 110; CANR 29, 57, 92

Mallowan, Agatha Christie
See Christie, Agatha (Mary Clarissa)

Maloff, Saul 1922- .... **CLC 5**
See also CA 33-36R

Malone, Louis
See MacNeice, (Frederick) Louis

Malone, Michael (Christopher)
1942- .... **CLC 43**
See also CA 77-80; CANR 14, 32, 57, 114

Malory, Sir Thomas 1410(?)-1471(?) . **LC 11, 88; WLCS**
See also BRW 1; BRWR 2; CDBLB Before 1660; DA; DAB; DAC; DAM MST; DLB 146; EFS 2; RGEL 2; SATA 59; SATA-Brief 33; TEA; WLIT 3

Malouf, (George Joseph) David
1934- .... **CLC 28, 86**
See also CA 124; CANR 50, 76; CN 7; CP 7; DLB 289; EWL 3; MTCW 2

Malraux, (Georges-)Andre
1901-1976 .... **CLC 1, 4, 9, 13, 15, 57**
See also BPFB 2; CA 21-22; 69-72; CANR 34, 58; CAP 2; DA3; DAM NOV; DLB 72; EW 12; EWL 3; GFL 1789 to the Present; MTCW 1, 2; RGWL 2, 3; TWA

Malthus, Thomas Robert
1766-1834 .... **NCLC 145**
See also DLB 107, 158; RGEL 2

Malzberg, Barry N(athaniel) 1939- ... **CLC 7**
See also CA 61-64; CAAS 4; CANR 16; CMW 4; DLB 8; SFW 4

Mamet, David (Alan) 1947- .. **CLC 9, 15, 34, 46, 91, 166; DC 4, 24**
See also AAYA 3, 60; AMWS 14; CA 81-84; CABS 3; CANR 15, 41, 67, 72, 129; CD 5; DA3; DAM DRAM; DFS 2, 3, 6, 12, 15; DLB 7; EWL 3; IDFW 4; MTCW 1, 2; RGAL 4

Mamoulian, Rouben (Zachary)
1897-1987 .... **CLC 16**
See also CA 25-28R; 124; CANR 85

Mandelshtam, Osip
See Mandelstam, Osip (Emilievich)
See also EW 10; EWL 3; RGWL 2, 3

Mandelstam, Osip (Emilievich)
1891(?)-1943(?) .... **PC 14; TCLC 2, 6**
See Mandelstam, Osip
See also CA 104; 150; MTCW 2; TWA

Mander, (Mary) Jane 1877-1949 ... **TCLC 31**
See also CA 162; RGEL 2

Mandeville, Bernard 1670-1733 .... **LC 82**
See also DLB 101

Mandeville, Sir John fl. 1350- ...... **CMLC 19**
See also DLB 146

Mandiargues, Andre Pieyre de .... **CLC 41**
See Pieyre de Mandiargues, Andre
See also DLB 83

Mandrake, Ethel Belle
See Thurman, Wallace (Henry)

Mangan, James Clarence
1803-1849 .... **NCLC 27**
See also RGEL 2

Maniere, J.-E.
See Giraudoux, Jean(-Hippolyte)

Mankiewicz, Herman (Jacob)
1897-1953 .... **TCLC 85**
See also CA 120; 169; DLB 26; IDFW 3, 4

Manley, (Mary) Delariviere
1672(?)-1724 .... **LC 1, 42**
See also DLB 39, 80; RGEL 2

Mann, Abel
See Creasey, John

Mann, Emily 1952- .... **DC 7**
See also CA 130; CAD; CANR 55; CD 5; CWD; DLB 266

Mann, (Luiz) Heinrich 1871-1950 ... **TCLC 9**
See also CA 106; 164, 181; DLB 66, 118; EW 8; EWL 3; RGWL 2, 3

Mann, (Paul) Thomas 1875-1955 .... **SSC 5, 70; TCLC 2, 8, 14, 21, 35, 44, 60; WLC**
See also BPFB 2; CA 104; 128; CANR 133; CDWLB 2; DA; DA3; DAB; DAC; DAM MST, NOV; DLB 66; EW 9; EWL 3; GLL 1; LATS 1:1; LMFS 1; MTCW 1, 2; NFS 17; RGSF 2; RGWL 2, 3; SSFS 4, 9; TWA

Mannheim, Karl 1893-1947 .... **TCLC 65**
See also CA 204

Manning, David
See Faust, Frederick (Schiller)
See also TCWW 2

Manning, Frederic 1882-1935 .... **TCLC 25**
See also CA 124; 216; DLB 260

Manning, Olivia 1915-1980 .... **CLC 5, 19**
See also CA 5-8R; 101; CANR 29; EWL 3; FW; MTCW 1; RGEL 2

Mano, D. Keith 1942- .... **CLC 2, 10**
See also CA 25-28R; CAAS 6; CANR 26, 57; DLB 6

Mansfield, Katherine . **SSC 9, 23, 38; TCLC 2, 8, 39; WLC**
See Beauchamp, Kathleen Mansfield
See also BPFB 2; BRW 7; DAB; DLB 162; EWL 3; EXPS; FW; GLL 1; RGEL 2; RGSF 2; SSFS 2, 8, 10, 11; WWE 1

Manso, Peter 1940- .... **CLC 39**
See also CA 29-32R; CANR 44

Mantecon, Juan Jimenez
See Jimenez (Mantecon), Juan Ramon

Mantel, Hilary (Mary) 1952- .... **CLC 144**
See also CA 125; CANR 54, 101; CN 7; DLB 271; RHW

Manton, Peter
See Creasey, John

Man Without a Spleen, A
See Chekhov, Anton (Pavlovich)

Manzoni, Alessandro 1785-1873 ... **NCLC 29, 98**
See also EW 5; RGWL 2, 3; TWA

Map, Walter 1140-1209 .... **CMLC 32**

Mapu, Abraham (ben Jekutiel)
1808-1867 .... **NCLC 18**

Mara, Sally
See Queneau, Raymond

Maracle, Lee 1950- .... **NNAL**
See also CA 149

Marat, Jean Paul 1743-1793 .... **LC 10**

Marcel, Gabriel Honore 1889-1973 . **CLC 15**
See also CA 102; 45-48; EWL 3; MTCW 1, 2

March, William 1893-1954 .... **TCLC 96**
See also CA 216

Marchbanks, Samuel
See Davies, (William) Robertson
See also CCA 1

Marchi, Giacomo
See Bassani, Giorgio

Marcus Aurelius
See Aurelius, Marcus
See also AW 2

Marguerite
See de Navarre, Marguerite

Marguerite d'Angouleme
See de Navarre, Marguerite
See also GFL Beginnings to 1789

Marguerite de Navarre
See de Navarre, Marguerite
See also RGWL 2, 3

Margulies, Donald 1954- .... **CLC 76**
See also AAYA 57; CA 200; DFS 13; DLB 228

Marie de France c. 12th cent. - ..... **CMLC 8; PC 22**
See also DLB 208; FW; RGWL 2, 3

Marie de l'Incarnation 1599-1672 ...... **LC 10**

Marier, Captain Victor
See Griffith, D(avid Lewelyn) W(ark)

Mariner, Scott
See Pohl, Frederik

Marinetti, Filippo Tommaso
1876-1944 .... **TCLC 10**
See also CA 107; DLB 114, 264; EW 9; EWL 3

Marivaux, Pierre Carlet de Chamblain de
1688-1763 .... **DC 7; LC 4**
See also GFL Beginnings to 1789; RGWL 2, 3; TWA

Markandaya, Kamala .... **CLC 8, 38**
See Taylor, Kamala (Purnaiya)
See also BYA 13; CN 7; EWL 3

Markfield, Wallace 1926-2002 .... **CLC 8**
See also CA 69-72; 208; CAAS 3; CN 7; DLB 2, 28; DLBY 2002

Markham, Edwin 1852-1940 .... **TCLC 47**
See also CA 160; DLB 54, 186; RGAL 4

Markham, Robert
See Amis, Kingsley (William)

Markoosie .... **NNAL**
See Patsauq, Markoosie
See also CLR 23; DAM MULT

Marks, J.
See Highwater, Jamake (Mamake)

Marks, J
See Highwater, Jamake (Mamake)

Marks-Highwater, J
See Highwater, Jamake (Mamake)

Marks-Highwater, J.
See Highwater, Jamake (Mamake)

Markson, David M(errill) 1927- .... **CLC 67**
See also CA 49-52; CANR 1, 91; CN 7

Marlatt, Daphne (Buckle) 1942- .... **CLC 168**
See also CA 25-28R; CANR 17, 39; CN 7; CP 7; CWP; DLB 60; FW

Marley, Bob .... **CLC 17**
See Marley, Robert Nesta

Marley, Robert Nesta 1945-1981
See Marley, Bob
See also CA 107; 103

Marlowe, Christopher 1564-1593 . **DC 1; LC 22, 47; PC 57; WLC**
See also BRW 1; BRWR 1; CDBLB Before 1660; DA; DA3; DAB; DAC; DAM DRAM, MST; DFS 1, 5, 13; DLB 62; EXPP; LMFS 1; RGEL 2; TEA; WLIT 3

Marlowe, Stephen 1928- .... **CLC 70**
See Queen, Ellery
See also CA 13-16R; CANR 6, 55; CMW 4; SFW 4

Marmion, Shakerley 1603-1639 .... **LC 89**
See also DLB 58; RGEL 2

Marmontel, Jean-Francois 1723-1799 .. **LC 2**

Maron, Monika 1941- .... **CLC 165**
See also CA 201

Marquand, John P(hillips)
1893-1960 .... **CLC 2, 10**
See also AMW; BPFB 2; CA 85-88; CANR 73; CMW 4; DLB 9, 102; EWL 3; MTCW 2; RGAL 4

Marques, Rene 1919-1979 .. **CLC 96; HLC 2**
See also CA 97-100; 85-88; CANR 78; DAM MULT; DLB 305; EWL 3; HW 1, 2; LAW; RGSF 2

Marquez, Gabriel (Jose) Garcia
See Garcia Marquez, Gabriel (Jose)

Marquis, Don(ald Robert Perry)
1878-1937 .... **TCLC 7**
See also CA 104; 166; DLB 11, 25; RGAL 4

Marquis de Sade
See Sade, Donatien Alphonse Francois

Marric, J. J.
See Creasey, John
See also MSW

Marryat, Frederick 1792-1848 .... **NCLC 3**
See also DLB 21, 163; RGEL 2; WCH

Marsden, James
See Creasey, John

Marsh, Edward 1872-1953 .... **TCLC 99**

Marsh, (Edith) Ngaio 1895-1982 .. **CLC 7, 53**
See also CA 9-12R; CANR 6, 58; CMW 4; CPW; DAM POP; DLB 77; MSW; MTCW 1, 2; RGEL 2; TEA

Marshall, Garry 1934- .... **CLC 17**
See also AAYA 3; CA 111; SATA 60

Marshall, Paule 1929- .. **BLC 3; CLC 27, 72; SSC 3**
See also AFAW 1, 2; AMWS 11; BPFB 2; BW 2, 3; CA 77-80; CANR 25, 73, 129; CN 7; DA3; DAM MULT; DLB 33, 157, 227; EWL 3; LATS 1:2; MTCW 1, 2; RGAL 4; SSFS 15

Marshallik
See Zangwill, Israel

Marsten, Richard
See Hunter, Evan

Marston, John 1576-1634 .... **LC 33**
See also BRW 2; DAM DRAM; DLB 58, 172; RGEL 2

Martel, Yann 1963- .... **CLC 192**
See also CA 146; CANR 114

Martha, Henry
See Harris, Mark

Marti, Jose
See Marti (y Perez), Jose (Julian)
See also DLB 290

Marti (y Perez), Jose (Julian)
1853-1895 .... **HLC 2; NCLC 63**
See Marti, Jose
See also DAM MULT; HW 2; LAW; RGWL 2, 3; WLIT 1

Martial c. 40-c. 104 .... **CMLC 35; PC 10**
See also AW 2; CDWLB 1; DLB 211; RGWL 2, 3

Martin, Ken
See Hubbard, L(afayette) Ron(ald)

Martin, Richard
See Creasey, John

Martin, Steve 1945- .... **CLC 30**
See also AAYA 53; CA 97-100; CANR 30, 100; DFS 19; MTCW 1

Martin, Valerie 1948- .... **CLC 89**
See also BEST 90:2; CA 85-88; CANR 49, 89

Martin, Violet Florence 1862-1915 .. **SSC 56; TCLC 51**

Martin, Webber
See Silverberg, Robert

Martindale, Patrick Victor
See White, Patrick (Victor Martindale)

Martin du Gard, Roger
1881-1958 .... **TCLC 24**
See also CA 118; CANR 94; DLB 65; EWL 3; GFL 1789 to the Present; RGWL 2, 3

Martineau, Harriet 1802-1876 ...... **NCLC 26, 137**
See also DLB 21, 55, 159, 163, 166, 190; FW; RGEL 2; YABC 2

Martines, Julia
See O'Faolain, Julia

Martinez, Enrique Gonzalez
See Gonzalez Martinez, Enrique

Martinez, Jacinto Benavente y
See Benavente (y Martinez), Jacinto

Martinez de la Rosa, Francisco de Paula
1787-1862 .... **NCLC 102**
See also TWA

Martinez Ruiz, Jose 1873-1967
See Azorin; Ruiz, Jose Martinez
See also CA 93-96; HW 1

Martinez Sierra, Gregorio
1881-1947 .... **TCLC 6**
See also CA 115; EWL 3

Martinez Sierra, Maria (de la O'LeJarraga)
1874-1974 .... **TCLC 6**
See also CA 115; EWL 3

Martinsen, Martin
See Follett, Ken(neth Martin)

Martinson, Harry (Edmund)
1904-1978 .... **CLC 14**
See also CA 77-80; CANR 34, 130; DLB 259; EWL 3

Martyn, Edward 1859-1923 .... **TCLC 131**
See also CA 179; DLB 10; RGEL 2

Marut, Ret
See Traven, B.

Marut, Robert
See Traven, B.

Marvell, Andrew 1621-1678 .... **LC 4, 43; PC 10; WLC**
See also BRW 2; BRWR 2; CDBLB 1660-1789; DA; DAB; DAC; DAM MST, POET; DLB 131; EXPP; PFS 5; RGEL 2; TEA; WP

Marx, Karl (Heinrich)
1818-1883 .... **NCLC 17, 114**
See also DLB 129; LATS 1:1; TWA

Masaoka, Shiki -1902 .... **TCLC 18**
See Masaoka, Tsunenori
See also RGWL 3

Masaoka, Tsunenori 1867-1902
See Masaoka, Shiki
See also CA 117; 191; TWA

Masefield, John (Edward)
1878-1967 .... **CLC 11, 47**
See also CA 19-20; 25-28R; CANR 33; CAP 2; CDBLB 1890-1914; DAM POET; DLB 10, 19, 153, 160; EWL 3; EXPP; FANT; MTCW 1, 2; PFS 5; RGEL 2; SATA 19

Maso, Carole 19(?)- .... **CLC 44**
See also CA 170; GLL 2; RGAL 4

Mason, Bobbie Ann 1940- ... **CLC 28, 43, 82, 154; SSC 4**
See also AAYA 5, 42; AMWS 8; BPFB 2; CA 53-56; CANR 11, 31, 58, 83, 125; CDALBS; CN 7; CSW; DA3; DLB 173; DLBY 1987; EWL 3; EXPS; INT CANR-31; MTCW 1, 2; NFS 4; RGAL 4; RGSF 2; SSFS 3, 8, 20; YAW

Mason, Ernst
See Pohl, Frederik

Mason, Hunni B.
See Sternheim, (William Adolf) Carl

Mason, Lee W.
See Malzberg, Barry N(athaniel)

Mason, Nick 1945- .... **CLC 35**

Mason, Tally
See Derleth, August (William)

Mass, Anna .... **CLC 59**

Mass, William
See Gibson, William

Massinger, Philip 1583-1640 .... **LC 70**
See also DLB 58; RGEL 2

Master Lao
See Lao Tzu

Masters, Edgar Lee 1868-1950 ...... **PC 1, 36; TCLC 2, 25; WLCS**
See also AMWS 1; CA 104; 133; CDALB 1865-1917; DA; DAC; DAM MST, POET; DLB 54; EWL 3; EXPP; MTCW 1, 2; RGAL 4; TUS; WP

Masters, Hilary 1928- .... **CLC 48**
See also CA 25-28R, 217; CAAE 217; CANR 13, 47, 97; CN 7; DLB 244

Mastrosimone, William 19(?)- .... **CLC 36**
See also CA 186; CAD; CD 5

Mathe, Albert
See Camus, Albert

Mather, Cotton 1663-1728 .... **LC 38**
See also AMWS 2; CDALB 1640-1865; DLB 24, 30, 140; RGAL 4; TUS

Mather, Increase 1639-1723 .... **LC 38**
See also DLB 24

Matheson, Richard (Burton) 1926- .. **CLC 37**
See also AAYA 31; CA 97-100; CANR 88, 99; DLB 8, 44; HGG; INT CA-97-100; SCFW 2; SFW 4; SUFW 2

Mathews, Harry 1930- .... **CLC 6, 52**
See also CA 21-24R; CAAS 6; CANR 18, 40, 98; CN 7

Mathews, John Joseph 1894-1979 .. **CLC 84; NNAL**
See also CA 19-20; 142; CANR 45; CAP 2; DAM MULT; DLB 175

Mathias, Roland (Glyn) 1915- .... **CLC 45**
See also CA 97-100; CANR 19, 41; CP 7; DLB 27

Matsuo Basho 1644-1694 .... **LC 62; PC 3**
See Basho, Matsuo
See also DAM POET; PFS 2, 7

Mattheson, Rodney
See Creasey, John

Matthews, (James) Brander
1852-1929 .... **TCLC 95**
See also DLB 71, 78; DLBD 13

Matthews, (James) Brander
1852-1929 .... **TCLC 95**
See also CA 181; DLB 71, 78; DLBD 13

Matthews, Greg 1949- .... **CLC 45**
See also CA 135

Matthews, William (Procter III)
1942-1997 .... **CLC 40**
See also AMWS 9; CA 29-32R; 162; CAAS 18; CANR 12, 57; CP 7; DLB 5

Matthias, John (Edward) 1941- .... **CLC 9**
See also CA 33-36R; CANR 56; CP 7

Matthiessen, F(rancis) O(tto)
1902-1950 .... **TCLC 100**
See also CA 185; DLB 63

Matthiessen, Peter 1927- ... **CLC 5, 7, 11, 32, 64**
See also AAYA 6, 40; AMWS 5; ANW; BEST 90:4; BPFB 2; CA 9-12R; CANR 21, 50, 73, 100; CN 7; DA3; DAM NOV; DLB 6, 173, 275; MTCW 1, 2; SATA 27

Maturin, Charles Robert
1780(?)-1824 .... **NCLC 6**
See also BRWS 8; DLB 178; HGG; LMFS 1; RGEL 2; SUFW

Matute (Ausejo), Ana Maria 1925- .. **CLC 11**
See also CA 89-92; CANR 129; CWW 2; EWL 3; MTCW 1; RGSF 2

Maugham, W. S.
See Maugham, W(illiam) Somerset

Maugham, W(illiam) Somerset
1874-1965 .. **CLC 1, 11, 15, 67, 93; SSC 8; WLC**
See also AAYA 55; BPFB 2; BRW 6; CA 5-8R; 25-28R; CANR 40, 127; CDBLB 1914-1945; CMW 4; DA; DA3; DAB; DAC; DAM DRAM, MST, NOV; DLB 10, 36, 77, 100, 162, 195; EWL 3; LAIT 3; MTCW 1, 2; RGEL 2; RGSF 2; SATA 54; SSFS 17

Maugham, William Somerset
See Maugham, W(illiam) Somerset

Maupassant, (Henri Rene Albert) Guy de
1850-1893 . **NCLC 1, 42, 83; SSC 1, 64;**
WLC
See also BYA 14; DA; DA3; DAB; DAC;
DAM MST; DLB 123; EW 7; EXPS; GFL
1789 to the Present; LAIT 2; LMFS 1;
RGSF 2; RGWL 2, 3; SSFS 4; SUFW;
TWA

Maupin, Armistead (Jones, Jr.)
1944- .... **CLC 95**
See also CA 125; 130; CANR 58, 101;
CPW; DA3; DAM POP; DLB 278; GLL
1; INT CA-130; MTCW 2

Maurhut, Richard
See Traven, B.

Mauriac, Claude 1914-1996 .... **CLC 9**
See also CA 89-92; 152; CWW 2; DLB 83;
EWL 3; GFL 1789 to the Present

Mauriac, Francois (Charles)
1885-1970 .... **CLC 4, 9, 56; SSC 24**
See also CA 25-28; CAP 2; DLB 65; EW
10; EWL 3; GFL 1789 to the Present;
MTCW 1, 2; RGWL 2, 3; TWA

Mavor, Osborne Henry 1888-1951
See Bridie, James
See also CA 104

Maxwell, William (Keepers, Jr.)
1908-2000 .... **CLC 19**
See also AMWS 8; CA 93-96; 189; CANR
54, 95; CN 7; DLB 218, 278; DLBY
1980; INT CA-93-96; SATA-Obit 128

May, Elaine 1932- .... **CLC 16**
See also CA 124; 142; CAD; CWD; DLB
44

Mayakovski, Vladimir (Vladimirovich)
1893-1930 .... **TCLC 4, 18**
See Maiakovskii, Vladimir; Mayakovsky,
Vladimir
See also CA 104; 158; EWL 3; MTCW 2;
SFW 4; TWA

Mayakovsky, Vladimir
See Mayakovski, Vladimir (Vladimirovich)
See also EW 11; WP

Mayhew, Henry 1812-1887 .... **NCLC 31**
See also DLB 18, 55, 190

Mayle, Peter 1939(?)- .... **CLC 89**
See also CA 139; CANR 64, 109

Maynard, Joyce 1953- .... **CLC 23**
See also CA 111; 129; CANR 64

Mayne, William (James Carter)
1928- .... **CLC 12**
See also AAYA 20; CA 9-12R; CANR 37,
80, 100; CLR 25; FANT; JRDA; MAI-
CYA 1, 2; MAICYAS 1; SAAS 11; SATA
6, 68, 122; SUFW 2; YAW

Mayo, Jim
See L'Amour, Louis (Dearborn)
See also TCWW 2

Maysles, Albert 1926- .... **CLC 16**
See also CA 29-32R

Maysles, David 1932-1987 .... **CLC 16**
See also CA 191

Mazer, Norma Fox 1931- .... **CLC 26**
See also AAYA 5, 36; BYA 1, 8; CA 69-72;
CANR 12, 32, 66, 129; CLR 23; JRDA;
MAICYA 1, 2; SAAS 1; SATA 24, 67,
105; WYA; YAW

Mazzini, Guiseppe 1805-1872 .... **NCLC 34**

McAlmon, Robert (Menzies)
1895-1956 .... **TCLC 97**
See also CA 107; 168; DLB 4, 45; DLBD
15; GLL 1

McAuley, James Phillip 1917-1976 .. **CLC 45**
See also CA 97-100; DLB 260; RGEL 2

McBain, Ed
See Hunter, Evan
See also MSW

McBrien, William (Augustine)
1930- .... **CLC 44**
See also CA 107; CANR 90

McCabe, Patrick 1955- .... **CLC 133**
See also BRWS 9; CA 130; CANR 50, 90;
CN 7; DLB 194

McCaffrey, Anne (Inez) 1926- .... **CLC 17**
See also AAYA 6, 34; AITN 2; BEST 89:2;
BPFB 2; BYA 5; CA 25-28R, 227; CAAE
227; CANR 15, 35, 55, 96; CLR 49;
CPW; DA3; DAM NOV, POP; DLB 8;
JRDA; MAICYA 1, 2; MTCW 1, 2; SAAS
11; SATA 8, 70, 116, 152; SATA-Essay
152; SFW 4; SUFW 2; WYA; YAW

McCall, Nathan 1955(?)- .... **CLC 86**
See also AAYA 59; BW 3; CA 146; CANR
88

McCann, Arthur
See Campbell, John W(ood, Jr.)

McCann, Edson
See Pohl, Frederik

McCarthy, Charles, Jr. 1933-
See McCarthy, Cormac
See also CANR 42, 69, 101; CN 7; CPW;
CSW; DA3; DAM POP; MTCW 2

McCarthy, Cormac .... **CLC 4, 57, 101**
See McCarthy, Charles, Jr.
See also AAYA 41; AMWS 8; BPFB 2; CA
13-16R; CANR 10; DLB 6, 143, 256;
EWL 3; LATS 1:2; TCWW 2

McCarthy, Mary (Therese)
1912-1989 .. **CLC 1, 3, 5, 14, 24, 39, 59;**
SSC 24
See also AMW; BPFB 2; CA 5-8R; 129;
CANR 16, 50, 64; DA3; DLB 2; DLBY
1981; EWL 3; FW; INT CANR-16;
MAWW; MTCW 1, 2; RGAL 4; TUS

McCartney, (James) Paul 1942- . **CLC 12, 35**
See also CA 146; CANR 111

McCauley, Stephen (D.) 1955- .... **CLC 50**
See also CA 141

McClaren, Peter .... **CLC 70**

McClure, Michael (Thomas) 1932- ... **CLC 6,**
10
See also BG 3; CA 21-24R; CAD; CANR
17, 46, 77, 131; CD 5; CP 7; DLB 16;
WP

McCorkle, Jill (Collins) 1958- .... **CLC 51**
See also CA 121; CANR 113; CSW; DLB
234; DLBY 1987

McCourt, Frank 1930- .... **CLC 109**
See also AMWS 12; CA 157; CANR 97;
NCFS 1

McCourt, James 1941- .... **CLC 5**
See also CA 57-60; CANR 98

McCourt, Malachy 1931- .... **CLC 119**
See also SATA 126

McCoy, Horace (Stanley)
1897-1955 .... **TCLC 28**
See also AMWS 13; CA 108; 155; CMW 4;
DLB 9

McCrae, John 1872-1918 .... **TCLC 12**
See also CA 109; DLB 92; PFS 5

McCreigh, James
See Pohl, Frederik

McCullers, (Lula) Carson (Smith)
1917-1967 .... **CLC 1, 4, 10, 12, 48, 100;**
SSC 9, 24; TCLC 155; WLC
See also AAYA 21; AMW; AMWC 2; BPFB
2; CA 5-8R; 25-28R; CABS 1, 3; CANR
18, 132; CDALB 1941-1968; DA; DA3;
DAB; DAC; DAM MST, NOV; DFS 5,
18; DLB 2, 7, 173, 228; EWL 3; EXPS;
FW; GLL 1; LAIT 3, 4; MAWW; MTCW
1, 2; NFS 6, 13; RGAL 4; RGSF 2; SATA
27; SSFS 5; TUS; YAW

McCulloch, John Tyler
See Burroughs, Edgar Rice

McCullough, Colleen 1938(?)- .. **CLC 27, 107**
See also AAYA 36; BPFB 2; CA 81-84;
CANR 17, 46, 67, 98; CPW; DA3; DAM
NOV, POP; MTCW 1, 2; RHW

McCunn, Ruthanne Lum 1946- .... **AAL**
See also CA 119; CANR 43, 96; LAIT 2;
SATA 63

McDermott, Alice 1953- .... **CLC 90**
See also CA 109; CANR 40, 90, 126; DLB
292

McElroy, Joseph 1930- .... **CLC 5, 47**
See also CA 17-20R; CN 7

McEwan, Ian (Russell) 1948- .... **CLC 13, 66,**
169
See also BEST 90:4; BRWS 4; CA 61-64;
CANR 14, 41, 69, 87, 132; CN 7; DAM
NOV; DLB 14, 194; HGG; MTCW 1, 2;
RGSF 2; SUFW 2; TEA

McFadden, David 1940- .... **CLC 48**
See also CA 104; CP 7; DLB 60; INT CA-
104

McFarland, Dennis 1950- .... **CLC 65**
See also CA 165; CANR 110

McGahern, John 1934- ... **CLC 5, 9, 48, 156;**
SSC 17
See also CA 17-20R; CANR 29, 68, 113;
CN 7; DLB 14, 231; MTCW 1

McGinley, Patrick (Anthony) 1937- . **CLC 41**
See also CA 120; 127; CANR 56; INT CA-
127

McGinley, Phyllis 1905-1978 .... **CLC 14**
See also CA 9-12R; 77-80; CANR 19;
CWRI 5; DLB 11, 48; PFS 9, 13; SATA
2, 44; SATA-Obit 24

McGinniss, Joe 1942- .... **CLC 32**
See also AITN 2; BEST 89:2; CA 25-28R;
CANR 26, 70; CPW; DLB 185; INT
CANR-26

McGivern, Maureen Daly
See Daly, Maureen

McGrath, Patrick 1950- .... **CLC 55**
See also CA 136; CANR 65; CN 7; DLB
231; HGG; SUFW 2

McGrath, Thomas (Matthew)
1916-1990 .... **CLC 28, 59**
See also AMWS 10; CA 9-12R; 132; CANR
6, 33, 95; DAM POET; MTCW 1; SATA
41; SATA-Obit 66

McGuane, Thomas (Francis III)
1939- .... **CLC 3, 7, 18, 45, 127**
See also AITN 2; BPFB 2; CA 49-52;
CANR 5, 24, 49, 94; CN 7; DLB 2, 212;
DLBY 1980; EWL 3; INT CANR-24;
MTCW 1; TCWW 2

McGuckian, Medbh 1950- .... **CLC 48, 174;**
PC 27
See also BRWS 5; CA 143; CP 7; CWP;
DAM POET; DLB 40

McHale, Tom 1942(?)-1982 .... **CLC 3, 5**
See also AITN 1; CA 77-80; 106

McHugh, Heather 1948- .... **PC 61**
See also CA 69-72; CANR 11, 28, 55, 92;
CP 7; CWP

McIlvanney, William 1936- .... **CLC 42**
See also CA 25-28R; CANR 61; CMW 4;
DLB 14, 207

McIlwraith, Maureen Mollie Hunter
See Hunter, Mollie
See also SATA 2

McInerney, Jay 1955- .... **CLC 34, 112**
See also AAYA 18; BPFB 2; CA 116; 123;
CANR 45, 68, 116; CN 7; CPW; DA3;
DAM POP; DLB 292; INT CA-123;
MTCW 2

McIntyre, Vonda N(eel) 1948- .... **CLC 18**
See also CA 81-84; CANR 17, 34, 69;
MTCW 1; SFW 4; YAW

McKay, Claude .... **BLC 3; HR 3; PC 2; TCLC 7, 41; WLC**
See McKay, Festus Claudius
See also AFAW 1, 2; AMWS 10; DAB; DLB 4, 45, 51, 117; EWL 3; EXPP; GLL 2; LAIT 3; LMFS 2; PAB; PFS 4; RGAL 4; WP

McKay, Festus Claudius 1889-1948
See McKay, Claude
See also BW 1, 3; CA 104; 124; CANR 73; DA; DAC; DAM MST, MULT, NOV, POET; MTCW 1, 2; TUS

McKuen, Rod 1933- .... **CLC 1, 3**
See also AITN 1; CA 41-44R; CANR 40

McLoughlin, R. B.
See Mencken, H(enry) L(ouis)

McLuhan, (Herbert) Marshall
1911-1980 .... **CLC 37, 83**
See also CA 9-12R; 102; CANR 12, 34, 61; DLB 88; INT CANR-12; MTCW 1, 2

McManus, Declan Patrick Aloysius
See Costello, Elvis

McMillan, Terry (L.) 1951- . **BLCS; CLC 50, 61, 112**
See also AAYA 21; AMWS 13; BPFB 2; BW 2, 3; CA 140; CANR 60, 104, 131; CPW; DA3; DAM MULT, NOV, POP; MTCW 2; RGAL 4; YAW

McMurtry, Larry (Jeff) 1936- .. **CLC 2, 3, 7, 11, 27, 44, 127**
See also AAYA 15; AITN 2; AMWS 5; BEST 89:2; BPFB 2; CA 5-8R; CANR 19, 43, 64, 103; CDALB 1968-1988; CN 7; CPW; CSW; DA3; DAM NOV, POP; DLB 2, 143, 256; DLBY 1980, 1987; EWL 3; MTCW 1, 2; RGAL 4; TCWW 2

McNally, T. M. 1961- .... **CLC 82**

McNally, Terrence 1939- .... **CLC 4, 7, 41, 91**
See also AMWS 13; CA 45-48; CAD; CANR 2, 56, 116; CD 5; DA3; DAM DRAM; DFS 16, 19; DLB 7, 249; EWL 3; GLL 1; MTCW 2

McNamer, Deirdre 1950- .... **CLC 70**

McNeal, Tom .... **CLC 119**

McNeile, Herman Cyril 1888-1937
See Sapper
See also CA 184; CMW 4; DLB 77

McNickle, (William) D'Arcy
1904-1977 .... **CLC 89; NNAL**
See also CA 9-12R; 85-88; CANR 5, 45; DAM MULT; DLB 175, 212; RGAL 4; SATA-Obit 22

McPhee, John (Angus) 1931- .... **CLC 36**
See also AMWS 3; ANW; BEST 90:1; CA 65-68; CANR 20, 46, 64, 69, 121; CPW; DLB 185, 275; MTCW 1, 2; TUS

McPherson, James Alan 1943- . **BLCS; CLC 19, 77**
See also BW 1, 3; CA 25-28R; CAAS 17; CANR 24, 74; CN 7; CSW; DLB 38, 244; EWL 3; MTCW 1, 2; RGAL 4; RGSF 2

McPherson, William (Alexander)
1933- .... **CLC 34**
See also CA 69-72; CANR 28; INT CANR-28

McTaggart, J. McT. Ellis
See McTaggart, John McTaggart Ellis

McTaggart, John McTaggart Ellis
1866-1925 .... **TCLC 105**
See also CA 120; DLB 262

Mead, George Herbert 1863-1931 . **TCLC 89**
See also CA 212; DLB 270

Mead, Margaret 1901-1978 .... **CLC 37**
See also AITN 1; CA 1-4R; 81-84; CANR 4; DA3; FW; MTCW 1, 2; SATA-Obit 20

Meaker, Marijane (Agnes) 1927-
See Kerr, M. E.
See also CA 107; CANR 37, 63; INT CA-107; JRDA; MAICYA 1, 2; MAICYAS 1; MTCW 1; SATA 20, 61, 99; SATA-Essay 111; YAW

Medoff, Mark (Howard) 1940- .... **CLC 6, 23**
See also AITN 1; CA 53-56; CAD; CANR 5; CD 5; DAM DRAM; DFS 4; DLB 7; INT CANR-5

Medvedev, P. N.
See Bakhtin, Mikhail Mikhailovich

Meged, Aharon
See Megged, Aharon

Meged, Aron
See Megged, Aharon

Megged, Aharon 1920- .... **CLC 9**
See also CA 49-52; CAAS 13; CANR 1; EWL 3

Mehta, Gita 1943- .... **CLC 179**
See also CA 225; DNFS 2

Mehta, Ved (Parkash) 1934- .... **CLC 37**
See also CA 1-4R, 212; CAAE 212; CANR 2, 23, 69; MTCW 1

Melanchthon, Philipp 1497-1560 .... **LC 90**
See also DLB 179

Melanter
See Blackmore, R(ichard) D(oddridge)

Meleager c. 140B.C.-c. 70B.C. ...... **CMLC 53**

Melies, Georges 1861-1938 .... **TCLC 81**

Melikow, Loris
See Hofmannsthal, Hugo von

Melmoth, Sebastian
See Wilde, Oscar (Fingal O'Flahertie Wills)

Melo Neto, Joao Cabral de
See Cabral de Melo Neto, Joao
See also CWW 2; EWL 3

Meltzer, Milton 1915- .... **CLC 26**
See also AAYA 8, 45; BYA 2, 6; CA 13-16R; CANR 38, 92, 107; CLR 13; DLB 61; JRDA; MAICYA 1, 2; SAAS 1; SATA 1, 50, 80, 128; SATA-Essay 124; WYA; YAW

Melville, Herman 1819-1891 ..... **NCLC 3, 12, 29, 45, 49, 91, 93, 123; SSC 1, 17, 46; WLC**
See also AAYA 25; AMW; AMWR 1; CDALB 1640-1865; DA; DA3; DAB; DAC; DAM MST, NOV; DLB 3, 74, 250, 254; EXPN; EXPS; LAIT 1, 2; NFS 7, 9; RGAL 4; RGSF 2; SATA 59; SSFS 3; TUS

Members, Mark
See Powell, Anthony (Dymoke)

Membreno, Alejandro .... **CLC 59**

Menander c. 342B.C.-c. 293B.C. .... **CMLC 9, 51; DC 3**
See also AW 1; CDWLB 1; DAM DRAM; DLB 176; LMFS 1; RGWL 2, 3

Menchu, Rigoberta 1959- .. **CLC 160; HLCS 2**
See also CA 175; DNFS 1; WLIT 1

Mencken, H(enry) L(ouis)
1880-1956 .... **TCLC 13**
See also AMW; CA 105; 125; CDALB 1917-1929; DLB 11, 29, 63, 137, 222; EWL 3; MTCW 1, 2; NCFS 4; RGAL 4; TUS

Mendelsohn, Jane 1965- .... **CLC 99**
See also CA 154; CANR 94

Menton, Francisco de
See Chin, Frank (Chew, Jr.)

Mercer, David 1928-1980 .... **CLC 5**
See also CA 9-12R; 102; CANR 23; CBD; DAM DRAM; DLB 13; MTCW 1; RGEL 2

Merchant, Paul
See Ellison, Harlan (Jay)

Meredith, George 1828-1909 .. **PC 60; TCLC 17, 43**
See also CA 117; 153; CANR 80; CDBLB 1832-1890; DAM POET; DLB 18, 35, 57, 159; RGEL 2; TEA

Meredith, William (Morris) 1919- .... **CLC 4, 13, 22, 55; PC 28**
See also CA 9-12R; CAAS 14; CANR 6, 40, 129; CP 7; DAM POET; DLB 5

Merezhkovsky, Dmitrii Sergeevich
See Merezhkovsky, Dmitry Sergeyevich
See also DLB 295

Merezhkovsky, Dmitry Sergeyevich
See Merezhkovsky, Dmitry Sergeyevich
See also EWL 3

Merezhkovsky, Dmitry Sergeyevich
1865-1941 .... **TCLC 29**
See Merezhkovsky, Dmitrii Sergeevich; Merezhkovsky, Dmitry Sergeevich
See also CA 169

Merimee, Prosper 1803-1870 ... **NCLC 6, 65; SSC 7, 77**
See also DLB 119, 192; EW 6; EXPS; GFL 1789 to the Present; RGSF 2; RGWL 2, 3; SSFS 8; SUFW

Merkin, Daphne 1954- .... **CLC 44**
See also CA 123

Merleau-Ponty, Maurice
1908-1961 .... **TCLC 156**
See also CA 114; 89-92; DLB 296; GFL 1789 to the Present

Merlin, Arthur
See Blish, James (Benjamin)

Mernissi, Fatima 1940- .... **CLC 171**
See also CA 152; FW

Merrill, James (Ingram) 1926-1995 .. **CLC 2, 3, 6, 8, 13, 18, 34, 91; PC 28**
See also AMWS 3; CA 13-16R; 147; CANR 10, 49, 63, 108; DA3; DAM POET; DLB 5, 165; DLBY 1985; EWL 3; INT CANR-10; MTCW 1, 2; PAB; RGAL 4

Merriman, Alex
See Silverberg, Robert

Merriman, Brian 1747-1805 .... **NCLC 70**

Merritt, E. B.
See Waddington, Miriam

Merton, Thomas (James)
1915-1968 . **CLC 1, 3, 11, 34, 83; PC 10**
See also AMWS 8; CA 5-8R; 25-28R; CANR 22, 53, 111, 131; DA3; DLB 48; DLBY 1981; MTCW 1, 2

Merwin, W(illiam) S(tanley) 1927- ... **CLC 1, 2, 3, 5, 8, 13, 18, 45, 88; PC 45**
See also AMWS 3; CA 13-16R; CANR 15, 51, 112; CP 7; DA3; DAM POET; DLB 5, 169; EWL 3; INT CANR-15; MTCW 1, 2; PAB; PFS 5, 15; RGAL 4

Metcalf, John 1938- .... **CLC 37; SSC 43**
See also CA 113; CN 7; DLB 60; RGSF 2; TWA

Metcalf, Suzanne
See Baum, L(yman) Frank

Mew, Charlotte (Mary) 1870-1928 .. **TCLC 8**
See also CA 105; 189; DLB 19, 135; RGEL 2

Mewshaw, Michael 1943- .... **CLC 9**
See also CA 53-56; CANR 7, 47; DLBY 1980

Meyer, Conrad Ferdinand
1825-1898 .... **NCLC 81; SSC 30**
See also DLB 129; EW; RGWL 2, 3

Meyer, Gustav 1868-1932
See Meyrink, Gustav
See also CA 117; 190

Meyer, June
See Jordan, June (Meyer)

Meyer, Lynn
See Slavitt, David R(ytman)

Meyers, Jeffrey 1939- .... **CLC 39**
　　See also CA 73-76, 186; CAAE 186; CANR
　　54, 102; DLB 111

Meynell, Alice (Christina Gertrude
　　Thompson) 1847-1922 .... **TCLC 6**
　　See also CA 104; 177; DLB 19, 98; RGEL
　　2

Meyrink, Gustav .... **TCLC 21**
　　See Meyer, Gustav
　　See also DLB 81; EWL 3

Michaels, Leonard 1933-2003 ..... **CLC 6, 25;**
　　SSC 16
　　See also CA 61-64; 216; CANR 21, 62, 119;
　　CN 7; DLB 130; MTCW 1

Michaux, Henri 1899-1984 .... **CLC 8, 19**
　　See also CA 85-88; 114; DLB 258; EWL 3;
　　GFL 1789 to the Present; RGWL 2, 3

Micheaux, Oscar (Devereaux)
　　1884-1951 .... **TCLC 76**
　　See also BW 3; CA 174; DLB 50; TCWW
　　2

Michelangelo 1475-1564 .... **LC 12**
　　See also AAYA 43

Michelet, Jules 1798-1874 .... **NCLC 31**
　　See also EW 5; GFL 1789 to the Present

Michels, Robert 1876-1936 .... **TCLC 88**
　　See also CA 212

Michener, James A(lbert)
　　1907(?)-1997 .. **CLC 1, 5, 11, 29, 60, 109**
　　See also AAYA 27; AITN 1; BEST 90:1;
　　BPFB 2; CA 5-8R; 161; CANR 21, 45,
　　68; CN 7; CPW; DA3; DAM NOV, POP;
　　DLB 6; MTCW 1, 2; RHW

Mickiewicz, Adam 1798-1855 . **NCLC 3, 101;**
　　PC 38
　　See also EW 5; RGWL 2, 3

Middleton, (John) Christopher
　　1926- .... **CLC 13**
　　See also CA 13-16R; CANR 29, 54, 117;
　　CP 7; DLB 40

Middleton, Richard (Barham)
　　1882-1911 .... **TCLC 56**
　　See also CA 187; DLB 156; HGG

Middleton, Stanley 1919- .... **CLC 7, 38**
　　See also CA 25-28R; CAAS 23; CANR 21,
　　46, 81; CN 7; DLB 14

Middleton, Thomas 1580-1627 ...... **DC 5; LC**
　　33
　　See also BRW 2; DAM DRAM, MST; DFS
　　18; DLB 58; RGEL 2

Migueis, Jose Rodrigues 1901-1980 . **CLC 10**
　　See also DLB 287

Mikszath, Kalman 1847-1910 .... **TCLC 31**
　　See also CA 170

Miles, Jack .... **CLC 100**
　　See also CA 200

Miles, John Russiano
　　See Miles, Jack

Miles, Josephine (Louise)
　　1911-1985 .... **CLC 1, 2, 14, 34, 39**
　　See also CA 1-4R; 116; CANR 2, 55; DAM
　　POET; DLB 48

Militant
　　See Sandburg, Carl (August)

Mill, Harriet (Hardy) Taylor
　　1807-1858 .... **NCLC 102**
　　See also FW

Mill, John Stuart 1806-1873 .... **NCLC 11, 58**
　　See also CDBLB 1832-1890; DLB 55, 190,
　　262; FW 1; RGEL 2; TEA

Millar, Kenneth 1915-1983 .... **CLC 14**
　　See Macdonald, Ross
　　See also CA 9-12R; 110; CANR 16, 63,
　　107; CMW 4; CPW; DA3; DAM POP;
　　DLB 2, 226; DLBD 6; DLBY 1983;
　　MTCW 1, 2

Millay, E. Vincent
　　See Millay, Edna St. Vincent

Millay, Edna St. Vincent 1892-1950 ..... **PC 6,**
　　61; TCLC 4, 49; WLCS
　　See Boyd, Nancy
　　See also AMW; CA 104; 130; CDALB
　　1917-1929; DA; DA3; DAB; DAC; DAM
　　MST, POET; DLB 45, 249; EWL 3;
　　EXPP; MAWW; MTCW 1, 2; PAB; PFS
　　3, 17; RGAL 4; TUS; WP

Miller, Arthur 1915- ...... **CLC 1, 2, 6, 10, 15,**
　　26, 47, 78, 179; DC 1; WLC
　　See also AAYA 15; AITN 1; AMW; AMWC
　　1; CA 1-4R; CABS 3; CAD; CANR 2,
　　30, 54, 76, 132; CD 5; CDALB 1941-
　　1968; DA; DA3; DAB; DAC; DAM
　　DRAM, MST; DFS 1, 3, 8; DLB 7, 266;
　　EWL 3; LAIT 1, 4; LATS 1:2; MTCW 1,
　　2; RGAL 4; TUS; WYAS 1

Miller, Henry (Valentine)
　　1891-1980 .... **CLC 1, 2, 4, 9, 14, 43, 84;**
　　WLC
　　See also AMW; BPFB 2; CA 9-12R; 97-
　　100; CANR 33, 64; CDALB 1929-1941;
　　DA; DA3; DAB; DAC; DAM MST, NOV;
　　DLB 4, 9; DLBY 1980; EWL 3; MTCW
　　1, 2; RGAL 4; TUS

Miller, Hugh 1802-1856 .... **NCLC 143**
　　See also DLB 190

Miller, Jason 1939(?)-2001 .... **CLC 2**
　　See also AITN 1; CA 73-76; 197; CAD;
　　CANR 130; DFS 12; DLB 7

Miller, Sue 1943- .... **CLC 44**
　　See also AMWS 12; BEST 90:3; CA 139;
　　CANR 59, 91, 128; DA3; DAM POP;
　　DLB 143

Miller, Walter M(ichael, Jr.)
　　1923-1996 .... **CLC 4, 30**
　　See also BPFB 2; CA 85-88; CANR 108;
　　DLB 8; SCFW; SFW 4

Millett, Kate 1934- .... **CLC 67**
　　See also AITN 1; CA 73-76; CANR 32, 53,
　　76, 110; DA3; DLB 246; FW; GLL 1;
　　MTCW 1, 2

Millhauser, Steven (Lewis) 1943- .... **CLC 21,**
　　54, 109; SSC 57
　　See also CA 110; 111; CANR 63, 114, 133;
　　CN 7; DA3; DLB 2; FANT; INT CA-111;
　　MTCW 2

Millin, Sarah Gertrude 1889-1968 ... **CLC 49**
　　See also CA 102; 93-96; DLB 225; EWL 3

Milne, A(lan) A(lexander)
　　1882-1956 .... **TCLC 6, 88**
　　See also BRWS 5; CA 104; 133; CLR 1,
　　26; CMW 4; CWRI 5; DA3; DAB; DAC;
　　DAM MST; DLB 10, 77, 100, 160; FANT;
　　MAICYA 1, 2; MTCW 1, 2; RGEL 2;
　　SATA 100; WCH; YABC 1

Milner, Ron(ald) 1938-2004 ..... **BLC 3; CLC**
　　56
　　See also AITN 1; BW 1; CA 73-76; CAD;
　　CANR 24, 81; CD 5; DAM MULT; DLB
　　38; MTCW 1

Milnes, Richard Monckton
　　1809-1885 .... **NCLC 61**
　　See also DLB 32, 184

Milosz, Czeslaw 1911- ...... **CLC 5, 11, 22, 31,**
　　56, 82; PC 8; WLCS
　　See also CA 81-84; CANR 23, 51, 91, 126;
　　CDWLB 4; CWW 2; DA3; DAM MST,
　　POET; DLB 215; EW 13; EWL 3; MTCW
　　1, 2; PFS 16; RGWL 2, 3

Milton, John 1608-1674 ..... **LC 9, 43, 92; PC**
　　19, 29; WLC
　　See also BRW 2; BRWR 2; CDBLB 1660-
　　1789; DA; DA3; DAB; DAC; DAM MST,
　　POET; DLB 131, 151, 281; EFS 1; EXPP;
　　LAIT 1; PAB; PFS 3, 17; RGEL 2; TEA;
　　WLIT 3; WP

Min, Anchee 1957- .... **CLC 86**
　　See also CA 146; CANR 94

Minehaha, Cornelius
　　See Wedekind, (Benjamin) Frank(lin)

Miner, Valerie 1947- .... **CLC 40**
　　See also CA 97-100; CANR 59; FW; GLL
　　2

Minimo, Duca
　　See D'Annunzio, Gabriele

Minot, Susan 1956- .... **CLC 44, 159**
　　See also AMWS 6; CA 134; CANR 118;
　　CN 7

Minus, Ed 1938- .... **CLC 39**
　　See also CA 185

Mirabai 1498(?)-1550(?) .... **PC 48**

Miranda, Javier
　　See Bioy Casares, Adolfo
　　See also CWW 2

Mirbeau, Octave 1848-1917 .... **TCLC 55**
　　See also CA 216; DLB 123, 192; GFL 1789
　　to the Present

Mirikitani, Janice 1942- .... **AAL**
　　See also CA 211; RGAL 4

Mirk, John (?)-c. 1414 .... **LC 105**
　　See also DLB 146

Miro (Ferrer), Gabriel (Francisco Victor)
　　1879-1930 .... **TCLC 5**
　　See also CA 104; 185; EWL 3

Misharin, Alexandr .... **CLC 59**

Mishima, Yukio ... **CLC 2, 4, 6, 9, 27; DC 1;**
　　SSC 4
　　See Hiraoka, Kimitake
　　See also AAYA 50; BPFB 2; GLL 1; MJW;
　　MTCW 2; RGSF 2; RGWL 2, 3; SSFS 5,
　　12

Mistral, Frederic 1830-1914 .... **TCLC 51**
　　See also CA 122; 213; GFL 1789 to the
　　Present

Mistral, Gabriela
　　See Godoy Alcayaga, Lucila
　　See also DLB 283; DNFS 1; EWL 3; LAW;
　　RGWL 2, 3; WP

Mistry, Rohinton 1952- ... **CLC 71, 196; SSC**
　　73
　　See also BRWS 10; CA 141; CANR 86,
　　114; CCA 1; CN 7; DAC; SSFS 6

Mitchell, Clyde
　　See Ellison, Harlan (Jay)

Mitchell, Emerson Blackhorse Barney
　　1945- .... **NNAL**
　　See also CA 45-48

Mitchell, James Leslie 1901-1935
　　See Gibbon, Lewis Grassic
　　See also CA 104; 188; DLB 15

Mitchell, Joni 1943- .... **CLC 12**
　　See also CA 112; CCA 1

Mitchell, Joseph (Quincy)
　　1908-1996 .... **CLC 98**
　　See also CA 77-80; 152; CANR 69; CN 7;
　　CSW; DLB 185; DLBY 1996

Mitchell, Margaret (Munnerlyn)
　　1900-1949 .... **TCLC 11**
　　See also AAYA 23; BPFB 2; BYA 1; CA
　　109; 125; CANR 55, 94; CDALBS; DA3;
　　DAM NOV, POP; DLB 9; LAIT 2;
　　MTCW 1, 2; NFS 9; RGAL 4; RHW;
　　TUS; WYAS 1; YAW

Mitchell, Peggy
　　See Mitchell, Margaret (Munnerlyn)

Mitchell, S(ilas) Weir 1829-1914 .... **TCLC 36**
　　See also CA 165; DLB 202; RGAL 4

Mitchell, W(illiam) O(rmond)
　　1914-1998 .... **CLC 25**
　　See also CA 77-80; 165; CANR 15, 43; CN
　　7; DAC; DAM MST; DLB 88

Mitchell, William (Lendrum)
　　1879-1936 .... **TCLC 81**
　　See also CA 213

Mitford, Mary Russell 1787-1855 ... **NCLC 4**
　　See also DLB 110, 116; RGEL 2

Mitford, Nancy 1904-1973 .... **CLC 44**
　See also BRWS 10; CA 9-12R; DLB 191;
　RGEL 2

Miyamoto, (Chujo) Yuriko
　1899-1951 .... **TCLC 37**
　See Miyamoto Yuriko
　See also CA 170, 174

Miyamoto Yuriko
　See Miyamoto, (Chujo) Yuriko
　See also DLB 180

Miyazawa, Kenji 1896-1933 .... **TCLC 76**
　See Miyazawa Kenji
　See also CA 157; RGWL 3

Miyazawa Kenji
　See Miyazawa, Kenji
　See also EWL 3

Mizoguchi, Kenji 1898-1956 .... **TCLC 72**
　See also CA 167

Mo, Timothy (Peter) 1950(?)- ... **CLC 46, 134**
　See also CA 117; CANR 128; CN 7; DLB
　194; MTCW 1; WLIT 4; WWE 1

Modarressi, Taghi (M.) 1931-1997 ... **CLC 44**
　See also CA 121; 134; INT CA-134

Modiano, Patrick (Jean) 1945- .... **CLC 18**
　See also CA 85-88; CANR 17, 40, 115;
　CWW 2; DLB 83, 299; EWL 3

Mofolo, Thomas (Mokopu)
　1875(?)-1948 .... **BLC 3; TCLC 22**
　See also AFW; CA 121; 153; CANR 83;
　DAM MULT; DLB 225; EWL 3; MTCW
　2; WLIT 2

Mohr, Nicholasa 1938- .... **CLC 12; HLC 2**
　See also AAYA 8, 46; CA 49-52; CANR 1,
　32, 64; CLR 22; DAM MULT; DLB 145;
　HW 1, 2; JRDA; LAIT 5; LLW 1; MAI-
　CYA 2; MAICYAS 1; RGAL 4; SAAS 8;
　SATA 8, 97; SATA-Essay 113; WYA;
　YAW

Moi, Toril 1953- .... **CLC 172**
　See also CA 154; CANR 102; FW

Mojtabai, A(nn) G(race) 1938- ..... **CLC 5, 9,
　15, 29**
　See also CA 85-88; CANR 88

Moliere 1622-1673 ..... **DC 13; LC 10, 28, 64;
　WLC**
　See also DA; DA3; DAB; DAC; DAM
　DRAM, MST; DFS 13, 18, 20; DLB 268;
　EW 3; GFL Beginnings to 1789; LATS
　1:1; RGWL 2, 3; TWA

Molin, Charles
　See Mayne, William (James Carter)

Molnar, Ferenc 1878-1952 .... **TCLC 20**
　See also CA 109; 153; CANR 83; CDWLB
　4; DAM DRAM; DLB 215; EWL 3;
　RGWL 2, 3

Momaday, N(avarre) Scott 1934- ...... **CLC 2,
　19, 85, 95, 160; NNAL; PC 25; WLCS**
　See also AAYA 11; AMWS 4; ANW; BPFB
　2; BYA 12; CA 25-28R; CANR 14, 34,
　68, 134; CDALBS; CN 7; CPW; DA;
　DA3; DAB; DAC; DAM MST, MULT,
　NOV, POP; DLB 143, 175, 256; EWL 3;
　EXPP; INT CANR-14; LAIT 4; LATS
　1:2; MTCW 1, 2; NFS 10; PFS 2, 11;
　RGAL 4; SATA 48; SATA-Brief 30; WP;
　YAW

Monette, Paul 1945-1995 .... **CLC 82**
　See also AMWS 10; CA 139; 147; CN 7;
　GLL 1

Monroe, Harriet 1860-1936 .... **TCLC 12**
　See also CA 109; 204; DLB 54, 91

Monroe, Lyle
　See Heinlein, Robert A(nson)

Montagu, Elizabeth 1720-1800 .... **NCLC 7,
　117**
　See also FW

Montagu, Mary (Pierrepont) Wortley
　1689-1762 .... **LC 9, 57; PC 16**
　See also DLB 95, 101; RGEL 2

Montagu, W. H.
　See Coleridge, Samuel Taylor

Montague, John (Patrick) 1929- ..... **CLC 13,
　46**
　See also CA 9-12R; CANR 9, 69, 121; CP
　7; DLB 40; EWL 3; MTCW 1; PFS 12;
　RGEL 2

Montaigne, Michel (Eyquem) de
　1533-1592 .... **LC 8, 105; WLC**
　See also DA; DAB; DAC; DAM MST; EW
　2; GFL Beginnings to 1789; LMFS 1;
　RGWL 2, 3; TWA

Montale, Eugenio 1896-1981 ... **CLC 7, 9, 18;
　PC 13**
　See also CA 17-20R; 104; CANR 30; DLB
　114; EW 11; EWL 3; MTCW 1; RGWL
　2, 3; TWA

Montesquieu, Charles-Louis de Secondat
　1689-1755 .... **LC 7, 69**
　See also EW 3; GFL Beginnings to 1789;
　TWA

Montessori, Maria 1870-1952 ...... **TCLC 103**
　See also CA 115; 147

Montgomery, (Robert) Bruce 1921(?)-1978
　See Crispin, Edmund
　See also CA 179; 104; CMW 4

Montgomery, L(ucy) M(aud)
　1874-1942 .... **TCLC 51, 140**
　See also AAYA 12; BYA 1; CA 108; 137;
　CLR 8, 91; DA3; DAC; DAM MST; DLB
　92; DLBD 14; JRDA; MAICYA 1, 2;
　MTCW 2; RGEL 2; SATA 100; TWA;
　WCH; WYA; YABC 1

Montgomery, Marion H., Jr. 1925- .... **CLC 7**
　See also AITN 1; CA 1-4R; CANR 3, 48;
　CSW; DLB 6

Montgomery, Max
　See Davenport, Guy (Mattison, Jr.)

Montherlant, Henry (Milon) de
　1896-1972 .... **CLC 8, 19**
　See also CA 85-88; 37-40R; DAM DRAM;
　DLB 72; EW 11; EWL 3; GFL 1789 to
　the Present; MTCW 1

Monty Python
　See Chapman, Graham; Cleese, John
　(Marwood); Gilliam, Terry (Vance); Idle,
　Eric; Jones, Terence Graham Parry; Palin,
　Michael (Edward)
　See also AAYA 7

Moodie, Susanna (Strickland)
　1803-1885 .... **NCLC 14, 113**
　See also DLB 99

Moody, Hiram (F. III) 1961-
　See Moody, Rick
　See also CA 138; CANR 64, 112

Moody, Minerva
　See Alcott, Louisa May

Moody, Rick .... **CLC 147**
　See Moody, Hiram (F. III)

Moody, William Vaughan
　1869-1910 .... **TCLC 105**
　See also CA 110; 178; DLB 7, 54; RGAL 4

Mooney, Edward 1951-
　See Mooney, Ted
　See also CA 130

Mooney, Ted .... **CLC 25**
　See Mooney, Edward

Moorcock, Michael (John) 1939- ...... **CLC 5,
　27, 58**
　See Bradbury, Edward P.
　See also AAYA 26; CA 45-48; CAAS 5;
　CANR 2, 17, 38, 64, 122; CN 7; DLB 14,
　231, 261; FANT; MTCW 1, 2; SATA 93;
　SCFW 2; SFW 4; SUFW 1, 2

Moore, Brian 1921-1999 ... **CLC 1, 3, 5, 7, 8,
　19, 32, 90**
　See Bryan, Michael
　See also BRWS 9; CA 1-4R; 174; CANR 1,
　25, 42, 63; CCA 1; CN 7; DAB; DAC;
　DAM MST; DLB 251; EWL 3; FANT;
　MTCW 1, 2; RGEL 2

Moore, Edward
　See Muir, Edwin
　See also RGEL 2

Moore, G. E. 1873-1958 .... **TCLC 89**
　See also DLB 262

Moore, George Augustus
　1852-1933 .... **SSC 19; TCLC 7**
　See also BRW 6; CA 104; 177; DLB 10,
　18, 57, 135; EWL 3; RGEL 2; RGSF 2

Moore, Lorrie .... **CLC 39, 45, 68**
　See Moore, Marie Lorena
　See also AMWS 10; DLB 234; SSFS 19

Moore, Marianne (Craig)
　1887-1972 .... **CLC 1, 2, 4, 8, 10, 13, 19,
　47; PC 4, 49; WLCS**
　See also AMW; CA 1-4R; 33-36R; CANR
　3, 61; CDALB 1929-1941; DA; DA3;
　DAB; DAC; DAM MST, POET; DLB 45;
　DLBD 7; EWL 3; EXPP; MAWW;
　MTCW 1, 2; PAB; PFS 14, 17; RGAL 4;
　SATA 20; TUS; WP

Moore, Marie Lorena 1957- .... **CLC 165**
　See Moore, Lorrie
　See also CA 116; CANR 39, 83; CN 7; DLB
　234

Moore, Thomas 1779-1852 .... **NCLC 6, 110**
　See also DLB 96, 144; RGEL 2

Moorhouse, Frank 1938- .... **SSC 40**
　See also CA 118; CANR 92; CN 7; DLB
　289; RGSF 2

Mora, Pat(ricia) 1942- .... **HLC 2**
　See also AMWS 13; CA 129; CANR 57,
　81, 112; CLR 58; DAM MULT; DLB 209;
　HW 1, 2; LLW 1; MAICYA 2; SATA 92,
　134

Moraga, Cherrie 1952- ...... **CLC 126; DC 22**
　See also CA 131; CANR 66; DAM MULT;
　DLB 82, 249; FW; GLL 1; HW 1, 2; LLW
　1

Morand, Paul 1888-1976 .... **CLC 41; SSC 22**
　See also CA 184; 69-72; DLB 65; EWL 3

Morante, Elsa 1918-1985 .... **CLC 8, 47**
　See also CA 85-88; 117; CANR 35; DLB
　177; EWL 3; MTCW 1, 2; RGWL 2, 3

Moravia, Alberto .... **CLC 2, 7, 11, 27, 46;
　SSC 26**
　See Pincherle, Alberto
　See also DLB 177; EW 12; EWL 3; MTCW
　2; RGSF 2; RGWL 2, 3

More, Hannah 1745-1833 ...... **NCLC 27, 141**
　See also DLB 107, 109, 116, 158; RGEL 2

More, Henry 1614-1687 .... **LC 9**
　See also DLB 126, 252

More, Sir Thomas 1478(?)-1535 .... **LC 10, 32**
　See also BRWC 1; BRWS 7; DLB 136, 281;
　LMFS 1; RGEL 2; TEA

Moreas, Jean .... **TCLC 18**
　See Papadiamantopoulos, Johannes
　See also GFL 1789 to the Present

Moreton, Andrew Esq.
　See Defoe, Daniel

Morgan, Berry 1919-2002 .... **CLC 6**
　See also CA 49-52; 208; DLB 6

Morgan, Claire
　See Highsmith, (Mary) Patricia
　See also GLL 1

Morgan, Edwin (George) 1920- .... **CLC 31**
　See also BRWS 9; CA 5-8R; CANR 3, 43,
　90; CP 7; DLB 27

Morgan, (George) Frederick
　1922-2004 .... **CLC 23**
　See also CA 17-20R; 224; CANR 21; CP 7

Morgan, Harriet
　See Mencken, H(enry) L(ouis)

Morgan, Jane
　See Cooper, James Fenimore

Morgan, Janet 1945- .... **CLC 39**
　See also CA 65-68

Morgan, Lady 1776(?)-1859 .... **NCLC 29**
See also DLB 116, 158; RGEL 2

Morgan, Robin (Evonne) 1941- .... **CLC 2**
See also CA 69-72; CANR 29, 68; FW;
GLL 2; MTCW 1; SATA 80

Morgan, Scott
See Kuttner, Henry

Morgan, Seth 1949(?)-1990 .... **CLC 65**
See also CA 185; 132

**Morgenstern, Christian (Otto Josef
Wolfgang)** 1871-1914 .... **TCLC 8**
See also CA 105; 191; EWL 3

Morgenstern, S.
See Goldman, William (W.)

Mori, Rintaro
See Mori Ogai
See also CA 110

Moricz, Zsigmond 1879-1942 .... **TCLC 33**
See also CA 165; DLB 215; EWL 3

Morike, Eduard (Friedrich)
1804-1875 .... **NCLC 10**
See also DLB 133; RGWL 2, 3

Mori Ogai 1862-1922 .... **TCLC 14**
See Ogai
See also CA 164; DLB 180; EWL 3; RGWL
3; TWA

Moritz, Karl Philipp 1756-1793 .... **LC 2**
See also DLB 94

Morland, Peter Henry
See Faust, Frederick (Schiller)

Morley, Christopher (Darlington)
1890-1957 .... **TCLC 87**
See also CA 112; 213; DLB 9; RGAL 4

Morren, Theophil
See Hofmannsthal, Hugo von

Morris, Bill 1952- .... **CLC 76**
See also CA 225

Morris, Julian
See West, Morris L(anglo)

Morris, Steveland Judkins 1950(?)-
See Wonder, Stevie
See also CA 111

Morris, William 1834-1896 . **NCLC 4; PC 55**
See also BRW 5; CDBLB 1832-1890; DLB
18, 35, 57, 156, 178, 184; FANT; RGEL
2; SFW 4; SUFW

Morris, Wright 1910-1998 .. **CLC 1, 3, 7, 18,
37; TCLC 107**
See also AMW; CA 9-12R; 167; CANR 21,
81; CN 7; DLB 2, 206, 218; DLBY 1981;
EWL 3; MTCW 1, 2; RGAL 4; TCWW 2

Morrison, Arthur 1863-1945 .... **SSC 40;
TCLC 72**
See also CA 120; 157; CMW 4; DLB 70,
135, 197; RGEL 2

Morrison, Chloe Anthony Wofford
See Morrison, Toni

Morrison, James Douglas 1943-1971
See Morrison, Jim
See also CA 73-76; CANR 40

Morrison, Jim .... **CLC 17**
See Morrison, James Douglas

Morrison, Toni 1931- ..... **BLC 3; CLC 4, 10,
22, 55, 81, 87, 173, 194**
See also AAYA 1, 22; AFAW 1, 2; AMWC
1; AMWS 3; BPFB 2; BW 2, 3; CA 29-
32R; CANR 27, 42, 67, 113, 124; CDALB
1968-1988; CLR 99; CN 7; CPW; DA;
DA3; DAB; DAC; DAM MST, MULT,
NOV, POP; DLB 6, 33, 143; DLBY 1981;
EWL 3; EXPN; FW; LAIT 2, 4; LATS
1:2; LMFS 2; MAWW; MTCW 1, 2; NFS
1, 6, 8, 14; RGAL 4; RHW; SATA 57,
144; SSFS 5; TUS; YAW

Morrison, Van 1945- .... **CLC 21**
See also CA 116; 168

Morrissy, Mary 1957- .... **CLC 99**
See also CA 205; DLB 267

Mortimer, John (Clifford) 1923- ..... **CLC 28,
43**
See also CA 13-16R; CANR 21, 69, 109;
CD 5; CDBLB 1960 to Present; CMW 4;
CN 7; CPW; DA3; DAM DRAM, POP;
DLB 13, 245, 271; INT CANR-21; MSW;
MTCW 1, 2; RGEL 2

Mortimer, Penelope (Ruth)
1918-1999 .... **CLC 5**
See also CA 57-60; 187; CANR 45, 88; CN
7

Mortimer, Sir John
See Mortimer, John (Clifford)

Morton, Anthony
See Creasey, John

Morton, Thomas 1579(?)-1647(?) .... **LC 72**
See also DLB 24; RGEL 2

Mosca, Gaetano 1858-1941 .... **TCLC 75**

Moses, Daniel David 1952- .... **NNAL**
See also CA 186

Mosher, Howard Frank 1943- .... **CLC 62**
See also CA 139; CANR 65, 115

Mosley, Nicholas 1923- .... **CLC 43, 70**
See also CA 69-72; CANR 41, 60, 108; CN
7; DLB 14, 207

Mosley, Walter 1952- .... **BLCS; CLC 97, 184**
See also AAYA 57; AMWS 13; BPFB 2;
BW 2; CA 142; CANR 57, 92; CMW 4;
CPW; DA3; DAM MULT, POP; DLB
306; MSW; MTCW 2

Moss, Howard 1922-1987 . **CLC 7, 14, 45, 50**
See also CA 1-4R; 123; CANR 1, 44; DAM
POET; DLB 5

Mossgiel, Rab
See Burns, Robert

Motion, Andrew (Peter) 1952- .... **CLC 47**
See also BRWS 7; CA 146; CANR 90; CP
7; DLB 40

Motley, Willard (Francis)
1909-1965 .... **CLC 18**
See also BW 1; CA 117; 106; CANR 88;
DLB 76, 143

Motoori, Norinaga 1730-1801 .... **NCLC 45**

Mott, Michael (Charles Alston)
1930- .... **CLC 15, 34**
See also CA 5-8R; CAAS 7; CANR 7, 29

Mountain Wolf Woman 1884-1960 . **CLC 92;
NNAL**
See also CA 144; CANR 90

Moure, Erin 1955- .... **CLC 88**
See also CA 113; CP 7; CWP; DLB 60

Mourning Dove 1885(?)-1936 .... **NNAL**
See also CA 144; CANR 90; DAM MULT;
DLB 175, 221

Mowat, Farley (McGill) 1921- .... **CLC 26**
See also AAYA 1, 50; BYA 2; CA 1-4R;
CANR 4, 24, 42, 68, 108; CLR 20; CPW;
DAC; DAM MST; DLB 68; INT CANR-
24; JRDA; MAICYA 1, 2; MTCW 1, 2;
SATA 3, 55; YAW

Mowatt, Anna Cora 1819-1870 ..... **NCLC 74**
See also RGAL 4

Moyers, Bill 1934- .... **CLC 74**
See also AITN 2; CA 61-64; CANR 31, 52

Mphahlele, Es'kia
See Mphahlele, Ezekiel
See also AFW; CDWLB 3; DLB 125, 225;
RGSF 2; SSFS 11

Mphahlele, Ezekiel 1919- ... **BLC 3; CLC 25,
133**
See Mphahlele, Es'kia
See also BW 2, 3; CA 81-84; CANR 26,
76; CN 7; DA3; DAM MULT; EWL 3;
MTCW 2; SATA 119

Mqhayi, S(amuel) E(dward) K(rune Loliwe)
1875-1945 .... **BLC 3; TCLC 25**
See also CA 153; CANR 87; DAM MULT

Mrozek, Slawomir 1930- .... **CLC 3, 13**
See also CA 13-16R; CAAS 10; CANR 29;
CDWLB 4; CWW 2; DLB 232; EWL 3;
MTCW 1

Mrs. Belloc-Lowndes
See Lowndes, Marie Adelaide (Belloc)

Mrs. Fairstar
See Horne, Richard Henry Hengist

M'Taggart, John M'Taggart Ellis
See McTaggart, John McTaggart Ellis

Mtwa, Percy (?)- .... **CLC 47**

Mueller, Lisel 1924- .... **CLC 13, 51; PC 33**
See also CA 93-96; CP 7; DLB 105; PFS 9,
13

Muggeridge, Malcolm (Thomas)
1903-1990 .... **TCLC 120**
See also AITN 1; CA 101; CANR 33, 63;
MTCW 1, 2

Muhammad 570-632 .... **WLCS**
See also DA; DAB; DAC; DAM MST

Muir, Edwin 1887-1959 . **PC 49; TCLC 2, 87**
See Moore, Edward
See also BRWS 6; CA 104; 193; DLB 20,
100, 191; EWL 3; RGEL 2

Muir, John 1838-1914 .... **TCLC 28**
See also AMWS 9; ANW; CA 165; DLB
186, 275

Mujica Lainez, Manuel 1910-1984 ... **CLC 31**
See Lainez, Manuel Mujica
See also CA 81-84; 112; CANR 32; EWL
3; HW 1

Mukherjee, Bharati 1940- ..... **AAL; CLC 53,
115; SSC 38**
See also AAYA 46; BEST 89:2; CA 107;
CANR 45, 72, 128; CN 7; DAM NOV;
DLB 60, 218; DNFS 1, 2; EWL 3; FW;
MTCW 1, 2; RGAL 4; RGSF 2; SSFS 7;
TUS; WWE 1

Muldoon, Paul 1951- .... **CLC 32, 72, 166**
See also BRWS 4; CA 113; 129; CANR 52,
91; CP 7; DAM POET; DLB 40; INT CA-
129; PFS 7

Mulisch, Harry (Kurt Victor)
1927- .... **CLC 42**
See also CA 9-12R; CANR 6, 26, 56, 110;
CWW 2; DLB 299; EWL 3

Mull, Martin 1943- .... **CLC 17**
See also CA 105

Muller, Wilhelm .... **NCLC 73**

Mulock, Dinah Maria
See Craik, Dinah Maria (Mulock)
See also RGEL 2

Munday, Anthony 1560-1633 .... **LC 87**
See also DLB 62, 172; RGEL 2

Munford, Robert 1737(?)-1783 .... **LC 5**
See also DLB 31

Mungo, Raymond 1946- .... **CLC 72**
See also CA 49-52; CANR 2

Munro, Alice 1931- .... **CLC 6, 10, 19, 50, 95;
SSC 3; WLCS**
See also AITN 2; BPFB 2; CA 33-36R;
CANR 33, 53, 75, 114; CCA 1; CN 7;
DA3; DAC; DAM MST, NOV; DLB 53;
EWL 3; MTCW 1, 2; RGEL 2; RGSF 2;
SATA 29; SSFS 5, 13, 19; WWE 1

Munro, H(ector) H(ugh) 1870-1916 .... **WLC**
See Saki
See also AAYA 56; CA 104; 130; CANR
104; CDBLB 1890-1914; DA; DA3;
DAB; DAC; DAM MST, NOV; DLB 34,
162; EXPS; MTCW 1, 2; RGEL 2; SSFS
15

Murakami, Haruki 1949- .... **CLC 150**
See Murakami Haruki
See also CA 165; CANR 102; MJW; RGWL
3; SFW 4

Murakami Haruki
See Murakami, Haruki
See also CWW 2; DLB 182; EWL 3

Murasaki, Lady
See Murasaki Shikibu

Murasaki Shikibu 978(?)-1026(?) ... **CMLC 1**
See also EFS 2; LATS 1:1; RGWL 2, 3

Murdoch, (Jean) Iris 1919-1999 ... **CLC 1, 2, 3, 4, 6, 8, 11, 15, 22, 31, 51**
See also BRWS 1; CA 13-16R; 179; CANR 8, 43, 68, 103; CDBLB 1960 to Present; CN 7; CWD; DA3; DAB; DAC; DAM MST, NOV; DLB 14, 194, 233; EWL 3; INT CANR-8; MTCW 1, 2; NFS 18; RGEL 2; TEA; WLIT 4

Murfree, Mary Noailles 1850-1922 .. **SSC 22; TCLC 135**
See also CA 122; 176; DLB 12, 74; RGAL 4

Murnau, Friedrich Wilhelm
See Plumpe, Friedrich Wilhelm

Murphy, Richard 1927- .... **CLC 41**
See also BRWS 5; CA 29-32R; CP 7; DLB 40; EWL 3

Murphy, Sylvia 1937- .... **CLC 34**
See also CA 121

Murphy, Thomas (Bernard) 1935- ... **CLC 51**
See also CA 101

Murray, Albert L. 1916- .... **CLC 73**
See also BW 2; CA 49-52; CANR 26, 52, 78; CSW; DLB 38

Murray, James Augustus Henry
1837-1915 .... **TCLC 117**

Murray, Judith Sargent
1751-1820 .... **NCLC 63**
See also DLB 37, 200

Murray, Les(lie Allan) 1938- .... **CLC 40**
See also BRWS 7; CA 21-24R; CANR 11, 27, 56, 103; CP 7; DAM POET; DLB 289; DLBY 2001; EWL 3; RGEL 2

Murry, J. Middleton
See Murry, John Middleton

Murry, John Middleton
1889-1957 .... **TCLC 16**
See also CA 118; 217; DLB 149

Musgrave, Susan 1951- .... **CLC 13, 54**
See also CA 69-72; CANR 45, 84; CCA 1; CP 7; CWP

Musil, Robert (Edler von)
1880-1942 .... **SSC 18; TCLC 12, 68**
See also CA 109; CANR 55, 84; CDWLB 2; DLB 81, 124; EW 9; EWL 3; MTCW 2; RGSF 2; RGWL 2, 3

Muske, Carol .... **CLC 90**
See Muske-Dukes, Carol (Anne)

Muske-Dukes, Carol (Anne) 1945-
See Muske, Carol
See also CA 65-68; 203; CAAE 203; CANR 32, 70; CWP

Musset, (Louis Charles) Alfred de
1810-1857 .... **NCLC 7**
See also DLB 192, 217; EW 6; GFL 1789 to the Present; RGWL 2, 3; TWA

Mussolini, Benito (Amilcare Andrea)
1883-1945 .... **TCLC 96**
See also CA 116

Mutanabbi, Al-
See al-Mutanabbi, Ahmad ibn al-Husayn Abu al-Tayyib al-Jufi al-Kindi

My Brother's Brother
See Chekhov, Anton (Pavlovich)

Myers, L(eopold) H(amilton)
1881-1944 .... **TCLC 59**
See also CA 157; DLB 15; EWL 3; RGEL 2

Myers, Walter Dean 1937- .. **BLC 3; CLC 35**
See also AAYA 4, 23; BW 2; BYA 6, 8, 11; CA 33-36R; CANR 20, 42, 67, 108; CLR 4, 16, 35; DAM MULT, NOV; DLB 33; INT CANR-20; JRDA; LAIT 5; MAICYA 1, 2; MAICYAS 1; MTCW 2; SAAS 2; SATA 41, 71, 109; SATA-Brief 27; WYA; YAW

Myers, Walter M.
See Myers, Walter Dean

Myles, Symon
See Follett, Ken(neth Martin)

Nabokov, Vladimir (Vladimirovich)
1899-1977 .... **CLC 1, 2, 3, 6, 8, 11, 15, 23, 44, 46, 64; SSC 11; TCLC 108; WLC**
See also AAYA 45; AMW; AMWC 1; AMWR 1; BPFB 2; CA 5-8R; 69-72; CANR 20, 102; CDALB 1941-1968; DA; DA3; DAB; DAC; DAM MST, NOV; DLB 2, 244, 278; DLBD 3; DLBY 1980, 1991; EWL 3; EXPS; LATS 1:2; MTCW 1, 2; NCFS 4; NFS 9; RGAL 4; RGSF 2; SSFS 6, 15; TUS

Naevius c. 265B.C.-201B.C. .... **CMLC 37**
See also DLB 211

Nagai, Kafu .... **TCLC 51**
See Nagai, Sokichi
See also DLB 180

Nagai, Sokichi 1879-1959
See Nagai, Kafu
See also CA 117

Nagy, Laszlo 1925-1978 .... **CLC 7**
See also CA 129; 112

Naidu, Sarojini 1879-1949 .... **TCLC 80**
See also EWL 3; RGEL 2

Naipaul, Shiva(dhar Srinivasa)
1945-1985 .... **CLC 32, 39; TCLC 153**
See also CA 110; 112; 116; CANR 33; DA3; DAM NOV; DLB 157; DLBY 1985; EWL 3; MTCW 1, 2

Naipaul, V(idiadhar) S(urajprasad)
1932- .... **CLC 4, 7, 9, 13, 18, 37, 105, 199; SSC 38**
See also BPFB 2; BRWS 1; CA 1-4R; CANR 1, 33, 51, 91, 126; CDBLB 1960 to Present; CDWLB 3; CN 7; DA3; DAB; DAC; DAM MST, NOV; DLB 125, 204, 207; DLBY 1985, 2001; EWL 3; LATS 1:2; MTCW 1, 2; RGEL 2; RGSF 2; TWA; WLIT 4; WWE 1

Nakos, Lilika 1903(?)-1989 .... **CLC 29**

Napoleon
See Yamamoto, Hisaye

Narayan, R(asipuram) K(rishnaswami)
1906-2001 . **CLC 7, 28, 47, 121; SSC 25**
See also BPFB 2; CA 81-84; 196; CANR 33, 61, 112; CN 7; DA3; DAM NOV; DNFS 1; EWL 3; MTCW 1, 2; RGEL 2; RGSF 2; SATA 62; SSFS 5; WWE 1

Nash, (Fredric) Ogden 1902-1971 . **CLC 23; PC 21; TCLC 109**
See also CA 13-14; 29-32R; CANR 34, 61; CAP 1; DAM POET; DLB 11; MAICYA 1, 2; MTCW 1, 2; RGAL 4; SATA 2, 46; WP

Nashe, Thomas 1567-1601(?) .... **LC 41, 89**
See also DLB 167; RGEL 2

Nathan, Daniel
See Dannay, Frederic

Nathan, George Jean 1882-1958 .... **TCLC 18**
See Hatteras, Owen
See also CA 114; 169; DLB 137

Natsume, Kinnosuke
See Natsume, Soseki

Natsume, Soseki 1867-1916 .... **TCLC 2, 10**
See Natsume Soseki; Soseki
See also CA 104; 195; RGWL 2, 3; TWA

Natsume Soseki
See Natsume, Soseki
See also DLB 180; EWL 3

Natti, (Mary) Lee 1919-
See Kingman, Lee
See also CA 5-8R; CANR 2

Navarre, Marguerite de
See de Navarre, Marguerite

Naylor, Gloria 1950- ..... **BLC 3; CLC 28, 52, 156; WLCS**
See also AAYA 6, 39; AFAW 1, 2; AMWS 8; BW 2, 3; CA 107; CANR 27, 51, 74, 130; CN 7; CPW; DA; DA3; DAM MST, MULT, NOV, POP; DLB 173; EWL 3; FW; MTCW 1, 2; NFS 4, 7; RGAL 4; TUS

Neff, Debra .... **CLC 59**

Neihardt, John Gneisenau
1881-1973 .... **CLC 32**
See also CA 13-14; CANR 65; CAP 1; DLB 9, 54, 256; LAIT 2

Nekrasov, Nikolai Alekseevich
1821-1878 .... **NCLC 11**
See also DLB 277

Nelligan, Emile 1879-1941 .... **TCLC 14**
See also CA 114; 204; DLB 92; EWL 3

Nelson, Willie 1933- .... **CLC 17**
See also CA 107; CANR 114

Nemerov, Howard (Stanley)
1920-1991 .... **CLC 2, 6, 9, 36; PC 24; TCLC 124**
See also AMW; CA 1-4R; 134; CABS 2; CANR 1, 27, 53; DAM POET; DLB 5, 6; DLBY 1983; EWL 3; INT CANR-27; MTCW 1, 2; PFS 10, 14; RGAL 4

Neruda, Pablo 1904-1973 .. **CLC 1, 2, 5, 7, 9, 28, 62; HLC 2; PC 4; WLC**
See also CA 19-20; 45-48; CANR 131; CAP 2; DA; DA3; DAB; DAC; DAM MST, MULT, POET; DLB 283; DNFS 2; EWL 3; HW 1; LAW; MTCW 1, 2; PFS 11; RGWL 2, 3; TWA; WLIT 1; WP

Nerval, Gerard de 1808-1855 ... **NCLC 1, 67; PC 13; SSC 18**
See also DLB 217; EW 6; GFL 1789 to the Present; RGSF 2; RGWL 2, 3

Nervo, (Jose) Amado (Ruiz de)
1870-1919 .... **HLCS 2; TCLC 11**
See also CA 109; 131; DLB 290; EWL 3; HW 1; LAW

Nesbit, Malcolm
See Chester, Alfred

Nessi, Pio Baroja y
See Baroja (y Nessi), Pio

Nestroy, Johann 1801-1862 .... **NCLC 42**
See also DLB 133; RGWL 2, 3

Netterville, Luke
See O'Grady, Standish (James)

Neufeld, John (Arthur) 1938- .... **CLC 17**
See also AAYA 11; CA 25-28R; CANR 11, 37, 56; CLR 52; MAICYA 1, 2; SAAS 3; SATA 6, 81, 131; SATA-Essay 131; YAW

Neumann, Alfred 1895-1952 .... **TCLC 100**
See also CA 183; DLB 56

Neumann, Ferenc
See Molnar, Ferenc

Neville, Emily Cheney 1919- .... **CLC 12**
See also BYA 2; CA 5-8R; CANR 3, 37, 85; JRDA; MAICYA 1, 2; SAAS 2; SATA 1; YAW

Newbound, Bernard Slade 1930-
See Slade, Bernard
See also CA 81-84; CANR 49; CD 5; DAM DRAM

Newby, P(ercy) H(oward)
1918-1997 .... **CLC 2, 13**
See also CA 5-8R; 161; CANR 32, 67; CN 7; DAM NOV; DLB 15; MTCW 1; RGEL 2

Newcastle
See Cavendish, Margaret Lucas

Newlove, Donald 1928- .... **CLC 6**
  See also CA 29-32R; CANR 25
Newlove, John (Herbert) 1938- .... **CLC 14**
  See also CA 21-24R; CANR 9, 25; CP 7
Newman, Charles 1938- .... **CLC 2, 8**
  See also CA 21-24R; CANR 84; CN 7
Newman, Edwin (Harold) 1919- ...... **CLC 14**
  See also AITN 1; CA 69-72; CANR 5
Newman, John Henry 1801-1890 . **NCLC 38, 99**
  See also BRWS 7; DLB 18, 32, 55; RGEL 2
Newton, (Sir) Isaac 1642-1727 ...... **LC 35, 53**
  See also DLB 252
Newton, Suzanne 1936- .... **CLC 35**
  See also BYA 7; CA 41-44R; CANR 14; JRDA; SATA 5, 77
New York Dept. of Ed. .... **CLC 70**
Nexo, Martin Andersen 1869-1954 .... **TCLC 43**
  See also CA 202; DLB 214; EWL 3
Nezval, Vitezslav 1900-1958 .... **TCLC 44**
  See also CA 123; CDWLB 4; DLB 215; EWL 3
Ng, Fae Myenne 1957(?)- .... **CLC 81**
  See also BYA 11; CA 146
Ngema, Mbongeni 1955- .... **CLC 57**
  See also BW 2; CA 143; CANR 84; CD 5
Ngugi, James T(hiong'o) . **CLC 3, 7, 13, 182**
  See Ngugi wa Thiong'o
Ngugi wa Thiong'o
  See Ngugi wa Thiong'o
  See also DLB 125; EWL 3
Ngugi wa Thiong'o 1938- ... **BLC 3; CLC 36, 182**
  See Ngugi, James T(hiong'o); Ngugi wa Thiong'o
  See also AFW; BRWS 8; BW 2; CA 81-84; CANR 27, 58; CDWLB 3; DAM MULT, NOV; DNFS 2; MTCW 1, 2; RGEL 2; WWE 1
Niatum, Duane 1938- .... **NNAL**
  See also CA 41-44R; CANR 21, 45, 83; DLB 175
Nichol, B(arrie) P(hillip) 1944-1988 . **CLC 18**
  See also CA 53-56; DLB 53; SATA 66
Nicholas of Cusa 1401-1464 .... **LC 80**
  See also DLB 115
Nichols, John (Treadwell) 1940- .... **CLC 38**
  See also AMWS 13; CA 9-12R, 190; CAAE 190; CAAS 2; CANR 6, 70, 121; DLBY 1982; LATS 1:2; TCWW 2
Nichols, Leigh
  See Koontz, Dean R(ay)
Nichols, Peter (Richard) 1927- .... **CLC 5, 36, 65**
  See also CA 104; CANR 33, 86; CBD; CD 5; DLB 13, 245; MTCW 1
Nicholson, Linda ed. .... **CLC 65**
Ni Chuilleanain, Eilean 1942- .... **PC 34**
  See also CA 126; CANR 53, 83; CP 7; CWP; DLB 40
Nicolas, F. R. E.
  See Freeling, Nicolas
Niedecker, Lorine 1903-1970 ..... **CLC 10, 42; PC 42**
  See also CA 25-28; CAP 2; DAM POET; DLB 48
Nietzsche, Friedrich (Wilhelm) 1844-1900 .... **TCLC 10, 18, 55**
  See also CA 107; 121; CDWLB 2; DLB 129; EW 7; RGWL 2, 3; TWA
Nievo, Ippolito 1831-1861 .... **NCLC 22**
Nightingale, Anne Redmon 1943-
  See Redmon, Anne
  See also CA 103
Nightingale, Florence 1820-1910 ... **TCLC 85**
  See also CA 188; DLB 166

Nijo Yoshimoto 1320-1388 .... **CMLC 49**
  See also DLB 203
Nik. T. O.
  See Annensky, Innokenty (Fyodorovich)
Nin, Anais 1903-1977 ..... **CLC 1, 4, 8, 11, 14, 60, 127; SSC 10**
  See also AITN 2; AMWS 10; BPFB 2; CA 13-16R; 69-72; CANR 22, 53; DAM NOV, POP; DLB 2, 4, 152; EWL 3; GLL 2; MAWW; MTCW 1, 2; RGAL 4; RGSF 2
Nisbet, Robert A(lexander) 1913-1996 .... **TCLC 117**
  See also CA 25-28R; 153; CANR 17; INT CANR-17
Nishida, Kitaro 1870-1945 .... **TCLC 83**
Nishiwaki, Junzaburo
  See Nishiwaki, Junzaburo
  See also CA 194
Nishiwaki, Junzaburo 1894-1982 .... **PC 15**
  See Nishiwaki, Junzaburo; Nishiwaki Junzaburo
  See also CA 194; 107; MJW; RGWL 3
Nishiwaki Junzaburo
  See Nishiwaki, Junzaburo
  See also EWL 3
Nissenson, Hugh 1933- .... **CLC 4, 9**
  See also CA 17-20R; CANR 27, 108; CN 7; DLB 28
Nister, Der
  See Der Nister
  See also EWL 3
Niven, Larry .... **CLC 8**
  See Niven, Laurence Van Cott
  See also AAYA 27; BPFB 2; BYA 10; DLB 8; SCFW 2
Niven, Laurence Van Cott 1938-
  See Niven, Larry
  See also CA 21-24R, 207; CAAE 207; CAAS 12; CANR 14, 44, 66, 113; CPW; DAM POP; MTCW 1, 2; SATA 95; SFW 4
Nixon, Agnes Eckhardt 1927- .... **CLC 21**
  See also CA 110
Nizan, Paul 1905-1940 .... **TCLC 40**
  See also CA 161; DLB 72; EWL 3; GFL 1789 to the Present
Nkosi, Lewis 1936- .... **BLC 3; CLC 45**
  See also BW 1, 3; CA 65-68; CANR 27, 81; CBD; CD 5; DAM MULT; DLB 157, 225; WWE 1
Nodier, (Jean) Charles (Emmanuel) 1780-1844 .... **NCLC 19**
  See also DLB 119; GFL 1789 to the Present
Noguchi, Yone 1875-1947 .... **TCLC 80**
Nolan, Christopher 1965- .... **CLC 58**
  See also CA 111; CANR 88
Noon, Jeff 1957- .... **CLC 91**
  See also CA 148; CANR 83; DLB 267; SFW 4
Norden, Charles
  See Durrell, Lawrence (George)
Nordhoff, Charles Bernard 1887-1947 .... **TCLC 23**
  See also CA 108; 211; DLB 9; LAIT 1; RHW 1; SATA 23
Norfolk, Lawrence 1963- .... **CLC 76**
  See also CA 144; CANR 85; CN 7; DLB 267
Norman, Marsha 1947- . **CLC 28, 186; DC 8**
  See also CA 105; CABS 3; CAD; CANR 41, 131; CD 5; CSW; CWD; DAM DRAM; DFS 2; DLB 266; DLBY 1984; FW
Normyx
  See Douglas, (George) Norman

Norris, (Benjamin) Frank(lin, Jr.) 1870-1902 .... **SSC 28; TCLC 24, 155**
  See also AAYA 57; AMW; AMWC 2; BPFB 2; CA 110; 160; CDALB 1865-1917; DLB 12, 71, 186; LMFS 2; NFS 12; RGAL 4; TCWW 2; TUS
Norris, Leslie 1921- .... **CLC 14**
  See also CA 11-12; CANR 14, 117; CAP 1; CP 7; DLB 27, 256
North, Andrew
  See Norton, Andre
North, Anthony
  See Koontz, Dean R(ay)
North, Captain George
  See Stevenson, Robert Louis (Balfour)
North, Captain George
  See Stevenson, Robert Louis (Balfour)
North, Milou
  See Erdrich, Louise
Northrup, B. A.
  See Hubbard, L(afayette) Ron(ald)
North Staffs
  See Hulme, T(homas) E(rnest)
Northup, Solomon 1808-1863 ...... **NCLC 105**
Norton, Alice Mary
  See Norton, Andre
  See also MAICYA 1; SATA 1, 43
Norton, Andre 1912- .... **CLC 12**
  See Norton, Alice Mary
  See also AAYA 14; BPFB 2; BYA 4, 10, 12; CA 1-4R; CANR 68; CLR 50; DLB 8, 52; JRDA; MAICYA 2; MTCW 1; SATA 91; SUFW 1, 2; YAW
Norton, Caroline 1808-1877 .... **NCLC 47**
  See also DLB 21, 159, 199
Norway, Nevil Shute 1899-1960
  See Shute, Nevil
  See also CA 102; 93-96; CANR 85; MTCW 2
Norwid, Cyprian Kamil 1821-1883 .... **NCLC 17**
  See also RGWL 3
Nosille, Nabrah
  See Ellison, Harlan (Jay)
Nossack, Hans Erich 1901-1978 .... **CLC 6**
  See also CA 93-96; 85-88; DLB 69; EWL 3
Nostradamus 1503-1566 .... **LC 27**
Nosu, Chuji
  See Ozu, Yasujiro
Notenburg, Eleanora (Genrikhovna) von
  See Guro, Elena (Genrikhovna)
Nova, Craig 1945- .... **CLC 7, 31**
  See also CA 45-48; CANR 2, 53, 127
Novak, Joseph
  See Kosinski, Jerzy (Nikodem)
Novalis 1772-1801 .... **NCLC 13**
  See also CDWLB 2; DLB 90; EW 5; RGWL 2, 3
Novick, Peter 1934- .... **CLC 164**
  See also CA 188
Novis, Emile
  See Weil, Simone (Adolphine)
Nowlan, Alden (Albert) 1933-1983 ... **CLC 15**
  See also CA 9-12R; CANR 5; DAC; DAM MST; DLB 53; PFS 12
Noyes, Alfred 1880-1958 ...... **PC 27; TCLC 7**
  See also CA 104; 188; DLB 20; EXPP; FANT; PFS 4; RGEL 2
Nugent, Richard Bruce 1906(?)-1987 ... **HR 3**
  See also BW 1; CA 125; DLB 51; GLL 2
Nunn, Kem .... **CLC 34**
  See also CA 159
Nwapa, Flora (Nwanzuruaha) 1931-1993 .... **BLCS; CLC 133**
  See also BW 2; CA 143; CANR 83; CD-WLB 3; CWRI 5; DLB 125; EWL 3; WLIT 2

Nye, Robert 1939- .... **CLC 13, 42**
See also BRWS 10; CA 33-36R; CANR 29, 67, 107; CN 7; CP 7; CWRI 5; DAM NOV; DLB 14, 271; FANT; HGG; MTCW 1; RHW; SATA 6

Nyro, Laura 1947-1997 .... **CLC 17**
See also CA 194

Oates, Joyce Carol 1938- .. **CLC 1, 2, 3, 6, 9, 11, 15, 19, 33, 52, 108, 134; SSC 6, 70; WLC**
See also AAYA 15, 52; AITN 1; AMWS 2; BEST 89:2; BPFB 2; BYA 11; CA 5-8R; CANR 25, 45, 74, 113, 129; CDALB 1968-1988; CN 7; CP 7; CPW; CWP; DA; DA3; DAB; DAC; DAM MST, NOV, POP; DLB 2, 5, 130; DLBY 1981; EWL 3; EXPS; FW; HGG; INT CANR-25; LAIT 4; MAWW; MTCW 1, 2; NFS 8; RGAL 4; RGSF 2; SSFS 17; SUFW 2; TUS

O'Brian, E. G.
See Clarke, Arthur C(harles)

O'Brian, Patrick 1914-2000 .... **CLC 152**
See also AAYA 55; CA 144; 187; CANR 74; CPW; MTCW 2; RHW

O'Brien, Darcy 1939-1998 .... **CLC 11**
See also CA 21-24R; 167; CANR 8, 59

O'Brien, Edna 1932- ..... **CLC 3, 5, 8, 13, 36, 65, 116; SSC 10, 77**
See also BRWS 5; CA 1-4R; CANR 6, 41, 65, 102; CDBLB 1960 to Present; CN 7; DA3; DAM NOV; DLB 14, 231; EWL 3; FW; MTCW 1, 2; RGSF 2; WLIT 4

O'Brien, Fitz-James 1828-1862 ..... **NCLC 21**
See also DLB 74; RGAL 4; SUFW

O'Brien, Flann .... **CLC 1, 4, 5, 7, 10, 47**
See O Nuallain, Brian
See also BRWS 2; DLB 231; EWL 3; RGEL 2

O'Brien, Richard 1942- .... **CLC 17**
See also CA 124

O'Brien, (William) Tim(othy) 1946- . **CLC 7, 19, 40, 103; SSC 74**
See also AAYA 16; AMWS 5; CA 85-88; CANR 40, 58, 133; CDALBS; CN 7; CPW; DA3; DAM POP; DLB 152; DLBD 9; DLBY 1980; LATS 1:2; MTCW 2; RGAL 4; SSFS 5, 15

Obstfelder, Sigbjoern 1866-1900 .... **TCLC 23**
See also CA 123

O'Casey, Sean 1880-1964 .... **CLC 1, 5, 9, 11, 15, 88; DC 12; WLCS**
See also BRW 7; CA 89-92; CANR 62; CBD; CDBLB 1914-1945; DA3; DAB; DAC; DAM DRAM, MST; DFS 19; DLB 10; EWL 3; MTCW 1, 2; RGEL 2; TEA; WLIT 4

O'Cathasaigh, Sean
See O'Casey, Sean

Occom, Samson 1723-1792 .... **LC 60; NNAL**
See also DLB 175

Ochs, Phil(ip David) 1940-1976 .... **CLC 17**
See also CA 185; 65-68

O'Connor, Edwin (Greene) 1918-1968 .... **CLC 14**
See also CA 93-96; 25-28R

O'Connor, (Mary) Flannery 1925-1964 .... **CLC 1, 2, 3, 6, 10, 13, 15, 21, 66, 104; SSC 1, 23, 61; TCLC 132; WLC**
See also AAYA 7; AMW; AMWR 2; BPFB 3; BYA 16; CA 1-4R; CANR 3, 41; CDALB 1941-1968; DA; DA3; DAB; DAC; DAM MST, NOV; DLB 2, 152; DLBD 12; DLBY 1980; EWL 3; EXPS; LAIT 5; MAWW; MTCW 1, 2; NFS 3; RGAL 4; RGSF 2; SSFS 2, 7, 10, 19; TUS

O'Connor, Frank .... **CLC 23; SSC 5**
See O'Donovan, Michael Francis
See also DLB 162; EWL 3; RGSF 2; SSFS 5

O'Dell, Scott 1898-1989 .... **CLC 30**
See also AAYA 3, 44; BPFB 3; BYA 1, 2, 3, 5; CA 61-64; 129; CANR 12, 30, 112; CLR 1, 16; DLB 52; JRDA; MAICYA 1, 2; SATA 12, 60, 134; WYA; YAW

Odets, Clifford 1906-1963 ..... **CLC 2, 28, 98; DC 6**
See also AMWS 2; CA 85-88; CAD; CANR 62; DAM DRAM; DFS 3, 17, 20; DLB 7, 26; EWL 3; MTCW 1, 2; RGAL 4; TUS

O'Doherty, Brian 1928- .... **CLC 76**
See also CA 105; CANR 108

O'Donnell, K. M.
See Malzberg, Barry N(athaniel)

O'Donnell, Lawrence
See Kuttner, Henry

O'Donovan, Michael Francis 1903-1966 .... **CLC 14**
See O'Connor, Frank
See also CA 93-96; CANR 84

Oe, Kenzaburo 1935- .. **CLC 10, 36, 86, 187; SSC 20**
See Oe Kenzaburo
See also CA 97-100; CANR 36, 50, 74, 126; DA3; DAM NOV; DLB 182; DLBY 1994; LATS 1:2; MJW; MTCW 1, 2; RGSF 2; RGWL 2, 3

Oe Kenzaburo
See Oe, Kenzaburo
See also CWW 2; EWL 3

O'Faolain, Julia 1932- .... **CLC 6, 19, 47, 108**
See also CA 81-84; CAAS 2; CANR 12, 61; CN 7; DLB 14, 231; FW; MTCW 1; RHW

O'Faolain, Sean 1900-1991 ...... **CLC 1, 7, 14, 32, 70; SSC 13; TCLC 143**
See also CA 61-64; 134; CANR 12, 66; DLB 15, 162; MTCW 1, 2; RGEL 2; RGSF 2

O'Flaherty, Liam 1896-1984 .... **CLC 5, 34; SSC 6**
See also CA 101; 113; CANR 35; DLB 36, 162; DLBY 1984; MTCW 1, 2; RGEL 2; RGSF 2; SSFS 5, 20

Ogai
See Mori Ogai
See also MJW

Ogilvy, Gavin
See Barrie, J(ames) M(atthew)

O'Grady, Standish (James) 1846-1928 .... **TCLC 5**
See also CA 104; 157

O'Grady, Timothy 1951- .... **CLC 59**
See also CA 138

O'Hara, Frank 1926-1966 .... **CLC 2, 5, 13, 78; PC 45**
See also CA 9-12R; 25-28R; CANR 33; DA3; DAM POET; DLB 5, 16, 193; EWL 3; MTCW 1, 2; PFS 8; 12; RGAL 4; WP

O'Hara, John (Henry) 1905-1970 . **CLC 1, 2, 3, 6, 11, 42; SSC 15**
See also AMW; BPFB 3; CA 5-8R; 25-28R; CANR 31, 60; CDALB 1929-1941; DAM NOV; DLB 9, 86; DLBD 2; EWL 3; MTCW 1, 2; NFS 11; RGAL 4; RGSF 2

O Hehir, Diana 1922- .... **CLC 41**
See also CA 93-96

Ohiyesa
See Eastman, Charles A(lexander)

Okada, John 1923-1971 .... **AAL**
See also BYA 14; CA 212

Okigbo, Christopher (Ifenayichukwu) 1932-1967 .... **BLC 3; CLC 25, 84; PC 7**
See also AFW; BW 1, 3; CA 77-80; CANR 74; CDWLB 3; DAM MULT, POET; DLB 125; EWL 3; MTCW 1, 2; RGEL 2

Okri, Ben 1959- .... **CLC 87**
See also AFW; BRWS 5; BW 2, 3; CA 130; 138; CANR 65, 128; CN 7; DLB 157, 231; EWL 3; INT CA-138; MTCW 2; RGSF 2; SSFS 20; WLIT 2; WWE 1

Olds, Sharon 1942- .. **CLC 32, 39, 85; PC 22**
See also AMWS 10; CA 101; CANR 18, 41, 66, 98, 135; CP 7; CPW; CWP; DAM POET; DLB 120; MTCW 2; PFS 17

Oldstyle, Jonathan
See Irving, Washington

Olesha, Iurii
See Olesha, Yuri (Karlovich)
See also RGWL 2

Olesha, Iurii Karlovich
See Olesha, Yuri (Karlovich)
See also DLB 272

Olesha, Yuri (Karlovich) 1899-1960 . **CLC 8; SSC 69; TCLC 136**
See Olesha, Iurii; Olesha, Iurii Karlovich; Olesha, Yury Karlovich
See also CA 85-88; EW 11; RGWL 3

Olesha, Yury Karlovich
See Olesha, Yuri (Karlovich)
See also EWL 3

Oliphant, Mrs.
See Oliphant, Margaret (Oliphant Wilson)
See also SUFW

Oliphant, Laurence 1829(?)-1888 .. **NCLC 47**
See also DLB 18, 166

Oliphant, Margaret (Oliphant Wilson) 1828-1897 .... **NCLC 11, 61; SSC 25**
See Oliphant, Mrs.
See also BRWS 10; DLB 18, 159, 190; HGG; RGEL 2; RGSF 2

Oliver, Mary 1935- .... **CLC 19, 34, 98**
See also AMWS 7; CA 21-24R; CANR 9, 43, 84, 92; CP 7; CWP; DLB 5, 193; EWL 3; PFS 15

Olivier, Laurence (Kerr) 1907-1989 . **CLC 20**
See also CA 111; 150; 129

Olsen, Tillie 1912- ... **CLC 4, 13, 114; SSC 11**
See also AAYA 51; AMWS 13; BYA 11; CA 1-4R; CANR 1, 43, 74, 132; CDALBS; CN 7; DA; DA3; DAB; DAC; DAM MST; DLB 28, 206; DLBY 1980; EWL 3; EXPS; FW; MTCW 1, 2; RGAL 4; RGSF 2; SSFS 1; TUS

Olson, Charles (John) 1910-1970 .. **CLC 1, 2, 5, 6, 9, 11, 29; PC 19**
See also AMWS 2; CA 13-16; 25-28R; CABS 2; CANR 35, 61; CAP 1; DAM POET; DLB 5, 16, 193; EWL 3; MTCW 1, 2; RGAL 4; WP

Olson, Toby 1937- .... **CLC 28**
See also CA 65-68; CANR 9, 31, 84; CP 7

Olyesha, Yuri
See Olesha, Yuri (Karlovich)

Olympiodorus of Thebes c. 375-c. 430 .... **CMLC 59**

Omar Khayyam
See Khayyam, Omar
See also RGWL 2, 3

Ondaatje, (Philip) Michael 1943- .... **CLC 14, 29, 51, 76, 180; PC 28**
See also CA 77-80; CANR 42, 74, 109, 133; CN 7; CP 7; DA3; DAB; DAC; DAM MST; DLB 60; EWL 3; LATS 1:2; LMFS 2; MTCW 2; PFS 8, 19; TWA; WWE 1

Oneal, Elizabeth 1934-
See Oneal, Zibby
See also CA 106; CANR 28, 84; MAICYA 1, 2; SATA 30, 82; YAW

Oneal, Zibby .... **CLC 30**
 See Oneal, Elizabeth
 See also AAYA 5, 41; BYA 13; CLR 13;
 JRDA; WYA

O'Neill, Eugene (Gladstone)
 1888-1953 ... **DC 20; TCLC 1, 6, 27, 49;**
 WLC
 See also AAYA 54; AITN 1; AMW; AMWC
 1; CA 110; 132; CAD; CANR 131;
 CDALB 1929-1941; DA; DA3; DAB;
 DAC; DAM DRAM, MST; DFS 2, 4, 5,
 6, 9, 11, 12, 16, 20; DLB 7; EWL 3; LAIT
 3; LMFS 2; MTCW 1, 2; RGAL 4; TUS

Onetti, Juan Carlos 1909-1994 ... **CLC 7, 10;**
 HLCS 2; SSC 23; TCLC 131
 See also CA 85-88; 145; CANR 32, 63; CD-
 WLB 3; CWW 2; DAM MULT, NOV;
 DLB 113; EWL 3; HW 1, 2; LAW;
 MTCW 1, 2; RGSF 2

O Nuallain, Brian 1911-1966
 See O'Brien, Flann
 See also CA 21-22; 25-28R; CAP 2; DLB
 231; FANT; TEA

Ophuls, Max 1902-1957 .... **TCLC 79**
 See also CA 113

Opie, Amelia 1769-1853 .... **NCLC 65**
 See also DLB 116, 159; RGEL 2

Oppen, George 1908-1984 ..... **CLC 7, 13, 34;**
 PC 35; TCLC 107
 See also CA 13-16R; 113; CANR 8, 82;
 DLB 5, 165

Oppenheim, E(dward) Phillips
 1866-1946 .... **TCLC 45**
 See also CA 111; 202; CMW 4; DLB 70

Opuls, Max
 See Ophuls, Max

Orage, A(lfred) R(ichard)
 1873-1934 .... **TCLC 157**
 See also CA 122

Origen c. 185-c. 254 .... **CMLC 19**

Orlovitz, Gil 1918-1973 .... **CLC 22**
 See also CA 77-80; 45-48; DLB 2, 5

Orris
 See Ingelow, Jean

Ortega y Gasset, Jose 1883-1955 ...... **HLC 2;**
 TCLC 9
 See also CA 106; 130; DAM MULT; EW 9;
 EWL 3; HW 1, 2; MTCW 1, 2

Ortese, Anna Maria 1914-1998 .... **CLC 89**
 See also DLB 177; EWL 3

Ortiz, Simon J(oseph) 1941- .... **CLC 45;**
 NNAL; PC 17
 See also AMWS 4; CA 134; CANR 69, 118;
 CP 7; DAM MULT, POET; DLB 120,
 175, 256; EXPP; PFS 4, 16; RGAL 4

Orton, Joe ...... **CLC 4, 13, 43; DC 3; TCLC**
 157
 See Orton, John Kingsley
 See also BRWS 5; CBD; CDBLB 1960 to
 Present; DFS 3, 6; DLB 13; GLL 1;
 MTCW 2; RGEL 2; TEA; WLIT 4

Orton, John Kingsley 1933-1967
 See Orton, Joe
 See also CA 85-88; CANR 35, 66; DAM
 DRAM; MTCW 1, 2

Orwell, George ...... **SSC 68; TCLC 2, 6, 15,**
 31, 51, 128, 129; WLC
 See Blair, Eric (Arthur)
 See also BPFB 3; BRW 7; BYA 5; CDBLB
 1945-1960; CLR 68; DAB; DLB 15, 98,
 195, 255; EWL 3; EXPN; LAIT 4, 5;
 LATS 1:1; NFS 3, 7; RGEL 2; SCFW 2;
 SFW 4; SSFS 4; TEA; WLIT 4; YAW

Osborne, David
 See Silverberg, Robert

Osborne, George
 See Silverberg, Robert

Osborne, John (James) 1929-1994 .... **CLC 1,**
 2, 5, 11, 45; TCLC 153; WLC
 See also BRWS 1; CA 13-16R; 147; CANR
 21, 56; CDBLB 1945-1960; DA; DAB;
 DAC; DAM DRAM, MST; DFS 4, 19;
 DLB 13; EWL 3; MTCW 1, 2; RGEL 2

Osborne, Lawrence 1958- .... **CLC 50**
 See also CA 189

Osbourne, Lloyd 1868-1947 .... **TCLC 93**

Osgood, Frances Sargent
 1811-1850 .... **NCLC 141**
 See also DLB 250

Oshima, Nagisa 1932- .... **CLC 20**
 See also CA 116; 121; CANR 78

Oskison, John Milton
 1874-1947 .... **NNAL; TCLC 35**
 See also CA 144; CANR 84; DAM MULT;
 DLB 175

Ossian c. 3rd cent. - .... **CMLC 28**
 See Macpherson, James

Ossoli, Sarah Margaret (Fuller)
 1810-1850 .... **NCLC 5, 50**
 See Fuller, Margaret; Fuller, Sarah Margaret
 See also CDALB 1640-1865; FW; LMFS 1;
 SATA 25

Ostriker, Alicia (Suskin) 1937- .... **CLC 132**
 See also CA 25-28R; CAAS 24; CANR 10,
 30, 62, 99; CWP; DLB 120; EXPP; PFS
 19

Ostrovsky, Aleksandr Nikolaevich
 See Ostrovsky, Alexander
 See also DLB 277

Ostrovsky, Alexander 1823-1886 .. **NCLC 30,**
 57
 See Ostrovsky, Aleksandr Nikolaevich

Otero, Blas de 1916-1979 .... **CLC 11**
 See also CA 89-92; DLB 134; EWL 3

O'Trigger, Sir Lucius
 See Horne, Richard Henry Hengist

Otto, Rudolf 1869-1937 .... **TCLC 85**

Otto, Whitney 1955- .... **CLC 70**
 See also CA 140; CANR 120

Otway, Thomas 1652-1685 ... **DC 24; LC 106**
 See also DAM DRAM; DLB 80; RGEL 2

Ouida .... **TCLC 43**
 See De la Ramee, Marie Louise (Ouida)
 See also DLB 18, 156; RGEL 2

Ouologuem, Yambo 1940- .... **CLC 146**
 See also CA 111; 176

Ousmane, Sembene 1923- ... **BLC 3; CLC 66**
 See Sembene, Ousmane
 See also BW 1, 3; CA 117; 125; CANR 81;
 CWW 2; MTCW 1

Ovid 43B.C.-17 .... **CMLC 7; PC 2**
 See also AW 2; CDWLB 1; DA3; DAM
 POET; DLB 211; RGWL 2, 3; WP

Owen, Hugh
 See Faust, Frederick (Schiller)

Owen, Wilfred (Edward Salter)
 1893-1918 ... **PC 19; TCLC 5, 27; WLC**
 See also BRW 6; CA 104; 141; CDBLB
 1914-1945; DA; DAB; DAC; DAM MST,
 POET; DLB 20; EWL 3; EXPP; MTCW
 2; PFS 10; RGEL 2; WLIT 4

Owens, Louis (Dean) 1948-2002 .... **NNAL**
 See also CA 137, 179; 207; CAAE 179;
 CAAS 24; CANR 71

Owens, Rochelle 1936- .... **CLC 8**
 See also CA 17-20R; CAAS 2; CAD;
 CANR 39; CD 5; CP 7; CWD; CWP

Oz, Amos 1939- ...... **CLC 5, 8, 11, 27, 33, 54;**
 SSC 66
 See also CA 53-56; CANR 27, 47, 65, 113;
 CWW 2; DAM NOV; EWL 3; MTCW 1,
 2; RGSF 2; RGWL 3

Ozick, Cynthia 1928- .... **CLC 3, 7, 28, 62,**
 155; SSC 15, 60
 See also AMWS 5; BEST 90:1; CA 17-20R;
 CANR 23, 58, 116; CN 7; CPW; DA3;
 DAM NOV, POP; DLB 28, 152, 299;
 DLBY 1982; EWL 3; EXPS; INT CANR-
 23; MTCW 1, 2; RGAL 4; RGSF 2; SSFS
 3, 12

Ozu, Yasujiro 1903-1963 .... **CLC 16**
 See also CA 112

Pabst, G. W. 1885-1967 .... **TCLC 127**

Pacheco, C.
 See Pessoa, Fernando (Antonio Nogueira)

Pacheco, Jose Emilio 1939- .... **HLC 2**
 See also CA 111; 131; CANR 65; CWW 2;
 DAM MULT; DLB 290; EWL 3; HW 1,
 2; RGSF 2

Pa Chin .... **CLC 18**
 See Li Fei-kan
 See also EWL 3

Pack, Robert 1929- .... **CLC 13**
 See also CA 1-4R; CANR 3, 44, 82; CP 7;
 DLB 5; SATA 118

Padgett, Lewis
 See Kuttner, Henry

Padilla (Lorenzo), Heberto
 1932-2000 .... **CLC 38**
 See also AITN 1; CA 123; 131; 189; CWW
 2; EWL 3; HW 1

Page, James Patrick 1944-
 See Page, Jimmy
 See also CA 204

Page, Jimmy 1944- .... **CLC 12**
 See Page, James Patrick

Page, Louise 1955- .... **CLC 40**
 See also CA 140; CANR 76; CBD; CD 5;
 CWD; DLB 233

Page, P(atricia) K(athleen) 1916- ...... **CLC 7,**
 18; PC 12
 See Cape, Judith
 See also CA 53-56; CANR 4, 22, 65; CP 7;
 DAC; DAM MST; DLB 68; MTCW 1;
 RGEL 2

Page, Stanton
 See Fuller, Henry Blake

Page, Stanton
 See Fuller, Henry Blake

Page, Thomas Nelson 1853-1922 .... **SSC 23**
 See also CA 118; 177; DLB 12, 78; DLBD
 13; RGAL 4

Pagels, Elaine Hiesey 1943- .... **CLC 104**
 See also CA 45-48; CANR 2, 24, 51; FW;
 NCFS 4

Paget, Violet 1856-1935
 See Lee, Vernon
 See also CA 104; 166; GLL 1; HGG

Paget-Lowe, Henry
 See Lovecraft, H(oward) P(hillips)

Paglia, Camille (Anna) 1947- .... **CLC 68**
 See also CA 140; CANR 72; CPW; FW;
 GLL 2; MTCW 2

Paige, Richard
 See Koontz, Dean R(ay)

Paine, Thomas 1737-1809 .... **NCLC 62**
 See also AMWS 1; CDALB 1640-1865;
 DLB 31, 43, 73, 158; LAIT 1; RGAL 4;
 RGEL 2; TUS

Pakenham, Antonia
 See Fraser, Antonia (Pakenham)

Palamas, Costis
 See Palamas, Kostes

Palamas, Kostes 1859-1943 .... **TCLC 5**
 See Palamas, Kostis
 See also CA 105; 190; RGWL 2, 3

Palamas, Kostis
 See Palamas, Kostes
 See also EWL 3

Palazzeschi, Aldo 1885-1974 .... **CLC 11**
See also CA 89-92; 53-56; DLB 114, 264;
EWL 3

Pales Matos, Luis 1898-1959 .... **HLCS 2**
See Pales Matos, Luis
See also DLB 290; HW 1; LAW

Paley, Grace 1922- .. **CLC 4, 6, 37, 140; SSC 8**
See also AMWS 6; CA 25-28R; CANR 13,
46, 74, 118; CN 7; CPW; DA3; DAM
POP; DLB 28, 218; EWL 3; EXPS; FW;
INT CANR-13; MAWW; MTCW 1, 2;
RGAL 4; RGSF 2; SSFS 3, 20

Palin, Michael (Edward) 1943- .... **CLC 21**
See Monty Python
See also CA 107; CANR 35, 109; SATA 67

Palliser, Charles 1947- .... **CLC 65**
See also CA 136; CANR 76; CN 7

Palma, Ricardo 1833-1919 .... **TCLC 29**
See also CA 168; LAW

Pamuk, Orhan 1952- .... **CLC 185**
See also CA 142; CANR 75, 127; CWW 2

Pancake, Breece Dexter 1952-1979
See Pancake, Breece D'J
See also CA 123; 109

Pancake, Breece D'J .... **CLC 29; SSC 61**
See Pancake, Breece Dexter
See also DLB 130

Panchenko, Nikolai .... **CLC 59**

Pankhurst, Emmeline (Goulden)
1858-1928 .... **TCLC 100**
See also CA 116; FW

Panko, Rudy
See Gogol, Nikolai (Vasilyevich)

Papadiamantis, Alexandros
1851-1911 .... **TCLC 29**
See also CA 168; EWL 3

Papadiamantopoulos, Johannes 1856-1910
See Moreas, Jean
See also CA 117

Papini, Giovanni 1881-1956 .... **TCLC 22**
See also CA 121; 180; DLB 264

Paracelsus 1493-1541 .... **LC 14**
See also DLB 179

Parasol, Peter
See Stevens, Wallace

Pardo Bazan, Emilia 1851-1921 .... **SSC 30**
See also EWL 3; FW; RGSF 2; RGWL 2, 3

Pareto, Vilfredo 1848-1923 .... **TCLC 69**
See also CA 175

Paretsky, Sara 1947- .... **CLC 135**
See also AAYA 30; BEST 90:3; CA 125;
129; CANR 59, 95; CMW 4; CPW; DA3;
DAM POP; DLB 306; INT CA-129;
MSW; RGAL 4

Parfenie, Maria
See Codrescu, Andrei

Parini, Jay (Lee) 1948- .... **CLC 54, 133**
See also CA 97-100, 229; CAAE 229;
CAAS 16; CANR 32, 87

Park, Jordan
See Kornbluth, C(yril) M.; Pohl, Frederik

Park, Robert E(zra) 1864-1944 ..... **TCLC 73**
See also CA 122; 165

Parker, Bert
See Ellison, Harlan (Jay)

Parker, Dorothy (Rothschild)
1893-1967 . **CLC 15, 68; PC 28; SSC 2; TCLC 143**
See also AMWS 9; CA 19-20; 25-28R; CAP
2; DA3; DAM POET; DLB 11, 45, 86;
EXPP; FW; MAWW; MTCW 1, 2; PFS
18; RGAL 4; RGSF 2; TUS

Parker, Robert B(rown) 1932- .... **CLC 27**
See also AAYA 28; BEST 89:4; BPFB 3;
CA 49-52; CANR 1, 26, 52, 89, 128;
CMW 4; CPW; DAM NOV, POP; DLB
306; INT CANR-26; MSW; MTCW 1

Parkin, Frank 1940- .... **CLC 43**
See also CA 147

Parkman, Francis, Jr. 1823-1893 .. **NCLC 12**
See also AMWS 2; DLB 1, 30, 183, 186,
235; RGAL 4

Parks, Gordon (Alexander Buchanan)
1912- .... **BLC 3; CLC 1, 16**
See also AAYA 36; AITN 2; BW 2, 3; CA
41-44R; CANR 26, 66; DA3; DAM
MULT; DLB 33; MTCW 2; SATA 8, 108

Parks, Suzan-Lori 1964(?)- .... **DC 23**
See also AAYA 55; CA 201; CAD; CD 5;
CWD; RGAL 4

Parks, Tim(othy Harold) 1954- ...... **CLC 147**
See also CA 126; 131; CANR 77; DLB 231;
INT CA-131

Parmenides c. 515B.C.-c.
450B.C. .... **CMLC 22**
See also DLB 176

Parnell, Thomas 1679-1718 .... **LC 3**
See also DLB 95; RGEL 2

Parr, Catherine c. 1513(?)-1548 .... **LC 86**
See also DLB 136

Parra, Nicanor 1914- ... **CLC 2, 102; HLC 2; PC 39**
See also CA 85-88; CANR 32; CWW 2;
DAM MULT; DLB 283; EWL 3; HW 1;
LAW; MTCW 1

Parra Sanojo, Ana Teresa de la
1890-1936 .... **HLCS 2**
See de la Parra, (Ana) Teresa (Sonojo)
See also LAW

Parrish, Mary Frances
See Fisher, M(ary) F(rances) K(ennedy)

Parshchikov, Aleksei 1954- .... **CLC 59**
See Parshchikov, Aleksei Maksimovich

Parshchikov, Aleksei Maksimovich
See Parshchikov, Aleksei
See also DLB 285

Parson, Professor
See Coleridge, Samuel Taylor

Parson Lot
See Kingsley, Charles

Parton, Sara Payson Willis
1811-1872 .... **NCLC 86**
See also DLB 43, 74, 239

Partridge, Anthony
See Oppenheim, E(dward) Phillips

Pascal, Blaise 1623-1662 .... **LC 35**
See also DLB 268; EW 3; GFL Beginnings
to 1789; RGWL 2, 3; TWA

Pascoli, Giovanni 1855-1912 .... **TCLC 45**
See also CA 170; EW 7; EWL 3

Pasolini, Pier Paolo 1922-1975 .. **CLC 20, 37, 106; PC 17**
See also CA 93-96; 61-64; CANR 63; DLB
128, 177; EWL 3; MTCW 1; RGWL 2, 3

Pasquini
See Silone, Ignazio

Pastan, Linda (Olenik) 1932- .... **CLC 27**
See also CA 61-64; CANR 18, 40, 61, 113;
CP 7; CSW; CWP; DAM POET; DLB 5;
PFS 8

Pasternak, Boris (Leonidovich)
1890-1960 ...... **CLC 7, 10, 18, 63; PC 6; SSC 31; WLC**
See also BPFB 3; CA 127; 116; DA; DA3;
DAB; DAC; DAM MST, NOV, POET;
DLB 302; EW 10; MTCW 1, 2; RGSF 2;
RGWL 2, 3; TWA; WP

Patchen, Kenneth 1911-1972 .... **CLC 1, 2, 18**
See also BG 3; CA 1-4R; 33-36R; CANR
3, 35; DAM POET; DLB 16, 48; EWL 3;
MTCW 1; RGAL 4

Pater, Walter (Horatio) 1839-1894 . **NCLC 7, 90**
See also BRW 5; CDBLB 1832-1890; DLB
57, 156; RGEL 2; TEA

Paterson, A(ndrew) B(arton)
1864-1941 .... **TCLC 32**
See also CA 155; DLB 230; RGEL 2; SATA
97

Paterson, Banjo
See Paterson, A(ndrew) B(arton)

Paterson, Katherine (Womeldorf)
1932- .... **CLC 12, 30**
See also AAYA 1, 31; BYA 1, 2, 7; CA 21-
24R; CANR 28, 59, 111; CLR 7, 50;
CWRI 5; DLB 52; JRDA; LAIT 4; MAI-
CYA 1, 2; MAICYAS 1; MTCW 1; SATA
13, 53, 92, 133; WYA; YAW

Patmore, Coventry Kersey Dighton
1823-1896 .... **NCLC 9; PC 59**
See also DLB 35, 98; RGEL 2; TEA

Paton, Alan (Stewart) 1903-1988 ...... **CLC 4, 10, 25, 55, 106; WLC**
See also AAYA 26; AFW; BPFB 3; BRWS
2; BYA 1; CA 13-16; 125; CANR 22;
CAP 1; DA; DA3; DAB; DAC; DAM
MST, NOV; DLB 225; DLBD 17; EWL
3; EXPN; LAIT 4; MTCW 1, 2; NFS 3,
12; RGEL 2; SATA 11; SATA-Obit 56;
TWA; WLIT 2; WWE 1

Paton Walsh, Gillian 1937- .... **CLC 35**
See Paton Walsh, Jill; Walsh, Jill Paton
See also AAYA 11; CANR 38, 83; CLR 2,
65; DLB 161; JRDA; MAICYA 1, 2;
SAAS 3; SATA 4, 72, 109; YAW

Paton Walsh, Jill
See Paton Walsh, Gillian
See also AAYA 47; BYA 1, 8

Patterson, (Horace) Orlando (Lloyd)
1940- .... **BLCS**
See also BW 1; CA 65-68; CANR 27, 84;
CN 7

Patton, George S(mith), Jr.
1885-1945 .... **TCLC 79**
See also CA 189

Paulding, James Kirke 1778-1860 ... **NCLC 2**
See also DLB 3, 59, 74, 250; RGAL 4

Paulin, Thomas Neilson 1949-
See Paulin, Tom
See also CA 123; 128; CANR 98; CP 7

Paulin, Tom 1949- .... **CLC 37, 177**
See Paulin, Thomas Neilson
See also DLB 40

Pausanias c. 1st cent. - .... **CMLC 36**

Paustovsky, Konstantin (Georgievich)
1892-1968 .... **CLC 40**
See also CA 93-96; 25-28R; DLB 272;
EWL 3

Pavese, Cesare 1908-1950 .... **PC 13; SSC 19; TCLC 3**
See also CA 104; 169; DLB 128, 177; EW
12; EWL 3; PFS 20; RGSF 2; RGWL 2,
3; TWA

Pavic, Milorad 1929- .... **CLC 60**
See also CA 136; CDWLB 4; CWW 2; DLB
181; EWL 3; RGWL 3

Pavlov, Ivan Petrovich 1849-1936 . **TCLC 91**
See also CA 118; 180

Pavlova, Karolina Karlovna
1807-1893 .... **NCLC 138**
See also DLB 205

Payne, Alan
See Jakes, John (William)

Paz, Gil
See Lugones, Leopoldo

Paz, Octavio 1914-1998 . **CLC 3, 4, 6, 10, 19, 51, 65, 119; HLC 2; PC 1, 48; WLC**
See also AAYA 50; CA 73-76; 165; CANR
32, 65, 104; CWW 2; DA; DA3; DAB;
DAC; DAM MST, MULT, POET; DLB
290; DLBY 1990, 1998; DNFS 1; EWL
3; HW 1, 2; LAW; LAWS 1; MTCW 1, 2;
PFS 18; RGWL 2, 3; SSFS 13; TWA;
WLIT 1

p'Bitek, Okot 1931-1982 .... **BLC 3; CLC 96; TCLC 149**
See also AFW; BW 2, 3; CA 124; 107; CANR 82; DAM MULT; DLB 125; EWL 3; MTCW 1, 2; RGEL 2; WLIT 2

Peacock, Molly 1947- .... **CLC 60**
See also CA 103; CAAS 21; CANR 52, 84; CP 7; CWP; DLB 120, 282

Peacock, Thomas Love
1785-1866 .... **NCLC 22**
See also BRW 4; DLB 96, 116; RGEL 2; RGSF 2

Peake, Mervyn 1911-1968 .... **CLC 7, 54**
See also CA 5-8R; 25-28R; CANR 3; DLB 15, 160, 255; FANT; MTCW 1; RGEL 2; SATA 23; SFW 4

Pearce, Philippa
See Christie, Philippa
See also CA 5-8R; CANR 4, 109; CWRI 5; FANT; MAICYA 2

Pearl, Eric
See Elman, Richard (Martin)

Pearson, T(homas) R(eid) 1956- .... **CLC 39**
See also CA 120; 130; CANR 97; CSW; INT CA-130

Peck, Dale 1967- .... **CLC 81**
See also CA 146; CANR 72, 127; GLL 2

Peck, John (Frederick) 1941- .... **CLC 3**
See also CA 49-52; CANR 3, 100; CP 7

Peck, Richard (Wayne) 1934- .... **CLC 21**
See also AAYA 1, 24; BYA 1, 6, 8, 11; CA 85-88; CANR 19, 38, 129; CLR 15; INT CANR-19; JRDA; MAICYA 1, 2; SAAS 2; SATA 18, 55, 97; SATA-Essay 110; WYA; YAW

Peck, Robert Newton 1928- .... **CLC 17**
See also AAYA 3, 43; BYA 1, 6; CA 81-84, 182; CAAE 182; CANR 31, 63, 127; CLR 45; DA; DAC; DAM MST; JRDA; LAIT 3; MAICYA 1, 2; SAAS 1; SATA 21, 62, 111; SATA-Essay 108; WYA; YAW

Peckinpah, (David) Sam(uel)
1925-1984 .... **CLC 20**
See also CA 109; 114; CANR 82

Pedersen, Knut 1859-1952
See Hamsun, Knut
See also CA 104; 119; CANR 63; MTCW 1, 2

Peeslake, Gaffer
See Durrell, Lawrence (George)

Peguy, Charles (Pierre)
1873-1914 .... **TCLC 10**
See also CA 107; 193; DLB 258; EWL 3; GFL 1789 to the Present

Peirce, Charles Sanders
1839-1914 .... **TCLC 81**
See also CA 194; DLB 270

Pellicer, Carlos 1897(?)-1977 .... **HLCS 2**
See also CA 153; 69-72; DLB 290; EWL 3; HW 1

Pena, Ramon del Valle y
See Valle-Inclan, Ramon (Maria) del

Pendennis, Arthur Esquir
See Thackeray, William Makepeace

Penn, Arthur
See Matthews, (James) Brander

Penn, William 1644-1718 .... **LC 25**
See also DLB 24

PEPECE
See Prado (Calvo), Pedro

Pepys, Samuel 1633-1703 ... **LC 11, 58; WLC**
See also BRW 2; CDBLB 1660-1789; DA; DA3; DAB; DAC; DAM MST; DLB 101, 213; NCFS 4; RGEL 2; TEA; WLIT 3

Percy, Thomas 1729-1811 .... **NCLC 95**
See also DLB 104

Percy, Walker 1916-1990 .... **CLC 2, 3, 6, 8, 14, 18, 47, 65**
See also AMWS 3; BPFB 3; CA 1-4R; 131; CANR 1, 23, 64; CPW; CSW; DA3; DAM NOV, POP; DLB 2; DLBY 1980, 1990; EWL 3; MTCW 1, 2; RGAL 4; TUS

Percy, William Alexander
1885-1942 .... **TCLC 84**
See also CA 163; MTCW 2

Perec, Georges 1936-1982 .... **CLC 56, 116**
See also CA 141; DLB 83, 299; EWL 3; GFL 1789 to the Present; RGWL 3

Pereda (y Sanchez de Porrua), Jose Maria de 1833-1906 .... **TCLC 16**
See also CA 117

Pereda y Porrua, Jose Maria de
See Pereda (y Sanchez de Porrua), Jose Maria de

Peregoy, George Weems
See Mencken, H(enry) L(ouis)

Perelman, S(idney) J(oseph)
1904-1979 .. **CLC 3, 5, 9, 15, 23, 44, 49; SSC 32**
See also AITN 1, 2; BPFB 3; CA 73-76; 89-92; CANR 18; DAM DRAM; DLB 11, 44; MTCW 1, 2; RGAL 4

Peret, Benjamin 1899-1959 .... **PC 33; TCLC 20**
See also CA 117; 186; GFL 1789 to the Present

Peretz, Isaac Leib
See Peretz, Isaac Loeb
See also CA 201

Peretz, Isaac Loeb 1851(?)-1915 ...... **SSC 26; TCLC 16**
See Peretz, Isaac Leib
See also CA 109

Peretz, Yitzkhok Leibush
See Peretz, Isaac Loeb

Perez Galdos, Benito 1843-1920 ..... **HLCS 2; TCLC 27**
See Galdos, Benito Perez
See also CA 125; 153; EWL 3; HW 1; RGWL 2, 3

Peri Rossi, Cristina 1941- .. **CLC 156; HLCS 2**
See also CA 131; CANR 59, 81; CWW 2; DLB 145, 290; EWL 3; HW 1, 2

Perlata
See Peret, Benjamin

Perloff, Marjorie G(abrielle)
1931- .... **CLC 137**
See also CA 57-60; CANR 7, 22, 49, 104

Perrault, Charles 1628-1703 .... **LC 2, 56**
See also BYA 4; CLR 79; DLB 268; GFL Beginnings to 1789; MAICYA 1, 2; RGWL 2, 3; SATA 25; WCH

Perry, Anne 1938- .... **CLC 126**
See also CA 101; CANR 22, 50, 84; CMW 4; CN 7; CPW; DLB 276

Perry, Brighton
See Sherwood, Robert E(mmet)

Perse, St.-John
See Leger, (Marie-Rene Auguste) Alexis Saint-Leger

Perse, Saint-John
See Leger, (Marie-Rene Auguste) Alexis Saint-Leger
See also DLB 258; RGWL 3

Perutz, Leo(pold) 1882-1957 .... **TCLC 60**
See also CA 147; DLB 81

Peseenz, Tulio F.
See Lopez y Fuentes, Gregorio

Pesetsky, Bette 1932- .... **CLC 28**
See also CA 133; DLB 130

Peshkov, Alexei Maximovich 1868-1936
See Gorky, Maxim
See also CA 105; 141; CANR 83; DA; DAC; DAM DRAM, MST, NOV; MTCW 2

Pessoa, Fernando (Antonio Nogueira)
1888-1935 ..... **HLC 2; PC 20; TCLC 27**
See also CA 125; 183; DAM MULT; DLB 287; EW 10; EWL 3; RGWL 2, 3; WP

Peterkin, Julia Mood 1880-1961 ...... **CLC 31**
See also CA 102; DLB 9

Peters, Joan K(aren) 1945- .... **CLC 39**
See also CA 158; CANR 109

Peters, Robert L(ouis) 1924- .... **CLC 7**
See also CA 13-16R; CAAS 8; CP 7; DLB 105

Petofi, Sandor 1823-1849 .... **NCLC 21**
See also RGWL 2, 3

Petrakis, Harry Mark 1923- .... **CLC 3**
See also CA 9-12R; CANR 4, 30, 85; CN 7

Petrarch 1304-1374 .... **CMLC 20; PC 8**
See also DA3; DAM POET; EW 2; LMFS 1; RGWL 2. 3

Petronius c. 20-66 .... **CMLC 34**
See also AW 2; CDWLB 1; DLB 211; RGWL 2, 3

Petrov, Evgeny .... **TCLC 21**
See Kataev, Evgeny Petrovich

Petry, Ann (Lane) 1908-1997 .. **CLC 1, 7, 18; TCLC 112**
See also AFAW 1, 2; BPFB 3; BW 1, 3; BYA 2; CA 5-8R; 157; CAAS 6; CANR 4, 46; CLR 12; CN 7; DLB 76; EWL 3; JRDA; LAIT 1; MAICYA 1, 2; MAIC-YAS 1; MTCW 1; RGAL 4; SATA 5; SATA-Obit 94; TUS

Petursson, Halligrimur 1614-1674 .... **LC 8**

Peychinovich
See Vazov, Ivan (Minchov)

Phaedrus c. 15B.C.-c. 50 .... **CMLC 25**
See also DLB 211

Phelps (Ward), Elizabeth Stuart
See Phelps, Elizabeth Stuart
See also FW

Phelps, Elizabeth Stuart
1844-1911 .... **TCLC 113**
See Phelps (Ward), Elizabeth Stuart
See also DLB 74

Philips, Katherine 1632-1664 . **LC 30; PC 40**
See also DLB 131; RGEL 2

Philipson, Morris H. 1926- .... **CLC 53**
See also CA 1-4R; CANR 4

Phillips, Caryl 1958- .... **BLCS; CLC 96**
See also BRWS 5; BW 2; CA 141; CANR 63, 104; CBD; CD 5; CN 7; DA3; DAM MULT; DLB 157; EWL 3; MTCW 2; WLIT 4; WWE 1

Phillips, David Graham
1867-1911 .... **TCLC 44**
See also CA 108; 176; DLB 9, 12, 303; RGAL 4

Phillips, Jack
See Sandburg, Carl (August)

Phillips, Jayne Anne 1952- .... **CLC 15, 33, 139; SSC 16**
See also AAYA 57; BPFB 3; CA 101; CANR 24, 50, 96; CN 7; CSW; DLBY 1980; INT CANR-24; MTCW 1, 2; RGAL 4; RGSF 2; SSFS 4

Phillips, Richard
See Dick, Philip K(indred)

Phillips, Robert (Schaeffer) 1938- .... **CLC 28**
See also CA 17-20R; CAAS 13; CANR 8; DLB 105

Phillips, Ward
See Lovecraft, H(oward) P(hillips)

Philostratus, Flavius c. 179-c.
244 .... **CMLC 62**

Piccolo, Lucio 1901-1969 .... **CLC 13**
See also CA 97-100; DLB 114; EWL 3

Pickthall, Marjorie L(owry) C(hristie)
1883-1922 .... **TCLC 21**
See also CA 107; DLB 92

Pico della Mirandola, Giovanni
1463-1494 .... **LC 15**
See also LMFS 1

Piercy, Marge 1936- .... **CLC 3, 6, 14, 18, 27,
62, 128; PC 29**
See also BPFB 3; CA 21-24R, 187; CAAE
187; CAAS 1; CANR 13, 43, 66, 111; CN
7; CP 7; CWP; DLB 120, 227; EXPP;
FW; MTCW 1, 2; PFS 9; SFW 4

Piers, Robert
See Anthony, Piers

Pieyre de Mandiargues, Andre 1909-1991
See Mandiargues, Andre Pieyre de
See also CA 103; 136; CANR 22, 82; EWL
3; GFL 1789 to the Present

Pilnyak, Boris 1894-1938 . **SSC 48; TCLC 23**
See Vogau, Boris Andreyevich
See also EWL 3

Pinchback, Eugene
See Toomer, Jean

Pincherle, Alberto 1907-1990 ...... **CLC 11, 18**
See Moravia, Alberto
See also CA 25-28R; 132; CANR 33, 63;
DAM NOV; MTCW 1

Pinckney, Darryl 1953- .... **CLC 76**
See also BW 2, 3; CA 143; CANR 79

Pindar 518(?)B.C.-438(?)B.C. .... **CMLC 12;
PC 19**
See also AW 1; CDWLB 1; DLB 176;
RGWL 2

Pineda, Cecile 1942- .... **CLC 39**
See also CA 118; DLB 209

Pinero, Arthur Wing 1855-1934 .... **TCLC 32**
See also CA 110; 153; DAM DRAM; DLB
10; RGEL 2

Pinero, Miguel (Antonio Gomez)
1946-1988 .... **CLC 4, 55**
See also CA 61-64; 125; CAD; CANR 29,
90; DLB 266; HW 1; LLW 1

Pinget, Robert 1919-1997 .... **CLC 7, 13, 37**
See also CA 85-88; 160; CWW 2; DLB 83;
EWL 3; GFL 1789 to the Present

Pink Floyd
See Barrett, (Roger) Syd; Gilmour, David;
Mason, Nick; Waters, Roger; Wright, Rick

Pinkney, Edward 1802-1828 .... **NCLC 31**
See also DLB 248

Pinkwater, Daniel
See Pinkwater, Daniel Manus

Pinkwater, Daniel Manus 1941- .... **CLC 35**
See also AAYA 1, 46; BYA 9; CA 29-32R;
CANR 12, 38, 89; CLR 4; CSW; FANT;
JRDA; MAICYA 1, 2; SAAS 3; SATA 8,
46, 76, 114; SFW 4; YAW

Pinkwater, Manus
See Pinkwater, Daniel Manus

Pinsky, Robert 1940- .... **CLC 9, 19, 38, 94,
121; PC 27**
See also AMWS 6; CA 29-32R; CAAS 4;
CANR 58, 97; CP 7; DA3; DAM POET;
DLBY 1982, 1998; MTCW 2; PFS 18;
RGAL 4

Pinta, Harold
See Pinter, Harold

Pinter, Harold 1930- .. **CLC 1, 3, 6, 9, 11, 15,
27, 58, 73, 199; DC 15; WLC**
See also BRWR 1; BRWS 1; CA 5-8R;
CANR 33, 65, 112; CBD; CD 5; CDBLB
1960 to Present; DA; DA3; DAB; DAC;
DAM DRAM, MST; DFS 3, 5, 7, 14;
DLB 13; EWL 3; IDFW 3, 4; LMFS 2;
MTCW 1, 2; RGEL 2; TEA

Piozzi, Hester Lynch (Thrale)
1741-1821 .... **NCLC 57**
See also DLB 104, 142

Pirandello, Luigi 1867-1936 .. **DC 5; SSC 22;
TCLC 4, 29; WLC**
See also CA 104; 153; CANR 103; DA;
DA3; DAB; DAC; DAM DRAM, MST;
DFS 4, 9; DLB 264; EW 8; EWL 3;
MTCW 2; RGSF 2; RGWL 2, 3

Pirsig, Robert M(aynard) 1928- ... **CLC 4, 6,
73**
See also CA 53-56; CANR 42, 74; CPW 1;
DA3; DAM POP; MTCW 1, 2; SATA 39

Pisarev, Dmitrii Ivanovich
See Pisarev, Dmitry Ivanovich
See also DLB 277

Pisarev, Dmitry Ivanovich
1840-1868 .... **NCLC 25**
See Pisarev, Dmitrii Ivanovich

Pix, Mary (Griffith) 1666-1709 .... **LC 8**
See also DLB 80

Pixerecourt, (Rene Charles) Guilbert de
1773-1844 .... **NCLC 39**
See also DLB 192; GFL 1789 to the Present

Plaatje, Sol(omon) T(shekisho)
1878-1932 .... **BLCS; TCLC 73**
See also BW 2, 3; CA 141; CANR 79; DLB
125, 225

Plaidy, Jean
See Hibbert, Eleanor Alice Burford

Planche, James Robinson
1796-1880 .... **NCLC 42**
See also RGEL 2

Plant, Robert 1948- .... **CLC 12**

Plante, David (Robert) 1940- . **CLC 7, 23, 38**
See also CA 37-40R; CANR 12, 36, 58, 82;
CN 7; DAM NOV; DLBY 1983; INT
CANR-12; MTCW 1

Plath, Sylvia 1932-1963 ..... **CLC 1, 2, 3, 5, 9,
11, 14, 17, 50, 51, 62, 111; PC 1, 37;
WLC**
See also AAYA 13; AMWR 2; AMWS 1;
BPFB 3; CA 19-20; CANR 34, 101; CAP
2; CDALB 1941-1968; DA; DA3; DAB;
DAC; DAM MST, POET; DLB 5, 6, 152;
EWL 3; EXPN; EXPP; FW; LAIT 4;
MAWW; MTCW 1, 2; NFS 1; PAB; PFS
1, 15; RGAL 4; SATA 96; TUS; WP;
YAW

Plato c. 428B.C.-347B.C. ... **CMLC 8; WLCS**
See also AW 1; CDWLB 1; DA; DA3;
DAB; DAC; DAM MST; DLB 176; LAIT
1; LATS 1:1; RGWL 2, 3

Platonov, Andrei
See Klimentov, Andrei Platonovich

Platonov, Andrei Platonovich
See Klimentov, Andrei Platonovich
See also DLB 272

Platonov, Andrey Platonovich
See Klimentov, Andrei Platonovich
See also EWL 3

Platt, Kin 1911- .... **CLC 26**
See also AAYA 11; CA 17-20R; CANR 11;
JRDA; SAAS 17; SATA 21, 86; WYA

Plautus c. 254B.C.-c. 184B.C. ...... **CMLC 24;
DC 6**
See also AW 1; CDWLB 1; DLB 211;
RGWL 2, 3

Plick et Plock
See Simenon, Georges (Jacques Christian)

Plieksans, Janis
See Rainis, Janis

Plimpton, George (Ames)
1927-2003 .... **CLC 36**
See also AITN 1; CA 21-24R; 224; CANR
32, 70, 103, 133; DLB 185, 241; MTCW
1, 2; SATA 10; SATA-Obit 150

Pliny the Elder c. 23-79 .... **CMLC 23**
See also DLB 211

Pliny the Younger c. 61-c. 112 ...... **CMLC 62**
See also AW 2; DLB 211

Plomer, William Charles Franklin
1903-1973 .... **CLC 4, 8**
See also AFW; CA 21-22; CANR 34; CAP
2; DLB 20, 162, 191, 225; EWL 3;
MTCW 1; RGEL 2; RGSF 2; SATA 24

Plotinus 204-270 .... **CMLC 46**
See also CDWLB 1; DLB 176

Plowman, Piers
See Kavanagh, Patrick (Joseph)

Plum, J.
See Wodehouse, P(elham) G(renville)

Plumly, Stanley (Ross) 1939- .... **CLC 33**
See also CA 108; 110; CANR 97; CP 7;
DLB 5, 193; INT CA-110

Plumpe, Friedrich Wilhelm
1888-1931 .... **TCLC 53**
See also CA 112

Plutarch c. 46-c. 120 .... **CMLC 60**
See also AW 2; CDWLB 1; DLB 176;
RGWL 2, 3; TWA

Po Chu-i 772-846 .... **CMLC 24**

Podhoretz, Norman 1930- .... **CLC 189**
See also AMWS 8; CA 9-12R; CANR 7,
78, 135

Poe, Edgar Allan 1809-1849 ..... **NCLC 1, 16,
55, 78, 94, 97, 117; PC 1, 54; SSC 1,
22, 34, 35, 54; WLC**
See also AAYA 14; AMW; AMWC 1;
AMWR 2; BPFB 3; BYA 5, 11; CDALB
1640-1865; CMW 4; DA; DA3; DAB;
DAC; DAM MST, POET; DLB 3, 59, 73,
74, 248, 254; EXPP; EXPS; HGG; LAIT
2; LATS 1:1; LMFS 1; MSW; PAB; PFS
1, 3, 9; RGAL 4; RGSF 2; SATA 23;
SCFW 2; SFW 4; SSFS 2, 4, 7, 8, 16;
SUFW; TUS; WP; WYA

Poet of Titchfield Street, The
See Pound, Ezra (Weston Loomis)

Pohl, Frederik 1919- .... **CLC 18; SSC 25**
See also AAYA 24; CA 61-64, 188; CAAE
188; CAAS 1; CANR 11, 37, 81; CN 7;
DLB 8; INT CANR-11; MTCW 1, 2;
SATA 24; SCFW 2; SFW 4

Poirier, Louis 1910-
See Gracq, Julien
See also CA 122; 126

Poitier, Sidney 1927- .... **CLC 26**
See also AAYA 60; BW 1; CA 117; CANR
94

Pokagon, Simon 1830-1899 .... **NNAL**
See also DAM MULT

Polanski, Roman 1933- .... **CLC 16, 178**
See also CA 77-80

Poliakoff, Stephen 1952- .... **CLC 38**
See also CA 106; CANR 116; CBD; CD 5;
DLB 13

Police, The
See Copeland, Stewart (Armstrong); Summers, Andrew James

Polidori, John William 1795-1821 . **NCLC 51**
See also DLB 116; HGG

Pollitt, Katha 1949- .... **CLC 28, 122**
See also CA 120; 122; CANR 66, 108;
MTCW 1, 2

Pollock, (Mary) Sharon 1936- .... **CLC 50**
See also CA 141; CANR 132; CD 5; CWD;
DAC; DAM DRAM, MST; DFS 3; DLB
60; FW

Pollock, Sharon 1936- .... **DC 20**

Polo, Marco 1254-1324 .... **CMLC 15**

Polonsky, Abraham (Lincoln)
1910-1999 .... **CLC 92**
See also CA 104; 187; DLB 26; INT CA-
104

Polybius c. 200B.C.-c. 118B.C. ...... **CMLC 17**
See also AW 1; DLB 176; RGWL 2, 3

Pomerance, Bernard 1940- .... **CLC 13**
See also CA 101; CAD; CANR 49, 134;
CD 5; DAM DRAM; DFS 9; LAIT 2

Ponge, Francis 1899-1988 .... **CLC 6, 18**
See also CA 85-88; 126; CANR 40, 86;
DAM POET; DLBY 2002; EWL 3; GFL
1789 to the Present; RGWL 2, 3

Poniatowska, Elena 1933- . **CLC 140; HLC 2**
See also CA 101; CANR 32, 66, 107; CD-
WLB 3; CWW 2; DAM MULT; DLB 113;
EWL 3; HW 1, 2; LAWS 1; WLIT 1

Pontoppidan, Henrik 1857-1943 .... **TCLC 29**
See also CA 170; DLB 300

Ponty, Maurice Merleau
See Merleau-Ponty, Maurice

Poole, Josephine .... **CLC 17**
See Helyar, Jane Penelope Josephine
See also SAAS 2; SATA 5

Popa, Vasko 1922-1991 .... **CLC 19**
See also CA 112; 148; CDWLB 4; DLB
181; EWL 3; RGWL 2, 3

Pope, Alexander 1688-1744 ...... **LC 3, 58, 60,**
64; PC 26; WLC
See also BRW 3; BRWC 1; BRWR 1; CD-
BLB 1660-1789; DA; DA3; DAB; DAC;
DAM MST, POET; DLB 95, 101, 213;
EXPP; PAB; PFS 12; RGEL 2; WLIT 3;
WP

Popov, Evgenii Anatol'evich
See Popov, Yevgeny
See also DLB 285

Popov, Yevgeny .... **CLC 59**
See Popov, Evgenii Anatol'evich

Poquelin, Jean-Baptiste
See Moliere

Porphyry c. 233-c. 305 .... **CMLC 71**

Porter, Connie (Rose) 1959(?)- .... **CLC 70**
See also BW 2, 3; CA 142; CANR 90, 109;
SATA 81, 129

Porter, Gene(va Grace) Stratton .. **TCLC 21**
See Stratton-Porter, Gene(va Grace)
See also BPFB 3; CA 112; CWRI 5; RHW

Porter, Katherine Anne 1890-1980 ... **CLC 1,**
3, 7, 10, 13, 15, 27, 101; SSC 4
See also AAYA 42; AITN 2; AMW; BPFB
3; CA 1-4R; 101; CANR 1, 65; CDALBS;
DA; DA3; DAB; DAC; DAM MST, NOV;
DLB 4, 9, 102; DLBD 12; DLBY 1980;
EWL 3; EXPS; LAIT 3; MAWW; MTCW
1, 2; NFS 14; RGAL 4; RGSF 2; SATA
39; SATA-Obit 23; SSFS 1, 8, 11, 16;
TUS

Porter, Peter (Neville Frederick)
1929- .... **CLC 5, 13, 33**
See also CA 85-88; CP 7; DLB 40, 289;
WWE 1

Porter, William Sydney 1862-1910
See Henry, O.
See also CA 104; 131; CDALB 1865-1917;
DA; DA3; DAB; DAC; DAM MST; DLB
12, 78, 79; MTCW 1, 2; TUS; YABC 2

Portillo (y Pacheco), Jose Lopez
See Lopez Portillo (y Pacheco), Jose

Portillo Trambley, Estela 1927-1998 .. **HLC 2**
See Trambley, Estela Portillo
See also CANR 32; DAM MULT; DLB
209; HW 1

Posey, Alexander (Lawrence)
1873-1908 .... **NNAL**
See also CA 144; CANR 80; DAM MULT;
DLB 175

Posse, Abel .... **CLC 70**

Post, Melville Davisson
1869-1930 .... **TCLC 39**
See also CA 110; 202; CMW 4

Potok, Chaim 1929-2002 ... **CLC 2, 7, 14, 26,**
112
See also AAYA 15, 50; AITN 1, 2; BPFB 3;
BYA 1; CA 17-20R; 208; CANR 19, 35,
64, 98; CLR 92; CN 7; DA3; DAM NOV;
DLB 28, 152; EXPN; INT CANR-19;
LAIT 4; MTCW 1, 2; NFS 4; SATA 33,
106; SATA-Obit 134; TUS; YAW

Potok, Herbert Harold -2002
See Potok, Chaim

Potok, Herman Harold
See Potok, Chaim

Potter, Dennis (Christopher George)
1935-1994 .... **CLC 58, 86, 123**
See also BRWS 10; CA 107; 145; CANR
33, 61; CBD; DLB 233; MTCW 1

Pound, Ezra (Weston Loomis)
1885-1972 .. **CLC 1, 2, 3, 4, 5, 7, 10, 13,**
18, 34, 48, 50, 112; PC 4; WLC
See also AAYA 47; AMW; AMWR 1; CA
5-8R; 37-40R; CANR 40; CDALB 1917-
1929; DA; DA3; DAB; DAC; DAM MST,
POET; DLB 4, 45, 63; DLBD 15; EFS 2;
EWL 3; EXPP; LMFS 2; MTCW 1, 2;
PAB; PFS 2, 8, 16; RGAL 4; TUS; WP

Povod, Reinaldo 1959-1994 .... **CLC 44**
See also CA 136; 146; CANR 83

Powell, Adam Clayton, Jr.
1908-1972 .... **BLC 3; CLC 89**
See also BW 1, 3; CA 102; 33-36R; CANR
86; DAM MULT

Powell, Anthony (Dymoke)
1905-2000 .... **CLC 1, 3, 7, 9, 10, 31**
See also BRW 7; CA 1-4R; 189; CANR 1,
32, 62, 107; CDBLB 1945-1960; CN 7;
DLB 15; EWL 3; MTCW 1, 2; RGEL 2;
TEA

Powell, Dawn 1896(?)-1965 .... **CLC 66**
See also CA 5-8R; CANR 121; DLBY 1997

Powell, Padgett 1952- .... **CLC 34**
See also CA 126; CANR 63, 101; CSW;
DLB 234; DLBY 01

Powell, (Oval) Talmage 1920-2000
See Queen, Ellery
See also CA 5-8R; CANR 2, 80

Power, Susan 1961- .... **CLC 91**
See also BYA 14; CA 160; CANR 135; NFS
11

Powers, J(ames) F(arl) 1917-1999 ..... **CLC 1,**
4, 8, 57; SSC 4
See also CA 1-4R; 181; CANR 2, 61; CN
7; DLB 130; MTCW 1; RGAL 4; RGSF
2

Powers, John J(ames) 1945-
See Powers, John R.
See also CA 69-72

Powers, John R. .... **CLC 66**
See Powers, John J(ames)

Powers, Richard (S.) 1957- .... **CLC 93**
See also AMWS 9; BPFB 3; CA 148;
CANR 80; CN 7

Pownall, David 1938- .... **CLC 10**
See also CA 89-92; 180; CAAS 18; CANR
49, 101; CBD; CD 5; CN 7; DLB 14

Powys, John Cowper 1872-1963 ... **CLC 7, 9,**
15, 46, 125
See also CA 85-88; CANR 106; DLB 15,
255; EWL 3; FANT; MTCW 1, 2; RGEL
2; SUFW

Powys, T(heodore) F(rancis)
1875-1953 .... **TCLC 9**
See also BRWS 8; CA 106; 189; DLB 36,
162; EWL 3; FANT; RGEL 2; SUFW

Prado (Calvo), Pedro 1886-1952 ... **TCLC 75**
See also CA 131; DLB 283; HW 1; LAW

Prager, Emily 1952- .... **CLC 56**
See also CA 204

Pratchett, Terry 1948- .... **CLC 197**
See also AAYA 19, 54; BPFB 3; CA 143;
CANR 87, 126; CLR 64; CN 7; CPW;
CWRI 5; FANT; SATA 82, 139; SFW 4;
SUFW 2

Pratolini, Vasco 1913-1991 .... **TCLC 124**
See also CA 211; DLB 177; EWL 3; RGWL
2, 3

Pratt, E(dwin) J(ohn) 1883(?)-1964 . **CLC 19**
See also CA 141; 93-96; CANR 77; DAC;
DAM POET; DLB 92; EWL 3; RGEL 2;
TWA

Premchand .... **TCLC 21**
See Srivastava, Dhanpat Rai
See also EWL 3

Preseren, France 1800-1849 .... **NCLC 127**
See also CDWLB 4; DLB 147

Preussler, Otfried 1923- .... **CLC 17**
See also CA 77-80; SATA 24

Prevert, Jacques (Henri Marie)
1900-1977 .... **CLC 15**
See also CA 77-80; 69-72; CANR 29, 61;
DLB 258; EWL 3; GFL 1789 to the
Present; IDFW 3, 4; MTCW 1; RGWL 2,
3; SATA-Obit 30

Prevost, (Antoine Francois)
1697-1763 .... **LC 1**
See also EW 4; GFL Beginnings to 1789;
RGWL 2, 3

Price, (Edward) Reynolds 1933- ... **CLC 3, 6,**
13, 43, 50, 63; SSC 22
See also AMWS 6; CA 1-4R; CANR 1, 37,
57, 87, 128; CN 7; CSW; DAM NOV;
DLB 2, 218, 278; EWL 3; INT CANR-
37; NFS 18

Price, Richard 1949- .... **CLC 6, 12**
See also CA 49-52; CANR 3; DLBY 1981

Prichard, Katharine Susannah
1883-1969 .... **CLC 46**
See also CA 11-12; CANR 33; CAP 1; DLB
260; MTCW 1; RGEL 2; RGSF 2; SATA
66

Priestley, J(ohn) B(oynton)
1894-1984 .... **CLC 2, 5, 9, 34**
See also BRW 7; CA 9-12R; 113; CANR
33; CDBLB 1914-1945; DA3; DAM
DRAM, NOV; DLB 10, 34, 77, 100, 139;
DLBY 1984; EWL 3; MTCW 1, 2; RGEL
2; SFW 4

Prince 1958- .... **CLC 35**
See also CA 213

Prince, F(rank) T(empleton)
1912-2003 .... **CLC 22**
See also CA 101; 219; CANR 43, 79; CP 7;
DLB 20

Prince Kropotkin
See Kropotkin, Peter (Aleksieevich)

Prior, Matthew 1664-1721 .... **LC 4**
See also DLB 95; RGEL 2

Prishvin, Mikhail 1873-1954 .... **TCLC 75**
See Prishvin, Mikhail Mikhailovich

Prishvin, Mikhail Mikhailovich
See Prishvin, Mikhail
See also DLB 272; EWL 3

Pritchard, William H(arrison)
1932- .... **CLC 34**
See also CA 65-68; CANR 23, 95; DLB
111

Pritchett, V(ictor) S(awdon)
1900-1997 ... **CLC 5, 13, 15, 41; SSC 14**
See also BPFB 3; BRWS 3; CA 61-64; 157;
CANR 31, 63; CN 7; DA3; DAM NOV;
DLB 15, 139; EWL 3; MTCW 1, 2;
RGEL 2; RGSF 2; TEA

Private 19022
See Manning, Frederic

Probst, Mark 1925- .... **CLC 59**
See also CA 130

Prokosch, Frederic 1908-1989 ...... **CLC 4, 48**
See also CA 73-76; 128; CANR 82; DLB
48; MTCW 2

Propertius, Sextus c. 50B.C.-c.
16B.C. .... **CMLC 32**
See also AW 2; CDWLB 1; DLB 211;
RGWL 2, 3

Prophet, The
See Dreiser, Theodore (Herman Albert)

Prose, Francine 1947- .... **CLC 45**
See also CA 109; 112; CANR 46, 95, 132;
DLB 234; SATA 101, 149

Proudhon
See Cunha, Euclides (Rodrigues Pimenta)
da

Proulx, Annie
See Proulx, E(dna) Annie

Proulx, E(dna) Annie 1935- ...... **CLC 81, 158**
See also AMWS 7; BPFB 3; CA 145;
CANR 65, 110; CN 7; CPW 1; DA3;
DAM POP; MTCW 2; SSFS 18

**Proust, (Valentin-Louis-George-Eugene)
Marcel** 1871-1922 ..... **SSC 75; TCLC 7,
13, 33; WLC**
See also AAYA 58; BPFB 3; CA 104; 120;
CANR 110; DA; DA3; DAB; DAC; DAM
MST, NOV; DLB 65; EW 8; EWL 3; GFL
1789 to the Present; MTCW 1, 2; RGWL
2, 3; TWA

Prowler, Harley
See Masters, Edgar Lee

Prus, Boleslaw 1845-1912 .... **TCLC 48**
See also RGWL 2, 3

Pryor, Richard (Franklin Lenox Thomas)
1940- .... **CLC 26**
See also CA 122; 152

Przybyszewski, Stanislaw
1868-1927 .... **TCLC 36**
See also CA 160; DLB 66; EWL 3

Pteleon
See Grieve, C(hristopher) M(urray)
See also DAM POET

Puckett, Lute
See Masters, Edgar Lee

Puig, Manuel 1932-1990 .... **CLC 3, 5, 10, 28,
65, 133; HLC 2**
See also BPFB 3; CA 45-48; CANR 2, 32,
63; CDWLB 3; DA3; DAM MULT; DLB
113; DNFS 1; EWL 3; GLL 1; HW 1, 2;
LAW; MTCW 1, 2; RGWL 2, 3; TWA;
WLIT 1

Pulitzer, Joseph 1847-1911 .... **TCLC 76**
See also CA 114; DLB 23

Purchas, Samuel 1577(?)-1626 .... **LC 70**
See also DLB 151

Purdy, A(lfred) W(ellington)
1918-2000 .... **CLC 3, 6, 14, 50**
See also CA 81-84; 189; CAAS 17; CANR
42, 66; CP 7; DAC; DAM MST, POET;
DLB 88; PFS 5; RGEL 2

Purdy, James (Amos) 1923- .... **CLC 2, 4, 10,
28, 52**
See also AMWS 7; CA 33-36R; CAAS 1;
CANR 19, 51, 132; CN 7; DLB 2, 218;
EWL 3; INT CANR-19; MTCW 1; RGAL
4

Pure, Simon
See Swinnerton, Frank Arthur

Pushkin, Aleksandr Sergeevich
See Pushkin, Alexander (Sergeyevich)
See also DLB 205

Pushkin, Alexander (Sergeyevich)
1799-1837 .... **NCLC 3, 27, 83; PC 10;
SSC 27, 55; WLC**
See Pushkin, Aleksandr Sergeevich
See also DA; DA3; DAB; DAC; DAM
DRAM, MST, POET; EW 5; EXPS; RGSF
2; RGWL 2, 3; SATA 61; SSFS 9; TWA

P'u Sung-ling 1640-1715 .... **LC 49; SSC 31**

Putnam, Arthur Lee
See Alger, Horatio, Jr.

Puzo, Mario 1920-1999 .... **CLC 1, 2, 6, 36,
107**
See also BPFB 3; CA 65-68; 185; CANR 4,
42, 65, 99, 131; CN 7; CPW; DA3; DAM
NOV, POP; DLB 6; MTCW 1, 2; NFS 16;
RGAL 4

Pygge, Edward
See Barnes, Julian (Patrick)

Pyle, Ernest Taylor 1900-1945
See Pyle, Ernie
See also CA 115; 160

Pyle, Ernie .... **TCLC 75**
See Pyle, Ernest Taylor
See also DLB 29; MTCW 2

Pyle, Howard 1853-1911 .... **TCLC 81**
See also AAYA 57; BYA 2, 4; CA 109; 137;
CLR 22; DLB 42, 188; DLBD 13; LAIT
1; MAICYA 1, 2; SATA 16, 100; WCH;
YAW

Pym, Barbara (Mary Crampton)
1913-1980 .... **CLC 13, 19, 37, 111**
See also BPFB 3; BRWS 2; CA 13-14; 97-
100; CANR 13, 34; CAP 1; DLB 14, 207;
DLBY 1987; EWL 3; MTCW 1, 2; RGEL
2; TEA

Pynchon, Thomas (Ruggles, Jr.)
1937- ...... **CLC 2, 3, 6, 9, 11, 18, 33, 62,
72, 123, 192; SSC 14; WLC**
See also AMWS 2; BEST 90:2; BPFB 3;
CA 17-20R; CANR 22, 46, 73; CN 7;
CPW 1; DA; DA3; DAB; DAC; DAM
MST, NOV, POP; DLB 2, 173; EWL 3;
MTCW 1, 2; RGAL 4; SFW 4; TUS

Pythagoras c. 582B.C.-c. 507B.C. . **CMLC 22**
See also DLB 176

Q
See Quiller-Couch, Sir Arthur (Thomas)

Qian, Chongzhu
See Ch'ien, Chung-shu

Qian, Sima 145B.C.-c. 89B.C. .... **CMLC 72**

Qian Zhongshu
See Ch'ien, Chung-shu
See also CWW 2

Qroll
See Dagerman, Stig (Halvard)

Quarrington, Paul (Lewis) 1953- ..... **CLC 65**
See also CA 129; CANR 62, 95

Quasimodo, Salvatore 1901-1968 .... **CLC 10;
PC 47**
See also CA 13-16; 25-28R; CAP 1; DLB
114; EW 12; EWL 3; MTCW 1; RGWL
2, 3

Quatermass, Martin
See Carpenter, John (Howard)

Quay, Stephen 1947- .... **CLC 95**
See also CA 189

Quay, Timothy 1947- .... **CLC 95**
See also CA 189

Queen, Ellery .... **CLC 3, 11**
See Dannay, Frederic; Davidson, Avram
(James); Deming, Richard; Fairman, Paul
W.; Flora, Fletcher; Hoch, Edward
D(entinger); Kane, Henry; Lee, Manfred
B(ennington); Marlowe, Stephen; Powell,
(Oval) Talmage; Sheldon, Walter J(ames);
Sturgeon, Theodore (Hamilton); Tracy,
Don(ald Fiske); Vance, John Holbrook
See also BPFB 3; CMW 4; MSW; RGAL 4

Queen, Ellery, Jr.
See Dannay, Frederic; Lee, Manfred
B(ennington)

Queneau, Raymond 1903-1976 ..... **CLC 2, 5,
10, 42**
See also CA 77-80; 69-72; CANR 32; DLB
72, 258; EW 12; EWL 3; GFL 1789 to
the Present; MTCW 1, 2; RGWL 2, 3

Quevedo, Francisco de 1580-1645 .... **LC 23**

Quiller-Couch, Sir Arthur (Thomas)
1863-1944 .... **TCLC 53**
See also CA 118; 166; DLB 135, 153, 190;
HGG; RGEL 2; SUFW 1

Quin, Ann (Marie) 1936-1973 .... **CLC 6**
See also CA 9-12R; 45-48; DLB 14, 231

Quincey, Thomas de
See De Quincey, Thomas

Quindlen, Anna 1953- .... **CLC 191**
See also AAYA 35; CA 138; CANR 73, 126;
DA3; DLB 292; MTCW 2

Quinn, Martin
See Smith, Martin Cruz

Quinn, Peter 1947- .... **CLC 91**
See also CA 197

Quinn, Simon
See Smith, Martin Cruz

Quintana, Leroy V. 1944- ...... **HLC 2; PC 36**
See also CA 131; CANR 65; DAM MULT;
DLB 82; HW 1, 2

Quiroga, Horacio (Sylvestre)
1878-1937 .... **HLC 2; TCLC 20**
See also CA 117; 131; DAM MULT; EWL
3; HW 1; LAW; MTCW 1; RGSF 2;
WLIT 1

Quoirez, Francoise 1935- .... **CLC 9**
See Sagan, Francoise
See also CA 49-52; CANR 6, 39, 73;
MTCW 1, 2; TWA

Raabe, Wilhelm (Karl) 1831-1910 . **TCLC 45**
See also CA 167; DLB 129

Rabe, David (William) 1940- .. **CLC 4, 8, 33;
DC 16**
See also CA 85-88; CABS 3; CAD; CANR
59, 129; CD 5; DAM DRAM; DFS 3, 8,
13; DLB 7, 228; EWL 3

Rabelais, Francois 1494-1553 .... **LC 5, 60;
WLC**
See also DA; DAB; DAC; DAM MST; EW
2; GFL Beginnings to 1789; LMFS 1;
RGWL 2, 3; TWA

Rabinovitch, Sholem 1859-1916
See Aleichem, Sholom
See also CA 104

Rabinyan, Dorit 1972- .... **CLC 119**
See also CA 170

Rachilde
See Vallette, Marguerite Eymery; Vallette,
Marguerite Eymery
See also EWL 3

Racine, Jean 1639-1699 .... **LC 28**
See also DA3; DAB; DAM MST; DLB 268;
EW 3; GFL Beginnings to 1789; LMFS
1; RGWL 2, 3; TWA

Radcliffe, Ann (Ward) 1764-1823 ... **NCLC 6,
55, 106**
See also DLB 39, 178; HGG; LMFS 1;
RGEL 2; SUFW; WLIT 3

Radclyffe-Hall, Marguerite
See Hall, (Marguerite) Radclyffe

Radiguet, Raymond 1903-1923 ...... **TCLC 29**
See also CA 162; DLB 65; EWL 3; GFL
1789 to the Present; RGWL 2, 3

Radnoti, Miklos 1909-1944 .... **TCLC 16**
See also CA 118; 212; CDWLB 4; DLB
215; EWL 3; RGWL 2, 3

Rado, James 1939- .... **CLC 17**
See also CA 105

Radvanyi, Netty 1900-1983
See Seghers, Anna
See also CA 85-88; 110; CANR 82

Rae, Ben
See Griffiths, Trevor

Raeburn, John (Hay) 1941- .... **CLC 34**
See also CA 57-60

Ragni, Gerome 1942-1991 .... **CLC 17**
See also CA 105; 134

Rahv, Philip .... **CLC 24**
See Greenberg, Ivan
See also DLB 137

Raimund, Ferdinand Jakob
1790-1836 .... **NCLC 69**
See also DLB 90

Raine, Craig (Anthony) 1944- .. **CLC 32, 103**
See also CA 108; CANR 29, 51, 103; CP 7;
DLB 40; PFS 7

Raine, Kathleen (Jessie) 1908-2003 .. **CLC 7, 45**
See also CA 85-88; 218; CANR 46, 109;
CP 7; DLB 20; EWL 3; MTCW 1; RGEL 2

Rainis, Janis 1865-1929 .... **TCLC 29**
See also CA 170; CDWLB 4; DLB 220;
EWL 3

Rakosi, Carl .... **CLC 47**
See Rawley, Callman
See also CA 228; CAAS 5; CP 7; DLB 193

Ralegh, Sir Walter
See Raleigh, Sir Walter
See also BRW 1; RGEL 2; WP

Raleigh, Richard
See Lovecraft, H(oward) P(hillips)

Raleigh, Sir Walter 1554(?)-1618 .... **LC 31, 39; PC 31**
See Ralegh, Sir Walter
See also CDBLB Before 1660; DLB 172;
EXPP; PFS 14; TEA

Rallentando, H. P.
See Sayers, Dorothy L(eigh)

Ramal, Walter
See de la Mare, Walter (John)

Ramana Maharshi 1879-1950 .... **TCLC 84**

Ramoacn y Cajal, Santiago
1852-1934 .... **TCLC 93**

Ramon, Juan
See Jimenez (Mantecon), Juan Ramon

Ramos, Graciliano 1892-1953 .... **TCLC 32**
See also CA 167; DLB 307; EWL 3; HW 2;
LAW; WLIT 1

Rampersad, Arnold 1941- .... **CLC 44**
See also BW 2, 3; CA 127; 133; CANR 81;
DLB 111; INT CA-133

Rampling, Anne
See Rice, Anne
See also GLL 2

Ramsay, Allan 1686(?)-1758 .... **LC 29**
See also DLB 95; RGEL 2

Ramsay, Jay
See Campbell, (John) Ramsey

Ramuz, Charles-Ferdinand
1878-1947 .... **TCLC 33**
See also CA 165; EWL 3

Rand, Ayn 1905-1982 ...... **CLC 3, 30, 44, 79; WLC**
See also AAYA 10; AMWS 4; BPFB 3;
BYA 12; CA 13-16R; 105; CANR 27, 73;
CDALBS; CPW; DA; DA3; DAC; DAM
MST, NOV, POP; DLB 227, 279; MTCW
1, 2; NFS 10, 16; RGAL 4; SFW 4; TUS;
YAW

Randall, Dudley (Felker) 1914-2000 . **BLC 3; CLC 1, 135**
See also BW 1, 3; CA 25-28R; 189; CANR
23, 82; DAM MULT; DLB 41; PFS 5

Randall, Robert
See Silverberg, Robert

Ranger, Ken
See Creasey, John

Rank, Otto 1884-1939 .... **TCLC 115**

Ransom, John Crowe 1888-1974 .. **CLC 2, 4, 5, 11, 24; PC 61**
See also AMW; CA 5-8R; 49-52; CANR 6,
34; CDALBS; DA3; DAM POET; DLB
45, 63; EWL 3; EXPP; MTCW 1, 2;
RGAL 4; TUS

Rao, Raja 1909- .... **CLC 25, 56**
See also CA 73-76; CANR 51; CN 7; DAM
NOV; EWL 3; MTCW 1, 2; RGEL 2;
RGSF 2

Raphael, Frederic (Michael) 1931- ... **CLC 2, 14**
See also CA 1-4R; CANR 1, 86; CN 7;
DLB 14

Ratcliffe, James P.
See Mencken, H(enry) L(ouis)

Rathbone, Julian 1935- .... **CLC 41**
See also CA 101; CANR 34, 73

Rattigan, Terence (Mervyn)
1911-1977 .... **CLC 7; DC 18**
See also BRWS 7; CA 85-88; 73-76; CBD;
CDBLB 1945-1960; DAM DRAM; DFS
8; DLB 13; IDFW 3, 4; MTCW 1, 2;
RGEL 2

Ratushinskaya, Irina 1954- .... **CLC 54**
See also CA 129; CANR 68; CWW 2

Raven, Simon (Arthur Noel)
1927-2001 .... **CLC 14**
See also CA 81-84; 197; CANR 86; CN 7;
DLB 271

Ravenna, Michael
See Welty, Eudora (Alice)

Rawley, Callman 1903-2004
See Rakosi, Carl
See also CA 21-24R; CANR 12, 32, 91

Rawlings, Marjorie Kinnan
1896-1953 .... **TCLC 4**
See also AAYA 20; AMWS 10; ANW;
BPFB 3; BYA 3; CA 104; 137; CANR 74;
CLR 63; DLB 9, 22, 102; DLBD 17;
JRDA; MAICYA 1, 2; MTCW 2; RGAL
4; SATA 100; WCH; YABC 1; YAW

Ray, Satyajit 1921-1992 .... **CLC 16, 76**
See also CA 114; 137; DAM MULT

Read, Herbert Edward 1893-1968 ..... **CLC 4**
See also BRW 6; CA 85-88; 25-28R; DLB
20, 149; EWL 3; PAB; RGEL 2

Read, Piers Paul 1941- .... **CLC 4, 10, 25**
See also CA 21-24R; CANR 38, 86; CN 7;
DLB 14; SATA 21

Reade, Charles 1814-1884 .... **NCLC 2, 74**
See also DLB 21; RGEL 2

Reade, Hamish
See Gray, Simon (James Holliday)

Reading, Peter 1946- .... **CLC 47**
See also BRWS 8; CA 103; CANR 46, 96;
CP 7; DLB 40

Reaney, James 1926- .... **CLC 13**
See also CA 41-44R; CAAS 15; CANR 42;
CD 5; CP 7; DAC; DAM MST; DLB 68;
RGEL 2; SATA 43

Rebreanu, Liviu 1885-1944 .... **TCLC 28**
See also CA 165; DLB 220; EWL 3

Rechy, John (Francisco) 1934- ...... **CLC 1, 7, 14, 18, 107; HLC 2**
See also CA 5-8R; 195; CAAE 195; CAAS
4; CANR 6, 32, 64; CN 7; DAM MULT;
DLB 122, 278; DLBY 1982; HW 1, 2;
INT CANR-6; LLW 1; RGAL 4

Redcam, Tom 1870-1933 .... **TCLC 25**

Reddin, Keith .... **CLC 67**
See also CAD

Redgrove, Peter (William)
1932-2003 .... **CLC 6, 41**
See also BRWS 6; CA 1-4R; 217; CANR 3,
39, 77; CP 7; DLB 40

Redmon, Anne .... **CLC 22**
See Nightingale, Anne Redmon
See also DLBY 1986

Reed, Eliot
See Ambler, Eric

Reed, Ishmael 1938- ..... **BLC 3; CLC 2, 3, 5, 6, 13, 32, 60, 174**
See also AFAW 1, 2; AMWS 10; BPFB 3;
BW 2, 3; CA 21-24R; CANR 25, 48, 74;
128; CN 7; CP 7; CSW; DA3; DAM
MULT; DLB 2, 5, 33, 169, 227; DLBD 8;
EWL 3; LMFS 2; MSW; MTCW 1, 2;
PFS 6; RGAL 4; TCWW 2

Reed, John (Silas) 1887-1920 .... **TCLC 9**
See also CA 106; 195; TUS

Reed, Lou .... **CLC 21**
See Firbank, Louis

Reese, Lizette Woodworth 1856-1935 . **PC 29**
See also CA 180; DLB 54

Reeve, Clara 1729-1807 .... **NCLC 19**
See also DLB 39; RGEL 2

Reich, Wilhelm 1897-1957 .... **TCLC 57**
See also CA 199

Reid, Christopher (John) 1949- .... **CLC 33**
See also CA 140; CANR 89; CP 7; DLB
40; EWL 3

Reid, Desmond
See Moorcock, Michael (John)

Reid Banks, Lynne 1929-
See Banks, Lynne Reid
See also AAYA 49; CA 1-4R; CANR 6, 22,
38, 87; CLR 24; CN 7; JRDA; MAICYA
1, 2; SATA 22, 75, 111; YAW

Reilly, William K.
See Creasey, John

Reiner, Max
See Caldwell, (Janet Miriam) Taylor
(Holland)

Reis, Ricardo
See Pessoa, Fernando (Antonio Nogueira)

Reizenstein, Elmer Leopold
See Rice, Elmer (Leopold)
See also EWL 3

Remarque, Erich Maria 1898-1970 . **CLC 21**
See also AAYA 27; BPFB 3; CA 77-80; 29-
32R; CDWLB 2; DA; DA3; DAB; DAC;
DAM MST, NOV; DLB 56; EWL 3;
EXPN; LAIT 3; MTCW 1, 2; NFS 4;
RGWL 2, 3

Remington, Frederic 1861-1909 ..... **TCLC 89**
See also CA 108; 169; DLB 12, 186, 188;
SATA 41

Remizov, A.
See Remizov, Aleksei (Mikhailovich)

Remizov, A. M.
See Remizov, Aleksei (Mikhailovich)

Remizov, Aleksei (Mikhailovich)
1877-1957 .... **TCLC 27**
See Remizov, Alexey Mikhaylovich
See also CA 125; 133; DLB 295

Remizov, Alexey Mikhaylovich
See Remizov, Aleksei (Mikhailovich)
See also EWL 3

Renan, Joseph Ernest 1823-1892 . **NCLC 26, 145**
See also GFL 1789 to the Present

Renard, Jules(-Pierre) 1864-1910 .. **TCLC 17**
See also CA 117; 202; GFL 1789 to the
Present

Renault, Mary .... **CLC 3, 11, 17**
See Challans, Mary
See also BPFB 3; BYA 2; DLBY 1983;
EWL 3; GLL 1; LAIT 1; MTCW 2; RGEL
2; RHW

Rendell, Ruth (Barbara) 1930- .. **CLC 28, 48**
See Vine, Barbara
See also BPFB 3; BRWS 9; CA 109; CANR
32, 52, 74, 127; CN 7; CPW; DAM POP;
DLB 87, 276; INT CANR-32; MSW;
MTCW 1, 2

Renoir, Jean 1894-1979 .... **CLC 20**
See also CA 129; 85-88

Resnais, Alain 1922- .... **CLC 16**

Revard, Carter (Curtis) 1931- .... **NNAL**
See also CA 144; CANR 81; PFS 5

Reverdy, Pierre 1889-1960 .... **CLC 53**
See also CA 97-100; 89-92; DLB 258; EWL
3; GFL 1789 to the Present

Rexroth, Kenneth 1905-1982 .... **CLC 1, 2, 6,
11, 22, 49, 112; PC 20**
See also BG 3; CA 5-8R; 107; CANR 14,
34, 63; CDALB 1941-1968; DAM POET;
DLB 16, 48, 165, 212; DLBY 1982; EWL
3; INT CANR-14; MTCW 1, 2; RGAL 4

Reyes, Alfonso 1889-1959 .... **HLCS 2; TCLC
33**
See also CA 131; EWL 3; HW 1; LAW

Reyes y Basoalto, Ricardo Eliecer Neftali
See Neruda, Pablo

Reymont, Wladyslaw (Stanislaw)
1868(?)-1925 .... **TCLC 5**
See also CA 104; EWL 3

Reynolds, John Hamilton
1794-1852 .... **NCLC 146**
See also DLB 96

Reynolds, Jonathan 1942- .... **CLC 6, 38**
See also CA 65-68; CANR 28

Reynolds, Joshua 1723-1792 .... **LC 15**
See also DLB 104

Reynolds, Michael S(hane)
1937-2000 .... **CLC 44**
See also CA 65-68; 189; CANR 9, 89, 97

Reznikoff, Charles 1894-1976 .... **CLC 9**
See also AMWS 14; CA 33-36; 61-64; CAP
2; DLB 28, 45; WP

Rezzori (d'Arezzo), Gregor von
1914-1998 .... **CLC 25**
See also CA 122; 136; 167

Rhine, Richard
See Silverstein, Alvin; Silverstein, Virginia
B(arbara Opshelor)

Rhodes, Eugene Manlove
1869-1934 .... **TCLC 53**
See also CA 198; DLB 256

R'hoone, Lord
See Balzac, Honore de

Rhys, Jean 1890-1979 .... **CLC 2, 4, 6, 14, 19,
51, 124; SSC 21, 76**
See also BRWS 2; CA 25-28R; 85-88;
CANR 35, 62; CDBLB 1945-1960; CD-
WLB 3; DA3; DAM NOV; DLB 36, 117,
162; DNFS 2; EWL 3; LATS 1:1; MTCW
1, 2; RGEL 2; RGSF 2; RHW; TEA;
WWE 1

Ribeiro, Darcy 1922-1997 .... **CLC 34**
See also CA 33-36R; 156; EWL 3

Ribeiro, Joao Ubaldo (Osorio Pimentel)
1941- .... **CLC 10, 67**
See also CA 81-84; CWW 2; EWL 3

Ribman, Ronald (Burt) 1932- .... **CLC 7**
See also CA 21-24R; CAD; CANR 46, 80;
CD 5

Ricci, Nino (Pio) 1959- .... **CLC 70**
See also CA 137; CANR 130; CCA 1

Rice, Anne 1941- .... **CLC 41, 128**
See Rampling, Anne
See also AAYA 9, 53; AMWS 7; BEST
89:2; BPFB 3; CA 65-68; CANR 12, 36,
53, 74, 100, 133; CN 7; CPW; CSW;
DA3; DAM POP; DLB 292; GLL 2;
HGG; MTCW 2; SUFW 2; YAW

Rice, Elmer (Leopold) 1892-1967 ...... **CLC 7,
49**
See Reizenstein, Elmer Leopold
See also CA 21-22; 25-28R; CAP 2; DAM
DRAM; DFS 12; DLB 4, 7; MTCW 1, 2;
RGAL 4

Rice, Tim(othy Miles Bindon)
1944- .... **CLC 21**
See also CA 103; CANR 46; DFS 7

Rich, Adrienne (Cecile) 1929- ... **CLC 3, 6, 7,
11, 18, 36, 73, 76, 125; PC 5**
See also AMWR 2; AMWS 1; CA 9-12R;
CANR 20, 53, 74, 128; CDALBS; CP 7;
CSW; CWP; DA3; DAM POET; DLB 5,
67; EWL 3; EXPP; FW; MAWW; MTCW
1, 2; PAB; PFS 15; RGAL 4; WP

Rich, Barbara
See Graves, Robert (von Ranke)

Rich, Robert
See Trumbo, Dalton

Richard, Keith .... **CLC 17**
See Richards, Keith

Richards, David Adams 1950- .... **CLC 59**
See also CA 93-96; CANR 60, 110; DAC;
DLB 53

Richards, I(vor) A(rmstrong)
1893-1979 .... **CLC 14, 24**
See also BRWS 2; CA 41-44R; 89-92;
CANR 34, 74; DLB 27; EWL 3; MTCW
2; RGEL 2

Richards, Keith 1943-
See Richard, Keith
See also CA 107; CANR 77

Richardson, Anne
See Roiphe, Anne (Richardson)

Richardson, Dorothy Miller
1873-1957 .... **TCLC 3**
See also CA 104; 192; DLB 36; EWL 3;
FW; RGEL 2

**Richardson (Robertson), Ethel Florence
Lindesay** 1870-1946
See Richardson, Henry Handel
See also CA 105; 190; DLB 230; RHW

Richardson, Henry Handel .... **TCLC 4**
See Richardson (Robertson), Ethel Florence
Lindesay
See also DLB 197; EWL 3; RGEL 2; RGSF
2

Richardson, John 1796-1852 .... **NCLC 55**
See also CCA 1; DAC; DLB 99

Richardson, Samuel 1689-1761 ...... **LC 1, 44;
WLC**
See also BRW 3; CDBLB 1660-1789; DA;
DAB; DAC; DAM MST, NOV; DLB 39;
RGEL 2; TEA; WLIT 3

Richardson, Willis 1889-1977 .... **HR 3**
See also BW 1; CA 124; DLB 51; SATA 60

Richler, Mordecai 1931-2001 .... **CLC 3, 5, 9,
13, 18, 46, 70, 185**
See also AITN 1; CA 65-68; 201; CANR
31, 62, 111; CCA 1; CLR 17; CWRI 5;
DAC; DAM MST, NOV; DLB 53; EWL
3; MAICYA 1, 2; MTCW 1, 2; RGEL 2;
SATA 44, 98; SATA-Brief 27; TWA

Richter, Conrad (Michael)
1890-1968 .... **CLC 30**
See also AAYA 21; BYA 2; CA 5-8R; 25-
28R; CANR 23; DLB 9, 212; LAIT 1;
MTCW 1, 2; RGAL 4; SATA 3; TCWW
2; TUS; YAW

Ricostranza, Tom
See Ellis, Trey

Riddell, Charlotte 1832-1906 .... **TCLC 40**
See Riddell, Mrs. J. H.
See also CA 165; DLB 156

Riddell, Mrs. J. H.
See Riddell, Charlotte
See also HGG; SUFW

Ridge, John Rollin 1827-1867 ...... **NCLC 82;
NNAL**
See also CA 144; DAM MULT; DLB 175

Ridgeway, Jason
See Marlowe, Stephen

Ridgway, Keith 1965- .... **CLC 119**
See also CA 172

Riding, Laura .... **CLC 3, 7**
See Jackson, Laura (Riding)
See also RGAL 4

Riefenstahl, Berta Helene Amalia 1902-2003
See Riefenstahl, Leni
See also CA 108; 220

Riefenstahl, Leni .... **CLC 16, 190**
See Riefenstahl, Berta Helene Amalia

Riffe, Ernest
See Bergman, (Ernst) Ingmar

Riggs, (Rolla) Lynn
1899-1954 .... **NNAL; TCLC 56**
See also CA 144; DAM MULT; DLB 175

Riis, Jacob A(ugust) 1849-1914 ..... **TCLC 80**
See also CA 113; 168; DLB 23

Riley, James Whitcomb 1849-1916 .... **PC 48;
TCLC 51**
See also CA 118; 137; DAM POET; MAI-
CYA 1, 2; RGAL 4; SATA 17

Riley, Tex
See Creasey, John

Rilke, Rainer Maria 1875-1926 .... **PC 2;
TCLC 1, 6, 19**
See also CA 104; 132; CANR 62, 99; CD-
WLB 2; DA3; DAM POET; DLB 81; EW
9; EWL 3; MTCW 1, 2; PFS 19; RGWL
2, 3; TWA; WP

Rimbaud, (Jean Nicolas) Arthur
1854-1891 ... **NCLC 4, 35, 82; PC 3, 57;
WLC**
See also DA; DA3; DAB; DAC; DAM
MST, POET; DLB 217; EW 7; GFL 1789
to the Present; LMFS 2; RGWL 2, 3;
TWA; WP

Rinehart, Mary Roberts
1876-1958 .... **TCLC 52**
See also BPFB 3; CA 108; 166; RGAL 4;
RHW

Ringmaster, The
See Mencken, H(enry) L(ouis)

Ringwood, Gwen(dolyn Margaret) Pharis
1910-1984 .... **CLC 48**
See also CA 148; 112; DLB 88

Rio, Michel 1945(?)- .... **CLC 43**
See also CA 201

Rios, Alberto (Alvaro) 1952- .... **PC 57**
See also AMWS 4; CA 113; CANR 34, 79;
CP 7; DLB 122; HW 2; PFS 11

Ritsos, Giannes
See Ritsos, Yannis

Ritsos, Yannis 1909-1990 .... **CLC 6, 13, 31**
See also CA 77-80; 133; CANR 39, 61; EW
12; EWL 3; MTCW 1; RGWL 2, 3

Ritter, Erika 1948(?)- .... **CLC 52**
See also CD 5; CWD

Rivera, Jose Eustasio 1889-1928 ... **TCLC 35**
See also CA 162; EWL 3; HW 1, 2; LAW

Rivera, Tomas 1935-1984 .... **HLCS 2**
See also CA 49-52; CANR 32; DLB 82;
HW 1; LLW 1; RGAL 4; SSFS 15;
TCWW 2; WLIT 1

Rivers, Conrad Kent 1933-1968 .... **CLC 1**
See also BW 1; CA 85-88; DLB 41

Rivers, Elfrida
See Bradley, Marion Zimmer
See also GLL 1

Riverside, John
See Heinlein, Robert A(nson)

Rizal, Jose 1861-1896 .... **NCLC 27**

Roa Bastos, Augusto (Antonio)
1917- .... **CLC 45; HLC 2**
See also CA 131; CWW 2; DAM MULT;
DLB 113; EWL 3; HW 1; LAW; RGSF 2;
WLIT 1

Robbe-Grillet, Alain 1922- .... **CLC 1, 2, 4, 6,
8, 10, 14, 43, 128**
See also BPFB 3; CA 9-12R; CANR 33,
65, 115; CWW 2; DLB 83; EW 13; EWL
3; GFL 1789 to the Present; IDFW 3, 4;
MTCW 1, 2; RGWL 2, 3; SSFS 15

Robbins, Harold 1916-1997 .... **CLC 5**
See also BPFB 3; CA 73-76; 162; CANR
26, 54, 112; DA3; DAM NOV; MTCW 1,
2

Robbins, Thomas Eugene 1936-
See Robbins, Tom
See also CA 81-84; CANR 29, 59, 95; CN
7; CPW; CSW; DA3; DAM NOV, POP;
MTCW 1, 2

Robbins, Tom .... **CLC 9, 32, 64**
See Robbins, Thomas Eugene
See also AAYA 32; AMWS 10; BEST 90:3;
BPFB 3; DLBY 1980; MTCW 2

Robbins, Trina 1938- .... **CLC 21**
See also CA 128

Roberts, Charles G(eorge) D(ouglas)
1860-1943 .... **TCLC 8**
See also CA 105; 188; CLR 33; CWRI 5;
DLB 92; RGEL 2; RGSF 2; SATA 88;
SATA-Brief 29

Roberts, Elizabeth Madox
1886-1941 .... **TCLC 68**
See also CA 111; 166; CLR 100; CWRI 5;
DLB 9, 54, 102; RGAL 4; RHW; SATA
33; SATA-Brief 27; WCH

Roberts, Kate 1891-1985 .... **CLC 15**
See also CA 107; 116

Roberts, Keith (John Kingston)
1935-2000 .... **CLC 14**
See also BRWS 10; CA 25-28R; CANR 46;
DLB 261; SFW 4

Roberts, Kenneth (Lewis)
1885-1957 .... **TCLC 23**
See also CA 109; 199; DLB 9; RGAL 4;
RHW

Roberts, Michele (Brigitte) 1949- .... **CLC 48,
178**
See also CA 115; CANR 58, 120; CN 7;
DLB 231; FW

Robertson, Ellis
See Ellison, Harlan (Jay); Silverberg, Robert

Robertson, Thomas William
1829-1871 .... **NCLC 35**
See Robertson, Tom
See also DAM DRAM

Robertson, Tom
See Robertson, Thomas William
See also RGEL 2

Robeson, Kenneth
See Dent, Lester

Robinson, Edwin Arlington
1869-1935 .... **PC 1, 35; TCLC 5, 101**
See also AMW; CA 104; 133; CDALB
1865-1917; DA; DAC; DAM MST,
POET; DLB 54; EWL 3; EXPP; MTCW
1, 2; PAB; PFS 4; RGAL 4; WP

Robinson, Henry Crabb
1775-1867 .... **NCLC 15**
See also DLB 107

Robinson, Jill 1936- .... **CLC 10**
See also CA 102; CANR 120; INT CA-102

Robinson, Kim Stanley 1952- .... **CLC 34**
See also AAYA 26; CA 126; CANR 113;
CN 7; SATA 109; SCFW 2; SFW 4

Robinson, Lloyd
See Silverberg, Robert

Robinson, Marilynne 1944- ...... **CLC 25, 180**
See also CA 116; CANR 80; CN 7; DLB
206

Robinson, Mary 1758-1800 .... **NCLC 142**
See also DLB 158; FW

Robinson, Smokey .... **CLC 21**
See Robinson, William, Jr.

Robinson, William, Jr. 1940-
See Robinson, Smokey
See also CA 116

Robison, Mary 1949- .... **CLC 42, 98**
See also CA 113; 116; CANR 87; CN 7;
DLB 130; INT CA-116; RGSF 2

Rochester
See Wilmot, John
See also RGEL 2

Rod, Edouard 1857-1910 .... **TCLC 52**

Roddenberry, Eugene Wesley 1921-1991
See Roddenberry, Gene
See also CA 110; 135; CANR 37; SATA 45;
SATA-Obit 69

Roddenberry, Gene .... **CLC 17**
See Roddenberry, Eugene Wesley
See also AAYA 5; SATA-Obit 69

Rodgers, Mary 1931- .... **CLC 12**
See also BYA 5; CA 49-52; CANR 8, 55,
90; CLR 20; CWRI 5; INT CANR-8;
JRDA; MAICYA 1, 2; SATA 8, 130

Rodgers, W(illiam) R(obert)
1909-1969 .... **CLC 7**
See also CA 85-88; DLB 20; RGEL 2

Rodman, Eric
See Silverberg, Robert

Rodman, Howard 1920(?)-1985 .... **CLC 65**
See also CA 118

Rodman, Maia
See Wojciechowska, Maia (Teresa)

Rodo, Jose Enrique 1871(?)-1917 .... **HLCS 2**
See also CA 178; EWL 3; HW 2; LAW

Rodolph, Utto
See Ouologuem, Yambo

Rodriguez, Claudio 1934-1999 .... **CLC 10**
See also CA 188; DLB 134

Rodriguez, Richard 1944- .... **CLC 155; HLC
2**
See also AMWS 14; CA 110; CANR 66,
116; DAM MULT; DLB 82, 256; HW 1,
2; LAIT 5; LLW 1; NCFS 3; WLIT 1

Roelvaag, O(le) E(dvart) 1876-1931
See Rolvaag, O(le) E(dvart)
See also CA 117; 171

Roethke, Theodore (Huebner)
1908-1963 .... **CLC 1, 3, 8, 11, 19, 46,
101; PC 15**
See also AMW; CA 81-84; CABS 2;
CDALB 1941-1968; DA3; DAM POET;
DLB 5, 206; EWL 3; EXPP; MTCW 1, 2;
PAB; PFS 3; RGAL 4; WP

Rogers, Carl R(ansom)
1902-1987 .... **TCLC 125**
See also CA 1-4R; 121; CANR 1, 18;
MTCW 1

Rogers, Samuel 1763-1855 .... **NCLC 69**
See also DLB 93; RGEL 2

Rogers, Thomas Hunton 1927- .... **CLC 57**
See also CA 89-92; INT CA-89-92

Rogers, Will(iam Penn Adair)
1879-1935 .... **NNAL; TCLC 8, 71**
See also CA 105; 144; DA3; DAM MULT;
DLB 11; MTCW 2

Rogin, Gilbert 1929- .... **CLC 18**
See also CA 65-68; CANR 15

Rohan, Koda
See Koda Shigeyuki

Rohlfs, Anna Katharine Green
See Green, Anna Katharine

Rohmer, Eric .... **CLC 16**
See Scherer, Jean-Marie Maurice

Rohmer, Sax .... **TCLC 28**
See Ward, Arthur Henry Sarsfield
See also DLB 70; MSW; SUFW

Roiphe, Anne (Richardson) 1935- .. **CLC 3, 9**
See also CA 89-92; CANR 45, 73; DLBY
1980; INT CA-89-92

Rojas, Fernando de 1475-1541 ... **HLCS 1, 2;
LC 23**
See also DLB 286; RGWL 2, 3

Rojas, Gonzalo 1917- .... **HLCS 2**
See also CA 178; HW 2; LAWS 1

Roland, Marie-Jeanne 1754-1793 .... **LC 98**

**Rolfe, Frederick (William Serafino Austin
Lewis Mary)** 1860-1913 .... **TCLC 12**
See Al Siddik
See also CA 107; 210; DLB 34, 156; RGEL
2

Rolland, Romain 1866-1944 .... **TCLC 23**
See also CA 118; 197; DLB 65, 284; EWL
3; GFL 1789 to the Present; RGWL 2, 3

Rolle, Richard c. 1300-c. 1349 ...... **CMLC 21**
See also DLB 146; LMFS 1; RGEL 2

Rolvaag, O(le) E(dvart) .... **TCLC 17**
See Roelvaag, O(le) E(dvart)
See also DLB 9, 212; NFS 5; RGAL 4

Romain Arnaud, Saint
See Aragon, Louis

Romains, Jules 1885-1972 .... **CLC 7**
See also CA 85-88; CANR 34; DLB 65;
EWL 3; GFL 1789 to the Present; MTCW
1

Romero, Jose Ruben 1890-1952 .... **TCLC 14**
See also CA 114; 131; EWL 3; HW 1; LAW

Ronsard, Pierre de 1524-1585 . **LC 6, 54; PC
11**
See also EW 2; GFL Beginnings to 1789;
RGWL 2, 3; TWA

Rooke, Leon 1934- .... **CLC 25, 34**
See also CA 25-28R; CANR 23, 53; CCA
1; CPW; DAM POP

Roosevelt, Franklin Delano
1882-1945 .... **TCLC 93**
See also CA 116; 173; LAIT 3

Roosevelt, Theodore 1858-1919 ..... **TCLC 69**
See also CA 115; 170; DLB 47, 186, 275

Roper, William 1498-1578 .... **LC 10**

Roquelaure, A. N.
See Rice, Anne

Rosa, Joao Guimaraes 1908-1967 ... **CLC 23;
HLCS 1**
See Guimaraes Rosa, Joao
See also CA 89-92; DLB 113, 307; EWL 3;
WLIT 1

Rose, Wendy 1948- . **CLC 85; NNAL; PC 13**
See also CA 53-56; CANR 5, 51; CWP;
DAM MULT; DLB 175; PFS 13; RGAL
4; SATA 12

Rosen, R. D.
See Rosen, Richard (Dean)

Rosen, Richard (Dean) 1949- .... **CLC 39**
See also CA 77-80; CANR 62, 120; CMW
4; INT CANR-30

Rosenberg, Isaac 1890-1918 .... **TCLC 12**
See also BRW 6; CA 107; 188; DLB 20,
216; EWL 3; PAB; RGEL 2

Rosenblatt, Joe .... **CLC 15**
See Rosenblatt, Joseph

Rosenblatt, Joseph 1933-
See Rosenblatt, Joe
See also CA 89-92; CP 7; INT CA-89-92

Rosenfeld, Samuel
See Tzara, Tristan

Rosenstock, Sami
See Tzara, Tristan

Rosenstock, Samuel
See Tzara, Tristan

Rosenthal, M(acha) L(ouis)
1917-1996 .... **CLC 28**
See also CA 1-4R; 152; CAAS 6; CANR 4,
51; CP 7; DLB 5; SATA 59

Ross, Barnaby
See Dannay, Frederic

Ross, Bernard L.
See Follett, Ken(neth Martin)

Ross, J. H.
See Lawrence, T(homas) E(dward)

Ross, John Hume
See Lawrence, T(homas) E(dward)

Ross, Martin 1862-1915
See Martin, Violet Florence
See also DLB 135; GLL 2; RGEL 2; RGSF 2

Ross, (James) Sinclair 1908-1996 ... **CLC 13; SSC 24**
See also CA 73-76; CANR 81; CN 7; DAC; DAM MST; DLB 88; RGEL 2; RGSF 2; TCWW 2

Rossetti, Christina (Georgina) 1830-1894 .... **NCLC 2, 50, 66; PC 7; WLC**
See also AAYA 51; BRW 5; BYA 4; DA; DA3; DAB; DAC; DAM MST, POET; DLB 35, 163, 240; EXPP; LATS 1:1; MAICYA 1, 2; PFS 10, 14; RGEL 2; SATA 20; TEA; WCH

Rossetti, Dante Gabriel 1828-1882 . **NCLC 4, 77; PC 44; WLC**
See also AAYA 51; BRW 5; CDBLB 1832-1890; DA; DAB; DAC; DAM MST, POET; DLB 35; EXPP; RGEL 2; TEA

Rossi, Cristina Peri
See Peri Rossi, Cristina

Rossi, Jean-Baptiste 1931-2003
See Japrisot, Sebastien
See also CA 201; 215

Rossner, Judith (Perelman) 1935- . **CLC 6, 9, 29**
See also AITN 2; BEST 90:3; BPFB 3; CA 17-20R; CANR 18, 51, 73; CN 7; DLB 6; INT CANR-18; MTCW 1, 2

Rostand, Edmond (Eugene Alexis) 1868-1918 .... **DC 10; TCLC 6, 37**
See also CA 104; 126; DA; DA3; DAB; DAC; DAM DRAM, MST; DFS 1; DLB 192; LAIT 1; MTCW 1; RGWL 2, 3; TWA

Roth, Henry 1906-1995 ..... **CLC 2, 6, 11, 104**
See also AMWS 9; CA 11-12; 149; CANR 38, 63; CAP 1; CN 7; DA3; DLB 28; EWL 3; MTCW 1, 2; RGAL 4

Roth, (Moses) Joseph 1894-1939 ... **TCLC 33**
See also CA 160; DLB 85; EWL 3; RGWL 2, 3

Roth, Philip (Milton) 1933- ... **CLC 1, 2, 3, 4, 6, 9, 15, 22, 31, 47, 66, 86, 119; SSC 26; WLC**
See also AMWR 2; AMWS 3; BEST 90:3; BPFB 3; CA 1-4R; CANR 1, 22, 36, 55, 89, 132; CDALB 1968-1988; CN 7; CPW 1; DA; DA3; DAB; DAC; DAM MST, NOV, POP; DLB 2, 28, 173; DLBY 1982; EWL 3; MTCW 1, 2; RGAL 4; RGSF 2; SSFS 12, 18; TUS

Rothenberg, Jerome 1931- .... **CLC 6, 57**
See also CA 45-48; CANR 1, 106; CP 7; DLB 5, 193

Rotter, Pat ed. .... **CLC 65**

Roumain, Jacques (Jean Baptiste) 1907-1944 .... **BLC 3; TCLC 19**
See also BW 1; CA 117; 125; DAM MULT; EWL 3

Rourke, Constance Mayfield 1885-1941 .... **TCLC 12**
See also CA 107; 200; YABC 1

Rousseau, Jean-Baptiste 1671-1741 ...... **LC 9**

Rousseau, Jean-Jacques 1712-1778 .... **LC 14, 36; WLC**
See also DA; DA3; DAB; DAC; DAM MST; EW 4; GFL Beginnings to 1789; LMFS 1; RGWL 2, 3; TWA

Roussel, Raymond 1877-1933 .... **TCLC 20**
See also CA 117; 201; EWL 3; GFL 1789 to the Present

Rovit, Earl (Herbert) 1927- .... **CLC 7**
See also CA 5-8R; CANR 12

Rowe, Elizabeth Singer 1674-1737 ..... **LC 44**
See also DLB 39, 95

Rowe, Nicholas 1674-1718 .... **LC 8**
See also DLB 84; RGEL 2

Rowlandson, Mary 1637(?)-1678 .... **LC 66**
See also DLB 24, 200; RGAL 4

Rowley, Ames Dorrance
See Lovecraft, H(oward) P(hillips)

Rowley, William 1585(?)-1626 .... **LC 100**
See also DLB 58; RGEL 2

Rowling, J(oanne) K(athleen) 1966- .... **CLC 137**
See also AAYA 34; BYA 11, 13, 14; CA 173; CANR 128; CLR 66, 80; MAICYA 2; SATA 109; SUFW 2

Rowson, Susanna Haswell 1762(?)-1824 .... **NCLC 5, 69**
See also DLB 37, 200; RGAL 4

Roy, Arundhati 1960(?)- .... **CLC 109**
See also CA 163; CANR 90, 126; DLBY 1997; EWL 3; LATS 1:2; WWE 1

Roy, Gabrielle 1909-1983 .... **CLC 10, 14**
See also CA 53-56; 110; CANR 5, 61; CCA 1; DAB; DAC; DAM MST; DLB 68; EWL 3; MTCW 1; RGWL 2, 3; SATA 104

Royko, Mike 1932-1997 .... **CLC 109**
See also CA 89-92; 157; CANR 26, 111; CPW

Rozanov, Vasilii Vasil'evich
See Rozanov, Vassili
See also DLB 295

Rozanov, Vasily Vasilyevich
See Rozanov, Vassili
See also EWL 3

Rozanov, Vassili 1856-1919 .... **TCLC 104**
See Rozanov, Vasilii Vasil'evich; Rozanov, Vasily Vasilyevich

Rozewicz, Tadeusz 1921- ...... **CLC 9, 23, 139**
See also CA 108; CANR 36, 66; CWW 2; DA3; DAM POET; DLB 232; EWL 3; MTCW 1, 2; RGWL 3

Ruark, Gibbons 1941- .... **CLC 3**
See also CA 33-36R; CAAS 23; CANR 14, 31, 57; DLB 120

Rubens, Bernice (Ruth) 1923-2004 . **CLC 19, 31**
See also CA 25-28R; CANR 33, 65, 128; CN 7; DLB 14, 207; MTCW 1

Rubin, Harold
See Robbins, Harold

Rudkin, (James) David 1936- .... **CLC 14**
See also CA 89-92; CBD; CD 5; DLB 13

Rudnik, Raphael 1933- .... **CLC 7**
See also CA 29-32R

Ruffian, M.
See Hasek, Jaroslav (Matej Frantisek)

Ruiz, Jose Martinez .... **CLC 11**
See Martinez Ruiz, Jose

Ruiz, Juan c. 1283-c. 1350 .... **CMLC 66**

Rukeyser, Muriel 1913-1980 . **CLC 6, 10, 15, 27; PC 12**
See also AMWS 6; CA 5-8R; 93-96; CANR 26, 60; DA3; DAM POET; DLB 48; EWL 3; FW; GLL 2; MTCW 1, 2; PFS 10; RGAL 4; SATA-Obit 22

Rule, Jane (Vance) 1931- .... **CLC 27**
See also CA 25-28R; CAAS 18; CANR 12, 87; CN 7; DLB 60; FW

Rulfo, Juan 1918-1986 .. **CLC 8, 80; HLC 2; SSC 25**
See also CA 85-88; 118; CANR 26; CD-WLB 3; DAM MULT; DLB 113; EWL 3; HW 1, 2; LAW; MTCW 1, 2; RGSF 2; RGWL 2, 3; WLIT 1

Rumi, Jalal al-Din 1207-1273 ...... **CMLC 20; PC 45**
See also RGWL 2, 3; WP

Runeberg, Johan 1804-1877 .... **NCLC 41**

Runyon, (Alfred) Damon 1884(?)-1946 .... **TCLC 10**
See also CA 107; 165; DLB 11, 86, 171; MTCW 2; RGAL 4

Rush, Norman 1933- .... **CLC 44**
See also CA 121; 126; CANR 130; INT CA-126

Rushdie, (Ahmed) Salman 1947- .... **CLC 23, 31, 55, 100, 191; WLCS**
See also BEST 89:3; BPFB 3; BRWS 4; CA 108; 111; CANR 33, 56, 108, 133; CN 7; CPW 1; DA3; DAB; DAC; DAM MST, NOV, POP; DLB 194; EWL 3; FANT; INT CA-111; LATS 1:2; LMFS 2; MTCW 1, 2; RGEL 2; RGSF 2; TEA; WLIT 4; WWE 1

Rushforth, Peter (Scott) 1945- .... **CLC 19**
See also CA 101

Ruskin, John 1819-1900 .... **TCLC 63**
See also BRW 5; BYA 5; CA 114; 129; CD-BLB 1832-1890; DLB 55, 163, 190; RGEL 2; SATA 24; TEA; WCH

Russ, Joanna 1937- .... **CLC 15**
See also BPFB 3; CA 5-28R; CANR 11, 31, 65; CN 7; DLB 8; FW; GLL 1; MTCW 1; SCFW 2; SFW 4

Russ, Richard Patrick
See O'Brian, Patrick

Russell, George William 1867-1935
See A.E.; Baker, Jean H.
See also BRWS 8; CA 104; 153; CDBLB 1890-1914; DAM POET; EWL 3; RGEL 2

Russell, Jeffrey Burton 1934- .... **CLC 70**
See also CA 25-28R; CANR 11, 28, 52

Russell, (Henry) Ken(neth Alfred) 1927- .... **CLC 16**
See also CA 105

Russell, William Martin 1947-
See Russell, Willy
See also CA 164; CANR 107

Russell, Willy .... **CLC 60**
See Russell, William Martin
See also CBD; CD 5; DLB 233

Russo, Richard 1949- .... **CLC 181**
See also AMWS 12; CA 127; 133; CANR 87, 114

Rutherford, Mark .... **TCLC 25**
See White, William Hale
See also DLB 18; RGEL 2

Ruyslinck, Ward .... **CLC 14**
See Belser, Reimond Karel Maria de

Ryan, Cornelius (John) 1920-1974 ..... **CLC 7**
See also CA 69-72; 53-56; CANR 38

Ryan, Michael 1946- .... **CLC 65**
See also CA 49-52; CANR 109; DLBY 1982

Ryan, Tim
See Dent, Lester

Rybakov, Anatoli (Naumovich) 1911-1998 .... **CLC 23, 53**
See Rybakov, Anatolii (Naumovich)
See also CA 126; 135; 172; SATA 79; SATA-Obit 108

Rybakov, Anatolii (Naumovich)
See Rybakov, Anatoli (Naumovich)
See also DLB 302

Ryder, Jonathan
See Ludlum, Robert

Ryga, George 1932-1987 .... **CLC 14**
See also CA 101; 124; CANR 43, 90; CCA 1; DAC; DAM MST; DLB 60

S. H.
See Hartmann, Sadakichi

S. S.
See Sassoon, Siegfried (Lorraine)

Sa'adawi, al- Nawal
See El Saadawi, Nawal
See also AFW; EWL 3
Saadawi, Nawal El
See El Saadawi, Nawal
See also WLIT 2
Saba, Umberto 1883-1957 .... **TCLC 33**
See also CA 144; CANR 79; DLB 114;
EWL 3; RGWL 2, 3
Sabatini, Rafael 1875-1950 .... **TCLC 47**
See also BPFB 3; CA 162; RHW
Sabato, Ernesto (R.) 1911- .... **CLC 10, 23;
HLC 2**
See also CA 97-100; CANR 32, 65; CD-
WLB 3; CWW 2; DAM MULT; DLB 145;
EWL 3; HW 1, 2; LAW; MTCW 1, 2
Sa-Carneiro, Mario de 1890-1916 . **TCLC 83**
See also DLB 287; EWL 3
Sacastru, Martin
See Bioy Casares, Adolfo
See also CWW 2
Sacher-Masoch, Leopold von
1836(?)-1895 .... **NCLC 31**
Sachs, Hans 1494-1576 .... **LC 95**
See also CDWLB 2; DLB 179; RGWL 2, 3
Sachs, Marilyn (Stickle) 1927- .... **CLC 35**
See also AAYA 2; BYA 6; CA 17-20R;
CANR 13, 47; CLR 2; JRDA; MAICYA
1, 2; SAAS 2; SATA 3, 68; SATA-Essay
110; WYA; YAW
Sachs, Nelly 1891-1970 .... **CLC 14, 98**
See also CA 17-18; 25-28R; CANR 87;
CAP 2; EWL 3; MTCW 2; PFS 20;
RGWL 2, 3
Sackler, Howard (Oliver)
1929-1982 .... **CLC 14**
See also CA 61-64; 108; CAD; CANR 30;
DFS 15; DLB 7
Sacks, Oliver (Wolf) 1933- .... **CLC 67**
See also CA 53-56; CANR 28, 50, 76;
CPW; DA3; INT CANR-28; MTCW 1, 2
Sackville, Thomas 1536-1608 .... **LC 98**
See also DAM DRAM; DLB 62, 132;
RGEL 2
Sadakichi
See Hartmann, Sadakichi
Sa'dawi, Nawal al-
See El Saadawi, Nawal
See also CWW 2
Sade, Donatien Alphonse Francois
1740-1814 .... **NCLC 3, 47**
See also EW 4; GFL Beginnings to 1789;
RGWL 2, 3
Sade, Marquis de
See Sade, Donatien Alphonse Francois
Sadoff, Ira 1945- .... **CLC 9**
See also CA 53-56; CANR 5, 21, 109; DLB
120
Saetone
See Camus, Albert
Safire, William 1929- .... **CLC 10**
See also CA 17-20R; CANR 31, 54, 91
Sagan, Carl (Edward) 1934-1996 .... **CLC 30,
112**
See also AAYA 2; CA 25-28R; 155; CANR
11, 36, 74; CPW; DA3; MTCW 1, 2;
SATA 58; SATA-Obit 94
Sagan, Francoise .... **CLC 3, 6, 9, 17, 36**
See Quoirez, Francoise
See also CWW 2; DLB 83; EWL 3; GFL
1789 to the Present; MTCW 2
Sahgal, Nayantara (Pandit) 1927- .... **CLC 41**
See also CA 9-12R; CANR 11, 88; CN 7
Said, Edward W. 1935-2003 .... **CLC 123**
See also CA 21-24R; 220; CANR 45, 74,
107, 131; DLB 67; MTCW 2
Saint, H(arry) F. 1941- .... **CLC 50**
See also CA 127

St. Aubin de Teran, Lisa 1953-
See Teran, Lisa St. Aubin de
See also CA 118; 126; CN 7; INT CA-126
Saint Birgitta of Sweden c.
1303-1373 .... **CMLC 24**
Sainte-Beuve, Charles Augustin
1804-1869 .... **NCLC 5**
See also DLB 217; EW 6; GFL 1789 to the
Present
**Saint-Exupery, Antoine (Jean Baptiste
Marie Roger) de** 1900-1944 .... **TCLC 2,
56; WLC**
See also BPFB 3; BYA 3; CA 108; 132;
CLR 10; DA3; DAM NOV; DLB 72; EW
12; EWL 3; GFL 1789 to the Present;
LAIT 3; MAICYA 1, 2; MTCW 1, 2;
RGWL 2, 3; SATA 20; TWA
St. John, David
See Hunt, E(verette) Howard, (Jr.)
St. John, J. Hector
See Crevecoeur, Michel Guillaume Jean de
Saint-John Perse
See Leger, (Marie-Rene Auguste) Alexis
Saint-Leger
See also EW 10; EWL 3; GFL 1789 to the
Present; RGWL 2
Saintsbury, George (Edward Bateman)
1845-1933 .... **TCLC 31**
See also CA 160; DLB 57, 149
Sait Faik .... **TCLC 23**
See Abasiyanik, Sait Faik
Saki .... **SSC 12; TCLC 3**
See Munro, H(ector) H(ugh)
See also BRWS 6; BYA 11; LAIT 2; MTCW
2; RGEL 2; SSFS 1; SUFW
Sala, George Augustus 1828-1895 . **NCLC 46**
Saladin 1138-1193 .... **CMLC 38**
Salama, Hannu 1936- .... **CLC 18**
See also EWL 3
Salamanca, J(ack) R(ichard) 1922- .. **CLC 4,
15**
See also CA 25-28R, 193; CAAE 193
Salas, Floyd Francis 1931- .... **HLC 2**
See also CA 119; CAAS 27; CANR 44, 75,
93; DAM MULT; DLB 82; HW 1, 2;
MTCW 2
Sale, J. Kirkpatrick
See Sale, Kirkpatrick
Sale, Kirkpatrick 1937- .... **CLC 68**
See also CA 13-16R; CANR 10
Salinas, Luis Omar 1937- ...... **CLC 90; HLC 2**
See also AMWS 13; CA 131; CANR 81;
DAM MULT; DLB 82; HW 1, 2
Salinas (y Serrano), Pedro
1891(?)-1951 .... **TCLC 17**
See also CA 117; DLB 134; EWL 3
Salinger, J(erome) D(avid) 1919- .. **CLC 1, 3,
8, 12, 55, 56, 138; SSC 2, 28, 65; WLC**
See also AAYA 2, 36; AMW; AMWC 1;
BPFB 3; CA 5-8R; CANR 39, 129;
CDALB 1941-1968; CLR 18; CN 7; CPW
1; DA; DA3; DAB; DAC; DAM MST,
NOV, POP; DLB 2, 102, 173; EWL 3;
EXPN; LAIT 4; MAICYA 1, 2; MTCW
1, 2; NFS 1; RGAL 4; RGSF 2; SATA 67;
SSFS 17; TUS; WYA; YAW
Salisbury, John
See Caute, (John) David
Sallust c. 86B.C.-35B.C. .... **CMLC 68**
See also AW; CDWLB 1; DLB 211;
RGWL 2, 3
Salter, James 1925- .. **CLC 7, 52, 59; SSC 58**
See also AMWS 9; CA 73-76; CANR 107;
DLB 130
Saltus, Edgar (Everton) 1855-1921 . **TCLC 8**
See also CA 105; DLB 202; RGAL 4
Saltykov, Mikhail Evgrafovich
1826-1889 .... **NCLC 16**
See also DLB 238:

Saltykov-Shchedrin, N.
See Saltykov, Mikhail Evgrafovich
Samarakis, Andonis
See Samarakis, Antonis
See also EWL 3
Samarakis, Antonis 1919-2003 .... **CLC 5**
See Samarakis, Andonis
See also CA 25-28R; 224; CAAS 16; CANR
36
Sanchez, Florencio 1875-1910 .... **TCLC 37**
See also CA 153; DLB 305; EWL 3; HW 1;
LAW
Sanchez, Luis Rafael 1936- .... **CLC 23**
See also CA 128; DLB 305; EWL 3; HW 1;
WLIT 1
Sanchez, Sonia 1934- .... **BLC 3; CLC 5, 116;
PC 9**
See also BW 2, 3; CA 33-36R; CANR 24,
49, 74, 115; CLR 18; CP 7; CSW; CWP;
DA3; DAM MULT; DLB 41; DLBD 8;
EWL 3; MAICYA 1, 2; MTCW 1, 2;
SATA 22, 136; WP
Sancho, Ignatius 1729-1780 .... **LC 84**
Sand, George 1804-1876 ..... **NCLC 2, 42, 57;
WLC**
See also DA; DA3; DAB; DAC; DAM
MST, NOV; DLB 119, 192; EW 6; FW;
GFL 1789 to the Present; RGWL 2, 3;
TWA
Sandburg, Carl (August) 1878-1967 . **CLC 1,
4, 10, 15, 35; PC 2, 41; WLC**
See also AAYA 24; AMW; BYA 1, 3; CA
5-8R; 25-28R; CANR 35; CDALB 1865-
1917; CLR 67; DA; DA3; DAB; DAC;
DAM MST, POET; DLB 17, 54, 284;
EWL 3; EXPP; LAIT 2; MAICYA 1, 2;
MTCW 1, 2; PAB; PFS 3, 6, 12; RGAL
4; SATA 8; TUS; WCH; WP; WYA
Sandburg, Charles
See Sandburg, Carl (August)
Sandburg, Charles A.
See Sandburg, Carl (August)
Sanders, (James) Ed(ward) 1939- .... **CLC 53**
See Sanders, Edward
See also BG 3; CA 13-16R; CAAS 21;
CANR 13, 44, 78; CP 7; DAM POET;
DLB 16, 244
Sanders, Edward
See Sanders, (James) Ed(ward)
See also DLB 244
Sanders, Lawrence 1920-1998 .... **CLC 41**
See also BEST 89:4; BPFB 3; CA 81-84;
165; CANR 33, 62; CMW 4; CPW; DA3;
DAM POP; MTCW 1
Sanders, Noah
See Blount, Roy (Alton), Jr.
Sanders, Winston P.
See Anderson, Poul (William)
Sandoz, Mari(e Susette) 1900-1966 .. **CLC 28**
See also CA 1-4R; 25-28R; CANR 17, 64;
DLB 9, 212; LAIT 2; MTCW 1, 2; SATA
5; TCWW 2
Sandys, George 1578-1644 .... **LC 80**
See also DLB 24, 121
Saner, Reg(inald Anthony) 1931- .... **CLC 9**
See also CA 65-68; CP 7
Sankara 788-820 .... **CMLC 32**
Sannazaro, Jacopo 1456(?)-1530 .... **LC 8**
See also RGWL 2, 3
Sansom, William 1912-1976 . **CLC 2, 6; SSC
21**
See also CA 5-8R; 65-68; CANR 42; DAM
NOV; DLB 139; EWL 3; MTCW 1;
RGEL 2; RGSF 2
Santayana, George 1863-1952 .... **TCLC 40**
See also AMW; CA 115; 194; DLB 54, 71,
246, 270; DLBD 13; EWL 3; RGAL 4;
TUS

Santiago, Danny .... **CLC 33**
See James, Daniel (Lewis)
See also DLB 122

Santmyer, Helen Hooven
1895-1986 .... **CLC 33; TCLC 133**
See also CA 1-4R; 118; CANR 15, 33;
DLBY 1984; MTCW 1; RHW

Santoka, Taneda 1882-1940 .... **TCLC 72**

Santos, Bienvenido N(uqui)
1911-1996 ... **AAL; CLC 22; TCLC 156**
See also CA 101; 151; CANR 19, 46; DAM
MULT; EWL; RGAL 4; SSFS 19

Sapir, Edward 1884-1939 .... **TCLC 108**
See also CA 211; DLB 92

Sapper .... **TCLC 44**
See McNeile, Herman Cyril

Sapphire
See Sapphire, Brenda

Sapphire, Brenda 1950- .... **CLC 99**

Sappho fl. 6th cent. B.C.- ... **CMLC 3, 67; PC
5**
See also CDWLB 1; DA3; DAM POET;
DLB 176; PFS 20; RGWL 2, 3; WP

Saramago, Jose 1922- ..... **CLC 119; HLCS 1**
See also CA 153; CANR 96; CWW 2; DLB
287; EWL 3; LATS 1:2

Sarduy, Severo 1937-1993 .... **CLC 6, 97;
HLCS 2**
See also CA 89-92; 142; CANR 58, 81;
CWW 2; DLB 113; EWL 3; HW 1, 2;
LAW

Sargeson, Frank 1903-1982 .... **CLC 31**
See also CA 25-28R; 106; CANR 38, 79;
EWL 3; GLL 2; RGEL 2; RGSF 2; SSFS
20

Sarmiento, Domingo Faustino
1811-1888 .... **HLCS 2**
See also LAW; WLIT 1

Sarmiento, Felix Ruben Garcia
See Dario, Ruben

Saro-Wiwa, Ken(ule Beeson)
1941-1995 .... **CLC 114**
See also BW 2; CA 142; 150; CANR 60;
DLB 157

Saroyan, William 1908-1981 ... **CLC 1, 8, 10,
29, 34, 56; SSC 21; TCLC 137; WLC**
See also CA 5-8R; 103; CAD; CANR 30;
CDALBS; DA; DA3; DAB; DAC; DAM
DRAM, MST, NOV; DFS 17; DLB 7, 9,
86; DLBY 1981; EWL 3; LAIT 4; MTCW
1, 2; RGAL 4; RGSF 2; SATA 23; SATA-
Obit 24; SSFS 14; TUS

Sarraute, Nathalie 1900-1999 .... **CLC 1, 2, 4,
8, 10, 31, 80; TCLC 145**
See also BPFB 3; CA 9-12R; 187; CANR
23, 66, 134; CWW 2; DLB 83; EW 12;
EWL 3; GFL 1789 to the Present; MTCW
1, 2; RGWL 2, 3

Sarton, (Eleanor) May 1912-1995 ..... **CLC 4,
14, 49, 91; PC 39; TCLC 120**
See also AMWS 8; CA 1-4R; 149; CANR
1, 34, 55, 116; CN 7; CP 7; DAM POET;
DLB 48; DLBY 1981; EWL 3; FW; INT
CANR-34; MTCW 1, 2; RGAL 4; SATA
36; SATA-Obit 86; TUS

Sartre, Jean-Paul 1905-1980 . **CLC 1, 4, 7, 9,
13, 18, 24, 44, 50, 52; DC 3; SSC 32;
WLC**
See also CA 9-12R; 97-100; CANR 21; DA;
DA3; DAB; DAC; DAM DRAM, MST,
NOV; DFS 5; DLB 72, 296; EW 12; EWL
3; GFL 1789 to the Present; LMFS 2;
MTCW 1, 2; RGSF 2; RGWL 2, 3; SSFS
9; TWA

Sassoon, Siegfried (Lorraine)
1886-1967 .... **CLC 36, 130; PC 12**
See also BRW 6; CA 104; 25-28R; CANR
36; DAB; DAM MST, NOV, POET; DLB
20, 191; DLBD 18; EWL 3; MTCW 1, 2;
PAB; RGEL 2; TEA

Satterfield, Charles
See Pohl, Frederik

Satyremont
See Peret, Benjamin

Saul, John (W. III) 1942- .... **CLC 46**
See also AAYA 10; BEST 90:4; CA 81-84;
CANR 16, 40, 81; CPW; DAM NOV,
POP; HGG; SATA 98

Saunders, Caleb
See Heinlein, Robert A(nson)

Saura (Atares), Carlos 1932-1998 .... **CLC 20**
See also CA 114; 131; CANR 79; HW 1

Sauser, Frederic Louis
See Sauser-Hall, Frederic

Sauser-Hall, Frederic 1887-1961 ...... **CLC 18**
See Cendrars, Blaise
See also CA 102; 93-96; CANR 36, 62;
MTCW 1

Saussure, Ferdinand de
1857-1913 .... **TCLC 49**
See also DLB 242

Savage, Catharine
See Brosman, Catharine Savage

Savage, Richard 1697(?)-1743 .... **LC 96**
See also DLB 95; RGEL 2

Savage, Thomas 1915-2003 .... **CLC 40**
See also CA 126; 132; 218; CAAS 15; CN
7; INT CA-132; SATA-Obit 147; TCWW
2

Savan, Glenn 1953-2003 .... **CLC 50**
See also CA 225

Sax, Robert
See Johnson, Robert

Saxo Grammaticus c. 1150-c.
1222 .... **CMLC 58**

Saxton, Robert
See Johnson, Robert

Sayers, Dorothy L(eigh) 1893-1957 . **SSC 71;
TCLC 2, 15**
See also BPFB 3; BRWS 3; CA 104; 119;
CANR 60; CDBLB 1914-1945; CMW 4;
DAM POP; DLB 10, 36, 77, 100; MSW;
MTCW 1, 2; RGEL 2; SSFS 12; TEA

Sayers, Valerie 1952- .... **CLC 50, 122**
See also CA 134; CANR 61; CSW

Sayles, John (Thomas) 1950- .... **CLC 7, 10,
14, 198**
See also CA 57-60; CANR 41, 84; DLB 44

Scammell, Michael 1935- .... **CLC 34**
See also CA 156

Scannell, Vernon 1922- .... **CLC 49**
See also CA 5-8R; CANR 8, 24, 57; CP 7;
CWRI 5; DLB 27; SATA 59

Scarlett, Susan
See Streatfeild, (Mary) Noel

Scarron 1847-1910
See Mikszath, Kalman

Schaeffer, Susan Fromberg 1941- ..... **CLC 6,
11, 22**
See also CA 49-52; CANR 18, 65; CN 7;
DLB 28, 299; MTCW 1, 2; SATA 22

Schama, Simon (Michael) 1945- ..... **CLC 150**
See also BEST 89:4; CA 105; CANR 39,
91

Schary, Jill
See Robinson, Jill

Schell, Jonathan 1943- .... **CLC 35**
See also CA 73-76; CANR 12, 117

Schelling, Friedrich Wilhelm Joseph von
1775-1854 .... **NCLC 30**
See also DLB 90

Scherer, Jean-Marie Maurice 1920-
See Rohmer, Eric
See also CA 110

Schevill, James (Erwin) 1920- .... **CLC 7**
See also CA 5-8R; CAAS 12; CAD; CD 5

Schiller, Friedrich von 1759-1805 ...... **DC 12;
NCLC 39, 69**
See also CDWLB 2; DAM DRAM; DLB
94; EW 5; RGWL 2, 3; TWA

Schisgal, Murray (Joseph) 1926- .... **CLC 6**
See also CA 21-24R; CAD; CANR 48, 86;
CD 5

Schlee, Ann 1934- .... **CLC 35**
See also CA 101; CANR 29, 88; SATA 44;
SATA-Brief 36

Schlegel, August Wilhelm von
1767-1845 .... **NCLC 15, 142**
See also DLB 94; RGWL 2, 3

Schlegel, Friedrich 1772-1829 .... **NCLC 45**
See also DLB 90; EW 5; RGWL 2, 3; TWA

Schlegel, Johann Elias (von)
1719(?)-1749 .... **LC 5**

Schleiermacher, Friedrich
1768-1834 .... **NCLC 107**
See also DLB 90

Schlesinger, Arthur M(eier), Jr.
1917- .... **CLC 84**
See also AITN 1; CA 1-4R; CANR 1, 28,
58, 105; DLB 17; INT CANR-28; MTCW
1, 2; SATA 61

Schlink, Bernhard 1944- .... **CLC 174**
See also CA 163; CANR 116

Schmidt, Arno (Otto) 1914-1979 ...... **CLC 56**
See also CA 128; 109; DLB 69; EWL 3

Schmitz, Aron Hector 1861-1928
See Svevo, Italo
See also CA 104; 122; MTCW 1

Schnackenberg, Gjertrud (Cecelia)
1953- .... **CLC 40; PC 45**
See also CA 116; CANR 100; CP 7; CWP;
DLB 120, 282; PFS 13

Schneider, Leonard Alfred 1925-1966
See Bruce, Lenny
See also CA 89-92

Schnitzler, Arthur 1862-1931 ..... **DC 17; SSC
15, 61; TCLC 4**
See also CA 104; CDWLB 2; DLB 81, 118;
EW 8; EWL 3; RGSF 2; RGWL 2, 3

Schoenberg, Arnold Franz Walter
1874-1951 .... **TCLC 75**
See also CA 109; 188

Schonberg, Arnold
See Schoenberg, Arnold Franz Walter

Schopenhauer, Arthur 1788-1860 .. **NCLC 51**
See also DLB 90; EW 5

Schor, Sandra (M.) 1932(?)-1990 ..... **CLC 65**
See also CA 132

Schorer, Mark 1908-1977 .... **CLC 9**
See also CA 5-8R; 73-76; CANR 7; DLB
103

Schrader, Paul (Joseph) 1946- .... **CLC 26**
See also CA 37-40R; CANR 41; DLB 44

Schreber, Daniel 1842-1911 .... **TCLC 123**

Schreiner, Olive (Emilie Albertina)
1855-1920 .... **TCLC 9**
See also AFW; BRWS 2; CA 105; 154;
DLB 18, 156, 190, 225; EWL 3; FW;
RGEL 2; TWA; WLIT 2; WWE 1

Schulberg, Budd (Wilson) 1914- .. **CLC 7, 48**
See also BPFB 3; CA 25-28R; CANR 19,
87; CN 7; DLB 6, 26, 28; DLBY 1981,
2001

Schulman, Arnold
See Trumbo, Dalton

Schulz, Bruno 1892-1942 .. **SSC 13; TCLC 5,
51**
See also CA 115; 123; CANR 86; CDWLB
4; DLB 215; EWL 3; MTCW 2; RGSF 2;
RGWL 2, 3

Schulz, Charles M(onroe)
1922-2000 .... **CLC 12**
See also AAYA 39; CA 9-12R; 187; CANR
6, 132; INT CANR-6; SATA 10; SATA-
Obit 118

Schumacher, E(rnst) F(riedrich)
    1911-1977 .... **CLC 80**
    See also CA 81-84; 73-76; CANR 34, 85

Schumann, Robert 1810-1856 ...... **NCLC 143**

Schuyler, George Samuel 1895-1977 .... **HR 3**
    See also BW 2; CA 81-84; 73-76; CANR
    42; DLB 29, 51

Schuyler, James Marcus 1923-1991 .. **CLC 5, 23**
    See also CA 101; 134; DAM POET; DLB
    5, 169; EWL 3; INT CA-101; WP

Schwartz, Delmore (David)
    1913-1966 ... **CLC 2, 4, 10, 45, 87; PC 8**
    See also AMWS 2; CA 17-18; 25-28R;
    CANR 35; CAP 2; DLB 28, 48; EWL 3;
    MTCW 1, 2; PAB; RGAL 4; TUS

Schwartz, Ernst
    See Ozu, Yasujiro

Schwartz, John Burnham 1965- .... **CLC 59**
    See also CA 132; CANR 116

Schwartz, Lynne Sharon 1939- .... **CLC 31**
    See also CA 103; CANR 44, 89; DLB 218;
    MTCW 2

Schwartz, Muriel A.
    See Eliot, T(homas) S(tearns)

Schwarz-Bart, Andre 1928- .... **CLC 2, 4**
    See also CA 89-92; CANR 109; DLB 299

Schwarz-Bart, Simone 1938- . **BLCS; CLC 7**
    See also BW 2; CA 97-100; CANR 117;
    EWL 3

Schwerner, Armand 1927-1999 .... **PC 42**
    See also CA 9-12R; 179; CANR 50, 85; CP
    7; DLB 165

**Schwitters, Kurt (Hermann Edward Karl
    Julius)** 1887-1948 .... **TCLC 95**
    See also CA 158

Schwob, Marcel (Mayer Andre)
    1867-1905 .... **TCLC 20**
    See also CA 117; 168; DLB 123; GFL 1789
    to the Present

Sciascia, Leonardo 1921-1989 .. **CLC 8, 9, 41**
    See also CA 85-88; 130; CANR 35; DLB
    177; EWL 3; MTCW 1; RGWL 2, 3

Scoppettone, Sandra 1936- .... **CLC 26**
    See Early, Jack
    See also AAYA 11; BYA 8; CA 5-8R;
    CANR 41, 73; GLL 1; MAICYA 2; MAI-
    CYAS 1; SATA 9, 92; WYA; YAW

Scorsese, Martin 1942- .... **CLC 20, 89**
    See also AAYA 38; CA 110; 114; CANR
    46, 85

Scotland, Jay
    See Jakes, John (William)

Scott, Duncan Campbell
    1862-1947 .... **TCLC 6**
    See also CA 104; 153; DAC; DLB 92;
    RGEL 2

Scott, Evelyn 1893-1963 .... **CLC 43**
    See also CA 104; 112; CANR 64; DLB 9,
    48; RHW

Scott, F(rancis) R(eginald)
    1899-1985 .... **CLC 22**
    See also CA 101; 114; CANR 87; DLB 88;
    INT CA-101; RGEL 2

Scott, Frank
    See Scott, F(rancis) R(eginald)

Scott, Joan .... **CLC 65**

Scott, Joanna 1960- .... **CLC 50**
    See also CA 126; CANR 53, 92

Scott, Paul (Mark) 1920-1978 ...... **CLC 9, 60**
    See also BRWS 1; CA 81-84; 77-80; CANR
    33; DLB 14, 207; EWL 3; MTCW 1;
    RGEL 2; RHW; WWE 1

Scott, Ridley 1937- .... **CLC 183**
    See also AAYA 13, 43

Scott, Sarah 1723-1795 .... **LC 44**
    See also DLB 39

Scott, Sir Walter 1771-1832 .... **NCLC 15, 69,
    110; PC 13; SSC 32; WLC**
    See also AAYA 22; BRW 4; BYA 2; CD-
    BLB 1789-1832; DA; DAB; DAC; DAM
    MST, NOV, POET; DLB 93, 107, 116,
    144, 159; HGG; LAIT 1; RGEL 2; RGSF
    2; SSFS 10; SUFW 1; TEA; WLIT 3;
    YABC 2

Scribe, (Augustin) Eugene 1791-1861 . **DC 5;
    NCLC 16**
    See also DAM DRAM; DLB 192; GFL
    1789 to the Present; RGWL 2, 3

Scrum, R.
    See Crumb, R(obert)

Scudery, Georges de 1601-1667 .... **LC 75**
    See also GFL Beginnings to 1789

Scudery, Madeleine de 1607-1701 .. **LC 2, 58**
    See also DLB 268; GFL Beginnings to 1789

Scum
    See Crumb, R(obert)

Scumbag, Little Bobby
    See Crumb, R(obert)

Seabrook, John
    See Hubbard, L(afayette) Ron(ald)

Seacole, Mary Jane Grant
    1805-1881 .... **NCLC 147**
    See also DLB 166

Sealy, I(rwin) Allan 1951- .... **CLC 55**
    See also CA 136; CN 7

Search, Alexander
    See Pessoa, Fernando (Antonio Nogueira)

Sebald, W(infried) G(eorg)
    1944-2001 .... **CLC 194**
    See also BRWS 8; CA 159; 202; CANR 98

Sebastian, Lee
    See Silverberg, Robert

Sebastian Owl
    See Thompson, Hunter S(tockton)

Sebestyen, Igen
    See Sebestyen, Ouida

Sebestyen, Ouida 1924- .... **CLC 30**
    See also AAYA 8; BYA 7; CA 107; CANR
    40, 114; CLR 17; JRDA; MAICYA 1, 2;
    SAAS 10; SATA 39, 140; WYA; YAW

Sebold, Alice 1963(?)- .... **CLC 193**
    See also AAYA 56; CA 203

Second Duke of Buckingham
    See Villiers, George

Secundus, H. Scriblerus
    See Fielding, Henry

Sedges, John
    See Buck, Pearl S(ydenstricker)

Sedgwick, Catharine Maria
    1789-1867 .... **NCLC 19, 98**
    See also DLB 1, 74, 183, 239, 243, 254;
    RGAL 4

Seelye, John (Douglas) 1931- .... **CLC 7**
    See also CA 97-100; CANR 70; INT CA-
    97-100; TCWW 2

Seferiades, Giorgos Stylianou 1900-1971
    See Seferis, George
    See also CA 5-8R; 33-36R; CANR 5, 36;
    MTCW 1

Seferis, George .... **CLC 5, 11**
    See Seferiades, Giorgos Stylianou
    See also EW 12; EWL 3; RGWL 2, 3

Segal, Erich (Wolf) 1937- .... **CLC 3, 10**
    See also BEST 89:1; BPFB 3; CA 25-28R;
    CANR 20, 36, 65, 113; CPW; DAM POP;
    DLBY 1986; INT CANR-20; MTCW 1

Seger, Bob 1945- .... **CLC 35**

Seghers, Anna .... **CLC 7**
    See Radvanyi, Netty
    See also CDWLB 2; DLB 69; EWL 3

Seidel, Frederick (Lewis) 1936- .... **CLC 18**
    See also CA 13-16R; CANR 8, 99; CP 7;
    DLBY 1984

Seifert, Jaroslav 1901-1986 . **CLC 34, 44, 93;
    PC 47**
    See also CA 127; CDWLB 4; DLB 215;
    EWL 3; MTCW 1, 2

Sei Shonagon c. 966-1017(?) .... **CMLC 6**

Sejour, Victor 1817-1874 .... **DC 10**
    See also DLB 50

Sejour Marcou et Ferrand, Juan Victor
    See Sejour, Victor

Selby, Hubert, Jr. 1928-2004 ..... **CLC 1, 2, 4,
    8; SSC 20**
    See also CA 13-16R; 226; CANR 33, 85;
    CN 7; DLB 2, 227

Selzer, Richard 1928- .... **CLC 74**
    See also CA 65-68; CANR 14, 106

Sembene, Ousmane
    See Ousmane, Sembene
    See also AFW; EWL 3; WLIT 2

Senancour, Etienne Pivert de
    1770-1846 .... **NCLC 16**
    See also DLB 119; GFL 1789 to the Present

Sender, Ramon (Jose) 1902-1982 ...... **CLC 8;
    HLC 2; TCLC 136**
    See also CA 5-8R; 105; CANR 8; DAM
    MULT; EWL 3; HW 1; MTCW 1; RGWL
    2, 3

Seneca, Lucius Annaeus c. 4B.C.-c.
    65 .... **CMLC 6; DC 5**
    See also AW 2; CDWLB 1; DAM DRAM;
    DLB 211; RGWL 2, 3; TWA

Senghor, Leopold Sedar 1906-2001 ... **BLC 3;
    CLC 54, 130; PC 25**
    See also AFW; BW 2; CA 116; 125; 203;
    CANR 47, 74, 134; CWW 2; DAM
    MULT, POET; DNFS 2; EWL 3; GFL
    1789 to the Present; MTCW 1, 2; TWA

Senior, Olive (Marjorie) 1941- .... **SSC 78**
    See also BW 3; CA 154; CANR 86, 126;
    CN 7; CP 7; CWP; DLB 157; EWL 3;
    RGSF 2

Senna, Danzy 1970- .... **CLC 119**
    See also CA 169; CANR 130

Serling, (Edward) Rod(man)
    1924-1975 .... **CLC 30**
    See also AAYA 14; AITN 1; CA 162; 57-
    60; DLB 26; SFW 4

Serna, Ramon Gomez de la
    See Gomez de la Serna, Ramon

Serpieres
    See Guillevic, (Eugene)

Service, Robert
    See Service, Robert W(illiam)
    See also BYA 4; DAB; DLB 92

Service, Robert W(illiam)
    1874(?)-1958 .... **TCLC 15; WLC**
    See Service, Robert
    See also CA 115; 140; CANR 84; DA;
    DAC; DAM MST, POET; PFS 10; RGEL
    2; SATA 20

Seth, Vikram 1952- .... **CLC 43, 90**
    See also BRWS 10; CA 121; 127; CANR
    50, 74, 131; CN 7; CP 7; DA3; DAM
    MULT; DLB 120, 271, 282; EWL 3; INT
    CA-127; MTCW 2; WWE 1

Seton, Cynthia Propper 1926-1982 .. **CLC 27**
    See also CA 5-8R; 108; CANR 7

Seton, Ernest (Evan) Thompson
    1860-1946 .... **TCLC 31**
    See also ANW; BYA 3; CA 109; 204; CLR
    59; DLB 92; DLBD 13; JRDA; SATA 18

Seton-Thompson, Ernest
    See Seton, Ernest (Evan) Thompson

Settle, Mary Lee 1918- .... **CLC 19, 61**
    See also BPFB 3; CA 89-92; CAAS 1;
    CANR 44, 87, 126; CN 7; CSW; DLB 6;
    INT CA-89-92

Seuphor, Michel
    See Arp, Jean

Sevigne, Marie (de Rabutin-Chantal)
1626-1696 .... **LC 11**
See Sevigne, Marie de Rabutin Chantal
See also GFL Beginnings to 1789; TWA

Sevigne, Marie de Rabutin Chantal
See Sevigne, Marie (de Rabutin-Chantal)
See also DLB 268

Sewall, Samuel 1652-1730 .... **LC 38**
See also DLB 24; RGAL 4

Sexton, Anne (Harvey) 1928-1974 ..... **CLC 2,
4, 6, 8, 10, 15, 53, 123; PC 2; WLC**
See also AMWS 2; CA 1-4R; 53-56; CABS
2; CANR 3, 36; CDALB 1941-1968; DA;
DA3; DAB; DAC; DAM MST, POET;
DLB 5, 169; EWL 3; EXPP; FW;
MAWW; MTCW 1, 2; PAB; PFS 4, 14;
RGAL 4; SATA 10; TUS

Shaara, Jeff 1952- .... **CLC 119**
See also CA 163; CANR 109

Shaara, Michael (Joseph, Jr.)
1929-1988 .... **CLC 15**
See also AITN 1; BPFB 3; CA 102; 125;
CANR 52, 85; DAM POP; DLBY 1983

Shackleton, C. C.
See Aldiss, Brian W(ilson)

Shacochis, Bob .... **CLC 39**
See Shacochis, Robert G.

Shacochis, Robert G. 1951-
See Shacochis, Bob
See also CA 119; 124; CANR 100; INT CA-
124

Shaffer, Anthony (Joshua)
1926-2001 .... **CLC 19**
See also CA 110; 116; 200; CBD; CD 5;
DAM DRAM; DFS 13; DLB 13

Shaffer, Peter (Levin) 1926- .. **CLC 5, 14, 18,
37, 60; DC 7**
See also BRWS 1; CA 25-28R; CANR 25,
47, 74, 118; CBD; CD 5; CDBLB 1960 to
Present; DA3; DAB; DAM DRAM, MST;
DFS 5, 13; DLB 13, 233; EWL 3; MTCW
1, 2; RGEL 2; TEA

Shakespeare, William 1564-1616 .... **WLC**
See also AAYA 35; BRW 1; CDBLB Be-
fore 1660; DA; DA3; DAB; DAC; DAM
DRAM, MST, POET; DFS 20; DLB 62,
172, 263; EXPP; LAIT 1; LATS 1:1;
LMFS 1; PAB; PFS 1, 2, 3, 4, 5, 8, 9;
RGEL 2; TEA; WLIT 3; WP; WS; WYA

Shakey, Bernard
See Young, Neil

Shalamov, Varlam (Tikhonovich)
1907-1982 .... **CLC 18**
See also CA 129; 105; DLB 302; RGSF 2

Shamloo, Ahmad
See Shamlu, Ahmad

Shamlou, Ahmad
See Shamlu, Ahmad

Shamlu, Ahmad 1925-2000 .... **CLC 10**
See also CA 216; CWW 2

Shammas, Anton 1951- .... **CLC 55**
See also CA 199

Shandling, Arline
See Berriault, Gina

Shange, Ntozake 1948- ... **BLC 3; CLC 8, 25,
38, 74, 126; DC 3**
See also AAYA 9; AFAW 1, 2; BW 2; CA
85-88; CABS 3; CAD; CANR 27, 48, 74,
131; CD 5; CP 7; CWD; CWP; DA3;
DAM DRAM, MULT; DFS 2, 11; DLB
38, 249; FW; LAIT 5; MTCW 1, 2; NFS
11; RGAL 4; YAW

Shanley, John Patrick 1950- .... **CLC 75**
See also AMWS 14; CA 128; 133; CAD;
CANR 83; CD 5

Shapcott, Thomas W(illiam) 1935- .. **CLC 38**
See also CA 69-72; CANR 49, 83, 103; CP
7; DLB 289

Shapiro, Jane 1942- .... **CLC 76**
See also CA 196

Shapiro, Karl (Jay) 1913-2000 ...... **CLC 4, 8,
15, 53; PC 25**
See also AMWS 2; CA 1-4R; 188; CAAS
6; CANR 1, 36, 66; CP 7; DLB 48; EWL
3; EXPP; MTCW 1, 2; PFS 3; RGAL 4

Sharp, William 1855-1905 .... **TCLC 39**
See Macleod, Fiona
See also CA 160; DLB 156; RGEL 2

Sharpe, Thomas Ridley 1928-
See Sharpe, Tom
See also CA 114; 122; CANR 85; INT CA-
122

Sharpe, Tom .... **CLC 36**
See Sharpe, Thomas Ridley
See also CN 7; DLB 14, 231

Shatrov, Mikhail .... **CLC 59**

Shaw, Bernard
See Shaw, George Bernard
See also DLB 190

Shaw, G. Bernard
See Shaw, George Bernard

Shaw, George Bernard 1856-1950 ..... **DC 23;
TCLC 3, 9, 21, 45; WLC**
See Shaw, Bernard
See also BRW 6; BRWC 1; BRWR 2; CA
104; 128; CDBLB 1914-1945; DA; DA3;
DAB; DAC; DAM DRAM, MST; DFS 1,
3, 6, 11, 19; DLB 10, 57; EWL 3; LAIT
3; LATS 1:1; MTCW 1, 2; RGEL 2; TEA;
WLIT 4

Shaw, Henry Wheeler 1818-1885 .. **NCLC 15**
See also DLB 11; RGAL 4

Shaw, Irwin 1913-1984 .... **CLC 7, 23, 34**
See also AITN 1; BPFB 3; CA 13-16R; 112;
CANR 21; CDALB 1941-1968; CPW;
DAM DRAM, POP; DLB 6, 102; DLBY
1984; MTCW 1, 21

Shaw, Robert 1927-1978 .... **CLC 5**
See also AITN 1; CA 1-4R; 81-84; CANR
4; DLB 13, 14

Shaw, T. E.
See Lawrence, T(homas) E(dward)

Shawn, Wallace 1943- .... **CLC 41**
See also CA 112; CAD; CD 5; DLB 266

Shchedrin, N.
See Saltykov, Mikhail Evgrafovich

Shea, Lisa 1953- .... **CLC 86**
See also CA 147

Sheed, Wilfrid (John Joseph) 1930- . **CLC 2,
4, 10, 53**
See also CA 65-68; CANR 30, 66; CN 7;
DLB 6; MTCW 1, 2

Sheehy, Gail 1937- .... **CLC 171**
See also CA 49-52; CANR 1, 33, 55, 92;
CPW; MTCW 1

Sheldon, Alice Hastings Bradley
1915(?)-1987
See Tiptree, James, Jr.
See also CA 108; 122; CANR 34; INT CA-
108; MTCW 1

Sheldon, John
See Bloch, Robert (Albert)

Sheldon, Walter J(ames) 1917-1996
See Queen, Ellery
See also AITN 1; CA 25-28R; CANR 10

Shelley, Mary Wollstonecraft (Godwin)
1797-1851 ...... **NCLC 14, 59, 103; WLC**
See also AAYA 20; BPFB 3; BRW 3;
BRWC 2; BRWS 3; BYA 5; CDBLB
1789-1832; DA; DA3; DAB; DAC; DAM
MST, NOV; DLB 110, 116, 159, 178;
EXPN; HGG; LAIT 1; LMFS 1, 2; NFS
1; RGEL 2; SATA 29; SCFW; SFW 4;
TEA; WLIT 3

Shelley, Percy Bysshe 1792-1822 .. **NCLC 18,
93, 143; PC 14; WLC**
See also BRW 4; BRWR 1; CDBLB 1789-
1832; DA; DA3; DAB; DAC; DAM MST,
POET; DLB 96, 110, 158; EXPP; LMFS
1; PAB; PFS 2; RGEL 2; TEA; WLIT 3;
WP

Shepard, Jim 1956- .... **CLC 36**
See also CA 137; CANR 59, 104; SATA 90

Shepard, Lucius 1947- .... **CLC 34**
See also CA 128; 141; CANR 81, 124;
HGG; SCFW 2; SFW 4; SUFW 2

Shepard, Sam 1943- .... **CLC 4, 6, 17, 34, 41,
44, 169; DC 5**
See also AAYA 1, 58; AMWS 3; CA 69-72;
CABS 3; CAD; CANR 22, 120; CD 5;
DA3; DAM DRAM; DFS 3, 6, 7, 14;
DLB 7, 212; EWL 3; IDFW 3, 4; MTCW
1, 2; RGAL 4

Shepherd, Michael
See Ludlum, Robert

Sherburne, Zoa (Lillian Morin)
1912-1995 .... **CLC 30**
See also AAYA 13; CA 1-4R; 176; CANR
3, 37; MAICYA 1, 2; SAAS 18; SATA 3;
YAW

Sheridan, Frances 1724-1766 .... **LC 7**
See also DLB 39, 84

Sheridan, Richard Brinsley
1751-1816 .... **DC 1; NCLC 5, 91; WLC**
See also BRW 3; CDBLB 1660-1789; DA;
DAB; DAC; DAM DRAM, MST; DFS
15; DLB 89; WLIT 3

Sherman, Jonathan Marc .... **CLC 55**

Sherman, Martin 1941(?)- .... **CLC 19**
See also CA 116; 123; CAD; CANR 86;
CD 5; DFS 20; DLB 228; GLL 1; IDTP

Sherwin, Judith Johnson
See Johnson, Judith (Emlyn)
See also CANR 85; CP 7; CWP

Sherwood, Frances 1940- .... **CLC 81**
See also CA 146, 220; CAAE 220

Sherwood, Robert E(mmet)
1896-1955 .... **TCLC 3**
See also CA 104; 153; CANR 86; DAM
DRAM; DFS 11, 15, 17; DLB 7, 26, 249;
IDFW 3, 4; RGAL 4

Shestov, Lev 1866-1938 .... **TCLC 56**

Shevchenko, Taras 1814-1861 .... **NCLC 54**

Shiel, M(atthew) P(hipps)
1865-1947 .... **TCLC 8**
See Holmes, Gordon
See also CA 106; 160; DLB 153; HGG;
MTCW 2; SFW 4; SUFW

Shields, Carol (Ann) 1935-2003 ...... **CLC 91,
113, 193**
See also AMWS 7; CA 81-84; 218; CANR
51, 74, 98, 133; CCA 1; CN 7; CPW;
DA3; DAC; MTCW 2

Shields, David (Jonathan) 1956- ...... **CLC 97**
See also CA 124; CANR 48, 99, 112

Shiga, Naoya 1883-1971 ..... **CLC 33; SSC 23**
See Shiga Naoya
See also CA 101; 33-36R; MJW; RGWL 3

Shiga Naoya
See Shiga, Naoya
See also DLB 180; EWL 3; RGWL 3

Shilts, Randy 1951-1994 .... **CLC 85**
See also AAYA 19; CA 115; 127; 144;
CANR 45; DA3; GLL 1; INT CA-127;
MTCW 2

Shimazaki, Haruki 1872-1943
See Shimazaki Toson
See also CA 105; 134; CANR 84; RGWL 3

Shimazaki Toson .... **TCLC 5**
See Shimazaki, Haruki
See also DLB 180; EWL 3

Shirley, James 1596-1666 .... **LC 96**
See also DLB 58; RGEL 2

Sholokhov, Mikhail (Aleksandrovich)
1905-1984 .... **CLC 7, 15**
See also CA 101; 112; DLB 272; EWL 3;
MTCW 1, 2; RGWL 2, 3; SATA-Obit 36

Shone, Patric
See Hanley, James

Showalter, Elaine 1941- .... **CLC 169**
See also CA 57-60; CANR 58, 106; DLB
67; FW; GLL 2

Shreve, Susan
See Shreve, Susan Richards

Shreve, Susan Richards 1939- .... **CLC 23**
See also CA 49-52; CAAS 5; CANR 5, 38,
69, 100; MAICYA 1, 2; SATA 46, 95, 152;
SATA-Brief 41

Shue, Larry 1946-1985 .... **CLC 52**
See also CA 145; 117; DAM DRAM; DFS
7

Shu-Jen, Chou 1881-1936
See Lu Hsun
See also CA 104

Shulman, Alix Kates 1932- .... **CLC 2, 10**
See also CA 29-32R; CANR 43; FW; SATA
7

Shuster, Joe 1914-1992 .... **CLC 21**
See also AAYA 50

Shute, Nevil .... **CLC 30**
See Norway, Nevil Shute
See also BPFB 3; DLB 255; NFS 9; RHW;
SFW 4

Shuttle, Penelope (Diane) 1947- .... **CLC 7**
See also CA 93-96; CANR 39, 84, 92, 108;
CP 7; CWP; DLB 14, 40

Shvarts, Elena 1948- .... **PC 50**
See also CA 147

Sidhwa, Bapsy (N.) 1938- .... **CLC 168**
See also CA 108; CANR 25, 57; CN 7; FW

Sidney, Mary 1561-1621 .... **LC 19, 39**
See Sidney Herbert, Mary

Sidney, Sir Philip 1554-1586 . **LC 19, 39; PC 32**
See also BRW 1; BRWR 2; CDBLB Before
1660; DA; DA3; DAB; DAC; DAM MST,
POET; DLB 167; EXPP; PAB; RGEL 2;
TEA; WP

Sidney Herbert, Mary
See Sidney, Mary
See also DLB 167

Siegel, Jerome 1914-1996 .... **CLC 21**
See Siegel, Jerry
See also CA 116; 169; 151

Siegel, Jerry
See Siegel, Jerome
See also AAYA 50

Sienkiewicz, Henryk (Adam Alexander Pius)
1846-1916 .... **TCLC 3**
See also CA 104; 134; CANR 84; EWL 3;
RGSF 2; RGWL 2, 3

Sierra, Gregorio Martinez
See Martinez Sierra, Gregorio

Sierra, Maria (de la O'LeJarraga) Martinez
See Martinez Sierra, Maria (de la
O'LeJarraga)

Sigal, Clancy 1926- .... **CLC 7**
See also CA 1-4R; CANR 85; CN 7

Siger of Brabant 1240(?)-1284(?) . **CMLC 69**
See also DLB 115

Sigourney, Lydia H.
See Sigourney, Lydia Howard (Huntley)
See also DLB 73, 183

Sigourney, Lydia Howard (Huntley)
1791-1865 .... **NCLC 21, 87**
See Sigourney, Lydia H.; Sigourney, Lydia
Huntley
See also DLB 1

Sigourney, Lydia Huntley
See Sigourney, Lydia Howard (Huntley)
See also DLB 42, 239, 243

Siguenza y Gongora, Carlos de
1645-1700 .... **HLCS 2; LC 8**
See also LAW

Sigurjonsson, Johann
See Sigurjonsson, Johann

Sigurjonsson, Johann 1880-1919 ... **TCLC 27**
See also CA 170; DLB 293; EWL 3

Sikelianos, Angelos 1884-1951 .... **PC 29; TCLC 39**
See also EWL 3; RGWL 2, 3

Silkin, Jon 1930-1997 .... **CLC 2, 6, 43**
See also CA 5-8R; CAAS 5; CANR 89; CP
7; DLB 27

Silko, Leslie (Marmon) 1948- .... **CLC 23, 74, 114; NNAL; SSC 37, 66; WLCS**
See also AAYA 14; AMWS 4; ANW; BYA
12; CA 115; 122; CANR 45, 65, 118; CN
7; CP 7; CPW 1; CWP; DA; DA3; DAC;
DAM MST, MULT, POP; DLB 143, 175,
256, 275; EWL 3; EXPP; EXPS; LAIT 4;
MTCW 2; NFS 4; PFS 9, 16; RGAL 4;
RGSF 2; SSFS 4, 8, 10, 11

Sillanpaa, Frans Eemil 1888-1964 ... **CLC 19**
See also CA 129; 93-96; EWL 3; MTCW 1

Sillitoe, Alan 1928- .. **CLC 1, 3, 6, 10, 19, 57, 148**
See also AITN 1; BRWS 5; CA 9-12R, 191;
CAAE 191; CAAS 2; CANR 8, 26, 55;
CDBLB 1960 to Present; CN 7; DLB 14,
139; EWL 3; MTCW 1, 2; RGEL 2;
RGSF 2; SATA 61

Silone, Ignazio 1900-1978 .... **CLC 4**
See also CA 25-28; 81-84; CANR 34; CAP
2; DLB 264; EW 12; EWL 3; MTCW 1;
RGSF 2; RGWL 2, 3

Silone, Ignazione
See Silone, Ignazio

Silver, Joan Micklin 1935- .... **CLC 20**
See also CA 114; 121; INT CA-121

Silver, Nicholas
See Faust, Frederick (Schiller)
See also TCWW 2

Silverberg, Robert 1935- .... **CLC 7, 140**
See also AAYA 24; BPFB 3; BYA 7, 9; CA
1-4R, 186; CAAE 186; CAAS 2; CANR
1, 20, 36, 85; CLR 59; CN 7; CPW; DAM
POP; DLB 8; INT CANR-20; MAICYA
1, 2; MTCW 1, 2; SATA 13, 91; SATA-
Essay 104; SCFW 2; SFW 4; SUFW 2

Silverstein, Alvin 1933- .... **CLC 17**
See also CA 49-52; CANR 2; CLR 25;
JRDA; MAICYA 1, 2; SATA 8, 69, 124

Silverstein, Shel(don Allan)
1932-1999 .... **PC 49**
See also AAYA 40; BW 3; CA 107; 179;
CANR 47, 74, 81; CLR 5, 96; CWRI 5;
JRDA; MAICYA 1, 2; MTCW 2; SATA
33, 92; SATA-Brief 27; SATA-Obit 116

Silverstein, Virginia B(arbara Opshelor)
1937- .... **CLC 17**
See also CA 49-52; CANR 2; CLR 25;
JRDA; MAICYA 1, 2; SATA 8, 69, 124

Sim, Georges
See Simenon, Georges (Jacques Christian)

Simak, Clifford D(onald) 1904-1988 . **CLC 1, 55**
See also CA 1-4R; 125; CANR 1, 35; DLB
8; MTCW 1; SATA-Obit 56; SFW 4

Simenon, Georges (Jacques Christian)
1903-1989 .... **CLC 1, 2, 3, 8, 18, 47**
See also BPFB 3; CA 85-88; 129; CANR
35; CMW 4; DA3; DAM POP; DLB 72;
DLBY 1989; EW 12; EWL 3; GFL 1789
to the Present; MSW; MTCW 1, 2; RGWL
2, 3

Simic, Charles 1938- .... **CLC 6, 9, 22, 49, 68, 130**
See also AMWS 8; CA 29-32R; CAAS 4;
CANR 12, 33, 52, 61, 96; CP 7; DA3;
DAM POET; DLB 105; MTCW 2; PFS 7;
RGAL 4; WP

Simmel, Georg 1858-1918 .... **TCLC 64**
See also CA 157; DLB 296

Simmons, Charles (Paul) 1924- .... **CLC 57**
See also CA 89-92; INT CA-89-92

Simmons, Dan 1948- .... **CLC 44**
See also AAYA 16, 54; CA 138; CANR 53,
81, 126; CPW; DAM POP; HGG; SUFW
2

Simmons, James (Stewart Alexander)
1933- .... **CLC 43**
See also CA 105; CAAS 21; CP 7; DLB 40

Simms, William Gilmore
1806-1870 .... **NCLC 3**
See also DLB 3, 30, 59, 73, 248, 254;
RGAL 4

Simon, Carly 1945- .... **CLC 26**
See also CA 105

Simon, Claude (Eugene Henri)
1913-1984 .... **CLC 4, 9, 15, 39**
See also CA 89-92; CANR 33, 117; CWW
2; DAM NOV; DLB 83; EW 13; EWL 3;
GFL 1789 to the Present; MTCW 1

Simon, Myles
See Follett, Ken(neth Martin)

Simon, (Marvin) Neil 1927- ... **CLC 6, 11, 31, 39, 70; DC 14**
See also AAYA 32; AITN 1; AMWS 4; CA
21-24R; CANR 26, 54, 87, 126; CD 5;
DA3; DAM DRAM; DFS 2, 6, 12, 18;
DLB 7, 266; LAIT 4; MTCW 1, 2; RGAL
4; TUS

Simon, Paul (Frederick) 1941(?)- ..... **CLC 17**
See also CA 116; 153

Simonon, Paul 1956(?)- .... **CLC 30**

Simonson, Rick ed. .... **CLC 70**

Simpson, Harriette
See Arnow, Harriette (Louisa) Simpson

Simpson, Louis (Aston Marantz)
1923- .... **CLC 4, 7, 9, 32, 149**
See also AMWS 9; CA 1-4R; CAAS 4;
CANR 1, 61; CP 7; DAM POET; DLB 5;
MTCW 1, 2; PFS 7, 11, 14; RGAL 4

Simpson, Mona (Elizabeth) 1957- ... **CLC 44, 146**
See also CA 122; 135; CANR 68, 103; CN
7; EWL 3

Simpson, N(orman) F(rederick)
1919- .... **CLC 29**
See also CA 13-16R; CBD; DLB 13; RGEL
2

Sinclair, Andrew (Annandale) 1935- . **CLC 2, 14**
See also CA 9-12R; CAAS 5; CANR 14,
38, 91; CN 7; DLB 14; FANT; MTCW 1

Sinclair, Emil
See Hesse, Hermann

Sinclair, Iain 1943- .... **CLC 76**
See also CA 132; CANR 81; CP 7; HGG

Sinclair, Iain MacGregor
See Sinclair, Iain

Sinclair, Irene
See Griffith, D(avid Lewelyn) W(ark)

Sinclair, Mary Amelia St. Clair 1865(?)-1946
See Sinclair, May
See also CA 104; HGG; RHW

Sinclair, May .... **TCLC 3, 11**
See Sinclair, Mary Amelia St. Clair
See also CA 166; DLB 36, 135; EWL 3;
RGEL 2; SUFW

Sinclair, Roy
See Griffith, D(avid Lewelyn) W(ark)

Sinclair, Upton (Beall) 1878-1968 ..... **CLC 1, 11, 15, 63; WLC**
See also AMWS 5; BPFB 3; BYA 2; CA
5-8R; 25-28R; CANR 7; CDALB 1929-
1941; DA; DA3; DAB; DAC; DAM MST,
NOV; DLB 9; EWL 3; INT CANR-7;
LAIT 3; MTCW 1, 2; NFS 6; RGAL 4;
SATA 9; TUS; YAW

Singe, (Edmund) J(ohn) M(illington) 1871-1909 .... WLC

Singer, Isaac
See Singer, Isaac Bashevis

Singer, Isaac Bashevis 1904-1991 .. CLC 1, 3, 6, 9, 11, 15, 23, 38, 69, 111; SSC 3, 53; WLC
See also AAYA 32; AITN 1, 2; AMW; AMWR 2; BPFB 3; BYA 1, 4; CA 1-4R; 134; CANR 1, 39, 106; CDALB 1941-1968; CLR 1; CWRI 5; DA; DA3; DAB; DAC; DAM MST, NOV; DLB 6, 28, 52, 278; DLBY 1991; EWL 3; EXPS; HGG; JRDA; LAIT 3; MAICYA 1, 2; MTCW 1, 2; RGAL 4; RGSF 2; SATA 3, 27; SATA-Obit 68; SSFS 2, 12, 16; TUS; TWA

Singer, Israel Joshua 1893-1944 .... TCLC 33
See also CA 169; EWL 3

Singh, Khushwant 1915- .... CLC 11
See also CA 9-12R; CAAS 9; CANR 6, 84; CN 7; EWL 3; RGEL 2

Singleton, Ann
See Benedict, Ruth (Fulton)

Singleton, John 1968(?)- .... CLC 156
See also AAYA 50; BW 2, 3; CA 138; CANR 67, 82; DAM MULT

Siniavskii, Andrei
See Sinyavsky, Andrei (Donatevich)
See also CWW 2

Sinjohn, John
See Galsworthy, John

Sinyavsky, Andrei (Donatevich) 1925-1997 .... CLC 8
See also Siniavskii, Andrei; Sinyavsky, Andrey Donatovich; Tertz, Abram
See also CA 85-88; 159

Sinyavsky, Andrey Donatovich
See Sinyavsky, Andrei (Donatevich)
See also EWL 3

Sirin, V.
See Nabokov, Vladimir (Vladimirovich)

Sissman, L(ouis) E(dward) 1928-1976 .... CLC 9, 18
See also CA 21-24R; 65-68; CANR 13; DLB 5

Sisson, C(harles) H(ubert) 1914-2003 .... CLC 8
See also CA 1-4R; 220; CAAS 3; CANR 3, 48, 84; CP 7; DLB 27

Sitting Bull 1831(?)-1890 .... NNAL
See also DA3; DAM MULT

Sitwell, Dame Edith 1887-1964 ..... CLC 2, 9, 67; PC 3
See also BRW 7; CA 9-12R; CANR 35; CDBLB 1945-1960; DAM POET; DLB 20; EWL 3; MTCW 1, 2; RGEL 2; TEA

Siwaarmill, H. P.
See Sharp, William

Sjoewall, Maj 1935- .... CLC 7
See Sjowall, Maj
See also CA 65-68; CANR 73

Sjowall, Maj
See Sjoewall, Maj
See also BPFB 3; CMW 4; MSW

Skelton, John 1460(?)-1529 ..... LC 71; PC 25
See also BRW 1; DLB 136; RGEL 2

Skelton, Robin 1925-1997 .... CLC 13
See Zuk, Georges
See also AITN 2; CA 5-8R; 160; CAAS 5; CANR 28, 89; CCA 1; CP 7; DLB 27, 53

Skolimowski, Jerzy 1938- .... CLC 20
See also CA 128

Skram, Amalie (Bertha) 1847-1905 .... TCLC 25
See also CA 165

Skvorecky, Josef (Vaclav) 1924- ...... CLC 15, 39, 69, 152
See also CA 61-64; CAAS 1; CANR 10, 34, 63, 108; CDWLB 4; CWW 2; DA3; DAC; DAM NOV; DLB 232; EWL 3; MTCW 1, 2

Slade, Bernard .... CLC 11, 46
See Newbound, Bernard Slade
See also CAAS 9; CCA 1; DLB 53

Slaughter, Carolyn 1946- .... CLC 56
See also CA 85-88; CANR 85; CN 7

Slaughter, Frank G(ill) 1908-2001 ... CLC 29
See also AITN 2; CA 5-8R; 197; CANR 5, 85; INT CANR-5; RHW

Slavitt, David R(ytman) 1935- ..... CLC 5, 14
See also CA 21-24R; CAAS 3; CANR 41, 83; CP 7; DLB 5, 6

Slesinger, Tess 1905-1945 .... TCLC 10
See also CA 107; 199; DLB 102

Slessor, Kenneth 1901-1971 .... CLC 14
See also CA 102; 89-92; DLB 260; RGEL 2

Slowacki, Juliusz 1809-1849 .... NCLC 15
See also RGWL 3

Smart, Christopher 1722-1771 . LC 3; PC 13
See also DAM POET; DLB 109; RGEL 2

Smart, Elizabeth 1913-1986 .... CLC 54
See also CA 81-84; 118; DLB 88

Smiley, Jane (Graves) 1949- ...... CLC 53, 76, 144
See also AMWS 6; BPFB 3; CA 104; CANR 30, 50, 74, 96; CN 7; CPW 1; DA3; DAM POP; DLB 227, 234; EWL 3; INT CANR-30; SSFS 19

Smith, A(rthur) J(ames) M(arshall) 1902-1980 .... CLC 15
See also CA 1-4R; 102; CANR 4; DAC; DLB 88; RGEL 2

Smith, Adam 1723(?)-1790 .... LC 36
See also DLB 104, 252; RGEL 2

Smith, Alexander 1829-1867 .... NCLC 59
See also DLB 32, 55

Smith, Anna Deavere 1950- .... CLC 86
See also CA 133; CANR 103; CD 5; DFS 2

Smith, Betty (Wehner) 1904-1972 .... CLC 19
See also BPFB 3; BYA 3; CA 5-8R; 33-36R; DLBY 1982; LAIT 3; RGAL 4; SATA 6

Smith, Charlotte (Turner) 1749-1806 .... NCLC 23, 115
See also DLB 39, 109; RGEL 2; TEA

Smith, Clark Ashton 1893-1961 .... CLC 43
See also CA 143; CANR 81; FANT; HGG; MTCW 2; SCFW 2; SFW 4; SUFW

Smith, Dave .... CLC 22, 42
See Smith, David (Jeddie)
See also CAAS 7; DLB 5

Smith, David (Jeddie) 1942-
See Smith, Dave
See also CA 49-52; CANR 1, 59, 120; CP 7; CSW; DAM POET

Smith, Florence Margaret 1902-1971
See Smith, Stevie
See also CA 17-18; 29-32R; CANR 35; CAP 2; DAM POET; MTCW 1, 2; TEA

Smith, Iain Crichton 1928-1998 .... CLC 64
See also BRWS 9; CA 21-24R; 171; CN 7; CP 7; DLB 40, 139; RGSF 2

Smith, John 1580(?)-1631 .... LC 9
See also DLB 24, 30; TUS

Smith, Johnston
See Crane, Stephen (Townley)

Smith, Joseph, Jr. 1805-1844 .... NCLC 53

Smith, Lee 1944- .... CLC 25, 73
See also CA 114; 119; CANR 46, 118; CSW; DLB 143; DLBY 1983; EWL 3; INT CA-119; RGAL 4

Smith, Martin
See Smith, Martin Cruz

Smith, Martin Cruz 1942- .. CLC 25; NNAL
See also BEST 89:4; BPFB 3; CA 85-88; CANR 6, 23, 43, 65, 119; CMW 4; CPW; DAM MULT, POP; HGG; INT CANR-23; MTCW 2; RGAL 4

Smith, Patti 1946- .... CLC 12
See also CA 93-96; CANR 63

Smith, Pauline (Urmson) 1882-1959 .... TCLC 25
See also DLB 225; EWL 3

Smith, Rosamond
See Oates, Joyce Carol

Smith, Sheila Kaye
See Kaye-Smith, Sheila

Smith, Stevie .... CLC 3, 8, 25, 44; PC 12
See Smith, Florence Margaret
See also BRWS 2; DLB 20; EWL 3; MTCW 2; PAB; PFS 3; RGEL 2

Smith, Wilbur (Addison) 1933- .... CLC 33
See also CA 13-16R; CANR 7, 46, 66, 134; CPW; MTCW 1, 2

Smith, William Jay 1918- .... CLC 6
See also AMWS 13; CA 5-8R; CANR 44, 106; CP 7; CSW; CWRI 5; DLB 5; MAICYA 1, 2; SAAS 22; SATA 2, 68, 154; SATA-Essay 154

Smith, Woodrow Wilson
See Kuttner, Henry

Smith, Zadie 1976- .... CLC 158
See also AAYA 50; CA 193

Smolenskin, Peretz 1842-1885 .... NCLC 30

Smollett, Tobias (George) 1721-1771 ... LC 2, 46
See also BRW 3; CDBLB 1660-1789; DLB 39, 104; RGEL 2; TEA

Snodgrass, W(illiam) D(e Witt) 1926- .... CLC 2, 6, 10, 18, 68
See also AMWS 6; CA 1-4R; CANR 6, 36, 65, 85; CP 7; DAM POET; DLB 5; MTCW 1, 2; RGAL 4

Snorri Sturluson 1179-1241 .... CMLC 56
See also RGWL 2, 3

Snow, C(harles) P(ercy) 1905-1980 ... CLC 1, 4, 6, 9, 13, 19
See also BRW 7; CA 5-8R; 101; CANR 28; CDBLB 1945-1960; DAM NOV; DLB 15, 77; DLBD 17; EWL 3; MTCW 1, 2; RGEL 2; TEA

Snow, Frances Compton
See Adams, Henry (Brooks)

Snyder, Gary (Sherman) 1930- . CLC 1, 2, 5, 9, 32, 120; PC 21
See also AMWS 8; ANW; BG 3; CA 17-20R; CANR 30, 60, 125; CP 7; DA3; DAM POET; DLB 5, 16, 165, 212, 237, 275; EWL 3; MTCW 2; PFS 9, 19; RGAL 4; WP

Snyder, Zilpha Keatley 1927- .... CLC 17
See also AAYA 15; BYA 1; CA 9-12R; CANR 38; CLR 31; JRDA; MAICYA 1, 2; SAAS 2; SATA 1, 28, 75, 110; SATA-Essay 112; YAW

Soares, Bernardo
See Pessoa, Fernando (Antonio Nogueira)

Sobh, A.
See Shamlu, Ahmad

Sobh, Alef
See Shamlu, Ahmad

Sobol, Joshua 1939- .... CLC 60
See Sobol, Yehoshua
See also CA 200

Sobol, Yehoshua 1939-
See Sobol, Joshua
See also CWW 2

Socrates 470B.C.-399B.C. .... CMLC 27

Soderberg, Hjalmar 1869-1941 ...... TCLC 39
See also DLB 259; EWL 3; RGSF 2

Soderbergh, Steven 1963- .... CLC 154
See also AAYA 43

Sodergran, Edith (Irene) 1892-1923
See Soedergran, Edith (Irene)
See also CA 202; DLB 259; EW 11; EWL 3; RGWL 2, 3

Soedergran, Edith (Irene)
1892-1923 .... **TCLC 31**
See Sodergran, Edith (Irene)

Softly, Edgar
See Lovecraft, H(oward) P(hillips)

Softly, Edward
See Lovecraft, H(oward) P(hillips)

Sokolov, Alexander V(sevolodovich) 1943-
See Sokolov, Sasha
See also CA 73-76

Sokolov, Raymond 1941- .... **CLC 7**
See also CA 85-88

Sokolov, Sasha .... **CLC 59**
See Sokolov, Alexander V(sevolodovich)
See also CWW 2; DLB 285; EWL 3; RGWL 2, 3

Solo, Jay
See Ellison, Harlan (Jay)

Sologub, Fyodor .... **TCLC 9**
See Teternikov, Fyodor Kuzmich
See also EWL 3

Solomons, Ikey Esquir
See Thackeray, William Makepeace

Solomos, Dionysios 1798-1857 .... **NCLC 15**

Solwoska, Mara
See French, Marilyn

Solzhenitsyn, Aleksandr I(sayevich)
1918- .. **CLC 1, 2, 4, 7, 9, 10, 18, 26, 34, 78, 134; SSC 32; WLC**
See Solzhenitsyn, Aleksandr Isaevich
See also AAYA 49; AITN 1; BPFB 3; CA 69-72; CANR 40, 65, 116; DA; DA3; DAB; DAC; DAM MST, NOV; DLB 302; EW 13; EXPS; LAIT 4; MTCW 1, 2; NFS 6; RGSF 2; RGWL 2, 3; SSFS 9; TWA

Solzhenitsyn, Aleksandr Isaevich
See Solzhenitsyn, Aleksandr I(sayevich)
See also CWW 2; EWL 3

Somers, Jane
See Lessing, Doris (May)

Somerville, Edith Oenone
1858-1949 .... **SSC 56; TCLC 51**
See also CA 196; DLB 135; RGEL 2; RGSF 2

Somerville & Ross
See Martin, Violet Florence; Somerville, Edith Oenone

Sommer, Scott 1951- .... **CLC 25**
See also CA 106

Sommers, Christina Hoff 1950- ...... **CLC 197**
See also CA 153; CANR 95

Sondheim, Stephen (Joshua) 1930- . **CLC 30, 39, 147; DC 22**
See also AAYA 11; CA 103; CANR 47, 67, 125; DAM DRAM; LAIT 4

Sone, Monica 1919- .... **AAL**

Song, Cathy 1955- .... **AAL; PC 21**
See also CA 154; CANR 118; CWP; DLB 169; EXPP; FW; PFS 5

Sontag, Susan 1933- .... **CLC 1, 2, 10, 13, 31, 105, 195**
See also AMWS 3; CA 17-20R; CANR 25, 51, 74, 97; CPW; DA3; DAM POP; DLB 2, 67; EWL 3; MAWW; MTCW 1, 2; RGAL 4; RHW; SSFS 10

Sophocles 496(?)B.C.-406(?)B.C. .... **CMLC 2, 47, 51; DC 1; WLCS**
See also AW 1; CDWLB 1; DA; DA3; DAB; DAC; DAM DRAM, MST; DFS 1, 4, 8; DLB 176; LAIT 1; LATS 1:1; LMFS 1; RGWL 2, 3; TWA

Sordello 1189-1269 .... **CMLC 15**

Sorel, Georges 1847-1922 .... **TCLC 91**
See also CA 118; 188

Sorel, Julia
See Drexler, Rosalyn

Sorokin, Vladimir .... **CLC 59**
See Sorokin, Vladimir Georgievich

Sorokin, Vladimir Georgievich
See Sorokin, Vladimir
See also DLB 285

Sorrentino, Gilbert 1929- .. **CLC 3, 7, 14, 22, 40**
See also CA 77-80; CANR 14, 33, 115; CN 7; CP 7; DLB 5, 173; DLBY 1980; INT CANR-14

Soseki
See Natsume, Soseki
See also MJW

Soto, Gary 1952- ... **CLC 32, 80; HLC 2; PC 28**
See also AAYA 10, 37; BYA 11; CA 119; 125; CANR 50, 74, 107; CLR 38; CP 7; DAM MULT; DLB 82; EWL 3; EXPP; HW 1, 2; INT CA-125; JRDA; LLW 1; MAICYA 2; MAICYAS 1; MTCW 2; PFS 7; RGAL 4; SATA 80, 120; WYA; YAW

Soupault, Philippe 1897-1990 .... **CLC 68**
See also CA 116; 147; 131; EWL 3; GFL 1789 to the Present; LMFS 2

Souster, (Holmes) Raymond 1921- .... **CLC 5, 14**
See also CA 13-16R; CAAS 14; CANR 13, 29, 53; CP 7; DA3; DAC; DAM POET; DLB 88; RGEL 2; SATA 63

Southern, Terry 1924(?)-1995 .... **CLC 7**
See also AMWS 11; BPFB 3; CA 1-4R; 150; CANR 1, 55, 107; CN 7; DLB 2; IDFW 3, 4

Southerne, Thomas 1660-1746 .... **LC 99**
See also DLB 80; RGEL 2

Southey, Robert 1774-1843 .... **NCLC 8, 97**
See also BRW 4; DLB 93, 107, 142; RGEL 2; SATA 54

Southwell, Robert 1561(?)-1595 .... **LC 108**
See also DLB 167; RGEL 2; TEA

Southworth, Emma Dorothy Eliza Nevitte
1819-1899 .... **NCLC 26**
See also DLB 239

Souza, Ernest
See Scott, Evelyn

Soyinka, Wole 1934- .. **BLC 3; CLC 3, 5, 14, 36, 44, 179; DC 2; WLC**
See also AFW; BW 2, 3; CA 13-16R; CANR 27, 39, 82; CD 5; CDWLB 3; CN 7; CP 7; DA; DA3; DAB; DAC; DAM DRAM, MST, MULT; DFS 10; DLB 125; EWL 3; MTCW 1, 2; RGEL 2; TWA; WLIT 2; WWE 1

Spackman, W(illiam) M(ode)
1905-1990 .... **CLC 46**
See also CA 81-84; 132

Spacks, Barry (Bernard) 1931- .... **CLC 14**
See also CA 154; CANR 33, 109; CP 7; DLB 105

Spanidou, Irini 1946- .... **CLC 44**
See also CA 185

Spark, Muriel (Sarah) 1918- ..... **CLC 2, 3, 5, 8, 13, 18, 40, 94; SSC 10**
See also BRWS 1; CA 5-8R; CANR 12, 36, 76, 89, 131; CDBLB 1945-1960; CN 7; CP 7; DA3; DAB; DAC; DAM MST, NOV; DLB 15, 139; EWL 3; FW; INT CANR-12; LAIT 4; MTCW 1, 2; RGEL 2; TEA; WLIT 4; YAW

Spaulding, Douglas
See Bradbury, Ray (Douglas)

Spaulding, Leonard
See Bradbury, Ray (Douglas)

Speght, Rachel 1597-c. 1630 .... **LC 97**
See also DLB 126

Spelman, Elizabeth .... **CLC 65**

Spence, J. A. D.
See Eliot, T(homas) S(tearns)

Spencer, Anne 1882-1975 .... **HR 3**
See also BW 2; CA 161; DLB 51, 54

Spencer, Elizabeth 1921- .... **CLC 22; SSC 57**
See also CA 13-16R; CANR 32, 65, 87; CN 7; CSW; DLB 6, 218; EWL 3; MTCW 1; RGAL 4; SATA 14

Spencer, Leonard G.
See Silverberg, Robert

Spencer, Scott 1945- .... **CLC 30**
See also CA 113; CANR 51; DLBY 1986

Spender, Stephen (Harold)
1909-1995 .... **CLC 1, 2, 5, 10, 41, 91**
See also BRWS 2; CA 9-12R; 149; CANR 31, 54; CDBLB 1945-1960; CP 7; DA3; DAM POET; DLB 20; EWL 3; MTCW 1, 2; PAB; RGEL 2; TEA

Spengler, Oswald (Arnold Gottfried)
1880-1936 .... **TCLC 25**
See also CA 118; 189

Spenser, Edmund 1552(?)-1599 ..... **LC 5, 39; PC 8, 42; WLC**
See also AAYA 60; BRW 1; CDBLB Before 1660; DA; DA3; DAB; DAC; DAM MST, POET; DLB 167; EFS 2; EXPP; PAB; RGEL 2; TEA; WLIT 3; WP

Spicer, Jack 1925-1965 .... **CLC 8, 18, 72**
See also BG 3; CA 85-88; DAM POET; DLB 5, 16, 193; GLL 1; WP

Spiegelman, Art 1948- .... **CLC 76, 178**
See also AAYA 10, 46; CA 125; CANR 41, 55, 74, 124; DLB 299; MTCW 2; SATA 109; YAW

Spielberg, Peter 1929- .... **CLC 6**
See also CA 5-8R; CANR 4, 48; DLBY 1981

Spielberg, Steven 1947- .... **CLC 20, 188**
See also AAYA 8, 24; CA 77-80; CANR 32; SATA 32

Spillane, Frank Morrison 1918-
See Spillane, Mickey
See also CA 25-28R; CANR 28, 63, 125; DA3; MTCW 1, 2; SATA 66

Spillane, Mickey .... **CLC 3, 13**
See Spillane, Frank Morrison
See also BPFB 3; CMW 4; DLB 226; MSW; MTCW 2

Spinoza, Benedictus de 1632-1677 .. **LC 9, 58**

Spinrad, Norman (Richard) 1940- ... **CLC 46**
See also BPFB 3; CA 37-40R; CAAS 19; CANR 20, 91; DLB 8; INT CANR-20; SFW 4

Spitteler, Carl (Friedrich Georg)
1845-1924 .... **TCLC 12**
See also CA 109; DLB 129; EWL 3

Spivack, Kathleen (Romola Drucker)
1938- .... **CLC 6**
See also CA 49-52

Spoto, Donald 1941- .... **CLC 39**
See also CA 65-68; CANR 11, 57, 93

Springsteen, Bruce (F.) 1949- .... **CLC 17**
See also CA 111

Spurling, (Susan) Hilary 1940- .... **CLC 34**
See also CA 104; CANR 25, 52, 94

Spyker, John Howland
See Elman, Richard (Martin)

Squared, A.
See Abbott, Edwin A.

Squires, (James) Radcliffe
1917-1993 .... **CLC 51**
See also CA 1-4R; 140; CANR 6, 21

Srivastava, Dhanpat Rai 1880(?)-1936
See Premchand
See also CA 118; 197

Stacy, Donald
See Pohl, Frederik

Stael
See Stael-Holstein, Anne Louise Germaine Necker
See also EW 5; RGWL 2, 3

Stael, Germaine de
See Stael-Holstein, Anne Louise Germaine Necker
See also DLB 119, 192; FW; GFL 1789 to the Present; TWA

Stael-Holstein, Anne Louise Germaine Necker 1766-1817 .... NCLC 3, 91
See Stael; Stael, Germaine de

Stafford, Jean 1915-1979 .. CLC 4, 7, 19, 68; SSC 26
See also CA 1-4R; 85-88; CANR 3, 65; DLB 2, 173; MTCW 1, 2; RGAL 4; RGSF 2; SATA-Obit 22; TCWW 2; TUS

Stafford, William (Edgar) 1914-1993 .... CLC 4, 7, 29
See also AMWS 11; CA 5-8R; 142; CAAS 3; CANR 5, 22; DAM POET; DLB 5, 206; EXPP; INT CANR-22; PFS 2, 8, 16; RGAL 4; WP

Stagnelius, Eric Johan 1793-1823 . NCLC 61

Staines, Trevor
See Brunner, John (Kilian Houston)

Stairs, Gordon
See Austin, Mary (Hunter)
See also TCWW 2

Stalin, Joseph 1879-1953 .... TCLC 92

Stampa, Gaspara c. 1524-1554 .... PC 43
See also RGWL 2, 3

Stampflinger, K. A.
See Benjamin, Walter

Stancykowna
See Szymborska, Wislawa

Standing Bear, Luther 1868(?)-1939(?) .... NNAL
See also CA 113; 144; DAM MULT

Stannard, Martin 1947- .... CLC 44
See also CA 142; DLB 155

Stanton, Elizabeth Cady 1815-1902 .... TCLC 73
See also CA 171; DLB 79; FW

Stanton, Maura 1946- .... CLC 9
See also CA 89-92; CANR 15, 123; DLB 120

Stanton, Schuyler
See Baum, L(yman) Frank

Stapledon, (William) Olaf 1886-1950 .... TCLC 22
See also CA 111; 162; DLB 15, 255; SFW 4

Starbuck, George (Edwin) 1931-1996 .... CLC 53
See also CA 21-24R; 153; CANR 23; DAM POET

Stark, Richard
See Westlake, Donald E(dwin)

Staunton, Schuyler
See Baum, L(yman) Frank

Stead, Christina (Ellen) 1902-1983 ... CLC 2, 5, 8, 32, 80
See also BRWS 4; CA 13-16R; 109; CANR 33, 40; DLB 260; EWL 3; FW; MTCW 1, 2; RGEL 2; RGSF 2; WWE 1

Stead, William Thomas 1849-1912 .... TCLC 48
See also CA 167

Stebnitsky, M.
See Leskov, Nikolai (Semyonovich)

Steele, Sir Richard 1672-1729 .... LC 18
See also BRW 3; CDBLB 1660-1789; DLB 84, 101; RGEL 2; WLIT 3

Steele, Timothy (Reid) 1948- .... CLC 45
See also CA 93-96; CANR 16, 50, 92; CP 7; DLB 120, 282

Steffens, (Joseph) Lincoln 1866-1936 .... TCLC 20
See also CA 117; 198; DLB 303

Stegner, Wallace (Earle) 1909-1993 .. CLC 9, 49, 81; SSC 27
See also AITN 1; AMWS 4; ANW; BEST 90:3; BPFB 3; CA 1-4R; 141; CAAS 9; CANR 1, 21, 46; DAM NOV; DLB 9, 206, 275; DLBY 1993; EWL 3; MTCW 1, 2; RGAL 4; TCWW 2; TUS

Stein, Gertrude 1874-1946 .... DC 19; PC 18; SSC 42; TCLC 1, 6, 28, 48; WLC
See also AMW; AMWC 2; CA 104; 132; CANR 108; CDALB 1917-1929; DA; DA3; DAB; DAC; DAM MST, NOV, POET; DLB 4, 54, 86, 228; DLBD 15; EWL 3; EXPS; GLL 1; MAWW; MTCW 1, 2; NCFS 4; RGAL 4; RGSF 2; SSFS 5; TUS; WP

Steinbeck, John (Ernst) 1902-1968 ... CLC 1, 5, 9, 13, 21, 34, 45, 75, 124; SSC 11, 37, 77; TCLC 135; WLC
See also AAYA 12; AMW; BPFB 3; BYA 2, 3, 13; CA 1-4R; 25-28R; CANR 1, 35; CDALB 1929-1941; DA; DA3; DAB; DAC; DAM DRAM, MST, NOV; DLB 7, 9, 212, 275, 309; DLBD 2; EWL 3; EXPS; LAIT 3; MTCW 1, 2; NFS 1, 5, 7, 17, 19; RGAL 4; RGSF 2; RHW; SATA 9; SSFS 3, 6; TCWW 2; TUS; WYA; YAW

Steinem, Gloria 1934- .... CLC 63
See also CA 53-56; CANR 28, 51; DLB 246; FW; MTCW 1, 2

Steiner, George 1929- .... CLC 24
See also CA 73-76; CANR 31, 67, 108; DAM NOV; DLB 67, 299; EWL 3; MTCW 1, 2; SATA 62

Steiner, K. Leslie
See Delany, Samuel R(ay), Jr.

Steiner, Rudolf 1861-1925 .... TCLC 13
See also CA 107

Stendhal 1783-1842 .. NCLC 23, 46; SSC 27; WLC
See also DA; DA3; DAB; DAC; DAM MST, NOV; DLB 119; EW 5; GFL 1789 to the Present; RGWL 2, 3; TWA

Stephen, Adeline Virginia
See Woolf, (Adeline) Virginia

Stephen, Sir Leslie 1832-1904 .... TCLC 23
See also BRW 5; CA 123; DLB 57, 144, 190

Stephen, Sir Leslie
See Stephen, Sir Leslie

Stephen, Virginia
See Woolf, (Adeline) Virginia

Stephens, James 1882(?)-1950 .... SSC 50; TCLC 4
See also CA 104; 192; DLB 19, 153, 162; EWL 3; FANT; RGEL 2; SUFW

Stephens, Reed
See Donaldson, Stephen R(eeder)

Steptoe, Lydia
See Barnes, Djuna
See also GLL 1

Sterchi, Beat 1949- .... CLC 65
See also CA 203

Sterling, Brett
See Bradbury, Ray (Douglas); Hamilton, Edmond

Sterling, Bruce 1954- .... CLC 72
See also CA 119; CANR 44, 135; SCFW 2; SFW 4

Sterling, George 1869-1926 .... TCLC 20
See also CA 117; 165; DLB 54

Stern, Gerald 1925- .... CLC 40, 100
See also AMWS 9; CA 81-84; CANR 28, 94; CP 7; DLB 105; RGAL 4

Stern, Richard (Gustave) 1928- ... CLC 4, 39
See also CA 1-4R; CANR 1, 25, 52, 120; CN 7; DLB 218; DLBY 1987; INT CANR-25

Sternberg, Josef von 1894-1969 .... CLC 20
See also CA 81-84

Sterne, Laurence 1713-1768 .... LC 2, 48; WLC
See also BRW 3; BRWC 1; CDBLB 1660-1789; DA; DAB; DAC; DAM MST, NOV; DLB 39; RGEL 2; TEA

Sternheim, (William Adolf) Carl 1878-1942 .... TCLC 8
See also CA 105; 193; DLB 56, 118; EWL 3; RGWL 2, 3

Stevens, Mark 1951- .... CLC 34
See also CA 122

Stevens, Wallace 1879-1955 . PC 6; TCLC 3, 12, 45; WLC
See also AMW; AMWR 1; CA 104; 124; CDALB 1929-1941; DA; DA3; DAB; DAC; DAM MST, POET; DLB 54; EWL 3; EXPP; MTCW 1, 2; PAB; PFS 13, 16; RGAL 4; TUS; WP

Stevenson, Anne (Katharine) 1933- .. CLC 7, 33
See also BRWS 6; CA 17-20R; CAAS 9; CANR 9, 33, 123; CP 7; CWP; DLB 40; MTCW 1; RHW

Stevenson, Robert Louis (Balfour) 1850-1894 ...... NCLC 5, 14, 63; SSC 11, 51; WLC
See also AAYA 24; BPFB 3; BRW 5; BRWC 1; BRWR 1; BYA 1, 2, 4, 13; CD-BLB 1890-1914; CLR 10, 11; DA; DA3; DAB; DAC; DAM MST, NOV; DLB 18, 57, 141, 156, 174; DLBD 13; HGG; JRDA; LAIT 1, 3; MAICYA 1, 2; NFS 11, 20; RGEL 2; RGSF 2; SATA 100; SUFW; TEA; WCH; WLIT 4; WYA; YABC 2; YAW

Stewart, J(ohn) I(nnes) M(ackintosh) 1906-1994 .... CLC 7, 14, 32
See Innes, Michael
See also CA 85-88; 147; CAAS 3; CANR 47; CMW 4; MTCW 1, 2

Stewart, Mary (Florence Elinor) 1916- .... CLC 7, 35, 117
See also AAYA 29; BPFB 3; CA 1-4R; CANR 1, 59, 130; CMW 4; CPW; DAB; FANT; RHW; SATA 12; YAW

Stewart, Mary Rainbow
See Stewart, Mary (Florence Elinor)

Stifle, June
See Campbell, Maria

Stifter, Adalbert 1805-1868 .. NCLC 41; SSC 28
See also CDWLB 2; DLB 133; RGSF 2; RGWL 2, 3

Still, James 1906-2001 .... CLC 49
See also CA 65-68; 195; CAAS 17; CANR 10, 26; CSW; DLB 9; DLBY 01; SATA 29; SATA-Obit 127

Sting 1951-
See Sumner, Gordon Matthew
See also CA 167

Stirling, Arthur
See Sinclair, Upton (Beall)

Stitt, Milan 1941- .... CLC 29
See also CA 69-72

Stockton, Francis Richard 1834-1902
See Stockton, Frank R.
See also CA 108; 137; MAICYA 1, 2; SATA 44; SFW 4

Stockton, Frank R. .... TCLC 47
See Stockton, Francis Richard
See also BYA 4, 13; DLB 42, 74; DLBD 13; EXPS; SATA-Brief 32; SSFS 3; SUFW; WCH

Stoddard, Charles
See Kuttner, Henry

Stoker, Abraham 1847-1912
See Stoker, Bram
See also CA 105; 150; DA; DA3; DAC;
DAM MST, NOV; HGG; SATA 29

Stoker, Bram . **SSC 62; TCLC 8, 144; WLC**
See Stoker, Abraham
See also AAYA 23; BPFB 3; BRWS 3; BYA
5; CDBLB 1890-1914; DAB; DLB 304;
LATS 1:1; NFS 18; RGEL 2; SUFW;
TEA; WLIT 4

Stolz, Mary (Slattery) 1920- .... **CLC 12**
See also AAYA 8; AITN 1; CA 5-8R;
CANR 13, 41, 112; JRDA; MAICYA 1,
2; SAAS 3; SATA 10, 71, 133; YAW

Stone, Irving 1903-1989 .... **CLC 7**
See also AITN 1; BPFB 3; CA 1-4R; 129;
CAAS 3; CANR 1, 23; CPW; DA3; DAM
POP; INT CANR-23; MTCW 1, 2; RHW;
SATA 3; SATA-Obit 64

Stone, Oliver (William) 1946- .... **CLC 73**
See also AAYA 15; CA 110; CANR 55, 125

Stone, Robert (Anthony) 1937- ... **CLC 5, 23,
42, 175**
See also AMWS 5; BPFB 3; CA 85-88;
CANR 23, 66, 95; CN 7; DLB 152; EWL
3; INT CANR-23; MTCW 1

Stone, Ruth 1915- .... **PC 53**
See also CA 45-48; CANR 2, 91; CP 7;
CSW; DLB 105; PFS 19

Stone, Zachary
See Follett, Ken(neth Martin)

Stoppard, Tom 1937- ... **CLC 1, 3, 4, 5, 8, 15,
29, 34, 63, 91; DC 6; WLC**
See also BRWC 1; BRWR 2; BRWS 1; CA
81-84; CANR 39, 67, 125; CBD; CD 5;
CDBLB 1960 to Present; DA; DA3;
DAB; DAC; DAM DRAM, MST; DFS 2,
5, 8, 11, 13, 16; DLB 13, 233; DLBY
1985; EWL 3; LATS 1:2; MTCW 1, 2;
RGEL 2; TEA; WLIT 4

Storey, David (Malcolm) 1933- . **CLC 2, 4, 5,
8**
See also BRWS 1; CA 81-84; CANR 36;
CBD; CD 5; CN 7; DAM DRAM; DLB
13, 14, 207, 245; EWL 3; MTCW 1;
RGEL 2

Storm, Hyemeyohsts 1935- ... **CLC 3; NNAL**
See also CA 81-84; CANR 45; DAM MULT

Storm, (Hans) Theodor (Woldsen)
1817-1888 .... **NCLC 1; SSC 27**
See also CDWLB 2; DLB 129; EW; RGSF
2; RGWL 2, 3

Storni, Alfonsina 1892-1938 . **HLC 2; PC 33;
TCLC 5**
See also CA 104; 131; DAM MULT; DLB
283; HW 1; LAW

Stoughton, William 1631-1701 .... **LC 38**
See also DLB 24

Stout, Rex (Todhunter) 1886-1975 ..... **CLC 3**
See also AITN 2; BPFB 3; CA 61-64;
CANR 71; CMW 4; DLB 306; MSW;
RGAL 4

Stow, (Julian) Randolph 1935- ... **CLC 23, 48**
See also CA 13-16R; CANR 33; CN 7;
DLB 260; MTCW 1; RGEL 2

Stowe, Harriet (Elizabeth) Beecher
1811-1896 .... **NCLC 3, 50, 133; WLC**
See also AAYA 53; AMWS 1; CDALB
1865-1917; DA; DA3; DAB; DAC; DAM
MST, NOV; DLB 1, 12, 42, 74, 189, 239,
243; EXPN; JRDA; LAIT 2; MAICYA 1,
2; NFS 6; RGAL 4; TUS; YABC 1

Strabo c. 64B.C.-c. 25 .... **CMLC 37**
See also DLB 176

Strachey, (Giles) Lytton
1880-1932 .... **TCLC 12**
See also BRWS 2; CA 110; 178; DLB 149;
DLBD 10; EWL 3; MTCW 2; NCFS 4

Stramm, August 1874-1915 .... **PC 50**
See also CA 195; EWL 3

Strand, Mark 1934- .... **CLC 6, 18, 41, 71**
See also AMWS 4; CA 21-24R; CANR 40,
65, 100; CP 7; DAM POET; DLB 5; EWL
3; PAB; PFS 9, 18; RGAL 4; SATA 41

Stratton-Porter, Gene(va Grace) 1863-1924
See Porter, Gene(va Grace) Stratton
See also ANW; CA 137; CLR 87; DLB 221;
DLBD 14; MAICYA 1, 2; SATA 15

Straub, Peter (Francis) 1943- ... **CLC 28, 107**
See also BEST 89:1; BPFB 3; CA 85-88;
CANR 28, 65, 109; CPW; DAM POP;
DLBY 1984; HGG; MTCW 1, 2; SUFW
2

Strauss, Botho 1944- .... **CLC 22**
See also CA 157; CWW 2; DLB 124

Strauss, Leo 1899-1973 .... **TCLC 141**
See also CA 101; 45-48; CANR 122

Streatfeild, (Mary) Noel
1897(?)-1986 .... **CLC 21**
See also CA 81-84; 120; CANR 31; CLR
17, 83; CWRI 5; DLB 160; MAICYA 1,
2; SATA 20; SATA-Obit 48

Stribling, T(homas) S(igismund)
1881-1965 .... **CLC 23**
See also CA 189; 107; CMW 4; DLB 9;
RGAL 4

Strindberg, (Johan) August
1849-1912 ... **DC 18; TCLC 1, 8, 21, 47;
WLC**
See also CA 104; 135; DA; DA3; DAB;
DAC; DAM DRAM, MST; DFS 4, 9;
DLB 259; EW 7; EWL 3; IDTP; LMFS
2; MTCW 2; RGWL 2, 3; TWA

Stringer, Arthur 1874-1950 .... **TCLC 37**
See also CA 161; DLB 92

Stringer, David
See Roberts, Keith (John Kingston)

Stroheim, Erich von 1885-1957 ..... **TCLC 71**

Strugatskii, Arkadii (Natanovich)
1925-1991 .... **CLC 27**
See Strugatsky, Arkadii Natanovich
See also CA 106; 135; SFW 4

Strugatskii, Boris (Natanovich)
1933- .... **CLC 27**
See Strugatsky, Boris (Natanovich)
See also CA 106; SFW 4

Strugatsky, Arkadii Natanovich
See Strugatskii, Arkadii (Natanovich)
See also DLB 302

Strugatsky, Boris (Natanovich)
See Strugatskii, Boris (Natanovich)
See also DLB 302

Strummer, Joe 1953(?)- .... **CLC 30**

Strunk, William, Jr. 1869-1946 ...... **TCLC 92**
See also CA 118; 164; NCFS 5

Stryk, Lucien 1924- .... **PC 27**
See also CA 13-16R; CANR 10, 28, 55,
110; CP 7

Stuart, Don A.
See Campbell, John W(ood, Jr.)

Stuart, Ian
See MacLean, Alistair (Stuart)

Stuart, Jesse (Hilton) 1906-1984 ... **CLC 1, 8,
11, 14, 34; SSC 31**
See also CA 5-8R; 112; CANR 31; DLB 9,
48, 102; DLBY 1984; SATA 2; SATA-
Obit 36

Stubblefield, Sally
See Trumbo, Dalton

Sturgeon, Theodore (Hamilton)
1918-1985 .... **CLC 22, 39**
See Queen, Ellery
See also AAYA 51; BPFB 3; BYA 9, 10;
CA 81-84; 116; CANR 32, 103; DLB 8;
DLBY 1985; HGG; MTCW 1, 2; SCFW;
SFW 4; SUFW

Sturges, Preston 1898-1959 .... **TCLC 48**
See also CA 114; 149; DLB 26

Styron, William 1925- .... **CLC 1, 3, 5, 11, 15,
60; SSC 25**
See also AMW; AMWC 2; BEST 90:4;
BPFB 3; CA 5-8R; CANR 6, 33, 74, 126;
CDALB 1968-1988; CN 7; CPW; CSW;
DA3; DAM NOV, POP; DLB 2, 143, 299;
DLBY 1980; EWL 3; INT CANR-6;
LAIT 2; MTCW 1, 2; NCFS 1; RGAL 4;
RHW; TUS

Su, Chien 1884-1918
See Su Man-shu
See also CA 123

Suarez Lynch, B.
See Bioy Casares, Adolfo; Borges, Jorge
Luis

Suassuna, Ariano Vilar 1927- .... **HLCS 1**
See also CA 178; DLB 307; HW 2; LAW

Suckert, Kurt Erich
See Malaparte, Curzio

Suckling, Sir John 1609-1642 . **LC 75; PC 30**
See also BRW 2; DAM POET; DLB 58,
126; EXPP; PAB; RGEL 2

Suckow, Ruth 1892-1960 .... **SSC 18**
See also CA 193; 113; DLB 9, 102; RGAL
4; TCWW 2

Sudermann, Hermann 1857-1928 .. **TCLC 15**
See also CA 107; 201; DLB 118

Sue, Eugene 1804-1857 .... **NCLC 1**
See also DLB 119

Sueskind, Patrick 1949- .... **CLC 44, 182**
See Suskind, Patrick

Suetonius c. 70-c. 130 .... **CMLC 60**
See also AW 2; DLB 211; RGWL 2, 3

Sukenick, Ronald 1932-2004 ..... **CLC 3, 4, 6,
48**
See also CA 25-28R; 209; 229; CAAE 209;
CAAS 8; CANR 32, 89; CN 7; DLB 173;
DLBY 1981

Suknaski, Andrew 1942- .... **CLC 19**
See also CA 101; CP 7; DLB 53

Sullivan, Vernon
See Vian, Boris

Sully Prudhomme, Rene-Francois-Armand
1839-1907 .... **TCLC 31**
See also GFL 1789 to the Present

Su Man-shu .... **TCLC 24**
See Su, Chien
See also EWL 3

Sumarokov, Aleksandr Petrovich
1717-1777 .... **LC 104**
See also DLB 150

Summerforest, Ivy B.
See Kirkup, James

Summers, Andrew James 1942- .... **CLC 26**

Summers, Andy
See Summers, Andrew James

Summers, Hollis (Spurgeon, Jr.)
1916- .... **CLC 10**
See also CA 5-8R; CANR 3; DLB 6

**Summers, (Alphonsus Joseph-Mary
Augustus) Montague**
1880-1948 .... **TCLC 16**
See also CA 118; 163

Sumner, Gordon Matthew .... **CLC 26**
See Police, The; Sting

Sun Tzu c. 400B.C.-c. 320B.C. ...... **CMLC 56**

Surrey, Henry Howard 1517-1574 ...... **PC 59**
See also BRW 1; RGEL 2

Surtees, Robert Smith 1805-1864 .. **NCLC 14**
See also DLB 21; RGEL 2

Susann, Jacqueline 1921-1974 .... **CLC 3**
See also AITN 1; BPFB 3; CA 65-68; 53-
56; MTCW 1, 2

Su Shi
See Su Shih
See also RGWL 2, 3

Su Shih 1036-1101 .... **CMLC 15**
See Su Shi
Suskind, Patrick .... **CLC 182**
See Sueskind, Patrick
See also BPFB 3; CA 145; CWW 2
Sutcliff, Rosemary 1920-1992 .... **CLC 26**
See also AAYA 10; BYA 1, 4; CA 5-8R;
139; CANR 37; CLR 1, 37; CPW; DAB;
DAC; DAM MST, POP; JRDA; LATS
1:1; MAICYA 1, 2; MAICYAS 1; RHW;
SATA 6, 44, 78; SATA-Obit 73; WYA;
YAW
Sutro, Alfred 1863-1933 .... **TCLC 6**
See also CA 105; 185; DLB 10; RGEL 2
Sutton, Henry
See Slavitt, David R(ytman)
Suzuki, D. T.
See Suzuki, Daisetz Teitaro
Suzuki, Daisetz T.
See Suzuki, Daisetz Teitaro
Suzuki, Daisetz Teitaro
1870-1966 .... **TCLC 109**
See also CA 121; 111; MTCW 1, 2
Suzuki, Teitaro
See Suzuki, Daisetz Teitaro
Svevo, Italo .... **SSC 25; TCLC 2, 35**
See Schmitz, Aron Hector
See also DLB 264; EW 8; EWL 3; RGWL
2, 3
Swados, Elizabeth (A.) 1951- .... **CLC 12**
See also CA 97-100; CANR 49; INT CA-
97-100
Swados, Harvey 1920-1972 .... **CLC 5**
See also CA 5-8R; 37-40R; CANR 6; DLB
2
Swan, Gladys 1934- .... **CLC 69**
See also CA 101; CANR 17, 39
Swanson, Logan
See Matheson, Richard (Burton)
Swarthout, Glendon (Fred)
1918-1992 .... **CLC 35**
See also AAYA 55; CA 1-4R; 139; CANR
1, 47; LAIT 5; SATA 26; TCWW 2; YAW
Swedenborg, Emanuel 1688-1772 ..... **LC 105**
Sweet, Sarah C.
See Jewett, (Theodora) Sarah Orne
Swenson, May 1919-1989 ...... **CLC 4, 14, 61,
106; PC 14**
See also AMWS 4; CA 5-8R; 130; CANR
36, 61, 131; DA; DAB; DAC; DAM MST,
POET; DLB 5; EXPP; GLL 2; MTCW 1,
2; PFS 16; SATA 15; WP
Swift, Augustus
See Lovecraft, H(oward) P(hillips)
Swift, Graham (Colin) 1949- ...... **CLC 41, 88**
See also BRWC 2; BRWS 5; CA 117; 122;
CANR 46, 71, 128; CN 7; DLB 194;
MTCW 2; NFS 18; RGSF 2
Swift, Jonathan 1667-1745 ..... **LC 1, 42, 101;
PC 9; WLC**
See also AAYA 41; BRW 3; BRWC 1;
BRWR 1; BYA 5, 14; CDBLB 1660-1789;
CLR 53; DA; DA3; DAB; DAC; DAM
MST, NOV, POET; DLB 39, 95, 101;
EXPN; LAIT 1; NFS 6; RGEL 2; SATA
19; TEA; WCH; WLIT 3
Swinburne, Algernon Charles
1837-1909 ... **PC 24; TCLC 8, 36; WLC**
See also BRW 5; CA 105; 140; CDBLB
1832-1890; DA; DA3; DAB; DAC; DAM
MST, POET; DLB 35, 57; PAB; RGEL 2;
TEA
Swinfen, Ann .... **CLC 34**
See also CA 202
Swinnerton, Frank Arthur
1884-1982 .... **CLC 31**
See also CA 108; DLB 34
Swithen, John
See King, Stephen (Edwin)

Sylvia
See Ashton-Warner, Sylvia (Constance)
Symmes, Robert Edward
See Duncan, Robert (Edward)
Symonds, John Addington
1840-1893 .... **NCLC 34**
See also DLB 57, 144
Symons, Arthur 1865-1945 .... **TCLC 11**
See also CA 107; 189; DLB 19, 57, 149;
RGEL 2
Symons, Julian (Gustave)
1912-1994 .... **CLC 2, 14, 32**
See also CA 49-52; 147; CAAS 3; CANR
3, 33, 59; CMW 4; DLB 87, 155; DLBY
1992; MSW; MTCW 1
Synge, (Edmund) J(ohn) M(illington)
1871-1909 .... **DC 2; TCLC 6, 37**
See also BRW 6; BRWR 1; CA 104; 141;
CDBLB 1890-1914; DAM DRAM; DFS
18; DLB 10, 19; EWL 3; RGEL 2; TEA;
WLIT 4
Syruc, J.
See Milosz, Czeslaw
Szirtes, George 1948- .... **CLC 46; PC 51**
See also CA 109; CANR 27, 61, 117; CP 7
Szymborska, Wislawa 1923- ... **CLC 99, 190;
PC 44**
See also CA 154; CANR 91, 133; CDWLB
4; CWP; CWW 2; DA3; DLB 232; DLBY
1996; EWL 3; MTCW 2; PFS 15; RGWL
3
T. O., Nik
See Annensky, Innokenty (Fyodorovich)
Tabori, George 1914- .... **CLC 19**
See also CA 49-52; CANR 4, 69; CBD; CD
5; DLB 245
Tacitus c. 55-c. 117 .... **CMLC 56**
See also AW 2; CDWLB 1; DLB 211;
RGWL 2, 3
Tagore, Rabindranath 1861-1941 .... **PC 8;
SSC 48; TCLC 3, 53**
See also CA 104; 120; DA3; DAM DRAM,
POET; EWL 3; MTCW 1, 2; PFS 18;
RGEL 2; RGSF 2; RGWL 2, 3; TWA
Taine, Hippolyte Adolphe
1828-1893 .... **NCLC 15**
See also EW 7; GFL 1789 to the Present
Talayesva, Don C. 1890-(?) .... **NNAL**
Talese, Gay 1932- .... **CLC 37**
See also AITN 1; CA 1-4R; CANR 9, 58;
DLB 185; INT CANR-9; MTCW 1, 2
Tallent, Elizabeth (Ann) 1954- .... **CLC 45**
See also CA 117; CANR 72; DLB 130
Tallmountain, Mary 1918-1997 .... **NNAL**
See also CA 146; 161; DLB 193
Tally, Ted 1952- .... **CLC 42**
See also CA 120; 124; CAD; CANR 125;
CD 5; INT CA-124
Talvik, Heiti 1904-1947 .... **TCLC 87**
See also EWL 3
Tamayo y Baus, Manuel
1829-1898 .... **NCLC 1**
Tammsaare, A(nton) H(ansen)
1878-1940 .... **TCLC 27**
See also CA 164; CDWLB 4; DLB 220;
EWL 3
Tam'si, Tchicaya U
See Tchicaya, Gerald Felix
Tan, Amy (Ruth) 1952- . **AAL; CLC 59, 120,
151**
See also AAYA 9, 48; AMWS 10; BEST
89:3; BPFB 3; CA 136; CANR 54, 105,
132; CDALBS; CN 7; CPW 1; DA3;
DAM MULT, NOV, POP; DLB 173;
EXPN; FW; LAIT 3, 5; MTCW 2; NFS
1, 13, 16; RGAL 4; SATA 75; SSFS 9;
YAW
Tandem, Felix
See Spitteler, Carl (Friedrich Georg)

Tanizaki, Jun'ichiro 1886-1965 ... **CLC 8, 14,
28; SSC 21**
See Tanizaki Jun'ichiro
See also CA 93-96; 25-28R; MJW; MTCW
2; RGSF 2; RGWL 2
Tanizaki Jun'ichiro
See Tanizaki, Jun'ichiro
See also DLB 180; EWL 3
Tanner, William
See Amis, Kingsley (William)
Tao Lao
See Storni, Alfonsina
Tapahonso, Luci 1953- .... **NNAL**
See also CA 145; CANR 72, 127; DLB 175
Tarantino, Quentin (Jerome)
1963- .... **CLC 125**
See also AAYA 58; CA 171; CANR 125
Tarassoff, Lev
See Troyat, Henri
Tarbell, Ida M(inerva) 1857-1944 . **TCLC 40**
See also CA 122; 181; DLB 47
Tarkington, (Newton) Booth
1869-1946 .... **TCLC 9**
See also BPFB 3; BYA 3; CA 110; 143;
CWRI 5; DLB 9, 102; MTCW 2; RGAL
4; SATA 17
Tarkovskii, Andrei Arsen'evich
See Tarkovsky, Andrei (Arsenyevich)
Tarkovsky, Andrei (Arsenyevich)
1932-1986 .... **CLC 75**
See also CA 127
Tartt, Donna 1963- .... **CLC 76**
See also AAYA 56; CA 142
Tasso, Torquato 1544-1595 .... **LC 5, 94**
See also EFS 2; EW 2; RGWL 2, 3
Tate, (John Orley) Allen 1899-1979 .. **CLC 2,
4, 6, 9, 11, 14, 24; PC 50**
See also AMW; CA 5-8R; 85-88; CANR
32, 108; DLB 4, 45, 63; DLBD 17; EWL
3; MTCW 1, 2; RGAL 4; RHW
Tate, Ellalice
See Hibbert, Eleanor Alice Burford
Tate, James (Vincent) 1943- ..... **CLC 2, 6, 25**
See also CA 21-24R; CANR 29, 57, 114;
CP 7; DLB 5, 169; EWL 3; PFS 10, 15;
RGAL 4; WP
Tate, Nahum 1652(?)-1715 .... **LC 109**
See also DLB 80; RGEL 2
Tauler, Johannes c. 1300-1361 ...... **CMLC 37**
See also DLB 179; LMFS 1
Tavel, Ronald 1940- .... **CLC 6**
See also CA 21-24R; CAD; CANR 33; CD
5
Taviani, Paolo 1931- .... **CLC 70**
See also CA 153
Taylor, Bayard 1825-1878 .... **NCLC 89**
See also DLB 3, 189, 250, 254; RGAL 4
Taylor, C(ecil) P(hilip) 1929-1981 .... **CLC 27**
See also CA 25-28R; 105; CANR 47; CBD
Taylor, Edward 1642(?)-1729 .... **LC 11**
See also AMW; DA; DAB; DAC; DAM
MST, POET; DLB 24; EXPP; RGAL 4;
TUS
Taylor, Eleanor Ross 1920- .... **CLC 5**
See also CA 81-84; CANR 70
Taylor, Elizabeth 1932-1975 ..... **CLC 2, 4, 29**
See also CA 13-16R; CANR 9, 70; DLB
139; MTCW 1; RGEL 2; SATA 13
Taylor, Frederick Winslow
1856-1915 .... **TCLC 76**
See also CA 188
Taylor, Henry (Splawn) 1942- .... **CLC 44**
See also CA 33-36R; CAAS 7; CANR 31;
CP 7; DLB 5; PFS 10
Taylor, Kamala (Purnaiya) 1924-2004
See Markandaya, Kamala
See also CA 77-80; 227; NFS 13

Author Index

Taylor, Mildred D(elois) 1943- .... **CLC 21**
  See also AAYA 10, 47; BW 1; BYA 3, 8;
  CA 85-88; CANR 25, 115; CLR 9, 59,
  90; CSW; DLB 52; JRDA; LAIT 3; MAI-
  CYA 1, 2; SAAS 5; SATA 135; WYA;
  YAW

Taylor, Peter (Hillsman) 1917-1994 .. **CLC 1,**
  4, 18, 37, 44, 50, 71; SSC 10
  See also AMWS 5; BPFB 3; CA 13-16R;
  147; CANR 9, 50; CSW; DLB 218, 278;
  DLBY 1981, 1994; EWL 3; EXPS; INT
  CANR-9; MTCW 1, 2; RGSF 2; SSFS 9;
  TUS

Taylor, Robert Lewis 1912-1998 .... **CLC 14**
  See also CA 1-4R; 170; CANR 3, 64; SATA
  10

Tchekhov, Anton
  See Chekhov, Anton (Pavlovich)

Tchicaya, Gerald Felix 1931-1988 .. **CLC 101**
  See Tchicaya U Tam'si
  See also CA 129; 125; CANR 81

Tchicaya U Tam'si
  See Tchicaya, Gerald Felix
  See also EWL 3

Teasdale, Sara 1884-1933 .... **PC 31; TCLC 4**
  See also CA 104; 163; DLB 45; GLL 1;
  PFS 14; RGAL 4; SATA 32; TUS

Tecumseh 1768-1813 .... **NNAL**
  See also DAM MULT

Tegner, Esaias 1782-1846 .... **NCLC 2**

Teilhard de Chardin, (Marie Joseph) Pierre
  1881-1955 .... **TCLC 9**
  See also CA 105; 210; GFL 1789 to the
  Present

Temple, Ann
  See Mortimer, Penelope (Ruth)

Tennant, Emma (Christina) 1937- .. **CLC 13,**
  52
  See also BRWS 9; CA 65-68; CAAS 9;
  CANR 10, 38, 59, 88; CN 7; DLB 14;
  EWL 3; SFW 4

Tenneshaw, S. M.
  See Silverberg, Robert

Tenney, Tabitha Gilman
  1762-1837 .... **NCLC 122**
  See also DLB 37, 200

Tennyson, Alfred 1809-1892 ... **NCLC 30, 65,**
  115; PC 6; WLC
  See also AAYA 50; BRW 4; CDBLB 1832-
  1890; DA; DA3; DAB; DAC; DAM MST,
  POET; DLB 32; EXPP; PAB; PFS 1, 2, 4,
  11, 15, 19; RGEL 2; TEA; WLIT 4; WP

Teran, Lisa St. Aubin de .... **CLC 36**
  See St. Aubin de Teran, Lisa

Terence c. 184B.C.-c. 159B.C. ...... **CMLC 14;**
  DC 7
  See also AW 1; CDWLB 1; DLB 211;
  RGWL 2, 3; TWA

Teresa de Jesus, St. 1515-1582 .... **LC 18**

Terkel, Louis 1912-
  See Terkel, Studs
  See also CA 57-60; CANR 18, 45, 67, 132;
  DA3; MTCW 1, 2

Terkel, Studs .... **CLC 38**
  See Terkel, Louis
  See also AAYA 32; AITN 1; MTCW 2; TUS

Terry, C. V.
  See Slaughter, Frank G(ill)

Terry, Megan 1932- .... **CLC 19; DC 13**
  See also CA 77-80; CABS 3; CAD; CANR
  43; CD 5; CWD; DFS 18; DLB 7, 249;
  GLL 2

Tertullian c. 155-c. 245 .... **CMLC 29**

Tertz, Abram
  See Sinyavsky, Andrei (Donatevich)
  See also RGSF 2

Tesich, Steve 1943(?)-1996 .... **CLC 40, 69**
  See also CA 105; 152; CAD; DLBY 1983

Tesla, Nikola 1856-1943 .... **TCLC 88**

Teternikov, Fyodor Kuzmich 1863-1927
  See Sologub, Fyodor
  See also CA 104

Tevis, Walter 1928-1984 .... **CLC 42**
  See also CA 113; SFW 4

Tey, Josephine .... **TCLC 14**
  See Mackintosh, Elizabeth
  See also DLB 77; MSW

Thackeray, William Makepeace
  1811-1863 .... **NCLC 5, 14, 22, 43; WLC**
  See also BRW 5; BRWC 2; CDBLB 1832-
  1890; DA; DA3; DAB; DAC; DAM MST,
  NOV; DLB 21, 55, 159, 163; NFS 13;
  RGEL 2; SATA 23; TEA; WLIT 3

Thakura, Ravindranatha
  See Tagore, Rabindranath

Thames, C. H.
  See Marlowe, Stephen

Tharoor, Shashi 1956- .... **CLC 70**
  See also CA 141; CANR 91; CN 7

Thelwell, Michael Miles 1939- .... **CLC 22**
  See also BW 2; CA 101

Theobald, Lewis, Jr.
  See Lovecraft, H(oward) P(hillips)

Theocritus c. 310B.C.- .... **CMLC 45**
  See also AW 1; DLB 176; RGWL 2, 3

Theodorescu, Ion N. 1880-1967
  See Arghezi, Tudor
  See also CA 116

Theriault, Yves 1915-1983 .... **CLC 79**
  See also CA 102; CCA 1; DAC; DAM
  MST; DLB 88; EWL 3

Theroux, Alexander (Louis) 1939- .... **CLC 2,**
  25
  See also CA 85-88; CANR 20, 63; CN 7

Theroux, Paul (Edward) 1941- ..... **CLC 5, 8,**
  11, 15, 28, 46
  See also AAYA 28; AMWS 8; BEST 89:4;
  BPFB 3; CA 33-36R; CANR 20, 45, 74,
  133; CDALBS; CN 7; CPW 1; DA3;
  DAM POP; DLB 2, 218; EWL 3; HGG;
  MTCW 1, 2; RGAL 4; SATA 44, 109;
  TUS

Thesen, Sharon 1946- .... **CLC 56**
  See also CA 163; CANR 125; CP 7; CWP

Thespis fl. 6th cent. B.C.- .... **CMLC 51**
  See also LMFS 1

Thevenin, Denis
  See Duhamel, Georges

Thibault, Jacques Anatole Francois
  1844-1924
  See France, Anatole
  See also CA 106; 127; DA3; DAM NOV;
  MTCW 1, 2; TWA

Thiele, Colin (Milton) 1920- .... **CLC 17**
  See also CA 29-32R; CANR 12, 28, 53,
  105; CLR 27; DLB 289; MAICYA 1, 2;
  SAAS 2; SATA 14, 72, 125; YAW

Thistlethwaite, Bel
  See Wetherald, Agnes Ethelwyn

Thomas, Audrey (Callahan) 1935- .... **CLC 7,**
  13, 37, 107; SSC 20
  See also AITN 2; CA 21-24R; CAAS 19;
  CANR 36, 58; CN 7; DLB 60; MTCW 1;
  RGSF 2

Thomas, Augustus 1857-1934 .... **TCLC 97**

Thomas, D(onald) M(ichael) 1935- . **CLC 13,**
  22, 31, 132
  See also BPFB 3; BRWS 4; CA 61-64;
  CAAS 11; CANR 17, 45, 75; CDBLB
  1960 to Present; CN 7; CP 7; DA3; DLB
  40, 207, 299; HGG; INT CANR-17;
  MTCW 1, 2; SFW 4

Thomas, Dylan (Marlais) 1914-1953 .... **PC 2,**
  52; SSC 3, 44; TCLC 1, 8, 45, 105;
  WLC
  See also AAYA 45; BRWS 1; CA 104; 120;
  CANR 65; CDBLB 1945-1960; DA; DA3;
  DAB; DAC; DAM DRAM, MST, POET;
  DLB 13, 20, 139; EWL 3; EXPP; LAIT
  3; MTCW 1, 2; PAB; PFS 1, 3, 8; RGEL
  2; RGSF 2; SATA 60; TEA; WLIT 4; WP

Thomas, (Philip) Edward 1878-1917 . **PC 53;**
  TCLC 10
  See also BRW 6; BRWS 3; CA 106; 153;
  DAM POET; DLB 19, 98, 156, 216; EWL
  3; PAB; RGEL 2

Thomas, Joyce Carol 1938- .... **CLC 35**
  See also AAYA 12, 54; BW 2, 3; CA 113;
  116; CANR 48, 114, 135; CLR 19; DLB
  33; INT CA-116; JRDA; MAICYA 1, 2;
  MTCW 1, 2; SAAS 7; SATA 40, 78, 123,
  137; SATA-Essay 137; WYA; YAW

Thomas, Lewis 1913-1993 .... **CLC 35**
  See also ANW; CA 85-88; 143; CANR 38,
  60; DLB 275; MTCW 1, 2

Thomas, M. Carey 1857-1935 .... **TCLC 89**
  See also FW

Thomas, Paul
  See Mann, (Paul) Thomas

Thomas, Piri 1928- .... **CLC 17; HLCS 2**
  See also CA 73-76; HW 1; LLW 1

Thomas, R(onald) S(tuart)
  1913-2000 .... **CLC 6, 13, 48**
  See also CA 89-92; 189; CAAS 4; CANR
  30; CDBLB 1960 to Present; CP 7; DAB;
  DAM POET; DLB 27; EWL 3; MTCW 1;
  RGEL 2

Thomas, Ross (Elmore) 1926-1995 .. **CLC 39**
  See also CA 33-36R; 150; CANR 22, 63;
  CMW 4

Thompson, Francis (Joseph)
  1859-1907 .... **TCLC 4**
  See also BRW 5; CA 104; 189; CDBLB
  1890-1914; DLB 19; RGEL 2; TEA

Thompson, Francis Clegg
  See Mencken, H(enry) L(ouis)

Thompson, Hunter S(tockton)
  1937(?)- .... **CLC 9, 17, 40, 104**
  See also AAYA 45; BEST 89:1; BPFB 3;
  CA 17-20R; CANR 23, 46, 74, 77, 111,
  133; CPW; CSW; DA3; DAM POP; DLB
  185; MTCW 1, 2; TUS

Thompson, James Myers
  See Thompson, Jim (Myers)

Thompson, Jim (Myers)
  1906-1977(?) .... **CLC 69**
  See also BPFB 3; CA 140; CMW 4; CPW;
  DLB 226; MSW

Thompson, Judith .... **CLC 39**
  See also CWD

Thomson, James 1700-1748 .... **LC 16, 29, 40**
  See also BRWS 3; DAM POET; DLB 95;
  RGEL 2

Thomson, James 1834-1882 .... **NCLC 18**
  See also DAM POET; DLB 35; RGEL 2

Thoreau, Henry David 1817-1862 .. **NCLC 7,**
  21, 61, 138; PC 30; WLC
  See also AAYA 42; AMW; ANW; BYA 3;
  CDALB 1640-1865; DA; DA3; DAB;
  DAC; DAM MST; DLB 1, 183, 223, 270,
  298; LAIT 2; LMFS 1; NCFS 3; RGAL
  4; TUS

Thorndike, E. L.
  See Thorndike, Edward L(ee)

Thorndike, Edward L(ee)
  1874-1949 .... **TCLC 107**
  See also CA 121

Thornton, Hall
  See Silverberg, Robert

Thorpe, Adam 1956- .... **CLC 176**
  See also CA 129; CANR 92; DLB 231

Thubron, Colin (Gerald Dryden)
1939- .... **CLC 163**
See also CA 25-28R; CANR 12, 29, 59, 95;
CN 7; DLB 204, 231

Thucydides c. 455B.C.-c. 395B.C. . **CMLC 17**
See also AW 1; DLB 176; RGWL 2, 3

Thumboo, Edwin Nadason 1933- .... **PC 30**
See also CA 194

Thurber, James (Grover)
1894-1961 .. **CLC 5, 11, 25, 125; SSC 1,
47**
See also AAYA 56; AMWS 1; BPFB 3;
BYA 5; CA 73-76; CANR 17, 39; CDALB
1929-1941; CWRI 5; DA; DA3; DAB;
DAC; DAM DRAM, MST, NOV; DLB 4,
11, 22, 102; EWL 3; EXPS; FANT; LAIT
3; MAICYA 1, 2; MTCW 1, 2; RGAL 4;
RGSF 2; SATA 13; SSFS 1, 10, 19;
SUFW; TUS

Thurman, Wallace (Henry)
1902-1934 .... **BLC 3; HR 3; TCLC 6**
See also BW 1, 3; CA 104; 124; CANR 81;
DAM MULT; DLB 51

Tibullus c. 54B.C.-c. 18B.C. .... **CMLC 36**
See also AW 2; DLB 211; RGWL 2, 3

Ticheburn, Cheviot
See Ainsworth, William Harrison

Tieck, (Johann) Ludwig
1773-1853 .... **NCLC 5, 46; SSC 31**
See also CDWLB 2; DLB 90; EW 5; IDTP;
RGSF 2; RGWL 2, 3; SUFW

Tiger, Derry
See Ellison, Harlan (Jay)

Tilghman, Christopher 1946- .... **CLC 65**
See also CA 159; CANR 135; CSW; DLB
244

Tillich, Paul (Johannes)
1886-1965 .... **CLC 131**
See also CA 5-8R; 25-28R; CANR 33;
MTCW 1, 2

Tillinghast, Richard (Williford)
1940- .... **CLC 29**
See also CA 29-32R; CAAS 23; CANR 26,
51, 96; CP 7; CSW

Timrod, Henry 1828-1867 .... **NCLC 25**
See also DLB 3, 248; RGAL 4

Tindall, Gillian (Elizabeth) 1938- ...... **CLC 7**
See also CA 21-24R; CANR 11, 65, 107;
CN 7

Tiptree, James, Jr. .... **CLC 48, 50**
See Sheldon, Alice Hastings Bradley
See also DLB 8; SCFW 2; SFW 4

Tirone Smith, Mary-Ann 1944- .... **CLC 39**
See also CA 118; 136; CANR 113; SATA
143

Tirso de Molina 1580(?)-1648 .... **DC 13;
HLCS 2; LC 73**
See also RGWL 2, 3

Titmarsh, Michael Angelo
See Thackeray, William Makepeace

**Tocqueville, Alexis (Charles Henri Maurice
Clerel Comte) de** 1805-1859 .. **NCLC 7,
63**
See also EW 6; GFL 1789 to the Present;
TWA

Toer, Pramoedya Ananta 1925- ...... **CLC 186**
See also CA 197; RGWL 3

Toffler, Alvin 1928- .... **CLC 168**
See also CA 13-16R; CANR 15, 46, 67;
CPW; DAM POP; MTCW 1, 2

Toibin, Colm
See Toibin, Colm
See also DLB 271

Toibin, Colm 1955- .... **CLC 162**
See Toibin, Colm
See also CA 142; CANR 81

Tolkien, J(ohn) R(onald) R(euel)
1892-1973 .... **CLC 1, 2, 3, 8, 12, 38;
TCLC 137; WLC**
See also AAYA 10; AITN 1; BPFB 3;
BRWC 2; BRWS 2; CA 17-18; 45-48;
CANR 36, 134; CAP 2; CDBLB 1914-
1945; CLR 56; CPW 1; CWRI 5; DA;
DA3; DAB; DAC; DAM MST, NOV,
POP; DLB 15, 160, 255; EFS 2; EWL 3;
FANT; JRDA; LAIT 1; LATS 1:2; LMFS
2; MAICYA 1, 2; MTCW 1, 2; NFS 8;
RGEL 2; SATA 2, 32, 100; SATA-Obit
24; SFW 4; SUFW; TEA; WCH; WYA;
YAW

Toller, Ernst 1893-1939 .... **TCLC 10**
See also CA 107; 186; DLB 124; EWL 3;
RGWL 2, 3

Tolson, M. B.
See Tolson, Melvin B(eaunorus)

Tolson, Melvin B(eaunorus)
1898(?)-1966 .... **BLC 3; CLC 36, 105**
See also AFAW 1, 2; BW 1, 3; CA 124; 89-
92; CANR 80; DAM MULT, POET; DLB
48, 76; RGAL 4

Tolstoi, Aleksei Nikolaevich
See Tolstoy, Alexey Nikolaevich

Tolstoi, Lev
See Tolstoy, Leo (Nikolaevich)
See also RGSF 2; RGWL 2, 3

Tolstoy, Aleksei Nikolaevich
See Tolstoy, Alexey Nikolaevich
See also DLB 272

Tolstoy, Alexey Nikolaevich
1882-1945 .... **TCLC 18**
See Tolstoy, Aleksei Nikolaevich
See also CA 107; 158; EWL 3; SFW 4

Tolstoy, Leo (Nikolaevich)
1828-1910 . **SSC 9, 30, 45, 54; TCLC 4,
11, 17, 28, 44, 79; WLC**
See Tolstoi, Lev
See also AAYA 56; CA 104; 123; DA; DA3;
DAB; DAC; DAM MST, NOV; DLB 238;
EFS 2; EW 7; EXPS; IDTP; LAIT 2;
LATS 1:1; LMFS 1; NFS 10; SATA 26;
SSFS 5; TWA

Tolstoy, Count Leo
See Tolstoy, Leo (Nikolaevich)

Tomalin, Claire 1933- .... **CLC 166**
See also CA 89-92; CANR 52, 88; DLB
155

Tomasi di Lampedusa, Giuseppe 1896-1957
See Lampedusa, Giuseppe (Tomasi) di
See also CA 111; DLB 177; EWL 3

Tomlin, Lily .... **CLC 17**
See Tomlin, Mary Jean

Tomlin, Mary Jean 1939(?)-
See Tomlin, Lily
See also CA 117

Tomline, F. Latour
See Gilbert, W(illiam) S(chwenck)

Tomlinson, (Alfred) Charles 1927- .... **CLC 2,
4, 6, 13, 45; PC 17**
See also CA 5-8R; CANR 33; CP 7; DAM
POET; DLB 40

Tomlinson, H(enry) M(ajor)
1873-1958 .... **TCLC 71**
See also CA 118; 161; DLB 36, 100, 195

Tonna, Charlotte Elizabeth
1790-1846 .... **NCLC 135**
See also DLB 163

Tonson, Jacob fl. 1655(?)-1736 .... **LC 86**
See also DLB 170

Toole, John Kennedy 1937-1969 ..... **CLC 19,
64**
See also BPFB 3; CA 104; DLBY 1981;
MTCW 1

Toomer, Eugene
See Toomer, Jean

Toomer, Eugene Pinchback
See Toomer, Jean

Toomer, Jean 1894-1967 .. **BLC 3; CLC 1, 4,
13, 22; HR 3; PC 7; SSC 1, 45; WLCS**
See also AFAW 1, 2; AMWS 3, 9; BW 1;
CA 85-88; CDALB 1917-1929; DA3;
DAM MULT; DLB 45, 51; EWL 3; EXPP;
EXPS; LMFS 2; MTCW 1, 2; NFS 11;
RGAL 4; RGSF 2; SSFS 5

Toomer, Nathan Jean
See Toomer, Jean

Toomer, Nathan Pinchback
See Toomer, Jean

Torley, Luke
See Blish, James (Benjamin)

Tornimparte, Alessandra
See Ginzburg, Natalia

Torre, Raoul della
See Mencken, H(enry) L(ouis)

Torrence, Ridgely 1874-1950 .... **TCLC 97**
See also DLB 54, 249

Torrey, E(dwin) Fuller 1937- .... **CLC 34**
See also CA 119; CANR 71

Torsvan, Ben Traven
See Traven, B.

Torsvan, Benno Traven
See Traven, B.

Torsvan, Berick Traven
See Traven, B.

Torsvan, Berwick Traven
See Traven, B.

Torsvan, Bruno Traven
See Traven, B.

Torsvan, Traven
See Traven, B.

Tourneur, Cyril 1575(?)-1626 .... **LC 66**
See also BRW 2; DAM DRAM; DLB 58;
RGEL 2

Tournier, Michel (Edouard) 1924- .... **CLC 6,
23, 36, 95**
See also CA 49-52; CANR 3, 36, 74; CWW
2; DLB 83; EWL 3; GFL 1789 to the
Present; MTCW 1, 2; SATA 23

Tournimparte, Alessandra
See Ginzburg, Natalia

Towers, Ivar
See Kornbluth, C(yril) M.

Towne, Robert (Burton) 1936(?)- ..... **CLC 87**
See also CA 108; DLB 44; IDFW 3, 4

Townsend, Sue .... **CLC 61**
See Townsend, Susan Lilian
See also AAYA 28; CA 119; 127; CANR
65, 107; CBD; CD 5; CPW; CWD; DAB;
DAC; DAM MST; DLB 271; INT CA-
127; SATA 55, 93; SATA-Brief 48; YAW

Townsend, Susan Lilian 1946-
See Townsend, Sue

Townshend, Pete
See Townshend, Peter (Dennis Blandford)

Townshend, Peter (Dennis Blandford)
1945- .... **CLC 17, 42**
See also CA 107

Tozzi, Federigo 1883-1920 .... **TCLC 31**
See also CA 160; CANR 110; DLB 264;
EWL 3

Tracy, Don(ald Fiske) 1905-1970(?)
See Queen, Ellery
See also CA 1-4R; 176; CANR 2

Trafford, F. G.
See Riddell, Charlotte

Traherne, Thomas 1637(?)-1674 .... **LC 99**
See also BRW 2; DLB 131; PAB; RGEL 2

Traill, Catharine Parr 1802-1899 .. **NCLC 31**
See also DLB 99

Trakl, Georg 1887-1914 .... **PC 20; TCLC 5**
See also CA 104; 165; EW 10; EWL 3;
LMFS 2; MTCW 2; RGWL 2, 3

Tranquilli, Secondino
See Silone, Ignazio
Transtroemer, Tomas Gosta
See Transtromer, Tomas (Goesta)
Transtromer, Tomas (Gosta)
See Transtromer, Tomas (Goesta)
See also CWW 2
Transtromer, Tomas (Goesta)
1931- .... **CLC 52, 65**
See Transtromer, Tomas (Goesta)
See also CA 117; 129; CAAS 17; CANR
115; DAM POET; DLB 257; EWL 3; PFS
21
Transtromer, Tomas Gosta
See Transtromer, Tomas (Goesta)
Traven, B. 1882(?)-1969 .... **CLC 8, 11**
See also CA 19-20; 25-28R; CAP 2; DLB
9, 56; EWL 3; MTCW 1; RGAL 4
Trediakovsky, Vasilii Kirillovich
1703-1769 .... **LC 68**
See also DLB 150
Treitel, Jonathan 1959- .... **CLC 70**
See also CA 210; DLB 267
Trelawny, Edward John
1792-1881 .... **NCLC 85**
See also DLB 110, 116, 144
Tremain, Rose 1943- .... **CLC 42**
See also CA 97-100; CANR 44, 95; CN 7;
DLB 14, 271; RGSF 2; RHW
Tremblay, Michel 1942- .... **CLC 29, 102**
See also CA 116; 128; CCA 1; CWW 2;
DAC; DAM MST; DLB 60; EWL 3; GLL
1; MTCW 1, 2
Trevanian .... **CLC 29**
See Whitaker, Rod(ney)
Trevor, Glen
See Hilton, James
Trevor, William .. **CLC 7, 9, 14, 25, 71, 116;**
SSC 21, 58
See Cox, William Trevor
See also BRWS 4; CBD; CD 5; CN 7; DLB
14, 139; EWL 3; LATS 1:2; MTCW 2;
RGEL 2; RGSF 2; SSFS 10
Trifonov, Iurii (Valentinovich)
See Trifonov, Yuri (Valentinovich)
See also DLB 302; RGWL 2, 3
Trifonov, Yuri (Valentinovich)
1925-1981 .... **CLC 45**
See Trifonov, Iurii (Valentinovich); Tri-
fonov, Yury Valentinovich
See also CA 126; 103; MTCW 1
Trifonov, Yury Valentinovich
See Trifonov, Yuri (Valentinovich)
See also EWL 3
Trilling, Diana (Rubin) 1905-1996 . **CLC 129**
See also CA 5-8R; 154; CANR 10, 46; INT
CANR-10; MTCW 1, 2
Trilling, Lionel 1905-1975 ..... **CLC 9, 11, 24;**
SSC 75
See also AMWS 3; CA 9-12R; 61-64;
CANR 10, 105; DLB 28, 63; EWL 3; INT
CANR-10; MTCW 1, 2; RGAL 4; TUS
Trimball, W. H.
See Mencken, H(enry) L(ouis)
Tristan
See Gomez de la Serna, Ramon
Tristram
See Housman, A(lfred) E(dward)
Trogdon, William (Lewis) 1939-
See Heat-Moon, William Least
See also CA 115; 119; CANR 47, 89; CPW;
INT CA-119
Trollope, Anthony 1815-1882 .... **NCLC 6, 33,**
101; SSC 28; WLC
See also BRW 5; CDBLB 1832-1890; DA;
DA3; DAB; DAC; DAM MST, NOV;
DLB 21, 57, 159; RGEL 2; RGSF 2;
SATA 22

Trollope, Frances 1779-1863 .... **NCLC 30**
See also DLB 21, 166
Trollope, Joanna 1943- .... **CLC 186**
See also CA 101; CANR 58, 95; CPW;
DLB 207; RHW
Trotsky, Leon 1879-1940 .... **TCLC 22**
See also CA 118; 167
Trotter (Cockburn), Catharine
1679-1749 .... **LC 8**
See also DLB 84, 252
Trotter, Wilfred 1872-1939 .... **TCLC 97**
Trout, Kilgore
See Farmer, Philip Jose
Trow, George W. S. 1943- .... **CLC 52**
See also CA 126; CANR 91
Troyat, Henri 1911- .... **CLC 23**
See also CA 45-48; CANR 2, 33, 67, 117;
GFL 1789 to the Present; MTCW 1
Trudeau, G(arretson) B(eekman) 1948-
See Trudeau, Garry B.
See also AAYA 60; CA 81-84; CANR 31;
SATA 35
Trudeau, Garry B. .... **CLC 12**
See Trudeau, G(arretson) B(eekman)
See also AAYA 10; AITN 2
Truffaut, Francois 1932-1984 ... **CLC 20, 101**
See also CA 81-84; 113; CANR 34
Trumbo, Dalton 1905-1976 .... **CLC 19**
See also CA 21-24R; 69-72; CANR 10;
DLB 26; IDFW 3, 4; YAW
Trumbull, John 1750-1831 .... **NCLC 30**
See also DLB 31; RGAL 4
Trundlett, Helen B.
See Eliot, T(homas) S(tearns)
Truth, Sojourner 1797(?)-1883 ...... **NCLC 94**
See also DLB 239; FW; LAIT 2
Tryon, Thomas 1926-1991 .... **CLC 3, 11**
See also AITN 1; BPFB 3; CA 29-32R; 135;
CANR 32, 77; CPW; DA3; DAM POP;
HGG; MTCW 1
Tryon, Tom
See Tryon, Thomas
Ts'ao Hsueh-ch'in 1715(?)-1763 .... **LC 1**
Tsushima, Shuji 1909-1948
See Dazai Osamu
See also CA 107
Tsvetaeva (Efron), Marina (Ivanovna)
1892-1941 .... **PC 14; TCLC 7, 35**
See also CA 104; 128; CANR 73; DLB 295;
EW 11; MTCW 1, 2; RGWL 2, 3
Tuck, Lily 1938- .... **CLC 70**
See also CA 139; CANR 90
Tu Fu 712-770 .... **PC 9**
See Du Fu
See also DAM MULT; TWA; WP
Tunis, John R(oberts) 1889-1975 ..... **CLC 12**
See also BYA 1; CA 61-64; CANR 62; DLB
22, 171; JRDA; MAICYA 1, 2; SATA 37;
SATA-Brief 30; YAW
Tuohy, Frank .... **CLC 37**
See Tuohy, John Francis
See also DLB 14, 139
Tuohy, John Francis 1925-
See Tuohy, Frank
See also CA 5-8R; 178; CANR 3, 47; CN 7
Turco, Lewis (Putnam) 1934- ..... **CLC 11, 63**
See also CA 13-16R; CAAS 22; CANR 24,
51; CP 7; DLBY 1984
Turgenev, Ivan (Sergeevich)
1818-1883 ..... **DC 7; NCLC 21, 37, 122;**
SSC 7, 57; WLC
See also AAYA 58; DA; DAB; DAC; DAM
MST, NOV; DFS 6; DLB 238, 284; EW
6; LATS 1:1; NFS 16; RGSF 2; RGWL 2,
3; TWA

Turgot, Anne-Robert-Jacques
1727-1781 .... **LC 26**
Turner, Frederick 1943- .... **CLC 48**
See also CA 73-76, 227; CAAE 227; CAAS
10; CANR 12, 30, 56; DLB 40, 282
Turton, James
See Crace, Jim
Tutu, Desmond M(pilo) 1931- .. **BLC 3; CLC
80**
See also BW 1, 3; CA 125; CANR 67, 81;
DAM MULT
Tutuola, Amos 1920-1997 ..... **BLC 3; CLC 5,
14, 29**
See also AFW; BW 2, 3; CA 9-12R; 159;
CANR 27, 66; CDWLB 3; CN 7; DA3;
DAM MULT; DLB 125; DNFS 2; EWL
3; MTCW 1, 2; RGEL 2; WLIT 2
Twain, Mark .... **SSC 6, 26, 34; TCLC 6, 12,
19, 36, 48, 59; WLC**
See Clemens, Samuel Langhorne
See also AAYA 20; AMW; AMWC 1; BPFB
3; BYA 2, 3, 11, 14; CLR 58, 60, 66; DLB
11; EXPN; EXPS; LAIT 2; MAWW; NCFS
4; NFS 1, 6; RGAL 4; RGSF 2; SFW 4;
SSFS 1, 7; SUFW; TUS; WCH; WYA;
YAW
Tyler, Anne 1941- . **CLC 7, 11, 18, 28, 44, 59,
103**
See also AAYA 18, 60; AMWS 4; BEST
89:1; BPFB 3; BYA 12; CA 9-12R; CANR
11, 33, 53, 109, 132; CDALBS; CN 7;
CPW; CSW; DAM NOV, POP; DLB 6,
143; DLBY 1982; EWL 3; EXPN; LATS
1:2; MAWW; MTCW 1, 2; NFS 2, 7, 10;
RGAL 4; SATA 7, 90; SSFS 17; TUS;
YAW
Tyler, Royall 1757-1826 .... **NCLC 3**
See also DLB 37; RGAL 4
Tynan, Katharine 1861-1931 .... **TCLC 3**
See also CA 104; 167; DLB 153, 240; FW
Tyndale, William c. 1484-1536 .... **LC 103**
See also DLB 132
Tyutchev, Fyodor 1803-1873 .... **NCLC 34**
Tzara, Tristan 1896-1963 ..... **CLC 47; PC 27**
See also CA 153; 89-92; DAM POET; EWL
3; MTCW 2
Uchida, Yoshiko 1921-1992 .... **AAL**
See also AAYA 16; BYA 2, 3; CA 13-16R;
139; CANR 6, 22, 47, 61; CDALBS; CLR
6, 56; CWRI 5; JRDA; MAICYA 1, 2;
MTCW 1, 2; SAAS 1; SATA 1, 53; SATA-
Obit 72
Udall, Nicholas 1504-1556 .... **LC 84**
See also DLB 62; RGEL 2
Ueda Akinari 1734-1809 .... **NCLC 131**
Uhry, Alfred 1936- .... **CLC 55**
See also CA 127; 133; CAD; CANR 112;
CD 5; CSW; DA3; DAM DRAM, POP;
DFS 11, 15; INT CA-133
Ulf, Haerved
See Strindberg, (Johan) August
Ulf, Harved
See Strindberg, (Johan) August
Ulibarri, Sabine R(eyes)
1919-2003 .... **CLC 83; HLCS 2**
See also CA 131; 214; CANR 81; DAM
MULT; DLB 82; HW 1, 2; RGSF 2
Unamuno (y Jugo), Miguel de
1864-1936 .. **HLC 2; SSC 11, 69; TCLC
2, 9, 148**
See also CA 104; 131; CANR 81; DAM
MULT, NOV; DLB 108; EW 8; EWL 3;
HW 1, 2; MTCW 1, 2; RGSF 2; RGWL
2, 3; SSFS 20; TWA
Uncle Shelby
See Silverstein, Shel(don Allan)
Undercliffe, Errol
See Campbell, (John) Ramsey

Underwood, Miles
See Glassco, John
Undset, Sigrid 1882-1949 ..... **TCLC 3; WLC**
See also CA 104; 129; DA; DA3; DAB; DAC; DAM MST, NOV; DLB 293; EW 9; EWL 3; FW; MTCW 1, 2; RGWL 2, 3
Ungaretti, Giuseppe 1888-1970 ... **CLC 7, 11, 15; PC 57**
See also CA 19-20; 25-28R; CAP 2; DLB 114; EW 10; EWL 3; PFS 20; RGWL 2, 3
Unger, Douglas 1952- .... **CLC 34**
See also CA 130; CANR 94
Unsworth, Barry (Forster) 1930- .... **CLC 76, 127**
See also BRWS 7; CA 25-28R; CANR 30, 54, 125; CN 7; DLB 194
Updike, John (Hoyer) 1932- . **CLC 1, 2, 3, 5, 7, 9, 13, 15, 23, 34, 43, 70, 139; SSC 13, 27; WLC**
See also AAYA 36; AMW; AMWC 1; AMWR 1; BPFB 3; BYA 12; CA 1-4R; CABS 1; CANR 4, 33, 51, 94, 133; CDALB 1968-1988; CN 7; CP 7; CPW 1; DA; DA3; DAB; DAC; DAM MST, NOV, POET, POP; DLB 2, 5, 143, 218, 227; DLBD 3; DLBY 1980, 1982, 1997; EWL 3; EXPP; HGG; MTCW 1, 2; NFS 12; RGAL 4; RGSF 2; SSFS 3, 19; TUS
Upshaw, Margaret Mitchell
See Mitchell, Margaret (Munnerlyn)
Upton, Mark
See Sanders, Lawrence
Upward, Allen 1863-1926 .... **TCLC 85**
See also CA 117; 187; DLB 36
Urdang, Constance (Henriette)
1922-1996 .... **CLC 47**
See also CA 21-24R; CANR 9, 24; CP 7; CWP
Uriel, Henry
See Faust, Frederick (Schiller)
Uris, Leon (Marcus) 1924-2003 ... **CLC 7, 32**
See also AITN 1, 2; BEST 89:2; BPFB 3; CA 1-4R; 217; CANR 1, 40, 65, 123; CN 7; CPW 1; DA3; DAM NOV, POP; MTCW 1, 2; SATA 49; SATA-Obit 146
Urista (Heredia), Alberto (Baltazar)
1947- .... **HLCS 1; PC 34**
See Alurista
See also CA 45-48, 182; CANR 2, 32; HW 1
Urmuz
See Codrescu, Andrei
Urquhart, Guy
See McAlmon, Robert (Menzies)
Urquhart, Jane 1949- .... **CLC 90**
See also CA 113; CANR 32, 68, 116; CCA 1; DAC
Usigli, Rodolfo 1905-1979 .... **HLCS 1**
See also CA 131; DLB 305; EWL 3; HW 1; LAW
Ustinov, Peter (Alexander)
1921-2004 .... **CLC 1**
See also AITN 1; CA 13-16R; 225; CANR 25, 51; CBD; CD 5; DLB 13; MTCW 2
U Tam'si, Gerald Felix Tchicaya
See Tchicaya, Gerald Felix
U Tam'si, Tchicaya
See Tchicaya, Gerald Felix
Vachss, Andrew (Henry) 1942- .... **CLC 106**
See also CA 118, 214; CAAE 214; CANR 44, 95; CMW 4
Vachss, Andrew H.
See Vachss, Andrew (Henry)
Vaculik, Ludvik 1926- .... **CLC 7**
See also CA 53-56; CANR 72; CWW 2; DLB 232; EWL 3
Vaihinger, Hans 1852-1933 .... **TCLC 71**
See also CA 116; 166

Valdez, Luis (Miguel) 1940- ..... **CLC 84; DC 10; HLC 2**
See also CA 101; CAD; CANR 32, 81; CD 5; DAM MULT; DFS 5; DLB 122; EWL 3; HW 1; LAIT 4; LLW 1
Valenzuela, Luisa 1938- .... **CLC 31, 104; HLCS 2; SSC 14**
See also CA 101; CANR 32, 65, 123; CDWLB 3; CWW 2; DAM MULT; DLB 113; EWL 3; FW; HW 1, 2; LAW; RGSF 2; RGWL 3
Valera y Alcala-Galiano, Juan
1824-1905 .... **TCLC 10**
See also CA 106
Valerius Maximus fl. 20- .... **CMLC 64**
See also DLB 211
Valery, (Ambroise) Paul (Toussaint Jules)
1871-1945 .... **PC 9; TCLC 4, 15**
See also CA 104; 122; DA3; DAM POET; DLB 258; EW 8; EWL 3; GFL 1789 to the Present; MTCW 1, 2; RGWL 2, 3; TWA
Valle-Inclan, Ramon (Maria) del
1866-1936 .... **HLC 2; TCLC 5**
See also CA 106; 153; CANR 80; DAM MULT; DLB 134; EW 8; EWL 3; HW 2; RGSF 2; RGWL 2, 3
Vallejo, Antonio Buero
See Buero Vallejo, Antonio
Vallejo, Cesar (Abraham)
1892-1938 .... **HLC 2; TCLC 3, 56**
See also CA 105; 153; DAM MULT; DLB 290; EWL 3; HW 1; LAW; RGWL 2, 3
Valles, Jules 1832-1885 .... **NCLC 71**
See also DLB 123; GFL 1789 to the Present
Vallette, Marguerite Eymery
1860-1953 .... **TCLC 67**
See Rachilde
See also CA 182; DLB 123, 192
Valle Y Pena, Ramon del
See Valle-Inclan, Ramon (Maria) del
Van Ash, Cay 1918-1994 .... **CLC 34**
See also CA 220
Vanbrugh, Sir John 1664-1726 .... **LC 21**
See also BRW 2; DAM DRAM; DLB 80; IDTP; RGEL 2
Van Campen, Karl
See Campbell, John W(ood, Jr.)
Vance, Gerald
See Silverberg, Robert
Vance, Jack .... **CLC 35**
See Vance, John Holbrook
See also DLB 8; FANT; SCFW 2; SFW 4; SUFW 1, 2
Vance, John Holbrook 1916-
See Queen, Ellery; Vance, Jack
See also CA 29-32R; CANR 17, 65; CMW 4; MTCW 1
Van Den Bogarde, Derek Jules Gaspard Ulric Niven 1921-1999 .... **CLC 14**
See Bogarde, Dirk
See also CA 77-80; 179
Vandenburgh, Jane .... **CLC 59**
See also CA 168
Vanderhaeghe, Guy 1951- .... **CLC 41**
See also BPFB 3; CA 113; CANR 72
van der Post, Laurens (Jan)
1906-1996 .... **CLC 5**
See also AFW; CA 5-8R; 155; CANR 35; CN 7; DLB 204; RGEL 2
van de Wetering, Janwillem 1931- ... **CLC 47**
See also CA 49-52; CANR 4, 62, 90; CMW 4
Van Dine, S. S. .... **TCLC 23**
See Wright, Willard Huntington
See also DLB 306; MSW
Van Doren, Carl (Clinton)
1885-1950 .... **TCLC 18**
See also CA 111; 168

Van Doren, Mark 1894-1972 .... **CLC 6, 10**
See also CA 1-4R; 37-40R; CANR 3; DLB 45, 284; MTCW 1, 2; RGAL 4
Van Druten, John (William)
1901-1957 .... **TCLC 2**
See also CA 104; 161; DLB 10; RGAL 4
Van Duyn, Mona (Jane) 1921- ...... **CLC 3, 7, 63, 116**
See also CA 9-12R; CANR 7, 38, 60, 116; CP 7; CWP; DAM POET; DLB 5; PFS 20
Van Dyne, Edith
See Baum, L(yman) Frank
van Itallie, Jean-Claude 1936- .... **CLC 3**
See also CA 45-48; CAAS 2; CAD; CANR 1, 48; CD 5; DLB 7
Van Loot, Cornelius Obenchain
See Roberts, Kenneth (Lewis)
van Ostaijen, Paul 1896-1928 .... **TCLC 33**
See also CA 163
Van Peebles, Melvin 1932- .... **CLC 2, 20**
See also BW 2, 3; CA 85-88; CANR 27, 67, 82; DAM MULT
van Schendel, Arthur(-Francois-Emile)
1874-1946 .... **TCLC 56**
See also EWL 3
Vansittart, Peter 1920- .... **CLC 42**
See also CA 1-4R; CANR 3, 49, 90; CN 7; RHW
Van Vechten, Carl 1880-1964 ... **CLC 33; HR 3**
See also AMWS 2; CA 183; 89-92; DLB 4, 9, 51; RGAL 4
van Vogt, A(lfred) E(lton) 1912-2000 . **CLC 1**
See also BPFB 3; BYA 13, 14; CA 21-24R; 190; CANR 28; DLB 8, 251; SATA 14; SATA-Obit 124; SCFW; SFW 4
Vara, Madeleine
See Jackson, Laura (Riding)
Varda, Agnes 1928- .... **CLC 16**
See also CA 116; 122
Vargas Llosa, (Jorge) Mario (Pedro)
1939- ... **CLC 3, 6, 9, 10, 15, 31, 42, 85, 181; HLC 2**
See Llosa, (Jorge) Mario (Pedro) Vargas
See also BPFB 3; CA 73-76; CANR 18, 32, 42, 67, 116; CDWLB 3; CWW 2; DA; DA3; DAB; DAC; DAM MST, MULT, NOV; DLB 145; DNFS 2; EWL 3; HW 1, 2; LAIT 5; LATS 1:2; LAW; LAWS 1; MTCW 1, 2; RGWL 2; SSFS 14; TWA; WLIT 1
Varnhagen von Ense, Rahel
1771-1833 .... **NCLC 130**
See also DLB 90
Vasiliu, George
See Bacovia, George
Vasiliu, Gheorghe
See Bacovia, George
See also CA 123; 189
Vassa, Gustavus
See Equiano, Olaudah
Vassilikos, Vassilis 1933- .... **CLC 4, 8**
See also CA 81-84; CANR 75; EWL 3
Vaughan, Henry 1621-1695 .... **LC 27**
See also BRW 2; DLB 131; PAB; RGEL 2
Vaughn, Stephanie .... **CLC 62**
Vazov, Ivan (Minchov) 1850-1921 . **TCLC 25**
See also CA 121; 167; CDWLB 4; DLB 147
Veblen, Thorstein B(unde)
1857-1929 .... **TCLC 31**
See also AMWS 1; CA 115; 165; DLB 246
Vega, Lope de 1562-1635 .... **HLCS 2; LC 23**
See also EW 2; RGWL 2, 3
Vendler, Helen (Hennessy) 1933- ... **CLC 138**
See also CA 41-44R; CANR 25, 72; MTCW 1, 2

Venison, Alfred
See Pound, Ezra (Weston Loomis)
Ventsel, Elena Sergeevna 1907-2002
See Grekova, I.
See also CA 154
Verdi, Marie de
See Mencken, H(enry) L(ouis)
Verdu, Matilde
See Cela, Camilo Jose
Verga, Giovanni (Carmelo)
1840-1922 .... **SSC 21; TCLC 3**
See also CA 104; 123; CANR 101; EW 7;
EWL 3; RGSF 2; RGWL 2, 3
Vergil 70B.C.-19B.C. ... **CMLC 9, 40; PC 12;**
WLCS
See Virgil
See also AW 2; DA; DA3; DAB; DAC;
DAM MST, POET; EFS 1; LMFS 1
Vergil, Polydore c. 1470-1555 .... **LC 108**
See also DLB 132
Verhaeren, Emile (Adolphe Gustave)
1855-1916 .... **TCLC 12**
See also CA 109; EWL 3; GFL 1789 to the
Present
Verlaine, Paul (Marie) 1844-1896 .. **NCLC 2,**
51; PC 2, 32
See also DAM POET; DLB 217; EW 7;
GFL 1789 to the Present; LMFS 2; RGWL
2, 3; TWA
Verne, Jules (Gabriel) 1828-1905 ... **TCLC 6,**
52
See also AAYA 16; BYA 4; CA 110; 131;
CLR 88; DA3; DLB 123; GFL 1789 to
the Present; JRDA; LAIT 2; LMFS 2;
MAICYA 1, 2; RGWL 2, 3; SATA 21;
SCFW; SFW 4; TWA; WCH
Verus, Marcus Annius
See Aurelius, Marcus
Very, Jones 1813-1880 .... **NCLC 9**
See also DLB 1, 243; RGAL 4
Vesaas, Tarjei 1897-1970 .... **CLC 48**
See also CA 190; 29-32R; DLB 297; EW
11; EWL 3; RGWL 3
Vialis, Gaston
See Simenon, Georges (Jacques Christian)
Vian, Boris 1920-1959(?) .... **TCLC 9**
See also CA 106; 164; CANR 111; DLB
72; EWL 3; GFL 1789 to the Present;
MTCW 2; RGWL 2, 3
Viaud, (Louis Marie) Julien 1850-1923
See Loti, Pierre
See also CA 107
Vicar, Henry
See Felsen, Henry Gregor
Vicente, Gil 1465-c. 1536 .... **LC 99**
See also DLB 287; RGWL 2, 3
Vicker, Angus
See Felsen, Henry Gregor
Vidal, (Eugene Luther) Gore 1925- .. **CLC 2,**
4, 6, 8, 10, 22, 33, 72, 142
See Box, Edgar
See also AITN 1; AMWS 4; BEST 90:2;
BPFB 3; CA 5-8R; CAD; CANR 13, 45,
65, 100, 132; CD 5; CDALBS; CN 7;
CPW; DA3; DAM NOV, POP; DFS 2;
DLB 6, 152; EWL 3; INT CANR-13;
MTCW 1, 2; RGAL 4; RHW; TUS
Viereck, Peter (Robert Edwin)
1916- .... **CLC 4; PC 27**
See also CA 1-4R; CANR 1, 47; CP 7; DLB
5; PFS 9, 14
Vigny, Alfred (Victor) de
1797-1863 .... **NCLC 7, 102; PC 26**
See also DAM POET; DLB 119, 192, 217;
EW 5; GFL 1789 to the Present; RGWL
2, 3
Vilakazi, Benedict Wallet
1906-1947 .... **TCLC 37**
See also CA 168

Villa, Jose Garcia 1914-1997 .... **AAL; PC 22**
See also CA 25-28R; CANR 12, 118; EWL
3; EXPP
Villa, Jose Garcia 1914-1997
See Villa, Jose Garcia
Villarreal, Jose Antonio 1924- .... **HLC 2**
See also CA 133; CANR 93; DAM MULT;
DLB 82; HW 1; LAIT 4; RGAL 4
Villaurrutia, Xavier 1903-1950 ...... **TCLC 80**
See also CA 192; EWL 3; HW 1; LAW
Villaverde, Cirilo 1812-1894 .... **NCLC 121**
See also LAW
Villehardouin, Geoffroi de
1150(?)-1218(?) .... **CMLC 38**
Villiers, George 1628-1687 .... **LC 107**
See also DLB 80; RGEL 2
Villiers de l'Isle Adam, Jean Marie Mathias
Philippe Auguste 1838-1889 ... **NCLC 3;**
SSC 14
See also DLB 123, 192; GFL 1789 to the
Present; RGSF 2
Villon, Francois 1431-1463(?) . **LC 62; PC 13**
See also DLB 208; EW 2; RGWL 2, 3;
TWA
Vine, Barbara .... **CLC 50**
See Rendell, Ruth (Barbara)
See also BEST 90:4
Vinge, Joan (Carol) D(ennison)
1948- .... **CLC 30; SSC 24**
See also AAYA 32; BPFB 3; CA 93-96;
CANR 72; SATA 36, 113; SFW 4; YAW
Viola, Herman J(oseph) 1938- .... **CLC 70**
See also CA 61-64; CANR 8, 23, 48, 91;
SATA 126
Violis, G.
See Simenon, Georges (Jacques Christian)
Viramontes, Helena Maria 1954- .... **HLCS 2**
See also CA 159; DLB 122; HW 2; LLW 1
Virgil
See Vergil
See also CDWLB 1; DLB 211; LAIT 1;
RGWL 2, 3; WP
Visconti, Luchino 1906-1976 .... **CLC 16**
See also CA 81-84; 65-68; CANR 39
Vitry, Jacques de
See Jacques de Vitry
Vittorini, Elio 1908-1966 .... **CLC 6, 9, 14**
See also CA 133; 25-28R; DLB 264; EW
12; EWL 3; RGWL 2, 3
Vivekananda, Swami 1863-1902 .... **TCLC 88**
Vizenor, Gerald Robert 1934- .... **CLC 103;**
NNAL
See also CA 13-16R, 205; CAAE 205;
CAAS 22; CANR 5, 21, 44, 67; DAM
MULT; DLB 175, 227; MTCW 2; TCWW
2
Vizinczey, Stephen 1933- .... **CLC 40**
See also CA 128; CCA 1; INT CA-128
Vliet, R(ussell) G(ordon)
1929-1984 .... **CLC 22**
See also CA 37-40R; 112; CANR 18
Vogau, Boris Andreyevich 1894-1938
See Pilnyak, Boris
See also CA 123; 218
Vogel, Paula A(nne) 1951- ... **CLC 76; DC 19**
See also CA 108; CAD; CANR 119; CD 5;
CWD; DFS 14; RGAL 4
Voigt, Cynthia 1942- .... **CLC 30**
See also AAYA 3, 30; BYA 1, 3, 6, 7, 8;
CA 106; CANR 18, 37, 40, 94; CLR 13,
48; INT CANR-18; JRDA; LAIT 5; MAI-
CYA 1, 2; MAICYAS 1; SATA 48, 79,
116; SATA-Brief 33; WYA; YAW
Voigt, Ellen Bryant 1943- .... **CLC 54**
See also CA 69-72; CANR 11, 29, 55, 115;
CP 7; CSW; CWP; DLB 120

Voinovich, Vladimir (Nikolaevich)
1932- .... **CLC 10, 49, 147**
See also CA 81-84; CAAS 12; CANR 33,
67; CWW 2; DLB 302; MTCW 1
Vollmann, William T. 1959- .... **CLC 89**
See also CA 134; CANR 67, 116; CPW;
DA3; DAM NOV, POP; MTCW 2
Voloshinov, V. N.
See Bakhtin, Mikhail Mikhailovich
Voltaire 1694-1778 . **LC 14, 79, 110; SSC 12;**
WLC
See also BYA 13; DA; DA3; DAB; DAC;
DAM DRAM, MST; EW 4; GFL Begin-
nings to 1789; LATS 1:1; LMFS 1; NFS
7; RGWL 2, 3; TWA
von Aschendrof, Baron Ignatz
See Ford, Ford Madox
von Chamisso, Adelbert
See Chamisso, Adelbert von
von Daeniken, Erich 1935- .... **CLC 30**
See also AITN 1; CA 37-40R; CANR 17,
44
von Daniken, Erich
See von Daeniken, Erich
von Hartmann, Eduard
1842-1906 .... **TCLC 96**
von Hayek, Friedrich August
See Hayek, F(riedrich) A(ugust von)
von Heidenstam, (Carl Gustaf) Verner
See Heidenstam, (Carl Gustaf) Verner von
von Heyse, Paul (Johann Ludwig)
See Heyse, Paul (Johann Ludwig von)
von Hofmannsthal, Hugo
See Hofmannsthal, Hugo von
von Horvath, Odon
See von Horvath, Odon
von Horvath, Odon
See von Horvath, Odon
von Horvath, Odon 1901-1938 .... **TCLC 45**
See von Horvath, Oedoen
See also CA 118; 194; DLB 85, 124; RGWL
2, 3
von Horvath, Oedoen
See von Horvath, Odon
See also CA 184
von Kleist, Heinrich
See Kleist, Heinrich von
von Liliencron, (Friedrich Adolf Axel)
Detlev
See Liliencron, (Friedrich Adolf Axel) De-
tlev von
Vonnegut, Kurt, Jr. 1922- . **CLC 1, 2, 3, 4, 5,**
8, 12, 22, 40, 60, 111; SSC 8; WLC
See also AAYA 6, 44; AITN 1; AMWS 2;
BEST 90:4; BPFB 3; BYA 3, 14; CA
1-4R; CANR 1, 25, 49, 75, 92; CDALB
1968-1988; CN 7; CPW 1; DA; DA3;
DAB; DAC; DAM MST, NOV, POP;
DLB 2, 8, 152; DLBD 3; DLBY 1980;
EWL 3; EXPN; EXPS; LAIT 4; LMFS 2;
MTCW 1, 2; NFS 3; RGAL 4; SCFW;
SFW 4; SSFS 5; TUS; YAW
Von Rachen, Kurt
See Hubbard, L(afayette) Ron(ald)
von Rezzori (d'Arezzo), Gregor
See Rezzori (d'Arezzo), Gregor von
von Sternberg, Josef
See Sternberg, Josef von
Vorster, Gordon 1924- .... **CLC 34**
See also CA 133
Vosce, Trudie
See Ozick, Cynthia
Voznesensky, Andrei (Andreievich)
1933- .... **CLC 1, 15, 57**
See Voznesensky, Andrey
See also CA 89-92; CANR 37; CWW 2;
DAM POET; MTCW 1

Voznesensky, Andrey
See Voznesensky, Andrei (Andreievich)
See also EWL 3

Wace, Robert c. 1100-c. 1175 .... **CMLC 55**
See also DLB 146

Waddington, Miriam 1917-2004 .... **CLC 28**
See also CA 21-24R; 225; CANR 12, 30;
CCA 1; CP 7; DLB 68

Wagman, Fredrica 1937- .... **CLC 7**
See also CA 97-100; INT CA-97-100

Wagner, Linda W.
See Wagner-Martin, Linda (C.)

Wagner, Linda Welshimer
See Wagner-Martin, Linda (C.)

Wagner, Richard 1813-1883 ..... **NCLC 9, 119**
See also DLB 129; EW 6

Wagner-Martin, Linda (C.) 1936- .... **CLC 50**
See also CA 159; CANR 135

Wagoner, David (Russell) 1926- .... **CLC 3, 5,
15; PC 33**
See also AMWS 9; CA 1-4R; CAAS 3;
CANR 2, 71; CN 7; CP 7; DLB 5, 256;
SATA 14; TCWW 2

Wah, Fred(erick James) 1939- .... **CLC 44**
See also CA 107; 141; CP 7; DLB 60

Wahloo, Per 1926-1975 .... **CLC 7**
See also BPFB 3; CA 61-64; CANR 73;
CMW 4; MSW

Wahloo, Peter
See Wahloo, Per

Wain, John (Barrington) 1925-1994 . **CLC 2,
11, 15, 46**
See also CA 5-8R; 145; CAAS 4; CANR
23, 54; CDBLB 1960 to Present; DLB 15,
27, 139, 155; EWL 3; MTCW 1, 2

Wajda, Andrzej 1926- .... **CLC 16**
See also CA 102

Wakefield, Dan 1932- .... **CLC 7**
See also CA 21-24R, 211; CAAE 211;
CAAS 7; CN 7

Wakefield, Herbert Russell
1888-1965 .... **TCLC 120**
See also CA 5-8R; CANR 77; HGG; SUFW

Wakoski, Diane 1937- ...... **CLC 2, 4, 7, 9, 11,
40; PC 15**
See also CA 13-16R, 216; CAAE 216;
CAAS 1; CANR 9, 60, 106; CP 7; CWP;
DAM POET; DLB 5; INT CANR-9;
MTCW 2

Wakoski-Sherbell, Diane
See Wakoski, Diane

Walcott, Derek (Alton) 1930- ... **BLC 3; CLC
2, 4, 9, 14, 25, 42, 67, 76, 160; DC 7;
PC 46**
See also BW 2; CA 89-92; CANR 26, 47,
75, 80, 130; CBD; CD 5; CDWLB 3; CP
7; DA3; DAB; DAC; DAM MST, MULT,
POET; DLB 117; DLBY 1981; DNFS 1;
EFS 1; EWL 3; LMFS 2; MTCW 1, 2;
PFS 6; RGEL 2; TWA; WWE 1

Waldman, Anne (Lesley) 1945- .... **CLC 7**
See also BG 3; CA 37-40R; CAAS 17;
CANR 34, 69, 116; CP 7; CWP; DLB 16

Waldo, E. Hunter
See Sturgeon, Theodore (Hamilton)

Waldo, Edward Hamilton
See Sturgeon, Theodore (Hamilton)

Walker, Alice (Malsenior) 1944- .... **BLC 3;
CLC 5, 6, 9, 19, 27, 46, 58, 103, 167;
PC 30; SSC 5; WLCS**
See also AAYA 3, 33; AFAW 1, 2; AMWS
3; BEST 89:4; BPFB 3; BW 2, 3; CA 37-
40R; CANR 9, 27, 49, 66, 82, 131;
CDALB 1968-1988; CN 7; CPW; CSW;
DA; DA3; DAB; DAC; DAM MST,
MULT, NOV, POET, POP; DLB 6, 33,
143; EWL 3; EXPN; EXPS; FW; INT

CANR-27; LAIT 3; MAWW; MTCW 1,
2; NFS 5; RGAL 4; RGSF 2; SATA 31;
SSFS 2, 11; TUS; YAW

Walker, David Harry 1911-1992 ...... **CLC 14**
See also CA 1-4R; 137; CANR 1; CWRI 5;
SATA 8; SATA-Obit 71

Walker, Edward Joseph 1934-2004
See Walker, Ted
See also CA 21-24R; 226; CANR 12, 28,
53; CP 7

Walker, George F. 1947- .... **CLC 44, 61**
See also CA 103; CANR 21, 43, 59; CD 5;
DAB; DAC; DAM MST; DLB 60

Walker, Joseph A. 1935- .... **CLC 19**
See also BW 1, 3; CA 89-92; CAD; CANR
26; CD 5; DAM DRAM, MST; DFS 12;
DLB 38

Walker, Margaret (Abigail)
1915-1998 .... **BLC; CLC 1, 6; PC 20;
TCLC 129**
See also AFAW 1, 2; BW 2, 3; CA 73-76;
172; CANR 26, 54, 76; CN 7; CP 7;
CSW; DAM MULT; DLB 76, 152; EXPP;
FW; MTCW 1, 2; RGAL 4; RHW

Walker, Ted .... **CLC 13**
See Walker, Edward Joseph
See also DLB 40

Wallace, David Foster 1962- ... **CLC 50, 114;
SSC 68**
See also AAYA 50; AMWS 10; CA 132;
CANR 59, 133; DA3; MTCW 2

Wallace, Dexter
See Masters, Edgar Lee

Wallace, (Richard Horatio) Edgar
1875-1932 .... **TCLC 57**
See also CA 115; 218; CMW 4; DLB 70;
MSW; RGEL 2

Wallace, Irving 1916-1990 .... **CLC 7, 13**
See also AITN 1; BPFB 3; CA 1-4R; 132;
CAAS 1; CANR 1, 27; CPW; DAM NOV,
POP; INT CANR-27; MTCW 1, 2

Wallant, Edward Lewis 1926-1962 ... **CLC 5,
10**
See also CA 1-4R; CANR 22; DLB 2, 28,
143, 299; EWL 3; MTCW 1, 2; RGAL 4

Wallas, Graham 1858-1932 .... **TCLC 91**

Waller, Edmund 1606-1687 .... **LC 86**
See also BRW 2; DAM POET; DLB 126;
PAB; RGEL 2

Walley, Byron
See Card, Orson Scott

Walpole, Horace 1717-1797 .... **LC 2, 49**
See also BRW 3; DLB 39, 104, 213; HGG;
LMFS 1; RGEL 2; SUFW 1; TEA

Walpole, Hugh (Seymour)
1884-1941 .... **TCLC 5**
See also CA 104; 165; DLB 34; HGG;
MTCW 2; RGEL 2; RHW

Walrond, Eric (Derwent) 1898-1966 .... **HR 3**
See also BW 1; CA 125; DLB 51

Walser, Martin 1927- .... **CLC 27, 183**
See also CA 57-60; CANR 8, 46; CWW 2;
DLB 75, 124; EWL 3

Walser, Robert 1878-1956 ..... **SSC 20; TCLC
18**
See also CA 118; 165; CANR 100; DLB
66; EWL 3

Walsh, Gillian Paton
See Paton Walsh, Gillian

Walsh, Jill Paton .... **CLC 35**
See Paton Walsh, Gillian
See also CLR 2, 65; WYA

Walter, Villiam Christian
See Andersen, Hans Christian

Walters, Anna L(ee) 1946- .... **NNAL**
See also CA 73-76

Walther von der Vogelweide c.
1170-1228 .... **CMLC 56**

Walton, Izaak 1593-1683 .... **LC 72**
See also BRW 2; CDBLB Before 1660;
DLB 151, 213; RGEL 2

Wambaugh, Joseph (Aloysius), Jr.
1937- .... **CLC 3, 18**
See also AITN 1; BEST 89:3; BPFB 3; CA
33-36R; CANR 42, 65, 115; CMW 4;
CPW 1; DA3; DAM NOV, POP; DLB 6;
DLBY 1983; MSW; MTCW 1, 2

Wang Wei 699(?)-761(?) .... **PC 18**
See also TWA

Warburton, William 1698-1779 .... **LC 97**
See also DLB 104

Ward, Arthur Henry Sarsfield 1883-1959
See Rohmer, Sax
See also CA 108; 173; CMW 4; HGG

Ward, Douglas Turner 1930- .... **CLC 19**
See also BW 1; CA 81-84; CAD; CANR
27; CD 5; DLB 7, 38

Ward, E. D.
See Lucas, E(dward) V(errall)

Ward, Mrs. Humphry 1851-1920
See Ward, Mary Augusta
See also RGEL 2

Ward, Mary Augusta 1851-1920 ... **TCLC 55**
See Ward, Mrs. Humphry
See also DLB 18

Ward, Peter
See Faust, Frederick (Schiller)

Warhol, Andy 1928(?)-1987 .... **CLC 20**
See also AAYA 12; BEST 89:4; CA 89-92;
121; CANR 34

Warner, Francis (Robert le Plastrier)
1937- .... **CLC 14**
See also CA 53-56; CANR 11

Warner, Marina 1946- .... **CLC 59**
See also CA 65-68; CANR 21, 55, 118; CN
7; DLB 194

Warner, Rex (Ernest) 1905-1986 ...... **CLC 45**
See also CA 89-92; 119; DLB 15; RGEL 2

Warner, Susan (Bogert)
1819-1885 .... **NCLC 31, 146**
See also DLB 3, 42, 239, 250, 254

Warner, Sylvia (Constance) Ashton
See Ashton-Warner, Sylvia (Constance)

Warner, Sylvia Townsend
1893-1978 .. **CLC 7, 19; SSC 23; TCLC
131**
See also BRWS 7; CA 61-64; 77-80; CANR
16, 60, 104; DLB 34, 139; EWL 3; FANT;
FW; MTCW 1, 2; RGEL 2; RGSF 2;
RHW

Warren, Mercy Otis 1728-1814 ..... **NCLC 13**
See also DLB 31, 200; RGAL 4; TUS

Warren, Robert Penn 1905-1989 .. **CLC 1, 4,
6, 8, 10, 13, 18, 39, 53, 59; PC 37; SSC
4, 58; WLC**
See also AITN 1; AMW; AMWC 2; BPFB
3; BYA 1; CA 13-16R; 129; CANR 10,
47; CDALB 1968-1988; DA; DA3; DAB;
DAC; DAM MST, NOV, POET; DLB 2,
48, 152; DLBY 1980, 1989; EWL 3; INT
CANR-10; MTCW 1, 2; NFS 13; RGAL
4; RGSF 2; RHW; SATA 46; SATA-Obit
63; SSFS 8; TUS

Warrigal, Jack
See Furphy, Joseph

Warshofsky, Isaac
See Singer, Isaac Bashevis

Warton, Joseph 1722-1800 .... **NCLC 118**
See also DLB 104, 109; RGEL 2

Warton, Thomas 1728-1790 .... **LC 15, 82**
See also DAM POET; DLB 104, 109;
RGEL 2

Waruk, Kona
See Harris, (Theodore) Wilson

Warung, Price .... **TCLC 45**
See Astley, William
See also DLB 230; RGEL 2
Warwick, Jarvis
See Garner, Hugh
See also CCA 1
Washington, Alex
See Harris, Mark
Washington, Booker T(aliaferro)
1856-1915 .... **BLC 3; TCLC 10**
See also BW 1; CA 114; 125; DA3; DAM
MULT; LAIT 2; RGAL 4; SATA 28
Washington, George 1732-1799 .... **LC 25**
See also DLB 31
Wassermann, (Karl) Jakob
1873-1934 .... **TCLC 6**
See also CA 104; 163; DLB 66; EWL 3
Wasserstein, Wendy 1950- ... **CLC 32, 59, 90,**
183; DC 4
See also CA 121; 129; CABS 3; CAD;
CANR 53, 75, 128; CD 5; CWD; DA3;
DAM DRAM; DFS 5, 17; DLB 228;
EWL 3; FW; INT CA-129; MTCW 2;
SATA 94
Waterhouse, Keith (Spencer) 1929- . **CLC 47**
See also CA 5-8R; CANR 38, 67, 109;
CBD; CN 7; DLB 13, 15; MTCW 1, 2
Waters, Frank (Joseph) 1902-1995 .. **CLC 88**
See also CA 5-8R; 149; CAAS 13; CANR
3, 18, 63, 121; DLB 212; DLBY 1986;
RGAL 4; TCWW 2
Waters, Mary C. .... **CLC 70**
Waters, Roger 1944- .... **CLC 35**
Watkins, Frances Ellen
See Harper, Frances Ellen Watkins
Watkins, Gerrold
See Malzberg, Barry N(athaniel)
Watkins, Gloria Jean 1952(?)- .... **CLC 94**
See also BW 2; CA 143; CANR 87, 126;
DLB 246; MTCW 2; SATA 115
Watkins, Paul 1964- .... **CLC 55**
See also CA 132; CANR 62, 98
Watkins, Vernon Phillips
1906-1967 .... **CLC 43**
See also CA 9-10; 25-28R; CAP 1; DLB
20; EWL 3; RGEL 2
Watson, Irving S.
See Mencken, H(enry) L(ouis)
Watson, John H.
See Farmer, Philip Jose
Watson, Richard F.
See Silverberg, Robert
Watts, Ephraim
See Horne, Richard Henry Hengist
Watts, Isaac 1674-1748 .... **LC 98**
See also DLB 95; RGEL 2; SATA 52
Waugh, Auberon (Alexander)
1939-2001 .... **CLC 7**
See also CA 45-48; 192; CANR 6, 22, 92;
DLB 14, 194
Waugh, Evelyn (Arthur St. John)
1903-1966 .. **CLC 1, 3, 8, 13, 19, 27, 44,**
107; SSC 41; WLC
See also BPFB 3; BRW 7; CA 85-88; 25-
28R; CANR 22; CDBLB 1914-1945; DA;
DA3; DAB; DAC; DAM MST, NOV,
POP; DLB 15, 162, 195; EWL 3; MTCW
1, 2; NFS 13, 17; RGEL 2; RGSF 2; TEA;
WLIT 4
Waugh, Harriet 1944- .... **CLC 6**
See also CA 85-88; CANR 22
Ways, C. R.
See Blount, Roy (Alton), Jr.
Waystaff, Simon
See Swift, Jonathan
Webb, Beatrice (Martha Potter)
1858-1943 .... **TCLC 22**
See also CA 117; 162; DLB 190; FW

Webb, Charles (Richard) 1939- .... **CLC 7**
See also CA 25-28R; CANR 114
Webb, Frank J. .... **NCLC 143**
See also DLB 50
Webb, James H(enry), Jr. 1946- ...... **CLC 22**
See also CA 81-84
Webb, Mary Gladys (Meredith)
1881-1927 .... **TCLC 24**
See also CA 182; 123; DLB 34; FW
Webb, Mrs. Sidney
See Webb, Beatrice (Martha Potter)
Webb, Phyllis 1927- .... **CLC 18**
See also CA 104; CANR 23; CCA 1; CP 7;
CWP; DLB 53
Webb, Sidney (James) 1859-1947 .. **TCLC 22**
See also CA 117; 163; DLB 190
Webber, Andrew Lloyd .... **CLC 21**
See Lloyd Webber, Andrew
See also DFS 7
Weber, Lenora Mattingly
1895-1971 .... **CLC 12**
See also CA 19-20; 29-32R; CAP 1; SATA
2; SATA-Obit 26
Weber, Max 1864-1920 .... **TCLC 69**
See also CA 109; 189; DLB 296
Webster, John 1580(?)-1634(?) ...... **DC 2; LC**
33, 84; WLC
See also BRW 2; CDBLB Before 1660; DA;
DAB; DAC; DAM DRAM, MST; DFS
17, 19; DLB 58; IDTP; RGEL 2; WLIT 3
Webster, Noah 1758-1843 .... **NCLC 30**
See also DLB 1, 37, 42, 43, 73, 243
Wedekind, (Benjamin) Frank(lin)
1864-1918 .... **TCLC 7**
See also CA 104; 153; CANR 121, 122;
CDWLB 2; DAM DRAM; DLB 118; EW
8; EWL 3; LMFS 2; RGWL 2, 3
Wehr, Demaris .... **CLC 65**
Weidman, Jerome 1913-1998 .... **CLC 7**
See also AITN 2; CA 1-4R; 171; CAD;
CANR 1; DLB 28
Weil, Simone (Adolphine)
1909-1943 .... **TCLC 23**
See also CA 117; 159; EW 12; EWL 3; FW;
GFL 1789 to the Present; MTCW 2
Weininger, Otto 1880-1903 .... **TCLC 84**
Weinstein, Nathan
See West, Nathanael
Weinstein, Nathan von Wallenstein
See West, Nathanael
Weir, Peter (Lindsay) 1944- .... **CLC 20**
See also CA 113; 123
Weiss, Peter (Ulrich) 1916-1982 .. **CLC 3, 15,**
51; TCLC 152
See also CA 45-48; 106; CANR 3; DAM
DRAM; DFS 3; DLB 69, 124; EWL 3;
RGWL 2, 3
Weiss, Theodore (Russell)
1916-2003 .... **CLC 3, 8, 14**
See also CA 9-12R; 189; 216; CAAE 189;
CAAS 2; CANR 46, 94; CP 7; DLB 5
Welch, (Maurice) Denton
1915-1948 .... **TCLC 22**
See also BRWS 8, 9; CA 121; 148; RGEL
2
Welch, James (Phillip) 1940-2003 ..... **CLC 6,**
14, 52; NNAL
See also CA 85-88; 219; CANR 42, 66, 107;
CN 7; CP 7; CPW; DAM MULT, POP;
DLB 175, 256; LATS 1:1; RGAL 4;
TCWW 2
Weldon, Fay 1931- . **CLC 6, 9, 11, 19, 36, 59,**
122
See also BRWS 4; CA 21-24R; CANR 16,
46, 63, 97; CDBLB 1960 to Present; CN
7; CPW; DAM POP; DLB 14, 194; EWL
3; FW; HGG; INT CANR-16; MTCW 1,
2; RGEL 2; RGSF 2

Wellek, Rene 1903-1995 .... **CLC 28**
See also CA 5-8R; 150; CAAS 7; CANR 8;
DLB 63; EWL 3; INT CANR-8
Weller, Michael 1942- .... **CLC 10, 53**
See also CA 85-88; CAD; CD 5
Weller, Paul 1958- .... **CLC 26**
Wellershoff, Dieter 1925- .... **CLC 46**
See also CA 89-92; CANR 16, 37
Welles, (George) Orson 1915-1985 .. **CLC 20,**
80
See also AAYA 40; CA 93-96; 117
Wellman, John McDowell 1945-
See Wellman, Mac
See also CA 166; CD 5
Wellman, Mac .... **CLC 65**
See Wellman, John McDowell; Wellman,
John McDowell
See also CAD; RGAL 4
Wellman, Manly Wade 1903-1986 ... **CLC 49**
See also CA 1-4R; 118; CANR 6, 16, 44;
FANT; SATA 6; SATA-Obit 47; SFW 4;
SUFW
Wells, Carolyn 1869(?)-1942 .... **TCLC 35**
See also CA 113; 185; CMW 4; DLB 11
Wells, H(erbert) G(eorge) 1866-1946 . **SSC 6,**
70; TCLC 6, 12, 19, 133; WLC
See also AAYA 18; BPFB 3; BRW 6; CA
110; 121; CDBLB 1914-1945; CLR 64;
DA; DA3; DAB; DAC; DAM MST, NOV;
DLB 34, 70, 156, 178; EWL 3; EXPS;
HGG; LAIT 3; LMFS 2; MTCW 1, 2;
NFS 17, 20; RGEL 2; RGSF 2; SATA 20;
SCFW; SFW 4; SSFS 3; SUFW; TEA;
WCH; WLIT 4; YAW
Wells, Rosemary 1943- .... **CLC 12**
See also AAYA 13; BYA 7, 8; CA 85-88;
CANR 48, 120; CLR 16, 69; CWRI 5;
MAICYA 1, 2; SAAS 1; SATA 18, 69,
114; YAW
Wells-Barnett, Ida B(ell)
1862-1931 .... **TCLC 125**
See also CA 182; DLB 23, 221
Welsh, Irvine 1958- .... **CLC 144**
See also CA 173; DLB 271
Welty, Eudora (Alice) 1909-2001 .. **CLC 1, 2,**
5, 14, 22, 33, 105; SSC 1, 27, 51; WLC
See also AAYA 48; AMW; AMWR 1; BPFB
3; CA 9-12R; 199; CABS 1; CANR 32,
65, 128; CDALB 1941-1968; CN 7; CSW;
DA; DA3; DAB; DAC; DAM MST, NOV;
DLB 2, 102, 143; DLBD 12; DLBY 1987,
2001; EWL 3; EXPS; HGG; LAIT 3;
MAWW; MTCW 1, 2; NFS 13, 15; RGAL
4; RGSF 2; RHW; SSFS 2, 10; TUS
Wen I-to 1899-1946 .... **TCLC 28**
See also EWL 3
Wentworth, Robert
See Hamilton, Edmond
Werfel, Franz (Viktor) 1890-1945 ... **TCLC 8**
See also CA 104; 161; DLB 81, 124; EWL
3; RGWL 2, 3
Wergeland, Henrik Arnold
1808-1845 .... **NCLC 5**
Wersba, Barbara 1932- .... **CLC 30**
See also AAYA 2, 30; BYA 6, 12, 13; CA
29-32R, 182; CAAE 182; CANR 16, 38;
CLR 3, 78; DLB 52; JRDA; MAICYA 1,
2; SAAS 2; SATA 1, 58; SATA-Essay 103;
WYA; YAW
Wertmueller, Lina 1928- .... **CLC 16**
See also CA 97-100; CANR 39, 78
Wescott, Glenway 1901-1987 .. **CLC 13; SSC**
35
See also CA 13-16R; 121; CANR 23, 70;
DLB 4, 9, 102; RGAL 4

Wesker, Arnold 1932- .... **CLC 3, 5, 42**
See also CA 1-4R; CAAS 7; CANR 1, 33;
CBD; CD 5; CDBLB 1960 to Present;
DAB; DAM DRAM; DLB 13; EWL 3;
MTCW 1; RGEL 2; TEA

Wesley, John 1703-1791 .... **LC 88**
See also DLB 104

Wesley, Richard (Errol) 1945- .... **CLC 7**
See also BW 1; CA 57-60; CAD; CANR
27; CD 5; DLB 38

Wessel, Johan Herman 1742-1785 .... **LC 7**
See also DLB 300

West, Anthony (Panther)
1914-1987 .... **CLC 50**
See also CA 45-48; 124; CANR 3, 19; DLB
15

West, C. P.
See Wodehouse, P(elham) G(renville)

West, Cornel (Ronald) 1953- .... **BLCS; CLC 134**
See also CA 144; CANR 91; DLB 246

West, Delno C(loyde), Jr. 1936- .... **CLC 70**
See also CA 57-60

West, Dorothy 1907-1998 .. **HR 3; TCLC 108**
See also BW 2; CA 143; 169; DLB 76

West, (Mary) Jessamyn 1902-1984 ... **CLC 7, 17**
See also CA 9-12R; 112; CANR 27; DLB
6; DLBY 1984; MTCW 1, 2; RGAL 4;
RHW; SATA-Obit 37; TCWW 2; TUS;
YAW

West, Morris
See West, Morris L(anglo)
See also DLB 289

West, Morris L(anglo) 1916-1999 ..... **CLC 6, 33**
See West, Morris
See also BPFB 3; CA 5-8R; 187; CANR
24, 49, 64; CN 7; CPW; MTCW 1, 2

West, Nathanael 1903-1940 .. **SSC 16; TCLC 1, 14, 44**
See also AMW; AMWR 2; BPFB 3; CA
104; 125; CDALB 1929-1941; DA3; DLB
4, 9, 28; EWL 3; MTCW 1, 2; NFS 16;
RGAL 4; TUS

West, Owen
See Koontz, Dean R(ay)

West, Paul 1930- .... **CLC 7, 14, 96**
See also CA 13-16R; CAAS 7; CANR 22,
53, 76, 89; CN 7; DLB 14; INT CANR-
22; MTCW 2

West, Rebecca 1892-1983 ... **CLC 7, 9, 31, 50**
See also BPFB 3; BRWS 3; CA 5-8R; 109;
CANR 19; DLB 36; DLBY 1983; EWL
3; FW; MTCW 1, 2; NCFS 4; RGEL 2;
TEA

Westall, Robert (Atkinson)
1929-1993 .... **CLC 17**
See also AAYA 12; BYA 2, 6, 7, 8, 9, 15;
CA 69-72; 141; CANR 18, 68; CLR 13;
FANT; JRDA; MAICYA 1, 2; MAICYAS
1; SAAS 2; SATA 23, 69; SATA-Obit 75;
WYA; YAW

Westermarck, Edward 1862-1939 . **TCLC 87**

Westlake, Donald E(dwin) 1933- . **CLC 7, 33**
See also BPFB 3; CA 17-20R; CAAS 13;
CANR 16, 44, 65, 94; CMW 4; CPW;
DAM POP; INT CANR-16; MSW;
MTCW 2

Westmacott, Mary
See Christie, Agatha (Mary Clarissa)

Weston, Allen
See Norton, Andre

Wetcheek, J. L.
See Feuchtwanger, Lion

Wetering, Janwillem van de
See van de Wetering, Janwillem

Wetherald, Agnes Ethelwyn
1857-1940 .... **TCLC 81**
See also CA 202; DLB 99

Wetherell, Elizabeth
See Warner, Susan (Bogert)

Whale, James 1889-1957 .... **TCLC 63**

Whalen, Philip (Glenn) 1923-2002 .... **CLC 6, 29**
See also BG 3; CA 9-12R; 209; CANR 5,
39; CP 7; DLB 16; WP

Wharton, Edith (Newbold Jones)
1862-1937 ... **SSC 6; TCLC 3, 9, 27, 53, 129, 149; WLC**
See also AAYA 25; AMW; AMWC 2;
AMWR 1; BPFB 3; CA 104; 132; CDALB
1865-1917; DA; DA3; DAB; DAC; DAM
MST, NOV; DLB 4, 9, 12, 78, 189; DLBD
13; EWL 3; EXPS; HGG; LAIT 2, 3;
LATS 1:1; MAWW; MTCW 1, 2; NFS 5,
11, 15, 20; RGAL 4; RGSF 2; RHW;
SSFS 6, 7; SUFW; TUS

Wharton, James
See Mencken, H(enry) L(ouis)

Wharton, William (a pseudonym) . **CLC 18, 37**
See also CA 93-96; DLBY 1980; INT CA-
93-96

Wheatley (Peters), Phillis
1753(?)-1784 ... **BLC 3; LC 3, 50; PC 3; WLC**
See also AFAW 1, 2; CDALB 1640-1865;
DA; DA3; DAC; DAM MST, MULT,
POET; DLB 31, 50; EXPP; PFS 13;
RGAL 4

Wheelock, John Hall 1886-1978 .... **CLC 14**
See also CA 13-16R; 77-80; CANR 14;
DLB 45

Whim-Wham
See Curnow, (Thomas) Allen (Monro)

White, Babington
See Braddon, Mary Elizabeth

White, E(lwyn) B(rooks)
1899-1985 .... **CLC 10, 34, 39**
See also AITN 2; AMWS 1; CA 13-16R;
116; CANR 16, 37; CDALBS; CLR 1, 21;
CPW; DA3; DAM POP; DLB 11, 22;
EWL 3; FANT; MAICYA 1, 2; MTCW 1,
2; NCFS 5; RGAL 4; SATA 2, 29, 100;
SATA-Obit 44; TUS

White, Edmund (Valentine III)
1940- .... **CLC 27, 110**
See also AAYA 7; CA 45-48; CANR 3, 19,
36, 62, 107, 133; CN 7; DA3; DAM POP;
DLB 227; MTCW 1, 2

White, Hayden V. 1928- .... **CLC 148**
See also CA 128; CANR 135; DLB 246

White, Patrick (Victor Martindale)
1912-1990 .... **CLC 3, 4, 5, 7, 9, 18, 65, 69; SSC 39**
See also BRWS 1; CA 81-84; 132; CANR
43; DLB 260; EWL 3; MTCW 1; RGEL
2; RGSF 2; RHW; TWA; WWE 1

White, Phyllis Dorothy James 1920-
See James, P. D.
See also CA 21-24R; CANR 17, 43, 65,
112; CMW 4; CN 7; CPW; DA3; DAM
POP; MTCW 1, 2; TEA

White, T(erence) H(anbury)
1906-1964 .... **CLC 30**
See also AAYA 22; BPFB 3; BYA 4, 5; CA
73-76; CANR 37; DLB 160; FANT;
JRDA; LAIT 1; MAICYA 1, 2; RGEL 2;
SATA 12; SUFW 1; YAW

White, Terence de Vere 1912-1994 ... **CLC 49**
See also CA 49-52; 145; CANR 3

White, Walter
See White, Walter F(rancis)

White, Walter F(rancis) 1893-1955 ... **BLC 3; HR 3; TCLC 15**
See also BW 1; CA 115; 124; DAM MULT;
DLB 51

White, William Hale 1831-1913
See Rutherford, Mark
See also CA 121; 189

Whitehead, Alfred North
1861-1947 .... **TCLC 97**
See also CA 117; 165; DLB 100, 262

Whitehead, E(dward) A(nthony)
1933- .... **CLC 5**
See also CA 65-68; CANR 58, 118; CBD;
CD 5

Whitehead, Ted
See Whitehead, E(dward) A(nthony)

Whiteman, Roberta J. Hill 1947- ...... **NNAL**
See also CA 146

Whitemore, Hugh (John) 1936- .... **CLC 37**
See also CA 132; CANR 77; CBD; CD 5;
INT CA-132

Whitman, Sarah Helen (Power)
1803-1878 .... **NCLC 19**
See also DLB 1, 243

Whitman, Walt(er) 1819-1892 .. **NCLC 4, 31, 81; PC 3; WLC**
See also AAYA 42; AMW; AMWR 1;
CDALB 1640-1865; DA; DA3; DAB;
DAC; DAM MST, POET; DLB 3, 64,
224, 250; EXPP; LAIT 2; LMFS 1; PAB;
PFS 2, 3, 13; RGAL 4; SATA 20; TUS;
WP; WYAS 1

Whitney, Phyllis A(yame) 1903- .... **CLC 42**
See also AAYA 36; AITN 2; BEST 90:3;
CA 1-4R; CANR 3, 25, 38, 60; CLR 59;
CMW 4; CPW; DA3; DAM POP; JRDA;
MAICYA 1, 2; MTCW 2; RHW; SATA 1,
30; YAW

Whittemore, (Edward) Reed, Jr.
1919- .... **CLC 4**
See also CA 9-12R, 219; CAAE 219; CAAS
8; CANR 4, 119; CP 7; DLB 5

Whittier, John Greenleaf
1807-1892 .... **NCLC 8, 59**
See also AMWS 1; DLB 1, 243; RGAL 4

Whittlebot, Hernia
See Coward, Noel (Peirce)

Wicker, Thomas Grey 1926-
See Wicker, Tom
See also CA 65-68; CANR 21, 46

Wicker, Tom .... **CLC 7**
See Wicker, Thomas Grey

Wideman, John Edgar 1941- ... **BLC 3; CLC 5, 34, 36, 67, 122; SSC 62**
See also AFAW 1, 2; AMWS 10; BPFB 4;
BW 2, 3; CA 85-88; CANR 14, 42, 67,
109; CN 7; DAM MULT; DLB 33, 143;
MTCW 2; RGAL 4; RGSF 2; SSFS 6, 12

Wiebe, Rudy (Henry) 1934- .. **CLC 6, 11, 14, 138**
See also CA 37-40R; CANR 42, 67, 123;
CN 7; DAC; DAM MST; DLB 60; RHW

Wieland, Christoph Martin
1733-1813 .... **NCLC 17**
See also DLB 97; EW 4; LMFS 1; RGWL
2, 3

Wiene, Robert 1881-1938 .... **TCLC 56**

Wieners, John 1934- .... **CLC 7**
See also BG 3; CA 13-16R; CP 7; DLB 16;
WP

Wiesel, Elie(zer) 1928- .... **CLC 3, 5, 11, 37, 165; WLCS**
See also AAYA 7, 54; AITN 1; CA 5-8R;
CAAS 4; CANR 8, 40, 65, 125; CDALBS;
CWW 2; DA; DA3; DAB; DAC; DAM
MST, NOV; DLB 83, 299; DLBY 1987;
EWL 3; INT CANR-8; LAIT 4; MTCW
1, 2; NCFS 4; NFS 4; RGWL 3; SATA
56; YAW

Wiggins, Marianne 1947- .... **CLC 57**
See also BEST 89:3; CA 130; CANR 60

Wigglesworth, Michael 1631-1705 .... **LC 106**
See also DLB 24; RGAL 4

Wiggs, Susan .... **CLC 70**
See also CA 201

Wight, James Alfred 1916-1995
See Herriot, James
See also CA 77-80; SATA 55; SATA-Brief 44

Wilbur, Richard (Purdy) 1921- ..... **CLC 3, 6, 9, 14, 53, 110; PC 51**
See also AMWS 3; CA 1-4R; CABS 2; CANR 2, 29, 76, 93; CDALBS; CP 7; DA; DAB; DAC; DAM MST, POET; DLB 5, 169; EWL 3; EXPP; INT CANR-29; MTCW 1, 2; PAB; PFS 11, 12, 16; RGAL 4; SATA 9, 108; WP

Wild, Peter 1940- .... **CLC 14**
See also CA 37-40R; CP 7; DLB 5

Wilde, Oscar (Fingal O'Flahertie Wills) 1854(?)-1900 .... **DC 17; SSC 11, 77; TCLC 1, 8, 23, 41; WLC**
See also AAYA 49; BRW 5; BRWC 1, 2; BRWR 2; BYA 15; CA 104; 119; CANR 112; CDBLB 1890-1914; DA; DA3; DAB; DAC; DAM DRAM, MST, NOV; DFS 4, 8, 9; DLB 10, 19, 34, 57, 141, 156, 190; EXPS; FANT; LATS 1:1; NFS 20; RGEL 2; RGSF 2; SATA 24; SSFS 7; SUFW; TEA; WCH; WLIT 4

Wilder, Billy .... **CLC 20**
See Wilder, Samuel
See also DLB 26

Wilder, Samuel 1906-2002
See Wilder, Billy
See also CA 89-92; 205

Wilder, Stephen
See Marlowe, Stephen

Wilder, Thornton (Niven) 1897-1975 .. **CLC 1, 5, 6, 10, 15, 35, 82; DC 1, 24; WLC**
See also AAYA 29; AITN 2; AMW; CA 13-16R; 61-64; CAD; CANR 40, 132; CDALBS; DA; DA3; DAB; DAC; DAM DRAM, MST, NOV; DFS 1, 4, 16; DLB 4, 7, 9, 228; DLBY 1997; EWL 3; LAIT 3; MTCW 1, 2; RGAL 4; RHW; WYAS 1

Wilding, Michael 1942- ...... **CLC 73; SSC 50**
See also CA 104; CANR 24, 49, 106; CN 7; RGSF 2

Wiley, Richard 1944- .... **CLC 44**
See also CA 121; 129; CANR 71

Wilhelm, Kate .... **CLC 7**
See Wilhelm, Katie (Gertrude)
See also AAYA 20; BYA 16; CAAS 5; DLB 8; INT CANR-17; SCFW 2

Wilhelm, Katie (Gertrude) 1928-
See Wilhelm, Kate
See also CA 37-40R; CANR 17, 36, 60, 94; MTCW 1; SFW 4

Wilkins, Mary
See Freeman, Mary E(leanor) Wilkins

Willard, Nancy 1936- .... **CLC 7, 37**
See also BYA 5; CA 89-92; CANR 10, 39, 68, 107; CLR 5; CWP; CWRI 5; DLB 5, 52; FANT; MAICYA 1, 2; MTCW 1; SATA 37, 71, 127; SATA-Brief 30; SUFW 2

William of Malmesbury c. 1090B.C.-c. 1140B.C. .... **CMLC 57**

William of Ockham 1290-1349 ..... **CMLC 32**

Williams, Ben Ames 1889-1953 ..... **TCLC 89**
See also CA 183; DLB 102

Williams, C(harles) K(enneth) 1936- .... **CLC 33, 56, 148**
See also CA 37-40R; CAAS 26; CANR 57, 106; CP 7; DAM POET; DLB 5

Williams, Charles
See Collier, James Lincoln

Williams, Charles (Walter Stansby) 1886-1945 .... **TCLC 1, 11**
See also BRWS 9; CA 104; 163; DLB 100, 153, 255; FANT; RGEL 2; SUFW 1

Williams, Ella Gwendolen Rees
See Rhys, Jean

Williams, (George) Emlyn 1905-1987 .... **CLC 15**
See also CA 104; 123; CANR 36; DAM DRAM; DLB 10, 77; IDTP; MTCW 1

Williams, Hank 1923-1953 .... **TCLC 81**
See Williams, Hiram King

Williams, Helen Maria 1761-1827 .... **NCLC 135**
See also DLB 158

Williams, Hiram Hank
See Williams, Hank

Williams, Hiram King
See Williams, Hank
See also CA 188

Williams, Hugo (Mordaunt) 1942- ... **CLC 42**
See also CA 17-20R; CANR 45, 119; CP 7; DLB 40

Williams, J. Walker
See Wodehouse, P(elham) G(renville)

Williams, John A(lfred) 1925- . **BLC 3; CLC 5, 13**
See also AFAW 2; BW 2, 3; CA 53-56; 195; CAAE 195; CAAS 3; CANR 6, 26, 51, 118; CN 7; CSW; DAM MULT; DLB 2, 33; EWL 3; INT CANR-6; RGAL 4; SFW 4

Williams, Jonathan (Chamberlain) 1929- .... **CLC 13**
See also CA 9-12R; CAAS 12; CANR 8, 108; CP 7; DLB 5

Williams, Joy 1944- .... **CLC 31**
See also CA 41-44R; CANR 22, 48, 97

Williams, Norman 1952- .... **CLC 39**
See also CA 118

Williams, Sherley Anne 1944-1999 ... **BLC 3; CLC 89**
See also AFAW 2; BW 2, 3; CA 73-76; 185; CANR 25, 82; DAM MULT, POET; DLB 41; INT CANR-25; SATA 78; SATA-Obit 116

Williams, Shirley
See Williams, Sherley Anne

Williams, Tennessee 1911-1983 . **CLC 1, 2, 5, 7, 8, 11, 15, 19, 30, 39, 45, 71, 111; DC 4; WLC**
See also AAYA 31; AITN 1, 2; AMW; AMWC 1; CA 5-8R; 108; CABS 3; CAD; CANR 31, 132; CDALB 1941-1968; DA; DA3; DAB; DAC; DAM DRAM, MST; DFS 17; DLB 7; DLBD 4; DLBY 1983; EWL 3; GLL 1; LAIT 4; LATS 1:2; MTCW 1, 2; RGAL 4; TUS

Williams, Thomas (Alonzo) 1926-1990 .... **CLC 14**
See also CA 1-4R; 132; CANR 2

Williams, William C.
See Williams, William Carlos

Williams, William Carlos 1883-1963 .... **CLC 1, 2, 5, 9, 13, 22, 42, 67; PC 7; SSC 31**
See also AAYA 46; AMW; AMWR 1; CA 89-92; CANR 34; CDALB 1917-1929; DA; DA3; DAB; DAC; DAM MST, POET; DLB 4, 16, 54, 86; EWL 3; EXPP; MTCW 1, 2; NCFS 4; PAB; PFS 1, 6, 11; RGAL 4; RGSF 2; TUS; WP

Williamson, David (Keith) 1942- ..... **CLC 56**
See also CA 103; CANR 41; CD 5; DLB 289

Williamson, Ellen Douglas 1905-1984
See Douglas, Ellen
See also CA 17-20R; 114; CANR 39

Williamson, Jack .... **CLC 29**
See Williamson, John Stewart
See also CAAS 8; DLB 8; SCFW 2

Williamson, John Stewart 1908-
See Williamson, Jack
See also CA 17-20R; CANR 23, 70; SFW 4

Willie, Frederick
See Lovecraft, H(oward) P(hillips)

Willingham, Calder (Baynard, Jr.) 1922-1995 .... **CLC 5, 51**
See also CA 5-8R; 147; CANR 3; CSW; DLB 2, 44; IDFW 3, 4; MTCW 1

Willis, Charles
See Clarke, Arthur C(harles)

Willy
See Colette, (Sidonie-Gabrielle)

Willy, Colette
See Colette, (Sidonie-Gabrielle)
See also GLL 1

Wilmot, John 1647-1680 .... **LC 75**
See Rochester
See also BRW 2; DLB 131; PAB

Wilson, A(ndrew) N(orman) 1950- .. **CLC 33**
See also BRWS 6; CA 112; 122; CN 7; DLB 14, 155, 194; MTCW 2

Wilson, Angus (Frank Johnstone) 1913-1991 . **CLC 2, 3, 5, 25, 34; SSC 21**
See also BRWS 1; CA 5-8R; 134; CANR 21; DLB 15, 139, 155; EWL 3; MTCW 1, 2; RGEL 2; RGSF 2

Wilson, August 1945- ... **BLC 3; CLC 39, 50, 63, 118; DC 2; WLCS**
See also AAYA 16; AFAW 2; AMWS 8; BW 2, 3; CA 115; 122; CAD; CANR 42, 54, 76, 128; CD 5; DA; DA3; DAB; DAC; DAM DRAM, MST, MULT; DFS 3, 7, 15, 17; DLB 228; EWL 3; LAIT 4; LATS 1:2; MTCW 1, 2; RGAL 4

Wilson, Brian 1942- .... **CLC 12**

Wilson, Colin 1931- .... **CLC 3, 14**
See also CA 1-4R; CAAS 5; CANR 1, 22, 33, 77; CMW 4; CN 7; DLB 14, 194; HGG; MTCW 1; SFW 4

Wilson, Dirk
See Pohl, Frederik

Wilson, Edmund 1895-1972 .. **CLC 1, 2, 3, 8, 24**
See also AMW; CA 1-4R; 37-40R; CANR 1, 46, 110; DLB 63; EWL 3; MTCW 1, 2; RGAL 4; TUS

Wilson, Ethel Davis (Bryant) 1888(?)-1980 .... **CLC 13**
See also CA 102; DAC; DAM POET; DLB 68; MTCW 1; RGEL 2

Wilson, Harriet
See Wilson, Harriet E. Adams
See also DLB 239

Wilson, Harriet E.
See Wilson, Harriet E. Adams
See also DLB 243

Wilson, Harriet E. Adams 1827(?)-1863(?) .... **BLC 3; NCLC 78**
See Wilson, Harriet; Wilson, Harriet E.
See also DAM MULT; DLB 50

Wilson, John 1785-1854 .... **NCLC 5**

Wilson, John (Anthony) Burgess 1917-1993
See Burgess, Anthony
See also CA 1-4R; 143; CANR 2, 46; DA3; DAC; DAM NOV; MTCW 1, 2; NFS 15; TEA

Wilson, Lanford 1937- .. **CLC 7, 14, 36, 197; DC 19**
See also CA 17-20R; CABS 3; CAD; CANR 45, 96; CD 5; DAM DRAM; DFS 4, 9, 12, 16, 20; DLB 7; EWL 3; TUS

Wilson, Robert M. 1941- .... **CLC 7, 9**
See also CA 49-52; CAD; CANR 2, 41; CD
5; MTCW 1

Wilson, Robert McLiam 1964- .... **CLC 59**
See also CA 132; DLB 267

Wilson, Sloan 1920-2003 .... **CLC 32**
See also CA 1-4R; 216; CANR 1, 44; CN 7

Wilson, Snoo 1948- .... **CLC 33**
See also CA 69-72; CBD; CD 5

Wilson, William S(mith) 1932- .... **CLC 49**
See also CA 81-84

Wilson, (Thomas) Woodrow
1856-1924 .... **TCLC 79**
See also CA 166; DLB 47

Wilson and Warnke eds. .... **CLC 65**

Winchilsea, Anne (Kingsmill) Finch
1661-1720
See Finch, Anne
See also RGEL 2

Windham, Basil
See Wodehouse, P(elham) G(renville)

Wingrove, David (John) 1954- .... **CLC 68**
See also CA 133; SFW 4

Winnemucca, Sarah 1844-1891 .... **NCLC 79;**
NNAL
See also DAM MULT; DLB 175; RGAL 4

Winstanley, Gerrard 1609-1676 .... **LC 52**

Wintergreen, Jane
See Duncan, Sara Jeannette

Winters, Janet Lewis .... **CLC 41**
See Lewis, Janet
See also DLBY 1987

Winters, (Arthur) Yvor 1900-1968 .... **CLC 4,**
8, 32
See also AMWS 2; CA 11-12; 25-28R; CAP
1; DLB 48; EWL 3; MTCW 1; RGAL 4

Winterson, Jeanette 1959- .... **CLC 64, 158**
See also BRWS 4; CA 136; CANR 58, 116;
CN 7; CPW; DA3; DAM POP; DLB 207,
261; FANT; FW; GLL 1; MTCW 2; RHW

Winthrop, John 1588-1649 .... **LC 31, 107**
See also DLB 24, 30

Wirth, Louis 1897-1952 .... **TCLC 92**
See also CA 210

Wiseman, Frederick 1930- .... **CLC 20**
See also CA 159

Wister, Owen 1860-1938 .... **TCLC 21**
See also BPFB 3; CA 108; 162; DLB 9, 78,
186; RGAL 4; SATA 62; TCWW 2

Wither, George 1588-1667 .... **LC 96**
See also DLB 121; RGEL 2

Witkacy
See Witkiewicz, Stanislaw Ignacy

Witkiewicz, Stanislaw Ignacy
1885-1939 .... **TCLC 8**
See also CA 105; 162; CDWLB 4; DLB
215; EW 10; EWL 3; RGWL 2, 3; SFW 4

Wittgenstein, Ludwig (Josef Johann)
1889-1951 .... **TCLC 59**
See also CA 113; 164; DLB 262; MTCW 2

Wittig, Monique 1935(?)-2003 .... **CLC 22**
See also CA 116; 135; 212; CWW 2; DLB
83; EWL 3; FW; GLL 1

Wittlin, Jozef 1896-1976 .... **CLC 25**
See also CA 49-52; 65-68; CANR 3; EWL
3

Wodehouse, P(elham) G(renville)
1881-1975 . **CLC 1, 2, 5, 10, 22; SSC 2;**
TCLC 108
See also AITN 2; BRWS 3; CA 45-48; 57-
60; CANR 3, 33; CDBLB 1914-1945;
CPW 1; DA3; DAB; DAC; DAM NOV;
DLB 34, 162; EWL 3; MTCW 1, 2;
RGEL 2; RGSF 2; SATA 22; SSFS 10

Woiwode, L.
See Woiwode, Larry (Alfred)

Woiwode, Larry (Alfred) 1941- ... **CLC 6, 10**
See also CA 73-76; CANR 16, 94; CN 7;
DLB 6; INT CANR-16

Wojciechowska, Maia (Teresa)
1927-2002 .... **CLC 26**
See also AAYA 8, 46; BYA 3; CA 9-12R;
183; 209; CAAE 183; CANR 4, 41; CLR
1; JRDA; MAICYA 1, 2; SAAS 1; SATA
1, 28, 83; SATA-Essay 104; SATA-Obit
134; YAW

Wojtyla, Karol
See John Paul II, Pope

Wolf, Christa 1929- .... **CLC 14, 29, 58, 150**
See also CA 85-88; CANR 45, 123; CD-
WLB 2; CWW 2; DLB 75; EWL 3; FW;
MTCW 1; RGWL 2, 3; SSFS 14

Wolf, Naomi 1962- .... **CLC 157**
See also CA 141; CANR 110; FW

Wolfe, Gene (Rodman) 1931- .... **CLC 25**
See also AAYA 35; CA 57-60; CAAS 9;
CANR 6, 32, 60; CPW; DAM POP; DLB
8; FANT; MTCW 1; SATA 118; SCFW 2;
SFW 4; SUFW 2

Wolfe, George C. 1954- .... **BLCS; CLC 49**
See also CA 149; CAD; CD 5

Wolfe, Thomas (Clayton)
1900-1938 ...... **SSC 33; TCLC 4, 13, 29,**
61; WLC
See also AMW; BPFB 3; CA 104; 132;
CANR 102; CDALB 1929-1941; DA;
DA3; DAB; DAC; DAM MST, NOV;
DLB 9, 102, 229; DLBD 2, 16; DLBY
1985, 1997; EWL 3; MTCW 1, 2; NFS
18; RGAL 4; TUS

Wolfe, Thomas Kennerly, Jr.
1931- .... **CLC 147**
See Wolfe, Tom
See also CA 13-16R; CANR 9, 33, 70, 104;
DA3; DAM POP; DLB 185; EWL 3; INT
CANR-9; MTCW 1, 2; SSFS 18; TUS

Wolfe, Tom .... **CLC 1, 2, 9, 15, 35, 51**
See Wolfe, Thomas Kennerly, Jr.
See also AAYA 8; AITN 2; AMWS 3; BEST
89:1; BPFB 3; CN 7; CPW; CSW; DLB
152; LAIT 5; RGAL 4

Wolff, Geoffrey (Ansell) 1937- .... **CLC 41**
See also CA 29-32R; CANR 29, 43, 78

Wolff, Sonia
See Levitin, Sonia (Wolff)

Wolff, Tobias (Jonathan Ansell)
1945- .... **CLC 39, 64, 172; SSC 63**
See also AAYA 16; AMWS 7; BEST 90:2;
BYA 12; CA 114; 117; CAAS 22; CANR
54, 76, 96; CN 7; CSW; DA3; DLB 130;
EWL 3; INT CA-117; MTCW 2; RGAL
4; RGSF 2; SSFS 4, 11

Wolfram von Eschenbach c. 1170-c.
1220 .... **CMLC 5**
See Eschenbach, Wolfram von
See also CDWLB 2; DLB 138; EW 1;
RGWL 2

Wolitzer, Hilma 1930- .... **CLC 17**
See also CA 65-68; CANR 18, 40; INT
CANR-18; SATA 31; YAW

Wollstonecraft, Mary 1759-1797 .... **LC 5, 50,**
90
See also BRWS 3; CDBLB 1789-1832;
DLB 39, 104, 158, 252; FW; LAIT 1;
RGEL 2; TEA; WLIT 3

Wonder, Stevie .... **CLC 12**
See Morris, Steveland Judkins

Wong, Jade Snow 1922- .... **CLC 17**
See also CA 109; CANR 91; SATA 112

Woodberry, George Edward
1855-1930 .... **TCLC 73**
See also CA 165; DLB 71, 103

Woodcott, Keith
See Brunner, John (Kilian Houston)

Woodruff, Robert W.
See Mencken, H(enry) L(ouis)

Woolf, (Adeline) Virginia 1882-1941 . **SSC 7;**
TCLC 1, 5, 20, 43, 56, 101, 123, 128;
WLC
See also AAYA 44; BPFB 3; BRW 7;
BRWC 2; BRWR 1; CA 104; 130; CANR
64, 132; CDBLB 1914-1945; DA; DA3;
DAB; DAC; DAM MST, NOV; DLB 36,
100, 162; DLBD 10; EWL 3; EXPS; FW;
LAIT 3; LATS 1:1; LMFS 2; MTCW 1,
2; NCFS 2; NFS 8, 12; RGEL 2; RGSF 2;
SSFS 4, 12; TEA; WLIT 4

Woollcott, Alexander (Humphreys)
1887-1943 .... **TCLC 5**
See also CA 105; 161; DLB 29

Woolrich, Cornell .... **CLC 77**
See Hopley-Woolrich, Cornell George
See also MSW

Woolson, Constance Fenimore
1840-1894 .... **NCLC 82**
See also DLB 12, 74, 189, 221; RGAL 4

Wordsworth, Dorothy 1771-1855 . **NCLC 25,**
138
See also DLB 107

Wordsworth, William 1770-1850 .. **NCLC 12,**
38, 111; PC 4; WLC
See also BRW 4; BRWC 1; CDBLB 1789-
1832; DA; DA3; DAB; DAC; DAM MST,
POET; DLB 93, 107; EXPP; LATS 1:1;
LMFS 1; PAB; PFS 2; RGEL 2; TEA;
WLIT 3; WP

Wotton, Sir Henry 1568-1639 .... **LC 68**
See also DLB 121; RGEL 2

Wouk, Herman 1915- .... **CLC 1, 9, 38**
See also BPFB 2, 3; CA 5-8R; CANR 6,
33, 67; CDALBS; CN 7; CPW; DA3;
DAM NOV, POP; DLBY 1982; INT
CANR-6; LAIT 4; MTCW 1, 2; NFS 7;
TUS

Wright, Charles (Penzel, Jr.) 1935- .. **CLC 6,**
13, 28, 119, 146
See also AMWS 5; CA 29-32R; CAAS 7;
CANR 23, 36, 62, 88, 135; CP 7; DLB
165; DLBY 1982; EWL 3; MTCW 1, 2;
PFS 10

Wright, Charles Stevenson 1932- ..... **BLC 3;**
CLC 49
See also BW 1; CA 9-12R; CANR 26; CN
7; DAM MULT, POET; DLB 33

Wright, Frances 1795-1852 .... **NCLC 74**
See also DLB 73

Wright, Frank Lloyd 1867-1959 .... **TCLC 95**
See also AAYA 33; CA 174

Wright, Jack R.
See Harris, Mark

Wright, James (Arlington)
1927-1980 .... **CLC 3, 5, 10, 28; PC 36**
See also AITN 2; AMWS 3; CA 49-52; 97-
100; CANR 4, 34, 64; CDALBS; DAM
POET; DLB 5, 169; EWL 3; EXPP;
MTCW 1, 2; PFS 7, 8; RGAL 4; TUS;
WP

Wright, Judith (Arundell)
1915-2000 .... **CLC 11, 53; PC 14**
See also CA 13-16R; 188; CANR 31, 76,
93; CP 7; CWP; DLB 260; EWL 3;
MTCW 1, 2; PFS 8; RGEL 2; SATA 14;
SATA-Obit 121

Wright, L(aurali) R. 1939- .... **CLC 44**
See also CA 138; CMW 4

Wright, Richard (Nathaniel)
1908-1960 ... **BLC 3; CLC 1, 3, 4, 9, 14,**
21, 48, 74; SSC 2; TCLC 136; WLC
See also AAYA 5, 42; AFAW 1, 2; AMW;
BPFB 3; BW 1; BYA 2; CA 108; CANR
64; CDALB 1929-1941; DA; DA3; DAB;

DAC; DAM MST, MULT, NOV; DLB 76, 102; DLBD 2; EWL 3; EXPN; LAIT 3, 4; MTCW 1, 2; NCFS 1; NFS 1, 7; RGAL 4; RGSF 2; SSFS 3, 9, 15, 20; TUS; YAW

Wright, Richard B(ruce) 1937- .... **CLC 6**
See also CA 85-88; CANR 120; DLB 53

Wright, Rick 1945- .... **CLC 35**

Wright, Rowland
See Wells, Carolyn

Wright, Stephen 1946- .... **CLC 33**

Wright, Willard Huntington 1888-1939
See Van Dine, S. S.
See also CA 115; 189; CMW 4; DLBD 16

Wright, William 1930- .... **CLC 44**
See also CA 53-56; CANR 7, 23

Wroth, Lady Mary 1587-1653(?) .... **LC 30; PC 38**
See also DLB 121

Wu Ch'eng-en 1500(?)-1582(?) .... **LC 7**

Wu Ching-tzu 1701-1754 .... **LC 2**

Wulfstan c. 10th cent. -1023 .... **CMLC 59**

Wurlitzer, Rudolph 1938(?)- .... **CLC 2, 4, 15**
See also CA 85-88; CN 7; DLB 173

Wyatt, Sir Thomas c. 1503-1542 . **LC 70; PC 27**
See also BRW 1; DLB 132; EXPP; RGEL 2; TEA

Wycherley, William 1640-1716 .... **LC 8, 21, 102**
See also BRW 2; CDBLB 1660-1789; DAM DRAM; DLB 80; RGEL 2

Wyclif, John c. 1330-1384 .... **CMLC 70**
See also DLB 146

Wylie, Elinor (Morton Hoyt)
1885-1928 .... **PC 23; TCLC 8**
See also AMWS 1; CA 105; 162; DLB 9, 45; EXPP; RGAL 4

Wylie, Philip (Gordon) 1902-1971 ... **CLC 43**
See also CA 21-22; 33-36R; CAP 2; DLB 9; SFW 4

Wyndham, John .... **CLC 19**
See Harris, John (Wyndham Parkes Lucas) Beynon
See also DLB 255; SCFW 2

Wyss, Johann David Von
1743-1818 .... **NCLC 10**
See also CLR 92; JRDA; MAICYA 1, 2; SATA 29; SATA-Brief 27

Xenophon c. 430B.C.-c. 354B.C. ... **CMLC 17**
See also AW 1; DLB 176; RGWL 2, 3

Xingjian, Gao 1940-
See Gao Xingjian
See also CA 193; RGWL 3

Yakamochi 718-785 .... **CMLC 45; PC 48**

Yakumo Koizumi
See Hearn, (Patricio) Lafcadio (Tessima Carlos)

Yamada, Mitsuye (May) 1923- .... **PC 44**
See also CA 77-80

Yamamoto, Hisaye 1921- .... **AAL; SSC 34**
See also CA 214; DAM MULT; LAIT 4; SSFS 14

Yamauchi, Wakako 1924- .... **AAL**
See also CA 214

Yanez, Jose Donoso
See Donoso (Yanez), Jose

Yanovsky, Basile S.
See Yanovsky, V(assily) S(emenovich)

Yanovsky, V(assily) S(emenovich)
1906-1989 .... **CLC 2, 18**
See also CA 97-100; 129

Yates, Richard 1926-1992 .... **CLC 7, 8, 23**
See also AMWS 11; CA 5-8R; 139; CANR 10, 43; DLB 2, 234; DLBY 1981, 1992; INT CANR-10

Yau, John 1950- .... **PC 61**
See also CA 154; CANR 89; CP 7; DLB 234

Yeats, W. B.
See Yeats, William Butler

Yeats, William Butler 1865-1939 . **PC 20, 51; TCLC 1, 11, 18, 31, 93, 116; WLC**
See also AAYA 48; BRW 6; BRWR 1; CA 104; 127; CANR 45; CDBLB 1890-1914; DA; DA3; DAB; DAC; DAM DRAM, MST, POET; DLB 10, 19, 98, 156; EWL 3; EXPP; MTCW 1, 2; NCFS 3; PAB; PFS 1, 2, 5, 7, 13, 15; RGEL 2; TEA; WLIT 4; WP

Yehoshua, A(braham) B. 1936- .. **CLC 13, 31**
See also CA 33-36R; CANR 43, 90; CWW 2; EWL 3; RGSF 2; RGWL 3

Yellow Bird
See Ridge, John Rollin

Yep, Laurence Michael 1948- .... **CLC 35**
See also AAYA 5, 31; BYA 7; CA 49-52; CANR 1, 46, 92; CLR 3, 17, 54; DLB 52; FANT; JRDA; MAICYA 1, 2; MAICYAS 1; SATA 7, 69, 123; WYA; YAW

Yerby, Frank G(arvin) 1916-1991 ..... **BLC 3; CLC 1, 7, 22**
See also BPFB 3; BW 1, 3; CA 9-12R; 136; CANR 16, 52; DAM MULT; DLB 76; INT CANR-16; MTCW 1; RGAL 4; RHW

Yesenin, Sergei Alexandrovich
See Esenin, Sergei (Alexandrovich)

Yesenin, Sergey
See Esenin, Sergei (Alexandrovich)
See also EWL 3

Yevtushenko, Yevgeny (Alexandrovich)
1933- ...... **CLC 1, 3, 13, 26, 51, 126; PC 40**
See Evtushenko, Evgenii Aleksandrovich
See also CA 81-84; CANR 33, 54; DAM POET; EWL 3; MTCW 1

Yezierska, Anzia 1885(?)-1970 .... **CLC 46**
See also CA 126; 89-92; DLB 28, 221; FW; MTCW 1; RGAL 4; SSFS 15

Yglesias, Helen 1915- .... **CLC 7, 22**
See also CA 37-40R; CAAS 20; CANR 15, 65, 95; CN 7; INT CANR-15; MTCW 1

Yokomitsu, Riichi 1898-1947 .... **TCLC 47**
See also CA 170; EWL 3

Yonge, Charlotte (Mary)
1823-1901 .... **TCLC 48**
See also CA 109; 163; DLB 18, 163; RGEL 2; SATA 17; WCH

York, Jeremy
See Creasey, John

York, Simon
See Heinlein, Robert A(nson)

Yorke, Henry Vincent 1905-1974 ..... **CLC 13**
See Green, Henry
See also CA 85-88; 49-52

Yosano Akiko 1878-1942 .... **PC 11; TCLC 59**
See also CA 161; EWL 3; RGWL 3

Yoshimoto, Banana .... **CLC 84**
See Yoshimoto, Mahoko
See also AAYA 50; NFS 7

Yoshimoto, Mahoko 1964-
See Yoshimoto, Banana
See also CA 144; CANR 98; SSFS 16

Young, Al(bert James) 1939- ... **BLC 3; CLC 19**
See also BW 2, 3; CA 29-32R; CANR 26, 65, 109; CN 7; CP 7; DAM MULT; DLB 33

Young, Andrew (John) 1885-1971 ...... **CLC 5**
See also CA 5-8R; CANR 7, 29; RGEL 2

Young, Collier
See Bloch, Robert (Albert)

Young, Edward 1683-1765 .... **LC 3, 40**
See also DLB 95; RGEL 2

Young, Marguerite (Vivian)
1909-1995 .... **CLC 82**
See also CA 13-16; 150; CAP 1; CN 7

Young, Neil 1945- .... **CLC 17**
See also CA 110; CCA 1

Young Bear, Ray A. 1950- ... **CLC 94; NNAL**
See also CA 146; DAM MULT; DLB 175

Yourcenar, Marguerite 1903-1987 ... **CLC 19, 38, 50, 87**
See also BPFB 3; CA 69-72; CANR 23, 60, 93; DAM NOV; DLB 72; DLBY 1988; EW 12; EWL 3; GFL 1789 to the Present; GLL 1; MTCW 1, 2; RGWL 2, 3

Yuan, Chu 340(?)B.C.-278(?)B.C. . **CMLC 36**

Yurick, Sol 1925- .... **CLC 6**
See also CA 13-16R; CANR 25; CN 7

Zabolotsky, Nikolai Alekseevich
1903-1958 .... **TCLC 52**
See Zabolotsky, Nikolay Alekseevich
See also CA 116; 164

Zabolotsky, Nikolay Alekseevich
See Zabolotsky, Nikolai Alekseevich
See also EWL 3

Zagajewski, Adam 1945- .... **PC 27**
See also CA 186; DLB 232; EWL 3

Zalygin, Sergei -2000 .... **CLC 59**

Zalygin, Sergei (Pavlovich)
1913-2000 .... **CLC 59**
See also DLB 302

Zamiatin, Evgenii
See Zamyatin, Evgeny Ivanovich
See also RGSF 2; RGWL 2, 3

Zamiatin, Evgenii Ivanovich
See Zamyatin, Evgeny Ivanovich
See also DLB 272

Zamiatin, Yevgenii
See Zamyatin, Evgeny Ivanovich

Zamora, Bernice (B. Ortiz) 1938- .. **CLC 89; HLC 2**
See also CA 151; CANR 80; DAM MULT; DLB 82; HW 1, 2

Zamyatin, Evgeny Ivanovich
1884-1937 .... **TCLC 8, 37**
See Zamiatin, Evgenii; Zamiatin, Evgenii Ivanovich; Zamyatin, Yevgeny Ivanovich
See also CA 105; 166; EW 10; SFW 4

Zamyatin, Yevgeny Ivanovich
See Zamyatin, Evgeny Ivanovich
See also EWL 3

Zangwill, Israel 1864-1926 ... **SSC 44; TCLC 16**
See also CA 109; 167; CMW 4; DLB 10, 135, 197; RGEL 2

Zappa, Francis Vincent, Jr. 1940-1993
See Zappa, Frank
See also CA 108; 143; CANR 57

Zappa, Frank .... **CLC 17**
See Zappa, Francis Vincent, Jr.

Zaturenska, Marya 1902-1982 ..... **CLC 6, 11**
See also CA 13-16R; 105; CANR 22

Zayas y Sotomayor, Maria de 1590-c.
1661 .... **LC 102**
See also RGSF 2

Zeami 1363-1443 .... **DC 7; LC 86**
See also DLB 203; RGWL 2, 3

Zelazny, Roger (Joseph) 1937-1995 . **CLC 21**
See also AAYA 7; BPFB 3; CA 21-24R; 148; CANR 26, 60; CN 7; DLB 8; FANT; MTCW 1, 2; SATA 57; SATA-Brief 39; SCFW; SFW 4; SUFW 1, 2

Zhang Ailing
See Chang, Eileen
See also CWW 2; RGSF 2

Zhdanov, Andrei Alexandrovich
1896-1948 .... **TCLC 18**
See also CA 117; 167
Zhukovsky, Vasilii Andreevich
See Zhukovsky, Vasily (Andreevich)
See also DLB 205
Zhukovsky, Vasily (Andreevich)
1783-1852 .... **NCLC 35**
See Zhukovsky, Vasilii Andreevich Ziegen-
hagen, Eric .... **CLC 55**
Zimmer, Jill Schary
See Robinson, Jill
Zimmerman, Robert
See Dylan, Bob
Zindel, Paul 1936-2003 ...... **CLC 6, 26; DC 5**
See also AAYA 2, 37; BYA 2, 3, 8, 11, 14;
CA 73-76; 213; CAD; CANR 31, 65, 108;
CD 5; CDALBS; CLR 3, 45, 85; DA;
DA3; DAB; DAC; DAM DRAM, MST,
NOV; DFS 12; DLB 7, 52; JRDA; LAIT
5; MAICYA 1, 2; MTCW 1, 2; NFS 14;
SATA 16, 58, 102; SATA-Obit 142; WYA;
YAW

Zinn, Howard 1922- .... **CLC 199**
See also CA 1-4R; CANR 2, 33, 90
Zinov'Ev, A. A.
See Zinoviev, Alexander (Aleksandrovich)
Zinov'ev, Aleksandr (Aleksandrovich)
See Zinoviev, Alexander (Aleksandrovich)
See also DLB 302
Zinoviev, Alexander (Aleksandrovich)
1922- .... **CLC 19**
See Zinov'ev, Aleksandr (Aleksandrovich)
See also CA 116; 133; CAAS 10
Zizek, Slavoj 1949- .... **CLC 188**
See also CA 201
Zoilus
See Lovecraft, H(oward) P(hillips)
Zola, Emile (Edouard Charles Antoine)
1840-1902 ...... **TCLC 1, 6, 21, 41; WLC**
See also CA 104; 138; DA; DA3; DAB;
DAC; DAM MST, NOV; DLB 123; EW
7; GFL 1789 to the Present; IDTP; LMFS
1, 2; RGWL 2; TWA
Zoline, Pamela 1941- .... **CLC 62**
See also CA 161; SFW 4

Zoroaster 628(?)B.C.-551(?)B.C. ... **CMLC 40**
Zorrilla y Moral, Jose 1817-1893 .... **NCLC 6**
Zoshchenko, Mikhail (Mikhailovich)
1895-1958 .... **SSC 15; TCLC 15**
See also CA 115; 160; EWL 3; RGSF 2;
RGWL 3
Zuckmayer, Carl 1896-1977 .... **CLC 18**
See also CA 69-72; DLB 56, 124; EWL 3;
RGWL 2, 3
Zuk, Georges
See Skelton, Robin
See also CCA 1
Zukofsky, Louis 1904-1978 ... **CLC 1, 2, 4, 7,
11, 18; PC 11**
See also AMWS 3; CA 9-12R; 77-80;
CANR 39; DAM POET; DLB 5, 165;
EWL 3; MTCW 1; RGAL 4
Zweig, Paul 1935-1984 .... **CLC 34, 42**
See also CA 85-88; 113
Zweig, Stefan 1881-1942 .... **TCLC 17**
See also CA 112; 170; DLB 81, 118; EWL
3
Zwingli, Huldreich 1484-1531 .... **LC 37**
See also DLB 179

Literary Criticism Series
Cumulative Topic Index

This index lists all topic entries in Gale's *Children's Literature Review* (CLR), *Classical and Medieval Literature Criticism* (CMLC), *Contemporary Literary Criticism* (CLC), *Drama Criticism* (DC), *Literature Criticism from 1400 to 1800* (LC), *Nineteenth-Century Literature Criticism* (NCLC), *Short Story Criticism* (SSC), and *Twentieth-Century Literary Criticism* (TCLC). The index also lists topic entries in the Gale Critical Companion Collection, which includes the following publications: *The Beat Generation* (BG), and *Harlem Renaissance* (HR).

Abbey Theatre in the Irish Literary Renaissance TCLC 154: 1-114
origins and development, 2-14
major figures, 14-30
plays and controversies, 30-59
artistic vision and significance, 59-114

Abolitionist Literature of Cuba and Brazil, Nineteenth-Century NCLC 132: 1-94
overviews, 2-11
origins and development, 11-23
sociopolitical concerns, 23-39
poetry, 39-47
prose, 47-93

Aborigine in Nineteenth-Century Australian Literature, The NCLC 120: 1-88
overviews, 2-27
representations of the Aborigine in Australian literature, 27-58
Aboriginal myth, literature, and oral tradition, 58-88

Aesopic Fable, The LC 51: 1-100
the British Aesopic Fable, 1-54
the Aesopic tradition in non-English-speaking cultures, 55-66
political uses of the Aesopic fable, 67-88
the evolution of the Aesopic fable, 89-99

African-American Folklore and Literature TCLC 126: 1-67
African-American folk tradition, 1-16
representative writers, 16-34
hallmark works, 35-48
the study of African-American literature and folklore, 48-64

Age of Johnson LC 15: 1-87
Johnson's London, 3-15
aesthetics of neoclassicism, 15-36
"age of prose and reason," 36-45
clubmen and bluestockings, 45-56
printing technology, 56-62
periodicals: "a map of busy life," 62-74
transition, 74-86

Age of Spenser LC 39: 1-70
overviews and general studies, 2-21
literary style, 22-34
poets and the crown, 34-70

AIDS in Literature CLC 81: 365-416

Alcohol and Literature TCLC 70: 1-58
overview, 2-8
fiction, 8-48
poetry and drama, 48-58

American Abolitionism NCLC 44: 1-73
overviews and general studies, 2-26
abolitionist ideals, 26-46
the literature of abolitionism, 46-72

American Autobiography TCLC 86: 1-115
overviews and general studies, 3-36
American authors and autobiography, 36-82
African-American autobiography, 82-114

American Black Humor Fiction TCLC 54: 1-85
characteristics of black humor, 2-13
origins and development, 13-38
black humor distinguished from related literary trends, 38-60
black humor and society, 60-75
black humor reconsidered, 75-83

American Civil War in Literature NCLC 32: 1-109
overviews and general studies, 2-20
regional perspectives, 20-54
fiction popular during the war, 54-79
the historical novel, 79-108

American Frontier in Literature NCLC 28: 1-103
definitions, 2-12
development, 12-17
nonfiction writing about the frontier, 17-30
frontier fiction, 30-45
frontier protagonists, 45-66
portrayals of Native Americans, 66-86
feminist readings, 86-98
twentieth-century reaction against frontier literature, 98-100

American Humor Writing NCLC 52: 1-59
overviews and general studies, 2-12
the Old Southwest, 12-42
broader impacts, 42-5
women humorists, 45-58

American Naturalism in Short Fiction SSC 77: 1-103
overviews and general studies, 2-30
major authors of American literary Naturalism, 30-102
Ambrose Bierce, 30

Stephen Crane, 30-53
Theodore Dreiser, 53-65
Jack London, 65-80
Frank Norris, 80-9
Edith Wharton, 89-102

American Novel of Manners TCLC 130: 1-42
history of the Novel of Manners in America, 4-10
representative writers, 10-18
relevancy of the Novel of Manners, 18-24
hallmark works in the Novel of Manners, 24-36
Novel of Manners and other media, 36-40

***American Mercury,* The** TCLC 74: 1-80

American Popular Song, Golden Age of TCLC 42: 1-49
background and major figures, 2-34
the lyrics of popular songs, 34-47

American Proletarian Literature TCLC 54: 86-175
overviews and general studies, 87-95
American proletarian literature and the American Communist Party, 95-111
ideology and literary merit, 111-17
novels, 117-36
Gastonia, 136-48
drama, 148-54
journalism, 154-9
proletarian literature in the United States, 159-74

American Realism NCLC 120: 89-246
overviews, 91-112
background and sources, 112-72
social issues, 172-223
women and realism, 223-45

American Renaissance SSC 64: 46-193
overviews and general studies, 47-103
major authors of short fiction, 103-92

American Romanticism NCLC 44: 74-138
overviews and general studies, 74-84
sociopolitical influences, 84-104
Romanticism and the American frontier, 104-15
thematic concerns, 115-37

American Western Literature TCLC 46: 1-100

definition and development of American Western literature, 2-7
characteristics of the Western novel, 8-23
Westerns as history and fiction, 23-34
critical reception of American Western literature, 34-41
the Western hero, 41-73
women in Western fiction, 73-91
later Western fiction, 91-9

American Writers in Paris TCLC 98: 1-156
overviews and general studies, 2-155

Anarchism NCLC 84: 1-97
overviews and general studies, 2-23
the French anarchist tradition, 23-56
Anglo-American anarchism, 56-68
anarchism: incidents and issues, 68-97

Animals in Literature TCLC 106: 1-120
overviews and general studies, 2-8
animals in American literature, 8-45
animals in Canadian literature, 45-57
animals in European literature, 57-100
animals in Latin American literature, 100-06
animals in women's literature, 106-20

Antebellum South, Literature of the NCLC 112:1-188
overviews, 4-55
culture of the Old South, 55-68
antebellum fiction: pastoral and heroic romance, 68-120
role of women: a subdued rebellion, 120-59
slavery and the slave narrative, 159-85

Anti-Americanism TCLC 158: 1-98
overviews and general studies, 3-18
literary and intellectual perspectives, 18-36
social and political reactions, 36-98

The Apocalyptic Movement TCLC 106: 121-69

Aristotle CMLC 31:1-397
philosophy, 3-100
poetics, 101-219
rhetoric, 220-301
science, 302-397

Art and Literature TCLC 54: 176-248
overviews and general studies, 176-93
definitions, 193-219
influence of visual arts on literature, 219-31
spatial form in literature, 231-47

Arthurian Literature CMLC 10: 1-127
historical context and literary beginnings, 2-27
development of the legend through Malory, 27-64
development of the legend from Malory to the Victorian Age, 65-81
themes and motifs, 81-95
principal characters, 95-125

Arthurian Revival NCLC 36: 1-77
overviews and general studies, 2-12
Tennyson and his influence, 12-43
other leading figures, 43-73
the Arthurian legend in the visual arts, 73-6

Australian Cultural Identity in Nineteenth-Century Literature NCLC 124: 1-164
overviews and general studies, 4-22
poetry, 22-67
fiction, 67-135
role of women writers, 135-64

Australian Literature TCLC 50: 1-94
origins and development, 2-21
characteristics of Australian literature, 21-33
historical and critical perspectives, 33-41
poetry, 41-58
fiction, 58-76

drama, 76-82
Aboriginal literature, 82-91

Beat Generation, The BG 1:1-562
the Beat Generation: an overview, 1-137
primary sources, 3-32
overviews and general studies, 32-47
Beat Generation as a social phenomenon, 47-65
drugs, inspiration, and the Beat Generation, 65-92
religion and the Beat Generation, 92-124
women of the Beat Generation, 124-36
Beat "scene": East and West, 139-259
primary sources, 141-77
Beat scene in the East, 177-218
Beat scene in the West, 218-59
Beat Generation publishing: periodicals, small presses, and censorship, 261-349
primary sources, 263-74
overview, 274-88
Beat periodicals: "little magazines," 288-311
Beat publishing: small presses, 311-24
Beat battles with censorship, 324-49
performing arts and the Beat Generation, 351-417
primary sources, 353-58
Beats and film, 358-81
Beats and music, 381-415
visual arts and the Beat Generation, 419-91
primary sources, 421-24
critical commentary, 424-90

Beat Generation, Literature of the TCLC 42: 50-102
overviews and general studies, 51-9
the Beat generation as a social phenomenon, 59-62
development, 62-5
Beat literature, 66-96
influence, 97-100

The Bell Curve Controversy CLC 91: 281-330

***Bildungsroman* in Nineteenth-Century Literature** NCLC 20: 92-168
surveys, 93-113
in Germany, 113-40
in England, 140-56
female *Bildungsroman,* 156-67

Bloomsbury Group TCLC 34: 1-73
history and major figures, 2-13
definitions, 13-7
influences, 17-27
thought, 27-40
prose, 40-52
and literary criticism, 52-4
political ideals, 54-61
response to, 61-71

The Bloomsbury Group TCLC 138: 1-59
representative members of the Bloomsbury Group, 9-24
literary relevance of the Bloomsbury Group, 24-36
Bloomsbury's hallmark works, 36-48
other modernists studied with the Bloomsbury Group, 48-54

The Blues in Literature TCLC 82: 1-71

Bly, Robert, *Iron John: A Book about Men and Men's Work* CLC 70: 414-62

The Book of J CLC 65: 289-311

Brazilian Literature TCLC 134: 1-126
overviews and general studies, 3-33
Brazilian poetry, 33-48
contemporary Brazilian writing, 48-76
culture, politics, and race in Brazilian writing, 76-100

modernism and postmodernism in Brazil, 100-25

British Ephemeral Literature LC 59: 1-70
overviews and general studies, 1-9
broadside ballads, 10-40
chapbooks, jestbooks, pamphlets, and newspapers, 40-69

Buddhism and Literature TCLC 70: 59-164
eastern literature, 60-113
western literature, 113-63

The *Bulletin* and the Rise of Australian Literary Nationalism NCLC 116: 1-121
overviews, 3-32
legend of the nineties, 32-55
Bulletin style, 55-71
Australian literary nationalism, 71-98
myth of the bush, 98-120

Businessman in American Literature TCLC 26: 1-48
portrayal of the businessman, 1-32
themes and techniques in business fiction, 32-47

The Calendar LC 55: 1-92
overviews and general studies, 2-19
measuring time, 19-28
calendars and culture, 28-60
calendar reform, 60-92

Captivity Narratives LC 82: 71-172
overviews, 72-107
captivity narratives and Puritanism, 108-34
captivity narratives and Native Americans, 134-49
influence on American literature, 149-72

Caribbean Literature TCLC 138: 60-135
overviews and general studies, 61-9
ethnic and national identity, 69-107
expatriate Caribbean literature, 107-23
literary historiography, 123-35

Catholicism in Nineteenth-Century American Literature NCLC 64: 1-58
overviews, 3-14
polemical literature, 14-46
Catholicism in literature, 47-57

Cavalier Poetry and Drama LC 107: 1-71
overviews, 2-36
Cavalier drama, 36-48
major figures, 48-70

Celtic Mythology CMLC 26: 1-111
overviews and general studies, 2-22
Celtic myth as literature and history, 22-48
Celtic religion: Druids and divinities, 48-80
Fionn MacCuhaill and the Fenian cycle, 80-111

Celtic Twilight See Irish Literary Renaissance

Censorship and Contemporary World Literature CLC 194: 1-80
overviews and general studies, 2-19
notorious cases, 19-59
censorship in the global context, 59-79

Censorship in Twentieth-Century Literature TCLC 154: 115-238
overviews and general studies, 117-25
censorship and obscenity trials, 125-61
censorship and sexual politics, 161-81
censorship and war, 181-207
political censorship and the state, 207-28
censorship and the writer, 228-38

Chartist Movement and Literature, The NCLC 60: 1-84
overview: nineteenth-century working-class fiction, 2-19
Chartist fiction and poetry, 19-73
the Chartist press, 73-84

Chicago Renaissance, The TCLC 154: 239-341
overviews and general studies, 240-60
definitions and growth, 260-82
the language debate, 282-318
major authors, 318-40

Child Labor in Nineteenth-Century Literature NCLC 108: 1-133
overviews, 3-10
climbing boys and chimney sweeps, 10-16
the international traffic in children, 16-45
critics and reformers, 45-82
fictional representations of child laborers, 83-132

Children's Literature, Nineteenth-Century NCLC 52: 60-135
overviews and general studies, 61-72
moral tales, 72-89
fairy tales and fantasy, 90-119
making men/making women, 119-34

Christianity in Twentieth-Century Literature TCLC 110: 1-79
overviews and general studies, 2-31
Christianity in twentieth-century fiction, 31-78

Chronicle Plays LC 89: 1-106
development of the genre, 2-33
historiography and literature, 33-56
genre and performance, 56-88
politics and ideology, 88-106

The City and Literature TCLC 90: 1-124
overviews and general studies, 2-9
the city in American literature, 9-86
the city in European literature, 86-124

Civic Critics, Russian NCLC 20: 402-46
principal figures and background, 402-9
and Russian Nihilism, 410-6
aesthetic and critical views, 416-45

The Cockney School NCLC 68: 1-64
overview, 2-7
Blackwood's Magazine and the contemporary critical response, 7-24
the political and social import of the Cockneys and their critics, 24-63

Colonial America: The Intellectual Background LC 25: 1-98
overviews and general studies, 2-17
philosophy and politics, 17-31
early religious influences in Colonial America, 31-60
consequences of the Revolution, 60-78
religious influences in post-revolutionary America, 78-87
colonial literary genres, 87-97

Colonialism in Victorian English Literature NCLC 56: 1-77
overviews and general studies, 2-34
colonialism and gender, 34-51
monsters and the occult, 51-76

Columbus, Christopher, Books on the Quincentennial of His Arrival in the New World CLC 70: 329-60

Comic Books TCLC 66: 1-139
historical and critical perspectives, 2-48
superheroes, 48-67
underground comix, 67-88
comic books and society, 88-122
adult comics and graphic novels, 122-36

Comedy of Manners LC 92: 1-75
overviews, 2-21
comedy of manners and society, 21-47
comedy of manners and women, 47-74

Commedia dell'Arte LC 83: 1-147
overviews, 2-7

origins and development, 7-23
characters and actors, 23-45
performance, 45-62
texts and authors, 62-100
influence in Europe, 100-46

Connecticut Wits NCLC 48: 1-95
overviews and general studies, 2-40
major works, 40-76
intellectual context, 76-95

Contemporary Black Humor CLC 196: 1-128
overviews and general studies, 2-18
black humor in American fiction, 18-28
development and history, 29-62
major authors, 62-115
technique and narrative, 115-127

Contemporary Feminist Criticism CLC 180: 1-103
overviews and general studies, 2-59
modern French feminist theory, 59-102

Contemporary Gay and Lesbian Literature CLC 171: 1-130
overviews and general studies, 2-43
contemporary gay literature, 44-95
lesbianism in contemporary literature, 95-129

Contemporary Southern Literature CLC 167: 1-132
criticism, 2-131

Crime in Literature TCLC 54: 249-307
evolution of the criminal figure in literature, 250-61
crime and society, 261-77
literary perspectives on crime and punishment, 277-88
writings by criminals, 288-306

Crime-Mystery-Detective Stories SSC 59:89-226
overviews and general studies, 90-140
origins and early masters of the crime-mystery-detective story, 140-73
hard-boiled crime-mystery-detective fiction, 173-209
diversity in the crime-mystery-detective story, 210-25

The Crusades CMLC 38: 1-144
history of the Crusades, 3-60
literature of the Crusades, 60-116
the Crusades and the people: attitudes and influences, 116-44

Cyberpunk TCLC 106: 170-366
overviews and general studies, 171-88
feminism and cyberpunk, 188-230
history and cyberpunk, 230-70
sexuality and cyberpunk, 270-98
social issues and cyberpunk, 299-366

Cyberpunk Short Fiction SSC 60: 44-108
overviews and general studies, 46-78
major writers of cyberpunk fiction, 78-81
sexuality and cyberpunk fiction, 81-97
additional pieces, 97-108

Czechoslovakian Literature of the Twentieth Century TCLC 42:103-96
through World War II, 104-35
de-Stalinization, the Prague Spring, and contemporary literature, 135-72
Slovak literature, 172-85
Czech science fiction, 185-93

Dadaism TCLC 46: 101-71
background and major figures, 102-16
definitions, 116-26
manifestos and commentary by Dadaists, 126-40
theater and film, 140-58
nature and characteristics of Dadaist writing, 158-70

Danish Literature See Twentieth-Century Danish Literature

Darwinism and Literature NCLC 32: 110-206
background, 110-31
direct responses to Darwin, 131-71
collateral effects of Darwinism, 171-205

Death in American Literature NCLC 92: 1-170
overviews and general studies, 2-32
death in the works of Emily Dickinson, 32-72
death in the works of Herman Melville, 72-101
death in the works of Edgar Allan Poe, 101-43
death in the works of Walt Whitman, 143-70

Death in Nineteenth-Century British Literature NCLC 68: 65-142
overviews and general studies, 66-92
responses to death, 92-102
feminist perspectives, 103-17
striving for immortality, 117-41

Death in Literature TCLC 78:1-183
fiction, 2-115
poetry, 115-46
drama, 146-81

Deconstruction TCLC 138: 136-256
overviews and general studies, 137-83
deconstruction and literature, 183-221
deconstruction in philosophy and history, 221-56

de Man, Paul, Wartime Journalism of CLC 55: 382-424

Detective Fiction, Nineteenth-Century NCLC 36: 78-148
origins of the genre, 79-100
history of nineteenth-century detective fiction, 101-33
significance of nineteenth-century detective fiction, 133-46
NCLC 148: 1-161
overviews, 3-26
origins and influences, 26-63
major authors, 63-134
Freud and detective fiction, 134-59

Detective Fiction, Twentieth-Century TCLC 38: 1-96
genesis and history of the detective story, 3-22
defining detective fiction, 22-32
evolution and varieties, 32-77
the appeal of detective fiction, 77-90

Detective Story See Crime-Mystery-Detective Stories

Dime Novels NCLC 84: 98-168
overviews and general studies, 99-123
popular characters, 123-39
major figures and influences, 139-52
socio-political concerns, 152-167

Disease and Literature TCLC 66: 140-283
overviews and general studies, 141-65
disease in nineteenth-century literature, 165-81
tuberculosis and literature, 181-94
women and disease in literature, 194-221
plague literature, 221-53
AIDS in literature, 253-82

El Dorado, The Legend of See Legend of El Dorado, The

The Double in Nineteenth-Century Literature NCLC 40: 1-95
genesis and development of the theme, 2-15
the double and Romanticism, 16-27

sociological views, 27-52
psychological interpretations, 52-87
philosophical considerations, 87-95

Dramatic Realism NCLC 44: 139-202
overviews and general studies, 140-50
origins and definitions, 150-66
impact and influence, 166-93
realist drama and tragedy, 193-201

Drugs and Literature TCLC 78: 184-282
overviews and general studies, 185-201
pre-twentieth-century literature, 201-42
twentieth-century literature, 242-82

Dystopias in Contemporary Literature CLC 168: 1-91
overviews and general studies, 2-52
dystopian views in Margaret Atwood's *The Handmaid's Tale* (1985), 52-71
feminist readings of dystopias, 71-90

Eastern Mythology CMLC 26: 112-92
heroes and kings, 113-51
cross-cultural perspective, 151-69
relations to history and society, 169-92

Ecocriticism and Nineteenth-Century Literature NCLC 140: 1-168
overviews, 3-20
American literature: Romantics and Realists, 20-76
American explorers and naturalists, 76-123
English literature: Romantics and Victorians, 123-67

Ecofeminism and Nineteenth-Century Literature NCLC 136: 1-110
overviews, 2-24
the local landscape, 24-72
travel writing, 72-109

Eighteenth-Century British Periodicals LC 63: 1-123
rise of periodicals, 2-31
impact and influence of periodicals, 31-64
periodicals and society, 64-122

Eighteenth-Century Travel Narratives LC 77: 252-355
overviews and general studies, 254-79
eighteenth-century European travel narratives, 279-334
non-European eighteenth-century travel narratives, 334-55

Electronic "Books": Hypertext and Hyperfiction CLC 86: 367-404
books vs. CD-ROMS, 367-76
hypertext and hyperfiction, 376-95
implications for publishing, libraries, and the public, 395-403

Eliot, T. S., Centenary of Birth CLC 55: 345-75

Elizabethan Drama LC 22: 140-240
origins and influences, 142-67
characteristics and conventions, 167-83
theatrical production, 184-200
histories, 200-12
comedy, 213-20
tragedy, 220-30

Elizabethan Prose Fiction LC 41: 1-70
overviews and general studies, 1-15
origins and influences, 15-43
style and structure, 43-69

The Emergence of the Short Story in the Nineteenth Century NCLC 140: 169-279
overviews, 171-74
the American short story, 174-214
the short story in Great Britain and Ireland, 214-235
stories by women in English, 235-45

the short story in France and Russia, 245-66
the Latin American short story, 266-77

Enclosure of the English Common NCLC 88: 1-57
overviews and general studies, 1-12
early reaction to enclosure, 12-23
nineteenth-century reaction to enclosure, 23-56 The Encyclopedists LC 26: 172-253
overviews and general studies, 173-210
intellectual background, 210-32
views on esthetics, 232-41
views on women, 241-52

English Abolitionist Literature of the Nineteenth Century NCLC 136: 111-235
overview, 112-35
origins and development, 135-42
poetry, 142-58
prose, 158-80
sociopolitical concerns, 180-95
English abolitionist literature and feminism, 195-233

English Caroline Literature LC 13: 221-307
background, 222-41
evolution and varieties, 241-62
the Cavalier mode, 262-75
court and society, 275-91
politics and religion, 291-306

English Decadent Literature of the 1890s NCLC 28: 104-200
fin de siècle: the Decadent period, 105-19
definitions, 120-37
major figures: "the tragic generation," 137-50
French literature and English literary Decadence, 150-7
themes, 157-61
poetry, 161-82
periodicals, 182-96

English Essay, Rise of the LC 18: 238-308
definitions and origins, 236-54
influence on the essay, 254-69
historical background, 269-78
the essay in the seventeenth century, 279-93
the essay in the eighteenth century, 293-307

English Mystery Cycle Dramas LC 34: 1-88
overviews and general studies, 1-27
the nature of dramatic performances, 27-42
the medieval worldview and the mystery cycles, 43-67
the doctrine of repentance and the mystery cycles, 67-76
the fall from grace in the mystery cycles, 76-88

The English Realist Novel, 1740-1771 LC 51: 102-98
overviews and general studies, 103-22
from Romanticism to Realism, 123-58
women and the novel, 159-175
the novel and other literary forms, 176-197

English Revolution, Literature of the LC 43: 1-58
overviews and general studies, 2-24
pamphlets of the English Revolution, 24-38
political sermons of the English Revolution, 38-48
poetry of the English Revolution, 48-57

English Romantic Hellenism NCLC 68: 143-250
overviews and general studies, 144-69
historical development of English Romantic Hellenism, 169-91
influence of Greek mythology on the Romantics, 191-229

influence of Greek literature, art, and culture on the Romantics, 229-50

English Romantic Poetry NCLC 28: 201-327
overviews and reputation, 202-37
major subjects and themes, 237-67
forms of Romantic poetry, 267-78
politics, society, and Romantic poetry, 278-99
philosophy, religion, and Romantic poetry, 299-324

The Epistolary Novel LC 59: 71-170
overviews and general studies, 72-96
women and the Epistolary novel, 96-138
principal figures: Britain, 138-53
principal figures: France, 153-69

Espionage Literature TCLC 50: 95-159
overviews and general studies, 96-113
espionage fiction/formula fiction, 113-26
spies in fact and fiction, 126-38
the female spy, 138-44
social and psychological perspectives, 144-58

European Debates on the Conquest of the Americas LC 67: 1-129
overviews and general studies, 3-56
major Spanish figures, 56-98
English perceptions of Native Americans, 98-129

European Romanticism NCLC 36: 149-284
definitions, 149-77
origins of the movement, 177-82
Romantic theory, 182-200
themes and techniques, 200-23
Romanticism in Germany, 223-39
Romanticism in France, 240-61
Romanticism in Italy, 261-4
Romanticism in Spain, 264-8
impact and legacy, 268-82

Exile in Literature TCLC 122: 1-129
overviews and general studies, 2-33
exile in fiction, 33-92
German literature in exile, 92-129

Existentialism and Literature TCLC 42: 197-268
overviews and definitions, 198-209
history and influences, 209-19
Existentialism critiqued and defended, 220-35
philosophical and religious perspectives, 235-41
Existentialist fiction and drama, 241-67

Ezra Pound Controversy TCLC 150: 1-132
politics of Ezra Pound, 3-42
anti-semitism of Ezra Pound, 42-57
the Bollingen Award controversy, 57-76
Pound's later writing, 76-104
criticism of *The Pisan Cantos*, 104-32

Familiar Essay NCLC 48: 96-211
definitions and origins, 97-130
overview of the genre, 130-43
elements of form and style, 143-59
elements of content, 159-73
the Cockneys: Hazlitt, Lamb, and Hunt, 173-91
status of the genre, 191-210

Fantasy in Contemporary Literature CLC 193: 137-250
overviews and general studies, 139-57
language, form, and theory, 157-91
major writers, 191-230
women writers and fantasy, 230-50

Fashion in Nineteenth-Century Literature NCLC 128: 104-93
overviews and general studies, 105-38
fashion and American literature, 138-46

fashion and English literature, 146-74
fashion and French literature, 174-92

The Faust Legend LC 47: 1-117

Fear in Literature TCLC 74: 81-258
overviews and general studies, 81
pre-twentieth-century literature, 123
twentieth-century literature, 182

Feminism in the 1990s: Commentary on Works by Naomi Wolf, Susan Faludi, and Camille Paglia CLC 76: 377-415

Feminist Criticism See Contemporary Feminist Criticism

Feminist Criticism in 1990 CLC 65: 312-60

Fifteenth-Century English Literature LC 17: 248-334
background, 249-72
poetry, 272-315
drama, 315-23
prose, 323-33

Fifteenth-Century Spanish Poetry LC 100:82-173
overviews and general studies, 83-101
the Cancioneros, 101-57
major figures, 157-72

Film and Literature TCLC 38: 97-226
overviews and general studies, 97-119
film and theater, 119-34
film and the novel, 134-45
the art of the screenplay, 145-66
genre literature/genre film, 167-79
the writer and the film industry, 179-90
authors on film adaptations of their works, 190-200
fiction into film: comparative essays, 200-23

Finance and Money as Represented in Nineteenth-Century Literature NCLC 76: 1-69
historical perspectives, 2-20
the image of money, 20-37
the dangers of money, 37-50
women and money, 50-69

Folklore and Literature TCLC 86: 116-293
overviews and general studies, 118-144
Native American literature, 144-67
African-American literature, 167-238
folklore and the American West, 238-57
modern and postmodern literature, 257-91

Food in Literature TCLC 114: 1-133
food and children's literature, 2-14
food as a literary device, 14-32
rituals invloving food, 33-45
food and social and ethnic identity, 45-90
women's relationship with food, 91-132

Food in Nineteenth-Century Literature NCLC 108: 134-288
overviews, 136-74
food and social class, 174-85
food and gender, 185-219
food and love, 219-31
food and sex, 231-48
eating disorders, 248-70
vegetarians, carnivores, and cannibals, 270-87

French Drama in the Age of Louis XIV LC 28: 94-185
overview, 95-127
tragedy, 127-46
comedy, 146-66
tragicomedy, 166-84

French Enlightenment LC 14: 81-145
the question of definition, 82-9
le siècle des lumières, 89-94
women and the salons, 94-105

censorship, 105-15
the philosophy of reason, 115-31
influence and legacy, 131-44

French New Novel TCLC 98: 158-234
overviews and general studies, 158-92
influences, 192-213
themes, 213-33

French Realism NCLC 52: 136-216
origins and definitions, 137-70
issues and influence, 170-98
realism and representation, 198-215

French Revolution and English Literature NCLC 40: 96-195
history and theory, 96-123
romantic poetry, 123-50
the novel, 150-81
drama, 181-92
children's literature, 192-5

French Symbolist Poetry NCLC 144: 1-107
overviews, 2-14
Symbolist aesthetics, 14-47
the Symbolist lyric, 47-60
history and influence, 60-105

Futurism, Italian TCLC 42: 269-354
principles and formative influences, 271-9
manifestos, 279-88
literature, 288-303
theater, 303-19
art, 320-30
music, 330-6
architecture, 336-9
and politics, 339-46
reputation and significance, 346-51

Gaelic Revival See Irish Literary Renaissance

Gates, Henry Louis, Jr., and African-American Literary Criticism CLC 65: 361-405

Gaucho Literature TCLC 158: 99-195
overviews and general studies, 101-43
major works, 143-95

Gay and Lesbian Literature CLC 76: 416-39

Gay and Lesbian Literature See also Contemporary Gay and Lesbian Literature

Generation of 1898 Short Fiction SSC 75: 182-287
overviews and general studies, 182-210
major short story writers of the Generation of 1898, 210-86
Azorín, 210-16
Emilia Pardo Bazán, 216-34
Vicente Blasco Ibáñez, 234-36
Gabriel Miró, 236-43
Miguel de Unamuno, 243-68
Ramon del Valle-Inclán, 268-86

German Exile Literature TCLC 30: 1-58
the writer and the Nazi state, 1-10
definition of, 10-4
life in exile, 14-32
surveys, 32-50
Austrian literature in exile, 50-2
German publishing in the United States, 52-7

German Expressionism TCLC 34: 74-160
history and major figures, 76-85
aesthetic theories, 85-109
drama, 109-26
poetry, 126-38
film, 138-42
painting, 142-7
music, 147-53
and politics, 153-8

The Ghost Story SSC 58: 1-142
overviews and general studies, 1-21

the ghost story in American literature, 21-49
the ghost story in Asian literature, 49-53
the ghost story in European and English literature, 54-89
major figures, 89-141

The Gilded Age NCLC 84: 169-271
popular themes, 170-90
Realism, 190-208
Aestheticism, 208-26
socio-political concerns, 226-70

Glasnost **and Contemporary Soviet Literature** CLC 59: 355-97

Gothic Drama NCLC 132: 95-198
overviews, 97-125
sociopolitical contexts, 125-58
Gothic playwrights, 158-97

Gothic Novel NCLC 28: 328-402
development and major works, 328-34
definitions, 334-50
themes and techniques, 350-78
in America, 378-85
in Scotland, 385-91
influence and legacy, 391-400

The Governess in Nineteenth-Century Literature NCLC 104: 1-131
overviews and general studies, 3-28
social roles and economic conditions, 28-86
fictional governesses, 86-131

The Grail Theme in Twentieth-Century Literature TCLC 142: 1-89
overviews and general studies, 2-20
major works, 20-89

Graphic Narratives CLC 86: 405-32
history and overviews, 406-21
the "Classics Illustrated" series, 421-2
reviews of recent works, 422-32

Graphic Novels CLC 177: 163-299
overviews and general studies, 165-198
critical readings of major works, 198-286
reviews of recent graphic novels, 286-299

Graveyard Poets LC 67: 131-212
origins and development, 131-52
major figures, 152-75
major works, 175-212

Greek Historiography CMLC 17: 1-49

Greek Mythology CMLC 26: 193-320
overviews and general studies, 194-209
origins and development of Greek mythology, 209-29
cosmogonies and divinities in Greek mythology, 229-54
heroes and heroines in Greek mythology, 254-80
women in Greek mythology, 280-320

Greek Theater CMLC 51: 1-58
criticism, 2-58

Hard-Boiled Fiction TCLC 118: 1-109
overviews and general studies, 2-39
major authors, 39-76
women and hard-boiled fiction, 76-109

The Harlem Renaissance HR 1: 1-563
overviews and general studies of the Harlem Renaissance, 1-137
primary sources, 3-12
overviews, 12-38
background and sources of the Harlem Renaissance, 38-56
the New Negro aesthetic, 56-91
patrons, promoters, and the New York Public Library, 91-121
women of the Harlem Renaissance, 121-37
social, economic, and political factors that

influenced the Harlem Renaissance, 139-240
primary sources, 141-53
overviews, 153-87
social and economic factors, 187-213
Black intellectual and political thought, 213-40
publishing and periodicals during the Harlem Renaissance, 243-339
primary sources, 246-52
overviews, 252-68
African American writers and mainstream publishers, 268-91
anthologies: *The New Negro* and others, 291-309
African American periodicals and the Harlem Renaissance, 309-39
performing arts during the Harlem Renaissance, 341-465
primary sources, 343-48
overviews, 348-64
drama of the Harlem Renaissance, 364-92
influence of music on Harlem Renaissance writing, 437-65
visual arts during the Harlem Renaissance, 467-563
primary sources, 470-71
overviews, 471-517
painters, 517-36
sculptors, 536-58
photographers, 558-63

Harlem Renaissance TCLC 26: 49-125
principal issues and figures, 50-67
the literature and its audience, 67-74
theme and technique in poetry, fiction, and drama, 74-115
and American society, 115-21
achievement and influence, 121-2

Havel, Václav, Playwright and President CLC 65: 406-63

Heroic Drama LC 91: 249-373
definitions and overviews, 251-78
politics and heroic drama, 278-303
early plays: Dryden and Orrery, 303-51
later plays: Lee and Otway, 351-73

Historical Fiction, Nineteenth-Century NCLC 48: 212-307
definitions and characteristics, 213-36
Victorian historical fiction, 236-65
American historical fiction, 265-88
realism in historical fiction, 288-306

Hollywood and Literature TCLC 118: 110-251
overviews and general studies, 111-20
adaptations, 120-65
socio-historical and cultural impact, 165-206
theater and hollywood, 206-51

Holocaust and the Atomic Bomb: Fifty Years Later CLC 91: 331-82
the Holocaust remembered, 333-52
Anne Frank revisited, 352-62
the atomic bomb and American memory, 362-81

Holocaust Denial Literature TCLC 58: 1-110
overviews and general studies, 1-30
Robert Faurisson and Noam Chomsky, 30-52
Holocaust denial literature in America, 52-71
library access to Holocaust denial literature, 72-5
the authenticity of Anne Frank's diary, 76-90
David Irving and the "normalization" of Hitler, 90-109

Holocaust, Literature of the TCLC 42: 355-450
historical overview, 357-61
critical overview, 361-70
diaries and memoirs, 370-95
novels and short stories, 395-425
poetry, 425-41
drama, 441-8

Homosexuality in Nineteenth-Century Literature NCLC 56: 78-182
defining homosexuality, 80-111
Greek love, 111-44
trial and danger, 144-81

Humors Comedy LC 85: 194-324
overviews, 195-251
major figures: Ben Jonson, 251-93
major figures: William Shakespeare, 293-324

Hungarian Literature of the Twentieth Century TCLC 26: 126-88
surveys of, 126-47
Nyugat and early twentieth-century literature, 147-56
mid-century literature, 156-68
and politics, 168-78
since the 1956 revolt, 178-87

Hysteria in Nineteenth-Century Literature NCLC 64: 59-184
the history of hysteria, 60-75
the gender of hysteria, 75-103
hysteria and women's narratives, 103-57
hysteria in nineteenth-century poetry, 157-83

Image of the Noble Savage in Literature LC 79: 136-252
overviews and development, 136-76
the Noble Savage in the New World, 176-221
Rousseau and the French Enlightenment's view of the noble savage, 221-51

Imagism TCLC 74: 259-454
history and development, 260
major figures, 288
sources and influences, 352
Imagism and other movements, 397
influence and legacy, 431

Immigrants in Nineteenth-Century Literature, Representation of NCLC 112: 188-298
overview, 189-99
immigrants in America, 199-223
immigrants and labor, 223-60
immigrants in England, 260-97

Incest in Nineteenth-Century American Literature NCLC 76: 70-141
overview, 71-88
the concern for social order, 88-117
authority and authorship, 117-40

Incest in Victorian Literature NCLC 92: 172-318
overviews and general studies, 173-85
novels, 185-276
plays, 276-84
poetry, 284-318

Indian Literature in English TCLC 54: 308-406
overview, 309-13
origins and major figures, 313-25
the Indo-English novel, 325-55
Indo-English poetry, 355-67
Indo-English drama, 367-72
critical perspectives on Indo-English literature, 372-80
modern Indo-English literature, 380-9
Indo-English authors on their work, 389-404

The Industrial Revolution in Literature NCLC 56: 183-273

historical and cultural perspectives, 184-201
contemporary reactions to the machine, 201-21
themes and symbols in literature, 221-73

The Irish Famine as Represented in Nineteenth-Century Literature NCLC 64: 185-261
overviews and general studies, 187-98
historical background, 198-212
famine novels, 212-34
famine poetry, 234-44
famine letters and eye-witness accounts, 245-61

Irish Literary Renaissance TCLC 46: 172-287
overview, 173-83
development and major figures, 184-202
influence of Irish folklore and mythology, 202-22
Irish poetry, 222-34
Irish drama and the Abbey Theatre, 234-56
Irish fiction, 256-86

Irish Nationalism and Literature NCLC 44: 203-73
the Celtic element in literature, 203-19
anti-Irish sentiment and the Celtic response, 219-34
literary ideals in Ireland, 234-45
literary expressions, 245-73

Irish Novel, The NCLC 80: 1-130
overviews and general studies, 3-9
principal figures, 9-22
peasant and middle class Irish novelists, 22-76
aristocratic Irish and Anglo-Irish novelists, 76-129

Israeli Literature TCLC 94: 1-137
overviews and general studies, 2-18
Israeli fiction, 18-33
Israeli poetry, 33-62
Israeli drama, 62-91
women and Israeli literature, 91-112
Arab characters in Israeli literature, 112-36

Italian Futurism See **Futurism, Italian**

Italian Humanism LC 12: 205-77
origins and early development, 206-18
revival of classical letters, 218-23
humanism and other philosophies, 224-39
humanism and humanists, 239-46
the plastic arts, 246-57
achievement and significance, 258-76

Italian Romanticism NCLC 60: 85-145
origins and overviews, 86-101
Italian Romantic theory, 101-25
the language of Romanticism, 125-45

Jacobean Drama LC 33: 1-37
the Jacobean worldview: an era of transition, 2-14
the moral vision of Jacobean drama, 14-22
Jacobean tragedy, 22-3
the Jacobean masque, 23-36

Jazz and Literature TCLC 102: 3-124

Jewish-American Fiction TCLC 62: 1-181
overviews and general studies, 2-24
major figures, 24-48
Jewish writers and American life, 48-78
Jewish characters in American fiction, 78-108
themes in Jewish-American fiction, 108-43
Jewish-American women writers, 143-59
the Holocaust and Jewish-American fiction, 159-81

Jews in Literature TCLC 118: 252-417
overviews and general studies, 253-97
representing the Jew in literature, 297-351
the Holocaust in literature, 351-416

Journals of Lewis and Clark, The NCLC 100: 1-88
    overviews and general studies, 4-30
    journal-keeping methods, 30-46
    Fort Mandan, 46-51
    the Clark journal, 51-65
    the journals as literary texts, 65-87

Kabuki LC 73: 118-232
    overviews and general studies, 120-40
    the development of Kabuki, 140-65
    major works, 165-95
    Kabuki and society, 195-231

Kit-Kat Club, The LC 71: 66-112
    overviews and general studies, 67-88
    major figures, 88-107
    attacks on the Kit-Kat Club, 107-12

Knickerbocker Group, The NCLC 56: 274-341
    overviews and general studies, 276-314
    Knickerbocker periodicals, 314-26
    writers and artists, 326-40

Künstlerroman TCLC 150: 133-260
    overviews and general studies, 135-51
    major works, 151-212
    feminism in the *Künstlerroman,* 212-49
    minority *Künstlerroman,* 249-59

Lake Poets, The NCLC 52: 217-304
    characteristics of the Lake Poets and their works, 218-27
    literary influences and collaborations, 227-66
    defining and developing Romantic ideals, 266-84
    embracing Conservatism, 284-303

Language Poets TCLC 126: 66-172
    overviews and general studies, 67-122
    selected major figures in language poetry, 122-72

Larkin, Philip, Controversy CLC 81: 417-64

Latin American Literature, Twentieth-Century TCLC 58: 111-98
    historical and critical perspectives, 112-36
    the novel, 136-45
    the short story, 145-9
    drama, 149-60
    poetry, 160-7
    the writer and society, 167-86
    Native Americans in Latin American literature, 186-97

Law and Literature TCLC 126: 173-347
    overviews and general studies, 174-253
    fiction critiquing the law, 253-88
    literary responses to the law, 289-346

Legend of El Dorado, The LC 74: 248-350
    overviews, 249-308
    major explorations for El Dorado, 308-50

The Levellers LC 51: 200-312
    overviews and general studies, 201-29
    principal figures, 230-86
    religion, political philosophy, and pamphleteering, 287-311

Literary Criticism in the Nineteenth Century, American NCLC 128: 1-103
    overviews and general studies, 2-44
    the trancendentalists, 44-65
    "young America," 65-71
    James Russell Lowell, 71-9
    Edgar Allan Poe, 79-97
    Walt Whitman, 97-102

Literary Expressionism TCLC 142: 90-185
    overviews and general studies, 91-138
    themes in literary expressionism, 138-61
    expressionism in Germany, 161-84

Literary Marketplace, The Nineteenth-Century NCLC 128: 194-368
    overviews and general studies, 197-228

    British literary marketplace, 228-66
    French literary marketplace, 266-82
    American literary marketplace, 282-323
    Women in the literary marketplace, 323-67

Literary Prizes TCLC 122: 130-203
    overviews and general studies, 131-34
    the Nobel Prize in Literature, 135-83
    the Pulitzer Prize, 183-203

Literature and Millenial Lists CLC 119: 431-67
    The Modern Library list, 433
    The Waterstone list, 438-439

Literature in Response to the September 11 Attacks CLC 174: 1-46
    Major works about September 11, 2001, 2-22
    Critical, artistic, and journalistic responses, 22-45

Literature of the American Cowboy NCLC 96: 1-60
    overview, 3-20
    cowboy fiction, 20-36
    cowboy poetry and songs, 36-59

Literature of the California Gold Rush NCLC 92: 320-85
    overviews and general studies, 322-24
    early California Gold Rush fiction, 324-44
    Gold Rush folklore and legend, 344-51
    the rise of Western local color, 351-60
    social relations and social change, 360-385

Literature of the Counter-Reformation LC 109: 213-56
    overviews and general studies, 214-33
    influential figures, 233-56

Living Theatre, The DC 16: 154-214

Luddism in Nineteenth-Century Literature NCLC 140: 280-365
    overviews, 281-322
    the literary response, 322-65

Lynching in Nineteenth-Century Literature NCLC 148: 162-247
    lynching in literature and music, 163-92
    Ida B. Wells-Barnett and the anti-lynching movement, 192-221
    resistance to lynching in society and the press, 221-46

Madness in Nineteenth-Century Literature NCLC 76: 142-284
    overview, 143-54
    autobiography, 154-68
    poetry, 168-215
    fiction, 215-83

Madness in Twentieth-Century Literature TCLC 50: 160-225
    overviews and general studies, 161-71
    madness and the creative process, 171-86
    suicide, 186-91
    madness in American literature, 191-207
    madness in German literature, 207-13
    madness and feminist artists, 213-24

Magic Realism TCLC 110: 80-327
    overviews and general studies, 81-94
    magic realism in African literature, 95-110
    magic realism in American literature, 110-32
    magic realism in Canadian literature, 132-46
    magic realism in European literature, 146-66
    magic realism in Asian literature, 166-79
    magic realism in Latin-American literature, 179-223
    magic realism in Israeli literature and the novels of Salman Rushdie, 223-38
    magic realism in literature written by women, 239-326

The Martin Marprelate Tracts LC 101: 165-240
    criticism, 166-240

Marxist Criticism TCLC 134: 127-57
    overviews and general studies, 128-67
    Marxist interpretations, 167-209
    cultural and literary Marxist theory, 209-49
    Marxism and feminist critical theory, 250-56

The Masque LC 63: 124-265
    development of the masque, 125-62
    sources and structure, 162-220
    race and gender in the masque, 221-64

Medical Writing LC 55: 93-195
    colonial America, 94-110
    enlightenment, 110-24
    medieval writing, 124-40
    sexuality, 140-83
    vernacular, 185-95

Memoirs of Trauma CLC 109: 419-466
    overview, 420
    criticism, 429

Metafiction TCLC 130: 43-228
    overviews and general studies, 44-85
    Spanish metafiction, 85-117
    studies of metafictional authors and works, 118-228

Metaphysical Poets LC 24: 356-439
    early definitions, 358-67
    surveys and overviews, 367-92
    cultural and social influences, 392-406
    stylistic and thematic variations, 407-38

Missionaries in the Nineteenth-Century, Literature of NCLC 112: 299-392
    history and development, 300-16
    uses of ethnography, 316-31
    sociopolitical concerns, 331-82
    David Livingstone, 382-91

Modern Essay, The TCLC 58: 199-273
    overview, 200-7
    the essay in the early twentieth century, 207-19
    characteristics of the modern essay, 219-32
    modern essayists, 232-45
    the essay as a literary genre, 245-73

Modern French Literature TCLC 122: 205-359
    overviews and general studies, 207-43
    French theater, 243-77
    gender issues and French women writers, 277-315
    ideology and politics, 315-24
    modern French poetry, 324-41
    resistance literature, 341-58

Modern Irish Literature TCLC 102: 125-321
    overview, 129-44
    dramas, 144-70
    fiction, 170-247
    poetry, 247-321

Modern Japanese Literature TCLC 66: 284-389
    poetry, 285-305
    drama, 305-29
    fiction, 329-61
    western influences, 361-87

Modernism TCLC 70: 165-275
    definitions, 166-184
    Modernism and earlier influences, 184-200
    stylistic and thematic traits, 200-229
    poetry and drama, 229-242
    redefining Modernism, 242-275

Muckraking Movement in American Journalism TCLC 34: 161-242
    development, principles, and major figures, 162-70
    publications, 170-9

social and political ideas, 179-86
targets, 186-208
fiction, 208-19
decline, 219-29
impact and accomplishments, 229-40

Multiculturalism CLC 189: 167-254
overviews and general studies, 168-93
the effects of multiculturalism on global literature, 193-213
multicultural themes in specific contemporary works, 213-53

Multiculturalism in Literature and Education CLC 70: 361-413

Music and Modern Literature TCLC 62: 182-329
overviews and general studies, 182-211
musical form/literary form, 211-32
music in literature, 232-50
the influence of music on literature, 250-73
literature and popular music, 273-303
jazz and poetry, 303-28

Mystery Story See Crime-Mystery-Detective Stories

Native American Literature CLC 76: 440-76

Natural School, Russian NCLC 24: 205-40
history and characteristics, 205-25
contemporary criticism, 225-40

Naturalism NCLC 36: 285-382
definitions and theories, 286-305
critical debates on Naturalism, 305-16
Naturalism in theater, 316-32
European Naturalism, 332-61
American Naturalism, 361-72
the legacy of Naturalism, 372-81

Negritude TCLC 50: 226-361
origins and evolution, 227-56
definitions, 256-91
Negritude in literature, 291-343
Negritude reconsidered, 343-58

Negritude TCLC 158: 196-280
overviews and general studies, 197-208
major figures, 208-25
Negritude and humanism, 225-29
poetry of Negritude, 229-47
politics of Negritude, 247-68
the Negritude debate, 268-79

New Criticism TCLC 34: 243-318
development and ideas, 244-70
debate and defense, 270-99
influence and legacy, 299-315

TCLC 146: 1-108
overviews and general studies, 3-19
defining New Criticism, 19-28
place in history, 28-51
poetry and New Criticism, 51-78
major authors, 78-108

New South, Literature of the NCLC 116: 122-240
overviews, 124-66
the novel in the New South, 166-209
myth of the Old South in the New, 209-39

The New World in Renaissance Literature LC 31: 1-51
overview, 1-18
utopia vs. terror, 18-31
explorers and Native Americans, 31-51

New York Intellectuals and *Partisan Review* TCLC 30: 117-98
development and major figures, 118-28
influence of Judaism, 128-39
Partisan Review, 139-57
literary philosophy and practice, 157-75
political philosophy, 175-87
achievement and significance, 187-97

The New Yorker TCLC 58: 274-357
overviews and general studies, 274-95

major figures, 295-304
New Yorker style, 304-33
fiction, journalism, and humor at *The New Yorker,* 333-48
the new *New Yorker,* 348-56

Newgate Novel NCLC 24: 166-204
development of Newgate literature, 166-73
Newgate Calendar, 173-7
Newgate fiction, 177-95
Newgate drama, 195-204

New Zealand Literature TCLC 134: 258-368
overviews and general studies, 260-300
Maori literature, 300-22
New Zealand drama, 322-32
New Zealand fiction, 332-51
New Zealand poetry, 351-67

Nigerian Literature of the Twentieth Century TCLC 30: 199-265
surveys of, 199-227
English language and African life, 227-45
politics and the Nigerian writer, 245-54
Nigerian writers and society, 255-62

Nihilism and Literature TCLC 110: 328-93
overviews and general studies, 328-44
European and Russian nihilism, 344-73
nihilism in the works of Albert Camus, Franz Kafka, and John Barth, 373-92

Nineteenth-Century Captivity Narratives NCLC 80:131-218
overview, 132-37
the political significance of captivity narratives, 137-67
images of gender, 167-96
moral instruction, 197-217

Nineteenth-Century Euro-American Literary Representations of Native Americans NCLC 104: 132-264
overviews and general studies, 134-53
Native American history, 153-72
the Indians of the Northeast, 172-93
the Indians of the Southeast, 193-212
the Indians of the West, 212-27
Indian-hater fiction, 227-43
the Indian as exhibit, 243-63

Nineteenth-Century Native American Autobiography NCLC 64: 262-389
overview, 263-8
problems of authorship, 268-81
the evolution of Native American autobiography, 281-304
political issues, 304-15
gender and autobiography, 316-62
autobiographical works during the turn of the century, 362-88

Nineteenth-Century Pornography NCLC 144: 108-202
nineteenth-century pornographers, 110-64
pornography and literature, 164-91
pornography and censorship, 191-201

Noh Drama LC 103: 189-270
overviews, 190-94
origins and development, 194-214
structure, 214-28
types of plays, 228-45
masks in Noh drama, 245-57
Noh drama and the audience, 257-69

Norse Mythology CMLC 26: 321-85
history and mythological tradition, 322-44
Eddic poetry, 344-74
Norse mythology and other traditions, 374-85

Northern Humanism LC 16: 281-356
background, 282-305
precursor of the Reformation, 305-14
the Brethren of the Common Life, the Devotio Moderna, and education, 314-40
the impact of printing, 340-56

Novel of Manners, The NCLC 56: 342-96
social and political order, 343-53
domestic order, 353-73
depictions of gender, 373-83
the American novel of manners, 383-95

Novels of the Ming and Early Ch'ing Dynasties LC 76: 213-356
overviews and historical development, 214-45
major works—overview, 245-85
genre studies, 285-325
cultural and social themes, 325-55

Nuclear Literature: Writings and Criticism in the Nuclear Age TCLC 46: 288-390
overviews and general studies, 290-301
fiction, 301-35
poetry, 335-8
nuclear war in Russo-Japanese literature, 338-55
nuclear war and women writers, 355-67
the nuclear referent and literary criticism, 367-88

Occultism in Modern Literature TCLC 50: 362-406
influence of occultism on literature, 363-72
occultism, literature, and society, 372-87
fiction, 387-96
drama, 396-405

Opium and the Nineteenth-Century Literary Imagination NCLC 20:250-301
original sources, 250-62
historical background, 262-71
and literary society, 271-9
and literary creativity, 279-300

Orientalism NCLC 96: 149-364
overviews and general studies, 150-98
Orientalism and imperialism, 198-229
Orientalism and gender, 229-59
Orientalism and the nineteenth-century novel, 259-321
Orientalism in nineteenth-century poetry, 321-63

The Oxford Movement NCLC 72: 1-197
overviews and general studies, 2-24
background, 24-59
and education, 59-69
religious responses, 69-128
literary aspects, 128-178
political implications, 178-196

The Parnassian Movement NCLC 72: 198-241
overviews and general studies, 199-231
and epic form, 231-38
and positivism, 238-41

Pastoral Literature of the English Renaissance LC 59: 171-282
overviews and general studies, 172-214
principal figures of the Elizabethan period, 214-33
principal figures of the later Renaissance, 233-50
pastoral drama, 250-81

Periodicals, Nineteenth-Century American NCLC 132: 199-374
overviews, chronology, and development, 200-41
literary periodicals, 241-83
regional periodicals, 283-317
women's magazines and gender issues, 317-47
minority periodicals, 347-72

Periodicals, Nineteenth-Century British NCLC 24: 100-65
overviews and general studies, 100-30
in the Romantic Age, 130-41
in the Victorian era, 142-54
and the reviewer, 154-64

Picaresque Literature of the Sixteenth and Seventeenth Centuries LC 78: 223-355
  context and development, 224-71
  genre, 271-98
  the picaro, 299-326
  the picara, 326-53

Plath, Sylvia, and the Nature of Biography CLC 86: 433-62
  the nature of biography, 433-52
  reviews of *The Silent Woman,* 452-61

Political Theory from the 15th to the 18th Century LC 36: 1-55
  overview, 1-26
  natural law, 26-42
  empiricism, 42-55

Polish Romanticism NCLC 52: 305-71
  overviews and general studies, 306-26
  major figures, 326-40
  Polish Romantic drama, 340-62
  influences, 362-71

Politics and Literature TCLC 94: 138-61
  overviews and general studies, 139-96
  Europe, 196-226
  Latin America, 226-48
  Africa and the Caribbean, 248-60

Popular Literature TCLC 70: 279-382
  overviews and general studies, 280-324
  "formula" fiction, 324-336
  readers of popular literature, 336-351
  evolution of popular literature, 351-382

The Portrayal of Jews in Nineteenth-Century English Literature NCLC 72: 242-368
  overviews and general studies, 244-77
  Anglo-Jewish novels, 277-303
  depictions by non-Jewish writers, 303-44
  Hebraism versus Hellenism, 344-67

The Portrayal of Mormonism NCLC 96: 61-148
  overview, 63-72
  early Mormon literature, 72-100
  Mormon periodicals and journals, 100-10
  women writers, 110-22
  Mormonism and nineteenth-century literature, 122-42
  Mormon poetry, 142-47

Post-apartheid Literature CLC 187: 284-382
  overviews and general studies, 286-318
  the post-apartheid novel, 318-65
  post-apartheid drama, 365-81

Postcolonial African Literature TCLC 146: 110-239
  overviews and general studies, 111-45
  ideology and theory, 145-62
  postcolonial testimonial literature, 162-99
  major authors, 199-239

Postcolonialism TCLC 114: 134-239
  overviews and general studies, 135-153
  African postcolonial writing, 153-72
  Asian/Pacific literature, 172-78
  postcolonial literary theory, 178-213
  postcolonial women's writing, 213-38

Postmodernism TCLC 90:125-307
  overview, 126-166
  criticism, 166-224
  fiction, 224-282
  poetry, 282-300
  drama, 300-307

Pre-Raphaelite Movement NCLC 20: 302-401
  overview, 302-4
  genesis, 304-12
  Germ and *Oxford and Cambridge Magazine,* 312-20
  Robert Buchanan and the "Fleshly School of Poetry," 320-31
  satires and parodies, 331-4
  surveys, 334-51
  aesthetics, 351-75

sister arts of poetry and painting, 375-94
influence, 394-9

Pre-romanticism LC 40: 1-56
  overviews and general studies, 2-14
  defining the period, 14-23
  new directions in poetry and prose, 23-45
  the focus on the self, 45-56

Pre-Socratic Philosophy CMLC 22: 1-56
  overviews and general studies, 3-24
  the Ionians and the Pythagoreans, 25-35
  Heraclitus, the Eleatics, and the Atomists, 36-47
  the Sophists, 47-55

Prison in Nineteenth-Century Literature, The NCLC 116: 241-357
  overview, 242-60
  romantic prison, 260-78
  domestic prison, 278-316
  America as prison, 316-24
  physical prisons and prison authors, 324-56

Protestant Hagiography and Martyrology LC 84: 106-217
  overview, 106-37
  John Foxe's *Book of Martyrs,* 137-97
  martyrology and the feminine perspective, 198-216

Protestant Reformation, Literature of the LC 37: 1-83
  overviews and general studies, 1-49
  humanism and scholasticism, 49-69
  the reformation and literature, 69-82

Psychoanalysis and Literature TCLC 38: 227-338
  overviews and general studies, 227-46
  Freud on literature, 246-51
  psychoanalytic views of the literary process, 251-61
  psychoanalytic theories of response to literature, 261-88
  psychoanalysis and literary criticism, 288-312
  psychoanalysis as literature/literature as psychoanalysis, 313-34

The Quarrel between the Ancients and the Moderns LC 63: 266-381
  overviews and general studies, 267-301
  Renaissance origins, 301-32
  Quarrel between the Ancients and the Moderns in France, 332-58
  Battle of the Books in England, 358-80

Racism in Literature TCLC 138: 257-373
  overviews and general studies, 257-326
  racism and literature by and about African Americans, 292-326
  theme of racism in literature, 326-773

Rap Music CLC 76: 477-50

Reader-Response Criticism TCLC 146: 240-357
  overviews and general studies, 241-88
  critical approaches to reader response, 288-342
  reader-response interpretation, 342-57

Realism in Short Fiction SSC 63: 128-57
  overviews and general studies, 129-37
  realist short fiction in France, 137-62
  realist short fiction in Russia, 162-215
  realist short fiction in England, 215-31
  realist short fiction in the United States, 231-56

Regionalism and Local Color in Short Fiction SSC 65: 160-289
  overviews and general studies, 163-205
  regionalism/local color fiction of the west, 205-42
  regionalism/local color fiction of the midwest, 242-57

regionalism/local color fiction of the south, 257-88

Renaissance Natural Philosophy LC 27: 201-87
  cosmology, 201-28
  astrology, 228-54
  magic, 254-86

Representations of Africa in Nineteenth-Century Literature NCLC 148: 248-351
  overview, 251-66
  Northeast and Central Africa, 266-76
  South Africa, 276-301
  West Africa, 301-49

Representations of the Devil in Nineteenth-Century Literature NCLC 100: 89-223
  overviews and general studies, 90-115
  the Devil in American fiction, 116-43
  English Romanticism: the satanic school, 143-89
  Luciferian discourse in European literature, 189-222

Restoration Drama LC 21: 184-275
  general overviews and general studies, 185-230
  Jeremy Collier stage controversy, 230-9
  other critical interpretations, 240-75

Revenge Tragedy LC 71: 113-242
  overviews and general studies, 113-51
  Elizabethan attitudes toward revenge, 151-88
  the morality of revenge, 188-216
  reminders and remembrance, 217-41

Revising the Literary Canon CLC 81: 465-509

Revising the Literary Canon TCLC 114: 240-84
  overviews and general studies, 241-85
  canon change in American literature, 285-339
  gender and the literary canon, 339-59
  minority and third-world literature and the canon, 359-84

Revolutionary Astronomers LC 51: 314-65
  overviews and general studies, 316-25
  principal figures, 325-51
  Revolutionary astronomical models, 352-64

Robin Hood, Legend of LC 19: 205-58
  origins and development of the Robin Hood legend, 206-20
  representations of Robin Hood, 220-44
  Robin Hood as hero, 244-56

Romantic Literary Criticism NCLC 144: 203-357
  background and overviews, 205-30
  literary reviews, 230-38
  the German Romantics, 238-81
  Wordsworth and Coleridge, 281-326
  variations on Romantic critical theory, 326-56

Rushdie, Salman, *Satanic Verses* Controversy CLC 55: 214-63; 59:404-56

Russian Nihilism NCLC 28: 403-47
  definitions and overviews, 404-17
  women and Nihilism, 417-27
  literature as reform: the Civic Critics, 427-33
  Nihilism and the Russian novel: Turgenev and Dostoevsky, 433-47

Russian Thaw TCLC 26: 189-247
  literary history of the period, 190-206
  theoretical debate of socialist realism, 206-11
  Novy Mir, 211-7
  Literary Moscow, 217-24
  Pasternak, *Zhivago,* and the Nobel prize, 224-7

poetry of liberation, 228-31
Brodsky trial and the end of the Thaw, 231-6
achievement and influence, 236-46

Salem Witch Trials LC 38: 1-145
overviews and general studies, 2-30
historical background, 30-65
judicial background, 65-78
the search for causes, 78-115
the role of women in the trials, 115-44

Salinger, J. D., Controversy Surrounding *In Search of J. D. Salinger* CLC 55: 325-44

Samizdat Literature TCLC 150: 261-342
overviews and general studies, 262-64
history and development, 264-309
politics and Samizdat, 309-22
voices of Samizdat, 322-42

Sanitation Reform, Nineteenth-Century NCLC 124: 165-257
overviews and general studies, 166
primary texts, 186-89
social context, 189-221
public health in literature, 221-56

Science and Modern Literature TCLC 90: 308-419
overviews and general studies, 295-333
fiction, 333-95
poetry, 395-405
drama, 405-19

Science in Nineteenth-Century Literature NCLC 100: 224-366
overviews and general studies, 225-65
major figures, 265-336
sociopolitical concerns, 336-65

Science Fiction, Nineteenth-Century NCLC 24: 241-306
background, 242-50
definitions of the genre, 251-56
representative works and writers, 256-75
themes and conventions, 276-305

Scottish Chaucerians LC 20: 363-412

Scottish Poetry, Eighteenth-Century LC 29: 95-167
overviews and general studies, 96-114
the Scottish Augustans, 114-28
the Scots Vernacular Revival, 132-63
Scottish poetry after Burns, 163-66

Sea in Literature, The TCLC 82: 72-191
drama, 73-9
poetry, 79-119
fiction, 119-91

Sea in Nineteenth-Century English and American Literature, The NCLC 104: 265-362
overviews and general studies, 267-306
major figures in American sea fiction—Cooper and Melville, 306-29
American sea poetry and short stories, 329-45
English sea literature, 345-61

Sensation Novel, The NCLC 80: 219-330
overviews and general studies, 221-46
principal figures, 246-62
nineteenth-century reaction, 262-91
feminist criticism, 291-329

Sentimental Novel, The NCLC 60: 146-245
overviews and general studies, 147-58
the politics of domestic fiction, 158-79
a literature of resistance and repression, 179-212
the reception of sentimental fiction, 213-44

September 11 Attacks See Literature in Response to the September 11 Attacks

Sex and Literature TCLC 82: 192-434
overviews and general studies, 193-216
drama, 216-63

poetry, 263-87
fiction, 287-431

Sherlock Holmes Centenary TCLC 26: 248-310
Doyle's life and the composition of the Holmes stories, 248-59
life and character of Holmes, 259-78
method, 278-79
Holmes and the Victorian world, 279-92
Sherlockian scholarship, 292-301
Doyle and the development of the detective story, 301-07
Holmes's continuing popularity, 307-09

Short Science Fiction, Golden Age of, 1938-1950 SSC 73: 1-145
overviews and general studies, 3-48
publishing history of Golden Age Short Science Fiction, 48-65
major Golden Age Short Science Fiction authors and editors
Isaac Asimov, 65-77
Ray Bradbury, 77-92
John W. Campbell, 92-106
Arthur C. Clarke, 106-15
Robert A. Heinlein, 115-29
Damon Knight, 129-40
Frederik Pohl, 141-43

Short-Short Fiction SSC 61: 311-36
overviews and general studies, 312-19
major short-short fiction writers, 319-35

The Silver Fork Novel NCLC 88: 58-140
criticism, 59-139

Slave Narratives, American NCLC 20: 1-91
background, 2-9
overviews and general studies, 9-24
contemporary responses, 24-7
language, theme, and technique, 27-70
historical authenticity, 70-5
antecedents, 75-83
role in development of Black American literature, 83-8

The Slave Trade in British and American Literature LC 59: 283-369
overviews and general studies, 284-91
depictions by white writers, 291-331
depictions by former slaves, 331-67

Social Conduct Literature LC 55: 196-298
overviews and general studies, 196-223
prescriptive ideology in other literary forms, 223-38
role of the press, 238-63
impact of conduct literature, 263-87
conduct literature and the perception of women, 287-96
women writing for women, 296-98

Social Protest Literature Outside England, Nineteenth-Century NCLC 124: 258-350
overviews and general studies, 259-72
oppression revealed, 272-306
literature to incite or prevent reform, 306-50

Socialism NCLC 88: 141-237
origins, 142-54
French socialism, 154-83
Anglo-American socialism, 183-205
Socialist-Feminism, 205-36

Southern Gothic Literature TCLC 142: 186-270
overviews and general studies, 187-97
major authors in southern Gothic literature, 197-230
structure and technique in southern Gothic literature, 230-50
themes in southern Gothic literature, 250-70

Southern Literature See Contemporary Southern Literature

Southern Literature of the Reconstruction NCLC 108: 289-369
overview, 290-91
reconstruction literature: the consequences of war, 291-321
old south to new: continuities in southern culture, 321-68

Spanish Civil War Literature TCLC 26: 311-85
topics in, 312-33
British and American literature, 333-59
French literature, 359-62
Spanish literature, 362-73
German literature, 373-75
political idealism and war literature, 375-83

Spanish Golden Age Literature LC 23: 262-332
overviews and general studies, 263-81
verse drama, 281-304
prose fiction, 304-19
lyric poetry, 319-31

Sparta in Literature CMLC 70: 145-271
overviews, 147-61
Spartan poetry, 161-72
the Spartan myth, 172-200
historical background, 200-27
Spartan society and culture, 227-69

Spasmodic School of Poetry NCLC 24: 307-52
history and major figures, 307-21
the Spasmodics on poetry, 321-7
Firmilian and critical disfavor, 327-39
theme and technique, 339-47
influence, 347-51

Sports in Literature TCLC 86: 294-445
overviews and general studies, 295-324
major writers and works, 324-402
sports, literature, and social issues, 402-45

Steinbeck, John, Fiftieth Anniversary of *The Grapes of Wrath* CLC 59: 311-54

Sturm und Drang NCLC 40: 196-276
definitions, 197-238
poetry and poetics, 238-58
drama, 258-75

Supernatural Fiction in the Nineteenth Century NCLC 32: 207-87
major figures and influences, 208-35
the Victorian ghost story, 236-54
the influence of science and occultism, 254-66
supernatural fiction and society, 266-86

Supernatural Fiction, Modern TCLC 30: 59-116
evolution and varieties, 60-74
"decline" of the ghost story, 74-86
as a literary genre, 86-92
technique, 92-101
nature and appeal, 101-15

Surrealism TCLC 30: 334-406
history and formative influences, 335-43
manifestos, 343-54
philosophic, aesthetic, and political principles, 354-75
poetry, 375-81
novel, 381-6
drama, 386-92
film, 392-8
painting and sculpture, 398-403
achievement, 403-5

Surrealism in Children's Literature CLR 103: 127-200
overviews and general studies, 130-52
critical analysis of surrealist children's authors and works, 152-99

Sylvia Beach and Company TCLC 158: 281-370
    overviews and general studies, 282-97
    Shakespeare and Company, 297-314
    the business of publishing, 315-40
    Sylvia Beach and James Joyce, 341-70

Symbolism, Russian TCLC 30: 266-333
    doctrines and major figures, 267-92
    theories, 293-8
    and French Symbolism, 298-310
    themes in poetry, 310-4
    theater, 314-20
    and the fine arts, 320-32

Symbolist Movement, French NCLC 20: 169-249
    background and characteristics, 170-86
    principles, 186-91
    attacked and defended, 191-7
    influences and predecessors, 197-211
    and Decadence, 211-6
    theater, 216-26
    prose, 226-33
    decline and influence, 233-47

Television and Literature TCLC 78: 283-426
    television and literacy, 283-98
    reading vs. watching, 298-341
    adaptations, 341-62
    literary genres and television, 362-90
    television genres and literature, 390-410
    children's literature/children's television, 410-25

Theater of the Absurd TCLC 38: 339-415
    "The Theater of the Absurd," 340-7
    major plays and playwrights, 347-58
    and the concept of the absurd, 358-86
    theatrical techniques, 386-94
    predecessors of, 394-402
    influence of, 402-13

Tin Pan Alley *See* American Popular Song, Golden Age of

Tobacco Culture LC 55: 299-366
    social and economic attitudes toward tobacco, 299-344
    tobacco trade between the old world and the new world, 344-55
    tobacco smuggling in Great Britain, 355-66

Transcendentalism, American NCLC 24: 1-99
    overviews and general studies, 3-23
    contemporary documents, 23-41
    theological aspects of, 42-52
    and social issues, 52-74
    literature of, 74-96

Travel Writing in the Nineteenth Century NCLC 44: 274-392
    the European grand tour, 275-303
    the Orient, 303-47
    North America, 347-91

Travel Writing in the Twentieth Century TCLC 30: 407-56
    conventions and traditions, 407-27
    and fiction writing, 427-43
    comparative essays on travel writers, 443-54

Treatment of Death in Children's Literature CLR 101: 152-201
    overviews and general studies, 155-80
    analytical and bibliographical reviews of death in children's literature, 180-97
    death of animals in children's literature, 197-200

Tristan and Isolde Legend CMLC 42: 311-404

Troubadours CMLC 66: 244-383
    overviews, 245-91
    politics, economics, history, and the troubadours, 291-344
    troubadours and women, 344-82

True-Crime Literature CLC 99: 333-433
    history and analysis, 334-407
    reviews of true-crime publications, 407-23
    writing instruction, 424-29
    author profiles, 429-33

Twentieth-Century Danish Literature TCLC 142: 271-344
    major works, 272-84
    major authors, 284-344

***Ulysses* and the Process of Textual Reconstruction** TCLC 26:386-416
    evaluations of the new *Ulysses,* 386-94
    editorial principles and procedures, 394-401
    theoretical issues, 401-16

Unconventional Family in Children's Literature CLR 102: 146-213
    overviews and general studies, 149-79
    analytical and bibliographical reviews, 179-97
    types of unconventional families: foster, adopted, homosexual, 197-212

Utilitarianism NCLC 84: 272-340
    J. S. Mill's Utilitarianism: liberty, equality, justice, 273-313
    Jeremy Bentham's Utilitarianism: the science of happiness, 313-39

Utopianism NCLC 88: 238-346
    overviews: Utopian literature, 239-59
    Utopianism in American literature, 259-99
    Utopianism in British literature, 299-311
    Utopianism and Feminism, 311-45

Utopian Literature, Nineteenth-Century NCLC 24: 353-473
    definitions, 354-74
    overviews and general studies, 374-88
    theory, 388-408
    communities, 409-26
    fiction, 426-53
    women and fiction, 454-71

Utopian Literature, Renaissance LC 32: 1-63
    overviews and general studies, 2-25
    classical background, 25-33
    utopia and the social contract, 33-9
    origins in mythology, 39-48
    utopia and the Renaissance country house, 48-52
    influence of millenarianism, 52-62

Vampire in Literature TCLC 46: 391-454
    origins and evolution, 392-412
    social and psychological perspectives, 413-44
    vampire fiction and science fiction, 445-53

Vernacular Bibles LC 67: 214-388
    overviews and general studies, 215-59
    the English Bible, 259-355
    the German Bible, 355-88

Victorian Autobiography NCLC 40: 277-363
    development and major characteristics, 278-88
    themes and techniques, 289-313
    the autobiographical tendency in Victorian prose and poetry, 313-47
    Victorian women's autobiographies, 347-62

Victorian Critical Theory NCLC 136: 236-379
    overviews and general studies, 237-86
    Matthew Arnold, 286-324
    Walter Pater and aestheticism, 324-36
    other Victorian critics, 336-78

Victorian Fantasy Literature NCLC 60: 246-384
    overviews and general studies, 247-91
    major figures, 292-366
    women in Victorian fantasy literature, 366-83

Victorian Hellenism NCLC 68: 251-376
    overviews and general studies, 252-78
    the meanings of Hellenism, 278-335
    the literary influence, 335-75

Victorian Illustrated Fiction NCLC 120: 247-356
    overviews and development, 128-76
    technical and material aspects of book illustration, 276-84
    Charles Dickens and his illustrators, 284-320
    William Makepeace Thackeray, 320-31
    George Eliot and Frederic Leighton, 331-51
    Lewis Carroll and John Tenniel, 351-56

Victorian Novel NCLC 32: 288-454
    development and major characteristics, 290-310
    themes and techniques, 310-58
    social criticism in the Victorian novel, 359-97
    urban and rural life in the Victorian novel, 397-406
    women in the Victorian novel, 406-25
    Mudie's Circulating Library, 425-34
    the late-Victorian novel, 434-51

Vietnamese Literature TCLC 102: 322-386

Vietnam War in Literature and Film CLC 91: 383-437
    overview, 384-8
    prose, 388-412
    film and drama, 412-24
    poetry, 424-35

Violence in Literature TCLC 98: 235-358
    overviews and general studies, 236-74
    violence in the works of modern authors, 274-358

Vorticism TCLC 62: 330-426
    Wyndham Lewis and Vorticism, 330-8
    characteristics and principles of Vorticism, 338-65
    Lewis and Pound, 365-82
    Vorticist writing, 382-416
    Vorticist painting, 416-26

Well-Made Play, The NCLC 80: 331-370
    overviews and general studies, 332-45
    Scribe's style, 345-56
    the influence of the well-made play, 356-69

Women's Autobiography, Nineteenth Century NCLC 76: 285-368
    overviews and general studies, 287-300
    autobiographies concerned with religious and political issues, 300-15
    autobiographies by women of color, 315-38
    autobiographies by women pioneers, 338-51
    autobiographies by women of letters, 351-68

Women's Diaries, Nineteenth-Century NCLC 48: 308-54
    overview, 308-13
    diary as history, 314-25
    sociology of diaries, 325-34
    diaries as psychological scholarship, 334-43
    diary as autobiography, 343-8
    diary as literature, 348-53

Women in Modern Literature TCLC 94: 262-425
    overviews and general studies, 263-86
    American literature, 286-304
    other national literatures, 304-33
    fiction, 333-94
    poetry, 394-407
    drama, 407-24

Women Writers, Seventeenth-Century LC 30: 2-58
    overview, 2-15
    women and education, 15-9

Topic Index

women and autobiography, 19-31
women's diaries, 31-9
early feminists, 39-58

World War I Literature TCLC 34: 392-486
overview, 393-403
English, 403-27
German, 427-50
American, 450-66
French, 466-74
and modern history, 474-82

World War I Short Fiction SSC 71: 187-347
overviews and general studies, 187-206

female short fiction writers of World War I,
206-36
Central Powers
Czechoslovakian writers of short fiction,
236-44
German writers of short fiction, 244-61
Entente/Allied Alliance
Australian writers of short fiction, 261-73
English writers of short fiction, 273-305
French writers of short fiction, 305-11
Associated Power: American writers of
short fiction, 311-46

Yellow Journalism NCLC 36: 383-456
overviews and general studies, 384-96
major figures, 396-413

Yiddish Literature TCLC 130: 229-364
overviews and general studies, 230-54
major authors, 254-305
Yiddish literature in America, 305-34
Yiddish and Judaism, 334-64

Young Playwrights Festival
1988 CLC 55: 376-81
1989 CLC 59: 398-403
1990 CLC 65: 444-8

SSC Cumulative Nationality Index

ALGERIAN

Camus, Albert **9**

AMERICAN

Abish, Walter **44**
Adams, Alice (Boyd) **24**
Aiken, Conrad (Potter) **9**
Alcott, Louisa May **27**
Algren, Nelson **33**
Anderson, Sherwood **1, 46**
Apple, Max (Isaac) **50**
Auchincloss, Louis (Stanton) **22**
Baldwin, James (Arthur) **10, 33**
Bambara, Toni Cade **35**
Banks, Russell **42**
Barnes, Djuna **3**
Barth, John (Simmons) **10**
Barthelme, Donald **2, 55**
Bass, Rick **60**
Beattie, Ann **11**
Bellow, Saul **14**
Benét, Stephen Vincent **10**
Berriault, Gina **30**
Betts, Doris (Waugh) **45**
Bierce, Ambrose (Gwinett) **9, 72**
Bowles, Paul (Frederick) **3**
Boyle, Kay **5**
Boyle, T(homas) Coraghessan **16**
Bradbury, Ray (Douglas) **29, 53**
Bradfield, Scott **65**
Bukowski, Charles **45**
Cable, George Washington **4**
Caldwell, Erskine (Preston) **19**
Calisher, Hortense **15**
Canin, Ethan **70**
Capote, Truman **2, 47**
Carver, Raymond **8, 51**
Cather, Willa (Sibert) **2, 50**
Chabon, Michael **59**
Chandler, Raymond (Thornton) **23**
Cheever, John **1, 38, 57**
Chesnutt, Charles W(addell) **7, 54**
Chopin, Kate **8, 68**
Cisneros, Sandra **32, 72**
Coover, Robert (Lowell) **15**
Cowan, Peter (Walkinshaw) **28**
Crane, Stephen (Townley) **7, 56, 70**
Davenport, Guy (Mattison Jr.) **16**
Davis, Rebecca (Blaine) Harding **38**
Dick, Philip K. **57**
Dixon, Stephen **16**
Dreiser, Theodore (Herman Albert) **30**
Dubus, André **15**
Dunbar, Paul Laurence **8**
Dybek, Stuart **55**
Elkin, Stanley L(awrence) **12**
Ellison, Harlan (Jay) **14**
Ellison, Ralph (Waldo) **26**
Fante, John **65**
Farrell, James T(homas) **28**
Fisher, Rudolph **25**

Fitzgerald, F(rancis) Scott (Key) **6, 31, 75**
Ford, Richard **56**
Freeman, Mary E(leanor) Wilkins **1, 47**
Gaines, Ernest J. **68**
Gardner, John (Champlin) Jr. **7**
Garland, (Hannibal) Hamlin **18**
Garrett, George (Palmer) **30**
Gass, William H(oward) **12**
Gibson, William (Ford) **52**
Gilchrist, Ellen (Louise) **14, 63**
Gilman, Charlotte (Anna) Perkins (Stetson) **13, 62**
Glasgow, Ellen (Anderson Gholson) **34**
Glaspell, Susan **41**
Gordon, Caroline **15**
Gordon, Mary **59**
Grau, Shirley Ann **15**
Hammett, (Samuel) Dashiell **17**
Harris, Joel Chandler **19**
Harrison, James (Thomas) **19**
Harte, (Francis) Bret(t) **8, 59**
Hawthorne, Nathaniel **3, 29, 39**
Heinlein, Robert A(nson) **55**
Hemingway, Ernest (Miller) **1, 25, 36, 40, 63**
Henderson, Zenna (Chlarson) **29**
Henry, O. **5, 49**
Howells, William Dean **36**
Hughes, (James) Langston **6**
Hurston, Zora Neale **4**
Huxley, Aldous (Leonard) **39**
Irving, Washington **2, 37**
Jackson, Shirley **9, 39**
James, Henry **8, 32, 47**
Jewett, (Theodora) Sarah Orne **6, 44**
Johnson, Denis **56**
Jones, Thom (Douglas) **56**
Kelly, Robert **50**
Kincaid, Jamaica **72**
King, Stephen (Edwin) **17, 55**
Lardner, Ring(gold) W(ilmer) **32**
Le Guin, Ursula K(roeber) **12, 69**
Ligotti, Thomas (Robert) **16**
Lish, Gordon (Jay) **18**
London, Jack **4, 49**
Lovecraft, H(oward) P(hillips) **3, 52**
Maclean, Norman (Fitzroy) **13**
Malamud, Bernard **15**
Marshall, Paule **3**
Mason, Bobbie Ann **4**
McCarthy, Mary (Therese) **24**
McCullers, (Lula) Carson (Smith) **9, 24**
Melville, Herman **1, 17, 46**
Michaels, Leonard **16**
Millhauser, Steven **57**
Murfree, Mary Noailles **22**
Nabokov, Vladimir (Vladimirovich) **11**
Nin, Anaïs **10**
Norris, (Benjamin) Frank(lin Jr.) **28**
Oates, Joyce Carol **6, 70**
O'Brien, Tim **74**
O'Connor, Frank **5**
O'Connor, (Mary) Flannery **1, 23, 61**
O'Hara, John (Henry) **15**

Olsen, Tillie **11**
Ozick, Cynthia **15, 60**
Page, Thomas Nelson **23**
Paley, Grace **8**
Pancake, Breece D'J **61**
Parker, Dorothy (Rothschild) **2**
Perelman, S(idney) J(oseph) **32**
Phillips, Jayne Anne **16**
Poe, Edgar Allan **1, 22, 34, 35, 54**
Pohl, Frederik **25**
Porter, Katherine Anne **4, 31, 43**
Powers, J(ames) F(arl) **4**
Price, (Edward) Reynolds **22**
Pynchon, Thomas (Ruggles Jr.) **14**
Roth, Philip (Milton) **26**
Salinger, J(erome) D(avid) **2, 28, 65**
Salter, James **58**
Saroyan, William **21**
Selby, Hubert Jr. **20**
Silko, Leslie (Marmon) **37, 66**
Singer, Isaac Bashevis **3, 53**
Spencer, Elizabeth **57**
Stafford, Jean **26**
Stegner, Wallace (Earle) **27**
Stein, Gertrude **42**
Steinbeck, John (Ernst) **11, 37, 77**
Stuart, Jesse (Hilton) **31**
Styron, William **25**
Suckow, Ruth **18**
Taylor, Peter (Hillsman) **10**
Thomas, Audrey (Callahan) **20**
Thurber, James (Grover) **1, 47**
Toomer, Jean **1, 45**
Trilling, Lionel **75**
Twain, Mark (Clemens, Samuel) **6, 26, 34**
Updike, John (Hoyer) **13, 27**
Vinge, Joan (Carol) D(ennison) **24**
Vonnegut, Kurt Jr. **8**
Walker, Alice (Malsenior) **5**
Wallace, David Foster **68**
Warren, Robert Penn **4, 58**
Welty, Eudora **1, 27, 51**
Wescott, Glenway **35**
West, Nathanael **16**
Wharton, Edith (Newbold Jones) **6**
Wideman, John Edgar **62**
Williams, William Carlos **31**
Wodehouse, P(elham) G(renville) **2**
Wolfe, Thomas (Clayton) **33**
Wolff, Tobias **63**
Wright, Richard (Nathaniel) **2**
Yamamoto, Hisaye **34**

ARGENTINIAN

Bioy Casares, Adolfo **17**
Borges, Jorge Luis **4, 41**
Cortázar, Julio **7, 76**
Valenzuela, Luisa **14**

AUSTRALIAN

Jolley, (Monica) Elizabeth **19**
Lawson, Henry (Archibald Hertzberg) **18**

Moorhouse, Frank **40**
White, Patrick (Victor Martindale) **39**
Wilding, Michael **50**

AUSTRIAN

Grillparzer, Franz **37**
Kafka, Franz **5, 29, 35, 60**
Musil, Robert (Edler von) **18**
Schnitzler, Arthur **15, 61**
Stifter, Adalbert **28**

BARBADIAN

Clarke, Austin C(hesterfield) **45**

BOTSWANAN

Head, Bessie **52**

BRAZILIAN

Lispector, Clarice **34**
Machado de Assis, Joaquim Maria **24**

CANADIAN

Atwood, Margaret (Eleanor) **2, 46**
Clarke, Austin C(hesterfield) **45**
Far, Siu Sin **62**
Gallant, Mavis **5, 78**
Hood, Hugh (John Blagdon) **42**
Laurence, (Jean) Margaret (Wemyss) **7**
Leacock, Stephen (Butler) **39**
Lewis, (Percy) Wyndham **34**
Metcalf, John **43**
Mistry, Rohinton **73**
Mukherjee, Bharati **38**
Munro, Alice **3**
Ross, (James) Sinclair **24**
Thomas, Audrey (Callahan) **20**

CHILEAN

Allende, Isabel **65**
Bombal, María Luisa **37**
Donoso (Yañez), José **34**

CHINESE

Chang, Eileen **28**
Lu Hsun **20**
P'u Sung-ling **31**

COLOMBIAN

García Márquez, Gabriel (Jose) **8**

CUBAN

Cabrera Infante, G(uillermo) **39**
Calvino, Italo **3, 48**
Carpentier (y Valmont), Alejo **35**

CZECH

Chapek, Karel **36**
Hašek, Jaroslav **69**
Kafka, Franz **5, 29, 35, 60**
Kundera, Milan **24**

DANISH

Andersen, Hans Christian **6, 56**
Dinesen, Isak **75**

EGYPTIAN

Idris, Yusuf **74**
Mahfouz, Naguib **66**

ENGLISH

Aldiss, Brian W(ilson) **36**
Ballard, J(ames) G(raham) **1, 53**
Barker, Clive **53**
Bates, H(erbert) E(rnest) **10**
Campbell, (John) Ramsey **19**
Carter, Angela (Olive) **13**
Chesterton, G(ilbert) K(eith) **1, 46**

Clarke, Arthur C(harles) **3**
Collier, John **19**
Conrad, Joseph **9, 67, 69**
Coppard, A(lfred) E(dgar) **21**
Crace, Jim **61**
de la Mare, Walter (John) **14**
Dickens, Charles (John Huffam) **17, 49**
Doyle, Arthur Conan **12**
du Maurier, Daphne **18**
Eliot, George **72**
Forster, E(dward) M(organ) **27**
Fowles, John (Robert) **33**
Galsworthy, John **22**
Gaskell, Elizabeth Cleghorn **25**
Gissing, George (Robert) **37**
Greene, Graham (Henry) **29**
Hardy, Thomas **2, 60**
Huxley, Aldous (Leonard) **39**
Isherwood, Christopher (William Bradshaw)
56
Jacobs, W(illiam) W(ymark) **73**
James, Montague (Rhodes) **16**
Jolley, (Monica) Elizabeth **19**
Kipling, (Joseph) Rudyard **5, 54**
Lawrence, D(avid) H(erbert Richards) **4, 19,
73**
Lee, Vernon **33**
Lessing, Doris (May) **6, 61**
Lowry, (Clarence) Malcolm **31**
Maugham, W(illiam) Somerset **8**
Morrison, Arthur **40**
Naipaul, V(idiadhar) S(urajprasad) **38**
Orwell, George **68**
Pritchett, V(ictor) S(awdon) **14**
Rhys, Jean **21, 76**
Saki (Munro, H. H.) **12**
Sansom, William **21**
Sayers, Dorothy **71**
Trollope, Anthony **28**
Warner, Sylvia Townsend **23**
Waugh, Evelyn (Arthur St. John) **41**
Wells, H(erbert) G(eorge) **6, 70**
White, Patrick (Victor Martindale) **39**
Wilding, Michael **50**
Wilde, Oscar (Fingal O'Flahertie Wills) **11,
77**
Wilson, Angus (Frank Johnstone) **21**
Wodehouse, P(elham) G(renville) **2**
Woolf, (Adeline) Virginia **7**
Zangwill, Israel **44**

FRENCH

Aymé, Marcel (Andre) **41**
Balzac, Honoré de **5, 59**
Barbey d'Aurevilly, Jules-Amédée **17**
Baudelaire, Charles **18**
Beauvoir, Simone (Lucie Ernestine Marie
Bertrand) de **35**
Beckett, Samuel (Barclay) **16, 74**
Camus, Albert **9, 76**
Colette, (Sidonie-Gabrielle) **10**
Duras, Marguerite **40**
Flaubert, Gustave **11, 60**
Gautier, Théophile **20**
Gide, André (Paul Guillaume) **13**
Jarry, Alfred **20**
Laforgue, Jules **20**
Lautréamont **14**
Maupassant, (Henri René Albert) Guy de **1,
64**
Mauriac, François (Charles) **24**
Mérimée, Prosper **7, 77**
Morand, Paul **22**
Nerval, Gérard de **18**
Nin, Anaïs **10**
Proust, Marcel **75**
Sartre, Jean-Paul **32**
Stendhal **27**
Villiers de l'Isle Adam, Jean Marie Mathias
Philippe Auguste **14**
Voltaire **12**

GERMAN

Arnim, Achim von (Ludwig Joachim von
Arnim) **29**
Boell, Heinrich (Theodor) **23**
Bukowski, Charles **45**
Goethe, Johann Wolfgang von **38**
Grimm, Jacob Ludwig Karl **36**
Grimm, Wilhelm Karl **36**
Hauptmann, Gerhart (Johann Robert) **37**
Hesse, Hermann **9, 49**
Hoffmann, E(rnst) T(heodor) A(madeus) **13**
Kleist, Heinrich von **22**
Kluge, Alexander **61**
Lenz, Siegfried **33**
Mann, (Paul) Thomas **5**
Storm, (Hans) Theodor (Woldsen) **27**
Tieck, (Johann) Ludwig **31**

INDIAN

Mukherjee, Bharati **38**
Narayan, R(asipuram) K(rishnaswami) **25**
Tagore, Rabindranath **48**

IRISH

Beckett, Samuel (Barclay) **16**
Bowen, Elizabeth (Dorothea Cole) **3, 28, 66**
Friel, Brian **76**
Higgins, Aidan **68**
Joyce, James (Augustine Aloysius) **3, 26, 44,
64**
Kiely, Benedict **58**
Lavin, Mary **4, 67**
Le Fanu, Joseph Sheridan **14**
McGahern, John **17**
Moore, George Augustus **19**
O'Brien, Edna **10, 77**
O'Faolain, Sean **13**
O'Flaherty, Liam **6**
Ross, Martin **56**
Somerville, Edith **56**
Stephens, James **50**
Stoker, Abraham **55, 62**
Trevor, William **21, 58**
Wilde, Oscar (Fingal O'Flahertie Wills) **11,
77**

ISRAELI

Agnon, S(hmuel) Y(osef Halevi) **30**
Appelfeld, Aharon **42**
Oz, Amos **66**

ITALIAN

Boccaccio, Giovanni **10**
Calvino, Italo **3, 48**
Ginzburg, Natalia **65**
Levi, Primo **12**
Moravia, Alberto **26**
Pavese, Cesare **19**
Pirandello, Luigi **22**
Svevo, Italo (Schmitz, Aron Hector) **25**
Verga, Giovanni (Carmelo) **21**

JAMAICAN

Senior, Olive (Marjorie) **78**

JAPANESE

Abe, Kobo **61**
Akutagawa, Ryunosuke **44**
Dazai Osamu **41**
Endo, Shūsaku **48**
Kawabata, Yasunari **17**
Oe, Kenzaburo **20**
Shiga, Naoya **23**
Tanizaki, Junichirō **21**

MEXICAN

Arreola, Juan José **38**
Castellanos, Rosario **39, 68**
Fuentes, Carlos **24**

Rulfo, Juan **25**

NEW ZEALANDER

Frame, Janet **29**
Mansfield, Katherine **9, 23, 38**

POLISH

Agnon, S(hmuel) Y(osef Halevi) **30**
Borowski, Tadeusz **48**
Conrad, Joseph **9, 71**
Peretz, Isaac Loeb **26**
Schulz, Bruno **13**
Singer, Isaac Bashevis **3, 53**

PUERTO RICAN

Ferré, Rosario **36**

RUSSIAN

Babel, Isaak (Emmanuilovich) **16, 78**
Bulgakov, Mikhail (Afanas'evich) **18**
Bunin, Ivan Alexeyevich **5**
Chekhov, Anton (Pavlovich) **2, 28, 41, 51**
Dostoevsky, Fedor Mikhailovich **2, 33, 44**
Gogol, Nikolai (Vasilyevich) **4, 29, 52**
Gorky, Maxim **28**
Kazakov, Yuri Pavlovich **43**
Leskov, Nikolai (Semyonovich) **34**
Nabokov, Vladimir (Vladimirovich) **11**

Olesha, Yuri **69**
Pasternak, Boris (Leonidovich) **31**
Pilnyak, Boris **48**
Platonov, Andrei (Klimentov, Andrei Platonovich) **42**
Pushkin, Alexander (Sergeyevich) **27, 55**
Solzhenitsyn, Aleksandr I(sayevich) **32**
Tolstoy, Leo (Nikolaevich) **9, 30, 45, 54**
Turgenev, Ivan (Sergeevich) **7, 57**
Zoshchenko, Mikhail (Mikhailovich) **15**

SCOTTISH

Davie, Elspeth **52**
Doyle, Arthur Conan **12**
Oliphant, Margaret (Oliphant Wilson) **25**
Scott, Walter **32**
Spark, Muriel (Sarah) **10**
Stevenson, Robert Louis (Balfour) **11, 51**

SOUTH AFRICAN

Gordimer, Nadine **17**
Head, Bessie **52**

SPANISH

Alarcón, Pedro Antonio de **64**
Cela, Camilo José **71**
Cervantes (Saavedra), Miguel de **12**
Pardo Bazán, Emilia **30**

Unamuno (y Jugo), Miguel de **11, 69**

SWEDISH

Lagervist, Par **12**

SWISS

Hesse, Hermann **9, 49**
Meyer, Conrad Ferdinand **30**
Keller, Gottfried **26**
Walser, Robert **20**

TRINIDADIAN

Naipaul, V(idiadhar) S(urajprasad) **38**

UKRAINIAN

Aleichem, Sholom **33**

URUGUAYAN

Onetti, Juan Carlos **23**

WELSH

Evans, Caradoc **43**
Lewis, Alun **40**
Machen, Arthur **20**
Thomas, Dylan (Marlais) **3, 44**

YUGOSLAVIAN

Andrić, Ivo **36**

Nationality Index

SSC-78 Title Index

"1933" (Gallant) **78**:272

"About Geneva" (Gallant) **78**:209-11, 238, 240

"Acceptance of Their Ways" (Gallant) **78**:190-91

Across the Bridge (Gallant) **78**:272-73, 284

"Afonka Bida" (Babel) **78**:5, 40, 47, 52, 116, 121, 126, 131-32, 138, 140, 143-45

"After the Battle" (Babel) **78**:13, 29, 48, 51, 122, 132, 164

"Argamak" (Babel) **78**:15, 29-30, 53, 65, 69-70, 75, 104, 122, 132-33, 137-38, 143, 145, 153-55, 157

"Arrival of the Snake-Woman" (Senior) **78**:312-13, 318-19, 326, 333, 337-39, 349-51, 367

Arrival of the Snake-Woman and Other Stories (Senior) **78**:314, 333-34, 336, 350-51, 364, 366

"Ascot" (Senior) **78**:307, 310, 333-34, 336, 341, 364

"The Assembly" (Gallant) **78**:246

"At St. Valentine's Church" (Babel)
See "In St. Valentine's Church"

"Autumn Day" (Gallant) **78**:176, 238, 243

"Awakening" (Babel) **78**:163

"Ballad" (Senior) **78**:307, 310, 318, 335, 338, 341, 365-66

"Baum, Gabriel (1935-)" (Gallant) **78**:258, 260, 283-85, 287-92

"Berestechko" (Babel) **78**:4-5, 14, 25-26, 41, 48-49, 63, 66-67, 75, 88, 90, 119, 126, 132, 159-60

"Bernadette" (Gallant) **78**:213, 242

"Between Zero and One" (Gallant) **78**:223

"The Biography of Matvey Rodionych Pavlichenko" (Babel) **78**:4-5, 11, 22, 40, 42, 49, 75, 90, 126, 130, 132, 157-59

"Bonaventure" (Gallant) **78**:248

"The Boy Who Loved Ice-Cream" (Senior) **78**:310

"The Brigade Commander" (Babel)
See "The Commander of II Brigade"

"Bright Thursdays" (Senior) **78**:307, 318, 334-35, 340-41, 365-66

"Buddenyj" (Babel) **78**:4

"The Case Against the Queen" (Senior) **78**:343

"The Catholic Church at Novograd" (Babel)
See "The Church at Novograd"

"The Cemetery at Kozin" (Babel) **78**:5, 25, 66-67, 86, 102, 117, 122, 158-59

"Chesniki" (Babel) **78**:10, 33, 48, 51, 58-59, 62, 132, 138, 159

"The Cho Choo Vine" (Senior) **78**:343

"The Chosen Husband" (Gallant) **78**:272

"The Church at Novograd" (Babel) **78**:4-5, 9, 15, 25, 34-35, 51-52, 54, 64, 76, 87, 132, 151, 159

Collected Stories (Babel) **78**:112

The Collected Stories of Isaac Babel (Babel) **78**:109

The Collected Stories of Mavis Gallant (Gallant) **78**:245-46, 258, 260, 269-70, 278, 284, 290

"The Colonel's Child" (Gallant) **78**:246

"Combrig 2" (Babel) **78**:138, 157

"The Commander of II Brigade" (Babel) **78**:47, 132

"The Concert Party" (Gallant) **78**:273

"Confirmation Day" (Senior) **78**:308, 318, 335, 341

"The Continuation of the Story of a Horse" (Babel)
See "The Story of a Horse Continued"

"Country of the One-Eye God" (Senior) **78**:300, 313, 341, 344, 346, 348-49, 364

"Crossing into Poland" (Babel)
See "Crossing the Zbruch"

"Crossing the Zbruch" (Babel) **78**:3-6, 13-14, 18, 20, 23-25, 30, 33-34, 38, 43, 47, 49, 51-53, 63, 65, 69, 72-73, 75-76, 98, 101, 103-4, 120, 122, 126, 128-30, 132, 138, 148, 151, 155, 157-58, 163

"A Day Like Any Other" (Gallant) **78**:170, 180, 242

"The Death of Dolgushov" (Babel) **78**:20, 29, 40, 49, 51, 53, 62, 77, 85, 122, 131-32, 144-45, 152, 157-58

Discerner of Hearts (Senior) **78**:343, 357

"Discourse on the Tachanka" (Babel) **78**:6, 48, 51, 87, 132, 138

"Do Angels Wear Brassieres?" (Senior) **78**:300, 311, 318-20, 323, 341, 365

"Eliya Isaakovich and Margarita Prokofyevna" (Babel) **78**:62

"An Emergency Case" (Gallant) **78**:211

The End of the World and Other Stories (Gallant) **78**:212

"Ernst in Civilian Clothes" (Gallant) **78**:171, 174-76, 178, 180-81

"Èskadronnyj Trunov" (Babel)
See "Squadron Commander Trunov"

"Evening" (Babel) **78**:10, 38, 42, 50, 61, 76, 104, 161-62

"The Fenton Child" (Gallant) **78**:245-46

"First Love" (Babel) **78**:109, 118-19

"Florida" (Gallant) **78**:272

"The Flowers of Spring" (Gallant) **78**:194-96

"A Flying Start" (Gallant) **78**:246-47, 249, 269

"Forain" (Gallant) **78**:273, 278-82

"The Four Seasons" (Gallant) **78**:246, 285, 290

"From Cloud to Cloud" (Gallant) **78**:272

From the Fifteenth District (Gallant) **78**:234, 285-86, 290

"Gedali" (Babel) **78**:5, 11, 13, 20, 27, 36, 41, 49, 66-67, 74-75, 102-3, 121, 126, 132, 144-45, 159, 161

"Ghedali" (Babel)
See "Gedali"

"Going Ashore" (Gallant) **78**:238, 241

"Good Morning and Goodbye" (Gallant) **78**:192, 194, 196, 198

"Goose" (Babel)
See "My First Goose"

"Grippes and Poche" (Gallant) **78**:268-70

Home Truths: Selected Canadian Stories (Gallant) **78**:197, 202-4, 210, 221-29, 232-33, 236-37, 243, 247-48, 290, 292

"How It Was Done in Odessa" (Babel) **78**:70, 74

"The Ice Wagon Going Down the Street" (Gallant) **78**:214, 236

"Ikh bylo deviat" (Babel)
See "There Were Nine"

"In Plain Sight" (Gallant) **78**:268-70

"In St. Valentine's Church" (Babel) **78**:40, 49-53, 58-59, 61, 86, 89, 132, 161

"In the Tunnel" (Gallant) **78**:248

In Transit (Gallant) **78**:211, 257, 260

"In Youth Is Pleasure" (Gallant) **78**:229

"Istoriia odnoi loshadi" (Babel)
See "The Story of a Horse"

"Italian Sunshine" (Babel) **78**:4, 35-36, 43, 49-51, 61, 63, 85, 90, 102, 132, 153, 158, 163

"Italy's Sun" (Babel)
See "Italian Sunshine"

"Its Image on the Mirror" (Gallant) **78**:215

"The Ivans" (Babel) **78**:5, 20, 38, 52, 57, 76, 85, 104, 117, 132, 144, 157, 160, 163-64

"Ivany" (Babel)
See "The Ivans"

"Iz knigi Konarmii" (Babel) **78**:155

"Izmena" (Babel)
See "Treason"

"Jorinda and Jorindel" (Gallant) **78**:192, 195, 197-98, 203-4

"The King" (Babel) **78**:74

"The Kiss" (Babel) **78**:155, 158-60

"Kladbishche v Kozine" (Babel)
See "The Cemetery at Kozin"

"Kombrig dva" (Babel)
See "Combrig 2"

Konarmiia (Babel) **78**:3-9, 13-15, 18, 20-21, 24, 26-34, 37-39, 41-54, 57-59, 62, 65-67, 69-79, 82, 85-91, 98, 101-2, 104-5, 108-9, 111-12, 115, 117-19, 122, 126-33, 135-40, 142-45, 147-49, 153, 155-63, 1664

"Konkin" (Babel) **78**:4, 8, 60, 104, 144, 163

"Konkin's Prisoner" (Babel) **78**:104, 126, 130, 132

"Kostol v Novograde" (Babel)
See "The Church in Novograd"

"The Kozino Cemetery" (Babel)
See "The Cemetery at Kozin"

"Larry" (Gallant) **78**:246-47, 249, 269

"The Latehomecomer" (Gallant) **78**:171, 173

"Lena" (Gallant) **78**:246

"A Letter" (Babel) **78**:4-5, 21-22, 39, 47, 49, 52, 54, 63, 85, 122, 126, 130, 132, 142-43, 145, 151, 157, 159, 163

"The Life and Adventures of Matvey Pavlichenko" (Babel)
See "The Biography of Matvey Rodionych Pavlichenko"

"The Life Story of Pavlichenko, Matvei Rodionych" (Babel)
See "The Biography of Matvey Rodionych Pavlichenko"

"Lily, Lily" (Senior) **78**:337, 366

"Liubka the Cossack" (Babel) **78**:66

"The Lizardy Man and His Lady" (Senior) **78**:343
"Love Orange" (Senior) **78**:303, 310, 364
"Luc and His Father" (Gallant) **78**:246-47, 249, 291
"Madeline's Birthday" (Gallant) **78**:195
"Malcolm and Bea" (Gallant) **78**:257-60
"Mlle Dias de Corta" (Gallant) **78**:273
"The Moabitess" (Gallant) **78**:213, 242
"Moj pervjy gus" (Babel)
    See "My First Goose"
"The Moslem Wife" (Gallant) **78**:290-91
"My First Goose" (Babel) **78**:4-6, 10-13, 20, 29, 42, 46-47, 49-50, 53-55, 65, 69, 76-78, 86, 88, 90-96, 121, 132, 138, 144-45, 149, 151, 162, 164
My Heart Is Broken (Gallant) **78**:212, 214-15, 242
"Nachalnik Konzapasa" (Babel)
    See "The Remount Officer"
"New Year's Eve" (Gallant) **78**:246
"The Novograd Church" (Babel)
    See "The Church at Novograd"
"Odessa" (Babel)
    See "How It Was Done in Odessa"
The Odessa Tales (Babel)
    See *Odesskie rasskazzy*
Odesskie rasskazzy (Babel) **78**:21-22
"The Old Place" (Gallant) **78**:242
"One Morning in June" (Gallant) **78**:238-40
The Other Paris (Gallant) **78**:209-10, 233-34
"The Other Paris" (Gallant) **78**:169, 176, 205, 233, 237-38, 242
"Overhead in a Balloon" (Gallant) **78**:246, 250, 253, 271
Overhead in a Balloon: Stories of Paris (Gallant) **78**:181, 234-36, 246-47, 249-55, 269-70, 273, 290-91
"A Painful Affair" (Gallant) **78**:246, 250, 269
"The Palace of Mothers" (Babel) **78**:63
"Pan Apolek" (Babel) **78**:4, 6, 8, 39, 50, 57, 77, 102, 132-33, 147-48, 151, 153
"Pavlichenko" (Babel)
    See "The Biography of Matvey Rodionych Pavlichenko"
The Pegnitz Junction (Gallant) **78**:291
"Perechod cerez Zbruc" (Babel)
    See "Crossing the Zbruch"
"Perexod cerez Zbruc" (Babel)
    See "Crossing the Zbruch"
"Pesnia" (Babel)
    See "The Song"
"The Picnic" (Gallant) **78**:237, 242
"Pis'mo" (Babel)
    See "A Letter"
"Poceluj" (Babel) **78**:15
"Poor Franzi" (Gallant) **78**:238-40, 242
"Posle boja" (Babel)
    See "After the Battle"
"Potselui" (Babel)
    See "The Kiss"
"Potter" (Gallant) **78**:246
"The Premature Infants" (Babel) **78**:63

"Prishchepa" (Babel) **78**:5, 11, 33, 126, 132, 158, 160
"Probuzhdenie" (Babel)
    See "Awakening"
"Put' v Brody" (Babel)
    See "The Road to Brody"
"The Rabbi" (Babel) **78**:5, 20, 29, 40-41, 54, 63, 66-68, 74-75, 100, 103-5, 120-22, 132, 144-45, 159
"The Rabbi's Son" (Babel) **78**:4, 20, 29, 40-41, 65-67, 69-70, 74-75, 98, 103-4, 111, 121-22, 132, 144-45, 159, 164
"Real Old Time T'ing" (Senior) **78**:307, 310, 321, 333-34, 341
"The Rebbe" (Babel)
    See "The Rabbi"
"The Rebbe's Son" (Babel)
    See "The Rabbi's Son"
"A Recollection" (Gallant) **78**:246
Red Calvary (Babel)
    See *Konarmiia*
"The Remission" (Gallant) **78**:234-36
"The Remount Officer" (Babel) **78**:23, 40, 49, 57, 61, 85, 118, 151, 158
"The Road to Brody" (Babel) **78**:18, 33, 39, 48, 52-54, 85, 117, 132, 159-60, 163
"Rue de Lille" (Gallant) **78**:246
"Salt" (Babel) **78**:4, 9-10, 42, 47, 50-51, 54, 63, 85, 117, 126, 130, 132, 142-45, 157-59
"Sandy the Christ" (Babel)
    See "Sashka the Christ"
"Sashka the Christ" (Babel) **78**:5, 28, 49, 52, 60, 62, 64, 76, 132, 137
"Saska-Xristos" (Babel)
    See "Sashka the Christ"
"Saturday" (Gallant) **78**:203
"Scarves, Beads, Sandals" (Gallant) **78**:268
"See the Tiki-Tiki Scatter" (Senior) **78**:322-23
The Selected Stories of Mavis Gallant (Gallant)
    See *The Collected Stories of Mavis Gallant*
"Señor Pinedo" (Gallant) **78**:170, 242, 262
"Singing" (Babel) **78**:62
"Smert Dolgushova" (Babel)
    See "The Death of Dolgushov"
"Sol'" (Babel)
    See "Salt"
"Solnce Italii" (Babel)
    See "Italian Sunshine"
"The Song" (Babel) **78**:49-50, 53-54, 86, 129, 132-33, 164
"Speck's Idea" (Gallant) **78**:235, 246-47, 250, 268, 271
"Squadron Commander Trunov" (Babel) **78**:14, 18, 20, 37, 41, 47, 51, 116-17, 119, 122, 126, 129, 156, 159-60, 163
"A State of Affairs" (Gallant) **78**:273, 278-83
"The Story of a Horse" (Babel) **78**:4-5, 46, 52, 75, 78, 85, 132, 155, 158, 164
"The Story of a Horse Continued" (Babel) **78**:20, 48, 75-76, 78-79, 83, 132, 157-58
"Summer Lightning" (Senior) **78**:334, 341
Summer Lightning and Other Stories (Senior) **78**:299, 305-7, 310-17, 323, 332-36, 340-41, 344, 364-66

"Sun of Italy" (Babel)
    See "Italian Sunshine"
"Swimming in the Ba'Ma Grass" (Senior) **78**:343
"Syn rabbi" (Babel)
    See "The Rabbi's Son"
"Tachanka" (Babel)
    See "Discourse on the Tachanka"
"Teaching about the Tachanka" (Babel)
    See "Discourse on the Tachanka"
"The Tenantry of Birds" (Senior) **78**:336, 366-67
"Thank You for the Lovely Tea" (Gallant) **78**:192, 195-98, 200, 203, 233-34, 248
"There Were Nine" (Babel) **78**:117
"There Were Ten" (Babel) **78**:117
"Three Brick Walls" (Gallant) **78**:192, 194, 196-97
"Timashenko and Mel'nikov" (Babel) **78**:79
"Treason" (Babel) **78**:4-5, 9-10, 22, 42, 117, 130, 132, 158
"Trunov" (Babel)
    See "Squadron Commander Trunov"
"The Two Grandmothers" (Senior) **78**:322, 366
"Two Ivans" (Babel)
    See "The Ivans"
"U sviatogo Valenta" (Babel)
    See "In St. Valentine's Church"
"Ucenie o tacanke" (Babel)
    See "Discourse on the Tachanka"
An Unmarried Man's Summer (Gallant)
    See *My Heart is Broken*
"Up North" (Gallant) **78**:192, 195, 198-99, 203
"Vasilisa the Beautiful" (Babel) **78**:144
"Vdova" (Babel)
    See "The Widow"
"Večer" (Babel)
    See "Evening"
"Vecher" (Babel)
    See "Evening"
"View from the Terrace" (Senior) **78**:312-13, 336
"Voices Lost in Snow" (Gallant) **78**:184-85
"When We Were Nearly Young" (Gallant) **78**:261-66
"The Widow" (Babel) **78**:5, 20, 51-52, 54, 58, 61-63, 132, 155, 158, 161
"Willi" (Gallant) **78**:171, 173-75, 178
"Wing's Chips" (Gallant) **78**:209-10
"A Wonderful Country" (Gallant) **78**:194, 196-97
"You Think I Mad, Miss?" (Senior) **78**:343
"Zamosc" (Babel) **78**:101-3, 118-19
"Zamoste" (Babel) **78**:5, 8, 17-18, 20, 26, 29-30, 38-39, 48, 50, 53, 63, 132, 155, 159, 161
"Zig-zag" (Senior) **78**:343, 357-58, 360-62
"Zisneopisanie Pavlicenki Matveja Rodionyca" (Babel)
    See "The Biography of Matvey Rodionych Pavlichenko"